CORPORATE TAKEOVERS
MODERN EMPIRICAL
DEVELOPMENTS

VOLUME 1

TAKEOVER ACTIVITY, VALUATION ESTIMATES,

AND SOURCES OF MERGER GAINS

CORPORATE TAKEOVERS
MODERN EMPIRICAL DEVELOPMENTS

VOLUME 1
TAKEOVER ACTIVITY, VALUATION ESTIMATES,
AND SOURCES OF MERGER GAINS

Edited by

B. ESPEN ECKBO
Tuck School of Business
Dartmouth College
Hanover, New Hampshire, USA

AMSTERDAM • BOSTON • HEIDELBERG • LONDON
NEW YORK • OXFORD • PARIS • SAN DIEGO
SAN FRANCISCO • SINGAPORE • SYDNEY • TOKYO
Academic Press is an imprint of Elsevier

ELSEVIER

Academic Press is an imprint of Elsevier
525 B Street, Suite 1900, San Diego, CA 92101-4495,USA
30Corporate Drive, Suite 400, Burlington, MA01803, USA
32 Jamestown Road, London, NW1 7BY, UK
Radarweg 29, PO Box 211, 1000 AE Amsterdam, The Netherlands

Material in the work originally appeared in *Handbook of Corporate Finance: Empirical Corporate Finance,
Volume 2* (Elsevier, B.V. 2007), *Journal of Corporate Finance* (Elsevier, B.V.), and *Journal of Financial
Economics (Elsevier, B.V.)*

Permissions may be sought directly from Elsevier's Science & Technology Rights Department in Oxford, UK: phone
(+44) (0) 1865 843830; fax (+44) (0) 1865 853333; email: permissions@elsevier.com. Alternatively you can submit
your request online by visiting the Elsevier web site at http://www.elsevier.com/locate/permissions, and selecting
Obtaining permission to use Elsevier material

Notice
No responsibility is assumed by the publisher for any injury and/or damage to persons or property as a matter of
products liability, negligence or otherwise, or from any use or operation of any methods, products, instructions or
ideas contained in the material herein. Because of rapid advances in the medical sciences, in particular,
independent verification of diagnoses and drug dosages should be made

ISBN 13: 978-0-12-382016-7 (set)
ISBN 13: 978-0-12-381983-3 (vol. 1)
ISBN 13: 978-0-12-381982-6 (vol. 2)

For information on all Academic Press publications
visit our website at *elsevierdirect.com*

Printed and bound in USA
10 11 12   10 9 8 7 6 5 4 3 2 1

Working together to grow
libraries in developing countries

www.elsevier.com | www.bookaid.org | www.sabre.org

ELSEVIER   BOOK AID
             International   Sabre Foundation

FOREWORD

This two-volume collection presents 44 empirical articles on corporate takeovers published by Elsevier Science. The two volumes form a coherent study of interesting empirical issues, theoretical propositions, econometric methodologies, and large-sample evidence in the field. The articles—with only five exceptions—were published since the millennium, so the collection is truly modern in scope. These articles reflect the significant shift toward greater sample sizes and increased transaction detail permitted by the Securities Data Company's (SDC) Merger and Acquisition Database over the past decade. As the collection provides a comprehensive status report on the modern scientific evidence on corporate takeovers, it is my hope that it will be useful as a graduate-level text for a course on corporate takeovers and as a convenient reference for those familiar with the main material.

The sole purpose of restricting the collection to Elsevier publications is to make the collection more cost effective in a world where most journal articles may be downloaded from the Web. Not surprisingly, most of the articles were originally published in the *Journal of Financial Economics*, the primary outlet for top research on takeovers since the late 1970s. However, the collection also includes six comprehensive review articles that previously appeared as chapters in two of Elsevier's *Handbook* Series, six articles from the *Journal of Corporate Finance*, and one previously published in the *Journal of Financial Intermediation*.

The body of research reprinted here builds on classic articles from the 1980s and 1990s. Given the general accessibility of those classic pieces, and my desire to report on modern developments, the seminal works predating year 2000 are excluded unless deemed absolutely necessary for the context. Also, the Elsevier restriction excludes (of course) work published in the *Journal of Finance* and the *Review of Financial Studies*. To mitigate those shortcomings, the reader will find a comprehensive discussion of more than 500 articles in the survey "Corporate Takeovers" by Betton et al. (2008), reprinted at the beginning of Volume 1. Moreover, although the focus of this collection is on corporate takeovers, Volume 1 also includes at the end a broad survey of more than 300 empirical articles on divestitures, spin-offs, leveraged buyouts, and other highly leveraged transactions in "Corporate Restructuring: Breakups and LBOs" by Eckbo and Thorburn (2008). In sum, the collection provides detailed references to the bulk of the empirical literature on takeovers and restructurings.

To make the collection as self-contained as possible, Volume 1 also includes two surveys on how to handle econometric issues when estimating valuation effects of voluntary corporate events. These surveys discuss sampling distributions and test statistics typically used in event studies, as well as criteria for reliability, specification, and power. Moreover, self-selection is endemic to voluntary corporate events, creating a statistical wedge between the population distribution and the distribution within a selected sample. Correcting for a potential self-selection bias is particularly relevant when drawing inferences about the determinants of event-induced abnormal stock returns from multivariate regressions, a technique used by most event studies today, including those reprinted here.

The collection focuses primarily on large-scale empirical research because it is in the empirical domain that one finds the major advances in the takeover literature over the past decade. However, to prepare the reader for key theoretical propositions, the collection also includes two comprehensive theoretical surveys on auctions and strategic bidding (in Volume 2). In addition, several of the empirical articles in Volume 2 develop their own, unique theoretical foundations for the hypotheses being tested. As a result, the careful reader of this collection will be able to acquire a good understanding of both the mainstream theoretical and empirical propositions existing in the takeover literature today.

The two volumes are organized as follows: Volume 1—Takeover Activity, Valuation Estimates, and Sources of Merger Gains—focuses on classical issues such as the existence and source of merger waves, empirical estimates of takeover announcement returns and the division of takeover gains between bidders and targets, and tests for potential sources of takeover gains (primarily involving estimation of industry wealth effects of takeovers).

Volume 2—Bidding Strategies, Financing, and Corporate Control—focuses on a range of special topics, ranging from theories and evidence on strategic bidding behavior (offer premiums, toeholds, bidder competition, winner's curse adjustments, and managerial overconfidence), issues arising when bidding for targets in bankruptcy auctions, effects of deal protection devices (termination agreements, poison pills), role of large shareholder voting in promoting takeover gains, deal financing issues (such as raising the cash used to pay for the target), managerial incentive effects of takeovers, governance spillovers from cross-border mergers, and returns to merger arbitrage.

In sum, this collection represents a "smorgasbord" of interesting topics, research methodologies, and empirical evidence. Bon appétit!

B. Espen Eckbo
Tuck School of Business at Dartmouth College
Hanover, New Hampshire
January 2010

CONTENTS OF VOLUMES

VOLUME 1: TAKEOVER ACTIVITY, VALUATION ESTIMATES, AND SOURCES OF MERGER GAINS

Part 5: Where Do Merger Gains Come From? Industry Wealth Effects of Takeovers

Part 6: Other Restructuring Activity: Breakups and Highly Leveraged Transactions

VOLUME 2: BIDDING STRATEGIES, FINANCING, AND CORPORATE CONTROL

CONTENTS OF VOLUME 1

INTRODUCTION TO CORPORATE TAKEOVERS: MODERN EMPIRICAL DEVELOPMENTS

B. ESPEN ECKBO
Tuck School of Business at Dartmouth, Hanover, New Hampshire, USA

Abstract

This two-volume collection of 44 recently published articles separate the empirical takeover literature into roughly two parts. Volume I, the first part, begins with a comprehensive overview of the empirical evidence, followed by introductions to the econometrics of event studies and various techniques for dealing with corporate self-selection issues. Volume I then delves into classic issues such as the nature of aggregate merger activity (merger waves), market valuation effects of merger announcements (the stock price performance of bidder and target firms), and the nature of the sources of merger gains in the context of industrial organization (much of it involving estimating the effects of mergers on industry competitors). Volume I ends with a review of restructuring transactions other than takeovers, such as divestitures, spin-offs, leveraged buyouts and other highly leveraged transactions.

Volume II, the second part, presents a series of specific deal-related topics—and provides reviews of both theory and associated empirical evidence. It begins with surveys of principles for optimal bidding in specific auction settings, followed by a review of actual takeover premiums and their determinants. Volume II then showcases recent empirical contributions on topics such as toehold bidding and winner's curse (does overbidding exist?), bidding for distressed targets (do bankruptcy auctions cause fire-sales?), effects of deal protection devices (do termination agreements and poison pills affect takeover premiums?), large shareholder voting on takeover outcomes (does institutional activism matter?), deal financing issues (does it matter how the bidder finances any cash payment for the target), managerial compensation effects of take-overs (what's in it for the CEO), governance spillovers from cross-border mergers (are there any?) and, finally, the returns to merger arbitrage activity (market efficiency and limits to arbitrage).

1. Volume I: Takeover activity, valuation estimates, and sources of merger gains

1.1. Surveys of takeover evidence and econometrics

Volume I begins with the survey "Corporate takeovers" by Betton et al. (2008) which covers empirical research reported by more than 500 articles. The survey covers topics ranging from the impact of statutory and regulatory restrictions on the acquisition process (disclosure and target defenses), strategic bidding behavior (preemption, markup pricing, bid jumps, toeholds, payment method choice, hostility), short- and long-run abnormal stock returns (CARs) to bidder and targets (size and division of takeover gains), to the origin and competitive effects of corporate combinations (efficiency, market power, and antitrust policy).

Importantly, the Betton et al. survey provides original empirical updates on both short- and long-horizon CARs using a sample of more than 35,000 takeover contests for US public targets from the period 1980–2005 (available on the SDC database). The main conclusions are listed in the survey's Table 15, in the form of 68 summary statements. Several of these conclusions are listed below when characterizing individual reprinted articles in the collection.[1]

The immediate stock price effect of a takeover announcement provides an important window into the economics of the corporate investment decision. Long-horizon returns also serve an important purpose as a way of examining market efficiency (conditional on some assumed return generating process). In "Econometrics of event studies," Kothari and Warner (2007) review methods for isolating the valuation impact of corporate events. The survey discusses sampling distributions and test statistics typically used in event studies, as well as criteria for reliability, specification, and power for both short- and long-horizon returns.

While much is known about the statistical properties of short-horizon event studies, the survey provides a critical review of potential pitfalls of long-horizon abnormal return estimates. Serious challenges related to model specification, skewness and cross-correlation remain. As Kothari-Warner also point out, events are likely to be associated with return-variance increases, which are equivalent to abnormal returns varying across sample securities. Misspecification induced by variance increases can cause the null hypothesis to be rejected too often unless the test statistic is adjusted to reflect the variance shift. Moreover, the authors emphasize the importance of paying close attention to specification issues for nonrandom samples of corporate events.

Self-selection is endemic to voluntary corporate events such as takeovers. The survey "Self-selection models in corporate finance" by Li and Prabhala (2007) reviews the relevant econometric issues with applications to takeovers and other corporate finance events. The statistical issue raised by self-selection is the wedge between the population distribution and the distribution within a selected sample,

---

[1] With the exception of the articles on cross-border mergers in Volume II, this two-volume collection focuses primarily on takeovers of US domiciled targets.

which renders standard linear (OLS/GLS) estimators biased and inconsistent. This issue is particularly relevant when drawing inferences about the determinants of event-induced CARs from multivariate regressions, a technique used by most event studies today. Cross-sectional regressions are typically run using samples that exclude none-vent firms. The standard solution is to include a scaled estimate of the event probability—the so-called inverse Mills ratio (the expected value of the true but unobservable regression error term)—as an additional variable in the cross-sectional regression.

Testing for the significance of the inverse Mills ratio is equivalent to testing whether the sample firms use private information when they self-select to undertake the event. Conversely, if one believes that the particular event being studied is induced by or reflect private information (market overpricing of equity, arrival of new investment projects, merger opportunities, etc.), then consistent estimation of the parameters in the cross-sectional regression requires the appropriate control for self-selection. What is appropriate generally depends on the specific application and should ideally be guided by economic theory. The Li and Prabhala survey also reviews related econometric techniques—including matching (treatment effect) models, panel data with fixed effects, and Bayesian self-selection models—with specific applications.

1.2. Aggregate takeover activity

Stock exchange delistings by US firms due to merger tend to occur in distinct waves—peaks of heavy activity followed by troughs of relatively few transactions.[2] Merger activity tends to be greatest in periods of general economic expansion. This is hardly surprising as external expansion through takeovers is just one of the available corporate growth strategies. Thus, aggregate takeover activity was relatively high in the late 1960s, throughout the 1980s, and again in the late 1990s. A majority of the mergers in the 1960s were between firms operating in unrelated industries (conglomerate mergers). The merger wave of the 1980s includes a number of mergers designed either to downsize or to specialize operations. Some of these corrected excessive conglomeration, others responded to excess capacity created by the 1970s recession (following the creation of the OPEC oil cartel), while yet others responded to the important advances in information and communication technologies. The 1980s also experienced the largest number of hostile bids in US history. The subsequent spread of strong takeover defenses in the late 1980s halted the use of hostile bids, and the late 1990s saw a "friendly" merger wave, with a primary focus on mergers with global strategic partners.

A complex set of factors are at play in any given merger wave. For example, merger waves may be affected by changes in legal and regulatory regimes, such as the stricter antitrust laws enacted in the United States in the early 1950s, and the deregulations of

---

[2] See Figure 1 in Betton et al. (2008), which shows the annual frequency distribution of delistings from 1926 through 2005.

the airline industry in 1970s and of the utility industry in 1992. The perhaps most compelling theory of merger waves rests on the technological link between firms in the same industry: a merger implementing a new technological innovation may, as news of the innovation spreads, induce follow-on takeovers among industry rivals for these to remain competitive.

In fact, there is substantial evidence of industry-clustering of mergers. In "Investigating the economic role of mergers," Andrade and Stafford (2004) find that mergers play both an expansionary and a contractionary role in industry restructurings. During the 1970s and 1980s, excess capacity tended to drive industry consolidation through merger, while peak capacity utilization triggered industry expansion through nonmerger investment (internal expansion). This phenomenon appears to have reversed itself in the 1990s, as industries with strong growth prospects, high profitability, and near capacity also experienced the most intense merger activity.[3]

The fact that merger waves are correlated with economic expansions and high stock market valuations has also spurred the development of models in which merger waves result from market overvaluation and managerial timing. The idea is that bull markets may lead bidders with overvalued stock as currency to purchase the assets of undervalued (or less overvalued) targets. In Shleifer and Vishny (2003), target managements accept overpriced bidder stock as they are assumed to have a short time horizon. In Rhodes-Kropf and Viswanathan (2004), target management accepts more bids from overvalued bidders during market valuation peaks because they overestimate synergies during these periods. In both models, the bidder gets away with selling overpriced stock.[4]

In "Valuation waves and merger activity," Rhodes-Kropf et al. (2005) find that merger waves coincide with high market-to-book (M/B) ratios.[5] If one views the M/B ratio as a proxy for market overvaluation, then this finding is consistent with the basic overvaluation arguments of Rhodes-Kropf and Viswanathan (2004) and Shleifer and Vishny (2003). In "What drives merger waves?," Harford (2005) contrasts behavioral explanations for merger waves with a neoclassical argument in which the key driver of merger waves is market liquidity. That is, under the neoclassical view, market liquidity is the fundamental driver of *both* M/B ratios and merger waves.[6]

Harford constructs a measure of aggregate capital liquidity based on interest rate (default) spreads and uses this measure in a horse race with M/B ratios in predicting industry merger waves. He finds that waves are preceded by deregulatory events and

---

[3] See also Mitchell and Mulherin (1996), Mulherin and Boone (2000), and Maksimovic and Phillips (2001).

[4] The model of Shleifer and Vishny (2003) assumes agents are irrational. In Rhodes-Kropf and Viswanathan (2004), rational (Bayesian) managers end up accepting too many all-stock merger bids when the stock market booms and too few when the market is low.

[5] See also Ang and Cheng (2006) and Dong et al. (2006).

[6] For example, Shleifer and Vishny (1992) argue that merger waves tend to occur in booms because increases in cash flows simultaneously raise fundamental values and relax financial constraints, bringing market values closer to fundamental values. Harford (1999) shows that firms that have built up large cash reserves are more prone to acquire other firms.

high capital liquidity. More importantly, he shows that the capital liquidity variable eliminates the ability of M/B ratios to predict industry merger waves. He concludes that aggregate merger waves are caused by the clustering of shock-driven industry merger waves, not by attempts to time the market.

Consistent with Hartford's conclusion, Betton et al. (2008) show that despite the market boom in the second half of the 1990s, the relative proportions of all-cash, all-stock, and mixed cash-stock offers in their sample of more than 15,000 merger bids did *not* change from the first half of the decade (Figure 7, p. 323). Also, during the 1996–2000 period with peak market valuations, the sum of all-cash and mixed cash-stock bids in mergers equals the number of all-stock merger bids. In sum, although the issue requires additional research, the existing evidence does not favor a behavioral explanation for merger waves.

Betton et al. also make the following descriptions concerning takeover activity:

- When organizing all SDC control bids into contest for US targets, there were a total of 35,727 control contests over the period 1980–2005. Of these, the initial bidder proposed a merger in 28,994 cases and made a public tender offer in another 4500 cases (the balance being 2224 controlling-block trades).
- In constant 2000 dollars, the merger deal was valued at $436 million on average (median $35 million), while the deal value of the average tender offer was $480 million (median $79 million).
- SDC provides information on the payment method for about half of the cases. Of these, 26% were all-cash deals, 37% were all-stock deals, and 37% were mixed cash-stock deals. All-cash and mixed offers have similar deal sizes, slightly above all-stock deals.
- A total of 590 initial bids are classified as "hostile" and another 435 deals are "unsolicited." Hostile bids have substantially higher than average deal values.
- In approximately 30% of all deals, the initial bidder and target operate in the same four-digit SIC industry (horizontal takeover). The two most active takeover sectors are Manufacturing, and Finance/Insurance/Real Estate.
- Two-thirds of the 35,727 initial bidders are public companies, while 37% of the targets are public. In 44% of the initial bids, a public bidder is pursuing a private target (the largest single group of takeovers), with an average deal value of $114 million (median $23 million). The total number of deals involving either a public bidder or target rose sharply in the 1990s.
- Of the 35,727 initial bidders, 11% were foreign companies (primarily Canada and the United Kingdom). Deals involving foreign bidders are relatively large.

1.3. Takeover gains

Volume I contains five recent papers significantly expanding our empirical knowledge of the size and division of takeover gains to bidder and target firms. In "Firm size and the gains from acquisitions," Moeller et al. (2004) find that, in a sample of 12,023 acquisitions by public firms from 1980 to 2001, the equally weighted abnormal announcement return is 1.1%, but acquiring-firm shareholders lose $25.2 million on average upon announcement. This disparity suggests the existence of a size effect in acquisition announcement returns. The announcement return for acquiring-firm share-holders is roughly two percentage points higher for small acquirers irrespective of the form of financing and whether the acquired firm is public or private. The size effect is robust to firm and deal characteristics, and it is not reversed over time.[7]

In "Why do private acquirers pay so little compared to public acquirers?," Bargeron et al. (2008) report that public target shareholders receive a 63% (14%) higher premium when the acquirer is a public firm rather than a private equity firm (private operating firm). The premium difference holds with the usual controls for deal and target characteristics, and it is highest when acquisitions by private bidders are compared to acquisitions by public companies with low managerial ownership. There is no significant difference between premiums paid by private equity firms and public firms when the public firms have high managerial ownership. Further, the premium paid by public bidders (not private bidders) increases with target managerial and institutional ownership. The authors note that unobservable target characteristics may be responsible for why some firms only attract the attention of private bidders or are ultimately more valuable for private equity bidders, and that further research is needed to help explain the premium difference.

In "The underpricing of private targets," Cooney et al. (2009) begin by noting that while the evidence of positive announcement returns to acquirers of private targets is pervasive and robust, explanations are sparse. They examine the relation between valuation changes of private firms and the announcement returns of their public acquirers. Using a sample of acquisitions of private firms that withdraw an initial public offering (IPO), they calculate the change in firm value from the planned IPO to the acquisition and find a positive relation between this valuation revision and acquirer announcement returns. Similar to other studies, acquirer announcement returns are positive, on average. However, positive acquirer announcement returns are mainly driven by targets that are acquired for more than their prior valuation. The authors argue that this relation is consistent with pricing effects associated with target valu-ation uncertainty as well as with behavioral biases in negotiation outcomes.

In "Gains in bank mergers: Evidence from the bond markets," Pena and Unal (2004) look at the effect of bank mergers on bondholder returns. In general, if the merger is synergistic, both bondholders and shareholders gain because firm value can increase by achieving economies of scale and scope and by eliminating less-efficient management. In nonsynergistic mergers, bondholders can still gain if the merger reduces cash flow volatility and leads to a lower risk of default.

---

[7] For early evidence on a size effect in bidder returns, see Asquith and Mullins (1983) and Eckbo and Thorburn (2000). Moeller et al. (2005) also demonstrate significant losses to relatively large acquirers.

   In the case of bank mergers there are at least two additional layers of complexity. First, the federal deposit insurer might consider the combined bank too big to fail (TBTF) as a result of the merger. This strategy allows all uninsured liabilities to have de facto insurance coverage and thereby maximizes the value of the implicit guarantees received from the government. Second, unlike nonfinancial firms, banks are subject to regulatory capital requirements. As a result, shareholders cannot simply increase leverage to make up for a merger that coinsures bondholders. Hence, even with no TBTF, bondholders could gain and shareholders could lose as bondholders expropriate some of the gains associated with the acquisition. The authors present evidence that the adjusted returns of merging banks bonds are positive and significant across premerger and announcement months. The cross-sectional evidence indicates that the primary determinants of merger-related bondholder gains are diversification gains, gains associated with achieving TBTF status, and, to a lesser degree, synergy gains. They make a similar conclusion after examining the acquiring banks credit spreads on new debt issues both before and after the merger. Moreover, the paper shows that a source of acquirer gains is lower cost of funds on postmerger debt issues.

   In "Do tender offers create value?," Bhagat et al. (2005) note that attempts to estimate the value effects of takeovers face two challenges. The first is the truncation dilemma. Given that not all takeover bids succeed, a short event window that extends only a few days past the bid announcement date estimates only a fraction of the value effects that would be brought about by a successful transaction. A long window that extends through successful completion of the transaction can capture the markets assessment of the full effect of takeover on value. However, this comes at the cost of introducing much greater noise and return benchmark errors. Adjusting for the truncation bias involves probability-weighting the announcement-induced stock returns.[8]

   The second challenge, the revelation bias, is that the bidders return on the announcement date reflects not just news about the value to be derived from combination, but also news about the stand-alone value of the bidder. To address these issues, Bhagat et al. estimate the stock markets perception of value improvements from tender offers using both conventional CARs at the time of the initial bid and two new approaches. They find that all approaches imply substantial value improvements. Furthermore, the new methods imply estimates of shareholder value improvement that are much larger than those implied by traditional methods.[9]

   Betton et al. (2008) summarize (in Table 15) some of their own large-sample evidence on bidder and target takeover gains as follows:

---

[8] See Betton and Eckbo (2000) for a first attempt to addresses this truncation bias using a structural estimation technique.

[9] To adjust for the revelation bias, Bhagat et al. extract information about value improvement from the stock returns associated with intervening events such as the announcement of a competing bid.

- The average target cumulative average CAR is positive and significant, both over the takeover preannouncement (run-up) period and the announcement period. The run-up constitutes about one-third of the total run-up plus announcement CAR. The largest target CAR occurs in all-cash offers.
- The average, value-weighted combined CAR to bidders and targets is positive and significant over both the run-up period and the announcement period.[10] For the overall sample, the sum of the combined CAR for the run-up- and announcement periods is a significant 1.79%.
- Bidder announcement period CARs average close to zero for the overall sample, with 49% of the bidders having negative CAR.[11] The combination large bidder (in the upper size quartile), payment in all-stock, and the target being a public company represent a "worst-case scenario" with average bidder announcement-period CAR of a significant −2.21%. The "best-case scenario" for the bidder is the combination of a small bidder (lower size-quartile), private target and *all-stock* as payment. This produces a significant average bidder announcement-period CAR of 6.46%.
- The major driver of negative bidder returns is not, as previously thought, the all-stock payment. Rather, the two key drivers are the target's status a public or private, and bidder size. Bidder announcement returns tend to be positive and significant when the acquirer is small and the target is a private firm, and negative for large acquirers bidding for public targets.
- Bidder size was particularly large in 1999 and 2000. These years were unusual relative to years before *and* years after. Cisco, with a (constant 2000 dollar) market capitalization of $180 billion was the dominant bidder in *both* the upper 1% and lower 1% tails of the distribution of bidder abnormal announcement returns. Removing Cisco from the sample reduces the aggregate bidder dollar wealth loss in 1999–2000 period by almost $100 billion.
- Studies of long-run CARs use either the matched-firm technique or Jensen's alpha (regression constant in an asset pricing model) to measure expected return to the merged firms in the sample. In the survey-sample of 15,298 successful takeovers completed during the period 1980–2003, long-run returns are significantly negative based on the matched-firm technique but insignificantly different from zero based on Jensen's alpha.
- The standard matched-firm procedure identifies firms that have significantly different factor loadings than the event firms—which undermines their role as "matches."
- A zero-investment portfolio strategy which is long in the merged firms and short in the matched firms fail to produce long-run CARs which are significantly different from zero, even for the sample of all-stock mergers.

---

[10] The average value-weighted sum of the announcement returns to *publicly traded* bidders and targets is also positive and significant. This confirms an important conclusion in the early survey by Jensen and Ruback (1983).

[11] Bidder announcement returns are subject to attenuation bias due to partial anticipation, and they reflect valuation impacts of factors beyond the value of the takeover per se (including revelations about bidder managerial quality and exogenous changes in industry conditions).

1.4. Sources of takeover gains

At the conclusion of their influential literature review, Jensen and Ruback (1983) admit that the sources of merger gains are "elusive." Volume I contains five papers attempting to shed light on the likely sources of merger gains. The first four of these use the methodology developed independently by Eckbo (1983) and Stillman (1983) and which combines traditional event studies in finance with models of industrial organization.

In "Horizontal mergers, collusion, and stockholder wealth," Eckbo (1983) develops and tests the hypothesis that horizontal mergers generate positive abnormal returns to stockholders of the bidder and target firms because they increase the probability of successful collusion among rival producers. Under the collusion hypothesis, *product market rivals* of the merging firms benefit from the merger since successful collusion limits output and raises product prices and/or lowers factor prices. Thus, a unique test of the collusion hypothesis is that events which increases the probability of a collusive merger (such as a merger proposal announcement) should cause a positive revaluation of the market value of the emerging firms' rivals, while subsequent events which decrease the probability of the collusive merger being consummated (such as a government challenge under antitrust laws) should reverse the positive effect (cause negative abnormal returns to the rivals).

Eckbo tests this proposition on a large sample of horizontal mergers in mining and manufacturing industries, including 55 mergers that were challenged by the government with violating antitrust laws (Section 7 of the Clayton Act). He also includes a control sample of vertical mergers taking place in the same industries (which by definition do not have horizontal anticompetitive effects). He finds that the antitrust law enforcement agencies (the US Department of Justice and the Federal Trade Commission) systematically select relatively profitable mergers for prosecution. More importantly, he finds that there is a small but positive (1.5%) industry wealth effect of the initial horizontal merger announcements. However, he also finds that rival firms receive a second *positive* market value boost when the government signals announce that it will seek to block the merger, which rejects the proposition that the mergers would have collusive effects.[12] Thus, Eckbo concludes against market power as representing the source of merger gains even for the cases where the antitrust authorities decided market power *was* a problem and that the mergers had to be stopped.[13]

The power of Eckbo's methodology to test the collusion hypothesis comes from having access to *both* probability-increasing (merger proposal) and probability-decreasing

---

[12] In Eckbo's sample, the government is successful in stopping the proposed merger in 80% of the cases it challenges.

[13] A horizontal merger *causes* a measurable increase in industry concentration. The classical market concentration doctrine holds that increases in concentration reliably increases the industry's market power and thus industry monopoly rents. Since the abnormal returns to industry rivals directly measures changes in industry rents, regressing the merger-induced rival abnormal returns on the change in industry concentration provides a powerful test of the market concentration doctrine. Eckbo (1985) and Eckbo (1992) perform this test and reject the doctrine.

(antitrust challenge) events for a given merger, *and* where the latter event is initiated by the antitrust authorities.[14] These test conditions are not available for merger samples more generally—where typically only the probability-increasing event (the merger proposal and/or the final merger agreement) is seen. Eckbo emphasizes strongly that finding a positive industry wealth effect of a probability-increasing event by itself is necessary but *not* sufficient to conclude in favor of the collusion hypothesis.

The reason for this ambiguity is that the net industry wealth effect of an efficient merger may be either positive or negative. On the one hand, scale-increasing efficient mergers tend to have a negative impact on the industry's equilibrium product price, which harms rival firms and by itself causes a negative industry wealth effect.[15] On the other hand, news of the merger may reveal positive information about the value of the resources controlled by the rival firms. That is, the merger may reveal increased demand for resources owned by other firms, causing a positive revaluation of these rivals. For example, the increased demand may lead to expectations of future merger activity, resulting in a positive "in-play" effect on rival firms from the announcement of the initial merger. In sum, the efficiency hypothesis does not restrict the abnormal returns to industry rivals.

Eckbo (1983) suggests that one should in principle be able to discriminate between the collusion and efficiency theories in single-event merger samples by examining the abnormal returns to the merging firms *corporate customers and suppliers of inputs.* For example, relative to the merger proposal announcement, corporate customers and suppliers should lose under the collusion hypothesis and gain under the efficiency hypothesis. Tests based on this notion are difficult since it is necessary to identify customers and suppliers who cannot switch their purchases/sales to other industries at a low cost (the customers/suppliers must to some extent be locked in).

The two papers "Sources of gains in horizontal mergers: Evidence from customers, suppliers, and rival firms" by Fee and Thomas (2004) and "Industry structure and horizontal takeovers: Analysis of wealth effects on rivals, suppliers, and corporate customers" by Shahrur (2005), follow Eckbo's original suggestion and expand the industry wealth effect estimation to upstream suppliers and downstream customers. They identify publicly traded suppliers and corporate customers using Compustat industry segment information. The major focus in both studies is the "buyer power" hypothesis, that is, the possibility that a horizontal merger increases the monopsony power of the combined firm over its input suppliers. In this case, the merger benefits the merging firms and (possibly) its industry rivals at the expense of upstream suppliers. Consumers benefit as well provided some of the increased monopsony rents are passed on downstream from the merging firms' industry. Both papers

---

[14] Several recent papers use the Eckbo-methodology to asses the likely anticompetitive effects of mergers reviewed under the competition laws of the European Union. See Section 6 in Betton et al. (2008) for a review.

[15] Rivals may minimize the negative product price impact by racing to adopt similar technological innovations as the merging firms—prompting industry merger waves.

conclude that the evidence is inconsistent with increased monopolistic collusion (they fail to identify a wealth loss to corporate customers), but consistent with improved efficiency and buying power of the merged firms.[16]

Eckbo (1983) also suggests that a positive industry wealth effect of horizontal merger announcements may simply reflect an increased probability that rival firms will become targets. Song and Walkling (2000) test this "in-play" effect on rival firms. An in-play effect follows naturally from the fact that rival firms uses similar production technologies and own some of the same (and possibly scarce) productive resources. A takeover may signal increased resource scarcity, causing a positive revaluation of every firm holding those resources. Song and Walkling increase the power to detect an in-play effect by focusing on cases where the merger announcements were particularly surprising ("dormant" industries with no merger announcement over the prior 12 months). The results of their study, as well as most of the earlier papers in this area, are consistent with the existence of a positive industry in-play (information) effect.[17]

Finally, in the paper, "Where do merger gains come from? Bank mergers from the perspective of insiders and outsiders," Houston et al. (2001) take the unusual approach of examining management estimates of projected cost savings and revenue enhancements to investigate the potential sources of takeover gains. They focus on large bank mergers as consolidation between banks removes geographic and product market entry restrictions—thus improving operating efficiency. The data on management projections allow identification of management's primary rationale for the acquisitions. The paper estimates the present value of the incremental earnings that management expects from the merger, and investigates the relation between these estimated gains and the change in the market value of the stock of the bidder and the target.

Houston et al. find that the primary source of management's expected merger-related gains is cost savings. Revenue enhancements are far less important as the paper's valuation of estimated revenue gains account for, on average, only 7% (median zero) of the total valuation gains implied by management's estimates. Moreover, under optimistic assumptions that incremental merger-related earnings are perpetual and grow at the inflation rate, the paper estimates that the average sample merger should increase the combined value of the bidder and target by 13%. Looking at the market's reaction to merger announcements, the paper finds that management's projected merger gains explain roughly 60% of the cross-sectional variation in the combined bidder and target stock returns. Interestingly, while valuation estimates of projected cost savings are positively related to the combined stock market returns of the bidder

---

[16] Fee and Thomas (2004) and Shahrur (2005) sample horizontal mergers. For a large-sample study of vertical mergers, with a focus on the potential for foreclosure following increased buying power, see Shenoy (2008). Eckbo (1983) samples both horizontal and vertical mergers but does not test for upstream buying power.

[17] Exceptions are Eckbo (1992), Akdogu (2009), and Becher et al. (2008) who find a negative industry wealth effect of multiindustry horizontal merger announcements in Canada, and in single-industry studies of the US telecommunications and utility firms, respectively.

and target, the valuation estimates of projected revenue increases are negatively related to these same stock market returns. Thus, the results suggest that cost savings represent the primary source of gains in the large majority of recent bank mergers and that managerial cost savings projections have significant capital market credibility.

1.5. Survey of other restructuring activity other than takeovers

Shocks to the corporate economic environment may give rise to severe organizational inefficiencies. For example, a vertically integrated firm may find that long-term contracts and/or spot market purchases of a key input have become more efficient. Or increased general capital market liquidity may have rendered internal capital markets a relatively costly divisional funding mechanism for conglomerates. High leverage may be optimal as financial innovations and expertise make it less expensive to manage financial distress. Financial innovations and general market liquidity may also render it optimal to securitize an entire division. The result is increased divisional managerial focus. In the survey "Corporate restructurings: Breakups and LBOs," Eckbo and Thorburn (2008b) refer to the transactions that implement these and other changes in asset composition, financial contracting, and ownership structure as "corporate restructurings."

The survey focuses on garden-variety restructuring procedures used to securitize and sell off part of the firm. It includes leveraged buyouts (LBOs) in which the entire firm is acquired by a financial buyer such as a buyout fund. The survey classifies corporate restructurings into two broad groups: breakups and highly leveraged transactions. Breakup transactions focus primarily on the separation of company assets and therefore include divestitures, spin-offs, equity carveouts, and tracking stock. Highly leveraged transactions involve a significant increase of debt in the firm's capital structure, either through a debt-financed special dividend in a leveraged recapitalization or in an LBO.

Corporate restructurings may be initiated by the firm's top-level management, by divisional managers, or by outside sponsors like buyout funds. Occasionally, the restructuring is defensive, arising in response to a control threat from the market for corporate control. Regardless of who initiates the transaction, the parties are seeking to improve operating efficiency, increase cash flow, and ultimately, enhance firm profitability. In breakup transactions, assets are transferred to higher value users, while highly leveraged transactions involve optimizing capital structure, improving managerial incentives and achieving tax efficiency.

The empirical evidence shows that the typical restructuring creates substantial value for shareholders, and there is evidence of improved operating performance. The value-drivers include elimination of costly cross-subsidizations characterizing internal capital markets, reduction in financing costs for subsidiaries through asset securitization and increased divisional transparency, improved (and more focused) investment programs, reduction in agency costs of free cash flow, implementation of executive compensation schemes with greater pay-performance sensitivity, and increased monitoring by lenders and LBO sponsors.

Buyouts after the turn of the century created value similar to LBOs of the 1980s. Recent developments include club deals (consortiums of LBO sponsors bidding together), fund-to-fund exits (LBO funds selling the portfolio firm to another LBO fund), a highly liquid (until mid-2007) leveraged loan market, and evidence of persistence in fund returns (perhaps because brand-sponsors borrow at better rates). Perhaps the greatest challenge to the restructuring literature is to achieve a modicum of integration of the analysis across transaction types. Another challenge is to produce precise estimates of the expected return from buyout investments in the presence of limited data on those portfolio companies that do not return to public status.

2. Volume II: Bidding strategies, financing, and corporate control

2.1. Surveys of bidding theory and takeover premiums

There is growing research interest in the details of the takeover process from the initial bid through the final contest outcome. Volume II begins with three survey articles covering the takeover bidding process: two surveys exposing optimal bidding theories—"Mergers and acquisitions: Strategic and informational issues" by Hirshleifer (1995) and "Auctions in corporate finance" by Dasgupta and Hansen (2007)—and the empirical review "Bidding strategies and takeover premiums" by Eckbo (2009).[1]

Figure 1 shows the six possible outcomes of an initial bid and their associated probabilities π_i ($i = 1, \ldots, 6$). It is useful to keep this contest tree structure in mind when thinking about theoretical bidding strategies. The time-line starts with the first bid—which may be an offer to negotiate a merger agreement or a tender offer directly to target shareholders.[2] The "contest" may be single-bid (first offer is accepted or rejected with no further observed bids) or multiple-bid (several bids and/or bid revisions are observed). The initial bidder may win, a rival bidder may win, or all bids may be rejected (no-bidder-wins).

The two surveys explain optimal bidding strategies given additional restrictions on the bidding environment. For example, as explained by Dasgupta and Hansen, auction models typically assume that the seller is a single decision maker credibly committed

[1] The latter review is also substantially contained in the discussion of strategic bidding issues found in Section 3 of Betton et al. (2008) (reprinted in Volume I of this collection).
[2] After signing a merger agreement, the target board is normally required to consider any new outside offers until target shareholders have voted to give final approval (the so-called "fiduciary out" clause). In other words, potential competition affects even signed merger agreements—thus the term "contest" to describe the takeover process also for merger proposals. In the data, the time from the initial offer to the effective takeover date averages 108 trading days (median 96) when the initial bid is a tender offer, and 71 days (median 49) for merger bids. In cases where there are more than one control bid for the target, the time from the first to the second bid averages 40 trading days (median 19).

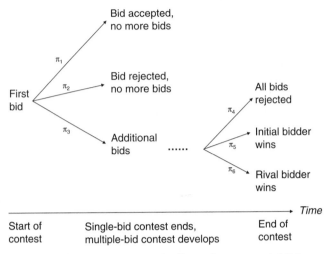

Fig. 1. Takeover contest structure, timeline, and outcome probabilities π.

to sell, and where alternative auction structures determine optimal bids and sales revenues. Hirshleifer focuses on bidding strategies when the seller consists of individual shareholders who may or may not coordinate their selling (share tendering) decisions. Lack of coordination may lead to free-rider problems (Grossman and Hart, 1980), while the existence of a large pivotal shareholder (e.g., management) may lead to issues of strategic defenses. Auction models typically imply that the probability of a successful bid (by the initial or a rival bidder) is equal to 1, while the success probability with multiple sellers and informational asymmetries among the transacting parties may be less than 1 but is assumed to be exogenously given in equilibrium.

As is apparent from the surveys, the typical theoretical settings are more restrictive than the type of contest games allowed in contest structures such as Figure 1. In particular, the "no-bidder-wins" outcome is an enigma to standard bidding theories where *some* bidder always wins.[3] In fact, despite an initial offer premium which average close to 50%,[4] the no-bidder-win outcome is surprisingly important in the data. As reviewed by Eckbo (2009), in samples exceeding 10,000 initial bids for US public targets from 1980 to 2005, the initial bidder wins the target in only two-thirds of cases. Surprisingly, the initial bidder wins *less* often when the initial bid is in the form of an invitation to negotiate a merger as opposed to a tender offer.

---

[3] Two bidding models which allow all bids to be optimally rejected by the target are Shleifer and Vishny (1986) and Giammarino and Heinkel (1986). There is also a growing auction literature assuming stochastic seller reserve prices, which allow no-bidder-wins outcomes.

[4] This premium average is measured relative to the target stock price 40 trading days prior to the initial bid.

The initial bidder is more likely to win when it has a toehold (ownership stake) in the target (Betton and Eckbo, 2000). Hostility substantially reduces the probability of winning, a rival bidder enters the contest, the rival wins the auction twice as often as the initial bidder. Moreover, the initial bidder wins less often when it is a private company, which is intuitive as it may be difficult to get shareholders of a public target to exchange their shares for nonlisted bidder shares. In sum, initiating a takeover is risky business. With the substantial resources committed to the takeover process, bidders obviously need to think strategically in order to maximize the expected value of bid initiation.

The growing empirical research on strategic bidding, some of which is reprinted in Volume II, seeks to answer a variety of questions: What determines the initial bid premium? If the initial bid is rejected, what should be the bid revision strategy (bid jump)? Do bidders fully account for the possibility of a winner's curse? Do bidders mark up the initially planned offer price in response to a run-up in the target stock price ("markup pricing")? Should the bidder acquire a toehold in the target, and is there evidence of toehold-induced (rational) overbidding in offer premiums? Do auction bids for financially distressed firms reflect a "fire-sale" discount? How does the choice of payment method affect bid premiums? How do offer premiums respond to a target defensive mechanism such as a poison pill?

Empirical tests of bidding theories are also important for the broader debate over bidder rationally and the efficiency of the market for corporate control. As discussed in Volume I, bidder CARs are typically small and often negative around takeover announcements. Roll (1986) was the first to suggest that bidder overconfidence or "hubris" may go a long way in explaining the surprisingly low bidder takeover gains. The relatively poor bidder performance remains a pervasive and puzzling phenomenon also today. Since part of the problem is one of properly estimating and interpreting bidder announcement returns, direct evidence on offer premiums and bidding behavior is of key interest in this debate.

2.2. Toeholds, winner's curse and overconfidence: do bidders behave strategically?

The substantial control premium typically observed in corporate takeovers makes a compelling case for acquiring targets hares (a toehold) in the market prior to launching a bid. Moreover, auction theory suggests that toehold bidding may yield a competitive advantage over rival bidders.[5] Nevertheless, with a sample exceeding 10,000 initial control bids for US public targets, Betton et al. (2009) show that toehold bidding has declined steadily since the early 1980s and is now surprisingly rare. At the same time, the average toehold is large when it occurs (20%), and toeholds are the norm in hostile bids.

To explain these puzzling observations, Betton et al. develop and test a two-stage takeover model where attempted merger negotiations are followed by open auction.

---

[5] If the toehold bidder loses to a rival, it gets to sell the toehold at a capital gain. If the toehold bidder wins, it needs to pay the full takeover premium on the remaining target shares only.

This formalizes the idea that merger negotiations occur in the "shadow" of an auction, and where the expected auction outcome (assuming optimal bidding behavior) affects the bargaining power of the negotiating parties. In their model, a toehold imposes a cost on target management, causing some targets to (rationally) reject merger negotiations. Optimal toeholds are therefore either zero (to avoid rejection costs) or greater than a threshold (so that toehold benefits offset rejection costs).

The toehold threshold estimate averages 9% across initial bidders, reflecting in part the bidders opportunity loss of a merger termination agreement. In the presence of market liquidity costs, a threshold of this size may well induce a broad range of bidders to select zero toehold. As predicted, the probability of toehold bidding decreases, and the toehold size increases, with the threshold estimate. The model also predicts a relatively high frequency of toehold bidding in hostile bids, as observed. Overall, these test results are consistent with rational bidder behavior with respect to the toehold decision.

In the vast majority of cases, there are no additional observed rival bids following the public announcement of the initial merger agreement. Boone and Mulherin (2007) show that the apparent lack of competition following the public announcement is somewhat deceptive as may targets invite multiple bidders to signal their interest in acquiring the target before selecting a negotiation partner. Nevertheless, given the substantial time between the signing of the merger proposal agreement, there should be ample opportunities for rival bidders to compete to break up a merger proposal which they judge to be too generous to the initial bidder.

Aktas et al. (2009) seek to determine whether acquirers in such friendly deals are truly insulated from competitive pressures. They study two countervailing influences: (1) potential but unobserved latent competition, the likelihood that rival bidders could appear, and (2) anticipated auction costs when negotiations fail. Using various proxies, they find that latent competition does increase the bid premium offered in negotiated deals, while auction costs reduce the premium as expected.

The winner's curse is a concept developed for auction settings where bidder valuations have a common component. At the extreme, every bidder has the *same* valuation for the auctioned item—a "pure" common value setting. An example would be a target where bidders are going to use the target resources simply as a financing vehicle for future investments by the bidder. Or, the change of control may allow the bidder to simply replace inefficient target management. A third example would be that the bidder is purchasing the target purely as a speculation in its future resale value. In a common-value setting, bidders receive private and noisy signals as to the true (common) value of the target. Bidding the full value of the signal would cause the bidder with the largest positive signal error to win and overpay (the "curse"). Optimal bidding takes this possibility into account by reducing the bid to the point where the expected value of the bid *conditional on winning* is nonnegative. Thus, testing for the presence of a winner's curse is equivalent to testing the hypothesis that bidders are rational (properly shave the bids).

Boone and Mulherin (2008) contrast the winner's curse hypothesis and the competitive market hypothesis as potential explanations for the observed returns to bidders in corporate takeovers. The authors posit that failing to properly adjust to the winner's curse will cause bidder returns to be inversely related to the level of competition in a given deal and to the uncertainty in the value of the target. They construct a measure of takeover competition based on the private auction process that occurs prior to the announcement of a takeover documented by Boone and Mulherin (2007). Controlling for endogeneity between bidder returns and the level of competition in takeover deals, they find that the returns to bidders are not significantly related to takeover competition. They also find that uncertainty in the value of the target does not reduce bidder returns. They infer from this that the break-even returns often observed to bidders in corporate takeovers stem not from the winner's curse but from the competitive market for targets that occurs predominantly prior to the public announcement of bids.

Malmendier and Tate (2008) ask whether CEO overconfidence helps to explain merger decisions. By definition, overconfident CEOs overestimate their ability to generate returns. As a result, they may overpay for target companies and undertake value-destroying mergers. The authors also argue that the effect of overconfidence should be strongest when the CEOs have access to internal financing (as outside financing would attract capital market monitoring in terms of the value of the deal). They test these predictions using two proxies for overconfidence: CEOs personal over-investment in their company and their press portrayal. They find that the odds of making an acquisition are 65% higher if the CEO is classified as overconfident. The effect is largest if the merger is diversifying and does not require external financing. The market reaction at merger announcement (-90 basis points) is significantly more negative than for nonoverconfident CEOs (-12 basis points). They also consider alternative interpretations including inside information, signaling, and risk tolerance. Overall, they conclude that the evidence corroborate the overconfidence explanation for mergers.

2.3. Auction bidding for bankrupt targets: do fire-sales exist?

Volume II contains four papers providing evidence on the acquisition of target firms that have filed for bankruptcy. Since bankruptcy law alters the bargaining position of the target, one expects the outcome for bidders to be different than for out-of-court acquisitions. The first two papers, Hotchkiss and Mooradian (1998) and Pulvino (1999), examine targets in Chapter 11 of the US Bankruptcy Code, where a decision to put the bankrupt firm up for sale is driven jointly by incumbent management and creditor committee votes. The final two papers, Eckbo and Thorburn (2008a, 2009), consider targets sold in the automatic auction bankruptcy system in Sweden. This code essentially eliminates the target's bargaining opportunities, and relies on bidder competition to maximize debt recovery and an efficient reallocation of the target assets.

An important research question is whether the form of a country's bankruptcy code distorts the efficient allocation of corporate resources. In particular, when introducing

Chapter 11 in 1978 lawmakers wished to give bankrupt firms ample time to restructure assets and financial claims under court protection.[6] The belief was—and still tends to be—that selling off distressed firms' assets under the time pressure of an auction will cause sales prices (and therefore debt recovery rates) to be low relative to their value in best alternative use.

Empirical evidence on this "fire-sale" hypothesis is, however, sparse. There are two issues. The first, which is addressed by the papers reprinted here, is to what extent bankruptcy auctions cause fire-sales. The second is whether the cost of a fire-sale exceeds the cost of a traditional Chapter 11 reorganization. Chapter 11 costs are significant, both because the average traditional reorganization takes close to 2 years and because personal managerial incentives may be to excessively continue economically failing firms. Over the past 10 years, we have seen a growing use of market-based mechanisms to lower the costs of Chapter 11 proceedings. These include "prepackaged" bankruptcies with a reorganization plan in place at filing, acquisition of distressed debt by "vulture" investors in order to make voting more efficient, and as studied by Hotchkiss and Mooradian (1998) voluntary sales in Chapter 11.[7]

Hotchkiss and Mooradian find that acquirers tend to be firms in the same industry as the target and to have some prior relationship with the target such as an ownership stake. Multiple bidders are not unusual indicating that the sales proceedings allow competition. They also report that the bankrupt targets in their sample on average are purchased at a 45% discount relative to prices paid for nonbankrupt targets in the same industry. However, they do not consider this as evidence of allocative inefficiency: "Although the transactions are at discount prices, the high proportion of acquirers operating in the same industry as the target, as well as the competitive bidding environment, does not support the conclusion that acquisitions in bankruptcy are sales to lower value users" (p. 243).[8] This conclusion is further supported by their finding that the postmerger cash flow performance of firms combined with bankrupt targets is better than that reported by Hotchkiss (1995) for firms emerging from Chapter 11. Hotchkiss and Mooradian also present evidence of positive and significant CARs to both bidders and bankrupt targets for the days surrounding the announcement of the acquisition.

---

[6] Chapter 11 grants the incumbent management exclusive rights within a limited time period (rolling 6 months) to propose a reorganization plan. If management fails to get creditor approval for the proposed plan, a new 6-month period may be granted, and so on.

[7] There are two ways in which a firm in Chapter 11 can sell substantially all of its assets: through a Section 363 (of the US Bankruptcy Code) sale or as part of a confirmed reorganization plan. Under a Section 363 sale, management must first obtain an offer and then notify the court, who in turn notifies creditors. The Bankruptcy Code invalidates no-shop agreements and allows creditors to retain advisors at the expense of the debtor firm to search for competing buyers. If there are several potential buyers, the court holds an auction. See Hotchkiss et al. (2008) for a broad review of empirical evidence on bankruptcy restructurings.

[8] Maksimovic and Phillips (1998) study divisional sales by firms in Chapter 11 and also conclude that buyers tend to be efficient.

Pulvino (1999) uses commercial aircraft transactions to determine whether prices obtained from asset sales are greater under US Chapter 11 reorganization than under Chapter 7 liquidation. His results indicate that prices obtained under both bankruptcy regimes are substantially lower than prices obtained by nondistressed airlines. Furthermore, there is no evidence that prices obtained by firms reorganizing under Chapter 11 are greater than those obtained by firms liquidating under Chapter 7. An analysis of aircraft sales indicates that Chapter 11 is also ineffective in limiting the number of aircraft sold at discounted prices. Pulvino's findings are interesting because they control for the industry in which the distressed sales take place. Since financial distress tends to be contagious within an industry, high-valuation industry rivals may themselves be financially constrained and unable to bid in the auction—which may be one reason for the discounted prices observed for distressed airline sales.

Eckbo and Thorburn (2008a, 2009) present the first comprehensive empirical analysis of the tendency for automatic bankruptcy auctions to induce fire-sale discounts in prices and debt recovery rates. In Sweden, filing firms are automatically turned over to a court-appointed trustee who organizes an open, cash-only auction. This mandatory auction system has an attractive simplicity. All debt claims are stayed during the auction period and the bids determine whether the firm will be continued as a going concern or liquidated piecemeal. As a result, the cross-sectional variation in auction prices is determined largely by demand-side conditions, which is ideal for the identification of fire-sale discounts.[9]

Eckbo and Thorburn (2008a) show that auction prices and debt recovery rate in *going concern sales* are unaffected by industry distress, and there is no evidence of lower prices when the buyer is an industry outsider. This conclusion holds also for cases where the buyer in the auction is a former manager/owner of the bankrupt firm (a saleback transaction), suggesting there is little scope for bypassing the discipline of the auction mechanism even if the buyer is the former target owner. The typical going concern auction attracts five interested bidders and three actual bids, which appears sufficient to counter potential fire-sale tendencies. Eckbo and Thorburn do, however, find a small (average 2%) price discount in auctions resulting in *piecemeal liquidation* of the target firm.

Eckbo and Thorburn (2009) develop the first structural test for the existence of auction overbidding, also using the context of going-concern sales of bankrupt firms in Sweden. They begin by noting that the main creditor (always a single bank) can neither bid in the auction nor refuse to sell in order to support a minimum price. Essentially, regulations try to ensure that the bank is a passive bystander to the auction process. However, Eckbo and Thorburn argue that the bank may increase its expected revenue by financing a bidder in return for a joint bid strategy. They derive the optimal coalition bid and show that it exceeds the bidder's private valuation (overbidding)

---

[9] A going-concern sale takes place by merging the assets and operations of the auctioned firm into the bidder firm, or into an empty corporate shell—much like a leveraged buyout transaction. Payment must be in cash, allowing the auction proceeds to be distributed to creditors strictly according to absolute priority.

by an amount that is increasing in the bank's ex ante debt impairment.[10] Since both the ex ante debt impairment and the final auction prices are observable quantities, the optimal coalition bid rule can be used to test for the existence of overbidding.

Eckbo and Thorburn find that bankbidder financing arrangements are common, and cross-sectional regressions show that winning bids are increasing in the bank-debt impairment as predicted. Also, while overbidding may in principle result in the coalition winning against a more efficient rival bidder, the evidence on postbankruptcy operating performance fails to support such allocative inefficiency effects. Since the fire-sale hypothesis and the overbidding hypothesis are effectively nested (flip sides of the same coin), it appears that creditor incentives help prevent fire-sales, in particular when the firm's debt is greatly impaired.

2.4. Do deal protection devices affect offer premiums?

A merger agreement is the result of negotiations between the bidder and target management teams. Merger negotiations protect the negotiating parties against opportunistic behavior. Before negotiations start, the parties sign agreements covering confidentiality, standstill, and nonsolicitation. The confidentiality agreement allows the target board to negotiate a sale of the firm without having to publicly disclose the proceedings, and it permits the target to open its books to the bidder. The standstill commits the bidder not to purchase target shares in the market during negotiations, while nonsolicitation ensures that neither the bidder nor the target tries to hire key employees away from the other firm. It is also common for the bidder to obtain tender agreements from target insiders, under which these insiders forsake the right to tender to a rival bidder.

Recent Delaware case law suggests that a merger agreement must include a "fiduciary out" clause enabling the target board to agree to a superior proposal if one is forthcoming from a third party. As a result, the target board cannot give its negotiating partner exclusionary rights to negotiate a control transfer: it must remain open to other bidders along the way. The resulting potential for bidder competition (even after the merger agreement has been signed but before the shareholder vote) has given rise to target termination agreements, starting in the mid-1980s. A termination agreement provides the bidder with a compensation in the form of a fixed fee ("breakup fee") or an option to purchase target shares at a discount ("lock-up option") should the target withdraw from the agreement.[11] As shown by the analysis in Betton et al. (2009), the

[10] It is instructive to think of the bankruptcy filing as creating an instant bank toehold equal to one when bank debt is impaired (100% bank ownership of the auctioned firm). As with toehold bidding in general (Betton et al., 2009), toeholds raise the bidder's reserve price above and beyond its private valuation—referred to as overbidding. Tests for auction overbidding based on creditor toeholds have the advantage that the toehold acquisition itself (i.e., the bankruptcy event) is exogenous to the creditor.
[11] The Delaware court views termination fees anywhere in the range of 2–5% of the transaction value as reasonable. Termination agreements sometimes allow a reduction in the breakup fee if the target strikes a competing deal within a 30/45 day time-frame. There are also cases where the deal includes a bidder termination agreement.

value of a target termination agreement may be substantial, and it may affect the initial bidder's optimal toehold strategy.

Does termination agreement affect offer premiums? Officer (2003) provides evidence on the effects of including a target termination fee in a merger contract. He tests the implications of the hypothesis that termination fees are used by self-interested target managers to deter competing bids and protect "sweetheart" deals with white knight bidders, presumably resulting in lower premiums for target shareholders. The alternative hypothesis is that target managers use termination fees to encourage bidder participation by ensuring that the bidder is compensated for the revelation of valuable private information released during merger negotiations.

Officer finds that merger deals with target termination fees involve significantly higher premiums and success rates than deals without such clauses. Furthermore, only weak support is found for the contention that termination fees deter competing bids. Overall, Officer's evidence suggests that termination fee use is at least not harmful, and is likely beneficial, to target shareholders.[12] It is worth noting that since deal protection devices such as termination agreements and toeholds are to some extent economic substitutes, it is important to control for the endogenous choice of bidder toeholds when considering premium effects of termination agreement (Betton et al., 2009).

A poison pill (also labeled "shareholder rights plan") is a permanent threat to dilute the value of a blockholder—typically defined as one holding 15% or more of the company's stock. The dilution takes place by allowing shareholders other than the blockholder to purchase (or exchange old for) new shares at half price. As this right is akin to a dividend, the pill may be adopted by the board anytime (including the day after receiving an unsolicited bid—a "morning after pill") and without shareholder vote. Since, to my knowledge, no bidder has yet triggered a pill, the perceived cost of triggering must be high, effectively forcing the would-be acquirer to negotiate with the target board and management. Should the target refuse to negotiate (appealing to the board's right to "just say no"), the only way around the pill appears to be to launch a proxy contest simultaneously with the offer. If the proxy contest succeeds, the bidder replaces the board with directors who are willing to rescind the pill. Board classification (staggered election of directors), however, prevents this strategy from working.

As summarized by Betton et al. (2008), the fraction of hostile bids (sum of unsolicited bids and bids where target is explicitly hostile) drops sharply after 1989, from more than 20% in the 1980s to less than 3% by the end of the 1990s. This drop coincides with the widespread adoption of poison pill plans by US publicly traded companies. Defenders of poison pills argue that a pill enhances shareholder wealth by improving the target's bargaining strength (conditional on receiving a bid). This argument suggests that poison pills should be associated with higher takeover premiums. However, the evidence in Comment and Schwert (1995) show that targets

---

[12] See also Bates and Lemmon (2003), an empirical evidence on termination agreements in a corporate governance context.

with poison pills receive offer premiums that are on average indistinguishable from offer premiums received by nonpill targets.[13]

What explains the surprising neutral impact of pills on observed offer premiums? Eckbo (2009) presents the following four alternative explanations:

H1: Poison pills do not convey bargaining power.
H2: Poison pills convey bargaining power and increases takeover premiums relative to what premiums would have been for the same target without a pill.
H3: Poison pills convey bargaining power which is used to benefit target management at the expense of target shareholders.
H4: Poison pills provide bargaining power, but "shadow" pills are as effective as adopted pills.

H1 maintains that pills are ineffective as a bargaining tool. For example, the bidder may believe that target board is not committed to trigger the pill. As pointed out by Schwert (2000), the definition of target "hostility" used in the literature probably captures plenty of targets that are ready to negotiate with or without the pill. Bidders that are able to look beyond the pill and determine whether negotiations are possible (based on observable target characteristic or on the bidder's own ability to persuade a hostile target management) may reach a final bargaining outcome that is largely indistinguishable from that observed in samples of ex ante "friendly" targets. This may also help explain why empirical evidence shows that the probability of receiving a bid (and ultimate bid success) is either unaffected or only slightly lower for targets with strong antitakeover defenses.[14]

H2–H4 maintain that pills convey bargaining power, but that a comparison of offer premiums in samples of firms with or without pills is difficult econometrically. For example, since pill adoptions are voluntary, they raise issues of endogeneity (H2). Controlling for self-selection is also difficult, however, because the marginal effect of a poison pill depends on the firm's entire governance system, including executive compensation (H3). Also, in order to isolate true premium effects of pills, empirical work relies on the existence of two samples, one representing "poison" and the other "placebo" effects (Comment and Schwert, 1995). This sampling procedure may simply be ineffective if as in H4 *all* firms effectively have ready access to the pill at any point in time (Coates, 2000).

Bates et al. (2008) find that board classification reduces the likelihood of receiving a takeover bid; however, the economic effect of bid deterrence on the value of the firm is quite small. Targets with classified boards appear to extract premiums equivalent to those of single-class boards. Moreover, shareholders of targets with a classified board realize bid returns that are equivalent to those of targets with a single class of directors, but receive a higher proportion of total bid surplus. Overall, the evidence in Bates et al.

---

[13] A similar result has been reported by studies, including Field and Karpoff (2002), Heron and Lie (2006), and Betton et al. (2009).
[14] Comment and Schwert (1995), Field and Karpoff (2002), Heron and Lie (2006).

is inconsistent with the conventional wisdom that board classification is an antitake-over device that facilitates managerial entrenchment.[15]

2.5. Large shareholder voting: does it improve takeover gains?

There is growing interest in the voting behavior of large shareholders—including managers and directors—in protecting their investment by influencing merger out-comes. Voting by large shareholders to approve mergers in which they hold shares in both the bidder and the target is a particularly interesting topic: these shareholders may effectively extract rents through the voting process.

Using a sample of 388 takeovers announced in the friendly environment of the 1990s, Moeller (2005) show that target shareholder control, proxied by low target chief executive officer share ownership, low fractions of inside directors, and the presence of large outside blockholders, is positively correlated with takeover premiums. Moeller concludes that targets with powerful CEOs receive lower takeover premiums.

Matvos and Ostrovsky (2008) show that institutional shareholders of acquiring companies on average do not lose money around public merger announcements, because they hold substantial stakes in the targets and make up for the losses from the acquirers with the gains from the targets. Depending on their holdings in the target, acquirer shareholders generally realize different returns from the same merger, some losing money, and others gaining. This conflict of interest is reflected in the mutual fund voting behavior: In mergers with negative acquirer announcement returns, cross-owners are significantly more likely to vote for the merger.

Greenwood and Schor (2009) begin by noting that recent work documents large positive abnormal returns when a hedge fund announces activist intentions regarding a publicly listed firm. They show that these returns are largely explained by the ability of activists to force target firms into a takeover. For a comprehensive sample of 13D filings by portfolio investors between 1993 and 2006, announcement returns and long-term abnormal returns are high for targets that are ultimately acquired, but not detectably different from zero for firms that remain independent. Firms targeted by activists are more likely than control firms to get acquired. Finally, activist investors' portfolios perform poorly during a period in which market wide takeover interest declined.

2.6. Does deal financing matter?

There is substantial theoretical work on the bidder's choice of payment method in takeovers. As reviewed by Eckbo (2009), the bidder's choice of payment method (cash

---

[15] Rose (2009) concludes that the presence of staggered boards have more of a detrimental impact of firm value when management is relatively entrenched. Also, Masulis et al. (2007) report that acquisition announcement-period stock returns are significantly lower for bidders with staggered boards, and suggest that board classification may reduce forced board turnover and quality.

vs. bidder shares) is potentially affected by factors such as corporate and personal taxes, information asymmetries between the bidder and the target (Eckbo et al., 1990; Fishman, 1989; Hansen, 1987; Myers and Majluf, 1984), capital structure and corporate control motives (Harris and Raviv, 1988; Jensen, 1986; Ross, 1977; Stulz, 1988), and behavioral issues (Rhodes-Kropf and Viswanathan, 2004; Shleifer and Vishny, 2003). Empirical evidence shows that offer premiums are greater for all-cash bids than for all-stock bids (Betton et al., 2009; Eckbo and Langohr, 1989; Franks et al., 1988; Huang and Walkling, 1987, and others), and that bidder announcement returns tend to be greater for all-cash bids than for all-stock bids (Asquith et al., 1987; Betton et al., 2009; Eckbo and Thorburn, 2000; Eckbo et al., 1990; Heron and Lie, 2004; Travlos, 1987, and others).

Much less work has been done examining the effects of the ways in which the bidder finances its cash payment to the target. Potential sources of the cash are retained earnings (financial slack), short-term debt (such as draw-down of a credit line), or issuances of debt or equity securities prior to the takeover. Integrating evidence on the cash financing is important in order to fully understand the deal financing choice, as the market reaction to the payment method conditions on this type of historical information. That is, while the market is aware of any prebid public security issues, the acquisition bid announcement possibly resolves uncertainty regarding the use of the issue proceeds. If this resolution is economically important, the source of financing for the cash portion of the bid will affect the market reaction to the takeover attempt. The collection reprints three empirical studies which touches on this issue. The empirical results indicate a prior-cash-financing-source component in acquisition announcement returns.

Bharadwaj and Shivdasani (2003) provide evidence on bank financing of 115 cash tender offers from the 1990s. Banks are found to extend financing in 70% of the tender offers and finance the entire tender offer in half of the takeovers. Bank financing of tender offers is more likely when internal cash reserves are low. Acquisitions that are entirely financed by banks are associated with large and significantly positive acquirer announcement returns. Announcement returns are also positively related to the fraction of the acquisition value financed by bank debt. The benefits of bank financing are found to be most pronounced for poorly performing acquirers and for acquirers facing substantial informational asymmetries. To explain these results, the authors suggest that bank debt performs an important certification and monitoring role for acquirers in tender offers.

Schlingemann (2004) reports that, after controlling for the form of payment, financing decisions during the year before a takeover play an important role in explaining the cross section of bidder gains. Bidder announcement period abnormal returns are positively and significantly related to the amount of ex ante equity financing. This relation is particularly strong for high Q firms. He further reports a negative and significant relation between bidder gains and free cash flow. This relation is particularly strong for firms classified as having poor investment opportunities. The amount of debt financing before a takeover announcement is not significantly related to bidder gains. Together, Schlingemann takes these findings as supportive of pecking-order theory of financing (Myers, 1984) and of the free cash flow hypothesis (Jensen, 1986).

Harford et al. (2009) use large investments such as acquisitions to examine firms' capital structure choices more generally. If firms have target capital structures, deviations from these targets should affect how bidders choose to finance acquisitions and how they adjust their capital structure following the acquisitions. They show that when a bidders leverage is over its target level, it is less likely to finance the acquisition with debt and more likely to finance the acquisition with equity. Also, they find a positive association between the merger-induced changes in target and actual leverage, and they show that bidders incorporate more than two-thirds of the change to the merged firms new target leverage. Following debt-financed acquisitions, managers actively move the firm back to its target leverage, reversing more than 75% of the acquisitions leverage effect within 5 years. Overall, the authors conclude that the results are consistent with a model of capital structure that includes a target level and adjustment costs.

2.7. Takeovers—what's in it for top executives?

Does the structure of CEO compensation packages affect the quality of takeover decisions? Or, as Lehn and Zhao (2006) puts it: "Are Bad Bidders Fired?" The presumption of the literature on optimal compensation is that a strong pay-performance sensitivity helps promote better acquisition decisions.[16] A key question is what package of capital gains, cash, and subsequent employment do target CEOs accept in exchange for relinquishing control. Another important issue is whether target CEOs sacrifice premiums paid to their own outside shareholders in return for a favorable "golden handshake." Walkling and Long (1984), Cotter and Zenner (1994), Wulf (2004), and Hartzell et al. (2004) all present evidence on acquisition-induced compensation of target firm CEOs. Hartzell et al. (2004) analyze a sample of 311 negotiated mergers between 1995 and 1997. They conclude from their evidence that "acquirers overtly pay certain CEOs to surrender managerial control over the firm's assets, or equivalently, that some CEOs 'purchase' executive jobs in the buyer by foregoing cash payments that they might otherwise have obtained" (p. 39). Also, they present some evidence indicating an inverse association between selling shareholder premia and unusual bonuses received by the target CEO as a reward to "step aside."[17]

There is evidence that target firms tend to underperform prior to becoming targets, that targets of hostile bids tend to show a prior history of value-decreasing acquisitions, and that CEO turnover increases after hostile bids. Moreover, Offenberg (2009) finds

---

[16] See, for example, Murphy (1999) and Aggarwal (2008) for comprehensive reviews of the literature on executive compensation and pay-performance sensitivity.

[17] As the authors recognize, since the study uses a sample of completed mergers only, it does not provide information on the sort of packages that other target CEOs turn down in attempted mergers that were not completed. Thus, the question of whether larger CEO packages come at the expense of target shareholders remains open.

evidence that CEOs of larger firm are more likely to be replaced following a series of poor acquisitions than CEOs of smaller firms. This indicates that the market for corporate control play a disciplinary role. On the other hand, with the spread of poison pill defense and subsequent decline of hostile takeovers after the 1980s, the market for corporate control may have become a "court of last resort"—with internal governance structures being the primary mechanism for disciplining poor managers.[18]

Lehn and Zhao (2006) show that managers who undertake value-reducing acquisitions in the period 1990–1998 face a significantly higher probability of being replaced than managers who make value-enhancing acquisitions, either by internal governance, takeovers, or bankruptcy. They also show that CEOs who cancel an acquisition after observing a reduction in their company's stock price face significantly lower replacement risk than their counterparts who proceed with value-reducing acquisitions. Among firms not subjected to takeover or bankruptcy, they find no association between a firm's governance characteristics and the probability that the CEO who make value-reducing acquisitions are replaced. Lehn and Zhao conclude that "corporate governance and the external market for corporate control generally work well in disciplining managers who pursue acquisitions to the detriment of their stockholders."

Several recent papers provide evidence on CEO compensation changes (other than turnover) following acquisition activity. Bliss and Rosen (2001) study bank mergers over the period 1985–1995, a period characterized by overcapacity and frequent mergers. Mergers are found to have a net positive effect on bidder firm CEO compensation, mainly via the effect of size on compensation. Compensation increases even if the merger causes the acquiring bank's stock price to decline (which is typical upon merger announcement). However, CEOs with more stock-based compensation are less likely to make an acquisition, suggesting that bank management are motivated by their compensation contracts.

Datta et al. (2001) study 1719 acquisitions over the period 1993–1998, and separate the acquirers into whether the equity-based compensation of their respective CEOs are above ("high") or below ("low") the median. While the market reaction to the merger announcements is insignificantly different from zero on average, it is significantly positive for bidder CEOs with high equity-based compensation and significantly negative when the equity-based compensation is low. Moreover, the compensation structure impacts the selection of target: high equity-based managers tend to seek out targets with relatively high M/B ratio (growth targets), whereas CEOs in the low incentive compensation group tend to acquire targets with low growth prospects. Thus, it appears that managers with high equity-based compensation are willing to take on riskier and more valuable acquisition projects that managers with low equity-based compensation.

---

[18] With data from 1979 through 1998, Kini et al. (2004) conclude that the corporate takeover market intercedes when internal control mechanisms are relatively weak of ineffective.

Grinstein and Hribar (2004) examine mergers and acquisitions (M&A) bonuses (typically all-cash) paid to CEOs of bidder firm after 327 large merger deals over the period 1993–1999. Bonuses are larger for larger deals. Other than size, measures of CEO "power" is the single most powerful variable explaining the cross-sectional variation in M&A bonuses. Much as in Bebchuk and Fried (2003), CEO power is measured as the CEO's ability to influence directors (and thereby the compensation decision). A CEO gains influence as a chairman of the board, as a member of the nominating committee, as the proportion of insiders on the board increases, and as board size increases.

Grinstein and Hribar find that the size and power variables explain much more of the variation in bonuses than variables capturing CEO skill, effort and performance. Moreover, the deal announcement-induced CAR is significantly lower (more negative) in the sample of CEOs with high power than with low power. Moeller (2005) also concludes that targets with powerful CEOs receive lower takeover premiums. However, Bauguess et al. (2009) present evidence that inside (managerial) ownership has a positive relation with target returns, whereas active-outside (nonmanaging director) ownership has a negative relation with target returns. They suggest that the latter effect reflects outsiders' willingness to share gains with the bidder.

Harford and Li (2007) also study how CEO pay and pay-performance sensitivity is affected by acquisitions. With a sample of 1508 mergers completed over the period 1993 and 2000, they show that bidding firm CEOs receive substantial rewards in the form of new stock and options grants following acquisitions. While a poorly performing acquisition reduces the value of the CEO's portfolio of stocks and options obtained prior to the acquisition, the new postacquisition grants more than compensate for this personal value-reduction. As a result, "CEO's pay and wealth are completely insensitive to poor postacquisition performance, but CEO's wealth remains sensitive to good postacquisition performance" (p. 919). Interestingly, they show that bidding firms with stronger boards retain the sensitivity of their CEO's compensation to poor postacquisition performance.

Harford and Li (2007) also document that compensation changes around major capital expenditures are much smaller and more sensitive to performance than those following acquisitions. That is, similarly to conclusions made by Andrade and Stafford (2004), external and internal expansion decisions are treated fundamentally differently by the board. This difference may be rooted in the greater degree of uncertainty and information asymmetry surrounding acquisitions, which may allow the CEO to demand (and receive) some degree of protection for the downside risk to her personal wealth.

There is some evidence on the role of board structure and director compensation in affecting the outcome of takeovers. Byrd and Hickman (1992) and Cotter et al. (1997) find that boards dominated by outsider directors increase value for their shareholders during an acquisition attempt. Harford (2003) document the effect of a takeover bid on target directors, both financially and in terms of its effect on the number of future board seats held by those directors. He finds that directors are rarely retained following a completed offer, and that target directors as a group hold fewer directorships after a takeover, suggesting that the target board seat is difficult to replace. Moreover, he shows that for outside directors, the direct financial impact of a completed merger is largely negative. In sum, failing as a monitor imposes a personal cost on outside directors.

Finally, Denis and Kruse (2000) examine the incidence of disciplinary events that reduce the control of current managers, and corporate restructuring among firms experiencing a large decline in operating performance during an active takeover period (1985–1988) and a less active period (1989–1992). They document a significant decline in the disciplinary events from the active to the less active period that is driven by a significant decline in disciplinary takeovers, those takeovers that result in a top executive change. Following the performance decline, however, there is a substantial amount of corporate restructuring, and a significant improvement in operating performance, during both the active and the less active takeover period. Denis and Kruse conclude that, although some managerial disciplinary events are related to overall takeover activity, the decline in takeover activity does not appear to result in fewer performance-enhancing restructurings following performance declines.

2.8. Cross-border mergers: positive governance spillover effects?

Rossi and Volpin (2004) study the determinants of M&A around the world by focusing on differences in laws and regulation across countries. They find that the volume of M&A activity is significantly larger in countries with better accounting standards and stronger shareholder protection. The probability of an all-cash bid decreases with the level of shareholder protection in the acquirer country. In cross-border deals, targets are typically from countries with poorer investor protection than their acquirers' countries, suggesting that cross-border transactions play a governance role by improving the degree of investor protection within target firms.

Martynova and Renneboog (2008) find that in cross-border acquisitions, the differences between the bidder and target corporate governance (measured by newly constructed indices capturing shareholder, minority shareholder, and creditor protection) have an important impact on the takeover returns. Their country-level corporate governance indices appear to capture well the changes in the quality of the national corporate governance regulations over the past 15 years. Their evidence suggests that when the bidder is from a country with a strong shareholder orientation (relative to the target), part of the total synergy value of the takeover result from the improvement in the governance of the target assets.

Martynova and Renneboog distinguish between complete takeovers, for which the corporate governance regulation of the bidder is imposed on the target (the positive spillover by law hypothesis), and partial takeovers, where improvements in the target corporate governance occur on voluntary basis (the spillover by control hypothesis). Their empirical analysis corroborates both spillover effects. In contrast, when the bidder is from a country with poorer shareholder protection, the negative spillover by law hypothesis states that the anticipated takeover gains will be lower as the poorer corporate governance regime of the bidder will be imposed on the target. The alternative bootstrapping hypothesis argues that poor governance bidders voluntarily bootstrap to the better-governance regime of the target. Martynova and Renneboog find some support for the bootstrapping effect.

Bris et al. (2008) also posit that cross-border mergers allow firms to alter the level of protection they provide to their investors, because target firms usually import the corporate governance system of the acquiring company by law. They construct measures of the change in investor protection induced by cross-border mergers in a sample of 7330 national industry years (spanning 39 industries in 41 countries in the period 1990–2001). They find that the Tobin's Q of an industry—including its unmerged firms—increases when firms within that industry are acquired by foreign firms coming from countries with better shareholder protection and better accounting standards. They present evidence that the transfer of corporate governance practices through cross-border mergers is Pareto improving. Firms that can adopt better practices willingly do so, and the market assigns more value to better protection.

2.9. Market efficiency and returns to merger arbitrage

After the announcement of a takeover bid, the target stock price adjusts upwards but typically still trades at a discount from the offer price. The difference between the offer price and the postannouncement market price is called the arbitrage spread. Merger arbitrage (or risk arbitrage) is a specialized investment strategy that tries to profit from this spread. Specifically, it is a bet on the likelihood that the proposed transaction closes. If the bid (or a rival bid) is successful and the target is acquired, the arbitrageur captures the price differential. If the takeover fails and the target remains independent, however, the target stock tends to fall back to prebid levels and the arbitrage position has to be closed at a loss. Since the position carries the transaction risk, it is not an arbitrage in the true (riskless) sense of the word. It is, however, designed to be neutral to subsequent market movements and to price fluctuations between the bidder and the target, would the deal succeed.

For a cash bid, a merger arbitrage position simply involves a long position in the target stock. When the acquisition is consummated, the target stock is exchanged for cash. With a positive arbitrage spread, the cash received at closing will exceed the initial investment in the target stock, hence generating a profit. In contrast, if the takeover fails and the target stock price falls, the speculative position has to be sold at a loss equal to the price decline in the target stock.

The arbitrage position in a stock-for-stock transaction is more complex, since target shareholders are offered acquirer stock as payment. Here, the arbitrage position consists of a long target stock and short acquirer stock in the same proportion as the exchange ratio. For example, with an offer of two acquirer shares for each target share, the arbitrage position is long one target share and short two acquirer shares. If the bid is subsequently revised, the arbitrage position must be adjusted to reflect the new exchange ratio. When the transaction closes, the arbitrageur receives in return for the target share the promised number of acquirer shares, which are used to cover the short position. The profit from a successful arbitrage position in a stock deal is the difference between the price of the short acquirer stock and the price of the target at the point in time when the position is established. If the bid fails, the arbitrageur will likely incur a loss from selling its target share holdings. The effect of closing out the short position in the acquirer is more uncertain: if the bidder stock falls, there may be an offsetting gain; and if the bidder stock appreciates, there may be additional losses.

Several empirical studies suggest that merger arbitrage strategies systematically generate excess risk-adjusted returns (Bhagat and Loewenstein, 1987; Jindra and Walkling, 2004; Larcker and Lys, 1987; Mitchell and Pulvino, 2001; Mitchell et al., 2004, and others). The literature proposes various explanations for the existence of these returns. One is that risk arbitrageurs may be compensated for carrying the risk of deal failure. Jensen (1986) points to three important roles played by merger arbitrageurs and for which they should be compensated: (i) they help value alternative offers; (ii) they provide risk-bearing services for investors who do not want the uncertainty associated with the outcome of the takeover offer; and (iii) they help resolve the free rider problems of small, diffuse shareholders who cannot organize to negotiate directly with competing bidders for the target. Moreover, transactions costs and other practical constraints may limit the possibilities to successfully implement an arbitrage strategy.

Hsieh and Walking (2005) examine the importance of merger arbitrageurs for the market for corporate control using a sample of 680 all-cash and all-stock takeover offers during the period 1992–1999. They find that arbitrage holdings increase in offers that are likely to be successful, and that these changes are positively correlated to the probability of bid success, bid premia, and arbitrage returns. They suggest that the former is evidence of the participation of passive arbitrageurs, whose accumulation of target stock does not affect the outcome of the deal, and the latter of the involvement of active arbitrageurs, who influence the outcome and the terms of the deal.

Baker and Savasoglu (2002) show that a diversified portfolio of risk arbitrage positions produces an abnormal return of 0.60.9% per month over the period from 1981 to 1996. They trace these profits to practical limits on risk arbitrage. In their model of risk arbitrage, arbitrageurs risk-bearing capacity is constrained by deal completion risk and the size of the position they hold. Consistent with this model, Baker and Savasoglu document that the returns to risk arbitrage increase in an ex ante measure of completion risk and target size. They also examine the influence of the general supply of arbitrage capital, measured by the total equity holdings of arbitrageurs, on arbitrage profits.

References

Aggarwal, R., 2008, "Executive Compensation and Incentives," In: B. E. Eckbo (Ed.), *Handbook of Corporate Finance: Empirical Corporate Finance*, Vol. 2, Chapter 17, Elsevier/North-Holland, Handbooks in Finance Series, pp. 497–538.

Akdogu, E., 2009, "Gaining a Competitive Edge Through Acquisitions: Evidence from the Telecommunications Industry," *Journal of Corporate Finance*, 15, 99–112.

Andrade, G. and E. Stafford, 2004, "Investigating the Economic Role of Mergers," *Journal of Corporate Finance*, 10, 1–36.

Ang, J. S. and Y. Cheng, 2006, "Direct Evidence on the Market-Driven Acquisition Theory," *Journal of Financial Research*, 29, 199–216.

Asquith, P. and D. W. Mullins, Jr., 1983, "The Impact of Initiating Dividend Payments on Shareholders Wealth," *Journal of Business*, 56, 77–96.

Asquith, P., R. Bruner and D. Mullins, 1987, "Merger Returns and the Form of Financing," *Proceedings of the Seminar on the Analysis of Securities Prices*, 34, 115–146.

Aktas, N., E. de Bodt and R. Roll, 2009, "Negotiations Under the Threat of an Auction," *Journal of Financial Economics*, forthcoming.

Baker, M. and S. Savasoglu, 2002, "Limited Arbitrage in Mergers and Acquisitions," *Journal of Financial Economics*, 64, 91–15.

Bargeron, L. L., F. P. Schlingemann, R. M. Stulz and C. Zutter, 2008, "Why Do Private Acquirers Pay So Little Compared to Public Acquirers?" *Journal of Financial Economics*, 89, 375–390.

Bates, T. H. and M. L. Lemmon, 2003, "Breaking Up is Hard to Do? An Analysis of Termination Fee Provisions and Merger Outcomes," *Journal of Financial Economics*, 69, 460–504.

Bates, T. W., D. A. Becher and M. L. Lemmon, 2008, "Board Classification and Managerial Entrenchment: Evidence from the Market for Corporate Control," *Journal of Financial Economics*, 87, 656–677.

Bauguess, S. W., S. B. Moeller, F. P. Schlingemenn and C. J. Zutter, 2009, "Ownership Structure and Target Returns," *Journal of Corporate Finance*, 15, 48–65.

Bebchuk, L. A. and J. M. Fried, 2003, "Executive Compensation as an Agency Problem," *Journal of Economic Perspectives*, 17, 71–92.

Becher, D. A, J. H. Mulherin and R. A. Walkling, 2008, "Industry Shocks and Merger Activity: An Analysis of U.S. Public Utilities," Working Paper, Drexel University.

Betton, S. and B. E. Eckbo, 2000, "Toeholds, Bid Jumps, and Expected Payoff in Takeovers," *Review of Financial Studies*, 13, 841–882.

Betton, S., B. E. Eckbo and K. S. Thorburn, 2008, "Corporate Takeovers," In: B. E. Eckbo (Ed.), *Handbook of Corporate Finance: Empirical Corporate Finance*, Vol. 2, Chapter 15, Elsevier/North-Holland, Handbooks in Finance Series, pp. 291–430.

Betton, S., B. E. Eckbo and K. S. Thorburn, 2009, "Merger Negotiations and the Toehold Puzzle," *Journal of Financial Economics*, 91, 158–178.

Bhagat, S., J. A. Brickley and U. Loewenstein, 1987, "The Pricing Effects of Interfirm Cash Tender Offers," *Journal of Finance*, 42 (4), 965–986.

Bhagat, S., M. Dong, D. Hirshleifer and R. Noah, 2005, "Do Tender Offers Create Value? New Methods and Evidence," *Journal of Financial Economics*, 76, 3–60.

Bharadwaj, A. and A. Shivdasani, 2003, "Valuation Effects of Bank Financing in Acquisitions," *Journal of Financial Economics*, 67, 113–148.

Bliss, R. T. and R. J. Rosen, 2001, "CEO Compensation and Bank Mergers," *Journal of Financial Economics*, 61, 107–138.

Boone, A. L. and J. H. Mulherin, 2007, "How Are Firms Sold?" *Journal of Finance*, 62, 847–875.

Boone, A. L. and J. H. Mulherin, 2008, "Do Auctions Induce a Winner's Curse? New Evidence from the Corporate Takeover Market," *Journal of Financial Economics*, 89, 1–19.

Bris, A., N. Brisley and C. Cabolis, 2008, "Adopting Better Corporate Governance: Evidence from Cross-Border Mergers," *Journal of Corporate Finance*, 14, 224–240.

Byrd, J. and K. Hickman, 1992, "Do Outside Directors Monitor Managers? Evidence from Tender Offer Bids," *Journal of Financial Economics*, 32, 195–222.

Coates, J. C., 2000, "Takeover Defenses in the Shadow of the Pill: A Critique of the Scientific Evidence," *Texas Law Review*, 79, 271–382.

Comment, R. and G. W. Schwert, 1995, "Poison or Placebo? Evidence on the Deterrent and Wealth Effects of Modern Antitakeover Measures," *Journal of Financial Economics*, 39, 3–43.

Cooney, J. W., T. Moeller and M. Stegemoller, 2009, "The Underpricing of Private Targets," *Journal of Financial Economics*, 93, 51–66.

Cotter, J and M Zenner, 1994, "How Managerial Wealth Affects the Tender Offer Process," *Journal of Financial Economics*, 35, 63–97.

Cotter, J., A. Shivdasani and M. Zenner, 1997, "Do Independent Directors Enhance Target Shareholder Wealth During Tender Offers?" *Journal of Financial Economics*, 43, 195–218.

Dasgupta, S. and R. G. Hansen, 2007, "Auctions in Corporate Finance," In: B. E. Eckbo (Ed.), *Handbook of Corporate Finance: Empirical Corporate Finance*, Vol. 1, Chapter 3, Elsevier/North-Holland, Handbooks in Finance Series, pp. 87–143.

Datta, S., M. Iskandar-Datt and K. Raman, 2001, "Executive Compensation and Corporate Acquisition Decisions," *Journal of Finance*, 56, 2299–2336.

Denis, D. J. and T. A. Kruse, 2000, "Managerial Discipline and Corporate Restructuring Following Performance Declines," *Journal of Financial Economics*, 55, 391–424.

Dong, M., D. Hisrshleifer, S. Richardson and S. H. Teoh, 2006, "Does Investor Misvaluation Drive the Takeover Market?" *Journal of Finance*, 61, 725–762.

Eckbo, B. E., 1983, "Horizontal Mergers, Collusion, and Stockholder Wealth," *Journal of Financial Economics*, 11, 241–272.

Eckbo, B. E., 1985, "Mergers and the Market Concentration Doctrine: Evidence from the Capital Market," *Journal of Business*, 58, 325–349.

Eckbo, B. E., 1992, "Mergers and the Value of Antitrust Deterrence," *Journal of Finance*, 47, 1005–1029.

Eckbo, B. E., 2009, "Bidding Strategies and Takeover Premiums: A Review," *Journal of Corporate Finance*, 15, 149–178.

Eckbo, B. E. and H. Langohr, 1989, "Information Disclosure, Method of Payment, and Takeover Premiums: Public and Private Tender Offers in France," *Journal of Financial Economics*, 24, 363–403.

Eckbo, B. E. and K. S. Thorburn, 2000, "Gains to Bidder Firms Revisited: Domestic and Foreign Acquisitions in Canada," *Journal of Financial and Quantitative Analysis*, 35, 1–25.

Eckbo, B. E. and K. S. Thorburn, 2008a, "Automatic Bankruptcy Auctions and Fire-Sales," *Journal of Financial Economics*, 89, 404–422.

Eckbo, B. E. and K. S. Thorburn, 2008b, "Corporate Restructuring: Breakups and LBOs," In: B. E. Eckbo (Ed.), *Handbook of Corporate Finance: Empirical Corporate Finance*, Vol. 2, Chapter 16, Elsevier/North-Holland, Handbooks in Finance Series, pp. 431–496.

Eckbo, B. E. and K. S. Thorburn, 2009, "Creditor Financing and Overbidding in Bankruptcy Auctions: Theory and Tests," *Journal of Corporate Finance*, 15, 10–29.

Eckbo, B. E., R. M. Giammarino and R. L. Heinkel, 1990, "Asymmetric Information and the Medium of Exchange in Takeovers: Theory and Tests," *Review of Financial Studies*, 3, 651–675.

Fee, C. E. and S. Thomas, 2004, "Sources of Gains in Horizontal Mergers: Evidence from Customers, Supplier, and Rival Firms," *Journal of Financial Economics*, 74, 423–460.

Field, L. C. and J. M. Karpoff, 2002, "Takeover Defenses at IPO Firms," *Journal of Finance*, 57, 1857–1889.

Fishman, M. J., 1989, "Preemptive Bidding and the Role of the Medium of Exchange in Acquisitions," *Journal of Finance*, 44, 41–57.

Franks, J. R., R. S. Harris and C. Mayer, 1988, "Means of Payment in Takeovers: Results for the U.K. and the U.S.," In: A. Auerbach (Ed.), *Corporate Takeovers*, NBER, University of Chicago Press, Chicago.

Giammarino, R. M. and R. L. Heinkel, 1986, "A Model of Dynamic Takeover Behavior," *Journal of Finance*, 41, 465–480.

Greenwood, R. and M. Schor, 2009, "Investor Activism and Takeovers," *Journal of Financial Economics*, 92, 362–375.

Grinstein, Y. and P. Hribar, 2004, "CEO Compensation and Incentives—Evidence from M&A Bonuses," *Journal of Financial Economics*, 73, 119–143.

Grossman, S. J. and O. D. Hart, 1980, "Takeover Bids, the Free-Rider Problem, and the Theory of the Corporation," *Bell Journal of Economics*, 11, 42–64.

Hansen, R. G., 1987, "A Theory for the Choice of Exchange Medium in the Market for Corporate Control," *Journal of Business*, 60, 75–95.

Harford, J, 1999, "Corporate Cash Reserves and Acquistions," *Journal of Finance*, 54 (6, December), 1969–1997.

Harford, J., 2003, "Takeover Bids and Target Directors' Incentives: The Impact of a Bid on Directors' Wealth and Board Seats," *Journal of Financial Economics*, 69, 51–83.

Harford, J., 2005, "What Drives Merger Waves?" *Journal of Financial Economics*, 77, 529–560.

Harford, J. and K. Li, 2007, "Decoupling CEO Wealth and Firm Performance: The Case of Acquiring CEOs," *Journal of Finance*, 62, 917–949.

Harford, J., S. Klasa and N. Walcott, 2009, "Do Firms Have Leverage Targets? Evidence from Acquisitions," *Journal of Financial Economics*, 93, 1–14.

Harris, M. and A. Raviv, 1988, "Corporate Control Contests and Capital Structure," *Journal of Financial Economics*, 20, 55–86.

Hartzell, J. C., E. Ofek and D. Yermack, 2004, "What's In It for Me? CEOs Whose Firms are Acquired," *Review of Financial Studies*, 17, 37–61.

Heron, R. A. and E. Lie, 2004, "A Comparison of the Motivations for and the Information Content of Different Types of Equity Offerings," *Journal of Business*, 77, 605–632.

Heron, R. A. and E. Lie, 2006, "On the Use of Poison Pill and Defensive Payouts by Takeover Targets," *Journal of Business*, 79, 1783–1807.

Hirshleifer, D., 1995, "Mergers and Acquisitions: Strategic and Informational Issues," In: R. A. Jarrow, V. Maksimovic and W. T. Ziemba (Eds.), *Finance, Vol. 9 of Handbooks in Operation Research and Management Science*, Chapter 26, North-Holland, pp. 839–885.

Hotchkiss, E. S., 1995, "Post-Bankruptcy Performance and Management Turnover," *Journal of Finance*, 50, 3–21.

Hotchkiss, E. S. and R. M. Mooradian, 1998, "Acquisitions as a Means of Restructuring Firms in Chapter 11," *Journal of Financial Intermediation*, 7, 240–262.

Hotchkiss, E. S., K. John, R. Mooradian and K. S. Thorburn, 2008, "Bankruptcy and the Resolution of Financial Distress," In: B. E. Eckbo (Ed.), *Handbook of Corporate Finance: Empirical Corporate Finance*, Vol. 2, Chapter 14, Elsevier/North-Holland, Handbooks in Finance Series, pp. 235–289.

Houston, J., C. James and M. Ryngaert, 2001, "Where Do Merger Gains Come from? Bank Mergers from the Perspective of Insiders and Outsiders," *Journal of Financial Economics*, 60, (2/3, May/June), 285–331.

Hsieh, J. and R. A. Walking, 2005, "Determinants and Implications of Arbitrage Holdings in Acquisitions," *Journal of Financial Economics*, 77, 605–648.

Huang, Y.-S. and R. A. Walkling, 1987, "Abnormal Returns Associated with Acquisition Announcements: Payment Method, Acquisition Form, and Managerial Resistance," *Journal of Financial Economics*, 19, 329–349.

Jensen, M. C., 1986, "Agency Costs of Free Cash Flow, Corporate Finance, and Takeovers," *American Economic Review*, 76, 323–329.

Jensen, M. C. and R. S. Ruback, 1983, "The Market for Corporate Control," *Journal of Financial Economics*, 11, 5–50.

Jindra, J. and R. A. Walkling, 2004, "Speculation Spreads and the Market Pricing of Proposed Acquisitions," *Journal of Corporate Finance*, 10, 495–526.

Kini, O., W. Kracaw and S. Mian, 2004, "The Nature and Discipline by Corporate Takeovers," *Journal of Finance*, 59, 1511–1552.

Kothari, S. P. and J. B. Warner, 2007, "Econometrics of Event Studies," In: B. E. Eckbo (Ed.), *Handbook of Corporate Finance: Empirical Corporate Finance*, Vol. 1, Chapter 1, Elsevier/North-Holland, Handbooks in Finance Series, pp. 3–36.

Larcker, D. F. and T. Lys, 1987, "An Empirical Analysis of the Incentives to Engage in Costly Information Acquisition: The Case of Risk Arbitrage," *Journal of Financial Economics*, 18, 111–126.

Lehn, K. and M. Zhao, 2006, "CEO Turnover After Acquisitions: Are Bad Bidders Fired?" *Journal of Finance*, 61, 1759–1811.

Li, K. and N. R. Prabhala, 2007, "Self-Selection Models in Corporate Finance," In: B. E. Eckbo (Ed.), *Handbook of Corporate Finance: Empirical Corporate Finance*, Vol. 1, Chapter 2, Elsevier/North-Holland, Handbooks in Finance Series, pp. 37–86.

Maksimovic, V. and G. Phillips, 1998, "Asset Efficiency and Reallocation Decisions of Bankrupt Firms," *Journal of Finance*, 53, 1495–1532.

Maksimovic, V. and G. Phillips, 2001, "The Market for Corporate Assets: Who Engages in Mergers and Asset Sales and Are There Efficiency Gains?" *Journal of Finance*, 56, 2019–2065.

Malmendier, U. and G. Tate, 2008, "Who Makes Acquisitions? CEO Overconfidence and the Market's Reaction," *Journal of Financial Economics*, 89, 20–43.

Martynova, M. and L. Renneboog, 2008, "Spillover of Corporate Governance Standards as a Takeover Synergy in Cross-Border Mergers and Acquisitions," *Journal of Corporate Finance*, 74, 200–223.

Masulis, R. W., C. Wand and F. Xie, 2007, "Corporate Governance and Acquirer Returns," *Journal of Finance*, 62, 1851–1889.

Matvos, G. and M. Ostrovsky, 2008, "Cross-Ownership, Returns, and Voting in Mergers," *Journal of Financial Economics*, 89, 391–403.

Mitchell, M. and J. H. Mulherin, 1996, "The Impact of Industry Shocks on Takeover and Restructuring Activity," *Journal of Financial Economics*, 41, 193–229.

Mitchell, M. and T. Pulvino, 2001, "Characteristics of Risk and Return in Risk Arbitrage," *Journal of Finance*, 56 (6), 2135–2175.

Mitchell, M., T. Pulvino and E. Stafford, 2004, "Price Pressure Around Mergers," *Journal of Finance*, 59 (1), 31–63.

Moeller, T., 2005, "Let's Make a Deal! How Shareholders Control Impacts Merger Payoff," *Journal of Financial Economics*, 76, 167–190.

Moeller, S. B., F. P. Schlingemann and R. M. Stulz, 2004, "Firm Size and the Gains from Acquisitions," *Journal of Financial Economics*, 73, 201–228.

Moeller, S. B., F. P. Schlingemann and R. M. Stulz, 2005, "Wealth Destruction on a Massive Scale? A Study of Acquiring Firm Returns in the Recent Merger Wave," *Journal of Finance*, 60, 757–782.

Mulherin, J. H. and A. L. Boone, 2000, "Comparing Acquisitions and Divestitures," *Journal of Corporate Finance*, 6, 117–139.

Murphy, K. J., 1999, "Executive Compensation," In: O. Ashenfelter and D. Card (Eds.), *Handbook of Labor Economics, Vol. 3b of Handbook of Labor Economics*, Chapter 38, Elsevier/North-Holland, pp. 2485–2563.

Myers, S. C., 1984, "The Capital Structure Puzzle," *Journal of Finance*, 39, 575–592.

Myers, S. C. and N. S. Majluf, 1984, "Corporate Financing and Investment Decisions When Firms Have Information That Investors Do Not Have," *Journal of Financial Economics*, 13, 187–221.

Offenberg, D., 2009, "Firm Size and the Effectiveness of the Market for Corporate Control," *Journal of Corporate Finance*, 15, 66–79.

Officer, M. S., 2003, "Termination Fees in Mergers and Acquisitions," *Journal of Financial Economics*, 69, 431–467.

Pena, M. F. and H. Unal, 2004, "Gains in Bank Mergers: Evidence from the Bond Markets," *Journal of Financial Economics*, 74, 149–179.

Pulvino, T., 1999, "Effects of Bankruptcy Court Protection on Asset Sales," *Journal of Financial Economics*, 52, 151–186.

Rhodes-Kropf, M. and S. Viswanathan, 2004, "Market Valuation and Merger Waves," *Journal of Finance*, 59, 2685–2718.

Rhodes-Kropf, M., D. T. Robinson and S. Viswanathan, 2005, "Valuation Waves and Merger Activity: The Empirical Evidence," *Journal of Financial Economics*, 77, 561–603.

Roll, R., 1986, "The Hubris Hypothesis of Corporate Takeovers," *Journal of Business*, 59, 437–467.

Rose, M. J., 2009, "Heterogeneous Impacts of Staggered Boards by Ownership Concentration," *Journal of Corporate Finance*, 15, 113–128.

Ross, S., 1977, "The Determination of Financial Structure: The Incentive Signalling Approach," *Bell Journal of Economics*, 8, 23–40.

Rossi, S. and P. F. Volpin, 2004, "Cross-country Determinants of Mergers and Acquisitions," *Journal of Financial Economics*, 74, 277–304.

Schlingemann, F. P., 2004, "Financing Decisions and Bidder Gains," *Journal of Corporate Finance*, 10, 683–701.

Schwert, G. W., 2000, "Hostility in Takeovers: In the Eyes of the Beholder?" *Journal of Finance*, 55, 2599–2640.

Shahrur, H., 2005, "Industry Structure and Horizontal Takeovers: Analysis of Wealth Effects on Rivals, Suppliers, and Corporate Customers," *Journal of Financial Economics*, 76, 61–98.

Shenoy, J., 2008, "An Examination of the Efficiency, Foreclsore, and Collusion Rationales for Vertical Takeovers," Working Paper, Georgia State University.

Shleifer, A. and R. W. Vishny, 1986, "Large Shareholders and Corporate Control," *Journal of Political Economy*, 94, 461–488.

Shleifer, A. and R. W. Vishny, 1992, "Liquidation Values and Debt Capacity: A Market Equilibrium Approach," *Journal of Finance*, 47, 1343–1366.

Shleifer, A. and R. W. Vishny, 2003, "Stock Market Driven Acquisitions," *Journal of Financial Economics*, 70, 295–311.

Song, M. H. and R. A. Walkling, 2000, "Abnormal Returns to Rivals of Acquisition Targets: A Test of the Acquisition Probability Hypothesis," *Journal of Financial Economics*, 55, 143–172.

Stillman, R., 1983, "Examining Antitrust Policy Toward Horizontal Mergers," *Journal of Financial Economics*, 11, 225–240.

Stulz, R., 1988, "Managerial Control of Voting Rights: Financing Policies and the Market for Corporate Control," *Journal of Financial Economics*, 20, 25–54.

Travlos, N. G., 1987, "Corporate Takeover Bids, Method of Payment, and Bidding Firms' Stock Returns," *Journal of Finance*, 42, 943–963.

Walkling, R. A. and M. S. Long, 1984, "Agency Theory, Managerial Welfare, and Takeover Bid Resistance," *RAND Journal of Economics*, xx, 54–68.

Wulf, J., 2004, "Do CEOs in Mergers Trade Power for Premium? Evidence from Mergers of Equals," *Journal of Law, Economics and Organization*, 20, 60–101.

PART 1

LITERATURE REVIEW AND EMPIRICAL UPDATES

Chapter 1

CORPORATE TAKEOVERS[*]

SANDRA BETTON

John Molson School of Business, Concordia University

B. ESPEN ECKBO

Tuck School of Business, Dartmouth College

KARIN S. THORBURN

Tuck School of Business, Dartmouth College

Contents

[*] Surveying the vast area of corporate takeovers is a daunting task, and we have undoubtedly missed many interesting contributions. We apologize to those who feel their research has been left out or improperly characterized, and welcome reactions and comments. Some of the material in Section 3 is also found in Eckbo (2009).

This article originally appeared in B. E. Eckbo (ed.), *Handbook of Corporate Finance: Empirical Corporate Finance*, Vol. 2, Ch. 15, pp. 291–430 (2008).
Corporate Takeovers, Volume 1
Edited by B. Espen Eckbo
Copyright © 2007 Elsevier B.V. All rights reserved.
DOI: 10.1016/B978-0-12-381983-3.00001-0

Abstract

This chapter surveys the recent empirical literature and adds to the evidence on takeover bids for US targets, 1980–2005. The availability of machine readable transaction databases have allowed empirical tests based on unprecedented sample sizes and detail. We review both aggregate takeover activity and the takeover process itself as it evolves from the initial bid through the final contest outcome. The evidence includes determinants of strategic choices such as the takeover method (merger vs. tender offer), the size of opening bids and bid jumps, the payment method, toehold acquisition, the response to target defensive tactics, and regulatory intervention (antitrust), and it offers links to executive compensation. The data provides fertile grounds for tests of everything ranging from signaling theories under asymmetric information to strategic competition in product markets and to issues of agency and control. The evidence is supportive of neoclassical merger theories. For example, regulatory and technological changes, and shocks to aggregate liquidity, appear to drive out market-to-book ratios as fundamental drivers of merger waves. Despite the market boom in the second half of the 1990s, the proportion of all-stock offers in more than 13,000 merger bids did not change from the first half of the decade. While some bidders experience large losses (particularly in the years 1999 and 2000), combined value-weighted announcement-period returns to bidders and targets are significantly positive on average. Long-run posttakeover abnormal stock returns are not significantly different from zero when using a performance measure that replicates a feasible portfolio trading strategy. There are unresolved econometric issues of endogeneity and self-selection.

Keywords

takeover, merger, tender offer, auction, offer premium, bidder gains, toeholds, markups, hostility, executive compensation, arbitrage, announcement return, long-run performance, monopoly, antitrust

JEL classification: G34

1. Introduction

Few economic phenomena attract as much public attention and empirical research as the various forms of transactions in what Manne (1965) dubbed "the market for corporate control." Corporate takeovers are among the largest investments that a company ever will undertake, thus providing a unique window into the value implications of important managerial decisions and bid strategies, and into the complex set of contractual devices and procedures that have evolved to enable the deals to go through. Empirical research in this area has focused on a wide range of topics including the impact of statutory and regulatory restrictions on the acquisition process (disclosure and target defenses), strategic bidding behavior (preemption, markup pricing, bid jumps, toeholds, payment method choice, hostility), short- and long-run abnormal stock returns to bidders and targets (size and division of takeover gains), and the origin and competitive effects of corporate combinations (efficiency, market power, and antitrust policy). In this survey, we review empirical research on each of these and related topics.

The structure of our survey differs from most earlier empirical reviews, where the focus tends to be on the final bid in completed takeovers.[1] We follow the approach begun by Betton and Eckbo (2000) and examine the entire takeover process as it evolves from the first bid through bid revision(s) and toward the final outcome (success or failure). This more detailed focus on the takeover process is also found in more recent publications.[2] We provide new empirical updates in some areas, using takeovers found in the Thomson Financial SDC database for the period 1980–2005. One limitation of the survey is that we do not discuss the general interplay between the market for corporate control, ownership structure, and corporate governance (with the exception of hostile bids).[3] We also limit the review to empirical studies of takeovers of US target firms.[4] Takeovers by financial buyers such as leveraged buyouts (LBOs) are surveyed in Eckbo and Thorburn (2008a).

Throughout, we use the term *takeover* generically for any acquisition of corporate control through the purchase of the voting stock of the target firm, regardless of whether the bid is in the form of a merger agreement or a tender offer. Moreover, in our vernacular, the first observed bid for a specific target starts a takeover "contest" whether or not subsequent bids actually materialize. All initial bids start a contest in the sense of attracting potential competition from rival bidders and/or incumbent target management. This is true even after signing a merger agreement as director fiduciary

---

[1] Jensen and Ruback (1983), Jarrell et al. (1988), Eckbo (1988), Andrade et al. (2001), and Martynova and Renneboog (2005, 2007).

[2] Bhagat et al. (2005), Boone and Mulherin (2007b), and Betton et al. (2009). See also the survey by Burkart and Panunzi (2008).

[3] Research on corporate ownership structure, managerial private benefits of control, shareholder activism and voting, etc. is surveyed in Becht et al. (2003), Dyck and Zingales (2004), and Adams and Ferreira (2007).

[4] See Martynova and Renneboog (2006) for the European takeover market.

duties require the target board to evaluate competing offers all the way until target shareholders have voted to accept the agreement (the fiduciary out). Also, we know from the data that a friendly merger negotiation is not a guarantee against the risk of turning the takeover process into an open auction for the target. The contest perspective helps us understand why initially friendly merger bids are sometimes followed by tender offers and vice versa, why we sometimes observe bid revisions even in the absence of rival bidders, why target hostility emerges even when the initial bidder appears to be friendly, and why the auction for the target sometimes fails altogether (no bidder wins).

We begin in Section 2, "Takeover activity," with a brief discussion of takeover waves, followed by a detailed description of the initial bids in an unprecedented sample consisting of more than 35,000 takeover contests for US public targets over the period 1980–2005. The description includes initial deal values, degree of actual competition (single-bid versus multiple-bid contests), success rates, the deal form (merger versus tender offer), payment method (cash, stock, or a mix), target attitude (hostile vs. neutral or friendly), product market connection (horizontal vs. nonhorizontal), public versus private status of the bidder and the target, time to second bid, and total contest duration. We also characterize the actual institutional environment in which firms are sold, including rules governing tender offers and various contractual innovations designed to support merger negotiations. Moreover, this section comments on the determinants of the choice between merger and tender offer, and it discusses the impact of mandatory disclosure rules on premiums in tender offers.

We then move to Section 3, "Bidding strategies." In theory, a complex set of factors determine the design of optimal bids.[5] These include auction design, the nature of bidder valuations, the private information environment, target ownership structure, and bidding costs. A key empirical challenge is to establish whether there is evidence of strategic bidding and/or signaling effects in the data. As the first mover in the takeover game, the initial bidder is in a unique position, so strategic bidding behavior is likely to be most evident in the first bid. Thus, our empirical analysis is structured around the actions of the first bidder making a control-offer for the target.

We begin Section 3 with a brief description of the classical free-rider model of Grossman and Hart (1980b) and of the standard auction setup in models with a single seller. This helps frame some of the subsequent empirical test results. We then review empirical work on strategic decisions, including the initial bidder's choice between merger and tender offer, the payment method, prebid acquisition of target shares in the market (toehold bidding), markup pricing following a prebid target stock price runup, takeover defenses, and acquisitions of formally bankrupt targets. This section focuses on how the various actions affect the initial and final offer premium.

---

[5] For surveys of takeover theories, see Spatt (1989), Hirshleifer (1995), Burkart and Panunzi (2008), and Dasguptha and Hansen (2007).

8

S. Betton et al.

In the first part of Section 4, "Takeover gains," we discuss estimates of the announcement effect of takeovers on the wealth of bidder and target shareholders. In their review of the empirical evidence from the 1960s and 1970s, Jensen and Ruback (1983) conclude that the average sum of the deal-related stock market gains to bidders and targets is significantly positive. Subsequent surveys have also made this conclusion (Andrade et al., 2001; Jarrell et al., 1988). On the other hand, as pointed out by Roll (1986) and strongly emphasized in Moeller et al. (2004), bidder deal-related abnormal returns are often negative. Drawing on Betton et al. (2008c), we show that the value-weighted sum of announcement-induced 3-day abnormal stock return to bidders and targets is significantly positive. This conclusion holds for the entire sample period 1980–2005 as well as for each of the 5-year subperiods. We also discuss the large bidder dollar losses from the period 1998–2001 that are the central focus of Moeller et al. (2004).

In the second part of Section 4, we review and update estimates of abnormal stock returns to merged firms over the 5-year period following successful completion of the takeover. We show that postmerger performance is on average negative if one benchmarks the returns with the returns to nonmerging firms matched on size and book-to-market (B/M) ratio. However, the abnormal performance is insignificantly different from zero when using standard asset pricing benchmarks. These conflicting inferences concerning long-run performance produced by the matched-firm technique and the "Jensen's alpha" (regression) procedure is reminiscent of the debate in the literature on security offerings.[6]

In Section 5, "Bondholders, executives, and arbitrageurs," we review empirical studies of the wealth implications of mergers for bondholders, for bidder and target executives and directors, and for arbitrageurs. Issues for bondholders include the potential for a wealth transfer from stockholders to bondholders as a result of the coinsurance effect of takeovers, and protection against event-risk. For executives, a key issue is the disciplinary role of the market for corporate control, and whether undertaking value-decreasing takeovers is costly in terms of increased turnover and/or reduced compensation. Merger (risk) arbitrage is an investment strategy that tries to profit from the spread between the offer price and the target stock price while the offer is outstanding. It is essentially a bet on the likelihood that the proposed transaction closes. Research documents the determinants of the arbitrage spreads, trading volumes, the role of transaction costs in establishing these positions, and the returns to arbitrage activity.

Finally, in Section 6, "Takeovers, competition, and antitrust," we broaden the focus to the industry of the bidder and target firms. The key empirical issue centers on the extent to which mergers are driven by opportunities for creating market power. While the potential for market power is most obvious for horizontal combinations (as recognized by the antitrust authorities), vertical mergers may generate buying power

[6] See the reviews by Ritter (2003) and Eckbo (2007).

vis-à-vis suppliers. We review empirical tests employing estimates of abnormal stock returns to the industry rivals of the merging firms. These estimates show that mergers tend to cause a wealth effect throughout the industry of the target firm. One consistent interpretation is that synergy gains generated by takeovers represent quasi-rents from scarce resources owned throughout the target industry. The alternative hypothesis—that the industry wealth effect represents the present value of monopoly rents from collusive behavior—is consistently rejected by the empirical studies. We end this section with a brief discussion of implications for antitrust policy.

The survey concludes in Section 7 with a summary of the key findings and some directions for future research.

2. Takeover activity

2.1. Merger waves

A merger wave is a clustering in time of successful takeover bids at the industry- or economy-wide level. This is shown in Figure 1 for US publicly traded firms over the period 1926–2006. The figure plots the annual fraction of all firms on the University of Chicago's Center for Research in Security Prices (CRSP) database in January of each year which delists from the stock exchange due to merger during the year. Looking back, aggregate takeover activity appears to occur in distinct waves—peaks of heavy activity followed by troughs of relatively few transactions.

Merger activity tends to be greatest in periods of general economic expansion. This is hardly surprising as external expansion through takeovers is just one of the available corporate growth strategies. As seen in Figure 1, aggregate takeover activity was relatively high in the late 1960s, throughout the 1980s, and again in the late 1990s. These waves are typically labeled the conglomerate merger wave of the 1960s, the refocusing wave of the 1980s, and the global wave or strategic merger wave of the 1990s.[7]

These labels indicate the character of the typical merger within the wave. Thus, a majority of the mergers in the 1960s were between firms operating in unrelated industries (conglomerate mergers). It is possible that the internal capital market created through conglomerate merger may have reduced financing costs for unrelated corporate entities.[8] On the other hand, since conglomerates tend to reduce (diversify) the risk of managerial human capital and to create "business empires" perhaps valued excessively by CEOs, the conglomerate wave may also reflect an agency problem.

---

[7] The merger wave of the late 1890s and early 1900s (not shown in Figure 1) has been referred to as the "Great merger wave" (O'Brien, 1988) or the monopolization wave (Stigler, 1950).

[8] Hubbard and Palia (1999) and Maksimovic and Phillips (2002). Maksimovic and Phillips (2007) reviews internal capital markets, while Eckbo and Thorburn (2008a) reviews breakup transactions that may follow excessive conglomeration.

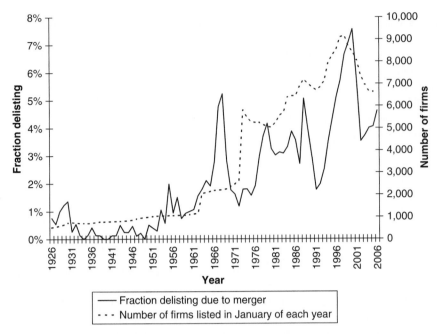

Fig. 1. Annual fraction of all publicly traded (CRSP) firms in January of each year which de lists due to merger during the year, 1926–2006.

The agency view is strengthened by the fact that executive compensation showed little sensitivity to firm performance at the time (Jensen and Murphy, 1990). Thus, value reducing diversifying mergers may have had little consequence for CEOs, leading to excessive conglomeration. However, estimates of abnormal stock returns around the conglomerate takeovers of the 1960s do not indicate that these investments were on average detrimental to shareholder wealth.[9]

The merger wave of the 1980s includes a number of mergers designed either to downsize or to specialize operations. Some of these corrected excessive conglomeration, others responded to excess capacity created by the 1970s recession (following the creation of the OPEC oil cartel), while yet others responded to the important advances in information and communication technologies (Jensen, 1986, 1993). The 1980s also experienced the largest number of hostile bids in US history. The subsequent spread of strong takeover defenses in the late 1980s halted the use of hostile bids, and the late 1990s saw a "friendly" merger wave, with a primary focus on mergers with global strategic partners.

A complex set of factors are at play in any given merger wave. For example, merger waves may be affected by changes in legal and regulatory regimes. Shleifer and

[9] Loderer and Martin (1990), Matsusaka (1993), and Akbulut and Matsusaka (2003).

Vishny (1991) suggest that the demand for conglomerate mergers in the 1960s may have been triggered by the stricter antitrust laws enacted in the early 1950s.[10] While this may have had an effect in the United States, it is interesting that countries with lax antitrust laws (Canada, Germany, and France) also experienced diversification waves in the 1960s (Matsusaka, 1996). Industry-specific deregulations may also create merger waves, such as deregulations of the airline industry in 1970s (Slovin et al., 1991; Spiller, 1983) and of the utility industry in 1992 (Becher et al., 2008; Jovanovic and Rousseau, 2004).

The perhaps most compelling theory of merger waves rests on the technological link between firms in the same industry. A merger implementing a new technological innovation may, as news of the innovation spreads, induce follow-on takeovers among industry rivals for these to remain competitive. This argument goes back at least to Coase (1937), who suggests that scale-increasing technological change is an important driver of merger activity. Jensen (1993) draws parallels between merger activity and the technological changes driving the great industrial revolutions of the nineteenth and twentieth centuries. Gort (1969) and Jovanovic and Rousseau (2002) use the related-technology notion to build theories of resource reallocations based on valuation discrepancies and Tobin's Q. Rhodes-Kropf and Robinson (2008) propose a search theory where bidders and targets match up based on the degree of complementarity of their resources.

There is substantial evidence of industry-clustering of mergers.[11] Andrade and Stafford (2004) find that mergers play both an expansionary and a contractionary role in industry restructurings. During the 1970s and 1980s, excess capacity tended to drive industry consolidation through merger, while peak capacity utilization triggered industry expansion through nonmerger investment (internal expansion). This phenomenon appears to have reversed itself in the 1990s, as industries with strong growth prospects, high profitability, and near capacity also experienced the most intense merger activity. Maksimovic and Phillips (2001) use performance improvements at the plant level to support the neoclassical reallocation theory of merger waves. Maksimovic et al. (2008) show that, for mergers in manufacturing industries, the acquirer on average closes or sells about half of the target firm's plants. Moreover, a simple neoclassical model of production helps predict the choice of which target plants to sell/close. The plants that are kept are often restructured, resulting in productivity increases. Servaes and Tamayo (2007) find that industry peers respond by financing and investment policies when another firm in the industry is the subject of a hostile takeover attempt, suggesting that firms in the same industry are linked by both technology and resource complementarities.

---

[10] One important antitrust development was the 1950 Celler-Kefauver amendment of the 1914 Clayton Act. See Section 6.

[11] Mitchell and Mulherin (1996), Mulherin and Boone (2000), Andrade, Mitchell, and Stafford (2001), Maksimovic and Phillips (2001), Andrade and Stafford (2004), and Harford (2005).

The fact that merger waves are correlated with economic expansions and high stock market valuations has also spurred the development of models in which merger waves result from market overvaluation and managerial timing. The idea is that bull markets may lead bidders with overvalued stock as currency to purchase the assets of under-valued (or less overvalued) targets. In Shleifer and Vishny (2003), target managements accept overpriced bidder stock as they are assumed to have a short time horizon. In Rhodes-Kropf and Viswanathan (2004), target management accepts more bids from overvalued bidders during market valuation peaks because they overestimate synergies during these periods. In both models, the bidder gets away with selling overpriced stock.

Eckbo et al. (1990) present a rational expectations model of the payment method in takeovers with two-sided information asymmetry (neither the bidder nor the target knows the true value of the shares of the other), in which the fraction of the deal paid in cash signals the bidder's true value. In equilibrium, the target receives correctly priced bidder stock as part of the payment. Their analysis suggests that the pooling equilibrium proposed by Shleifer and Vishny (2003) is sensitive to the possibility of mixed offers. As shown in Figure 7 below, mixed offers represent a substantial portion of all take-overs: during the period 1980 through 2005, there were nearly as many mixed cash-stock offers as there were all-stock bids. Moreover, despite the market boom in the second half of the 1990s, the relative proportions of all-cash, all-stock, and mixed cash-stock offers in more than 15,000 merger bids did not change from the first half of the decade. Also, during the 1996–2000 period with peak market valuations, the sum of all-cash and mixed cash-stock bids in mergers equals the number of all-stock merger bids.

Rhodes-Kropf et al. (2005), Ang and Cheng (2006), and Dong et al. (2006) find that merger waves coincide with high market-to-book (M/B) ratios. One argument is that the M/B ratio is a reliable proxy for market overvaluation and that investor misvaluations tend to drive merger waves. High market valuations may be a fundamental driver of merger waves as bidders attempt to sell overpriced stock to targets (and succeed). Rhodes-Kropf and Viswanathan (2004) present an interesting model in which *rational* (Bayesian) managers accept too many all-stock merger bids when the stock market booms and too few when the market is low. They assume that the market's pricing error has two components, one economy-wide and another that is firm-specific. When receiv-ing a bid, the target attempts to filter out the market-wide error component. The Bayesian update puts some weight on there being high synergies in the merger, so when the market-wide overvaluation is high, the target is more likely to accept the offer. In other words, bids tend to look better in the eyes of the target when the market is overvalued.

Harford (2005) contrasts these predictions with a neoclassical argument in which the driver of merger waves is market liquidity. That is, under the neoclassical view, market liquidity is the fundamental driver of *both* M/B ratios and merger waves.[12] Harford

---

[12] For example, Shleifer and Vishny (1992) argue that merger waves tend to occur in booms because increases in cash flows simultaneously raise fundamental values and relax financial constraints, bringing market values closer to fundamental values. Harford (1999) shows that firms that have built up large cash reserves are more prone to acquire other firms.

(2005) constructs a measure of aggregate capital liquidity based on interest rate (default) spreads and uses this measure in a "horse race" with M/B ratios in predicting industry merger waves. He finds that waves are preceded by deregulatory events and high capital liquidity. More importantly, he shows that the capital liquidity variable eliminates the ability of M/B ratios to predict industry merger waves. He concludes that aggregate merger waves are caused by the clustering of shock-driven industry merger waves, not by attempts to time the market.

Patterns of merger waves notwithstanding, predicting individual target firms with any accuracy has proven difficult.[13] Probability estimates are sensitive to the choice of size and type of control sample. Firm size consistently predicts targets across most studies, while results are mixed for other commonly used variables, including factors capturing growth, leverage, M/B ratios, and ownership structure.

2.2. Takeover contests, 1980–2005

As discussed in Section 2.3, after signing a merger agreement, the target board is normally required to consider new outside offers until target shareholders have given final approval of the takeover (the so-called fiduciary out clause). This means that no bidder can expect to lock up the target through negotiations but must be prepared for potential competition. All initial bidders, whether the initial bid is in the form of a merger or a tender offer, face this potential competition. We therefore refer to all initial bids as initiating a *control contest* whether or not multiple bids actually emerge ex post.

The "contest tree" in Figure 2 shows the potential outcomes of any initial bid. In the first round of the contest, one of three outcomes will occur: (1) the bid is accepted by the target and the contest ends; (2) the bid is rejected and the contest ends; or (3) the bid is followed by one or more rival bids and/or bid revisions before the contest ends. After two or more rounds of bidding, one of three final outcomes will occur: (4) the initial bidder wins control; (5) a rival bidder wins control; or (6) no bidder wins control (the target remains independent). Later in this chapter, we use this contest-tree structure to organize successive bids for the same target and to describe recent bidding activity.

2.2.1. Initial bidders and offer characteristics

We collect bids from the Thomson Financial SDC mergers and acquisitions database. SDC provides records of individual bids based on information in the news and securities and exchange (SEC) filings by the bidder and target firms. As shown by Boone and Mulherin (2007b), targets increasingly initiate takeovers through a process

---

[13] Hasbrouck (1985), Palepu (1986), Mork et al. (1988), Mikkelson and Partch (1989), Ambrose and Megginson (1992), Shivdasani (1993), Comment and Schwert (1995), and Cremers et al. (2008).

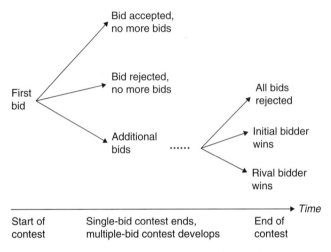

Fig. 2. Takeover contest structure and outcomes.

where they privately solicit several potentially interested bidders and select a negoti-ating partner among the respondents. The initial bidder identified by the SDC may well have emerged from such a process. However, we follow standard practice and use the first *official* (public) bid for the target to start the contest.

The bids are by US or foreign bidders for a US public or private target announced between January 1980 and December 2006. We start by downloading all mergers (SDC deal form M), acquisition of majority (AM) interest, acquisition of partial (AP) interest, and acquisition of remaining (AR) interest.[14] This results in a total of 70,548 deals (bids). We then use the SDC tender flag to identify which of the bids are tender offers and control-block trades.[15] Next, we organize the 70,548 bids into control contests, where a target is identified using the CUSIP number. A control bid is defined as a merger or acquisition (tender offer) of majority interest where the bidder holds less than 50% of the target shares at announcement.[16] The control contest begins with the first control bid for a given target and continues until 126 trading days have passed without any additional offer (including acquisitions of minority interests). Each time an additional offer for the target is identified, the 126 trading day search window rolls forward.

---

[14] We exclude all transactions classified as exchange offers, acquisition of assets, acquisition of certain assets, buybacks, recaps, and acquisition (of stock).

[15] This identification proceeds as follows: If the tender flag is "no" and the deal form is a merger, then the deal is a merger. If the tender flag is "no" and the deal form is "acquisition of majority interest" *and* the effective date of the deal equals the announcement date, then the deal is classified as a control-block trade. If the tender flag is "yes," or if the tender flag is "no" and it is not a block trade, then the deal is a tender offer.

[16] If information on the bidder's prior ownership in the target is missing from SDC, we assume that the prior shareholding is zero.

A control bid is successful if SDC's deal status field states "completed." For successful contests, the formal contest ending date is the earlier of SDC's effective conclusion date and target delisting date. Unsuccessful contests (no bid is successful) end with the offer date of the last control bid or partial acquisition plus 126 trading days (given that there were no more bids in the 126-day period).[17] This selection process produces a total of 35,727 contests. Control contests may be single-bid, multiple-bid but single bidder, or multiple bidder. A multiple-bid contest occurs either because there are multiple bidders or because the initial bidder submits a bid revision. Bid revisions are shown on SDC as a difference between the initial and final offer price within one SDC deal entry. For multiple-bidder contests, the identity of the successful bidder is determined by comparing the CUSIP of the successful bidder with the CUSIP of the initial control bidder. If they are the same, then the initial bidder is successful; otherwise a rival bidder is successful.

Tables 1–3 and Figures 3–6 describe the central characteristics of the total sample of 35,727 initial bids and their outcomes. Table 1 shows how the total sample is split between initial merger bids (28,994), tender offers (4500), and control-block trades (2224). Panel A of Figure 3 shows the annual distribution of the initial merger bids and tender offers, confirming the peak activity periods also shown earlier in Figure 1. The number of merger bids exceeds the number of tender offers by a factor of at least 3 in every sample year and by a factor of 7 for the total period. The relative frequency of tender offers peaked in the second half of the 1980s.

The SDC deal value, converted to constant 2000 dollars using the Consumer Price Index of the Bureau of Labor Statistics (Series Id: CUUR0000SA0), averages $436 million for initial merger bids, and $480 million for initial tender offers.[18] The distribution of deal values is highly skewed, with a median of only $35 million for mergers and $79 million for tender offers, respectively. The annual deal values plotted in Panel A of Figure 3 show that tender offers have somewhat greater deal values in the first half of the sample period, and that merger bids have slightly greater deal values than tender offers in the years 1998–2000.

Table 1 also provides information on the initial bidder's choice of payment method, the target's reaction to the initial bid, and the product-market relationship between the initial bidder and the target. SDC provides payment information for 53% of the sample bids. Of these, 26% (4798) are classified as all-cash bids, in 37% the method of payment is all-stock, and for 37% the bidder pays with a mix of cash, bidder stock, and/or other (typically debt) securities. In terms of average deal size, mixed and all-stock offers have similar sizes ($538 and $493 million, respectively), while all-cash bids are somewhat lower with $310 million. SDC classifies 590 initial bids as hostile and another 435 bids as unsolicited. All other bids are grouped here as friendly— including bids for which SDC does not provide a classification. The hostile bids are by

---

[17] We removed a single contest due to missing target name, 23 contests due to multiple successful bids, and 36 contests where the target was a Prudential-Bache fund.
[18] SDC deal values are available for 17,367 of the merger bids and for 3267 of the tender offers.

Table 1

Total number of takeover contests and characteristics of the initial control bid, 1980–2005

Control bids (mergers and tender offers) and their characteristics are from SDC. Control contests begin with the first control bid for a company and continue until 126 trading days have passed without any offer (including acquisitions of minority interests). Each time an offer for the target is identified, the 126 trading day search window rolls forward. Multiple-bid contests occur when there are either multiple control bidders or the initial bidder revises the bid. Successful offers are identified as completed by the SDC status variable. Initial deal values provided by SDC for the first control offer in the contest are restated in constant 2000 dollars using the Consumer Price Index obtained from the Bureau of Labor Statistics (Series Id: CUUR0000SA0).

	Number of contests				Number of successful contests				Initial deal values			
			Multiple bids				Multiple bids			(millions of 2000 constant $)		
								Multiple bidders					
	All contests	Single bid	Single bidder	Multiple bidders	Single bid	Single bidder	Initial bidder	Rival bidder	Number	Mean	S.D.	Median
All cotests	35,727	33,836	671	1220	26,012	476	732	646	21,476	419.43	2610.1	36.39
Initial deal form												
Merger bid	28,994	27,663	481	850	21,087	349	481	462	17,367	426.33	2838.2	34.57
Tender offer	4509	3955	188	366	2707	125	246	183	3267	481.36	1384.3	79.01
Block trade	2224	2218	2	4	2218	2	5	1	842	36.95	93.1	8.45
Initial payment method												
All-cash	4798	4114	268	416	3424	160	266	209	4798	309.54	1130.1	54.82
All-stock	6983	6699	161	123	5708	146	181	62	6983	492.89	3747.1	33.56
Mixed cash-sec.	6995	6516	172	307	5672	133	221	167	6995	538.41	2410.9	38.56
No payment data	16,951	16,507	70	374	11,208	37	64	208	2700	116.50	621.3	19.45
Initial attitude												
Hostile	590	207	153	230	35	72	16	133	560	1611.8	4055.0	301.06
Unsolicited	435	272	38	125	3	5	6	84	362	608.92	2729.9	103.19
Friendly	34,702	33,357	480	865	25,974	399	600	429	20,554	383.61	2549.4	33.94
Initial offer												
Horizontal	10,452	10,043	154	255	7953	130	198	128	6080	562.48	3172.0	40.17

Panel A: Number of initial control bids by type

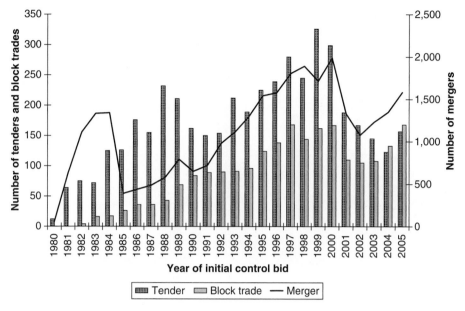

Panel B: Average deal value by type of initial control bid

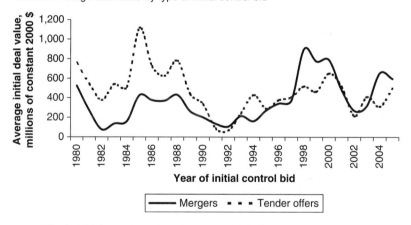

Fig. 3. Initial control bids for US targets, 1980–2005: merger, tender offer, or block trade.

far the largest in terms of size, with an average deal size of $1612 million versus $609 million for unsolicited offers and $384 million for the average friendly deal.

The last panel in Table 1 shows that 10,452 or 29% of all bids are horizontal (defined as the initial bidder and the target operate in the same four-digit Standard Industrial Classification (SIC) industry). With an average deal value of $562 million, the typical horizontal bid is somewhat larger than the sample average deal size. Figure 4

Panel A: Number of contests by time period and industry sector

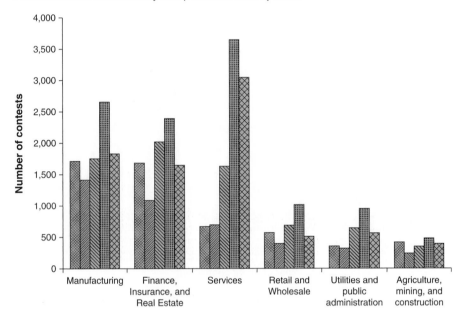

Panel B: % of horizontal deals

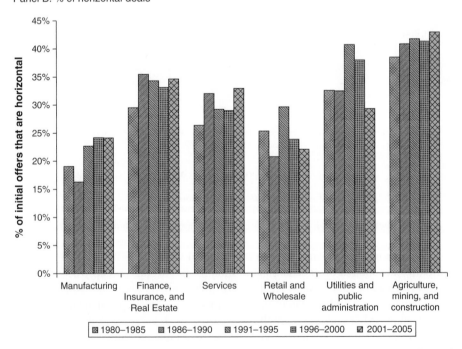

Fig. 4. Initial control bids for US targets, 1980–2005, by two-digit SIC target industry sector and four-digit SIC horizontal within sector.

complements the industry information by listing the total number of bids (Panel A) and the fraction of horizontal initial bids (Panel B) by broad industry sectors and by time period. The industry sectors are Manufacturing; Finance, Insurance, and Real Estate; Services; Retail, and Wholesale; Utilities and Public Administration; and Agriculture, Mining, and Construction. The two first sectors (Manufacturing, and Finance, Insurance, and Real Estate) are by far the most takeover-intensive sectors in every one of the five 5-year subperiods covering the total sample. The only exception is that Services experienced a peak takeover-intensity during 1996–2005. The percentage of the takeover bids that are horizontal tends to be somewhat greater for the least takeover-intensive sectors such as Utilities and Public Administration, and Agriculture, Mining and Construction.

Table 2 and Figure 5 list the sample according to the public status of the target and initial bidder. Of the total sample of 35,727 initial bidders, 67% (24,058) are publicly traded. There are a total of 13,185 publicly traded targets, of which 8259 receive initial bids from a public bidder. Not surprisingly, these are also the largest deals, with an average of $957 million in constant 2000 dollars (median $116 million). The largest single group is public bidders initiating a contest for a private target, with a total of 15,799 initial bids (44% of the sample). These deal values are typically small, with an average deal value of $66 million (median $16 million). There is also a group of 4482 private bidder/private targets, comprising 13% of the total database and with an average deal value of $114 million (median $23 million).

Panel A of Figure 5 plots the number and total deal value (in constant 2000 dollars) for public and private target deals over the sample period, while Panel B repeats the plot based on the bidder being either public or private. The number of deals with public targets (Panel A) and with public bidders (Panel B) both increase sharply in the second half of the 1990s. The average deal values when the target is private (Panel A) is small and stable over the entire sample period. Deal values for private bidders (Panel B) are also relatively low, but fluctuate over time in direct proportion to the number of public targets in this group.

Recall that our sampling procedure requires the target but not the bidder to be a US firm. The last panel of Table 2 shows how the bidders split according to nationality. A total of 3882 or 11% of the total sample of initial bidders are domiciled outside of the United States. Of these, 1044 bidders are from Canada, 716 from the United Kingdom, and the remaining 2122 are from a variety of other nations. Interestingly, contests initiated by a foreign bidder are on average large, with a mean of $701 million (median 41 million) when the bidder is from the United Kingdom, and $649 million (median $78 million) when the bidder is from the group of "other" countries.

2.2.2. Duration, time to second bid, and success rates

Recall that, starting with the initial offer, we identify the final bid in the contest when 126 trading days have passed without any new offer. Table 3 provides information on the duration of the 25,166 successful contests initiated by a merger or a tender offer.

Table 2

Bidder and target public status and initial bidder nationality in takeover contests, 1980–2005

Control bids (mergers and tender offers) and their characteristics are from SDC. Control contests begin with the first control bid for a company and continue until 126 trading days have passed without any offer (including acquisitions of minority interests). Each time an offer for the target is identified, the 126 trading day search window rolls forward. Multiple bid contests occur when there are either multiple control bidders or the initial bidder revises the bid. Successful offers are identified as completed by the SDC status variable. Initial deal values provided by SDC for the first control offer in the contest are restated in constant 2000 dollars using the Consumer Price Index obtained from the Bureau of Labor Statistics (Series Id: CUUR0000SA0). Bidder nationality and the public status of target and initial bidder is from SDC. "Other bidder" status includes unknown (268), joint-venture (115), individual (54), mutual (23), and government (19).

	Number of contests				Number of successful contests					Initial deal values (millions of 2000 constant $)			
			Multiple bids				Multiple bids						
								Multiple bidders					
	All contests	Single bid	Single bidder	Multiple bidders	Single bid	Single bidder	Initial bidder	Rival bidder		Number	Mean	S.D.	Median
Public target and status of initial bidder													
Public bidder	8259	7364	397	498	5822	321	449	248		7088	957.38	4337.4	115.75
Private bidder	3656	3012	180	464	1710	93	162	263		2424	388.07	1523.9	61.65
Other bidder	1270	1125	47	98	841	32	55	52		986	502.83	1806.4	84.87
Private target and status of initial bidder													
Public bidder	15,799	15,675	29	95	12,467	23	45	51		9269	66.28	233.7	26.06
Private bidder	4482	4429	5	48	3413	4	15	27		940	111.41	323.1	22.92
Other bidder	2261	2231	13	17	1759	3	6	5		769	86.26	416.5	16.84
Nation of initial bidder													
United States	31,845	30,184	613	1048	23,399	431	648	555		19,249	404.56	2632.0	35.97
Canada	1044	1011	10	23	688	5	9	11		590	222.09	933.4	11.13
United Kingdom	716	681	5	30	574	4	18	14		514	701.45	3364.2	41.43
Other international	2122	1960	43	119	1351	36	57	66		1123	649.00	2409.7	77.88

Panel A: Deal values by target public status

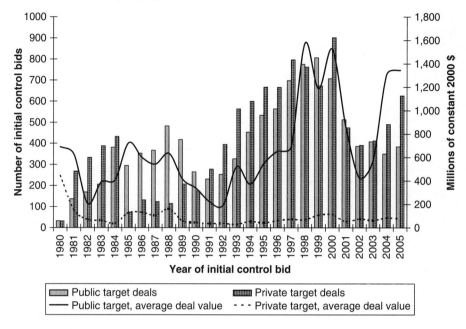

Panel B: Deal values by initial bidder public status

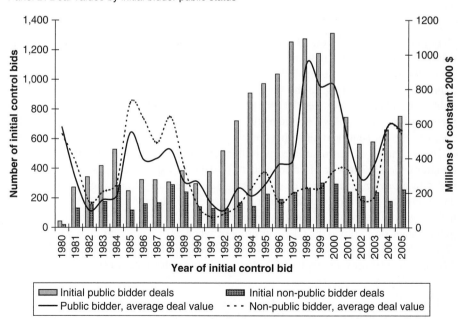

Fig. 5. Initial control bids for US targets, by public status of bidder and target, 1980–2005.

Table 3

Distribution of the time to completion of control contests for successful US target firms, classified by the type of initial offer and the public status of the bidder and target firms. Total sample of 25,166 successful targets, 1980–2005

Control contests begin with the first control bid for a company and continue until 126 trading days have passed without any offer (including acquisitions of minority interests). Each time an offer for the target is identified, the 126 trading day search window rolls forward. The table reports the number of trading days from the date of the initial control bid to the effective merger date reported by the SDC. The effective date is the date target shareholders approve the merger agreement.

Public status						Trading days from initial control bid to effective data	
						Quartiles	
Target	Bidder	No. of observation	Mean	Median	Lowest	Highest
Entire sample		25,166	64.62	42	0	100
Merger		22,030	62.42	39	0	100
Public	Public	5147	107.92	96	63	136
Public	Private	1766	97.84	86	42	136
Private	Public	11,131	48.42	19	0	73
Private	Private	3986	27.09	0	0	28
Tender		3136	80.06	52	30	98
Public	Public	1257	71.44	49	31	85
Public	Private	1030	97.8	67	34	123
Private	Public	533	73.61	43	21	84
Private	Private	316	67.38	41	19	92

Duration is measured from the date of the initial bid to the effective date of the takeover. The effective date is the day of target shareholder approval of the deal. Given the stringent disclosure rules governing public offer, it is important to separate public from private firms. In the group where both the initial bidder and the target are public, the duration averages 108 trading days (median 96) when the initial bid is a merger offer and 71 days (median 49) when the initial bid is a tender offer. This confirms the conventional view that tender offers are quicker than merger negotiations.

These results are comparable to Betton and Eckbo (2000), who report contest durations for 1353 tender offer contest, 1971–1990. Of these contests, 62% are single bid with an average duration of 40 trading days (median 29 and highest quartile 52 days). For the multibid contests, the average (median) duration is 70 (51) days. Thus, there is very little change in duration from the 1980s. Also, Table 3 shows clearly that a public target slows down the takeover process, whether or not the initial bid is a merger or a tender offer. Contests have the shortest duration when both firms are private: 27 days (median 0) for mergers and 67 days (median 41) for tender offers.[19]

---

[19] A contest duration of zero results when the initial offer is announced and accepted on the same day. This is possible in some private deals, provided bidder shareholders do not need to vote on a share issue to pay for the target, and provided the target vote is quick due, say, to high shareownership concentration.

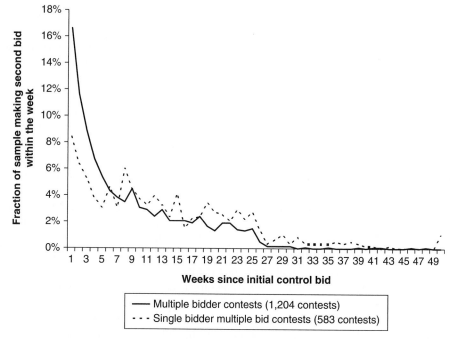

Fig. 6. Weeks from first to second bid in 1787 contests with multiple bids for US targets, 1980–2005. For the 1204 contests with multiple bidders, the time from the initial to the second bid averages 5.7 calendar weeks (40 trading days) with a median of 3.7 weeks. For the 583 contests with a single bidder making multiple bids, the average time to the first bid revision is 9 weeks (63 trading days) with a median of 7.6 weeks. Under the 1968 Williams Act, any given tender offer must be open for at least 20 days, and a new bid extends the minimum period accordingly.

Figure 6 shows the distribution of the number of weeks from the initial to the second bid in 1787 of the 1891 multibid contests in our sample (Table 1). In general, the expected time to arrival of a second bid depends on the cost to rival bidders of becoming informed of their own valuation of the target, as well as the time it takes to file a formal offer. For some rival bidders, the initial bid may have been largely anticipated based on general industry developments or prior rumors of the target being in play. However, in general, the observed time to the second bid sheds some light on the likelihood that rival bidders have ready access to the resources required to generate takeover gains.

For the 1204 contests with multiple bidders, the time from the initial to the second bid averages 5.7 calendar weeks (29 trading days), with a median of 3.7 weeks. For the 583 contests with a single bidder making multiple bids, the average time to the first bid revision is 9 weeks (45 trading days) with a median of 7.6 weeks.[20] Thus, the time to

---

[20] Under the 1968 Williams Act, any given tender offer must be open for at least 20 days, and a new bid extends the minimum period accordingly.

the second bid is, on average, shorter when a rival bidder enters than when the second bid represents a bid revision by the initial bidder. These findings are comparable to those in Betton and Eckbo (2000), who report a mean of 2 weeks (14 trading days) and a highest quartile of 6 week days from the first to the second bid for their sample of 518 multibid tender offer contests.

Several studies provide estimates of the probability that the target will be successfully acquired by *some* bidder (the initial or a rival) following takeover bids. Given our contest focus (Figure 2), we are particularly interested in the probability that the *initial* bidder wins (possible after multiple bid rounds). Betton et al. (2009) estimate this probability using 7470 initial merger bids and tender offers. They find that this probability is higher when the initial bidder has a toehold in the target and when the initial bid is all-cash (rather than all-stock or mixed cash-stock), when the bid is a tender offer (rather than merger), and when the bidder is a public company. The probability is also increasing in the prebid target stock price runup (the average cumulative target abnormal return from day -42 through day -2 relative to the initial offer day), when the target is traded on the NYSE or the Amex, and when the bidder and target are horizontally related in product markets. Finally, the probability that the initial bidder wins the contest is lower if the target has a poison pill and if the target reaction is hostile. The negative impact of the presence of a poison pill is interesting, for it suggests that pills deter some bids. We return to this issue in Section 3.5.

Finally, Table 1 implies that the probability that all bids fail in a contest is 23% when the contest is initiated by merger and 28% when the initial bid is a tender offer. Thus, as noted by Betton et al. (2009) as well, merger negotiations are risky for the initial bidder. They are particularly risky when the initial bidder is private. As shown in Table 2, the probability that all bids fail is as high as 40% when the initial bidder is private and the target is public and the bidder approaches with a merger offer.

2.3. Merger negotiation versus public tender offer

2.3.1. Merger agreement and deal protection devices

A merger agreement is the result of negotiations between the bidder and target management teams. The agreement sets out how the bidder will settle any noncash portion of the merger payment. Frequently used contingent payment forms include stock swaps (discussed extensively in Section 3.2), collars, and clawbacks and earn-outs.[21] Contingent payment forms allow bidder and target shareholders to share the risk that the target and/or bidder shares are overvalued ex ante. Both parties typically supply fairness opinions as part of the due diligence process.[22]

Whenever the bidder pays the target in the form of bidder stock, the merger agreement specifies the exchange ratio (the number of bidder shares to be exchanged

---

[21] Officer (2004), Officer (2006), Kohers and Ang (2000), and Cain et al. (2005).

[22] Kisgen et al. (2006), Makhija and Narayanan (2007), and Chen and Sami (2006).

for each target share). A collar provision provides for changes in the exchange ratio should the level of the bidder's stock price change before the effective date of the merger. This helps insulate target stockholders from volatility in the bidder's stock price. Collar bids may have floors and caps (or both), which define a range of bidder stock prices within which the exchange ratio is held fixed, and outside of which the exchange ratio is adjusted up or down. Thus, floors and caps guarantee the target a minimum and maximum payment.

The total payment to target shareholders may also be split between an upfront payment and additional future payments that are contingent upon some observable measure of performance (earnouts, often over a 3-year period). This helps close the deal when the bidder is particularly uncertain about the true ability of the target to generate cash flow. It provides target managers with an incentive to remain with the firm over the earnout period, which may be important to the bidder. The downside is that the earnout may distort the incentives of target managers (an emphasis on short-term over long-term cash flows), and it may induce the new controlling shareholder (the bidder) to manipulate earnings in order to lower the earnout payment. Thus, earnouts are not for everyone.

Merger negotiations protect the negotiating parties against opportunistic behavior while bargaining takes place. Before negotiations start, the parties sign agreements covering confidentiality, standstill, and nonsolicitation. The confidentiality agreement allows the target board to negotiate a sale of the firm without having to publicly disclose the proceedings, and it permits the target to open its books to the bidder. The standstill commits the bidder not to purchase target shares in the market during negotiations, while nonsolicitation ensures that neither the bidder nor the target tries to hire key employees away from the other firm. It is also common for the bidder to obtain tender agreements from target insiders, under which these insiders forsake the right to tender to a rival bidder (Bargeron, 2005).

Delaware case law suggests that a merger agreement must include a fiduciary out clause enabling the target board to agree to a superior proposal if one is forthcoming from a third party.[23] As a result, the target board cannot give its negotiating partner exclusive rights to negotiate a control transfer: it must remain open to other bidders along the way. The resulting potential for bidder competition (after the merger agreement has been signed but before the shareholder vote) has given rise to target termination agreements, starting in the mid-1980s. A termination agreement provides the bidder with compensation in the form of a fixed fee (breakup fee) or an option to purchase target shares or assets at a discount (lockup option) should the target withdraw from the agreement (Bates and Lemmon, 2003; Boone and Mulherin,

---

[23] *Omnicare Inc. vs. NCS Healthcare Inc.*, 818 A.2d 914 (Del. 2003). Delaware law is important as approximately 60% of all publicly traded companies in the United States are incorporated in the state of Delaware. Moreover, decisions in the Delaware Supreme Court tend to set a precedence for court decisions in other states.

2007a; Burch, 2001; Officer, 2003).[24] As discussed in Section 3.3, the value of a target termination agreement may be substantial, and it may affect the initial bidder's optimal toehold strategy.

When merger negotiations close, the bidder seeks SEC approval for any share issue required in the deal, and a merger prospectus is worked out. Writing the prospectus typically takes from 30 to 90 days, so the target shareholder vote is typically scheduled 3–6 months following the signing of the initial merger proposal.[25] The New York Stock Exchange requires that the shareholders of the bidder firm must also be allowed to vote on the merger if the agreement calls for the bidder to increase the number of shares outstanding by at least 20% in order to pay for the target.

2.3.2. Mandatory disclosure and tender offer premiums

In contrast to the merger process, a public tender offer is relatively quick. A tender offer is an offer made by the bidder directly to target shareholders to purchase target shares The offer specifies the price per target share, the method of payment (cash, securities, or a mix of the two), whether the offer is restricted to less than 100% of the target shares, conditions for accepting tendered shares (e.g., all or nothing or any or all), and how long the offer is outstanding. The 1968 Williams Act, the main federal law governing public tender offers, requires an orderly auction mechanism: the tender offer must be open for a minimum of 20 business days; competing bid and material bid revisions automatically extend the offer period by 10 days; target shareholders may withdraw all tendered shares for any reason (typically in response to a higher bid) within 15 days; and the bidder must purchase target shares on a pro rata basis among those who tendered their shares.[26]

The 1968 Williams Act also requires public information disclosure.[27] These provisions of the Act were in part a response to perceived takeover abuses in the 1960s, such

---

[24] The Delaware court views termination fees anywhere in the range of 2–5% of the transaction value as reasonable. Termination agreements sometimes allow a reduction in the breakup fee if the target strikes a competing deal within a 30/45-day time frame. There are also cases where the deal includes a bidder termination agreement.

[25] During this waiting period, the bidder also performs a due diligence on key assumptions behind the merger agreement. If the bidder receives 90% of the target shares in a prior tender offer, the bidder can force a merger without calling for a vote among the remaining minority target shareholders (so-called short-form merger).

[26] Note that, contrary to takeover regulations in many Western countries (Berglof and Burkart, 2003), the Williams Act does not include a mandatory bid rule. A mandatory bid rule requires the bidder to proceed with an offer for 100% of the target shares after acquiring a certain stake in the target (Burkart and Panunzi, 2003). Mandatory bid rules do, however, exist in certain states, including Pennsylvania and Maine. The mandatory bid price varies with jurisdiction but is typically a function of the price(s) the bidder paid for the initial stake.

[27] A tender offer is disclosed through a 14D filing with the SEC. Also, regardless of any plans to acquire the target, an investor purchasing 5% or more of the target shares must file Form 13D with the SEC within a 10-day period. The 13D includes statements concerning the purchaser's intention with respect to the eventual purchase of control. Antifraud provisions were added to the Williams Act in 1970 to back up these disclosure requirements.

as "creeping takeovers" and "Saturday night raids" where the bidder quickly gained control of the target shares using all-cash purchases in the market and privately from blockholders. While the stated intention of the Act is to protect target shareholders, a concern for potential bidders is that the mandatory disclosure rules also act to increase the ability of potential rival bidders to compete for the target. As pointed out by Grossman and Hart (1980a) and Jarrell and Bradley (1980), an active market for corporate control presupposes that initial bidders expect to have an advantage over potential rivals when search costs are sunk. Mandatory disclosure rules that increase expected competition among bidders possibly raise offer premiums and therefore deter some bids.[28]

Did the disclosure provisions of the Williams Act raise tender offer premiums? Jarrell and Bradley (1980) examine this issue and find that the average cash tender offer premium increased from 32% to nearly 53% following passage of the Act in 1968. Consistent with higher premium costs, Schipper and Thompson (1983) present evidence indicating that a sample of frequent acquirers earned significantly negative abnormal returns over the months surrounding announcements of the introduction of the Williams Act. Also, Asquith et al. (1983), Loderer and Martin (1990), and others report that gains to bidder firms in mergers are on average lower after 1968.

Nathan and O'Keefe (1989) find that the premium increase after introduction of the Williams Act is not restricted to cash tender offers: Cash *mergers* experienced an increase in the average premium from 30% to 67%, while security exchange mergers saw the average premium increase from 30% to 54%. They also show that the majority of the increase in the average offer premium takes place after 1972. This delay is puzzling and raises the question of whether the premium increase is due to the Williams Act or to some other economic phenomenon.

The Williams Act introduced both disclosure rules and a minimum 20-day offer period. Providing rival bidders with time to respond to the initial bid (the 20-day wait period) is obviously key to increased competition. Thus, studies of the Williams Act cannot isolate the premium impact of the disclosure rules. Specifically, these studies do not answer the fundamental question of whether the introduction of disclosure rules affects offer premiums in an environment where rival bidders already have time to respond.

Eckbo and Langohr (1989) provide evidence on this question using a different institutional setting. In 1970, France introduced mandatory disclosure rules for public tender offers—much like those in the Williams Act. The difference is that France had already established a minimum (4-week) tender offer period much earlier (in 1966). Eckbo and Langohr (1989) find that the average offer premium in successful cash tender offers increased from 34% to nearly 61% after the 1970 disclosure regulations.

---

[28] However, severe penalties on the release of false (or misleading) information may benefit some bidder firms by making their otherwise voluntarily disclosed information more credible (Eckbo and Langohr, 1989). This positive effect is greater the lower the correlation between rival bidders' private valuations of the target (i.e., the more unique the bidder's contribution to total synergy creation).

Since the minimum tender offer period remained at 1 month throughout their sample period, this indicates that disclosure requirements *alone* can cause a substantial increase in average offer premiums. Eckbo and Langohr (1989) also study a contemporaneous control sample of privately negotiated controlling-block trades, exempt from the 1970 disclosure regulations. Premiums in these alternative control acquisitions did not increase subsequent to the 1970 regulations.

2.3.3. Determinants of the merger choice

What are some of the determinants of the choice between merger negotiations and a public tender offer? From the bidder's point of view, two immediate advantages of the tender offer process is speed of execution (supported empirically by Table 3) and the fact that it does not require prior approval by—or even prior contact with—target management. Thus, the tender offer is an option for bidders who believe the target will refuse to negotiate ex ante, or should negotiations break down ex post.[29] Also, many tender offers involve prior contact and even negotiations with the target management (Comment and Jarrell, 1987). Negotiated tender offers may help resolve bargaining issues (e.g., difference of opinions on what constitutes a reasonable bid price), and the arm's length transaction implied by a public tender offer helps protect target managements against charges ex post that they "sold out" to the bidder.

As discussed in Section 3.5, the target takeover defenses developed in the 1980s, in particular the poison pill, have significantly raised the cost to the bidder of launching a hostile tender offer. This is evidenced by a substantial decline in the frequency of hostile bids over the past 20 years. In today's legal environment, it is likely that virtually *all* bidders (also those who intend to replace incumbent target management) prefer to approach the target management with a proposal to negotiate. Again, an initially friendly approach preserves the option of making a hostile tender offer down the line. Moreover, a significant benefit of a friendly cooperative approach is that it gives the bidder access to the target books, a crucial factor in pricing.

Systematic empirical evidence on the choice of merger versus tender offer is only beginning to emerge. Kohers et al. (2007) study 2610 completed mergers and 795 successful tender offers for the period 1984–1999. They find that the probability of a tender offer is more likely when the form of payment is all-cash, when the target is defensive, and has high institutional ownership, and when there are multiple bidders. The tender offer form is less likely between two "glamor" companies (i.e., when the bidder and target have low book-to-market (B/M) ratios), and for deals after the 1980s.

Betton et al. (2008a) study the *initial* bidder's choice between merger and tender offer for 4618 merger bids and 1638 tender offers for public US target firms from 1980 through 2002. They separate public bidders (3119) from private bidders (1438) and test

---

[29] Berkovitch and Khanna (1991), Aktas et al. (2007), and Betton et al. (2009) present models in which a tender offer (auction) is an explicit outside option in merger negotiations.

for differences in their choices. They show that bidder and target B/M values drive the merger choice only when these ratios exceed the median B/M of the respective industry rivals. Public bidders are significantly less likely to select merger over tender offer when the B/M values of the target or of the bidder exceed their respective industry medians. For private bidders, however, this glamor effect does not exist: private bidders are *more* likely to select merger over tender offer when the target's B/M exceeds its industry median (data on private bidders' B/M values are not available). In the 1980s, public bidders were less likely to choose merger, while private bidders were more likely to select this acquisition form. While the target's asset size and target hostility both reduce a public bidder's likelihood of selecting a merger, these factors do not influence the choice of private bidders. Moreover, the greater the concentration of the target's industry, the less likely both public and private bidders are to select merger over tender offer.

3. Bidding strategies

3.1. Modeling the takeover process

Before reviewing the empirical evidence on various bidding strategies, it is instructive to briefly characterize the two most common theoretical settings used to model takeover bids. This in turn helps us understand the various empirical hypotheses and their relevance for actual takeover activity.

3.1.1. Free riders and postoffer dilution

An early workhorse in the theoretical takeover literature is the free-rider model of Grossman and Hart (1980b) and Bradley (1980). They analyze the incentives of dispersed, noncooperative target shareholders to accept a tender offer from a single bidder and the resulting inefficiency of the takeover market. To illustrate, suppose the target's preoffer (stand-alone) share price is equal to 0 and that it is common knowledge that the posttakeover share price will equal $v > 0$. The value-increase v may be thought of as synergy gains resulting from the bidder taking control of the target. The bidder makes a conditional unrestricted bid b for 50% of the target shares (sufficient to transfer control of the target to the bidder).[30] A risk-neutral target shareholder tenders only if the offer price exceeds the expected value of her share if she retains it:

$$\text{Tender if } b \geq \Pr(\text{Success}|i \text{ Retain})v \tag{1}$$

where $\Pr(\cdot)$ denotes the probability that the offer succeeds given that the shareholder does not tender.[31]

---

[30] "Conditional" means no shares will be purchased if less than 50% are tendered. "Unrestricted" means any or all tendered shares above 50% will be purchased.
[31] We are ignoring taxes. For example, when b is paid in cash, the offer may trigger a capital gains tax liability.

By inspection of Equation (1), the target shareholder is more willing to tender the lower is the posttakeover value v, and the more she believes that retaining reduces the takeover's probability of success. As the number of target shareholder becomes larger, however, the probability that any single shareholder is pivotal for the outcome of the bid becomes arbitrarily small. For such shareholders, the tender criterion in Equation (1) reduces to:

Tender if $b \geq v$ (2)

Since the bidder has no economic incentive to make the bid in Equation (2), these shareholders are in effect free-riding on a decision by others to tender. Of course, if all shareholders behave this way, the takeover opportunity never materializes.[32]

Making *every* target shareholder pivotal by a conditional and restricted offer for 100% is unlikely to help. Because the bidder gains control after receiving 50% of the shares, refusing to purchase those shares if she is one share short of 100% is not credible. Also, allowing the bidder to be better informed than target shareholders (about v) does not solve the problem. Individual target shareholders now demand an offer price $b \geq E(v|\text{Offer})$ in order to tender, where the right-hand side is the expected valuation of the bidder given that he makes an offer. An offer below this expectation leads target shareholders to infer that $b < v$ and therefore to retain their shares. In this case, there does not exist a rational expectations (perfect Bayesian) equilibrium in which the bidder expects to make a profit from the takeover.[33]

There are a number of ways to mitigate the free-rider problem so that the bidder gains on the acquired target shares. Two frequently mentioned mechanisms are post-takeover dilution (Grossman and Hart, 1980b) and pretakeover toehold acquisition (Shleifer and Vishny, 1986b). Posttakeover dilution reduces the "back-end" value of the takeover and may be enforced through a two-tiered tender offer. The first tier is a bid b while the back end is a minority buyout (enforced by the bidder after acquiring control in the front end) at a lower value $v^d < v$. Alternatively, if fair price rules prevent the minority buyout to take place at a price below the front-end price, the bidder may resort to self-dealing ("asset tunneling"), which is harmful to minority shareholders after the takeover. Examples of such dilution techniques are asset sales at prices below market value, transfer pricing favorable to the majority shareholder, excessive compensation schemes, and so on. These schemes create a wedge between the posttakeover share value to the acquirer and minority shareholders and enable the

---

[32] Just as the free-rider problem can discourage value-increasing bids, value-reducing bids—bids where the posttakeover value of the target is less than its preoffer value—may be encouraged due to a "pressure-to-tender" problem (Bebchuk, 1985): Conditional on the offer succeeding, tendering may dominate retaining and receiving an even lower value. Thus, paradoxically, there may be "pressure-to-tender" when the bidder is value-reducing. The root cause of this result is, as above, that each target shareholder bases the tendering decision on a comparison between b and v, ignoring the pretakeover value.

[33] Hirshleifer and Titman (1990) prove the existence of a separating equilibrium in which the offer price fully reveals v.

acquirer to make a profit. Although such transfers may enhance the ex ante efficiency of the takeover market, they are controversial and legally difficult to enforce ex post.[34]

A firm contemplating making a bid for the target may also decide to purchase target shares—a toehold—in the market at the prebid (no-information) target share price. The implications of such toehold acquisitions for optimal bidding are discussed in detail later in this chapter. In the context of the free-rider problem, the important point is that the toehold bidder may gain on the toehold while making zero profits on the shares acquired in the formal takeover bid. Let δ denote the fraction of the target posttakeover value that may be diluted ex post, and α the fraction of the target shares held by the bidder prior to the offer, respectively. The bidder makes the conditional unrestricted offer of

$$b^* = (1 - \delta)v \tag{3}$$

which yields a bidder profit of

$$v - (1 - \alpha)b^* = \alpha v + (1 - \alpha)(v - b^*) = \alpha v + (1 - \alpha)\delta v \tag{4}$$

The first term, αv, is the gain on the toehold shares, while the second term is the profits on the shares purchased in the takeover. The second term, $(1 - \alpha)\delta v$, shows that dilution is costly for the bidder in that it also reduces the value of the bidder's toehold shares. Thus, the larger the initial stake α, the lower the controlling shareholder's incentive to dilute ex post. In other words, a corporate insider with a larger equity stake is more prone to act in the outside (minority) shareholders' interest (Burkart et al., 1998; Jensen and Meckling, 1976).

What is the empirical relevance of the free-rider problem in corporate takeovers? The most direct way to evaluate this question is to look at the frequency of (pivotal) blockholders in corporate shareownership structures. A large blockholder likely accounts for the possibility that her tendering decision affects the probability that the offer will succeed. In this case, shareholders are willing to tender at a price lower than indicated by expression (1) above (Bagnoli and Lipman, 1988; Holmstrom and Nalebuff, 1992).[35]

The evidence on corporate ownership structures around the world suggests that the existence or one or more large blockholder is the rule rather than the exception.[36]

---

[34] Djankov et al. (2008) survey the opportunities for corporate insiders around the world to dilute minority shareholder value through self-dealings deemed *legal* under a country's corporate laws. Under the European Takeover Directive (article 14), member-states may grant acquirers a squeeze-out right, that is, the right to compel posttakeover minority shareholders to sell their shares after the acquirer has purchased 90% of the target shares.

[35] In Holmstrom and Nalebuff (1992), there are N target shareholders of equal size, and the bidder needs K of these to tender in order to acquire control. They show that there exists a mixed strategy equilibrium where the takeover succeeds and the bidder makes a positive expected profit. In this equilibrium, individual target shareholders tender with a probability $p = K/N$. Expected profits go to zero when N becomes large.

[36] Following the early international evidence of La et al. (1999), detailed information on corporate ownership structures has appeared for East Asia (Claessens et al., 2000), Western Europe (Faccio and Lang, 2002; Franks et al., 2005), and the United States (Dlugosz et al., 2006; Helwege et al., 2007; Holderness, 2009; Holderness et al., 1999).

In the United States and elsewhere, small and midsized publicly traded companies typically have one or more large shareholder (defined as a minimum 5% holding).[37] In largecap firms, individual (or family) blockholdings are less frequent in the United States; however, large blocks held by financial institutions such as pension funds are common for our large firms. As highlighted by Holderness (2009), the evidence challenges the view—originating with Berle and Means (1932)—that US ownership is largely dispersed, and it suggests that free-rider problems in takeovers may be a rarity.[38]

A more indirect way to evaluate the empirical relevance of free-rider problems is to examine characteristics of observed takeover bids. For example, the unequal distribution of takeover gains between target and bidder firms—with most, if not all, of the total gains typically accruing to the target—is often cited in support of the existence of the free-rider problem (Burkart and Panunzi, 2008; Hirshleifer, 1995). However, as discussed in Section 4, there are a number of alternative and plausible reasons for the observed uneven distribution of takeover gains. Moreover, toehold bidding—perhaps the most obvious way to mitigate expected free-rider problems—is extremely rare in control-oriented acquisitions (Betton et al., 2009).

3.1.2. Auction with single seller

A second workhorse in the theoretical literature on takeover bidding is the competitive auction. Here, the bidder faces a single seller in the form of a large target shareholder or a target management with sufficient authority to commit to selling in the auction. As noted by Dasgupta and Hansen (2007), auction theory plays an important prescriptive role: to inform a company's board or regulators about the impact of selling processes or rules on shareholder wealth, efficiency, and welfare. They also note that, for such prescriptions to be useful, the auction model must reasonably mimic the actual takeover bidding environment. One important characteristic of any auction is the seller's commitment to stick to the rules of the game. For auction-theoretic results to

---

[37] The definition of a block varies in the literature from 5% to 20%. Note that a relatively small block may become pivotal depending on the ownership distribution of the remaining shares. A natural empirical measure of "pivotal" is the Shapley transformation of the block (Shapley, 1953). The Shapley value is the probability that the block will be pivotal, computed using all possible shareholder coalitions (with the block) in which the coalition determines the voting outcome. See, for example, Eckbo and Verma (1994) and Zingales (1994) for applications in corporate finance.

[38] Holderness (2009) studies a random sample of 10% of the firms trading on the NYSE, Amex, and NASDAQ. Large shareholders (which include institutional holdings) on average own 39% of the voting power of the common stock. Moreover, 96% of the firms have at least one 5%+ blockholder, and the average holding of the largest blockholder is 26%. Holderness also reports that 89% of the firms in the S&P 500 Index have large blockholders. Thus, free-rider problems are unlikely. Whether the evidence also challenges the seriousness of the Berle-Means warnings of agency costs associated with delegated management in public firms is, of course, a different issue. It is possible that a large block held by a financial institution (as opposed to an individual investor) carries with it serious agency problems when seen from the point of view of the firm's individual shareholders.

apply, the seller must be trying to secure the best price for the firm's shareholders by committing to a selling mechanism.[39] As noted earlier, since a publicly traded target's board of directors has a fiduciary obligation to accept the highest offer (provided the board has placed the target "in play"), a takeover is arguably much like an auction even if the target initially negotiates a merger agreement.

The typical assumption is of an open, ascending (English) auction with zero entry and bidding costs, and where the winning bidder pays the second-highest bid.[40] Bidder valuations v (synergies) are private knowledge, but the seller knows the probability distribution function over v, $G(v)$. Since bidders tend to have different skill levels in terms of managing the target assets, it is often assumed that the valuations v are uncorrelated across bidders—a "private value." Alternatively, bidder valuations may be correlated—a "common value" environment that requires bidders to shave their bids in anticipation of the "winners curse."[41]

It is also commonly assumed that the bidder's outside option is status quo. That is, the payoff to the bidder is zero when losing the auction. This assumption is effectively relaxed when the bidder has a toehold[42] or a target termination agreement, or when the takeover is a response to changes in industry competition (Akdogu, 2007; Molnar, 2008; Morellec and Zhdanov, 2005). The toehold provides a positive payoff when the toehold bidder loses to a rival (who purchases the toehold). A termination contract also pays off when the bidder loses and no other bidder wins (the target remains independent). Also, a worsening of the competitive industry equilibrium can place the unsuccessful bidder at a competitive disadvantage vis-à-vis the winner.

3.2. The payment method choice

As discussed earlier (Table 1), the payment method in takeovers includes all-stock payment, various debt securities, mixes of securities and cash, and all-cash payment.[43] As Table 1 shows for the total sample, 26% of the initial bidders use the all-cash

---

[39] For example, in a first-price auction, in which bidders optimally shave their bids, the seller must be able to commit not to allow further bid revisions by the losing bidder (who, after losing, may want to submit a bid higher than the winning bid).

[40] With zero entry and bidding costs, optimal bid increments are infinitesimal, so the winning bidder pays the second highest price whether or not the auction is defined formally at a first-price or second-price auction.

[41] In a common-value setting, bidders receive private and noisy signals as to the true (common) value of the target. Bidding the full value of the signal would cause the bidder with the largest positive signal error to win and overpay (the "curse"). Optimal bidding takes this possibility into account by reducing the bid to the point where the expected value of the bid *conditional on winning* is nonnegative. Thus, testing for the presence of a winner's curse is equivalent to testing the hypothesis that bidders are irrational (cannot compute). See Boone and Mulherin (2007b) for same evidence inconsistent with this hypothesis. In a private value setting, bidders know their true valuations and thus do not face a winner's curse.

[42] Burkart (1995), Bulow et al. (1999), and Betton et al. (2009).

[43] The cash amount is typically financed using accumulated retained earnings (financial slack) or debt issues prior to the takeover.

method while the groups of all-stock and mixed offers each cover 37% of the initial bids. Figure 7 plots the fraction of all initial bids that are in the form of each of these three payment methods over the 1980–2005 period. Use of the various payment methods clearly differs between merger bids (Panel A) and tender offers (Panel B): the majority of tender offers use all-cash or a mix of cash and stock, while the majority of merger bids are in the form of all-stock (with the exception of the 1980–1985 period when 90% of the initial merger bids offered a mix of cash and securities).

Notice that in the two subperiods 1990–1995 and 1996–2000, the percentage of all-stock offers in initial merger bids was approximately 55% in *both* periods. This means that (1) nearly half of the initial merger bids in the 1990s used some cash as payment, and (2) the percentage of all-stock merger bids remained unaffected by the significant runup in overall market valuations in the 1996–2000 period.

Table 4 summarizes a number of economic hypotheses and related empirical evidence concerning the choice of payment method. The associated empirical evidence is a combination of determinants of the probability of a specific payment method choice (e.g., all-cash versus all-stock), and announcement-induced abnormal stock returns as a function of the payment method. The hypotheses deal with tax effects, deal financing costs under asymmetric information, agency and corporate control motives, and behavioral arguments. These hypotheses are not necessarily mutually exclusive, so a given payment choice may reflect elements of several theories.

3.2.1. Taxes

The US Internal Revenue Code (IRC) requires target shareholders to immediately pay capital gains taxes in an all-cash purchase. If the merger qualifies as a tax-free reorganization under Section 368 of IRC, for example by using all-stock as method of payment, target shareholder capital gains taxes are deferred until the shares received in the deal are sold. Mixed cash-stock offers are treated as either all-cash bids or the stock part is treated as an all-stock bid depending on the cash portion and other characteristics of the deal. There is a carry-over of the tax basis in the target to the acquiring company, unless a 338 election is made. Under a 338 election, there is a step-up of the tax-basis of the target assets to the price paid in the takeover (Bruner, 2004). Such elections imply a capital gains tax in the target, and are used only in rare circumstances such as when there are substantial target net operating losses (NOLs) due to expire, or when the target is a subsidiary.

Given these differences in the tax treatment, there is little doubt that taxes play an important role in the bidder's choice of payment method. The more difficult empirical issue is whether the bidder in all-cash offers must pay target shareholders a compensation up front both for the realization of a potential capital gains tax penalty and for the value of the target's unused tax benefits. This depends, of course, on the relative bargaining power of the bidder and the target and is therefore transaction specific. For example, targets that have low-cost substitute ways of capitalizing on unused tax benefits will force bidders to pay for these in the deal (Gilson et al., 1988).

Panel A: Distribution of mergers by time period and method of payment

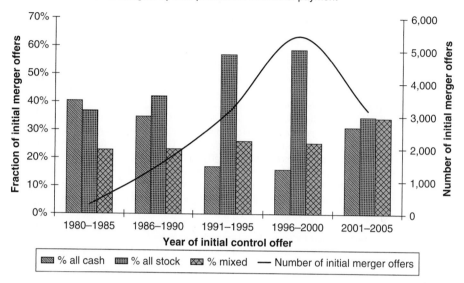

Panel B: Distribution of tender offers by time period by method of payment

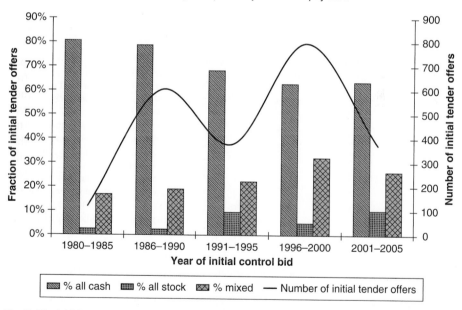

Fig. 7. The initial control bidder's use of all-cash, all-stock, and mixed cash-stock as method of payment. Total sample of 13,503 merger bids and 2678 tender offers with SDC information on payment method. US targets, 1980–2005.

Table 4

Selected hypotheses and US evidence concerning the choice of payment method in takeovers

Theories	Hypotheses	Evidence
A. Taxes and the payment method		
US Internal Revenue Code, Section 368 governing statutory merger. Gilson et al. (1988)	H1: *Cash deals may be relatively costly as the implied capital gains tax penalty forces higher target premiums.* In a cash-for-stock deal, target shareholders pay capital gains tax immediately (the deal is taxable if target shareholders receive less than 50% of the deal in bidder stock). The buyer steps up the tax basis with the takeover premium. In a Stock deal, however, target capital gains taxes are deferred until shares received are sold. No step-up of tax basis for buyer. Buyer in stock deal may make a Section 338 election to be treated as cash deal (Bruner, 2004).	Carleton et al. (1983): Probability of stock offer increases in bidder's M/B ratio. Huang and Walkling (1987), Hayn (1989): Target announcement returns in US deals higher for taxable than tax-deferred transactions. Franks et al. (1988): Reach similar conclusion for control-oriented takeovers in the United Kingdom. However, the all-cash premium effect is present also before the introduction on capital gains taxes. Eckbo and Langohr (1989): Find higher target premiums in all-cash tenders offers for control as well as for minority buyouts in France. Brown and Ryngaert (1991): Find empirical support for their proposition that stock should not be used by bidders selecting taxable offers.
B. The payment method choice motivated by asymmetric information		
Myers and Majluf (1984)	H2: *One-sided information asymmetry: Investor concern with adverse selection produces a negative market reaction to the news of a stock deal.*	Travlos (1987), Asquith et al. (1987), Servaes (1991), Brown and Ryngaet (1991), Smith and Kim (1994), Martin (1996), Emery and Switzer (1999), Heron and Lie (2004), Schlingemann (2004) and many others show that bidder announcement-induced abnormal stock returns are on average negative in all-stock offers for public targets. However, bidder announcement returns are nonnegative in all-stock offers for private targets (Bradley and Sundaram, 2006; Chang, 1998; Fuller et al., 2002; Moeller et al., 2004; Officer et al., 2009).
Hansen (1987), Fishman (1989)	H3: *Two-sided information asymmetry: Paying with securities induce targets to make more efficient accept/reject decisions than with cash. Stock offers are less likely when (i) the bidder has a relatively large total equity size, and (ii) when the target undervalues the bidder's shares.*	Hansen (1987): Probability of stock offer increases in bidder's asset size as well as in the size of its liabilities.

(Continued)

Table 4 (*Continued*)

Theories	Hypotheses	Evidence
	The value of a stock offer is contingent on the true values of both the bidder and the target. A cash offer that undervalues the target will be rejected, while an equivalent stock offer may be accepted because the stock offer will rise in value ex post. This ex post price effect is smaller the smaller the size of bidder's total equity relative to the target's.	Chemmanur and Paeglis (2003): Probability of stock offer increases in a measure of market mispricing of bidder shares and falls as the dispersion of analyst forecast of bidder earnings increases.
	The more the target undervalues the bidder's stock, the more costly a given stock offer, and the more likely the bidder is to use cash.	Betton and Eckbo (2000): Probability that the target accepts the initial bid in tender offer contests is lower for stock offers than for cash bids. Travlos (1987): Bidder's announcement-induced abnormal stock returns lower for stock offers than for cash bids.
Eckbo et al. (1990) Berkovitch and Narayanan (1990)	H4: *Two-sided information asymmetry where bidders in equilibrium choose a mix of cash and stock. There exists a fully revealing separating equilibrium in which the greater the proportion of the deal paid in cash, the greater the true value of the bidder.*	Eckbo et al. (1990), Eckbo and Thorburn (2000): The average announcement-induced abnormal stock returns to bidders are highest for all-cash deals, lowest for all-stock deals, with mixed cash-stock deals in between.
	In Eckbo et al. (1990), target adverse selection pushes the bidder towards using stock as payment method, while target undervaluation of bidder shares pushes the bidder towards cash. The market uses the proportion of the deal paid in cash to separate low-value from high-value bidders. In equilibrium, bidder announcement-induced abnormal stock returns are an increasing and convex function of the cash portion of the deal.	Eckbo et al. (1990): In cross-sectional regressions, bidder announcement-induced abnormal stock returns are increasing in the cash portion of the deal as predicted. However, the data rejects convexity.
	In Berkovitch and Narayanan (1990), the bidder's choice of cash-stock mix affects target returns as well. Greater potential bidder competition raises the optimal amount of cash, and with actual competition all but the lowest type make all-cash offers.	Betton et al. (2008c): Shows frequent use of mixed cash-stock offers in tender offers (see Moreover, there is evidence that multiple bids raise the use of cash, however, the amount of stock used in competitive contests remains significantly Figure 7).

C. Capital structure and corporate control motives for the payment method choice

Rose (1977) Jensen (1986) Harris and Raviv (1988)	H5: *The payment method is selected as part of a broader capital structure choice. Moreover, some bidder managements select (possibly debt financed)*	Capital structure: The cash portion of the bid must be financed internally or by a previous security issue. Schlingemann (2004), Toffanin (2005) find a link

(*Continued*)

Table 4 (*Continued*)

Theories	Hypotheses	Evidence
Stulz (1988)	*cash over stock as payment method in order to avoid diluting their private benefits of control in the merged firm.* In Rose (1977) increased leverage raises expected managerial-specific bankruptcy costs. In Jensen (1986), paying with cash drains free-cash flow and reduces agency costs.	between the market reaction to takeover announcements and financing decision in the previous year. Yook (2003) find greater bidder gains in all-cash offers when the takeover causes downgrading of the merged firm's debt (due to increased leverage). The results are consistent with agency costs of free cash flow (Jensen, 1986).
	In Harris and Raviv (1988), Stulz (1988), managers act to protect private benefits of control.	Control: Amihud et al. (1990), Martin (1996), Ghosh and Ruland (1998) find that bidder management shareholdings in the United States have negative effect on stock financing. Studying European mergers, Faccio and Masulis (2005) find that corporate control incentives to choose cash are particularly strong when in bidder firms with relatively concentrated shareownership structures. Martynova and Renneboog (2006) finds a link between the quality of a country's corporate governance system and the market reaction to stock as payment form.

D. Behavioral motives for the payment method choice

Shleifer and Vishny (2003)	H6: *Bidders are able to sell overpriced stock to less overpriced targets.*	The propensity of all-stock offers increases with M/B ratios (Ang and Cheng, 2006; Dong et al., 2006; Rhodes-Kropf et al., 2005). This supports the behavioral argument provided M/B is a fundamental driver of takeovers.
Rhodes-Kropf and Viswanathan (2004)	Bidders attempt to cash in on a temporary market overvaluation of their stocks. In Shleifer and Vishny they succeed because targets have "short time horizon."	Harford (2005): A macroeconomic measure of capital liquidity (interest rate spreads) drives merger activity and drives out M/B as a predictor of merger activity. This is inconsistent with the behavioral argument.
	In Rhodes-Kropf and Viswanathan (2004) they succeed because targets accept more bids from overvalued bidders during market valuation peaks because they tend overestimate synergies during these periods.	Betton et al. (2008c): There are nearly as many mixed cash-stock offers as all-stock offers, also in the recent period of high market valuations and peak merger activity (1996–2000). Mixed offers are an enigma in the model of Shleifer and Vishny (2003). The fact that the substantial market runup prior to year 2000 did not induce a greater use of all-stock offers as a proportion of all merger bids is inconsistent with the behavioral argument.

Hypothesis H1 in Table 4 holds that targets will receive higher offer premiums in all-cash bids than in all-stock offers, where the difference is compensation for the capital gains tax penalty inherent in the cash bid. Early studies that classify takeover premiums according to the payment method include Huang and Walkling (1987) and Hayn (1989) on US data, and Franks et al. (1988) and Eckbo and Langohr (1989) on acquisitions in the United Kingdom and France, respectively. This evidence shows that takeover premiums are indeed significantly greater in all-cash deals than in all-stock offers, which is consistent with H1. Also, Brown and Ryngaert (1991) find empirical support for their hypothesis that stocks are less likely to be found in taxable offers (offers where less than 50% of the offer is to be paid in bidder stock).

On the other hand, Franks et al. (1988) show that takeover premiums in the United Kingdom were greater in cash deals even *before* the introduction of capital gains taxes. Moreover, Eckbo and Langohr (1989) argue that for a tax compensation to induce tendering behavior, it must be included in the value of the option to tender (as opposed to keeping) the target shares. They approximate this option value with the difference between the offer price and the expected postoffer target share price, and they find that this difference is indistinguishable across all-stock and all-cash offers. They also how that the larger total premium in all-cash offers carries over to minority buyouts that convey few if any bidder tax benefits (as the two firms are already consolidated for counting purposes). This evidence does not support the view that the larger takeover premiums observed in all-cash deals are driven by the tax hypothesis H1.

3.2.2. Information asymmetries

Hypotheses H2-H4 in Panel B of Table 4 suggest that the payment method choice may be economically important—and give rise to premium effects—even in the absence of taxes. When the bidder and target are asymmetrically informed about the true value of their respective shares, the payment method may cause information revelation and affect both the division of synergy gains and the probability that the offer is successful. Hypothesis H2 is motivated by the adverse selection argument of Myers and Majluf (1984) and the associated financing "pecking order" suggested by Myers (1984). H2 focuses on the implication for the market's reaction to the all-stock versus all-cash announcement: Equity issues to relatively uninformed target shareholders may cause a negative market reaction as investors hedge against the possibility that the bidder's stock is overpriced.

There is substantial empirical evidence that seasoned equity offerings (SEOs) are on average met with a negative market reaction (approximately -3%)—even when the SEOs are fully underwritten by reputable investment banks. This is consistent with the hypothesis that outside investors are somewhat nervous that the typical equity issue may be overpriced—despite the substantial due diligence effort and reputational risk exposure of underwriters. The evidence on takeovers indicates that all-equity acquisition announcements also tend to cause a statistically significant (approximately) 1%

price bidder price drop when the target is a public company.[44] However, bidder announcement returns are nonnegative (or even positive) in all-stock offers for *private* targets.[45]

Hansen (1987), Fishman (1989), and Eckbo et al. (1990) provide theoretical analyses that also incorporate adverse selection but where the bidder's choice of payment method is modeled explicitly. An important insight of Hansen (1987) is that ex post means of payments such as stock can increase the seller's revenue beyond what cash payments can do.[46] This point is easily illustrated using our second-price, independent private value auction with two bidders ($v_1 > v_2$). If bidder 1 (B1) wins with an all-cash offer, the target receives v_2 (the second price). Alternatively, with all-stock as the payment method, the bidder offers the target the ownership fraction z_i in the merged firm. Suppose B1 and B2 have the same stand-alone value v. The optimal bid is the fraction z_i, which satisfies

$$(v + v_i)(1 - z_i) = v \tag{5}$$

or $z_i = v_i/(v + v_i)$. This leaves each bidder with a postacquisition value equal to the preacquisition (stand-alone) value. If B1 wins, the target receives

$$z_2(v + v_1) = \frac{v + v_1}{v + v_2} v_2 > v_2 \tag{6}$$

since $v_1 \geq v_2$. In other words, the all-stock offer extracts a higher revenue from the winning bidder than does the all-cash bid, resulting in more efficient sell/don't sell decisions by the target.[47]

Another insight is that all-stock payment may increase the expected deal value for the bidder if there is little or no uncertainty concerning the true bidder value. Consider a single bidder B who has all the bargaining power. Denote B's with-synergy value as $v_B \equiv v + v_i$. Assume that v_B is known to everyone and that B only knows the probability distribution over the true target value, $v_T \in [\underline{v}_T, \bar{v}_T]$, where $\underline{v}_T < \bar{v}_T$. Moreover, suppose B's strategy is to ensure bid success.[48] The all-cash offer is therefore $c = \bar{v}_T$.

---

[44] Travlos (1987), Asquith et al. (1987), Servaes (1991), Brown and Ryngaert (1991), Martin (1996), Emery and Switzer (1999), Heron and Lie (2004), and Schlingemann (2004). Because the level of communication between bidder and target management teams in merger negotiations is greater than that between underwriters and the market in SEOs, the potential for adverse selection is also smaller, thus the smaller price drop in all-equity bids than in SEOs.

[45] Chang (1998), Fuller et al. (2002), Moeller et al. (2004), Bradley and Sundaram (2006), and Officer et al. (2009). Faccio et al. (2006) find a similar positive bidder announcement effect of all-stock offers in Europe.

[46] See also Hansen (1985), DeMarzo et al. (2005), and Dasgupta and Hansen (2007) for a review.

[47] In Fishman (1989), the alternative to cash is a debt instrument secured in the *target's* asset. This also eliminates target uncertainty about the true value of the bidder's payment for all-security offers and leads to efficient target accept/reject decisions.

[48] This bid strategy is maintained in the model of Eckbo et al. (1990b). In Hansen (1987), high-value bidders separate themselves by lowering their all-stock offers z, which is costly as it reduces the probability that the target will accept. The signaling cost is the reduction in the bidder's expected synergy gains from a reduction in z.

This means that B expects to overpay for the target by the amount $\bar{v}_T - E(v_T|\text{accept})$, where the expectation is conditional on the target accepting the bid. The corresponding all-stock offer solves $z(v_B + \bar{v}_T) = \bar{v}_T$, or $z = \bar{v}_T/(v_B + \bar{v}_T)$. The expected overpayment cost is now

$$z[v_B + E(v_T|\text{accept})] - E(v_T|\text{accept}) = \frac{v_B}{v_B + \bar{v}_T}[\bar{v}_T - E(v_T|\text{accept})] \tag{7}$$

Since $v_B/(v_B + \bar{v}_T) < 1$, the expected overpayment cost of securities is less than that of cash, reflecting the contingent nature of stock as payment form (payment in shares causes the target to share in the overpayment ex post). Cash, on the other hand, precommits the bidder to a target value ex ante.

If we also allow v_B to be private information (two-sided information asymmetry), then the above preference for a stock offer is reversed provided the bidder shares are sufficiently undervalued by the target. With two-sided information asymmetry, let $\hat{v}_B$ denote target beliefs about bidder value. In this case, the all-stock offer which guarantees success solves $z(\hat{v}_B + \hat{v}_T) = \hat{v}_T$, and the difference between the expected overpayment cost of an all-stock and an all-cash offer becomes

$$\bar{v}_T = \frac{(v_B - \hat{v}_B) - (\bar{v}_T - E(v_T|\text{accept}))}{v_B + E(v_T|\text{accept})} \tag{8}$$

which is positive or negative depending on whether the target undervalues $(v_B - \hat{v}_B > 0)$ or overvalues $(v_B - \hat{v}_B < 0)$ the bidder shares, respectively. Consistent with this, Chemmanur and Paeglis (2003) find that the probability of a stock offer falls when measures of bidder share underpricing increase.

As discussed earlier (see Figure 7), mixed cash-stock offers are pervasive across the entire sample period. Eckbo et al. (1990) and Berkovitch and Narayanan (1990) model equilibrium mixed offers.[49] In the separating equilibrium of Eckbo et al. (1990), bidder types are separated by the fraction of the total target payment that is paid in cash. Consistent with a separating equilibrium, Eckbo et al. (1990) and Eckbo and Thorburn (2000) find that abnormal announcement returns are, on average, highest in all-cash offers and lowest in all-stock deals, with mixed offers in between.[50]

Eckbo et al. (1990) present cross-sectional regressions tests of their signaling model. To illustrate, let γ_j denote the announcement-induced bidder abnormal return. The separating equilibrium implies that

$$\gamma_j = h_j\left(\frac{c_j}{v_T}\right), \quad h_j', h_j'' > 0, \tag{9}$$

---

[49] In Hansen (1987) and Fishman (1989), bidders select between all-stock and all-cash offers but do not mix the two.

[50] These two studies use mergers in Canada where offering less than 50% of the deal in cash does not trigger capital gains taxes. In the United States, the tax code confounds the analysis as it in of itself discourages mixed offers where the cash portion exceeds 50% (Brown and Ryngaert, 1991).

where c_j is the cash payment, v_T is the average prebid target value, and the superscripts h'_j and h''_j denote first and second derivatives, respectively. That is, in the separating equilibrium, the market reaction to the takeover announcement is an increasing and convex function of the cash portion of the deal. The cross-sectional regression tests confirm the "increasing" part, but fails to identify a significant second derivative (convexity). Additional empirical tests are required to sort out why convexity fails.

3.2.3. Capital structure and control motives

Under hypothesis H5 in Panel C of Table 4, the payment method is selected as part of a broader capital structure choice. Moreover, some bidder managements select cash over stock to avoid diluting private benefits of control. Attempts to link the payment method choice to financing sources for the cash portion of the bid are only starting to emerge. For example, Yook (2003) finds greater bidder gains in all-cash offers when the takeover causes downgrading of the merged firm's debt (due to increased leverage). He interprets this as consistent with the free-cash flow argument of Jensen (1986).

Schlingemann (2004) and Toffanin (2005) examine whether the market reaction to the payment method choice is a function of the type of cash financing. While the market is aware of any prebid public security issues, the acquisition bid announcement possibly resolves uncertainty regarding use of the issue proceeds. If this resolution is economically important, the source of financing for the cash portion of the bid will affect the market reaction to the takeover attempt. The empirical results indicate a prior-cash-financing-source component in acquisition announcement returns.

Schlingemann (2004) reports that, after controlling for the form of payment, financing decisions during the year before a takeover play an important role in explaining the cross section of bidder gains. Bidder announcement-period abnormal returns are positively and significantly related to the amount of ex ante equity financing. This relation is particularly strong for high q firms. He further reports a negative and significant relation between bidder gains and free cash flow. This relation is particularly strong for firms classified as having poor investment opportunities. The amount of debt financing before a takeover announcement is not significantly related to bidder gains. Interestingly. Toffanin (2005) finds that the well-known positive market reaction to all-cash bids requires the cash to have been financed either using internal funds (retained earnings) or borrowing. All-cash acquisitions financed by a prior equity issue earn zero or negative abnormal returns.

Early theories incorporating private benefits of control in the contexts of takeovers and capital structure choice are Stulz (1988) and Harris and Raviv (1988). In our context, an all-cash offer preserves the bidder's control position, while an all-stock offer may significantly dilute this position (e.g., a merger of equals). The potential for control dilution may therefore drive the use of cash. Several empirical papers examine the payment method choice from this angle. For example, Amihud et al. (1990), Martin (1996), and Ghosh and Ruland (1998) all find that bidder management shareholdings in the United States have negative effects on stock financing. Similarly, studying

European mergers, Faccio and Masulis (2005) find that corporate control incentives to choose cash are particularly strong in bidder firms with relatively concentrated share ownership structures. Overall, corporate control motives are likely to play a role in some all-cash mergers. Martynova and Renneboog (2006), who also examine acquisitions in Europe, find a link between the quality of a country's corporate governance system and the market reaction to stock as payment form. All-stock offers are more likely in countries with greater levels of shareholder rights protection.

3.2.4. Behavioral arguments for all-stock

The hypothesis here is that bidders are able to sell overpriced stock to less overpriced targets (H6). We discussed this hypothesis in Section 2.1 on merger waves and so will provide only a summary here. In the model of Shleifer and Vishny (2003), bidders succeed in selling overpriced stock to target managers with a short time horizon. In Rhodes-Kropf and Viswanathan (2004), bidders succeed as targets (rationally) accept more bids from overvalued bidders during market valuation peaks because they tend to overestimate synergies during these periods. Empirically, the propensity to select all-stock offers increases with M/B ratios. If one views the M/B ratio as a proxy for stock overvaluation, then this empirical regularity supports the behavioral argument for all-stock selections.[51] On the other hand, Harford (2005) finds that a macroeconomic measure of capital liquidity (interest rate spreads) drives merger activity and drives out M/B as a predictor of merger activity. This finding reduces the likelihood that market overvaluation systematically drives the bidder's selection of all-stock as the payment method.

Earlier we reported that there are nearly as many mixed cash-stock offers as all-stock offers, even in the recent period of high market valuations and peak merger activity (1996–2000). Because mixing cash and stock increases the ability of under-valued bidders to separate out from the pool of overvalued bidders (Eckbo et al., 1990), the substantial presence of mixed offers undermines the pooling equilibrium of Shleifer and Vishny (2003). Also, our finding in Figure 7 that the substantial market runup prior to year 2000 did not induce greater use of all-stock offers as a proportion of all merger bids further undermines the behavioral argument. In sum, while some bidders undoubtedly get away with selling overpriced stock to their targets, additional research is needed to systematically contrast behavioral to rational theories of the payment method choice in takeovers.

3.3. Toehold bidding

In this section, we first discuss optimal bids when the initial bidder has a toehold and has also negotiated a termination agreement. We then review the empirical evidence on toehold bidding.

---

[51] Rhodes-Kropf et al. (2005), Ang and Cheng (2006), and Dong et al. (2006).

3.3.1. Optimal bids

We use a standard auction setting with two risk-neutral bidders. The bidders have private valuations that are independent and identical distributed (i.i.d.) with distribution and density functions $G(v)$ and $g(v)$, respectively. The initial bidder (B1) has toehold $\alpha \in [0, 0.5)$ acquired at the normalized pretakeover target share price of zero. B1 has negotiated a merger agreement with the target management that includes a termination fee $t \in (0, v)$. A rival bidder (B2) challenges the agreement and forces an open auction. The termination fee is paid by B2 if B2 wins, or by the target if neither B1 nor B2 wins (the target remains independent). The no-bidder-wins outcome occurs with an exogenous probability θ.[52]

Since the termination fee represents a claim of t on the target, the fee reduces B2's private valuation to $v_2 - t$. B2's optimal bid is therefore $b_2^* = v_2 - t$: bidding less risks foregoing a profitable takeover, while bidding more risks overpaying for the target. Given B2's optimal bid, and noting that the net termination fee paid to B1 if B2 wins is $(1 - \alpha)t$, B1's expected profits from bidding b is

$$E(\Pi) = \{(v)G(b+t) - (1-\alpha) \int_t^{b+t} (v_2 - t)g(v_2)\mathrm{d}v_2 \\ + (t + \alpha b)[1 - G(b+t)]\}(1 - \theta) + t(1-\alpha)\theta \tag{10}$$

The right-hand side is the sum of four components. The first three (inside the curly bracket) are, respectively, B1's expected private value, the expected payment for the target, and the expected value from selling the toehold α and receiving t when B2 wins the auction. The fourth term is the expected payoff when no bidder wins. Using Equation (10), the first-order condition for profit maximization, $\partial E(\Pi)/\partial b = 0$, implies an optimal bid for B1 of [53]

$$b_1^* = v_1 - t + \alpha h(b_1^*) \tag{11}$$

where $h(b_1^*) \equiv 1 - G(b_1^*)/g(b_1^*)$. Notice the following from Equation (11):

- The toehold induces overbidding, that is, a bid greater than the private valuation v_1. This means that B1 may win even if B2 is the higher valuation bidder (when $v_1 < v_2 < b_1^*$).
- The effect of the termination fee is to induce underbidding. For example, a bidder with zero toehold and a termination agreement walks away from the target when

---

[52] The probability θ captures exogenous factors that may derail merger negotiations or cause all bidders to abandon a takeover auction. For example, the market may revise upwards its estimate of the target's standalone value during the contest, causing the takeover to be unprofitable for both B1 and B2. Betton et al. (2009) report that close to 30% of takeover contests end up in the no-bidder-wins state. This issue is discussed further below.

[53] To ensure uniqueness, $G(v)$ must be twice continuously differentiable and satisfy the monotonicity condition $\partial (1 - G(v))/\partial g(v) \geq 0$.

rival bids exceed $v_1 - t$ (quitting means receiving t while continued bidding implies an expected profit of less than t).

- Since B1's optimal bid is increasing in the toehold, the probability that B1 wins the auction is also increasing in the toehold. This gives economic content to the frequently heard notion among practitioners that toehold bidding is "aggressive" toward the target.
- When $\alpha = 1$, the optimal bid b_1^* is equivalent to the optimal reserve price by a monopolist seller in a take-it-or-leave-it offer (Eckbo and Thorburn, 2009).

Bulow et al. (1999) and Dasgupta and Tsui (2003) examine toehold bidding in a pure common-value setting where both B1 and B2 have toeholds but of unequal size (asymmetric toeholds). Toehold bidding also induces overbidding in a common-value setting, and these researchers show that holding B1's toehold constant, B2's probability of winning goes to zero as B2's toehold becomes arbitrarily small. Even small differences in toeholds can produce significant benefits for the bidder with the greater toehold. Moreover, the expected winning sales price is decreasing in the difference between the toeholds of B1 and B2. This suggests an incentive on the part of the target to sell a toehold to B2—and for B2 to purchase a toehold—in order to even the playing field. Consistent with this, Betton and Eckbo (2000) find that when a rival bidder enters a takeover contest with a toehold, the toehold size is on average roughly the same size as that of the initial bidder (approximately 5%).

3.3.2. The toehold puzzle

A priori, there is a compelling case for acquiring a toehold prior to initiating a takeover bid. The toehold not only reduces the number of shares that must be purchased at the full takeover premium, but it may also be sold at an even greater premium should a rival bidder enter the contest and win the target. This expected toehold gain raises the bidder's valuation of the target, which in turn helps overcome free-rider problems and makes the toehold bidder a more aggressive competitor in the presence of rivals. Early empirical research supports the existence of toehold benefits. Walkling (1985), Jennings and Mazzeo (1993), and Betton and Eckbo (2000) show that toehold bidding increases the probability of winning the target. Consistent with entry deterrence effects of toeholds, Betton and Eckbo (2000) also find that toeholds are associated with lower offer premiums in winning bids.

However, toehold bidding has in fact been declining dramatically over the past two decades and is now surprisingly rare. This decline is apparent in Figure 8, which plots toehold data from Betton et al. (2009). The toeholds in Figure 8 include target shares held by the bidder long term as well as shares purchased within 6 months of the actual offer date (short-term toeholds). Betton et al. (2009) report a sample-wide toehold frequency of 13%. Moreover, the sample-wide frequency of short-term toeholds—defined as target shares purchased within 6 months of the offer—is only 2%. In sum,

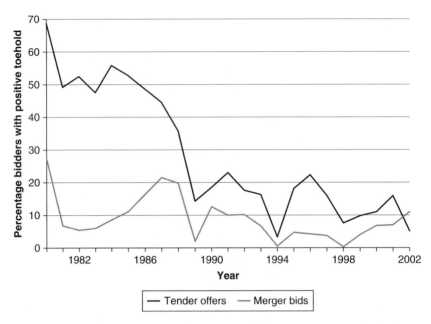

Fig. 8. Annual percentage of initial control bidders with a positive toehold in the target, classified by the type of the initial bid. US public targets. Data source: Betton et al. (2009).

toehold benefits notwithstanding, toeholds acquired as part of an active bidding strategy are almost nonexistent.

Presumably, rational bidders avoid toeholds as a response to large toehold costs. Several potential sources of toehold costs have been suggested in the literature, ranging from mandatory information disclosure and market illiquidity to costs associated with target management resistance to the takeover. Consider first the argument that mandatory disclosure rules make toeholds too costly because they reveal the bidder's intentions early in the takeover process. As discussed above, toehold purchases of 5% or more have triggered mandatory disclosure requirements (13d filings with the SEC) since the 1968 Williams Act. Also, under the 1976 Hart-Scott-Rodino (HSR) Antitrust Improvements Act, share acquisitions exceeding a certain threshold ($60 million in 2007) trigger notification to the antitrust agencies.

As shown in Figure 8, however, toehold bidding was relatively common in the early 1980s. The passage of disclosure rules in the 1970s cannot explain this time-series pattern. Also, the decline in toehold bidding has occurred despite a steady increase in market liquidity over the entire sample period.[54] Furthermore, Betton et al. (2009)

---

[54] Small toeholds, for which concerns with liquidity and disclosure are unimportant, can also have significant investment value as they retain many of the strategic benefits of larger ones. Toehold benefits arise as long as the toehold is greater than that of the rival bidder (Bulow et al., 1999; Dasgupta and Tsui, 2004).

report that the average toehold size (when positive) is as large as 20%, and 13% for short-term toeholds. It is difficult to explain the observed bimodal toehold distribution (centered on either zero or large toeholds) by appealing to general market illiquidity.

Goldman and Qian (2005) point to a toehold cost when entrenched target management successfully thwarts the takeover bid. In their model, entrenched target managements may resist a bidder in order to retain the private benefits of control. The degree of target entrenchment is unknown ex ante and, in equilibrium, is signaled ex post through the size of the bidder's toehold in successfully resisted offers. Successful resistance causes the target share price to drop, and the price drop is greater the greater the bidder's toehold. Bidders trade off expected toehold benefits (greater success probability) with expected toehold costs (greater target price decline when the bid fails), causing some bidders to select small or even zero toeholds. However, the evidence in Betton et al. (2009) rejects the predicted negative correlation between the sizes of bidder toeholds and target price declines conditional on all bids failing. The potential for a toehold loss in the event that all bids fail following target resistance does not appear to explain the toehold puzzle.

Betton et al. (2009) develop and test a model in which toehold costs arise endogenously. The takeover game starts with the initial bidder approaching the target with an invitation to negotiate a merger. In line with the fiduciary out requirement discussed earlier, a merger agreement is always followed by a period during which the target board is required to consider any rival bids (until the shareholder vote). The expected outcome of this open auction period determines the outcome of merger negotiations. Since a toehold affects the expected auction outcome (recall the optimal bid in Equation (11)), it also affects the willingness of entrenched target managements to accept the bidder's invitation to negotiate. If the target management rejects negotiations, the bidder foregoes the benefit of the termination agreement and incurs resistance costs during the takeover process.

These toehold-induced bidder costs make it optimal for some bidders to approach the target without a toehold. That is, the expected toehold cost creates a *toehold threshold* (a minimum toehold size), below which the optimal toehold is zero. Betton et al. (2009) show that the toehold threshold averages 9% in the data, which is consistent with the observed bimodal distribution of observed toeholds (centered on zero or large toeholds). That is, some bidders find that the toehold threshold is too costly to purchase in the market (e.g., due to market illiquidity) and select zero toehold. The key model prediction is that the likelihood of toehold bidding decreases in the toehold threshold estimate (the expected opportunity loss of the termination agreement), which the empirical evidence supports.

The threshold model is also consistent with another stylized fact: toeholds are much more common in hostile than in friendly takeovers. While 11% of initial bidders have toehold when the target is friendly, 50% of the initial bidders in hostile contests have toeholds. The threshold theory suggests that one should observe toehold bidding when the opportunity cost of the toehold is relatively low. A special case is when the opportunity cost is *zero,* which occurs whenever the target's optimal resistance strategy is independent of the toehold. That is, if target management is expected to resist regardless of toeholds, acquiring a toehold is always optimal.[55] Thus, the toehold threshold model predicts a higher toehold frequency in hostile bids, and it is consistent with the observed decline in the frequency of toehold bidding over the 1990s (Figure 8). This decline coincides with a general reduction in hostile bids due to a widespread adoption of strong takeover defenses such as poison pills.

Finally, in the absence of synergistic opportunities with the target ($v = 0$), the owner of a toehold may contemplate making a (false) bid in an attempt to put the target in play. The idea is to try to sell the toehold to a potential rival bidder or (anonymously) to an unwitting market anticipating a successful takeover. Bagnoli and Lipman (1996) present a model with a single bidder selling the toehold shares to individual noise traders through a market maker before calling off the takeover bid. While charges of price manipulation go back at least to the greenmail episodes of the late 1970s, systematic empirical evidence on the feasibility of this type of price manipulation is virtually nonexistent. The context of hostile bids is potentially interesting since hostility may induce the target to produce a white knight committed to purchase the toehold.

3.4. Bid jumps and markup pricing

In this section we examine evidence on the size of bid jumps in multiple-bid contests and investigate how prebid target runups affect the initial and final offer prices. Also, an interesting question is whether target runups and markup pricing deter toehold acquisitions by the initial bidder.

3.4.1. Preemption and bid jumps

As indicated earlier, the high premiums observed in takeovers are consistent with the hypothesis that takeover benefits are partly common to several potential bidders. This is likely when takeover benefits emanate, for example, from replacing inefficient target management or using voting control to extract value from ex post minority share-holders in the merged firm. These and other forms of bidder-target complementarities often do not require specialized resources owned by a single potential bidder firm. As a result, the first bidder is concerned that the initial bid will alert potential rivals to a profit opportunity. The empirical issue is whether this possibility affects observed bid strategies.

Fishman (1988) analyzes this issue assuming that bidders must pay an investigation cost to identify their respective private valuations of the target. If both bidders enter (so that both investigation costs are sunk), an open English auction with costless bidding ensues and produces the "ratchet" solution $\min[v_1, v_2]$ (Hirshleifer, 1995). However, there exists an initial bid that deters the second bidder from paying the investigation

---

[55] Similarly, toehold bidding occurs when the target's optimal strategy is to never resist.

cost and entering the auction. The high initial (all-cash) bid signals that the initial bidder has a relatively high private valuation for the target, which reduces rival bidders' expected value of winning. For a sufficiently large investigation cost, the expected value is negative and the rival does not enter.

Testing preemption arguments is difficult since one obviously cannot observe deterred bids nor bidder private valuations in observed bids. One must look to auxiliary or related predictions, and the following four categories of results seem relevant. First, entry is rapid when it occurs: the average number of trading days between the first and second control bid is 40 in our sample (Figure 6) and 15 days in Betton and Eckbo (2000). This suggests that the rival bidder's investigation process required to establish its own valuation of the target is not very time-consuming in these cases. Also, some rivals may have completed much of the evaluation prior to the initial bid. Observing the initial bid event may produce a sufficient target valuation estimate to make a bid.

Second, auction outcomes are sensitive to bidder asymmetries. One important form of bidder asymmetry is the size of bidder toeholds. Even small toehold differences can have a large impact on entry and competition. Empirically, Betton and Eckbo (2000) find that when a rival bidder enters a takeover contest with a positive toehold, the toehold size is on average of roughly the same size as that of the initial bidder (approximately 5%). It is as if the rival bidder realizes the initial bidder's toehold advantage and wants to neutralize it upon entry.

Third, both Betton and Eckbo (2000) and Betton et al. (2009) report that the average offer premium in single-bidder successful tender offer contests (the first node in Figure 2) is slightly higher than the average *initial* offer premium in contests that developed into multiple bids. This is consistent with the argument that the premiums in single-bid successful contests are preemptive in the sense of Fishman (1988). However, the premium effect is weak: the probability of rival bidder entry appears unaffected by the initial offer premium (Betton et al., 2008b).

Fourth, Betton and Eckbo (2000) report evidence of significant bid jumps throughout the tender offer contests. For example, the average jump from the initial to the second bid price in the contest is 10%, implying a 31% change in the initial offer premium. The jump from the first to the final bid average 14% (a 65% revision in the initial offer premium), and the average bid jump throughout the entire contest, is 5% (average premium increments of 17%). The evidence of significant bid jumps throughout the contest is consistent with the presence of bidding costs. This in turn supports the notion in Fishman (1988) that initial bidders may strategically raise the first bid in an attempt to deter competition.[56]

---

[56] See also Hirshleifer and Ping (1990) and Daniel and Hirshleifer (2008) for discussions of the implication of bidding costs for optimal bidding strategies.

3.4.2. Runups and markups

We now turn to the markup pricing phenomenon first documented by Schwert (1996). Initial takeover bids are typically preceded by substantial target stock price runups. The runup reflects takeover rumors generated from various public sources, such as Schedule 13(d) filings with SEC disclosing stake purchases of 5% or more in the target, media speculations, and street talk. The conventional view is that runups reflect takeover rumors based on information that is already known to the bidder.[57] If this view is correct, the runup anticipates an already planned offer premium and does not require a premium revision before the offer is made.

This is not the only possible scenario, however. Schwert (1996) begins his paper with the following question:

> Suppose that you are planning to bid for control of a company and, before you can announce the offer, the price of the target firm's stock begins to rise coincident with unusually high trading volume. You have not been buying the target company's stock, and there is no reliable evidence to show who has been buying. Do you go forward with the offer exactly as you had planned? Or do you take into account the recent movement in the target's stock price and adjust your bidding strategy? (pp. 153–154)

Bidders need a plan for how to react to the runup before making the initial bid. Moreover, such a plan requires an understanding of the true nature of the prebid target runup. For example, it is possible that the target runup represents an increase in the target's fundamental (stand-alone) value, in which case the target management may demand a higher price. If so, the bidder may be forced to mark up the offer price to reflect the higher target stock price on the day before the offer is made.

To examine the extent of markup pricing, Schwert (1996) writes the total offer premium as $Premium \equiv Markup + Runup$, where $Runup$ is the cumulative target abnormal stock return from day -42 through day -1 relative to the first bid for the target (day 0), and $Markup$ is the cumulative abnormal target stock return from day 0 through day 126 (or until delisting, whatever comes first). He then estimates the coefficient b in the following cross-sectional regression:

$$Premium_i = a + b \ Runup_i + u_i \qquad (12)$$

where u is an error term. With a sample of 1814 mergers and tender offers from the period 1975–1991, Schwert finds a statistically significant $b = 1.13$ for the total sample (with a t-value of 2.88 for the null hypothesis of $b = 1$). In other words, in the total sample, a dollar runup in the target stock price raises the total offer premium by approximately a dollar. Under the more conventional view of the runup, $Markup$ and $Runup$ are substitutes (predicting $b = 0$ in regression (12)), which Schwert's evidence rejects.

---

[57] Jarrell and Poulsen (1989) and King and Padalko (2005) conclude that runups are primarily a result of public information. Meulbroek (1992) and Schwert (1996) find greater target runups in cases where the SEC subsequently alleges insider trading.

Schwert's estimate of the markup is impacted by events occurring *after* the initial offer, such as the entry of rival bidders and bid revisions by the initial bidder, target management resistance, and ultimate target shareholder voting outcomes. Betton et al. (2008b) use the initial offer price p_{initial} to measure the initial markup directly as $Markup = \ln(p_{\text{initial}}/p_{-1})$, where p_{-1} is the target share price on the day prior to the initial bid. The runup is measured as $Runup = \ln(p_{-1}/p_{-42})$. With a sample of 6000 initial takeover bids for US public targets from the period 1980–2002, they estimate the coefficient b' in the following regression,

$$\text{Markup}_i = a' + b' \, \text{Runup}_i + cX + u_i \tag{13}$$

where X is a set of bidder- and target-specific deal characteristics. Betton, Eckbo, and Thorburn find that $b' = -0.18$ for the total sample (*t*-value of -15.44). Thus, in the cross section of bids, a dollar increase in the target runup is associated with an increase in the average initial offer price by $\$0.82$.[58] They also show that the degree of substitution between the markup and the runup is greater when the bidder purchases a target toehold in the runup period, and they conclude that target runups are an unlikely explanation for the sparsity of toehold purchases by initial bidders in the runup period.

Is markup pricing costly in the sense of reducing bidder synergies? To examine this issue, Betton et al. (2008b) estimate the following cross-sectional regression with bidder takeover-induced abnormal stock returns, BCAR, as dependent variable:

$$\text{BCAR}_i = a_b + b_b \, \text{Runup}_i + c_b X_i + u_i \tag{14}$$

where *Runup* is the *target* runup (as before). The coefficient b_b is positive and highly significant in a sample exceeding 4000 public bidders. That is, greater target runups are simultaneously associated with markup pricing and greater bidder synergies from the takeover.

Since target synergies are also (obviously) increasing in target runups, the positive estimate of b_b means that the runup is a proxy for *total* synergies in the cross section. This finding affects the interpretation of the coefficients b and b' in Equations (12) and (13). To illustrate, suppose takeover rumors allow market investors to not only identify the target but also to distinguish targets with high and low expected total synergies. Moreover, suppose competition always forces bidders to grant target shareholders (in the form of a takeover premium) a fixed portion of the total synergies. Bidders expecting the takeover to be profitable now also expect a high prebid runup, and mark up the initial offer price ex ante (before the runup). This also produces a markup that is independent of the runup ex post ($b = 1$), although there are no actual bid revisions following the runup. Ultimately, distinguishing between this total synergy hypothesis and Schwert (1996)'s ex post markup proposition requires evidence on

---

[58] If one changes the dependent variable in Equation (13) to the total initial offer premium, $\ln(p_{\text{initial}}/p_{-42})$, the slope coefficient changes to $1 + b' = 0.82$.

actual offer price changes made by the initial bidder during the runup period. However, either scenario is consistent with a positive association with target runups and bidder takeover gains.

3.5. Takeover defenses

In this section, we briefly characterize the legal basis for target takeover defenses, and then we examine the empirical evidence on the shareholder wealth effects of antitakeover measures, in particular poison pills, classified boards, and defensive payouts (greenmail). Figure 9 shows the annual frequency of the sample of 1052 unfriendly (unsolicited and outright hostile) initial bids previously listed in Table 1.

Since target hostility may simply represent posturing to improve the target's bargaining position, several definitions of hostility exist (Schwert, 2000). The SDC definition probably casts a relatively wide net, as all it ensures is that (1) the bidder (and not the target) initiates the takeover and (2) the target board is initially unprepared and/or unwilling to enter into merger negotiations. Specifically, the SDC classification does *not* necessarily mean that the target is dead set against negotiations, nor does it mean that it is going to implement defensive tactics. However, target defensive actions

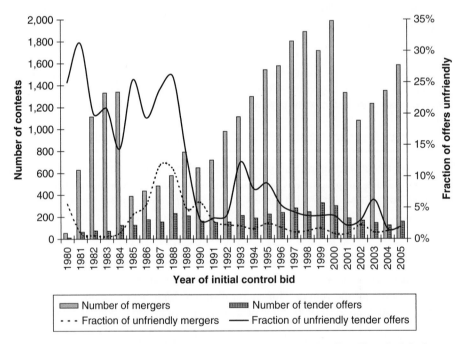

Fig. 9. Target attitude toward the initial control bidder in mergers and tender offers. The attitude is shown as "unfriendly" ($N = 1025$) if the SDC lists the offer as either "hostile" or "unsolicited." All other offers are shown as "friendly" ($N = 34,702$). US targets, 1980–2005.

are more likely in this sample than in cases where initial bids are classified by SDC as solicited or friendly. Notice also that the SDC definition allows a hostile initial bid to be in the form of either a merger or a tender offer (although, as shown in Figure 9, unfriendly initial bids are typically in the form of a tender offer). An example of an initially hostile merger bid is a "bear hug," in which the bidder invites the target to negotiate while reminding the target board that the bidder is likely to pursue a tender offer should the board refuse negotiations.

As shown in Figure 9, the fraction of bids that are unfriendly is relatively high throughout the 1980s and then drops sharply after 1989. Comment and Schwert (1995) analyze the drop in hostility, which is closely associated with the spread of takeover defenses and the development of state antitakeover statutes (control share and business combinations laws). Given this close association, it is natural to view the drop as being caused by increased managerial entrenchment afforded by strong takeover defenses. Comment and Schwert (1995), however, argue that the emergence of takeover defenses played only a minor role in ending the 1980s merger wave. They point instead to the development of a general economic recession beginning in 1989, which caused a collapse in net new lending to the nonfinancial sector by commercial banks from $33 billion in 1989 to $2 billion in 1990. Commercial banks were the dominant providers of bridge or transaction financing for large, cash acquisitions at the time. Takeover activity was also generally reduced as a result of a drop in the availability of long-term and subordinated financing, in part due to government intervention in the junk bonds in 1989.[59]

While the overall credit crunch undoubtedly slowed the economy and reduced takeover activity, there is also little doubt that the sharp reduction in *unfriendly* takeovers in large part reflects the legal certification and spread of strong antitakeover measures. Indeed, Jensen (1993) argues that the regulatory attack on the junk bond market around 1989 in of itself may be understood as a broadly organized defensive tactic against unwanted takeovers.[60] While the combination of a poison pill and staggered board is not viewed as a draconian defense in the eyes of the law (see below), there can be no question that these measures when used in combination effectively bar or seriously delay a hostile bid. As discussed in the following, however, the overall degree of deterrence remains unclear from the empirical literature.

---

[59] "In August 1989, Congress passed the Financial Institutions Reform, Recovery and Enforcement Act (FIR-REA), which penalized savings and loans for holding junk bonds and mandated their sale, while regulators issued guidelines barring commercial bank participation in highly leveraged transactions (including all acquisition loans that raised liabilities to 75% of assets, or doubled the debt ratio while raising it to 50% of assets). The junk bond market crashed in September 1989" (Comment and Schwert, 1995, p. 9).

[60] The critical view many business leaders had of the junk bond market is illustrated by the sentiment expressed by J. Richard Munro, chairman and CEO of Time, Inc., in a speech in 1989: "Notwithstanding television ads to the contrary, junk bonds are designed as the currency of 'casino economics' ... they've been used not to create new plants or jobs or products but to do the opposite: to dismantle existing companies so the players can make their profit. This isn't the Seventh Cavalry coming to the rescue. It's a scalping party" (Munro, 1989, p. 472).

3.5.1. Legal basis for defensive measures

In this section, we summarize certain aspects of the highly complex case law governing takeover defenses.[61] We focus on Delaware case law since a majority of US public companies (and more than 60% of the Fortune 500 firms) are incorporated in the state of Delaware.

Delaware case law sanctions the right of a board to "just say no" to an unsolicited takeover bid and to defend itself against that bid if necessary to remain an independent corporation. The case law rests on director fiduciary duties and the judicially developed principle referred to as the business judgment rule. Director fiduciary duties include duty of care and duty of loyalty. Duty of care is typically satisfied as long as the board examines fairness opinions of a bid and spends a minimum amount of board time discussing the value of the proposed deal.[62] Duty of loyalty is typically satisfied as long as the proposed deal does not imply a personal benefit for directors. Moreover, the presence of a majority of independent directors is viewed as a strong indication of the satisfaction of duty of loyalty.

The business judgment rule presumes, when director action is challenged, that the director of a corporation acted on an informed basis, in good faith, and in the best interest of the company. If the board is found to have acted this way, a court will not substitute its judgment for that of the board, and the court is inclined to find some rational purpose for the board action. In the context of a takeover bid, the board may determine in good faith that the continuing independence of the corporation is in the long-term best interests of the corporation and its stockholders. The board "is under no obligation, in the abstract, to submit to an external summons to the auction block or otherwise transfer control of corporate assets."[63]

A board may even be legally required to oppose an offer that it believes is not in the best interest of the corporation and its stockholders.[64] The board is not obligated to accept an offer simply because it represents a premium over a current market price. Refusal of such an offer is not *prima facie* evidence of a breach of fiduciary duty,[65] *except* when a sale of control of the corporation has been decided. If a determination is made to enter into a sale of control transaction, the fiduciary duties of the directors are enhanced and the directors have an obligation to seek the transaction offering the best value (which may mean highest price) reasonably available to stockholders—the so-called Revlon-duties.[66]

---

[61] We have benefited greatly from conversations with John G. Gorman, partner in the law firm Luse Gorman Pomerenk & Schtik, P.C. (Washington, DC). For comprehensive reviews of federal and state rules governing corporate control changes, see, for example, Wasserstein (2000), Lipton and Steinberger (2004), and Gaughan (2007).

[62] The standard for determining breach of the duty of care is generally considered to be gross negligence. *Smith vs. Van Gorkam*, 488 A.2d 858 (Del. 1985).

[63] *Paramount Communications, Inc. vs. Time, Inc.*, 571 A.2d 1140 (Del. 1990).

[64] *Gilbert vs. El Paso Co.*, 575A.2d 1131 (Del. 1990).

[65] *Pogostin vs. Rice*, 480 A.2d 619 (Del. 1984).

[66] See *Revlon, Inc. vs. MacAndrews and Forbes Holdings, Inc.*, 506 A.2d 182 (Del. 1986), and *Paramount Communications, Inc. vs. QVC Network, Inc.*, 637 A.2d 34 (Del. 1994).

Case law sanctions a wide range of target defensive mechanisms against an unsolicited bid. However, the courts have noted that given the "omnipresent-specter that a board may be acting primarily in its own interests, there is an enhanced duty which calls for judicial examination at the threshold before the protections of the business judgment rule may be conferred."[67] This modified business judgment rule requires that the board initially establishes that (i) it had reasonable grounds for believing there was a danger to corporate policy and effectiveness, and (ii) the measure adopted in response to the threat was reasonable in relation to the threat posed.[68]

If the board's defensive response is not draconian (i.e., it is neither coercive nor preclusive) but within the range of reasonableness given the perceived threat, the board is protected by the modified business judgment rule. The following excerpt from the Unitrin decision, the leading case on a board of directors' ability to use defensive measures to prevent a hostile takeover, illustrates the court's mind-set:[69]

> Proper and proportionate defensive responses are intended and permitted to thwart perceived threats. When a corporation is not for sale, the board of directors is the defender of the metaphorical medieval corporate bastion and the protector of the corporation's shareholders. The fact that a defensive action must not be coercive or preclusive does not prevent a board from responding defensively before a bidder is at the corporate gate .... Thus, continuing with the medieval metaphor, if a board reasonably perceives that a threat is on the horizon, it has broad authority to respond with a panoply of individual or combined defensive precautions, e.g., staffing the barbican, raising the drawbridge, and lowering the portcullis. Stated more directly, depending upon the circumstances, the board may respond to a reasonably perceived threat by adopting individually or sometimes in combination: advance notice by-laws, supermajority voting provisions, shareholder rights plans, repurchase programs, etc.

A defense that is deemed preclusive because it frustrates, impedes, or disenfranchises a shareholder vote will be held to the so-called Blasius standard of compelling justification[70] and is unlikely to be upheld.[71] For example, a stock repurchase designed primarily to preclude a third party from winning a proxy contest for the selection of directors may not pass the Blasius standard. Also, defensive measures have not fared

---

[67] *Unocal Corp. vs. Mesa Petroleum Co.*, 493 A.2d 946 (Del. 1985).

[68] The burden of proving reasonable grounds as to the danger to corporate policy and effectiveness can be met by showing good faith and reasonable investigation. A board's ability to show the reasonableness of the response adopted is enhanced when a majority of the board consists of outside, independent directors, or when the actions taken precede an actual threatened change in control. An "inadequate" offer price can be a reasonably perceived threat. The concern that shareholders may be ignorant of the true value of the company may be considered by the board, and the interests of long-term shareholders versus short-term speculators (such as arbitrageurs) may be taken into account.

[69] *Unitrin, Inc. vs. American General Corp.*, 651 A.2d 1361 (Del. 1995).

[70] *Blasius Indus., Inc. vs. Atlas Corp.*, 564 A.2d 651, 660 (Del. 1988).

[71] *MM Companies vs. Liquid Audio, Inc.*, 813 A.2d 1118 (Del. 2003). In this case, the court invalidated the board's decision to add two new directors to prevent the acquirer from obtaining board control at the subsequent shareholder meeting. The Blasius standard "is to be applied sparingly, and only in circumstances in which self-interested or faithless fiduciaries act to deprive stockholders of a full and fair opportunity to participate and to thwart what appears to be the will of a majority of stockholders" (MONY Group, Inc. Shareholder Litigation, Del. (class action that was settled)).

well in court when the defense has involved a transaction in which existing management will have an equity interest or where the purpose is to favor one party over
another.

3.5.2. Defenses and offer premiums

Following the reference made by Manne (1965) to the "external" and "internal"
market for corporate control, several authors have similarly categorized antitakeover
provisions.[72] The external control market involves takeover bids and specific target
responses, while the internal market involves general board actions and shareholder
voting. Examples of internal antitakeover provisions are classified (staggered) board
(directors are divided into separate classes—typically three—and elected to overlapping terms), unequal voting rights (e.g., two classes of common stock, one with zero
voting rights), and various restrictions on shareholder rights to amend company charter
and bylaws, to act by written consent, and to call special meetings. Examples of
external antitakeover provisions include antigreenmail provisions (prohibition on
paying greenmail—the targeted repurchase of a single shareholder's stockholding at
a premium), supermajority requirements to approve a merger, blank check preferred
stock (used to implement a poison pill), fair price provisions (requires a large shareholder to pay a minimum price set by formula for all shares acquired in the back end of
a two-tiered acquisition), and poison pills or shareholder rights plans.

The development of the poison pill is tied directly to the history of greenmail.
Following several occurrences of greenmail payments during the late 1970s and early
1980s, Unocal made what turned out to be a landmark decision to reverse the
greenmail payment. In 1983, Mr. T. Boone Pickens Jr. and his Mesa Partners II,
who held 13.6% of Unocal's stock, made an $8.1 billion takeover bid for Unocal.
The offer was for $54 a share in cash for 37% of Unocals stock and $54 a share in
junior securities for the rest. Unocal's board responded by offering to exchange $72 a
share in senior securities for 50.1% of the company's total shares, but barred the Mesa
group from participating in the stock repurchase. Delaware Supreme Court upheld
Unocal's right to undertake the targeted repurchase.[73]

Attorney Martin Lipton of Wachtell, Lipton, Rosen & Katz was a key legal strategist
working for Unocal. Subsequently, Mr. Lipton's law firm proceeded to develop the
"shareholder rights plan"—popularly referred to as the poison pill—which is an
ongoing commitment to trigger what in essence is a reverse greenmail payment.[74]
When adopting the poison pill, the corporation issues to its stockholders (usually by
means of a dividend) certain rights to purchase stock. The rights are out of the money
(the exercise price exceeds the then market price) and not exercisable until a triggering

---

[72] Jarrell and Poulsen (1987), Danielsen and Karpoff (1998), Gompers et al. (2003), and Moussawi (2004).
Bebchuk et al. (2002) summarize case law concerning antitakeover provisions.
[73] *Unocal Corp. vs. Mesa Petroleum Co*, 493 A.2d 946 (Del. 1985).
[74] Mr. Lipton's law firm became a dominant supplier of poison pills to US public companies thereafter.

event. The triggering event is that someone acquires a certain percentage (e.g., 15%) of the firm's voting shares. Pending their exercise, the rights may be redeemed for a nominal value by the board. If triggered, the rights give each holder, other than the stockholder who triggered the pill, the right to purchase shares of the issuing corporation (flip-in) or of the acquirer (flip-over) at a deep discount (e.g., 50%) to the market price. The board may offer pills without prior stockholder approval, and the pills may be issued after having received a hostile bid ("morning after" pill).[75]

In 1985, the Delaware Supreme Court upheld Household International's adoption of a shareholder rights plan as reasonable under the Unocal standard, even though the company did not face a hostile threat.[76] Subsequently, Delaware has upheld the right of a board to refuse to redeem a pill in the face of an all-cash, noncoercive tender offer, even though a majority of the company's stockholders had tendered their shares to the bidder.[77] On the other hand, Delaware courts have invalidated the so-called dead-hand poison pill, which attempted to provide that only incumbent directors could redeem the rights, thus preventing newly elected directors from unwinding the pill.[78] This is an important decision, as one (though costly) way to circumvent the pill is to launch a proxy contest simultaneously with the hostile offer, in the hope of winning enough board seats to have the board rescind the pill and let the offer go through.

The combination of a hostile bid and a proxy contest does not work if the target board is classified or staggered. For example, if only one-third of the board is up for election, the hostile bidder cannot win the majority needed to rescind the pill. Indeed, as argued by Bebchuk et al. (2002, 2004) and Bebchuk and Cohen (2005), board classification may in and of itself constitute an antitakeover device. Bebchuk and Cohen (2005) examine the cross-sectional relationship between board classification and firm value, and find that board classification is negatively correlated with industry-adjusted Tobin's Q. Also, Masulis et al. (2007) find that acquisition announcement-period stock returns are significantly lower for bidders with staggered boards, possibly because board classification reduces forced board turnover and quality. On the other hand, Bates et al. (2008) find that board classification does not reduce the probability that a firm, once it is targeted, is ultimately acquired. Moreover, targets with classified boards appear to extract premiums equivalent to those of single-class boards. However, they do find that board classification is associated with a small reduction in the probability of receiving a takeover bid. Rose (2009) also concludes that the presence of staggered boards has more of a detrimental impact on firm value when management is relatively entrenched.

---

[75] Pill adoption does not require a shareholder vote since it is akin to a dividend payment. Recently, there has been a growing demand from large institutional shareholders such as pension funds to allow shareholders to vote on pill adoptions.

[76] *Moran vs. Household International, Inc.*, 500A.2d 1346 (Del. 1985).

[77] *Moore Corp., Ltd. vs. Wallace Computer Services, Inc.*, 907 F. Supp. 1545 (D. Del. 1995).

[78] *Quickturn Design Systems, Inc. vs. Shapiro* 721 A.2d 1281 (Del. 1998). This version of the pill had been upheld under Georgia Law, but also invalidated under New York law.

The ambiguities in interpreting the overall consequences for shareholders of a defensive measure such as a staggered board are also present in the debate over the poison pill defense. There is substantial empirical evidence that targets that have adopted poison pills receive offer premiums that are, on average, indistinguishable from offer premiums received by nonpill targets.[79] This evidence is consistent with the following four alternative hypotheses:

H1 Poison pills are irrelevant for determining final takeover premiums.

H2 Poison pills convey bargaining power, which increases the final takeover premium relative to what the premium would have been for the same target without a pill.

H3 Poison pills convey bargaining power that is used to benefit target management at the expense of target shareholders.

H4 Poison pills provide bargaining power, but "shadow" pills are as effective as adopted pills.

Hypotheses H2–H4 maintain that pills do convey bargaining power but that a comparison of offer premiums in samples of firms with or without pills is difficult from an econometric point of view. Pill adoptions are voluntary, which raises complex issues of endogeneity (H2). Controlling for self-selection is difficult because the marginal effect of a poison pill depends on the firm's entire governance system, including executive compensation (H3).[80] Also, in order to isolate the true premium effects of pills, empirical work relies on the existence of two samples, one representing "poison" and the other "placebo" effects (Comment and Schwert, 1995). This sampling is difficult, if not impossible, if, as in H4, *all* firms effectively have ready access to the pill (Coates, 2000).

H1 maintains that pills may simply be ineffective and therefore irrelevant for final offer premiums. At first blush, H1 seems to be rejected by the fact that no bidder (to our knowledge) has yet triggered a pill. However, why trigger an ineffective pill if the trigger itself is costly—also to target management? Consider the failed 1996 takeover attempt by US Surgical Corporation of medical device maker Circon Corporation. Exercising the Circon pill would have required Circon shareholders to pay approximately $800 million in cash into a company with a pretakeover total equity value of $150 million. In return for this massive (and expensive) cash infusion, Circon shareholders would lose a 70% takeover premium and stood to gain only $10 million from the resulting dilution of US Surgical's shareholding in Circon. In general, a pill with this structure may lack credibility and therefore have little effect on bargaining outcomes.[81]

---

[79] Comment and Schwert (1995), Field and Karpoff (2002), Heron and Lie (2006), and Betton et al. (2009).

[80] Compensation effects of takeovers are discussed in Section 5.2. Heron and Lie (2006) find that the targets of hostile bids are more likely to adopt poison pills when they have classified boards, suggesting that the two antitakeover devices are interdependent.

[81] In the Circon case, Circon chairman and CEO Richard Auhll appeared to be protecting large private benefits of control. Using information on SDC, approximately half of all pills are cash pills (the exercise price is paid in cash rather than by an exchange of securities.

Moreover, the definition of target "hostility" used in the literature probably captures many targets that are ready to negotiate with or without the pill (Schwert, 2000). Bidders that are able to look beyond the pill and determine whether negotiations are possible (based on observable target characteristics or on the bidder's own ability to persuade a hostile target management) may reach a final bargaining outcome that is largely indistinguishable from that observed in samples of ex ante "friendly" targets. Empirical evidence shows that the probability of receiving a bid (and ultimate bid success) is either unaffected or slightly lower for targets with strong antitakeover defenses.[82]

Finally, several studies estimate the valuation effects of antitakeover charter amendments (which require a shareholder vote), with data primarily from the 1980s. An advantage of studying charter amendments is that the market reaction isolates the net present value of the expected impact of the antitakeover measures on all future takeover activity. A disadvantage, however, is that the lengthy process toward a vote at the share-holder meeting leaks information and leads the market to partially anticipate the event, thus reducing power to register significant changes in market expectations. There is also some controversy over which event date is the most appropriate: the shareholder meeting date, the proxy announcement date, or the proxy mailing date (Bhagat and Jefferis, 1991). Also, as with studies of poison pills, it is important but difficult to properly account for the endogenous nature of the amendment choice, as it is part of the amending firm's entire governance system.[83]

Since the amendments must pass a shareholder vote, a natural null hypothesis is that these serve the interests of shareholders. Under this hypothesis, a takeover amendment increases the expected future takeover premium (the change in the probability of a takeover times the change in the premium conditional on a takeover). For example, the amendments may help resolve a target shareholder coordination (holdout) problem and increase the expected takeover price, especially in a two-tier tender offer setting (DeAngelo and Rice, 1983). Or, in the context of optimal contracting, the amendment decreases the expected future takeover premium in return for greater managerial incentives to invest in firm-specific human capital (Shleifer and Vishny, 1989). The main alternative hypothesis is that the amendments further entrench incumbent management (with insufficient offsetting benefits) and that the voting mechanism is unable to prevent the management proposal from passing.[84]

Early studies of share price effects of fair price amendments, classified boards, supermajority requirements, and other "shark repellents" adopted by publicly traded

---

[82] Comment and Schwert (1995), Field and Karpoff (2002), and Heron and Lie (2006).

[83] Malekzadeh et al. (1998) and Bhagat and Jefferis (2002).

[84] It is well understood that a vote may not necessarily safeguard shareholder interests. See, for example, Austen-Smith and O'Brien (1986), Jarrell and Poulsen (1987), Brickley et al. (1988), and Gordon and Pound (1993) for evidence of voting on antitakeover amendments. Since the 1980s, increasing institutional shareholder activism has made it more difficult for incumbents to secure shareholder support for defensive measures.

firms find a zero or small negative market reaction. These include DeAngelo and Rice (1983), Linn and McConnell (1983), and Jarrell and Poulsen (1987). Fair-price amendments (the bulk of the sample amendments) are met with an insignificant market reaction, while board classification elicits significantly negative abnormal stock returns. Jarrell and Poulsen (1987) also find that the amendments having the most negative effects are adopted by firms with the lowest percentage of institutional holdings and the greatest percentage of insider holdings. Malatesta and Walkling (1988) distinguish between takeover defenses that do or do not require shareholder approval, and conclude that defenses that are not ratified by a shareholder vote reduce shareholder wealth. Ryngaert (1988) also finds evidence that poison pill adoptions reduce shareholder value, as do news of court decisions upholding poison pill defenses. More recent studies of the market reaction to antitakeover amendments tend to confirm the conclusions of this literature, also after providing a more detailed picture of the interaction with the adopting firm's corporate governance and ownership structures.[85]

Finally, a number of papers examine the valuation effects of greenmail—the precursor to the poison pill—and antigreenmail charter amendments. As indicated above, greenmail refers to an arrangement in which a company repurchases the stock held by a large shareholder, usually at a substantial above-market price. In return, the large stockholder signs a standstill agreement committing not to purchase additional target shares or launch a control bid for typically a 10-year period. Bradley and Wakeman (1983), Dann and DeAngelo (1983), and Mikkelson and Ruback (1991) find that the announcement of greenmail transactions are associated with significantly negative abnormal stock returns of approximately -2%. Mikkelson and Ruback (1991) find that the market reaction is negative only if the stockholder signs a standstill agreement or if it aborts a control contest.[86] Mikkelson and Ruback (1985) show that the total abnormal stock return from the initial 13D filing by the toehold investor until he receives the greenmail payment is significantly positive. In other words, the greenmail payment and standstill do not eliminate all gains from having had a significant blockholder in the firm's ownership structure.

Eckbo (1990b) and Bhagat and Jefferis (1991) present evidence on antigreenmail charter amendments. The typical amendment prohibits the firm from repurchasing some or all of the common (voting) stock of an *interested shareholder*—normally defined as a shareholder who owns 5% or more of the outstanding common stock and who acquired this ownership position within the past 2–3 years. Virtually all firms retain the option to pay greenmail as long as (1) two-thirds or more of the *disinterested shareholders* approve of the action, or (2) if the shares are repurchased at a fair price, usually defined as an average of the stock's trading prices over the 90 days immediately preceding the share repurchase.

---

[85] Mahoney and Mahoney (1993), McWilliams and Sen (1997), and Sundaramurthy et al. (1997).
[86] They also report that even with the standstill, 40% of the firms paying greenmail experience a control change within the subsequent 3 years.

The market reaction to greenmail prohibitions represents the value of the *option* to pay greenmail in the future. If the option value is negative, the market reaction to the amendment will be positive. The option value is negative if the sum of the repurchase premium (greenmail payment), the marginal increase in agency costs from success-fully rebuffing future hostile takeover bids, and the increased likelihood of receiving purely extortive bids (bids designed exclusively to generate greenmail payments) exceed the expected benefits. Thus, evidence of a positive market reaction to the greenmail prohibition would support the widely held view that greenmail payments harm nonselling shareholders.[87]

For a subsample where the antigreenmail amendment is proposed by itself (without other simultaneous antitakeover proposals), Eckbo (1990b) has found the average market reaction to the charter amendments to be weakly negative. The market reacts negatively to the greenmail prohibition if the value of the unrestricted option to pay greenmail is positive. However, cross-sectional regressions further indicate that the market reaction is strongly positive when the firm has experienced a recent stock price runup along with takeover rumors. Eckbo (1990b) concludes that the option to pay greenmail is costly when the firm likely has been identified as a target, in which case the antigreenmail amendment removes a possible barrier to the pending takeover.

3.6. Targets in bankruptcy

In this section, we consider evidence on the acquisitions of target firms that have filed for bankruptcy. Since bankruptcy law alters the bargaining position of the target, one expects the outcome for bidders to be different from that for out-of-court acquisitions. We begin with targets in Chapter 11 of the US Bankruptcy Code, where a decision to put the bankrupt firm up for sale is driven jointly by incumbent management and creditor committee votes. We then consider targets sold in the automatic auction bankruptcy system in Sweden. This code essentially eliminates the target's bargaining opportunities and relies on bidder competition to maximize debt recovery and an efficient reallocation of the target assets.

3.6.1. Chapter 11 targets

Beginning with US bankruptcies, there is growing use of market-based mechanisms to lower the costs of traditional Chapter 11 proceedings. These include prepackaged bankruptcies with a reorganization plan in place at filing (Betker, 1995; Lease et al., 1996), acquisition of distressed debt by "vulture" investors in order to make voting more efficient (Hotchkiss and Mooradian, 1997), and voluntary sales in Chapter 11 (Hotchkiss

---

[87] It is not, however, the only possible interpretation. In the asymmetric information model of Shleifer and Vishny (1986a), greenmail payments increase the intrinsic value of the firm while at the same time causing the firm's stock price to fall.

and Mooradian, 1998; Maksimovic and Phillips, 1998). Baird and Rasmussen (2003) report that more than half of all large Chapter 11 cases resolved in 2002 used the auction mechanism in one form or another, and that another quarter were prepacks.

Hotchkiss and Mooradian (1998) study acquisitions of targets in Chapter 11. There are two ways in which a firm in Chapter 11 can sell substantially all of its assets: through a Section 363 (of the US Bankruptcy Code) sale or as part of a confirmed reorganization plan. Under a Section 363 sale, management must first obtain an offer and then notify the court, which in turn notifies creditors. The Bankruptcy Code invalidates no-shop agreements and allows creditors to retain advisers at the expense of the debtor firm to search for competing buyers. If there are several potential buyers, the court holds an auction.

Chapter 11 grants the incumbent management exclusive rights within a limited time period (rolling 6 months) to propose a reorganization plan. As a consequence, hostile acquisitions are difficult and the targets will be more likely for firms whose management has already been replaced or for which managerial private benefits of control are small. It is also possible that management is willing to put the target up for sale when it has private information that the target assets are of relatively low quality. Furthermore, since acquisition bids are subject to creditor approval (just as for any other reorganization plan), complex debt structure makes it more difficult to generate the necessary votes. Thus, targets are also likely to have relatively simple capital structures.

Hotchkiss and Mooradian (1998) start with 1200 public companies that filed for Chapter 11 between October 1970 and December 1992. Using SEC and Compustat information, they identify 339 firms that reorganized as independent public companies and 111 firms that were acquired by another operating company. Of these, 55 acquirers are publicly traded firms. Target firms spend a median time in bankruptcy of 14 months, compared to 17 months for independently reorganized firms. They find little evidence that acquired firms have unusually simple capital structures (although they tend to have less public debt) or that incumbent management is particularly entrenched. Acquirers tend to be firms in the same industry as the target and have some prior relationship with the target such as an ownership stake. Of the 55 takeovers, 18 transactions have multiple bidders.

Hotchkiss and Mooradian (1998) also report that the bankrupt targets on average are purchased at a 45% discount relative to prices paid for nonbankrupt targets in the same industry. However, they do not consider this as evidence of allocative inefficiency: "Although the transactions are at discount prices, the high proportion of acquirers operating in the same industry as the target, as well as the competitive bidding environment, does not support the conclusion that acquisitions in bankruptcy are sales to lower value users" (p. 243). This conclusion is further supported by their finding that the postmerger cash flow performance of firms combined with bankrupt targets is better than that reported by Hotchkiss (1995) for firms emerging from Chapter 11. Finally, there is evidence of positive and significant abnormal stock returns to both bidders and bankrupt targets for the days surrounding the announcement of the acquisition.

3.6.2. Bankruptcy auctions and fire sales

Next, we consider bankruptcies in Sweden's mandatory auction system. Here, a firm filing for bankruptcy is turned over to a court-appointed trustee who puts the firm up for sale in an auction. This mandatory auction system has an attractive simplicity. All debt claims are stayed during the auction period and the bids determine whether the firm will be continued as a going concern or liquidated piecemeal. A going-concern sale takes place by merging the assets and operations of the auctioned firm into the bidder firm, or into an empty corporate shell—much like a leveraged buyout transaction. Payment must be in cash, allowing the auction proceeds to be distributed to creditors strictly according to absolute priority.

As surveyed by Hotchkiss et al. (2008), bid premiums observed in the mandatory auction bankruptcy system in Sweden provide an important empirical perspective on the viability auctions as a mechanism for resolving bankruptcy. Proponents of the market-oriented auction system point to costs associated with conflicts of interests and excessive continuation of operations due to managerial control over the restructuring process in Chapter 11.[88] These costs most likely explain the trend toward increased use of market-based mechanisms in the United States. On the other hand, opponents of an auction-based system argue that the time pressure of an auction system is costly as it may cause excessive liquidation and fire sales of economically viable firms when potential bidders in the auction are themselves financially constrained.

A series of papers study the Swedish auction system using a sample of 260 auctioned firms.[89] The average auctioned firm has $5 million in sales and assets of $2 million ($8 million and $4 million, respectively, in 2007 dollars), and it has an average of 45 employees.[90] Thorburn (2000) reports that the auctions are quick—lasting an average of 2 months—and relatively cost-efficient. Moreover, three-quarters of the filing firms survive the auction as a going concern, which is similar to the survival rate of Chapter 11 cases. In going-concern sales, the buyer typically rehires lower level employees. Top management fares less well: Eckbo and Thorburn (2003) find that while the buyer rehires the old management to run the restructured company in about one-half of the going-concern sales, the old management typically experiences a median wealth decline of -47% relative to managers of nonbankrupt firms. They argue that this expected personal bankruptcy cost, along with the loss of private benefits of control, counteract shareholder risk-shifting incentives when the firm is in severe financial distress (Jensen and Meckling, 1976). That is, if the CEO's objective includes being rehired by the buyer in the auction, she may implement a relatively

---

[88] See, for example, Baird (1986), Bebchuk (1988), Jensen (1989), Aghion et al. (1992), Bebchuk and Chang (1992), Bradley and Rosenzweig (1992), and Baird (1993). Hotchkiss (1995) finds that firms emerging from Chapter 11 tend to underperform their industry rivals which is consistent with excessive continuation.

[89] Thorburn (2000), Strömberg (2000), and Eckbo and Thorburn (2003, 2008b, 2009).

[90] A majority of Chapter 11 filings are also by small private firms: Chang and Schoar (2007) report average sales of $2 million and 22 employees in a large and representative sample of Chapter 11 filings between 1989 and 2003. Bris et al. (2006) report that the median firm filing for Chapter 11 has assets of $1 million.

conservative investment policy to preserve the possibility of a going-concern sale in the auction.

Does the auction mechanism induce an efficient reallocation of the resources of the bankrupt firm? First, Eckbo and Thorburn (2003) show that firms sold as going-concerns typically perform at par with industry rivals. Second, Eckbo and Thorburn (2008b) fail to find auction fire-sale discounts in going-concern sales. That is, the auction produces auction premiums (and postbankruptcy operating performance) in going-concern sales that are independent of fire-sale conditions such as industry-wide financial distress, industry leverage, and whether or not the buyer is an industry insider or outsider.

Third, Eckbo and Thorburn (2008b) find that prepackaged auctions (where the buyer has been identified prior to filing) tend to produce prices consistent with the hypothesis that the contracting parties are concerned with preempting piecemeal liquidation. Stromberg (2000) shows that salebacks to the previous owner-manager tend to increase during periods of high industry financial distress, which further helps preempt liquidation. Eckbo and Thorburn (2008b) document that prices paid in salebacks are as high as prices in nonsaleback going-concern transactions, which fails to support arguments that salebacks carry an inherent conflict of interest with junior creditors.

3.6.3. Testing for auction overbidding

Eckbo and Thorburn (2009) develop and test the argument that creditor incentives may induce auction overbidding. Recall from Section 3.3 that toehold bidding raises the optimal bid above the bidder's own private valuation of the target, for example, as shown in Equation (11). In the sample of Swedish bankruptcies, the main creditor is always a single bank. Thus, the toehold analogy is that the bankruptcy event effectively creates an instant "creditor toehold" of $\alpha = 1$ when the creditor's debt is impaired at filing. The question is whether the existence of this creditor toehold leads to overbidding in the auction. Given the importance of toehold bidding in the takeover literature, we outline the main test procedure and results below.

Swedish bank regulations prevent the bank from bidding directly in the auction. However, Eckbo and Thorburn (2009) report that the bank often finances the winning bidder and uses this observation to motivate the following proposition: Bank financing allows the bank to induce bidder 1 to submit a bid b_c^* that involves overbidding and is jointly optimal for both parties.[91] As in Section 3.3, overbidding forces a wealth transfer from bidder 2 to the bank-bidder coalition when bidder 2 wins the auction. This rent transfer raises auction revenue and the bank's expected debt recovery rate.

Suppose the bank forms a coalition with bidder 1. Continuing the notation from Section 3.3, the coalition's optimal bid is as follows:

---

[91] The bank may induce the bidder to bear the expected overpayment cost by granting a lower interest on the loan. Eckbo and Thorburn (2009) show that there exists a positive transfer from the bank to bidder 1 which makes coalition formation incentive compatible for both parties.

$$
b_c^* = \begin{cases} v_1 + h(b_c) & \text{if} \quad v_1 \leq f - h(b_c) & \text{(unconstrained overbidding)} \\ f & \text{if} \quad f - h(b_c) < v_1 < f & \text{(constrained overbidding)} \\ v_1 & \text{if} \quad v_1 \geq f & \text{(no overbidding)} \end{cases} \tag{15}
$$

where f is the face value of the bank's debt claim. Note that the unconstrained overbidding price is identical to the bid in Equation (11) but with $\alpha = 1$ and a termination fee $t = 0$. A value of $\alpha = 1$ follows because the bank, being the secured creditor with an impaired debt claim, is effectively the seller of the auctioned firm. Thus, the bank has a creditor toehold equal to 1. As shown by Hotchkiss and Mooradian (2003) as well (in the context of Chapter 11 sales), a creditor toehold induces overbidding in exactly the same manner as a bidder toehold outside of bankruptcy.

What makes this overbidding theory testable is the constraining effect of the bank-debt face value f.[92] To illustrate, let l denote the piecemeal liquidation value of the bankrupt firm, and suppose l is public knowledge at the beginning of the auction. Since l is the sum of the value of the firm's assets if sold individually, it constitutes a price floor in the auction of the firm as a going-concern. Let $r \equiv l/f \in [0, 1]$ denote the bank's debt recovery if the firm is liquidated piecemeal. r is a measure of the bank's debt impairment: low values of r indicate that the bank's debt is highly impaired. For low values of r, the bank-bidder coalition fully overbids (unconstrained overbidding). However, as the value of r increases, the amount of overbidding becomes constrained by f: the coalition optimally overbids *only* to the extent that overbidding does not benefit junior creditors. If the valuation of the bank's coalition partner is such that $v_1 > f$, the bank will receive full debt recovery even without overbidding, so the optimal coalition bid is simply $b_c^* = v_1$.

Eckbo and Thorburn (2009) prove that the greater the liquidation recovery rate r, the lower is the incentive to overbid and, in turn, the lower is the expected premium paid by the winning bidder. They use a professional estimate of the piecemeal liquidation value l, published by the bankruptcy trustee at the beginning of the auction.[93] They find that when the firm is sold as a going-concern, final auction premiums are higher the lower is the liquidation recovery rate, as predicted by overbidding. Equally important, in subsamples where the theory implies zero overbidding incentive, the cross-sectional regressions reject overbidding. That is, final auction premiums are unaffected by the liquidation recovery rate when the auction leads to the target being liquidated piecemeal (in which case the going-concern premium is zero), or when the bank's collateral exceeds the face value ($l > f$) so the bank's debt is not impaired.

---

[92] This testable restriction does not exist for takeovers outside of bankruptcy. Extant empirical evidence on toehold-induced overbidding is therefore indirect. For example, theory implies that overbidding increases the probability of winning, which is supported by studies of corporate takeover bids with equity toeholds (Betton and Eckbo, 2000).

[93] Bidders appear to rely on this estimate as well: when the auction does lead to piecemeal liquidation, the average price paid by the winning bidder is close to (on average 8% above) the trustee's estimate. In contrast, when the bankrupt firm is purchased as a going-concern, the average auction premium more than doubles the trustee's piecemeal liquidation value estimate.

Overbidding results in allocative inefficiency whenever the bank-bidder coalition wins against a higher valuation bidder. To examine this possibility, Eckbo and Thorburn (2009) estimate the postbankruptcy operating performance of firms sold as going-concerns conditional on the bank-bidder coalition having large overbidding incentives and winning the auction. While this is the most powerful subsample to look for ex post allocative inefficiency, they show that the postbankruptcy operating performance in this subsample is at par with or exceeds that of industry rivals. Overall, they conclude from this that the bank's coalition partner tends to be efficient in terms of restructuring and operating the bankrupt firm's asset.

3.7. Offer premium summary

Reflecting restrictions on the availability of actual offer prices, the bulk of the empirical studies on takeovers are content to use target cumulative abnormal stock returns around the takeover bid as a proxy for the actual offer premium. Obviously, target abnormal stock returns present noisy estimates of offer premiums because they incorporate the probability of bid failure and competition at the initial offer date, and they must be estimated over a long event window to capture the final premium. Thus, it is difficult to properly sort out how bidders determine offer premiums unless one employs offer price data directly.

Several papers study offer prices directly. Bradley (1980) provides the first systematic offer price analysis in the context of public tender offers. Walkling (1985) uses offer premiums to predict tender offer success. Eckbo and Langohr (1989) examine the effect of disclosure rules and method of payment (cash versus stock) on tender offer premiums. Betton and Eckbo (2000) examine bid jumps and offer premium determinants in tender offers. Officer (2003, 2004), Bates and Lemmon (2003), and Bargeron (2005) examine the premium effects of deal protection devices such as termination and share-tendering agreements. Betton et al. (2009) study the premium effects of toehold bidding, while Betton et al. (2008b) are the first to estimate the effect of target runups on markups in initial and final offer prices. Chatterjee et al. (2008) study the effect of divergence of opinion on bid prices, while Levi et al. (2008) examine whether CEO and director gender affect takeover premiums.

Table 5 shows the cross-sectional determinants of both the initial and final offer premiums. The offer price data used for this table is from Betton et al. (2008b), and covers a total of 4889 targets. The premiums are defined as $\ln(p_{initial}/p_{-42})$ and $\ln(p_{final}/p_{-42})$, respectively, where $p_{initial}$ is the initial offer price, p_{final} is the final offer price in the contest, and p_{-42} is the stock price on day -42 adjusted for splits and dividends. The sample is restricted to targets in the period 1980–2002 with a stock price $\geq\$1$ and a market capitalization $\geq\$10$ million. As shown in the first two rows of the table, the mean (median) value of the initial offer premium is 43% (37%), which increases to 48% (39%) by the time of the final bid.

Table 5

Determinants of the offer premium in 4889 control contests for US public targets, 1980–2002

The table shows OLS estimates of the initial and final offer premium, defined as $\ln(p_{initial}/p_{-42})$ and $\ln(p_{final}/p_{-42})$, respectively, where $p_{initial}$ is the initial offer price, p_{final} is the final offer price in the contest, and p_{-42} is the stock price on day -42 adjusted for splits and dividends. Amihud liquidity is the average value of $|R_i|/(p_i S_i)$ over days $i \in \{-250, -42\}$, where R_i is the % holding period return, p_i is the closing price and S_i is the number of shares traded. Industry is the four-digit SIC code in CRSP. The sample is 4889 control bids 1980–2002 for US targets with a stock price $\geq \$1$ and a market capitalization $\geq \$10$ million. The p-values are in parenthesis. The data is from Betton et al. (2009).

	Initial offer premium		Final offer premium	
Mean	0.43		0.48	
Median	0.37		0.39	
S.D.	0.46		0.47	
Intercept	0.296 (0.000)	0.256 (0.000)	0.296 (0.000)	0.254 (0.000)
A. Target characteristics				
Size: ln of target market capitalization on day -42	−0.030 (0.000)	−0.027 (0.000)	−0.030 (0.000)	−0.027 (0.000)
Target B/M > industry median	0.025 (0.000)	0.029 (0.000)	0.024 (0.000)	0.029 (0.000)
Target runup: $\ln(p_{-1}/p_{-42})$	0.808 (0.000)	0.811 (0.000)	0.808 (0.000)	0.811 (0.000)
Amihud liquidity	8.55 (0.311)	13.29 (0.114)	8.71 (0.302)	13.46 (0.110)
Poison pill dummy	−0.016 (0.606)	0.000 (0.990)	−0.016 (0.604)	−0.001 (0.987)
B. Bidder characteristics				
Positive toehold (vs. zero toehold)	−0.023 (0.032)	−0.025 (0.024)	−0.023 (0.032)	−0.025 (0.024)
Acquirer public (vs. private)	0.015 (0.079)	0.023 (0.008)	0.015 (0.072)	0.023 (0.007)
Horizontal takeover (same industry)	−0.004 (0.608)	−0.004 (0.664)	−0.004 (0.618)	−0.004 (0.673)
C. Deal characteristics				
Tender offer (vs. merger)	−0.061 (0.000)	−0.066 (0.000)	−0.061 (0.000)	−0.066 (0.000)
All-cash consideration (vs. stock or mixed)	0.019 (0.017)	0.021 (0.012)	0.019 (0.017)	0.021 (0.012)
Hostile target response (vs. friendly or neutral)	0.020 (0.185)	0.020 (0.185)	0.019 (0.216)	0.019 (0.216)
Multiple bidders (vs. single-bidder contest)			0.009 (0.497)	0.008 (0.501)
Announced in 1980–1989 (vs. 1990–2002)	−0.016 (0.056)		−0.017 (0.050)	
Year fixed effects	No	Yes	No	Yes
Adjusted R2	0.424	0.436	0.423	0.436
F-value	300.3 (0.000)	115.3 (0.000)	277.2 (0.000)	111.9 (0.000)

The explanatory variables, which are grouped into target characteristics, bidder characteristics, and deal characteristics, cover the types of decisions discussed throughout Section 3. We alternately use a time dummy for offers taking place in the early sample period (1980–1989) and year fixed effects. Notice also that the information in these variables is known at the time the offer premium was set. We include the variable hostile target response as a determinant of the initial offer premium because we believe this information is basically known at the outset. However, the variable multiple bidders obviously are not and are included as a determinant of the final offer premium only.

Not surprisingly (given the relative paucity of multiple-bid contests in the total sample of 4889), the explanatory variables have similar coefficients and level of significance for both the initial and final offer premiums. In the order of the discussion of this section, the initial and final offer premiums are

1. significantly *higher* when the bidder is a public company and significantly *lower* if the initial bid is a tender offer (Section 2.3);
2. significantly *greater* when the method of payment is all cash (Section 3.2);
3. significantly *lower* when the bidder has a positive toehold (Section 3.3);
4. significantly *greater* the greater the target runup $\ln(p_{-1}/p_{-42})$ prior to the initial bid (Section 3.4);[94]
5. *unaffected* by either the presence of a target poison pill or target hostility to the initial bid (Section 3.5).

Table 5 further shows that the initial and final offer premiums are decreasing in target total equity capitalization on day -42, and they are greater if the target's B/M ratio exceeds the industry median B/M (i.e., if the target has few growth options relative to industry rivals). Offer premiums are unaffected by target stock liquidity, by the presence of multiple bidders, and by whether the bidder and target are horizontally related in product markets. Finally, offer premiums have increased from the 1980s.[95]

Officer (2003) and Bates and Lemmon (2003) show that offer premiums are significantly greater when the SDC indicates the existence of a target termination agreement, while Bargeron (2005) finds lower premiums in the presence of a target board/management tender agreement. Moeller (2005) presents evidence indicating that powerful entrenched target CEOs reduce takeover premiums. Chatterjee et al. (2008) find that takeover premiums are larger the greater the disagreement between the earnings forecasts of financial analysts following the target. Levi et al. (2008) use

---

[94] The coefficient on the runup variable is 0.80. This means that a dollar increase in the target runup causes the bidder to raise the offer price by 80 cents on average. Betton et al. (2008b) also show that offer markups (either $\ln(p_{initial}/p_{-1})$ or $\ln(p_{final}/p_{-1})$) are significantly decreasing in the runup. Thus, there is partial substitution between runups and markups.

[95] Since most of the hostile bids occurred in the 1980s, this is consistent with the finding that offer premiums in hostile bids are no lower than those for nonhostile offers.

RiskMetrics Group data on board structure and find that bid premiums are affected by the gender composition of the board. Specifically, bid premiums are lower when the bidder CEO is female, and the higher the target board's proportion of female directors (provided that the female directors are independent appointees).

Several of the variables used to explain the offer premium are themselves endogenous choice variables (payment method, toehold, hostility, termination agreements, bidder's public status). Some of the reported effects appear robust to endogeneity.[96] One variable that does *not* appear to be robust is "tender offer." The inclusion of other variables (such as toeholds and hostility) tends to affect conclusions as to whether offer premiums are higher, the same, or lower in tender offers than in merger bids. Additional specification analysis is needed to fully sort out the endogenous from truly exogenous forces in the data.

4. Takeover gains

In this section, we present estimates of abnormal stock returns to bidders and targets around takeover contests, as well as in the postmerger period. Given the large number of papers providing abnormal returns estimates in takeovers, we limit the review to more recent studies with large samples of 1000 or more bidder firms, such as those listed in Table 6. Studies are included in the table only if announcement-induced abnormal returns to bidders are in fact reported. This excludes large-sample studies such as Schwert (1996) and Bates and Lemmon (2003), where the main focus is on targets or some other deal aspect and where bidder returns may be estimated and used for purposes of cross-sectional regressions—but average announcement returns are not reported. It also excludes almost all studies before SDC became available as a convenient online data source.[97]

4.1. Econometric caveats

Abnormal stock returns measure only the unanticipated component of the total economic effect of the event. Given the difficulty in predicting target firms, partial anticipation of the bid announcement does not pose much of an econometric problem for studies of target takeover gains. Most researchers agree that one captures most, if not all, of the total target gains by comparing the offer price to the preoffer target share price within 2 months of the first bid. As illustrated in this section, the bulk of the target preoffer runup typically actually occurs within 10 days of the bid.

---

[96] Betton and Eckbo (2000), Officer (2003), and Betton et al. (2009) use systems of equations and various corrections for self-selection. See Li and Prabhala (2007) for a survey of self-selection models in corporate finance.

[97] Two exceptions in Table 6 are Loderer and Martin (1990) and Betton and Eckbo (2000), who use large hand-collected samples.

Table 6

Large-sample ($N > 1000$) estimates of announcement-induced average cumulative abnormal stock returns (ACAR) to US bidders

Study	Sample	Average announcement return: ACAR (day $\tau1$, day $\tau2$) =
Loderer and Martin (1990)	$N = 1135$ completed mergers, 274 completed tender offers, and 3296 "other" acquisitions (not classifiable as merger or tender offer) by public acquirers, where the offer is announced in the Wall Street Journal, 1996–1984.	ACAR(−5, 0) is 1.7%* for 970 cases 1966–1968, 0.57%* for 3401 cases 1960–1980, and −0.1% for 801 cases 1981–1984. Bidder announcement returns smaller for larger bidders and decreasing in the relative size of the target firm.
Betton and Eckbo (2000)	Initial and rival bidders in $N = 1353$ tender offer contests for public targets, 1971–1990.	(1) Day 0 is the initial bid date: ACAR(−60, 0) is 1.3% for initial bidders and 2.2% for rival bidders. (2) Day 0 is the second bid date: ACAR(−60, 0) is 1.2% for initial bidders, and 6.1%* for rivals.
Fuller et al. (2002)	$N = 3135$ takeovers, 1990–2000, by 539 public acquirers with at least 5 successful control bids within 3 years. Minimum deal size is $1 million.	ACAR(−2, 2) is 1.8%* for total sample of bidders, −1.0%* when target is public, 2.1%* when target is private, and 2.8%* when target is a subsidiary.
Akbulut and Matsusaka (2003)	$N = 3466$ successful mergers between public firms, 1950–2002	ACAR(−2, 1) is 1.2%* for "related" acquisitions (bidder and target have at least one three-digit SIC code in common) and 1.1%* for unrelated acquisition.
Officer (2003, 2004)	$N = 2511$ attempted mergers and tender offers between public firms, 1988–2000 (Officer, 2003)	ACAR(−3, 3) is −1.2%* for the total sample.
Moeller et al. (2004, 2005)	$N = 12,023$ acquisitions, 1980–2001. Minimum deal value is $1 million and 1% of the acquirer's assets.	ACAR(−1, 1) is 1.1%* for total sample, 2.3%* for small acquirers, and 0.1% for large acquireres. Using dollar values, bidders loose a total of $221 billion in market capitalization over day −1 to +1. This aggregate loss is driven by a small number of very large deals concentrated to the 1998–2001 period.
Bhagat et al. (2005)	$N = 1018$ tender offers for public targets.	ACAR(−5, 5) is 0.2% with a median dollar return of −1.2 million.
Song and Walkling (2005)	$N = 3389$ acquisitions, 1985–2001. Minimum deal value is $10 million.	ACAR(−1, 0) for the first bidder after a 12-month dormant period in the industry is 0.7%*, and 0.04% for subsequent bidders. Consistent with an attenuation effect of partial anticipation of takeover activity.
Bradley and Sundaram (2006)	$N = 12,476$ completed acquisitions by 4116 public companies, 1990–2000	ACAR(−2, 2) is 1.4% for the total sample, −0.7% for public targets, and 1.9% when the target is private. Bidding firms experience a large stock price runup over the 2 years period preceding the bid. This runup is greater for stock bids than for cash bids.

(Continued)

Table 6 (*Continued*)

Study	Sample	Average announcement return: ACAR (day $\tau 1$, day $\tau 2$) =
Savor (2006)	$N = 1484$ (159 failed and 1335 successful) merger bids, 1990–2000. The bid is nonhostile and all-cash (359 successful cases) or all-equity (976 successful cases). Minimum deal size is 5% of bidder market value.	ACAR(-1, 1) is $-3.5\%^*$ for all-stock bidders and 1.0%* for all-cash bidders. Similar results for the full sample of failed acquirers.
Dong et al. (2006)	$N = 3137$ merger bids and tender offers between public firms, 1978–2000	ACAR(-1, 1) ranges from -0.2% (when target is ranked as relatively "undervalued") to -1.8 (when target is ranked as relatively "over-valued")%
Moeller et al. (2007)	$N = 4322$ all-cash and all-stock bids, 1980–2002. Minimum deal value is $1 million and 1% of the acquirer's assets.	ACAR(-1, 1) for the total sample is 0.8%. When target is public, ACAR(-1, 1) is -2.3% in all-stock deals and 0.7% in all-cash deals. When the target is private, ACAR(-1, 1) is 3.4% in all-stock deals.
Bargeron et al. (2008)	$N = 1292$ completed all-cash takeovers of US public targets by private and public bidders, 1990–2005	Average target announcement CAR(-1, 1) is 32% for public bidders and 22% for private bidders.
Betton et al. (2007, 2008b)	$N = 10,806$ initial control bids for public targets: 7076 merger bids from 1980 to 2002 and 3730 tender offers from 1973 to 2002	ACAR(-1, 10 is $-1.2\%^*$ for total sample and $-0.15\%^*$ if the bidder has a toehold. In Betton et al. (2008b), ACAR(-1, 1) is $-1.9\%^*$ for merger offers, and an insignificant 0.3% for tender offers.
Betton et al. (2008c)	$N = 15,987$ initial control bids by public bidders for public or private targets, 1980–2005: 13,985 merger bids and 1468 tender offers.	ACAR(-1, 1) is 0.69% with a significantly negative z-statistic of -3.9 for initial bidders in mergers, and 0.76 (insignificant) for initial bidders in tender offers. Large public bidders acquiring public targets and paying with all-cash produces ACAR(-1, 1) of $-2.2\%^*$. Small public bidders acquiring private targets in all-stock offers produces ACAR(-1, 1) of 6.5%*. Details are in Tables 7–9 in this survey.
Hackbarth and Morellec (2008)	$N = 1086$ completed takeovers between public firms, 1985–2002. Minimum transaction value of $50 mill., and regulated and financial firms are excluded.	ACAR(-1, 1) is $-0.5\%^*$. Bidder risk changes around the acquisition events are found to be consistent with a neoclassical investment model.

*Significant at 10% level.

It is also widely understood that partial anticipation can severely complicate estimation of gains from bidding. Any partial anticipation must somehow be accounted for to avoid underestimating the value implications. In simple environments with only a single possible event, the announcement effect equals the valuation effect times 1 minus the probability that the merger event will occur. It is thus attenuated toward zero, creating a bias against rejection of the null of zero gains from bidding. Malatesta and Thompson (1985) directly model the information arrival process and conclude that bidder stock returns include a component due to partial anticipation of future acquisition activity. Eckbo et al. (1990) model the probability of the takeover event and conclude that this probability affects estimates of bidder takeover gains. The conclusion from these studies is that partial anticipation of bidding activity is an important empirical issue when the researcher fails to reject the hypothesis of zero abnormal stock returns to bidders.

Another approach to dealing with partial anticipation is through various sampling techniques. For example, Schipper and Thompson (1983) sample firms that announce entire acquisition programs. Since this announcement capitalizes a whole series of future expected acquisitions (rather than responding to a single-acquisition announcement), power to detect true acquisition gains is enhanced. Their evidence is consistent with the hypothesis that future expected acquisitions have positive net present value as a group. Song and Walkling (2000, 2005) select takeover announcements that follow a dormant period—with no previous takeovers in the industry of the bidder for a minimum of 12 months. Presumably, these announcements come as a relative surprise to the market, adding power to reject the null of zero bidder abnormal returns. Perhaps as a direct result, the authors report significantly positive bidder announcement returns.

Takeover announcements may also reveal new information about the quality of the bidder's management team—regardless of the value of the proposed acquisition per se. This further confounds the interpretation of bidder announcement returns as gains from merger activity. One approach is to formally model the signaling problem and test for its existence using cross-sectional regressions with bidder announcement returns as dependent variable (Eckbo et al., 1990). Fuller et al. (2002) approach this issue by selecting a sample of frequent acquirers (firms that acquire five or more targets within a 3-year period). This sampling strategy helps control for certain bidder characteristics in the cross section.

Finally, because bidder managers time takeovers based on private information, consistent estimation of parameters in cross-sectional models with bidder returns as the dependent variable requires a correction for self-selection (Eckbo et al., 1990). While such cross-sectional regressions are commonly presented in the literature, this (or other equivalent) correction is rarely implemented. However, the recent review of Li and Prabhala (2007) is likely to increase general awareness of the importance of providing unbiased estimates in these cross-sectional models.[98]

4.2. Runup- and announcement-period returns

We estimate the average daily abnormal stock return for firm j over event window k as the event parameter AR_{jk} in the value-weighted market model

---

[98] Note that self-selection poses an econometric issue in cross-sectional regressions with the target abnormal return as dependent variable only to the extent that the target self-selects the timing of the acquisition.

$$r_{jt} = \alpha_j + \beta_j r_{mt} + \sum_{k=1}^{K} AR_{jk} d_{kt} + \varepsilon_{jt}, \quad t = \text{day}\{-293, \ldots, \text{end}\} \tag{16}$$

where r_{jt} is the return (in logarithmic form) to firm j over day t, r_{mt} is the value-weighted market return, and d_{kt} is a dummy variable that takes a value of 1 if day t is in the kth event window and 0 otherwise.[99] This conditional event parameter estimation yields identical abnormal return estimates as the more standard residual analysis technique, but is more efficient in terms of using the available return data. Moreover, the regression easily incorporates variable-length event windows across takeovers, and it produces estimates of standard errors of the abnormal returns directly.[100]

Day 0 is the day of the initial control bid, and the ending date is the earlier of the day of the control last bid in the contest plus 126 trading days and the effective date + 126. If the target delisting date is between the date of the last control bid and the effective date, then the contest end is set to the target delisting date. The runup and announcement abnormal returns are estimated using three event windows ($K = 3$). The three event windows are $[-41, -2]$ (the runup period), $[-1, 1]$ (the announcement period), and $[2, \text{end}]$. The estimation uses ordinary least squares (OLS) with White's heteroskedastic-consistent covariance matrix and requires a minimum of 100 days of nonmissing returns during the estimation period.

The cumulative abnormal return (CAR) to firm j over event period k is

$$CAR_{jk} = \omega_k AR_{jk} \tag{17}$$

where ω_k is the number of trading days in the event window. In a sample of N firms, the average cumulative abnormal return (ACAR) is

$$ACAR_k = \frac{1}{N} \sum_j CAR_{jk} \tag{18}$$

The z-values are determined as

$$z = \frac{1}{\sqrt{N}} \sum_j \frac{AR_{jk}}{\sigma AR_{jk}} \tag{19}$$

and σAR_{jk} is the estimated standard error of AR_{jk}. Under the null of ACAR $= 0$, $z \sim N(0, 1)$ for large N. The combined bidder and target abnormal returns are determined by weighting the bidder and target abnormal returns by the market capitalization on day -42.

[99] The return analysis is limited to ordinary shares. Missing returns are dealt with as follows: A succession of less than six missing returns are backfilled by allocating the cumulative return equally over the missing days. For example, if there are three missing days and then a return of 10%, each missing day and the subsequent nonmissing day would be allocated a return on 2.5%.
[100] For reviews of event study econometrics, and the conditional event parameter approach used here, see Thompson (1985, 1995), MacKinlay (1997), and Kothari and Warner (2007).

The twin Tables 7 and 8 detail the average abnormal return estimates (CAR) for the runup period $(-42, -2)$, the announcement period $(-1, 1)$, classified by market capitalization (Panel B), the public status of the bidder and target firms (Panel C), merger versus tender offer (Panel D), the payment method (Panel E), and, finally, the time period (Panel F). CAR is shown for the target, the initial bidder, and the value-weighted sum of the bidder and target CARs. For illustrative purposes, Figure 10 plots the daily CARs from day -40 through day 10 relative to the initial offer announcement, classified by the public status of the bidder and target.[101] The CARs to targets are somewhat greater when the bidder is public than when the bidder is private. Moreover, bidder returns are somewhat greater when the target is private than when the target is public.

Several overall conclusions emerge from the results in Tables 7 and 8 that are broadly consistent with the conclusions from the extant literature, including those listed in Table 6:

(1) *Target CARs*

(a) The average target CAR is positive and significant in all samples, over both the runup and the announcement period.
(b) The runup typically constitutes about one-third of the total runup plus announcement CAR. The largest target CAR occurs in all-cash offers (Panel E), where the sum of the runup and the announcement CAR is 28%.

(2) *Combined CARs (value-weighted)*

(a) The average combined CAR is positive and significant over the runup period for 9 of the 10 sample categories, and insignificant for the lowest size-quartile bidders (Panel B). The average combined runup-period CAR for the total sample of 4803 cases is 0.7% with a z-value of 4.3.
(b) The average combined CAR is positive and significant for the announcement period for 8 of the 10 samples, insignificant in one (Panel E, for bidders in the lowest size quartile), and significantly negative in one (Panel E, when the payment method is all-stock). The average combined announcement-period CAR for the total sample of 4803 cases is 1.06% with a z-value of 14.6.
(c) For the total sample (Panel A), the sum of the combined CAR for the runup and announcement periods is a significant 1.79%.

(3) *Bidder CARs*

(a) Announcement-period CAR is 0.73% for the total sample, but with a negative and significant z-statistic of -2.53.[102] The median CAR is -0.05%, and the percentage of bidders with negative CAR is 49%.

---

[101] The cumulative abnormal returns shown in the graph are estimated by including a dummy variable for each of the days in the $(-42, +10)$ interval and adding the estimated dummy coefficients.
[102] The average CAR and its z-statistic may differ in sign.

Table 7

Cumulative abnormal stock returns (CAR) to targets and bidders (individually and combined) relative to the initial bid date. Sample of control contests for US targets, 1980–2005

See the next for the details of the abnormal return estimation. The average market capitalization on day -42 for the target (VB), and for the ratio VT/VB. are reported in brackets (in $1000). Day 0 is the day of the initial control bid. The combined bidder and target abnormal returns are determined by weighting the bidder and target abnormal returns by the market capitalization on day -42.

	Target CAR			Initial bidder CAR			Combined CAR		
	N (average VT	Runup $(-41, -2)$	Ann'ct $(-1, 1)$	N (average VB	Runup $(-41, -2)$	Ann'ct $(-1, 1)$	N (average VT/VB)	Runup $(-41, -2)$	Ann'ct $(-1, 1)$
A. Entire sample									
Mean	$9298 ($641,951)	0.0680	0.1461	15,987 (3,752,262)	0.0049	0.0073	4.803 (0.4445)	0.0072	0.0106
Median		0.0516	0.1234		−0.0024	−0.0005		0.0070	0.006
Z		25.2701	102.2990		−2.1463	−2.5297		4.2496	14.605
% Positive		0.6231	0.8271		0.4924	0.4939		0.5259	0.5640
B. Subsamples based on market capitalization on day -42									
Lowest quartile									
Mean	2324 (11,207)	0.01019	0.1472	3995 (28,762)	0.0492	0.0404	1200 (0.0195)	0.0009	−0.000
Median		0.0708	0.1200		0.0154	0.0087		−0.0005	−0.001
Z		11.9283	46.8157		5.5730	21.7874		0.5042	0.1303
% Positive		0.6248	0.7900		0.5357	0.5827		0.4958	0.4858
Highest quartile									
Mean	2323 (2,372,966)	0.0365	0.1327	10,480 (5,698,863)	−0.0122	−0.0049	1201 (1.3891)	0.0155	0.0279
Median		0.0385	0.1156		−0.0073	−0.0035		0.0149	0.019
Z		11.2752	51.6770		−6.0704	−17.5109		4.1736	15.032
% Positive		0.6117	0.8429		0.4757	0.4599		0.5612	0.6295
C. Subsamples based on the public status of the bidder and target firms									
Public target									
Mean	9298	0.0680	0.1461	6301	0.0065	−0.0087	4803	0.0072	0.0106
Median		0.0516	0.1234		0.0012	−0.0066		0.0070	0.0067
Z		25.2701	102.2990		0.5387	−19.0462		4.2496	14.6057
% Positive		0.6231	0.8271		0.5034	0.4269		0.5259	0.5640
Private target									
Mean				9686	0.0040	0.0176			
Median					−0.0051	0.0029			
Z					−3.1918	12.1118			
% Positive					0.4852	0.5375			

(b) The average announcement-period bidder CAR is significantly positive for the lowest bidder size-quartile (Panel B), when the target is private (Panel C), in all-cash bids (Panel E), and in the period 1991–1995 (Panel F). It is

Table 8

Cumulative abnormal announcement returns in control contests (continued from Table 7)

		Target CAR			Initial bidder CAR			Combined CAR	
	N	Runup (−41, −2)	Ann'ct (−1,1)	N	Runup (−41, −2)	Ann'ct (−1,1)	N	Runup (−41, −2)	Ann'ct (−1, 1)
D. Subsamples based on form of initial bid									
Merger									
Mean	6836	0.0619	0.1338	13,995	0.0050	0.0069	3939	0.0071	0.0060
Median		0.0481	0.1134		−0.0024	−0.0008		0.0070	0.0037
Z		20.7051	88.2153		−2.2479	−3.8858		3.5536	7.7429
% Positive		0.6181	0.8212		0.4921	0.4920		0.5268	0.5380
Tender offer									
Mean	2320	0.0868	0.1881	1468	0.0060	0.0076	837	0.0090	0.0335
Median		0.0693	0.1707		0.0006	0.0011		0.0073	0.0232
Z		14,9492	52.7321		0.5420	0.9110		2.6312	18.4987
% Positive		0.6427	0.8573		0.5014	0.5123		0.5245	0.6941
E. Subsamples based on method of payment of initial offer									
All-cash									
Mean	2846	0.0765	0.2023	1857	−0.0039	0.0081	996	0.0011	0.0285
Median		0.0523	0.1797		−0.0027	0.0025		0.0039	0.0170
Z		15.0345	65.3668		−1.1140	7.7136		1.4279	18.6150
% Positive		0.6283	0.8949		0.4890	0.5315		0.5120	0.6837
E. Subsamples based on method of payment of initial offer									
All-stock									
Mean	2163	0.0680	0.1396	5189	0.0096	0.0025	1909	0.0092	−0.0030
Median		0.0533	0.1215		−0.0003	−0.0044		0.0083	−0.0016
Z		12.6045	46.7639		0.8922	−10.0304		3.0591	−1.5634
% Positive		0.6301	0.8174		0.4993	0.4531		0.5343	0.4819
F. Subsamples based on time period of initial offer									
1991–1995									
Mean	1601	0.0608	0.1344	3654	0.0102	0.0169	941	0.0012	0.0131
Median		0.0485	0.1141		−0.0027	0.0017		0.0019	0.0079
Z		9.0822	43.3055		−0.9762	6.6646		0.4272	6.0191
% Positive		0.6121	0.8189		0.4910	0.5216		0.5090	0.5770
1996–2000									
Mean	3008	0.0818	0.1564	5464	0.0039	0.0074	1816	0.0099	0.0072
Median		0.0674	0.1372		−0.0017	−0.0008		0.0108	0.0052
Z		16.6761	56.6973		−0.3038	−1.4063		3.6605	5.9602
% Positive		0.6483	0.8328		0.4941	0.4929		0.5391	0.5435

significantly negative for bidders in the highest size-quartile (Panel F), when the target is public (Panel C), when the initial bid is a merger (Panel D), and when the payment method is all-stock (Panel E).

(c) The runup period bidder CAR is positive but largely insignificant, typically in the range 0.05–0.10%. Bidders in the lowest size quartile have a significantly

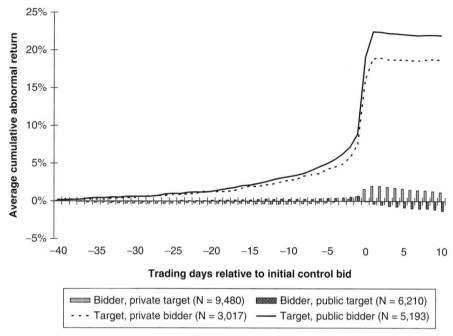

Fig. 10. Percent average cumulative abnormal stock returns to targets and initial bidders from day −40 through day 10 relative to the initial control bid. US targets 1980–2005.

positive average runup of 4.9%, and the average runup is a significant −1.2% for bidders in the highest quartile (Panel B). In these two subsamples, the runup is greater than the announcement return (and of the same sign).

This confirms several of the conclusions of the studies listed in Table 6, in particular Fuller et al. (2002), Moeller et al. (2004, 2005), Bradley and Sundaram (2006), Savor (2006), Moeller et al. (2007), Bargeron et al. (2008), and Betton et al. (2007, 2008b,c). Table 9 further highlights the impact of key offer characteristics on bidder announce-ment returns. The combination of large bidder (here in the upper-size quartile), payment in all-stock, and the target being a public company represents a worst-case scenario with average bidder announcement-period CAR of −2.21%. The best-case scenario is the combination of a small bidder (lower size-quartile), private target, and, again, *all-stock* as payment. This produces an average bidder announcement-period CAR of 6.46%. Thus, a major driver of negative bidder returns is not, as previously thought, the all-stock payment. Rather, the two key drivers appear to be the target's status as public or private and the bidder size. As shown next, bidder size was particularly large in 1999 and 2000, which suggests that the bidder size effect may also represent a unique time-period effect.

Table 9

Summary of initial bidder 3-day announcement-period abnormal returns, 1980–2005

Initial bidder cumulative abnormal returns for the window −1, 1 relative to the initial control bid. Large bidders are bidders in the upper quartile of market capitalization on day −42 (in constant 2000 dollars) and small bidders are bidders in the lower quartile of market capitalization on day −42. The cutoff values for the upper and lower quartiles are $134 million and $2.2 billion respectively. The method of payment is determined from the SDC 100% cash or 100% stock consideration field. The public status of the target is determined from SDC.

Sample	Public targets		Private targets	
	N	CAR(−1, 1)	N	CAR(−1, 1)
A. Large bidders				
All-stock	769	−0.0221*	445	0.0010
All-cash	439	−0.0030*	88	0.0026*
B. Small bidders				
All-stock	495	−0.0006	872	0.0646*
All-cash	190	0.0306*	184	0.0176*

*Represents significance at the 1% level (two-sided test)

4.3. Dollar returns

Figure 11 presents an annual scatter plot of the 3-day announcement-period bidder abnormal returns CAR(−1, 1) (Panel A) and the raw bidder dollar change from closing of day −2 to closing of day 1. As first noticed by Moeller et al. (2004, 2005), the distributions of the CAR(−1, 1) and the dollar change are dramatically different. Betton et al. (2008c) extend the sample period to 2005 and discover that the period 1998–2000 is unusual not only relative to the pre-1998 period, but also relative to the post-2000 years. Figure 12 further illuminates the role and effect of bidder size. Panel A plots bidder market values (in constant 2000 dollars) as of day −2. Clearly, bidders in the 1998–2000 period were unusually large.

Betton et al. (2008c) examine the distribution of dollar differences in Figure 11B. They identify 125 firms in the lower 1% and 129 firms in the upper 1%. In *both* groups, the dominant sector was manufacturing and the dominant firm was Cisco. Cisco appears with 62 deals in the total sample, with an average (constant dollar) market capitalization of $180 billion. Other frequent acquirers are Union Planters with 40 deals (market cap $2.5 billion) and BancOne with 40 deals (market cap $8.1 billion).[103] Of these 62 deals made by Cisco, 26 appear in the group with the highest 1%

---

[103] The largest bidders are CitiGroup (market cap $245 billion and two deals), Microsoft (market cap $190 billion and seven deals).

Panel A: Cumulative abnormal return (−1,1)

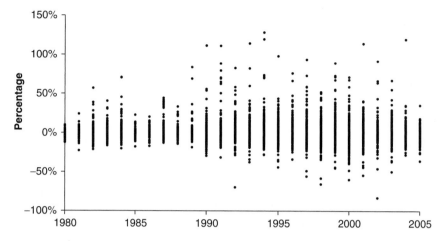

Panel B: Dollar change (−2,1)

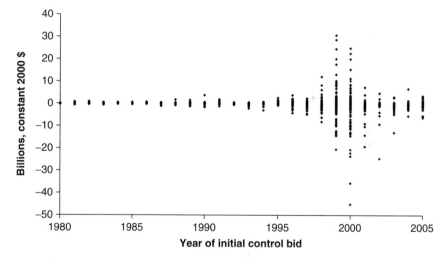

Fig. 11. Announcement-period abnormal returns and dollar-changes for 12,898 successful initial bidders, 1980–2005. Panel A is a scatter plot of the announcement period abnormal stock returns, CAR(−1, 1). Panel B is a scatter plot of the bidders' announcement-period dollar changes. Dollar changes are calculated as the change in market capitalization from day −2 to day 1 (relative to initial control bid) and converted to constant 2000 dollars using the CPI.

Panel C: Market value day −2

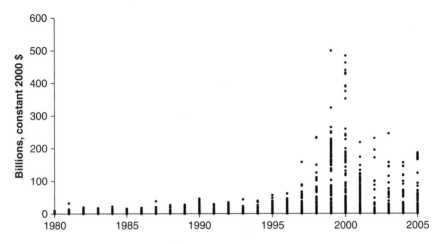

Panel D: Aggregate dollar abnormal returns

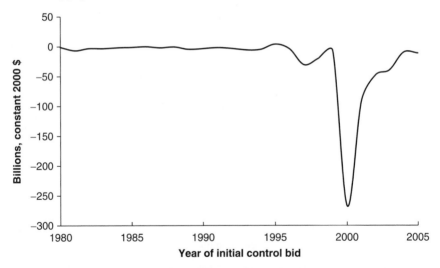

Fig. 12. The market values and announcement-period aggregate dollar abnormal return to 12,898 successful initial bidders, 1980–2005. Panel C is a scatter plot of the market value in constant 2000 dollars of successful initial bidders on day −2 relative to the initial control bid announcement. Panel D is a plot of the aggregate dollar abnormal returns earned by successful initial bidders over the window (−2, 1) Aggregate dollar abnormal returns are calculated by multiplying the bidder market capitalization on day −2 by the cumulative abnormal return and then summing over the year.

CAR(−1, 1), with 10 bids in 99 and 6 bids in 2000.[104] Furthermore, Cisco appears 17 times in the lower 1% group (distributed evenly over the 3-year period 1999–2001).[105]

Panel D in Figure 12 plots the aggregate dollar CAR(−1, 1) for each sample year (combining Panel A of Figure 11 and Panel C, Figure 12). The large negative spike in the years 1999 and 2000 is what Moeller et al. (2005) characterize as a "wealth destruction on a massive scale." It is massive indeed; yet, it is important not to forget that it is caused by a few very large firms that decided to bid in this particular period and that, on average, made value-decreasing acquisitions. Note that Panel D of Figure 12 does not eliminate overlapping abnormal returns to frequent acquirers (which may be one reason why the spike is greater here than in Moeller et al., 2005). Also, removing Cisco from the sample changes the minimum of the spike to −$198 billion from −$267 billion. The ultimately unanswered question is whether the spike is a bidder size effect or a year fixed effect (or a combination of the two). At this point, there appears to be no explanation for why the large firms decided to enter the market for corporate control in 1998–2001, and then only to leave again.

Finally, Figure 13 shows the frequency distribution for the dollar announcement abnormal return for the total sample of successful initial bidders, classified by the time period and the method of payment (all-stock or all-cash). Panel A covers the total sample, while Panel B is restricted to the 1995–2005 period. There is very little difference between the two panels (in both panels, all-stock offers are slightly skewed relative to all-cash bids). Thus, the distribution in Panel B is not noticeably affected by the extreme cases from the 1998–2000 period. Until we reach a better understanding of the unique 1998–2000 period, estimates of the expected gains from bidding are best obtained from overall distributions such as those in Figure 13.

4.4. Estimating expected bidder gains

Referring back to Figure 2, let CAR_s and CAR_f denote average bidder gains conditional on the offer succeeding or failing, respectively. Moreover, let $\pi(x_j)$ denote the market's estimate of the probability that an offer by bidder j will succeed conditional on the offer characteristics x_j. As discussed in Section 3, important offer characteristics include the offer premium, toehold, payment method, and hostility. The bid announcement causes rational investors to impound the *expected* bidder takeover gain into the bidder's share price, generating the following announcement return:

$$CAR(-1, 1) = CAR_s \pi(x) + CAR_f(1 - \pi(x)) \tag{20}$$

The empirical objective is to estimate the bidder gain CAR_s from successful takeovers. The common procedure is to form the average cumulative return in the

---

[104] The next most common bidders in the upper 1% group are Johnson & Johnson with six cases and Tyco with five cases.
[105] The next most common bidder in the lower 1% group is Lucent with six bids.

Panel A: Successful initial bidders 1980–2005

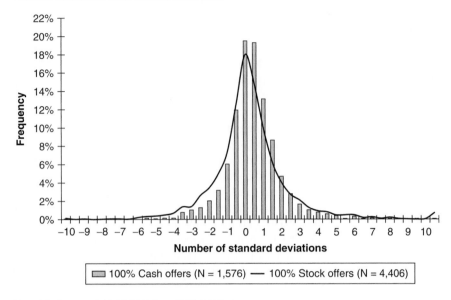

Panel B: Successful initial bidders 1995–2005

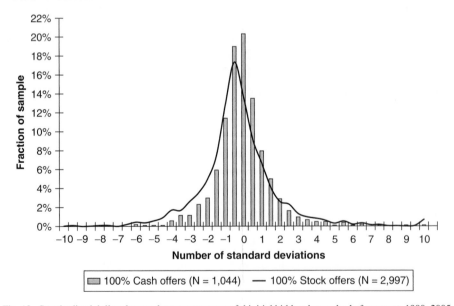

Fig. 13. Standardized dollar abnormal returns to successful initial bidders by method of payment, 1980–2005 (Panel A) and 1995–2005 (Panel B). Dollar abnormal returns are calculated as the change in market capitalization (in constant 2000 dollars) from day −2 to day 1 relative to initial control bid. Dollar abnormal returns are then standardized by the historical average and standard deviation of nonoverlapping 3-day dollar market value changes measured over the period −293 to −42 relative to the initial control bid. Sample windows are (−45, −42), (−48, −45), etc.

subsample of ex post successful bids. This average is either the average CAR$(-1, 1)$ for successful bids or the average abnormal bidder return cumulated all the way through the end of the contest (at which point $\pi = 1$). Note that, since these ex post averages necessarily restrict the sample to successful bids, they ignore information in the abnormal returns to ultimately unsuccessful bids. Also, cumulation to the end of the contest (typically, 6 months for mergers) adds noise relative to that of the 3-day estimate CAR$(-1, 1)$.

Betton and Eckbo (2000) develop an alternative estimation procedure that exploits the information in *all* initial bids (also the ultimately unsuccessful ones) in order to extract an estimate of CAR$_s$. The idea is to view Equation (20) as a cross-sectional regression where CAR$_s(-1, 1)$ is the dependent variable, $\pi(x_j)$ is the regressor, and CAR$_s$ and CAR$_f$ are estimated directly as regression parameters. Using a sample of 1353 initial tender offers (both successful and unsuccessful), Betton and Eckbo (2000) find that the parameter CAR$_s$ for bidders is statistically insignificantly different from zero. Thus, the expected net bidder return from initiating tender offers is nonnegative. Moreover, they estimate CAR$_f$ to be significantly positive, which they suggest in part reflects the expected gain to the unsuccessful bidder from selling its toehold in the target to the ultimately winning (rival) bidder.[106]

This alternative estimation procedure also allows one to test the effect on bidder expected returns of changing one or more of the offer parameters in the vector x. That is, when estimated, the right-hand side of Equation (20) forms the predicted (conditional) alue $E[\text{CAR}(-1, 1)|x]$. As modeled in Equation (20), changes in x affect bidder expected gains by changing $\pi(x)$. Tests of the bidder valuation impact of changing the offer parameters x amount to testing whether the partial derivative of $E[\text{CAR}(-1, 1)|x]$ with respect to x is significantly different from zero. For example, both Betton and Eckbo (2000) and Betton et al. (2009) report that this partial derivative with respect to the bidder's toehold is positive and significant.

4.5. Posttakeover (long-run) abnormal returns

Several studies report evidence of postmerger underperformance, particularly when using the matched-firm buy-and-hold technique (implemented below). For example, Rau and Vermaelen (1998) find that merged firms with low B/M ratio tend to underperform, while Loughran and Vijh (1997) report underperformance when the merger is paid in stock (while all-cash mergers overperform). Moeller et al. (2004) report insignificant long-run (36-month) postmerger performance. Harford (2005) finds some evidence suggestive of relatively poor postmerger performance for the largest bidders. Moeller et al. (2005) find significantly negative long-run buy-and-hold returns to portfolios of "large loss deal" bidders. Rosen (2006) reports evidence that mergers

---

[106] In Betton and Eckbo (2000), 48% of all initial bidders have a positive toehold. Their sample period is 1971–1990, with the largest toehold frequency prior to the mid-1980s (consistent with Figure 8).

that take place during periods of high general merger activity tend to have high premerger share prices followed by low postmerger performance.

There are at least three possible explanations for the postmerger underperformance. First, under behavioral arguments, the market slowly corrects its overvaluation of the merged firms' shares (Baker et al., 2007; Shleifer and Vishny, 2003). Second, a neoclassical argument is that the merger is a response to a negative industry shock and that the merged firm performs better than it would have without the merger— which may still be worse than the premerger performance (Harford, 2005). Third, the apparent underperformance is an artifact of the econometric methodology itself. The rest of this section sheds light on the third hypothesis.

We begin the long-run abnormal return analysis with the matched firm technique, and then we show results when returns are risk-adjusted using factor regressions applied to portfolios of merged firms.[107] Our sample drops to 15,298 mergers after imposing the following additional restrictions: (1) The sample period is 1980–2003 to allow a minimum of 3 years of postmerger stock returns. (2) The merged firm is found on CRSP and is listed on NYSE/AMEX/Nasdaq for at least 1 year following the year of the effective date of the merger. (3) The merged firm must have Compustat information on equity B/M ratio to allow selection of a matched firm based on size and B/M.[108]

4.5.1. Buy-and-hold returns

The typical buy-and-hold experiment involves buying the merged firm's stock in the month following the merger completion month (effective merger date) and holding the stock for a period of 3–5 years or until delisting, whichever comes first. In a sample of N issues, the average return over a holding period of T months is computed as the average cumulative (T-period) return, also referred to as $\overline{\text{BHR}}$ (for buy-and-hold return):

$$\overline{\text{BHR}} \equiv \sum_{i=1}^{N} w_i \left[\prod_{t=\tau_i}^{T_i} (1 + R_{it}) - 1 \right] \tag{21}$$

where R_{it} denotes the return to stock i over month t and w_i is stock i's weight in forming the average holding-period return $\omega_i = 1/N$ when equal-weighting). The effective holding period for stock i is T_i, where T_i in the analysis below is either 5 years or the

---

[107] We thank Øyvind Norli for his generous programming assistance. The econometric methodology implemented below is identical to the one used by Eckbo et al. (2007) when estimating the long-run performance following security offerings.

[108] Book value is defined as "the Compustat book value of stockholders equity, plus balance sheet deferred taxes and investment tax credits (if available), minus the book value of preferred stock. Depending on availability, we use the redemption, liquidation, or par value (in that order) to estimate the value of preferred stock" (Fama and French, 1993, p. 8). If available on Compustat, the book value of equity is also measured at the end of the year prior to the year of the acquisition. If this book value is not available, we use the first available book value on Compustat starting with the acquisition year and ending with the year following the acquisition year.

time until delisting or the occurrence of a new merger, whichever comes first).[109, 110] The matched-firm technique equates the *expected* return to merged firms with the *realized* return to a nonmerging firm, usually matched on firm characteristics such as industry, size, and B/M ratio. The abnormal or unexpected return BHAR is then

$$BHAR_{Issuer} \equiv BHR_{Issuer} - BHR_{Matched\ firm} \tag{22}$$

Table 10 shows average 5-year percent buy-and-hold returns for our sample and for firms matched on size and B/M. The matched firms are selected from all CRSP-listed companies at the end of the year prior to the year of the merger completion and companies that are not in our sample of mergers for a period of 5 years prior to the offer date. Moreover, the matching procedure is as follows: We first select the subset of firms that have equity market values within 30% of the equity market value of the merged firm. This subset is then ranked according to B/M ratios. The size and B/M matched firm is the firm with the B/M ratio, measured at the end of the year prior to the merger year, that is closest to the merged firm's ratio. Matched firms are included for the full 5-year holding period or until they are delisted, whichever occurs sooner. If a match delists, a new match is drawn from the *original* list of candidates described earlier.

Table 10 shows that, when using either the total sample period 1980–2003 or the subperiod 1990–2003, merged firms on average underperform their matched firms whether $\overline{BHR}$ is formed using equal weights or value weights. For the total sample period, the difference between the equal-weighted $\overline{BHR}$ for merged and matched firms is -21.9% and -17.1% with value-weighting, both with *p*-values of 0.00. About 20% of the sample mergers take place in the 1980s, and here the underperformance is evident only for equal-weighted $\overline{BHR}$. For the subperiod 1990–2003, the underperformance

---

[109] Kothari and Warner (1997), Barber and Lyon (1997), and Lyon et al. (1999) provide simulation-based analysis of the statistical properties of test statistics based on long-run return metrics such as $\overline{BHR}$. Kothari and Warner (2007) survey the main statistical conclusions from this analysis.

[110] An alternative to BHR is to estimate the average monthly return to a strategy of investing in the stocks of merged firms and hold these for up to T periods. The T-period return would then be formed as the *cumulative average* (portfolio) return, or

$$\overline{CMR} \equiv \prod_{t=\pi}^{T} \left[1 + \frac{1}{\omega_t} \sum_{i=1}^{N_t} R_{it} \right] - 1$$

As noted by Kothari and Warner (2007), depending on the return generating process, the statistical properties of $\overline{BHR}$ and $\overline{CMR}$ can be very different. Notice also that while $\overline{CMR}$ represents the return on a feasible investment strategy, $\overline{BHR}$ does not. You obtain CMR by investing one dollar in the first security issue at the beginning of the sample period, and then successively rebalancing this initial investment to include subsequent issues as they appear (and N increases), all with a T-period holding period. In contrast, $\overline{BHR}$ is formed in event time—and thus presumes prior knowledge of the magnitude of N. Thus, estimates of $\overline{CMR}$ are better suited than estimates of $\overline{BHR}$ to address the question of whether investors have an incentive to take advantage of a potential market mispricing of merged firms' securities. Most of the empirical studies using the matched firm technique report results based on $\overline{BHR}$, which we follow here. In the subsequent section, we discuss portfolio benchmark returns based on asset pricing models, which use the return concept $\overline{CMR}$ on a monthly basis, that is, without the T-period cumulation.

Table 10

Percent average 5-year buy-and-hold stock returns ($\overline{\text{BHR}}$) for merged firms, nonmerging matched firms, and the difference between merged and matched firms, 1980–2006

Buy-and-hold percent returns are defined as:

$$\overline{\text{BHR}} \equiv \sum_{i=1}^{N} w_i \left[\prod_{t=\tau_i}^{T_i} (1 + R_{it}) - 1 \right] \times 100.$$

The sampling of merged firms starts in February 1980 and ends in December 2003, while the return holding period is allowed to continue to December 2006. The total sample of merged firms with information on matched firms is 15,298. The nonmerging matched firms are firms that did not merge in the previous 5-year period and have similar total equity size and B/M ratio. When equal-weighting, $\omega_i \equiv 1/N$, and when value-weighting, $\omega_i = \text{MV}_i/\text{MV}$, where MV_i is the firm's common stock market value at the start of the holding period and $\text{MV}_i = \sum_i \text{MV}_i$. The abnormal buy-and-hold returns shown in the column marked "Diff." represent the difference between the BHR in the "Merged" and "Match" columns. "N" is the total number of issues. The p-values for equal-weighted abnormal returns are p-values of the t-statistic using a two-sided test of no difference in average 5-year buy-and-hold returns for issuer and matching firms. The p-values for the value-weighted abnormal returns are computed using where ω is a vector of value weights and x is the corresponding vector of differences in buy-and-hold returns for issuer and match. Assuming that x is distributed normal $N(\mu, \sigma^2)$ and that σ^2 can be consistently estimated using $\sum_i \omega_i (x_i - \bar{x})^2$, where $\bar{x} = \sum_i \omega_i x_i$, U is distributed $N(0, 1)$.

Merger sample period	N	Equal-weighted $\overline{\text{BHR}}$				Value-weighted $\overline{\text{BHR}}$			
		Merged	Matched	Diff.	$P(t)$	Merged	Matched	Diff.	$P(t)$
1980–2003	15,298	62.6%	84.6	−21.9	0.000	32.6	49.6	−17.1	0.000
1980–1989	3815	83.6	95.1	−11.5	0.003	102.0	113.9	−12.0	0.120
1990–2003	11,483	55.7	81.1	−25.4	0.000	26.7	44.2	−17.5	0.000

estimates are again highly significant and slightly greater than for the total period −25.4% using the equal-weighted estimate of $\overline{\text{BHR}}$.

4.5.2. Portfolio performance estimation

An alternative to the buy-and-hold matched firm technique is to form portfolios of event firms rolling forward in calendar time and to estimate portfolio performance. Monthly portfolio (excess) returns are regressed on a set of risk factors presumed to generate expected returns. The regression intercept—or alpha—is the measure of average monthly abnormal return. We estimate alphas in a model with the following five risk factors:

$$r_{pt} = \alpha_p + \beta_1 \text{RM} + \beta_2 \text{SMB}_t + \beta_3 \text{HML} + \beta_4 \text{UMD} + \beta_5 \text{LMH} + e_t \qquad (23)$$

where r_{pt} is the excess return to an equal-weighted portfolio of issuers, RM is the excess return on the CRSP value-weighted market index. SMB and HML are the Fama and French (1993) size and B/M factors. UMD is a momentum factor inspired by

Carhart (1997) and constructed as the return difference between the one-third highest and the one-third lowest CRSP performers over the past 12 months. LMH is the Eckbo and Norli (2005) turnover factor, defined as a portfolio long in low-turnover stocks and short in high-turnover stocks.

We report estimates for three different portfolios: (1) the merging firms, (2) the nonmerging matched firms, and (3) the zero-investment portfolio that is long in merged firms and short in matched firms. The zero-investment portfolio has the advantage that it controls for any omitted risk factor with identical factor betas across issuer and matched firm, effectively combining the matched-firm and asset pricing techniques. For example, suppose the true set of risk factors is given by the vector F and that only a subset F_1 of this vector is included in the regression model, with the complement vector F_2 omitted. Let B denote merged firm and M matched firm. The merger-match zero-investment portfolio regression is then

$$r_B - r_M = (\alpha_B - \alpha_M) + (\beta_{1B} - \beta_{1M})F_1 + \varepsilon \tag{24}$$

where $\varepsilon = (\beta_{2B} - \beta_{2M})F_2 + u$, where u is a white noise error term. The definition of a "good" match is that β_B is close to β_M. Given a good match, the zero-investment portfolio will have both a small alpha and values of beta close to zero. Alternatively, if the matching technique fails to control for important risk factors, then the zero-investment portfolio will contain significant factor loadings.

Table 11 reports the alphas and factor loadings (betas) for our three portfolios and the five-factor model. Portfolio formation starts in 1980 and ends in 2003. The table shows estimates for both equal weighting and value weighting of the firms in the portfolios. Given the large portfolios, the R^2 are high, approximately 0.94. Notice also that the zero-investment portfolios receive R^s of close to 0.20, with several significant factor loadings, indicating that the usual size and B/M matching procedure typically yields firms that have different expected returns than the event firms. This in turn means that the "abnormal" return reported earlier in Table 11 in part reflects differences in *expected* returns for merged and matched firms.

The key result in Table 11 is that the alphas for the portfolio of merged firms are small and statistically insignificant for both equal- and value-weighted portfolios. Thus, we cannot reject the hypothesis of zero abnormal postmerger performance. Four of the five factor-mimicking portfolios have significant factor loadings, with the turnover-based factor producing a factor loading that is significant at the 10% level for equal-weighted portfolio returns.

Table 11 also shows that the empirical factor model misprices the equal-weighted portfolio of matched firms. The alpha of this portfolio is 0.23 with a p-value of 0.003. As a result, the portfolio of merged firms underperforms the matched portfolio (the alpha for the zero-investment portfolio is -0.15 with a p-value of 0.05). When equal-weighting returns, the factor model's mispricing of the matched-firm portfolio is less significant, and now the alpha of the zero-investment portfolio is insignificantly different from zero.

Table 11

Alphas and factor loadings for 5-year rolling portfolios of merged firms, nonmerging matched firms, and long-short merged-matched firms, 1980–2006

The merged-matched portfolio is a zero-investment portfolio that is long in the merged firms and short in the nonmerging matched firms. The portfolios are either equal-weighted ("EW") or value-weighted ("VW"). The nonmerging matched firms are firms that did not merge in the previous 5-year period and have similar total equity size and B/M ratio. The portfolios are formed starting in February 1980: a firm is added to the portfolio in the month following the month of the effective merger date and held for the minimum of 5 years and until delisting. The merger sampling stops in 12/2003, yielding a total of 15,298 successful mergers with data on size and B/M matched firms. The abnormal return estimation ends in December 2006. Abnormal returns are estimated using the following asset pricing model:

$$r_{pt} = \alpha_p + \beta_1 RM + \beta_2 SMB_t + \beta_3 HML + \beta_4 UMD + \beta_5 LMH + e_t$$

where r_{pt} is the portfolio excess return, RM is the excess return on the CRSP value-weighted market index, SMB and HML are the Fama and French (1993) size and B/M factors, UMD is a momentum factor constructed as the returns difference between the one-third highest and the one-third lowest CRSP performers over the past 12 months, and LMH is the Eckbo and Norli (2005) turnover factor (a portfolio long in low-turnover stocks and short in high-turnover stocks). The coefficients are estimated using OLS. Standard errors are computed using the heteroskedasticity consistent estimator of White (1980). The numbers in parentheses are p-values. R^2 is the adjusted R-squared.

Portfolio	α_p	RM	SMB	HML	UMD	LMH	R^2
EW-merger	0.08 (0.434)	1.05 (0.000)	0.62 (0.000)	0.26 (0.000)	−0.28 (0.000)	−0.13 (0.070)	0.943
EW-match	0.23 (0.003)	0.97 (0.000)	0.52 (0.000)	0.24 (0.000)	−0.19 (0.000)	−0.14 (0.019)	0.949
EW-zero	−0.15 (0.050)	0.09 (0.000)	0.11 (0.000)	0.02 (0.333)	−0.09 (0.000)	0.01 (0.785)	0.239
VW-merger	0.02 (0.838)	1.07 (0.000)	−0.08 (0.029)	−0.10 (0.016)	−0.05 (0.028)	−0.01 (0.828)	0.935
VW-match	0.11 (0.076)	1.00 (0.000)	−0.14 (0.000)	−0.06 (0.016)	−0.02 (0.266)	0.07 (0.100)	0.949
VW-zero	−0.09 (0.288)	0.06 (0.017)	0.06 (0.027)	−0.03 (0.386)	−0.03 (0.181)	−0.09 (0.071)	0.170

In sum, when using the rolling portfolio technique, there is no evidence of abnormal stock returns following mergers. Moreover, our evidence that matched firms have significantly different factor loadings than merged firms undermines the notion that the underperformance reported in Table 10 represents truly negative abnormal stock returns.

5. Bondholders, executives, and arbitrageurs

5.1. Takeovers and bondholder wealth

Corporate mergers affect the wealth of the target and the acquiring firms' senior claimholders for the same reasons that they affect stockholders. Merger-induced synergies add security to outstanding bonds and therefore increase bond values, while value-reducing mergers reduce bond value. In addition, bondholders benefit from any coinsurance effect from combining the less than perfectly correlated cash flows of the bidder and target firms.[111] The coinsurance effect means that a merger that generates no synergies, and where the bidder firm neither overpays for the target nor manages to sell overpriced bidder stock to the target, nevertheless causes a wealth transfer from stockholders to bondholders (Galai and Masulis, 1976). The magnitude of this wealth transfer depends on the sensitivity of the bond payments to changes in firm value (bond risk), with greater potential valuation impact on ex ante riskier bonds.[112] The coinsurance effect also reduces the risk of firm-specific human capital. This argument has led to a concern that entrenched managers seek empire building through conglomerate merger activity primarily in order to hedge the risk of their firm-specific human capital.

A difficulty facing bond studies is the lack of access to high-frequency data on bond values, particularly prior to the 1980s. One of the primary data sources is the Lehman Brothers Fixed Income Database. Most bonds do not have published transaction prices, and many of the reported prices are matrix prices. Matrix prices are reported when the bond does not trade or a dealer quote is unavailable. The matrix consists of prices of similar bonds that did trade, based on characteristics such as bond rating and maturity. Obviously, the effect of a merger does not show up in matrix prices (for other bonds), reducing power to reject the null of no price impact of the merger.

Kim and McConnell (1977) examine 2286 mergers but find price data for 44 bonds of 39 firms only. In their sample of 2870 mergers, Asquith and Kim (1982) find prices for 62 bonds, while the sample in Eger (1983) includes 33 acquirer bonds and 6 target bonds. The Dennis and McConnell (1986) bond sample contains 67 bonds of 39 acquirers and 27 bonds for 21 targets. Maquieira et al. (1998) identify a large sample of 504 acquirer bonds and 124 target bonds of firms involved in 260 stock-for-stock mergers (the bulk of which took place prior to 1980). More recently, Billett et al. (2004) examine 940 mergers and acquisitions from the period 1979–1997, identifying 818 bonds of 265 target firms and 3083 bonds of 831 acquiring firms. Moreover, Penas and Unal (2004) use a sample of 282 bonds in 66 mergers between commercial banks during the period 1991–1997.[113]

The early studies found mixed evidence for the wealth effects of mergers on bidder bonds: excess bond returns (typically computed as the difference between monthly total return and the return on a bond index matched on rating and remaining maturity) are significantly positive in Eger (1983) and Maquieira et al. (1998); insignificant in Kim and McConnell (1977) and Asquith and Kim (1982); and negative (marginally

---

[111] Levy and Sarnat (1970), Lewellen (1971), and Higgins and Schall (1975).

[112] There is also a maturity effect: When the bonds of the bidder and target firms have different maturities, the shorter maturity bonds effectively gain seniority after the merger. This seniority effect is valuable because of the larger merged firm's asset base.

[113] Warga and Welch (1993) also use this Lehman Brothers Fixed Income Database to study the bond wealth effects of leveraged buyouts, while Eberhart and Siddique (2002) use these bond data in their study of long-run bond returns following securities offerings. See Eckbo and Thorburn (2008a) and Eckbo et al. (2007) for reviews.

significant) in Dennis and McConnell (1986). Billett et al. (2004) find zero or negative bidder bond excess returns, while Penas and Unal (2004) document significantly positive bidder bond returns for their sample of commercial bank mergers.

Early studies of target bond returns report insignificant excess returns to *target* bonds. This finding is surprising, as one would expect target bondholders to benefit from the typically large asset-base increase that comes with a merger with a bidder that is often several times larger than the target. However, with improved data, both Billett et al. (2004) and Penas and Unal (2004) report significantly positive excess returns to target bonds. This finding may also reflect the increased use of event risk covenants in bonds issued in the 1990s.[114] Penas and Unal (2004) conclude that the bond market views bank mergers as default-risk-reducing events. Billett et al. (2004) conclude that there is no evidence of wealth transfers in the data, or that positive synergies expected from the corporate combinations tend to overshadow any wealth transfer that do exist.

5.2. Takeovers and executive compensation

Does the structure of CEO compensation packages affect the quality of takeover decisions? Or, as Lehn and Zhao (2006) put it: "Are Bad Bidders Fired?" The literature on optimal compensation presumes that a strong pay-performance sensitivity helps promote better acquisition decisions.[115] There is evidence that target firms tend to underperform prior to becoming targets.[116] Moreover, Mitchell and Lehn (1990), Martin and McConnell (1991), Agrawal and Walkling (1994), and Kini et al. (1995, 2004) document that targets of hostile bids tend to show a prior history of value-decreasing acquisitions and that CEO turnover increases after hostile bids. Offenberg (2009) finds evidence that CEOs of larger firms are more likely to be replaced following a series of poor acquisitions than CEOs of smaller firms. This is consistent with a disciplinary role played by the market for corporate control.

With the spread of the poison pill defense and the subsequent decline of hostile takeovers after the 1980s, the market for corporate control may have become a court of last resort—with internal governance structures being the primary mechanism for disciplining poor managers.[117] Huson et al. (2001) find that changes in the intensity of the takeover market over the period 1976–1994 are *not* associated with changes in the sensitivity of CEO turnover to firm performance. Their evidence suggests that changes in external and internal governance mechanisms have not significantly

[114] Atypical event risk covenant for mergers requires the company to repurchase the outstanding bonds at the full principal amount plus accrued interest, effectively insuring the bond against potentially value-decreasing control events (Lehn and Poulsen, 1992; Nash et al., 2003).
[115] See, for example, Murphy (1999) and Aggarwal (2008) for comprehensive reviews of the literature on executive compensation and pay-performance sensitivity.
[116] Asquith (1983) and Malatesta (1983). There is also evidence of poor operating performance prior to divisional sales. See Eckbo and Thorburn (2008a) for a review.
[117] Mikkelson and Partch (1997) and Holmstrom and Kaplan (2001).

changed the likelihood that the CEO of a poorly performing firm will be replaced. They also suggest that the effectiveness of internal monitoring mechanisms is not dependent on the intensity of the takeover market. With data from 1979 through 1998, Kini et al. (2004) conclude that the corporate takeover market intercedes when internal control mechanisms are relatively weak or ineffective.

Lehn and Zhao (2006) show that managers who undertake value-reducing acquisitions in the period 1990–1998 face a significantly higher probability of being replaced than managers who make value-enhancing acquisitions, either by internal governance, takeovers, or bankruptcy. They also show that CEOs who cancel an acquisition after observing a reduction in their company's stock price face significantly lower replacement risk than their counterparts who proceed with value-reducing acquisitions. Among firms not subjected to takeover or bankruptcy, they find no association between a firm's governance characteristics and the probability that the CEOs who make value-reducing acquisitions are replaced.

Lehn and Zhao (2006) conclude that "corporate governance and the external market for corporate control generally work well in disciplining managers who pursue acquisitions to the detriment of their stockholders." Moreover, they interpret their evidence of a lack of association between the CEO replacement probability and specific governance characteristics following bad takeovers as an indication that governance structures are on average optimally chosen. While this is one possible interpretation, an alternative view (which they recognize) is that governance structure is irrelevant as to the firing decision for the sample firms. Given the endogeneity of the governance structure (where the CEO herself plays a role), additional research is necessary to discriminate between these two positions.[118]

Lehn and Zhao (2006) also present evidence of relevance for the "market-driven acquisition" hypothesis of Shleifer and Vishny (2003) discussed above. This hypothesis implies that acquisitions that are followed by poor long-run bidder stock returns may nevertheless be in the interest of bidder stockholders, provided the alternative of no merger would have been even worse. For example, it is tempting (with hindsight) to characterize AOL/Time Warner merger as a successful attempt by AOL's CEO Stephen Case to use overvalued stock as currency to acquire Time Warner's "hard" assets:

> From our perspective, the central feature of this acquisition is not technological synergies, but rather the attempt by the management of the overvalued AOL to buy the hard assets of Time Warner to avoid even worse returns in the long run. In this acquisition, as in other deals involving high-technology acquirers with overvalued stock prices, long-run acquirer returns appear to be poor. However, according to our model, these returns are not as negative as they would have been had the acquisitions not taken place. When future writers condemn the merger spree of the late 1990s as manifesting misguided policies on the part of acquirers, they should focus on the alternative of not making these acquisitions. (Shleifer and Vishny, 2003, p. 295)

The market-driven acquisition hypothesis implies that the bidder prefers cash as payment method when bidder stock is sufficiently undervalued. Cash acquisitions must

---

[118] Himmelberg et al. (1999), Bhagat and Jefferis (2002), and Hermalin and Weisbach (2003).

generate value through synergies (as opposed to selling overvalued stock) for the bidder management to act in their shareholders' interest. Thus, while poor bidder performance following all-stock mergers is consistent with bidder value-maximizing behavior, poor performance following all-cash mergers is not.

Lehn and Zhao (2006) find a significant inverse relation between long-run returns after acquisitions and the probability that CEOs are replaced. More importantly, CEOs of acquiring firms with negative bidder returns are equally likely to be replaced, regardless of whether they used stock or cash as the method of payment in the acquisition. This finding challenges the prediction of Shleifer and Vishny (2003) and instead suggests that stock acquisitions (as well as cash acquisitions) associated with negative long-run bidder returns are destructive of value.

Several recent papers provide evidence on CEO compensation changes (other than turnover) following acquisition activity. Bliss and Rosen (2001) study bank mergers over the period 1985–1995, a period characterized by overcapacity and frequent mergers. Mergers are found to have a net positive effect on bidder firm CEO compensation, mainly via the effect of size on compensation. Compensation increases even if the merger causes the acquiring bank's stock price to decline (which is typical upon merger announcement). However, CEOs with more stock-based compensation are less likely to make an acquisition, suggesting that bank managers are motivated by their compensation contracts.

Datta et al. (2001) study 1719 acquisitions over the period 1993–1998 and separate the acquirers into whether the equity-based compensation of their respective CEOs is above (high) or below (low) the median. While the market reaction to the merger announcements is insignificantly different from zero on average, it is significantly positive for bidder CEOs with high equity-based compensation and significantly negative when the equity-based compensation is low. Moreover, the compensation structure impacts the target selection: high equity-based managers tend to seek out targets with relatively high M/B ratio (growth targets), whereas CEOs in the low-incentive compensation group tend to acquire targets with low growth prospects. Thus, it appears that managers with high equity-based compensation are willing to take on riskier and more valuable acquisition projects than managers with low equity-based compensation.

Grinstein and Hribar (2004) examine M&A bonuses (typically all-cash) paid to CEOs of bidder firm after 327 large merger deals over the period 1993–1999. Bonuses are larger for larger deals. Other than size, CEO power is the single most powerful variable explaining the cross-sectional variation in M&A bonuses. Much as in Bebchuk and Fried (2003), CEO power is measured as the CEO's ability to influence directors (and thereby the compensation decision). A CEO gains influence as a chairman of the board, as a member of the nominating committee, as the proportion of insiders on the board increases, and as board size increases. The size and power variables explain much more of the variation in bonuses than variables capturing CEO skill, effort, and performance. Moreover, the deal announcement-induced abnormal stock return is significantly lower (more negative) in the sample of CEOs with high power than those with low power. Moeller (2005) also concludes that targets with powerful CEOs receive lower takeover premiums. However, Bauguess et al. (2009) present evidence that inside (managerial) ownership has a positive relation with target returns, whereas active-outside (nonmanaging director) ownership has a negative relation with target returns. They suggest that the latter effect reflects outsiders' willingness to share gains with the bidder.

Harford and Li (2007) also study how CEO pay and pay-performance sensitivity are affected by acquisitions. With a sample of 1508 mergers completed over the period 1993–2000, they show that bidding firm CEOs receive substantial rewards in the form of new stock and options grants following acquisitions. While a poorly performing acquisition reduces the value of the CEO's portfolio of stocks and options obtained prior to the acquisition, the new postacquisition grants more than compensate for this personal value reduction. As a result, "CEO's pay and wealth are completely insensitive to poor postacquisition performance, but CEO's wealth remains sensitive to good postacquisition performance" (p. 919). Interestingly, they show that bidding firms with stronger boards retain the sensitivity of their CEO's compensation to poor postacquisition performance.

Harford and Li (2007) also document that compensation changes around major capital expenditures are much smaller and more sensitive to performance than those following acquisitions. That is, similar to conclusions made by Andrade and Stafford (2004), external and internal expansion decisions are treated fundamentally differently by the board. This difference may be rooted in the greater degree of uncertainty and information asymmetry surrounding acquisitions, which may allow the CEO to demand (and receive) some degree of protection for the downside risk to her personal wealth.

Walkling and Long (1984), Cotter and Zenner (1994), Wulf (2004), and Hartzell et al. (2004) all present evidence on acquisition-induced compensation of *target* firm CEOs. Hartzell et al. (2004) analyze a sample of 311 negotiated mergers between 1995 and 1997. A key question is what package of capital gains, cash, and subsequent employment do target CEOs accept in exchange for relinquishing control? Another important issue is whether target CEOs sacrifice premiums paid to their own outside shareholders in return for a favorable golden handshake.[119] Consistent with earlier studies, they conclude that "acquirers overtly pay certain CEOs to surrender managerial control over the firm's assets, or equivalently, that some CEOs 'purchase' executive jobs in the buyer by foregoing cash payments that they might otherwise have obtained" (p. 39). Also, they present some evidence of an inverse association between selling shareholder premia and unusual bonuses received by the target CEO as a reward to "step aside." However, since their study uses a sample of completed mergers only, it does not provide information on the sort of packages that other target CEOs turn down in attempted mergers that were not completed. Thus, as the authors

---

[119] Yermack (2006) presents evidence on severance packages more generally, in a sample of "Fortune 500" companies.

recognize, the study does not conclusively indicate that the large CEO packages come at the expense of target shareholders.

Finally, there is some evidence that board structure and director compensation affect the outcome of takeovers. Byrd and Hickman (1992) and Cotter et al. (1997) find that boards dominated by outsider directors increase value for their shareholders during an acquisition attempt. Harford (2003) documents the effect of a takeover bid on target directors, both financially and in terms of its effect on the number of future board seats held by those directors. He finds that directors are rarely retained following a completed offer and that target directors as a group hold fewer directorships after a takeover, suggesting that the target board seat is difficult to replace. Moreover, he shows that for outside directors, the direct financial impact of a completed merger is largely negative. In sum, failing as a monitor imposes a personal cost on outside directors.

5.3. Merger arbitrage

5.3.1. Arbitrage positions

After the announcement of a takeover bid, the target stock price adjusts upward but typically still trades at a discount from the offer price. The difference between the offer price and the postannouncement market price is called the arbitrage spread. Merger arbitrage (or risk arbitrage) is a specialized investment strategy that tries to profit from this spread. Specifically, it is a bet on the likelihood that the proposed transaction closes. If the bid (or a rival bid) is successful and the target is acquired, the arbitrageur captures the price differential. If the takeover fails and the target remains independent, however, the target stock tends to fall back to prebid levels and the arbitrage position has to be closed at a loss. Since the position carries the transaction risk, it is not an arbitrage in the true (riskless) sense of the word. It is, however, designed to be neutral to subsequent market movements and to price fluctuations between the bidder and the target if the deal succeeds.

For a cash bid, a merger arbitrage position simply involves a long position in the target stock. When the acquisition is consummated, the target stock is exchanged for cash. With a positive arbitrage spread, the cash received at closing will exceed the initial investment in the target stock, hence generating a profit. In contrast, if the takeover fails and the target stock price falls, the speculative position has to be sold at a loss equal to the price decline in the target stock.

The arbitrage position in a stock-for-stock transaction is more complex, since target shareholders are offered acquirer stock as payment. Here, the arbitrage position consists of a long target stock and a short acquirer stock in the same proportion as the exchange ratio. For example, with an offer of two acquirer shares for each target share, the arbitrage position is long one target share and short two acquirer shares. If the bid is subsequently revised, the arbitrage position must be adjusted to reflect the new exchange ratio. When the transaction closes, the arbitrageur receives in return for the target share the promised number of acquirer shares, which are used to cover the short position. The profit from a successful arbitrage position in a stock deal is the difference between the price of the short acquirer stock and the price of the target at the point in time when the position is established. If the bid fails, the arbitrageur will likely incur a loss from selling its target share holdings. The effect of closing out the short position in the acquirer is more uncertain: if the bidder stock falls, there may be an offsetting gain; and if the bidder stock appreciates, there may be additional losses.

Jindra and Walkling (2004) examine arbitrage spreads for 362 cash tender offers of publicly traded US targets between 1981 and 1995. They document large cross-sectional variations in the initial arbitrage spread, with one-quarter of the targets exhibiting a negative spread (i.e., a trading price exceeding the offer price) and an average spread of 2% (median 2%). Arbitrage spreads are greater for lengthier contests and smaller for hostile targets, and they suggest that spreads reflect market anticipation of the duration and price resolution of the offer.

5.3.2. Arbitrage gains

The magnitude of arbitrage returns depends on several factors, including the size of the arbitrage spread, the probability that the deal closes, the length of time that the arbitrageur must hold the position, and the target stock price development, if the deal fails. Several empirical studies document that merger arbitrage strategies tend to generate substantial excess returns. The largest abnormal returns have been documented for cash tender offers. For a sample of 295 cash tender offers from 1962 to 1980, Bhagat et al. (1987) document an average target excess return of 2% from 2 days after the tender offer announcement to the day prior to the expiration of the offer (on average 29 days). Dukes et al. (1992) analyze 761 cash tender offers identified from 14D-1 filings in 1971–1985. They find average daily raw returns of 0.5%, or holding-period returns of 25%, for the average arbitrage-position holding period of 52 days. Jindra and Walkling (2004) report an abnormal monthly return of 2% for investments in the target stock from the day after the initial bid until bid resolution. Although continuous reinvestment at similar returns is unlikely, these studies indicate annualized excess returns ranging from 25% to over 100%.

Studies involving a mix of cash and stock, as well as tender and merger offers, also document positive, though smaller returns to merger arbitrage. Larcker and Lys (1987) examine a sample of 111 13-D filings in 1977–1983 that state arbitrage or participation in a takeover proposal as the purpose of the investment and are associated with an acquisition offer. They show that an arbitrage position held from the announcement date to the resolution of the offer (median of 31 days) generates a cumulative excess return of on average 5% (median 3%). Karolyi and Shannon (1999) study 37 takeover bids for Canadian publicly traded targets in 1997. They find an average abnormal return to a merger arbitrage strategy of 5% over a 57-day average investment period. Baker and Savasoglu (2002) report monthly abnormal returns of almost 1% from a merger arbitrage strategy for a portfolio of 1901 US takeover offers between 1981 and 1996.

The studies reviewed above collectively suggest that merger arbitrage strategies systematically generate excess risk-adjusted returns. The literature proposes various explanations for the existence of these returns. One is that risk arbitrageurs may be compensated for carrying the risk of deal failure. Jensen (1986) points to three important roles played by merger arbitrageurs for which they should be compensated: (1) they help value alternative offers; (2) they provide risk-bearing services for investors who do not want the uncertainty associated with the outcome of the takeover offer; and (3) they help resolve the free-rider problems of small, diffuse shareholders who cannot organize to negotiate directly with competing bidders for the target. Moreover, transactions costs and other practical constraints may limit the possibilities of successfully implementing an arbitrage strategy.

Larcker and Lys (1987) argue that the excess returns constitute compensation to arbitrageurs for assembling costly information related to the outcome of the bid. They show that the ex post fraction of successful bids is significantly higher than the success probability implied by the arbitrage spread, suggesting that arbitrageurs have gathered private information about the deal outcome. In contrast, Cornelli and Li (2002) argue that the private information may be endogenous to the creation of the arbitrage position itself. The probability of offer success is positively related to the increased participation of arbitrageurs, since they are more likely to tender their target shares. The arbitrageur's investment in the target will therefore create an informational advantage, which can explain the profits earned by arbitrageurs. The model in Cornelli and Li (2002) predicts that the more liquid the stock, the easier it is to hide trades and the larger the arbitrage profits.[120]

Hsieh and Walking (2005) examine the importance of merger arbitrageurs for the market for corporate control using a sample of 680 all-cash and all-stock takeover offers during the period 1992–1999. They find that arbitrage holdings increase in offers that are likely to be successful, and suggest that this is evidence of the participation of passive arbitrageurs, whose accumulation of target stock does not affect the outcome of the deal. Hsieh and Walkling further find that these changes in arbitrage holdings are positively correlated to the probability of bid success, bid premia, and arbitrage returns. They interpret this as evidence of the involvement of active arbitrageurs, who influence the outcome and the terms of the deal.

5.3.3. Limits to arbitrage

The significance of transactions costs in limiting profits from merger arbitrage is investigated by Mitchell and Pulvino (2001). For a sample of 4750 mergers from 1963 to 1998, they document annual excess returns to merger arbitrage of 10% when ignoring transactions costs. When accounting for transactions costs, such as brokerage commissions and the price impact of trading, the annual excess returns are reduced to

---

[120] Gomes (2001) makes a similar argument where the entry of merger arbitrageurs creates large blocks of target shares that can hold out to a freeze out and hence forces the bidder to offer a higher preemptive bid.

4%. Thus, transactions costs appear to limit but not entirely eliminate the excess profits generated by merger arbitrage strategies. Mitchell and Pulvino (2001) further show that merger arbitrage returns are correlated with market returns in a nonlinear way. Specifically, the returns are positively correlated in down markets but uncorrelated in flat and appreciating markets. They suggest that the excess returns are compensation to arbitrageurs for providing liquidity, especially during severe market downturns.

Arbitrage activity may be limited in practice because these investments are risky and require capital (Shleifer and Vishny, 1997). It is obvious that merger arbitrage in cash offers require capital, since the investor takes a long position in the target stock. Because the lender of a stock typically demands the short-sale proceeds as collateral, merger arbitrage positions require capital in stock-for-stock transactions too. Baker and Savasoglu (2002) propose that the capacity of arbitrageurs to carry risk is limited by the transaction risk and the size of their arbitrage position. They report that merger arbitrage returns increase with target size and a measure for the ex ante deal completion risk. Moreover, there is some evidence that subsequent arbitrage profits are negatively related to changes in the supply of arbitrage capital.

Although merger arbitrage tends to be a profitable strategy, these trading strategies periodically generate large losses, primarily caused by unexpected deal failure (Baker and Savasoglu, 2002). Such liquidity events could affect the available supply of risk capital and hence the presence of arbitrageurs in subsequent deals. Officer (2007) examines the direct effect of two liquidity events—large arbitrage losses and the announcement of large deals-on arbitrage spreads. For a sample of 4593 all-cash and all-stock offers in 1985–2004, he finds that risk returns are negatively related to big arbitrage losses, but this is attributable to the deal itself and has no contagion to other deals or spreads on pending deals. Overall, Officer (2007) finds little evidence indicating that large losses would cause withdrawal of arbitrage funds to the extent that it affects pricing in other merger and acquisition transactions.

Trading volumes typically increase in connection with the announcement of a takeover offer. Estimates of the target ownership by merger arbitrageurs following a takeover announcement ranges from 15% (Hsieh and Walking, 2005) to 35% (Officer, 2007). Yet, Geczy et al. (2002) suggest that merger arbitrage strategies may be limited by short-selling constraints. They show that it is relatively expensive to borrow acquirer stock compared to other company stocks, in particular when the acquirer is small.

Mitchell et al. (2004) study the effects of merger arbitrage for 2130 mergers announced between 1994 and 2000. They document a substantial arbitrage activity after the announcement of a takeover offer. In the announcement month, the acquiring firm's short interest increases with a median of 40% in fixed-exchange-ratio stock mergers (i.e., where the exchange ratio is determined in the merger agreement). Interestingly, there is no corresponding change in the short interest for mergers where the arbitrage position does not involve a concurrent shorting of the acquirer stock, such as cash mergers or floating-exchange-ratio mergers (where the acquirer offers stock equivalent to a specific dollar value). The level of short interest falls dramatically when the merger closes. Also, the announcement effect of stock mergers is related to the change in short interest that occurs in the month of the announcement, suggesting a relationship between the arbitrage spread and the level of arbitrage activity.

To single out the effect of arbitrage trading activity, Mitchell et al. (2004) further examine a subsample of 64 floating-exchange-ratio mergers. During the pricing period, which typically lasts 10 days and ends 5 days prior to merger closing, the corresponding number of acquirer stock is determined. In this type of stock mergers, the short selling of acquirer stock typically takes place during the pricing period. Since most of the deal uncertainty has already been resolved at this point, the effect of the short-selling pressure is no longer confounded with the revelation of new information about the merger. Importantly, the short interest increases significantly and there is a negative abnormal drift in the acquirer stock price of 3% during the pricing period for the floating-exchange-ratio mergers. Mitchell et al. (2004) conclude that the short-selling by merger arbitrageur causes downward price pressure that accounts for almost half of the negative announcement return for acquirers in stock-financed mergers.

Overall, mergers and acquisitions of publicly traded firms attract substantial merger arbitrage activity. Such merger arbitrage strategies, betting on the closing of the transaction, seem to systematically generate positive excess returns. These returns reflect limits to arbitrage from transaction costs as well as compensation for carrying transaction risk.

6. Takeovers, competition, and antitrust

In Section 4, we concluded that the typical merger produces significantly positive combined announcement-induced abnormal stock returns to bidders and targets. A standard interpretation is that the wealth effect is the present value of future expected increases in the merging firms' operating margins (the spread between future revenues and costs). In this section, we review studies that attempt to tease out whether the wealth effect predominantly originates in cost reductions (efficiency effects) or in revenue increases (market power effects).

6.1. Efficiency versus market power: predictions

Eckbo (1983) and Stillman (1983) develop a test approach based on stock prices rather than product price data to infer the anticompetitive significance of horizontal mergers.[121] On the one hand, the (combined) abnormal stock returns to the bidder, and the target cannot be used to discriminate between efficiency and market power hypotheses: these returns represent the *net* effect of expected cost reductions and revenue increases. On the other hand, merger-induced changes in expected future product and factor

---

[121] Examples of merger studies examining product price and output data are Barton and Sherman (1984) on microfilm; Borenstein (1990), Werden et al. (1991), Kim and Singal (1993), and Singal (1996) on airlines; Akhavein et al. (1997), Prager and Hannan (1998), and Focarelli and Panetta (2003) on banking; and Dafny (2005) on hospital mergers.

prices translate into abnormal stock returns to industry rivals (as well as upstream suppliers and downstream customers) of the merging firms. In particular, a collusive, anticompetitive merger raises the product price and thus benefits the nonmerging rivals as well. This means that evidence of a negative industry wealth effect of a merger announcement is inconsistent with the merger having collusive, anticompetitive effects on its industry.

A positive industry wealth effect is necessary but not sufficient to conclude in favor of the collusion hypothesis. The reason is that the industry wealth effect of an efficient merger may be either positive or negative. On the one hand, scale-increasing efficient mergers tend to have a negative impact on the industry's equilibrium product price, which harms rival firms and by itself causes a negative industry wealth effect.[122] On the other hand, news of the merger may reveal positive information about the value of the resources controlled by the rival firms. That is, the merger may reveal increased demand for resources owned by other firms, causing a positive revaluation of these rivals. For example, the increased demand may lead to expectations of future merger activity, resulting in a positive "in-play" effect on rival firms from the announcement of the initial merger. In sum, the efficiency hypothesis does not restrict the abnormal returns to industry rivals.

As summarized in Table 12, which is reproduced here from Eckbo and Wier (1985), these predictions can be refined further by distinguishing between public announcements that either increase or decrease the probability of a merger in the industry. The table adds predatory pricing as a variant of the market power hypothesis. The predation theory holds that the merger provides an incentive for the bidder firm to increase output and drive product prices down until rivals exit—at which point output is cut back to the monopoly level. Thus, both predation and productive efficiency arguments predict a lowering of the product price (albeit in the short run under the predation argument), which harms rivals.

An event decreasing the probability of the merger is the announcement of a decision by US antitrust authorities (Department of Justice or Federal Trade Commission) to challenge the proposed merger with violation of antitrust laws (Section 7 of the 1914 Clayton Act).[123] As is seen in Table 12, the only pattern of abnormal stock returns to rival firms at once inconsistent with the market power hypothesis and consistent with the efficiency hypothesis is one where the rivals experience nonnegative returns in response to *both* probability-increasing and probability-decreasing events. Moreover, the collusion hypothesis is rejected unless one observes positive rival returns to

---

[122] Rivals may minimize the negative product price impact by racing to adopt similar technological innovations as the merging firms—prompting industry merger waves.

[123] Section 7 of the Clayton Act replaced Section 2 of the 1890 Sherman Act as the principal federal antitrust law regulating corporate mergers and acquisitions. A *potential* threat to competition constitutes an offense under this law, and it is not necessary to prove a horizontal relationship between the combining firms. Further-more, anticipated or demonstrated economic efficiencies are not a defense against the illegality of a merger that may lessen competition.

Table 12

Predicted abnormal returns to merging firms and their industry rivals under market power and productive efficiency hypotheses, classified by whether the event increases or decreases the probability of merger in the industry

Examples of positive information effects on rival firms are the case where the merger announcement reveals possibilities for efficiency gains also available to nonmerging rivals and the case where the merger signals an increase in demand for resources generally owned throughout the industry of the merging firms.

Theory predicting the source of the merger gains	Abnormal returns to merging firms	Abnormal returns to industry rivals
A. Events increasing the probability of merger (e.g., initial merger proposal announcement)		
Market power:		
(1) Collusion	Positive (monopoly rents)	Positive (monopoly rents)
(2) Predatory pricing	Positive (monopoly rents)	Negative (costs of price war)
Productive efficiency:		
(3) Productivity increase	Positive (cost savings)	Negative (competitive disadvantage)
(4) Information	Positive (undervalued resources)	Zero or Positive (undervalued resources and/or opportunities for productivity increases)
B. Events decreasing the probability of merger (e.g., antitrust complaint blocks the merger)		
Market power:		
(1) Collusion	Negative (loss of monopoly rents)	Negative (loss of monopoly rents)
(2) Predatory pricing	Negative (loss of monopoly rents)	Positive (avoiding price war)
Productive efficiency:		
(3) Productivity increase	Negative (loss of cost savings)	Positive (avoiding competitive disadvantage)
(4) Information	Zero (information already out)	Zero (information already out)

the initial merger proposal followed by negative returns to news of the antitrust action. The predation theory is rejected unless a price pattern opposite to the pattern under the collusion theory is observed.

This shows that information on the abnormal return to rival firms in principle has the power to test market power hypotheses. This is true even if a given merger has a combination of productive efficiency and market power effects (so the rival firm performance reflects the net effect of the two). Tests of the predictions in Table 12 do, however, presume that collusion and predation are mutually exclusive market power effects (since you would otherwise be netting out positive and negative rival effects at both announcements). It is common in the theoretical literature, as well as in the practice of antitrust policy, to treat these two market power theories as separate.

Further refinements of the predictions in Table 12 are possible. Schumann (1993) suggests that market power theories may have different implications for rivals with small versus large market shares. Fee and Thomas (2004) and Shahrur (2005) follow the

Table 13

Predicted abnormal returns to merging firms, rivals, customers, and suppliers. Source: Shahrur (2005)

	Productive efficiency	Collusion	Buyer power
Merging firms:	Positive	Positive	Positive[a]
	More-efficient production will result in higher infra-marginal rents to the merging firms	Higher likelihood of collusion will result in increased monopoly rents to the merging firms (Eckbo, 1983)	Lower input prices due to intensified competition among suppliers (Snyder, 1996)
Rivals:	Unrestricted	Positive	Positive[a]
	Positive: information regarding industry-wide restructuring. *Negative*: more-intense competition in the industry due to a new, more-efficient combined firm (Eckbo, 1983)	Higher likelihood of collusion will result in increased monopoly rents to rival firms (Eckbo, 1983)	Lower input prices due to more intense competition among suppliers (Snyder, 1996)
Customers:	Unrestricted[b]	Negative	Unrestricted[c]
	Positive: scale-increasing mergers. *Negative*: scale-decreasing mergers	Restricted output in the takeover industry results in lower demand for suppliers' output	*Positive*: benefit from lower input costs for merging firms. *Negative*: supplier underinvestment
Suppliers:	Unrestricted[b]	Negative	Negative[a]
	Positive: scale-increasing mergers. *Negative*: scale-decreasing mergers and/or more-efficient combined firm	Restricted output in the takeover industry results in lower demand for suppliers' output	The increased buyer power of the merging firms will intensify competition among suppliers (Snyder, 1996)

[a]Efficient mergers can be of the scale-increasing or the scale-decreasing types (see, e.g., Andrade and Stafford, 2004; Eckbo, 1992). If the merger is expansionary in nature, it should benefit customers. Suppliers can benefit from a scale-increasing merger as long as the positive effect of expansion is not outweighed by the adverse effect of the increased efficiency of the combined firm. Finally, an efficient merger of the scale-decreasing type can hurt customers and suppliers.

[b]Snyder (1996) shows that by creating a larger buyer, a horizontal merger can result in more intense competition among suppliers, which will benefit the merging firms and their rivals at the expense of suppliers.

[c]Customers may benefit from the increased buyer power if some of the gains resulting from lower input prices are passed on to them because of competition in the takeover industry. Customers can also suffer if the increased buyer power induces suppliers to underinvest.

suggestion of Eckbo (1983) to examine the wealth effects of mergers also for customers and suppliers. The two papers develop similar predictions, reproduced here as Table 13 from Table 1 in Shahrur (2005). The major focus in these two studies is on the buyer power hypothesis (last column)—that is, the possibility that the merger increases the monopsony power of the combined firm over its input suppliers. In this case, the merger benefits the merging firms and (possibly) its industry rivals at the expense of upstream suppliers. Consumers benefit as well, provided some of the increased monopsony rents are passed on downstream from the merging firms' industry. Evidence on customer performance also helps resolve a possible ambiguity from looking at rival firm performance alone. For example, while evidence of a positive rival firm performance in response to the merger proposal announcement does not discriminate between collusion and efficiency, collusion is rejected if customers also benefit.

Tests of predictions such as those in Tables 12 and 13 are likely to pick up an in-play effect in the abnormal returns to rival firms in response to merger announcements. The in-play effect, which motivates the positive information effect predicted by hypothesis (4) of Table 12, occurs when the merger event increases the probability that the rivals may become targets. An in-play effect follows naturally from the fact that rival firms use similar production technologies and own some of the same (and possibly scarce) productive resources. A takeover may signal increased resource scarcity, causing a positive revaluation of every firm holding those resources. The findings of most of the studies discussed below are consistent with such a positive industry information effect.[124]

Banerjee and Eckard (1998) and Fridolson and Stennek (2005) suggest that since a successful merger bid eliminates rival firms as potential merger partners for the target, there could be a negative out-of-play effect for these rivals. Such a negative effect might attenuate a positive effect due to market power. In their sample of largely conglomerate takeovers (where there arguably are no market power effects), Betton and Eckbo (2000) document *positive* rival firm performance when the rival learns that it has lost the target. While the idea of an out-of-play effect is interesting and consistent with formal competitive takeover models such as Akdogu (2007) and Molnar (2008), we are unaware of evidence favoring a significant out-of-play effect on rival firms.

6.2. Effects of merger on rival firms

Table 14 lists a number of empirical studies providing estimates of the industry wealth effects of horizontal mergers, beginning with Eckbo (1983) and Stillman (1983). Eckbo (1983) examines intra-industry wealth effects of 191 horizontal mergers in the United States between 1963 and 1978, 65 of which were challenged by either the Department of Justice (DOJ) or the Federal Trade Commission (FTC) with violating Section 7 of the Clayton Act. A sample of 68 vertical mergers, of which 11 were challenged, is also examined. For each merger, a set of horizontal competitors of the merging firms that were listed on the NYSE or the American Stock Exchange (ASE) at the time of the merger proposal announcement is identified.

The rivals are defined based on overlapping five-digit SIC codes. For the challenged mergers, the relevant product market is the one identified in court records as being the market "threatened" by the "anticompetitive" merger. For unchallenged mergers, the

---

[124] Exceptions are Eckbo (1992), Akdogu (2009), and Becher et al. (2008), who find a negative industry wealth effect of multi-industry horizontal merger announcements in Canada, and in single-industry studies of the US telecommunications and utility firms, respectively.

Table 14

Stock market studies examining industry wealth effects of horizontal mergers

Study	Merger sample	Selection of industry rival, customers and suppliers	Key findings
Stillman (1983)	11 US horizontal mergers challenged by DOJ or FTC with violating Section 7 of the Clayton Act, 1964–1972	Rival firms identified in antitrust litigation reports and antitrust enforcement agency fact memoranda	Zero average abnormal returns to rivals. Results inconsistent with market power effects of the sample mergers
Eckbo (1983)	191 US horizontal and 68 vertical mergers between mining or manufacturing firms operating nationally, 1963–1978. 65 horizontal and 11 vertical mergers were challenged by DOJ or FTC under Section 7	Rival firms selected from the major target industry using a five-digit SIC-based product classification procedure created by the author. For challenged mergers, the relevant industry is identified using court documents	Rival firms earn zero or positive abnormal returns in response to both the initial merger proposal announcement and the subsequent antitrust complaint. Results inconsistent with the market power (collusion) effects of the horizontal mergers
Eckbo and Wier (1985)	82 US challenged horizontal mergers, 1963–1981, including 65 from Eckbo (1983). 17 Cases occurred after the passage of the 1978 Hart-Scott-Rodino Antitrust Improvements Act	Two sets of rivals: one based on five-digit SIC codes as in Eckbo (1983), and another identified in antitrust litigation reports	Rival firm performance inconsistent with market power either before or after 1978. This conclusion holds for both sets of rivals
Eckbo (1985)	266 US merger proposals (196 horizontal, 98 challenged), including those in Eckbo (1983) and Eckbo and Wier (1985), 1963–1981	Rivals selected using the five-digit SIC code procedure of Eckbo (1983)	Industry wealth effect negatively related to merger-induced increase in industry concentration. Inconsistent with predictions of the Market Concentration Doctrine
Eckbo (1992)	471 merger proposals (312 horizontal), 266 between US firms and 205 between Canadian firms, 1963–1982. 80 of the US horizontal mergers were challenged under Section 7, none of the Canadian mergers were challenged	Rivals for both US and Canadian mergers identified using the five-digit SIC code procedure of Eckbo (1983)	No evidence of market power despite no antitrust deterrence of anticompetitive mergers in Canada until 1985. Industry wealth effect negatively related to merger-induced increase in industry concentration.
Schumann (1993)	37 acquisitions challenged by the FTC, 1981–1987	Rival firms identified using antitrust litigation reports	Positive rival firm performance at merger proposal and zero or positive at antitrust complaint. At the complaint, rival returns lower the greater the merger-induced change in concentration
Fee and Thomas (2004)	554 proposed (four-digit SIC) US horizontal mergers between publicly traded firms	Identifies single- and multiple-segment rivals in same four-digit horizontal	Evidence inconsistent with increased monopolistic collusion, but consistent with

(Continued)

Table 14 (*Continued*)

Study	Merger sample	Selection of industry rival, customers and suppliers	Key findings
	from SDC, 39 challenged under Section 7, 391 deals completed, 1981–1997	industry using Compustat industry segment information. The segment information also helps identify customers and suppliers	improved efficiency and buying power of merged firm
Shahrur (2005)	463 successful (four-digit SIC) US horizontal mergers and tender offers from SDC, 1987–1999	Identifies single-segment rivals, and customer and supplier firms, using Compustat industry segment information	Evidence inconsistent with increased monopolistic collusion, but consistent with improved efficiency and buying power of merged firm
Aktas et al. (2007)	290 proposed horizontal mergers in the European Union, of which 55 were subjected to "in-depth investigation" for potential antitrust violation. Bidder is a non-EU firm in 104 cases	Rival firms identified in same country and industrial sector as target using Hoover's Online Database, European Commission Web Site, and Datastream	Negative rival abnormal performance around merger proposal announcements. Suggests the sample mergers enhance industry competitiveness
Bhattahcaryya and Nain (2006)	615 successful (four-digit SIC) US horizontal mergers, 1989–2000, from SDC	Use Bureau of Economic Analysis benchmark Input-Output tables to identify the fraction of the supplier industry's output sold to the merging industry	Conclude with increased buying power based on postmerger decline in supplier product prices
Akdogu (2009)	$N = 275$, of which 115 (four-digit SIC) US horizontal takeover bids in the telecommunications industry, 1996-2005	Rivals firms identified using SDC and CRSP, using SIC code 4813	Evidence of negative industry wealth effect of the acquisition bids. Conclude that acquirers are on average expected to gain competitive advantage from the takeovers.
Becher et al. (2008)	384 successful mergers between electric utilities, 1980–2004	Rival firms are all public utilities with assets >$500 mill.	Evidence inconsistent with market power but consistent with efficiency (synergy) effects of the horizontal mergers
Shenoy (2008)	453 successful vertical mergers, 1981–2004	Use Bureau of Economic Analysis benchmark Input-Output tables to identify the main customer industries and rivals. Customer portfolios based on single-segment firms	Evidence fail to support market power but consistent with vertical mergers having efficiency effects

relevant product market is the target's major product line, as defined in Standard & Poor's Registry of Corporations. As shown by Eckbo and Wier (1985), the empirical results based on the five-digit SIC rivals are robust: They duplicate the tests using rivals identified by the DOJ or the FTC as being relevant competitors, and they draw the same inferences. To test the hypotheses in Table 12, the paper reports estimates of the abnormal stock returns to the merging firms and their horizontal rivals relative to (i) the merger proposal announcement and (ii) the subsequent announcement that the DOJ or the FTC has filed a Section 7 complaint against the horizontal merger.

Eckbo (1983) reports that the observed sequence of abnormal returns across the proposal and antitrust complaint announcements does not follow the pattern predicted by the collusion hypothesis. Rivals of the 65 horizontal challenged mergers earn small but significantly positive abnormal returns around the merger proposal announcement, followed by zero or positive abnormal returns in response to the antitrust complaint announcement.[125] The antitrust complaint causes a negative average abnormal return of −10% to the *merging* firms. This means that the antitrust complaint comes as a surprise to the market, which in turn means that the complaint announcement has the requisite power to test the market power hypothesis using rival firm returns.

This pattern of abnormal return to rival firms is inconsistent with the predictions as summarized in Table 12 of the collusion hypothesis, but it is jointly consistent with the efficiency and information arguments. Stillman (1983) performs a similar set of tests on 11 horizontal, challenged mergers for the period 1964–1972 and finds zero average abnormal rival stock returns relative to both merger announcements and antitrust complaints. Thus, both Eckbo and Stillman conclude against the market power hypothesis. Eckbo (1983) also reports that the average intra-industry wealth effect of unchallenged horizontal mergers is indistinguishable from the average intra-industry wealth effect of unchallenged vertical mergers. Since vertical mergers are unlikely to have collusive effects, this further supports the view that the horizontal unchallenged mergers in the sample were not expected to be anticompetitive.

Schumann (1993) also examines the effect of horizontal merger proposals and antitrust complaints on rival firms. His sample consists of 37 cases from 1981 to 1987 that were challenged by the FTC, a period with less antitrust intervention than in the sample periods of the earlier studies. Rival firms are identified using antitrust litigation reports, much as in Eckbo and Wier (1985). The results for the total sample, which indicates significantly positive rival returns at the proposal announcement and zero at the time of the antitrust complaint, are "remarkably similar to those reported in Eckbo (1983) and Eckbo and Wier (1985)" (Schumann, 1993, p. 681). For a subsample of 97 rivals with available data on market shares, Schumann also reports that rivals in the smallest market-share quartile have the largest abnormal returns and that these are

---

[125] The industry wealth effect of the merger is estimated by first forming an equal-weighted portfolio of the rivals of a given target and then estimating the portfolio abnormal return. Let $AR(t_1, t_2)$ denote the average of these portfolio estimates, where the period of cumulation is $t_2 - t_1 + 1$ days around the event-announcement day (day 0). Eckbo (1983) reports $AR(-1, 1) = 0.10\%$ and $AR(-10, 5) = 1.17\%$ relative to the merger proposal (significant at the 5% level), and an insignificant $AR(-1, 1) = 0.17\%$ relative to the antitrust complaint announcement. Eckbo (1983) also reports that complaints by the FTC cause a significantly *positive* industry wealth effect of $AR(0) = 0.74\%$.

significantly positive at both the proposal and complaint events. Following the predictions in Table 12, these findings contradict the collusion (market power) hypothesis.

Several studies also document significantly negative abnormal returns to rival firm portfolios in response to the announcement of horizontal mergers. Eckbo (1992) finds a negative industry wealth effect of horizontal merger announcements in Canada. Aktas et al. (2007) study horizontal mergers in the European Union, several of which were subjected to a preliminary antitrust review. They report significantly negative rival abnormal returns. Akdogu (2009) finds negative rival abnormal returns in response to horizontal takeover bids in the US telecommunications industry. Becher et al. (2008) document a significantly negative industry wealth effect in a large sample of horizontal mergers between US electric utilities. All of these studies reject the market power hypothesis and conclude that the typical sample merger would likely enhance efficiency.

6.3. Effects of merger on suppliers and customers

Fee and Thomas (2004) and Shahrur (2005) estimate the effect of horizontal mergers on rivals and, in particular, on upstream suppliers and downstream customers, over the period 1981–1999. These two studies provide new tests of market power theories based directly on the wealth effects for suppliers and customers. Moreover, by revisiting abnormal returns to rivals during a time period with relatively lax US antitrust enforcement in the merger area, they provide a perspective on the generality of the findings of earlier studies on industry wealth effects.

Starting with the evidence on rival firms, both studies report a statistically significant, positive industry wealth effect in response to the merger proposal announcement. Abnormal returns to portfolios of single-segment rival firms average 0.54% in Fee and Thomas (2004) and 0.39% in Shahrur (2005). These results are close to the early results in Eckbo (1983), and to those in Song and Walkling (2000). The evidence confirms that the composition of the rival firm portfolios in this literature yields sufficient power to register industry wealth effects of horizontal mergers.[126] Moreover, Eckbo (1983) as well as Fee and Thomas (2004) report significantly positive rival firm abnormal returns in response to news of antitrust action against the proposed merger.[127] Thus, consistent with the earlier literature, Fee and Thomas (2004) reject the collusion hypothesis for the horizontal-merger gains.

Fee and Thomas (2004) and Shahrur (2005) identify customer and supplier information using Compustat's industry segment files. These files record information mandated by Federal Accounting Standards Board (FASB) rule No. 14 during their sample period. Under this rule, firms are required to report financial information for any industry segment comprising more than 10% of consolidated yearly sales, assets, or profits.[128]

---

[126] See Eckbo (1983, 1989, 1992), McAfee and Williams (1988), and Schumann (1993) for discussions of power issues in the selection of rivals.
[127] Shahrur (2005) does not study antitrust events.
[128] After 1998, SFAS No. 131 governs required segment disclosures.

This reporting requirement also discloses the identity of any customer representing more than 10% of the total sales, as well as the company segment that was primarily responsible for those sales. Both studies also use sales data to identify suppliers and customers that are particularly dependent on the industry of the merged firm.

Under the monopoly (collusion) hypothesis, the merging firms and their rivals gain at the expense of customers. Fee and Thomas (2004) and Shahrur (2005) reject this hypothesis because they find no systematic evidence of customer losses, even for customers that are particularly reliant on the merging firm's industry. There is also evidence that the mergers with the largest gains to the merging firms also produce gains to customers. As Fee and Thomas (2004) conclude, "Taken together, the customer and rival results are strongly inconsistent with the monopolistic collusion hypothesis" (p. 457). Shahrur (2005) states that "Our overall evidence suggests that the lenient antitrust policy in recent years does not appear to have resulted in predominantly anticompetitive takeovers" (p. 95). These results support the conclusion in Eckbo (1992) that, when it comes to the need to use antitrust policy to strongly deter potentially anticompetitive mergers, "Judging from the evidence, there simply isn't much to deter" (p. 1028).

Fee and Thomas (2004) and Shahrur (2005) find some evidence of losses to upstream suppliers of the merging firms and conclude that horizontal merger tends to increase buying power. Increased buying power follows if the merger increases monopsony power or if it forces upstream suppliers to be more efficient. Fee and Thomas (2004) argue that if the source of buying power is upstream efficiency, then the losses to suppliers will be asymmetric—with losses only to those suppliers that are not retained postmerger. That is, those suppliers that lose a bidding competition postmerger would suffer. Fee and Thomas do in fact find that the wealth effect for suppliers depends significantly on the supplier's ability to retain its product-market relationship with the merged entity. Only the suppliers that are terminated experience negative abnormal returns around the merger announcement and significant negative cash flow changes postmerger. Suppliers that are retained experience increases in market share and do not show evidence of abnormal stock returns or changes in operating performance. The authors therefore conclude that the effect of the merger on suppliers reflects efficiency-increasing buying power. Shahrur (2005) reaches a similar conclusion: "Along with the evidence in Fee and Thomas (2004), our results suggest that industry consolidations can help increase the efficiency of upstream industries" (p. 96).

Bhattahcaryya and Nain (2006) and Shenoy (2008) also focus on vertical buying power. Bhattahcaryya and Nain (2006) sample 615 successful horizontal mergers and fail to find a significant announcement effect on the horizontal rivals. However, they find evidence of a reduction in the product price paid to upstream suppliers, which is consistent with increased buying power. Moreover, they find some evidence indicating that the upstream suppliers, perhaps feeling the squeeze from the increased buying power, restructure to counter the effect of the downstream horizontal merger. The authors suggest that the net effect of all this may have been to leave the market value of the horizontal rivals of the merging firms unchanged. Finally, Shenoy (2008) studies the industry wealth effects of 453 successful *vertical* mergers and concludes that these on average have efficiency effects. This evidence is also consistent with the effects of vertical mergers first reported by Eckbo (1983).

6.4. Some implications for antitrust policy

6.4.1. The market concentration doctrine

The US government selects Section 7, Clayton Act, cases against horizontal mergers largely on the basis of market share and industry concentration.[129] The government agencies' reliance on structural standards for selection of merger cases is rooted in one of the oldest propositions in industrial economics: the market concentration doctrine. This doctrine holds that the level of industry concentration is a *reliable* index of the industry's market power. The empirical implication is that a relatively high level of industry concentration, which in the presence of entry barriers is believed to facilitate intra-industry collusion or dominant-firm pricing, should be associated with relatively large industry-wide monopoly rents.

A horizontal merger produces a measurable change in the industry's level of concentration and a change in the risk-adjusted present value of industry rents that is directly associated with the concentration change. Under the market concentration doctrine, this change in industry rents is positively correlated with the change in concentration. This value-based test in the *changes* of the two variables (industry rents and concentration) allows more specific inferences than can be drawn from a correlation between the levels of (accounting) profits and concentration.

Eckbo (1985, 1992) provides empirical tests of the market concentration doctrine by estimating cross-sectional regressions of the following form:

$$AR_i = \alpha_0 + \alpha_1 CR_i + \alpha_2 dCR_i + \beta' Z_i + e_i \tag{25}$$

where CR_t is a measure of the premerger level of concentration in the industry where the horizontal merger is taking place, dCR_t is the change in concentration caused by the merger, Z_i is a set of firm- and industry-specific control variables, and AR_i is the abnormal return to an equal-weighted portfolio of the rivals of the merging firms around the merger proposal announcement. Under the market concentration doctrine, and assuming the sample includes some anticompetitive mergers, one should find that $\alpha_2 > 0$. This is because the AR of rivals of an anticompetitive merger represents

---

[129] The Justice Department's Merger Guidelines of 1968 state market shares that were likely to trigger an antitrust complaint. The critical aggregate market shares varied according to the four-firm market concentration ratios. For example, a merger between two firms each having 4% of the sales in a market with a four-firm concentration ratio of 75% or more was likely to be challenged. The department's 1982 Merger Guidelines use the Herfindahl Index of concentration and are somewhat less restrictive than the old guidelines, but their focus is also on market structure.

increased monopoly rents, and the market concentration doctrine holds that the increase in monopoly rents will be larger the larger the increase in concentration caused by the merger. Furthermore, under the stronger proposition embedded in antimerger policy, which holds that a merger is more likely to have anticompetitive effects the larger the premerger *level* of concentration, one should also find evidence of $\alpha_1 > 0$.

While the form of Equation (25) is similar in spirit to the regression models typically estimated in the "structure-conduct-performance" (industrial organization) literature, there are some notable qualitative differences: For example, while the dependent variable AR measures directly the market value of the increase in industry profits expected to follow from the (merger-induced) increase in industry concentration, the tradition has been to regress an accounting measure of the level of industry profits on the level of concentration. The traditional approach has been criticized on the grounds that accounting profits are a poor proxy for economic profits and that any cross-sectional variation in the level of industry profits can simply reflect differences in risk. This criticism does not apply here, since AR is measured using market values and represents a risk-adjusted change in the level of industry rents. Equally important is the fact that since Equation (25) is specified in the form of changes in the central variables, α_2 can be meaningfully interpreted without specifying a complete structural model relating the level of industry profits to concentration.

Eckbo (1985, 1992) uses the four-firm concentration ratio (CR_4) of the major four-digit SIC industry of the target firm to represent CR, while the change in the industry's Herfindahl Index (dH) measures dCR.[130] While data on CR_4 is generally available, the market shares of the bidder and target firms, which yield dH, were collected from case-related court records and publications. In the sample of challenged mergers in Eckbo (1985), the average level of CR_4 is 58% (ranging from 6% to 94%), while the average value of dH is 3.3% (ranging from 0.02% to 24.2%).

Both studies report a statistically significant negative coefficient on dH. In Eckbo (1985), increasing dH by 1% implies a reduction of 0.42% in the abnormal returns to the average portfolio of rival firms. Similar results emerge when one uses the abnormal returns to the *merging* firms as dependent variable. The author notes that since the regressions of the type in Equation (25) are based on challenged mergers, the results are biased in favor of the market concentration doctrine. Despite this potential bias, there is no evidence supporting the doctrine.[131]

---

[130] $CR_4 \equiv \sum_{i=1}^{4} s_i$, and $H \equiv \sum_{i=1}^{n} s_i^2$, where s_i is the market share of firm i (in CR_4 the sum is over the four firms with the largest market shares) and n is the total number of firms in the industry. The change in the Herfindahl Index caused by the merger between firms i and j in the same industry is therefore given by $dH = 2s_i S_j$.

[131] "[T]he evidence systematically rejects the antitrust doctrine even for values of industry concentration and market shares which, over the past four decades, have been considered critical in determining the probability that a horizontal merger will have anticompetitive effects" (Eckbo, 1992, p. 1028).

6.4.2. Did the 1978 antitrust improvements act improve antitrust?

The 1976 HSR Antitrust Improvements Act significantly increased the legal powers of the law enforcement agencies to obtain private information needed for judging a merger's anticompetitive impact before filing a complaint. The HSR Act addressed two perceived handicaps borne by the agencies charged with enforcing Section 7 of the Clayton Act. First, under the 1962 Antitrust Civil Process Act, the DOJ could not require third parties, such as competitors and trade associations, to provide information about corporate acquisitions until after a Section 7 complaint had been filed. This frequently caused the DOJ to drop an investigation altogether for lack of information or to file a "skeleton" complaint based on scanty data. HSR established the right of the DOJ to issue Civil Investigative Demands to the merging firms and to other parties not directly involved in the merger prior to filing a complaint. Second, until the HSR Act, the government could not require postponement of proposed acquisitions pending investigation. HSR required firms planning mergers to prenotify the FTC and the DOJ of the transaction, providing the agencies with time and information to prepare a case before merger consummation.

According to the FTC,[132] the notification requirements and delay assure that "virtually all significant mergers or acquisitions occurring in the United States will be reviewed by the antitrust agencies prior to the consummation of the transaction." Moreover, the information provided by the parties "usually is sufficient for the enforcement agencies to make a prompt determination of the existence of any antitrust problems raised by the transaction." These assurances notwithstanding, Eckbo and Wier (1985) compare the anticompetitive significance of horizontal mergers challenged before and under HRS and find no significant difference in their effect on rival firms. Moreover, they conclude that the pattern of abnormal stock returns to the industry rivals is inconsistent with the mergers having collusive anticompetitive effects both before and under the HSR. Based on this, they argue that HSR is unlikely to have significantly increased the precision with which defendants are chosen by the antitrust agencies.

Why would the antitrust process, which many believe is designed to protect consumer interests, result in blocking efficient mergers? Bittlingmayer and Hazlett (2000) suggest bureaucratic self-interest, political extraction, and private benefits. In this context, it is important to keep in mind that, while preventing efficient mergers harms consumers, the *rivals* of the merging firms benefit as they avoid having to face competition from an increasingly efficient merged firm. The rivals can indeed form a politically strong interest group in situations where they perceive a significant threat to their existing industry equilibrium. This industry capture theory is highlighted by Posner (1969) who asserts that the FTC is significantly impaired in its task of promoting the public interest; Posner claims that its investigations are initiated "at the behest of corporations, trade associations, and trade unions whose motivation is at best

---

[132] 6 FTC Ann. Rep. to Cong. concerning HSR ACT 11 (1983).

to shift the costs of their private litigation to the taxpayer and at worst to harass competitors" (p. 88).

A case in point is Chrysler's vocal opposition to the joint venture between GM and Toyota in 1983. At the time the venture was announced, Chrysler demanded publicly that the FTC take action to stop the venture because it would "harm competition" in the automobile industry. An alternative interpretation of Chrysler's opposition is that it suspected the venture would make GM a tougher competitor, placing Chrysler at a competitive disadvantage. In fact, Eckbo (1990a) finds significant abnormal returns of −9% to Chrysler upon the announcement of the GM-Toyota joint venture. More recent cases in point include the airline industry, where Slovin et al. (1991) conclude that Civil Aeronautics Board interventions during 1965 to 1988 reduced competition and favored collusion among existing carriers. Bittlingmayer and Hazlett (2000) study the effect on the software and computer industry of 54 antitrust enforcement actions against Microsoft over the period 1991–1997, and strongly reject the thesis that these actions would enhance efficiency. Also, Aktas et al. (2007), who study rival firm performance following antitrust interventions against mergers in the European Union, find evidence consistent with antitrust policy being used to protect EU firms from outside competition.

Since the anticompetitive significance of a horizontal merger does not represent a directly observable characteristic, policy makers are forced to rely on largely untested theories to justify their decisions. As noted by Stigler (1982), the economics profession has supplied "precious little" in the way of *tested* knowledge to support the market share and concentration criteria that (still) form the basis for US antimerger policy. As long as those responsible for antimerger policy continue to insist on rigid structural standards for evaluating the competitive effects of mergers, it is reasonable, given the evidence, that special interest groups, including those representing relatively inefficient producers and/or a rigid workforce, will continue to exploit antitrust policy toward merger.

7. Summary and conclusions

Table 15 summarizes key findings across the various topics we have surveyed. Here, we draw broad inferences from these findings and point to interesting but unresolved issues.

7.1. Takeover activity

While there are clear patterns of merger waves in the data, there is little agreement on the basic sources of the waves. Under neoclassical theories, basic sources include industry-specific technological and demand shocks, regulatory changes, and liquidity constraints. Under behavioral arguments, mergers are driven by attempts to sell overpriced assets and securities and herding behavior. There is evidence that regulatory changes and liquidity factors predict industry waves. There is also evidence of

Table 15

Summary of empirical results on corporate takeovers, classified by research topic

Topic

A. Takeover activity

(1)   Merger waves (clustering of takeovers) tend to occur in periods of market booms. They occurred in the late 1800s and early 1900s ("the monopolization wave"), the late 1960s ("the conglomerate wave"), the mid 1980s ("the refocusing wave"), and the late 1990s ("the strategic/global wave").

(2)   There is substantial evidence of industry-clustering of mergers. Regulatory changes and macroeconomic liquidity variables are better predictors of industry merger waves than are M/B ratios.

(3)   In the period 1996–2000, when market valuations were particularly high, the sum of all-cash and mixed cash-stock bids was equal to the number of all-stock bids. Also, in this period, the proportion all-stock offers was the same as during the previous 5-year periods.

(4)   Despite strong merger patterns, predicting target firms with any accuracy has proven difficult.

(5)   Target firms increasingly initiate the takeover process by soliciting bid indications from a set of potential negotiating partners. The bidder that is selected is recorded as the first bidder in SEC registration documents and therefore by data bases such as SDC (Thomson Financial).

(6)   When organizing all SDC control bids into contest for US targets, there were a total of 35,727 control contests. Of these, the initial bidder proposed a merger in 28,994 cases and made a public tender offer in another 4500 cases (the balance being 2224 controlling-block trades).

(7)   In constant 2000 dollars, the merger deal was valued at $436 million on average (median ($35 mill.), while the deal value of the average tender offer was $480 (median $79 mill.).

(8)   SDC provides information on the payment method for about half of the cases. Of these, 26% were all-cash deals, 37% were all-stock deals, and 37% were mixed cash-stock deals. All-cash and mixed offers have similar deal sizes, slightly above all-stock deals.

(9)   A total of 590 initial bids are classified as "hostile" and another 435 deals are "unsolicited." Hostile bids have substantially higher than average deal values.

(10) In approximately 30% of all deals, the initial bidder and target operate in the same four-digit SIC industry (horizontal takeover). The two most active takeover sectors are Manufacturing, and Finance/Insurance/Real Estate.

(11) Two-thirds of the 35,727 initial bidders are public companies, while 37% of the targets are public. In 44% of the initial bids, a public bidder is pursuing a private target (the largest single group of takeovers), with an average deal value of $114 mill (median $23 mill.). The total number of deals involving either a public bidder or target rose sharply in the 1990s.

(12) Of the 35,727 initial bidders, 11% were foreign companies (primarily Canada and the United Kingdom). Deals involving foreign bidders are relatively large.

(13) The time from the initial offer to the effective takeover date averages 108 trading days (median 96) when the initial bid is a tender offer, and 71 days (median 49) for merger bids. In cases where there are more than one control bid for the target, the time from the first to the second bid averages 40 trading days (median 19).

(14) The likelihood that the initial bidder wins the target is higher when the bidder has a toehold, when the payment method is all-cash, when the bid form is tender offer, and when the bidder is a public company. The probability of winning is lower for targets with poison pills, and when the target reaction is negative. All bids fail (no bidder wins) in 22% of the cases, with a greater failure probability for private bidders.

B. The payment method

(15) Bidders initiating takeover bids for US targets over the period 1980–2005 offered all-cash as payment in 26% of the cases, all-stock in 37%, and a mix of stock of cash in 37%.

(Continued)

Table 15 (*Continued*)

Topic

(16) The majority of tender offers are all-cash or a mix of cash and stock. While the majority of merger bids are in the form of all-stock (with the exception of the 1980–1985 period where most merger bids offered a mixed cash-stock payment).

(17) In the two subperiods 1990–1995 and 1996–2000, the percentage all-stock offers in initial merger bids were approximately 55% in both period. This means that (1) nearly half of the initial merger bids in the 1990s use some cash as payment, and (2) the percentage all-stock merger bids remained unaffected by the significant runup in overall market valuations in the 1996–2000 period.

(18) The payment method choice is in part determined by tax considerations, the degree of information asymmetry between the bidder and the target, the degree of market mispricing of bidder stock, and by corporate control considerations. Stock offers are more likely the greater the bidder's asset size and M/B ratio. Stock offers are less likely the greater the bidder management's shareholdings and the greater the dispersion in analyst forecast of bidder earnings.

(19) Offer premiums are greater in all-cash offers than in all-stock offers. The probability that the initial bidder wins the target is lower for all-stock offers than for cash offers.

(20) When the target is public, bidder announcement returns are on average negative in all-stock offers and greater in all-cash and mixed cash-stock offers than in all-stock offers. Moreover, bidder announcement-induced stock returns are increasing in the cash-portion of the (mixed) offer.

(21) When the target is a private company, stock offers generate positive bidder announcement returns that are as high—if not higher—than for all-cash bids.

C. Toehold bidding:

(22) The frequency of toehold bidding in friendly mergers and tender offers has fallen dramatically since the 1980s. Over the 1990–2002 period, 7% of bidders initiating a takeover had toeholds, and only 2% had toeholds acquired in the market shortly prior to launching the bid.

(23) Toehold bidding remains common in hostile bids (50% frequency).

(24) Toeholds are large when they exist: on average 20%.

(25) Toehold bidders tend to pay lower offer premiums and win the target more often than zero-toehold bidders.

(26) The presence of a bidder toehold attenuates the drop in the target share price when all bids fail.

(27) Since bidder toehold benefits mirror target toehold costs (lower offer price, greater probability of target management being replaced) toehold bidding may be viewed as aggressive by the target. Thus, approaching the target with a toehold may cause some otherwise friendly targets to refuse negotiations. Consistent with this, the data indicates a significantly negative association between the likelihood of the initial bidder approaching with a toehold and the expected value of resistance costs (including the opportunity loss of a termination agreement).

D. Bid jumps and markup pricing

(28) The average offer premium in successful single-bid takeover contests is somewhat higher than the average initial offer premium in multibid contests. This is consistent with the greater premium preempting competition in ex post successful single-bid cases.

(29) Bid revisions are substantial, with an average bid jump from the first to the second bid in the contest of 10% (a 31% change in the offer premium).

(30) A dollar increase in the preoffer target share price runup causes the initial bidder to mark up the total offer premium by $0.80.

(31) (31) Markup pricing notwithstanding, bidder takeover gains are increasing in the target runup. Thus, takeovers with greater target runups are more profitable for both bidder and target firms, which may also explain why bidders agree to (partial) markup pricing.

(32) Toehold acquisitions during the runup period bidder increase the target runup. When the toehold is acquired by the initial bidder, however, the markup is reduced. No such markup reduction is observed when the toehold is acquired by another investor.

(Continued)

Table 15 (*Continued*)

Topic

E. Takeover defenses

(33) The presence of a majority of independent directors on the board of the target is viewed by the court as a strong indication of satisfaction of the fiduciary duty of loyalty.

(34) Delaware case law sanctions the right to "just say no" to an unsolicited takeover bid. That is, the board may determine in good faith that the continuing independence of the corporation is in the long-term best interest of the corporation and its stockholders.

(35) If the board's defensive response is not "draconian" (i.e., it is neither coercive nor preclusive) but "within the range of reasonableness" given the perceived threat, the board is protected by the business judgment rule. A defense that is deemed preclusive because it frustrates, impedes or disenfranchises a shareholder vote is unlikely to be upheld.

(36) The twin defense of staggered board election and a poison pill ("shareholder rights plan") is "draconian" in the eyes of many economists but not the court. However, "dead hand" pills (where only directors not up for election may vote to rescind the pill) have been struck down.

(37) The fraction of "hostile" (sum of unsolicited bids and bids where target is explicitly hostile) drops sharply after 1989, from more than 20% in the 1980s to less than 3% by the end of the 1990s.

(38) Offer premiums are no lower for targets with poison pills.

(39) There is a small but significantly negative market reaction to the adoption of strong antitakeover amendments such as poison pills and staggered board. The market reacts positively to antigreenmail amendments provided these occur when a takeover is rumored.

F. Targets in bankruptcy

(40) There is a trend towards market-based mechanisms for resolving Chapter 11 cases, including sale of the firm to a bidder. Target firms that are sold spend less time in Chapter 11, which lowers bankruptcy costs. Acquirers tend to be in the same industry, and premiums paid are on average lower than in takeovers of nonbankrupt firm in the same industry.

(41) Premiums paid for targets sold in mandatory, open, first-price, all-cash bankruptcy auctions in Sweden suggest the possibility that the auction mechanism may work well for the typical Chapter 11 case as well (which is of a similar size as the Swedish sample firm).

(42) The average mandatory auction receives three bids and lasts 2 months; three-quarters of the auctioned firms are sold as going concern; the prices paid in these going-concern sales do not exhibit fire-sale discounts; and competition among bidders appear to force insiders to pay premiums comparable to those paid by outsiders.

(43) The bankrupt firm's major creditor (bank) often finances a bidder in the auction, which pushes the auction towards overbidding. Postbankruptcy operating performance is found to be at par with nonbankrupt industry rivals, regardless of overbidding incentives, suggesting that the auction leads to a relatively efficient restructuring of the target firm.

G. Offer premiums

(44) Large-sample evidence on offer premiums are only starting to emerge. This evidence indicates that both the initial and final offer premiums are
- greater after the 1980s;
- greater for public bidders;
- greater in all-cash offers;
- lower for toehold bidders;
- increasing in the target runup (markup pricing);
- decreasing in target total equity capitalization and grater if the target's B/M ratio exceeds the industry median M/B ratio;
- greater in the presence of substantial dispersion in analysts' earnings forecasts;

(*Continued*)

Table 15 (*Continued*)

Topic

- lower when the bidder CEO is female, and the higher the target board's proportion of female directors (provided that the female directors are independent appointees);
- unaffected by either the presence of a target poison pill or target hostility to the initial bid.

H. Takeover gains

(45) The average target cumulative average abnormal stock return (CAR) is positive and significant, both over the runup period and the announcement period. The runup constitutes about one-third of the total runup plus announcement CAR. The largest target CAR occurs in all-cash offers.

(46) The average, value-weighted combined CAR to bidders and targets is positive and significant over both the runup period and the announcement period. For the overall sample used here, the sum of the combined CAR for the runup- and announcement periods is a significant 1.79%.

(47) Bidder announcement-period CARs average close to zero for the overall sample, with 49% of the bidders having negative CAR. The combination large bidder (here in the upper size quartile), payment in all-stock, and the target being a public company represents a "worst-case scenario" with average bidder announcement-period CAR of a significant -2.21%. The "best-case scenario" for the bidder is the combination of a small bidder (lower size-quartile), private target and all-stock as payment. This produces a significant average bidder announcement-period CAR of 6.46%.

(48) The major driver of negative bidder returns is not, as previously thought, the all- stock payment. Rather, the two key drivers are the target's status a public or private, and bidder size.

(49) Bidder size was particularly large in 1999 and 2000. These years were unusual relative to years before and years after. Cisco, with a (constant 2000 dollar) market capitalization of $180 billion was the dominant bidder in both the upper 1% and lower 1% tails of the distribution of bidder abnormal announcement returns. Removing Cisco from the sample reduces the aggregate bidder dollar wealth loss in 1999–2000 period by almost $100 billion.

(50) Studies of long-run abnormal stock returns use either the matched-firm technique or Jensen's alpha (regression constant in an asset pricing model) to measure expected return to the merged firms in the sample. With 15,298 successful takeovers completed during the period 1980–2003, we show that long-run returns are significantly negative based on the matched-firm technique and insignificantly different from zero based Jensen's alpha.

(51) The standard matched-firm procedure identifies firms that have significantly different factor loadings than the event firms—which undermines their role as "matches."

(52) A zero-investment portfolio strategy which is long in the merged firms and short in the matched firms fail to produce long-run abnormal stock returns which are significantly different from zero, even for the sample of all-stock mergers.

I. Bondholders, management, and arbitrageurs

(53) Studies of excess returns to bondholders of bidder and target firms find zero or negative gains to bidder bondholders and positive gains to target bondholders. There is no evidence of a wealth transfer from stockholders to bondholders due to a coinsurance effect of mergers. As of the 1990s, target bondholders are often fully protected via event risk covenants.

(54) Some target firms, particularly those receiving hostile bids, underperform prior to becoming targets. Moreover, CEO turnover increases after hostile bids. These findings indicate a disciplinary role played by the market for corporate control. There is, however, indications that this external control mechanism represents a "court of last resort."

(55) There is evidence that managers undertaking value-reducing acquisitions face a greater probability of being replaced than do managers undertaking value-increasing acquisitions. That is, bad bidders risk being fired.

(56) There is evidence that CEO compensation (other than turnover) changes following acquisition activity. The market reaction to merger announcements tends to be positive and greater for CEOs with above-average equity-based compensation, suggesting that compensation affects the quality of managerial investment decisions.

(*Continued*)

Table 15 (*Continued*)

Topic

(57) CEOs with high equity-based compensation tend to seek out targets with relatively high M/B ratios (growth firms). This is consistent with high equity compensation inducing risk-taking behavior.

(58) Empirical measures of CEO "power" helps explain the cross-sectional variation in M&A bonuses. Deal announcement induced abnormal stock returns tend to be lower for CEOs with greater "power," suggesting that power may be misused.

(59) While a poorly performing acquisition reduces the value of the CEO's portfolio of stocks and options, there is evidence that the value of postacquisition grants more than compensates for this value reduction. This indicates that CEOs face combination of low downside risk and high upside potential from making good acquisition decisions.

(60) There is evidence that some target firm CEOs may be sacrificing takeover premium in return for a "golden handshake" from the bidder (to step aside and relinquish control).

(61) There is evidence that boards dominated by outside directors tend to increase value for their shareholders during an acquisition attempt. Target directors are rarely retained after a completed takeover, and their number of board seats and income levels tend to drop. This indicates that failing as a monitor imposes a personal cost on directors.

(62) There is substantial evidence of increased trading activity in the bidder and target shares following merger announcements. In all-cash offers, merger (risk) arbitrageurs purchase target shares without shorting the bidder shares. In all-stock deals, arbitrageurs short the bidder stock using the exchange rate. If the exchange ratio is floating, the short sales are postponed until the final pricing has been set and the floating ratio has been fixed.

(63) There are substantial (risk-adjusted) returns to merger arbitrage strategies. Moreover, the short selling activity appears to put downward pressure on the acquirer stock price that may account for almost half of the negative announcement return for acquirers of stock-financed mergers.

J. Mergers, competition and antitrust

(64) Merger-induced changes in product and factor prices directly translate into abnormal stock returns to the merging firms' industry rivals, upstream suppliers and downstream customers. Market power theories (collusion, predation, buying power) and productive neoclassical efficiency theories make empirically testable predictions for these abnormal stock returns. Such tests complement and extend traditional product price analysis seen in industrial economics.

(65) The power of tests based on stock returns depend on the accurate identification of related firms (rivals, customers, suppliers). Since much of the available evidence indicates significant contagion effects of horizontal merger announcements on these related firms, the tests appear to have sufficient power. Related firms are identified using four-digit SIC codes, Compustat industry segment information, and the Bureau of Economic Analysis Input Output tables.

(66) The tests utilize two sets of samples: Mergers that have been challenged with violation of antitrust laws (or, in the European Union, reviewed for such violation), and nonchallenged mergers. For challenged mergers, the tests exploit two events with (typically) opposing implications for the industry wealth effects, thus increasing power to reject.

(67) The empirical studies typically conclude against horizontal market power effects of horizontal mergers, whether or not these were challenged. That is, the observed wealth effects on horizontal rivals and downstream (corporate) customers do not support increased market power. Some studies find traces of monopsony (buying power) effects vis-à-vis upstream suppliers.

(68) A horizontal merger causes a measurable increase in industry concentration (equal to twice the product of the market shares of the bidder and target when using the Herfindahl measure of concentration). The classical market concentration doctrine holds that increases in concentration reliably increases the industry's market power and thus industry monopoly rents. Since the abnormal returns to industry rivals directly measures changes in industry rents, regressing the merger-induced rival abnormal returns on the change in industry concentration provides a powerful test of the market concentration doctrine. Empirical tests reject the doctrine.

greater average M/B ratios during periods of merger waves, which may (but need not) indicate overvaluation. On the other hand, additional research is needed on the extent to which bidders select stock as payment in response to M/B ratios and on whether the presence of mixed cash-stock offers (which are typically as frequent as all-stock offers) are consistent with equilibria in which targets willingly accept overpriced bidder shares.

Perhaps the most straightforward way to advance our understanding of aggregate merger activity is to model the takeover process from basic, microeconomic principles. One does not get something from nothing—so this requires imposing various restrictive (but hopefully testable) assumptions on production technologies and market structures. The theoretical literature on the optionality of corporate investments is a promising avenue, as are models of industry competition in which industry shocks force rival firms to restructure. Empirical research tailored to such modeling efforts is only starting to emerge.

Important stylized facts from the aggregate takeover activity in the 1980–2005 period include (1) the stability of horizontal combinations at 30–40% of the total takeover population, (2) negotiations (as opposed to open auction) as the preferred route to acquiring control, (3) the sharp drop-off in hostile takeovers after 1988, (4) the large increase in volume and deal values involving public bidders toward the end of the 1990s, (5) the predominance of all-cash and mixed cash-stock offers in tender offers, (6) the rise of mixed stock-cash offers to become the most frequently used payment method in mergers by 2001, and (7) the dramatic fall in toehold bidding since the mid-1980s.

Additional research is needed to sort out the competing theories for the sharp drop in hostile takeovers and what this drop means for the market for corporate control to function effectively as the court of last resort. While takeover activity depends on market liquidity factors (and thus fell during the credit crunch of the late 1980s), it is also important to establish how draconian antitakeover devices such as the staggered board and poison pill defense contributed to the fall.

The choice between merger and tender offer is interesting but has received little attention. There is some evidence that this decision is impacted by industry competition. This is hardly surprising as the likelihood of attracting rival competition in an auction setting depends on industry structure as well as asset characteristics. This is a fertile area for future research, both empirical and theoretical, and it ultimately links back to our understanding of takeover waves. Moreover, there are some indications that the target (and not the bidder) is increasingly initiating takeovers and thus determines the acquisition form. The economics of the selection process behind target-initiated deals is an exciting area for future research.

7.2. Bidding strategies and offer premiums

Bidders initiating takeover bids for US targets over the period 1980–2005 offered all-cash as payment in 26% of the cases, all-stock in 37%, and a mix of stock of cash in 37%. The majority of tender offers are all-cash or a mix of cash and stock. While the majority of merger bids are in the form of all-stock (with the exception of the 1980–1985 period where most merger bids offered a mixed cash-stock payment). As pointed out earlier, all-cash and mixed cash-stock offers are predominant in tender offers. Moreover, mixed stock-cash offers rose to become the most frequently used payment method in mergers by 2001. In the two subperiods 1990–1995 and 1996–2000, the percentage of all-stock offers in initial merger bids was approximately 55% in *both* period. This means that (1) nearly half of the initial merger bids in the 1990s use some cash as payment, and (2) the fraction of merger bids where the payment is all-stock remained unaffected by the significant runup in overall market valuations in the 1996–2000 period.

The choice of payment method is strategic for several reasons, including tax effects, its impact on the conditional expected value of the bid to asymmetrically informed bidders and targets, and corporate control considerations. The evidence indicates that stock offers are more likely the greater the bidder's asset size and M/B ratio. Stock offers are less likely the greater the bidder management's shareholdings and the greater the dispersion in analyst forecast of bidder earnings. Moreover, offer premiums are greater in all-cash offers than in all-stock offers, and the probability that the initial bidder wins the target is lower for all-stock offers than for cash offers.

The pervasive negative market reaction to all-stock merger bids by public bidders is typically compared to the average negative market reaction to SEOs. The comparison is appealing since the timing of the equity issue is determined endogenously by the issuer in both events, and thus involves some degree of adverse selection. On the other hand, in terms of the *issue method,* stock swaps in mergers are closer to private placements than they are to an underwritten SEO—and there is substantial evidence that the market reaction to private placement is positive on average (Eckbo et al., 2007). Moreover, the market reaction to merger stock swaps is positive when the target is private. Also, formal tests of signaling theories for the payment method choice have received mixed success. Additional research is needed to establish the empirical relevance of asymmetric information arguments for the strategic payment choice.

The dramatic fall in toehold bidding coincides with the rise of structural takeover defenses beginning in the 1980s. In theory, toehold bidding conveys the substantial strategic advantage of rival bidders, particularly in a common-value setting. Since many of these advantages come at the expense of the *target*, some targets may be reluctant to negotiate if the bidder has a toehold. If so, acquiring a toehold prior to attempting friendly merger negotiations may backfire: if the target refuses, the bidder foregoes not only things like a termination agreement but also the opportunity to examine the target books—which is crucial for pricing the merger.

Another way to put this is that a toehold must be large to be worth it—larger than 10% by some (conservative) estimates. This argument may go a long way in explaining the dual observation that toeholds are large (on average 20%) when they exist and that they occur mostly in hostile bids. An interesting and hitherto unexplored empirical issue is whether toeholds are important in other jurisdictions, in particular those with highly concentrated shareownership and a set of takeover regulations and corporate governance practices that differ from those in the United States.

The average offer premium in successful single-bid takeover contests is somewhat higher than the average initial offer premium in multibid contests. While this is consistent with the greater premium preempting competition in ex post successful single-bid cases, systematic empirical tests of preemption are almost nonexistent. Bid revisions are substantial when the initial bid attracts competition and/or is revised by the initial bidder. The average bidjump from the first to the second bid in the contest is 1% points, a 31% change in the offer premium.

Another interesting jump is the markup of the offer price above the target stock price on the day before the offer is announced. There is substantial evidence that a dollar increase in the preoffer target share price runup causes the initial bidder to mark up the total offer premium by almost a dollar ($0.80). Interestingly, *bidder* takeover gains are also found to be increasing in the target runup, which raises issues concerning the true nature of the markup pricing phenomenon itself. It appears that takeovers with greater prebid target runups are more profitable for *both* bidder and target firms, which may explain why bidders agree to the (partial) markup.

A useful approach to investigating the markup pricing phenomenon further is to document in much greater detail the bidder's pricing process during merger negotiations. An analogy here may be the structure of the pricing process in SEOs and in initial public offerings. Which parties are involved? What role do fairness reports play for the pricing process? If bidders, in fact, react by revising the offer price in response to the target runup, how is the runup analyzed? Is the reverse causality at play, that is, is the offer price set high ex ante in profitable takeovers, which when rumored drives the runup in the target price ex post?

Delaware case law sanctions the right to "just say no" to an unsolicited takeover bid. Moreover, if the board's defensive response is not draconian (i.e., it is neither coercive nor preclusive), the board is protected by the business judgment rule. The twin defense of staggered board election and a poison pill (shareholder rights plan) is draconian in the eyes of many economists but not the court. However, "dead-hand" pills (where only incumbent directors may vote to rescind the pill) have been struck down.

There is a small but significantly negative market reaction to the adoption of strong antitakeover amendments such as poison pills and staggered board. The market reacts positively to antigreenmail amendments provided these occur when a takeover is rumored. Offer premiums appear to be as high (if not higher) for targets with poison pills than targets with no pill in place. Since pills can be adopted any time, and in particular in response to a bid ("morning after pill"), the power of tests that compare offer premiums in pill-targets with no-pill-targets is questionable and should be examined further. Understanding the true economic effects of defenses such as staggered boards and poison pills is important, not the least for the ongoing public policy debate over antitakeover measures.

There is a trend toward market-based mechanisms for resolving Chapter 11 cases, including sale of the firm to a bidder. Target firms that are sold spend less time in

Chapter 11, which lowers bankruptcy costs. Acquirers tend to be in the same industry, and premiums paid are on average lower than in takeovers of nonbankrupt firms in the same industry. Premiums paid for targets sold in mandatory, open, first-price, all-cash bankruptcy auctions in Sweden suggest the possibility that the auction mechanism may also work well for the typical Chapter 11 case (which is of a similar size as the Swedish sample firms). Importantly, the Swedish auction prices do not exhibit fire-sale discounts, contradicting a central presumption behind the creation of Chapter 11 back in 1978. The growing use of auction-related mechanisms in the United States is likely to have lowered bankruptcy costs. By how much remains an important question for future research.

Large-sample evidence on offer premiums is only starting to emerge. This evidence indicates that both the initial and final offer premiums were greater after the 1980s; greater for public bidders; greater in all-cash offers; lower for toehold bidders; increasing in the target runup (markup pricing); decreasing in target total equity capitalization and greater if the target's B/M ratio exceeds the industry median M/B ratio; greater in the presence of substantial dispersion in analysts' earnings forecasts; lower when the bidder CEO is female, and the higher the target board's proportion of female directors (provided that the female directors are independent appointees); and unaffected by either the presence of a target poison pill or target hostility to the initial bid.

Several variables used by researchers to explain the offer premium are themselves endogenous choice variables (payment method, toehold, hostility, termination agreements, bidder's public status). Some of the effects stated earlier appear robust to corrections for endogeneity (including systems of equations and Heckman procedures). One variable that does *not* appear to be robust, however, is tender offer. The inclusion of other variables (such as toeholds and hostility) appears to affect conclusions as to whether offer premiums are higher, the same, or lower in tender offers than in merger bids. Additional work is needed to sort this issue out—and may also affect the conclusion so far that poison pills have a neutral effect on offer premiums.

7.3. Takeover gains

Becoming a target is a significant surprise event; thus target total gains are measured relatively precisely by the offer premium (typically, relative to the target market price 2 months prior to the first offer announcement) or, alternatively, by target CARs over the same period. Consistent with the evidence on offer premiums (above), the average target cumulative average abnormal stock return (CAR) is positive and significant, over both the runup and the announcement period. The target runup constitutes about one-third of the total runup plus announcement CAR. The largest target CAR occurs in all-cash offers.

The average, value-weighted combined CAR to bidders and targets is positive and significant over both the runup period and the announcement period. For the overall sample used here, the sum of the combined CAR for the runup and announcement periods is a significant 1.79%. Bidder announcement-period CARs average close to zero for the overall sample, with 49% of the bidders having negative CAR. The combination large bidder (here in the upper size quartile), payment in all-stock, and the target being a public company represents a worst-case scenario, with average bidder announcement-period CAR of a significant −2.21%. The best-case scenario for the bidder is the combination of a small bidder (lower size-quartile), private target, and *all-stock* as payment. This produces a significant average bidder announcement-period CAR of 6.46%.

The major driver of negative bidder returns is not, as previously thought, the all-stock payment. Rather, the two key drivers are the target's status as public or private and bidder size. Bidder size was particularly large in 1999 and 2000. These years were unusual relative to years before *and* years after. Cisco, with a market capitalization of $180 billion (constant 2000 dollars) was the dominant bidder in *both* the upper 1% and lower 1% tails of the distribution of bidder abnormal announcement returns. Removing Cisco from the sample reduces the aggregate bidder dollar wealth loss in the 1999–2000 period by almost $100 billion. An important but unanswered question is whether the negative spike is truly a bidder size effect or a year effect (or a combination of two). At this point, there appears to be no explanation for why the large firms decided to enter the market for corporate control in 1998–2001, only then to leave again.

Studies of long-run abnormal stock returns use either the matched-firm technique or Jensen's alpha (regression constant in an asset pricing model) to measure expected return to the merged firms in the sample. With 15,298 successful takeovers completed during 1980–2003, we show that long-run returns are significantly negative based on the matched-firm technique but insignificantly different from zero-based Jensen's alpha. Of the two methods, only the latter can actually be replicated using a portfolio investment strategy. We also show that the standard matched-firm procedure identifies firms that have significantly different factor loadings than the event firms—which undermines their role as "matches." A zero-investment portfolio strategy that is long in the merged firms and short in the matched firms fails to produce long-run abnormal stock returns that are significantly different from zero, even for the sample of all-stock mergers. Overall, the long-run performance evidence presented here does not support the hypothesis that merged firms underperform.

7.4. Bondholders, executives and arbitrage

Studies of bondholder returns have suffered from limited access to data on bond market values. However, bond data are improving. Recent studies of excess returns to bondholders of bidder and target firms find zero or negative gains to bidder bondholders and positive gains to target bondholders. There is no evidence of a wealth transfer from stockholders to bondholders due to a coinsurance effect of mergers. As of the 1990s, target bondholders are often fully protected via event risk covenants. Bondholder wealth effects of a variety of corporate control decisions seem a fertile area for future research.

There is evidence that managers undertaking value-reducing acquisitions face a greater probability of being replaced than do managers undertaking value-increasing acquisitions. That is, bad bidders risk being fired. Some target firms, particularly those receiving hostile bids, underperform prior to becoming targets. However, CEO turnover increases after hostile bids, indicating a disciplinary role played by the market for corporate control. There is also evidence that CEO compensation (other than turnover) changes following acquisition activity. The market reaction to merger announcements tends to be positive and greater for CEOs with above-average equity-based compensation, suggesting that compensation affects the quality of managerial investment decisions.

CEOs with high equity-based compensation tend to seek out targets with relatively high M/B ratios (growth firms). This is consistent with high equity compensation inducing risk-taking behavior. Moreover, while a poorly performing acquisition reduces the value of the CEO's portfolio of stocks and options, there is evidence that the value of postacquisition grants more than compensates for this value reduction. This indicates that CEOs face the combination of low downside risk and high upside potential from making good acquisition decisions.

There is also some evidence that target firm CEOs may be sacrificing takeover premium in return for a golden handshake from the bidder (to step aside and relinquish control). Empirical measures of CEO power help explain the cross-sectional variation in M&A bonuses. Moreover, deal announcement-induced abnormal stock returns tend to be lower for CEOs with greater power, suggesting that power may be misused. This raises the question of what role boards play in monitoring takeover activity. There is evidence that boards dominated by outside directors tend to increase value for their shareholders during an acquisition attempt. Target directors are rarely retained after a completed takeover, and their number of board seats and income levels tend to drop. This suggests that failing as a monitor imposes a personal cost on directors, which helps align the interest of directors and shareholders.

Merger arbitrage (or risk arbitrage) is a specialized investment strategy that tries to profit from the spread between the offer price and the target stock market price conditional on the offer having been made. It is essentially a (risky) bet on the likelihood that the proposed transaction will go through. Arbitrage gains depend on several factors, including the size of the arbitrage spread, the probability that the deal closes, the length of time that the arbitrageur must hold the position, and the target stock price development if the deal fails. Average gains are significantly positive, with the largest abnormal returns reported for cash tender offers. In addition to bearing deal failure risk, merger arbitrageurs provide a service in terms of providing deal-related information, liquidity, and helping resolve the free rider problems among small, diffuse target shareholders. Transaction costs, such as brokerage commissions and price impact of trading, limit arbitrage returns. There is evidence that short-selling by merger arbitrageur causes downward price pressure that accounts for almost half of the negative announcement return for acquirers in stock-financed mergers.

7.5. Competition and antitrust

Merger-induced changes in product and factor prices directly translate into abnormal stock returns to the merging firms' industry rivals, upstream suppliers, and downstream customers. Market power theories (collusion, predation, buying power) and productive neoclassical efficiency theories make empirically testable predictions for these abnormal stock returns. Such tests complement and extend the traditional product price analysis seen in industrial economics. The empirical studies typically conclude against the horizontal market power effects of horizontal mergers. That is, the observed wealth effects on horizontal rivals and downstream (corporate) customers do not support increased market power. Some studies find traces of monopsony (buying power) effects vis-à-vis upstream suppliers.

A horizontal merger causes a measurable increase in industry concentration (equal to twice the product of the market shares of the bidder and target when using the Herfindahl measure of concentration). The classical market concentration doctrine holds that an increase in concentration reliably increases the industry's market power and thus industry monopoly rents. Since the abnormal returns to industry rivals directly measure changes in industry rents, regressing the merger-induced rival abnormal returns on the change in industry concentration provides a powerful test of the market concentration doctrine. Empirical tests reject the doctrine.

The power of tests based on stock returns depends on the accurate identification of related firms (rivals, customers, suppliers). Since much of the available evidence indicates significant contagion effects of horizontal merger announcements on these related firms, the tests appear to have sufficient power. Related firms are identified using four-digit SIC codes, Compustat industry segment information, and the Bureau of Economic Analysis Input-Output tables. The tests utilize two sets of samples: mergers that have been challenged with violation of antitrust laws (or, in the European Union, reviewed for such violation) and nonchallenged mergers. For challenged mergers, the tests exploit two events with (typically) opposing implications for the industry wealth effects, thus increasing power to reject.

In the future the interaction of industrial and financial economics, where econometric methods traditionally used in corporate finance are applied to interesting phenomena in industrial economics, is likely to increase in importance. While most of the attention thus far has centered on testing theories of monopoly, the econometric method applies equally well to an examination of alternative efficiency theories of corporate investment. For example, an industry-based theory of merger waves may be couched in terms of the valuation effects for related firms and may be tested using the event study methodology. Similarly, behavioral arguments for things like clustering of merger activity and postmerger underperformance have hitherto untested implications for the event-induced valuation effect across industry rivals.

References

Adams, R. and D. Ferreira, 2007, "One Share, One Vote: The Empirical Evidence," Working Paper, University of Queensland and London School of Economics & Political Science.

Aggarwal, R., 2008, "Executive Compensation," In B. E. Eckbo (Ed.), *Handbook of Corporate Finance: Empirical Corporate Finance*, Vol. 2, Chapter 17, Elsevier/North-Holland, Amsterdam, Handbooks in Finance Series.

Aghion, P., O. Hart and J. Moore, 1992, "The Economics of Bancruptcy Reform," *Journal of Law, Economics and Organization*, 8, 523–546.

Agrawal, A. and R. A. Walkling, 1994, "Executive Careers and Compensation Surrounding Takeover Bids," *Journal of Finance*, 49, 985–1014.

Akbulut, M. E. and J. G. Matsusaka, 2003, "Fifty Years of Diversification Announcements," Working Paper, Marshall School of Business, University of Southern California.

Akdogu, E., 2009, "Gaining a Competitive Edge Through Acquisitions: Evidence from the Telecommunications Industry," *Journal of Corporate Finance*, 15, 99–112.

Akdogu, E., 2007, "Value-maximizing Managers, Value-increasing Mergers and Overbidding," Working Paper, Southern Methodist University.

Akhavein, J. D., A. N. Berger and D. B. Humphrey, 1997, "The Effects of Megamergers on Efficiency and Prices: Evidence from a Bank Profit Function," *Review of Industrial Organization*, 12, 95–139.

Akhavein, J. D., A. N. Berger and D. B. Humphrey, 2007, "Negotiation under the Threat of an Auction: Friendly Deals, ex ante Competition and Bidder Returns," Working Paper, University of California, Los Angeles.

Aktas, N., E. deBodt and R. Roll, 2007, "Is European M&A Regulation Protectionist?" *Economic Journal*, 117, 1096–1121.

Ambrose, K. W. and W. L. Megginson, 1992, "The Role of Asset Structure, Ownership Structure and Takeover Defenses in Determining Acquisition Likelihood," *Journal of Financial and Quantitative Analysis*, 27, 575–589.

Amihud, Y., B. Lev and N. Travlos, 1990, "Corporate Control and the Choice of Investment Financing: The Case of Corporate Acquisitions," *Journal of Finance*, 45, 603–616.

Andrade, G. and E. Stafford, 2004, "Investigating the Economic Role of Mergers," *Journal of Corporate Finance*, 10, 1–36.

Andrade, G., M. Mitchell and E. Stafford, 2001, "New Evidence and Perspectives on Mergers," *Journal of Economic Perspectives*, 15, 103–120.

Ang, J. S. and Y. Cheng, 2006, "Direct Evidence on the Market-driven Acquisition Theory," *Journal of Financial Research*, 29, 199–216.

Asquith, P., 1983, "Merger Bids, Uncertainty and Stockholder Returns," *Journal of Financial Economics*, 11, 51–83.

Asquith, P. and E. H. Kim, 1982, "The Impact of Merger Bids on the Participating Firms' Security Holders," *Journal of Finance*, 37, 1209–1228.

Asquith, P., R. Bruner and D. Mullins, 1983, "The Gains to Bidding Firms from Merger," *Journal of Financial Economics*, 11, 121–139.

Asquith, P., R. Bruner and D. Mullins, 1987, "Merger Returns and the Form of Financing," *Proceedings of the Seminar on the Analysis of Securities Prices*, 34, 115–146.

Austen-Smith, D. and P. O'Brien, 1986, "Takeover Defenses and Shareholder Voting," Working Paper, Sloan School of Management, Massachusetts Institute of Technology.

Bagnoli, M. and B. L. Lipman, 1988, "Successful Takeover Without Exclusion," *Review of Financial Studies*, 1, 89–110.

Bagnoli, M. and B. L. Lipman, 1996, "Stock Price Manipulation Through Takeover Bids," *RAND Journal of Economics*, 27, 124–147.

Baird, D. G., 1986, "The Uneasy Case for Corporate Reorganizations," *Journal of Legal Studies*, 15, 127–147.

Baird, D. G., 1993, "Revisiting Auctions in Chapter 11," *Journal of Law and Economics*, 36, 633–653.

Baird, D. G. and R. K. Rasmussen, 2003, "Chapter 11 at Twilight," *Stetson Law Review*, 56, 673–699.

Baker, M. and S. Savasoglu, 2002, "Limited Arbitrage in Mergers and Acquisitions," *Journal of Financial Economics*, 64, 91–15.

Baker, M., R. S. Ruback and J. Wurgler, 2007, "Behavioral Corporate Finance," In B. E. Eckbo (Ed.), *Handbook of Corporate Finance: Empirical Corporate Finance*, Vol. 1, Chapter 4, Elsevier/North-Holland, Amsterdam, Handbooks in Finance Series.

Banerjee, A. and W. E. Eckard, 1998, "Are Mega-Mergers Anticompetitive? Evidence from the First Great Merger Wave," *RAND Journal of Economics*, 29, 803–827.

Barber, B. M. and J. D. Lyon, 1997, "Detecting Long-run Abnormal Stock Returns: The Empirical Power and Specification of Test Statistics," *Journal of Financial Economics*, 43, 341–372.

Bargeron, L., 2005, "Do Shareholder Tender Agreements Inform or Expropriate Shareholders?" Working Paper, University of Pittsburgh.

Bargeron, L., F. P. Schlingemann, R. M. Stulz and C. Zutter, 2008, "Why Do Private Acquirers Pay So Little Compared to Public Acquirers?" *Journal of Financial Economics*, 89, 375–390.

Barton, D. M. and R. Sherman, 1984, "The Price and Profit Effect of Horizontal Merger: A Case Study," *Journal of Industrial Economics*, 33, 165–177.

Bates, T. H. and M. L. Lemmon, 2003, "Breaking Up Is Hard to do? An Analysis of Termination Fee Provisions and Merger Outcomes," *Journal of Financial Economics*, 69, 460–504.

Bates, T. W., D. A. Becher and M. L. Lemmon, 2008, "Board Classification and Managerial Entrenchment: Evidence from the Market for Corporate Control," *Journal of Financial Economics*, 87, 656–677.

Bauguess, S. W., S. B. Moeller, F. P. Schlingemenn and C. J. Zutter, 2009, "Ownership Structure and Target Returns," *Journal of Corporate Finance*, 15, 48–65.

Bebchuk, L. A., 1985, "Toward Undistorted Choice and Equal Treatment in Corporate Takeovers," *Harvard Law Review*, 98, 1695–1808.

Bebchuk, L. A., 1988, "A New Approach to Corporate Reorganizations," *Harvard Law Review*, 101, 775–804.

Bebchuk, L. A. and H. F. Chang, 1992, "Bargaining and the Division of Value in Corporate Reorganization," *Journal of Law, Economics and Organization*, 8, 253–279.

Bebchuk, L. A. and A. Cohen, 2005, "The Costs of Entrenched Boards," *Journal of Financial Economics*, 78, 409–433.

Bebchuk, L. A. and J. M. Fried, 2003, "Executive Compensation as an Agency Problem," *Journal of Economic Perspectives*, 17, 71–92.

Bebchuk, L. A., J. C. Coates and G. Subramanian, 2002, "The Powerful Anti-takeover Force of Staggered Boards: Theory, Evidence and Policy," *Stanford Law Review*, 54, 887–951.

Bebchuk, L. A., A. Cohen and A. Ferrell, 2004, "What Matters in Corporate Governance?" Working Paper, Harvard University.

Becher, D. A., J. H. Mulherin and R. A. Walkling, 2008, "Industry Shocks and Merger Activity: An Analysis of U.S. Public Utilities," Working Paper, Drexel University.

Becht, M., P. Bolton and A. Roll, 2003, "Corporate Governance and Control," In M. Harris and R. Stulz (Eds.), *George Constantinides*, Vol. 1, Chapter 1, North-Holland, Amsterdam, Handbook of the Economics of Finance, pp. 1–109.

Berglof, E. and M. Burkart, 2003, "European Takeover Regulation," *Economic Policy*, 36, 171–213.

Berkovitch, E. and N. Khanna, 1991, "A Theory of Acquisition Markets: Mergers versus Tender Offers, and Golden Parachutes," *Review of Financial Studies*, 4, 149–174.

Berkovitch, E. and M. Narayanan, 1990, "Competition and the Medium of Exchange in Takeovers," *Review of Financial Studies*, 3 (2), 153–174.

Berle, A. A. Jr. and G. C. Means, 1932, *The Modern Corporation and Private Property*, Macmillan, New York.

Betker, B. L., 1995, "An Empirical Examination of Prepackaged Bankruptcy," *Financial Management*, 24, 3–18.

Betton, S. and B. E. Eckbo, 2000, "Toeholds, Bid Jumps, and Expected Payoff in Takeovers," *Review of Financial Studies*, 13, 841–882.

Betton, S., B. E. Eckbo and K. S. Thorburn, 2009, "Merger Negotiations and the Toehold Puzzle," *Journal of Financial Economics*, 91, 158–178.

Betton, S., B. E. Eckbo and K. S. Thorburn, 2008a, "Does Industry Competition Affect Takeover Bids?" Working Paper, Tuck School of Business, Dartmouth.

Betton, S., B. E. Eckbo and K. S. Thorburn, 2008b, "Markup Pricing Revisited," Working Paper, Tuck School of Business, Dartmouth.

Betton, S., B. E. Eckbo and K. S. Thorburn, 2008c, "Massive Wealth Destruction? Bidder Gains Revisited," Working Paper, Tuck School of Business, Dartmouth.

Bhagat, S. and R. H. Jefferis, 1991, "Voting Power in the Proxy Process: The Case of Antitakeover Charter Amendments," *Journal of Financial Economics*, 30, 193–226.

Bhagat, S. and R. H. Jefferis, 2002, *The Econometrics of Corporate Governance Studies*, MIT Press, Cambridge, MA.

Bhagat, S. J., A. Brickley and U. Loewenstein, 1987, "The Pricing Effects of Interfirm Cash Tender Offers," *Journal of Finance*, 42 (4), 965–986.

Bhagat, S., M. Dong, D. Hirshleifer and R. Noah, 2005, "Do Tender Offers Create Value? New Methods and Evidence," *Journal of Financial Economics*, 76, 3–60.

Bhattahcaryya, S. and A. Nain, 2006, "Horizontal Acquisitions and Buying Power: A Product Market Approach," Working Paper, Ross School of Business, University of Michigan.

Billett, M. T., T.-H. D. King and F. C. Mauer, 2004, "Bondholder Wealth Effects in Mergers and Acquisitions: New Evidence from the 1980s and 1990s," *Journal of Finance*, 59, 107–135.

Bittlingmayer, G. and T. W. Hazlett, 2000, "DOS *kapital:* Has Antitrust Action Againt Microsoft Created Value in the Computer Industry?" *Journal of Financial Economics*, 55, 329–359.

Bliss, R. T. and R. J. Rosen, 2001, "CEO Compensation and Bank Mergers," *Journal of Financial Economics*, 61, 107–138.

Boone, A. L. and J. H. Mulherin, 2007a, "Do Termination Provisions Truncate the Takeover Bidding Process?" *Review of Financial Studies*, 20, 461–489.

Boone, A. L. and J. H. Mulherin, 2007b, "How Are Firms Sold?" *Journal of Finance*, 62, 847–875.

Boone, A. L. and J. H. Mulherin, 2008, "Do Auctions Induce a Winner's Curse? New Evidence from the Corporate Takeover Market," *Journal of Financial Economics*, 89, 1–19.

Borenstein, S., 1990, "Airline Mergers, Airport Dominance, and Market Power," *American Economic Review*, 80, 400–404.

Bradley, M., 1980, "Interfirm Tender Offers and the Market for Corporate Control," *Journal of Business*, 53, 345–376.

Bradley, M. and M. Rosenzweig, 1992, "The Untenable Case for Chapter 11," *Yale Law Journal*, 101, 1043–1095.

Bradley, M. and A. Sundaram, 2006, "Acquisitions and Performance: A Re-assessment of the Evidence," Working Paper, Duke University.

Bradley, M. and L. M. Wakeman, 1983, "The Wealth Effects of Targeted Share Repurchases," *Journal of Financial Economics*, 11, 301–328.

Brickley, J., R. Lease and C. Smith, 1988, "Ownership Structure and Voting on Takeover Amendments," *Journal of Financial Economics*, 20, 267–293.

Bris, A., I. Welch and N. Zhu, 2006, "The Costs of Bankruptcy: Chapter 7 Liquidation versus Chapter 11 Reorganization," *Journal of Finance*, 61, 1253–1303.

Brown, D. T. and M. D. Ryngaert, 1991, "The Mode of Acquisition in Takeovers: Taxes and Asymmetric Information," *Journal of Finance*, 46, 653–669.

Bruner, R. F., 2004, *Applied Mergers & Acquisitions*, John Wiley & Sons, Hoboken, NJ.

Bulow, J., M. Huang and P. Klemperer, 1999, "Toeholds and Takeovers," *Journal of Political Economy*, 107, 427–454.

Burch, T., 2001, "Locking Out Rival Bidders: The Use of Lockup Options in Corporate Mergers," *Journal of Financial Economics*, 60, 103–141.

Burkart, M., 1995, "Initial Shareholdings and Overbidding in Takeover Contests," *Journal of Finance*, 50, 1491–1515.

Burkart, M. and F. Panunzi, 2003, "Mandatory Bids, Squeeze-out, Sell-out and the Dynamics of the Tender Offer Process," Working Paper, European Corporate Governance Institute.

Burkart, M. and F. Panunzi, 2008, "Takeovers," In Ph. H. X. Freicas and C. Mayer (Ed.), *Financial Markets and Institutions: An European Perspective*, Chapter 9, Oxford University Press.

Burkart, M., D. Gromb and F. Panunzi, 1998, "Why Takeover Premia Protect Minority Shareholders," *Journal of Political Economy*, 106, 647–677.

Byrd, J. and K. Hickman, 1992, "Do Outside Directors Monitor Managers? Evidence from Tender Offer Bids," *Journal of Financial Economics*, 32, 195–222.

Cain, M. D., D. Denis and D. K. Denis, 2005, "Earnouts: A Study of Contracting in Acquisition Agreements," Working Paper, Purdue University.

Carhart, M. M., 1997, "On the Persistence in Mutual Fund Performance," *Journal of Finance*, 52, 57–82.

Carleton, W., D. Guilkey, R. Harris and J. Stewart, 1983, "An Empirical Analysis of the Role of the Medium of Exchange in Mergers," *Journal of Finance*, 38, 57–82.

Chang, S., 1998, "Takeovers of Privately Held Targets, Methods of Payment, and Bidder Returns," *Journal of Finance*, 53, 773–784.

Chang, T. and A. Schoar, 2007, "The Effect of Judicial Bias in Chapter 11 Reorganization," Working Paper, Massachusetts Institute of Technology.

Chatterjee, S., K. John and A. Yan, 2008, "Takeover Premium and Divergence of Opinions," Working Paper, School of Business, Fordham University.

Chemmanur, T. J. and I. Paeglis, 2003, "The Choice of the Medium of Exchange in Acquisitions: A Direct Test of the Double-sided Asymmetric Information Hypothesis," Working Paper, Boston College.

Chen, L. H. and H. Sami, 2006, "Does the Use of Fariness Opinions Impair the Acquirers' Abnormal return? The Litigation Risk Effect," Working Paper, Arizona State University.

Claessens, S., S. Djankov and L. H. P. Lang, 2000, "The Separation of Ownership and Control in East Asian Corporations," *Journal of Financial Economics*, 58, 81–112.

Coase, R., 1937, "The Nature of the Firm," *Economica*, 4, 386–405.

Coates, J. C., 2000, "Takeover Defenses in the Shadow of the Pill: A Critique of the Scientific Evidence," *Texas Law Review*, 79, 271–382.

Comment, R. and G. Jarrell, 1987, "Two-Tier and Negotiated Tender Offers: The Imprisonment of the Free-riding Shareholder," *Journal of Financial Economics*, 19, 283–310.

Comment, R. and G. W. Schwert, 1995, "Poison or Placebo? Evidence on the Deterrent and Wealth Effects of Modern Antitakeover Measures," *Journal of Financial Economics*, 39, 3–43.

Cornelli, F. and D. D. Li, 2002, "Risk Arbitrage in Takeovers," *Review of Financial Studies*, 15 (3), 837–868.

Cotter, J. and M. Zenner, 1994, "How Managerial Wealth Affects the Tender Offer Process," *Journal of Financial Economics*, 35, 63–97.

Cotter, J., A. Shivdasani and M. Zenner, 1997, "Do Independent Directors Enhance Target Shareholder Wealth During Tender Offers?" *Journal of Financial Economics*, 43, 195–218.

Cremers, K., J. Martijn, V. B. Nair and K. John, 2008, "Takeovers and the Cross-section of Returns," *Review of Financial Studies*, 22, 1409–1445.

Dafny, L., 2005, "Estimation and Identification of Merger Effects: An Application to Hospital Mergers," NBER Working Paper No. W11673.

Daniel, K. and D. Hirshleifer, 2008, "A Theory of Costly Sequential Bidding," Working Paper, Anderson Graduate School of Management, University of California, Los Angeles.

Danielsen, M. G. and J. M. Karpoff, 1998, "On the Uses of Corporate Governance Provisions," *Journal of Corporate Finance*, 4, 347–371.

Dann, L. Y. and H. DeAngelo, 1983, "Standstill Agreements, Privately Negotiated Stock Repurchases, and the Market for Corporate Control," *Journal of Financial Economics*, 11(April), 275–300.

Dasgupta, S. and R. G. Hansen, 2007, "Auctions in Corporate Finance," In B. E. Eckbo (Ed.), *Handbook of Corporate Finance: Empirical Corporate Finance*, Vol. 1, Chapter 3, Elsevier/North-Holland, Amsterdam, Handbooks in Finance Series, pp. 87–143.

Dasgupta, S. and K. Tsui, 2003, "A 'Matching Auction' for Targets with Heterogeneous Bidders," *Journal of Financial Intermediation*, 12, 331–364.

Dasgupta, S. and K. Tsui, 2004, "Auctions with Cross-Shareholdings," *Economic Theory*, 24, 163–194.

Datta, S., M. Iskandar-Datt and K. Raman, 2001, "Executive Compensation and Corporate Acquisition Decisions," *Journal of Finance*, 56, 2299–2336.

DeAngelo, H. and E. M. Rice, 1983, "Antitakeover Charter Amendments and Stockholder Wealth," *Journal of Financial Economics*, 11, 329–359.

DeMarzo, P. M., I. Kremer and A. Skrzypacz, 2005, "Bidding with Securities: Auctions and Security Design," *American Economic Review*, 95, 936–959.

Dennis, D. and J. McConnell, 1986, "Corporate Mergers and Security Returns," *Journal of Financial Economics*, 16 (2, June), 143–187.

Djankov, S., R. La Porta, F. Lopez-de-Silanes and A. Shleifer, 2008, "The Law and Economics of Self-Dealing," *Journal of Financial Economics*, 88, 430–465.

Dlugosz, J., R. Fahlenbrach, P. A. Gompers and A. Metrick, 2006, "Large Blocks of Stock: Prevalence, Size, and Measurement," *Journal of Corporate Finance*, 12, 594–618.

Dong, M., D. Hirshleifer, S. Richardson and S. H. Teoh, 2006, "Does Investor Misvaluation Drive the Takeover Market?" *Journal of Finance*, 61, 725–762.

Dukes, W. P., C. J. Frohlich and C. K. Ma, 1992, "Risk Arbitrage in Tender Offers," *Journal of Portfolio Management*, 18 (4), 47–55.

Dyck, A. and L. Zingales, 2004, "Private Benefits of Control: An International Comparison," *Journal of Finance*, 59, 533–596.

Eberhart, A. C. and A. Siddique, 2002, "The Long-Term Performance of Corporate Bonds (and Stocks) Following Seasoned Equity Offerings," *Review of Financial Studies*, 15, 1385–1406.

Eckbo, B. E., 1983, "Horizontal Mergers, Collusion, and Stockholder Wealth," *Journal of Financial Economics*, 11, 241–272.

Eckbo, B. E., 1985, "Mergers and the Market Concentration Doctrine: Evidence from the Capital Market," *Journal of Business*, 58, 325–349.

Eckbo, B. E., 1988, "The Market for Corporate Control: Policy Issues and Capital Market Evidence," In R. S. Khemani, D. Shapiro and W. T. Stanbury (Eds.), *Mergers, Corporate Concentration and Corporate Power in Canada*, Chapter 7, Canadian Institute for Research on Public Policy, Montreal, pp. 143–225.

Eckbo, B. E., 1989, "The Role of Stock Market Studies in Formulating Antitrust Policy Towards Horizontal Mergers," *Quarterly Journal of Business and Economics*, 28, 22–38.

Eckbo, B. E., 1990a, "Competition and Wealth Effects of Horizontal Mergers," In M. Mathewson, M. Trebilcock and M. Walker (Eds.), *The Law and Economics of Competition Policy*, Chapter 9, The Fraser Institute, pp. 297–332.

Eckbo, B. E., 1990b, "Valuation Effects of Greenmail Prohibitions," *Journal of Financial and Quantitative Analysis*, 25, 491–505.

Eckbo, B. E., 1992, "Mergers and the Value of Antitrust Deterrence," *Journal of Finance*, 47, 1005–1029.

Eckbo, B. E., 2009, "Bid Strategies and Takeover Premiums: A Review," *Journal of Corporate Finance*, 15, 149–178.

Eckbo, B. E. and H. Langohr, 1989, "Information Disclosure, Method of Payment, and Takeover Premiums: Public and Private Tender Offers in France," *Journal of Financial Economics*, 24, 363–403.

Eckbo, B. E. and Ø. Norli, 2005, "Liquidity Risk, Leverage and Long-Run IPO Returns," *Journal of Corporate Finance*, 11, 1–35.

Eckbo, B. E. and K. S. Thorburn, 2000, "Gains to Bidder Firms Revisited: Domestic and Foreign Acquisitions in Canada," *Journal of Financial and Quantitative Analysis*, 35, 1–25.

Eckbo, B. E. and K. S. Thorburn, 2003, "Control Benefits and CEO Discipline in Automatic Bankruptcy Auctions," *Journal of Financial Economics*, 69, 227–258.

Eckbo, B. E. and K. S. Thorburn, 2008, "Automatic Bankruptcy Auctions and Fire-Sales," *Journal of Financial Economics*, 89, 404–422.

Eckbo, B. E. and K. S. Thorburn, 2008a, "Corporate Restructuring: Breakups and LBOs," In B. E. Eckbo (Ed.), *Handbook of Corporate Finance: Empirical Corporate Finance*, Vol. 2, Chapter 16, Elsevier/ North-Holland, Amsterdam, Handbooks in Finance Series.

Eckbo, B. E. and K. S. Thorburn, 2009, "Creditor Financing and Overbidding in Bankruptcy Auctions," *Journal of Corporate Finance*, 15, 10–29.

Eckbo, B. E. and S. Verma, 1994, "Managerial Shareownership, Voting Power, and Cash Dividend Policy," *Journal of Corporate Finance*, 1, 33–62.

Eckbo, B. E. and P. Wier, 1985, "Antimerger Policy under the Hart-Scott-Rodino Act: A Reexamination of the Market Power Hypothesis," *Journal of Law and Economics*, 28 (1, April), 119–150.

Eckbo, B. E., Maksimovic V. and J. Williams, 1990a, "Consistent Estimation of Cross-sectional Models in Event Studies," *Review of Financial Studies*, 3, 343–365.

Eckbo, B. E., Ronald M. G. and R. L. Heinkel, 1990b, "Asymmetric Information and the Medium of Exchange in Takeovers: Theory and Tests," *Review of Financial Studies*, 3, 651–675.

Eckbo, B. E., R. W. Masulis and Ø. Norli, 2007, "Security Offerings," In B. E. Eckbo (Ed.), *Handbook of Corporate Finance: Empirical Corporate Finance*, Vol. 1, Chapter 6, Elsevier/North-Holland, Amsterdam, Handbooks in Finance Series.

Eger, C. E., 1983, "An Empirical Test of the Redistribution Effect in Pure Exchange Mergers," *Journal of Financial and Quantitative Analysis*, 4, 547–572.

Emery, G. and J. Switzer, 1999, "Expected Market Reaction and the Choice of Method of Payment for Acquisitions," *Financial Management*, 28 (4), 73–86.

Faccio, M. and L. H. P. Lang, 2002, "The Ultimate Ownership of Western European Corporations," *Journal of Financial Economics*, 65, 365–395.

Faccio, M. and R. W. Masulis, 2005, "The Choice of Payment Method in European Mergers and Acquisitions," *Journal of Finance*, 60, 1345–1388.

Faccio, M., J. J. McConnell and D. Stolin, 2006, "Returns to Acquirers of Listed and Unlisted Targets," *Journal of Financial and Quantitative Analysis*, 41, 197–220.

Fama, E. F. and K. R. French, 1993, "Common Risk Factors in the Returns on Stocks and Bonds," *Journal of Financial Economics*, 43, 3–56.

Fee, C. E. and S. Thomas, 2004, "Sources of Gains in Horizontal Mergers: Evidence from Customers, Supplier, and Rival Firms," *Journal of Financial Economics*, 74, 423–460.

Field, L. C. and J. M. Karpoff, 2002, "Takeover Defenses at IPO Firms," *Journal of Finance*, 57, 1857–1889.

Fishman, M. J., 1988, "A Theory of Preemptive Takeover Bidding," *RAND Journal of Economics*, 19, 88–101.

Fishman, M. J., 1989, "Preemptive Bidding and the Role of the Medium of Exchange in Acquisitions," *Journal of Finance*, 44, 41–57.

Focarelli, D. and F. Panetta, 2003, "Are Mergers Beneficial to Consumers? Evidence from the Market for Bank Deposits," *American Economic Review*, 93, 1151–1171.

Franks, J. R., R. S. Harris and C. Mayer, 1988, "Means of Payment in Takeovers: Results for the U.K. and the U.S.," In A. Auerbach (Ed.), *Corporate Takeovers*, NBER, University of Chicago Press, Chicago.

Franks, J., C. P. Mayer and S. Rossi, 2005, "Ownership: Evolution and Regulation," Working Paper, London Business School.

Fridolfson, S.-O. and J. Stennek, 2005, "Why Mergers Reduce Profits, and Raise Share Prices-a Theory of Preemptive Mergers," *Journal of the European Economic Association*, 3, 1083–1104.

Fuller, K., J. Netter and M. Stegemoller, 2002, "What do Returns to Acquiring Firms Tell Us? Evidence from Firms that Make Many Acquisitions," *Journal of Finance*, 57, 1763–1793.

Galai, D. and R. W. Masulis, 1976, "The Option Pricing Model and the Risk Factor of Stock," *Journal of Financial Economics*, 3, 53–81.

Gaughan, P. A., 2007, *Mergers, Acquisitions, and Corporate Restructurings*, 4th edition, John Wiley & Sons, Hoboken, NJ.

Geczy, C. C., D. K. Musto and A. V. Reed, 2002, "Stocks are Special Too: An Analysis of the Equity Lending Market," *Journal of Financial Economics*, 66, 241–269.

Ghosh, A. and W. Ruland, 1998, "Managerial Ownership and the Method of Payment for Acquisitions, and Executive Job Retention," *Journal of Finance*, 53 (2), 785–797.

Gilson, R. J., M. S. Scholes and M. A. Wolfson, 1988, "Taxation and the Dynamics of Corporate Control: The Uncertain Case for Tax-Motivated Acquisitions," In J. C. Coffe, L. Lowenstein and S. Rose-Ackerman (Eds.), *Knights, Raiders and Targets: The Impact of the Hostile Takeover*, Oxford University Press, New York.

Goldman, E. and J. Qian, 2005, "Optimal Toeholds in Takeover Contests," *Journal of Financial Economics*, 77, 321–346.

Gomes, A., 2001, "Takeovers, Freezeouts and Risk Arbitrage," Working Paper, University of Pennsylvania.

Gompers, P., J. Ishi and A. Metrick, 2003, "Corporate Governance and Equity Prices," *Quarterly Journal of Economics*, 118, 107–155.

Gordon, L. A. and J. Pound, 1993, "Information, Ownership Structure, and Shareholder Voting: Evidence from Shareholder-Sponsored Corporate Governance Proposals," *Journal of Finance*, 68, 697–718.

Gort, M., 1969, "An Economic Disturbance Theory of Mergers," *Quarterly Journal of Economics*, 83, 624–642.

Grinstein, Y. and P. Hribar, 2004, "CEO Compensation and Incentives-Evidence from M&A Bonuses," *Journal of Financial Economics*, 73, 119–143.

Grossman, S. and O. Hart, 1980a, "Disclosure Law and Takeover Bids," *Journal of Finance*, 35, 323–334.

Grossman, S. J. and O. D. Hart, 1980b, "Takeover Bids, the Free-Rider Problem, and the Theory of the Corporation," *Bell Journal of Economics*, 11, 42–64.

Hackbarth, D. and E. Morellec, 2008, "Stock Returns in Mergers and Acquisitions," *Journal of Finance*, 63, 1213–1252.

Hansen, R. G., 1985, "Auctions with Contingent Payments," *American Economic Review*, 75, 862–865.

Hansen, R. G., 1987, "A Theory for the Choice of Exchange Medium in the Market for Corporate Control," *Journal of Business*, 60, 75–95.

Harford, J., 1999, "Corporate Cash Reserves and Acquistions," *Journal of Finance*, 54 (6, December), 1969–1997.

Harford, J., 2003, "Takeover Bids and Target Directors' Incentives: The Impact of a Bid on Directors' Wealth and Board Seats," *Journal of Financial Economics*, 69, 51–83.

Harford, J., 2005, "What Drives Merger Waves?" *Journal of Financial Economics*, 77, 529–560.

Harford, J. and K. Li, 2007, "Decoupling CEO Wealth and Firm Performance: The Case of Acquiring CEOs," *Journal of Finance*, 62, 917–949.

Harris, M. and A. Raviv, 1988, "Corporate Control Contests and Capital Structure," *Journal of Financial Economics*, 20, 55–86.

Hartzell, J. C., E. Ofek and D. Yermack, 2004, "What's in It for Me? CEOs Whose Firms are Acquired," *Review of Financial Studies*, 17, 37–61.

Hasbrouck, J., 1985, "The Characteristics of Takeover Targets," *Journal of Banking and Finance*, 9, 351–362.

Hayn, C. 1989, "Tax Attributes as Determinants of Shareholder Gains in Corporate Acquisitions," *Journal of Financial Economics*, 23, 121–153.

Helwege, J., C. Pirinsky and R. M. Stulz, 2007, "Why Do Firms Become Widely Held? An Analysis of the Dynamics of Corporate Ownership?" *Journal of Finance*, 62, 995–1028.

Hermalin, B. E. and M. S. Weisbach, 2003, "Boards of Directors as an Endogenously Determined Institution: A Survey of the Economic Literature," *Federal Reserve Bank of New York Economic Policy Review*, 9, 7–26.

Heron, R. A. and E. Lie, 2004, "A Comparison of the Motivations for and the Information Content of Different Types of Equity Offerings," *Journal of Business*, 77, 605–632.

Heron, R. A. and E. Lie, 2006, "On the Use of Poison Pill and Defensive Payouts by Takeover Targets," *Journal of Business*, 79, 1783–1807.

Higgins, R. C. and L. D. Schall, 1975, "Corporate Bankruptcy and Conglomerate Merger," *Journal of Finance*, 30, 93–111.

Himmelberg, C., R. G. Hubbard and D. Palia, 1999, "Understanding the Determinants of Manager Ownership and the Link between Ownership and Firm Performance," *Journal of Financial Economics*, 53, 353–384.

Hirshleifer, D., 1995, "Mergers and Acquisitions: Strategic and Informational Issues," In R. A. Jarrow and V. M. W. T. Ziemba (Eds.), *Finance*, Vol. 9, Chapter 26, North-Holland, Amsterdam, Handbooks in Operation Research and Management Science, pp. 839–885.

Hirshleifer, D. and I. P. L. Ping, 1990, "Facilitation of Competing Bids and the Price of a Takeover Target," *Review of Financial Studies*, 2, 587–606.

Hirshleifer, D. and S. Titman, 1990, "Share Tendering Strategies and the Success of Hostile Takeover Bids," *Journal of Political Economy*, 98, 295–324.

Holderness, C. G., 2009, "The Myth of Diffuse Ownership in the United States," *Review of Financial Studies*, 22, 1377–1408.

Holderness, C. G., R. S. Kroszner and D. P. Sheehan, 1999, "Were the Good Old Days that Good? Changes in Management Stock Ownership Since the Great Depression," *Journal of Finance*, 54, 435–469.

Holmstrom, B. and S. Kaplan, 2001, "Corporate Governance and Merger Activity in the U.S.: Making Sense of the 1980's and 1990's," Working Paper, NBER No. W8220.

Holmstrom, B. and B. Nalebuff, 1992, "To the Raider Goes the Surplus? A Reexamination of the Free Rider Problem," *Journal of Economics and Management Strategy*, 1, 37–62.

Hotchkiss, E. S., 1995, "Post-bankruptcy Performance and Management Turnover," *Journal of Finance*, 50, 3–21.

Hotchkiss, E. S. and R. M. Mooradian, 1997, "Vulture Investors and the Market for Control of Distressed Firms," *Journal of Financial Economics*, 43, 401–432.

Hotchkiss, E. S. and R. M. Mooradian, 1998, "Acquisitions as a Means of Restructuring Firms in Chapter 11," *Journal of Financial Intermediation*, 7, 240–262.

Hotchkiss, E. S. and R. M. Mooradian, 2003, "Auctions in Bankruptcy," *Journal of Corporate Finance*, 9, 555–574.

Hotchkiss, E. S., K. John, R. Mooradian and K. S. Thorburn, 2008, "Bankruptcy and the Resolution of Financial Distress," In B. E. Eckbo (Ed.), *Handbook of Corporate Finance: Empirical Corporate Finance*, Vol. 2, Chapter 14, Elsevier/North-Holland, Amsterdam, Handbooks in Finance Series.

Hsieh, J. and R. A. Walking, 2005, "Determinants and Implications of Arbitrage Holdings in Acquisitions," *Journal of Financial Economics*, 77, 605–648.

Huang, Y.-S. and R. A. Walkling, 1987, "Abnormal Returns Associated with Acquisition Announcements: Payment Method, Acquisition Form, and Managerial Resistance," *Journal of Financial Economics*, 19, 329–349.

Hubbard, G. and D. Palia, 1999, "A Re-examination of the Conglomerate Merger Wave in the 1960's: An Internal Capital Markets View," *Journal of Finance*, 54, 1131–1152.

Huson, M. R., R. Parrino and L. Starks, 2001, "Internal Monitoring Mechanism and CEO Turnover: A Long-term Perspective," *Journal of Finance*, 56, 2265–2297.

Jarrell, G. A. and M. Bradley, 1980, "The Economic Effects of Federal and State Regulations of Cash Tender Offers," *Journal of Law and Economics*, 23 (2, October), 371–407.

Jarrell, G. A. and A. B. Poulsen, 1987, "Shark Repellents and Stock Prices: The Effects of Antitakeover Amendments since 1980," *Journal of Financial Economics*, 19, 127–168.

Jarrell, G. A. and A. B. Poulsen, 1989, "Stock Trading before the Announcement of Tender Offers: Insider Trading or Market Anticipation?" *Journal of Law, Economics and Organization*, 5, 225–248.

Jarrell, G. A., J. A. Brickley and J. M. Netter, 1988, "The Market for Corporate Control: The Empirical Evidence Since 1980," *Journal of Economic Perspectives*, 2, 49–68.

Jennings, R. H. and M. A. Mazzeo, 1993, "Competing Bids, Target Management Resistance, and the Structure of Takeover Bids," *Review of Financial Studies*, 6, 883–910.

Jensen, M. C., 1986, "Agency Costs of Free Cash Flow, Corporate Finance, and Takeovers," *American Economic Review*, 76, 323–329.

Jensen, M. C., 1989, "Eclipse of the Public Corporation," *Harvard Business Review*, September–October, 61–74.

Jensen, M., 1993, "The Modern Industrial Revolution, Exit, and the Failure of Internal Control Systems," *Journal of Finance*, 48 (July), 831–880.

Jensen, M. C. and W. Meckling, 1976, "Theory of the Firm: Managerial Behavior, Agency Costs, and Capital Structure," *Journal of Financial Economics*, 3, 305–360.

Jensen, M. C. and K. J. Murphy, 1990, "Performance Pay and Top-Management Incentives," *Journal of Political Economy*, 98, 225–264.

Jensen, M. C. and R. S. Ruback, 1983, "The Market for Corporate Control," *Journal of Financial Economics*, 11, 5–50.

Jindra, J. and R. A. Walkling, 2004, "Speculation Spreads and the Market Pricing of Proposed Acquisitions," *Journal of Corporate Finance*, 10, 495–526.

Jovanovic, B. and P. L. Rousseau, 2002, "The Q-Theory of Mergers," *American Economic Review*, 92, 198–204.

Jovanovic, B. and P. L. Rousseau, 2004, "Mergers as Reallocation," Working Paper, New York University.

Karolyi, G. A. and J. Shannon, 1999, "Where's the Risk in Risk Arbitrage?" *Canadian Investment Review*, 12, 11–18.

Kim, E. H. and J. J. McConnell, 1977, "Corporate Mergers and the Co-insurance of Corporate Debt," *Journal of Finance*, 32, 349–365.

Kim, E. H. and V. Singal, 1993, "Mergers and Market Power: Evidence from the Airline Industry," *American Economic Review*, 83, 549–569.

King, M. R. and M. Padalko, 2005, "Pre-bid Run-ups Ahead of Canadian Takeovers: How Big is the Problem?" Working Paper 2005–3, Bank of Canada.

Kini, O., W. Kracaw and S. Mian, 1995. "Corporate Takeovers, Firm Performance, and Board Composition," *Journal of Corporate Finance*, 1, 383–412.

Kini, O., W. Kracaw and S. Mian, 2004, "The Nature and Discipline by Corporate Takeovers," *Journal of Finance*, 59, 1511–1552.

Kisgen, D. J., J. Qian and W. Song, 2006, "Are Fairness Opinions Fair? The Case of Mergers and Acquisitions," Working Paper, Boston College.

Kohers, N. and J. Ang, 2000, "Earnouts in Mergers: Agreeing to Disagree and Agreeing to Stay," *Journal of Business*, 73, 445–476.

Kohers, N., G. Kohers and T. Kohers, 2007, "Glamour, Value, and the Form of Takeover," *Journal of Economics and Business*, 59, 74–87.

Kothari, S. P. and J. B. Warner, 1997, "Measuring Long-horizon Security Price Performance," *Journal of Financial Economics*, 301–339.

Kothari, S. P. and J. B. Warner, 2007, "Econometrics of Event Studies," In B. E. Eckbo (Ed.), *Handbook of Corporate Finance: Empirical Corporate Finance*, Vol. 1, Chapter 1, Elsevier/North-Holland, Amsterdam, Handbooks in Finance Series.

La, P. R., F. Lopez-de-Silanes and A. Shleifer, 1999, "Corporate Ownership Around the World," *Journal of Finance*, 54, 471–518.

Larcker, D. F. and T. Lys, 1987, "An Empirical Analysis of the Incentives to Engage in Costly Information Acquisition: The Case of Risk Arbitrage," *Journal of Financial Economics*, 18, 111–126.

Lease, R., J. McConnell and E. Tashjian, 1996, "Prepacks: An Empirical Analysis of Prepackaged Bankruptcies," *Journal of Financial Economics*, 40, 135–162.

Lehn, K. and A. B. Poulsen, 1992, "Contractual Resolution of Bondholder-Stockholder Conflicts in Leveraged Buyouts," *Journal of Law and Economics*, 34, 645–673.

Lehn, K. and M. Zhao, 2006, "CEO Turnover After Acquisitions: Are Bad Bidders Fired?" *Journal of Finance*, 61, 1759–1811.

Levi, M., K. Li and F. Zhang, 2008, "Mergers and Acquisitions: The Role of Gender," Working Paper, Sauder School of Business, University of British Columbia.

Levy, H. and H. Sarnat, 1970, "Diversification, Portfolio Analysis, and the Uneasy Case for Conglomerate Mergers," *Journal of Finance*, 25, 795–802.

Lewellen, W., 1971, "A Pure Financial Rationale for the Conglomerate Merger," *Journal of Finance*, May.

Li, K. and N. R. Prabhala, 2007, "Self-Selection Models in Corporate Finance," In B. E. Eckbo (Ed.), *Handbook of Corporate Finance: Empirical Corporate Finance*, Vol. 1, Chapter 2, Elsevier/North-Holland, Amsterdam, Handbooks in Finance Series.

Linn, S. and J. McConnell, 1983, "An Empirical Investigation of the Impact of Anti-Takeover Amendments on Common Stock Prices," *Journal of Financial Economics*, 11, 361–400.

Lipton, M. and E. H. Steinberger, 2004, *Takeovers & Freezeouts*, Vol. 1, Law Journal Press, New York.

Loderer, C. and K. Martin, 1990, "Corporate Acquisitions by Listed Firms: The Experience of Comprehensive Sample," *Financial Management*, 19, 17–33.

Loughran, T. and A. M. Vijh, 1997, "Do Long-term Shareholders Benefit from Corporate Acquisitions?" *Journal of Finance*, 52, 1765–1790.

Lyon, J. D., B. M. Barber and C.-L. Tsai, 1999, "Improved Methods for Tests of Long-run Abnormal Stock Returns," *Journal of Finance*, 54, 165–201.

MacKinlay, A. C., 1997, "Event Studies in Economics and Finance," *Journal of Economic Literature*, 35, 13–39.

Mahoney, J. H. and J. T. Mahoney, 1993, "An Empirical Investigation of the Effect of Corporate Charter Amendments on Stockholder Wealth," *Strategic Management Journal*, 14, 17–31.

Makhija, A. K. and R. P. Narayanan, 2007, "Fairness Opinions in Mergers and Acquisitions," Working Paper, Ohio State University.

Maksimovic, V. and G. Phillips, 1998, "Asset Efficiency and Reallocation Decisions of Bankrupt Firms," *Journal of Finance*, 53, 1495–1532.

Maksimovic, V. and G. Phillips, 2001, "The Market for Corporate Assets: Who Engages in Mergers and Asset Sales and are There Efficiency Gains?" *Journal of Finance*, 56, 2019–2065.

Maksimovic, V. and G. Phillips, 2002, "Do Conglomerate Firms Allocate Resources Inefficiently across Industries?" *Journal of Finance*, 57, 721–768.

Maksimovic, V. and G. Phillips, 2007, "Conglomerate Firms and Internal Capital Markets," In B. E. Eckbo (Ed.), *Handbook of Corporate Finance: Empirical Corporate Finance*, Vol. 1, Chapter 8, Elsevier/North-Holland, Amsterdam, Handbooks in Finance Series, pp. 423–479.

Maksimovic, V., G. Phillips and N. R. Prabhala, 2008, "Post-Merger Restructuring and the Boundaries of the Firm," Working Paper, University of Maryland.

Malatesta, P., 1983, "The Wealth Effect of Merger Activity and the Objective Functions of Merging Firms," *Journal of Financial Economics*, 11 (1–4, April), 155–181.

Malatesta, P. and R. Thompson, 1985, "Partially Anticipated Events: A Model of Stock Price Reaction with an Application to Corporate Acquisitions," *Journal of Financial Economics*, 14, 237–250.

Malatesta, P. H. and R. A. Walkling, 1988, "Poison Pill Securities: Stockholder Wealth, Profitability, and Ownership Structure," *Journal of Financial Economics*, 20, 347–376.

Malekzadeh, A. R, V. B. McWilliams and N. Sen, 1998, "Implications of CEO Structural Ownership Powers, Board Ownership and Composition on the Market's Reaction to Antitakeover Charter Amendments," *Journal of Applied Business Research*, 14, 54–62.

Manne, H. G., 1965, "Mergers and the Market for Corporate Control," *Journal of Political Economy*, 73, 110–120.

Maquieira, C. P., W. L. Megginson and L. A. Nail, 1998, "Wealth Creation Versus Wealth Redistribution in Pure Stock-for-stock Mergers," *Journal of Financial Economics*, 48, 3–33.

Martin, K., 1996, "The Method of Payment in Corporate Acquisitions, Investment Opportunities, and Management Ownership," *Journal of Finance*, 51, 1227–1246.

Martin, K. J. and J. McConnell, 1991, "Corporate Performance, Corporate Takeovers, and Management Turnover," *Journal of Finance*, June, 671–687.

Martynova, M. and L. Renneboog, 2005, "Takeover Waves: Triggers, Performance and Motives," Working Paper, Tilburg University.

Martynova, M. and L. Renneboog, 2006, "Mergers and Acquisitions in Europe," In L. Renneboog (Ed.), *Advances in Corporate Finance and Asset Pricing*, Chapter 2, Elsevier, pp. 13–75.

Martynova, M. and L. Renneboog, 2007, "Sources of Transaction Financing in Corporate Takeovers," Working Paper, Tilburg University.

Masulis, R. W., C. Wand and F. Xie, 2007, "Corporate Governance and Acquirer Returns," *Journal of Finance*, 62, 1851–1889.

Matsusaka, J. G., 1993, "Takeover Motives During the Conglomerate Merger Wave," *RAND Journal of Economics*, 24, 357–379.

Matsusaka, J. G., 1996, "Did Tough Antitrust Enforcement Cause the Diversification of American Corporations?" *Journal of Financial and Quantitative Analysis*, 31, 283–294.

McAfee, R. and M. Williams, 1988, "Can Event Studies Detect Anticompetitive Mergers?" *Economics Letters*, 28, 199–203.

McWilliams, V. B. and N. Sen, 1997, "Board Monitoring and Antitakeover Amendments," *Journal of Financial and Quantitative Analysis*, 32, 491–505.

Meulbroek, L., 1992, "An Empirical Analysis of Illegal Insider Trading," *Journal of Finance*, 47, 1661–1699.

Mikkelson, W. H. and M. M. Partch, 1989, "Managers' Voting Rights and Corporate Control," *Journal of Financial Economics*, 25, 263–290.

Mikkelson, W. and M. Partch, 1997, "The Decline of Takeovers and Disciplinary Managerial Turnover," *Journal of Financial Economics*, 44, 205–228.

Mikkelson, W. H and R. S. Ruback, 1985, "An Empirical Analysis of the Interfirm Equity Investment Process," *Journal of Financial Economics*, 14, 523–553.

Mikkelson, W. H. and R. S. Ruback, 1991, "Targeted Repurchases and Common Stock Returns," *RAND Journal of Economics*, 22 (4), 544–561.

Mitchell, M. and K. Lehn, 1990, "Do Bad Bidders Become Good Targets?" *Journal of Political Economy*, 98, 372–398.

Mitchell, M. and J. H. Mulherin, 1996, "The Impact of Industry Shocks on Takeover and Restructuring Activity," *Journal of Financial Economics*, 41, 193–229.

Mitchell, M. and T. Pulvino, 2001, "Characteristics of Risk and Return in Risk Arbitrage," *Journal of Finance*, 56 (6), 2135–2175.

Mitchell, M., T. Pulvino and E. Stafford, 2004, "Price Pressure Around Mergers," *Journal of Finance*, 59 (1), 31–63.

Moeller, T., 2005, "Let's Make a Deal! How Shareholders Control Impacts Merger Payoff," *Journal of Financial Economics*, 76, 167–190.

Moeller, S. B., F. P. Schlingemann and R. M. Stulz, 2004, "Firm Size and the Gains from Acquisitions," *Journal of Financial Economics*, 73, 201–228.

Moeller, S. B., F. P. Schlingemann and R. M. Stulz, 2005, "Wealth Destruction on a Massive Scale? A Study of Acquiring Firm Returns in the Recent Merger Wave," *Journal of Finance*, 60, 757–782.

Moeller, S. B., F. P. Schlingemann and R. M. Stulz, 2007, "How do Diversity of Opinion and Information Asymmetry Affect Acquirer Returns?" *Review of Financial Studies*, 20, 2047–2078.

Molnar, J., 2008, "Preemptive Horizontal Mergers: Theory and Evidence," Working Paper, Bank of Finland.

Morellec, E. and A. Zhdanov, 2005, "The Dynamics of Mergers and Aquisitions," *Journal of Financial Economics*, 77, 649–672.

Mork, R., A. Shleifer and R. W. Vishny, 1988, "Characteristics of Targets of Hostile and Friendly Takeovers," In A. J. Auerbach (Ed.), *Corporate Takeovers: Causes and Consequences*. National Bureau of Economic Research, Chicago, IL.

Moussawi, R., 2004, "Shareholders and Antitakeover Provisions," Working Paper, University of Texas, Dallas.

Mulherin, J. H. and A. L. Boone, 2000, "Comparing Acquisitions and Divestitures," *Journal of Corporate Finance*, 6, 117–139.

Munro, J. R., 1989, "Takeovers: The Myths Behind the Mystique," *Vital Speeches*, May 15.

Murphy, K. J., 1999, "Executive Compensation," In O. Ashenfelter and D. Card (Eds.), *Handbook of Labor Economics*, Vol. 3b, Chapter 38, Elsevier/North-Holland, Amsterdam, Handbooks in Labor Economics, pp. 2485–2563.

Myers, S. C., 1984, "The Capital Structure Puzzle," *Journal of Finance*, 39, 575–592.

Myers, S. C. and N. S. Majluf, 1984, "Corporate Financing and Investment Decisions when Firms Have Information that Investors do not Have," *Journal of Financial Economics*, 13, 187–221.

Nash, R., J. Netter and A. B. Poulsen, 2003, "Determinants of Contractual Relations between Shareholders and Bondholders: Investment Opportunities and Restrictive Covenants," *Journal of Corporate Finance*, 9, 201–232.

Nathan, K. S. and T. B. O'Keefe, 1989, "The Rise in Takeover Premiums: An Exploratory Study," *Journal of Financial Economics*, 23, 101–119.

O'Brien, A. P., 1988, "Factory Size, Economies of Scale, and the Great Merger Wave of 1898–1902," *Journal of Economic History*, 48, 639–649.

Offenberg, D., 2009, "Firm Size and the Effectiveness of the Market for Corporate Control," *Journal of Corporate Finance*, 15, 66–79.

Officer, M. S., 2003, "Termination Fees in Mergers and Acquisitions," *Journal of Financial Economics*, 69, 431–467.

Officer, M. S., 2004, "Collars and Renegotiations in Mergers and Acquisitions," *Journal of Finance*, 59, 2719–2743.

Officer, M. S., 2006, "The Market Pricing of Implicit Options in Merger Collars," *Journal of Business*, 79, 115–136.

Officer, M. S., 2007, "The Price of Corporate Liquidity: Acquisition Discounts for Unlisted Targets," *Journal of Financial Economics*, 83, 571–598.

Officer, M. S., A. B. Poulsen and M. Stegemoller, 2009, "Information Asymmetry and Acquirer Returns," *Review of Financial Studies*, 13, 467–493.

Palepu, K. G., 1986, "Predicting Takeover Targets: A Methodological and Empirical Analysis," *Journal of Accounting and Economics*, 8, 3–35.

Penas, M. F. and H. Unal, 2004, "Gain from Bank Mergers: Evidence from the Bond Markets," *Journal of Financial Economics*, 74, 149–179.

Posner, R., 1969, "The Federal Trade Commission," *University of Chicago Law Review*, 37, 47–89.

Prager, R. A. and T. H. Hannan, 1998, "Do Substantial Horizontal Mergers Generate Significant Price Effects? Evidence from the Banking Industry," *Journal of Industrial Economics*, 46, 433–452.

Rau, P. R. and T. Vermaelen, 1998, "Glamour, Value and the Post-Acquisition Performance of Acquiring Firms," *Journal of Financial Economics*, 49, 223–253.

Rhodes-Kropf, M. and D. T. Robinson, 2008, "The Market for Mergers and the Boundaries of the Firm," *Journal of Finance* 63, 1169–1211.

Rhodes-Kropf, M. and S. Viswanathan, 2004, "Market Valuation and Merger Waves," *Journal of Finance*, 59, 2685–2718.

Rhodes-Kropf, M., D. T. Robinson and S. Viswanathan, 2005, "Valuation Waves and Merger Activity: The Empirical Evidence," *Journal of Financial Economics*, 77, 561–603.

Ritter, J. R., 2003, "Investment Banking and Security Issuance," In G. Constantinides, M. Harris, and R. Stulz (Eds.), *Handbook of the Economics of Finance: Corporate Finance*, Chapter 5, Elsevier/North-Holland, Amsterdam, Handbooks in Labor Economics, pp. 254–304.

Roll, R., 1986, "The Hubris Hypothesis of Corporate Takeovers," *Journal of Business*, 59, 437–467.

Rose, S., 1977, "The Determination of Financial Structure: The Incentive Signalling Approach," *Bell Journal of Economics*, 8, 23–40.

Rose, M. J., 2009, "Heterogeneous Impacts of Staggered Boards by Ownership Concentration," *Journal of Corporate Finance*, 15, 113–128.

Rosen, R. J., 2006, "Merger Momentum and Investor Sentiment: The Stock Market Reaction to Merger Announcements," *Journal of Business*, 79, 987–1017.

Ryngaert, M., 1988, "The Effect of Poison Pill Securities on Stockholder Wealth," *Journal of Financial Economics*, 20, 377–417.

Savor, P., 2006, "Do Stock Mergers Create Value for Acquirers?" Working Paper, Wharton School of Business.

Schipper, K. and R. Thompson, 1983, "Evidence on the Capitalized value of Merger Activity for Acquiring Firms," *Journal of Financial Economics*, 11, 85–119

Schlingemann, F. P., 2004, "Financing Decisions and Bidder Gains," *Journal of Corporate Finance*, 10, 683–701.

Schumann, L., 1993, "Patterns of Abnormal Returns and the Competitive Effects of Horizontal Mergers," *Review of Industrial Organization*, 8, 679–696.

Schwert, G. W., 1996, "Markup Pricing in Mergers and Acquisitions," *Journal of Financial Economics*, 41, 153–192.

Schwert, G. W., 2000, "Hostility in Takeovers: In the Eyes of the Beholder?" *Journal of Finance*, 55, 2599–2640.

Servaes, H., 1991, "Tobin's q and the Gains from Takeovers," *Journal of Finance*, 46, 409–419.

Servaes, H. and A. Tamayo, 2007, "Waking up the Neighbors: How Industry Peers Respond to Control Threats?" Working Paper, London Business School.

Shahrur, H., 2005, "Industry Structure and Horizontal Takeovers: Analysis of Wealth Effects on Rivals, Suppliers, and Corporate Customers," *Journal of Financial Economics*, 76, 61–98.

Shapley, L., 1953, "A Value for N-Person Games," In H. Kuhnand and A. Tucker (Eds.), *Contributions to the Theory of Games*, Vol. II, Chapter 28, Princeton University Press, Princeton, Annals of Mathematics Studies, pp. 307–317.

Shenoy, J., 2008, "An Examination of the Efficiency, Foreclosure, and Collusion Rationales for Vertical Takeovers," Working Paper, Georgia State University.

Shivdasani, A., 1993, "Board Composition, Ownership Structure, and Hostile Takeovers," *Journal of Accounting and Economics*, 16, 167–198.

Shleifer, A. and R. W. Vishny, 1986a, "Greenmail, White Knights, and Shareholders' Interest," *RAND Journal of Economics*, 17, 293–309.

Shleifer, A. and R. W. Vishny, 1986b, "Large Shareholders and Corporate Control," *Journal of Political Economy*, 94, 461–488.

Shleifer, A. and R. W. Vishny, 1989, "Management Entrenchment: The Case of Manager-Specific Investments," *Journal of Financial Economics*, 25, 123–139.

Shleifer, A. and R. W. Vishny, 1991, "Takeovers in the 60s and the 80s: Evidence and Implications," *Strategic Management Journal*, 12, 51–59.

Shleifer, A. and R. W. Vishny, 1992, "Liquidation Values and Debt Capacity: A Market Equilibrium Approach," *Journal of Finance*, 47, 1343–1366.

Shleifer, A. and R. W. Vishny, 1997, "The Limits ofArbitrage," *Journal of Finance*, 52 (1), 35–55.

Shleifer, A. and R. Vishny, 2003, "Stock Market Driven Acquisitions," *Journal of Financial Economics*, 70, 295–311.

Singal, V., 1996, "Airline Mergers and Competition: An Integration of Stock and Product Market Effects," *Journal of Business*, 69, 233–268.

Slovin, M. B., M. E. Sushka and C. D. Hudson, 1991, "Deregulation, Contestability, and Airline Acquisitions," *Journal of Financial Economics*, 30, 231–251.

Smith, R. L. and J.-H. Kim, 1994, "The Combined Effect of Free Cash Flow and Financial Slack on Bidder and Target Stock Return," *Journal of Business*, 67, 281–310.

Snyder, C. M., 1996, "A Dynamic Theory of Countervailing Power," *RAND Journal of Economics*, 27, 747–769.

Song, M. H. and R. A. Walkling, 2000, "Abnormal Returns to Rivals of Acquisition Targets: A Test of the Acquisition Probability Hypothesis," *Journal of Financial Economics*, 55, 143–172.

Song, M. H. and R. A. Walkling, 2005, "Anticipation, Acquisitions and Bidder Returns," Working Paper, LeBow College of Business.

Spatt, C., 1989, "Discussion: Strategic Analyses of Takeover Bids," In S. Bhattacharya and G. Constantinides (Eds.), *Financial Markets and Incomplete Information: Frontiers of Modern Financial Theory*, Vol. 2, North-Holland, Amsterdam, pp. 106–121.

Spiller, P. T., 1983, "The Differential Effect of Airline Regulation on Individual Firms and Markets: An Empirical Analysis," *Journal of Law and Economics*, 26, 655–689.

Stigler, G. J., 1950, "Monopoly and Oligopoly Power by Merger," *American Economic Review*, 40, 23–34.

Stigler, G. J., 1982, "The Economist and the Problem of Monopoly," *American Economic Review*, 72, 1–11.

Stillman, R., 1983, "Examining Antitrust Policy Toward Horizontal Mergers," *Journal of Financial Economics*, 11, 225–240.

Strömberg, P., 2000, "Conflicts of Interests and Market Illiquidity in Bankruptcy Auctions: Theory and Tests," *Journal of Finance*, 55, 2641–2692.

Stulz, R., 1988, "Managerial Control of Voting Rights: Financing Policies and the Market for Corporate Control," *Journal of Financial Economics*, 20, 25–54.

Sundaramurthy, C., J. M. Mahoney and J. T. Mahoney, 1997, "Board Structure, Antitakeover Provisions, and Stockholder Wealth," *Strategic Management Journal*, 18, 231–245.

Thompson, R., 1985, "Conditioning the Return-Generating Process on Firm-Specific Events: A Discussion of Event Study Methods," *Journal of Financial and Quantitative Analysis*, 20, 151–168.

Thompson, R., 1995, "Empirical Methods in Event Studies in Corporate Finance," In R. A. Jarrow, V. Maksimovic and W. T. Ziemba (Eds.), *Finance*, Vol. 9, Chapter 29, North-Holland, Amsterdam, Handbooks in Operation Research and Management Science, pp. 963–992.

Thorburn, K. S., 2000, "Bankruptcy Auctions: Costs, Debt Recovery, and Firm Survival," *Journal of Financial Economics*, 58, 337–368.

Toffanin, M., 2005, "Examining the Implications of Financing Choice for Cash Acquisitions," Concordia University, Master of Science Dissertation, Unpublished.

Travlos, N. G., 1987, "Corporate Takeover Bids, Method of Payment, and Bidding Firms' Stock Returns," *Journal of Finance*, 42, 943–963.

Walkling, R., 1985, "Predicting Tender Offer Success: A Logistic Analysis," *Journal of Financial and Quantitative Analysis*, 20, 461–478.

Walkling, R. A. and M. S. Long, 1984, "Agency Theory, Managerial Welfare, and Takeover Bid Resistance," *RAND Journal of Economics*, 15, 54–68.

Warga, A. and I. Welch, 1993, "Bondholder Losses in Leveraged Buyouts," *Review of Financial Studies*, 6, 959–982.

Wasserstein, B., 2000, *Big Deal: Mergers and Acquisitions in the Digital Age*, Warner Books, New York.

Werden, G. J., A. S. Joskow and R. Johnson, 1991, "The Effects of Mergers on Price and Output: Two Case Studies from the Airline Industry," *Managerial and Decision Economics*, 12, 341–352.

White, H., 1980, "A Heteroskedasticity-consistent Covariance Matrix Estimator and a Direct Test for Heteroscedasticity," *Econometrica*, 48, 817–838.

Wulf, J., 2004, "Do CEOs in Mergers Trade Power for Premium? Evidence from Mergers of Equals," *Journal of Law, Economics and Organization*, 20, 60–101.

Yermack, D., 2006, "Golden Handshakes: Separation Pay for Retired and Dismissed CEOs," *Journal of Accounting and Economics*, 41, 237–256.

Yook, K. C., 2003, "Larger Returns to Cash Acquisitions: Signaling Effect or Leverage Effect?" *Journal of Business*, 76, 477–498.

Zingales, L., 1994, "The Value of the Voting Right: Study of the Milan Stock Exchange Experience," *Review of Financial Studies*, 7, 125–148.

PART 2

ECONOMETRICS OF VOLUNTARY CORPORATE EVENTS

Chapter 2

ECONOMETRICS OF EVENT STUDIES[*]

S.P. KOTHARI

Sloan School of Management, E52–325, Massachusetts Institute of Technology, 50 Memorial Drive, Cambridge, Massachusetts, USA

JEROLD B. WARNER

William E. Simon Graduate School of Business Administration, University of Rochester, Rochester, New York, USA

Contents

* We thank Espen Eckbo, Jon Lewellen, Adam Kolasinski, and Jay Ritter for insightful comments, and Irfan Safdar and Alan Wancier for research assistance.

This article originally appeared in B. E. Eckbo (ed.), *Handbook of Corporate Finance: Empirical Corporate Finance*, Vol. 1, Ch. 1, pp. 3–36 (2007).
Corporate Takeovers, Volume 1
Edited by B. Espen Eckbo

Abstract

The number of published event studies exceeds 500, and the literature continues to grow. We provide an overview of event study methods. Short-horizon methods are quite reliable. While long-horizon methods have improved, serious limitations remain. A challenge is to continue to refine long-horizon methods. We present new evidence illustrating that properties of event study methods can vary by calendar time period and can depend on event sample firm characteristics such as volatility. This reinforces the importance of using stratified samples to examine event study statistical properties.

Keywords

event study, abnormal returns, short-horizon tests, long-horizon tests, cross-sectional tests, risk adjustment

JEL classification: G14

1. Introduction and background

This chapter focuses on the design and statistical properties of event study methods. Event studies examine the behavior of firms' stock prices around corporate events.[1] A vast literature on event studies written over the past several decades has become an important part of financial economics. Prior to that time, "there was little evidence on the central issues of corporate finance. Now we are overwhelmed with results, mostly from event studies" (Fama, 1991, p. 1600). In a corporate context, the usefulness of event studies arises from the fact that the magnitude of abnormal performance at the time of an event provides a measure of the (unanticipated) impact of this type of event on the wealth of the firms' claimholders. Thus, event studies focusing on announcement effects for a short-horizon around an event provide evidence relevant for understanding corporate policy decisions.

Event studies also serve an important purpose in capital market research as a way of testing market efficiency. Systematically nonzero abnormal security returns that persist after a particular type of corporate event are inconsistent with market efficiency. Accordingly, event studies focusing on long horizons following an event can provide key evidence on market efficiency (Brown and Warner, 1980; Fama, 1991).

Beyond financial economics, event studies are useful in related areas. For example, in the accounting literature, the effect of earnings announcements on stock prices has received much attention. In the field of law and economics, event studies are used to examine the effect of regulation, as well as to assess damages in legal liability cases.

The number of published event studies easily exceeds 500 (see Section 2), and continues to grow. A second and parallel literature, which concentrates on the methodology of event studies, began in the 1980s. Dozens of papers have now explicitly studied statistical properties of event study methods. Both literatures are mature.

From the methodology papers, much is known about how to do—and how not to do—an event study. While the profession's thinking about event study methods has evolved over time, there seems to be relatively little controversy about statistical properties of event study methods. The conditions under which event studies provide information and permit reliable inferences are well-understood.

This chapter highlights key econometric issues in event study methods, and summarizes what we know about the statistical design and the interpretation of event study experiments. Based on the theoretical and empirical findings of the methodology literature, we provide clear guidelines both for producers and consumers of event studies. Rather than provide a comprehensive survey of event study methods, we seek

---

[1] We discuss event studies that focus only on the mean stock price effects. Many other types of event studies also appear in the literature, including event studies that examine return variances (e.g., Beaver, 1968; Patell, 1976), trading volume (e.g., Beaver, 1968; Campbell and Wasley, 1996), operating (accounting) performance (e.g., Barber and Lyon, 1996), and earnings management via discretionary accruals (e.g., Dechow et al., 1995; Kothari et al., 2005).

to sift through and synthesize existing work on the subject. We provide many references and borrow heavily from the contributions of published papers. Two early papers that cover a wide range of issues are by Brown and Warner (1980, 1985). More recently, an excellent chapter in the textbook of Campbell et al. (1997) is a careful and broad outline of key research design issues. These standard references are recommended reading, but predate important advances in our understanding of event study methods, in particular on long-horizon methods. We provide an updated and much needed overview, and include a bit of new evidence as well.

Although much emphasis will be on the statistical issues, we do not view our mission as narrowly technical. As financial economists, our ultimate interest is in how to best specify and test interesting economic hypotheses using event studies. Thus, the econometric and economic issues are interrelated, and we will try to keep sight of the interrelation.

In Section 2, we briefly review the event study literature and describe the changes in event study methodology over time. In Section 3 we discuss how to use events studies to test economic hypotheses. We also characterize the properties of the event study tests and how these properties depend on variables such as security volatility, sample size, horizon length, and the process generating abnormal returns. Section 4 is devoted to issues most likely encountered when conducting long-horizon event studies. The main issues are risk adjustment, cross-correlation in returns, and changes in volatility during the event period.

2. The event study literature: basic facts

2.1. The stock and flow of event studies

To quantify the enormity of the event study literature, we conducted a census of event studies published in 5 leading journals: the *Journal of Business* (JB), *Journal of Finance* (JF), *Journal of Financial Economics* (JFE), *Journal of Financial and Quantitative Analysis* (JFQA), and the *Review of Financial Studies* (RFS). We began in 1974, the first year the JFE was published.

Table 1 reports the results for the years 1974–2000. The total number of papers reporting event study results is 565. Since many academic and practitioner-oriented journals are excluded, these figures provide a lower bound on the size of the literature. The number of papers published per year increased in the 1980s, and the flow of papers has since been stable. The peak years are 1983 (38 papers), 1990 (37 papers), and 2000 (37 papers). All five journals have significant representation. The JFE and JF lead, with over 200 papers each.

Table 1 makes no distinction between long-horizon and short-horizon studies. While the exact definition of "long horizon" is arbitrary, it generally applies to event windows of 1 year or more. Approximately 200 of the 565 event studies listed in

Table 1

Event studies, by year and journal

For each journal, all papers that contain an event study are included. Survey and methodological papers are excluded.

Year	Journal of business	Journal of finance	Journal of financial economics	Journal of financial and quant. analysis	Review of financial studies	Grand total
1974	2		2	1		5
1975		2	2	1		5
1976		5	1	1		7
1977		5	5	1		11
1978	1	5	4	1		11
1979		7		2		9
1980	3	4	2	2		11
1981	1	3	4	2		10
1982	1	6	2	1		10
1983	2	14	18	4		38
1984		5	5	1		11
1985	2	4	7	2		15
1986	2	7	14	4		27
1987		7	18	1		26
1988	1	4	7	5	1	18
1989		11	11	1	1	24
1990	5	17	7	6	2	37
1991	5	17	2	4	1	29
1992	4	13	9	4	1	31
1993	5	7	5	5	3	25
1994	1	10	10	5		26
1995	1	8	14	11	2	36
1996	1	7	10	5	3	26
1997	3	8	12	3		26
1998	1	14	11	3		29
1999	1	7	12	1	4	25
2000	2	15	13	5	2	37
Totals	44	212	207	82	20	565

Table 1 use a maximum window length of 12 months or more, with no obvious time trend in the year by year proportion of studies reporting a long-horizon result.

No survey of these 565 event study papers is attempted here. For the interested reader, the following are some examples of event study surveys. MacKinlay (1997) and Campbell et al. (1997) document the origins and breadth of event studies. The relation of event studies to tests of market efficiency receives considerable attention in Fama (1991), and in recent summaries of long-horizon tests in Kothari and Warner (1997) and Fama (1998). Smith (1986) presents reviews of event studies of financing decisions. Jensen and Ruback (1983), Jensen and Warner (1988), and

Jarrell et al. (1988) survey corporate control events. Recently, Kothari (2001) reviews event studies in the accounting literature.

2.2. Changes in event study methods: the big picture

Even the most cursory perusal of event studies done over the past 30 years reveals a striking fact: the basic statistical format of event studies has not changed over time. It is still based on the table layout in the classic stock split event study of Fama et al. (1969). The key focus is still on measuring the sample securities' mean and cumulative mean abnormal return around the time of an event.

Two main changes in methodology have taken place, however. First, the use of daily (and sometimes intraday) rather than monthly security return data has become prevalent, which permits more precise measurement of abnormal returns and more informative studies of announcement effects. Second, the methods used to estimate abnormal returns and calibrate their statistical significance have become more sophisticated. This second change is of particular importance for long-horizon event studies. The changes in long-horizon event study methods reflect new findings in the late 1990s on the statistical properties of long-horizon security returns. The change also parallels developments in the asset pricing literature, particularly the Fama-French three-factor model.

While long-horizon methods have improved, serious limitations of long-horizon methods have been brought to light and still remain. We now know that inferences from long-horizon tests "require extreme caution" (Kothari and Warner, 1997, p. 301) and even using the best methods "the analysis of long-run abnormal returns is treacherous" (Lyon et al., 1999, p. 165). These developments underscore and dramatically strengthen earlier warnings (e.g., Brown and Warner, 1980, p. 225) about the reliability—or lack of reliability—of long-horizon methods. This contrasts with short-horizon methods, which are relatively straightforward and trouble-free. As a result, we can have more confidence and put more weight on the results of short-horizon tests than long-horizon tests. Short-horizon tests represent the "cleanest evidence we have on efficiency" (Fama, 1991, p. 1602), but the interpretation of long-horizon results is problematic. As discussed later, long-horizon tests are highly susceptible to the joint-test problem, and have low power.

Of course these statements about properties of event study tests are very general. To provide a meaningful basis for assessing the usefulness of event studies—both short- and long-horizon—it is necessary to have a framework that specifies: (i) the economic and statistical hypotheses in an event study, and (ii) an objective basis for measuring and comparing the performance of event study methods. Section 3 lays out this framework, and summarizes general conclusions from the methodology literature. In the remainder of the chapter, additional issues and problems are considered with more specificity.

3. Characterizing event study methods

3.1. An event study: the model

An event study typically tries to examine return behavior for a sample of firms experiencing a common type of event (e.g., a stock split). The event might take place at different points in calendar time or it might be clustered at a particular date (e.g., a regulatory event affecting an industry or a subset of the population of firms). Let $t = 0$ represent the time of the event. For each sample security i, the return on the security for time period t relative to the event, R_{it}, is:

$$R_{it} = K_{it} + e_{it},\tag{1}$$

where K_{it} is the "normal" (i.e., expected or predicted return given a particular model of expected returns), and e_{it} is the component of returns which is abnormal or unexpected.[2] Given this return decomposition, the abnormal return, e_{it}, is the difference between the observed return and the predicted return:

$$e_{it} = R_{it} - K_{it}.\tag{2}$$

Equivalently, e_{it} is the difference between the return conditional on the event and the expected return unconditional on the event. Thus, the abnormal return is a direct measure of the (unexpected) change in securityholder wealth associated with the event. The security is typically a common stock, although some event studies look at wealth changes for firms' preferred or debt claims.

A model of normal returns (i.e., expected returns unconditional on the event but conditional on other information) must be specified before an abnormal return can be defined. A variety of expected return models (e.g., market model, constant expected returns model, capital asset pricing model) have been used in event studies.[3] Across alternative methods, both the bias and precision of the expected return measure can differ, affecting the properties of the abnormal return measures. Properties of different methods have been studied extensively, and are discussed later.

3.2. Statistical and economic hypotheses

3.2.1. Cross-sectional aggregation

An event study seeks to establish whether the cross-sectional distribution of returns at the time of an event is abnormal (i.e., systematically different from predicted). Such an exercise can be conducted in many ways. One could, for example, examine the entire distribution of abnormal returns. This is equivalent comparing the distributions of actual with the distribution of predicted returns and asking whether the distributions

---

[2] This framework is from Brown and Warner (1980) and Campbell et al. (1997).
[3] For descriptions of each of these models, see Brown and Warner (1985) or Campbell et al. (1997).

are the same. In the event study literature, the focus almost always is on the mean of the distribution of abnormal returns. Typically, the specific null hypothesis to be tested is whether the mean abnormal return (sometimes referred to as the average residual, AR) at time t is equal to zero. Other parameters of the cross-sectional distribution (e.g., median, variance) and determinants of the cross-sectional variation in abnormal returns are sometimes studied as well. The focus on mean effects, that is, the first moment of the return distribution, makes sense if one wants to understand whether the event is, on average, associated with a change in security holder wealth, and if one is testing economic models and alternative hypotheses that predict the sign of the average effect. For a sample of N securities, the cross-sectional mean abnormal return for any period t is:

$$AR_t = \frac{1}{N} \sum_{i=1}^{N} e_{it}. \tag{3}$$

3.2.2. Time-series aggregation

It is also of interest to examine whether mean abnormal returns for periods around the event are equal to zero. First, if the event is partially anticipated, some of the abnormal return behavior related to the event should show up in the preevent period. Second, in testing market efficiency, the speed of adjustment to the information revealed at the time of the event is an empirical question. Thus, examination of postevent returns provides information on market efficiency.

In estimating the performance measure over any multiperiod interval (e.g., time 0 through $+6$), there are a number of methods for time-series aggregation over the period of interest. The cumulative average residual method (CAR) uses as the abnormal performance measures the sum of each month's average abnormal performance. Later, we also consider the buy-and-hold method, which first compounds each security's abnormal returns and then uses the mean compounded abnormal return as the performance measure. The CAR starting at time t_1 through time t_2 (i.e., horizon length $L = t_2 - t_1 + 1$) is defined as:

$$CAR(t_1,t_2) = \sum_{t=t_1}^{t_2} AR_t. \tag{4}$$

Both CAR and buy-and-hold methods test the null hypothesis that mean abnormal performance is equal to zero. Under each method, the abnormal return measured is the same as the returns to a trading rule that buys sample securities at the beginning of the first period, and holds through the end of the last period. CARs and buy-and-hold abnormal returns (BHAR) correspond to security holder wealth changes around an event. Further, when applied to postevent periods, tests using these measures provide information about market efficiency, since systematically nonzero abnormal returns following an event are inconsistent with efficiency and imply a profitable trading rule (ignoring trading costs).

3.3. Sampling distributions of test statistics

For a given performance measure, such as the CAR, a test statistic is typically computed and compared to its assumed distribution under the null hypothesis that mean abnormal performance equals zero.[4] The null hypothesis is rejected if the test statistic exceeds a critical value, typically corresponding to the 5% or 1% tail region (i.e., the test level or size of the test is 0.05 or 0.01). The test statistic is a random variable because abnormal returns are measured with error. Two factors contribute to this error. First, predictions about securities' unconditional expected returns are imprecise. Second, individual firms' realized returns at the time of an event are affected for reasons unrelated to the event, and this component of the abnormal return does not average to literally zero in the cross-section.

For the CAR shown in Equation (4), a standard test statistic is the CAR divided by an estimate of its standard deviation.[5] Many alternative ways to estimate this standard deviation have been examined in the literature (see, e.g., Campbell et al., 1997). The test statistic is given by:

$$\frac{\text{CAR}(t_1,t_2)}{[\sigma^2(t_1,t_2)]^{1/2}}, \tag{5}$$

where

$$\sigma^2(t_1,t_2) = L\sigma^2(\text{AR}_t) \tag{6}$$

and $\sigma^2(\text{AR}_t)$ is the variance of the one-period mean abnormal return. Equation (6) simply says that the CAR has a higher variance the longer is L, and assumes time-series independence of the one-period mean abnormal return. The test statistic is typically assumed unit normal in the absence of abnormal performance. This is only an approximation, however, since estimates of the standard deviation are used.

The test statistic in Equation (5) is well-specified provided the variance of one-period mean abnormal return is estimated correctly. Event-time clustering renders the independence assumption for the abnormal returns in the cross-section incorrect (see Bernard, 1987; Collins and Dent, 1984; Petersen, 2005, and more detailed discussion in Section 4 below). This would bias the estimated standard deviation downward and the test statistic given in Equation (5) upward. To address the bias, the significance of the event-period average abnormal return can be and often is gauged using the variability of the time series of event portfolio returns in the period preceding or

---

[4] Standard tests are "classical" rather than "Bayesian." A Bayesian treatment of event studies is beyond the scope of this chapter.

[5] An alternative would be a test statistic that aggregates standardized abnormal returns, which means each observation is weighted in inverse proportion of the standard deviation of the estimated abnormal return. The standard deviation of abnormal returns is estimated using time-series return data on each firm. While a test using standardized abnormal returns is in principle superior under certain conditions, empirically in short-horizon event studies it typically makes little difference (see Brown and Warner, 1980, 1985).

after the event date. For example, the researcher can construct a portfolio of event firms and obtain a time series of daily abnormal returns on the portfolio for a number of days (e.g., 180 days) around the event date. The standard deviation of the portfolio returns can be used to assess the significance of the event-window average abnormal return. The cross-sectional dependence is accounted for because the variability of the portfolio returns through time incorporates whatever cross-dependence that exists among the returns on individual event securities.

The portfolio return approach has a drawback, however. To the extent the event period is associated with increased uncertainty, that is, greater return variability, the use of historical or postevent time-series variability might understate the true variability of the event-period abnormal performance. An increase in event-period return variability is economically intuitive. The event might have been triggered by uncertainty-increasing factors and/or the event itself causes uncertainty in the economic environment for the firm. In either case, the event-period return variability is likely to exceed that during other time periods for the event firms. Therefore, the statistical significance of the event-window abnormal performance would be overstated if it is evaluated on the basis of historical variability of the event-firm portfolio returns (Brown and Warner, 1980, 1985; Collins and Dent, 1984). One means of estimating the likely increase in the variability of event-period returns is to estimate the cross-sectional variability of returns during the event and nonevent periods. The ratio of the variances during the event period and nonevent periods might serve as an estimate of the degree of increase in the variability of returns during the event period, which can be used to adjust for the bias in the test statistic calculated ignoring the increased event-period uncertainty.[6]

3.4. Criteria for "reliable" event study tests

Using the test statistics, errors of inference are of two types. A Type I error occurs when the null hypothesis is falsely rejected. A Type II error occurs when the null is falsely accepted. Accordingly, two key properties of event study tests have been investigated. The first is whether the test statistic is correctly specified. A correctly specified test statistic yields a Type I error probability equal to the assumed size of the test. The second concern is power, that is, a test's ability to detect abnormal performance when it is present. Power can be measured as one minus the probability of a Type II error. Alternatively, it can be measured as the probability that the null hypothesis will be rejected given a level of Type I error and level of abnormal performance. When comparing tests that are well-specified, those with higher power are preferred.

---

[6] Use of nonparametric tests of significance, as suggested in Corrado (1989), might also be effective in performing well-specified tests in the presence of increased event-period uncertainty.

3.5. Determining specification and power

3.5.1. The joint-test problem

While the specification and power of a test can be statistically determined, economic interpretation is not straightforward because all tests are joint tests. That is, event study tests are well-specified only to the extent that the assumptions underlying their estimation are correct. This poses a significant challenge because event study tests are joint tests of whether abnormal returns are zero and of whether the assumed model of expected returns (i.e., the CAPM, market model, etc.) is correct. Moreover, an additional set of assumptions concerning the statistical properties of the abnormal return measures must also be correct. For example, a standard *t*-test for mean abnormal performance assumes, among other things, that the mean abnormal performance for the cross-section of securities is normally distributed. Depending on the specific *t*-test, there may be additional assumptions that the abnormal return data are independent in time series or cross-section. The validity of these assumptions is often an empirical question. This is particularly true for small samples, where one cannot rely on asymptotic results or the central limit theorem.

3.5.2. Brown-Warner simulation

To directly address the issue of event study properties, the standard tool in event study methodology research is simulation procedures that use actual security return data. The motivation and specific research design is initially laid out in Brown and Warner (1980, 1985), and has been followed in almost all subsequent methodology research.

Much of what is known about general properties of event study tests comes from such large-scale simulations. The basic idea behind the event study simulations is simple and intuitive.[7] Different event study methods are simulated by repeated application of each method to samples that have been constructed through a random (or stratified random) selection of securities and random selection of an event date to each. If performance is measured correctly, these samples should show no abnormal performance, on average. This makes it possible to study test statistic specification, that is, the probability of rejecting the null hypothesis when it is known to be true. Further, various levels of abnormal performance can be artificially introduced into the samples. This permits direct study of the power of event study tests, that is, the ability to detect a given level of abnormal performance.

3.5.3. Analytical methods

Simulation methods seem both natural and necessary to determine whether event study test statistics are well-specified. Once it has been established using simulation methods

---

[7] This characterization of simulation is from Brown and Warner (1985, p. 4).

that a particular test statistic is well-specified, analytical procedures have also been used to complement simulation procedures. Although deriving a power function analytically for different levels of abnormal performance requires additional distributional assumptions, the evidence in Brown and Warner (1985, p. 13) is that analytical and simulation methods yield similar power functions for a well-specified test statistic. As illustrated below, these analytical procedures provide a quick and simple way to study power.

3.6. A quick summary of our knowledge

3.6.1. Qualitative properties

Table 2 highlights, in qualitative terms, what is known about the properties of event study tests. The table shows the characteristics of event study methods along three dimensions: specification, power against specific types of alternative hypotheses, and the sensitivity of specification to assumptions about the return generating process. The table also shows how these properties can differ sharply for short and long-horizon studies. Much of the remainder of the chapter deals with the full details of this table.

From Table 2, horizon length has a big impact on event study test properties. First, short-horizon event study methods are generally well-specified, but long-horizon methods are sometimes very poorly specified. While much is understood about how to reduce misspecification in long-horizon studies (see Section 4), no procedure in whose specification researchers can have complete confidence has yet been developed. Second, short-horizon methods are quite powerful if (but only if) the abnormal performance is concentrated in the event window. For example, a precise event date

Table 2

General characterization of properties of event study test methods

Criterion	Length of event window Short (<12 months)	Long (12 months or more)
Specification	Good	Poor/Moderate
Power when abnormal performance is:		
Concentrated in event window	High	Low
Not concentrated in event window	Low	Low
Sensitivity of test statistic specification to assumptions about the return generating process:		
Expected returns, unconditional on event	Low	High
Cross-sectional and time-series dependence of sample abnormal returns	Low/Moderate	Moderate/High
Variance of abnormal returns, conditional on event	High	High
Sensitivity of power to:		
Sample size	High	High
Firm characteristics (e.g., size, industry)	High	High

is known for earnings announcements, but insider trading events might be known to have occurred only sometime during a one-month window. In contrast to the short-horizon tests, long-horizon event studies (even when they are well-specified) generally have low power to detect abnormal performance, both when it is concentrated in the event window and when it is not. That power to detect a given level of abnormal performance is decreasing in horizon length is not surprising, but the empirical magnitudes are dramatic (see below). Third, with short-horizon methods the test statistic specification is not highly sensitive to the benchmark model of normal returns or assumptions about the cross-sectional or time-series dependence of abnormal returns. This contrasts with long-horizon methods, where specification is quite sensitive to assumptions about the return generating process.

Along several lines, however, short- and long-horizon tests show similarities, and these results are easy to show using either simulation or analytical procedures. First, a common problem shared by both short- and long-horizon studies is that when the variance of a security's abnormal returns conditional on the event increases, test statistics can easily be misspecified, and reject the null hypothesis too often. This problem was first brought to light and has been studied mainly in the context of short-horizon studies (Brown and Warner, 1985; Corrado, 1989). A variance increase is indistinguishable from abnormal returns differing across sample securities at the time of an event, and would be expected for an event. Thus, this issue is likely to be empirically relevant both in a short- and long-horizon context as well. Second, power is higher with increasing sample size, regardless of horizon length. Third, power depends on the characteristics of firms in the event study sample. In particular, firms experiencing a particular event can have nonrandom size and industry characteristics. This is relevant because individual security variances (and abnormal return variances) exhibit an inverse relation to firm size and can vary systematically by industry. Power is inversely related to sample security variance: the noisier the returns, the harder to extract a given signal. As shown below, differences in power by sample type can be dramatic.

3.6.2. Quantitative results

To provide additional texture on Table 2, below we show specific quantitative estimates of power. We do so using the test statistic shown previously in Equations (5) and (6), using two-tailed tests at the 0.05 significance level.[8] Since this test statistic is well-specified, at least at short horizons, the power functions are generated using analytic (rather than simulation) procedures. The estimates are for illustrative purposes only, however, and only represent "back of the envelope" estimates. The figures and the test statistic on which they are based assume independence of the returns (both through

---

[8] This format for displaying power functions is similar to Campbell et al. (1997, pp. 168–172). Our test statistic and procedures are the same as for their test statistic J1, but as discussed below we use updated variance inputs.

time and in the cross-section), and that all securities within a sample have the same standard deviation. The power functions also assume that return and abnormal return variances are the same (i.e., the model of abnormal returns is the "mean-adjusted returns" model of Brown and Warner, 1980).

3.6.3. Volatility

In calculating the test statistic in an event study, a key input required here is the individual security return (or abnormal return) variance (or standard deviation). To determine a reasonable range of standard deviations, we estimate daily standard deviations for all CRSP listed firms from 1990 to 2002. Specifically, for each year, we: (i) calculate each stock's standard deviation, and (ii) assign firms to deciles ranked by standard deviation. From each decile, the averages of each year's mean and median values are reported in Table 3. The mean daily standard deviation for all firms is 0.053. This is somewhat higher than the value of 0.026 reported by Brown and Warner (1985, p. 9) for NYSE/AMEX firms and the value of 0.035 reported by Campbell and Wasley (1993, p. 79) for NASDAQ firms. The differences reflect that individual stocks have become more volatile over time (Campbell et al., 2001). This is highly relevant because it suggests that the power to detect abnormal performance for events over 1990–2002 is lower than for earlier periods. From Table 3, there is wide variation across the deciles. Firms in decile 1 have a mean daily standard deviation of 0.014,

Table 3

Standard deviation of daily returns on individual securities using all CRSP common-stock securities from 1990 to 2002

For each year, firms are ranked by their estimated daily standard deviation. Firms with missing observations are excluded. The numbers under mean and median columns represent the average of the annual mean and median values for the firms in each decile and for all firms. The number of firms in each decile ranges from 504 in 2002 to 673 in 1997.

Decile	Standard deviation Mean	Median
1	0.014	0.014
2	0.019	0.019
3	0.023	0.023
4	0.028	0.028
5	0.033	0.033
6	0.039	0.039
7	0.046	0.046
8	0.055	0.055
9	0.069	0.068
10	0.118	0.098
All firms	0.053	0.053

compared to 0.118 for decile 10. The figure of 0.118 for decile 10 seems very high, although this is likely to represent both very small firms and those with low stock prices. Further, there is a strong negative empirical relation between volatility and size. Our qualitative results apply if ranking is by firm size, so Table 3 is not simply picking up measurement error in volatility.

3.6.4. Results

Figure 1 shows how, for a sample comprised of securities of average risk and 10% abnormal performance, the power to detect abnormal performance falls with horizon length. This level of abnormal performance seems economically highly significant. If the abnormal performance is concentrated entirely in one day (and the day in known with certainty), a sample of only six stocks detects this level of abnormal performance 100% of the time. In contrast, if the same abnormal performance occurs over six months, a sample size of 200 is required to detect the abnormal performance even 65% of the time. These various rejection frequencies are lower than those using pre-1990 volatilities (not reported), although this is not surprising.

Figure 2A–C show related results using a one-day horizon for samples whose individual security standard deviations correspond to the average standard deviation for: the lowest decile (Figure 2A); all firms (Figure 2B); and the highest decile (Figure 2C). For decile 1 firms, with 1% abnormal performance a 90% rejection rate

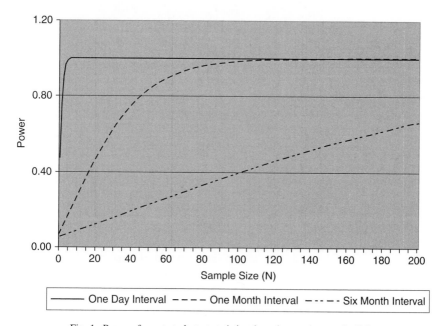

Fig. 1. Power of event study test statistic when abnormal return is 10%.

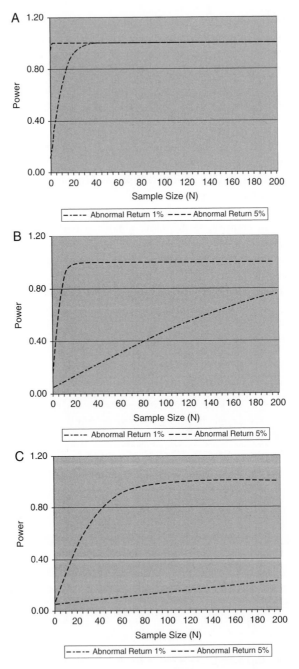

Fig. 2. (A) Power of event study for firms in the lowest volatility decile. (B) Power of event study for firms with average volatility. (C) Power of event study for firms in the highest volatility decile.

requires only 21 stocks. For firms in decile 10, even with 5% abnormal performance a 90% rejection rate requires 60 stocks. These comparisons may distort the differences in actual power if high variance firms are less closely followed and events are bigger surprises. When the effect of events differs cross-sectionally, analysis of test properties (i.e., power and specification) is more complicated.

Collectively, our results illustrate that power against alternative hypotheses can be sensitive to calendar time period and sample firm characteristics, and highlight the importance already recognized in the profession of studying test statistic properties for samples stratified by firm characteristics. A complete analysis of these issues would focus on abnormal return (rather than return) volatility, and study how specification (and abnormal return distributional properties such as skewness) varies across time and firm characteristics.

3.7. Cross-sectional tests

This section's focus thus far has been event study tests for mean stock price effects. These tests represent the best understood class of event study tests. To provide a more complete picture of event-related tests, we briefly call attention to cross-sectional tests. These tests examine how the stock price effects of an event are related to firm characteristics. For a cross-section of firms, abnormal returns are compared to (e.g., regressed against) firm characteristics. This provides evidence to discriminate among various economic hypotheses.

Cross-sectional tests are a standard part of almost every event study. They are relevant even when the mean stock price effect of an event is zero. In addition, they are applicable regardless of horizon length. They are simple to do, but as discussed below, "one must be careful in interpreting the results" (Campbell et al., 1997, p. 174).

One reason that abnormal returns vary cross-sectionally is that the economic effect of the event differs by firm. For such a situation, Sefcik and Thompson (1986) examine the statistical properties of cross-sectional regressions. They are concerned with the effects of cross-sectionally correlated abnormal returns and heteroscedasticity in the abnormal returns. They argue that accounting for each appears to be potentially important for inferences, and they suggest procedures to deal with these issues.

Abnormal returns also vary cross-sectionally because the degree to which the event is anticipated differs by firm. For example, for firms that are more closely followed (e.g., more analysts), events should be more predictable, all else equal. Further, events are endogenous, reflecting a firm's self-selection to choose the event, which in turn reflects insiders' information. Recognizing these factors, and recognizing that it is the unexpected information provided by an event that determines the stock price effect, has numerous consequences. For example, standard estimates of cross-sectional coefficients can be biased (Eckbo et al., 1990). Appropriate procedures for treating self-selection and partial anticipation issues is the subject of an entire chapter by Li and Prabhala (2007).

Quite apart from the issues discussed in the context of Li and Prabhala, there are several additional dimensions where our understanding of cross-sectional tests is incomplete, and where additional work is potentially fruitful. One area concerns the power of cross-sectional procedures. While specification of cross-sectional regression methods (i.e., biases in regression coefficients) has received much attention, the power of alternative procedures to detect underlying cross-sectional effects has received less study.

A related point is that a simple type of cross-sectional procedure is to form portfolios based on firm characteristics, and compare portfolio abnormal returns. Such procedures are common, but methodological comparisons to cross-sectional regressions would prove useful. Portfolio procedures seem less amenable to multivariate comparisons than do regression procedures, but the relative empirical merits of each in an event-study context have not been investigated.

We also note that some studies focus not on the stock price effect of an event, but on predicting a corporate event (e.g., management turnover, or a security issue of a particular type), sometimes using past stock prices as one explanatory variable. These tests use cross-sectional methods in the sense that the cross-section includes both event and nonevent firms. Typically, discrete choice models (e.g., probit or logit model) relate whether or not the event occurred to firm-specific characteristics. This seems intuitive, since we would like to know what factors led the firm to have the event. These methods complement standard event study methods. Methodological work on prediction models could enhance our understanding of how to best to use information about events to test economic hypotheses about firm behavior.

Finally, additional important issues to consider in an event study are: (i) whether the event was partially anticipated by market participants (e.g., a governance-related regulation might be anticipated following corporate scandals or CEO turnover is likely in the case of a firm experiencing steep stock-price decline and poor accounting performance), and (ii) whether the partial anticipation is expected to vary cross-sectionally in a predictable fashion (e.g., market participants might anticipate that managers of firms experiencing high price run-ups are likely to make value-destroying stock acquisitions, but the negative announcement effect of an actual merger announcement might have been largely anticipated for the firms who have experienced relatively high prior price run-up). These issues arising from the nature of information arrival, partial anticipation of events, and cross-sectional variation in the degree of anticipation are also beyond the scope of this chapter. Interested readers will find treatments in Malatesta and Thompson (1985), Eckbo et al. (1990), and, especially, Thompson (1995) of considerable interest.

4. Long-horizon event studies

All event studies, regardless of horizon length, must deal with several basic issues. These include risk adjustment and expected/abnormal return modeling (Section 4.2), the aggregation of security-specific abnormal returns (Section 4.3), and the calibration of the statistical significance of abnormal returns (Section 4.4). These issues become critically important with long horizons. The remainder of this chapter focuses on efforts in the long-horizon literature to deal with the issues.

4.1. Background

Long-horizon event studies have a long history, including the original stock split event study by Fama et al. (1969). As evidence inconsistent with the efficient markets hypothesis started to accumulate in the late seventies and early eighties, interest in long-horizon studies intensified. Evidence on the postearnings announcement effect (Ball and Brown, 1968; Jones and Litzenberger, 1970), size effect (Banz, 1981), and earnings yield effect (Basu, 1977, 1983) contributed to skepticism about the CAPM as well as market efficiency. This evidence prompted researchers to develop hypotheses about market inefficiency stemming from investors' information processing biases (DeBondt and Thaler, 1985, 1987) and limits to arbitrage (De Long et al., 1990a,b; Shliefer and Vishny, 1997).

The "anomalies" literature and the attempts to model the anomalies as market inefficiencies has led to a burgeoning field known as behavioral finance. Research in this field formalizes (and tests) the security pricing implications of investors' information processing biases.[9] Because the behavioral biases might be persistent and arbitrage forces might take a long time to correct the mispricing, a vast body of literature hypothesizes and studies abnormal performance over long horizons of one-to-five years following a wide range of corporate events. The events might be one-time (unpredictable) phenomena like an initial public offering or a seasoned equity offering, or they may be recurring events such as earnings announcements.

Many long-horizon studies document apparent abnormal returns spread over long horizons. The literature on long-horizon security price performance following corporate events is summarized extensively in many studies, including Fama (1998), Kothari and Warner (1997), Schwert (2001), and Kothari (2001). Whether the apparent abnormal returns are due to mispricing, or simply the result of measurement problems, is a contentious and unresolved issue among financial economists. The methodological research in the area is important because it demonstrates how easy it is to conclude there is abnormal performance when none exists. Before questions on mispricing can be answered, better methods than currently exist are required.

We summarize some of the salient difficulties and the state-of-the-art event study methods for estimating long-horizon security price performance. More detailed discussions appear in Barber and Lyon (1997), Kothari and Warner (1997), Fama (1998),

---

[9] See Shleifer (2000), Barberis et al. (1998), Daniel et al. (1998), Daniel et al. (2002), Hirshleifer (2001), and Hong and Stein (1999).

Brav (2000), Lyon et al. (1999), Mitchell and Stafford (2000), Jegadeesh and Karceski (2004), Viswanathan and Wei (2004), Eckbo et al. (2006), and Petersen (2005).

4.2. Risk adjustment and expected returns

In long-horizon tests, appropriate adjustment for risk is critical in calculating abnormal price performance. This is in sharp contrast to short-horizon tests in which risk adjustment is straightforward and typically unimportant. The error in calculating abnormal performance due to errors in adjusting for risk in a short-horizon test is likely to be small. Daily expected returns are about 0.05% (i.e., annualized about 12–13%). Therefore, even if the event-firm portfolio's beta risk is misestimated by 50% (e.g., estimated beta risk of 1.0 when true beta risk is 1.5), the error in the estimated abnormal error is small relative to the abnormal return of 1% or more that is typically documented in short-window event studies. Not surprisingly, Brown and Warner (1985) conclude that simple risk-adjustment approaches to conducting short-window event studies are quite effective in detecting abnormal performance.

In multiyear long-horizon tests, risk-adjusted return measurement is the Achilles heel for at least two reasons. First, even a small error in risk adjustment can make an economically large difference when calculating abnormal returns over horizons of one year or longer, whereas such errors make little difference for short horizons. Thus, the precision of the risk adjustment becomes far more important in long-horizon event studies. Second, it is unclear which expected return model is correct, and therefore estimates of abnormal returns over long horizons are highly sensitive to model choice. We now discuss each of these problems in turn.

4.2.1. Errors in risk adjustment

Such errors can make an economically nontrivial difference in measured abnormal performance over one-year or longer periods. The problem of risk adjustment error is exacerbated in long-horizon event studies because the potential for such error is greater for longer horizons. In many event studies, (i) the event follows unusual prior performance (e.g., stock splits follow good performance), or (ii) the event sample consists of firms with extreme (economic) characteristics (e.g., low market capitalization stocks, low-priced stocks, or extreme book-to-market stocks), or (iii) the event is defined on the basis of unusual prior performance (e.g., contrarian investment strategies in DeBondt and Thaler, 1985; Lakonishok et al., 1994). Under these circumstances, accurate risk estimation is difficult, with historical estimates being notoriously biased because prior economic performance negatively impacts the risk of a security. Therefore, in long-horizon event studies, it is crucial that abnormal-performance measurement be on the basis of postevent, not historical risk estimates (Ball and Kothari, 1989; Ball et al., 1995; Chan, 1988; Chopra et al., 1992). However, how the postevent risk should be estimated is itself a subject of considerable debate, which we summarize below in an attempt to offer guidance to researchers.

4.2.2. Model for expected returns

The question of which model of expected returns is appropriate remains an unresolved issue. As noted earlier, event studies are joint tests of market efficiency and a model of expected returns (e.g., Fama, 1970). On a somewhat depressing note, Fama (1998, p. 291) concludes that "all models for expected returns are incomplete descriptions of the systematic patterns in average returns," which can lead to spurious indications of abnormal performance in an event study. With the CAPM as a model of expected returns being thoroughly discredited as a result of the voluminous anomalies evidence, a quest for a better-and-improved model began. The search culminated in the Fama and French (1993) three-factor model, further modified by Carhart (1997) to incorporate the momentum factor.[10] However, absent a sound economic rationale motivating the inclusion of the size, book-to-market, and momentum factors, whether these factors represent equilibrium compensation for risk or they are an indication of market inefficiency has not been satisfactorily resolved in the literature (see, e.g., Brav and Gompers, 1997). Fortunately, from the standpoint of event study analysis, this flaw is not fatal. Regardless of whether the size, book-to-market, and momentum factors proxy for risk or indicate inefficiency, it is essential to use them when measuring abnormal performance. The purpose of an event study is to isolate the incremental impact of an event on security price performance. Since the price performance associated with the size, book-to-market, and momentum characteristics is applicable to all stocks sharing those characteristics, not just the sample of firms experiencing the event (e.g., a stock split), the performance associated with the event itself must be distinguished from that associated with other known determinants of performance, such as the aforementioned four factors.[11]

4.3. Approaches to abnormal-performance measurement

While postevent risk-adjusted performance measurement is crucial in long-horizon tests, actual measurement is not straightforward. Two main methods for assessing and calibrating postevent risk-adjusted performance are used: characteristic-based matching approach and the Jensen's alpha approach, which is also known as the calendar-time portfolio approach (Eckbo et al., 2000; Fama, 1998; Mitchell and Stafford, 2000). Analysis and comparison of the methods is detailed below. Despite an extensive literature, there is still no clear winner in a horse race. Both have low power against economically interesting null hypotheses, and neither is immune to misspecification.

---

[10] More recently, considerable evidence suggests the importance of a liquidity factor in determining expected returns (Brennan and Subrahmanyam, 1996; Pastor and Stambaugh, 2003; Sadka, 2006). However, still others have begun to question the usefulness of the liquidity factor (see Chordia et al., 2006; Ng et al., 2006).

[11] See Kothari et al. (2005) for an extended discussion.

4.3.1. BHAR approach

In recent years, following the works of Ikenberry et al. (1995), Barber and Lyon (1997), Lyon et al. (1999), the characteristic-based matching approach (or also known as the BHAR) has been widely used. Mitchell and Stafford (2000, p. 296) describe BHAR returns as "the average multiyear return from a strategy of investing in all firms that complete an event and selling at the end of a prespecified holding period versus a comparable strategy using otherwise similar nonevent firms." An appealing feature of using BHAR is that buy-and-hold returns better resemble investors' actual investment experience than periodic (monthly) rebalancing entailed in other approaches to measuring risk-adjusted performance.[12] The joint-test problem remains in that any inference on the basis of BHAR hinges on the validity of the assumption that event firms differ from the "otherwise similar nonevent firms" only in that they experience the event. The researcher implicitly assumes an expected return model in which the matched characteristics (e.g., size and book-to-market) perfectly proxy for the expected return on a security. Since corporate events themselves are unlikely to be random occurrences, that is, they are unlikely to be exogenous with respect to past performance and expected returns, there is a danger that the event and nonevent samples differ systematically in their expected returns notwithstanding the matching on certain firm characteristics. This makes matching on (unobservable) expected returns more difficult, especially in the case of event firms experiencing extreme prior performance.

Once a matching firm or portfolio is identified, BHAR calculation is straightforward. A T-month BHAR for event firm i is defined as:

$$\text{BHAR}_i(t, T) = \prod_{t=1 \text{ to } T} (1 + R_{i,t}) - \prod_{t=1 \text{ to } T} (1 + R_{B,t}), \tag{7}$$

where R_B is the return on either a nonevent firm that is matched to the event firm i, or it is the return on a matched (benchmark) portfolio.[13] If the researcher believes that the Carhart (1997) four-factor model is an adequate description of expected returns, then firm-specific matching might entail identifying a nonevent firm that is closest to an event firm on the basis of firm size (i.e., market capitalization of equity), book-to-market ratio, and past one-year return. Alternatively, characteristic portfolio matching would identify the portfolio of all nonevent stocks that share the same quintile ranking on size, book-to-market, and momentum as the event firm (see Daniel et al., 1997 or Lyon et al., 1999, for details of benchmark portfolio construction). The return on the matched portfolio is the benchmark portfolio return, R_B. For the sample of event firms,

---

[12] Apart from similarity with the actual investment experience, the BHAR approach also avoids biases arising from security microstructure issues when portfolio performance is measured with frequent rebalancing (see Ball et al., 1995; Blume and Stambaugh, 1983; Roll, 1983). The latter biases are also reduced if value-weight portfolio performance is examined.

[13] See Mitchell and Stafford (2000) for details.

the mean BHAR is calculated as the (equal- or value-weighted) average of the individual firm BHARs.

4.3.2. Jensen-alpha approach

The Jensen-alpha approach (or the calendar-time portfolio approach) to estimating risk-adjusted abnormal performance is an alternative to the BHAR calculation using a matched-firm approach to risk adjustment. Jaffe (1974) and Mandelker (1974) introduced a calendar-time methodology to the financial-economics literature, and it has since been advocated by many, including Fama (1998) and Mitchell and Stafford (2000).[14] The distinguishing feature of the most recent variants of the approach is to calculate calendar-time portfolio returns for firms experiencing an event, and calibrate whether they are abnormal in a multifactor (e.g., CAPM or Fama-French three factors) regression. The estimated intercept from the regression of portfolio returns against factor returns is the postevent abnormal performance of the sample of event firms.

To implement the Jensen-alpha approach, assume a sample of firms experiences a corporate event (e.g., an IPO or an SEO).[15] The event might be spread over several years or even many decades (the sample period). Also assume that the researcher seeks to estimate price performance over two years ($T = 24$ months) following the event for each sample firm. In each calendar month over the entire sample period, a portfolio is constructed comprising all firms experiencing the event within the previous T months. Because the number of event firms is not uniformly distributed over the sample period, the number of firms included in a portfolio is not constant through time. As a result, some new firms are added each month and some firms exit each month. Accordingly, the portfolios are rebalanced each month and an equal- or value-weighted portfolio excess return is calculated. The resulting time series of monthly excess returns is regressed on the CAPM market factor, or the three (Fama and French, 1993) factors, or the four (Carhart, 1997) factors as follows:

$$R_{pt} - R = a_p + b_p(R_{mt} - R) + s_p\text{SMB}_t + h_p\text{HML}_t + m_p\text{UMD}_t + e_{pt}, \tag{8}$$

where

- R_{pt} is the equal- or value-weighted return for calendar month t for the portfolio of event firms that experienced the event within the previous T months;
- R_{ft} is the risk-free rate;
- R_{mt} is the return on the CRSP value-weight market portfolio;
- SMB_{pt} is the difference between the return on the portfolio of "small" stocks and "big" stocks;

---

[14] For a variation of the Jensen-alpha approach, see Ibbotson (1975) *returns across time and securities* (RATS) methodology, which is used in Ball and Kothari (1989) and others.
[15] The description here is based on Mitchell and Stafford (2000).

- HML$_{pt}$ is the difference between the return on the portfolio of "high" and "low" book-to-market stocks;
- UMD$_{pt}$ is the difference between the return on the portfolio of past one-year "winners" and "losers";
- a_p is the average monthly abnormal return (Jensen alpha) on the portfolio of event firms over the T-month postevent period;
- b_p, s_p, h_p, and m_p are sensitivities (betas) of the event portfolio to the four factors.

Inferences about the abnormal performance are on the basis of the estimated a_p and its statistical significance. Since a_p is the average monthly abnormal performance over the T-month postevent period, it can be used to calculate annualized postevent abnormal performance.

Recent work on the implications of using the Jensen-alpha approach is mixed. For example, Mitchell and Stafford (2000) and Brav and Gompers (1997) favor the Jensen-alpha approach. However, Loughran and Ritter (2000) argue against using the Jensen-alpha approach because it might be biased toward finding results consistent with market efficiency. Their rationale is that corporate executives time the events to exploit mispricing, but the Jensen-alpha approach, by forming calendar-time portfolios, underweights managers' timing decisions and overweights other observations. In the words of Loughran and Ritter (2000, p. 362): "If there are time-varying misvaluations that firms capitalize on by taking some action (a supply response), there will be more events involving larger misvaluations in some periods than in others... In general, tests that weight firms equally should have more power than tests that weight each time period equally." Since the Jensen-alpha (i.e., calendar-time) approach weights each period equally, it has lower power to detect abnormal performance if managers time corporate events to coincide with misvaluations. As a means of addressing the problem, Fama (1998) advocates weighting calendar months by their statistical precision, which varies with sample size. Countering the criticism of Loughran and Ritter (2000) and Eckbo et al. (2000) point out another problem with the buy-and-hold abnormal return methods. The latter is not a feasible portfolio strategy because the total number of securities is not known in advance.[16]

4.4. Significance tests for BHAR and jensen-alpha measures

The choice between the matched-firm BHAR approach to abnormal return measurement and the calendar-time Jensen-alpha approach (also known as the calendar-time

---

[16] The BHAR approach is also criticized for "pseudo-timing" because BHAR mechanically produces underperformance following a clustering of issues experiencing a common event, for example, an IPO, in an up or down market (Eckbo and Norli, 2005; Schultz, 2003). The criticism assumes that those seeking to exploit the event-related market inefficiency do not have market-timing ability. The question of pseudo-timing and return predictability is a topic of intense current interest and appears currently unresolved (Baker et al., 2004, 2006; Boudoukh et al., 2006; Cochrane, 2006; Goyal and Welch, 2003, 2005).

portfolio approach) hinges on the researcher's ability to accurately gauge the statistical significance of the estimated abnormal performance using the two approaches. Unbiased standard errors for the distribution of the event-portfolio abnormal returns are not easy to calculate, which leads to test misspecification. Assessing the statistical significance of the event portfolio's BHAR has been particularly difficult because (i) long-horizon returns depart from the normality assumption that underlies many statistical tests; (ii) long-horizon returns exhibit considerable cross-correlation because the return horizons of many event firms overlap and also because many event firms are drawn from a few industries; and (iii) volatility of the event firm returns exceeds that of matched firms because of event-induced volatility. We summarize below the econometric inferential issues encountered in performing long-horizon tests and some of the remedies put forward in recent studies.

4.4.1. Skewness

Long-horizon buy-and-hold returns, even after adjusting for the performance of a matched firm (or portfolio), tend to be right skewed. The right-skewness of buy-and-hold returns is not surprising because the lower bound is -100% and returns are unbounded on the upside. Skewness in abnormal returns imparts a skewness bias to long-horizon abnormal-performance test statistics (see Barber and Lyon, 1997). Brav (2000, p. 1981) concludes that "with a skewed-right distribution of abnormal returns, the Student t-distribution is asymmetric with a mean smaller than the zero null." While the right-skewness of individual firms' long-horizon returns is undoubtedly true, the extent of skewness bias in the test statistic for the hypothesis that mean abnormal performance for the portfolio of event firms is zero is expected to decline with sample size.[17] Fortunately, the sample size in long-horizon event studies is often several hundred observations (e.g., Byun and Rozeff, 2003; Teoh et al., 1998). Therefore, if the BHAR observations for the sample firms are truly independent, as assumed in using a t-test, the Central Limit Theorem's implication that "the sum of a large number of independent random variables has a distribution that is approximately normal" should apply (Ross, 1976, p. 252). The right-skewness of the distribution of long-horizon abnormal returns on event *portfolios*, as documented in, for example, Brav (2000) and Mitchell and Stafford (2000), appears to be due largely to the lack of independence arising from overlapping long-horizon return observations in event portfolios. That is, skewness in portfolio returns is in part a by-product of cross-correlated data rather than a direct consequence of skewed firm-level buy-and-hold abnormal (or raw) returns.

---

[17] Simulation evidence in Barber and Lyon (1997) on skewness bias is based on samples consisting of 50 firms and early concern over skewness bias as examined in Neyman and Pearson (1928) and Pearson (1929a,b) also refers to skewness bias in small samples.

4.4.2. Cross-correlation

4.4.2.1. The Issue Specification bias arising due to cross-correlation in returns is a serious problem in long-horizon tests of price performance. Brav (2000, p. 1979) attributes the misspecification to the fact that researchers conducting long-horizon tests typically "maintain the standard assumptions that abnormal returns are independent and normally distributed although these assumptions fail to hold even approximately at long horizons."[18] The notion that economy-wide and industry-specific factors would generate contemporaneous comovements in security returns is the cornerstone of portfolio theory and is economically intuitive and empirically compelling. Interestingly, the cross-dependence, although muted, is also observed in risk-adjusted returns.[19] The degree of cross-dependence decreases in the effectiveness of the risk-adjustment approach and increases in the homogeneity of the sample firms examined (e.g., sample firms clustered in one industry). Cross-correlation in abnormal returns is largely irrelevant in short-window event studies when the event is not clustered in calendar-time. However, in long-horizon event studies, even if the event is not clustered in calendar-time, cross-correlation in abnormal returns cannot be ignored (Brav, 2000; Jegadeesh and Karceski, 2004; Mitchell and Stafford, 2000). Long-horizon abnormal returns tend to be cross-correlated because: (i) abnormal returns for subsets of the sample firms are likely to share a common calendar period due to the long measurement period; (ii) corporate events like mergers and share repurchases exhibit waves (for rational economic reasons as well as opportunistic actions on the part of the shareholders and/or management); and (iii) some industries might be over-represented in the event sample (e.g., merger activity among technology stocks).

If the test statistic in an event study is calculated ignoring cross-dependence in data, even a fairly small amount of cross-correlation in data will lead to serious misspecification of the test. In particular, the test will reject the null of no effect far more often than the size of the test (Bernard, 1987; Collins and Dent, 1984; Mitchell and Stafford, 2000). The overrejection is caused by the downward biased estimate of the standard deviation of the cross-sectional distribution of BHAR for the event sample of firms.

4.4.2.2. Magnitude of Bias To get an idea of approximate magnitude of the bias, we begin with the cross-sectional standard deviation of the event firms' abnormal returns, AR, assuming equal variances and pairwise covariances across all sample firms' abnormal returns:

$$\sigma_{AR} = \left[\frac{1}{N}\sigma^2 + \frac{N-1}{N}\rho_{i,j}\sigma^2\right]^{1/2}, \tag{9}$$

---

[18] Also see Barber and Lyon (1997), Kothari and Warner (1997), Fama (1998), Lyon et al. (1999), Mitchell and Stafford (2000), and Jegadeesh and Karceski (2004).
[19] See Schipper and Thompson (1983), Collins and Dent (1984), Sefcik and Thompson (1986), Bernard (1987), Mitchell and Stafford (2000), Brav (2000), and Jegadeesh and Karceski (2004).

where N is the number of sample firms, σ^2 is the variance of abnormal returns, which is assumed to be the same for all firms; and $\rho_{i,j}$ is the correlation between firm i and js abnormal returns, which is also assumed to be the same across all firms. The second term in the square brackets in Equation (9) is due to the cross-dependence in the data, and it would be absent if the standard deviation is calculated assuming independence in the data. The bias in the standard deviation assuming independence is given by the ratio of the "true" standard deviation allowing for dependence to the standard deviation assuming independence:

$$\frac{\sigma_{AR}(\text{Dependence})}{\sigma_{AR}(\text{Independence})} = [1 + (N-1)\rho_{i,j}]^{1/2}. \tag{10}$$

The ratio in Equation (10) is the factor by which the standard error in a test for the significance of abnormal performance is understated and therefore the factor by which the test statistic (e.g., t-statistic) itself is overstated. The ratio is increasing in the pairwise cross-correlation, $\rho_{i,j}$. Empirical estimates of the average pairwise correlation between annual BHARs of event firms are about 0.02 to 0.03 (see Mitchell and Stafford, 2000). The average pairwise correlation in multiyear BHARs is likely to be greater than that for annual returns because Bernard (1987, Table 1) reports that the average cross-correlations increase with return horizon. Assuming the average pairwise cross-sectional correlation to be only 0.02, for a sample of 100, the ratio in Equation (4) is 1.73, and it increases with both sample size and the degree of cross-correlation. Since the sample size in many long-horizon event studies is a few hundred securities, and the BHAR horizon is three-to-five years, even a modest degree of average cross-correlation in the data can inflate the test statistics by a factor of two or more. Therefore, accounting for cross-correlation in abnormal returns is crucial to drawing accurate statistical inferences in long-horizon event studies. Naturally, this has been a subject of intense interest among researchers.

4.4.2.3. Potential solutions One simple solution to the potential bias due to cross-correlation is to use the Jensen-alpha approach. It is immune to the bias arising from cross-correlated (abnormal) returns because of the use of calendar-time portfolios. Whatever the correlation among security returns, the event portfolio's time series of returns in calendar time accounts for that correlation. That is, the variability of portfolio returns is influenced by the cross-correlation in the data. The statistical significance of the Jensen alpha is based on the time-series variability of the portfolio return residuals. Since returns in an efficient market are serially uncorrelated (absent nontrading), on this basis the independence assumption in calculating the standard error and the t-statistic for the regression intercept (i.e., the Jensen alpha) seems quite appropriate. However, the evidence is that this method is misspecified in nonrandom samples (Lyon et al., 1999, Table 10). This is unfortunate, given that the method seems simple and direct. The reasons for the misspecification are unclear (see Lyon et al., 1999). Appropriate calibration under calendar-time methods probably warrants further investigation.

In the BHAR approach, estimating standard errors that account for the cross-correlation in long-horizon abnormal returns is not straightforward. As detailed below, there has been much discussion, and some interesting progress. Statistically precise estimates of pairwise cross-correlations are difficult to come by for the lack of availability of many time-series observations of long-horizon returns to accurately estimate the correlations (see Bernard, 1987). The difficulty is exacerbated by the fact that only a portion of the postevent-period might overlap with other firms. Researchers have developed bootstrap- and pseudoportfolio-based statistical tests that might account for the cross-correlations and lead to accurate inferences.

4.4.2.4. Cross-correlation and skewness   Lyon et al. (1999) develop a bootstrapped skewness-adjusted *t*-statistic to address the cross-correlation and skewness biases. The first step in the calculation is the skewness-adjusted *t*-statistic (see Johnson, 1978). This statistic adjusts the usual *t*-statistic by two terms that are a function of the skewness of the distribution of abnormal returns (see Equation (5) in Lyon et al., 1999, p. 174). Notwithstanding the skewness adjustment, the adjusted *t*-statistic indicates overrejection of the null and thus warrants a further refinement. The second step, therefore, is to construct a bootstrapped distribution of the skewness-adjusted *t*-statistic (Lyon et al., 1999; Sutton, 1993). To bootstrap the distribution, a researcher must draw a large number (e.g., 1000) of resamples from the original sample of abnormal returns and calculate the skewness-adjusted *t*-statistic using each resample. The resulting empirical distribution of the test statistics is used to ascertain whether the skewness-adjusted *t*-statistic for the original event sample falls in the $\alpha\%$ tails of the distribution to reject the null hypothesis of zero abnormal performance.

The pseudoportfolio-based statistical tests infer statistical significance of the event sample's abnormal performance by calibrating against an empirical distribution of abnormal performance constructed using repeatedly sampled pseudoportfolios.[20] The empirical distribution of average abnormal returns on the pseudoportfolios is under the null hypothesis of zero abnormal performance. The empirical distribution is generated by repeatedly constructing matched firm samples with replacement. The matching is on the basis of characteristics thought to be correlated with the expected rate of return. Following the Fama and French (1993) three-factor model, matching on size and book-to-market as expected return determinants is quite common (e.g., Byun and Rozeff, 2003; Gompers and Lerner, 2003; Lyon et al., 1999). For each matched-sample portfolio, an average buy-and-hold abnormal performance is calculated as the raw return minus the benchmark portfolio return. It is quite common to use 1000–5000 resampled portfolios to construct the empirical distribution of the average abnormal returns on the matched-firm samples. This distribution yields empirical 5 and 95% cutoff probabilities against which the event-firm sample's performance is calibrated to

---

[20] See, for example, Brock et al. (1992), Ikenberry et al. (1995), Ikenberry et al. (1996), Lee (1997), Lyon et al. (1999), Mitchell and Stafford (2000), and Byun and Rozeff (2003).

infer whether or not the event-firm portfolio buy-and-hold abnormal return is statistically significant.

Unfortunately, the two approaches described above, which are aimed at correcting the bias in standard errors due to cross-correlated data, are not quite successful in their intended objective. Lyon et al. find pervasive test misspecification in nonrandom samples. Because the sample of firms experiencing a corporate event is not selected randomly by the researcher, correcting for the bias in the standard errors stemming from the nonrandomness of the event sample selection is not easy. In a strident criticism of the use of bootstrap- and pseudoportfolio-based tests, Mitchell and Stafford (2000, p. 307) conclude that long-term event studies often incorrectly "claim that bootstrapping solves all dependence problems. However, that claim is not valid. Event samples are clearly different from random samples. Event firms have chosen to participate in a major corporate action, while nonevent firms have chosen to abstain from the action. An empirical distribution created by randomly selecting firms with similar size-BE/ME characteristics does not replicate the covariance structure underlying the original event sample. In fact, the typical bootstrapping approach does not even capture the cross-sectional correlation structure related to industry effects ...." Jegadeesh and Karceski (2004, pp. 1–2) also note that the Lyon et al. (1999) approach is misspecified because it "assumes that the observations are cross-sectionally uncorrelated. This assumption holds in random samples of event firms, but is violated in nonrandom samples. In nonrandom samples where the returns for event firms are positively correlated, the variability of the test statistics is larger than in a random sample. Therefore, if the empiricist calibrates the distribution of the test statistics in random samples and uses the empirical cutoff points for nonrandom samples, the tests reject the null hypothesis of no abnormal performance too often."

4.4.2.5. Autocorrelation   To overcome the weaknesses in prior tests, Jegadeesh and Karceski (2004) propose a correlation and heteroskedasticity-consistent test. The key innovation in their approach is to estimate the cross-correlations using a monthly time series of portfolio long-horizon returns (see Jegadeesh and Karceski, 2004, Section II. A for details). Because the series is monthly, but the monthly observations contain long-horizon returns, the time series exhibits autocorrelation that is due to overlapping return data. The autocorrelation is, of course, due to cross-correlation in return data. The autocorrelation is expected to be positive for $H - 1$ lags, where H is the number of months in the long horizon. The length of the time series of monthly observations depends on the sample period during which corporate events being examined take place. Because of autocorrelation in the time series of monthly observations, the usual t-statistic that is a ratio of the average abnormal return to the standard deviation of the time series of the monthly observations would be understated. To obtain an unbiased t-statistic, the covariances (i.e., the variance-covariance matrix) should be taken into account. Jegadeesh and Karceski (2004) use the Hansen and Hodrick (1980) estimator of the variance-covariance matrix assuming homoskedasticity. They also use a heteroskedasticity-consistent estimator that "generalizes White's heteroskedasticity-consistent estimator and allows for serial covariances to be non-zero" (p. 8). In both random and nonrandom (industry) samples the Jegadeesh and Karceski (2004) tests perform quite well, and we believe these might be the most appropriate to reduce misspecification in tests of long-horizon event studies.

4.4.3. The bottom line

Despite positive developments in BHAR calibration methods, two general long-horizon problems remain. The first concerns power. Jegadeesh and Karceski (2004) report that their tests show no increase in power relative to that of the test employed in previous research, which already had low power. For example, even with seemingly huge cumulative abnormal performance (25% over 5 years) in a sample of 200 firms, the rejection rate of the null is typically under 50% (see their Table 6).

Second, specification issues remain. For example, as discussed earlier (Section 3.6), events are generally likely to be associated with variance increases, which are equivalent to abnormal returns varying across sample securities. Previous literature shows that variance increases induce misspecification, and can cause the null hypothesis to be rejected far too often. Thus, whether a high level of measured abnormal performance is due to chance or mispricing (or a bad model) is still difficult to empirically determine, unless the test statistic is adjusted downward to reflect the variance shift. Solutions to the variance shift issue include such intuitive procedures as forming subsamples with common characteristics related to the level of abnormal performance (e.g., earnings increase vs. decrease subsamples). With smaller subsamples, however, specification issues unrelated to variance shifts become more relevant. Moreover, the importance of examining specification for nonrandom samples cannot be overemphasized.

Given the various power and specification issues, a challenge that remains for the profession is to continue to refine long-horizon methods. Whether calendar time, BHAR methods or some combination can best address long-horizon issues remains an open question.

References

Baker, M., R. Talliaferro and J. Wurgler, 2004, "Pseudo Market Timing and Predictive Regression," Working Paper #10823, National Bureau of Economic Research.

Baker, M., R. Talliaferro and J. Wurgler, 2006, "Predicting Returns with Managerial Decision Variables: Is There a Large-Sample Bias?," *Journal of Finance*, 61, 1711–1730.

Ball, R. and P. Brown, 1968, "An Empirical Evaluation of Accounting Income Numbers," *Journal of Accounting Research*, 6, 159–177.

Ball, R. and S. Kothari, 1989, "Nonstationary Expected Returns: Implications for Tests of Market Efficiency and Serial Correlation in Returns," *Journal of Financial Economics*, 25, 51–74.

Ball, R., S. Kothari and J. Shanken, 1995, "Problems in Measuring Portfolio Performance: An Application to Contrarian Investment Strategies," *Journal of Financial Economics*, 38, 79–107.

Banz, R., 1981, "The Relationship Between Return and Market Value of Common Stocks," *Journal of Financial Economics*, 9, 3–18.

Barber, B. and J. Lyon, 1996, "Detecting Abnormal Operating Performance: The Empirical Power and Specification of Test Statistics," *Journal of Financial Economics*, 41, 359–399.

Barber, B. and J. Lyon, 1997, "Detecting Long-Run Abnormal Stock Returns: The Empirical Power and Specification of Test Statistics," *Journal of Financial Economics*, 43, 341–372.

Barberis, N., A. Shleifer and R. Vishny, 1998, "A Model of Investor Sentiment," *Journal of Financial Economics*, 49, 307–343.

Basu, S., 1977, "The Investment Performance of Common Stocks in Relation to Their Price-Earnings Ratios: A Test of the Efficient Markets Hypothesis," *Journal of Finance*, 32, 663–682.

Basu, S., 1983, "The Relationship Between Earnings Yield, Market Value, and Returns for NYSE Common Stocks: Further Evidence," *Journal of Financial Economics*, 12, 129–156.

Beaver, W., 1968, "The Information Content of Annual Earnings Announcements," *Journal of Accounting Research Supplement*, 6, 67–92.

Bernard, V., 1987, "Cross-Sectional Dependence and Problems in Inference in Market-Based Accounting Research," *Journal of Accounting Research*, 25, 1–48.

Blume, M. and R. Stambaugh, 1983, "Biases in Computed Returns: An Application to the Size Effect," *Journal of Financial Economics*, 12, 387–404.

Boudoukh, J., M. Richardson and R. Whitelaw, 2006, "The Myth of Long-Horizon Predictability," Working Paper, New York University.

Brav, A., 2000, "Inference in Long-Horizon Event Studies: A Bayesian Approach with Application to Initial Public Offerings," *Journal of Finance*, 55, 1979–2016.

Brav, A. and P. Gompers, 1997, "Myth or Reality? The Long-Run Underperformance of Initial Public Offerings: Evidence from Venture and Nonventure Capital-Backed Companies," *Journal of Finance*, 52, 1791–1821.

Brennan, M. and A. Subrahmanyam, 1996, "Market Microstructure and Asset Pricing: On the Compensation for Illiquidity in Stock Returns," *Journal of Financial Economics*, 41, 441–464.

Brock, W., J. Lakonishok and B. LeBaron, 1992, "Simple Trading Rules and the Stochastic Properties of Stock Returns," *Journal of Finance*, 47, 1731–1764.

Brown, S. and J. Warner, 1980, "Measuring Security Price Performance," *Journal of Financial Economics*, 8, 205–258.

Brown, S. and J. Warner, 1985, "Using Daily Stock Returns: The Case of Event Studies," *Journal of Financial Economics*, 14, 3–31.

Byun, J. and M. Rozeff, 2003, "Long-Run Performance After Stock Splits: 1927 to 1996," *Journal of Finance*, 58, 1063–1085.

Campbell, C. and C. Wasley, 1993, "Measuring Security Price Performance Using Daily NASDAQ Returns," *Journal of Financial Economics*, 33, 73–92.

Campbell, C. and C. Wasley, 1996, "Measuring Abnormal Trading Volume for Samples of NYSE/ASE and NASDAQ Securities Using Parametric and Nonparametric Test Statistics," *Review of Quantitative Finance and Accounting*, 6, 309–326.

Campbell, J., A. Lo and A. C. MacKinlay, 1997, *The Econometrics of Financial Markets*, Princeton University Press, Princeton, NJ.

Campbell, J., M. Lettau, B. Malkiel and Y. Xu, 2001, "Have Individual Stocks Become More Volatile? An Empirical Exploration of Idiosyncratic Risk," *Journal of Finance*, 56, 1–43.

Carhart, M., 1997, "On Persistence in Mutual Fund Performance," *Journal of Finance*, 52, 57–82.

Chan, K., 1988, "On the Contrarian Investment Strategy," *Journal of Business*, 61, 147–163.

Chopra, N., J. Lakonishok and J. Ritter, 1992, "Measuring Abnormal Performance: Does the Market Overreact," *Journal of Financial Economics*, 32, 235–268.

Chordia, T., A. Goyal, G. Sadka, R. Sadka and L. Shivakumar, 2006, "Liquidity and the Post-Earnings-Announcement Drift," Working Paper, LBS.

Cochrane, J., 2006, "The Dog That Did Not Bark: A Defense of Return Predictability," Working Paper, University of Chicago and NBER.

Collins, D. and W. Dent, 1984, "A Comparison of Alternative Testing Methodologies Used in Capital Market Research," *Journal of Accounting Research*, 22, 48–84.

Corrado, C., 1989, "A Nonparametric Test for Abnormal Security-Price Performance in Event Studies," *Journal of Financial Economics*, 23, 385–395.

Daniel, K., M. Grinblatt, S. Titman and R. Wermers, 1997, "Measuring Mutual Fund Performance with Characteristic-Based Benchmarks," *Journal of Finance*, 52, 1035–1058.

Daniel, K., D. Hirshleifer and A. Subrahmanyam, 1998, "Investor Psychology and Security Market Under- and Overreactions," *Journal of Finance*, 53, 1839–1885.

Daniel, K., D. Hirshleifer and S. Teoh, 2002, "Investor Psychology in Capital Markets: Evidence and Policy Implications," *Journal of Monetary Economics*, 49, 139–209.

DeBondt, W. and R. Thaler, 1985, "Does the Stock Market Overreact?," *Journal of Finance*, 40, 793–805.

DeBondt, W. and R. Thaler, 1987, "Further Evidence of Investor Overreaction and Stock Market Seasonality," *Journal of Finance*, 42, 557–581.

Dechow, P., R. Sloan and A. Sweeney, 1995, "Detecting Earnings Management," *The Accounting Review*, 70, 3–42.

De Long, J., A. Shleifer, R. Vishny and R. Waldman, 1990a, "Noise Trader Risk in Financial Markets," *Journal of Political Economy*, 98, 703–738.

De Long, J., A. Shleifer, R. Vishny, R. Waldman, 1990b, "Positive Feedback Investment Strategies and Destabilizing Rational Speculation," *Journal of Finance*, 45, 375–395.

Eckbo, B. and O. Norli, 2005, "Liquidity Risk, Leverage and Long-Run IPO Returns," *Journal of Corporate Finance*, 11, 1–35.

Eckbo, B., V. Maksimovic and J. Williams, 1990, "Consistent Estimation of Cross-Sectional Models in Event Studies," *Review of Financial Studies*, 3, 343–365.

Eckbo, B., R. Masulis and O. Norli, 2000, "Seasoned Public Offerings: Resolution of the 'New Issues Puzzle'," *Journal of Financial Economics*, 56, 251–291.

Eckbo, B., R. Masulis and O. Norli, 2006, "Security Offerings," In B. E. Eckbo (Ed.), *Handbook of Corporate Finance: Empirical Corporate Finance*, Vol. 1, Chapter 6, Elsevier/North-Holland, Amsterdam, Handbook in Finance Series.

Fama, E., 1970, "Efficient Capital Markets: A Review of Theory and Empirical Work," *Journal of Finance*, 25, 383–417.

Fama, E., 1991, "Efficient Capital Markets: II," *Journal of Finance*, 46, 1575–1617.

Fama, E., 1998, "Market Efficiency, Long-Term Returns, and Behavioral Finance," *Journal of Financial Economics*, 49, 283–306.

Fama, E. and K. French, 1993, "Common Risk Factors in the Returns on Stocks and Bonds," *Journal of Financial Economics*, 33, 3–56.

Fama, E., L. Fisher, M. Jensen and R. Roll, 1969, "The Adjustment of Stock Prices to New Information," *International Economic Review*, 10, 1–21.

Gompers, P. and J. Lerner, 2003, "The Really Long-Run Performance of Initial Public Offerings: The Pre-Nasdaq Evidence," *Journal of Finance*, 58, 1355–1392.

Goyal, A. and I. Welch, 2003, "Predicting the Equity Premium with Dividend Ratios," *Management Science*, 49, 639–654.

Goyal, A. and I. Welch, 2005, "A Comprehensive Look at the Empirical Performance of Equity Premium Prediction," Working Paper, Brown University.

Hansen, L. and R. Hodrick, 1980, "Forward Rates as Optimal Predictors of Future Spot Rates: An Econometric Analysis," *Journal of Political Economy*, 88, 829–853.

Hirshleifer, D., 2001, "Investor Psychology and Asset Pricing," *Journal of Finance*, 56, 1533–1598.

Hong, H. and J. Stein, 1999, "A Unified Theory of Underreaction, Momentum Trading, and Overreaction in Asset Markets," *Journal of Finance*, 54, 2143–2184.

Ibbotson, R., 1975, "Price Performance of Common Stock New Issues," *Journal of Financial Economics*, 2, 235–272.

Ikenberry, D., J. Lakonishok and T. Vermaelen, 1995, "The Underreaction to Open Market Share Repurchases," *Journal of Financial Economics*, 39, 181–208.

Ikenberry, D., G. Rankine and E. Stice, 1996, "What Do Stock Splits Really Signal?," *Journal of Financial and Quantitative Analysis*, 31, 357–376.

Jaffe, J., 1974, "Special Information and Insider Trading," *Journal of Business*, 47, 411–428.

Jarrell, G., J. Brickley and J. Netter, 1988, "The Market for Corporate Control—The Empirical Evidence Since 1980," *Journal of Economic Perspectives*, 2, 49–68.

Jegadeesh, N. and J. Karceski, 2004, "Long-Run Performance Evaluation: Correlation and Heteroskedasticity-Consistent Tests," Working Paper, Emory University.

Jensen, M. and R. Ruback, 1983, "The Market for Corporate Control—The Scientific Evidence," *Journal of Financial Economics*, 11, 5–50.

Jensen, M. and J. Warner, 1988, "The Distribution of Power Among Corporate Managers, Shareholders, and Directors," *Journal of Financial Economics*, 20, 3–24.

Johnson, N., 1978, "Modified t Tests and Confidence Intervals for Symmetrical Populations," *Journal of American Statistical Association*, 73, 536–544.

Jones, C. and R. Litzenberger, 1970, "Quarterly Earnings Reports and Intermediate Stock Price Trends," *Journal of Finance*, 25, 143–148.

Kothari, S., 2001, "Capital Markets Research in Accounting," *Journal of Accounting and Economics*, 31, 105–231.

Kothari, S. and J. Warner, 1997, "Measuring Long-Horizon Security Price Performance," *Journal of Financial Economics*, 43, 301–339.

Kothari, S., A. Leone and C. Wasley, 2005, "Performance-Matched Discretionary accruals," *Journal of Accounting and Economics*, 39, 163–197.

Lakonishok, J., A. Shleifer and R. Vishny, 1994, "Contrarian Investment, Extrapolation, and Risk," *Journal of Finance*, 49, 1541–1578.

Lee, I., 1997, "Do Firms Knowingly Sell Overvalued Equity?," *Journal of Finance*, 52, 1439–1466.

Li, K. and N. Prabhala, 2007, "Self-Selection Models in Corporate Finance," In B. E. Eckbo (Ed.), *Handbook of Corporate Finance: Empirical Corporate Finance*, Vol. 1, Chapter 2, Elsevier/North-Holland, Amsterdam.

Loughran, T. and J. Ritter, 2000, "Uniformly Least Powerful Tests of Market Efficiency," *Journal of Financial Economics*, 55, 361–389.

Lyon, J., B. Barber and C. Tsai, 1999, "Improved Methods of Tests of Long-Horizon Abnormal Stock Returns," *Journal of Finance*, 54, 165–201.

MacKinlay, A. C., 1997, "Event Studies in Economics and Finance," *Journal of Economic Literature*, 35, 13–39.

Malatesta, P. and R. Thompson, 1985, "Partially Anticipated Events: A Model of Stock Price Reactions with an Application to Corporate Acquisitions," *Journal of Financial Economics*, 14, 237–250.

Mandelker, G., 1974, "Risk and Return: The Case of Merging Firms," *Journal of Financial Economics*, 1, 303–335.

Mitchell, M. and E. Stafford, 2000, "Managerial Decisions and Long-Term Stock Price Performance," *Journal of Business*, 73, 287–329.

Neyman, J. and E. Pearson, 1928, "On the Use and Interpretation of Certain Test Criteria for Purposes of Statistical Inference, Part I," *Biometrika*, 20A, 175–240.

Ng, J., T. Rusticus and R. Verdi, 2006, "Implications of Transaction Costs for the Post-Earnings-Announcement Drift," Working Paper, MIT Sloan School of Management.

Pastor, L. and R. Stambaugh, 2003, "Liquidity Risk and Expected Stock Returns," *Journal of Political Economy*, 111, 642–685.

Patell, J., 1976, "Corporate Forecasts of Earnings Per Share and Stock Price Behavior: Empirical Tests," *Journal of Accounting Research*, 14, 246–276.

Pearson, E., 1929a, "The Distribution of Frequency Constants in Small Samples from Symmetrical Distributions," *Biometrika*, 21, 356–360.

Pearson, E., 1929b, "The Distribution of Frequency Constants in Small Samples from Non-Normal Symmetrical and Skew Populations," *Biometrika*, 21, 259–286.

Petersen, M., 2005, "Estimating Standard Errors in Finance Panel Data Sets: Comparing Approaches," Working Paper, Northwestern University.

Roll, R., 1983, "On Computing Mean Returns and the Small Firm Premium," *Journal of Financial Economics*, 12, 371–386.

Ross, S., 1976, *A First Course in Probability*, Macmillan, New York.

Sadka, R., 2006, "Momentum and Post-Earnings-Announcement Drift Anomalies: The Role of Liquidity Risk," *Journal of Financial Economics*, 80, 309–349.

Schipper, K. and R. Thompson, 1983, "The Impact of Merger-Related Relationships on the Shareholders of Acquiring Firms," *Journal of Accounting Research*, 21, 184–221.

Schultz, P., 2003, "Pseudo Market Timing and the Long-Run Underperformance of IPOs," *Journal of Finance*, 58, 483–517.

Schwert, G. W., 2001, "Anomalies and Market Efficiency," In G. Constantinides, M. Harris, R. Stulz (Eds.), *Handbook of the Economics of Finance*, pp. 939–974, North-Holland, Amsterdam.

Sefcik, S. and R. Thompson, 1986, "An Approach to Statistical Inference in Cross-Sectional Models with Security Abnormal Returns as Dependent Variables," *Journal of Accounting Research*, 24, 316–334.

Shleifer, A., 2000, *Inefficient Markets: An Introduction to Behavioral Finance*, Oxford University Press, London.

Shliefer, A. and R. Vishny, 1997, "The Limits of Arbitrage," *Journal of Finance*, 52, 35–55.

Smith, C., 1986, "Investment Banking and the Capital Acquisition Process," *Journal of Financial Economics*, 15, 3–29.

Sutton, C., 1993, "Computer-Intensive Methods for Tests About the Mean of an Asymmetrical Distribution," *Journal of American Statistical Association*, 88, 802–808.

Teoh, S., I. Welch and T. Wong, 1998, "Earnings Management and the Long-Run Performance of Initial Public Offerings," *Journal of Finance*, 53, 1935–1974.

Thompson, R., 1995, "Empirical Methods of Event Studies in Corporate Finance," In R. Jarrow, V. Maksimovic, B. Ziemba (Eds.), *Finance. Series of Handbooks in Operations Research and Management Science*, pp. 1017–1072, North-Holland, Amsterdam.

Viswanathan, S. and B. Wei, 2004, "Endogenous Event and Long Run Returns," Working Paper, Duke University.

Chapter 3

SELF-SELECTION MODELS IN CORPORATE FINANCE[*]

KAI LI

Sauder School of Business, University of British Columbia, Vancouver, British Columbia, Canada

NAGPURNANAND R. PRABHALA

Robert H. Smith School of Business, University of Maryland, College Park, Maryland, USA

Contents

[*] We thank N.K. Chidambaran, Craig Doidge, Espen Eckbo, Andrew Karolyi, Gordon Phillips, Vojislav Maksimovic, Jeffrey Smith, and Xinlei Zhao without implicating them for any errors or omissions, which remain ours. Li acknowledges the financial support from the Social Sciences and Humanities Research Council of Canada, and the W.M. Young Chair in Finance from the Sauder School of Business at UBC. Li also wishes to thank the support and hospitality of the MIT Sloan School of Management where she completed most of her work on this chapter.

This article originally appeared in B. E. Eckbo (ed.), *Handbook of Corporate Finance: Empirical Corporate Finance*, Vol. 1, Ch. 2, pp. 37–86 (2007).
Corporate Takeovers, Volume 1
Edited by B. Espen Eckbo
DOI: 10.1016/B978-0-12-381983-3.00003-4

Abstract

Corporate finance decisions are not made at random, but are usually deliberate decisions by firms or their managers to *self-select* into their preferred choices. This chapter reviews econometric models of self-selection. The review is organized into two parts. The first part reviews econometric models of self-selection, focusing on the key assumptions of different models and the types of applications they may be best suited for. Part two reviews empirical applications of selection models in the areas of corporate investment, financing, and financial intermediation. We find that self-selection is a rapidly growing area in corporate finance, partly reflecting its recognition as a pervasive feature of corporate finance decisions, but more importantly, the increasing recognition of selection models as unique tools for understanding, modeling, and testing the role of private information in corporate finance.

Keywords

selection, private information, switching regression, treatment effect, matching, propensity score, Bayesian selection methods, panel data, event study, underwriting, investment banking, diversification

JEL classification: C24, C25

1. Introduction

Corporate finance concerns the financing and investment choices made by firms and a broad swathe of decisions within these broad choices. For instance, firms pick their target capital structure, and to achieve the target, must make several choices including issue timing of security issues, structural features of the securities issued, the investment bank chosen to underwrite it, and so on. These choices are not usually random, but are deliberate decisions by firms or their managers to *self-select* into their preferred choices. This chapter reviews econometric models of self-selection. We review the approaches used to model self-selection in corporate finance and the substantive findings obtained by implementing selection methods.

Self-selection has a rather mixed history in corporate finance. The fact that there is self-selection is probably not news; indeed, many papers at least implicitly acknowledge its existence. However, the literature differs on whether to account for self-selection using formal econometric methods, and why one should do so. One view of self-selection is that it is an errant nuisance, a "correction" that must be made to prevent other parameter estimates from being biased. Selection is itself of little economic interest under this view. In other applications, self-selection is itself of central economic interest, because models of self-selection represent one way of incorporating and controlling for unobservable private information that influences corporate finance decisions. Both perspectives find expression in the literature, although an increasing emphasis in recent work reflects the positive view in which selection models are used to construct interesting tests for private information.

Our review is organized into two parts. Part I focuses on econometric models of self-selection. We approach selection models from the viewpoint of a corporate finance researcher who is implementing selection models in an empirical application. We formalize the notion of self-selection and overview several approaches towards modeling it, including reduced form models, structural approaches, matching methods, fixed effect estimators, and Bayesian methods. As the discussion clarifies, the notion of selection is not monolithic. No single model universally models or accounts for all forms of selection, so there is no one "fix" for selection. Instead, there are a variety of approaches, each of which makes its own economic and statistical assumptions. We focus on the substantive economic assumptions underlying the different approaches to illustrate what each can and cannot do and the type of applications a given approach may be best suited for. We do not say much on estimation, asymptotic inference, or computational issues, but refer the reader to excellent texts and articles on these matters.

Part II of our review examines corporate finance applications of self-selection models. We cover a range of topics such as mergers and acquisitions, stock splits, equity offerings, underwriting, analyst behavior, share repurchases, and venture capital. Our objective is to illustrate the wide range of corporate finance settings in which selection arises and the different econometric approaches employed in modeling it.

Here, we focus on applications published in the last decade or so, and on articles in which self-selection is a major component of the overall results.[1]

2. Modeling self-selection

This portion of our review discusses econometric models of self-selection. Our intention is not to summarize the entire range of available models and their estimation. Rather, we narrow our focus to models that have been applied in the corporate finance literature, and within these models, we focus on the substantive assumptions made by each specification. From the viewpoint of the empirical researcher, this is the first order issue in deciding what approach suits a given application in corporate finance. We do not touch upon asymptotic theory, estimation, and computation. These important issues are well covered in excellent textbooks.[2]

We proceed as follows. Section 1 describes the statistical issue raised by self-selection, the wedge between the population distribution and the distribution within a selected sample. Sections 2–6 develop the econometric models that can address selection. Section 2 discusses a baseline model for self-selection, the "Heckman" selection model analyzed in Heckman (1979), a popular modeling choice in corporate finance.[3] We discuss identification issues related to the model, which are important but not frequently discussed or justified explicitly in corporate finance applications. Because the Heckman setting is so familiar in corporate finance, we use it to develop a key point of this survey, the analogy between econometric models of self-selection and private information models in corporate finance. Section 3 considers switching regressions and structural self-selection models. While these models generalize the Heckman selection model in some ways, they also bring additional baggage in terms of economic and statistical assumptions that we discuss.

We then turn to other approaches towards modeling selection. Section 4 discusses matching models, which are methods *du jour* in the most recent applications. The popularity of matching models can be attributed to their relative simplicity, easy interpretation of coefficients, and minimal structure with regard to specification. However, these gains come at a price. Matching models make the strong economic assumption that unobservable private information is irrelevant. This assumption may not be realistic in many corporate finance applications. In contrast, selection models explicitly model and incorporate private information. A second point we develop is that while matching methods are often motivated by the fact that they yield easily

---

[1] Our attempt is to capture the overall flavor of self-selection models as they stand in corporate finance as of the writing. We apologize to any authors whose work we have overlooked: no slight is intended.

[2] The venerable reference, Maddala (1983), continues to be remarkably useful, though its notation is often (and annoyingly, to the empirical researcher) different from that used in other articles and software packages. Newer material is covered in Wooldridge (2002) and Greene (2003).

[3] Labeling any one model as "the" Heckman model surely does disservice to the many other contributions of James Heckman. We choose this label following common usage in the literature.

interpretable *treatment effects*, selection methods also estimate treatment effects with equal ease. Our review of methodology closes by briefly touching upon fixed effect models in Section 5 and Bayesian approaches to selection in Section 6.

2.1. Self-selection: the statistical issue

To set up the self-selection issue, assume that we wish to estimate parameters j of the regression

$$Y_i = X_i \beta + \varepsilon_i \tag{1}$$

for a population of firms. In Equation (1), Y_i is the dependent variable, which is typically an *outcome* such as profitability or return. The variables explaining outcomes are X_i, and the error term is ε_i. If ε_i satisfies usual classical regression conditions, standard OLS/GLS procedures consistently estimate β.

Now consider a subsample of firms who self-select choice E. For this subsample, Equation (1) can be written as

$$Y_i \mid E = X_i \beta + \varepsilon_i \mid E. \tag{2}$$

The difference between Equations (2) and (1) is at the heart of the self-selection problem. Equation (1) is a specification written for the population but Equation (2) is written for a subset of firms, those that self-select choice E. If self-selecting firms are not random subsets of the population, the usual OLS/GLS estimators applied to Equation (2), are no longer consistent estimators of β.

Accounting for self-selection consists of two steps. Step 1 specifies a model for self-selection, using economic theory to model why some firms select E while others do not. While this specification step is not often discussed extensively in applications, it is critical because the assumptions involved ultimately dictate what econometric model should be used in the empirical application. Step 2 ties the random variable(s) driving self-selection to the outcome variable Y.

2.2. The baseline Heckman selection model

2.2.1. The econometric model

Early corporate finance applications of self-selection are based on the model analyzed in Heckman (1979). We spend some time developing this model because most other specifications used in the finance literature can be viewed as extensions of the Heckman model in various directions.

In the conventional perspective of self-selection, the key issue is that we have a regression such as Equation (1) that is well specified for a population but it must be estimated using subsamples of firms that self-select into choice E. To estimate population parameters from self-selected subsamples, we first specify a self-selection mechanism. This usually takes the form of a probit model in which firm i chooses E if the net benefit from doing so, a scalar W_i, is positive. Writing the selection variable W_i as a function of explanatory variables Z_i, which are assumed for now to be exogenous,[4] we have the system

$$C = E \equiv W_i = Z_i\gamma + \eta_i > 0, \tag{3}$$

$$C = NE \equiv W_i = Z_i\gamma + \eta_i \leq 0, \tag{4}$$

$$Y_i = X_i\beta + \varepsilon_i, \tag{5}$$

where Z_i denotes publicly known information influencing a firm's choice, γ is a vector of probit coefficients, and η_i is orthogonal to public variables Z_i. In the standard model, Y_i is observed only when a firm picks one of E or NE (but not both), so Equation (5) would require the appropriate conditioning. Assuming that η_i and ε_i are bivariate normal, the likelihood function and the maximum likelihood estimators for Equations (3)–(5) follow, although a simpler two-step procedure (Greene, 1981; Heckman, 1979) is commonly used for estimation. Virtually all applied work is based on the bivariate normal structure discussed above.

2.2.2. Self-selection and private information

In the above setup, self-selection is a nuisance problem. We model it because not doing so leads to inconsistent estimates of parameters β in regression (1). Self-selection is, by itself, of little interest. However, this situation is frequently reversed in corporate finance, because tests for self-selection can be viewed as tests of private information theories. We develop this point in the context of the Heckman (1979) model outlined above, but we emphasize that this private information interpretation is more general.

We proceed as follows. Following a well-established tradition in econometrics, Section 2.2.1 presents selection as an omitted variable problem. Section 2.2.2 interprets the omitted variable as a proxy for unobserved private information. Thus, including the omitted self-selection variable controls for and tests for the significance of private information in explaining ex post outcomes of corporate finance choices.

2.2.2.1. Selection: an omitted variable problem Suppose that firm i self-selects choice E. For firm i, we can take expectations of Equation (5) and write

$$Y_i \mid E = X_i\beta + (\varepsilon_i \mid Z_i\gamma + \eta_i > 0) \tag{6}$$

$$Y_i \mid E = X_i\beta + \pi(\eta_i \mid Z_i\gamma + \eta_i > 0) + v_i. \tag{7}$$

---

[4] Thus, we preclude for now the possibility that Z includes the outcome variable Y. This restriction can be relaxed at a cost, as we show in later sections.

Equation (7) follows from the standard result that $\varepsilon_i|\eta_i = \pi\eta_i + v_i$, where π is the coefficient in the regression of ε_i on η_i, and v_i is an orthogonal zero-mean error term.[5] Given the orthogonality and zero-mean properties of v_i, we can take expectations of Equation (7) and obtain the regression model

$$E(Y_i \mid E) = X_i\beta + \pi E(\eta_i \mid Z_i\gamma + \eta_i > 0) \tag{8}$$

and a similar model for firms choosing not to announce E,

$$E(Y_i \mid NE) = X_i\beta + \pi E(\eta_i \mid Z_i\gamma + \eta_i \leq 0). \tag{9}$$

Equations (8) and (9) can be compactly rewritten as

$$E(Y_i \mid C) = X_i\beta + \pi\lambda_C(Z_i\gamma) \tag{10}$$

where $C \in \{E, NE\}$ and $\lambda_C(\cdot)$ is the conditional expectation of η_i given C. In particular, if η and ε are bivariate normal, as is standard in the bulk of the applied work, $\lambda_E(\cdot) = \phi(\cdot)/\Phi(\cdot)$ and $\lambda_{NE}(\cdot) = -\phi(\cdot)/[1 - \Phi(\cdot)]$ (Greene, 2003, p. 759).

A comparison of Equations (1) and (10) clarifies why self-selection is an omitted variable problem. In the population regression in Equation (1), regressing outcome Y on X consistently estimates β. However, in self-selected samples, consistent estimation requires that we include an additional variable, the inverse Mills ratio $\lambda_C(\cdot)$. Thus, the process of correction for self-selection can be viewed as including an omitted variable.

2.2.2.2. *The omitted variable as private information*   In the probit models (3) and (4), η_i is the part of W_i not explained by public variables Z_i. Thus, η_i can be viewed as the private information driving the corporate financing decision being modeled. The ex ante expectation of η_i should be zero, and it is so, given that it has been defined as an error term in the probit model.

Ex post after firm i selects $C \in \{E, NE\}$, the expectations of η_i can be updated. The revised expectation, $E(\eta_i|C)$, is thus an updated estimate of the firm's private information. If we wished to test whether the private information in a firm's choice affected postchoice outcomes, we would regress outcome Y on $E(\eta_i|C)$. But $E(\eta_i|C) = \lambda_C(\cdot)$ is the inverse Mills ratio term that we add anyway to adjust for self-selection. Thus, correcting for self-selection is equivalent to testing for private information. The omitted variable used to correct for self-selection, $\lambda_C(\cdot)$, is an estimate of the private information underlying a firm's choice and testing its significance is a test of whether private information possessed by a firm explains ex post outcomes. In fact, a two-step procedure most commonly used to estimate selection models follows this logic.[6]

---

[5] Note that $\pi = \rho_{\eta\varepsilon}\sigma_\varepsilon$ where $\rho_{\eta\varepsilon}$ is the correlation between ε and η, and σ_ε^2 is the variance of ε.

[6] Step 1 estimates the probit models (3) and (4) to yield estimates of γ, say $\hat{\gamma}$, and hence the private information function $\lambda_C(Z_i\,\hat{\gamma})$. In step 2, we substitute the estimated private information in lieu of its true value in equation (10) and estimate it by OLS. Standard errors must be corrected for the fact that γ is estimated in the second step, along the lines of Heckman (1979), Greene (1981), and Murphy and Topel (1985).

Our main purpose of incorporating the above discussion of the Heckman model is to highlight the dual nature of self-selection "corrections." One can think of them as a way of accounting for a statistical problem. There is nothing wrong with this view. Alternatively, one can interpret self-selection models as a way of testing private information hypotheses, which is perhaps an economically more useful perspective of selection models in corporate finance. Selection models are clearly useful if private information is one's primary focus, but even if not, the models are useful as means of controlling for potential private information effects.

2.2.3. Specification issues

Implementing selection models in practice poses two key specification issues: the need for exclusion restrictions and the assumption that error terms are bivariate normal. While seemingly innocuous, these issues, particularly the exclusion question, are often important in empirical applications, and deserve some comment.

2.2.3.1. Exclusion restrictions In estimating Equations (3)–(5), researchers must specify two sets of variables: those determining selection (Z) and those determining the outcomes (X). An issue that comes up frequently is whether the two sets of variables can be identical. This knotty issue often crops up in practice. For instance, consider the self-selection event E in Equations (3) and (4) as the decision to acquire a target and suppose that the outcome variable in Equation (5) is postdiversification productivity. Variables such as firm size or the relatedness of the acquirer and the target could explain the acquisition decision. The same variables could also plausibly explain the ex post productivity gains from the acquisition. Thus, these variables could be part of both Z and X in Equations (3)–(5). Similar arguments can be made for several other explanatory variables: they drive firms' decision to self-select into diversification and the productivity gains after diversification. Do we need exclusion restrictions so that there is at least one variable driving selection, an instrument in Z that is not part of X?

Strictly speaking, exclusion restrictions are not necessary in the Heckman selection model because the model is identified by nonlinearity. The selection-adjusted outcome regression (10) regresses Y on X and $\lambda_C(Z'\gamma)$. If $\lambda_C(\bullet)$ were a linear function of Z, we would clearly need some variables in Z that are not part of X or the regressors would be collinear.[7] However, under the assumption of bivariate normal errors, $\lambda_C(\bullet)$ is a nonlinear function. As Heckman and Navarro-Lozano (2004) note, collinearity between the outcome regression function (here and usually the linear function $X_i\beta$) and the selection "control" function $\lambda_C(\bullet)$ is not a generic feature, so some degree of

---

[7] In this case, having a variable in X that is not part of Z does not help matters. If $\lambda_C(\bullet)$ is indeed linear, it is spanned by X whenever Z is spanned by X. Thus, we require extra variables that explain the decision to self-select but are unrelated to the outcomes following self-selection.

nonlinearity will probably allow the specification to be estimated even when there are no exclusion restrictions.

In practice, the identification issue is less clear-cut. The problem is that while $\lambda_C(\cdot)$ is a nonlinear function, it is roughly linear in parts of its domain. Hence, it is entirely possible that $\lambda_C(z'\gamma)$ has very little variation relative to the remaining variables in Equation (10), that is, X. This issue can clearly arise when the selection variables Z and outcome variables X are identical. However, it is important to realize that merely having extra instruments in Z may not solve the problem. The quality of the instruments also matters. Near-multicollinearity could still arise when the extra instruments in Z are weak and have limited explanatory power.

What should one do if there appears to be a multicollinearity issue? It is tempting to recommend that the researcher impose additional exclusion restrictions so that self-selection instruments Z contain unique variables not spanned by outcome variables X. Matters are, of course, a little more delicate. Either the exclusions make sense, in which case these should have been imposed in the first place. Alternatively, the restrictions are not reasonable, in which case it hardly makes sense to force them on a model merely to make it estimable. In any event, as a practical matter, it seems reasonable to always run diagnostics for multicollinearity while estimating selection models whether one imposes exclusion restrictions or not.

The data often offer one degree of freedom that can be used to work around particularly thorny cases of collinearity. Recall that the identification issue arises mainly because of the 1/0 nature of the selection variable W_i, which implies that we do not observe the error term η_i and we must take its expectation, which is the inverse Mills ratio term. However, if we could observe the *magnitude* of the selection variable W_i, we would introduce an independent source of variation in the selection correction term and in effect observe the private information η_i itself and use it in the regression in lieu of the inverse Mills ratio. Exclusion restrictions are no longer needed. This is often more than just a theoretical possibility. For instance, in analyzing a sample of firms that have received a bank loan, we do observe the bank loan amount conditional on a loan being made. Likewise, in analyzing equity offerings, we observe the fact that a firm made an equity offering and also the size of the offer. In hedging, we do observe (an estimate of) the extent of hedging given that a firm has hedged. This introduces an independent source of variation into the private information variable, freeing one from the reliance on nonlinearity for identification.

2.2.3.2. Bivariate normality   A second specification issue is that the baseline Heckman model assumes that errors are bivariate normal. In principle, deviations from normality could introduce biases in selection models, and these could sometimes be serious (for an early illustration, see Goldberger, 1983). If nonnormality is an issue, one alternative is to assume some specific nonnormal distribution (Lee, 1983; Maddala, 1983, Chapter 9.3). The problem is that theory rarely specifies a particular alternative distribution that is more appropriate. Thus, whether one uses a nonnormal distribution and the type of the distribution should be used are often driven by empirical features of the data. One approach that works around the need to specify parametric structures is to use semiparametric methods (e.g., Newey et al., 1990). Here, exclusion restrictions are necessary for identification.

Finance applications of nonnormal selection models remain scarce, so it is hard at this point of time to say whether nonnormality is a first order issue deserving particular attention in finance. In one application to calls of convertible bonds (Scruggs, 2007), the data were found to be nonnormal, but nonnormality made little difference to the major conclusions.

2.3. Extensions

We review two extensions of the baseline Heckman self-selection model, switching regressions and structural selection models. The first allows some generality in specifying regression coefficients across alternatives, while the second allows bidirectional simultaneity between self-selection and postselection outcomes.[8] Each of these extensions generalizes the Heckman model by allowing some flexibility in specification. However, it should be emphasized that the additional flexibility that is gained does not come for free. The price is that the alternative approaches place additional demands on the data or require more stringent economic assumptions. The plausibility and feasibility of these extra requirements should be carefully considered before selecting any alternative to the Heckman model for a given empirical application.

2.3.1. Switching regressions

As in Section 2, a probit model based on exogenous variables drives firms' self-selection decisions. The difference is that the outcome is now specified separately for firms selecting E and NE, so the single outcome regression (5) in system (3)–(5) is now replaced by two regressions. The complete model is as follows:

$$C = E \equiv Z_i \gamma + \eta_i > 0, \tag{11}$$

$$C = NE \equiv Z_i \gamma + \eta_i \leq 0, \tag{12}$$

$$Y_{E,i} = X_{E,i} \beta_E + \varepsilon_{E,i}, \tag{13}$$

$$Y_{NE,i} = X_{NE,i} \beta_{NE} + \varepsilon_{NE,i}, \tag{14}$$

where $C \in \{E, NE\}$. Along with separate outcome regression parameter vectors β_E and β_{NE}, there are also two covariance coefficients for the impact of private information on

---

[8] For instance, in modeling corporate diversification as a decision involving self-selection, structural models would allow self-selection to determine postdiversification productivity changes, as in the standard setup, but also allow anticipated productivity changes to impact the self-selection decision.

outcomes, the covariance between private information η and ε_E and that between η and ε_{NE}. Two-step estimation is again straightforward, and is usually implemented assuming that the errors $\{\eta_i, \varepsilon_{E,i}, \varepsilon_{NE,i}\}$ are trivariate normal.[9]

Given the apparent flexibility in specifying two outcome regressions (13) and (14) compared to the one outcome regression in the standard selection model, it is natural to ask why we do not always use the switching regression specification. There are three issues involved. First, theory should say whether there is a single population regression whose LHS and RHS variables are observed conditional on selection, as in the Heckman model, or whether we have two regimes in the population and the selection mechanism dictates which of the two we observe. In some applications, the switching regression is inappropriate: for instance, it is not consistent with the equilibrium modeled in Acharya (1988). A second issue is that the switching regression model requires us to observe outcomes of firms' choices in both regimes. This may not always be feasible because we only observe outcomes of firms self-selecting E but have little data on firms that choose not to self-select. For instance, if we were analyzing stock market responses to merger announcements as in Eckbo et al. (1990), implementing switching models literally requires us to obtain a sample of would-be acquirers that had never announced to the market and the market reaction on the dates that the markets realize that there is no merger forthcoming. These data may not always be available (Prabhala, 1997).[10] A final consideration is statistical power: imposing restrictions such as equality of coefficients $\{\beta, \pi\}$ for E and NE firms (when valid), lead to greater statistical power.

A key advantage of the switching regression framework is that we obtain more useful estimates of (unobserved) counterfactual outcomes. Specifically, if firm i chooses E, we observe outcome $Y_{E,i}$. However, we can ask what the outcome might have been had firm i chosen NE, the unobserved counterfactual, and what the gain is from firm i's having made choice E rather than NE. The switching regression framework provides an estimate. The net benefit from choosing E is the outcome of choosing E less the counterfactual had it chosen NE, that is, $Y_{E,i} - Y_{NE,i} = Y_{E,i} - X_i \beta_{NE} - \pi_{NE} \lambda_{NE} (Z_i \gamma)$. The *expected* gain for firm i is $X_i (\beta_E - \beta_{NE}) + (\pi_E \lambda_E(\cdot) - \pi_{NE} \lambda_{NE}(\cdot))$.[11]

---

[9] Write Equations (13) and (14) in regression form as

$$Y_{C,i} = X_{C,i} \beta_C + \pi_C \lambda_C(Z_i \gamma), \tag{15}$$

where $C \in \{E, NE\}$. The two-step estimator follows: the probit models (11) and (12) gives estimates of γ and hence the inverse Mills ratio $\lambda_C(\cdot)$ which is fed into regression (15) to give parameters $\{\beta_E, \beta_{NE}, \pi_E, \pi_{NE}\}$. As before, standard errors in the second step regression require adjustment because $\lambda_C(Z\hat{\gamma})$ is a generated regressor (Maddala, 1983, pp. 226–227).

[10] Li and McNally (2004) and Scruggs (2007) describe how we can use Bayesian methods to update priors on counterfactuals. More details on their approach are given in Section 6.

[11] This expression stands in contrast to the basic Heckman setup. There, in Equation (9), $\beta_E = \beta_{NE}$ and $\pi_E = \pi_{NE}$, so the expected difference is $\pi(\lambda_E(\cdot) - \lambda_{NE}(\cdot))$. There, the sign of the expected difference is fixed: it *must* equal to the sign of π because $\lambda_E(\cdot) - \lambda_{NE}(\cdot)) > 0$. Additionally, the expected difference in the setup of Section 2 does not vary with β or variables X that are not part of Z: here, it does. In short, the counterfactual choices that could be made but were not are less constrained in the switching regression setup.

We return to the counterfactuals issue when we deal with treatment effects and propensity scores. We make this point at this stage only to emphasize that selection models do estimate treatment effects. This fact is often not apparent when reading empirical applications, especially those employing matching methods.

2.3.2. Simultaneity in self-selection models

The models considered thus far presume that the variables Z explaining the self-selection decision (Equations (3) and (4) or Equations (11) and (12)) are exogenous. In particular, the bite of this assumption is to preclude the possibility that the decision to self-select choice C does not directly depend on the anticipated outcome from choosing C. This assumption is sometimes too strong in corporate finance applications. For instance, suppose we are interested in studying the diversification decision and that the outcome variable to be studied is firm productivity. The preceding models would assume that postmerger productivity does *not* influence the decision to diversify. If firms' decisions to diversify depend on their anticipated productivity changes, as theory might suggest (Maksimovic and Phillips, 2002), the assumption that Z is exogenous is incorrect.

The dependence of the decision to self-select on outcomes and the dependence of outcomes on the self-selection decision is essentially a problem of simultaneity. Structural selection models can account for simultaneity. We review two modeling choices. Roy (1951) model places few demands on the data but it places tighter restrictions on the mechanism by which self-selection occurs. More elaborate models are less stringent on the self-selection mechanism, but they demand more of the data, specifically instruments, exactly as in conventional simultaneous equations models.

2.3.2.1. The Roy model   The Roy model hardwires the dependence of self-selection on postselection outcomes. Firms self-select E or NE depending on which of the two alternatives yields the higher outcome. Thus, $\{E, Y_E\}$ is observed for firm i if $Y_{E,i} > Y_{NE,i}$. If, on the other hand, $Y_{NE,i} \geq Y_{E,i}$, we observe $\{NE, Y_{NE,i}\}$. The full model is

$$C = E \equiv Y_{E,i} > Y_{NE,i}, \tag{16}$$

$$C = NE \equiv Y_{E,i} \leq Y_{NE,i}, \tag{17}$$

$$Y_{E,i} = X_i \beta_E + \varepsilon_{E,i}, \tag{18}$$

$$Y_{NE,i} = X_i \beta_{NE} + \varepsilon_{NE,i}, \tag{19}$$

where the ε's are (as usual) assumed to be bivariate normal. The Roy model is no more demanding of the data than standard selection models. Two-step estimation is again fairly straightforward (Maddala, 1983, Chapter 9.1).

The Roy selection mechanism is rather tightly specified on two dimensions. One, the model exogenously imposes the restriction that firms selecting E would experience worse outcomes had they chosen NE and vice versa. This is often plausible. However, it is unclear whether this should be a hypothesis that one wants to test or a restriction that one imposes on the data. Two, the outcome differential is the *only* driver of the self-selection decision in the Roy setup. Additional flexibility can be introduced by loosening the model of self-selection. This extra flexibility is allowed in models to be described next, but it comes at the price of requiring additional exclusion restrictions for model identification.

2.3.2.2. Structural self-selection models   In the standard Heckman and switching regression models, the explanatory variables in the selection equation are exogenous. At the other end of the spectrum is the Roy model of Section 3.2.1, in which self-selection is driven solely by the endogenous variable. The interim case is one where selection is driven by both exogenous and outcome variables. This specification is

$$C = E \equiv Z_i\gamma + \delta(Y_{E,i} - Y_{NE,i}) + \eta_i > 0, \tag{20}$$

$$C = NE \equiv Z_i\gamma + \delta(Y_{E,i} - Y_{NE,i}) + \eta_i \leq 0, \tag{21}$$

$$Y_{E,i} = X_i\beta_E + \varepsilon_{E,i}, \tag{22}$$

$$Y_{NE,i} = X_i\beta_{NE} + \varepsilon_{NE,i}. \tag{23}$$

The structural model generalizes the switching regression model of Section 3.1, by incorporating the extra explanatory variable $Y_{E,i} - Y_{NE,i}$, the net outcome gain from choosing E over NE, in the selection decision, and generalizes the Roy model by permitting exogenous variables Z_i to enter the selection equation. Estimation of the system (20)–(23) follows the route one typically treads in simultaneous equations systems estimation—reduced form estimation followed by a step in which we replace the dependent variables appearing in the RHS by their fitted projections. A trivariate normal assumption is standard (Maddala, 1983, pp. 223–239). While structural self-selection models have been around for a while in the labor economics literature, particularly those studying unionism and the returns to education (see Maddala, 1983, Chapter 8), applications in finance are of very recent origin.

The structural self-selection model clearly generalizes every type of selection model considered before. The question is why one should not always use it. Equivalently, what additional restrictions or demands does it place on the data? Because it is a type of the switching regression model, it comes with all the baggage and informational requirements of the switching regression. As in simultaneous equations systems, instruments must be specified to identify the model. In the diversification example at the beginning of this section, the identification requirement demands that we have at least one instrument that determines whether a firm diversifies but does not determine the ex post productivity of the diversifying firm. The quality of one's estimates depends on the strength of the instrument, and all the caveats and discussion of Section 2.3.1 apply here.

2.4. Matching models and self-selection

This section reviews matching models, primarily those based on propensity scores. Matching models are becoming increasingly common in applied work. They represent an attractive means of inference because they are simple to implement and yield readily interpretable estimates of "treatment effects." However, matching models are based on fundamentally different set of assumptions relative to selection models. Matching models assume that unobserved private information is irrelevant to outcomes. In contrast, unobserved private information is the essence of self-selection models. We discuss these differences between selection and matching models as well as specific techniques used to implement matching models.

To clarify the issues, consider the switching regression selection model of Section 3.1, but relabel the choices to be consistent with the matching literature. Accordingly, firms are *treated* and belong to group *E* or *untreated* and belong to group *NE*. This assignment occurs according to the probit model

$$\Pr(E \mid Z) = \Pr(Z\gamma + \eta) > 0, \tag{24}$$

where Z denotes explanatory variables, γ is a vector of parameters and we drop firm subscript i for notational convenience. The probability of being untreated is $1 - \Pr(E|Z)$. We write postselection outcomes as Y_E for treated firms and Y_{NE} for untreated firms, and for convenience, write

$$Y_E = X_E\beta_E + \varepsilon_E, \tag{25}$$

$$Y_{NE} = X_{NE}\beta_{NE} + \varepsilon_{NE}, \tag{26}$$

where (again suppressing subscript i) ε_C denotes error terms, X_C denotes explanatory variables, β_C denotes parameter vectors, and $C \in \{E, NE\}$. We emphasize that the basic setup is identical to that of a switching regression of Section 3.1.

2.4.1. Treatment effects

Matching models focus on estimating *treatment effects*. A treatment effect, loosely speaking, is the value added or the difference in outcome when a firm undergoes treatment *E* relative to not undergoing treatment, that is, choosing *NE*. Selection models such as the switching regression specification (Equations (11)–(14)) estimate treatment effects. Their approach is indirect. In selection models, we estimate a vector of parameters and covariances in the selection equations and use these parameters to estimate treatment effects. In contrast, matching models go directly to treatment effect estimation, setting aside the step of estimating parameters of regression structures specified in selection models.

The key question in the matching literature is whether treatment effects are significant. In the system of Equations (24)–(26), this question can be posed statistically in a number of ways.

- At the level of an individual firm i, the effectiveness of a treatment can be judged by asking whether $E(Y_{E,i} - Y_{NE,i}) = 0$.
- For the group of treated firms, the effectiveness of the treatment for treated firms is assessed by testing whether the *treatment effect on treated* (TT), equals zero, that is, whether $E[(Y_E - Y_{NE})|C = E] = 0$.
- For the population as a whole whether treated or not, we test the significance of the *average treatment effect* (ATE) by examining whether $E(Y_E - Y_{NE}) = 0$.

The main issue in calculating any of the treatment effects discussed above, whether by selection or matching models, is the fact that unchosen counterfactuals are not observed. If a firm i chooses E, we observe outcome of its choice $Y_{E,i}$. However, because firm i chose E, we do not explicitly observe the outcome $Y_{NE,i}$ that would occur had the firm instead made the counterfactual choice NE. Thus, the difference $Y_{E,i} - Y_{NE,i}$ is never directly observed for any particular firm i, so its expectation—whether at the firm level, or across treated firms, or across treated and untreated firms—cannot be calculated directly. Treatment effects can, however, be obtained via selection models or by matching models, using different identifying assumptions. We discuss selection methods first and then turn to matching methods.

2.4.2. Treatment effects from selection models

Self-selection models obtain treatment effects by first estimating parameters of the system of Equations (24)–(26). Given the parameter estimates, it is straightforward to estimate treatment effects described in Section 4.1, as illustrated, for example, in Section 3.1 for the switching regression model. The key identifying assumption in selection models is the specification of the variables entering selection and outcome Equations, that is, variables X and Z in Equations (24)–(26).

Two points deserve emphasis. The first is that the entire range of selection models discussed in Section 2 through Section 3.2 can be used to estimate treatment effects. This point deserves special mention because in received corporate finance applications, the tendency has been to report estimates of matching models and as a robustness check, an accompanying estimate of a selection model. With virtually no exception, the selection model chosen for the robustness exercise is the Heckman model of Section 2. However, there is no a priori reason to impose this restriction—any other model, including the switching regression models or the structural models, can be used, and perhaps ought to at least get a hearing. The second point worth mentioning is that unlike matching models, selection models always explicitly test for and incorporate the effect of unobservable private information, through the inverse Mills ratio term, or more generally, through *control functions* that model private information (Heckman and Navarro-Lozano, 2004).

2.4.3. Treatment effects from matching models

In contrast to selection models, matching models begin by assuming that private information is irrelevant to outcomes.[12] Roughly speaking, this is equivalent to imposing zero correlation between private information η and outcome Y_E in Equations (24)–(26).

Is irrelevance of private information a reasonable assumption? It clearly depends on the specific application. The assumption is quite plausible if the decision to obtain treatment E is done through an exogenous randomization process. It becomes less plausible when the decision to choose E is an endogenous choice of the decision maker, which is probably close to many corporate finance applications except perhaps for exogenous shocks such as regulatory changes.[13] If private information can be ignored, matching methods offer two routes to estimate treatment effects: dimension-by-dimension matching and propensity score matching.

2.4.3.1. Dimension-by-dimension matching

If private information can be ignored, the differences in firms undergoing treatment E and untreated NE firms only depend on observable attributes X. Thus, the treatment effect for any firm i equals the difference between its outcome and the outcome for a firm $j(i)$ that matches it on all observable dimensions, Formally, the treatment effect equals $Y_{i,E} - Y_{j(i),NE}$, where $j(i)$ is such that $X_{i,k} = X_{j(i),k}$ for all K relevant dimensions, that is, $\forall k, k = 1, 2, \ldots, K$. Other measures such as TT and ATE defined in Section 4.1 follow immediately.[14]

Dimension-by-dimension matching methods have a long history of usage in empirical corporate finance, as explained in Chapter 1 (Kothari and Warner, 2007) in this book. Virtually all studies routinely match on size, industry, the book-to-market ratio, and so on. The "treatment effect" is the matched-pair difference in outcomes. There is nothing inherently wrong with these methods. They involve the same economic assumptions as other matching methods based on propensity scores used in recent applications. In fact, dimension-by-dimension matching imposes less structure and probably represents a reasonable first line of attack in typical corporate finance applications.

Matching on all dimensions and estimating the matched-pair differences in outcomes poses two difficulties. One is that characteristics are not always exactly matched in corporate finance applications. For instance, we often match firm size or

---

[12] See, for example, Wooldridge (2002) for formal expressions of this condition.

[13] Of course, even here, if unobservable information guides company responses to such shocks, irrelevance of unobservables is still not a good assumption.

[14] One could legitimately ask why we need to match dimension by dimension when we have a regression structure such as Equations (25) and (26). The reason is that dimension-by-dimension matching is still consistent when the data come from the regressions, but dimension-by-dimension matching is also consistent with other data generating mechanisms. If one is willing to specify Equations (25) and (26), the treatment effect is immediately obtained as the difference between the fitted values in the two equations.

book-to-market ratios with 30% calipers. When matches are inexact, substantial biases could build up as we traverse different characteristics being matched. A second issue that proponents of matching methods frequently mention is dimensionality. When the number of dimensions to be matched goes up and the matching calipers become fine (e.g., size and prior performance matched within 5% rather than 30%, and four-digit rather than two-digit SIC matches), finding matches becomes difficult or even infeasible. When dimension-by-dimension matching is not feasible, a convenient alternative is methods based on propensity scores. We turn to these next.

2.4.3.2. Propensity score matching   Propensity score (PS) matching methods handle the problems caused by dimension-by-dimension matching by reducing it to a problem of matching on a single one: the probability of undergoing treatment E. The probability of treatment is called the *propensity score*. Given a probability model such as Equation (24), the treatment effect equals the outcome for the treated firm minus the outcome for an untreated firm with equal treatment probability. The simplicity of the estimator and its straightforward interpretation makes the propensity score estimator attractive.

It is useful to review the key assumptions underlying the propensity score method. Following Rosenbaum and Rubin (1983), suppose that the probability model in Equation (24) satisfies

- PS1: $0 < \Pr(E|Z) < 1$.
- PS2: Given Z, outcomes Y_E, Y_{NE} do not depend on whether the firm is in group $E(NE)$.

Assumption (PS1) requires that at each level of the explanatory variable Z, some firms should pick E and others pick NE. This constraint is frequently imposed in empirical applications by requiring that treated and untreated firms have common support.

Assumption (PS2) is the *strong ignorability* or conditional independence condition. It requires that unobserved private information should not explain outcome differentials between firms choosing E and those choosing NE. This is a crucial assumption. As Heckman and Navarro-Lozano (2004) show, even fairly mild departures can trigger substantial biases in treatment effect estimates.

Given assumptions (PS1) and (PS2), Rosenbaum and Rubin (1983) show that the treatment effect is the difference between outcomes of treated and untreated firms having identical treatment probabilities (or propensity scores). Averaging across different treatment probabilities gives an ATE across the population.[15]

---

[15] This discussion points to another distinction between PS and selection methods. The finest level to which PS methods can go is the propensity score or the probability of treatment. Because many firms can have the same propensity score, PS methods do not estimate treatment effects at the level of the individual firm, while selection methods can do so.

2.4.3.3. Implementation of PS methods   In light of Rosenbaum and Rubin (1983), the treatment effect is the difference between outcomes of treated and untreated firms with identical propensity scores. One issue in implementing matching is that we need to know propensity scores, that is, the treatment probability $\Pr(E|Z)$. This quantity is not ex ante known but it must be estimated from the data, using, for instance, probit, logit, or other less parametrically specified approaches. The corresponding treatment effects are also estimated with error and the literature develops standard error estimates (e.g., Dehejia and Wahba, 1999; Heckman et al., 1998; Wooldridge, 2002, Chapter 18).

A second implementation issue immediately follows. What variables do we include in estimating the probability of treatment? While self-selection models differentiate between variables determining outcomes and variables determining probability of being treated (X and Z, respectively, in Equations (24)–(26)), matching models make no such distinction. Roughly speaking, either a variable determines the treatment probability, in which case it should be used in estimating treatment probability, or it does not, in which case it should be randomly distributed across treated and untreated firms and is averaged out in computing treatment effects. Thus, for matching models, the prescription is to use all relevant variables in estimating propensity scores.[16]

A third issue is estimation error. In principle, matching demands that treated firms be compared to untreated firms with the same treatment probability. However, treatment probabilities must be estimated, so exact matching based on the true treatment probability is usually infeasible. A popular approach, following Dehejia and Wahba (1999), divides the data into several probability bins. The treatment effect is estimated as the average difference between the outcomes of E and NE firms within each bin. Heckman et al. (1998) suggest taking the weighted average of untreated firms, with weights declining inversely in proportion to the distance between the treated and untreated firms. For statistical reasons, Abadie and Imbens (2004) suggest that the counterfactual outcomes should be estimated not as the actual outcomes for a matched untreated firm, but as the fitted value in a regression of outcomes on explanatory variables.[17]

2.5. Panel data with fixed effects

In self-selection models, the central issue is that unobserved attributes that lead firms to self-select could explain variation in outcomes. In panel data settings, we have multiple observations on the same firm over different periods. If the unobservable attributes are fixed over time, we can control for them by including firm fixed effects. Applications of fixed effect models in corporate finance include Himmelberg et al. (1999), Palia (2001),

---

[16] This statement is not, of course, a recommendation to engage in data snooping. For instance, in fitting models to estimate propensity scores, using quality of fit as a model selection criterion leads to difficulties, as pointed out by Heckman and Navarro-Lozano (2004).

[17] The statistical properties of different estimators has been extensively discussed in the econometrics literature, most recently in a review issue devoted to the topic (Symposium on the Econometrics of Matching, *Review of Economics and Statistics* 86 (1), 2004).

Schoar (2002), Bertrand and Mullainathan (2003), and Çolak and Whited (2007). There are undoubtedly many more. One question is whether the use of such fixed effect models alleviates self-selection issues. Not necessarily, as we discuss next.

There are two main issues with using firm fixed effects to rule out unobservables. One is that the unobservables should be time invariant. When time invariant effects exist and ought to be controlled for, fixed effect models are effective. However, time invariance is unlikely to be an appropriate modeling choice for corporate events where unobservables are not only time varying but also related to the event under consideration. Furthermore, unobservables often have a causal role in precipitating the corporate finance event being studied. For instance, in the framework of Maksimovic and Phillips (2002), firms diversify or focus because they receive an unobserved shock that alters the optimal scope of the firm. Thus, in studying conglomerate diversification or spinoffs, the central unobservable of importance is the scope-altering shock. It is time varying and it leads to the event of interest—diversification. Including time-invariant firm fixed effects does nothing to address such event-related unobservable shocks. This point also applies to the difference-in-difference methods related to fixed effects. They do not account for event-related self-selection. Such methods are just not designed to capture time-varying and event-related unobservables, which are, in contrast, the central focus of selection models.[18]

A second issue with fixed effect models is statistical power. Models with fixed effects rely on time variation in RHS variables and LHS outcomes for a given firm. Thus, fixed effect models often have limited power when the underlying variables vary slowly over time. In this scenario, causal effects, if any, are primarily manifested in the cross-section rather than time series. Zhou (2001) presents an argument on these lines with an empirical application. Thus, it appears especially important to take a more careful look at the lack of power as an explanation for insignificant results when using fixed effects. It should also be pointed out that the regression R^2 in fixed effects regressions could easily lead to misleading impressions of the strength of an economic relation.[19]

2.6. Bayesian self-selection models

Thus far, our discussion covered inference via classical statistical methods. An alternative approach towards estimating selection models involves Bayesian methods.

---

[18] A related issue is the use of period-by-period estimates of Heckman-style selection models in panel data. Imposing such a structure imposes the assumption that the period-by-period disturbances are pairwise uncorrelated with next-period disturbances, which may not necessarily be realistic.

[19] Most cross-sectional studies in corporate finance with reasonable sample sizes report a modest R^2 when there are no fixed effects. However when one adds fixed effects, there is often an impressive improvement in R^2 (see, e.g., Campa and Kedia, 2002; Villalonga, 2004, for interesting illustrations of this point). The high R^2 should not be misattributed to the explanatory power of the included variables, because they often arise due to the (ultimately unexplained) fixed effects.

These techniques often represent an elegant way of handling selection models that are computationally too burdensome to be practical for classical methods. We review the Bayesian approach briefly and illustrate their potential value by discussing a class of selection models based on Markov Chain Monte Carlo (MCMC) simulations (see Poirier (1995) for a more in-depth comparison between Bayesian and classical statistical inferences).

2.6.1. Bayesian methods

The Bayesian approach begins by specifying a prior distribution over parameters that must be estimated. The prior reflects the information known to the researcher without reference to the dataset on which the model is estimated. In time series context, a prior can be formed by looking at out of sample historical data. In most empirical corporate finance applications, which are cross-sectional in nature, researchers tend to be agnostic and use noninformative diffuse priors.

Denote the parameters to be estimated by θ and the prior beliefs about these parameters by the density $p(\theta)$. If the observed sample is y, the posterior density of θ given the sample can be written as

$$p(\theta \mid y) = \frac{P(y \mid \theta)p(\theta)}{p(y)}, \tag{27}$$

where $p(y \mid \theta)$ denotes the likelihood function of the econometric model being estimated. Given the prior and the econometric model, Equation (27) employs Bayes rule to generate the posterior distribution $p(\theta|y)$ about parameter θ. The posterior density $p(\theta|y)$ summarizes what one learns about θ after seeing the data. It is the central object of interest that Bayesian approaches wish to estimate.

A key difficulty in implementing Bayesian methods is the computation of the posterior. Except for a limited class of priors and models, posteriors do not have closed-form analytic expressions, which poses computational difficulties in implementing Bayesian models. However, recent advances in computational technology and more importantly, the advent of the Gibbs sampler and the Metropolis-Hastings algorithm, which are specific implementations of MCMC methods, simplify implementation of fairly complex Bayesian models. In some cases, it even provides a viable route for model estimation where classical methods prove to be computationally intractable. Chib and Greenberg (1996) and Koop (2003) provide more detailed discussions of these issues.

2.6.2. Bayesian methods for selection models

To illustrate the implementation of the Bayesian approach to selection models, consider the switching regression model of Section 3.1. For notational convenience, rewrite this model as the system of equations

$$I = 1_{Z_i\gamma+\eta_i>0}, \tag{28}$$

$$Y_{E,i} = X_{E,i}\beta_E + \varepsilon_{E,i}, \tag{29}$$

$$Y_{NE,i} = X_{NE,i}\beta_{NE} + \varepsilon_{NE,i}, \tag{30}$$

where $1_{\{\cdot\}}$ denotes the indicator function and the other notation follows that in Section 3.1. As before, assume that the errors are trivariate normal with the probit error variance in Equation (28) normalized to unity.

The critical unobservability issue, as discussed in Section 4, is that if a firm self-selects E, we observe the outcome $Y_{E,i}$. However, we do not observe the counterfactual $Y_{NE,\ i}$ that would have occurred had firm i chosen NE instead of E. Following Tanner and Wong (1987), a Bayesian estimation approach generates counterfactuals by augmenting the observed data with simulated observations of the unobservables through a "data augmentation" step. When augmented data are generated in a manner consistent with the structure of the model, the distribution of the augmented data converges to the distribution of the observed data. The likelihood of both the observed and the augmented data can be used as a proxy for the likelihood of the observed data. Conditional on the observed and augmented data and given a prior on parameters γ, β and the error covariances, approximate posteriors for the model parameters can be obtained by using standard simulation methods. The additional uncertainty introduced by simulating unobserved data can then be integrated out (Gelfand and Smith, 1990) to obtain posteriors conditional on only the observed data.

Explicitly modeling the unobserved counterfactuals offers advantages in the context of selection models. The counterfactuals that are critical in estimating treatment effects are merely the augmented data that are anyway employed in Bayesian estimation. The augmented data also reveal deficiencies in the model that are not identified by simple tests for the existence of selectivity bias. In addition, one can obtain exact small sample distributions of parameter estimates that are particularly useful when sample sizes are small to moderate, such as self-selection involving relatively infrequent events. Finally, we can impose parameter constraints without compromising estimation. In later sections, we review empirical applications that employ the Bayesian approach towards estimating counterfactuals (Li and McNally, 2004; Scruggs, 2007). We also illustrate an application to a matching problem (Sørensen, 2007) in which the tractability of the conditional distributions given subsets of parameters leads to computationally feasible estimators in a problem where conventional maximum likelihood estimators are relatively intractable.

3. Empirical applications

This part reviews empirical applications of self-selection models in corporate finance. We limit our scope to papers in which self-selection is an important element of the econometric approach or substantive findings. We begin with applications in event-studies. Here, the specifications are related to but differ from standard selection models. We then review applications in security offerings and financial intermediation, where more conventional selection models are used to characterize how private information affects debt issue pricing. We then turn to the diversification discount literature, where a range of methods have been used to address self-selection issues. The remaining sections include a collection of empirical applications based on selection and propensity score based matching methods. A last section covers Bayesian techniques. As will be clear from the review, most applications are relatively recent and involve a reasonably broad spectrum of approaches. In most cases, the model estimates suggest that unobserved private information is an important determinant of corporate finance choices.

3.1. Event studies

Event studies are a staple of empirical corporate finance. Hundreds of studies routinely report the stock market reactions to announcements such as mergers, stock splits, dividend announcements, equity issues, etc. Evidence in these studies has been used as a basis for testing and generating a wealth of theories, policies, and regulations. Chapter 1 in this volume (Kothari and Warner, 2007) overviews the literature.

Self-selection entered the event-study literature relatively recently. Its main use has been as a tool to model private information revealed in events. The basic idea is that when firms announce events, they reveal some latent "private" information. If the private information has value, it should explain the announcement effects associated with an event. Selection models are convenient tools to model the information revelation process and estimate "conditional" announcement effects.

3.1.1. Conditional announcement effects: Acharya (1988)

Acharya (1988) introduces the self-selection theme to event-studies, using a version of the standard Heckman specification to model calls of convertible bonds. In Acharya's model, firms decide whether to call an outstanding convertible bond (event E) or not (event NE) according to a probit model, viz.,

$$E \text{ if } W_i = Z_i\gamma + \eta_i > 0, \tag{31}$$

$$NE \text{ if } W_i = Z_i\gamma + \eta_i \leq 0, \tag{32}$$

where Z denotes known observables and η, the probit error term, is private information. Ex ante, private information has zero mean, but ex post, once the firm has announced E or NE, markets update expectations. If the private information affects stock prices, the stock price reaction γ to the firm's choice should be related to the updated value of private information. Assuming that (η, γ) are bivariate normal with mean, variances, and correlation equal to $(0, 0, 1, \sigma_y^2, \rho)$, we can write

$$E(y \mid E) = \pi E\left(\eta_i \mid \eta_i > -Z_i'\gamma\right) = \pi \lambda_E\left(Z_i'\gamma\right), \tag{33}$$

where $\pi = \rho \sigma_\varepsilon$ and $\lambda_E\left(Z_i'\gamma\right) = \pi \phi(Z_i'\gamma)/\Phi(Z_i'\gamma)$, the inverse Mills ratio. Equation (33) gives the *conditional* announcement effect associated with event E. It is a specialized version of the Heckman (1979) model (e.g., Equation (10)) in which there are no regressors other than the inverse Mills ratio.[20]

The empirical application in Acharya (1988) is conversion-forcing calls of convertible bonds (event E) while NE denotes the decision to delay forced conversion. Acharya finds that the coefficient π in Equation (33) is statistically significant, suggesting that the markets do react to the private information revealed in the call. The coefficient is negative, consistent with the Harris and Raviv (1985) signaling model. A legitimate question is whether testing for the significance of unconditional announcement effects and running a linear regression on characteristics Z could yield inferences equivalent to those from Acharya's model. Acharya (1993) offers simulation evidence and the question is formally analyzed in Prabhala (1997). Self-selection models add most value when one has samples of firms that chose *not* to announce E because these methods offer a natural way of exploiting the information in samples of silent nonannouncers.

3.1.2. Two announcements on the same date: Nayak and Prabhala (2001)

In the Acharya model, there is one announcement on an event-date. Nayak and Prabhala (2001) analyze a specification in which two announcements are made on the same date. They present a model to recover the individual impact of each announcement from the observed announcement effects, which reflect the combined impact of both announcements made on one date.

The empirical application in Nayak and Prabhala is to stock splits, 80% of which are announced jointly with dividends. Nayak and Prabhala model the joint decisions about whether to split a stock and whether to increase dividends using a bivariate probit model, which can be specified as

$$\text{SPL}_i = \gamma_s Z_{si} + \psi_{si}, \tag{34}$$

$$\text{DIV}_i = \gamma_d Z_{di} + \psi_{di}. \tag{35}$$

If SPL_i exceeds zero, a firm splits, and if DIV_i exceeds zero, it increases dividends. The private information components of these two latent variables are ψ_{si} and ψ_{di}, and these have potentially nonzero correlation ρ_{sd}. The announcement effect from the two decisions is

$$E(\text{AR}_{sdi}) = \gamma_{sd} + \beta_d E(\psi_{di} \mid C, S) + \beta_s E(\psi_{si} \mid C, S). \tag{36}$$

---

[20] The absence of other regressors is dictated by the condition that announcement effects should not be related to ex ante variables under the efficient markets hypothesis.

The question of substantive interest is to decompose the joint split-dividend announcement effect into a portion due to the dividend information implicit in a split and the portion unrelated to the dividend information in the split. This decomposition cannot be inferred directly from Equation (36) because the term relating to splits ($\beta_d E$ ($\psi_{di} \mid C, S$)) incorporates both the dividend and the nondividend portion of the information in splits. However, this decomposition is facilitated by writing the split information ψ_{si} into dividend and nondividend components. Accordingly, write $\psi_{si} = \rho_{sd}\psi_{di} + \psi_{s-d,i}$, in which case the joint announcement effect is

$$E(AR_{sdi} \mid C, S) = \gamma_{sd} + (\alpha_d - \rho_{sd}\alpha_{s-d})E(\psi_{di} \mid C, S) + \alpha_{s-d}E(\psi_{si} \mid C, S), \quad (37)$$

where α_d and α_{s-d} denote the reaction to the dividend and pure split components of the information in splits. Given these, Nayak and Prabhala show that the market's reaction to a hypothetical "pure" split unaccompanied by a dividend is

$$E(AR_{si}) = \left(1 - \rho_{sd}^2\right)\alpha_{s-d}\psi_{si} + \rho_{sd}\alpha_d\psi_{si}. \quad (38)$$

The first component in Equation (38) represents the market's reaction to pure split information orthogonal to dividends and the second represents the reaction to the dividend information implied by a split. Estimating the model is carried out using a two-step procedure.[21] Using a sample of splits made between 1975 and 1994 divided into two subsamples of 10 years each, Nayak and Prabhala report that about 46% of split announcement effects are due to information unrelated to the dividend information in splits.

The Nayak and Prabhala analysis has interesting implications for sample selection in event-studies. In many cases, an event is announced together with secondary information releases. For instance, capital expenditure, management, or compensation announcements may be made together with earnings releases, creating noisy samples. The conventional remedy for this problem is to pick samples in which the primary announcement of interest is not accompanied by a secondary announcement by firms. However, the analysis in Nayak and Prabhala suggests that this remedy may not cure the ill, since markets can form expectations about and price secondary announcements even when they are not explicitly announced on the event-date. A different approach is to model both announcements and extract the information content of each. Selection methods are useful tools in this regard because they explicitly model and incorporate the latent information from multiple announcements.

3.1.3. Takeovers: Eckbo et al. (1990)

Eckbo et al. (1990)—henceforth EMW—propose variants of the "truncated regression" specification, rather than the Heckman selection model used in Acharya (1988)

---

[21] The parameter p_sd is obtained as the correlation coefficient in the bivariate probit models (34) and (35). The inverse Mills ratios for Equation (37) follow (they require modification from standard expressions to incorporate nonzero correlation between bivariate latent variables). The other coefficients can be estimated from regression (37).

model to analyze announcement effects. Their empirical application is to takeovers, the subject of Chapter 15 (Betton et al., 2008).

EMW develop two models for announcement effects. In both models, managers announce event E if the stock market gain, $y_i = x_i\gamma + \eta_i$ is positive. As before, η_i is private information, normally distributed with mean zero and variance ω^2 and x_i denotes publicly known variables. In model (1), event E completely surprises the capital markets. In this case, the bidder's announcement effect is

$$F(x_i) = E(y_i \mid y_i = x_i\gamma + \eta_i > 0)$$
$$= x_i\gamma + \omega \frac{\phi(x_i\gamma/\omega)}{\Phi(x_i\gamma/\omega)}. \tag{39}$$

In model (2), the market learns about the impending takeover on a prior rumor date. The probability that the takeover will be announced is the probability that the takeover gain is positive, that is, $\Pr(x_i\gamma + \eta_i > 0) = \Phi(x_i\gamma/\omega)$. If the takeover occurs, the gain is $F(x_i)$, while the absence of the takeover is assumed to lead to zero gain. Thus, the expected stock return on the rumor date is $F(x_i)\Phi(x_i\gamma/\omega)$. On the actual merger announcement date, the takeover probability rises to 1 and the announcement effect is

$$G(x_i) = \left[x_i\gamma + \omega \frac{\phi(x_i\gamma/\omega)}{\Phi(x_i\gamma/\omega)}\right][1 - \Phi(x_i\gamma/\omega)]. \tag{40}$$

The EMW expression in Equation (40) is different from the Acharya model because EMW assume that private information has value only conditional on the takeover E, but has no value if there is no takeover. Thus, EMW model the real gains specific to mergers rather than nonspecific information modeled by Acharya. In the actual empirical application, EMW find that bidder gains decrease with the size of the bidder relative to the target, the concentration of firms in the industry, and the number of previous takeovers in the industry. As a model diagnostic, they show that OLS estimates differ from those of the nonlinear model (40), which is supported by Vuong (1989) test statistics. EMW also report that ω^2 is significant, indicating that bidders' private information is valued by capital markets.

The EMW framework has been widely applied in other event-studies with cross-sectional regressions. Eckbo (1990) examines the valuation effects of greenmail prohibitions and finds that the precommitment not to pay greenmail is value enhancing. Maksimovic and Unal (1993) estimate the after-market price performance of public offers in thrift conversions recognizing that management's choice of issue size reflects the value of growth opportunities and conflicts of interest between managers and investors. Servaes (1994) relates takeover announcement effects to excess capital expenditure. Hubbard and Palia (1995) find an increasing and then decreasing relation between merger announcement effects and managerial ownership levels. Bohren et al. (1997) use it to explain why rights flotations are not favored over public offerings despite the greater direct costs of the latter. Li and McNally (2006) apply the EMW method to open market share repurchases in Canada and find evidence supporting a signaling interpretation of repurchase announcement effects. We study one particular extension of EMW, Eckbo (1992), in greater detail next.

3.1.4. Takeover deterrence: Eckbo (1992)

Eckbo (1992) extends the EMW framework to account for the fact that regulatory challenges and court decisions on these could affect merger gains. To the extent these decisions also involved unobserved private information, they introduce additional selection bias terms into the final specification. Eckbo develops these models and applies them to horizontal mergers and price effects of rivals not involved in takeovers.

As in EMW, horizontal mergers occur if the acquirer's share of the synergy gains, $y_j = x_j\,\gamma + n_j > 0$. Under the EMW assumptions, the model for the announcement effects is Equation (40). Additionally, regulators can choose whether to initiate antitrust actions or not, and subsequently courts can decide whether to stop a merger or not. These actions are modeled using additional probit models.

$$R = x_i\phi_r + \eta_r > 0, \tag{41}$$

$$C = x_i\phi_c + \eta_c > 0. \tag{42}$$

Merger gains are realized if mergers are not challenged or they are challenged but challenges are unsuccessful. Assuming that challenges have a cost c proportional to merger gains, conditional announcement effects of merger announcements can be written as

$$E(\text{AR}_i \mid E) = \left[(1 - p_{ri}p_{ci}) \left(x_i\gamma + \omega\, \frac{\phi(x_i\gamma/\omega)}{\Phi(x_i\gamma/\omega)} \right) - p_{ri}c \right]$$
$$\times\, [1 - \Phi(x_i\gamma/\omega)]. \tag{43}$$

Eckbo applies the truncated regression models to US and Canadian data. For Canadian data, Eckbo uses the EMW models (39) and (40) because there is no regulatory overhang. He uses Equation (43) in US horizontal mergers where regulatory overhang exists. The explanatory variables include the ratio of the market values of the bidder and target firms, the number of nonmerging rival firms in the industry of the horizontal merger, the premerger level of and merger-induced change in industry concentration. Eckbo finds that bidder gains are positively related to the premerger concentration ratio and are negatively related to the merger-induced changes in the concentration ratio. These do not support the collusion explanation for merger gains. In an interesting innovation, Eckbo also estimates the models for nonmerging rivals. He reports similar and even sharper findings in challenged deals where court documents identify rivals more precisely. Changes in concentration are negatively related to rival gains in the regulatory overhang free environment in Canada, further refuting the collusion hypothesis.

3.2. The pricing of public debt offerings

Companies making a debt issue must make several decisions related to the offering such as the terms and structure of the offering, the type of the underwriter for the issue. Private information held by the issuer or the intermediaries participating in the offering could affect the choices made by firms. If such information has value, it affects the prices at which issues can be sold. A fairly wide range of self-selection models have been used to address the existence of private information and its effect on the pricing of debt issues. We review some of the applications and the key findings that emerge.

3.2.1. Bank underwritings and the Glass-Steagall Act: Puri (1996)

The choice of an underwriter is an area that has been extensively analyzed using self-selection models. An early application is Puri (1996), who investigates the information in a firm's choice between commercial banks and investment banks as underwriters of public debt offerings. Commercial banks are often thought to possess private information about their borrowers. If they use the private information positively, commercial bank underwritten offerings should be priced higher (the "certification" hypothesis). Alternatively, banks could use their information negatively to palm off their lemons to the market, in which case the markets should discount commercial bank underwritten offerings (the "conflicts of interest" hypothesis). Selection models are natural avenues to examine the nature of these private information effects.

Puri models the private information in the underwriter choice using a probit model, viz.,

$$C = \text{CB} \equiv W_i = Z_i \gamma + \eta_i > 0, \tag{44}$$

$$C = \text{IB} \equiv W_i = Z_i \gamma + \eta_i \leq 0, \tag{45}$$

where CB denotes a commercial bank, IB denotes an investment bank, and η_i is the private information in offering i. Markets price issue i at yield y_i where

$$y_i = x_i \beta + \varepsilon_i, \tag{46}$$

$$E(y_i \mid C) = X_i \beta + \pi \lambda_C(Z_i \gamma). \tag{47}$$

Equation (47) follows from Equation (46) and the assumption that ε and η are bivariate normal. The above system is, of course, the standard Heckman model of Section 2, so the sign of the covariance coefficient π determines the impact of private information on offer yields. If $\pi > 0$, markets demand higher yield for CB offerings, consistent with a conflicts of interest hypothesis, while $\pi < 0$ supports the certification hypothesis.

The data in Puri (1996) are debt and preferred stock issues prior to the passage of the 1933 Glass-Steagall Act. She includes issue size, credit rating, syndicate size, whether the security is exchange listed, whether it is collateralized, and the age of the issuer as determinants of the offer yield. She finds that $\pi < 0$, consistent with the certification hypothesis. Additionally, π is more negative for information sensitive securities, where the conflicts of interest hypothesis predicts the more *positive* coefficient.[22] Gande et al. (1997, 1999) report similar findings for debt issues offered after the 1989 relaxation of the Glass-Steagall Act. Underwritings by commercial banks convey positive information that improves the prices at which debt offerings can be sold.[23]

3.2.2. Underwriting syndicate structure: Song (2004)

Song (2004) analyzes debt offerings as in Puri (1996) and Gande et al. (1997, 1999) but there are some important differences in her specifications. Song uses a switching regression instead of the Heckman model. Second, she focuses on the effect of the syndicate structure rather than the commercial/investment banking dichotomy on debt issue spreads.

In Song's model, commercial banks could enter as lead underwriters or be part of a hybrid syndicate with investment banks. Alternatively, issues could be underwritten by a pure investment bank syndicate. For each outcome, we observe the yield of the debt offering, which is modeled as a function of public information and (implicitly) the private information conveyed in the firm's choice of a syndicate structure. The resulting specification is a variant of the switching regression model of Section 3.1, and can be written as

$$A_i = 1 \text{ if } (-Z_{Ai}\gamma_A + \eta_{Ai}) > 0, \tag{48}$$

$$B_i = 1 \text{ if } (-Z_{Bi}\gamma_B + \eta_{Bi}) > 0, \tag{49}$$

$$C_i = 1 \text{ if } (-Z_{Ci}\gamma_C + \eta_{Ci}) > 0, \tag{50}$$

$$Y_{1i} = X_{1i}\beta_1 + \eta_{1i}, \tag{51}$$

$$Y_{2i} = X_{2i}\beta_2 + \eta_{2i}, \tag{52}$$

$$Y_{3i} = X_{3i}\beta_3 + \eta_{3i}, \tag{53}$$

where we have adapted Song's notation for consistency with the rest of this chapter.[24] In Equations (48)–(50), the counterfactuals are $A = 0, B = 0$, and $C = 0$, respectively.

---

[22] Of course, it is possible that investors paid more for bank underwritten issues but were fooled into doing so. Puri (1994) rules out this hypothesis by showing that bank underwritten offerings defaulted less than nonbank issues.

[23] Chiappori and Salanie (2000) use similar methods to analyze the role of private information in insurance markets. Liu and Malatesta (2006) is a recent application of self-selection models to seasoned equity offerings. They analyze the availability of a credit rating on the underpricing and announcement effects of SEOs.

[24] Song's usage of signs for coefficients and error terms illustrates some confusing notation in the limited dependent variable literature. Her notation follows Maddala (1983) where the selection criterion is often written as $z\gamma - \eta > 0$, while the more modern textbook convention is to use $z\gamma + \eta > 0$.

In Song's model $A_i = 1$ if a lead investment bank invites a commercial bank to participate in the syndicate. $B_i = 1$ if the commercial bank joins the syndicate, and zero otherwise. $C_i = 1$ if a commercial bank led syndicate is chosen and $C_i = 0$ if a pure investment bank syndicate is chosen. Thus, a hybrid syndicate is observed (regime 1) when $A_i = 1$ and $B_i = 1$; a pure investment bank syndicate (regime 2) is observed when $A_i = 0$ and $C_i = 0$, while a commercial bank led syndicate (regime 3) is observed when $B_i = 0$ and $C_i = 1$.[25] Song assumes that the latent errors η are i.i.d. normal, correlated with yields Y with regression coefficients σ_{wj} where $\omega \in \{A, B, C\}$ and $j \in \{1, 2, 3\}$. The yields in each regime can be expressed in regression form as

$$E(y_{1i} \mid A_i = 1, B_i = 1) = X_{1i}\beta_1 + \sigma_{A1} \frac{\phi(Z_{Ai}\gamma_A)}{1 - \Phi(Z_{Ai}\gamma_A)} + \sigma_{B1} \frac{\phi(Z_{Bi}\gamma_B)}{1 - \Phi(Z_{Bi}\gamma_B)}, \quad (54)$$

$$E(y_{2i} \mid A_i = 0, C_i = 0) = X_{2i}\beta_2 - \sigma_{A2} \frac{\phi(Z_{Ai}\gamma_A)}{\Phi(Z_{Ai}\gamma_A)} - \sigma_{C2} \frac{\phi(Z_{Ci}\gamma_C)}{\Phi(Z_{Ci}\gamma_C)}, \quad (55)$$

$$E(y_{3i} \mid B_i = 0, C_i = 1) = X_{3i}\beta_3 - \sigma_{B3} \frac{\phi(Z_{Bi}\gamma_B)}{\Phi(Z_{Bi}\gamma_B)} + \sigma_{C3} \frac{\phi(Z_{Ci}\gamma_C)}{1 - \Phi(Z_{Ci}\gamma_C)}. \quad (56)$$

Song's sample comprises 2345 bond issues offered between January 1991 and December 1996. In the first-step probit estimates, Song reports that compared to pure investment bank syndicates, hybrid syndicates underwrite small firms that have made smaller debt issues in the past, have low S&P stock rankings, invest less, and use more bank debt. These findings are reminiscent of those in Gande et al. (1997, 1999) that commercial banks underwrite informationally sensitive companies. Compared to commercial bank led syndicates, hybrid syndicates underwrite smaller firms with lower stock rankings that issue to refinance debt and lower ranked firms, consistent with the claim that these underwritings potentially alleviate conflicts of interest with commercial banks. Only two out of six private information coefficients in Equations (54)–(56) are significant. Pricing benefits are seen in pure investment banking syndicates (Equation (55)) where excluding a commercial bank leads to higher yields, consistent with a certification hypothesis. On the other hand, picking an investment bank to run the syndicate increases yields, because the coefficient σ_{C2} in the same Equation (55) is positive. Thus, the ex ante effect of awarding a syndicate to an investment bank cannot be a priori signed.

Relative to prior work, Song (2004) has very different sample, sample period, and explanatory variables, not to mention the changes in underwriter classification, which is based on syndicate structure rather than on classification into commercial/investment bank or on bank reputation. Thus, it is hard to pinpoint the specific value added by her elaborate selection model. In addition, absent additional diagnostics, it is also

---

[25] Song does not explicitly write out the extensive form of the model she estimates. It is unclear whether pure investment bank syndicates should also include the node at which an investment bank is awarded the mandate and chooses to invite a commercial bank but the bank declines to join.

difficult to interpret whether the general insignificance of most selection terms reflects coefficients that are truly zero, the lack of power, perhaps due to collinearity, or perhaps an unmodeled correlation between errors in Equations (48)–(50) that are assumed to be i.i.d. for the purposes of estimation. As Song points out, additional data may not help shed light on interpretation or robustness because there have been structural changes in the banking industry since 1996, due to several mergers and further relaxation of the Glass-Steagall Act.

3.2.3. Underwriter reputation: Fang (2005)

Like the other papers reviewed in this section, Fang (2005) also studies the role of underwriter choice in explaining at issue bond spreads. Unlike the other papers in the section, however, Fang draws on an earlier literature and classifies underwriters by reputation rather than by organization into commercial or investment banks. Fang examines whether the information in the choice of a reputed underwriter impacts underwriting spreads and yields.

Fang uses a probit specification to model underwriter-issuer matching. If issue i is underwritten by a reputed underwriter, the yield is $Y_{E,i}$ and if not, the yield is $Y_{NE,i}$. Yields are specified as a function of regressors x_i with different regression coefficients across the two choices. Thus, Fang's model is exactly the switching regression of Section 3.1. Fang also estimates an auxiliary regression where the dependent variable is gross spread rather than offer yield.

Fang finds that reputed underwriters underwrite higher grade, less risky issues of large and frequent issuers, and are more likely to be associated with longer maturity callable issues that she interprets as being more complex. The self-selection term in the yield equation is negative. Thus, the unobserved information that leads firms to choose reputed underwriters leads to lower bond yields or better offer prices. In the specification analyzing gross spreads, Fang finds that issue size increases fees more rapidly but risk variables matter less for reputed underwriters, indicating greater marginal costs and superior risk bearing capacity of reputed underwriters. Most importantly, the coefficient for the inverse Mills ratio in the gross spread equation is positive, suggesting that reputed underwriters charge greater fees to issuers.

Taken together, the yield and gross spread specifications show that reputed underwriters charge issuers greater fees and lower the offer yields (i.e., increase the offer price) to borrowers. Fang shows that the benefit of lowered debt yields typically outweighs the higher commissions paid by issuers. The pattern of results is shown to strengthen in lower yield bonds, so that reputation matters more for more informationally sensitive issues.

3.2.4. Debt covenants: Goyal (2005)

While the papers reviewed in this section study and model information in underwriter choice, Goyal (2005) examines the information in the choice of covenants attached to debt issues. Goyal argues that commercial banks often enjoy franchise value because of regulations that deter free entry. Banks with more valuable franchises are less likely to engage in excessive risk taking, so they should have less need to include covenants in their debt issues. This incentive is recognized and priced by the market, and the pricing differential again feeds back into firms' decisions about whether to include covenants. In other words, the decision to include covenants influences and is influenced by the expected pricing benefits from doing so. Goyal implements the structural self-selection model of Section 3.2 to model the simultaneity.

Goyal estimates the structural model on a sample of 415 subordinated debt issues made by firms between 1975 and 1994. He finds that yields are negatively related to franchise value. This finding is consistent with the hypothesis that banks with greater franchise value have less incentives to take risk, latent information that is recognized and priced by financial markets. The inverse Mills ratio term is significant in the noncovenant subsample but not in the sample with restrictive covenants. In the equation explaining whether firms use covenants or not, the coefficient for the yield differential with/without covenants is significant in explaining covenant choice, suggesting that anticipated pricing benefits do influence whether firms select covenants or not in their debt issues. Many of Goyal's results are more prominent in the 1981–1988 subperiod, when the risk-taking activity in the United States was more elevated.[26]

3.2.5. Discussion

The public debt issue pricing area is interesting for the wide range of selection models employed. One issue, however, is that it is a little difficult to place the literature in perspective because the sources of self-selection modeled vary across papers. An additional issue is, of course, that there is probably self-selection on other dimensions as well, such as maturity, collateral, or the callability of an issue, not speaking of the decision to issue debt in the first place. This raises another thorny question, one that probably has no easy answer. What dimensions of self-selection should one control for in a given empirical application? Modeling every source of selection seems infeasible, while studying some sources of bias while ignoring others also seems a little ad hoc. Embarking on a purely empirical search for sources of selection that matter is certainly undesirable, smacking of data snooping. A happy middle way is likely to emerge as the literature matures.

3.3. Other investment banking applications

3.3.1. Underwriter compensation in IPOs: Dunbar (1995)

Dunbar (1995) presents an interesting application of a Roy (1951) style self-selection model to the study of underwriter compensation. Some IPO issuers offer warrants to

---

[26] Reisel (2004) provides an interesting extension, a structural self-selection model applied to debt covenants included in industrial bonds.

compensate their underwriters while other issuers do not. Dunbar examines the role of self-selection in explaining this choice, and in particular, whether firms choose the alternative that minimizes their underwriting costs.

Let W denote the decision to use warrants to compensate underwriters and N if not, subscripts w and n denote the costs if warrants are used or not, respectively, U denote underpricing costs and C the other costs of going public. If firm i chooses underwriter warrant compensation, we observe the pair $\{U_{wi}, C_{wi}\}$ while we observe $\{U_{ni}, C_{ni}\}$ if it chooses just straight cash compensation. The key self-selection issue is that we observe the choice made by firm i but not the costs of the alternative not chosen by firm i. Without knowing the unchosen counterfactuals, we cannot tell how much a company saved by choosing to include or exclude warrants to compensate its underwriters.

Dunbar models the decision to use warrants using a probit model

$$W = \xi(U_{ni} + C_{ni} - U_{wi} - C_{wi}) - \varepsilon_i > 0, \tag{57}$$

$$N = \xi(U_{ni} + C_{ni} - U_{wi} - C_{wi}) - \varepsilon_i \leq 0. \tag{58}$$

The expression in parentheses in Equation (57) is the reduction in offering costs if warrants are used as compensation instead of straight cash compensation. Each component of costs is written as a function of observables and unobservables as follows:

$$U_{ni} = X_{ni}\beta_n + \varepsilon_{uni}, \tag{59}$$

$$U_{wi} = X_{wi}\beta_w + \varepsilon_{uwi}, \tag{60}$$

$$C_{ni} = Z_{ni}\gamma_n + \varepsilon_{cni}, \tag{61}$$

$$C_{wi} = Z_{wi}\gamma_w + \varepsilon_{cwi}. \tag{62}$$

Assuming that the errors in Equations (59)–(62) are i.i.d. normal but potentially correlated with the probit error term, Dunbar's system is a version of the Roy (1951) self-selection model.

Dunbar reports that variables such as offering size, underwriter reputation, and a hot issue dummy explain underpricing in the warrant and cash compensation samples. The self-selection term is significant in the nonwarrant sample but not in the warrant compensation sample. Most interesting are Dunbar's estimates of unobserved counterfactuals. For firms that do not use warrants, underpricing (other costs) would be 11.6% (19.2%) on average had warrants been used compared to actual underpricing (other costs) of 12.8% (9.8%). For firms that do use warrants, underpricing (other costs) would be 36.4% (14.6%) if warrants had not been used, compared to actual costs of 23.3% (23.9%). While warrants are associated with high underpricing in reduced form cross-sectional regressions, it is incorrect to conclude that warrants result in higher underpricing. Estimates of the self-selection model indicates that the use of warrants actually *reduces* underpricing compared to what it would be without warrants. Firms appear to use warrants to reduce underpricing costs.

3.3.2. Analyst coverage: Ljungqvist et al. (2006)

Ljungqvist et al. (2006) examine the relation between the decision to award an underwriting mandate to a bank and the coverage offered by the bank's analyst. The self-selection issue in Ljungqvist et al. is that banks self-select on whether they cover a stock or not. If the bank covers a stock, we observe the nature of the stock recommendation and we can tie it to the decision to award an underwriting mandate. However, if a bank does not elect to cover a stock, we do not know what the nature of its recommendation might have been had it chosen to cover the stock. Ljungqvist et al. model this source of self-selection in testing whether a firm with more positive coverage of a firm is more likely to win the firm's underwriting mandates.

Ljungqvist et al. model the probability that bank j covers firm i's stock as a probit model

$$y_C = \begin{cases} 1 & \text{if } y_C^* = X_C \beta_C + u_C > 0, \\ 0 & \text{if } y_C^* = X_C \beta_C + u_C \le 0, \end{cases} \tag{63}$$

where all subscripts are suppressed for notational convenience. If there is coverage, the tie between coverage and the award of an underwriting mandate is established by the equations

$$\left. \begin{aligned} y_A &= \beta_A X_A + u_A \\ y_L &= I_{\beta L X_L + \delta_L y_A + u_L > 0} \end{aligned} \right\} \text{ if } y_C^* > 0 \tag{64}$$

If there is no coverage, we have

$$\left. \begin{aligned} y_A &= 0 \\ y_L &= I_{\beta_{LNC} X_L + u_{LNC} > 0} \end{aligned} \right\} \text{ if } y_C^* \le 0, \tag{65}$$

where y_A is the nature of an analyst's recommendation, y_L is a 1/0 dummy for whether an underwriting mandate is awarded to a bank, I is the 1/0 indicator function, and X's are explanatory variables. Equations (63)–(65) represent a switching regression system, similar to the type analyzed in Section 3.1. The difference here is that we have two recursive equations observed in each regime instead of just one regression in Section 3.1.

Ljungqvist et al. find that the decision to cover a stock is positively related to the type of coverage offered by an analyst for debt underwriting transactions. Prior relationships in the underwriting and loan markets are the other most significant explanatory variables. There is no evidence that the type of coverage influences the decision to award equity underwriting mandates. Even when it is significant, the coefficient for analyst recommendation β_A in Equation (64) is negative. Ljungqvist et al. interpret this finding as evidence that even if analysts are overly biased, issuers refrain from using them for underwriting.

The analysis of Ljungqvist et al. has appealing features. The choice of instruments is carefully motivated, with both economic intuition and tests for instrument strength suggested by Staiger and Stock (1997). Their analysis also suggests some natural extensions. One issue is that the very decision to cover a stock—rather than the type of coverage—might affect the probability of winning an underwriting mandate. A second and perhaps more difficult issue is that of cross-sectional correlation. The 16,000+ transactions in the Ljungqvist et al. sample occur over overlapping periods, which leads to commonality across transactions and potential cross-sectional correlation in the disturbance terms.

3.4. Diversification discount

The scope of the firm is an issue that has occupied economists since Coase (1933). One issue in this literature has been whether firms should diversify or not. While the question can be examined from several perspectives, a now well developed literature in finance investigates the diversification question from a valuation perspective. Does diversification impact firm value, and if so, in what direction, and why does diversification have this effect? Our review of this literature focuses on self-selection explanations for diversification. Chapter 8 (Maksimovic and Phillips, 2007) provides a more complete review of the now vast literature on diversification.

The recent finance literature on diversification begins with the empirical observation that diversified firms trade below their imputed value, which is the weighted average value of stand-alone firms in the same businesses as the divisions of the diversified firm (see, e.g., Berger and Ofek, 1995; Lang and Stulz, 1994; Servaes, 1996). The difference between the actual and imputed values is called the diversification discount. The existence of a diversification discount is frequently interpreted as a value destroying consequence of diversification, although there is no consensus on the issue (e.g., Chevalier, 2000; Graham et al., 2002). We review three papers that discuss the role of self-selection in explaining the source of diversification discount.

3.4.1. Unobservables and the diversification discount: Campa and Kedia (2002)

Campa and Kedia (2002) argue that firms self-select into becoming diversified and that self-selection explains the diversification discount. They model the decision to become diversified using a probit model

$$D_{it} = 1 \text{ if } Z_{it}\gamma + \eta_{it} > 0, \tag{66}$$

$$D_{it} = 0 \text{ if } Z_{it}\gamma + \eta_{it} \leq 0, \tag{67}$$

where D_{it} is a diversification dummy that takes the value of 1 if the firm operates in more than one segment, and 0 otherwise, and Z_{it} is a set of explanatory variables. The notations are adapted to match that in Section 2. Excess value V_{it} is specified as

$$V_{it} = d_0 + d_1 X_{it} + d_2 D_{it} + \varepsilon_{it}, \tag{68}$$

where X_{it} is a set of exogenous observable characteristics of firm i at time t. Coefficient d_2 is the key parameter of interest. If it is negative, becoming diversified causes the diversification discount. If not, the diversification discount could not be due to diversification. Under the assumption that the error terms in Equations (67) and (68) are bivariate normal, the system is akin to and is estimated just like the basic Heckman selection model.[27]

In the empirical application, Campa and Kedia measure the LHS variable in Equation (68), as the difference between the actual value of the firm and the sum of the imputed value of each of its segments. Segment imputed values are estimated using multipliers based on market value to sales or market value to book value of assets of peer firms. The explanatory variables for Equation (68) include profitability, size, capital expenditure, and leverage. The additional instruments used in the probit specification Equations (66) and (67) include industry instruments such as the fraction of firms (or their sales) in an industry that are diversified, time instruments, macroeconomic indicators such as the overall economic growth and economic expansion/contraction, and firm specific instruments such as being listed on a major exchange or being included in a stock index. Campa and Kedia extensively discuss their choices for instruments.

Campa and Kedia show that in OLS specifications, d_2 is negative, so that diversified firms do appear to trade at a discount. However, once they include the inverse Mills ratio to correct for self-selection, the coefficient d_2 becomes positive. The negative sign seen in OLS estimates is soaked up by the coefficient for the inverse Mills ratio. This indicates that diversified firms possess private information that makes them self-select into being diversified. The information is negatively associated with value and leads to the diversification discount. After accounting for unobserved private information, there is no diversification discount: in fact, there is a premium, implying that diversification may well be in shareholders best interests.

The flip in the sign of d_2 when the selection term is introduced does raise the question of robustness of results, particularly with respect to potential collinearity between the dummy variable for diversification and the inverse Mills ratio that corrects for selection. Campa and Kedia address this issue by reporting several other models, including a simultaneous questions system that instruments the diversification dummy D_{it} and evidence based on a sample of refocusing firms. The main results are robust: there is indeed a diversification discount as found by Lang and Stulz (1994) or Berger and Ofek (1995) when using OLS estimates. However, this discount is not due to diversification, but by private information that leads firms to become diversified. In fact, the Campa and Kedia self-selection estimates suggest that diversified firms trade at a premium relative to their value had they not diversified.

---

[27] Compared to the standard Heckman model, there is one additional variable in the second stage Equation (68), specifically, the dummy variable D_{it}. The Heckman model with the additional dummy variable is called a "treatment effects" model. The panel data setting also requires the additional assumption that the unobserved errors be i.i.d. period by period. Campa and Kedia estimate fixed effects models as an alternative to Heckman style selection models to handle the panel structure of the data.

3.4.2. Observables and the discount: Villalonga (2004)

While Campa and Kedia (2002) attribute the diversification discount to unobservables causing firms to diversify, Villalonga (2004) offers an explanation based on differences in observables. Villalonga uses a longitudinal rather than cross-sectional analysis, focusing on *changes* in excess value around diversification rather than the level of the excess value itself.

Villalonga's main sample comprises 167 cases where firms move from being one segment to two segments. She tracks the changes in the diversification discount around the diversification event compared to a control group of nondiversifying firms, using propensity score (PS) based matching to construct matched control firms. Following the methods discussed in Section 4.3.2, Villalonga fits a probit model to estimate the probability that a given firm will diversify using variables similar to those in Campa and Kedia (2002). She matches each diversifying firm with a nondiversifying firm with a similar propensity score, that is, diversifying probability. Her final sample has five quintiles of firms based on their estimated propensity scores and having a common support.

Villalonga estimates the "treatment effect" caused by diversification as the difference between the change in excess value of a diversifying firm and the excess value change of a comparable nondiversifying firms with the closest propensity score. She reports that while the treatment effect is negative, it is not significant whether she uses the Dehejia and Wahba (1999) or the Abadie and Imbens (2004) technique for estimation. Villalonga also reports similar findings when using a Heckman correction, presumably a treatment effect model on the lines of Campa and Kedia (2002).[28]

Two aspects of Villalonga's results deserve comment. One issue is perhaps semantic, the use of the term *causal inference*. In reading the work, one could easily come away with the impression that matching methods somehow disentangle causality from correlation. This is incorrect. Matching methods rule out correlation by arbitrary fiat: causality is an *assumption* rather than a statistically tested output of these methods. This fact is indeed acknowledged by Villalonga but easy to overlook given the prominence attached to the term "causal inference" in the paper.

A second issue is that some point estimates of treatment effects are insignificant but not very different in economic magnitude from those in Lang and Stulz (1994) and Berger and Ofek (1995)—and indeed, from the baseline industry-adjusted estimates that Villalonga herself reports. Thus, in fairness to Lang and Stulz and Berger and Ofek, Villalonga's results do not necessarily refute their earlier work. Nevertheless,

---

[28] In reviewing applications, we often found references to "the" Heckman model or "standard" Heckman models to be quite confusing. Campa and Kedia (2002) and Çolak and Whited (2007) use it to denote a treatment effects model, and focus on the coefficient for the diversification dummy variable. However, the Heckman (1979) model is not a treatment effects model. Also, it is not clear from the papers whether the coefficient of interest is the coefficient for the dummy variable in a treatment effects model or for the inverse Mills ratio term. It is perhaps a better practice not to use labels but instead describe fully the specification being estimated.

Villalonga's work does make an important point. Specifically, the statistical significance of discount based on industry/size matching methods is not a given fact, but is an open question in light of her results.

3.4.3. Refocusing and the discount: Çolak and Whited (2007)

If one accepts the diversification discount as a fact, then the question is what causes the discount. One view is that conglomerates (i.e., diversified firms) follow inefficient investment policies, subsidizing inefficient divisions with cash flow from the efficient divisions. Çolak and Whited (2007) evaluate the efficiency of investment in conglomerate and nonconglomerate firms by comparing investments made by focusing firms with those made by firms that do not focus. The focusing sample in Çolak and Whited (2007) consists of 267 divestitures and 154 spinoffs between 1981 and 1996. Control nonfocusing firms are multisegment firms in similar businesses that do not focus in years -3 through $+3$ where year 0 is the focusing event for a sample point.

The main specification used in Çolak and Whited (2007) employs propensity scores to match focusing and nonfocusing firms. As in standard propensity score method implementations, Çolak and Whited (2007) estimate the propensity score as the probability that a given firm will focus in the period ahead. The probit estimates broadly indicate that firms are more likely to focus if they are larger, have less debt, diversity in segments (entropy), and have had recent profit shocks.

The central issue in Çolak and Whited is, of course, on change in investment efficiency after a focusing activity. Çolak and Whited use several measures of change in investment efficiency, including investment Q-sensitivity, the difference in adjusted investment to sales ratio between high and low growth segments, and the relative value added, which is akin to weighted investment in high minus low Q segments. Çolak and Whited find that the changes in these measures are not significant relative to changes in firms that do not focus and that have similar propensity scores, using the Dehejia and Wahba (1999) matching procedure and the Abadie and Imbens (2004) implementation. There is no evidence that post-spinoff efficiency improves once the focusing firms are matched by propensity score to the nonfocusing firms.

For robustness, Çolak and Whited also report estimates of a treatment effects model, Equation (68) of Campa and Kedia (2002). There is little evidence for efficiency gains, except for one case in which the investment efficiency has a significance level of 10% for focusing firms. This could, however, arise due to pure chance given the wide number of dependent variables and specifications examined. While the paper does not report the coefficient for the inverse Mills ratio in the treatment effects model, Toni Whited confirms to us in private communication, that this selection term *is* significant. This suggests that self-selection is the main explanation for why firms experience efficiency gains after focusing. The unobserved private information that leads firms to focus explains postfocusing improvements in efficiency; controlling for self-selection, there is little evidence of any additional efficiency gains.

3.4.4. Discussion

A key advantage of the diversification discount literature is that it has reasonably similar datasets, so it is easier to see the changes due to different econometric approaches. By the same token, it becomes easier to raise additional questions on model choice. We raise these questions here for expositional convenience, but emphasize that the questions are general in nature and not particular to the diversification discount literature.

One issue is statistical power. The diversification discount is significant using conventional industry-size matching but it is insignificant using PS based matching methods. Is this because the latter lack power? Çolak and Whited offer some welcome Monte Carlo evidence with respect to their application, simulating data with sample sizes, means, covariance matrix, and covariates with third and fourth moments equal to that observed in the actual data. They confirm that their tests have appropriate size, and at the level of the treatment effects in the sample, there is a better than 20% chance of detecting the observed treatment effect. More on these lines would probably be useful.

A second issue is the use of PS based matching methods as primary means of inference about treatment effects. There are good reasons to be uncomfortable with such an approach. The main issue is that propensity score methods assume that private information is irrelevant. However, this assumption is probably violated to at least some degree in most corporate finance applications. In fact, in the diversification literature, private information does empirically matter. Thus, using PS methods as the primary specification seems inappropriate without strong arguments as to why firms' private information is irrelevant. Heckman and Navarro-Lozano (2004) stress and show explicitly that even small deviations from this assumption can introduce significant bias. Thus, the practice followed in the finance literature of reporting private information specifications in conjunction with matching models is probably appropriate, although more full discussion on reconciling the results from different approaches would be useful.

A final comment is about the self-selection specifications used to control for private information. While the literature has used versions of the baseline Heckman (1979) model, we emphasize that this restriction is neither necessary nor desirable. Other models, such as switching regressions and structural models are viable alternatives for modeling self-selection and private information. Because these models come with their own additional requirements, it is not clear that they would always be useful, but these issues are ultimately empirical.

3.5. Other applications of selection models

3.5.1. Accounting for R&D: Shehata (1991)

Shehata (1991) applies self-selection models to analyze the accounting treatment of research and development (R&D) expenditures chosen by firms during the period of the introduction of FASB ruling SFAS No. 2. This ruling pushed firms to expense rather than defer R&D expenditures. Other studies examined the issue by comparing observed changes in R&D expenditures for a sample of capitalizing firms with those of expensing firms. If firms self-select into the choice they prefer, it is inappropriate to treat the choice as exogenous and assess its impact by comparing differences between capitalizers and expensers. Shehata uses a switching regression instead.

Shehata uses a probit specification to model how firms choose an accounting method, and two regressions to determine the level of the R&D expenditure, one for each accounting choice. This is, of course, the switching regression system of Section 3.1. Shehata estimates the system using standard two-step methods. As discussed in Section 3.1, one useful feature of the system is the estimation of counterfactuals: what the R&D spending would be for firms that expensed had they elected to defer and vice versa. Shehata reports that capitalizers are small, highly leveraged, have high volatility of R&D expenditures, more variable earnings, and spend a significant portion of their income on R&D activities. The second stage regression shows that the two groups of firms behave differently with respect to R&D spending. For instance, R&D is a nonlinear function of size and is related to the availability of internally generated funds for capitalizers but the size relation is linear and internally generated funds do not matter for expensers. Thus, it is more appropriate to use a switching regression specification rather than the Heckman (1979) setup to model selection.

The inverse Mills ratio that corrects for self-selection matters in the second stage regression for both groups. Thus, standard OLS estimates tend to understate the impact of SFAS No. 2 on R&D expenditures. Finally, Shehata (1991) reports predictions of the expected values of R&D expenditures for both expensing and capitalizing samples had they elected to be in the other group. The mean value of R&D for each group is lower under the unchosen alternative. The decline is more pronounced for the capitalizing group, where it declines from \$ 0.69 mm to \$ 0.37 mm, while the decline is from \$ 0.85 mm to \$ 0.79 mm for the expensing group.

3.5.2. Bankruptcy costs: Bris et al. (2006)

Bris et al. (2006) analyze the relative costs of bankruptcy under the Chapters 11 and 7 procedures in the United States, codes that are discussed more fully in Chapter 14 (John et al., 2008). The sample consists of close to 300 bankruptcy filings in Arizona and Southern New York, the largest sample in the literature as of this writing.

The specification is the basic Heckman model of Section 2, with treatment effects in some specifications. Step 1 is a probit specification that models the choice between Chapters 11 and 7, conditional on deciding to file for bankruptcy. Bris et al. show that the procedural choice is related to firm characteristics such as size, managerial ownership, and the structure of debt including variables such as the number of creditors, whether the debt is secured or not, and the presence of banks as a company creditor. Step 2 involves modeling the costs of bankruptcy. Bris et al. analyze four metrics to specify the LHS dependent variable: the change in value of the estate during bankruptcy; the time spent in bankruptcy; the expenses submitted to and approved by the bankruptcy court; and the recovery rates of creditors. These are modeled as a function of a comprehensive set of regressors that include linear and nonlinear functions of firm size, various proxies for the structure of the filing firm and managerial ownership. Because the variables in the two stages are similar, the study essentially relies on nonlinearity for identification.

Bris et al. find no evidence that firms that were more likely to self-select into Chapter 11 were any faster or slower in completing the bankruptcy process. Controlling for self-selection, Chapter 11 cases consumed more fees, not because Chapter 11 is intrinsically the more expensive procedure, but because of intrinsic differences in firms that choose to reorganize under this code. After controlling for self-selection, Chapter 11 emerges as the cheaper mechanism, and Bris et al. report that self-selection explains about half of the variation in bankruptcy expenses. With self-selection controls, Chapter 11 cases had higher recovery rates than Chapter 7 cases. In sum, selection has a significant impact on estimates of reorganization costs under different bankruptcy codes. After controlling for selection, Chapter 7 takes almost as long, consumes no less and probably more in professional fees, and creditors rarely receive as much, so there is little evidence that it is more efficient than Chapter 11 reorganizations.

3.5.3. Family ownership and value: Villalonga and Amit (2006)

Villalonga and Amit (2006) examine the effect of family ownership, control, and management on value for a sample of Fortune 500 firms from 1994 to 2000. The specification is a standard Heckman style selection model of Section 2 with a treatment effect.

The first step is a probit specification that models whether a firm remains family owned or not. Family ownership is defined as firms in which the founding family owns at least 5% of shares or holds the CEO position. In the second step, value, proxied by Tobin's Q, is regressed on a dummy variable for family ownership, industry dummy variables, the Gompers et al. (2003) shareholder rights index, firm-specific variables from COMPUSTAT, outside block ownership and proportion of nonfamily outside directors, and, of course, the inverse Mills ratio that corrects for self-selection. To assist in identification, Villalonga and Amit include two additional instruments in the selection equation lagged Q and idiosyncratic risk. Idiosyncratic risk is presumably related to family ownership but not to Q if only systematic risk is priced by the market.

Villalonga and Amit report that family ownership has a positive effect on value in the overall sample and in subsamples in which the founder is the CEO. Interestingly, the sign is negative when the founder is not the CEO. Villalonga and Amit interpret their findings as evidence that the benefits of family ownership are lost when the family retains control in the postfounder generation. Their results strengthen when they incorporate a control for self-selection. In the self-selection specification, the inverse Mills ratio is significant and negative in the overall specification and subsamples in which the CEO is the founder. In these samples, family ownership appears to be associated with unobserved attributes that are negatively related to value. These unobserved attributes positively impact value if the founder is not the CEO.[29]

3.6. Other applications of matching methods

3.6.1. Bank debt versus bonds: Bharath (2004)

Debt financing by a corporation gives rise to conflicts of interest between creditors and shareholders that can reduce the value of the firm. Such conflicts are limited more effectively in bank loans than in public debt issues if banks monitor. Bharath (2004) measures the size of agency costs by calculating the yield spread between corporate bonds and bank loans (the Bond-Bank spread) of the same firm at the same point in time. To quantify the difference, Bharath needs to match bonds with bank loans of the same firm at the same point in time and having substantively identical terms. The matching problem is complicated by the fact that bank loans and public bonds are contractually very different on multiple dimensions such as credit rating, seniority, maturity, and collateral.

Bharath argues that because bank loans and bonds are matched at the same point of time and for the same firm, matching based on observables should adequately control for differences between bank debt and public debt. Thus, propensity score based matching methods are appropriate tools to control for differences between bank loans and public debt. Bharath uses the propensity score matched difference between bank and bond credit spreads as the treatment effect, or the value added by banks. The spread can be interpreted as the value added by banks in enforcing better investment policies, or more generally, as the price of the "specialness" of banks due to their ability to monitor, generate information, or better renegotiate loans, or even perhaps other explanations such as monopoly rents.

Using a sample of over 15,000 yield observations, Bharath finds that the Bond-Bank spread is negative for high credit quality firms and positive for low credit quality firms. He interprets his findings as being consistent with the view that for high-quality firms, the benefits of bank monitoring are outweighed by the costs of bank holdup. This causes the spread to be negative, indicating that bank debt offers few benefits for high-quality firms. For low-quality firms, the opposite is true, causing the spread to be positive. The magnitude of the potential agency costs mitigated by banks is more important for poor quality firms, justifying the decision to borrow from banks.

---

[29] An interesting question raised by this study is survivorship (e.g., Brown et al., 1995). Perhaps family owned firms that survived and made it to Fortune 500 status are of better quality, and hence these firms are valued more. This question can perhaps be resolved by looking at broader samples that incorporate smaller firms outside the Fortune 500 universe. Bennedsen et al. (2006) take a step in this direction.

3.6.2. *Matching and long-run performance: Cheng (2003) and Li and Zhao (2006)*

A vast literature on market efficiency examines the long-run stock return after events such as IPOs, SEOs, share repurchases, listing changes, etc. The semistrong version of the efficient markets hypothesis predicts that long-run returns should be zero on average. However, several papers report empirical evidence against the efficiency hypothesis (Fama, 1998). In most studies, postevent buy-and-hold returns are systematically positive or negative relative to benchmarks over periods of 3-5 years. Chapter 1 (Kothari and Warner, 2007) offers an overview of this literature. We focus on applications of matching models to assess long-run performance.

To test whether abnormal returns are zero or not, one needs a model of benchmark returns. As discussed in Chapter 1, the standard approach, is to match an event firm with a nonevent firm on between two and four characteristics that include size, book-to-market, past returns, and perhaps industry. This method runs into difficulties when the number of dimensions becomes large and the calipers become fine, when it becomes difficult to generate matching firms. Propensity score (PS) based matching methods reviewed in Section 4.3.2 are potentially useful alternatives in this scenario. Two recent papers, Cheng (2003) and Li and Zhao (2006) use PS methods to reexamine the long-term performance of stock returns after SEOs. Both papers find that while characteristic-by-characteristic matching results in significant long-term abnormal returns after SEOs, abnormal returns are insignificant if one uses propensity score based matching methods instead.

Cheng (2003) studies SEOs offered between 1970 and 1997 for which necessary COMPUSTAT data are available on firm characteristics. She finds significant buy-and-hold abnormal returns of between -6% and -14% over 3–5 years in the full sample and various subsamples when matches are constructed on size, industry and book-to-market. She then uses three logit models, one for each decade, to predict the probability of issuance. Several firm characteristics such as size, book-to-market, industry, R&D, exchange, as well as 11-month past returns predict the issuance decision. Cheng matches each issuer with a nonissuer in the SEO year with a similar propensity score (i.e., predicted probability). She finds little evidence of significant abnormal returns except for one subsample in the 1970s.

Li and Zhao undertake an exercise similar to that in Cheng (2003) for issuers from 1986 to 1997. They show that characteristic-by-characteristic matching produces inadequate matches between issuers and nonissuers in terms of average size.[30] They estimate propensity scores with size, book-to-market, and past returns in three quarters prior to issuance, one model per year, and add interaction terms for better predictions and delete firms as necessary to have a common support. In their final sample, conventional matching gives average 3-year buy-and-hold abnormal returns of -16%, but this drops to an insignificant -4% with PS matching.

---

[30] Medians are not reported, so it is hard to assess the role of outliers.

Cheng (2003) and Li and Zhao (2006) emphasize that PS methods are merely substitutes for characteristic-by-characteristic matching of observables. This perspective is probably appropriate. The main issue in these applications is the data driven nature of the exercise in fitting probit models. Characteristics and interaction terms are added as needed to achieve balance in characteristics and propensity scores. While we recognize that a reasonable probit model seems necessary to place faith in treatment effect estimates, the search required to achieve balance, however transparent, nevertheless raises data dredging concerns and even inconsistency of estimates (Heckman and Navarro-Lozano, 2004). The general use of PS methods in studies of long-term stock return or operating performance as an alternative to methods studied in Barber and Lyon (1996, 1997), Barber et al. (1999), and Kothari and Warner (1997) remains an open question.

3.7. Bayesian methods

3.7.1. Matching: Sørensen (2007)

Investors differ in their abilities to select good investments, and in their ability to take a given investment and monitor and manage it so as to add value to what they invest in. A key question in the venture capital literature is the differentiation of selection from value-addition. To what extent are better performing venture capitalists more successful because of their ability to select good investments rather than their ability to value-add to their investments? Sørensen (2007) employs a matching-selection model to separate these two influences, using Bayesian MCMC (Markov Chain Monte Carlo) methods to estimate it.

In Sørensen's model, there is a set of venture capital investors indexed by i. Each investor evaluates a set of potential investments indexed by j and ultimately invests (i.e., becomes the lead investor) in a subset of these. Once an investment occurs, its outcome is specified as the variable *IPO* which equals one if the investment results in a public offering and zero otherwise. In Sørensen's model, feasible investments for each investor are partly determined by the characteristics of the other agents in the market. These characteristics are related to the investment decision but unrelated to the investment outcome, so they provide the exogenous variation used for identification of the model. On the other hand, this type of sorting also causes interaction between investment decisions by different venture capitalists, which leads to a dimensionality problem and considerable numerical difficulties in estimation. Bayesian methods offer feasible routes for estimation.

Sørensen specifies normally distributed and diffuse prior beliefs with prior variances that are over 300 times the posterior variance. He assumes that error terms for different deals are independent. There are three sets of exogenous variables. The characteristics of the company includes the stage of development of the company and industry dummies. The characteristics of the venture capital investor include his experience and amount of capital he has available. The characteristic of the market is the year of the investment. There are two parameters of central interest. One is the access of better venture capitalists to deal flow, which is captured by the experience of the venture capitalist. The other is the synergy between venture capitalists and their target investments or the value added by venture capitalists, which is captured by the correlation between the private information in the decision to invest and the probability of going public.

Sørensen's final sample includes 1666 investments made by 75 venture capitalists between 1975 and 1995 in the states of California and Massachusetts. Experience is proxied by the total and stage-of-life-cycle-specific number of deals done since 1975. Sørensen reports a number of interesting findings. He finds evidence for sorting. Experienced investors are more likely to have access to the better deals whose probability of going public (and doing so faster) increases by about two-thirds. This type of sorting explains about 60% of the increased probability of success, leaving about 40% for the synergies, or the value added by venture capital investors. Sørensen explains why one might get different results from estimating a standard selection model compared to one with sorting.

3.7.2. Switching regressions: Li and McNally (2004) and Scruggs (2007)

Li and McNally (2004) and Scruggs (2007) offer interesting applications of Bayesian methods to estimate switching regression models of self-selection. Both papers emphasize that the value of the Bayesian approach is not merely the difference in philosophy or technique; rather, the techniques offer insights not readily available through classical methods. The application in Li and McNally (2004) is the choice of a mechanism to effect share repurchases, while the application in Scruggs relates to whether convertibles are called with or without standby underwriting arrangements. For convenience, we focus on Li and McNally, but substantially similar insights on methodology are offered in the work by Scruggs.[31]

Share repurchases started becoming popular in the 1980s as a way to return excess cash to shareholders in lieu of dividends. Repurchases tend to be more flexible in timing and quantity relative to the fixed cash flow stream expected by markets when companies raise dividends. Share repurchases can be implemented in practice as a direct tender offer or more open-ended open market repurchases. Li and McNally (2004) investigate the choice between the two mechanisms and their impact on share price reactions to announcements of repurchases using Bayesian self-selection methods.

Li and McNally propose the following system of equations to analyze the choice of a repurchase mechanism:

$$I^* = Z_i \gamma + \eta_i, \tag{69}$$

---

[31] Wald and Long (2006) present an application of switching regression using classical estimation methods. They analyze the effect of state laws on capital structure.

$$p_1^* = X_1\beta_1 + \varepsilon_1, \tag{70}$$

$$p_2^* = X_2\beta_2 + \varepsilon_2, \tag{71}$$

$$y_1^* = W_1\alpha_1 + v_1, \tag{72}$$

$$R_1^* = V_1\theta_1 + u_1, \tag{73}$$

$$R_2^* = V_2\theta_2 + u_2, \tag{74}$$

where I^* is an unobserved latent variable representing the incremental utility of tender offers over open market repurchases, p_1^*, y_1^*, R_1^* are the percentage of shares sought, tender premium and announcement effects under the tender offer regime, and p_2^*, R_2^* are the proportion sought and announcement effects in an open market repurchase regime. The error terms in Equations (69)–(74) are assumed to have a multivariate normal distribution.

The system of Equations (69)–(74) represents a switching regression system discussed in Section 3.1, but with more than one regression in each regime. The key issue in estimating the system is the lack of information on unobserved counterfactuals. We observe outcomes in the repurchase technique actually chosen by a firm but do not explicitly observe what would happen if the firm had chosen the alternative technique instead. Li and McNally employ MCMC methods that generate counterfactuals as a natural by-product of the estimation procedure. This approach involves a data augmentation step in which the observed data are supplemented with counterfactuals generated consistent with the model structure. The priors about parameters are updated and posteriors obtained using standard simulation methods after which the additional uncertainty due to the data augmentation step can be integrated out. Observations on counterfactual choices and outcomes are generated as part of the estimation procedure. These can be directly used to examine the impact of choosing a given type of repurchase mechanism not just in isolation, but also relative to the impact of choosing the unchosen alternative.

The sample in Li and McNally comprises 330 fixed price tender offers, 72 Dutch auction tender offers, and 1197 open market repurchases covering time periods from 1962 to 1988. In terms of findings, Li and McNally report that firms choose the tender offer mechanism when they have financial slack and large shareholders that monitor management. Firms prefer the open market repurchase in times of market turbulence or weak business conditions. Unobserved private information affects both the type of the repurchase program and the repurchase terms and is reflected in the stock market announcement effects. The estimates of counterfactuals are quite interesting. For instance, if the open market repurchasers had opted for tender offers, the proportion of shares sought would have been 36% (vs. actual of about 7%) and the tender premium would have been 33% compared to 0% actuals, and the 5-day announcement effect would be 16% compared to the actual announcement effect of 2.2%. Likewise, tender offer firms would have repurchased 10.6% (actual = 19.7%) and experienced announcement effects of 3.7% (actual $= 10.2\%$). Firms appear to have a comparative advantage in their chosen repurchase mechanisms.

4. Conclusions

Our review suggests that self-selection is a growth area in empirical corporate finance. The rapidly expanding number of applications undoubtedly reflects the growing recognition in the finance profession that self-selection is an important and pervasive feature of corporate finance decisions. The range of econometric models in use is also growing as techniques diffuse from the econometrics literature to finance. However, the key issue in implementing self-selection models still remains the choice of specification, particularly the economic assumptions that make one model or another more appropriate for a given application. One size does not fit all. Each self-selection model addresses a different kind of problems, places its own demands on the type of data needed, and more importantly, carries its own baggage of economic assumptions. The plausibility of these assumptions is perhaps the primary criterion to guide what is used in empirical applications.

References

Abadie, A. and G. Imbens, 2004, "Simple and Bias-Corrected Matching Estimators for Average Treatment Effects," Working Paper, Harvard University.

Acharya, S., 1988, "A Generalized Econometric Model and Tests of a Signaling Hypothesis with Two Discrete Signals," *Journal of Finance*, 43, 413–429.

Acharya, S., 1993, "Value of Latent Information: Alternative Event Study Methods," *Journal of Finance*, 48, 363–385.

Barber, B. and J. Lyon, 1996, "Detecting Abnormal Operating Performance: The Empirical Power and Specification of Test Statistics," *Journal of Financial Economics*, 41, 359–400.

Barber, B. and J. Lyon, 1997, "Detecting Long-Run Abnormal Stock Returns: The Empirical Power and Specification of Test Statistics," *Journal of Financial Economics*, 43, 341–372.

Barber, B., J. Lyon and C. Tsai, 1999, "Improved Methods for Tests of Long-Run Abnormal Stock Returns," *Journal of Finance*, 54, 165–201.

Bennedsen, M., K. Nielsen, F. Perez-Gonzalez and D. Wolfenzon, 2006, "Inside the Family Firm: The Role of Family in Succession Decisions and Performance," Working Paper, New York University.

Berger, P. G. and E. Ofek, 1995, "Diversification's Effect on Firm Value," *Journal of Financial Economics*, 37, 39–65.

Bertrand, M. and S. Mullainathan, 2003, "Enjoying the Quiet Life? Corporate Governance and Managerial Preferences," *Journal of Political Economy*, 111, 1043–1075.

Betton, S., E. Eckbo and K. Thorburn, 2008, "Takeovers, Restructurings, and Corporate Control," in B. E. Eckbo (Ed.), *Handbook of Corporate Finance: Empirical Corporate Finance*, vol. 2, Chapter 15, pp. 291–495. Elsevier/North-Holland, Amsterdam.

Bharath, S., 2004, "Agency Costs, Bank Specialness and Renegotiation," Working Paper, Stephen M. Ross School of Business, University of Michigan.

Bohren, O., B. E. Eckbo and D. Michalsen, 1997, "Why Underwrite Rights Offerings? Some New Evidence," *Journal of Financial Economics*, 46, 223–261.

Bris, A., N. Zhu and I. Welch, 2006, "The Cost of Bankruptcy: Chapter 7 Liquidation Versus Chapter 11 Reorganization," *Journal of Finance*, 61, 1253–1303.

Brown, S., W. Goetzmann and S. Ross, 1995, "Survival," *Journal of Finance*, 50, 853–873.

Campa, J. M. and S. Kedia, 2002, "Explaining the Diversification Discount," *Journal of Finance*, 57, 1731–1762.

Cheng, Y., 2003, "Propensity Score Matching and the New Issues Puzzle," Working Paper, Florida State University.

Chevalier, J., 2000, "Why Do Firms Undertake Diversifying Mergers? An Examination of the Investment Policies of Merging Firms," Working Paper, Yale School of Management.

Chiappori, P. and B. Salanie, 2000, "Testing for Asymmetric Information in Insurance Markets," *Journal of Political Economy*, 108, 56–78.

Chib, S. and E. Greenberg, 1996, "Markov Chain Monte Carlo Simulation Methods in Econometrics," *Econometric Theory*, 12, 409–431.

Coase, R. H., 1933, "The Nature of the Firm," *Economica*, 4, 386–405.

Çolak, G. and T. M. Whited, 2007, "Spin-Offs, Divestitures, and Conglomerate Investment," *Review of Financial Studies*, 20, 557–595.

Dehejia, R. H. and S. Wahba, 1999, "Casual Effects in Non-Experimental Studies: Re-Evaluating the Evaluation of Training Programs," *Journal of American Statistical Association*, 94, 1053–1062.

Dunbar, C. G., 1995, "The Use of Warrants As Underwriter Compensation in Initial Public Offerings," *Journal of Financial Economics*, 38, 59–78.

Eckbo, B. E., 1990, "Valuation Effects of Greenmail Prohibitions," *Journal of Financial and Quantitative Analysis*, 25, 491–505.

Eckbo, B. E., 1992, "Mergers and the Value of Antitrust Deterrence," *Journal of Finance*, 47, 1005–1029.

Eckbo, B. E., V. Maksimovic and J. Williams, 1990, "Consistent Estimation of Cross-Sectional Models in Event Studies," *Review of Financial Studies*, 3, 343–365.

Fama, E., 1998, "Market Efficiency, Long-Term Returns, and Behavioral Finance," *Journal of Financial Economics*, 49, 283–306.

Fang, L. H., 2005, "Investment Bank Reputation and the Price and Quality of Underwriting Services," *Journal of Finance*, 60, 2729–2761.

Gande, A., M. Puri, A. Saunders and I. Walter, 1997, "Bank Underwriting of Debt Securities: Modern Evidence," *Review of Financial Studies*, 10, 1175–1202.

Gande, A., M. Puri and A. Saunders, 1999, "Bank Entry, Competition, and the Market for Corporate Securities Underwriting," *Journal of Financial Economics*, 54, 165–195.

-Gelfand, A. E. and A. F. M. Smith, 1990, "Sampling Based Approaches to Calculating Marginal Densities," *Journal of American Statistical Association*, 85, 398–409.

Goldberger, A., 1983, "Abnormal Selection Bias," In S. Karlin, T. Amemiya and L. Goodman (Eds.), *Studies in Econometrics, Time Series, and Multivariate Statistics*, Academic Press, New York.

Gompers, P. A., J. L. Ishii and A. Metrick, 2003, "Corporate Governance and Equity Prices," *Quarterly Journal of Economics*, 118, 107–155.

Goyal, V. K., 2005, "Market Discipline of Bank Risk: Evidence from Subordinate Debt Contracts," *Journal of Financial Intermediation*, 14, 318–350.

Graham, J. R., M. L. Lemmon and J. G. Wolf, 2002, "Does Corporate Diversification Destroy Value?," *Journal of Finance*, 57, 695–720.

Greene, W., 1981, "Sample Selection Bias as a Specification Error: Comment," *Econometrica*, 49, 795–798.

Greene, W., 2003, *Econometric Analysis*. 5th edition, Prentice-Hall, New York.

Harris, M. and A. Raviv, 1985, "A Sequential Signaling Model of Convertible Debt Call Policy," *Journal of Finance*, 40, 1263–1282.

Heckman, J. J., 1979, "Sample Selection As a Specification Error," *Econometrica*, 47, 153–161.

Heckman, J. J. and S. Navarro-Lozano, 2004, "Using Matching, Instrumental Variables, and Control Functions to Estimate Economic Choice Models," *Review of Economics and Statistics*, 86, 30–57.

Heckman, J. J., H. Ichimura and P. Todd, 1998, "Matching As an Econometric Evaluation Estimator," *Review of Economic Studies*, 65, 261–294.

Himmelberg, C., R. Hubbard and D. Palia, 1999, "Understanding the Determinants of Managerial Ownership and the Link Between Ownership and Performance," *Journal of Financial Economics*, 53, 353–384.

Hubbard, R. G. and D. Palia, 1995, "Benefits of Control, Managerial Ownership, and the Stock Returns of Acquiring Firms," *RAND Journal of Economics*, 26, 782–792.

John, K., E. Hotchkiss, R. C. Mooradian and K. Thorburn, 2008, "Bankruptcy and the Resolution of Financial Distress," in B. E. Eckbo (Ed.), *Handbook of Corporate Finance: Empirical Corporate Finance*, vol. 2, Chapter 14, pp. 235–237. Elsevier/North-Holland, Amsterdam.

Koop, G., 2003, *Bayesian Econometrics*, John Wiley & Sons, New York.

Kothari, S. P. and J. B. Warner, 1997, "Measuring Long-Horizon Security Price Performance," *Journal of Financial Economics*, 43, 301–339.

Kothari, S. P. and J. B. Warner, 2007, "Econometrics of Event Studies," in B. E. Eckbo (Ed.), *Handbook of Corporate Finance: Empirical Corporate Finance*, vol. 1, Chapter 1, this volume, Elsevier/North-Holland, Amsterdam.

Lang, L. H. P. and R. M. Stulz, 1994, "Tobin's Q, Corporate Diversification, and Firm Performance," *Journal of Political Economy*, 102, 1248–1280.

Lee, L. F., 1983, "Generalized Econometric Models with Selectivity," *Econometrica*, 51, 507–512.

Li, K. and W. McNally, 2004, "Open Market Versus Tender Offer Share Repurchases: A Conditional Event Study," Working Paper, Sauder School of Business UBC. Available at http://finance.sauder.ubc.ca/~kaili/buyback. pdf.

Li, K. and W. McNally, 2006, "The Information Content of Canadian Open Market Repurchase Announcements," *Managerial Finance (A Special Issue on Payout Policy)*, 33, 65–80.

Li, X. and X. Zhao, 2006, "Is There an SEO Puzzle?," *Journal of Empirical Finance*, 13, 351–370.

Liu, Y. and P. Malatesta, 2006, "Credit Ratings and the Pricing of Seasoned Equity Offerings," Working Paper, University of Washington.

Ljungqvist, A., F. Marston and W. J. Wilhelm Jr., 2006, "Competing for Securities Underwriting Mandates: Banking Relationships and Analyst Recommendations," *Journal of Finance*, 61, 301–340.

Maddala, G. S., 1983, *Limited-Dependent and Qualitative Variables in Econometrics*, Cambridge University Press, Cambridge.

Maksimovic, V. and G. Phillips, 2002, "Do Conglomerate Firms Allocate Resources Efficiently?," *Journal of Finance*, 57, 721–767.

Maksimovic, V. and G. Phillips, 2007, "Conglomerate Firms and Internal Capital Markets," in B. E. Eckbo (Ed.), *Handbook of Corporate Finance: Empirical Corporate Finance*, vol. 1, Chapter 8, this volume, Elsevier/North-Holland, Amsterdam.

Maksimovic, V. and H. Unal, 1993, "Issue Size Choice and "Underpricing" in Thrift Mutual-to-Stock Conversions," *Journal of Finance*, 48, 1659–1692.

Murphy, K. and R. Topel, 1985, "Estimation and Inference in Two Step Econometric Models," *Journal of Business and Economic Statistics*, 3, 370–379.

Nayak, S. and N. R. Prabhala, 2001, "Disentangling the Dividend Information in Splits: A Decomposition Using Conditional Event-Study Methods," *Review of Financial Studies*, 14, 1083–1116.

Newey, W., J. Powell and J. Walker, 1990, "Semi-Parametric Estimation of Selection Models," *American Economic Review*, 80, 324–328.

Palia, D., 2001, "The Endogeneity of Managerial Compensation in Firm Valuation: A Solution," *Review of Financial Studies*, 14, 735–764.

Poirier, D. J., 1995, *Intermediate Statistics and Econometrics*, MIT Press, Cambridge.

Prabhala, N. R., 1997, "Conditional Methods in Event Studies and an Equilibrium Justification for Standard Event-Study Procedures," *Review of Financial Studies*, 10, 1–38.

Puri, M., 1994, "The Long-Term Default Performance of Bank Underwritten Securities Issues," *Journal of Banking and Finance*, 18, 397–418.

Puri, M., 1996, "Commercial Banks in Investment Banking: Conflict of Interest or Certification Role?," *Journal of Financial Economics*, 40, 373–401.

Reisel, N., 2004, "On the Value of Restrictive Covenants: An Empirical Investigation of Public Bond Issues," Working Paper, Rutgers University.

Rosenbaum, R. and D. Rubin, 1983, "The Central Role of the Propensity Score in Observational Studies for Causal Effects," *Biometrika*, 70, 41–55.

Roy, A. D., 1951, "Some Thoughts on the Distribution of Earnings," *Oxford Economic Papers*, 3, 135–146.

Schoar, A., 2002, "The Effect of Diversification on Firm Productivity," *Journal of Finance*, 62, 2379–2403.

Scruggs, J. T., 2007, "Estimating the Cross-Sectional Market Response to an Endogenous Event: Naked vs. Underwritten Calls of Convertible Bonds," *Journal of Empirical Finance*, 14, 220–247.

Servaes, H., 1994, "Do Takeover Targets Overinvest?," *Review of Financial Studies*, 7, 253–277.

Servaes, H., 1996, "The Value of Diversification During the Conglomerate Merger Wave," *Journal of Finance*, 51, 1201–1225.

Shehata, M., 1991, "Self-Selection Bias and the Economic Consequences of Accounting Regulation: An Application of Two-Stage Switching Regression to SFAS No. 2," *Accounting Review*, 66, 768–787.

Song, W., 2004, "Competition and Coalition Among Underwriters: The Decision to Join a Syndicate," *Journal of Finance*, 59, 2421–2444.

Sørensen, M., 2007, "How Smart is Smart Money? An Empirical Two-Sided Matching Model of Venture Capital," *Journal of Finance*, 62, 2725–2762.

Staiger, D. and J. H. Stock, 1997, "Instrumental Variables Regression with Weak Instruments," *Econometrica*, 65, 557–586.

Tanner, M. A. and W. H. Wong, 1987, "The Calculation of Posterior Distributions by Data Augmentation," *Journal of the American Statistical Association*, 82, 528–550.

Villalonga, B., 2004, "Does Diversification Cause the "Diversification Discount"?," *Financial Management*, 33, 5–27.

Villalonga, B. and R. Amit, 2006, "How Do Family Ownership, Control, and Management Affect Firm Value?," *Journal of Financial Economics*, 80, 385–417.

Vuong, Q., 1989, "Likelihood Ratio Tests for Model Selection and Non-Nested Hypotheses," *Econometrica*, 57, 307–333.

Wald, J. and M. Long, 2006, "The Effect of State Laws on Capital Structure," *Journal of Financial Economics*, 83, 297–319.

Wooldridge, J., 2002, *Econometric Analysis of Cross Section and Panel Data*, MIT Press, Cambridge.

Zhou, X., 2001, "Understanding the Determinants of Managerial Ownership and the Link Between Ownership and Performance: Comment," *Journal of Financial Economics*, 62, 559–571.

PART 3

MERGER WAVES: WHAT DRIVES AGGREGATE TAKEOVER ACTIVITY?

Chapter 4

INVESTIGATING THE ECONOMIC ROLE OF MERGERS*

GREGOR ANDRADE

Harvard Business School, Soldiers Field, Boston, Massachusetts, USA

ERIK STAFFORD

Harvard Business School, Soldiers Field, Boston, Massachusetts, USA

Contents

* This paper was previously titled: "Investigating the Characteristics and Determinants of Mergers and Other Forms of Investment." We thank several anonymous referees, seminar participants at Wharton, Duke, Stanford, NYU and MIT, as well as Judy Chevalier, Doug Diamond, Eugene Fama, J.B. Heaton, Laurie Hodrick, Anil Kashyap, Owen Lamont, Raghuram Rajan, Robert Vishny, Tuomo Vuolteenaho, and Luigi Zingales for helpful comments and discussion, and Fai Tong Chung for assisting with data collection. We are particularly indebted to Steve Kaplan and Mark Mitchell for their support and valuable insights.

This article originally appeared in the *Journal of Corporate Finance*, Vol. 10, pp. 1–36 (2004).
Corporate Takeovers, Volume 1
Edited by B. Espen Eckbo
DOI: 10.1016/B978-0-12-381983-3.00004-6

Abstract

We investigate the economic role of mergers by performing a comparative study of mergers and internal corporate investment at the industry and firm levels. We find strong evidence that merger activity clusters through time by industry, whereas internal investment does not. Mergers play both an "expansionary" and "contractionary" role in industry restructuring. During the 1970s and 1980s, excess capacity drove industry consolidation through mergers, while peak capacity utilization triggered industry expansion through nonmerger investments. In the 1990s, this phenomenon is reversed, as industries with strong growth prospects, high profitability, and near capacity experience the most intense merger activity.

Keywords

mergers, acquisitions, restructuring, corporate governance

JEL classification: G34

1. Introduction

This paper investigates the economic role of corporate mergers and acquisitions by studying both the firm and industry-level forces that motivate them. We classify these forces broadly as either "expansionary," in which case mergers are similar in spirit to internal investment, adding to the capital stock of a firm or industry; or "contractionary," whereby mergers facilitate consolidation and reduction of the asset base.

From the point of view of the acquiring company, the first-order effect of mergers is a net addition to the firm's stock of assets. This has two implications. Firstly, a significant portion of merger activity should be explained by factors that motivate firms to expand and grow. Secondly, mergers and internal investment should be related, since they are similar ways of adding to a firm's asset base and productive capacity. Therefore, the choice between investing internally and acquiring another firm boils down to considering the relative net benefits of the alternatives.

Industry-wide forces can also precipitate mergers, for example, a reaction to a change in the industry structure, in response to some fundamental shock. This somewhat intuitive view has gained prominence in recent years. Jensen (1993) proposes that most merger activity since the mid-1970s has been caused by technological and supply shocks, which resulted in excess productive capacity in many industries. He argues that mergers are the principal way of removing this excess capacity, as faulty internal governance mechanisms prevent firms from "shrinking" themselves. Mitchell and Mulherin (1996) document that a substantial portion of takeover activity in the 1980s could be explained by industries reacting to major shocks, such as deregulation, increased foreign competition, financial innovations, and oil price shocks. In addition, Morck et al. (1988) suggest that hostile takeovers are "responses to adverse industry-wide shocks."

When mergers are due to industry-wide causes, their association with expansion becomes less clear-cut. In particular, at the industry level, the immediate effect of own-industry mergers is the reallocation of existing assets. Clearly, this reallocation can occur in the context of an industry-wide expansion, as firms may attempt to increase their size and scale in order to afford large capital investments.[1] However, it is also clear that to the extent that mergers within an industry allow firms to remove duplicate functions and rationalize operations, they often result in an overall decrease in the industry's asset base. These are two fundamentally different types of merger activity, and the tension between their effects on industry-level productive capacity, growth in one case and neutral or reduction in the other, suggests that merger activity can be decomposed into two fundamental roles: "expansion" and "contraction."

While the notion that mergers play different economic roles has been previously cited, and to some extent intuitively held by many merger researchers, there is scant empirical work linking these disparate roles. This paper is aimed at filling this gap. We

---

[1] This explanation is often cited as the main reason behind the media and telecommunications mergers of the 1990s.

examine the determinants of mergers and internal corporate investment, within a framework that allows us to test for the incidence of different types of mergers, expansionary or contractionary, over time and across industries. Also, by performing the analysis both at the industry and firm level, we can empirically verify our premise that merger activity is related to both firm-specific and industry-wide causes.

Given our previous definitions, we test for the expansionary role of mergers at the firm and industry level by determining the extent to which mergers and internal investment both respond to the same external incentives to add assets. In particular, this story predicts that both merger and nonmerger investment should be increasing in estimates of growth opportunities, such as Tobin's q. We also expect that the incentives to expand are stronger in times when existing capacity is near exhaustion, and thus both merger and nonmerger investment should be positively related to capacity utilization. In contrast, the contractionary role implies that merger activity should be negatively related to capacity utilization, particularly at the industry level.

Regression analysis on the industry-level determinants of merger and nonmerger investment finds that industry capacity utilization has significant and opposite effects on merger and nonmerger investment. Excess capacity drives industry consolidation through mergers, while peak capacity utilization induces industry expansion through nonmerger investments.[2] Further analysis reveals that the negative relationship between mergers and capacity utilization is restricted to the 1970s and 1980s, while in the 1990s, the relation is positive and significant, indicating that the role of mergers in facilitating expansion and contraction changes over time. The evidence suggests that in the mid-1970s and 1980s, as the economy adjusted to a variety of shocks to capacity and competition (see Mitchell and Mulherin, 1996), industries restructured and consolidated via mergers. However, during the 1990s, merger activity appears more related to industry expansion, as industries near capacity, with high q, and increased profitability are more likely to experience intense merger activity. In addition, we find a strong positive relation between industry shocks and own-industry mergers in the 1990s. This is consistent with recent findings by Mulherin and Boone (2000) and Andrade et al. (2001) who each find significantly higher merger activity in recently deregulated industries in the 1990s.

We also perform clustering tests, which indicate significant time series clustering of mergers by industry of the acquirer. In particular, industry rankings of merger activity are essentially independent through time, while similar rankings for nonmerger forms of investment show strong persistence from one 5-year subperiod to the next. Also, on average, half of an industry's mergers occur within a span of 5 years during our sample period from 1970 to 1994. This evidence is suggestive of mergers resulting from industry shocks, unlike nonmerger investments. These results on acquirer industry clustering are similar to those found for target firms by Mitchell and Mulherin (1996),

---

[2] The positive relation between internal investment and industry capacity utilization is also reported in Kovenock and Phillips (1997).

and for both mergers and divestitures in the 1990s by Mulherin and Boone (2000). In a separate test, we find that in four out of five subperiods, industry rankings of merger and nonmerger investment are independent of each other, indicating a lack of either complementarity or substitutability between merger and other types of investment.

At the firm level, we find further evidence of an important expansionary component to mergers. In particular, we find that firms classified as "high q" are significantly more likely to undertake both mergers and nonmerger investment projects than "low q" firms, as would be predicted by the q-theory of investment. Moreover, we find a strong positive relation between sales growth and both mergers and nonmerger investment. Therefore, both merger and nonmerger investments seem to respond similarly to firm-level incentives to grow.

The sample used in our study is described in Section 2. Section 3 characterizes industry-level merger and nonmerger investment activity. Section 4 reports firm-level analysis. Section 5 summarizes our results and concludes.

2. Data sources and sample description

One of the main difficulties in performing industry-level empirical work is deciding on relevant industry classifications and allocating firms to them. Both CRSP and Compustat report SIC codes for most firms they cover, but these data are fraught with errors. In fact, recent studies (see, e.g., Guenther and Rosman, 1994; Kahle and Walkling, 1996; and the CRSP documentation manuals) indicate that more than one-third of firms on both databases do not match at the two-digit level of SIC code, which for many industries is already an excessive level of aggregation.[3] In addition, since Compustat only reports current SIC codes, while CRSP reports historical classifications, matching worsens as one goes further back in time.[4]

The data set we use for this paper is based on the universe of firms and industries covered by Value Line from 1970 to 1994. This provides a ready-made, widely accepted industry classification scheme, allowing us to sidestep the problems with SIC codes mentioned above. For each year during the sample period, we compile a list of all firms and their industry assignments from the fourth quarter edition of Value Line (see Appendix A for details on this procedure).

We exclude all firms classified under: (1) foreign industries (e.g., "Japanese Diversified," or "Canadian Energy"), (2) ADR's, (3) REIT's, and (4) investment funds and/or companies. We also eliminate six firms that were not in Compustat, as well as 67 firms that were classified as "Unassigned" or "Recent Additions" in some years but

---

[3] For example, SIC code 2800 includes firms which produce chemicals, drugs, and toiletries and cosmetics, all of which we classify separately.

[4] However, this should not lead one to conclude that since CRSP reports historical SIC codes, that it must be the preferred classification source, because as Kahle and Walkling (1996) show, Compustat classifies current firms more accurately. In fact, CRSP SIC code allocations have so many mistakes that they effectively offset any advantage from having historical numbers.

were not subsequently assigned to an industry. There are also 30 firms that, for at least 1 year, Value Line placed in two different industries, which we randomly assign to one of them. The resulting sample contains 2969 firms, representing 37,147 firm-years.

Merger data consist of a subset of the CRSP Merger Database including all mergers between CRSP-listed firms over the 1970–1994 period. The database includes transaction announcement and completion dates obtained from the Wall Street Journal Index for most mergers, where completion is defined as the earliest date in which control (+50% interest) is achieved. For 196 deals where a completion date is not available, it is estimated as 4 months following the announcement, which corresponds to the median time period elapsed between announcement and completion for the mergers that report both dates. We assign each merger a value based on the total market value of the target at completion, defined as the sum of total book debt and preferred stock [Compustat items 9, 34, and 56], market equity capitalization [from CRSP], less excess cash, estimated as total cash in the balance sheet [Compustat item 1] in excess of 5.5% of sales,[5] with all balance sheet items as of precompletion fiscal year-end (see Appendix C for a listing of Compustat data items used in this paper). Targets in the financial sector are valued only at market equity. In addition, for 612 target firms not available in Compustat, we hand-collect capitalization figures from the annual Moody's Industrial, OTC, Transportation and Utilities manuals. As a result, only 66 mergers are not assigned a value, and are therefore excluded from the analysis. Our method for assigning deal values allows us to maximize use of the sample by not requiring the parties involved to disclose the price of the transaction. On the other hand, it assumes that the acquirer obtains 100% of the target at the completion date. While that may be true for most mergers in the sample, there are some for which the completion date merely represents acquisition of control, which was later followed by a "clean-up merger" at a different price. In addition, we exclude leveraged buyouts and other going private deals, which were very common in the 1980s. This is because our analysis focuses on acquirers that can and do engage in both mergers and nonmerger investment, rather than firms whose sole purpose is to perform takeovers.[6]

Finally, we search through the merger data set for deals where the acquirer belonged to our industry sample at the time of the merger completion and the deal was completed after 1969. This procedure yields 1711 mergers, of which 1682 have estimated values that are allocated to the respective acquirer in the fiscal year of completion. Table A2 in Appendix B shows how the mergers are distributed by industry and year. In addition, for each of these mergers, we attempt to allocate the target firm to an industry at the time of the initial merger announcement, by searching in Value Line, or by matching combinations of CRSP, Compustat and Dun and Bradstreet Million Dollar Directory SIC codes (see Appendix B for details on the target industry assignment procedure). For the subset of target firms assigned to an

---

[5] 5.5% corresponds to the median ratio of cash to sales for all firms on Compustat from 1970 to 1994.
[6] Excluding LBO's and other going-private deals makes our merger series different at the aggregate level from the ones used by other authors, who include all takeovers of domestic targets.

industry, we classify the merger as diversifying or own industry by comparing acquirer and target industry classifications at announcement. Diversifying mergers are defined as deals where the industry of the acquirer and the target differ, while the opposite is true for own-industry merger. In total, 1536 targets are successfully assigned to an industry, resulting in 656 diversifying and 880 own-industry mergers.

3. Mergers and nonmerger investment at the industry level

The goal of this section is to gain insights into the industry-level forces behind merger and nonmerger investment. Specifically, we test (1) the degree to which mergers and nonmerger investment are related to shocks to industry structure, (2) whether mergers tend to occur in times of industry-wide excess capacity, and (3) whether mergers tend to occur in times of strong industry growth prospects.

Most industry-level empirical analysis we perform is based on industry-wide measures of annual merger and investment "intensities," which we define as the total value of merger and investment activity in the industry, scaled by the total book assets of all firms in the industry at year-end. This method is useful in two respects: (1) the intensities can be compared across time, industries, and types of merger and nonmerger investment, since they are fairly insensitive to changes and/or differences in industry composition,[7] and (2) at the firm level, investment is aimed at replacing depreciated assets and/or adding new assets, therefore, it is natural to scale investment by some measure of the capital stock in place.[8] We estimate annual industry-level intensities for six types of expenditures: (1) Merger, (2) Diversifying Merger, (3) Own-Industry Merger, (4) CAPX (Capital expenditures), (5) R&D (research and development), and (6) NonMerger Investment (defined as the sum of CAPX, R&D and advertising expenses). For merger-related intensities (1, 2, and 3 above), the denominator in the intensity measure includes all firms reporting nonmissing book assets, whereas for nonmerger investment intensities (4, 5, and 6), we also require firms to report nonmissing CAPX to ensure that the same firms are included in the numerator and denominator. When calculating the nonmerger investment intensities, R&D and advertising are set to zero whenever missing.

Table 1 reports summary statistics on the total level of investment by our sample firms between 1970 and 1994. This total includes both merger and nonmerger investment, as defined above.[9] The table also displays the percentage of total investment

---

[7] Furthermore, these intensities are later used as dependent variables in panel regressions, in which case the scaling provides a rough but somewhat effective means of controlling for heteroscedasticity.

[8] See Kaplan and Zingales (1997) and Mitchell and Mulherin (1996) for recent examples of empirical studies where proxies for firm value scale investment and merger expenditures.

[9] Aggregate investment peaks in the early 1980's but that is due mainly to changes in the composition of Value Line over the sample period. In particular, starting in the early 1980's, the banking and brokerage industries have constituted a larger portion of the sample relative to early periods (see Table A1 in Appendix A). As these industries perform little nonmerger investment (especially CAPX and R&D), they reduce the overall level of investment in the total sample.

Table 1

Summary statistics on real investment expenditures by sample firms, and comparison of industry-level investment intensity rankings across 5-year subperiods from 1970 to 1994

Total investment expenditures include both merger and nonmerger investment, and are reported in constant 1994 dollars. Comparisons between pairs of consecutive subperiods are based on Spearman's rank correlation coefficient. Industry rankings are based on investment intensities that are calculated for each industry as the average over the subperiod of the annual ratio of total investment of each type by firms in the industry to the total book assets of the industry at year-end. Industry merger values are the total value of all transactions in the CRSP Merger Database involving acquirers in the industry. Capital expenditures (CAPX), research and development (R&D) and advertising include all sample firms with Compustat data. Nonmerger investment is the sum of CAPX, R&D, and advertising. CAPX rankings exclude financial sector firms. R&D rankings include only industries related to manufacturing and mining. p-Values are in parentheses.

Summary statistics

	1970–1974	1975–1979	1980–1984	1985–1989	1990–1994
Real total investment (merger and nonmerger) in billions of 1994 dollars	$1377	$1954	$2340	$2291	$2168
Merger as of total investment (%)	3.8	4.9	9.4	12.5	7.9

Subperiod correlations

	Spearman's rank correlation coefficient			
	1970–1974 vs. 1975–1979	1975–1979 vs. 1980–1984	1980–1984 vs. 1985–1989	1985–1989 vs. 1990–1994
Merger	0.376 (0.006)	0.331 (0.015)	0.114 (0.403)	0.175 (0.198)
CAPX	0.830 (0.000)	0.860 (0.000)	0.659 (0.000)	0.729 (0.000)
R&D	0.970 (0.000)	0.969 (0.000)	0.949 (0.000)	0.931 (0.000)
Nonmerger investment	0.883 (0.000)	0.912 (0.000)	0.853 (0.000)	0.855 (0.000)

made up of merger activity. Note that the relative importance of merger activity changes over time. This is seen more clearly in Figure 1, which plots the average ratio of merger to total investment expenditures for our sample firms on an annual basis.[10] Firm-level expenditures on mergers relative to internal investment increased dramatically in the late 1980s, not surprising considering the period corresponds to a well-known economy-wide merger wave. However, it is interesting that even during the recession that followed in the early 1990s, merger activity remained at a significantly higher level than in the 1970s. Perhaps this represents a shift in the overall propensity of firms to acquire others, which

[10] Both Table 1 and Figure 1 understate total merger activity, given the way we identify merger in this study. In particular, we only look at merger between Value Line acquirers and CRSP-listed targets. We ignore foreign acquirers and targets, acquisitions of plants and divisions, as well as LBO's and other going-private transactions.

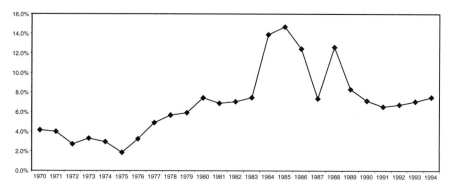

Fig. 1. Merger activity as the percentage of total firm-level investment (average across all firms).

would also be consistent with the subsequent explosion in merger activity of the late 1990s, the largest merger wave ever (see Andrade et al., 2001).

3.1. Historical patterns in industry merger and nonmerger investment

Mitchell and Mulherin (1996) document significant clustering of target firms by industry during the 1980s.[11] In this subsection, we test for such industry clustering in both merger and nonmerger investment activity. In contrast to those authors, we look at the industry of the acquirer, not the target. A finding that mergers cluster by industry over time would support the claim that, to some extent, merger activity is a result of industry shocks.

We divide the sample period (1970–1994) into five equal subperiods, and calculate industry-level subperiod intensities for all six of the investment measures defined above, by averaging the annual intensities within each subperiod.[12] Then, each of the industry-level investment intensity series is ranked within each subperiod, and we compare the rankings over time and across forms of investment.[13] Therefore, we are testing whether the relative ranking across industries, for each form of investment, is persistent over time.

---

[11] There is also evidence of clustering in earlier periods. Nelson (1959) identifies pronounced differences in takeover rates across industries over time, using data for the first half of the century. Gort (1969) confirms those results with data on takeovers in the 1950s, and suggests they are caused by "economic disturbances" due to rapid changes in technology and/or stock prices.

[12] We also estimate business cycle-based subperiods, using NBER's classification of expansions and contractions. This resulted in five cycles during our sample period: 1970–1974, 1975–1979, 1980–1982, 1983–1990, and 1991–1994 (this last period is not a complete cycle, since it has been a period of expansion only). Changing the subperiod definition did not impact the results, and the inferences remained unaltered, therefore, only the equal subperiods are reported.

[13] For CAPX and R&D rankings, we exclude certain industries because: (1) Compustat does not report CAPX or R&D expense for them, or (2) by the very nature of their business, these firms do not perform R&D investment. As a result, CAPX rankings exclude firms in the financial sector, while the R&D rankings include only manufacturing and mining firms.

For each of merger, CAPX, R&D and nonmerger investment, we analyze the stability of rankings over time. We perform a Spearman's rank correlation test for each pair of consecutive subperiods (see Gibbons, 1985 for details). Since the null hypothesis is that the rankings are independent each period, rejection indicates a strong level of stability in the rankings. Table 1 reports our results.

The first thing to note is the striking contrast between the stability of merger and nonmerger rankings across subperiods. While industry merger rankings, particularly in the 1980s, exhibit little correlation from one subperiod to the next, the rankings for CAPX, R&D and total nonmerger investment intensity are nearly constant.[14] This is evident not only from the puny p-values, but the magnitude of the test statistics themselves, which can be loosely interpreted as correlation coefficients. The industry-rank correlations average 0.25 across subperiods for mergers and 0.88 for nonmerger investment. Additionally, the average industry has approximately 50% of its mergers occur within a 5-year subperiod over the 25-year sample period (see Table A2 in Appendix B). These results suggest strong time series clustering of industry merger activity, while rejecting the notion of clustering for nonmerger investment. The result that nonmerger investment does not cluster by industry is important, as it strengthens the restructuring interpretation of the evidence on mergers. In some sense, if both merger and nonmerger investment clustered, we would be hard pressed to argue that mergers play a distinct restructuring role, one that cannot be fulfilled by other forms of investment.[15]

Given the markedly different historical patterns in merger and nonmerger investment, it is interesting to check whether at each point in time there is any relation, positive or negative, between the two. In particular, we want to know whether there is any evidence of complementarity or substitutability between internal and external investment, or its components. Towards that goal, within each subperiod, we compare the rankings between the following sets of investment intensity pairs: (1) merger and nonmerger investment, (2) diversifying merger and nonmerger investment, (3) own-industry merger and nonmerger investment, and (4) diversifying merger and own-industry merger. The statistical procedure used is again the Spearman's rank correlation test. Note that under the null hypothesis, the rankings within each subperiod are independent—a rejection indicates some complementarity or substitutability between investment forms, depending on the sign.

Table 2 contains our results for these tests. In general, the merger and nonmerger investment intensities are independent within subperiods. Therefore, there is no persistent evidence that firms merge conditionally on high levels of internal investment in

[14] If depreciation rates differ greatly across industries but are fairly constant through time, it can be argued that the stability in CAPX and nonmerger investment intensity rankings is partly due to industries replacing depreciated assets.
[15] A separate implication of the results on industry clustering is that merger event studies are poorly specified statistically. The assumption of independence across events is certainly violated, and is likely even more severe a problem for long-term performance studies (see Mitchell and stafford, 2000).

Table 2

Comparison within subperiods of industry-level investment intensity rankings across investment types

Subperiods are 5-year intervals from 1970 to 1994. Comparisons are based on Spearman's rank correlation coefficients. Industry rankings are based on investment intensities that are calculated for each industry as the average over the subperiod of the annual ratio of total investment of each type by firms in the industry to the total book assets of the industry at year-end. Industry merger values are the total value of all transactions in the CRSP Merger Database involving acquirers in the industry. Capital expenditures (CAPX), research and development (R&D) and advertising include all sample firms with Compustat data. Nonmerger investment is the sum of CAPX, R&D, and advertising. CAPX rankings exclude financial sector firms. R&D rankings include only industries related to manufacturing, mining and utilities. *p*-Values are in parentheses.

Investment comparison	1970–1974	1975–1979	1980–1984	1985–1989	1990–1994
Merger vs. nonmerger investment	0.009 (0.950)	−0.021 (0.875)	0.210 (0.123)	0.308 (0.024)	0.057 (0.677)
Diversifying merger vs. nonmerger investment	−0.069 (0.614)	−0.265 (0.051)	0.032 (0.813)	0.287 (0.035)	−0.031 (0.822)
Own-industry merger vs. nonmerger investment	−0.008 (0.954)	0.107 (0.432)	0.073 (0.593)	0.108 (0.429)	0.064 (0.639)
Diversifying merger vs. own-industry merger	0.259 (0.057)	0.005 (0.972)	−0.039 (0.777)	−0.112 (0.409)	−0.184 (0.177)

the industry, during our sample period. There is some indication that merger and nonmerger investment in the late 1980s are complements, apparently driven by diversifying mergers. In other words, the industries that experienced high levels of merger activity in the late 1980s were also industries that were expanding via internal investment. Note that in addition, we find virtually no relation between own-industry and diversifying mergers, suggesting that it is important to analyze these separately.

In short, during the 1970–1994 sample period, merger intensities differed significantly through time by industry, and showed little relation to nonmerger investment within any given subperiod. The picture that emerges is one where industry nonmerger investment is fairly stable through time, while there are periods of intense merger activity at the industry level, perhaps in response to changing industry conditions that bring about broad restructuring.

3.2. Panel regressions: the determinants of industry merger and nonmerger investment

In this section, we search for more specific evidence on the expansionary and contractionary motives for mergers by examining the relation between annual industry-level merger and nonmerger investment activity, industry capacity utilization, shocks, and proxies for growth opportunities. The regression framework allows us to control for other determinants of merger and nonmerger investment, such as business conditions and industry structure characteristics. The dependent variables in our panel regressions are "merger," "own-industry merger," and "nonmerger investment" intensities. For the merger-based dependent variable, we have the problem that in many industry years there are no mergers, as can be seen in Table A2 (Appendix B). Therefore, the intensity measure is censored at zero, which makes ordinary least-squares (OLS) estimates inconsistent. We account for this by fitting Tobit specifications, which are designed to explicitly correct for this type of censoring.[16] For the nonmerger-based dependent variables, censoring is not a problem, and simple OLS regressions are estimated. To allow comparable inferences from both Tobit and OLS specifications, only raw Tobit coefficients are reported, that is, not conditioned on the dependent variable being strictly positive (for a discussion on this point, see Greene, 1993).

From Compustat, we create the following set of annual industry-level explanatory variables, which are all constructed as ratios of sums over firms in the industry at year-end[17]:

Variable	Definition	Requirements for inclusion of firm
Tobin's q (q)[18]	[book assets + market equity − book equity]/book assets	market equity, book equity > 0 book assets > 0
Cash flow (CF)	EBITDA/sales	sales > 0
Sales growth (SALESGRO)	$[\text{sales}(t)/\text{cpi}(t)]/[\text{sales}(t-2)/\text{cpi}(t-2)] - 1$	sales(t and $t-2$) > 0, presence in industry at time t
Shock	abs[sales growth (t) − mean(sales growth in all t)]	same as sales growth
Industry concentration (INDCONC)[19]	sum[(sales/total industry sales)^2]	sales > 0[20]

[16] See Greene (1993) and Maddala (1983) for detailed discussions on Tobit estimation techniques, the form of the likelihood function, and the asymptotic variance matrix.

[17] Summing over all numerator and denominator firms before creating the ratio makes these independent variables "value-weighted" measures.

[18] This definition of q is flawed in many respects: (1) it assumes replacement value of assets and market value of liabilities is well proxied by book value, (2) it assumes average and marginal q are the same, (3) it ignores tax effects. Still, it is easy to calculate and it's minimal data requirements allow for maximal coverage on Compustat, which likely explains why it is commonly found in the macro and finance literatures (see Blanchard et al., 1994; Kaplan and Zingales, 1997 for recent examples).

[19] We use the natural logarithm of INDCONC in all of our regressions. The industry concentration measure that we use is also known as the Hirshman-Herfindahl Index.

[20] For years, where less then two-thirds of the firms in the industry reported positive sales, we estimated the INDCONC using one of the following procedures: (1) if 1970 or 1994 is missing, we regress the valid INDCONC's on a time trend and predict the missing values for those 2 years, otherwise (2) we linearly interpolate using INDCONC's available on dates surrounding the missing year.

Note that the above definition of 2-year sales growth is somewhat biased, since it only includes firms that are present at time t. Therefore, it underestimates industry growth if there has been entry, and industry decline if there has been exit. The same goes for the "shock" variable, which is based on the sales growth calculation.

From CITIBASE, we obtain industry capacity utilization rates (CAPUTIL). Only figures for manufacturing, mining and utilities are available, therefore service and financial industries are assigned "missing" codes for this variable. Also, since the capacity utilization ratios are reported on the basis of two-digit SIC codes for the most part, wherever our industries are more finely classified than the figures on CITIBASE, we assign the same capacity utilization figure for all the industries covered by the classification (e.g., both the electrical equipment and electronics industries are given the CITIBASE "Electrical Equipment" capacity utilization rate).

All regression specifications exclude three financial sector industries[21] because: (a) Compustat does not report CAPX for these firms, making nonmerger investment invalid, and (b) differences in accounting and the nature of the businesses themselves make it difficult to define variables comparable to cash flow (CF), capacity, etc. In addition, the explanatory variables are always as of the beginning of the period, that is, lagged by 1 year. This is done to accommodate the fact that variables such as q are forward looking, so their effect must precede the investment, as well as the more practical point that depending on how investment is financed or a merger accounted for, accounting-based variables such as profitability and sales growth may be affected by the merger or investment itself, generating a spurious correlation. Finally, all regression specifications include both year and industry dummy variables.

Our choice of independent variables is motivated by the need to control for other factors which theory suggests should influence investment activity. On the other hand, since some of these theories, such as q-theory, are meant to describe firm-level investment, arguably they are better suited to the firm-level analysis of Section 4. Still, to the extent that growth prospects are correlated across firms in an industry, we might expect to see some industry-wide effects, and therefore the variables are included in the industry-level specifications. For example, assuming q-theory is well specified at the industry level, all forms of investment should be positively related to q. This is captured in our "base" specification, where q is measured as a continuous variable. However, another interpretation of the theory suggests that firms with good growth opportunities should be investing, while firms with poor growth opportunities should not. It is not clear what can be said about the relation between investment and q, conditional on having good or bad growth prospects. Therefore, we present specifications that also include the "high q" and "low q" dummy variables, which are meant to identify the industries with good and poor growth opportunities. Each year, we sort the industries on the basis of q, classifying the bottom third as "low q" and the top third as "high q," and then assigning them to dummy variables of the same name. In addition,

---

[21] They are: (1) Bank and Thrift, (2) Brokerage, Leasing and Financial Services, and (3) Insurance.

this classification scheme helps get around some of the empirical problems with measures of q. Since our estimates of q likely have measurement error, we are more comfortable making inferences based on the broader classifications. This will be particularly important for the firm level analysis in Section 4, where measurement errors are more severe.

We also include a measure of industry profitability and CF, which not only captures some measure of industry business conditions, but also helps pick up elements of growth prospects and "real q" that our noisy estimate of q might fail to measure.

Industrial organization theory suggests that the level of merger activity is affected by changing industry characteristics and/or conditions. Therefore, to control for differences in industry structure, we include the natural logarithm of the market concentration index (INDCONC).

We attempt to capture "shocks" to the industry by including lagged sales growth and the absolute deviation of sales growth from its long-term mean (our shock variable). This is arguably a very weak proxy, since it primarily captures shocks to demand, and fails to identify technological shocks that primarily affect costs of production, as well as any forward-looking industry changes, such as anticipated deregulation.

All of the regressions are estimated with independent variables measured both in levels and as deviations from their industry's time series mean. The level regressions are meant to capture the marginal effect of the industry-level variables on merger/ investment intensity across all industries and time, while the industry-adjusted variables are designed to capture the marginal effect of the independent variables during periods when they are unusually high or low relative to the historical average for that industry.

Table 3 displays our results for both the entire panel of 55 industries, and the restricted panel of industries for which CAPUTIL data is available. The regression results are largely consistent with there being an important industry-restructuring component to merger activity. We find opposite signs on the capacity utilization coefficient for merger and nonmerger investment. Consistent with the claim by Jensen (1993) that recent mergers have been largely motivated by the need to eliminate excess capacity, we find a significantly negative relation between own-industry merger and utilization rates. We also find some evidence that mergers are related to industry shocks. Mitchell and Mulherin (1996) show that industry shocks motivate industry restructuring and account for a significant portion of takeover activity from the target's perspective. Based on that evidence, we expect a positive relation between shocks and own-industry mergers, as industries undergoing restructuring consolidate, and indeed, find the effect of SHOCK to be restricted to own-industry mergers.

The positive and significant coefficient on q, which is predicted by q-theory, only appears in the specifications involving nonmerger forms of investment. All of the coefficients on q, as well as the high and low q dummy variables, are significant and of the predicted sign for the nonmerger investment specifications, both in levels and industry-adjusted. Together with the positive relation between nonmerger investment

Table 3

Results for both the entire sample of 55 industries and the restricted panel with available capacity utilization data

Panel refers to 55 industries and 25 years covering 1970–1994. Annual (type) merger/investment intensities are calculated for each industry as the ratio of total value of (type) acquisitions/investments over the year by firms in the industry to the total book value of assets in the industry at year-end. Mergers are determined to be diversifying if the target and acquirer are in different industries at the time of announcement, or own industry if both parties are in the same industry. Industry capital expenditures (CAPX), research and development (R&D), and advertising are based on sample firms with Compustat data. Nonmerger investment is the sum of CAPX, R&D, and advertising. q is estimated as the ratio of the industry's total market value of assets (book value of assets + market value of common equity − book value of common equity) to its total book value of assets. Low (high) q is a dummy variable equal to one if the industry's q is below the 33rd (above the 67th) percentile of all industry q's during the year. Cash flow (CF) is a dummy variable equal to one if the industry's CF is above the 67th percentile of all industry CFs during the year. High CF is calculated as the sum across firms in the industry of EBITDA divided by the sum across firms in the industry of sales. Sales growth is the 2-year growth rate in industry sales, based on the firms assigned to the industry in year t. Industry shock is calculated as the absolute value of the deviation of industry sales growth from the mean sales growth for the industry over the sample period. The industry market concentration index is the natural logarithm of the sum of squared market shares (based on sales) calculated each year for each industry. Capacity utilization is the percentage of total industry capacity utilized (available for manufacturing, mining, and utilities). All specifications include year and industry dummies, although not reported. Industry-adjusted independent variables are net of the industry's own time series mean. N refers to the number of observations. t-Statistics are in parentheses. All coefficients are multiplied by 1000.

	Levels			Industry-adjusted		
(a) Ordinary least squares panel regressions of annual nonmerger investment intensities on industry-level variables						
Low q		−13.28 (−5.71)***	−9.08 (−3.44)***		−17.07 (−5.92)***	−16.27 (−4.97)***
High q		6.26 (2.62)***	9.54 (3.05)***		8.74 (2.62)***	22.87 (5.52)***
Q	11.54 (5.84)***	7.59 (3.61)***	−0.19 (−0.08)	38.06 (17.31)***	26.60 (9.29)***	21.76 (6.90)***
Cash flow	151.55 (5.59)***	130.21 (4.83)***	−2.40 (−0.06)	65.70 (3.47)***	73.67 (3.95)***	93.04 (3.59)***
Sales growth	26.40 (4.88)***	19.98 (3.68)***	27.04 (3.26)***	26.66 (3.53)***	15.56 (2.05)**	−0.07 (−0.01)
Industry shock	−4.57 (−0.57)	−1.25 (−0.16)	−4.77 (−0.45)			
Industry concentration	2.89 (1.01)	4.45 (1.57)	2.80 (0.63)	13.82 (8.18)***	13.58 (8.17)***	20.51 (10.82)***
Capacity utilization			0.78 (4.62)***			0.40 (1.86)*
R^2	0.76	0.77	0.83	0.34	0.37	0.54
N	1297	1297	699	1297	1297	699
(b) TOBIT panel regressions of annual merger intensities on industry-level variables						
Low q		−0.06 (−0.02)	1.55 (0.34)		−2.65 (−0.82)	−3.14 (−0.89)
High q		6.37 (1.50)	2.16 (0.41)		4.50 (1.21)	5.44 (1.24)

(Continued)

Table 3 (*Continued*)

	Levels			Industry-adjusted		
Q	0.33 (0.09)	-1.64 (-0.43)	0.75 (0.19)	4.16 (1.67)*	0.64 (0.19)	3.93 (1.16)
Cash flow	55.95 (1.14)	46.96 (0.95)	30.15 (0.46)	52.72 (2.57)**	53.94 (2.62)***	28.18 (1.04)
Sales growth	16.68 (1.63)	14.73 (1.42)	40.90 (2.83)***	15.66 (1.83)*	12.39 (1.41)	33.48 (2.61)***
Industry shock	25.11 (1.69)*	25.99 (1.75)*	29.27 (1.59)			
Industry concentration	-25.92 (-4.87)***	-25.91 (-4.85)***	-21.62 (-2.66)***	-7.38 (-3.97)***	-7.59 (-4.07)***	-5.22 (-2.48)**
Capacity utilization			-0.47 (-1.60)			-0.39 (-1.62)
Log-likelihood	828.31	829.44	554.42	753.24	754.59	535.55
N	1298	1298	700	1298	1298	700

(c) TOBIT panel regressions of annual own-industry merger intensities on industry-level variables

	Levels		Industry-adjusted		
Low q	0.07 (0.02)	-1.57 (-0.34)		-1.25 (-0.40)	-6.07 (-1.67)*
High q	2.11 (0.50)	5.11 (0.93)		-1.83 (-0.50)	3.65 (0.83)
Q	0.51 (0.14)	0.26 (0.07)	3.57 (1.49)	4.04 (1.29)	0.58 (0.17)
Cash flow	25.97 (0.54)	45.09 (0.68)	56.47 (2.79)***	57.27 (2.82)***	67.20 (2.37)**
Sales growth	14.92 (1.46)	41.65 (2.83)***	-1.24 (-0.15)	-1.04 (-0.12)	36.68 (2.84)***
Industry shock	26.79 (1.84)*	17.53 (0.95)			
Industry concentration	-13.43 (-2.52)**	-5.25 (-0.63)	-3.38 (-1.88)*	-3.31 (-1.83)*	0.51 (0.24)
Capacity utilization		-0.55 (-1.96)**			-0.65 (-2.65)***
Log-likelihood	560.16	392.82	466.67	466.84	373.80
N	1298	700	1298	1298	700

Statistical significance at the 1%, 5%, and 10% levels are denoted by ***, **, and *, respectively.

and capacity utilization, this evidence suggests that there is a strong industry-wide component to firm-level growth prospects. We find no relation between merger intensity and q, although it is not clear that q-theory predicts such a relation for the industry in the first place.

We also find a strong positive relationship between merger and nonmerger investment and both CF, as proxied by EBITDA/sales, and sales growth. This result is broadly consistent with the previous evidence on the link between CF and investment at the firm level (for a recent discussion see Kaplan and Zingales, 1997). It should be noted that EBITDA/sales and sales growth might proxy for components of "real q" which our measure for q does not capture. Alternatively, a positive relation between investment and CF is consistent with some degree of capital market imperfection, which forces industries to rely primarily on internally generated funds in order to invest.

The opposite signs of the coefficient on INDCONC for merger and nonmerger investment intensity in the industry-adjusted specifications suggest an interesting interpretation. When industries are particularly concentrated, relative to their historical average, expansion is likely to occur via internal investment. On the other hand, the negative coefficient on INDCONC in the merger regressions suggests that high levels of industry concentration deter firms from pursuing acquisitions, perhaps due to antitrust regulations or even just a lack of targets. However, we caution that this latter result might also be due to problems with the coverage of our merger sample. We implicitly assume that all zero merger intensities represent no mergers in the industry over the year. Failure to identify mergers increases the probability of small industries (in terms of number of firms) reporting zero transactions in a given year. Since INDCONC is roughly inversely related to the number of firms, the negative relation between merger intensity and INDCONC might be spurious. Still, we do not believe that the significance of INDCONC is completely driven by measurement errors, as our merger sample is quite comprehensive.

The overall results suggest that mergers, particularly own-industry mergers, appear to play a key role in affecting major industry change. Own-industry mergers seem to follow industry shocks, and occur in times of excess capacity, consistent with the hypothesized contractionary motive for mergers. On the other hand, periods of peak utilization and good growth prospects require capacity expansion via increased internal investment. However, one must be careful not to generalize the results to all own-industry mergers through time. Jensen (1993) for example, explicitly notes that the industry restructuring role should refer primarily to mergers from the mid-1970s through the late 1980s, as this is the time "when excess capacity began to proliferate in the worldwide economy." Morck et al. (1988) suggest that a key determinant of merger, takeover and LBO activity in the 1980s is the need to restructure industries that have experienced adverse economic shocks. We allow for the possibility that the contractionary role of mergers is period specific, by splitting the panel regressions by decade. Table 4 reports the results for these decade-by-decade specifications. For most variables, results are qualitatively consistent over the 1970s, 1980s, and 1990s. While

Table 4

Panel regressions of annual industry investment intensities on industry-level variables split by decade—independent variables in LEVELS

Panel refers to 55 industries and 25 years covering 1970–1994. Annual (type) merger/investment intensities are calculated for each industry as the ratio of total value of (type) acquisitions/investments over the year by firms in the industry to the total book value of assets in the industry at year-end. Mergers are determined to be diversifying if the target and acquirer are in different industries, or own industry if both parties are in the same industry. Industry capital expenditures (CAPX), research and development (R&D) and advertising are based on sample firms with Compustat data. Nonmerger investment is the sum of CAPX, R&D, and advertising. q is estimated as the ratio of the industry's total market value of assets (book value of assets + market value of common equity − book value of common equity) to its total book value of assets. Low (high) q is a dummy variable equal to one if the industry's q is below the 33rd (above the 67th) percentile of all industry q's during the year. Cash flow (CF) is calculated as the sum across firms in the industry of EBITDA divided by the sum across firms in the industry of sales. High CF is a dummy variable equal to one if the industry's CF is above the 67th percentile of all industry CFs during the year. Sales growth (SALESGRO) is the 2-year growth rate in industry sales, based on the firms assigned to the industry in year t. SHOCK is calculated as the absolute value of the deviation of industry sales growth from the mean sales growth for the industry over the sample period. The industry market concentration index (INDCONC) is the natural logarithm of the sum of squared market shares (based on sales) calculated each year for each industry. Capacity utilization (CAPUTIL) is the percentage of total industry capacity utilized (available for manufacturing, mining, and utilities). All specifications include year and industry dummies, although not reported. N refers to the number of observations. Specifications involving nonmerger investment intensities are estimated using OLS, while merger-related specifications employ TOBIT. t-Statistics are in parentheses. All coefficients are multiplied by 1000.

	Nonmerger investment			Mergers			Own-industry mergers		
	1970–1979	1980–1989	1990–1994	1970–1979	1980–1989	1990–1994	1970–1979	1980–1989	1990–1994
Low q	−0.73 (−0.17)	−9.42 (−1.98)**	5.40 (1.27)	−0.23 (−0.03)	14.02 (1.45)	−1.36 (−0.11)	−0.17 (−0.02)	2.63 (0.30)	−70.16 (−2.45)**
High q	9.54 (1.76)*	0.59 (0.12)	−0.03 (−0.01)	−0.15 (−0.02)	−5.94 (−0.58)	12.82 (1.00)	2.30 (0.25)	3.17 (0.36)	115.58 (2.42)**
Q	1.18 (0.42)	34.26 (3.23)***	35.49 (5.81)***	7.53 (1.71)*	50.99 (2.38)**	−40.06 (−1.78)*	4.28 (0.94)	19.61 (1.04)	−307.81 (−2.73)***
CF	72.98 (0.99)	−11.79 (−0.20)	38.15 (0.50)	125.91 (1.08)	−2.62 (−0.02)	335.14 (1.33)	76.85 (0.62)	77.84 (0.67)	2498.30 (2.50)**
SALESGRO	−10.79 (−0.82)	10.50 (0.87)	29.23 (1.71)*	19.25 (0.89)	45.28 (1.81)*	34.13 (0.66)	17.15 (0.74)	27.34 (1.24)	11.99 (0.14)

SHOCK	12.20 (0.70)	−8.87 (−0.56)	21.20 (1.04)	34.58 (1.20)	40.80 (1.21)	7.27 (0.12)	51.61 (1.66)*	−20.79 (−0.68)	681.25 (2.39)**
INDCONC	−5.51 (−0.36)	−1.98 (−0.22)	12.84 (1.18)	10.46 (0.44)	−11.67 (−0.61)	−41.55 (−1.16)	14.48 (0.56)	12.04 (0.72)	−93.56 (−1.48)
CAPUTIL	0.71 (2.88)***	0.57 (2.15)**	0.99 (3.06)***	−0.83 (−2.04)**	−0.38 (−0.68)	2.05 (1.84)*	−0.79 (−1.83)*	−0.55 (−1.10)	9.61 (2.34)**
N	279	280	140	280	280	140	280	280	140

Statistical significance at the 1%, 5%, and 10% levels are denoted by ***, **, and *, respectively.

statistical significance might be concentrated in just one decade, the signs tend to be preserved throughout. One major exception is industry capacity utilization. In particular, in specifications involving either mergers or own-industry mergers, the sign on CAPUTIL is negative (and sometimes statistically significant) during the 1970s and 1980s, while positive (and sometimes significant) in the 1990s. Note also the strongly positive sign on the high q dummy and CF for own-industry mergers during the 1990s. These results are consistent with Jensen (1993) and Morck et al. (1988), and suggest that the restructuring role for mergers is important during the 1970s and 1980s, as industries react to excess capacity by merging. However, during the 1990s merger activity appears more related to industry expansion, as industries with high q, increased profitability and near capacity, are more likely to experience increased merger activity.

4. Mergers and nonmerger investment at the firm level

At the firm level, the net effect of a merger or an internal investment is largely the same, namely an increase in the firm's asset base and/or productive capacity. Therefore, we hypothesize that from the point of view of the investor—acquirer, both merger and nonmerger investment will respond similarly to external incentives to invest. This section documents this expansionary motive for mergers, by examining the determinants of both corporate merger and nonmerger investment. Moreover, we gain insights into the previously identified contractionary motive for mergers by analyzing the premerger characteristics of the acquirer and target companies, with the overall goal of better understanding who the buyers and sellers are.

4.1. Defining investment events

The decision to merge is inherently a "lumpy" one—mergers are discrete events, and as such cannot be modeled by a continuous variable. Therefore, to better capture the merger versus nonmerger investment decisions of firms, we need to "discretize" the latter. For this purpose, we define a set of individual investment "events," which we calculate as "abnormal" firm-level changes in nonmerger investment expenditures (relative to some trend). The rationale is that these large 1-year changes in investment are more likely to be the result of discrete choices by the firms, making them more comparable to mergers.

For each firm in the sample with at least 2 years of valid data on Compustat, we calculate a series of annual nonmerger investment intensities, defined (as in Section 3) as the ratio of the sum of CAPX, R&D and advertising expense to the year-end total book assets of the firm. Firm-years with missing CAPX or book assets are excluded. We define annual "abnormal" investment as a deviation from the firm's average nonmerger investment, that is, for firm j in year t:

$$(\text{abnormal non} - \text{merger investment})_{jt}$$
$$= (\text{non} - \text{merger intensity})_{jt} - \text{mean}(\text{non} - \text{merger intensity})_j$$

Next, we combine all abnormal nonmerger investment figures across firms and years into one panel, and rank them. The upper tail of this distribution, more than one standard deviation above the mean, is defined as the set of nonmerger events, which we will compare to mergers.[22] Note that this definition of events only includes large positive changes in nonmerger investment, so that they represent net additions to assets. A total of 3876 events are classified by this procedure.

In an attempt to remain consistent with the above definition of investment events, we also exclude all mergers where the target value was less than 1% of the total value of the acquirer at the end of the precompletion year. Again, the idea is to focus on a set of events which likely result from important individual decisions by firms, rather than normal day-to-day operations. This trimming results in 1090 merger events, with 645 classified as own industry and 363 as diversifying.[23]

4.2. Logit analysis on the determinants of merger and nonmerger events

The main econometric tool used in this section is the logit regression, which is designed specifically to analyze the determinants of discrete dependent variables, as is the case with our events. We create four panels of dependent variables, each of which consists of a set of dummy variables for different types of events. They are:

1. NON_MERGER = 1 for nonmerger event, 0 otherwise
2. DIV_MERGER = 1 for diversifying merger event, 0 otherwise
3. OWNIND_MERGER = 1 for own-industry merger event, 0 otherwise
4. MERGER = 1 for merger event, 0 otherwise

We refrain from defining all the independent variables, due to their similarity to the definitions used in Section 3 at the industry level. The key differences are: (1) all variables are now estimated at the firm level; (2) we no longer include INDCONC and SHOCK, the latter because it requires a long time series of sales growth to be estimated, something most individual firms do not have; (3) we include a measure of the excess returns earned by the firm's stock during the year (STOCKRET); and (4) since we do not have firm-level capacity utilization rates, we replace them with a sales to total book assets ratio, under the assumption that variations in this measure over time should be correlated with the "intensity" of asset use. Brealey and Myers (1996) state that "a high ratio (of sales to total assets) could indicate that the firm is working close to capacity." We adjust the sales to assets ratio for each firm-year by subtracting the median sales to assets ratio across all years of the industry, which is meant to adjust for differences in accounting and/or steady-state capacity utilization rates across industries.

---

[22] A plot of the ranked abnormal nonmerger investment panel revealed the following properties of the distribution: (1) centered around zero, (2) near-perfect symmetry, (3) slightly "fatter" tails than a normal of similar mean and variance.

[23] The actual numbers of merger-related events used in the estimation are slightly smaller because some of the firms had missing values for the explanatory variables.

Capital structure can also play a role in influencing investment activity. In particular, higher leverage can lead to underinvestment (Myers, 1977) or reduce overinvestment in firms with excess free CF (Jensen, 1986). In addition, both the agency costs of free CF and the financial constraints literature have found that measures of leverage appear significantly in investment regressions. Therefore, our specifications include measures of firm-level financial leverage (BOOKLEV), estimated as the ratio of book debt plus preferred stock to book equity.

In order to reduce measurement error in the independent variables due to potential mistakes in the data reported by Compustat, we trim 1% off the tails (0.5% each) of all explanatory variables separately, which results in a small loss of firm-years with investment events (approximately 200), but a significant improvement in the maximized likelihood values for the fitted models. Finally, as is the case in Section 3, all regression specifications: (a) exclude three financial sector industries, (b) include dummy variables for year and industry (except Fama-MacBeth specifications), and (c) contain beginning-of-period values for the independent variables.

Table 5 displays the results for this section. It is divided into four panels (a through d), one for each of the dependent variables defined above. Explanatory variables can be expressed both in "levels" and in "industry-adjusted" form, where the latter are calculated as deviations from the firm's industry median for the same year, and the table displays results for both types. For all logit specifications, we report adjusted coefficients that are designed to measure the marginal impact of each explanatory variable[24] (see Greene, 1993, ch. 21). One of the problems with large panel data sets is that often the standard errors are poorly estimated, and usual inference techniques are not valid, because the estimated covariance matrix fails to account for crosscorrelations between dependent variables and/or residuals across time. In order to partially account for this, and therefore test the robustness of our logit p-values to these estimation problems, we reestimate each specification using the procedure pioneered by Fama and MacBeth (see Fama, 1976). Our Fama-MacBeth procedure involves estimating annual cross-sectional OLS regressions, which results in a time series of coefficient estimates for each independent variable. The mean and standard error of this time series of estimates of each coefficient, allows us to construct a t-statistic for that coefficient, and test whether it significantly differs from zero. These results are displayed in Table 5 under the headings "Fama-MacBeth Levels" and "Fama-MacBeth Industry-Adjusted."

In order to make statements about firms' decisions based on the estimated coefficients of our regressions, we implicitly assume that in every firm-year, firms could have undertaken any form of investment. Therefore, a value of zero for the event dummy variable actually represents a decision not to invest. This assumption could be false if either: (a) there are missing mergers in our sample or (b) firms were prevented

[24] In constructing the adjusted logit coefficients—"slopes"—we evaluate all the independent variables at their sample averages This procedure is meant to improve comparability between the logit estimates and their Fama-MacBeth counterparts, although the relationship is not perfect due to the existence of dozens of dummy variables in our various specifications.

Table 5

Logit analysis of the determinants of merger and nonmerger events

Base specifications are estimated via LOGIT (we report adjusted coefficients—"slopes"—evaluated at the average value of the independent variables). Fama-MacBeth specifications are estimated via ordinary least squares, and involve estimating annual cross-sectional regressions, resulting in a time series for each coefficient, from which the mean is reported. Each independent variable is trimmed 1% (0.5% from each tail). Dependent variables are dummy variables set to 1 if the firm participated in the event during the year, and 0 otherwise. A firm is determined to have participated in a nonmerger investment event if the firm's abnormal nonmerger investment intensity is more than 1 standard deviation above the sample mean abnormal nonmerger investment intensity across all firms and all years. Firm abnormal nonmerger investment intensity is the deviation in nonmerger investment intensity from its mean estimated over all years available for the firm. Nonmerger investment intensity is estimated for each firm-year as the ratio of the sum of CAPX, R&D and advertising expense to total book assets. Mergers are classified as diversifying if the target and acquirer are in different industries at the time of announcement, and own industry if both parties are in the same industry. Industry-adjusted independent variables for each firm-year are calculated as deviations from the industry median for that year. q is estimated as the ratio of the firm's total market value of assets (book value of assets + market value of common equity – book value of common equity) to its total book value of assets. Low (high) q is a dummy variable equal to one if the firm's q is below the 33rd (above the 67th) percentile of all firm q's during the year. Cash flow (CF) is calculated as EBITDA divided by sales. High CF is a dummy variable equal to one if the firm's q is below the 33rd (above the 67th percentile of all firm CFs during the year. AGENCY is the product of Low q and High CF. Book leverage (BOOKLEV) is calculated as the ratio of the firm's debt (long-term debt + short-term debt + preferred stock) to the firm's book value of common equity. Sales growth (SALESGRO) is the 2-year growth rate. Stock return (STOCKRET) is the net-of-market annual return for the firm's common stock. Capacity utilization (CAPUTIL) is proxied by the deviation of the firm's ratio of sales to book assets from the industry median over the entire period. All specifications include industry dummies and LOGIT specifications also include year dummies. p-Values referring to unadjusted coefficients are reported in parentheses for the LOGIT specifications. t-Statistics are reported in parentheses for the Fama-MacBeth specifications, based on the standard error of the time series mean of each coefficient. All coefficients are multiplied by 1000. Statistical significance at the 1%, 5%, and 10% levels are denoted by ***, **, and *, respectively.

(a) Panel regressions of annual individual firm nonmerger investment events on firm-level independent variables from 1970 to 1994

	Levels (LOGIT)			Fama-MacBeth Levels (OLS)			Industry-adjusted (LOGIT)			Fama-MacBeth industry-adjusted (OLS)		
	1	2	3	1	2	3	1	2	3	1	2	3
Low q		−160.7 (0.00)***	−115.2 (0.00)***		−9.5 (−2.04)**	−6.0 (−1.12)		−187.2 (0.00)***	−148.6 (0.00)***		−9.4 (−2.01)**	−5.9 (−1.06)
High q		59.5 (0.00)***	62.5 (0.00)***		18.3 (2.79)***	18.4 (2.81)***		115.0 (0.00)***	117.7 (0.00)***		19.9 (2.92)***	20.0 (2.93)***
AGENCY			−33.9 (0.00)***			−18.0 (−2.42)**			−29.5 (0.00)***			−20.1 (−2.40)**

(Continued)

Table 5 (*Continued*)

	Levels (LOGIT)			Fama-MacBeth Levels (OLS)			Industry-adjusted (LOGIT)			Fama-MacBeth industry-adjusted (OLS)		
	1	2	3	1	2	3	1	2	3	1	2	3
q	230.0 (0.00)***	51.7 (0.32)	46.9 (0.37)	15.5 (2.88)***	3.3 (0.53)	3.1 (0.50)	17.5 (0.00)***	−6.8 (0.16)	−6.9 (0.15)	15.7 (2.84)***	2.4 (0.35)	2.2 (0.32)
CF	494.3 (0.00)***	433.4 (0.00)***	462.6 (0.00)***	316.6 (7.96)***	301.8 (7.43)***	312.0 (7.44)***	13.3 (0.00)***	10.6 (0.00)***	11.4 (0.00)***	316.4 (6.87)***	300.7 (6.47)***	311.2 (6.45)***
BOOKLEV	−13.8 (0.47)	−9.1 (0.63)	−8.0 (0.67)	2.1 (0.80)	2.3 (0.84)	2.3 (0.87)	−7.1 (0.13)	−4.7 (0.31)	−4.1 (0.36)	2.0 (0.75)	2.1 (0.78)	2.2 (0.80)
SALESGRO	54.6 (0.00)***	48.8 (0.00)***	49.0 (0.00)***	35.6 (2.68)***	30.9 (2.39)**	31.1 (2.39)**	15.8 (0.00)***	13.2 (0.00)***	13.4 (0.00)***	30.0 (2.21)**	24.8 (1.93)*	25.2 (1.96)**
SALESGRO2	−3.0 16.0 (0.00)***	14.1 (0.00)***	14.2 (0.00)***	44.5 (5.25)***	42.8 (5.28)***	43.0 (5.28)***	17.5 (0.00)***	15.0 (0.00)***	15.1 (0.00)***	45.6 (5.32)***	43.7 (5.33)***	44.0 (5.33)***
CAPUTIL	21.7 (0.00)***	18.8 (0.00)***	18.9 (0.00)***	23.3 (5.31)***	22.0 (4.98)***	21.9 (4.95)***	15.0 (0.00)***	11.5 (0.00)***	11.7 (0.00)***	22.9 (5.34)***	21.5 (5.05)***	21.3 (5.01)***
Number observed	28,592	28,592	28,592				28,580	28,580	28,580			
Number of events	2810	2810	2810			2805	2805	2805	2805			

(b) Panel regressions of annual individual firm own-industry merger events on firm-level independent variables from 1970 to 1994

	Levels (LOGIT)			Fama-MacBeth Levels (OLS)			Industry-adjusted (LOGIT)			Fama-MacBeth industry-adjusted (OLS)		
	1	2	3	1	2	3	1	2	3	1	2	3
Low q		−22.1 (0.57)	−58.8 (0.16)		−2.7 (−1.53)	−4.8 (−2.74)***		−28.4 (0.47)	−66.7 (0.11)		−3.6 (−1.90)*	−5.5 (−2.99)***
High q		28.6 (0.46)	29.6 (0.45)		1.7 (0.61)	1.8 (0.64)		49.6 (0.19)	51.1 (0.18)		2.1 (0.79)	2.1 (0.82)
AGENCY			39.5 (0.01)***			11.1 (3.05)***			41.5 (0.01)***			10.1 (2.61)***
q	90.0 (0.41)	19.9 (0.88)	34.7 (0.79)	−0.2 (−0.09)	−1.1 (−0.49)	−1.0 (−0.43)	9.0 (0.36)	−1.1 (0.93)	−0.1 (0.99)	0.4 (0.26)	−1.0 (−0.54)	−0.9 (−0.48)
CF	−74.8 (0.41)	−92.8 (0.32)	−151.9 (0.12)	−16.6 (−1.21)	−18.6 (−1.35)	−25.2 (−1.76)*	−3.0 (0.34)	−3.9 (0.23)	−6.0 (0.08)*	−18.6 (−1.37)	−21.2 (−1.57)	−27.7 (−1.95)*

	Levels (LOGIT)			Fama-MacBeth Levels (OLS)			Industry-adjusted (LOGIT)			Fama-MacBeth industry-adjusted (OLS)		
	1	2	3	1	2	3	1	2	3	1	2	3
BOOKLEV	−37.0 (0.41)	−34.8 (0.43)	−38.5 (0.38)	0.2 (0.19)	0.3 (0.30)	0.2 (0.25)	−5.5 (0.60)	−4.6 (0.65)	−5.8 (0.58)	−0.3 (0.40)	−0.2 (0.33)	−0.3 (−0.37)
SALESGRO	49.3 (0.00)***	48.3 (0.00)***	48.0 (0.00)***	13.6 (2.53)**	13.1 (2.38)**	12.3 (2.24)**	18.3	17.8	17.6	14.5 (2.74)***	13.5 (2.48)***	12.8 (2.35)**
SALESGRO^2	−4.9 (0.35)	−4.8 (0.36)	−4.8 (0.36)	−3.7 (−1.03)	−3.5 (−0.92)	−3.1 (−0.82)	5.7	5.6	5.5	−3.6 (−0.97)	−3.1 (−0.79)	−2.7 (−0.71)
STOCKRET	3.5 (0.34)	3.2 (0.40)	3.1 (0.41)	3.9 (1.06)	3.3 (0.91)	3.1 (0.84)	1.8 (0.67)	1.2 (0.78)	1.1 (0.80)	3.4 (0.97)	2.7 (0.76)	2.5 (0.70)
CAPUTIL	−19.3 (0.01)***	−20.0 (0.00)***	−20.0 (0.00)***	−5.5 (−2.76)***	−5.9 (−2.91)***	−5.9 (−2.88)***	−18.4 (0.00)***	−19.4 (0.00)***	−19.3 (0.00)***	−6.1 (−3.19)***	−6.5 (−3.41)***	−6.4 (−3.40)***
Number observed	28,512	28,512	28,512				28,501	28,501	28,501			
Number of events	594	594	594	592	592	592						

(c) Panel regressions of annual individual firm diversifying merger events on firm-level independent variables from 1970 to 1994

	Levels (LOGIT)			Fama-MacBeth Levels (OLS)			Industry-adjusted (LOGIT)			Fama-MacBeth industry-adjusted (OLS)		
	1	2	3	1	2	3	1	2	3	1	2	3
Low q		−118.0 (0.03)**	−114.9 (0.05)**		−3.8 (−2.68)***	−3.6 (−2.23)**		−127.1 (0.02)**	−127.0 (0.03)**		−3.8 (−2.67)***	−3.8 (−2.29)**
High q		33.6 (0.50)	33.7 (0.50)		0.9 (0.37)	0.8 (0.33)		47.0 (0.33)	47.0 (0.33)		1.7 (0.73)	1.6 (0.69)
AGENCY			−3.1 (0.89)			−1.6 (−0.55)			−0.1 (1.00)			−0.5 (−0.16)
q	1.7 (0.99)	−144.0 (0.39)	−144.8 (0.38)	1.4 (0.91)	−0.9 (−0.58)	−1.0 (−0.60)	1.0 (0.93)	−13.5 (0.35)	−13.5 (0.35)	1.4 (0.83)	−1.3 (−0.80)	−1.3 (−0.82)
CF	126.5 (0.26)	79.9 (0.49)	83.1 (0.48)	−2.9 (−0.33)	−6.5 (−0.70)	−4.9 (−0.52)	3.1 (0.43)	1.3 (0.75)	1.3 (0.75)	−1.8 (−0.19)	−5.8	−5.1
BOOKLEV	−153.4 (0.04)***	−146.0 (0.05)**	−146.1 (0.05)**	−0.7 (−1.07)	−0.8 (−1.14)	−0.8 (−1.18)	−29.9 (0.07)*	−27.7 (0.09)*	−27.7 (0.09)*	−0.6 (−0.75)	−0.6 (−0.77)	−0.6 (−0.82)
SALESGRO	55.8 (0.00)***	52.9 (0.01)***	52.9 (0.01)***	11.9 (3.62)***	11.2 (3.52)***	11.2 (3.51)***	24.5 (0.00)***	23.5 (0.00)***	23.5 (0.00)***	12.3 (3.48)***	11.4 (3.29)***	11.4 (3.27)***
SALESGRO^2	3.2 (0.30)	3.4 (0.27)	3.4 (0.27)	−4.5 (−2.31)**	−3.9 (−2.08)**	−3.9 (−2.03)**	−2.8 (−0.54)	−3.1 (−0.51)	−3.1 (−0.51)	−4.6 (−2.09)**	−4.0 (−1.81)*	−3.9 (−1.76)*
STOCKRET	10.0 (0.03)**	8.9 (0.05)**	8.9 (0.05)**	7.1 (3.33)***	6.5 (3.23)***	6.5 (3.23)***	11.5 (0.02)**	10.1 (0.05)**	10.1 (0.05)**	7.4 (3.66)***	6.7 (3.51)***	6.7 (3.52)***

(Continued)

Table 5 (*Continued*)

	Levels (LOGIT)			Fama-MacBeth Levels (OLS)			Industry-adjusted (LOGIT)			Fama-MacBeth industry-adjusted (OLS)		
	1	2	3	1	2	3	1	2	3	1	2	3
CAPUTIL	-4.4 (0.59)	-6.2 (0.46)	-6.2 (0.46)	-2.6 (-1.69)*	-3.0 (-1.89)*	-3.0 (-1.90)*	-4.4 (0.56)	-6.4 (0.41)	-6.4 (0.41)	-2.1 (-1.29)	-2.5 (-1.51)	-2.5 (-1.52)
Number observed	28,512	28,512	28,512				28,501	28,501	28,501			
Number of events	333	333	333				332	332	332			

(d) Panel regressions of annual individual firm merger events on firm-level independent variables from 1970 to 1994

	Levels (LOGIT)			Fama-MacBeth Levels (OLS)			Industry-adjusted (LOGIT)			Fama-MacBeth industry-adjusted (OLS)		
	1	2	3	1	2	3	1	2	3	1	2	3
Low q		-63.2 (0.04)**	-81.7 (0.01)***		-8.3 (-3.26)***	-9.7 (-3.47)***		-69.6 (0.02)**	-90.1 (0.01)***		-8.9 (-3.48)***	-10.5 (-3.58)***
High q		23.2 (0.44)	23.2 (0.44)		0.9 (0.27)	0.8 (0.25)		36.5 (0.21)	36.7 (0.21)		1.8 (0.65)	1.8 (0.64)
AGENCY			20.2 (0.11)			7.5 (1.53)			22.4 (0.07)*			7.7 (1.51)
q	44.8 (0.58)	-49.4 (0.62)	-42.9 (0.67)	0.6 (0.23)	-2.3 (-0.73)	-2.2 (-0.70)	5.9 (0.43)	-4.7 (0.60)	-4.2 (0.63)	1.7 (0.60)	-2.0 (-0.66)	-1.9 (-0.65)
CF	-30.6 (0.66)	-60.6 (0.40)	-87.2 (0.24)	-26.4 (-1.44)	-33.0 (-1.83)*	-36.8 (-2.07)**	-1.5 (0.53)	-2.7 (0.27)	-3.7 (0.14)	-27.4 (-1.43)	-34.7 (-1.86)*	-39.3 (-2.09)**
BOOKLEV	-72.1 (0.05)**	-69.6 (0.05)**	-70.5 (0.05)**	-0.8 (-0.67)	-0.8 (-0.67)	-0.9 (-0.72)**	-12.4 (0.14)	-11.6 (0.16)	-12.0 (0.15)	-1.3 (-1.18)	-1.4 (-1.21)	-1.4 (-1.29)
SALESGRO	56.4 (0.00)***	54.6 (0.00)***	54.5 (0.00)***	27.3 (3.65)***	26.0 (3.43)***	25.4 (3.35)***	22.5 (0.00)***	21.8 (0.00)***	21.8 (0.00)***	29.5 (4.08)***	27.6 (3.77)***	27.1 (3.69)***
SALESGRO^2	-0.6 (0.81)	-0.5 (0.85)	-0.5 (0.85)	-7.4 (-1.58)	-6.8 (-1.41)	-6.4 (-1.33)	3.2 (0.07)*	3.1 (0.08)*	3.1 (0.09)*	-7.9 (-1.66)	-6.9 (-1.43)	-6.5 (-1.35)
STOCKRET	6.2 (0.03)**	5.5 (0.05)**	5.5 (0.05)**	11.6 (2.47)**	10.3 (2.25)**	10.2 (2.21)**	6.4 (0.04)**	5.5 (0.08)*	5.5 (0.09)*	11.2 (2.60)**	9.7 (2.28)**	9.6 (2.24)**
CAPUTIL	-15.6 (0.00)***	-16.9 (0.00)***	-16.9 (0.00)***	-9.5 (-2.94)***	-10.3 (-3.18)***	-10.3 (-3.19)***	-14.3 (0.00)***	-15.7 (0.00)***	-15.8 (0.00)***	-9.6 (-2.87)***	-10.4 (-3.13)***	-10.4 (-3.16)***
Number observed	28,592	28,592	28,592				28,580	28,580	28,580			
Number of events	995	995	995				991	991	991			

from engaging in certain types of investment, for whatever reason. In an attempt to test the robustness of our results, we reestimate some of the MERGER and NONMERGER logit specifications, restricting the sample to firms that at some point engaged in each. The results are mostly unchanged, so we do not report these restricted sample estimates.

As in Section 3, for each dependent variable, the first model we run (which is labeled "1" in Table 5) includes q as a continuous variable, and corresponds to the traditional interpretation of q-theory as predicting that investment should increase with q. However, as we noted before, our reading of the theory suggests that the decision to invest based on q is really a discrete one, that is, if q exceeds a certain threshold, investment should be undertaken, otherwise not. Empirically, this can be accomplished by classifying firms based on whether q exceeds that threshold or not. Another problem with the continuous measure of q is that there is likely to be a significant measurement error in our estimate of q, so we feel more confident grouping companies into broad categories, rather than relying on the estimates directly. As a result, each year we sort all firms by q and classify them as "high q" or "low q," depending on whether they fall in the top third or bottom third of the distribution. Based on this classification, we create dummy variables which are included in models "2" and "3."

Finally, we define an "AGENCY" dummy variable, which corresponds to those firms which, in a given year, belong to both "low q" and "high CF" (the latter corresponds to firms in the top third of the annual cross-section of firm cash-flow margins). By including this variable, we can test the prediction of the agency costs of free CF theory that firms with poor growth or investment prospects, but available CF, will overinvest. This test should be especially powerful in the models that include our "low q" dummy in addition to AGENCY, since here we are isolating the marginal effect of higher CF on the investment patterns of companies with no growth opportunities. The agency cost of free CF theory implies a significantly positive sign on AGENCY in these regressions.

The first striking results to emerge from Table 5 are the consistently positive signs on "high q" and negative signs on "low q," across all forms of investment, merger and nonmerger. While the significance level varies across specifications, with "high q" appearing as significant in the nonmerger investment regressions, and "low q" in the various merger-related specifications,[25] we consider the results to be supportive of the hypothesis that mergers have an important expansionary role.

---

[25] The "high q" and "low q" dummy variables measure marginal effects of q relative to the middle third of the distribution. As we already pointed out, q-theory predicts that firms with q above a certain threshold should be investing, but due to the measurement error in our proxy, we cannot say where this "cut-off" value lies within our estimated values. For example, if the threshold is relatively low, then we would expect that all the "high q" and most "middle third" companies should be investing heavily. In that case, only the coefficient on "low q" would be significant (and negative), while the estimate on "high q" would be statistically insignificant, since there would be no marginal impact in going from the "middle third" to "high q." The opposite would be the case if the threshold is relatively high. Therefore, we consider that if either "low q" is significantly negative or "high q" is significantly positive, that is consistent with q-theory.

The results on AGENCY are more inconsistent across investment types. For both diversifying mergers and nonmerger investment, the coefficient estimates on AGENCY are negative, although only significant in the latter case. As stated above, this appears to be inconsistent with the basic predictions of the agency costs of free CF theory. In the case of diversifying mergers, the negative coefficient on "low q" and the weakly negative sign on AGENCY should serve to mitigate the concerns that these transactions are the result of rampant agency problems within the acquirers. Previous empirical evidence (e.g., Morck et al., 1990) has indicated that most diversifying mergers are value decreasing, a claim which cannot be addressed in our paper, as we focus on the decision to invest, rather than how much to spend. However, even if acquirers overpay and/or destroy value when diversifying, our evidence suggests that this is not necessarily related to a deliberate desire to overbuild and invest in negative NPV projects, simply due to an overabundance of available CF. In fact, the strongly positive coefficient estimates on SALESGRO and STOCKRET for these diversifying acquisitions are more consistent with managerial optimism rather than malice (see Heaton, 1999).

For own-industry mergers, the AGENCY dummy is significantly positive across all specifications. In conjunction with the results discussed above, we could interpret this as implying that own-industry mergers are the only type of major corporate investment activities motivated by costly agency problems within the firm. This might be evidence of a desire to increase market power, or self-serving behavior by managers, who wish to become dominant players in an industry, irrespective of the cost. However, an alternative interpretation of the results is suggested by the view, already expressed, that many of these own-industry mergers are precipitated by the need for industry contraction. In this case, in declining industries (low q) requiring consolidation, it is not surprising that the relatively cash-flow-rich companies (high CF) are the acquirers. For example, if Jensen's (1993) view is correct, then excess capacity generated by productivity shocks could induce both low values of q (since capital needs to exit, not enter these industries) and higher expenditures on own-industry acquisitions. We cannot distinguish between these two interpretations, that is, agency costs of free CF or industry restructuring, although we do find evidence (see Section 4.3) that in own-industry mergers, acquirers tend to be more profitable and have higher q than target companies.

The significant and opposite signs on CAPUTIL are consistent with our evidence in Section 3.2 that own-industry mergers are often a tool for restructuring, where industries with excess capacity undergo consolidation via mergers. The picture that emerges is that own-industry mergers often arise from the need to restructure the industry, perhaps in reaction to some shock. On the other hand, firms that initiate significant internal expansions can be characterized as having had strong operating performance and healthy growth prospects as evidenced by the positive relation between nonmerger investment events and sales growth, profitability, and excess returns.

Jensen (1993) suggests that this excess capacity motivation for mergers was predominantly a mid-1970s and 1980s phenomenon. As in Section 3, we explicitly allow for this possibility by splitting the sample by decade, and rerunning the logit regressions for each subperiod separately. The results, reported in Table 6, bear out Jensen's prediction, that is, the negative relationship between capacity utilization and either merger or own-industry merger, is restricted to the 1970s and 1980s, while the relationship is positive (and sometimes significant) in the 1990s. This evidence, combined with that of Section 3, strengthens our view that mergers can play two different roles for acquirers, contraction or expansion, and that while the former was more important through the late 1980s, as economic conditions forced a massive reallocation of assets among companies, the latter role seems to better describe merger activity in the 1990s.

Finally, we emphasize the remarkable consistency in the results discussed above across estimation methods. Whether one focuses on "Levels" or "Industry-Adjusted" specifications, the direction and significance of the coefficients is stable, and the same occurs with the "Fama-MacBeth" regressions, which occasionally lead to higher significance levels than the panel logits themselves. This stability and consistency gives us confidence that the effects we uncover are real, irrespective of whether the reader agrees with the interpretations we ascribe to them.

4.3. Acquirer and target characteristics

In this section, we analyze the relative characteristics of acquirer and target companies in different types of mergers. For all mergers used in the regressions of Section 4.2, we compile data on a variety of financial variables for both the acquirer and the target companies, as of the last fiscal year before deal closing. These variables are then differenced for each transaction (acquirer minus target), with the median values of these differences reported in Table 7, together with p-values for the test that these median differences are equal to zero.[26] The table contains three panels, for mergers, own-industry mergers and diversifying mergers, respectively. Each panel reports statistics on differences in characteristics both in absolute levels and industry-adjusted, where we subtract the industry median characteristic from the firm's.

Evidence on diversifying mergers is somewhat tricky to interpret. On one hand, acquirers have higher CFs, consistent with diversifying acquisitions being related to agency problems in firms with excess cash. On the other hand, these acquirers also have higher leverage, which goes against the agency story. In addition, these results do not survive in the industry-adjusted analysis.

The most interesting results pertain to own-industry mergers, as they tie in directly to the industry contraction role discussed above. Table 7 reports that for the subsample of own-industry deals, acquirers have significantly higher q, CFs, and lagged stock

[26] The results are qualitatively similar for means of differences (rather than medians), although statistical significance is sometimes less, due to outliers in the observations, which is why we prefer the nonparametric Wilcoxon signed rank test for medians reported in Table 7.

Table 6

Panel regressions of annual individual firm investment events on firm-level variables split by decade

Base specifications are estimated via LOGIT (we report adjusted coefficients—"slopes"—evaluated at the average value of the independent variables). Each independent variable is trimmed 1% (0.5% from each tail) to remove the effect of outliers. Dependent variables are dummy variables set to 1 if the firm participated in the event during the year, and 0 otherwise. A firm is determined to have participated in a nonmerger investment event if the firm's abnormal nonmerger investment intensity is more than 1 standard deviation above the sample mean abnormal nonmerger investment intensity across all firms and all years. Firm abnormal nonmerger investment intensity is the deviation in nonmerger investment intensity from its mean estimated over all years available for the firm. Nonmerger investment intensity is estimated for each firm-year as the ratio of the sum of CAPX, R&D and advertising expense to total book assets. Merger events are transactions in the CRSP Merger Database involving acquirers in the sample, and where the estimated target value exceeded 1% of the total market value of the acquirer at the end of the precompletion fiscal year. Mergers are classified as diversifying if the target and acquirer are in different industries at the time of announcement, and own-industry if both parties are in the same industry. q is estimated as the ratio of the firm's total market value of assets (book value of assets + market value of common equity − book value of common equity) to its total book value of assets. Low (high) q is a dummy variable equal to one if the firm's q is below the 33rd (above the 67th) percentile of all firm's q during the year. Cash flow (CF) is calculated as EBITDA divided by sales. High CF is a dummy variable equal to one if the firm's CF is above the 67th percentile of all firm CFs during the year. AGENCY is the product of low q and high CF. Book leverage (BOOKLEV) is calculated as the ratio of the firm's debt (long-term debt + short-term debt + preferred stock) to the firm's book value of common equity. Sales growth (SALESGRO) is the 2-year growth rate. Stock return (STOCKRET) is the net-of-market annual return for the firm's common stock. Capacity utilization (CAPUTIL) is proxied by the deviation of the firm's ratio of sales to book assets from the industry median over the entire period. All specifications include industry and year dummy variables. p-Values referring to unadjusted coefficients are reported in parentheses for the LOGIT specifications. All coefficients are multiplied by 1000. Statistical significance at the 1%, 5%, and 10% levels are denoted by ***, **, and *, respectively.

	Event = Merger			Event = Diversifying merger			Event = Own-industry merger			Event = Nonmerger investment		
	1970–1979	1980–1989	1990–1994	1970–1979	1980–1989	1990–1994	1970–1979	1980–1989	1990–1994	1970–1979	1980–1989	1990–1994
Low q	−60.1 (0.23)	−56.5 (0.24)	−508.5 (0.00)***	−24.7 (0.81)	−62.9 (0.43)	−682.1 (0.00)***	−25.7 (0.67)	−79.7 (0.21)	−459.6 (0.02)**	−27.9 (0.02)**	−117.7 (0.00)***	−23.1 (0.72)
High q	32.0 (0.49)	47.9 (0.29)	−127.3 (0.18)	173.8 (0.04)**	5.3 (0.94)	−215.0 (0.14)	−4.4 (0.94)	81.0 (0.19)	31.9 (0.81)	18.7 (0.05)**	91.8 (0.00)***	−19.9 (0.72)
AGENCY	8.3 (0.50)	14.0 (0.55)	75.9 (0.13)	−41.3 (0.21)	−3.2 (0.94)	124.3 (0.08)*	23.4 (0.08)*	36.2 (0.22)	61.8 (0.44)	28.7 (0.43)	−7.7 (0.31)	−45.8 (0.19)
q	201.1 (0.11)	−519.1 (0.01)***	18.2 (0.96)	329.5 (0.12)	−574.2 (0.05)**	74.4 (0.88)	188.8 (0.22)	−597.8 (0.04)**	−10.7 (0.98)	−0.3 (0.94)	80.9 (0.31)	162.6 (0.23)
CF	−77.9 (0.56)	94.8 (0.36)	−427.7 (0.03)**	−99.7 (0.70)	323.8 (0.04)**	−313.8 (0.27)	−42.9 (0.79)	−34.5 (0.81)	−437.8 (0.12)	1893.3 (0.00)***	289.4 (0.00)***	711.1 (0.00)***

BOOKLEV	−18.3 (0.74)	−148.5 (0.01)***	34.5 (0.68)	−4.1 (0.97)	−242.9 (0.02)**	−172.6 (0.40)	−29.9 (0.67)	−126.6 (0.10)	149.5 (0.13)	2.7 (0.01)***	−70.6 (0.02)**	−114.7 (0.05)**
SALESGRO	27.8 (0.29) 57.0 (0.00)***	71.4 (0.00)***	13.9 (0.81) 67.6 (0.00)***	51.7 (0.12)	13.6 (0.67) 54.5 (0.12)	68.1 (0.01)***	47.5 (0.00)***	55.1 (0.00)***	−43.9 (0.05)**			
SALESGRO^2	−1.6 (0.71)	−0.4 (0.91) 2.9 (0.70)	−36.9 (0.95)	4.6 (0.22)	7.2 (0.36)	0.0 (1.00)	−9256.7 (0.91)	−60.8 (0.95)	0.0 (0.33)	−1.7 (0.42)	−2.9 (0.58)	
STOCKRET	4.9 (0.40) 8.1 (0.06)*	2.1 (0.51)	17.0 (0.10) 7.1 (0.31)	7.8 (0.07)*	2.8 (0.70)	7.7 (0.17)	−6.1 (0.25)	58.5 (0.00)***	17.2 (0.00)***	11.4 (0.02)**		
CAPUTIL	−10.8 (0.33)	−28.7 (0.01)*** 14.0 (0.04)**	−20.2 (0.29)	0.3 (0.98)	9.9 (0.37)	−4.8 (0.73)	−45.5 (0.00)***	12.2 (0.18)	28.4 (0.00)***	21.6 (0.00)***	42.7 (0.00)***	
Number observed	10,994	12,003 5595	10,965	11,961	5586	10,965	11,961	5586	10,994	12,003	5595	
Number of events	413	476 106	114	170	49	275	271	48	1111	1366	333	

Table 7

Differences in acquirer and target premerger characteristics

Medians of differences between acquirer and target characteristics in the last fiscal year before transaction closing. Merger events are transactions in the CRSP Merger Database where the estimated target value exceeded 1% of the total market value of the acquirer at the end of the precompletion fiscal year. Mergers are classified as diversifying if the target and acquirer are in different industries, and own industry if both parties are in the same industry. Industry-adjusted independent variables for each firm-year are calculated as deviations from the industry median for that year. q is estimated as the ratio of the firm's total market value of assets (book value of assets + market value of common equity − book value of common equity) to its total book value of assets. Cash flow (CF) is calculated as EBITDA divided by sales. Book leverage (BOOKLEV) is calculated as the ratio of the firm's debt (long-term debt + short-term debt + preferred stock) to the firm's book value of common equity. Market leverage (MKTLEV) is similar to BOOKLEV, but the denominator is the firm's market value of common equity. Sales growth (SALESGRO) is the 2-year growth rate. Stock return (STOCKRET) is the net-of-market annual return for the firm's common stock. Capacity utilization (CAPUTIL) is proxied by the deviation of the firm's ratio of sales to book assets from the industry median over the entire period. p-Values for the Wilcoxon signed rank test for each coefficient are reported in parentheses.

| | Median acquirer characteristics | Panel 1 | | Panel 2 | | Panel 3 | |
| | | All mergers | | Own-industry mergers | | Diversifying mergers | |
		Levels	Industry-adjusted	Levels	Industry-adjusted	Levels	Industry-adjusted
q	1.142	0.021 (0.40)	0.053 (0.03)	0.097 (0.00)	0.097 (0.00)	−0.023 (0.05)	0.020 (0.78)
CF	0.133	0.013 (0.00)	0.008 (0.00)	0.015 (0.00)	0.015 (0.00)	0.011 (0.00)	0.004 (0.10)
BOOKLEV	0.606	0.034 (0.09)	−0.010 (0.60)	−0.057 (0.01)	−0.057 (0.01)	0.075 (0.00)	0.042 (0.19)
MKTLEV	0.434	0.010 (0.89)	−0.022 (0.04)	−0.060 (0.00)	−0.060 (0.00)	0.046 (0.07)	0.019 (0.86)
SALESGRO	0.116	−0.003 (0.64)	0.021 (0.07)	0.010 (0.47)	0.010 (0.47)	−0.010 (0.90)	0.025 (0.08)
STOCKRET	0.022	0.053 (0.21)	0.132 (0.02)	0.184 (0.00)	0.184 (0.00)	−0.061 (0.26)	0.051 (0.83)
CAPUTIL	0.005	−0.067 (0.00)	−0.064 (0.00)	−0.025 (0.06)	−0.025 (0.06)	−0.090 (0.00)	−0.084 (0.00)

returns, as well as lower leverage and capacity utilization, than their target companies. That is, within a given industry, the acquirers are firms that are better performers, at least in relative terms, and also have the ability to carry out the acquisition, in the sense of more debt capacity, and the operational slack to absorb their targets, consistent with the findings in Maksimovic and Phillips (2001). These mergers are also more likely to generate value, given the results of Lang et al. (1989) that mergers between high q and acquirers and low q targets result in the most overall gains. Overall, our findings suggest that industry restructuring results in a transfer of assets to the relatively effective users, and that the contractionary role of mergers leads to a more efficient allocation of resources and capacity within industries and the economy.

5. Conclusion

There is a growing empirical literature documenting that mergers are efficient means for assets to be reallocated within the economy. Large sample evidence on combined acquirer and target stock returns, as well as postmerger operating performance,[27] suggests that mergers on average increase value, and lead to improved profitability in subsequent years. Song and Walkling (2000) report that stock prices in a given industry tend to appreciate upon an announcement of a takeover, presumably in expectation of other mergers to come, and consistent with mergers being a tool for industries to generate synergies by consolidating and restructuring. In a recent paper, Maksimovic and Phillips (2001) show that mergers and acquisitions on average result in productivity gains for the assets acquired, and that the buyers tend to be relatively more productive firms. Our results add to the literature on the efficiency of merger activity, by suggesting a mechanism by which mergers help firms and industries grow and restructure, particularly in response to shocks.

Overall, our analysis indicates that mergers play a dual economic role. On one hand, mergers, like internal investments, are a means for companies to increase their capital base, in response to good growth prospects. Both merger and nonmerger investment are positively related to the firm's Tobin's q and sales growth. On the other hand, mergers appear to facilitate industry contraction. The clustering of mergers by industry suggests that mergers are often a response to industry shocks. Our finding that own-industry mergers are negatively related to capacity utilization during the 1970s and 1980s, is consistent with the view that mergers are an effective means for industries with excess capacity to rationalize and induce exit. In addition, we find that within these contracting industries, acquirers tend to be the firms with better performance, perhaps even better management, and lower leverage and capacity utilization, suggesting that this industry rationalization and asset reallocation results in improved efficiency.

---

[27]   See Healy et al. (1992) on operating performance, as well as Jarrell et al. (1988) and Andrade et al. (2001) for a review of the literature on announcement returns and long-term profitability.

Appendix A: Procedure for creating industries

Value Line industry classifications have not remained static since 1970, with industries dividing or merging over time. In order to create a single set of industries that could be followed continuously from 1970 to 1994, we generate a subset of 55 industry classifications, to which firms in Value Line are allocated.

We include each firm in our sample up to 3 years before its addition, in which case, the firm is included in the industry where it first appears, and up to 3 years after its exclusion, with the firm remaining in the last industry to which it belonged. This procedure mitigates some of the problems caused by increases in overall Value Line coverage in the early 1970s, which can be seen in the first few columns of Table A1.

For most cases, the following guidelines are followed in transforming Value Line industries into "our" industries:

- Most industries which exist in the same form throughout the entire 1970–1994 period, that is, no other industries are merged into them or split off from them, are kept intact.
- Industries which differ merely by geographic classifications (e.g., "Utilities (East)" and "Utilities (West)"), or where the product lines seem particularly similar (e.g., "Auto Parts (OEM)" and "Auto Parts (Replacement)"), are merged.
- Some industries that are separate as of 1994, but are merged in earlier periods, and where reclassification is straightforward (e.g., "Computers" and "Office Equipment"), are split up in the early periods. Companies which existed both pre- and postsplit are assigned to their postsplit industry, while for companies that only exist presplit, a description of the firm's product line from Value Line is used for classification.
- There are some subsets of firms that Value Line includes in different industries at various points in time (e.g., "Forest Products" firms are first included in "Building" and later become part of the "Paper and Forest Products" industry). In these cases, we transfer firms from their early period classifications to their later ones (e.g., all "Forest Products" firm are classified with "Paper Products" firms for the entire sample period). This also requires reading descriptions of firms which only exist in the early years, and deciding where to allocate them.
- In total, 60 firms are allocated manually after reading their descriptions on Value Line.

Table A1

Value Line sample by year and industry classification.

Includes all firms on Value Line from 1970 to 1994 which had data on COMPUSTAT and were not classified as: (1) foreign industries, (2) ADR's, (3) REIT's, (4) investment companies or funds, (5) "Unassigned." Industries are based on actual industry classifications from Value Line, with some modifications to adjust for changes in Value Line coverage, such as additions, deletions and mergers of industries and reclassifications of subsets of industries in different years (see Appendix A for details).

Industry Number	Industry Name	1970	1971	1972	1973	1974	1975	1976	1977	1978	1979	1980	1981	1982	1983	1984	1985	1986	1987	1988	1989	1990	1991	1992	1993	1994
1	Advertising, publishing and newspaper	24	27	27	31	32	36	36	38	39	38	38	40	40	41	39	40	40	38	34	34	35	37	37	36	36
2	Aerospace and defense	21	22	21	20	20	24	24	27	26	26	30	31	30	32	33	33	33	30	31	31	32	29	32	35	34
3	Air transport	16	16	15	15	15	17	17	17	19	23	23	25	24	25	24	24	20	19	17	14	14	11	11	11	11
4	Apparel and shoe	35	40	38	39	38	38	39	40	38	36	34	37	39	38	35	34	30	30	26	29	25	25	24	22	23
5	Auto and truck	5	5	6	6	6	5	5	6	6	6	6	6	7	6	9	9	8	7	6	5	4	4	4	4	4
6	Auto parts	29	32	32	33	31	31	31	30	26	25	25	25	24	24	23	21	23	22	23	21	19	19	18	18	19
7	Bank and Thrift	46	48	48	60	63	64	65	70	71	71	71	74	73	70	67	78	86	82	81	84	90	89	85	82	80
8	Beverage	21	21	22	24	23	24	24	23	22	22	23	19	16	14	13	11	10	9	9	10	9	10	10	11	13
9	Broadcasting and cable TV	7	6	6	6	5	8	8	8	8	7	7	11	15	16	15	16	14	12	12	11	10	10	10	10	10
10	Brokerage, leasing, and financial services	15	27	28	25	25	24	22	23	22	20	18	17	16	27	26	27	28	32	37	35	34	36	40	42	41
11	Building materials, cement, furniture and homebuilding	53	61	62	70	64	67	74	74	72	73	68	66	68	66	65	68	70	76	68	64	59	59	57	57	54
12	Chemical	43	44	45	45	46	47	52	52	48	49	49	53	52	54	55	52	53	53	56	58	65	64	62	62	63
13	Coal and alternate energy	8	7	7	6	6	9	9	11	11	10	12	12	11	11	10	10	9	11	9	7	8	7	7	5	4
14	Computer	8	18	18	19	19	19	23	25	25	27	30	34	40	50	52	50	57	59	61	54	55	58	62	66	72
15	Diversified	27	39	37	39	38	36	37	34	35	35	39	43	44	42	44	45	44	53	56	51	52	52	51	49	49
16	Drug	20	20	20	21	23	21	21	22	20	20	19	20	20	21	21	20	23	24	24	21	19	19	22	27	27
17	Drugstore	5	12	12	14	14	16	17	15	15	15	14	10	10	12	10	8	8	7	7	9	9	9	9	9	10
18	Electrical equipment and home appliance	41	45	44	45	46	49	49	48	49	46	46	45	43	43	43	41	34	32	30	27	25	25	25	25	24
19	Electronics and semiconductor	30	31	30	29	28	32	34	32	34	39	45	46	51	46	47	51	52	49	53	55	54	54	52	54	52
20	Food processing	54	56	57	56	57	62	66	67	64	61	60	59	57	55	53	50	48	46	45	45	46	45	44	44	41
21	Food wholesalers and grocery stores	20	25	26	27	27	25	25	24	23	25	25	29	32	34	30	29	29	28	30	25	30	30	28	28	29
22	Hotel and gaming	7	8	8	12	12	14	13	14	15	14	12	12	12	13	14	14	13	14	15	15	15	15	15	16	15
23	Household products	7	9	8	8	8	8	10	12	11	10	10	10	10	9	11	11	12	11	10	10	10	11	11	12	12

(*Continued*)

Table A1 (Continued)

Industry Number	Industry Name	1970	1971	1972	1973	1974	1975	1976	1977	1978	1979	1980	1981	1982	1983	1984	1985	1986	1987	1988	1989	1990	1991	1992	1993	1994
24	Industrial services (including environmental)	5	10	10	17	16	19	18	18	16	18	19	19	22	20	20	23	24	23	29	35	38	41	42	41	38
25	Insurance	20	25	26	33	33	41	42	45	47	47	46	47	43	41	41	42	41	43	46	49	49	48	49	49	50
26	Machine tool	15	15	15	17	17	18	17	17	16	16	15	15	14	14	14	13	11	15	11	11	9	8	9	7	7
27	Machinery	67	67	64	70	70	74	73	72	71	70	69	67	69	64	60	60	53	46	45	46	47	45	46	45	47
28	Manufactured housing, and recreational vehicles	8	7	8	9	9	8	10	11	11	11	11	11	9	9	9	8	10	8	9	8	7	7	7	8	8
29	Maritime	7	7	8	9	8	7	9	8	8	7	8	7	8	8	12	12	8	6	6	6	5	5	5	5	5
30	Medical services	0	0	0	3	3	4	5	3	4	9	9	8	10	10	9	11	10	10	12	9	10	11	12	15	14
31	Medical supplies	11	14	13	14	12	12	15	18	18	21	26	25	23	25	24	23	27	32	33	36	39	45	43	42	42
32	Metal fabricating	20	20	20	21	21	21	18	19	19	19	20	20	18	18	18	20	18	19	16	16	14	14	14	13	13
33	Metals and mining	43	43	43	45	44	44	43	40	36	34	36	33	33	33	32	31	31	28	28	28	28	30	29	28	27
34	Natural gas	43	48	48	46	44	44	48	50	51	50	54	50	53	52	53	54	50	50	49	48	47	48	47	47	47
35	Office equipment and supplies	12	12	12	14	15	17	17	16	18	15	15	15	15	15	14	15	17	19	20	21	21	21	21	21	22
36	Oilfield services and equipment	10	12	13	15	14	19	19	19	23	29	27	32	34	33	34	32	26	21	19	20	19	17	18	18	17
37	Packaging and container	19	21	21	26	26	26	27	27	23	22	22	23	25	24	19	19	17	17	16	18	17	17	17	13	13
38	Paper and forest products	18	19	19	20	19	22	25	26	26	27	28	27	25	25	28	29	25	28	30	30	29	29	29	29	30
39	Petroleum	41	46	43	46	49	54	58	64	62	63	64	63	61	54	47	45	45	45	46	42	42	44	42	42	42
40	Precision instrument	23	27	28	28	28	31	31	32	36	35	22	23	27	26	26	24	26	11	25	25	24	23	22	22	20
41	Railroad	19	18	17	16	16	16	17	17	17	17	14	13	13	13	12	15	10	11	11	11	10	6	10	9	12
42	Real estate	5	8	8	14	14	13	12	13	13	11	12	12	10	9	12	15	14	14	11	10	8	6	5	0	0
43	Recreation	15	17	19	22	21	24	22	21	21	22	20	18	20	18	18	19	21	22	22	21	19	19	20	20	19
44	Restaurant	3	4	4	4	4	13	19	17	19	17	16	16	15	16	18	16	21	20	21	18	19	17	17	19	19
45	Retail (special lines)	8	11	12	13	13	13	16	17	16	17	18	15	18	20	23	26	32	36	43	49	54	53	54	53	52
46	Retail store	33	38	37	40	39	41	38	38	36	42	42	38	33	32	35	36	32	31	29	26	25	24	24	27	27
47	Steel	31	30	29	28	27	31	32	31	31	30	31	31	29	29	26	25	24	20	20	24	26	26	24	22	25
48	Telecommunications	11	12	12	12	12	13	13	14	14	14	16	17	20	22	30	32	34	36	34	35	36	33	33	33	35
49	Textile	19	19	12	22	22	21	21	18	19	20	19	17	14	15	12	11	9	9	11	10	9	4	4	9	11
50	Tire and rubber	10	10	10	11	11	12	12	12	12	12	12	12	13	13	11	11	11	8	4	4	4	4	4	4	5
51	Tobacco	11	11	10	10	10	9	9	9	9	9	8	8	7	7	7	8	8	8	9	8	8	9	9	9	9
52	Toiletries and cosmetics	14	12	12	11	11	12	13	14	15	15	15	15	16	16	15	14	11	12	11	10	9	9	10	10	9
53	Toys	6	8	8	8	8	7	7	8	10	11	10	10	6	6	5	6	6	5	6	7	7	6	7	6	4
54	Trucking and transportation leasing	16	18	17	20	20	21	21	23	23	18	21	17	13	12	11	12	14	17	12	12	12	12	12	11	12
55	Utilities	91	94	94	95	95	97	96	98	98	97	96	97	97	96	95	97	97	97	101	102	103	101	101	101	100
	Total	1196	1322	1317	1409	1397	1486	1524	1549	1537	1543	1545	1547	1547	1544	1523	1539	1526	1526	1525	1510	1511	1509	1507	1504	1504

Appendix B: Procedure for assigning industries to merger targets

In an attempt to assign an industry to all the targets in mergers where the acquirer belonged to the sample, a total of 1711 transactions, we follow these steps in order (Table A2):

(1) Check if the target is in Value Line, and assign it's corresponding industry. This results in 572 classifications.
(2) Create a conversion table of SIC codes to our industry classifications. This is based on our reading the descriptions of all four-digit SIC codes from the Standard Industrial Classification Manual (1987). For most cases, the appropriate industry assignment is obvious, but in case of doubt, we classify the four-digit code as "missing."
(3) Using the conversion table, assign industries to the remaining targets on the basis of both their CRSP and Compustat SIC codes. If the industries match, assign the target to it, which results in 456 additional classifications
(4) Hand-collect primary SIC codes for remaining unclassified targets from Dun and Bradstreet's Million Dollar Directory. Using the conversion table, assign industries to the targets found in the Directory. This results in 537 additional classifications.

Table A2

Mergers by acquirers in Value Line during the 1970–1994 period.

Includes all deals where target was in CRSP and a transaction value could be estimated. Mergers are assigned to the industry of the acquirer in the year of completion. This sample is a subset of the CRSP Merger Database, including all mergers between CRSP-listed firms in the 1958–1994 period. Industries are based on actual industry classifications from Value Line, with some modifications to adjust for changes in Value Line coverage and classification, such as additions, deletions and mergers of industries, as well as reclassifications of subsets of industries in different years (see Appendix A for details).

Industry Number	Industry Name	1970	1971	1972	1973	1974	1975	1976	1977	1978	1979	1980	1981	1982	1983	1984	1985	1986	1987	1988	1989	1990	1991	1992	1993	1994	Total
1	Advertising, publishing and newspaper	0	1	0	2	1	0	0	3	4	7	1	1	0	0	3	1	1	3	2	0	2	0	1	1	0	34
2	Aerospace and defense	0	1	0	0	1	0	2	3	3	2	5	0	0	2	3	3	4	2	0	2	1	1	0	0	0	35
3	Air transport	1	1	1	1	0	0	0	0	0	2	2	0	1	0	0	3	6	5	4	0	0	0	0	0	1	26
4	Apparel and shoe	0	0	1	1	0	2	1	0	1	3	1	1	1	0	3	0	1	4	2	1	0	0	0	0	1	20
5	Auto and truck	0	0	0	0	0	1	0	0	0	0	1	0	0	0	1	2	0	2	2	1	1	0	0	0	0	13
6	Auto parts	2	0	1	0	0	2	2	0	5	3	3	2	3	0	0	1	2	1	0	1	1	0	0	1	0	31
7	Bank and thrift	2	0	0	3	3	2	1	4	1	0	1	1	12	9	8	8	24	18	14	12	13	10	23	31	21	217
8	Beverage	2	0	2	3	1	0	1	4	3	1	0	1	3	1	0	1	1	0	2	2	0	0	1	0	0	28
9	Broadcasting and cable TV	0	0	0	0	1	1	0	1	2	0	0	0	3	1	0	0	2	2	2	1	1	0	1	0	2	18
10	Brokerage, leasing and financial services	0	0	1	1	1	1	1	2	2	3	4	1	3	0	0	1	3	1	5	2	3	1	2	0	0	36
11	Building materials, cement, furniture and homebuilding	1	1	0	0	0	1	0	3	5	4	4	1	2	2	3	3	2	3	3	0	0	0	1	0	0	41
12	Chemical	3	2	2	3	3	1	1	4	5	3	4	8	3	7	1	6	2	4	3	3	1	0	0	1	0	68
13	Coal and alternate energy	0	0	0	0	3	0	0	0	2	0	1	0	0	0	0	0	0	2	2	3	0	0	0	1	0	10
14	Computer	0	0	0	0	0	1	2	2	3	1	3	2	2	0	3	1	1	4	4	3	1	4	2	5	0	44
15	Diversified	3	5	4	5	6	8	11	2	8	4	3	3	4	5	12	10	3	6	2	2	3	1	2	0	0	113
16	Drug	0	1	0	0	0	0	0	1	3	3	1	0	2	2	0	0	3	3	1	2	0	0	0	3	0	34
17	Drugstore	0	1	1	0	0	0	1	2	0	0	0	0	0	0	0	0	0	0	0	0	0	0	0	0	0	6
18	Electrical Equipment and home appliance	3	1	1	1	1	5	3	2	4	5	3	1	2	2	0	3	2	3	4	6	2	0	0	2	0	59
19	Electronics and semiconductor	0	1	1	1	0	1	2	1	3	0	0	4	0	0	2	0	0	3	0	2	0	0	0	0	1	24
20	Food processing	0	2	0	5	5	3	2	5	14	4	4	3	3	1	3	4	2	2	0	5	2	1	0	1	0	72
21	Food wholesalers and grocery stores	0	0	0	0	1	0	1	0	0	2	0	1	0	2	2	2	2	0	2	0	0	0	1	0	0	17
22	Hotel and gaming	0	0	0	0	0	0	0	0	0	0	1	0	2	0	0	1	2	0	0	1	0	1	0	0	0	8
23	Household Products	0	1	1	2	0	0	1	1	0	1	0	0	0	1	0	1	1	2	0	0	3	0	2	1	1	18
24	Industrial services (including environmental)	0	0	0	0	0	0	0	0	1	0	0	1	0	0	0	0	3	3	2	1	3	2	1	0	0	15

#	Industry	Column values (cross-industry merger counts)	Total
25	Insurance	1, 0, 0, 0, 0, 0, 0, 0, 2, 1, 0, 0, 10, 5, 8, 9, 2, 1, 5, 2, 0, 2, 0, 0, 1	68
26	Machine tool	0, 0, 0, 0, 0, 0, 0, 0, 1, 1, 1, 0, 1, 1, 0, 0, 0, 0, 0, 0, 0, 0, 0, 0, 0	6
27	Machinery	2, 2, 1, 1, 2, 2, 5, 4, 10, 9, 4, 4, 2, 2, 2, 0, 3, 1, 1, 1, 0, 0, 1, 2, 0	60
28	Manufactured housing and recreational vehicles	0, 0, 0, 0, 0, 0, 0, 0, 0, 0, 0, 0, 0, 0, 0, 0, 0, 0, 0, 0, 0, 0, 0, 0, 0	1
29	Maritime	0, 0, 0, 0, 0, 0, 0, 0, 1, 1, 0, 0, 2, 0, 0, 0, 0, 0, 0, 0, 0, 0, 0, 0, 0	2
30	Medical services	0, 0, 0, 0, 0, 0, 0, 2, 1, 1, 1, 0, 2, 2, 3, 0, 3, 1, 0, 2, 1, 0, 1, 2, 1	18
31	Medical supplies	0, 0, 2, 2, 0, 0, 1, 0, 2, 2, 2, 3, 3, 2, 3, 1, 0, 0, 0, 2, 1, 0, 3, 3, 0	32
32	Metal fabricating	0, 0, 0, 0, 0, 0, 2, 0, 2, 2, 0, 2, 0, 0, 1, 0, 0, 0, 1, 0, 0, 0, 0, 0, 0	12
33	Metals and mining	1, 2, 0, 2, 1, 0, 2, 0, 1, 0, 4, 1, 0, 2, 2, 2, 0, 2, 0, 1, 2, 0, 2, 0, 0	25
34	Natural gas	0, 3, 1, 1, 0, 0, 5, 0, 0, 2, 4, 2, 0, 7, 7, 4, 0, 0, 4, 5, 0, 0, 5, 0, 0	45
35	Office Equipment and supplies	0, 0, 0, 0, 0, 0, 1, 0, 2, 0, 1, 0, 0, 0, 0, 1, 0, 1, 0, 0, 0, 2, 0, 0, 0	8
36	Oilfield services and equipment	0, 0, 1, 0, 1, 0, 0, 0, 2, 2, 2, 1, 2, 0, 0, 2, 0, 1, 0, 0, 0, 0, 1, 0, 1	13
37	Packaging and container	1, 0, 0, 1, 1, 0, 3, 3, 3, 0, 2, 3, 3, 3, 2, 1, 1, 0, 0, 0, 0, 1, 0, 3, 0	29
38	Paper and forest products	0, 0, 0, 0, 2, 2, 1, 3, 2, 1, 2, 1, 2, 1, 2, 3, 3, 1, 1, 0, 1, 0, 3, 0, 0	25
39	Petroleum	1, 1, 0, 1, 3, 3, 6, 2, 6, 7, 3, 4, 3, 1, 0, 4, 1, 2, 2, 3, 1, 0, 4, 1, 0	53
40	Precision instrument	0, 0, 1, 1, 4, 1, 2, 1, 2, 3, 0, 2, 1, 0, 2, 1, 0, 1, 1, 3, 0, 0, 0, 1, 1	23
41	Railroad	2, 1, 1, 0, 0, 0, 3, 0, 3, 0, 3, 3, 0, 0, 0, 0, 0, 0, 0, 0, 0, 0, 0, 0, 0	27
42	Real estate	0, 0, 0, 0, 0, 0, 0, 0, 0, 1, 0, 0, 0, 0, 0, 0, 0, 0, 0, 0, 0, 0, 0, 0, 0	3
43	Recreation	0, 0, 2, 2, 0, 0, 5, 2, 2, 0, 0, 1, 0, 0, 0, 0, 0, 0, 0, 2, 0, 0, 2, 0, 0	19
44	Restaurant	0, 0, 0, 0, 0, 0, 0, 0, 0, 0, 0, 0, 0, 0, 0, 0, 0, 0, 0, 0, 0, 0, 3, 0, 0	3
45	Retail (special lines)	1, 1, 0, 1, 0, 0, 3, 1, 0, 0, 2, 0, 1, 2, 1, 3, 2, 0, 2, 2, 0, 0, 0, 1, 0	17
46	Retail store	2, 0, 2, 3, 0, 3, 3, 3, 2, 5, 2, 3, 2, 5, 3, 2, 2, 0, 4, 1, 4, 0, 2, 0, 1	46
47	Steel	0, 0, 0, 0, 1, 0, 0, 0, 1, 0, 2, 0, 0, 1, 0, 2, 0, 2, 1, 0, 0, 0, 0, 2, 0	12
48	Telecommunications	0, 0, 0, 1, 0, 1, 3, 1, 5, 4, 4, 3, 3, 4, 0, 3, 7, 0, 0, 0, 0, 6, 2, 3, 0	54
49	Textile	0, 0, 0, 0, 0, 0, 0, 1, 0, 0, 0, 0, 0, 0, 0, 0, 0, 0, 1, 0, 0, 2, 3, 2, 0	8
50	Tire and rubber	1, 0, 0, 1, 0, 0, 2, 0, 0, 0, 0, 0, 0, 0, 1, 1, 0, 1, 2, 0, 0, 0, 0, 0, 0	9
51	Tobacco	0, 0, 0, 0, 0, 0, 1, 2, 3, 0, 0, 0, 1, 1, 0, 0, 2, 1, 0, 0, 0, 0, 0, 0, 0	17
52	Toiletries and cosmetics	2, 0, 0, 0, 1, 1, 1, 1, 1, 0, 0, 0, 1, 0, 0, 2, 2, 0, 0, 0, 0, 0, 0, 0, 0	12
53	Toys	0, 0, 0, 0, 0, 0, 0, 0, 1, 0, 0, 0, 0, 0, 0, 0, 0, 0, 0, 0, 0, 1, 1, 1, 0	10
54	Trucking and transportation leasing	2, 2, 0, 0, 1, 0, 0, 1, 0, 0, 1, 1, 0, 0, 1, 1, 1, 0, 1, 1, 0, 0, 0, 0, 0	11
55	Utilities	0, 0, 0, 1, 0, 0, 0, 0, 0, 1, 1, 0, 0, 2, 0, 3, 3, 1, 2, 2, 1, 3, 2, 2, 2	27
	Total	35, 28, 23, 46, 41, 42, 57, 87, 118, 111, 92, 73, 86, 58, 71, 99, 108, 94, 88, 67, 57, 43, 54, 70, 34	

Appendix C: Compustat data items

The following Compustat data items were used to construct the industry-level and firm-level variables in Sections 3 and 4:

Variable name	Compustat data item number
Advertising	45
CAPX	128
R&D	46
Cash	1
Sales	12
Total assets	6
Book equity	60
Market equity	199×25
EBITDA	13
Debt in current liabilities	34
Long-term debt	9
Preferred stock—redemption value	56

References

Andrade, G., M. Mitchell and E. Stafford, 2001, "New Evidence and Perspectives on Mergers," *Journal of Economic Perspectives*, 15, 103–120.

Blanchard, O., F. Lopez-de-Silanes and A. Shleifer, 1994, "What Do Firms Do with Cash Windfalls?" *Journal of Financial Economics*, 36, 337–360.

Brealey, R. and S. Myers, 1996, *Principles of Corporate Finance*, 5th edition, McGraw-Hill, New York, NY.

Fama, E., 1976, *Foundations of Finance*, Basic, New York.

Gibbons, J., 1985, *Nonparametric Statistical Inference*, 2nd edition, Marcel Dekker, New York, NY.

Gort, M., 1969, "An Economic Disturbance Theory of Mergers," *Quarterly Journal of Economics*, 83, 624–642.

Greene, W., 1993, *Econometric Analysis*, 2nd edition, Macmillan, New York, NY.

Guenther, D. and A. Rosman, 1994, "Differences between Compustat and CRSP SIC Codes and Related Effects on Research," *Journal of Accounting and Economics*, 18, 115–128.

Healy, P., K. Palepu and R. Ruback, 1992, "Does Corporate Performance Improve After Mergers?" *Journal of Financial Economics*, 31, 135–175.

Heaton, J. B., 1999, "Managerial Optimism and Corporate Finance," Working Paper, University of Chicago.

Jarrell, G., J. Brickley and J. Netter, 1988, "The Market for Corporate Control: The Empirical Evidence Since 1980," *Journal of Economic Perspectives*, 2, 49–68.

Jensen, M., 1986, "Agency Costs of Free Cash Flow, Corporate Finance and Takeovers," *American Economic Review*, 76, 323–329.

Jensen, M., 1993, "The Modern Industrial Revolution, Exit, and Control Systems," *Journal of Finance*, 48, 831–880.

Kahle, K. and R. Walkling, 1996, "The Impact of Industry Classifications on Financial Research," *Journal of Financial and Quantitative Analysis*, 31, 309–335.

Kaplan, S. and L. Zingales, 1997, "Do Financing Constraints Explain Why Investment is Correlated With Cash Flow?" *Quarterly Journal of Economics*, 112, 169–215.

Kovenock, D. and G. Phillips, 1997, "Capital Structure and Product Market Behavior: An Examination of Plant Exit and Investment Decisions," *Review of Financial Studies*, 10, 767–803.

Lang, L., R. Stulz and R. Walkling, 1989, "Managerial Performance, Tobin's q, and the Gains from Successful Tender Offers," *Journal of Financial Economics*, 24, 137–154.

Maddala, G., 1983, *Limited Dependent and Qualitative Variables in Econometrics*, Cambridge University Press, New York, NY.

Maksimovic, V. and G. Phillips, 2001, "The Market for Corporate Assets: Who Engages in Mergers and Asset Sales and are there Efficiency Gains?" *Journal of Finance*, 56, 2019–2065.

Mitchell, M. and J. Mulherin, 1996, "The Impact of Industry Shocks on Takeover and Restructuring Activity," *Journal of Financial Economics*, 41, 193–229.

Mitchell, M. and E. Stafford, 2000, "Managerial Decisions and Long-Term Stock Price Performance," *Journal of Business*, 73, 287–329.

Morck, R., A. Shleifer and R. Vishny, 1988, "Characteristics of Targets of Hostile and Friendly Takeovers," In A. J. Auerbach (Ed.), *Corporate Takeovers: Causes and Consequences*, University of Chicago Press/ NBER, Chicago, IL.

Morck, R., A. Shleifer and R. Vishny, 1990, "Do Managerial Objectives Drive Bad Acquisitions?" *Journal of Finance*, 45, 31–48.

Mulherin, J. and A. Boone, 2000, "Comparing Acquisitions and Divestitures," *Journal of Corporate Finance*, 6, 117–139.

Myers, S., 1977, "Determinants of Corporate Borrowing," *Journal of Financial Economics*, 5, 147–175.

Nelson, R., 1959, *Merger Movements in American Industry, 1895–1956*, Princeton University Press/NBER, Princeton, NJ.

Song, M. and R. Walkling, 2000, "Abnormal Returns to Rivals of Acquisition Targets: A Test of the "Acquisition Probability Hypothesis"," *Journal of Financial Economics*, 55, 143–172.

Chapter 5

VALUATION WAVES AND MERGER ACTIVITY: THE EMPIRICAL EVIDENCE[*]

MATTHEW RHODES-KROPF

Graduate School of Business, Columbia University, New York, USA

DAVID T. ROBINSON

Fuqua School of Business, Duke University, Durham, North Carolina, USA

S. VISWANATHAN

Fuqua School of Business, Duke University, Durham, North Carolina, USA

Contents

* We thank Audra Boone, Serguey Braguinsky, Arturo Bris, B. Espen Eckbo, Larry Glosten, John Graham, John Hand, Boyan Jovanovic, Steve Kaplan, Pete Kyle, Per Olsson, Stephen Penman, Gordon Phillips, Jay Ritter, Jeremy Stein, René Stulz, Jayanti Sunder, Paolo Volpin, Ira Weiss, and Jeff Wurgler, for useful discussions and ideas. We also thank workshop participants at Carnegie-Mellon, Columbia, Dartmouth, Duke, UCLA, UNC, the NBER, 2003 EFA meetings, 2004 NYU Five-Star Conference, 2003 Texas Finance Festival, 2004 AFA meetings, and 2004 Indiana FEA Conference for insightful comments. We are also grateful for the comments of an anonymous referee.

This article originally appeared in the *Journal of Financial Economics*, Vol. 77, pp. 561–603 (2005).
Corporate Takeovers, Volume 1
Edited by B. Espen Eckbo
DOI: 10.1016/B978-0-12-381983-3.00005-8

Abstract

To test recent theories suggesting that valuation errors affect merger activity, we develop a decomposition that breaks the market-to-book ratio (*M/B*) into three components: the firm-specific pricing deviation from short-run industry pricing; sector-wide, short-run deviations from firms' long-run pricing; and long-run pricing to book. We find strong support for recent theories by Rhodes-Kropf and Viswanathan [Rhodes-Kropf, M. and S. Viswanathan, 2004, "Market valuation and merger waves," *Journal of Finance*, 59, 2685–2718] and Shleifer and Vishny [Shleifer, A. and R. Vishny, 2003, "Stock market driven acquisitions," *Journal of Financial Economics*, 70, 295–311], which predict that misvaluation drives mergers. So much of the behavior of *M/B* is driven by firm-specific deviations from short-run industry pricing, that long-run components of *M/B* run counter to the conventional wisdom: *Low* long-run value-to-book firms buy *high* long-run value-to-book firms. Misvaluation affects who buys whom, as well as method of payment, and combines with neoclassical explanations to explain aggregate merger activity.

Keywords

mergers and acquisitions, merger waves, valuation

JEL classification: G34, G14

1. Introduction

The goal of this paper is to test the effect of misvaluation on merger activity. The last 125 years of business history indicate that periods of high M/B ratios coincide with periods of intense merger activity, especially for stock-financed deals.[1] This fact is open to two interpretations. Under the neoclassical view, this fact is evidence that assets are being redeployed toward more productive uses.[2] In contrast, if financial markets value firms incorrectly or managers have information not held by the market, this result can be interpreted as evidence that acquisition frenzies are driven by overvaluation. Indeed, the fact that each of the last five great merger waves on record ended with a precipitous decline in equity prices has led many to believe that misvaluation drives merger activity.

While this idea is compelling, it seems inconsistent with a broader equilibrium that endogenizes the target's response to the offer. To put it simply, why is the target fooled? Why would a value-maximizing target knowingly accept overvalued currency in a takeover offer?

Two recent theories offer answers to this question and, thus, to the role that valuation waves play in merger activity. Rhodes-Kropf and Viswanathan (2004, henceforth RKV) propose a rational theory based on correlated misinformation. In the RKV world, errors in valuing potential takeover synergies are correlated with overall valuation error. Merger waves occur during valuation waves because ex post, targets have mistakenly overestimated synergies. Shleifer and Vishny (2003, henceforth SV) propose a theory based on an irrational stock market and self-interested target managers who can cash out quickly. SV posit that target managers do not maximize long-term shareholder value; they instead maximize their own short-run gain. Because these theories, although economically very different, do not model the source of the misvaluation, they yield parallel empirical predictions on the link between misvaluation and merger waves.

In this paper we test the empirical predictions of RKV and SV and find strong support for the idea that misvaluation shapes merger activity. We show that misvaluation affects the level of merger activity, the decision to be an acquirer or target, and the transaction medium. To guard against the possible alternative interpretations for our findings, we run a battery of empirical horseraces between misvaluation and standard neoclassical explanations of takeover. Even if we attribute all spikes in merger activity to neoclassically motivated industry shocks, our results indicate that misvaluation is critical for understanding who buys whom in merger transactions.

To explore misvaluation empirically, we decompose M/B into two parts:

$$\text{Market to book} \equiv \text{market to value} \times \text{value to book.} \tag{1}$$

---

[1] See Maksimovic and Phillips (2001) or Jovanovic and Rousseau (2001) for recent evidence.
[2] See Servaes (1991) and Lang et al. (1989) for market reaction evidence consistent with this view.

If we had an accurate measure of value, we could assign labels to each of the two pieces on the right-hand side of Equation (1). The first piece would measure the discrepancy between price and true value, and would therefore measure misvaluation. This could be the result of a behavioral anomaly or asymmetric information between informed insiders and the rest of the market. In either case, the second piece would capture true value to book, which would then measure growth opportunities in a manner that is unadulterated by misvaluation.

Any breakdown of M/B rests critically on particular measures of value. We use sector-level, cross-sectional regressions of firm-level market equities on firm fundamentals each year to derive a series of such measures. Average R^2 values indicate that this approach explains between 80% and 94% of within-sector variation in firm-level market values at a point in time. We then use the resulting regression coefficients to generate measures of value. These coefficients have natural interpretations as time-varying valuation multiples and account for variation in the market's expectations of returns and growth over time and across industries.

Because RKV stresses the difference between sector-wide and firm-specific misvaluation, our empirical implementation of Equation (1) breaks M/B into three components: firm-specific error, time-series sector error, and long-run value to book. By exploiting the panel structure of our data, we measure *firm-specific error* with firm-specific deviations from valuations implied by contemporaneous sector multiples. This captures the idea that a firm could have an idiosyncratic misvaluation component. We measure *time-series sector error* by differences that arise when contemporaneous multiples differ from long-run multiples. This captures the idea that sectors, or entire markets, could be overheated, and thus that firms in the same sector could share a common misvaluation component. The final piece is long-run value-to-book, which relates values implied by long-run valuation multiples to book value. This captures long-run growth opportunities.

Using this breakdown, we find support for each prediction of RKV and SV. Our results show the following:

- Acquiring firms are priced significantly higher than targets. The valuation difference is roughly 20% of the target's log M/B ratio.
- While the difference in M/B between acquirers and targets is large, it is dwarfed by differences in firm-specific error. Roughly 60% of the acquirer's M/B is attributable to firm-specific error. Almost none of the target's M/B is attributable to firm-specific error.
- Acquirers and targets cluster in sectors with high time-series sector error. Thus, acquirers and targets appear to share a common misvaluation component.
- Cash targets are undervalued (they have negative firm-specific error) while stock targets are slightly overvalued. Cash acquirers are less overvalued than stock acquirers.
- Increasing firm-specific error raises the probability that a firm will be involved in a merger, that it will be an acquirer, and that it uses stock. In contrast, M/B alone has

no effect on the probability of merger once we control for year fixed effects. Similarly, sector-wide takeover activity increases with time-series sector error. This is especially true for stock merger intensity.

- When we examine long-run value to book, we find that *low* value-to-book firms buy *high* value-to-book firms. The long-run value-to-book component of *M/B* for targets is three to five times higher than that for acquirers.

- Misvaluation explains about 15% of merger activity at the sector level. Thus, while misvaluation is important for understanding patterns of merger activity at the industry level, neoclassical factors such as industry productivity shocks also play an important role.

- While roughly 40% of the total dollar volume of merger activity occurs during these merger waves, highly overvalued bidders are responsible for the bulk of these mergers. During merger waves, as much as 65% of merger activity comes from the quintile of most overvalued bidders. Thus, while neoclassical explanations are important for understanding merger activity at the sector level, misvaluation is critical for understanding who buys whom, regardless of whether the merger occurs during a time when productivity shocks could have caused a spike in merger activity.

Two alternative interpretations of our results that acquirers have higher firm-specific errors than targets exist. The first is that misvaluation matters. Overvalued firms buy less-overvalued firms in sectors that are themselves overvalued. Alternatively, one could view our decomposition as a refinement of Q theory, in which valuations implied by sector multiples provide better estimates of replacement costs than traditional accounting measures.

However, this second view must confront an unexpected finding, one that is a puzzle for existing theory. Namely, *low* long-run value-to-book firms buy *high* long-run value-to-book firms. Long-run value to book for targets is three to five times higher than that for acquirers. Thus, so much of the 'high buys low' effect in the overall *M/B* ratio is driven by short-run valuation dynamics that the long-run components go in the opposite direction. This suggests that short-run misvaluation stemming from asymmetric information or behavioral phenomena masks Jensen (1986) agency-style motivations for takeover.[3]

Our robustness tests control for a number of potential neoclassical explanations. First, our misvaluation measures drive out Q theory-based proxies for merger activity. Further, the "high buys low" result commonly offered as evidence in favor of Q oriented explanations of merger activity is stronger in failed deals than in successful ones. In contrast, misvaluation is higher in successful deals. Second, our misvaluation measures explain about 15% of sectoral merger activity based on the classification of

---

[3] See Rhodes-Kropf and Robinson (2004) for a model that nests the standard Q theory of mergers as a special case, but is also consistent with these findings.

economic shocks in Harford (2005). However, within these periods of economic flux, the bulk of acquirers come from the highest misvaluation decile. Thus, even during periods when economic shocks have caused spikes in merger activity at the industry level (Mitchell and Mulherin, 1996), misvaluation is still critical for understanding who buys whom and how they finance the acquisition. Based on these robustness tests, we conclude that while neoclassical explanations are important, misvaluation plays a significant role in determining merger activity.

This paper is related to a number of distinct literatures. It adds to a large empirical literature that examines trends in merger and acquisition activity (see Andrade et al., 2001; Holmstrom and Kaplan, 2001, for recent surveys). Our technique for calculating the pieces of our decomposition draws on the value-relevance literature in accounting (see Barth et al., 2001; Penman, 1998; or Francis and Schipper, 1999 for recent examples). Our results linking valuation to merger waves complement contemporaneous empirical work by Harford (2005). In related work, Dong et al. (2005) and Ang and Chen (2004) follow a similar idea to that in this paper, but use analyst's estimates of future earnings instead of our regression-based approach. Recent work by Moeller et al. (2005) shows that the merger wave of the late 1990s destroyed almost 10 times the dollar value per share as did mergers occurring during the merger wave of the 1980s, while Moeller et al. (2004) show that the bulk of this occurred with large acquirers. Our analysis of misvaluation and transaction size complements these findings.

The remainder of the paper is organized as follows. In Section 2, we review current theories relating valuation waves to merger waves and determine our testable predictions. In Section 3, we describe the data. Sections 4 and 5 describe the conditional regression multiples approach in detail, and compare it to alternative specifications for value. Section 6 presents our findings. In Section 7 we run an empirical horserace between misvaluation and neoclassical explanations for merger activity. Section 8 concludes.

2. Theoretical background and testable implications

If firms use stock as an acquisition currency when their stock is overvalued, and this is widely known, then why are targets fooled? In this section, we review the main features of SV and RKV, which offer answers to this question. Then we explore their empirical implications.

In RKV, private information on both sides rationally leads to a correlation between stock merger activity and market valuation. In their theory, misvaluation has a market- or sector-wide component as well as a firm-specific component. The target's and bidding firm's private information tells them whether they are over- or undervalued, but they cannot separately identify the sources of the misvaluation. A rational target correctly adjusts bids for potential overvaluation but, as a Bayesian, puts some weight on high synergies as well. When the market-wide overvaluation is high, the estimation error associated with the synergy is high, too, so the offer is more likely to be accepted.

Thus, when the market is overvalued, the target is more likely to overestimate the synergies because it underestimates the component of misvaluation that it shares with the bidders.

In contrast, SV posit inefficient capital markets and differences in managerial time-horizons as the key drivers of merger activity. They hypothesize that short-run managers sell their firm for stock in a long-run manager's firm when both firms are overvalued, even though the transaction price gives the short-run manager less than he knows his firm will be worth in the long run. The short-run manager then sells his stock. The market is assumed to be irrational and therefore does not react to this deception or exploitation.

2.1. Relative value predictions

In both models, overvaluation leads to mergers. Therefore, the central prediction of either theory is

Empirical Prediction 1 *Overvalued firms use stock to buy relatively undervalued firms when both firms are overvalued.*

In SV this occurs because the overvalued short-run managers wish to sell out while their stock is overvalued. The acquirer is also overvalued because only long-run managers whose companies are more overvalued have room in their stock price to overpay for a target that is also overvalued and still make money in the long run.

In RKV, if the bidding firm has a large firm-specific overvaluation then it is more likely to win because the target cannot fully distinguish between a large synergy and a large firm-specific error. Furthermore, if the market or sector is overvalued, then the target is more likely to accept an offer because, although the target makes the correct adjustment for potential market or sector overvaluation, as a Bayesian, the target puts some weight on high synergies as well. Therefore, an overvalued market leads to an overestimation of the synergies.

The above logic from both papers also suggests that

Empirical Prediction 2 *Overall merger activity will be higher in overvalued markets. On average, firms in overvalued sectors should use stock to buy firms in relatively less overvalued sectors.*

The theories differ only slightly in their predictions about cash mergers. SV suggest that firms should use only cash to buy an undervalued firm because there is no role for true synergies in their model. In RKV, cash targets should be less overvalued than stock targets but could still be overvalued if high synergies outweigh the overvaluation. Furthermore, in both theories stock-financed deals are more likely to be completed when acquirers are more overvalued, therefore cash acquirers on average should be less overvalued than stock acquirers. Overall the theories suggest that cash mergers are driven by undervaluation or synergies or both, while stock mergers are driven by overvaluation. Thus, the theories suggest that

Empirical Prediction 3 *Cash targets are more undervalued than stock targets. Cash acquirers are less overvalued than stock acquirers.*

2.2. Merger intensity predictions

The first three predictions relate to levels of relative misvaluation across types of transactions conditional on a merger. The SV and RKV theories also demonstrate how misvaluation can cause merger waves. Thus, the predictions from theory should also be stated in terms of how increases in misvaluation cause increases in merger activity. For the theories to have empirical relevance, merger activity should be more likely conditional on high valuation errors. Therefore, theory leads to

Empirical Prediction 4 *Increasing misvaluation increases the probability that a firm is in a merger, is the acquirer, and uses stock as the method of payment.*

In both theories, the greater a firm's overvaluation, the more likely it is to win the bidding for a target. RKV also predict that even the probability of being a target should increase with sector overvaluation. This is because, in RKV, targets make mistakes evaluating synergies that are correlated with sector-wide misvaluation.

Prediction 4 is about individual firms. A similar prediction should hold at the sector-level about aggregate merger intensity.

Empirical Prediction 5 *Increasing sector misvaluation increases merger activity, and the use of stock as method of payment, in that sector.*

These predictions allow us to examine the importance of valuation, and the components of valuation, in merger activity. However, a number of other prominent explanations exist for merger waves. For example, Holmstrom and Kaplan (2001) argue that corporate governance issues led to the merger waves of the 1980s and 1990s. Andrade et al. (2001) and Mulherin and Boone (2000) argue that deregulation caused the 1990s wave. Gorton et al. (2000) suggest that mergers are a defensive mechanism by managers. Jovanovic and Rousseau (2001, 2002) argue that technological changes caused the waves of the 1900s, 1920s, 1980s, and 1990s, but not the 1960s. Therefore, to understand better how much merger activity can be attributed to misvaluation, and how much can be explained by more neoclassically oriented explanations, we not only test these empirical predictions but also provide a battery of robustness checks and empirical horse races to ensure that our findings are not simply capturing more conventional explanations.

3. Data and trends in merger activity

Our sample includes all merger activity between publicly traded bidders and targets listed on the Securities Data Corporation (SDC) Merger and Acquisition Database between 1978 and 2001. Because our sample includes only publicly traded firms, this excludes transactions such as leveraged buyouts (LBOs) and management buyouts (MBOs). We then match these data with Compustat fiscal year-end accounting data and stock price data from the Center for Research in Securities Prices (CRSP) to obtain a final sample.

We use the following conventions to merge data from the three sources. First, to calculate *M/B*, we match fiscal year-end data from Compustat with CRSP market values occurring 3 months afterward. Because firms have different fiscal year-end dates, this involves compensating for Compustat's year-of-record scheme, so that the year of the data corresponds to the year in which the accounting information was filed. Then, we associate this CRSP and Compustat observation with an SDC merger announcement if the announcement occurs at least 1 month after the date of the CRSP market value. If a merger announcement occurs between the fiscal year-end and 1 month after the CRSP market value, we associate the merger announcement with the previous year's accounting information.

Table 1 reports the time series of merger announcements over our sample. While the SDC data span from 1978 to 2001, our data conventions associate the earliest mergers with fiscal year 1977 and the latest with fiscal year 2000. Requiring both firms to be on CRSP and Compustat, we have announcements from 4325 acquirers corresponding to 4025 target firms. (The difference owes to withdrawn or failed offers in multibidder takeover battles.) As the table shows, in many instances the SDC data do not indicate the method of payment of the transaction: Our sample contains 799 mixed payment, 1218 all stock, and 1542 all cash transactions.

Using Compustat, we calculate a variety of size, performance, and leverage ratios. Market value is CRSP market equity plus Compustat book assets (item 6) minus deferred taxes (item 74) minus book equity (item 60). In addition, we obtain the following size-related measures: Total Plant, Property, Equipment (item 8), Total Cash (item 1), Long-term Debt (item 9), capital expenditures (CAPEX) (item 128), and Net Income (item 172). Return on assets and equity are calculated by dividing net income in year t by assets (item 6) or book equity (item 60) in year $t - 1$. For leverage measures, we obtain the Current Ratio (items 4/5), Quick Ratio [items $(4 - 3)/5$], market leverage $(1 - $ market equity/market value), and book leverage $(1 - $ book equity/total book assets). Finally, the announcement and closing dates of mergers, the method of payment (when available), and a dummy for whether the merger was withdrawn were taken from SDC and merged to the data from Compustat and CRSP.

Table 2 provides a comparison of these summary statistics based on whether or not a firm was involved in a merger and, if so, whether it was an acquirer or a target. Firms are flagged as merger observations in Table 2 in the year that a merger event is announced, therefore firms that ultimately are involved in mergers will be grouped in the nonmerger category in the years in which they have no merger activity. Along virtually any conceivable size dimension, merger observations are larger than the typical nonmerger firm on Compustat. However, this difference is driven by the fact that acquirers are much larger than average; target firms are about the same size, or a little smaller, than the average Compustat firm.

Table 1

Characteristics of merger sample

Mergers come from SDC merger database and are required to have acquirer and target information on the
Center for Research in Securities Prices (CRSP) and Compustat tapes. (Withdrawn deals are included.) Mean
size is the average transaction value in millions of US dollars as reported by SDC. All stock and all cash refer
to transactions that are known to be paid in 100% stock or cash, respectively. Mixed payment transactions
include combinations of stock, cash, and derivative securities. Transactions of unknown type are omitted
from the method-of-payment columns.

Year	Acquirers	Targets	All stock	All cash	Mixed	Mean size
1977	11	9	4	7	0	434.7
1978	11	11	1	4	0	88.3
1979	18	21	0	3	0	310.2
1980	61	44	1	4	0	856.5
1981	63	55	0	0	0	270.6
1982	95	94	2	9	1	307.8
1983	104	109	7	34	4	251.6
1984	113	110	17	55	16	406.2
1985	144	145	14	81	15	300.1
1986	164	168	25	95	25	273.7
1987	141	135	20	70	18	175.0
1988	141	123	28	66	15	362.6
1989	101	103	19	49	13	274.4
1990	108	90	31	32	16	233.8
1991	99	83	24	43	16	227.9
1992	170	147	51	69	27	460.4
1993	255	219	96	98	34	259.5
1994	315	284	100	124	58	568.8
1995	367	342	141	116	78	716.7
1996	413	411	157	116	103	713.4
1997	426	409	154	127	104	1840.1
1998	451	410	160	160	104	1420.9
1999	395	363	124	137	95	1665.7
2000	159	140	42	43	57	993.9
Total	4325	4025	1218	1542	799	839.4

The market-to-book ratios for firms involved in mergers are considerably higher
than those for nonmerger firms. When we compare acquirers and targets, we find that
M/B is significantly higher for acquirers than for targets. However, average M/B ratios
for targets are statistically larger than for nonmerger firms. Thus, the conventional
wisdom that high M/B buys low M/B is somewhat misguided: High M/B firms buy
lower M/B firms, but these targets have higher M/B ratios than the average firm. This is
a first hint that mergers occur when both firms are overvalued, which is our main
relative value prediction.

Table 2

Characteristics of merger and nonmerger firms

Summary statistics for size, performance, and leverage taken from Compustat between 1977 and 2000 to match the availability of the SDC data. Merger observations are firms appearing on the SDC as either a bidder or target in the period 1977–2001. Observations are required to have book-to-market ratios below 100 and market equity larger than $10 million. Market value of assets is market value of equity (CRSP price × shares outstanding) + book assets (d6) − book equity (d60) − deferred taxes (d74). Quick ratio is (d4 − d3)/ d5. Current ratio is d4/d5. Leverage is debt to total assets: market leverage is 1 − market equity/market value; book leverage is 1 − book equity/book value. The column *t*(diff.) reports the *t*-statistic for the hypothesis *H* (0): nonmerger − merger = 0, or target − acquirer = 0, correcting for unequal variance across groups. Performance measures are winsorized to remove influential outliers.

Variable	Nonmerger	Merger	*t*(diff.)	Target	Acquirer	*t*(diff.)
Sample size	102,527	8350		4025	4325	
Size measures						
Market value (assets)	2700.32	10,743.50	−17.62	2425.89	18,486.55	−18.66
Book assets	2352.61	6936.98	−14.95	2017.70	11,516.44	−16.44
Market equity	889.40	5421.84	−16.15	789.94	9733.78	−16.79
Book equity	487.24	1467.56	−19.13	338.49	2518.64	−22.85
PP&E	515.42	1121.06	−12.52	319.76	1869.88	−17.06
Long-term debt	377.09	976.55	−12.65	308.85	1596.73	−14.53
Capital expenditure	93.97	271.89	−13.02	66.67	466.12	−15.37
Net income	53.72	223.37	−17.17	32.09	401.63	−19.90
Performance measures						
Return on assets	0.0267	0.0297	−1.78	0.005	0.052	−14.98
Return on equity	0.0796	0.1019	−6.97	0.046	0.152	−17.46
Market/book	2.75	3.13	−9.86	2.81	3.43	−7.89
Leverage measures						
Leverage (book)	0.54	0.58	−14.09	0.56	0.59	−7.00
Leverage (market)	0.43	0.44	−3.16	0.44	0.44	0.08
Quick ratio	2.46	2.21	5.25	2.42	2.00	5.43
Current ratio	3.15	2.76	7.97	3.01	2.52	6.17

To say more about the tendency for mergers to cluster in particular sectors at a point in time (as in Andrade et al., 2001; or Mitchell and Mulherin, 1996), we use industry classifications provided by Eugene Fama and Kenneth French. These are described in Table 3, which reports verbal descriptions along with firm counts and aggregate valuation and merger statistics. The firm counts indicate that sector-year regressions, discussed in Section 5, do not suffer from small sample problems.

The summary statistics from this section expand on existing results linking *M/B* to merger activity: High *M/B* firms are involved in mergers; the very highest *M/B* firms buy higher-than-average *M/B* firms. To build on these findings, we next discuss a technique for decomposing the *M/B* ratio that allows us to attach separate interpretations to these findings in terms of a firm-specific value component, a sector value component, and long-run value to book.

Table 3

Industry characteristics used in subsequent valuation models

Industry definitions are taken from Fama and French. Observations describe the minimum, mean, and maximum number of observations per year in each industry. All averages are equally weighted. Merger activity is measured by the number of firms involved in mergers in a given industry.

| Industry | Observations per year | | | Average multiples | | | Merger activity | | |
	Mean	Min.	Max.	p/e	M/B	Average market equity	Acquirers	Targets	Total
(1) Consumer nondurables	406	336	495	19.37	2.43	792.1	242	196	438
(2) Consumer durables	180	142	227	15.99	2.45	1033.4	106	99	205
(3) Manufacturing	796	639	904	16.51	2.44	445.4	453	377	830
(4) Energy	323	205	477	23.52	3.83	1454.4	161	141	302
(5) Chemicals	144	115	174	16.85	5.79	1211.7	104	80	184
(6) Computers, software, etc.	1037	388	1811	19.05	5.48	780	788	782	1570
(7) Telephone and TV	165	66	333	31.53	6.96	3948.8	233	156	389
(8) Utilities	191	103	222	12.74	1.5	987.4	103	84	187
(9) Wholesale	687	532	883	22.47	2.81	430.1	286	331	617
(10) Medical	489	133	838	17.57	8.29	1205.4	401	378	779
(11) Finance	630	298	897	16.9	6.42	812.5	983	908	1891
(12) Everything else	914	521	1268	17.43	3.9	552.7	465	493	958

4. Decomposing market to book

This section and the next discuss the two methodological innovations that we use to study how valuation waves affect merger waves. The theories of SV and RKV both suggest that a merger is more likely when a firm's market value, M, is greater than its true value, V. Therefore, both theories implicitly suggest that a firm's market-to-book ratio should be broken into two components: market value-to-true value, M/V, and true value-to-book, V/B. Thus, for any measure of value, we can use the following algebraic identity to decompose the market-to-book ratio:

$$m - b \equiv (m - v) + (v - b), \qquad (2)$$

where m is market value, b is book value, and v is some measure of fundamental, or true value, all expressed in logarithms. (We use lowercase letters to denote values expressed in logs and uppercase letters to denote the same values expressed in standard units.) Inserting a measure of value into the market-to-book ratio thus allows us to separate $\ln(M/B)$ into two components: a measure of price to fundamentals, $\ln(M/V)$, and a measure of fundamentals to book value, $\ln(V/B)$.

For the sake of argument, assume that a perfect measure of v exists. Then, if markets perfectly anticipate future growth opportunities, discount rates, and cash flows, there would be no scope for pricing error to contaminate M/B, the term $m - v$ would always be equal to 0, and the term $v - b$ would be trivially equal to $\ln(M/B)$ at all times.

If markets potentially make mistakes in estimating discounted future cash flows or, as in RKV, markets do not have all the information known by managers, then price-to-true value, $m - v$, captures the part of $\ln(M/B)$ that is associated with misvaluation. This perhaps does or does not correspond to an asset-pricing sense of mispricing, depending on whether the information in v is known to the market. If the market price does not reflect true value, then $\ln(M/V)$ will be positive in times of overvaluation, and negative in times of undervaluation.

RKV takes the breakdown of $m_{it} - b_{it}$ further to suggest that one component of $m - v$ is shared by all firms in a given sector or market, while another component of $m - v$ is firm-specific. Thus, we separate $\ln(M/B)$ into three components: (1) the difference between observed price and a valuation measure that reflects time-t fundamentals (firm-specific error); (2) the difference between valuation conditional on time-t fundamentals and a firm-specific valuation that reflects long-run value (time-series sector error); and (3) the difference between valuation based on long-run value and book value (long-run value to book).

Our approach to estimating v conceptually involves expressing v as a linear function of firm-specific accounting information at a point in time, θ_{it}, and a vector of conditional accounting multiples, α. Thus, writing $v(\theta_{it}; \alpha)$ as the predicted value based on some vector of multiples α, we can rewrite Equation (2) as:

$$m_{it} - b_{it} = \underbrace{m_{it} - v(\theta_{it}; \alpha_{jt})}_{\text{firm}} + \underbrace{v(\theta_{it}; \alpha_{jt}) - v(\theta_{it}; \alpha_j)}_{\text{sector}} + \underbrace{v(\theta_{it}; \alpha_j) - b_{it}}_{\text{long-run}} \tag{3}$$

The key difference in the $v(\theta_{it};7)$ expressions is that time-t multiples are represented as α_{jt} while long-run multiples are represented by α_j. The first term is the difference between market value and fundamental value conditional on time t and sector j valuation effects, $m_{it} - v(\theta_{it}; \alpha_{jt})$. We call this firm-specific error. Thus, if the market is overheated at time t, this will show up in α_{jt} and therefore in $v(\theta_{it}; \alpha_{jt})$. Likewise, if industry j is hot relative to other industries at time t, this, too, will appear in α_{jt}. This means that the firm-specific error, $m_{it} - v(\theta_{it}; \alpha_{jt})$, captures purely firm-specific deviations from fundamental value, because the v term captures all deviations common to a sector at a point in time.

The second component of $\ln(M/B)$ is time-t fundamental value to long-run value, $v(\theta_{it}; \alpha_{jt}) - v(\theta_{it}; \alpha_j)$. We call this time-series sector error, because the function $v(\theta_{it}; \alpha_j)$ captures sector-specific valuation that does not vary over time. When time-series sector error, $v(\theta_{it}; \alpha_{jt}) - v(\theta_{it}; \alpha_j)$, is high, the sector-wide valuation wave is near its peak. The parameters in α_j in some sense capture the long-run multiples for industry j. The final component is the difference between long-run value and book, $v(\theta_{it}; \alpha_j) - b_{it}$. Each of these three components varies at the firm-year level and involve valuation multiples that vary across industries and over time. Thus, $v(\theta_{it}; \alpha_j)$ varies over time at the firm level as accounting information changes (i.e., θ_{it} varies over t holding i constant), and varies across firms within an industry as their accounting data differ (i.e., θ_{it} varies over i at a particular time t).

5. Estimating market value

To use our decomposition of M/B, we must estimate the pieces of the decomposition that relate to time-t fundamental value and true value. This subsection describes our approach to calculating $v(\theta_{it}; \alpha_{jt})$ and $v(\theta_{it}; \alpha_j)$.

Our starting point is the definition of firm value, $\mathbf{M}_t$, as the present value of expected free cash flows (FCF):

$$\mathbf{M}_t = \int_t^\infty e^{-\int_t^\tau r(\eta)\mathrm{d}\eta} \mathbf{FCF}\, \mathrm{d}\tau, \tag{4}$$

where $r(\eta)$ is a potentially time-varying discount rate. Following an idea that goes back to Marshall, we can rewrite the present value of FCFs as the value of the assets in place plus the economic value added. In accounting terms the value of a firm is the book value of the assets plus the residual income generated by those assets:

$$\mathbf{M}_t = \mathbf{B}_t + \int_t^\infty e^{-\int_t^\tau r(\eta)\mathrm{d}\eta} \mathbf{RI}\, \mathrm{d}\tau, \tag{5}$$

where RI is residual income, defined as the excess of the economic flows arising from the assets over their opportunity cost. By defining residual income as the difference between the return on equity (ROE) and the cost of capital, both multiplied by the previous period's capital stock, we can write Equation (5) in discrete time as

$$\mathbf{M}_t = \mathbf{B}_t + \mathrm{E}_t \sum_{\tau=t+1}^\infty \frac{(\mathrm{ROE}_\tau - r_\tau)\mathbf{B}_{\tau-1}}{(1+r_\tau)^\tau}. \tag{6}$$

There are a number of ways of implementing Equation (6) to get a measure of value. One approach is to use analyst's forecasts as proxies for expected future ROE values. Lee et al. (1999) use this approach to study the intrinsic value of the Dow, and Dong et al. (2005) use this approach to study the relation between M/B and merger activity. However, as Ritter and Warr (2002) point out, the particular form of the perpetuity calculation used by Dong et al. (2005) rests on a number of assumptions that make it difficult to conclude that mispricing (not differences in growth opportunities) is responsible for their findings. Moreover, their emphasis on behavioral explanations makes it difficult to see the impact of other theories.

To avoid these and other shortcomings, we take a different approach to obtain a measure of value. Our strategy is to impose identifying restrictions on Equation (6). This approach does not rely on analysts' forecasts that could include expectations of future merger activity, it does not bias our sample toward large transactions, and it allows us to recover the market's estimates of growth and discount rates. Depending on the identifying assumptions imposed, Equation (6) yields to a variety of econometric specifications.

5.1. Model 1: market value and book value

We begin with a simple model linking market equity to book equity alone. To link current values of market equity to current values of book, two identifying restrictions are sufficient. The first is that expected future ROE is a constant multiple of expected future discount rates ($E_t(ROE_\tau) = \lambda E_t r_\tau \forall \ \tau > t$). This assumption can be motivated in terms of markup pricing or in terms of the potential for competitive entry or techno-logical change to force expectations of future profitability to be multiples of discount rates. The second assumption is that book equity is expected to grow at a constant rate over time. In that case, we can express Equation (6) as

$$\mathbf{M}_t = \alpha_{0t} + \alpha_{1t}\mathbf{B}_t, \tag{7}$$

where the particular values of α_{0t} and α_{1t} depend on the particular identifying assumptions imposed. For example, if we assume that perfect competition forces the ROE equal to its opportunity cost at all points in time ($\lambda = 1$ in the discussion above), then we no longer need to assume constant expected growth in book equity, and we have $\alpha_{0t} = 0$ and $\alpha_{1t} = 1$ for all t. In general, the α_{0t} and α_{1t} will be proportional to discount rates (costs of capital) and growth rates, which likely vary over time.

To account explicitly for the possibility that discount rates and growth rates vary over time and across industries, we estimate Equation (7) through the following equation for Model 1:

$$\mathbf{m}_{it} = \alpha_{0jt} + \alpha_{1jt}\mathbf{b}_{it} + \varepsilon_{it}. \tag{8}$$

This is estimated in logs (hence the lowercase letters) to account for the right-skewness in the accounting data. To implement Equation (8), we group firms according to the 12 Fama and French industries and perform annual, cross-sectional regressions for each industry in question. By estimating separate equations for each industry-year, we do not require the growth rates or discount rates embedded in our multiples to be constant over time. This addresses concerns about time-varying risk premia and expected growth opportunities raised by Ang and Liu (2001) and Feltham and Ohlson (1999).

Equation (8) is not an asset-pricing equation; it does not relate expected returns to a particular set of priced risk factors in the economy. Nevertheless, because multiples reflect discount rates and expected growth rates, the α coefficients naturally embody risk characteristics of the average firm in the industry.

The industry classifications used for these regressions are discussed in Table 3. To interpret Equation (8), consider an industry average M/B multiple from Table 3. Equation (8) breaks this multiple into two pieces. Since the equation is estimated in logs, the first piece, α_{0jt}, is the average market value associated with a firm with \$1 million book equity in industry j, year t. This term captures the amount of market value attributed to all firms on average, in a given industry at a point in time, regardless of their book value relative to other firms in their industry. This can be interpreted as the value of intangibles priced into the average firm in a sector at a point in time, because under ordinary least squares $\hat{\alpha}_{0jt} = \bar{m}_{jt} - \hat{\alpha}_{jt}\bar{b}_{jt}$. The second piece of the M/B multiple is the coefficient on book, α_{1jt}, which then measures the multiple associated with incremental book equity.

To generate estimates of $v(\theta_{it}; \alpha_{jt})$ and $v(\theta_{it}; \alpha_j)$, we use fitted values from Equation (8) above:

$$v(\mathbf{B}_{it}; \hat{\alpha}_{0jt}, \hat{\alpha}_{1jt}) = \hat{\alpha}_{0jt} + \hat{\alpha}_{1jt}\mathbf{b}_{it} \tag{9}$$

for each firm. To obtain $v(\theta_{it}; \bar{\alpha}_j)$, we average over time to obtain $1/T \sum \hat{\alpha}_{jt} = \bar{\alpha}_j$ for each set of parameters $\{\alpha\}$, then calculate

$$v(\mathbf{B}_{it}; \bar{\alpha}_{0j}, \bar{\alpha}_{1j}) = \bar{\alpha}_{0j} + \bar{\alpha}_{1j}\mathbf{b}_{it}. \tag{10}$$

The time-series averages from Model 1 are presented in the upper panel of Table 4. The variable $\bar{\alpha}_{0j}$ is recorded as $E_t(\hat{\alpha}_0)$, and varies considerably across industries. Moreover, the magnitudes of $E_t(\hat{\alpha}_0)$ are consistent with interpretations as capitalized intangible value, given the industry descriptions. For example, utilities and consumer nondurables have the lowest values of $E_t(\hat{\alpha}_0)$, while telephone and TV, computers, and medicine have the highest values of intangibles according to our estimation scheme. Moreover, the values of $\bar{\alpha}_j$ are generally the highest in the same industries in which the constant terms are the lowest, suggesting that in these industries tangible book assets are most highly correlated with value. Finally, the average R^2 values are high across all industries, even in a simple model of log market value on log book value.

5.2. Model 2: market value, book value, and net income

Recent scholarship in accounting has pointed to the importance of net income for explaining cross-sectional variation in market values. Examining the value-relevance of various accounting measures via equations similar in spirit to Equation (8) has a long tradition in the accounting literature. That literature is far too large to discuss fully here, but Holthausen and Watts (2001), Kothari and Zimmerman (1995), Kothari (2001), and Barth et al. (2001) contain excellent surveys of this literature and debates about the conclusions that can be drawn from it. A number of authors (e.g., Amir and Lev, 1996; Lev, 1997) have argued that the value relevance of accounting has declined, in part because of the rise in importance of intangible assets that are not captured in book equity. Collins et al. (1997) counter that accounting information continues to be important in the face of intangibles, pointing instead to the increasing importance of net income for explaining cross-sectional variation in market value.

To develop a valuation model that includes net income as well as book value, we can impose slightly less restrictive assumptions on Equation (6). For example, if we

Table 4

Conditional regression multiples

Fama and French 12 industry classifications are reported across the top. Output from valuation regressions are reported in each row. Each model is estimated cross-sectionally at the industry-year level. The subscripts j and t denote industry and year, respectively. The variable $E_t(\hat{\alpha}_0)$ is the time-series average of the constant term for each regression. $E_t(\hat{\alpha}_k)$ is the time-series average multiple from the regression associated with the kth accounting variable. Fama-MacBeth standard errors are printed below average point estimates. Finally, the time-series average R^2 is reported for each industry. Regressions are run annually for each industry from 1977 to 2000. This regression uses natural logs of market (M) and book value (B), natural log of the absolute value of net income (NI), and an indicator interacted with log net income (NI$^+$) to separately estimate net income for firms with negative net income (in Model 2), and leverage (Lev). Natural logs are denoted with lowercase letters.

Parameter	Fama and French industry classification											
	1	2	3	4	5	6	7	8	9	10	11	12
Model 1: $m_{it} = \alpha_{0jt} + \alpha_{1jt} b_{it} + \varepsilon_i$												
$E_t(\hat{\alpha}_0)$	0.98	1.65	1.19	1.46	1.47	1.70	2.06	0.66	1.13	1.97	1.16	1.70
	0.06	0.11	0.06	0.08	0.09	0.07	0.12	0.10	0.07	0.05	0.07	0.05
$E_t(\hat{\alpha}_1)$	0.87	0.71	0.81	0.79	0.83	0.77	0.74	0.92	0.85	0.77	0.80	0.72
	0.01	0.02	0.01	0.01	0.01	0.02	0.01	0.01	0.01	0.01	0.01	0.01
R^2	0.68	0.65	0.74	0.80	0.77	0.68	0.76	0.88	0.72	0.73	0.75	0.65
Model 2: $m_{it} = \alpha_{0jt} + \alpha_{1jt} b_{it} + \alpha_{2jt} ni_{it}^+ + \alpha_{3jt}(I_{(<0)} ni^+)_{it} + \varepsilon_i$												
$E_t(\hat{\alpha}_0)$	1.86	2.39	1.79	1.87	2.26	2.24	2.31	1.21	1.87	2.29	1.83	2.17
	0.06	0.13	0.05	0.08	0.06	0.07	0.07	0.09	0.06	0.06	0.05	0.05
$E_t(\hat{\alpha}_1)$	0.47	0.35	0.51	0.62	0.39	0.49	0.55	0.66	0.50	0.54	0.49	0.48
	0.02	0.03	0.02	0.02	0.03	0.03	0.03	0.04	0.02	0.02	0.02	0.01
$E_t(\hat{\alpha}_2)$	0.38	0.38	0.33	0.18	0.46	0.33	0.21	0.27	0.37	0.28	0.32	0.26
	0.02	0.02	0.02	0.02	0.04	0.02	0.05	0.04	0.02	0.02	0.01	0.01
$E_t(\hat{\alpha}_3)$	−0.35	−0.35	0.22	−0.15	−0.23	−0.22	0.18	−0.03	−0.25	0.02	−0.14	−0.18
	0.04	0.10	0.04	0.04	0.07	0.04	0.06	0.04	0.05	0.05	0.06	0.05
R^2	0.73	0.71	0.78	0.82	0.82	0.73	0.79	0.89	0.77	0.77	0.79	0.68

Model 3: $m_{it} = \alpha_{0jt} + \alpha_{1jt}b_{it} + \alpha_{2jt}ni_{it}^{+} + \alpha_{3jt}I_{(<0)}(ni^{+})_{it} + \alpha_{4jt}Lev_{it} + \varepsilon_i$

$E_t(\hat{\alpha}_0)$	2.39	2.56	2.20	2.35	2.38	2.55	2.91	2.15	2.44	2.68	2.21	2.60
	0.04	0.11	0.05	0.06	0.11	0.05	0.10	0.13	0.05	0.04	0.04	0.05
$E_t(\hat{\alpha}_1)$	0.64	0.56	0.64	0.66	0.64	0.59	0.60	0.85	0.62	0.61	0.58	0.60
	0.01	0.02	0.01	0.02	0.05	0.02	0.03	0.03	0.01	0.02	0.01	0.01
$E_t(\hat{\alpha}_2)$	0.27	0.30	0.27	0.23	0.31	0.29	0.26	0.12	0.28	0.26	0.30	0.25
	0.01	0.02	0.01	0.02	0.04	0.01	0.04	0.03	0.01	0.01	0.01	0.01
$E_t(\hat{\alpha}_3)$	0.08	0.05	0.10	0.00	0.13	-0.03	0.27	0.17	0.01	-0.09	-0.16	0.00
	0.03	0.06	0.03	0.04	0.06	0.04	0.05	0.04	0.04	0.05	0.05	0.04
$E_t(\hat{\alpha}_4)$	-2.59	-2.36	-2.09	-2.13	-2.43	-2.55	-2.27	-2.52	-2.11	-2.42	-1.06	-2.15
	0.05	0.09	0.07	0.15	0.19	0.11	0.18	0.23	0.06	0.10	0.05	0.09
R^2	0.84	0.80	0.86	0.88	0.90	0.83	0.87	0.94	0.86	0.85	0.82	0.80

assume that book value and net income are growing at constant rates, we can rewrite Equation (6) as

$$\mathbf{M}_t = \alpha_0 + \alpha_1 \mathbf{B}_t + \alpha_2 \mathbf{NI}_t. \tag{11}$$

Because net income is sometimes negative, we estimate the following equation for Model 2:

$$\mathbf{m}_{it} = \alpha_{0jt} + \alpha_{1jt}\mathbf{b}_{it} + \alpha_{2jt}\ln(\mathbf{NI})_{it}^+ + \alpha_{3jt}I_{(<0)}\ln(\mathbf{NI})_{it}^+ + \varepsilon_{it}, \tag{12}$$

where $\mathbf{NI}^+$ stands for the absolute value of net income and $I_{(<0)}\ln(\mathbf{NI})_{it}^+$ is an indicator function for negative net income observations. Because this equation is estimated in logs, and net income is often negative, this setup allows for net income to enter into the estimation without discarding all the firms with negative net income at a point in time. By estimating separate sets of parameters $\{\alpha_2\}$ and $\{\alpha_3\}$ for positive and negative net income, we allow negative net income observations to enter into the estimation without contaminating the earnings multiple interpretation of α_2. Thus, if firms in a given industry are penalized for having negative net income in a given year, the α_{3jt} parameter is negative.

To obtain $v(\theta_{it}; \hat{\alpha}_{jt})$ and $v(\theta_{it}; \hat{\alpha}_j)$ using Equation (12), we perform calculations analogous to Equation (9):

$$\begin{aligned} v(\mathbf{B}_{it}, \mathbf{NI}_{it}; \hat{\alpha}_{0jt}, \hat{\alpha}_{1jt}, \hat{\alpha}_{2jt}, \hat{\alpha}_{3jt}) &= \hat{\alpha}_{0jt} + \hat{\alpha}_{1jt}\mathbf{b}_{it} + \hat{\alpha}_{2jt}\ln(\mathbf{NI})_{it}^+ \\ &\quad + \hat{\alpha}_{3jt}I_{(<0)}\ln(\mathbf{NI})_{it}^+ \end{aligned} \tag{13}$$

for each firm. To obtain $v(\theta_{it};\alpha_j)$ under Model 2, we average over time to obtain $1/T\sum\alpha_{jt} = \bar{\alpha}_j$ for α_k, $k = 0, 1, 2, 3$, then calculate

$$\begin{aligned} v(\mathbf{B}_{it}, \mathbf{NI}_{it}; \hat{\alpha}_{0j}, \hat{\alpha}_{1j}, \hat{\alpha}_{2j}, \hat{\alpha}_{3j}) &= \hat{\alpha}_{0j} + \hat{\alpha}_{1j}\mathbf{b}_{it} + \hat{\alpha}_{2j}\ln(\mathbf{NI})_{it}^+ \\ &\quad + \hat{\alpha}_{3j}I_{(<0)}\ln(\mathbf{NI})_{it}^+. \end{aligned} \tag{14}$$

The second panel of Table 4 reports time-series average values of the $\{\alpha_j\}$ for each industry. The cross-industry comparisons match Model 1, except that the addition of net income to the model uniformly increases average R^2 values. In addition, the interpretations of the loadings on the income variables make intuitive sense: The loading on net income for positive net income realizations is positive and about the same order of magnitude as the loading on the absolute value of the negative net income observations. The other noteworthy feature of this model is that including net income reduces the loading on book value; presumably this is arising from the time-series properties of net income.

5.3. Model 3: market value, book value, net income and leverage

Models 1 and 2 implicitly impose the restriction that firms be priced against the average multiples for firms in that industry-year. To account for the fact that within-industry differences in leverage could potentially influence this, we estimate a third model in which leverage also appears. Accounting for leverage allows for the fact that firms with higher or lower than industry-average leverage have a different cost of capital, forcing them to differ from industry average multiples. Thus, Model 3 is

$$m_{it} = \alpha_{0jt} + \alpha_{1jt}\mathbf{b}_{it} + \alpha_{2jt}\ln(\mathbf{NI})_{it}^{+} + \alpha_{3jt}I_{(<0)}\ln(\mathbf{NI})_{it}^{+} + \alpha_{4jt}\mathbf{LEV}_{it} + \varepsilon_{it}, \qquad (15)$$

where $\mathbf{LEV}_{it}$ is the leverage ratio. As in Models 1 and 2, this regression is estimated cross-sectionally in each industry-year, allowing the α_k, $k = 0, \ldots, 4$ to vary both over time and across industries. Cross-sectional and time-series variation in the parameters, in particular, captures the fact that some industries could be able to sustain high debt loads, while in other industries the optimal capital structure could be more tilted toward equity.

The third panel of Table 4 presents summary statistics for Model 3. Not surprisingly, the loading on leverage is negative and highly significant (Fama-MacBeth standard errors are reported below point estimates). Moreover, the value of intangibles rises when we account for cross-sectional differences in leverage. Finally, the average R^2 values range between 80% and 94%, indicating that accounting information and leverage alone explain the vast majority of cross-sectional variation in market values within a given industry at a given time.

Looking across the three models reported in Table 4, it is generally easy to reject the null hypothesis that the average $\alpha_0 = 0$. There is less time-series volatility in the loadings on accounting variables for each industry than on the α_0 terms, however, which suggests that while discount rates and growth rates vary a great deal across industries, they are less variable within industries over time.

5.4. Discussion

Table 5 summarizes our decomposition methodology by identifying each component of our M/B decomposition and describing how it is calculated. Although the multiples used in our decomposition are calculated first at the industry-year level, and then at the long-run industry level, our valuation approach applies these multiples to firm-specific, time-varying accounting information. Therefore, each component of the decomposition varies across firms and over time as the underlying accounting fundamentals change. Based on this approach, we can offer the following interpretations of our decomposition.

The term $m_{it} - v(\theta_{it}; \hat{\alpha}_{jt})$ is the regression error obtained from annual, industry-level, cross-sectional regressions. We label this piece *firm-specific error*. Because the multiples obtained from annual, cross-sectional regressions contain time-varying market expectations of industry average growth rates and discounts rates, firm-specific error can be interpreted either as one component of misvaluation or as firm-specific deviations from contemporaneous, industry-average growth and discount rates. Because average regression error is zero by construction, our valuation measure prices firms correctly on average relative to their industry valuation.

Table 5

Defining the components of the decomposed market-to-book ratio

This table is a guide to the analysis presented in Tables 6–13. In Table 6, the variables below correspond to firm-level variables. In the merger intensity regression tables (Table 10), the same notation refers to annual industry average values, because the unit of observation is an intensity of merger activity in an industry-year.

M/B component	Definition
$m_{it} - b_{it}$	The natural log of the market-to-book ratio for firm i at time t
$\bar{m}_t - \bar{b}_t$	In Table 10, this notation refers to sector-average market-to-book in year t
$v(\theta_{it}; \alpha_{jt})$	The fundamental value of the firm obtained by applying annual, sector-average regression multiples to firm-level accounting values. The individual time t values of the αs from Table 4 are used to obtain this number. Using Model 2, for instance, we would have $v = \hat{\alpha}_{0jt} + \hat{\alpha}_{1jt} \ln(\mathbf{B})_{it}$
$v(\theta_{it}; \bar{\alpha}_j)$	The fundamental value of the firm obtained by applying long-run industry average multiples to firm-level accounting values. The long-run average values of α_j from Table 4 are used to obtain this number. Using Model 2, for instance, $v = \bar{\alpha}_{0j} + \bar{\alpha}_{1j} \ln(\mathbf{B})_{it}$
$m_{it} - v(\theta_{it}; \alpha_{jt})$	The component of $m_{it} - b_{it}$ that results from firm-specific deviations from valuations implied by sector valuation multiples calculated at time t. This is called firm-specific error
$v(\theta_{it}; \alpha_{jt}) - v(\theta_{it}; \bar{\alpha}_j)$	The component of $m_{it} - b_{it}$ that results from valuations implied by current sector multiples deviating from valuations implied by long-run multiples. In Table 6, this notation refers to firm-level observations calculated by applying sector multiples to firm-specific accounting information. This is called time-series sector error
$\bar{v}(\alpha_{jt}) - \bar{v}(\bar{\alpha}_j)$	In Table 10, this notation refers to sector average time-series sector error
$v(\theta_{it}; \bar{\alpha}_j) - b_{it}$	The component of $m_{it} - b_{it}$ that is attributable to the difference between valuations implied by long-run multiples and current book values. In Table 6, this notation refers to firm-level observations calculated by applying long-run sector multiples to firm-specific accounting information. This is called long-run value to book
$\bar{v}(\alpha_{jt}) - \bar{b}_t$	In Table 10, this notation refers to sector average long-run value to book

The term $v(\theta_{it}; \hat{\alpha}_{jt}) - v(\theta_{it}; \hat{\alpha}_j)$ captures the portion of M/B that is attributable to short-run industry multiples deviating from their long-run average values. We label this piece *time-series sector error*. If short-run multiples are higher than average, then, when we apply them to a firm's accounting information, the resulting valuation exceeds what we would find by using lower, long run average multiples instead. This difference reflects the fact that an entire sector could be overheated at a point in time. This is an inherently backward-looking calculation, because we are using ex post knowledge about valuation levels to discover when prices were high. This information could not possibly be incorporated into prices at time t. It was not in investors' information sets at time t, unless we assume a particular form of stationarity in asset prices. Thus, accepting the interpretation that this measure proxies for misvaluation does not require one to believe that assets were mispriced in an asset-pricing sense. It does not rest on the inability of market participants to make full use of available information. This measure could proxy for knowledge held by the management that was unknown to the market at the time. Thus, this form of misvaluation could be a part of a completely rational model, as it is in RKV. This measure can also be interpreted, along with firm-specific error, as another component of mispricing.

Finally, $v(\theta_{it}; \hat{\alpha}_j) - b_{it}$ represents long-run value to book. This is the portion of M/B that cannot be attributed to firm-specific deviations from industry average values or to industry-wide waves in valuation levels. The multiples used in this component of the breakdown are in some sense the Fama and MacBeth (1973) multiples for a given industry and thus reflect the long-run average growth rates and discount rates that should apply to the average firm in the industry. This long-run value-to-book measure varies over time and across firms, but this variation is attributable solely to firm-specific variation in accounting fundamentals. Valuation effects that arise from hot industry effects or firm-specific misvaluation have been purged from this measure.

Naturally, these interpretations rest on a correct measure of v. Because we are estimating v, we face the standard joint hypothesis problem: It is impossible to distinguish empirically between a purely behavioral explanation for misvaluation and one based on rational behavior in the presence of asymmetric information. However, distinctions can be drawn between these two theories and a class of explanations based on the idea that mergers occur as an efficient response to reorganization opportunities (see, e.g., Gort, 1969; Jovanovic and Rousseau, 2002). Therefore, we conduct an empirical horse race between these two groups of explanations at the end of the paper. The conclusions of that horse race suggest that our misvaluation measures are not a proxy for Q-based variables.

6. Tests and findings

We now use our methodology to test the predictions discussed in Section 2. Because the SV and RKV theories explicitly link misvaluation levels to merger waves, we proceed in two steps. First, we examine the valuation characteristics of the sample of firms that participated in mergers. In Section 6.1 we examine the relative value predictions. Second, we also study whether times of high aggregate valuation errors are times of high merger activity. These merger intensity predictions are tested in Section 6.2.

6.1. Testing relative value predictions

The first row of Table 6 reports differences in $m_{it} - b_{it}$ ratios by target, acquirer, and method of payment. From this we see that it is not the case that high M/B buys low M/B, but that high M/B targets are bought by even higher M/B acquirers. This finding is driven by the characteristics of targets in stock transactions. In this group, both acquirers and targets have significantly higher M/B ratios than in other method-of-payment categories. When we examine cash-only or mixed payment transactions, we find no difference in M/B between target firms and nonmerger firms.

The remainder of Table 6 reports the results of using the fitted values from Models 1, 2, and 3 to break market-to-book into its three components: $m_{it} - v(\theta_{it}; \hat{\alpha}_{jt})$, firm-specific error; $v(\theta_{it}; \hat{\alpha}_{jt}) - v(\theta_{it}; \bar{\alpha}_j)$, time-series sector error; and $v(\theta_{it}; \bar{\alpha}_j) - b_{it}$, long-run value-to-book. Because the table is in logs, the three components of M/B for each model add to the $\ln(M/B)$ ratio reported in the top row. Table 6 reports values for all mergers (4025 mergers) but also breaks the sample into 100% cash transactions (1542 mergers), 100% stock transactions (1218 mergers), and mixed transactions (799 mergers). (SDC omits method of payment for many mergers. We include missing method-of-payment transactions in the overall column but exclude them from any column that reports results by transaction type.) Within each group, Table 6 reports whether the difference between the target and the acquirer is significant.

Looking across models, we can compare how they attribute total M/B with its various components. For example, merger targets in cash acquisitions have an $m_{it} - b_{it}$ of 0.61. Model 1 attributes 0.59 of this to long-run value-to-book, 0.13 of this to sector-specific misvaluation, and the remaining -0.11 to firm-specific error. By comparison, Models 2 and 3 attribute 0.58 and 0.62 to long-run value-to-book, a slightly smaller 0.12 and 0.06 to sector-specific misvaluation, and a slightly larger -0.09 and -0.08 to firm-specific error, respectively. Overall the breakdown of M/B across the three models is remarkably consistent. Since the results are robust to different models, in what follows we will discuss the results only for Model 3.

Table 6 allows us to test the first three predictions from the theory. The first prediction says that overvalued firms buy relatively undervalued firms when both firms are overvalued. This means that firm-specific error should be lower for targets than acquirers,

$$\underbrace{m_{it} - v(\theta_{it}; \hat{\alpha}_{jt})}_{\text{target}} < \underbrace{m_{it} - v(\theta_{it}; \hat{\alpha}_{jt})}_{\text{acquirer}}, \tag{16}$$

but that the total of firm-specific and time-series sector error for firms in mergers should be greater than firms not involved in mergers:

$$\underbrace{m_{it} - v(\theta_{it}; \hat{\alpha}_{jt}) + v(\theta_{it}; \hat{\alpha}_{jt}) - v(\theta_{it}; \bar{\alpha}_j)}_{\text{Target or acquirer}}$$

$$> \underbrace{m_{it} - v(\theta_{it}; \hat{\alpha}_{jt}) + v(\theta_{it}; \hat{\alpha}_{jt}) - v(\theta_{it}; \bar{\alpha}_j)}_{\text{Nonmerger}} \tag{17}$$

This result should hold for the entire sample, but particularly for stock-financed acquisitions. Furthermore, cash targets should more undervalued than stock targets, and cash acquirers should be less overvalued than stock acquirers:

$$\underbrace{m_{it} - v(\theta_{it}; \hat{\alpha}_{jt})}_{\text{Cash target or acquirer}} < \underbrace{m_{it} - v(\theta_{it}; \hat{\alpha}_{jt})}_{\text{Stock target or acquirer}} . \tag{18}$$

Table 6

Decomposing market to book at the firm-level

The data comprise 102,527 nonmerger firm-level observations between 1977 and 2000 plus 8350 firm-level merger observations, corresponding to 4025 merger events occurring between bidders and targets listed on CRSP, Compustat, and SDC. The column labeled t(diff.) reports the t-statistic for the test $H(0)$: nonmerger $-$ merger $= 0$, or $H(0)$: target $-$ acquirer $= 0$. The data include 1899 known all cash transactions, 968 known mixed payment transactions, and 1436 known all stock transactions. Each model regresses log market equity on accounting information in annual, cross-sectional, industry-level regressions described in Table 4. Model 1 corresponds to $\ln(M_{it}) = \alpha_{0jt} + \alpha_{1jt}\ln(B)_{it}$; Model 2 adds net income; Model 3 adds leverage. See Table 5 for descriptions of the components of each model.

Valuation com−ponent	Overall comparison			Only mergers			Only all cash			Only mixed			Only all stock		
	Nonmerger	Merger	t(diff.)	Tar.	Acq.	t(diff.)	Tar.	Acq.	t(diff.)	Tar.	Acq.	t(diff.)	Tar.	Acq.	t(diff.)
$m_{it} - b_{it}$	0.59	0.76	−15.81	0.69	0.83	−6.95	0.61	0.79	−5.13	0.61	0.77	−3.29	0.87	1.12	−6.97
Model 1															
$m_{it} - v(\theta_{it}; \alpha_{jt})$	0.02	0.26	−26.81	0.01	0.50	−25.12	−0.11	0.49	−18.34	0.04	0.46	−9.20	0.11	0.64	−16.60
$v(\theta_{it}; \alpha_{jt}) - v(\theta_{it}; \bar{\alpha}_j)$	0.07	0.15	−27.70	0.13	0.18	−8.08	0.13	0.19	−6.10	0.14	0.17	−2.54	0.18	0.26	−7.09
$v(\theta_{it}; \bar{\alpha}_j) - b_{it}$	0.54	0.34	33.64	0.54	0.16	37.91	0.59	0.11	29.61	0.43	0.14	12.95	0.58	0.23	18.97
Model 2															
$m_{it} - v(\theta_{it}; \alpha_{jt})$	−0.01	0.22	−24.48	0.02	0.41	−22.00	−0.09	0.38	−15.45	0.04	0.39	−8.27	0.11	0.57	−15.65
$v(\theta_{it}; \alpha_{jt}) - v(\theta_{it}; \bar{\alpha}_j)$	0.06	0.15	−26.19	0.12	0.18	−9.11	0.12	0.19	−7.16	0.14	0.17	−2.65	0.17	0.25	−6.90
$v(\theta_{it}; \bar{\alpha}_j) - b_{it}$	0.54	0.39	22.69	0.55	0.25	24.77	0.58	0.22	17.53	0.43	0.20	8.00	0.60	0.30	13.30
Model 3															
$m_{it} - v(\theta_{it}; \alpha_{jt})$	−0.01	0.18	−25.21	0.03	0.32	−20.21	−0.08	0.29	−15.01	0.17	0.29	−3.46	0.05	0.44	−16.09
$v(\theta_{it}; \alpha_{jt}) - v(\theta_{it}; \bar{\alpha}_j)$	0.03	0.10	−24.20	0.07	0.12	−8.73	0.06	0.14	−8.40	0.08	0.12	−3.97	0.12	0.17	−5.21
$v(\theta_{it}; \bar{\alpha}_j) - b_{it}$	−0.57	0.48	10.69	0.58	0.39	12.52	0.62	0.37	9.97	0.36	0.36	0.20	0.71	0.51	6.94

We find support in the data for each of these predictions. Regarding Model 3, firm-specific error is higher for acquirers than targets in the overall merger sample (0.32 for acquirers, but only 0.03 for targets) and for stock-financed mergers (0.44 for acquirers, but only 0.05 for targets). We also find that both firm-specific and time-series sector errors are greater for firms involved in mergers than those not in mergers (0.18 firm-specific error in Model 3 is greater than the −0.01 for nonmerger firms, and the time-series sector error of 0.10 for merger-firms exceeds the 0.03 for nonmerger firms).

The second prediction is that acquirers should come from sectors that are more overvalued than targets. Thus, time-series sector error, $v(\theta_{it}; \hat{\alpha}_{jt}) - v(\theta_{it}; \bar{\alpha}_j)$, should be greater for acquirers than targets. This effect holds for each of the three models and across each type of method of payment. For example, in Model 3, the time-series sector error for mixed payment acquirers is 0.12, while it is only 0.08 for mixed payment targets. For stock transactions, acquirers have an average time-series sector error of 0.17, while targets have an average of only 0.12. This relationship also holds for cash transactions.

The last prediction that can be tested with Table 6 is Empirical Prediction 3. This also holds for all models. First, cash targets are more undervalued than stock targets. For example, in Model 3, the firm-specific error for stock targets (0.05) is larger than that of cash targets (−0.08). The same is true of time-series sector error for stock and cash targets (0.12 for stock targets is greater than 0.06 for cash targets).

In addition, firm-specific error is higher for stock acquirers than cash acquirers. From Model 3, the stock acquirer firm-specific error is 0.44, while for cash acquirers it is only 0.29. Time-series sector error of 0.17 for stock acquirers exceeds the 0.14 for cash acquirers. Although the theory does not discuss mixed payment acquisitions, by extension it would seem that all stock acquirers should be more overvalued than mixed payment acquirers, which is supported by the data [0.44 (stock) versus 0.29 (mixed) for firm-specific, and 0.17 (stock) versus 0.12 (mixed) for sector-specific]. All reported inequalities are statistically significant.

We can say little about predictions for mixed offers because, except for Eckbo et al. (1990), little theoretical work models the use of mixed offers. If mixed offers allow the under and overvalued acquirers to separate, as suggested by Eckbo et al. (1990), then we might expect the predictions of RKV and SV not to hold for mixed offers. However, under a loose interpretation of RKV and SV we might expect mixed offers to fall between all cash and all stock offers.

Thus, to the extent that firm-specific error and time-series sector error proxy for misvaluation, Table 6 provides strong support for the central predictions of SV and RKV. It shows that merger firms are more overvalued than nonmerger firms, that bidders are more overvalued than targets, and that method of payment determines whether a target is over- or undervalued. In cash acquisitions, targets are undervalued on average. In stock acquisitions, targets are overvalued. These latter findings support the idea that correlated misvaluation leads overvalued targets to accept takeover bids from overvalued bidders precisely because they overestimate the expected synergies.

6.1.1. Do low growth firms acquire high growth?

Table 6 also contains a new finding that is not predicted by either efficient markets or
the possibility of misvaluation. Although high M/B firms buy low M/B, this difference
between bidders and targets is driven by firm-specific deviations from short-run
average value, not from fundamental differences between targets' and acquirers'
long-run pricing. To see this in Table 6, compare the top row of the table, which
reports $\ln(M/B)$ with the bottom row of each model, which reports long-run value-to-
book. For example, the average $\log(M/B)$ of acquirers is 0.83 and the average $\log(M/B)$
of targets is 0.69, while, in Model 3, the average long-run value to book of acquirers is
0.39; targets, 0.58. In all of our models, we find that *low* long-run value-to-book firms
acquire *high* long-run value-to-book targets, both in stock-financed and cash-financed
transactions.

   Thus, while it is true that high M/B acquirers buy lower M/B targets, so much of this
is driven by short-run valuation dynamics that the long-run value-to-book measures
work in the opposite direction. Long-run value is not lower due to the merger. Long-
run value is a function of premerger accounting variables and long-run industry-wide
valuation multiples. Thus, a low long-run value arises from an industry with low long-
run pricing.[4] This has important implications for questions relating to mergers, corporate governance, and economic efficiency.

   The low buys high long-run value finding is a puzzle for existing theory. Under a
strict efficient markets interpretation, Q theory would suggest that merger activity
spikes when expected growth opportunities are high. However, these growth opportunities appear transient as the targets will be priced higher than the acquirer in the
long run. Thus, the short-run changes in growth rates or discount rates seem to mask
underlying long-run fundamentals that go in the opposite direction. In a long run sense,
firms with low growth opportunities acquire targets that have better long-run growth
opportunities.

   This finding is reminiscent of Jensen (1986) motivations for mergers activity,
because it suggests that firms with low growth prospects use acquisitions as a way of
buying growth when the market's growth expectations are overblown. However, the
fact that two countervailing effects are at work (high M/B buys low M/B, but low long-
run value-to-book buys high long-run value to book) means that rational explanations
cannot explain our findings unless it contains some element of asymmetric information
as a key ingredient.

---

[4] The accounting treatment of a recent merger would lead to distortions in the value of serial acquirers. To
guard against this possibility, we discarded all multiple acquirers and repeated our analysis. This has no
effect on the magnitude or significance of our results. We thank René Stulz for pointing out this possibility.

6.1.2. Robustness checks on relative value predictions

Table 6 contains striking evidence in support of the idea that temporary firm-specific and industry-specific fluctuations in value drive acquisition activity. However, a number of potential alternative explanations could be clouding the results in Table 6. Tables 7 and 8 provide robustness checks and further extensions to our primary relative value predictions.

One concern with the preceding analysis is that the results are being driven by the late 1990s, when valuations were high and our long-run value calculations are the most backward-looking. To see why late 1990s mergers might be a problem for our analysis, consider a typical merger occurring in 1999. During this period, valuations were at all-time highs. Thus, $m_{it} - b_{it}$ is likely to be large, and α_{jt} values are likely to be above their long-term values, which toward the end of the sample are mostly backward-looking (an $\bar{\alpha}$ contains only 2 years of forward-looking data in 1999). Moreover, because this period was a time of intense merger activity, such mergers could make up a disproportionate fraction of our sample.

To control for this possibility, Table 7 includes a column that repeats Table 6 except that only mergers occurring prior to 1996 are included. Thus, while $\bar{\alpha}$ is calculated using data out to 2001, the latest merger is in 1996, meaning that every merger in Table 7 has at least 5 years of forward-looking data built into $\bar{\alpha}$. The results are virtually unchanged. The main difference is that the long-run value-to-book measures are higher in Table 7 than in Table 6 for Models 1 and 2. This shows that our results are not being solely driven by events in the late 1990s, when our long-run multiples are the most backward-looking.[5]

Table 7 includes a number of additional robustness checks. The fact that we get the same results when we split mergers according to whether they were within or across industry shows that our results cannot be attributed to explanations based on industry expansion or contraction.[6] Another potential concern is that firms at risk for LBO were systematically misvalued by our valuation technique because they had low growth prospects. This is not the case; excluding any firm that was ever in an LBO does not affect our findings. (Because our sample only includes deals between publicly traded firms, no LBO transaction is actually in our merger sample, but some firms were nevertheless also on the SDC LBO database at other points in their history.) Finally, what if misvaluations correct between the announcement and consummation of the merger, and the terms of the deal adjust? Evidence from Hietala et al. (2003) indicates that the terms of a transaction can change considerably if there is a long period of time

---

[5] To guard against the possibility that isolated industries are influencing our decompositions, we summarized our breakdown on an industry by industry basis. Performing the means tests industry-by-industry also has the feature that because the sample sizes are much smaller, the *t*-statistics are not overstated by assumptions about independence. None of *t*-statistics become insignificant.

[6] See Andrade and Stafford (2004). For brevity we have omitted results broken out by method of payment, but they match what is reported in Table 6.

Table 7

Robustness of firm-level market-to-book decompositions

This table reproduces Table 6, except that it presents results from isolated subsamples to control for alternative explanations. Pre-1996 only means that only transactions occurring before 1996 are used. Within-industry and across-industry describe whether the bidder and target belong to the same Fama and French 48 Industry classification. No LBO firms indicates that no transaction is included involving a firm that was, at some point, involved in a leveraged buyout, whether before or after the merger in our sample (LBO transactions per se are excluded by our sample selection criteria). Quick-closing deals is the subsample of transactions that are effective within 30 days of the announcement date.

Valuation component	Pre-1996 only			Within industry			Across industry			No LBO firms			Quick-closing deals		
	Tar.	Acq.	t(diff.)	Tar.	Acq.	t(diff.)	Tar.	Acq.	t(diff.)	Tar.	Acq.	t(diff.)	Tar.	Acq.	t(diff.)
$m_{it} - b_{it}$	0.6	0.73	−5.87	0.63	0.8	−7.25	0.76	0.83	−2.29	0.69	0.83	−6.95	0.69	0.72	−0.48
Model 1															
$m_{it} - v(\theta_{it}; \alpha_{jt})$	−0.03	0.43	−23.01	0	0.47	−20.81	0.07	0.58	−16.72	0.01	0.5	−25.12	0.02	0.49	−8.34
$v(\theta_{it}; \alpha_{jt}) - v(\theta_{it}; \bar{\alpha}_j)$	0.08	0.09	−1.98	0.13	0.19	−14.65	0.12	0.17	−6.48	0.13	0.18	−8.08	0.08	0.12	−2.94
$v(\theta_{it}; \bar{\alpha}_j) - b_{it}$	0.56	0.21	28.63	0.5	0.14	43.93	0.57	0.08	35.81	0.54	0.16	37.91	0.59	0.1	18.43
Model 2															
$m_{it} - v(\theta_{it}; \alpha_{jt})$	−0.02	0.36	−20.07	0	0.39	−17.67	0.08	0.47	−13.91	0.02	0.41	−22	0.01	0.39	−7.04
$v(\theta_{it}; \alpha_{jt}) - v(\theta_{it}; \bar{\alpha}_j)$	0.06	0.08	−2.96	0.12	0.19	−14.51	0.11	0.17	−7.03	0.12	0.18	−9.11	0.06	0.13	−3.93
$v(\theta_{it}; \bar{\alpha}_j) - b_{it}$	0.56	0.29	18.24	0.51	0.22	23.36	0.57	0.19	21.24	0.55	0.25	24.77	0.62	0.2	11.65
Model 3															
$m_{it} - v(\theta_{it}; \alpha_{jt})$	0.02	0.29	−17.3	0.04	0.31	−14.96	0.05	0.37	−13.8	0.03	0.32	−20.21	−0.02	0.28	−6.98
$v(\theta_{it}; \alpha_{jt}) - v(\theta_{it}; \bar{\alpha}_j)$	0.04	0.05	−2.26	0.07	0.13	−10.67	0.06	0.12	−7.43	0.07	0.12	−8.73	0.02	0.09	−5.05
$v(\theta_{it}; \bar{\alpha}_j) - b_{it}$	0.55	0.39	8.43	0.51	0.36	10.41	0.65	0.34	14.12	0.58	0.39	12.52	0.69	0.35	7.72

between announcement and eventual success of the merger. The fact that we obtain our main findings in a sample of transactions that close within 30 days of announcement suggest that misvaluation is unlikely to be driven away through protracted renegotiation.[7]

Table 8 provides additional robustness checks by showing that our results hold across all transaction size. This table reports our breakdown of $m_{it} - b_{it}$ according to transaction quintiles. Q1 are the smallest transactions; these deals involve small targets and are most often straight cash deals. Moving rightward in the table, toward Q5, deal size and the size of the target increases. In addition, the relative fraction of straight cash deals drops.

As transaction size increases, a number of distinct effects appear. Among the quintile of largest transactions (Q5), it is no longer the case that the $m_{it} - b_{it}$ of the acquirer is statistically larger than that of the target. However, even though the *M/B* values are roughly equal, it is still the case that the misvaluation differences between acquirers and targets are large and statistically significant. Moreover, low long-run value-to-book firms acquire higher long-run value-to-book firms.

Another striking feature of Table 8 is the pronounced change in the target's firm-specific misvaluation moving from Q1 to Q5. For the smallest transactions (groups Q1 and Q2), target firm-specific misvaluation is negative and very large. Moving toward Q5, the firm-specific misvaluation of the target increases, growing positive between Q3 and Q4. The long-run value-to-book measures move in the opposite direction.

Finally, this table reports a row that adds together the sector-specific and long-run values into a single number. This is presented to guard against the possible criticism that our long-run value measure is inappropriate, because it uses forward-looking data. Even if we attribute all sector-specific valuation to long-run value, we still find that low value-to-book firms acquire high value-to-book firms.

In summary, this table shows that our decomposition results hold for all transaction sizes. In addition, the table removes the possibility that the decomposition results follow mechanically from differences in $m_{it} - b_{it}$ across targets and bidders. The results hold when differences in $m_{it} - b_{it}$ are large or small.

6.2. Overvaluation and takeover intensity

Now we turn the analysis from the previous section around and ask whether increases in valuation levels cause increases in merger activity. We approach this in two steps. First, at the firm level, we explore how valuation error affects the probability of being involved in a merger. Second, at the sector level, we relate aggregate merger activity to

---

[7] Another possible concern is that our valuation models are failing to price large firms well. In unreported robustness tests, we have replicated Table 6 for models that include squared and cubic terms for book value to capture nonlinearities in size. In addition, we have repeated Table 6 using models that scale by shares outstanding, so that all variables are measured on a per share basis. These are omitted for brevity but are available upon request.

Table 8

Transaction size and the components of market to book

This table presents the same market-to-book decomposition results as Tables 6 and 7, but it sorts the results according to transaction size. Q1 is the quintile of smallest transactions; Q5 is the largest transactions. Approximately 800 firms of each type (acquirers, targets) are in each quintile. The t-statistics assume unequal variances across groups. The fourth row of each model adds the results of the second and third rows to show that the low buys high long-run value-to-book result holds even after accounting for time-series sector error.

Valuation component	Quintile 1 (smallest)			Quintile 2			Quintile 3			Quintile 4			Quintile 5 (largest)		
	Tar.	Acq.	t(diff.)	Tar.	Acq.	t(diff.)	Tar.	Acq.	t(diff.)	Tar.	Acq.	t(diff.)	Tar.	Acq.	t(diff.)
$m_{it} - b_{it}$	0.69	0.86	−2.85	0.55	0.75	−4.19	0.54	0.82	−6.40	0.68	0.94	−6.11	0.92	0.93	−0.15
Model 1															
$m_{it} - v(\theta_{it}; \alpha_{jt})$	−0.23	0.34	−10.72	−0.32	0.31	−15.24	−0.19	0.45	−16.99	0.07	0.65	−15.64	0.51	0.80	−6.46
$v(\theta_{it}; \alpha_{jt}) - v(\theta_{it}; \bar{\alpha}_j)$	0.10	0.14	−2.47	0.09	0.14	−3.83	0.11	0.18	−5.24	0.14	0.20	−4.73	0.20	0.25	−3.30
$v(\theta_{it}; \bar{\alpha}_j) - b_{it}$	0.82	0.39	15.81	0.78	0.30	22.00	0.62	0.19	22.14	0.47	0.09	20.11	0.21	−0.12	16.73
$V(\theta_{it}; \alpha_{jt}) - b_{it}$	0.92	0.52	12.39	0.87	0.44	17.25	0.73	0.37	15.61	0.61	0.30	13.69	0.41	0.14	11.45
Model 2															
$m_{it} - v(\theta_{it}; \alpha_{jt})$	−0.19	0.26	−9.22	−0.26	0.25	−13.81	−0.16	0.39	−16.28	0.09	0.55	−13.27	0.45	0.67	−5.17
$v(\theta_{it}; \alpha_{jt}) - v(\theta_{it}; \bar{\alpha}_j)$	0.07	0.13	−3.30	0.08	0.14	−4.44	0.10	0.18	−5.60	0.14	0.20	−4.58	0.20	0.25	−3.55
$v(\theta_{it}; \bar{\alpha}_j) - b_{it}$	0.81	0.47	9.30	0.73	0.36	12.89	0.61	0.26	13.72	0.46	0.19	11.40	0.27	0.01	10.81
$V(\theta_{it}; \alpha_{jt}) - b_{it}$	0.88	0.60	7.18	0.81	0.50	10.18	0.71	0.44	9.81	0.59	0.39	7.72	0.47	0.26	7.47
Model 3															
$m_{it} - v(\theta_{it}; \alpha_{jt})$	−0.18	0.19	−8.87	−0.18	0.20	−12.22	−0.09	0.31	−13.77	0.08	0.44	−12.65	0.37	0.48	−3.63
$v(\theta_{it}; \alpha_{jt}) - v(\theta_{it}; \bar{\alpha}_j)$	0.02	0.09	−4.89	0.04	0.09	−3.68	0.06	0.12	−5.21	0.09	0.14	−4.59	0.14	0.19	−4.12
$v(\theta_{it}; \bar{\alpha}_j) - b_{it}$	0.85	0.59	5.63	0.69	0.47	6.10	0.58	0.39	5.52	0.51	0.36	4.88	0.42	0.26	5.20
$V(\theta_{it}; \alpha_{jt}) - b_{it}$	0.87	0.67	4.00	0.73	0.55	4.72	0.64	0.51	3.46	0.60	0.50	2.84	0.56	0.45	3.02

overall levels of valuation error. This allows us to test Empirical Predictions 4 and 5 directly. We address the question of whether valuation error affects the probability of an individual firm being involved in a merger. This is presented in Section 6.2.1. In Section 6.2.2, we examine aggregate merger intensity.

6.2.1. Firm-level intensity regressions

Panel A of Table 9 presents tests of the probability that a firm is involved in a merger as a function of its valuation characteristics. The panel reports probit regressions in which the dependent variable is 1 if the firm in question was involved in a merger (either as an acquirer or a target), 0 otherwise. Column 1 shows that firms are more likely to be in mergers when their $m_{it} - b_{it}$ is high, corroborating widely cited evidence linking valuation levels to merger intensity. However, this effect is not robust to the inclusion of year fixed effects, as Column 2 demonstrates. In Column 2, the loading on $m_{it} - b_{it}$ diminishes, and loses statistical significance, indicating that the $m_{it} - b_{it}$ variable is picking up mostly time trends in overall valuation levels, not differences across firms in their probability of merger.

Columns 3-8 repeat the analysis of Columns 1 and 2 but replace $m_{it} - b_{it}$ with the components of our decomposition. No matter which model we use, firm-specific error and time-series sector error have a positive and statistically significant effect on the probability that a firm is involved in a merger, while long-run value to book has a negative, significant effect. Introducing year fixed effects eliminates the significance of the sector valuation error, but neither the firm-specific error nor the long-run value to book is affected. These findings hold across each of the three models.

In Panel B of Table 9, we focus only on the sample of mergers and test the difference between acquirers and targets. Specifically, we report results from probit regressions in which the dependent variable is 1 if the firm is an acquirer and 0 if it is a target. Because the fraction of acquirers in the sample does not vary over time, year fixed effects would have no effect on the results and are therefore omitted. This allows us to examine whether our decomposition explains the difference between acquirers and targets. It shows that a firm is much more likely to be an acquirer if it has higher firm-specific or time-series sector error. Increasing long-run value to book decreases the probability that a firm is an acquirer. These results are highly statistically significant across each of the three models. While $\ln(M/B)$ is important for predicting whether a firm is an acquirer, our decomposition produces much stronger results, because the individual components of $\ln(M/B)$ affect this probability differently.

Panel C of Table 9 relates our decomposition to method of payment. It reports probit regressions in which the dependent variable is 1 if the acquisition was 100% stock-financed, 0 otherwise. It shows that high $\ln(M/B)$ firms are more likely to use stock. Each element of the decomposition has a positive, significant affect on this probability. This supports the findings of Martin (1996), which relates q to method of payment. It also supports the predictions of RKV and SV.

Table 9

Firm-level merger intensity regressions

This table reports probit regressions of merger activity on valuation characteristics. The dependent variable in Panel A is a dummy for whether the firm in question is involved a merger (this includes acquirers and targets). Panel A uses the entire intersection of Compustat and SDC. Panels B and C focus only on the sample of merger observations.

Valuation component	Baseline		Model 1		Model 2		Model 3	
	(1)	(2)	(3)	(4)	(5)	(6)	(7)	(8)
Panel A: Merger = 1, nonmerger = 0								
$m_{it} - b_{it}$	0.088 (15.95)	−0.034 (1.19)						
$m_{it} - v(\theta_{it}; \alpha_{jt})$			0.153 (23.63)	0.119 (3.26)	0.162 (22.86)	0.151 (3.74)	0.209 (24.13)	0.206 (4.02)
$v(\theta_{it}; \alpha_{jt}) - v(\theta_{it}; \bar\alpha_j)$			0.671 (30.95)	0.075 (0.72)	0.537 (27.36)	−0.011 (0.12)	0.722 (28.38)	−0.233 (1.90)
$v(\theta_{it}; \bar\alpha_j) - b_{it}$			−0.392 (31.90)	−0.462 (7.32)	−0.174 (17.63)	−0.317 (5.63)	−0.083 (10.59)	−0.125 (3.28)
Log likelihood	−29492	−14867	−28189	−14831	−28631	−14840	−28782	−14850
χ^2	258.14	1.43	2864.90	71.43	1857.24	53.46	1555.31	32.78
Panel B: Acquirer = 1, target = 0								
$m_{it} - b_{it}$	0.097 (6.86)							
$m_{it} - v(\theta_{it}; \alpha_{jt})$			0.279 (16.77)		0.302 (17.60)		0.379 (18.00)	
$v(\theta_{it}; \alpha_{jt}) - v(\theta_{it}; \bar\alpha_j)$			0.208 (3.81)		0.226 (4.71)		0.491 (8.39)	
$v(\theta_{it}; \bar\alpha_j) - b_{it}$			−0.974 (30.13)		−0.526 (20.15)		−0.229 (11.27)	
Log likelihood	−5758		−4971		−5302		−5483	
χ^2	46.84		1621.19		937.73		575.22	
Panel C: Stock = 1, not stock = 0								
$m_{it} - b_{it}$	0.232 (14.35)	0.179 (10.11)						
$m_{it} - v(\theta_{it}; \alpha_{jt})$			0.158 (8.99)	0.141 (7.94)	0.174 (9.20)	0.151 (7.98)	0.146 (6.33)	0.116 (5.02)
$v(\theta_{it}; \alpha_{jt}) - v(\theta_{it}; \bar\alpha_j)$			0.707 (13.33)	0.404 (6.52)	0.636 (12.88)	0.374 (6.81)	0.643 (10.53)	0.373 (5.70)
$v(\theta_{it}; \bar\alpha_j) - b_{it}$			0.326 (10.55)	0.331 (10.44)	0.239 (9.06)	0.225 (8.35)	0.236 (10.87)	0.219 (9.92)
Log likelihood	−4891	−4676	−4839	−4658	−4843	−4662	−4852	−4660
χ^2	215.28	102.11	320.36	167.68	292.50	144.09	274.03	148.17
Fixed effects?		Year		Year		Year		Year

These findings show that positive firm-level deviations from industry pricing increase the probability that a firm is involved in a merger, that a firm is an acquirer, and that the acquisition is financed with stock. Thus, this table offers strong support for Empirical Prediction 4.

6.2.2. Sector-level intensity regressions

To test Empirical Prediction 5 we regress merger activity in sector j, year t, on a variety of aggregate valuation measures. These are reported in Table 10.

In Panel A, the dependent variable is a count of the total merger activity in sector j during year t. The first five columns regress this measure of merger activity on the average $\ln(M/B)$ in that sector, which is denoted $\bar{m}_t - \bar{b}_t$. Columns 6-10 instead regress this measure on average time-series sector error, $\bar{v}(\alpha_{jt}) - \bar{v}(\alpha_j)$, and long-run value-to-book, $\bar{v}(\alpha_{jt}) - \bar{b}_t$. The independent variables are obtained by averaging the firm-level data (this includes Compustat nonmerger firms as well as firms engaged in merger activity) down to the sector level each year. In particular, because firm-specific error is zero at the sector-year level, this means that $\bar{m}_t$ is equal to $\bar{v}(\alpha_{jt})$.

The results from Column 1 indicate that merger activity loads positively and significantly on $\ln(M/B)$. Because this regression includes sector fixed effects, the interpretation is that sectors experience more merger activity as their valuation levels increase. In Column 2, however, introducing year fixed effects destroys this result. In other words, once we control for the fact that in some years all sectors simultaneously experience high levels of valuation and high levels of merger activity, we no longer find that increases in industry valuation levels lead to increases in merger activity. Thus, we cannot rule out the alternative explanation that some external factor such as deregulation or industry consolidation is responsible for both changes in overall $\ln(M/B)$ and changes in merger activity. This mirrors the finding in Table 9 which shows that firm-level $\ln(M/B)$ does not predict increased probability of merger once we control for year effects.

In Columns 6 and 7, we repeat these regressions but replace $\bar{m}_t - \bar{b}_t$ with average time-series sector error, $\bar{v}(\alpha_{jt}) - \bar{v}(\alpha_j)$, and long-run value-to-book, $\bar{v}(\alpha_{jt}) - \bar{b}_t$. From these regressions, we see that the inclusion of sector and year fixed effects does not destroy the significance of our decomposition. In both cases, we see that increases in average sector valuation error lead to increases in merger activity. Because we control for sector and year fixed effects, the interpretation is that sectors with larger increases in valuation (relative to other sectors) experience greater increases in merger activity.

At the same time, sector-average long-run value to book is negatively associated with sector-level merger activity. This gives us a better understanding of why the overall $\bar{m}_t - \bar{b}_t$ are so tenuous. The result indicates that $\bar{m}_t - \bar{b}_t$ is smearing two offsetting effects: short-run sector-level average valuation error, which is positively associated with merger activity, and sector-average long-run value to book, which is negatively related to it. Taken separately, each effect is statistically significant,

Table 10

Valuation waves, merger intensity, and method of payment

In Panel A the dependent variable is the count of merger announcements in sector j, year t. In Panel B, the dependent variable is the count of 100% stock-financed merger announcements, as reported by SDC. Table 5 describes the independent variables, with the exception of total mergers. [Note that $\bar{m}_t = \bar{v}(\alpha_{jt})$] "Total mergers, year t" is the total number of mergers across all sectors in year t, while "Total mergers, year j" is the total number of mergers across all years for sector j. Each regression contains 300 observations. Double asterisks (**) denote significance at the 1% level single asterisk (*) denote 5%.

Valuation component	Using market to book alone (Columns 1-5)					Using M/B decomposition (Columns 6-10)				
	(1)	(2)	(3)	(4)	(5)	(6)	(7)	(8)	(9)	(10)
Panel A: Dependent variable is merger count in industry j, year t										
$\bar{m}_t - \bar{b}_t$	24.673	12.676	24.640	8.260	19.117					
	(3.82)**	(1.82)	(3.81)**	(1.24)	(3.06)**					
$\bar{v}(\alpha_{jt}) - \bar{v}(\bar{\alpha}_j)$						54.675	39.079	54.539	42.197	56.096
						(6.97)**	(4.11)**	(6.93)**	(4.10)**	(6.59)**
$\bar{v}(\bar{\alpha}_j) - \bar{b}_t$						−27.281	−21.054	−27.077	−17.403	−18.655
						(2.73)**	(2.04)*	(2.69)**	(2.02)*	(2.23)*
Total mergers, year t			0.004 (0.83)		0.005 (0.94)			0.001 (0.27)		0.002 (0.42)
Total mergers, sector j				0.013	0.012				0.015	0.015
				(5.25)**	(4.69)**				(6.05)**	(5.98)**
Fixed effects	Sector	Sector, year	Sector	Year	None	Sector	Sector, year	Sector	Year	None
R^2	0.05	0.20	0.05	0.12	0.13	0.16	0.25	0.16	0.18	0.23

Panel B: Dependent variable is stock-financed merger count in industry j, year t

$\bar{m}_t - \bar{b}_t$	8.733 (2.83)**	5.165 (1.52)	8.713 (2.82)**	3.395 (1.04)	6.668 (2.23)*				
$\bar{v}(\alpha_{jt}) - \bar{v}(\alpha_j)$						20.067 (5.23)**	15.822 (3.37)**	19.911 (5.17)**	18.132 (3.57)**	21.246 (5.12)**
$\bar{v}(\alpha_j) - \bar{b}_t$						−10.961 (2.24)*	−8.449 (1.66)	−10.728 (2.18)*	−7.721 (1.82)	−8.255 (2.02)*
Total mergers, year t			0.002		0.003 (1.16)			0.001 (0.63)		0.002 (0.74)
Total mergers, sector j				0.006 (4.59)**	0.005 (4.33)**				0.007 (5.26)**	0.006 (5.31)**
Fixed effects	Sector	Sector, year	Sector	Year	None	Sector	Sector, year	Sector	Year	None
R^2	0.03	0.14	0.03	0.09	0.10	0.10	0.18	0.10	0.14	0.17

but because they partially offset one another, this destroys the overall sector-average ln (M/B) effect when we control for sector and year fixed effects.

Because fixed effects seem to be important for understanding how valuation (and valuation error) affects merger activity, the remaining columns of Panel A explore possible explanations for the economic forces that year and sector fixed effects are capturing. In Columns 3 and 8 we replace the year fixed effect with a count of the total number of mergers across all sectors in year t. This is intended to capture the idea that in some years merger activity spikes across all sectors. Introducing this variable does not drive out sector-average $\bar{m}_t - \bar{b}_t$, but at the same time this variable does not have a statistically significant relation to sector-level merger activity once we control for valuation level. Thus, we can conclude that while there are spikes in overall, economy-wide merger activity, these spikes do not explain away the relation between sector-level merger activity and sector-level valuation error.

Columns 4 and 9 drop the sector fixed effects and replace them with the total count of merger activity in that sector over the entire sample period. Like a sector fixed effect, this variable takes on only one value per sector, but instead of a dummy variable for each sector, the variable is higher for sectors that experience a great deal of merger activity. This variable is positive and highly significant, and it diminishes the loading on $\bar{m}_t - \bar{b}_t$ by a factor of 3. This indicates that sectors in which mergers are common have an increased sensitivity to changes in valuation (or valuation error). Finally, Columns 5 and 10 drop all fixed effects and include both sector-wide and year-total merger activity. In general, these regressions do not capture as much variation in merger activity as ones including year and sector fixed effects, indicating that the fixed effects are capturing more than just localized spikes in merger activity.

In Panel B we replace the dependent variable with the count of 100% stock-financed merger transactions and repeat the analysis conducted in Panel A. This allows us to test the second part of Empirical Prediction 5, which relates specifically to the frequency of stock-financed mergers as a function of aggregate valuation error. The results largely mirror the findings from Panel A. In particular, we again find that year fixed effects drive out market to book, but not our aggregate sector misvaluation measure. Again, $\bar{m}_t - \bar{b}_t$ smears two off-setting effects, a positive relation between sector misvaluation and merger activity, and a negative relation between long-run value to book and merger activity. Thus, taken together, Table 10 provides strong support for Empirical Prediction 5, relating aggregate merger activity to aggregate valuation error.

An alternative interpretation that does not make use of the SV and RKV predictions is that aggregate merger intensity is a function of growth opportunities. Our findings suggest that merger intensity spikes when short-run growth opportunities are high. The strongest evidence for this finding comes from Column 7, which shows that sectors with relative increases in valuation error experience relative increases in merger activity. However, the long-run growth opportunities go in the opposite direction; they are negatively associated with merger intensity, as well as the use of stock. This suggests that the Martin (1996) finding relating q to method of payment is probably driven by short-run Q variation (or by misvaluation), not by long-run measures of investment opportunities.

Finally, the inclusion of a variable that measures overall, economy-wide merger activity in a given year helps us to guard against a potential objection to our analysis, which is that there have been only a very small number of merger waves in our sample period of 1977–2001. If this were the case, then we would find a strong positive loading on the total number of mergers in year t, and this effect would drive down the significance of the loading on average sector valuation error. Instead, our results indicate that industries experience valuation-specific merger waves that differ from the overall, economy-wide trends in merger activity, corroborating evidence in Mitchell and Mulherin (1996) and Harford (2005), which shows that mergers cluster in time at the industry level.

7. A horse race between competing theories of merger activity

The neoclassical explanation for merger activity is that mergers are an efficient response to reorganization opportunities that arise as a result of some underlying economic event (see, e.g., Gort, 1969). The economic shock in question could come from a variety of sources: industry overcapacity, the advent of a new technology, changing regulatory attitudes, or changes in access to capital markets that alter the optimal operating scale of firms. Explanations along these lines could account for some of our findings if mergers cluster when opportunities for reorganization are rich, which in turn are periods of high valuation because markets bid up prices in anticipation of the restructuring.

To guard against the possibility that neoclassical explanations are responsible for our findings, we use two approaches. The first approach is based on arguments made by Jovanovic and Rousseau (2002) and others, who say that dispersion in Tobin's Q reflects opportunities for organizational change. This Q theory of mergers suggests that some exogenous economic shock occurs in an industry. Some firms are well positioned to take advantage of this shock, while others are not, thus creating fruitful opportunities for reorganization. The stylized fact that mergers involve high M/B bidders acquiring lower M/B targets is often offered as support for Q theoretic explanations for merger activity.

Given the wide range of potential causes for economic shocks, the problem with the Q dispersion measure is that it could fail to capture many sources of organizational flux. Therefore, our second approach is to partition the data into two periods: an economic shock sample, and a normal sample. Our classification of economic shocks follows the merger wave classification discussed in Harford (2005). Under this strategy, we assume that all large spikes in merger activity are caused by some form of economic shock, and we ask whether misvaluation is still important for explaining merger activity.

The first approach probably gives too little weight to the neoclassical story by looking only at one potential neoclassical explanation for merger activity. The second approach could give too much weight to the neoclassical story, because it attributes neoclassical explanations, ex post, to all mergers that occurred during times of extreme merger activity. However, by running both types of empirical horse races, we can better see whether our misvaluation story stands up to alternative explanations. We explore the Q theory of mergers alternative by comparing failed and successful acquisitions. The horse race pits misvaluation against the ex post classification of economic shocks.

7.1. Comparing failed and successful mergers

Our first horse race comes from comparing successful acquisitions with failed acquisitions. Because assets are being efficiently reorganized, a Q-based explanation would give a higher chance of completion to a merger between two firms with a larger disparity in M/B. Thus, if Tobin's Q explains merger activity, then we would expect the bidder/target Q differential to be higher among successful deals than among failed deals. On the other hand, if misvaluation is driving merger activity, then we expect misvaluation levels to be higher in completed deals, and lower in failed deals.

Table 11 reports the same breakdown as in Table 6 but splits the sample according to whether or not the deal was successful. The Q difference between bidder and target is higher in failed deals, not in successful deals. However, the absolute valuation levels are lower in failed deals. (Targets that are later successfully acquired have higher firm-specific error in the withdrawn deal than targets which are never subsequently taken over.) Moreover, when we decompose the M/B ratio and compare success and failure, we see that failed deals have lower misvaluation, not higher misvaluation. Long-run q is higher in failed deals than in successful deals.

This cross-sectional horse race speaks against two alternatives. First, efficient asset redeployment is unlikely to be responsible for our findings, because Q dispersion is higher in failed deals than in successful ones. Instead, misvaluation seems to be at work, because overall valuation levels are higher in successful than in failed bids, and more of the level is attributable to misvaluation in successful deals as well. Second, it seems unlikely that our analysis is simply capturing *ex ante* valuation differences that vanish between the announcement and consummation of the merger, because the overall misvaluation level is higher in deals that go through than in ones that are withdrawn.

7.2. Can Q dispersion explain merger intensity?

Next, we conduct a horse race based on the merger intensity predictions by introducing dispersion in M/B as a proxy for reorganization opportunities. The measure of Q dispersion we use is the within-industry standard deviation in $m_{it} - b_{it}$ in a given year. Jovanovic and Rousseau (2001) argue that high levels of Q dispersion reflect the fact that there are opportunities to reshuffle assets from low-productivity to high-productivity uses. Thus, if the reorganization story were at work, we would expect Q dispersion to predict merger intensity and to drive out our measures of misvaluation.

Table 11

Failed versus successful targets

This table repeats the decomposition of the market-to-book ratio but examines targets and acquirers according to whether the deal was successful (success) or whether it was withdrawn for any reason (failed).

Valuation component	All transactions			Only all cash deals			Only all stock deals		
	Success	Failed	t(diff.)	Success	Failed	t(diff.)	Success	Failed	t(diff.)
Targets:									
$m_{it} - b_{it}$	0.71	0.58	3.45	0.64	0.43	4.09	0.87	0.89	−0.18
Model 1									
$Mit - v(\theta_{it}; \alpha_{jt})$	0.02	−0.00	0.62	−0.10	−0.22	2.40	0.12	0.14	−0.24
$v(\theta_{it}; \alpha_{jt}) - v(\theta_{it}; \bar{\alpha}_j)$	0.13	0.11	1.92	0.13	0.13	0.29	0.18	0.14	2.30
$v(\theta_{it}; \bar{\alpha}_j) - b_{it}$	0.56	0.47	4.41	0.61	0.52	2.67	0.57	0.62	−1.05
Model 2									
$m_{it} - v(\theta_{it}; \alpha_{jt})$	0.03	−0.00	0.93	−0.07	−0.17	2.10	0.12	0.10	0.23
$v(\theta_{it}; \alpha_{jt}) - v(\theta_{it}; \bar{\alpha}_j)$	0.12	0.10	2.00	0.11	0.12	−0.14	0.18	0.11	2.84
$v(\theta_{it}; \bar{\alpha}_j) - b_{it}$	0.56	0.49	3.06	0.60	0.48	2.73	0.58	0.68	−1.93
Model 3									
$m_{it} - v(\theta_{it}; \alpha_{jt})$	0.03	0.05	−0.86	−0.08	−0.09	0.31	0.06	0.04	0.32
$v(\theta_{it}; \alpha_{jt}) - v(\theta_{it}; \bar{\alpha}_j)$	0.07	0.06	1.72	0.06	0.07	−0.79	0.13	0.07	3.11
$v(\theta_{it}; \bar{\alpha}_j) - b_{it}$	0.60	0.47	4.47	0.65	0.44	4.04	0.70	0.79	−1.54
Acquirers:									
$m_{it} - b_{it}$	0.85	0.74	2.32	0.80	0.72	1.29	1.14	1.02	1.48
Model 1									
$m_{it} - v(\theta_{it}; \alpha_{jt})$	0.53	0.31	5.49	0.52	0.30	3.78	0.67	0.40	3.96
$v(\theta_{it}; \alpha_{jt}) - v(\theta_{it}; \bar{\alpha}_j)$	0.19	0.12	5.93	0.20	0.14	3.20	0.27	0.15	5.84
$v(\theta_{it}; \bar{\alpha}_j) - b_{it}$	0.13	0.31	−8.39	0.08	0.28	−5.77	0.19	0.47	−7.08
Model 2									
$m_{it} - v(\theta_{it}; \alpha_{jt})$	0.44	0.25	5.13	0.41	0.22	3.62	0.60	0.37	3.80
$v(\theta_{it}; \alpha_{jt}) - v(\theta_{it}; \bar{\alpha}_j)$	0.19	0.12	5.80	0.20	0.13	3.28	0.27	0.16	4.64
$v(\theta_{it}; \bar{\alpha}_j) - b_{it}$	0.22	0.38	−6.51	0.20	0.36	−4.17	0.27	0.50	−5.07
Model 3									
$m_{it} - v(\theta_{it}; \alpha_{jt})$	0.34	0.23	3.76	0.30	0.19	2.53	0.46	0.29	3.48
$v(\theta_{it}; \alpha_{jt}) - v(\theta_{it}; \bar{\alpha}_j)$	0.13	0.07	5.48	0.14	0.11	2.16	0.18	0.10	4.23
$v(\theta_{it}; \bar{\alpha}_j) - b_{it}$	0.38	0.45	−2.20	0.36	0.42	−1.12	0.49	0.64	−2.57

Columns 1 and 2 of Table 12 support the neoclassical, optimal reorganization theory for mergers. When we include dispersion in q in a regression with ln(*M/B*), Q dispersion comes in positive and statistically significant, which indicates that mergers are more likely in times when there is dispersion in valuation.

However, the explanatory power of Q dispersion disappears when we introduce our valuation decomposition. In Column 3, Q dispersion becomes statistically insignificant. This suggests that the short-run valuation dynamics that our decomposition

Table 12

A horse race between competing theories of merger

Q dispersion is the standard deviation in $\ln(mb)$ within an industry in a given year. All other variables are defined in Table 5. Columns 4 and 5 use only the observations for which the industry valuation $[\bar{v}(\alpha_{jt}) - \bar{v}(\bar{\alpha}_j)]$ was below its time-series median. Columns 6 and 7 only use observations above the industry median valuation. The mean value (S.D.) of Q dispersion is 0.897 (0.260) in the low-valuation subsample and 0.839 (0.298) in the high valuation subsample.

Independent variable	Full sample period			Low valuation		High valuation	
	(1)	(2)	(3)	(4)	(5)	(6)	(7)
$\bar{m}_t - \bar{b}_t$	26.729	23.988		18.228		21.800	
	(4.31)	(3.73)		(2.54)		(1.78)	
Q dispersion	14.007	20.426	4.773 (0.50)	16.716	14.049	7.786	−9.189
	(1.65)	(2.10)		(2.03)	(1.55)	(0.51)	(0.47)
$[\bar{v}(\alpha_{jt}) - \bar{v}(\bar{\alpha}_j)]$			53.829		49.383		117.355
			(6.70)		(4.09)		(4.78)
$\bar{v}(\bar{\alpha}_j) - \bar{b}_t$			−26.277		1.541		−46.934
			(2.57)		(0.13)		(2.95)
Sample size	299	299	299	144	144	155	155
R^2	0.07	0.06	0.16	0.07	0.15	0.02	0.17
Industry fixed effects?		Yes	Yes		Yes		Yes

captures are not being driven by the fact that the market anticipates reorganization opportunities and compounds them into prices.

The results from the left-hand portion of Table 12 guard against the explanation that valuation is merely a by-product of Q dispersion, which in turn reflects the root cause of merger activity. To push this further, we split each industry time series into periods that are above and below the median level of sector misvaluation for that industry, and we reexamine the ability of Q dispersion to explain merger activity.

The right half of Table 12 reports these results. Comparing Columns 4 and 6, we see that Q dispersion predicts merger activity only in the low valuation subsample. During high misvaluation periods, Q dispersion is not statistically significant. To ensure that this is not being driven by the fact that Q dispersion was low in the high value period, we checked the mean and standard deviation of the Q dispersion variable in each subsample. They are roughly the same (0.897 in the low sample, 0.839 in the high sample, with standard deviations of 0.26 and 0.298, respectively), indicating that this is not being driven by a problem of limited variance in one subsample. This suggests that while Q dispersion could reflect some underlying economic force that drives merger activity, many mergers occur during periods of high misvaluation that are unrelated to these forces. The large and statistically significant loadings on sector misvaluation suggest that misvaluation drives merger activity. The fact that Q dispersion works in times of low misvaluation, but not high misvaluation, indicates that misvaluation is not simply capturing liquidity.

7.3. Economic shocks as an alternative explanation for merger intensity

One problem with the previous analysis is that many potential neoclassical explanations exist for merger activity that do not involve dispersion in Tobin's Q. Thus, we could be giving too little weight to neoclassical explanations for merger activity. To guard against this potential objection, this section conducts a horse race using a measure designed to capture a broad range of potential neoclassical *ex ante* motivations for merger.

To do this, we use the classification of merger waves conducted by Harford (2005). The Harford (2005) technique builds on Mitchell and Mulherin (1996) and starts with the null hypothesis that merger activity is more or less uniformly distributed over time for each industry (though industries could differ in their overall level of merger activity). The technique then classifies an industry as undergoing a merger wave if, during a 2-year window, an industry experiences so many mergers that it is statistically unlikely to have come from this null distribution. Harford (2005) then goes back and pinpoints the economic shocks (deregulation, the advent of new technology, consolidation, etc.) that precipitated each spike in merger activity.

Because Harford (2005) provides the likely rationale behind each merger wave from a variety of possible neoclassical motivations, our approach is to examine whether our misvaluation measures continue to explain mergers once we control for this classification. Because this measure was developed independently of our analysis, it is unlikely to be mechanically related to any of the measures we develop here and thus provides an independent measure of neoclassically motivated merger activity.

First, we relate economic shocks to sector-level misvaluation measures. This is done in Panel A of Table 13, in which we run probit regressions of merger waves on industry average valuation and misvaluation. The first row indicates that merger waves are generally times of high overall valuations; the average industry market-to-book ratio is statistically significant and explains about 7% of the variation in merger waves.

The next two rows replace the average market-to-book ratio with average sector misvaluation and average sector long-run growth. These variables explain about twice as much of the variation in merger waves as does the log market-to-book ratio. Both variables are statistically significant for predicting whether a sector is in a merger wave.

Examining R^2 values across the three regressions illustrates an important point. While our regressions explain about twice as much variation in merger waves as does market to book, the regressions indicate that merger waves are being driven by much more than just sector-level misvaluation. A crude interpretation of Panel A is that, while sector-level misvaluation is a crucial determinant of merger waves, it leaves 85% of merger waves unexplained. This is indirect evidence favoring Mitchell and

Table 13

Misvaluation and merger activity during economic shocks

Panel A reports probit regressions that predict whether a sector is experiencing a merger wave based on levels of valuation ($m_{it} - b_{it}$) and misvaluation [$v(\alpha_{jt}) - v(\bar{\alpha}_j)$]. Merger wave is defined in Harford (2005), which details when industries have experienced economic shocks that induced merger waves. Pseudo R^2 values as well as χ^2 values of significance are reported. Standard errors appear in italics below point estimates[1]. The regressions are based on 1187 industry-year observations across 48 Fama and French industries over the 1978–2001 time period. In Panels B and C, merger activity is reported by firm-specific misvaluation quantile for the entire sample (Panel B) and for the subsample of observations that occur during merger waves (Panel C). Dollar volume is reported in billions of nominal US dollars. Merger wave observations account for 12% of firm-years and 6.5% of industry-years in our sample.

	$m_{it} - b_{it}$	$v(\alpha_{jt}) - v(\bar{\alpha}_j)$	$v(\bar{\alpha}_j) - b_{it}$	R^2	χ^2
Panel A: Probability of merger wave based on valuation					
Pr(merger wave)	0.94			7.37	39.24
	0.16				
Pr(merger wave)		3.31		15.28	81.33
		0.47			
Pr(merger wave)		3.37	0.46	16.01	85.18
		0.47	*0.23*		

Merger statist	Lowest quintile (%)	20–50th percentile (%)	50–80th percentile (%)	Highest quintile (%)	Total
Panel B: Distribution of mergers across misvaluation quantiles					
Acquisitions	8.21	17.57	32.02	42.20	4325
Dollar volume	5.08	10.01	25.02	59.89	6112
Stock acquisitions	5.75	12.64	34.07	47.54	1218
Panel C: Merger/misvaluation distribution during economic shocks					
Acquisitions	10.78	13.05	27.24	48.92	881
(Percent of overall total)					(20)
Dollar volume	4.92	12.65	16.68	65.75	2391
(Percent of overall total)					(39)
Stock acquisitions	7.92	10.85	28.15	53.08	341
(Percent of overall total)					(28)

Mulherin (1996), Mulherin and Boone (2000), Andrade et al. (2001), and others who argue that economic shocks from a variety of potential sources are responsible for spikes in merger activity at the sector level.

At the same time, this evidence leaves open the question of who buys whom during merger waves. For this, we turn to Panels B and C of Table 13. In Panel B, we provide several statistics of merger activity broken down according to the quantile of firm-specific misvaluation that the acquirer came from when the acquisition was announced. Panel B shows that the quintile of the most overvalued firms is responsible for 42% of merger transactions and an even larger fraction (47%) of stock-financed transactions. This quintile is responsible for nearly 60% of the dollar volume of merger transactions.

In Panel C we repeat Panel B but focus only on the transactions that occur during Harford (2005) merger waves. Even though merger waves only comprise 70 of the roughly 1100 industry-years, 20% of overall activity and 39% of merger dollar volume occurs during these periods. Nevertheless, we see from the breakdown across misvaluation quantiles that misvaluation continues to be important, even during economic shock periods. Almost 50% of the transactions, and over 65% of the dollar volume, comes from acquirers in the top misvaluation quintile. The top misvaluation quintile is responsible for over one-half of stock-financed merger activity during periods of economic shocks.

Taken together, these results allow us to compare the neoclassical explanation for merger activity with misvaluation. The results show that while sector misvaluation is an important determinant of merger waves, many other factors are also important. Misvaluation is by no means the whole story at the sector level. Yet at the firm level, misvaluation is critical for understanding who participates in these merger waves. Even when the merger is part of a merger wave that is being driven by neoclassical considerations, most merger activity is the work of misvalued firms. While roughly one-fifth of the transactions and almost one-half the dollar volume of mergers occurs in the relatively uncommon periods of economic shocks, the vast majority of transactions (whether or not they occur during these periods) involve highly overvalued bidders.

8. Summary and conclusions

This paper uses regression techniques to decompose the M/B ratio into components that track misvaluation at the firm and sector levels and a component that tracks long-run growth opportunities. This decomposition allows us to test recent theories arguing misvaluation drives merger activity. To summarize our main findings, our breakdown of M/B finds the following:

- Acquirers with high firm-specific error use stock to buy targets with relatively lower firm-specific error at times when both firms benefit from positive time-series sector error.

- Cash targets are undervalued relative to stock targets. Cash acquirers are less overvalued than stock acquirers.
- Merger intensity is highly positively correlated with short-run deviations in valuation from long-run trends, especially when stock is used as the method of payment. This holds for individual firms, as well as at the aggregate level.
- After controlling for firm-specific and time-series sector error, we find that low long-run value-to-book firms actually buy high long-run value-to-book targets.

Therefore, while it is generally true that higher *M/B* firms acquire targets with lower *M/B*, so much of this is driven by short-run deviations in fundamentals, both at the firm and sector level, that the results for fundamental value go in the opposite direction. The component of *M/B* attributable to fundamental value to book either has no effect or is negatively correlated with the intensity of merger activity over time.

The fact that *low* long-run value firms buy *high* long-run value targets is a puzzle for most theories of merger activity. What causes this finding? One possibility is that managers who face high short-run valuations acquire targets with high long-run value to substantiate the market's beliefs. Another is that value-maximizing, but low-skilled, managers of low-valued firms acquire managerial talent from outside, and try to adapt their organization to the newly acquired talent. Yet another possibility is that low-value managers acquire higher value targets as' a way of further entrenching themselves. Sorting through these possibilities is a task for future theoretical and empirical research.

Pitting our predictions against neoclassical, Q oriented explanations for merger activity reveals that a significant fraction of merger activity is explained by misvaluation. Q theory suggests that successful transactions have large market-to-book differences between bidder and target. However, we find that failed transactions have larger differences than completed transactions, while successful deals display higher levels of misvaluation. Even in industries that appear to have experienced an economic shock, most acquirers come from the highest misvaluation quintile. Therefore, our findings support misvaluation theories based either on behavioral explanations or on asymmetric information between otherwise rational managers and markets. Economic shocks could well be the fundamental drivers of merger activity, but misvaluation affects how these shocks are propagated through the economy. Misvaluation affects who buys whom, as well as the method of payment they use to conduct the transaction.

References

Amir, E. and B. Lev, 1996, "Value-Relevance of Nonfinancial Information: The Wireless Communications Industry," *Journal of Accounting and Economics*, 22, 3–30.

Andrade, G. and E. Stafford, 2004, "Investigating the Economic Role of Mergers," *Journal of Corporate Finance*, 10, 1–36.

Andrade, G., M. Mitchell and E. Stafford, 2001, "New Evidence and Perspectives on Mergers," *Journal of Economic Perspectives*, 15 (2), 103–120.

Ang, J. and Y. Chen, 2004, "Direct Evidence on the Market-Driven Acquisitions Theory," Unpublished Working Paper, Florida State University, Tallahassee, FL.

Ang, A. and J. Liu, 2001, "A General Affine Earnings Valuation Model," *Review of Accounting Studies*, 6, 397–425.

Barth, M. E., W. H. Beaver and W. R. Landsman, 2001, "The Relevance of the Value-Relevance Literature for Financial Accounting Standard Setting: Another View," *Journal of Accounting and Economics*, 31, 77–104.

Collins, D. W., E. L. Maydew and I. S. Weiss, 1997, "Changes in the Value-Relevance of Earnings and Book Values over the Past 40 Years," *Journal of Accounting and Economics*, 24, 39–67.

Dong, M., D. Hirshleifer, S. Richardson and S. H. Teoh, 2005, "Does Investor Misvaluation Drive the Takeover Market?" *Journal of Finance*, forthcoming.

Eckbo, B. E., R. M. Giammarino and R. L. Heinkel, 1990, "Asymmetric Information and the Medium of Exchange in Takeovers: Theory and Tests," *Review of Financial Studies*, 3, 651–675.

Fama, E. and J. MacBeth, 1973, "Risk, Return, and Equilibrium: Empirical Tests," *Journal of Political Economy*, 81 (3), 607–636.

Feltham, G. and J. Ohlson, 1999, "Valuation and Clean Surplus Accounting for Operating and Financial Activities," *Contemporary Accounting Research*, 74 (2), 165–183.

Francis, J. and K. Schipper, 1999, "Have Financial Statements Lost Their Relevance?" *Journal of Accounting Research*, 37 (2), 319–352.

Gort, M., 1969, "An Economic Disturbance Theory of Mergers," *Quarterly Journal of Economics*, 83, 624–642.

Gorton, G., M. Kahl and R. Rosen, 2000, "Eat or Be Eaten: A Theory of Mergers and Merger Waves," Unpublished Working Paper, University of Pennsylvania, Philadelphia, PA.

Harford, J., 2005, "What Drives Merger Waves?" *Journal of Financial Economics*, forthcoming.

Hietala, P., S. N. Kaplan and D. Robinson, 2003, "What is the Price of Hubris? Using Takeover Battles to Infer Overpayments and Synergies," *Financial Management*, 32 (3), 1–32.

Holmstrom, B. and S. N. Kaplan, 2001, "Corporate Governance and Merger Activity in the United States: Making Sense of the 1980s and 1990s," *Journal of Economic Perspectives*, 15, 121–144.

Holthausen, R. W. and R. L. Watts, 2001, "The Relevance of the Value-Relevance Literature for Financial Accounting Standard Setting," *Journal of Accounting and Economics*, 31, 3–75.

Jensen, M., 1986, "Agency Costs of Free Cash Flow, Corporate Finance and Takeovers," *American Economic Review*, 76, 323–329.

Jovanovic, B. and P. Rousseau, 2001, "Mergers and Technological Change: 1885–2001," Unpublished Working Paper, New York University, New York.

Jovanovic, B. and P. Rousseau, 2002, "The *q*-Theory of Mergers," *American Economic Review, Papers and Proceedings*, 92 (2), 198–204.

Kothari, S., 2001, "Capital Markets Research in Accounting," *Journal of Accounting and Economics*, 31, 105–231.

Kothari, S. and J. L. Zimmerman, 1995, "Price and Return Models," *Journal of Accounting and Economics*, 20, 155–192.

Lang, L., R. Stulz and R. Walkling, 1989, "Managerial Performance, Tobin's *q*, and the Gains from Successful Tender Offers," *Journal of Financial Economics*, 24, 137–154.

Lee, C., J. Myers and B. Swaminathan, 1999, "What is the Intrinsic Value of the Dow?" *Journal of Finance*, 54 (5), 1693–1741.

Lev, B., 1997, "The Boundaries of Financial Reporting and How to Extend Them," Unpublished Working Paper, New York University, New York.

Maksimovic, V. and G. Phillips, 2001, "The Market for Corporate Assets: Who Engages in Mergers and Asset Sales and are There Efficiency Gains?" *The Journal of Finance*, 56 (6), 2019–2065.

Martin, K., 1996, "The Method of Payment in Corporate Acquisitions, Investment Opportunities, and Managerial Ownership," *Journal of Finance*, 51, 1227–1246.

Mitchell, M. L. and J. H. Mulherin, 1996, "The Impact of Industry Shocks on Takeover and Restructuring Activity," *Journal of Financial Economics*, 41, 193–229.

Moeller, S., F. Schlingemann and R. Stulz, 2004, "Firm Size and Gains from Acquisition," *Journal of Financial Economics*, 73, 201–228.

Moeller, S., F. Schlingemann and R. Stulz, 2005, "Wealth Destruction on a Massive Scale? An Analysis of Acquiring-Firm Returns During the Recent Merger Wave," *Journal of Finance*, 60, 757–782.

Mulherin, H. and A. Boone, 2000, "Comparing Acquisitions and Divestitures," *Journal of Corporate Finance*, 6 (2), 117–139.

Penman, S., 1998, "Combining Earnings and Book Value in Equity Valuation," *Contemporary Accounting Research*, 15 (3), 291–324.

Rhodes-Kropf, M. and D. T. Robinson, 2004, "The Market for Mergers and the Boundaries of the Firm," Unpublished Working Paper, Columbia University and Duke University, New York, and Durham, NC.

Rhodes-Kropf, M. and S. Viswanathan, 2004, "Market Valuation and Merger Waves," *Journal of Finance*, 59, 2685–2718.

Ritter, J. and R. Warr, 2002, "The Decline of Inflation and the Bull Market of 1982–1999," *Journal of Financial and Quantitative Analysis*, 37 (1), 29–61.

Servaes, H., 1991, "Tobin's q and the Gains from Takeovers," *Journal of Finance*, 46 (1), 409–419.

Shleifer, A. and R. Vishny, 2003, "Stock Market Driven Acquisitions" *Journal of Financial Economics*, 70, 295–311.

Chapter 6

WHAT DRIVES MERGER WAVES?[*]

JARRAD HARFORD

University of Washington Business School, Seattle, Washington, USA

Contents

* I thank John Chalmers, Larry Dann, Harry DeAngelo, Vidhan Goyal, Alan Hess, Jon Karpoff, Paul Malatesta, Wayne Mikkelson, Harold Mulherin, Ed Rice, Husayn Shahrur, an anonymous referee, and seminar participants at Babson College, Penn State, Purdue, Vanderbilt, Duke, the Universities of Arkansas, Southern California, and Utah, the University of Oregon research roundup, the 2001 Pacific Northwest Finance Conference, and the 2004 AFA meetings for comments. Sandy Klasa provided excellent research assistance. I gratefully acknowledge the contribution of Thomson Financial for providing earnings per share forecast data, available through I/B/E/S. This paper is partially derived from an earlier paper that circulated under the title, ''Efficient and distortional components to industry merger waves.''

This article originally appeared in the *Journal of Financial Economics*, Vol. 77, pp. 529–560 (2005).
Corporate Takeovers, Volume 1
Edited by B. Espen Eckbo
DOI: 10.1016/B978-0-12-381983-3.00006-X

Abstract

Aggregate merger waves could be due to market timing or to clustering of industry shocks for which mergers facilitate change to the new environment. This study finds that economic, regulatory and technological shocks drive industry merger waves. Whether the shock leads to a wave of mergers, however, depends on whether there is sufficient overall capital liquidity. This macro-level liquidity component causes industry merger waves to cluster in time even if industry shocks do not. Market-timing variables have little explanatory power relative to an economic model including this liquidity component. The contemporaneous peak in divisional acquisitions for cash also suggests an economic motivation for the merger activity.

Keywords

mergers and acquisitions, takeover, merger waves, behavioral, capital liquidity

JEL classification: G34

1. Introduction

Recent debate about the cause of merger waves has highlighted the fact that merger waves are correlated with high stock market valuations. Authors such as Shleifer and Vishny (2003) and Rhodes-Kropf and Viswanathan (2004) develop models in which merger waves result from managerial timing of market overvaluations of their firms. More neoclassical explanations of merger waves, dating at least to Gort (1969) and more recently examined by Mitchell and Mulherin (1996), argue that merger waves result from shocks to an industry's economic, technological, or regulatory environment. This study asks whether a clustering of mergers at the aggregate level is due to a combination of industry shocks for which mergers facilitate change to the new environment, or whether such clustering is due to market timing.

The results presented here support a neoclassical explanation of merger waves: merger waves occur in response to specific industry shocks that require large scale reallocation of assets. However, these shocks are not enough on their own. There must be sufficient capital liquidity to accommodate the asset reallocation. The increase in capital liquidity and reduction in financing constraints that is correlated with high asset values must be present for the shock to propagate a wave. Variables that separately measure capital liquidity and market valuations suggest that the observed relation between high stock market valuations and merger waves has been misattributed to behavioral misvaluation factors. Rather, the relation is actually driven by the higher capital liquidity (lower transaction costs) that accompanies an economic expansion.

Thus, the explanation for merger waves is intuitive: merger waves require both an economic motivation for transactions and relatively low transaction costs to generate a large volume of transactions. The influence of this macro-level liquidity factor causes industry merger waves to cluster in time even if industry shocks do not.

This study proceeds by using a sample of industry-level merger waves in the 1980s and 1990s to test the behavioral and neoclassical hypotheses about the causes of merger waves. The first test examines the characteristics of the industries before merger waves. The set of characteristics is designed to capture economic shocks to an industry's operating environment. One potential economic characteristic, the market-to-book (M/B) ratio, is ambiguous because it is also claimed by the behavioral hypothesis. However, the behavioral models rely on both high valuations and dispersion in valuations, so I include the cross-sectional standard deviation of the M/B ratio, the average 1- and 3-year stock returns, and the cross-sectional standard deviation of those returns.

Since economic shocks could have different effects across firms and, further, since different shocks across industries could have different average directional implications, I use the median absolute change in the economic characteristics to measure economic shocks. I find that waves are directly preceded by abnormally large absolute changes in most of the economic characteristics studied. As for the behavioral variables, M/B ratios are also abnormally high and the 1- and 3-year returns are marginally high, but the standard deviations of these measures are not.

Building on this first set of tests, I employ successive logit models to predict the start of an industry merger wave. Industry median M/B alone has some predictive power. However, once it is included with the economic variables, it becomes insignificant. The industry-specific economic shock measures predict waves, but only when capital liquidity is also high. An index of major deregulatory events and a measure of capital liquidity adds sharply to the predictive power of the model. Finally, on their own, the behavioral variables (prior industry return, the standard deviation of this return, and including M/B in this set) have only a fair ability to predict merger waves, and they add only marginally to the predictive power of the neoclassical model, which uses industry-specific shocks, deregulation, and liquidity.

Following the examination of the causes of industry-level merger waves, the next step is to connect the industry-level waves to aggregate merger activity. I show that the vast majority of activity in aggregate merger waves is being driven by the clustering of the industry merger waves identified here. Further, a model of aggregate merger activity that takes into account industry shocks and overall capital liquidity further supports the role of these factors rather than behavioral ones in causing aggregate clustering of merger activity.

One prediction distinguishing between the behavioral and neoclassical hypotheses of merger waves centers on acquisitions of firms' divisions for cash. Since the neoclassical hypothesis predicts that capital will be reallocated as quickly and efficiently as possible, it follows that not all transactions will be for whole firms and that not all transactions will use stock as the method of payment. Under the behavioral hypothesis, there is no underlying reason for a merger wave other than the desire by managers to use overvalued stock to acquire the assets of less overvalued firms. Thus, while stock swap mergers are predicted by the behavioral hypothesis, cash-financed partial-firm (divisional) acquisitions are not. Consequently, in the next set of tests, I examine the relation between firm-level and partial-firm-level acquisition activity. There is a strong time-series correlation between the proportion of an industry involved in firm-level mergers and the proportion involved in partial-firm acquisitions. This correlation holds even when only stock swap mergers are compared to cash partial-firm acquisitions. Further, at the firm level, being a bidder (even a stock bidder) strongly predicts being a partial-firm acquirer (even for cash). These results are directly implied by the neoclassical explanation of merger waves, but are inconsistent with the behavioral explanation.

The focus of the behavioral hypothesis on asset misvaluation warrants a further examination of the returns surrounding merger waves. Using the Fama (1998) calendar-time approach, I examine the returns of the portfolios of firms in each industry over the 20-year sample period. Fama-French three-factor adjusted returns in the period immediately before, during, or following a wave are not significantly different from the returns of nonwave periods. Only unadjusted value-weighted returns show the typically observed pattern of relatively high returns before and during a wave followed by relatively low returns after the wave. This finding is not robust to equal weighting, suggesting that if anything, it is large firms that experience poor postwave performance. The evidence does not suggest that managers in these industries are taking advantage of temporary mispricing of their industries, but rather, that the capital liquidity that a business expansion and accompanying bull market provide allows industry-level merger waves to occur. Examining only the returns of bidders, I find that there is some evidence in the value-weighted returns of postbid underperformance by bidders in waves using stock. This finding is also not robust to equal weighting.

The tests conclude with an examination of changes in operating performance, a valuation measure, and analyst forecasts following mergers. I argue that augmenting traditional operating performance tests with changes in analyst forecasts mitigates the benchmarking problem typical of these tests, specifically, that the empiricist cannot observe the expected performance absent a merger to compare it to postmerger performance. I present evidence that changes in both forecasts and actual operating performance following mergers in waves are not worse than (and by some measures are better than) changes following nonwave mergers.

The next section briefly reviews the literature and establishes the framework for testing the hypotheses. Section 3 describes the data and identification of merger waves. Section 4 presents the empirical tests and results, and Section 5 concludes.

2. Literature review and hypothesis development

It is well known that merger waves exist (see, e.g., Brealey and Myers, 2003). Mitchell and Mulherin (1996) document clear clustering of waves within industries and tie that clustering to various technological, economic, or regulatory shocks to those industries. They suggest that a systematic analysis of industry shocks and merger activity may shed light on understanding merger waves. The industry-level clustering of mergers is confirmed for the 1990s in Mulherin and Boone (2000) and Andrade et al. (2001). Nonetheless, there is no consensus as to why merger waves occur. The competing explanations can be broadly categorized into two groups: neoclassical and behavioral.

2.1. Neoclassical hypothesis

Neoclassical explanations of rational merger waves (see, e.g., Gort, 1969) are based on an economic disturbance that leads to industry reorganization. Coase (1937) is one of the earliest to argue that technological change leads to mergers. More recently, Jovanovic and Rousseau (2001, 2002) put forth models under which technological change and subsequent increased dispersion in q ratios lead to high-q firms taking over low-q firms in waves. Maksimovic and Phillips (2001) use performance improvements at the plant-level to support a neoclassical theory of merger waves.

Building on recent work on capital liquidity, this paper suggests a role for capital liquidity in a neoclassical hypothesis of merger waves. Eisfeldt and Rampini (2003) show that variation in capital liquidity strongly impacts the degree of total (industrial, household, and labor) capital reallocation in the economy and further that the degree of capital liquidity is cyclical. While they do not explicitly study market valuations, I argue that because higher market valuations relax financing constraints, market valuations are an important component of capital liquidity. Shleifer and Vishny (1992) make a similar argument in a study of asset liquidity, showing that in order for transactions to occur, buyers who intend to employ the asset in its first-best use must be relatively unconstrained. This allows prices offered to be close to fundamental values. Shleifer and Vishny hypothesize that the reason merger waves always occur in booms is because increases in cash flows simultaneously increase fundamental values and relax financial constraints, bringing prices closer to fundamental values. Empirical evidence by Harford (1999) supports this argument by showing that firms that have built up large cash reserves are more active in the acquisition market. Recently, Schlingemann et al. (2002) show that industry-specific asset liquidity is important in determining which assets will be divested.

To summarize, under the neoclassical hypothesis, once a technological, regulatory, or economic shock to an industry's environment occurs, the collective reaction of firms inside and outside the industry is such that industry assets are reallocated through mergers and partial-firm acquisitions. This activity clusters in time as managers simultaneously react and then compete for the best combinations of assets. The capital liquidity argument modifies the neoclassical hypothesis of waves to predict that only when sufficient capital liquidity exists to accommodate the reallocation of assets, will an industry shock generate a merger wave. Thus, even if industry shocks do not cluster in time, the importance of capital liquidity means that industry merger waves as reactions to shocks will cluster in time to create aggregate merger waves.

2.2. Behavioral hypothesis

Recent theoretical work has addressed the observed positive correlation between stock valuations and merger activity, which has been noted by Golbe and White (1988), among others. Shleifer and Vishny (2003) argue that we observe clustering in merger activity because a substantial portion of merger activity is driven by stock market valuations. They posit that bull markets lead groups of bidders with overvalued stock to use the stock to buy real assets of undervalued targets through mergers. Coupled with sufficiently high misperceived merger synergies in the marketplace, Shleifer and Vishny's model allows for (less) overvalued targets as well, relying mainly on dispersion in valuations. Target managers with short time horizons are willing to accept the bidder's temporarily overvalued equity. Overvaluation in the aggregate or in certain industries would lead to wave-like clustering in time. Contemporaneously, Rhodes-Kropf and Viswanathan (2004) develop a model of rational managerial behavior and uncertainty about sources of misvaluation that also would lead to a correlation between market performance and merger waves. In their model, rational targets without perfect information will accept more bids from overvalued bidders during market valuation peaks because they overestimate synergies during these periods. The greater transaction flow produces a merger wave. Their model differs from that of Shleifer and

Vishny in that target managers rationally accept overvalued equity because of imperfect information about the degree of synergies rather than shorter time horizons. Nonetheless, because both explanations rely at least partly on bidders taking advantage of temporary misvaluations and also on dispersion in misvaluations in the market, they can be grouped as behavioral hypotheses.

In a follow-up empirical study, Rhodes-Kropf et al. (2004) show that aggregate merger waves occur when market valuations, measured as M/B ratios, are high relative to true valuations, estimated using residual income models or industry multiples. However, they note that their results are consistent with both the behavioral mispricing stories and the interpretation that merger activity spikes when growth opportunities are high or when firm-specific discount rates are low. This latter interpretation is similar to a neoclassical hypothesis with a capital liquidity component. Nonetheless, further tests lead them to favor a mispricing explanation. Dong et al. (2003) and Ang and Cheng (2003) also use accounting numbers to estimate a fundamental value and find evidence consistent with the behavioral explanation of merger activity. Verter (2002) confirms that the level and dispersion of stock market valuations are correlated with merger activity, especially mergers for stock. While Rhodes-Kropf et al. (2004) recognize alternative interpretations of their evidence and try to distinguish between competing explanations, the other studies that examine the behavioral hypothesis tend to only provide evidence consistent with behavioral explanations, rather than considering both neoclassical and behavioral hypotheses and then formally rejecting the neoclassical.

2.3. Specific predictions

The behavioral hypothesis asserts that mergers happen when managers use overvalued stock to buy the assets of lower valued firms. To generate a merger wave, this requires waves of high valuations for enough firms. Consequently, the behavioral hypothesis makes the following predictions: (1) Merger waves will occur following periods of abnormally high stock returns or M/B ratios, especially when dispersion in those returns or ratios is large; (2) Industries undergoing waves will experience abnormally poor returns following the height of the wave; (3) As there is no economic driver to the wave, identifiable economic or regulatory shocks will not systematically precede the wave; (4) The method of payment in a wave should be overwhelmingly that of stock, such that cash mergers should not increase in frequency during waves; and, as a corollary; (5) Because the wave is being driven by the acquisition of real assets with overvalued stock, partial-firm (divisional) transactions for cash should not be common and they should be especially rare by firms that are bidding for other firms with stock.

Alternatively, the neoclassical hypothesis asserts that merger waves occur when industries react to shocks to their operating environment. If the efficient response to a shock requires a reallocation of assets, then some firms acquire either all or part of the assets of other firms through mergers and partial-firm transactions. Observable economic or regulatory shocks will precede waves. The method of payment will be either stock or cash, and partial-firm transactions for cash will be observed. The same firm might engage in both a stock swap merger and a cash partial-firm transaction. The capital liquidity component of this explanation predicts that credit constraints will be low and/or asset values will be high.

One can also use postmerger operating performance to distinguish between the neoclassical and behavioral explanations. Some authors, such as Shleifer and Vishny (2003), argue that the neoclassical hypothesis is lacking because it predicts performance improvements following a merger and the extant evidence on this is mixed at best (see Agrawal and Jaffe, 2003, for a review of the evidence). However, when the neoclassical hypothesis is applied to merger waves, it does not necessarily predict that raw performance will improve following mergers in a wave. The neoclassical hypothesis predicts that performance of the combined firms will be better than it would have been without the merger. In many circumstances, prior performance is a reasonable proxy for performance without the merger. In a merger wave, however, this proxy is much worse than usual because in a wave, the firms are responding to an industry shock.

Due to the changes the industry is undergoing and the endogeneity of the choice to merge, the contemporaneous performance of the industry also is a problematic proxy. All firms are likely to restructure in some way (either externally or internally) in response to the industry shock, and thus there is no reason to expect that the performance of the merging parties should outperform the benchmark. One could observe a performance decline following a merger, but relative to what would have happened in the absence of the merger, this result may be the better outcome. Thus, the neoclassical hypothesis predicts that performance will improve relative to the unobservable unmerged performance. Any empirical test of this hypothesis implicitly tests the joint hypothesis that the empirical benchmark is a good proxy for the unobservable benchmark and that performance improves relative to this benchmark. I argue that using traditional proxies for the unobservable benchmark is likely to lead to the rejection of the first part of the joint hypothesis.

Although I believe that the joint hypothesis problem makes examination of operating performance changes inherently problematic, in the interest of completeness I report the results of such tests. To mitigate the joint hypothesis problem, I use both traditional industry benchmarks and analyst forecasts. Using I/B/E/S data, I compare analyst forecasts of the sample firms' long-term performance before the announcement of the merger to forecasts made after the completion of the merger. Under the assumption that analysts have already incorporated the expected impact of the industry shock into their forecasts prior to the merger, the premerger forecast should be a good proxy for the unobservable unmerged performance.

The neoclassical hypothesis predicts that analyst performance forecasts will increase postmerger. One can also derive a prediction under the behavioral hypothesis. Because in the behavioral framework mergers in waves have no underlying economic rationale and no real synergies, there are no benefits to offset the costs of integration. Thus, the merged firm should endure especially poor postmerger operating performance.

Table 1

Predictions of the neoclassical and behavioral hypotheses for merger waves

	Neoclassical	Behavioral	Finding
Cause of industry wave	Regulatory or economic shock accompanied by capital liquidity	Overvaluation and dispersion of valuation within industry	Regulatory and economic shocks accompanied by capital liquidity
Cause of aggregate wave	Multiple simultaneous industry waves clustering because of macro liquidity factor	Overvaluation and dispersion in the aggregate	Multiple simultaneous industry waves clustering because of macro liquidity factor
Cash partial-firm acquisitions	Increase during wave; could be made by stock bidders	Do not increase during wave; are not made by stock bidders	Increase during waves and are made by stock bidders
Prewave returns and market-to-book ratios	High if capital liquidity is tied to asset valuation	High	High
Dispersion in prewave returns	No prediction	High	Normal
Postwave returns	No prediction	Low	Normal
Measures of tight credit	Low if capital liquidity is important	No prediction	Low
Postmerger operating performance	Better than without a merger	Worse in waves	Similar/better in waves

Under the null of the behavioral hypothesis, performance forecasts following mergers in waves should be worse than average.

Table 1 summarizes the predictions of the behavioral and neoclassical hypotheses of merger waves. The table also previews the empirical findings of Section 4.

3. Data and merger wave identification

I start with all merger or tender-offer bids recorded by Thomson Financial's Securities Data Company (SDC) between 1981 and 2000 with a transaction value of at least $50 million. I assign each bidder and target to one of 48 industry groups based on their SIC code recorded by SDC at the time of the announcement.[1] Because the 1980s and 1990s were characterized by two distinct aggregate merger waves, with a substantial trough surrounding the 1990–1991 recession, I split the sample into the 1980s and 1990s. Based on Mitchell and Mulherin's (1996) study of 2-year wave periods, waves in this

---

[1] These industry groupings are the same 48 groups used in Fama and French (1997), and are detailed in the appendix of that paper.

paper will be 24 months. Thus, for each industry, I calculate the highest 24-month concentration of merger bids involving firms in that industry in each decade.[2] This 24-month period is identified as a potential wave. Taking the total number of bids over the entire decade for a given industry, I simulate 1000 distributions of that number of occurrences of industry member involvement in a bid over a 120-month period by randomly assigning each occurrence to a month where the probability of assignment is 1/120 for each month. I then calculate the highest 24-month concentration of activity from each of the 1000 draws. Finally, I compare the actual concentration of activity from the potential wave to the empirical distribution of 1000 peak 24-month concentrations. If the actual peak concentration exceeds the 95th percentile from that empirical distribution, that period is coded as a wave. For example, 36% of the 161 bids in the health care industry in the 1990s occurred within one 24-month period starting in May 1996. Out of 1000 simulated distributions of 161 bids across a 10-year period, the 95th percentile of maximum concentration within any 24-month period is 27%. Thus, the cluster of bids in the health care industry starting in May 1996 is coded as a wave.

The end result is 35 waves from 28 industries (seven of which have two distinct waves, one in the 1980s and one in the 1990s). The industries and their waves are described in Table 2. Over the 20-year sampling period, the average number of bids any one of these 28 industries sees in a 24-month nonwave period is 7.8 while the average number of bids it sees during a 24-month wave is 34.3.

4. Results

I start with an examination of the two sets of factors predicted by the behavioral and neoclassical hypotheses to be associated with merger waves. One set of factors captures economic shocks to an industry's operating environment. These factors are: cash flow margin on sales (cash flow scaled by sales), asset turnover (sales divided by beginning-of-period assets), research and development (scaled by beginning-of-period assets), capital expenditures (scaled by beginning-of-period assets), employee growth, return on assets (ROA), and sales growth. These variables are motivated by papers such as Healy et al. (1992), who look at efficiency measures affecting performance around mergers and Mitchell and Mulherin (1996), who examine sales, employment, and regulatory shocks and industry merger activity in the 1980s. One other potential economic characteristic, the *M/B* ratio, is ambiguous because it is also claimed by the behavioral hypothesis. The set of factors chosen to more directly examine the behavioral hypothesis' reliance on market timing includes the cross-sectional standard

---

[2] If the bidder is in industry X and the target is in industry Y, then the bid will count toward merger activity in that month for both industry X and Y. If the bidder and target are both in industry X, then the bid will count once toward the merger activity for industry X for that month (it will not be double counted). Multiple bids for a single target within a 2-month period only count as one contest when calculating merger activity in that industry.

Table 2

Industries with merger waves

The industries and starting dates of the merger waves comes from the procedure described in Section 3. The reasons for the wave come from Lexis-Nexis searches of news reports analyzing the merger activity at the time of the wave.

Industry	Date wave started and reason given
Aircraft	January 1999
	Big, older fleets require increased maintenance, repair and overhaul
	Increasingly outsourced from carriers, who want "one-stop shops"
Banking	August 1985
	Deregulation allows interstate banking, particularly in California
	October 1996
	Deregulation and information technology (IT)
Business services	October 1986
	Partially IT-driven mergers as IT becomes important
	September 1998
	Fragmented, smaller players combine, share cost structures, offer more complete line of services to customers—industry grows as outsourcing takes off
Business supplies	January 1997
	Paper and pulp industry consolidates from fragmented price takers to gain market power and avoid costly duplication of capital intensive production facilities
Candy and soda	April 1992
	Snapple and other noncarbonated beverages make strides, leading to activity to beat or buy them
Chemicals	March 1995
	Large cash flows, over capacity in production, need to consolidate research
Communication	November 1987
	Deregulation: Break-up of AT&T in 1984 followed by entry into long distance, investment in fiber optic capacity, etc.
	July 1997
	Deregulation: Telecommunications Act in 1996, consolidation, technological changes
Computers	July 1998
	Internet
Consumer goods	August 1986
	Mature market and the need to offer full line leads to consolidation
Electrical equipment	June 1986
	Several companies seek growth through acquisition to compete better with industry leaders Westinghouse and General Electric
Electronic equipment	January 1999
	OEM's growth leads to demand for electronic equipment manufacturers to shift from small regional players to larger global players capable of infrastructure, IT, etc. to grow with their customers
Entertainment	October 1987
	Deregulation allows firms to own many stations
	March 1998
	Studios seek diversified production sources and strong libraries; Telecom Act of 1996 relaxes media ownership limits
Food products	January 1999
	Retail consolidation pushes distribution consolidation and/or sale of distributors to bigger retailers who want to buy rather than build distribution channels

(Continued)

Table 2 (*Continued*)

Industry	Date wave started and reason given
Healthcare	May 1996
	Service providers consolidate to have bargaining power with HMOs
Insurance	November 1998
	Bigger is safer, leading to consolidation, especially in reinsurers
Machinery	May 1996
	Large manufacturers decreased number of suppliers they were willing to deal with in bid to improve efficiency. This forced consolidation in a number of capital goods industries—many smaller players were bought in "roll-up" deals
Measuring and control equipment	November 1998
	Depression in semiconductor industry (big customer)
Medical equipment	November 1998
	Two motives: first, acquisitions in core areas to grow, then acquisitions outside core areas to offer broad products to increasingly consolidated customer base (hospitals)
Personal services	February 1996
	Consolidation in legal and funeral services industries
Petroleum and natural gas	June 1997
	Increasing prices, record drilling, increasing costs lead drive to increase size to be more efficient
Pharmaceutical products	October 1998
	Midsized companies merge to garner size necessary to fund increasingly large costs of development
Restaurants, hotels, motels	March 1985
	Saturation and similarity, trends toward take-out, competition from supermarket delis
	December 1996
	Operators such as Starwood have buying sprees. Others buy properties to gain sufficient bulk to compete in corporate account business market
Retail	October 1986
	Shift to specialty stores as aging department stores consolidated; value of land and buildings in revitalized urban centers
	August 1996
	Strong growth and impact of Internet
Shipbuilding, railroad equipment	August 1998
	Shrinking defense budgets finally forced the issue of overcapacity in the industry
Steel works	September 1997
	Collapse in demand from Asia leads to falling prices forcing consolidation
Transportation	August 1986
	Mostly still working out issues following deregulation
	July 1997
	End of Interstate Commerce Commission, overcapacity in shipping, open-skies agreements, railroad consolidation started with a few big mergers and then forced responses to balance
Utilities	November 1997
	Deregulation in some markets plus elimination of a law prohibiting mergers between noncontiguous providers
Wholesale	June 1996
	Simultaneous consolidation in several wholesale sectors as growth slows and firms move to add breadth, take advantage of new IT ability, grow by acquisition

deviation of the *M/B* ratio and the average 1- and 3-year stock returns and cross-sectional standard deviation of those returns.

4.1. Univariate evidence

The tests examine the above two sets of industry characteristics before merger waves. All variables are examined in the year prior to the start of an industry's merger wave. Thus, out of 28 industries each with a 20-year history, there are 35 industry-years preceding the start of a merger wave. The results are summarized in Table 3. Since economic shocks could have different effects across firms, and further, since different shocks across industries could have different average directional implications, I use the median absolute change in each of the above variables to measure economic shocks. The number presented in the table is the mean, across all industries, of this industry-specific median in the year immediately preceding the start of the merger wave. For each industry, I also rank the time series of 20 shock observations into quartiles and present the cross-industry mean rank of the shock in the prewave year. The table shows that changes to profitability, asset turnover, R&D, capital expenditures, employee growth, ROA, and sales growth are all abnormally high prior to waves. The time-series ranks show that the prewave changes were high for the average industry, and the (untabulated) medians establish that the changes were at least in the third quartile of the industry's own history of changes.

Turning to the variables that are related to both the behavioral and neoclassical hypotheses, one sees that *M/B*, the change in *M/B*, and the intraindustry dispersion of *M/B* are all abnormally high in the year preceding a wave. The stock return variables motivated by behavioral hypothesis are less conclusive. While all are relatively high before the start of a wave, they are not significantly abnormally high relative to each industry's history of returns. I examined the pattern of returns further and found that while returns are higher than average before an industry merger wave, the relation is weak because the highest returns for most industries do not precede their waves. Thus, the strongest relation between a measure of valuation and waves found here is for *M/B* rather than returns.

Shocks to an industry environment can also come from major regulatory changes. Panel B of Table 3 documents major deregulatory events over the sample period and identifies which industries were affected by those events. A comparison of the panel and the starts of the waves suggests a relation which will be explored further in the next section.

Applying the capital liquidity arguments advanced by Shleifer and Vishny (1992) and Eisfeldt and Rampini (2003) to merger waves suggests that a macro component which proxies for capital liquidity should help explain waves. One proxy is provided by the Federal Reserve Senior Loan Officer (SLO) survey. The Federal Reserve surveys SLOs across the nation on a quarterly basis, asking them whether over the previous quarter they had tightened or eased credit standards for commercial lending.

Table 3

(Panel A) Measures of economic shocks and stock valuation

The state of the industry in the year before a merger wave is summarized. Several variables are used to measure economic shocks to the industry: net income/sales (profitability), asset turnover, R&D, capital expenditures, employee growth, ROA, and sales growth. The median absolute change in each of above variables is computed for each industry-year. Market-to-book and dispersion in market-to-book are either economic variables or misvaluation proxies. Stock valuation is also addressed by the median prior 1- and 3-year compounded return for firms in the industry along with the intraindustry dispersion of that return. For all variables, the number presented in the table is the mean, across all industries, of this industry-specific median in the year immediately preceding the start of the merger wave (there are 35 industry-year observations for this prewave year). For each industry, the 20-year time series of shock observations is ranked into quartiles and the cross-industry mean rank of the shock in the prewave year is presented. A test is performed on the average difference between a rank of 2.5 (middle) and the ranking of the prewave year within its own industry time series. The p-value for the hypothesis that this difference is zero is presented in brackets.

Economic shocks (variables related to the neoclassical hypotheses)	Mean	Rank	Stock valuation (variables related to the behavioral hypotheses)	Mean	Rank
Net income/sales	0.030	2.83	3-year return	0.638	2.66
H_0: Rank = 2.5		[0.100]	H_0: Rank = 2.5		[0.372]
Asset turnover	0.096	2.77	σ(3-year return)	1.317	2.60
H_0: Rank = 2.5		[0.076]	H_0: Rank = 2.5		[0.372]
R&D	0.004	2.86	1-year return	0.132	2.66
H_0: Rank = 2.5		[0.007]	H_0: Rank = 2.5		[0.328]
Capital expenditures	0.023	2.80	σ (1-year Return)	0.566	2.74
H_0: Rank = 2.5		[0.109]	H_0: Rank = 2.5		[0.152]
Employee growth	0.128	2.97	Market-to-book variables (related to both hypotheses)		
H_0: Rank = 2.5		[0.008]	Market-to-book	1.563	3.14
ROA	0.040	2.80	H_0: Rank = 2.5		[0.001]
H_0: Rank = 2.5		[0.066]	Industry σ(market-to-book)	1.201	3.11
Sales growth	0.128	3.03	H_0: Rank = 2.5		[0.001]
H_0: Rank = 2.5		[0.003]	Change in market-to-book	0.022	2.86
			H_0: Rank = 2.5		[0.055]

(Panel B) This table lists the major deregulatory initiatives during the sample period and is constructed from Viscusi et al. (2000), Economics of Regulation and Antitrust, Tables 10.2 and 10.3

Year	Deregulatory event	Industry affected
1981	Decontrol of crude oil and refined petroleum products (executive order)	Petrol and natural gas
	Deregulation of radio (FCC)	Entertainment
1982	Garn-St. Germain Depository Institutions Act	Banking
	AT&T settlement	Communications
1984	Cable Television Deregulation Act	Entertainment
	Shipping Act	Transportation
1987	Elimination of fairness doctrine (FCC)	Entertainment
1989	Natural Gas Wellhead Decontrol Act of 1989	Petrol and natural gas
1991	Federal Deposit Insurance Corporation Improvement Act	Banking
1992	Cable Television Consumer Protection and Competition	Entertainment
	Energy Policy Act	Petrol and natural gas
	FERC Order 636	Utilities
1993	Elimination of state regulation of cellular telephone rates	Communications
	Negotiated Rates Act	Transportation
1994	Trucking Industry and Regulatory Reform Act	Transportation
	Interstate Banking and Branching Efficiency Act	Banking
1995	Interstate Commerce Commission Termination Act	Transportation
1996	Telecommunications Act	Communications
	FERC Order 888	Utilities

Lown et al. (2000) show that the SLO survey forecasts not only commercial loan growth but also overall economic activity and narrower measures such as inventory investment and industrial production. They find evidence of a series of events characteristic of a credit crunch—credit standards tighten, commercial loans contract sharply, and output falls. Unfortunately, the Federal Reserve did not ask the question between 1984 and 1990. Nonetheless, Lown et al. (2000) find that the degree to which the SLO survey reports tightening is strongly correlated with the spread between the average interest rate on commercial and industrial (C&I) loans and the Federal Funds rate. This spread has been collected consistently over the entire sample period. I do not argue that the availability of C&I credit has a direct causal effect for merger activity. Indeed, equity mergers do not require access to the credit markets. Instead, I assert that, based on the results of the Lown et al. paper, the rate spread may be used as a proxy for overall liquidity or ease of financing (in whatever form) in the economy. In the neoclassical model with transaction costs, the rate spread will be correlated with transaction costs. Based on the argument that higher asset values accommodate capital liquidity in an industry, the empirical specifications to test the model will also include an industry-specific interaction variable that accounts for the valuation levels in the industry.

The four-quarter moving average of the rate spread is plotted against aggregate merger activity in Figure 1. The figure displays an inverse relation (with a slight lag) between the rate spread and aggregate merger activity. A decrease in the rate spread precedes an increase in merger activity and an increase in the rate spread signals the end of a merger wave. Figure 1 also contains bars showing the timing of individual industry merger waves. Industry merger waves tend to cluster when the rate spread is relatively low, creating aggregate merger waves.

One might expect the transaction costs proxy, the rate spread, to be correlated with some of the key variables in the behavioral models. Figure 2 shows that the level of the rate spread is correlated with both overall median M/B and the 3-year compounded return on the S&P 500 index. However, as suggested by Figure 2, the rate spread leads the M/B ratio. Decreases in the rate spread lead to increases in the M/B ratio; the correlation between lagged changes in the rate spread and current changes in the M/B ratio is a significant -0.38. The reverse is not true; the correlation between lagged changes in the M/B ratio and current changes in the rate spread is an insignificant -0.03. This is consistent with the evidence presented in Lown et al. (2000) on the effects of changes in the ease of credit on overall economic growth. A decrease in the rate spread leads to increased economic growth, potentially lower risk-premiums, and as shown later, greater merger and acquisition activity. All of these would have the effect of causing an increase in M/B ratios.

The only correlation between changes in the rate spread and the S&P500 return is a marginally significant lagged positive relation, which is opposite of what would need to be present for the rate spread to simply be capturing the stock return effects of a market-timing explanation. The correlation between lagged S&P500 returns and

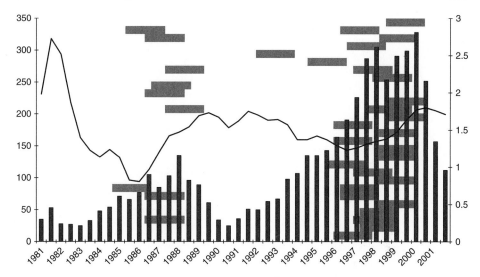

Fig. 1. Capital liquidity, industry merger waves, and aggregate merger activity. The line is the spread between the average rate charged for commercial and industrial loans and the fed funds rate, reported in the Federal Reserve's Survey of Terms of Business Lending (right axis). This spread is measured in percentage points and proxies for low capital liquidity. The horizontal bars mark the timing of the industry-level merger wave periods in this study (e.g., the top-most bar represents an industry-level merger wave starting in the latter half of 1998 and ending in the first half of 2000). The vertical bars represent the total number of merger bids with a transaction value of at least $50 million in 2002 dollars (left axis).

current changes in the rate spread is 0.39. Thus, after periods of strong growth, the rate spread starts to rise. While these results should mitigate concerns about the relation between the liquidity variable and traditional behavioral variables, one might still harbor doubts. In the multivariate tests, I attempt to control for the behavioral variables in testing the explanatory power of the liquidity variable.

The results thus far present definite indications that economic factors drive merger waves. Observable economic and deregulatory shocks precede industry merger waves and those merger waves cluster when transaction costs are low enough so that capital liquidity is relatively high. Nonetheless, if one counts the level and dispersion of *M/B* as behavioral hypothesis variables, then the evidence on them is still consistent with a role for the behavioral explanation. In the next test, I distinguish between these two interpretations by employing successive logit models to predict merger waves. The successive logits will also bear on the interpretation of the relation between the rate spread and the behavioral variables. Since the behavioral variables will be included in the regression, if the rate spread is actually a proxy for those variables, it will be insignificant. If, instead, the behavioral variables are simply capturing effects correlated with the rate spread, then they will be insignificant.

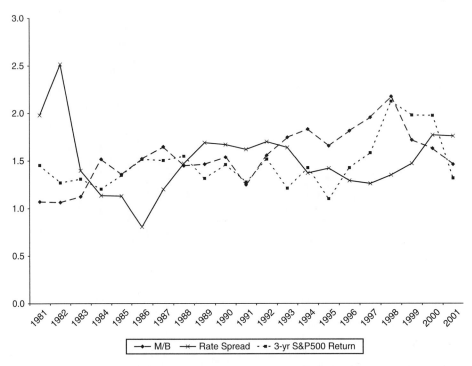

Fig. 2. Time-series relation between the rate spread variable and variables commonly used in behavioral explanations of merger waves. The rate spread is the spread between the average commercial and industrial loan rate and the Fed Funds rate, as collected by the Federal Reserve in its Survey of Terms of Business Lending. This spread is measured in percentage points and proxies for low capital liquidity. The *M/B* time series is the median *M/B* ratio of all firms on Compustat each year. Finally, 3-year S&P500 Return is one plus the compounded prior 3-year return on the S&P500 index. All series are scaled to use the left axis (e.g., 1.5 represents a rate spread of 1.5 percentage points, a median *M/B* ratio of 1.5, and 50% compound return on the S&P500 index).

4.2. Logit models

Table 4 presents the results of estimating logit models of merger wave starts. The sample is all 48 industries for the 20-year sample period. The explanatory variables come from those analyzed in Table 3. One problem with the industry-specific economic shock variables is that they are highly correlated within an industry and cause multicollinearity if simultaneously included in a regression model. To address this problem, I extract the first principal component from the seven economic shock variables (profitability, asset turnover, R&D, capital expenditures, employee growth, ROA, and sales growth). The capital liquidity part of the neoclassical hypothesis predicts that these shocks will be less likely to propagate a wave when liquidity is low. High liquidity years would be years in which the rate spread is below its time-series median and the industry's *M/B* ratio is simultaneously above its time-series

Table 4

Predicting merger waves

Logit models are used to predict when an industry will have a merger wave. The sample is 48 industries, each over 20 years (1981–2000). The dependent variable in the first four columns is equal to one if the industry-year is the beginning of a merger wave in that industry. The explanatory variables are measured at the end of year $t - 1$. Market-to-book is the industry median market-to-book ratio, 3-year return and σ(3-year return) are the median return in the industry for the 3 years ending at the end of year $t - 1$ and the intraindustry standard deviation of that return, and the C&I loan rate spread (spread above the fed funds rate) proxies for low capital liquidity. There is also a dummy variable selecting years that were preceded by a major deregulatory event. The economic shock index is the first principal component of the seven economic shock variables in the first column of Table 3. The shock index is also interacted with a dummy variable selecting years when market-to-book ratios are below their industry-specific time-series median or the C&I rate spread is above its time-series median (years of low capital liquidity).

The last three columns regress an indicator for aggregate merger activity on aggregate versions of the independent variables. There are 20 observations, one for each year from 1981 to 2000. The dependent variable identifies whether aggregate merger activity is in the top, middle, or bottom third of the time series of merger activity over the sample period. Aggregate merger activity is defined as the fraction of firms in the population involved in merger activity (as a target or bidder) in a given year. Years in the top third can be thought of as merger wave years (the years are 1986–1988 and 1996–1999). The independent variables are weighted averages of the industry-level variables for that year, where the weights are the number of firms in the industry. For example, the economic shock index is the average economic shock index across all industries, weighted by the number of firms in each industry.

	(1)	(2)	(3)	(4)	(5)	(6)	(7)
Intercept	-4.445	-4.450	-2.980	-3.320	-0.713	3.499	2.306
	[<0.0001]	[<0.0001]	[<0.0001]	[<0.0001]	[0.074]	[0.001]	[0.173]
M/B_{t-1}	0.847	0.840		0.165	2.172		0.520
	[0.017]	[0.031]		[0.745]	[0.002]		[0.297]
3-year return$_{t-1}$		0.152		-0.109	1.027		0.426
		[0.736]		[0.850]	[0.216]		[0.463]
σ(3-year return)$_{t-1}$		-0.059		0.250	-0.790		0.015
		[0.846]		[0.492]	[0.203]		[0.973]
C&I rate spread$_{t-1}$			-0.521	-0.567		-1.079	-0.998
			[0.032]	[0.026]		[0.004]	[0.011]
Deregulatory event$_{t-1}$			1.872	1.930		3.313	2.166
			[0.025]	[0.023]		[0.291]	[0.488]
Econ shock index$_{t-1}$			0.452	0.369		1.137	1.000
			[0.007]	[0.091]		[0.001]	[0.003]
Econ shock index$_{t-1}$* (tight capital)			-0.917	-0.881		-0.290	-0.205
			[0.001]	[0.002]		[0.083]	[0.268]
Adj. R^2					0.356	0.774	0.786
Pseudo-R^2	0.016	0.017	0.151	0.154			
Correlation of prediction with waves	0.079	0.075	0.240	0.248			

median. Thus, low liquidity years would be all other years. The economic shock principal component will enter the logit models both on its own and interacted with a dummy identifying low liquidity years.

The first column of Table 4 shows that industry *M/B* by itself has some ability to predict merger waves.[3] The second column adds the industry 3-year return and intraindustry standard deviation of this return for the full set of variables motivated by behavioral explanations.[4] For each model, one can correlate the actual occurrence of a wave in a given industry-year with the probability of a wave generated by the model. These correlations are tabulated in the last row of the table. Column 2 reports that the correlation between the behavioral-predicted probability of a merger wave and the actual occurrence of a merger wave is 0.08, significant at the 4% level.

In Column 3, the model is estimated using only the economic variables. Notably, the shock variable is positive and significant, but the shock variable interacted with the dummy variable for low liquidity is negative and significant (and the sum of the two is insignificant). Both the deregulation indicator variable and the rate spread variable are strongly significant. The deregulatory variable is consistent with similar findings in Mitchell and Mulherin (1996) for the 1980s. These results confirm the univariate results supporting the neoclassical hypothesis. The correlation between the predicted probabilities of this model and the actual occurrence of a wave is 0.24, significant at less than the 1% level.

Finally, the full model is estimated in Column 4. The stock return and standard deviation of stock return remain insignificant and *M/B* becomes insignificant. The fact that *M/B* predicts merger waves is generally cited as evidence in favor of the behavioral hypothesis. However, Column 5 shows that the *M/B* variable is subsumed by the shock and rate spread variables. This suggests that the *M/B* variable is in fact proxying for lower transaction costs that come with greater capital liquidity. The results for the neoclassical variables are qualitatively unchanged. The correlation between the predicted probabilities of the full model and the actual waves is 0.25, significant at better than the 1% level. The addition of the behavioral variables (even counting *M/B* as a behavioral variable) to the neoclassical variables increases the correlation between the probabilities and actual waves by only 0.01, from 0.24 to 0.25. The results of the full model support the neoclassical hypothesis over the behavioral one. They further suggest that variables associated with behavioral explanations are actually proxying for an important economic condition that is necessary, but not sufficient, for merger waves: capital liquidity.

---

[3] The intraindustry standard deviation of market-to-book is too highly correlated with the industry median level of market-to-book for both to enter the specification at the same time. When the specifications are estimated replacing the level of market-to-book with the standard deviation, the results for the standard deviation are qualitatively the same, but with marginally higher *p*-values than the results tabulated for the level. The other results are unaffected.

[4] In separate regressions, I substitute the 1-year return level and standard deviation for the 3-year return variables. The coefficients are not significant.

4.3. Relation between industry merger waves and aggregate merger activity

The next question is whether clustering of merger activity at the aggregate level is caused by clustering of industry-level merger waves. Figure 3 shows the relation between aggregate merger activity and the timing and fraction of bids occurring in the industry-level merger waves identified here. It is clear from the figure that aggregate merger waves occur when industry-level merger waves cluster in time and that the total merger activity in these waves is driven by bids in the industries undergoing waves. As a formal test of this observation, the correlation between the fraction of bids in industries undergoing industry-specific waves and the total number of merger transactions in the economy is computed to be a highly significant 0.85. This strongly suggests that industry-level merger waves explain aggregate clustering of merger activity.

As a further test of the relation between the neoclassical explanation of industry-level merger waves and overall aggregate merger activity, I try to predict aggregate merger waves using a specification analogous to those used to predict industry merger waves. In the aggregate merger waves specification, the dependent variable identifies whether aggregate merger activity is in the top, middle, or bottom third of the time series of merger activity over the sample period. Aggregate merger activity is defined

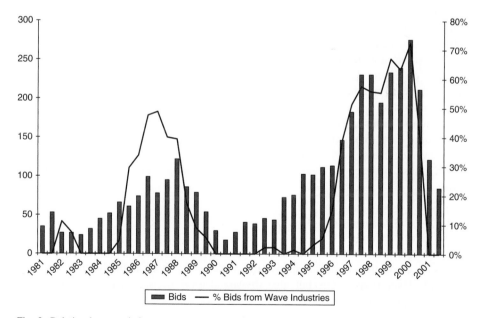

Fig. 3. Relation between industry merger waves and aggregate merger activity. The height of each bar represents the number of bids, shown on the left axis, with a deal value of at least $50 million (2002 dollars) across all industries in that year. The line indicates the percent of all bids, shown on the right axis, in each year that involved one of the industries undergoing a merger wave in that year.

as the fraction of firms in the population involved in merger activity (as a target or bidder) in a given year. Years in the top third can be thought of as merger wave years (the years are 1986–1988 and 1996–1999). The independent variables are industry-weighted analogs of the independent variables in the logit models of Table 4. Thus, the median M/B ratio is the weighted average of the 48 industry median M/B ratios, where the weights are the fraction of the total population of firms in an industry. Similarly, the industry shock variable is the weighted average of the shock index across industries. Thus, a large realization of this variable corresponds to a large fraction of the total population of firms being exposed to industry-level shocks. The results are presented in Columns 5-7 of Table 4.

There are only 20 observations, so the significance levels are reduced. Nonetheless, the results confirm at the aggregate level the primary inferences from the industry wave regressions. When only behavioral variables are included, the M/B ratio is significantly positively related to industry merger activity. The 3-year stock return is positive, but insignificant, and the standard deviation of that return is insignificantly negative. Column 6 presents the results for the neoclassical variables. The shock variable shows that when a larger proportion of firms are exposed to industry-level shocks, an aggregate merger wave occurs. The variable interacting industry-level shocks with periods of low capital liquidity is negative and significant. Also, a high rate spread reduces aggregate merger activity. Notably, deregulation is positive, but not significant in the aggregate model. Column 7 shows that once the neoclassical and behavioral variables are included together, the magnitude of the M/B ratio drops substantially, and it becomes insignificant, but the industry shock variable and the rate spread variable remain significant.[5]

Based on Figure 3, the correlation between industry merger waves and aggregate merger activity, and the results of Table 4, I conclude that aggregate merger waves can be understood as a clustering of industry merger waves. When a large portion of the population of firms is exposed to shocks at an industry level during a time of low transaction costs brought about by relatively high capital liquidity, an aggregate merger wave occurs. In the following subsections, I examine further tests that attempt to distinguish between behavioral and neoclassical explanations for industry merger waves.

4.4. Partial-firm acquisitions

One distinguishing prediction of the two hypotheses centers around partial-firm acquisitions. Because the efficient response to an economic shock is likely to involve not only firm-level transactions but also divisional-level transactions, the neoclassical

---

[5] With aggregated variables, one might be concerned about multicollinearity between the market-to-book ratio and the variable interacting economic shocks with tight liquidity. When I remove the interaction variable, the significance of the market-to-book ratio increases marginally, but remains insignificant.

hypothesis predicts that partial-firm acquisitions will spike during merger waves. Many of these transactions occur via cash payments. It is harder to produce such a prediction from the behavioral hypothesis, which relies on managers taking advantage of stock price errors to acquire other firms using overvalued stock. Partial-firm acquisitions for stock could fit into these models, but not those for cash.

Figure 4 summarizes the firm-level and partial-firm-level acquisition activity prior, during, and after a merger wave in the sample of 28 industries with merger waves. It is clear that, as implied by the neoclassical hypothesis, partial-firm acquisition activity, even that for cash, follows the pattern of firm-level acquisition activity. Panel A of Table 5 shows the average across all 48 industries of the time-series correlations between merger activity and partial-firm acquisition activity in a given year, defined as the proportion of an industry involved in merger activity and partial-firm acquisition activity, respectively. Not only is total firm-level merger activity correlated with total partial-firm-level activity, but also the stock swap only merger activity is correlated with the cash partial-firm-level activity. While both the neoclassical and behavioral hypotheses can explain an increase in stock swap merger activity constituting a wave, only the neoclassical one explains the accompanying increase in cash mergers and cash partial-firm transactions.

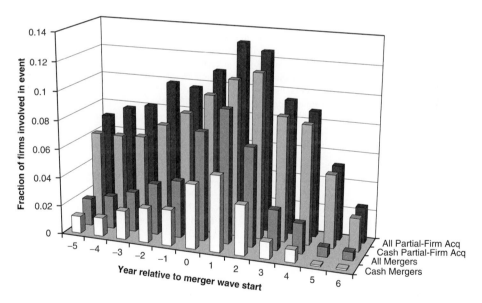

Fig. 4. Merger and partial-firm acquisition activity around an industry merger wave. The fractions of firms in an industry that are involved in a merger or partial-firm acquisition (e.g., acquisition of a division) during the industry merger wave (years 0 and 1) and for 5 years on either side of the merger wave are presented. The first contains only mergers where cash is the method of payment, while the second row presents the data for all mergers. The third row presents only partial-firm acquisitions paid for with cash and the last row has all partial-firm acquisitions.

Table 5

(Panel A) The relation between merger activity and partial-firm acquisitions

The simple correlations between the fraction of firms in an industry that bid in a firm-level merger and are buyers in a partial-firm-level acquisition over any 12-month period are presented. Partial-firm does not mean transactions for less than 100% of a selling firm's outstanding equity. Rather, it refers to divisional transactions (outright purchases of an operational piece of the selling firm). The merger and partial-firm transactions are also split according to whether the method of payment was cash or stock. The correlations are calculated separately for all 48 industries and the cross-industry mean correlation is presented here along with its p-value, in brackets.

	Stock mergers	Cash mergers	Total partial-firm	Stock partial-firm	Cash partial-firm
Total mergers	0.728	0.902	0.369	0.179	0.341
	[0.000]	[0.000]	[0.000]	[0.000]	[0.000]
Stock mergers		0.535	0.176	0.218	0.109
		[0.000]	[0.000]	[0.000]	[0.019]
Cash mergers			0.331	0.124	0.273
			[0.000]	[0.008]	[0.000]
Total partial-firm				0.312	0.890
				[0.000]	[0.000]
Stock partial-firm					0.159
					[0.000]

(Panel B) Logit models to predict which firms will be buyers in partial-firm acquisitions

The dependent variable takes a value of 1 in years in which the firm is a buyer in at least one partial-firm transaction, and is 0 otherwise. In the first column, this variable is 1 for buyers in any partial-firm acquisition and in the final two columns it is 1 only for buyers in cash partial-firm acquisitions. The independent variables include three dummy variables indicating whether the firm was a bidder in a merger in that year, a cash bidder, or a stock bidder. The C&I rate spread for the year and a dummy variable set to 1 if the year is during the industry's merger wave are included in the specification. The remaining control variables are all measured in the prior year and are: cash to total assets, asset turnover, size (the log of sales), market-to-book of assets, cash flow scaled by beginning-of-period assets, leverage (total debt scaled by assets), and the 1-year stock return.

	All partial acquisitions	Cash partial acquisitions	
Intercept	−2.811	−3.429	−4.299
	[<0.0001]	[<0.0001]	[<0.0001]
$Bidder_t$	0.863	0.906	
	[<0.0001]	[<0.0001]	
Cash bidder$_t$			0.874
			[0.009]
Stock bidder$_t$			1.743
			[<0.0001]
C&I rate spread$_t$	−0.637	−0.492	−0.503
	[<0.0001]	[<0.0001]	[<0.0001]
In-wave dummy$_t$	9.128	3.378	3.378
	[<0.0001]	[<0.0001]	[<0.0001]
$Cash_{t-1}$	−0.196	−0.046	−0.036
	[0.017]	[0.651]	[0.727]

(Continued)

Table 5 (*Continued*)

	All partial acquisitions	Cash partial acquisitions	
Asset turnover$_{t-1}$	−0.257	−0.425	−0.427
	[<0.0001]	[<0.0001]	[<0.0001]
Size$_{t-1}$	0.336	0.303	0.307
	[<0.0001]	[<0.0001]	[<0.0001]
Market-to-book$_{t-1}$	0.017	0.015	0.015
	[0.000]	[0.012]	[0.010]
Cash flows$_{t-1}$	0.117	0.360	0.359
	[0.067]	[<0.0001]	[<0.0001]
Leverage$_{t-1}$	0.069	0.149	0.147
	[0.174]	[0.010]	[0.011]
Stock return$_{t-1}$	0.079	0.076	0.076
	[<0.0001]	[<0.0001]	[<0.0001]
Pseudo-R^2	0.132	0.106	0.105
Firm-years	108,183	108,183	108,183

It is possible that there is a behavioral set of firms engaging in stock swap mergers and a different set of firms making partial-firm transactions. Therefore, Panel B of Table 5 presents a specification designed to test whether bidders in mergers are also buyers in partial-firm transactions. The sample is all firms in the 48 industries, although the results are the same if the sample is restricted to the 28 industries with merger waves. The table presents logit models for partial-firm buying activity. All three columns show that, like mergers, partial-firm transactions are also more common when the rate spread is lower. Further, as predicted by the neoclassical hypothesis, partial-firm transactions are more likely during merger waves. The first column shows that bidding in a given year predicts that the same firm will also be a buyer in a partial-firm transaction. The second column shows that bidding also predicts being a cash buyer in a partial-firm transaction. Finally, the last column shows that being a bidder in a stock swap merger strongly predicts being a cash buyer in a partial-firm acquisition. These results, while directly implied by the neoclassical hypothesis, are at odds with the behavioral hypothesis.

4.5. Long-run returns

One of the implications of the behavioral hypothesis is that long-run returns should be poor following merger waves. Previous studies of long-run returns following mergers have found evidence of significant underperformance for subsets of bidders. Rau and Vermaelen (1998) find that low book-to-market "glamor" firms underperform following acquisitions and Loughran and Vijh (1997) find that firms that use stock as the method of payment experience long-run underperformance. However, a recent paper by Mitchell and Stafford (2000) which reviews the long-run return literature questions the common methodology of calculating buy-and-hold returns and forming event-time portfolios. They show that positive cross-correlations for event firms, especially in dealing with events that cluster in time and industry such as mergers, invalidates the bootstrapping approach used for statistical inference in this methodology. Instead, they implement a calendar portfolio approach advocated by Fama (1998). This approach does not suffer from the above problems. The method can be summarized as follows. First, each month, form a portfolio consisting of all firms in the treatment sample. Calculate the 1-month value-weighted and equally weighted returns for that portfolio. Repeat this each month. Finally, regress each vector of 1-month returns on the monthly Fama-French factor realizations and examine the intercept. A significant intercept is evidence of abnormal performance. Loughran and Ritter (2000) argue that one should weight the monthly observations by the number of firms in the monthly portfolio, and that equally weighted returns are more likely to pick up abnormal performance than are value-weighted returns. I use weighted least squares estimation and present both value-weighted and equally weighted return results. The sample is the 28 wave industries.

In Table 6, I examine the returns both of the overall industry and of the bidders specifically. The behavioral hypothesis predicts that waves will occur during times of high valuation for the industry, so we would expect to see abnormally high returns prior to and possibly during a wave and abnormally low returns following a wave. The first four columns examine the returns for the whole industry. Applying the Fama (1998) methodology, each month a portfolio of all firms in the industry is formed and the 1-month return for that portfolio is calculated. The time series of monthly returns for each industry is regressed separately and the cross-industry median coefficients are presented along with their *p*-values. The first two columns show that, relative to the Fama-French three-factor portfolios, the industries do not exhibit abnormal performance around merger waves. Column 3 shows that the unadjusted returns are relatively high before and during a wave and relatively low following a wave. Since the pattern of high then low returns is not abnormal relative to market conditions, this evidence suggests that managers in these industries are not taking advantage of temporary mispricing of their industries. Rather, the capital liquidity that a business expansion and overall bull market provide allows industry-level merger waves to occur. Regardless, Column 4 shows that this result is not robust to equally weighted portfolio returns.

Panel B presents results for bidders only. The sample is all bidders in the 28 wave industries, whether their bids took place during a wave or not. Implementing the calendar-time approach to test for postevent long-run returns requires that each month, one form a portfolio of all firms that have made a bid in the prior 36 months. Using these monthly portfolios, one proceeds as before, calculating a vector of monthly returns and regressing that vector on explanatory variables. Columns 1 and 2 examine the general result from the extant literature that bidders in stock-financed mergers underperform in the 3 years following the merger. The results are mixed. In the value-weighted specification, the stock bidders significantly underperform the cash bidders (who are represented by the intercept), but because the cash bidders have a positive point estimate, a test of the net abnormal performance ($+0.25 - 0.40 =$

Table 6

(Panel A) Calendar time-based regressions of long-run stock return performance for the 28 industries

The dependent variables in the VW and EW columns are the value-weighted and equally weighted returns, respectively, for month *t* of the portfolio of merged companies. Market, small minus big, and high minus low are the monthly factor realizations of the Fama and French (1993) factors. The estimation procedure is described in Section 4. Abnormal performance is detected in the intercept or dummy variable. The regressions are estimated separately for the time series of each of the 28 industries over the entire sample period. The median coefficient estimates from those 28 regressions and the *p*-values for a test of whether the median is different from zero are presented here. Prewave is a dummy variable identifying the 12 months immediately prior to a merger wave, In-wave is a dummy variable identifying the 24-month wave period, and postwave is a dummy variable identifying the 36 months following the end of the wave.

	VW	EW	VW	EW
Intercept	0.139	−0.016	*0.751*	*0.787*
	[0.459]	[0.845]	*[0.001]*	*[0.001]*
Prewave	0.155	0.069	*0.895*	−0.159
	[0.447]	[0.665]	*[0.001]*	[0.627]
In-wave	−0.149	−0.134	*1.195*	0.415
	[0.998]	[0.511]	*[0.001]*	[0.150]
Postwave	0.185	0.351	*−0.865*	−0.610
	[0.669]	[0.260]	*[0.072]*	[0.103]
Market	*1.024*	0.994		
	[0.001]	*[0.001]*		
Small minus big	0.052	*0.892*		
	[0.275]	*[0.001]*		
High minus low	−0.065	*0.196*		
	[0.301]	*[0.001]*		

(Panel B) Calendar time-based regressions of long-run stock return performance following a completed merger

The calendar-time estimation is described in Section 4. Stock is a dummy variable taking the value of 1 for mergers in which stock was the method of payment and 0 otherwise. In-wave stock and nonwave stock dummies identify stock-payment mergers taking place inside or outside and industry merger wave. Market, small minus big, and high minus low are the monthly factor realizations of the Fama and French (1993) factors. The observations are monthly returns for time series of portfolios containing bidders in different categories. The number of observations varies depending on the number of different samples considered and the number of calendar months in the estimation. In Columns 1 and 2, there are 237 total months in the time series of returns for the portfolio of cash bidders and 248 for the portfolio of stock bidders. In Columns 3 and 4, there are 248 months of data for portfolios of nonwave stock bidders, 215 months of data for portfolios of wave stock bidders, and the remaining 237 observations are the time series of months for the cash bidders. Columns headed VW use value-weighted returns and those headed EW use equally weighted returns as the dependent variables. The *p*-values from heteroskedasticity-consistent tests of the coefficients are presented.

	VW	EW	VW	EW
Intercept	0.254	−0.213	0.233	−0.223
	[0.132]	[0.280]	[0.166]	[0.254]
Stock	*−0.396*	−0.179		
	[0.057]	[0.567]		

(Continued)

Table 6 (*Continued*)

	UV	EW	VW	EW
In-wave stock			−0.667	−0.458
			[0.021]	[0.352]
Nonwave stock			−0.258	−0.074
			[0.230]	[0.783]
Market	1.044	1.239	1.057	1.252
	[<0.001]	[<0.001]	[<0.001]	[<0.001]
Small minus big	−0.179	0.341	−0.180	0.336
	[<0.001]	[<0.001]	[<0.001]	[<0.001]
High minus low	−0.047	0.372	−0.004	0.382
	[0.323]	[<0.001]	[0.922]	[<0.001]
Adj. R^2	0.904	0.844	0.878	0.824
N	485	485	700	700

−0.15) of the stock bidders reveals it to be insignificantly different from zero. In the equally weighted specification, the net abnormal performance of the stock bidders (−0.21 − 0.18 = −0.39) is also insignificantly different from zero.

The next two columns split the stock bidders into those whose bids took place in a wave and those whose did not. Again, the results are mixed for the equally and value-weighted portfolios. The value-weighted approach reveals evidence of underperformance and that it is concentrated in the wave bidders. The total underperformance for stock bidders in waves (0.23 − 0.67 = −0.44) is significant, but is not significantly different from that for nonwave stock bidders (0.23 − 0.26 = −0.03). The equally weighted approach finds no underperformance for either wave or nonwave stock bidders. The mixed results for the two weighting approaches suggest that only large bidders experience poor postmerger performance. This is consistent with the findings of Moeller et al. (2004), who, in a comprehensive look at the 1980–2001 period, find that large acquirers destroy billions in value while small acquirers actually create value in mergers. The findings for large wave bidders can be interpreted as consistent with Rosen (2004), who finds that bidders in ''hot'' merger markets have lower long-run performance.

The results provide only weak support for the behavioral hypothesis, especially given that the behavioral models were designed to explain the previously observed rise and fall pattern in the bidder's stock price. The only evidence of underperformance for wave bidders comes in the value-weighted specification, and even in that specification, the performance of wave bidders is not significantly different from that of nonwave bidders. Further, the finding is not robust to changing to equally weighted portfolios.

4.6. Operating performance

As noted before, because benchmark performance is inherently unobservable in merger waves, tests of the neoclassical hypothesis using operating performance face the problem of actually testing a joint hypothesis that performance improves relative to what it would have been and that the empirical proxy for that unobservable benchmark is valid.[6] None of the behavioral papers explicitly make predictions regarding operating performance, but one can derive a prediction that the costs of integrating two firms with no real combined synergies (and hence no operational motive to merge) would produce particularly poor postmerger operating performance for mergers in waves.

Despite the inherent noisiness of operating performance tests, in the interest of completeness, Table 7 presents results of operating performance regressions. The model regresses postmerger industry-adjusted operating performance on premerger industry-adjusted operating performance and a dummy variable set to 1 if the merger occurred in a wave and 0 otherwise. This test is based on Healy et al. (1992). As in that study, the intercept in this regression will capture the average postmerger change in the performance measure. The dummy variable will indicate whether waves are different from other periods. The slope coefficient is expected to be less than one because of mean-reversion in industry-adjusted operating performance (see Barber and Lyon, 1996). Because of the clustering of merger activity at the industry level, the observations in these regressions are not independent. Thus, I report the results of grouped-mean (the between estimator, described in Greene, 1993, p. 472) regressions as well as those for the full data set.

The results in the table show no evidence that changes in actual performance following mergers in waves are worse than during other periods. The only significant coefficients on the wave dummy is for sales growth, which is positive. The grouped-means results do not change the overall inferences; there are no cases in which mergers in waves perform significantly worse than those outside waves. Instead, postmerger changes in sales growth remains significantly greater inside waves.

I make two attempts to control for the unobservable benchmark problem in operating performance tests. First, I attempt to identify waves in which the benchmark performance is likely to be particularly poor. To do so, I create a subsample of waves that respond to contractionary shocks, defined as shocks such that the prewave change in sales growth and ROA are both negative and below their medians. I reestimate the operating performance regressions including a dummy for contractionary waves. The results on asset turnover are affected by the benchmarking problem. Controlling for contractionary waves, the coefficient on the wave dummy is positive and significant. None of the other inferences are changed by the inclusion of the contraction dummy.

Second, I use I/B/E/S data on analyst forecasts of long-term growth as a proxy for expected performance absent the merger. I collect the last forecasts for both the bidder and target prior to the announcement of the bid. Even if the industry has undergone a shock that changes expected performance, this change in expectations should be incorporated into analyst projections at the time. I compare the average of the bidder

[6] Maksimovic and Phillips (2001) find efficiency gains following mergers and interpret the evidence as supportive of a neoclassical model of resource allocation. They use plant-level data, which is arguably less susceptible to the benchmarking problem.

Table 7

Operating performance and analyst forecast changes following mergers

This table presents the results of regressions where the dependent variable is a measure of postmerger industry-adjusted operating performance or valuation (average of years +1 to +3 relative to merger completion) and the independent variables are the corresponding premerger (average of years −3 to −1 relative to the announcement) industry-adjusted performance or valuation measure and a dummy variable taking the value of 1 for mergers taking place during a wave and 0 otherwise. LTG forecast is the forecast long-term earnings growth (in %) and it comes from the I/B/E/S summary analyst forecast measure of long-term growth immediately before announcement and after completion of the merger. The bottom panel also contains a dummy variable taking the value of 1 when the wave is classified as contractionary, meaning that the prewave shock to sales growth and ROA for the industry were both negative and below their respective medians. OLS regressions based on all observations and on group means are presented. The p-values are in brackets.

Individual observations

	Profitability	Asset turnover	ROA	Sales growth	M/B	LTG forecast
Intercept	−0.016	0.017	−0.015	−0.003	−0.035	0.410
	[0.073]	[0.094]	[<0.0001]	[0.683]	[0.289]	[0.067]
Premerger Measure	0.590	0.608	0.449	0.159	0.362	0.986
	[<0.0001]	[<0.0001]	[<0.0001]	[<0.0001]	[<0.0001]	[<0.0001]
In-wave	−0.010	0.024	0.004	0.024	0.069	0.372
	[0.522]	[0.148]	[0.424]	[0.043]	[0.194]	[0.059]
Adj. R^2	0.330	0.517	0.296	0.032	0.204	0.895
Obs	1323	1323	1323	1323	1323	613
Intercept	−0.016	0.017	−0.015	−0.003	−0.035	0.433
	[0.073]	[0.095]	[<0.0001]	[0.691]	[0.289]	[0.054]
Premerger Measure	0.590	0.609	0.449	0.157	0.362	0.984
	[<0.0001]	[<0.0001]	[<0.0001]	[<0.0001]	[<0.0001]	[<0.0001]
In-wave	−0.004	0.031	0.006	0.035	0.065	0.292
	[0.813]	[0.081]	[0.294]	[0.007]	[0.266]	[0.169]
Contraction	−0.025	−0.033	−0.007	−0.048	0.020	0.346
	[0.383]	[0.296]	[0.428]	[0.033]	[0.846]	[0.329]
Adj. R^2	0.330	0.517	0.296	0.035	0.204	0.895
Obs	1323	1323	1323	1323	1323	613

Group means

	Profitability	Asset turnover	ROA	Sales growth	M/B	LTG forecast
Intercept	−0.008	0.025	−0.014	0.004	−0.020	0.548
	[0.503]	[0.106]	[0.004]	[0.718]	[0.686]	[0.114]
Premerger Measure	0.970	0.482	0.243	0.029	0.319	0.975
	[<0.0001]	[<0.0001]	[0.070]	[0.814]	[0.001]	[<0.0001]
In-wave	−0.005	0.021	0.003	0.027	0.073	0.390
	[0.804]	[0.396]	[0.657]	[0.092]	[0.272]	[0.084]
Adj. R^2	0.479	0.450	0.028	0.022	0.220	0.972
Obs	56	56	56	56	56	56
Intercept	−0.008	0.025	−0.014	0.006	−0.016	0.631
	[0.513]	[0.107]	[0.003]	[0.618]	[0.732]	[0.070]
Premerger Measure	0.988	0.487	0.254	0.004	0.309	0.969
	[<0.0001]	[<0.0001]	[0.048]	[0.976]	[0.001]	[<0.0001]
In-wave	0.003	0.026	0.005	0.039	0.070	0.306
	[0.880]	[0.324]	[0.558]	[0.021]	[0.330]	[0.198]
Contraction	−0.035	−0.023	−0.006	−0.052	0.019	0.396
	[0.351]	[0.616]	[0.675]	[0.071]	[0.876]	[0.320]
Adj. R^2	0.489	0.438	0.022	0.062	0.207	0.969
Obs	59	59	59	59	59	57

and target prebid forecasts, weighted by their market values, to the first forecast made for long-term growth of the combined firm following consummation of the merger. I report the results of this regression in Columns 6 and 12 of Table 7.

The results show that analyst forecast revisions following mergers in waves are significantly greater than those outside of waves; Columns 6 and 12 show that the revisions in the long-term growth rate forecast are almost 40 basis points higher inside a wave than outside. The positive coefficient remains significant even after a correction for the independence problem using group means. In the specifications that include the contraction dummy, the contraction dummy is not significant, and the significance of the wave coefficient drops, but the intercepts are positive, indicating a general expectation of performance improvement following mergers that is no different for mergers in waves.

Overall, the operating performance results show that mergers inside waves produce no worse, and by some measures better, postmerger operating performance. Further, when I control for the benchmarking problem, the results either show that mergers in general are seen to have performance improvements or that wave mergers have either better or no different performance from mergers outside waves. These results, while consistent with the neoclassical explanation, cannot be reconciled with the behavioral explanations of merger waves.

4.7. Contractionary waves

In the previous subsection, I separate waves preceded by contractionary shocks from all others. In untabulated tests, I examine whether more can be learned from using such a separation in the other tests. For example, contractionary shocks requiring consolidation in the industry can be met only through merger, but those that do not can be met either through internal expansion or reorganization through merger (the classic buy vs. build decision). Expansion through merger will only be optimal if the transaction costs of merger are low enough. Thus, under the neoclassical hypothesis, one might expect the ability of contractionary shocks to propagate a wave to be less sensitive to capital liquidity than other shocks would be. I repeat the logit models in Table 4 for industry waves, separating shocks into contractionary versus noncontractionary categories. The results support the conjecture: the coefficient interacting capital liquidity and contractionary shocks is smaller than that for other shocks, and its p-value is 0.15.

I also examine long-run returns following contractionary and noncontractionary waves and find no difference. One could argue that the behavioral explanation would predict that waves preceded by expansionary shocks should produce worse long-run returns if those waves are driven by market valuations that have overreacted to positive shocks. The fact that the long-run postmerger returns are equivalent in contractionary versus noncontractionary waves is consistent with bidders having similar motivations to merge in each type of wave. The neoclassical hypothesis predicts such similar motivation while the behavioral hypothesis does not.

5. Conclusion

Recent explanations of merger waves as the outcome of attempts to time market misvaluations have refocused the literature on an old question: what causes merger waves? In this paper, I examine two general classes of explanations: the neoclassical model, in which industries responding to shocks reorganize through mergers and acquisitions, and thereby create a clustering of merger activity; and, the behavioral model, in which rational managers take advantage of consistent pricing errors in the market to buy real assets with overvalued stock. While there has been some evidence in the extant literature supporting each of the above explanations, most prior work tests the implications of only one of the explanations, rather than directly attempting to distinguish between the two. The tests in this paper directly compare the two explanations and support the neoclassical model, as modified to include a role for capital liquidity. It is the importance of capital liquidity that causes individual industry-level merger waves to cluster in time to create aggregate-level merger waves. Further, the relation between asset values and merger activity that is the motivation of the behavioral hypothesis reflects the capital liquidity effect rather than any misvaluation effect.

Overall, the view supported here is that shocks, be they economic, regulatory, or technological, cause industry merger waves. Not all shocks will propagate a wave; sufficient capital liquidity must be present to accommodate the necessary transactions. This macro-level liquidity component causes industry merger waves to cluster even if industry shocks do not. While it would be disingenuous to claim that there are no mergers driven by managers timing the market, such mergers are not the cause of waves. Rather, aggregate merger waves are caused by the clustering of shock-driven industry merger waves, not by attempts to time the market.

References

Agrawal, A. and J. Jaffe, 2003, "Do Takeover Targets Underperform? Evidence from Operating and Stock Returns," *Journal of Financial and Quantitative Analysis*, 38, 721–746.
Andrade, G., M. Mitchell and E. Stafford, 2001, "New Evidence and Perspectives on Mergers," *Journal of Economic Perspectives*, 15, 103–120.
Ang, J. and Y. Cheng, 2003, "Direct Evidence on the Market-Driven Acquisitions Theory," Unpublished Working Paper, Florida State University.
Barber, B. and J. Lyon, 1996, "Detecting Abnormal Operating Performance: The Empirical Power and Specification of Test Statistics," *Journal of Financial Economics*, 41, 359–399.
Brealey, R. and S. Myers, 2003, *Principles of Corporate Finance*, McGraw-Hill, New York.
Coase, R., 1937, "The Nature of the Firm," *Economica*, 4, 386–405.
Dong, M., D. Hirshleifer, S. Richardson and S. H. Teoh, 2003, "Does Investor Misvaluation Drive the Takeover Market?" Unpublished Working Paper, Ohio State University.
Eisfeldt, A. and A. Rampini, 2003, "Capital Reallocation and Liquidity," Unpublished Working Paper, Northwestern University.
Fama, E., 1998, "Market Efficiency, Long-Term Returns, and Behavioral Finance," *Journal of Financial Economics*, 49, 283–306.

Fama, E. and K. French, 1993, "Common Risk Factors in the Returns on Stocks and Bonds," *Journal of Financial Economics*, 33, 3–56.

Fama, E. and K. French, 1997, "Industry Costs of Equity," *Journal of Financial Economics*, 43, 153–193.

Golbe, D. L. and L. J. White, 1988, "A Time Series Analysis of Mergers and Acquisitions in the U.S. Economy," In: A. Auerbach (Ed.), *Corporate Takeovers: Causes and Consequences*, NBER: University of Chicago Press, Chicago, 265–302.

Gort, M., 1969, "An Economic Disturbance Theory of Mergers," *Quarterly Journal of Economics*, 83, 623–642.

Greene, W., 1993, *Econometric Analysis*, Prentice-Hall, Englewood Cliffs, NJ.

Harford, J., 1999, "Corporate Cash Reserves and Acquisitions," *Journal of Finance*, 54, 1969–1997.

Healy, P., K. Palepu and R. Ruback, 1992, "Does Corporate Performance Improve After Mergers?" *Journal of Financial Economics*, 31, 135–175.

Jovanovic, B. and P. Rousseau, 2001, "Mergers and Technological Change: 1885–1998," Unpublished Working Paper, Vanderbilt University.

Jovanovic, B. and P. Rousseau, 2002, "The Q-Theory of Mergers," *American Economic Review*, 92, 198–204.

Loughran, T. and J. Ritter, 2000, "Uniformly Least Powerful Tests of Market Efficiency," *Journal of Financial Economics*, 55, 361–389.

Loughran, T. and A. Vijh, 1997, "Do Long-Term Shareholders Benefit from Corporate Acquisitions?" *Journal of Finance*, 52, 1765–1790.

Lown, C., D. Morgan and S. Rohatgi, 2000, "Listening to Loan Officers: The Impact of Commercial Credit Standards on Lending and Output," *FRBNY Economic Policy Review*, July.

Maksimovic, V. and G. Phillips, 2001, "The Market for Corporate Assets: Who Engages in Mergers and Asset Sales and Are There Efficiency Gains?" *Journal of Finance*, 56, 2019–2065.

Mitchell, M. and J. H. Mulherin, 1996, "The Impact of Industry Shocks on Takeover and Restructuring Activity," *Journal of Financial Economics*, 41, 193–229.

Mitchell, M. and E. Stafford, 2000, "Managerial Decisions and Long-Term Stock Price Performance," *Journal of Business*, 73, 287–329.

Moeller, S., F. Schlingemann and R. Stulz, 2004, "Firm Size and the Gains from Acquisitions," *Journal of Financial Economics*, 73, 201–228.

Mulherin, J. H. and A. Boone, 2000, "Comparing Acquisitions and Divestitures," *Journal of Corporate Finance*, 6, 117–139.

Rau, P. R. and T. Vermaelen, 1998, "Glamour, Value and the Post-Acquisition Performance of Acquiring Firms," *Journal of Financial Economics*, 49, 223–253.

Rhodes-Kropf, M. and S. Viswanathan, 2004, "Market Valuation and Merger Waves," *Journal of Finance*, 59.

Rhodes-Kropf, M., D. Robinson and S. Viswanathan, 2004, "Valuation Waves and Merger Activity: The Empirical Evidence," *Journal of Financial Economics*, forthcoming.

Rosen, R., 2004, "Merger Momentum and Investor Sentiment: The Stock Market Reaction to Merger Announcements," *Journal of Business*, forthcoming.

Schlingemann, F., R. Stulz and R. Walkling, 2002, "Divestitures and the Liquidity of the Market for Corporate Assets," *Journal of Financial Economics*, 64, 117–144.

Shleifer, A. and R. Vishny, 1992, "Liquidation Values and Debt Capacity," *Journal of Finance*, 32, 337–347.

Shleifer, A. and R. Vishny, 2003, "Stock Market Driven Acquisitions," *Journal of Financial Economics*, 70, 295–311.

Verter, G., 2002, *Timing Merger Waves*, Harvard University, Mimeo.

Viscusi, W., J. Vernon and J. Harrington, 2000, *Economics of Regulation and Antitrust*, The MIT Press, Cambridge, MA.

PART 4

WHAT DETERMINES THE SIZE AND DIVISION OF TAKEOVER GAINS?

Chapter 7

FIRM SIZE AND THE GAINS FROM ACQUISITIONS[*]

SARA B. MOELLER

Cox School of Business, Southern Methodist University, Dallas, Texas, USA

FREDERIK P. SCHLINGEMANN

Katz Graduate School of Business, University of Pittsburgh, Pittsburgh, Pennsylvania, USA

RENÉ M. STULZ

Department of Finance, Fisher College of Business, The Ohio State University, Columbus, Ohio, USA

Contents

[*] We thank Evrim Akdogu, Harry DeAngelo, Hemang Desai, Eugene Fama, David Hirshleifer, Cliff Holderness, Bengt Holmstrom, Jin-Lung (Jim) Hsieh, Paul Malatesta, Jeffry Netter, Bill Schwert, Mike Stegemoller, Vish Viswanathan, Ralph Walking, seminar participants at Boston College and the Federal Reserve Bank of New York, and an anonymous referee for useful comments.

This article originally appeared in the *Journal of Financial Economics*, Vol. 73, pp. 201–228 (2004).
Corporate Takeovers, Volume 1
Edited by B. Espen Eckbo
DOI: 10.1016/B978-0-12-381983-3.00007-1

Abstract

We examine a sample of 12,023 acquisitions by public firms from 1980 to 2001. The equally weighted abnormal announcement return is 1.1%, but acquiring-firm shareholders lose $25.2 million on average upon announcement. This disparity suggests the existence of a size effect in acquisition announcement returns. The announcement return for acquiring-firm shareholders is roughly 2% points higher for small acquirers irrespective of the form of financing and whether the acquired firm is public or private. The size effect is robust to firm and deal characteristics, and it is not reversed over time.

Keywords

acquisitions, bidder, size effect, organizational form

JEL classification: G31, G32, G34

1. Introduction

In this paper, we examine the gains to shareholders of firms that announce acquisitions of public firms, private firms, or subsidiaries of other firms. We consider these different types of acquisitions together since corporations making such acquisitions could be acquiring similar assets.[1] Typically, acquisitions are sizable investments for the firms that undertake them. We form a sample of all such purchases over $1 million by public firms from 1980 to 2001 recorded by the Securities Data Corporation. After imposing some additional sampling criteria, we obtain a sample of 12,023 acquisitions. Such a comprehensive sample has not been studied before. The equally weighted average announcement return for acquiring-firm shareholders in our sample is 1.1%, representing a gain of $5.61 per $100 spent on acquisitions. If the capital markets' assessment is unbiased, this gain represents the economic benefit of the acquisition for the shareholders of the acquiring firm together with the stock-price impact of other information released or inferred by investors when firms make acquisition announcements.

The equally weighted average announcement return implies that the wealth of acquiring-firm shareholders increases when acquisitions are announced. Strikingly, however, the average dollar change in the wealth of acquiring-firm shareholders when acquisition announcements are made is negative. From 1980 to 2001, the sample firms spent roughly $3.4 trillion on acquisitions and the wealth of the shareholders of these firms fell by $303 billion dollars (in 2001 dollars), for a dollar abnormal return, defined in Malatesta (1983) as the abnormal return times the firm's equity capitalization cumulated over the event window, of −$25.2 million per acquisition. The dollar abnormal return can differ in sign from the percentage abnormal return if the percentage abnormal return differs in sign for large and small firms. This is the case here. We define small firms in a given year to be firms whose capitalization falls below the 25th percentile of NYSE firms that year. Acquisitions by small firms are profitable for their shareholders, but these firms make small acquisitions with small dollar gains. Large firms make large acquisitions that result in large dollar losses. Acquisitions thus result in losses for shareholders in the aggregate because the losses incurred by large firms are much larger than the gains realized by small firms. Roughly, shareholders from small firms earn $9 billion from the acquisitions made during the period 1980–2001, whereas the shareholders from large firms lose $312 billion. Though it is common to focus on equally weighted returns in event studies, it follows from these numbers that value-weighted returns lead to a different assessment of the profitability of acquisitions. The value-weighted return is −1.18%.

---

[1] Kaplan and Weisbach (1992) have a sample of 282 large acquisitions. They find that almost 44% of the acquisitions are subsequently divested. Two hundred and sixteen of their acquisitions are acquisitions of public companies. The acquired assets are then spun off in some cases and acquired by other companies in most cases. Hence, in their sample, the same assets most likely are first organized as a public firm and then as a division. In this paper, we use the term subsidiary acquisition to denote the acquisition of a subsidiary, division, or branch.

After documenting that small firms are good acquirers and large firms are not, we examine possible explanations for this size effect, defined as the difference between the abnormal returns of small acquirers and large acquirers. First, roughly one quarter of the firms acquiring public firms are small whereas half of the firms acquiring private firms are small. If acquiring private firms is more profitable than acquiring public firms, this could explain the size effect. Fuller et al. (2002) show for a sample of firms that make five or more acquisitions in the 1990s that abnormal returns are higher for firms acquiring private firms or subsidiaries than for firms acquiring public firms. Second, small firms are more likely to pay for acquisitions with cash than with equity. Travlos (1987) and others show that acquisitions of public firms paid for with equity are accompanied by lower announcement returns. However, Chang (1998) and Fuller et al. (2002) show that acquisitions of private firms paid for with equity do not have lower announcement returns than private acquisitions paid for with cash. Third, small and large acquirers have different characteristics. The literature has shown that a number of acquiring-firm and deal characteristics are related to announcement returns for public-firm acquisitions. For instance, Lang et al. (1991) and Servaes (1991) show that high q bidders have higher announcement abnormal returns for tender offer acquisitions and public-firm acquisitions, respectively, and Maloney et al. (1993) find that bidders with higher leverage have higher abnormal returns. We find that controlling for a wide variety of acquiring-firm and deal characteristics does not alter the size effect. In all of our regressions, the estimate of the size effect is positive and significantly different from zero at the 1% probability level.

A number of explanations have been offered for why the stock-price of firms announcing an acquisition can be negative. Roll (1986) hypothesizes that managers of bidding firms may suffer from hubris, so they overpay. Travlos (1987) points out that firms with poor returns generally pay with equity, and Myers and Majluf (1984) show that firms that issue equity signal that the market overvalues their assets in place (the equity signaling hypothesis). A related hypothesis, formalized by McCardle and Viswanathan (1994) and Jovanovic and Braguinsky (2002), is that firms make acquisitions when they have exhausted their internal growth opportunities (the growth opportunities signaling hypothesis). Jensen (1986) argues that empire-building managements would rather make acquisitions than increase payouts to shareholders (the free cash flow hypothesis). Recently, Dong et al. (2002) show that firms with higher valuations have worse announcement returns. This could be because highly valued acquirers communicate to the market that these high valuations are not warranted by fundamentals, perhaps because they are undertaking efforts to acquire less overvalued assets with more overvalued equity (the overvaluation hypothesis).[2] Finally, Mitchell et al. (2004) show that there is a price pressure effect on the stock-price of the bidder for acquisitions paid for with equity because of the activities of arbitrageurs (the arbitrageur hypothesis).

---

[2] Shleifer and Vishny (2003) provide a model in which overvalued firms find it advantageous to acquire less overvalued firms to lock in real assets, but they make no predictions about abnormal returns.

For these hypotheses to explain the size effect for some or all types of acquisitions, they have to be more pertinent for large firms than for small firms. This is not implausible. Generally, the incentives of managers in small firms are better aligned with those of shareholders than is the case in large firms. In particular, Demsetz and Lehn (1985) find that managers in small firms typically have more firm ownership than managers in large firms. Managers of large firms might be more prone to hubris, perhaps because they are more important socially, have succeeded in growing the firm, or simply face fewer obstacles in making acquisitions because their firm has more resources. A firm may be large because its equity is highly valued, so a large firm is more likely to be overvalued. A firm that is further along in its lifecycle might be more likely to be large and to have exhausted its growth opportunities. Agency costs of free cash flow occur when a firm no longer has growth opportunities, which could be more likely for large firms than for small firms. Finally, arbitrageurs are unlikely to use their resources for a merger when the acquirer is a small firm because it will be too difficult and costly to establish large short positions.

We investigate whether these hypotheses are helpful in understanding the size effect. We provide evidence that managers of large firms pay more for acquisitions. The premium paid increases with firm size after controlling for firm and deal characteristics. Large firms are also more likely to complete an offer. This is consistent with hubris being more of a problem for large firms. We find that the combined dollar return of the acquired and acquiring firms for acquisitions of public firms is positive and significant for small firms but significantly negative for large firms. In other words, there are no dollar synergy gains for acquisitions by large firms given how synergy gains are typically computed (following the method proposed by Bradley et al., 1988), but there are dollar synergy gains for acquisitions by small firms. Percentage synergy returns are positive for acquisitions by large firms as well as by small firms, but they are significantly higher for acquisitions by small firms. Of course, the synergy gain estimate for acquisitions by large firms could be made negative by the adverse information revealed about the acquirer through the acquisition announcement rather than by the adverse impact on shareholder wealth of the acquisition itself, although it is not clear why large acquirers reveal relatively more adverse information than do small acquirers.

We also provide evidence that is inconsistent with the overvaluation hypothesis. In contrast to the market value of a firm's equity, the book value of a firm's assets is unlikely to be correlated with the overvaluation of the firm's stock-price. Consequently, if the size effect is due to the fact that large firms tend to be overvalued, it should disappear when we use the book value of the firm's assets as a size measure. Nonetheless, we find that the size effect holds when we use the book value of a firm's assets instead of the firm's market value of equity. Though the outcome of the acquisitions by large firms is consistent with the existence of agency costs of managerial discretion, there is little support for the free cash flow hypothesis. Finally, we investigate the hypothesis that the market makes systematic mistakes in evaluating acquisitions that it rectifies over time. In this case, acquisitions by small firms would be followed by negative abnormal returns and acquisitions by large firms would be followed by positive abnormal returns. This explanation cannot account for the size effect. The market seems fairly efficient in incorporating the information conveyed by acquisition announcements in the stock-price.

The paper is organized as follows. In Section 2 we describe our sample and document that abnormal returns for acquisition announcements are significantly positive and negatively correlated with firm size. In Section 3, we demonstrate that the size effect is robust to firm and deal characteristics. In Section 4, we investigate possible explanations for the size effect. We conclude in Section 5.

2. Announcement returns for successful acquisitions

To estimate the shareholder gains from acquisitions, we consider acquisition announcements that are successful and result in a completed transaction. In Sections 3 and 4, we include unsuccessful acquisition announcements to investigate whether this focus introduces a bias in our analysis and find that it does not. We first describe our sample and then estimate the gains to shareholders.

2.1. The sample

The sample of acquisitions comes from the Securities Data Company's (SDC) US Mergers and Acquisitions Database. We select domestic mergers and acquisitions with announcement dates between 1980 and 2001. We consider only acquisitions in which acquiring firms end up with all the shares of the acquired firm or subsidiary, and we require the acquiring firm to control less than 50% of the shares of the target firm before the announcement. We further require that (1) the transaction is completed, (2) the deal value is greater than $1 million, (3) a public or private US firm or a nonpublic subsidiary of a public or private firm are acquired, and (4) the acquirer is a public firm listed on the Center for Research in Security Prices (CRSP) and Compustat during the event window. Deal value is defined by SDC as the total value of consideration paid by the acquirer, excluding fees and expenses. After collecting these acquisitions, we eliminate those in which the deal value relative to the market value of the acquirer is less than 1%. The market value of the acquirer is defined as the sum of the market value of equity, long-term debt, debt in current liabilities, and the liquidating value of preferred stock. We also require that the number of days between the announcement and completion dates is between 0 and 1000.

Our requirements yield a sample of 12,023 successful offers. Slightly more than half of the acquisitions are by large firms, which we define as those with a market capitalization above the 25th percentile of NYSE firms in the year in which the acquisition is announced. Table 1 shows the number of acquisitions by year. The number of acquisitions does not increase monotonically through time: it falls in 1990 and in recent years. The number of acquisitions in the 1990s is dramatically larger than

Table 1

Sample distribution by announcement year and acquirer size

The sample contains all completed US mergers and acquisitions between 1980 and 2001 listed on SDC where the publicly traded acquiring firm gains control of a public, private, or subsidiary target whose transaction value is at least $1 million and 1% of the acquirer's market value. Small (large) acquirers have a market capitalization equal to or less (greater) than the market capitalization of the 25th percentile of NYSE firms in the same year.

Announcement Year	Acquirer size		
	Large	Small	All
1980	16	6	22
1981	83	30	113
1982	93	56	149
1983	111	103	214
1984	170	111	281
1985	125	32	157
1986	187	58	245
1987	173	43	216
1988	151	74	225
1989	166	138	304
1990	164	92	256
1991	156	148	304
1992	220	255	475
1993	277	356	633
1994	411	393	804
1995	394	502	896
1996	523	553	1076
1997	689	828	1517
1998	827	681	1508
1999	649	466	1115
2000	582	303	885
2001	353	275	628
All	6520	5503	12,023

in the 1980s. In our tests, we will often use time dummies to take into account these changes. Interestingly, though there are normally fewer acquisitions by small firms than by large firms, this is not the case for most of the 1990s.

2.2. The gains to acquiring-firm shareholders

The most traditional way to evaluate bidder returns is to estimate abnormal percentage returns with standard event study methods (following Brown and Warner, 1985). We estimate these abnormal returns over the 3-day event window $(-1, +1)$ using market model benchmark returns with the CRSP equally weighted index returns. The parameters for the market model are estimated over the $(-205, -6)$ interval, and the p-values are estimated using the time-series and cross-sectional variation of abnormal returns. We also calculate abnormal returns by subtracting the value-weighted CRSP market return from the firm's return. Our results are not sensitive to using either definition of abnormal returns.

The equally weighted abnormal return for our sample of successful offers is given in the first row of Table 2. It is 1.10% and highly significant. The median abnormal return is 0.36% and is also significant. On average, therefore, shareholders of acquiring companies benefit from acquisitions. This result is quite different from the result obtained in samples restricted to acquisitions of public companies, since authors studying such samples typically find that shareholders do not gain from acquisitions; Andrade et al. (2001) report insignificant negative abnormal returns from 1973 to 1998.

The equally weighted abnormal return gives the same weight to a company with a capitalization of $100 million dollars and a company with a capitalization of $100 billion dollars. Yet a given abnormal return has much more of an economic impact if earned by the larger firm. Any assessment of the economic significance of gains to acquiring-firm shareholders should put more weight on the return of a company with a

Table 2

Announcement abnormal returns and dollar abnormal returns: sorted by acquirer size

The sample contains all completed US mergers and acquisitions between 1980 and 2001 listed on SDC where the publicly traded acquiring firm gains control of a public, private, or subsidiary target whose transaction value is at least $1 million and 1% of the acquirer's market value. Small (large) acquirers have a market capitalization equal to or less (greater) than the market capitalization of the 25th percentile of NYSE firms in the same year. $CAR_{(-1, +1)}$ denotes the 3-day cumulative abnormal return (in percent) measured using the market model. $ANPV_{(\$2001)}$ denotes the inflation-adjusted (base 2001 dollars) abnormal dollar returns in millions, defined as the gross change in the value of the acquirer's equity minus the predicted change from the market model. The value-weighted cumulative abnormal return, $VWCAR_{(-1, +1)}$, is the sum of the dollar abnormal returns across acquirers divided by the aggregate market capitalization of acquirers. ANPV/TV is the abnormal dollar return divided by the total transaction value reported by SDC and represents the dollar gain per dollar spent on acquisitions. The final row for each subgroup lists the number of observations. The difference tests are based on *t*-tests for equality in means and a Wilcoxon-test for equality of medians. Median values are in brackets. The sum of the abnormal dollar returns across acquisitions is reported in italics.

	All (1)	Large (2)	Small (3)	Difference (2)–(3)
$CAR_{(-1, +1)}$	1.102[a] [0.362][a]	0.076 [−0.027]	2.318[a] [0.940][a]	−2.242[a] [−0.967][a]
$ANPV_{(\$2001)}$	−25.2[a] [0.5][a]	−47.9[a] [−0.1][a]	1.7[a] [0.6]	−49.6[a] [−0.7][a]
	−$302,742	*−$312,061*	*$9319*	
$VWCAR_{(-1, +1)}$	−1.177	−1.249	1.272	
ANPV/TV	5.613[b] [1.874][a]	2.961 [−0.152]	8.755[a] [3.791][a]	−5.794 [−3.943][a]
n	12,023	6520	5503	

[a]Statistical significance at the 1% level.
[b]Statistical significance at the 5% level.

capitalization of $100 billion dollars than on one with a capitalization of $100 million dollars. One possible approach is to estimate the dollar abnormal return made by acquiring-firm shareholders. This measure, introduced by Malatesta (1983), subtracts from the gross change in the value of the acquirer's equity the predicted change from the market model. The second row of Table 2 shows that the average dollar abnormal return for our sample is −$25.2 million in 2001 dollars. This negative average dollar abnormal return is not caused by a few sample years. There are only 7 years where the average dollar abnormal return is positive (1982, 1984, 1990, 1991, 1993, 1995, and 1996). Aggregating the dollar abnormal returns across firms, we find that the aggregate loss amounts to $303 billion in 2001 dollars over our sample period. In our sample, the equally weighted abnormal return and the equally weighted dollar abnormal return have opposite signs. Such a situation can arise when there is a size effect. If large firms and small firms have different announcement returns, a value-weighted average abnormal return should reflect the announcement returns of large firms. The value-weighted average abnormal return is presented in the third row. It corresponds simply to the sum of the dollar abnormal returns across acquirers divided by the aggregate market capitalization of acquirers. As expected, the value-weighted average abnormal return is negative (−1.18%).

The existence of a size effect in acquiring-firm abnormal returns can be established by dividing the sample into small and large acquiring firms. Table 2 shows that large firms have an insignificant equally weighted abnormal return of 0.08% and a value-weighted abnormal return of −1.25%. In contrast, small firms have an equally weighted abnormal return of 2.32%, significantly higher than that of large firms, and a value-weighted abnormal return of 1.27%.

A legitimate concern is that announcements might be more unexpected for small firms than for large firms. As a result, the announcement returns of large firms would be pulled towards zero compared to small firms. If this were the case, however, the size effect would be even larger for the type of acquisitions where the abnormal return of large firms is negative.

3. Is the size effect explained by firm and deal characteristics?

We first show how firm and deal characteristics differ between large and small acquirers. We then explore whether these differences explain why the abnormal returns of large and small acquirers differ. To do that, we compare abnormal returns for similar deals across large and small acquirers and then use multivariate regressions.

3.1. The relation of acquiring-firm size to firm and deal characteristics

Table 3 shows deal and acquiring-firm characteristics for our sample. We report the information for the whole sample and for large and small firms. The dollar value of acquisitions is much larger for large firms than small firms. This is not surprising, but

Table 3

Summary statistics: sorted by acquirer size

The sample contains all completed US mergers and acquisitions between 1980 and 2001 as listed by SDC where the publicly traded acquiring firm gains control of a public, private, or subsidiary target whose transaction value is at least $1 million and 1% of the acquirer's market value. Small (large) acquirers have a market capitalization equal to or less (greater) than the market capitalization of the 25th percentile of NYSE firms in the same year. The transaction value ($ million) is the total value of consideration paid by the acquirer, excluding fees and expenses. Relative size is the transaction value divided by the equity market capitalization of the acquirer at the end of the fiscal year prior to the acquisition announcement. Competed deals have at least one other bidder for the same target. The liquidity index for the target is calculated as the value of all corporate control transactions for $1 million or more reported by SDC for each year and two-digit SIC code divided by the total book value of assets of all Compustat firms in the same two-digit SIC code and year. The number of days to completion is measured as the number of calendar days between the announcement and effective dates. The cash (equity) in payment is the percent cash (equity) payment of the transaction value. Pure cash (equity) deals are when 100% of the consideration is cash (equity). Acquisitions are defined as tender offers, hostile, and competed deals as reported by SDC. Conglomerate deals involve targets with a two-digit SIC code other than that of the bidder. The percent public, private, and subsidiary targets are the proportions in each sample. In Panel B, Cash includes cash and marketable securities and debt is total assets minus the book value of equity. The firm market value is total book assets minus the book value of equity plus market capitalization. Tobin's q is defined as the firm market value divided by the book value of assets. Operating cash flow (OCF) is sales minus the cost of goods sold, sales and general administration, and working capital change. Book-to-market is defined as in Fama and French (1993). Median values are in brackets.

	Large	Small	All
Panel A: Deal characteristics			
Transaction value (TV)	450.10 [75.70]	29.70[a] [11.50][a]	257.67 [31.00]
TV/assets	0.1041 [0.0412]	0.2811[a] [0.0955][a]	0.1851 [0.0614]
Relative size	0.1928 [0.0803]	0.5016[a] [0.1863][a]	0.3342 [0.1185]
Competed deals	0.0183	0.0049[a]	0.0121
Days to completion	92.70 [68.00]	68.10[a] [35.00][a]	81.45 [52.00]
Liquidity index for target	0.1099 [0.0450]	0.1039[b] [0.0480][a]	0.1072 [0.0453]
Cash in payment (%)	51.25	57.17[a]	53.96
Equity in payment (%)	35.55	28.31[a]	32.23
Pure cash deals (%)	40.09	40.85	40.44
Pure equity deals (%)	28.45	20.04[a]	24.60
Hostile deals (%)	0.63	0.25[a]	00.46
Tender offers (%)	6.04	1.45[a]	03.94
Conglomerate deals (%)	40.54	43.65[a]	41.96
Public target (%)	30.08	12.38[a]	21.97
Private target (%)	38.19	56.21[a]	46.44
Subsidiary target (%)	31.73	31.42	31.59
Panel B: Acquirer characteristics			
Cash/assets (book)	0.1445 [0.0663]	0.1607[a] [0.0730][a]	0.1519 [0.0684]
Assets (book)	4618.6 [959.5]	214.6[a] [74.4][a]	2602.9 [302.2]
Assets (market)	6744.5 [1687.3]	256.0[a] [130.7][a]	3774.7 [530.4]
Equity (market)	3072.6 [806.7]	92.2[a] [72.8][a]	1708.5 [263.2]
Debt/assets (book)	0.4667 [0.4620]	0.4707 [0.4452][c]	0.4686 [0.4548]

(*Continued*)

Table 3 (*Continued*)

	Large	Small	All
Debt/assets (market)	0.2872 [0.2650]	0.3333[a] [0.2925][a]	0.3092 [0.2782]
Tobin's *q*	2.5136 [1.5402]	1.8629[a] [1.3515][a]	2.2158 [1.4461]
OCF/assets (market)	0.1141 [0.0896]	0.1464 [0.0907]	0.1286 [0.0902]
Book-to-market	0.4805 [0.4270]	0.6354[a] [0.5425][a]	0.5514 [0.4757]

[a]Statistical significance between large and small at the 1% level.
[b]Statistical significance between large and small at the 10% level.
[c]Statistical significance between large and small at the 5% level.

what is surprising is that the acquisitions by small firms are larger relative to firm market value (defined as book value of assets minus book value of equity plus market value of equity) or relative to their market value of equity, than are the acquisitions by large firms. Asquith et al. (1983) show that bidder returns increase in the ratio of the target's equity capitalization to the bidder's equity capitalization. This ratio is larger for small acquirers, so that we will have to investigate whether this characteristic helps explain the size effect. It also takes longer for large firms to complete an acquisition than for small firms. This may not be surprising since regulatory issues are typically more important for large firms.

We expect competition for a target to decrease the return to the acquirer. We use as a proxy for competition whether multiple firms make a public bid for the same target. With this proxy, competition is rare, but it is more frequent for large acquirers than for small acquirers. However, our measure suffers from the fact that while sometimes there are multiple potential acquirers, the competition among them takes place privately. Boone and Mulherin (2002) show that, in the 1990s, an acquisition by one public bidder can follow a private auction in which many firms participate. Here our measure of competition would indicate no competition, even though there might have been strong competition in the private auction. Another problem with our proxy for competition is that in a competitive market, a firm might choose to increase the premium offered to deter competition. Hence, we might conclude that there is no competition when in fact potential competition strongly impacts the premium. An alternative proxy for competition is whether a particular acquisition takes place in an active mergers and acquisitions market. As a measure of how active the market for mergers and acquisitions is in an industry, we use (following Schlingemann et al., 2002) the value of all corporate control deals in a particular year and two-digit SIC code divided by the book value of all assets in the corresponding year and two-digit SIC code. We find the mean value for this liquidity index to be marginally higher for large firms than for small firms, but the opposite occurs with medians.

Earlier research shows that equity offers for the acquisition of public firms have lower returns (e.g., Travlos, 1987). In contrast, equity offers for the acquisition of private firms have higher abnormal returns (e.g., Chang, 1998; Fuller et al., 2002). Cash is used more frequently in acquisitions by small firms. Using the SDC definition of hostility, hostile offers have lower abnormal returns (see Schwert, 2000). Few offers are hostile in our sample, but small firms are half as likely to make a hostile offer. Similarly, small firms are much less likely to make tender offers than large firms. Though not reported in Table 3, small firms are never white knights in our sample, while large firms sometimes are. Morck et al. (1990) show that acquirers of public firms have lower abnormal returns for diversifying acquisitions. We define a transaction as diversifying if the target and acquirer have different two-digit SIC codes (using the SIC codes reported by SDC). Small firms are more likely to make diversifying acquisitions than are large firms. Though we do not report this information in Table 3, large firms that acquire public firms are more likely to use options in their offer, make an offer with a collar, have termination fees, and face litigation in the acquisition process.

Next we provide information on the organizational form of the assets acquired. Zingales (1995) presents a model in which the acquirer of a private firm or a subsidiary faces a different bargaining situation than the acquirer of a public firm. With the acquisition of a public firm, the free-rider problem identified by Grossman and Hart (1980) comes into play, so that the shareholders of public firms get a better deal when their firm is acquired than do the shareholders of private firms. However, the owners of private firms or subsidiaries might be more likely to be looking to sell them, either to exit or to raise funds. In such cases, the acquirer might benefit from providing a liquidity service. Most of the existing empirical evidence on acquisitions is on acquisitions of public firms. However, there is evidence that the abnormal return associated with the announcement of acquisitions of private firms and subsidiaries is higher. Fuller et al. (2002) show this for a sample of repeat acquirers in the 1990s and Chang (1998) shows this for a sample of firms acquiring private firms with equity. In our sample, almost half of the acquisitions are private-firm acquisitions. Public-firm acquisitions represent less than one quarter of the sample. Large firms are more than twice as likely as small firms to acquire a public firm. It could therefore be that the size effect is explained by the fact that large firms are more likely to acquire a public firm. In the following, it will therefore be important for us to investigate whether the size effect holds irrespective of the organizational form of the acquired firm. The probability that a subsidiary will be acquired is roughly the same for a small and a large firm.

Panel B of Table 3 provides characteristics of the acquiring firm. Free cash flow theory predicts that firms with empire-building managers and poor investment opportunities prefer to invest the firm's excess cash flow rather than pay it to shareholders. Such firms accumulate excess cash, so that firms with excess cash are more likely to make poor acquisitions (see Harford, 1999). However, small firms have a higher mean and median ratio of cash to total assets, which deepens the puzzle of the size effect. Maloney et al. (1993) show that firms with higher leverage make better acquisitions and small firms have higher leverage than large firms. We also estimate Tobin's q using the market value of the firm's assets divided by the book value. As mentioned earlier, the existing evidence is that firms with higher q values make better acquisitions. Small firms have lower q values than large firms, so that differences in q cannot explain the size effect. Finally, we report the equity book-to-market (BM) ratio, computed as in Fama and French (1993). Dong et al. (2002) argue that firms with low BM ratios are more likely to be overvalued. Small firms have higher BM ratios. There is no significant difference between the operating cash flows of large and small firms.

3.2. Abnormal returns, firm size, deal characteristics, and firm characteristics

We show in Table 4 how abnormal returns differ between large and small firms depending on the organizational form of the assets acquired and the form of payment. We report both abnormal returns and dollar abnormal returns for the rows without the size breakout to show that abnormal returns and dollar abnormal returns can lead to different conclusions because of the size effect. When we compare small firms and large firms, we only report equally weighted (and not dollar or value-weighted) abnormal returns to save space since we already take into account size differences by splitting the sample.

We find that acquisitions have positive abnormal returns irrespective of how they are financed, but the dollar abnormal return is significantly negative when equity is used in payment. For each type of financing, there is a significant difference between small and large firms that ranges from 1.478% for acquisitions paid with cash to 2.986% for those paid with equity only. Strikingly, small firms have significant positive abnormal returns in excess of 2% for each type of financing.

In Panel B, we show that acquisitions of private firms have significantly positive abnormal returns. The highest abnormal returns are for equity and mixed offers as one would expect from the results of Chang (1998) and Fuller et al. (2002). Turning to public targets in Panel C, the abnormal return is significantly negative for the whole sample. Cash offers have an insignificant positive abnormal return, but the other acquisitions have a significant negative abnormal return. The only negative abnormal return for small firms in Table 4 is when they acquire public targets with equity only. Large firms have a significant negative abnormal return for each form of financing— even cash. Finally, we report results for acquisitions of subsidiaries. The abnormal returns are significant irrespective of how the acquisition is financed. Acquisitions of subsidiaries are the most profitable acquisitions, followed by acquisitions of private firms.

3.3. Does size proxy for acquiring-firm and deal characteristics?

The comparisons in Table 4 ignore that firms and deals differ in other dimensions than in the form of financing and the organizational form of assets. To take into account other determinants of abnormal returns, we estimate a multiple regression.

In Table 5, regression (1) uses all the acquisitions for which we have data, regardless of the type of acquisition, and controls for acquiring-firm and deal characteristics.

Table 4

Announcement abnormal returns sorted by organizational form of acquired assets, form of payment, and size

The sample contains all completed US mergers and acquisitions between 1980 and 2001 as listed by SDC where the publicly traded acquiring firm gains control of a public, private, or subsidiary target whose transaction value is at least $1 million and 1% of the acquirer's market value. Small (large) acquirers have a market capitalization equal to or less (greater) than the market capitalization of the 25th percentile of NYSE firms in the same year. Each row includes the mean 3-day cumulative abnormal return (%). Inflation-adjusted dollar abnormal returns (base 2001, $ million), defined as the gross change in the value of the acquirer's equity minus the predicted change from the market model, are reported in brackets for the "All" rows with the number of observations listed below. The groups mixed, equity, and cash are defined as transactions paid for with a mix of cash, equity, and other considerations, all equity, and all cash, respectively. Difference tests are based on t-tests for equality in means.

	Mixed (1)	Equity (2)	Cash (3)	All (4)	Difference tests		
					(1)–(2)	(2)–(3)	(1)–(3)
Panel A: Full sample							
All	1.452[a]	0.153[a]	1.377[a]	1.102[a]	1.300[a]	−1.223[a]	0.076
	[−22.0][a]	[−79.5][a]	[5.1]	[−25.2][a]	[57.5][a]	[−84.6][a]	[−27.2][a]
	n = 4203	n = 2958	n = 4862	n = 12,023			
Small	2.620[a]	2.026[a]	2.171[a]	2.318[a]	0.594	−0.146	0.449
Large	0.227	−0.960[a]	0.693[a]	0.076	1.187[a]	−1.653[a]	−0.466[a]
Difference	2.394[a]	2.986[a]	1.478[a]	2.242[a]			
Panel B: Private targets							
All	1.799[a]	1.493[a]	1.208[a]	1.496[a]	0.305	0.286	0.591[b]
	[−3.5]	[−9.2]	[1.2]	[−3.0]	[6.7]	[−10.4]	[−3.7]
	n = 1970	n = 1553	n = 2060	n = 5583			
Small	2.395[a]	2.701[a]	1.519[a]	2.138[a]	−0.306	1.182[a]	0.875[b]
Large	0.781[a]	0.502[a]	0.813[a]	0.697[a]	0.279	−0.311	−0.032
Difference	1.614[a]	2.199[a]	0.706[b]	1.441[a]			
Panel C: Public targets							
All	−0.401[a]	−2.023[a]	0.364	−1.022[a]	1.622[a]	−2.387[a]	−0.765[c]
	[−101.2][a]	[−183.3][a]	[−33.1]	[−128.2][a]	[82.1]	[−150.2][c]	[−68.1]
	n = 1047	n = 1199	n = 396	n = 2642			
Small	2.010[a]	−0.747[a]	2.843[a]	0.920[a]	2.757[a]	−3.589[a]	−0.833
Large	−1.315[a]	−2.445[a]	−0.418[a]	−1.697[a]	1.130[a]	−2.027[a]	−0.897[b]
Difference	3.325[a]	1.698[a]	3.260[a]	2.616[a]			
Panel D: Subsidiary targets							
All	2.513[a]	2.721[a]	1.688[a]	2.002[a]	−0.207	1.033[c]	0.825[a]
	[15.4][a]	[−5.3]	[14.8][c]	[13.9][a]	[20.7]	[−20.1]	[0.6]
	n = 1186	n = 206	n = 2406	n = 3798			
Small	3.353[a]	5.394[a]	2.857[a]	3.190[a]	−2.040	2.537[b]	0.497
Large	1.587[a]	−0.058	0.854[a]	1.009[a]	1.645[b]	−0.912	0.733[a]
Difference	1.767[a]	5.452[c]	2.003[a]	2.181[a]			

[a]Statistical significance at the 1% level.
[b]Statistical significance at the 5% level.
[c]Statistical significance at the 10% level.

Table 5

Cross-sectional regression analysis of announcement abnormal returns

The sample contains all completed US mergers and acquisitions between 1980 and 2001 as listed by SDC where the publicly traded acquiring firm gains control of a public, private, or subsidiary target whose transaction value is at least $1 million and 1% of the acquirer's market value. The dependent variable is the 3-day cumulative abnormal return measured using the market model. Private, public, small, conglomerates, tender offer, hostile, competed, all equity, and all cash are dummy variables that take the value one for acquisitions of private firms, of public firms, by firms whose capitalization is below the 25th percentile of NYSE firms that year, of firms in another two-digit SIC code than the acquirer, if the acquisition is a tender offer, if it is hostile according to SDC, if there is more than one bidder, if only equity is used to pay for the acquisition, and if only cash is used, respectively. The transaction value ($ million) is the total value of consideration paid by the acquirer, excluding fees and expenses. Relative size is the transaction value divided by the equity market capitalization of the acquirer at the end of the fiscal year prior to the acquisition announcement. The liquidity index for the target is calculated as the value of all corporate control transactions for $1 million or more reported by SDC for each year and two-digit SIC code divided by the total book value of assets of all Compustat firms in the same two-digit SIC code and year. Tobin's q is defined as the firm market value divided by the book value of assets. Operating cash flow (OCF) is sales minus the cost of goods sold, sales and general administration, and working capital change. Significance is based on White-adjusted standard errors with p-values reported below each coefficient.

	Sample				
	All (1)	All (2)	All (3)	Small (4)	Large (5)
Intercept	0.0150[a]	0.0503[a]	0.0465[a]	0.0316[a]	0.0184[a]
	0.000	0.001	0.001	0.001	0.001
Private	−0.0037[b]	−0.0042[b]	−0.0043[c]	−0.0058	−0.0016
	0.085	0.051	0.045	0.104	0.443
Public	−0.0320[a]	−0.0297[a]	−0.0297[a]	−0.0242[a]	−0.0311[a]
	0.000	0.001	0.001	0.002	0.001
Small	0.0159[a]				
	0.000				
In equity (market)		−0.0051[a]			
		0.001			
In assets (book)			−0.0050[a]		
			0.001		
Conglomerate	−0.0036[b]	−0.0039[c]	−0.0037[c]	−0.0038	−0.0045[c]
	0.051	0.033	0.042	0.236	0.016
Tender offer	0.0153[a]	0.0153[a]	0.0154[a]	0.0201	0.0147[a]
	0.001	0.001	0.001	0.175	0.001
Hostile	−0.0116	−0.0109	−0.0109	−0.0387	0.0052
	0.195	0.221	0.222	0.129	0.553
Competed	−0.0067	−0.0054	−0.0056	−0.0302[b]	0.0005
	0.299	0.391	0.375	0.057	0.944
All equity	−0.0029	−0.0027	−0.0033	0.0001	−0.0073[c]
	0.341	0.380	0.276	0.982	0.021
All cash	−0.0039[c]	−0.0031	−0.003	−0.0046	−0.0053[c]
	0.047	0.112	0.129	0.173	0.011

(*Continued*)

Table 5 (*Continued*)

	Sample				
	All (1)	All (2)	All (3)	Small (4)	Large (5)
Relative size	0.0119[a]	0.0110[a]	0.0112[a]	0.0126[a]	−0.0072[b]
	0.001	*0.001*	*0.001*	*0.001*	*0.056*
Tobin's q	−0.0007[b]	−0.0005	−0.001[a]	−0.0008	−0.0007
	0.064	*0.213*	*0.006*	*0.251*	*0.117*
Debt/assets$_{(mkt.)}$	0.0007	−0.0003	0.0133[c]	0.0021	0.0029
	0.876	*0.952*	*0.013*	*0.784*	*0.542*
Liquidity index	−0.0089[a]	−0.0073[c]	−0.0077[b]	−0.0156[c]	−0.0058[c]
	0.003	*0.014*	*0.009*	*0.021*	*0.040*
OCF/assets$_{(mkt.)}$	0.0006	0.0003	0.0005	−0.0003	0.0017
	0.811	*0.905*	*0.853*	*0.929*	*0.635*
N	9712	9712	9712	4583	5129
Adjusted-R^2	0.052	0.055	0.055	0.04	0.04

[a]Statistical significance at the 1% level.
[b]Statistical significance at the 10% level.
[c]Statistical significance at the 5% level.

To capture the size effect, we use a dummy variable that equals one if the acquiring firm is small. Controlling for firm and deal characteristics, we find that the abnormal return of an acquisition is 1.59% points higher if it involves a small acquirer. Keeping everything else the same, firms that make acquisitions of private firms and public firms have significantly lower abnormal returns than firms that make acquisitions of subsidiaries. Whether an acquisition is paid for with equity is not correlated with abnormal returns when the whole sample is used.

Cash acquisitions have significantly lower abnormal returns. This is surprising in light of the evidence for public acquisitions. The reason for this result is that acquisitions of private firms financed with equity or with a mix of securities have higher abnormal returns, while acquisitions of public firms in general have lower abnormal returns. There are two plausible explanations for the higher abnormal returns of all-equity and mixed offers. First, the ownership of the private firm being acquired is normally highly concentrated, so that the owners of the firm can obtain inside information about the true value of the equity they receive as payment for their shares. This conveys favorable information about the true value of the acquirer's shares as in the analysis of private placements of equity by Hertzel and Smith (1993). Second, the owners of the private firm become large shareholders of the acquirer, so that they have incentives to monitor the management of the acquiring firm as suggested by Chang (1998) and Fuller et al. (2002). In a regression not reported here, we find that the abnormal return for acquisitions of private firms does not increase more with the size of the transaction when it is financed with equity only, which is inconsistent with the monitoring hypothesis, which proposes that the incentives to monitor increase with the large shareholder's stake.

Following Asquith et al. (1983), bidder return regressions generally control for the size of the target relative to the size of the acquirer for acquisitions of public firms, to adjust for the impact of an acquisition on the equity market capitalization of the acquiring firm. If a dollar spent on acquisitions has the same positive return irrespective of the size of the acquisition the abnormal return should increase in the size of the target relative to the size of the acquirer. However, if an acquisition is paid for with equity, a larger acquisition will result in a greater increase in the number of shares outstanding at completion of the acquisition, so that if there is a downward-sloping demand for the shares of the acquirers, the abnormal return will fall with the relative size of the acquisition. In the literature, the relative size variable is often significant, but the sign of the coefficient varies across studies. For instance, the relative size is positive in Asquith et al. (1983) but negative in Travlos (1987). Since the relative size variable falls as bidder size increases, all else equal, it follows that bidder returns are negatively related to bidder size when the variable has a positive coefficient.[3] Regression (1) uses relative size, defined as the sum of all consideration paid, excluding fees and costs, divided by the market value of equity of the acquirer as an explanatory variable. This variable has a significant coefficient of 0.0119. The significance of the coefficient on the size dummy variable does not depend on whether we control for the value of the target relative to the value of the acquirer, but adding the relative size variable to the regression reduces the magnitude of the coefficient on the size dummy variable from 0.199 (not reported) to 0.0159. In any case, the size effect is not the same as the relative size effect.

The coefficients of the other variables in regression (1) are similar to those of earlier studies, with some exceptions. As in Morck et al. (1990), conglomerate acquisitions have lower abnormal returns. Acquiring-firm shareholders gain more with tender offers. Almost all tender offers are acquisitions of public firms paid for with cash. Consequently, an acquisition of a public firm paid for with cash through a tender offer has a higher abnormal return than an acquisition of a public firm paid for with equity in a merger. Our proxy for q has a negative significant coefficient, which is surprising since the earlier literature (see Lang et al., 1989; Servaes, 1991) shows a positive relation between abnormal returns and q, but the effect is economically trivial.[4] As expected, acquisitions in industries with more mergers and acquisitions activity, that is,

---

[3] Schwert (2000) finds a positive coefficient on bidder size when examining cumulative abnormal returns from day 63 before the announcement to day 126 after the announcement. His abnormal returns are market model abnormal returns assuming an intercept of zero. The average bidder size in Schwert (2000) is much higher than in our study. Using our sample until 1996, our abnormal returns, and Schwert's (2000) explanatory variables (using only SDC information for hostility), we find that the coefficient on bidder size becomes positive, but insignificant, when we eliminate firms with assets below $250 million.

[4] Earlier evidence by Servaes (1991) for acquisitions of public firms and by Lang et al. (1989) for tender offers shows that high q bidders have higher abnormal returns. If we consider only large-firm acquisitions and use a dummy variable for firms with q below the sample median (regressions not reported), the dummy variable is significantly negative for cash acquisitions in the 1980s, which is consistent with the earlier literature, but the dummy variable is not significant in the 1990s.

industries with a high liquidity index, have lower abnormal returns. Potential competition therefore lowers returns to acquiring-firm shareholders. Finally, the coefficient on leverage, defined as the firm's total debt over the firm's market value, is insignificant, which is surprising in light of Maloney et al. (1993).

In Table 4, we split the sample into large and small firms, but in a regression we can use a continuous measure of size. In regression (2), we replace the size dummy with the logarithm of the market capitalization of the acquiring firm's equity. This coefficient is negative and significant, providing further evidence of the size effect.

We estimate regression (1) for each type of organizational form of the acquired firm and for each type of financing separately to make sure that the size effect is pervasive across types of acquisitions, and this is indeed the case (results not reported). The lowest estimate of the size effect, 1.25%, is for acquisitions of private firms, and the highest estimate, 3.49%, is for acquisitions of public firms. All estimates are significant at better than the 1% level. When we turn to acquisitions of public firms or acquisitions financed with equity, the relative size variable becomes insignificant. We also investigate whether the size effect is robust to controlling for year and industry effects. After adding dummy variables for two-digit SIC code-based major industry classification for acquired firms or acquirers, as well as year dummies, we find that the impact of size remains unaffected (regressions not reported in the table).

As explained earlier, our sample uses only completed offers. At the time of the acquisition, investors do not know whether the acquisition will succeed. The problem with taking into account offers that do not succeed is that the data on uncompleted acquisitions are likely to be much better for acquisitions of public firms because such offers have to be made to public shareholders. Nevertheless, we estimate our regressions using both completed and unsuccessful offers. Though we do not report these regressions, none of our conclusions concerning the size effect depend on whether we use only successful acquisitions or also include unsuccessful acquisitions.

4. Why do large firms have lower announcement abnormal returns than small firms?

In this section, we explore whether the hypotheses advanced to explain the negative abnormal returns associated with acquisitions are more pertinent for acquisitions by large firms. We first examine whether the overvaluation, equity signaling, growth opportunities signaling, and free cash flow hypotheses can explain the size effect. This would require these hypotheses to predict lower returns for acquisitions by large firms, but the hypotheses would not apply to acquisitions by small firms or at least would apply less to them. We then examine whether large firms are more prone to overpay and to undertake offers with negative synergy. Finally, we investigate long-run returns following acquisitions by small and large firms.

4.1. Can overvaluation, signaling, or agency explain the size effect?

We saw in Table 3 that large firms have a higher Tobin's q proxy and a lower BM ratio than small firms. Dong et al. (2002) and others believe that these variables proxy for overvaluation. Since by definition large firms have a high equity capitalization, it could simply be that they are more likely to be overvalued. When they announce the acquisition, they might signal something about their true value to the market, especially when they use equity. The overvaluation hypothesis of Dong et al. (2002) seems hard to disentangle from the equity signaling hypothesis and the growth opportunities signaling hypothesis.

If size proxies for overvaluation, either because of market inefficiency as in Dong et al. (2002) or because of private information as in the signaling hypotheses, equity market capitalization should explain more of the abnormal returns than will the book value of assets. An increase in the stock-price necessarily increases a firm's equity market capitalization, but it does not necessarily increase the book value of a firm's assets. To examine this hypothesis, we use the log of book value of firm assets as our size measure in regression (3) in Table 5. We find that the coefficient on the book value of assets is negative and significant and the adjusted-R^2 of regression (3) is essentially the same as the adjusted-R^2 of regression (2). This evidence is not supportive of the hypothesis that size proxies for overvaluation.

Another way to examine whether the overvaluation and signaling hypotheses explain the size effect is to estimate regression (1) separately for small and large firms. If these hypotheses are relevant for large firms but not small ones, regression (1) would have a size effect because it is misspecified, in that the variables that influence bidder returns do so differentially for large and small firms. Regressions (4) and (5) in Table 5 estimate regression (1) separately for small and large firms. Only one variable has a significantly different impact on small and large firms: the coefficient on the relative size of the acquisition. The relative size coefficient is significantly positive for small firms and significantly negative for large firms. The signaling hypotheses do not predict this difference in the sign of the relative size coefficient. However, if large acquirers systematically overpay for acquisitions, a negative association between bidder gains and bidder size is expected. This suggests that the hubris hypothesis might be relevant for large firms but not small ones. We investigate this possibility more directly for public offers below using premium data for these offers. Finally, if acquisitions are positive net present value projects for small firms, larger acquisitions would lead to a higher net present value and hence a larger abnormal return if the net present value per dollar invested does not depend on the size of the acquisition. The opposite would be the case for large firms if acquisitions are negative net present value project for these firms.

Mitchell et al. (2004) provide evidence that arbitrageurs put pressure on the stock-price of the acquiring firm for all-equity offers for public firms. This is because they establish long positions in target stock and short positions in bidder stock. This price pressure effect should be larger as the size of the acquisition relative to the market capitalization of the bidder increases. From our regressions, this is not the case for the sample as a whole. However, when we estimate our regression for the sample of offers by large firms for public firms paid for with equity, we find a coefficient of −0.061, significant at the 1% level. In contrast, the coefficient on small firms is insignificant and much closer to zero. This evidence is consistent with the hypothesis of Mitchell et al. (2004) applying to large but not small firms.

We also examine, but do not report the estimated regressions, whether the size effect is simply the result that young firms are small. It is not implausible that growth opportunities would be more important for young firms than older ones. However, when we add the age of the firm, measured as the number of years the firm's stock returns have been reported by CRSP, that variable is insignificant.

4.2. Do large firms overpay?

Roll's hubris hypothesis predicts that managers are overconfident and overpay. When Malmendier and Tate (2002) measure overconfidence by the options a manager has left unexercised, they find evidence that overconfident managers make more acquisitions and that abnormal returns are lower. There are good reasons to think that managers of large firms might be more prone to overconfidence. Such managers might have made the firm large or, if not, they might have to overcome more obstacles to become CEOs than managers of small firms. Since we have data on premiums for public offers, we can investigate whether large firms pay more.

As reported by Officer (2003), the data on premiums have a number of problems. SDC reports three pieces of information on premiums. First, they provide the value of the different components of the offer (i.e., the aggregate value of cash, stock, and other securities offered by the bidder to the target shareholders). Second, they provide the initial offer price. Third, they list the terminal offer price. Unfortunately, the premium data are not available for all acquisitions of publicly traded firms. Further, while the components data are available for roughly three-quarters of our sample and the terminal offer price is available for a slightly larger number of acquisitions, the initial offer price is not provided by SDC for more than half of our sample. Since we are interested in understanding the announcement abnormal returns, the best approach is to use the components data, which are available at the time of the announcement. The premium is then defined as the value of the components divided by the market value of the target 50 days prior to the announcement day. We follow Officer (2003) and truncate the premium so that it takes values between zero and two. Alternatively, we follow Schwert (2000) and define the premium as the market model residual for the target firm cumulated over the period starting 63 days prior to the announcement to 126 days after the announcement day.

The mean and median premiums are larger for acquisitions by large firms than for those by small firms when we estimate the premium using the components data and using the target market model residuals. The mean (median) premium for acquisitions by large firms is 68% (61%). In contrast, the mean (median) premium for acquisitions by small firms is 62% (52%). The difference in premiums between acquisitions by large and small firms is significant at the 5% level for the means and medians. However, this result depends on how the premium is computed. In particular, if the premium is computed using the initial or terminal price, it does not hold. This may not be surprising because the sample using the initial price has fewer small firms and the terminal price is affected by stock returns over the life of the offer, which themselves might depend on firm size.

There is ample evidence in the literature that firm and deal characteristics affect the premium paid by the bidder (see, for recent papers, Officer, 2003; Schwert, 2000). It could therefore be that large firms pay more because they acquire targets or enter deals that require a large premium rather than because they are large firms. In Table 6, regression (1) relates the components-based premium paid to firm and deal characteristics using similar specifications as in the recent literature. The variables we use have the same impact on the premium as they do in other papers. Since we lose almost 600 acquisitions and end up with a sample that is biased towards large firms, we use the logarithm of equity market capitalization as our size measure so that we can capture meaningful variation in firm size. There is a strong size effect in the regressions whether estimated using a dummy variable (not reported) or the natural logarithm of the acquirer's equity market capitalization.[5] The size effect holds in regressions in which the dependent variable is a premium computed using the initial price, the terminal price, or the market model cumulated residuals.

If large firms pay more, presumably they should have more success in making acquisitions. Otherwise, it would mean that acquiring-firm size just proxies for firm or deal characteristics that affect the premium but are ignored in our premium regression. Of the offers made by small firms, 13.67% are unsuccessful. In contrast, large firms fail 11.05% of the time. Again, however, firm and deal characteristics affect outcomes. We therefore estimate logistic regressions predicting the outcome of the deal in regressions (2) and (3) in Table 6. We use variables similar to those used in recent studies (see e.g., Officer, 2003; Schwert, 2000). We estimate one regression without the toehold variable since presumably this variable is endogenously determined and one regression with the toehold variable. The results are similar to those obtained for the premiums. We find that large firms are significantly more likely to succeed when they attempt to acquire a public company.

The evidence on premiums and probability of success is consistent with hubris being more of a factor for the managers of large firms. Could this explain the size effect? We add the premium offered to the abnormal return regression for public offers. Doing so reduces the sample size. When we estimate regression (1) of Table 5 on the reduced sample, the coefficient on the size dummy corresponds to an abnormal return difference between small and large firms of 2.63%. The difference becomes 2.68% when we add the premium as an explanatory variable in the regression. When we estimate the regression separately for large and small firms, the coefficient on the premium is significant and negative for large firms, but insignificant and close to zero for small

---

[5] Officer (2003) uses the natural logarithm of the acquirer's equity market capitalization in his premium regressions and reports a significant positive coefficient also.

Table 6

Determinants of the bidder premium and the probability of success

The sample for this table contains all offers by US firms to acquire publicly traded US firms between 1980 and 2001 as listed by SDC where the publicly traded acquiring firm gains control of a public target whose transaction value is at least $1 million and 1% of the acquirer's market value. In model (1), the dependent variable in an OLS regression is the premium, defined as the aggregate value of cash, stock, and other securities offered by the bidder to the target shareholders divided by the market value of equity of the target 50 days prior to the takeover announcement. Premium values that are less than zero or larger than two are eliminated. In models (2) and (3) the dependent variable in a logistic regression is equal to one if the bid is classified by SDC as successful and zero otherwise. The variable ln(Equity) is the natural logarithm of the market value of equity. Toehold is a dummy variable equal to one if the acquirer holds at least 5% of the target shares and zero otherwise. Conglomerates, tender offer, hostile, competed, and all cash are dummy variables that take value one for acquisitions of firms in another two-digit SIC code than the acquirer, if the acquisition is a tender offer, if it is hostile according to SDC, if there is more than one bidder, and if only cash is used, respectively. Significance is based on White-adjusted standard errors for model (1) and quasi-ML robust standard errors for models (2) and (3) with p-values reported below each coefficient. For models (2) and (3) the pseudo-R^2 is reported and P(success) denotes the base case predicted probability of success.

	(1) (OLS)	(2) (Logistic)	(3) (Logistic)
Intercept	0.8379[a]	1.7579[b]	1.9381[a]
	0.000	*0.012*	*0.005*
Premium		0.1207	0.0874
		0.525	*0.638*
All cash	−0.1478[a]	−0.586[a]	−0.6401[a]
	0.000	*0.006*	*0.002*
Toehold	−0.1063	2.1977[b]	
	0.113	*0.011*	
ln(Equity$_{\text{(bidder)}}$)	0.0343[a]	0.4169[a]	0.401[a]
	0.000	*0.001*	*0.001*
ln(Equity$_{\text{(target)}}$)	−0.0329[a]	−0.1827[b]	−0.1862[b]
	0.001	*0.020*	*0.017*
Tender offer	0.1346[a]	1.7541[a]	1.8846[a]
	0.000	*0.001*	*0.001*
Hostile	0.0326	−3.2637[a]	−3.1851[a]
	0.392	*0.001*	*0.001*
Conglomerate	−0.0499[b]	−0.5197[a]	−0.462[a]
	0.016	*0.002*	*0.005*
Tobin's $q_{\text{(bidder)}}$	0.0091	−0.0467[c]	−0.0466[c]
	0.103	*0.077*	*0.076*
Tobin's $q_{\text{(target)}}$	−0.0117	0.0514	0.0469
	0.195	*0.481*	*0.510*
Compete	0.0437	−1.6784[a]	−1.7312[a]
	0.250	*0.001*	*0.001*
P(success)		0.886	0.882
n	1761	1761	1761
Adjusted-R^2 [pseudo-R^2]	0.039	0.292	0.284

[a]Statistical significance at the 1% level.
[b]Statistical significance at the 5% level.
[c]Statistical significance at the 10% level.

firms. Consequently, the greater premium paid by large firms decreases the average abnormal return of large firms. If a large premium is more likely to reflect overpayment for large firms than for small firms, it would explain why the coefficient on the premium is not significant for the sample as a whole but is significant for large firms.

4.3. Do small firm acquisitions have synergy gains?

Large firms pay more. If a firm pays too much, it just redistributes wealth from the shareholders of the acquiring firm to the shareholders of the acquired firm. Overpayment therefore does not affect the wealth of diversified shareholders. However, an acquisition that reduces the total value of the acquired and acquiring firms makes diversified shareholders worse off. Alternatively, an acquisition that has a synergy gain increases the combined value of the acquired and acquiring firms. Bradley et al. (1988) show that on average, acquisitions have a synergy gain for their sample of tender offer acquisitions in the 1970s and 1980s. We examine here whether the synergy gains from acquisitions by small firms differ from the synergy gains from acquisitions by large firms.

We measure the impact of the acquisition announcement on the combined value of the acquiring and acquired firm in percent and in dollars following the method of Bradley et al. (1988). We start by forming a time-series of portfolio returns in event-time for each sample transaction, where the portfolio is a value-weighted average of the target and bidder return accounting for a toehold if SDC reports one. The percentage gain over an event window, $CARC_i$, is defined as the cumulative abnormal return over the event window for the portfolio. Abnormal returns are defined as market model residuals, with the parameters estimated over the $(-205, -6)$ event window relative to the announcement day. The change in the capitalization of the acquiring and acquired firms over an event window, $\$CARC_i$, is defined as the combined value of the acquiring and acquired firms multiplied by the abnormal return.

Table 7 reports the results for the percentage and dollar change in the combined value of the acquiring and acquired firms. For the whole sample, the average cumulative portfolio abnormal return is a significant 1.35%. The dollar abnormal return is a loss of $42.417 million with a t-statistic of -1.701. When we turn to the sample of large firms, we find a significant average abnormal return of 0.68%. The dollar abnormal return represents a loss of $55.501 million with a t-statistic of -1.747. In contrast, the portfolio return for small firms is 3.80% with a z-statistic of 8.254 and is significantly higher (p-value < 0.001) than for large firms. The dollar abnormal return is $5.337 million with a t-statistic of 4.908.

The acquisition announcements of large firms are consistent with the existence of negative synergies. In other words, the firm resulting from the merger is worth less than the constituent firms on their own. In contrast, announcements by small firms exhibit positive synergies when using the percentage abnormal return measure.

4.4. Postevent stock-price performance

So far, we have assumed that the market incorporates information in stock-prices efficiently, so that the announcement return is an unbiased estimate of the impact of

Table 7

Synergy gains: sorted by acquirer size

The sample for this table contains all completed US mergers and acquisitions between 1980 and 2001 as listed by SDC where the publicly traded acquiring firm gains control of a public target whose transaction value is at least $1 million and 1% of the acquirer's market value. The percentage synergy gain, CARC, follows Bradley et al. (1988) and is defined as the cumulative abnormal return over the $(-1, +1)$ event window for a value-weighted portfolio of the target and bidder return. The weights for the bidder and the target are based on the market value of equity 2 days prior to the announcement. The target weight adjusts for the percentage of target shares held by the acquirer prior to the announcement of the deal. Abnormal returns are defined as market model residuals, where the parameters are estimated over the $(-205, -6)$ event window relative to the announcement day. The dollar value synergistic gain over an event window, $CARC_i$, is defined as CARC times the sum of the market value of equity for the bidder and the target in million dollars, adjusted for the percentage of target shares held by the acquirer prior to the announcement of the deal. The z-statistics are based on cross-sectional and time-series variation (see Bradley et al., 1988) and the t-statistic is based on only cross-sectional variation.

	All	Large	Small
CARC	1.352[a]	0.700[a]	3.803[a]
z-statistic	8.091	4.062	8.254
$CARC	−$42.417[b]	−$55.501[b]	$5.337[a]
t-statistic	−1.701	−1.747	4.908

[a]Statistical significance at the 1% level.
[b]Statistical significance at the 10% level.

an acquisition on the wealth of acquiring-firm shareholders. If this is not the case, it could be that the size effect is reversed over time and disappears. To examine this possibility, we compare long-term returns following acquisition announcements for small and large firms separately using the calendar-time approach recommended by Fama (1998).

For each calendar month we form an equally weighted portfolio of firms that made an acquisition in the past 3 years, measured relative to the completion date of the transaction, provided that there are at least ten such firms, both for the whole sample of acquisitions of a particular type and separately for large and small firms. The time-series of portfolio returns net of the risk-free return over the sample period is regressed on the four factors from the Fama and French (1992, 1993) and Carhart (1997) models. The intercept reflects the average monthly abnormal return for the sample. The difference between small and large acquirers' abnormal returns is calculated as the intercept in a regression of the return of a long position in the portfolio of small acquirers and a simultaneous short position in the portfolio of large acquirers.

In Table 8, we report the postevent long-term results for the whole sample and various subsamples. For the whole sample, the monthly abnormal return is 0.018% and insignificant. Long-term abnormal returns would be a source of concern if taking into account these returns would change the conclusions we draw from the announcement

Table 8

Calendar-time postevent monthly abnormal returns

The sample for this table contains all completed US mergers and acquisitions between 1980 and 2001 as listed by SDC where the publicly traded acquiring firm gains control of a public, private, or subsidiary target whose transaction value is at least $1 million and 1% of the acquirer's market value. Each monthly abnormal return is calculated using a time-series regression, where the dependent variable is the equally weighted portfolio return in each calendar month of all bidders within each subgroup that have an event during the 36 months prior to the measurement month. The independent variables are the Fama and French (1993) and Carhart (1997) factors. At least ten firms per month per subgroup must exist to calculate a portfolio return for that subgroup and month. The intercept of the time-series regression for each subgroup is the monthly abnormal return (in percentage). The sample is divided into size (i.e., large, small), organizational form (i.e., private, public, subsidiary), and the form of payment (i.e., mixed, equity, cash). Difference denotes the intercept of the regression of the returns on a long position in the small and a short position in the large firms. For each cell *p*-values are reported in italics.

Form	Payment	All	Large	Small	Difference
Panel A: Whole sample					
All	All	0.018	0.076	−0.031	−0.132
		0.848	*0.420*	*0.846*	*0.426*
Panel B: Sorted by organizational form of acquired assets					
Private	All	0.029	0.273[a]	−0.266	−0.588[b]
		0.815	*0.035*	*0.150*	*0.006*
Public	All	0.040	0.045	0.155	0.058
		0.697	*0.675*	*0.433*	*0.778*
Subsidiary	All	0.000	−0.021	0.092	0.084
		0.999	*0.844*	*0.589*	*0.641*
Panel C: Sorted by form of payment					
All	Mix	−0.004	−0.008	−0.002	−0.028
		0.741	*0.944*	*0.991*	*0.886*
All	Equity	0.178	0.293[c]	0.016	−0.349
		0.209	*0.060*	*0.948*	*0.205*
All	Cash	0.104	0.080	0.143	0.057
		0.346	*0.472*	*0.402*	*0.734*
Panel D: Sorted by organizational form of acquired assets and form of payment					
Private	Mix	−0.065	0.177	−0.257	−0.482[c]
		0.659	*0.251*	*0.234*	*0.059*
	Equity	0.287	0.539[a]	−0.234	−0.763[a]
		0.138	*0.018*	*0.433*	*0.034*
	Cash	0.206	0.235	0.054	−0.158
		0.154	*0.140*	*0.785*	*0.464*
Public	Mix	−0.092	−0.092	0.032	0.027
		0.447	*0.452*	*0.905*	*0.924*
	Equity	0.189	0.152	0.820[a]	0.324
		0.191	*0.320*	*0.030*	*0.344*
	Cash	0.396[a]	0.287[c]	0.764[a]	0.348
		0.012	*0.091*	*0.027*	*0.362*
Subsidiary	Mix	0.105	0.078	0.186	0.109

(*Continued*)

Table 8 (*Continued*)

Form	Payment	All	Large	Small	Difference
		0.449	*0.585*	*0.392*	*0.648*
	Equity	0.316	0.162	0.173	−0.056
		0.391	*0.693*	*0.772*	*0.934*
	Cash	0.012	0.002	0.087	0.095
		0.917	*0.986*	*0.647*	*0.635*

[a]Statistical significance at the 5% level.
[b]Statistical significance at the 1% level.
[c]Statistical significance at the 10% level.

returns. There is no consistent pattern of this happening. Very few subsamples have significant long-term returns. Private-firm acquisitions by large firms have positive long-term abnormal returns, while private-firm acquisitions by small firms have negative, yet insignificant, long-term abnormal returns. The difference between these abnormal returns is significant at the 1% level. Acquisitions of public firms paid for with cash have significant positive abnormal returns.

5. Conclusion

We have shown that small firms fare significantly better than large firms when they make an acquisition announcement. Overall, the abnormal return associated with acquisition announcements for small firms exceeds the abnormal return associated with acquisition announcements for large firms by 2.24% points. Except for acquisitions of public firms paid for with equity, small firms gain significantly when they announce an acquisition. Large firms experience significant shareholder wealth losses when they announce acquisitions of public firms irrespective of how the acquisition is financed. We find that this size effect is robust. It holds (1) in the 1980s as well as in the 1990s, (2) across subsamples of acquisitions constructed based on the form of payment or the organizational form of the assets acquired, and (3) in regressions that control for firm and deal characteristics. There is no evidence that the size effect is reversed over time. Large firms offer larger acquisition premiums than small firms and enter acquisitions with negative dollar synergy gains. The evidence is therefore consistent with managerial hubris playing more of a role in the decisions of large firms. Further work is therefore required to investigate how the size effect relates to managerial incentives and firm governance.

References

Andrade, G., M. Mitchell and E. Stafford, 2001, "New Evidence and Perspectives on Mergers," *Journal of Economic Perspectives*, 15, 103–120.
Asquith, P., R. Bruner and D. Mullins, 1983, "The Gains to Bidding Firms from Merger," *Journal of Financial Economics*, 11, 121–139.

Boone, A. L. and H. J. Mulherin, 2002, "Corporate Restructuring and Corporate Auction," Unpublished Working Paper, Claremont College, Claremont, CA.

Bradley, M., A. Desai and E. H. Kim, 1988, "Synergistic Gains from Corporate Acquisitions and Their Division Between the Stockholders of Target and Acquiring Firms," *Journal of Financial Economics*, 21, 3–40.

Brown, S. J. and J. B. Warner, 1985, "Using Daily Stock Returns: The Case of Event Studies," *Journal of Financial Economics*, 14, 3–31.

Carhart, M. M., 1997, "On the Persistence in Mutual Fund Performance," *Journal of Finance*, 52, 57–82.

Chang, S., 1998, "Takeovers of Privately Held Targets, Method of Payment, and Bidder Returns," *Journal of Finance*, 53, 773–784.

Demsetz, H. and K. Lehn, 1985, "The Structure of Corporate Ownership: Causes and Consequences," *Journal of Political Economy*, 1155–1177.

Dong, M., D. Hirshleifer, S. Richardson and S. H. Teoh, 2002, "Does Investor Misevaluation Drive the Takeover Market?," Unpublished Working Paper, The Ohio State University, Columbus, OH.

Fama, E. F., 1998, "Market Efficiency, Long-Term Returns, and Behavioral Finance," *Journal of Financial Economics*, 49, 283–306.

Fama, E. F. and K. French, 1992, "The Cross-Section of Expected Stock Returns," *Journal of Finance*, 47, 427–465.

Fama, E. F. and K. French, 1993, "Common Risk-Factors in the Returns on Stocks and Bonds," *Journal of Financial Economics*, 33, 3–56.

Fuller, K., J. Netter and M. Stegemoller, 2002, "What Do Returns to Acquiring Firms Tell Us? Evidence from Firms that Make Many Acquisitions," *Journal of Finance*, 57, 1763–1794.

Grossman, S. and O. Hart, 1980, "Takeover Bids, the Free Rider Problem and the Theory of the Corporation," *Bell Journal of Economics*, 10, 20–32.

Harford, J., 1999, "Corporate Cash Reserves and Acquisitions," *Journal of Finance*, 54 (6), 1969–1997.

Hertzel, M. G. and R. L. Smith, 1993, "Market Discounts and Shareholder Gains for Placing Equity Privately," *Journal of Finance*, 48, 459–485.

Jensen, M. C., 1986, "Agency Costs of Free Cash Flow, Corporate Finance, and Takeovers," *American Economic Review*, 76, 323–329.

Jovanovic, B. and S. Braguinsky, 2002, "Bidder Discounts and Target Premia in Takeovers," NBER Working Paper #9009, NBER, Cambridge, MA.

Kaplan, S. and M. S. Weisbach, 1992, "The Success of Acquisitions: Evidence from Divestitures," *Journal of Finance*, 47 (1), 107–138.

Lang, L. H. P., R. M. Stulz and R. A. Walkling, 1989, "Managerial Performance, Tobin's Q, and the Gains from Successful Tender Offers," *Journal of Financial Economics*, 24, 137–154.

Lang, L. H. P., R. M. Stulz and R. A. Walkling, 1991, "A Test of the Free Cash Flow Hypothesis: The Case of Bidder Returns," *Journal of Financial Economics*, 29, 315–336.

Malatesta, P., 1983, "The Wealth Effect of Merger Activity and the Objective Function of Merging Firms," *Journal of Financial Economics*, 11, 155–182.

Malmendier, U. and G. A. Tate, 2002, "Who Makes Acquisitions? CEO Overconfidence and the Market's Reaction," Unpublished Working Paper, Harvard Business School, Cambridge, MA.

Maloney, M. T., R. E. McCormick and M. L. Mitchell, 1993, "Managerial Decision Making and Capital Structure," *Journal of Business*, 66, 189–217.

McCardle, K. F. and S. Viswanathan, 1994, "The Direct Entry Versus Takeover Decision and Stock Price Performance Around Takeovers," *Journal of Business*, 67, 1–43.

Mitchell, M., T. Pulvino and E. Stafford, 2004, "Price Pressure Around Mergers," *Journal of Finance*, 59, 31–63.

Morck, R., A. Shleifer and R. W. Vishny, 1990, "Do Managerial Objectives Drive Bad Acquisitions?," *Journal of Finance*, 45, 31–48.

Myers, S. C. and N. S. Majluf, 1984, "Corporate Financing and Investment Decisions When Firms have Information that Investors Do Not have," *Journal of Financial Economics*, 13, 187–221.

Officer, M., 2003, "Termination Fees in Mergers and Acquisitions," *Journal of Financial Economics*, 69, 431–467.

Roll, R., 1986, "The Hubris Hypothesis of Corporate Takeovers," *Journal of Business*, 59, 197–216.

Schlingemann, F. P., R. M. Stulz and R. A. Walkling, 2002, "Divestitures and the Liquidity of the Market for Corporate Assets," *Journal of Financial Economics*, 64, 117–144.

Schwert, G. W., 2000, "Hostility in Takeovers: In the Eyes of the Beholder?," *Journal of Finance*, 55, 2599–2640.

Servaes, H., 1991, "Tobin's Q, Agency Costs, and Corporate Control: An Empirical Analysis of Firm Specific Parameters," *Journal of Finance*, 46, 409–419.

Shleifer, A. and R. W. Vishny, 2003, "Stock Market Driven Acquisitions," *Journal of Financial Economics*, 70, 295–311.

Travlos, N. G., 1987, "Corporate Takeover Bids, Method of Payment, and Bidding Firm's Stock Returns," *Journal of Finance*, 52, 943–963.

Zingales, L., 1995, "Insider Ownership and the Decision to go Public," *Review of Economic Studies*, 62, 425–448.

Chapter 8

WHY DO PRIVATE ACQUIRERS PAY SO LITTLE COMPARED TO PUBLIC ACQUIRERS?*

LEONCE L. BARGERON

Katz Graduate School of Business, University of Pittsburgh, Pittsburgh, Pennsylvania, USA

FREDERIK P. SCHLINGEMANN

Katz Graduate School of Business, University of Pittsburgh, Pittsburgh, Pennsylvania, USA

CHAD J. ZUTTER

Katz Graduate School of Business, University of Pittsburgh, Pittsburgh, Pennsylvania, USA

RENÉ M. STULZ

Fisher College of Business, The Ohio State University and NBER, Columbus, Ohio, USA

Contents

* Part of this research was conducted while Stulz was visiting the University of Southern California. We thank Henrik Cronqvist, Ken French, Jeff Gordon, Calvin Johnson, Steve Kaplan, an anonymous referee, seminar participants at the University of Pittsburgh and the Ohio State University, and participants at the 2007 New York Society of Quantitative Analysts Conference for valuable comments. Manoj Kulchania provided useful research assistance.

This article originally appeared in the *Journal of Financial Economics*, Vol. 89, pp. 375–390 (2008).
Corporate Takeovers, Volume 1
Edited by B. Espen Eckbo
DOI: 10.1016/B978-0-12-381983-3.00008-3

Abstract

Using the longest event window, we find that public target shareholders receive a 63% (14%) higher premium when the acquirer is a public firm rather than a private equity firm (private operating firm). The premium difference holds with the usual controls for deal and target characteristics, and it is highest (lowest) when acquisitions by private bidders are compared to acquisitions by public companies with low (high) managerial ownership. Further, the premium paid by public bidders (not private bidders) increases with target managerial and institutional ownership.

Keywords

private equity acquisitions, target abnormal returns

JEL classification: G30, G34

1. Introduction

The significant participation of private firms in general and private equity firms in particular in the market for corporate control over recent years has drawn much attention in the press. In 2005, 15% of the total deal value of US mergers and acquisitions came from private equity deals and 18 of the top 100 deals were private equity deals.[1]

Though the press has emphasized the relative importance and growing role of private bidders in the takeover market, academic research has devoted little attention to these bidders. For example, we know of no systematic evidence on whether the gains to target shareholders differ when the acquirer is a private firm rather than a public firm. Yet both academics and the press have suggested reasons why private bidders might behave differently from public bidders. Academics have emphasized that the incentives of private equity firm managers are much more high-powered than those of public firms (see, e.g., Jensen, 1989). There is much debate in the press about whether private equity firms get away with paying lower premiums because target management colludes with the acquirers.[2] In this paper, we provide evidence on how the premiums paid by private acquirers compare to the premiums paid by public companies.

Since a private firm does not have publicly traded equity to offer in an acquisition, it is not surprising that most acquisitions by private firms are cash deals. Therefore, to make an apples-to-apples comparison, it is necessary to compare premiums for cash offers by private firms to premiums for cash offers by public firms. Using a sample of completed cash-only deals during the period 1980–2005 consisting of 453 deals by private bidders and 1214 deals by public bidders, we find a sizable difference in premiums between the two types of acquisitions, measured as in Schwert (1996) from preannouncement runup to completion. In our sample, the average premium for target shareholders when the bidder is a public firm is 46.5%. The average premium when the acquirer is a private operating company is 40.9%, and it is only 28.5% when the acquirer is a private equity firm, so that the premium for an acquisition by a public firm is 63.3% higher than for an acquisition by a private equity firm. Similar results hold for other premium measures.

Why are there such differences in the gains to target shareholders between acquisitions by public firms versus private firms? The simplest explanation is that public firms and private firms acquire different types of firms. With such an explanation, target shareholders do not necessarily receive less if a private firm acquires their firm than they would if a public firm made the acquisition. One might also argue that acquisitions by public firms generate more shareholder wealth because public firms are operating companies, so that such acquisitions would have synergy gains that are

---

[1] These statistics from Mergerstat are cited in "A high-water mark?" by Tim Reason, CFO Magazine, January 1, 2006.

[2] See, for example, Newsweek, April 24, 2006.

shared with the target. Similarly, private equity firms acquire firms for which synergy gains are nonexistent, and hence premiums for the acquired firms are not driven as high as the premiums that public firms pay.

Nonetheless, we find that for most premium measures private operating companies pay less than public firms (47.9% of the private bidders in our sample are operating companies). Whether private operating companies pay more than private equity companies depends on the measure of the premium used. If we use a premium estimated from the preannouncement runup to completion, private operating companies pay more than private equity companies. If, instead, we use a 3-day announcement return, there is no premium difference. Further, when we take into account target and deal characteristics, private operating companies pay less for acquisitions than public companies irrespective of the premium measure, but whether they pay more than private equity firms depends on the premium measure used. It is clear, however, that there is support for an important role for synergy gains in explaining the premium difference when we use premiums estimated over a long window.

A vast literature shows that differences in firm and deal characteristics help explain differences in target gains. Controlling for target and deal characteristics does not reduce the difference in target premiums between private acquisitions and public acquisitions. If observable target and deal characteristics do not explain the difference in premiums, either target and deal characteristics we cannot observe with our dataset explain the difference or private bidders and public bidders make different offers for similar firms. There are at least two possible explanations for why offers would depend on the organizational form of the bidder. First, failure of an offer has more adverse consequences for managers of public firms than for managers of private firms.[3] In particular, public firms might have to reveal more information about their strategy in the process of making an offer, which could possibly help competitors and perhaps make it more likely that an unsuccessful acquirer becomes a target. However, Lehn and Zhao (2006) find that managers are more likely to keep their jobs if they cancel an offer to which the market has reacted poorly instead of going through with the acquisition. Second, as advanced by Jensen (1989) and others, agency problems might be more serious in many public firms than in private firms. There is a long tradition in finance, starting with Berle and Means (1932), questioning whether managers with low firm ownership make decisions that go against the interests of shareholders. This tradition emphasizes the potential for managers to gain from acquisitions that do not benefit shareholders. In particular, managers can gain in prestige from managing larger firms, receive more perks, be better compensated, and be safer from hostile takeovers.

To address the agency view, we examine the difference in target premiums between private bidders and public bidders with highly concentrated managerial ownership

---

[3] We thank Jeff Gordon for this suggestion.

(defined broadly as ownership by insiders). The difference in target shareholder gains is highest when acquisitions by private equity firms are compared to acquisitions by public firms with managerial ownership of less than or equal to 1% and insignificant when private equity firm acquisitions are compared to acquisitions by public firms with managerial ownership in excess of 50%. In addition, private firms differ from the bidding behavior of public firms in that private firms are much less reluctant to walk away from a deal than are public firms—while 37.4% of the offers by private firms are withdrawn, only 16.9% of the offers by public firms are withdrawn. This evidence is consistent with the hypothesis that failure is more costly for public firms, but it could also reflect greater agency costs in the typical public firm relative to private firms or a greater willingness of private firms to make offers that have little chance of success.

We also investigate the hypothesis that target shareholders are somehow cheated in acquisitions by private firms because target managers are willing to sell to private bidders at a lower price. Such an argument makes sense if a private acquirer can offer the promise of continued employment to target managers along with the possibility of a large payoff if they improve the firm enough that it eventually goes public again. With this hypothesis, however, we expect that the difference in shareholder gains falls as the share ownership of target managers increases because, as their stake increases, they lose more from a low acquisition premium. We also expect the premium difference to fall as institutional ownership increases because institutional shareholders have greater ability and incentives to force management to seek improvements in the premium offered. We find that target shareholder gains are higher for firms with greater managerial ownership, but only for our long-horizon premium estimates. When we allow the relation between the shareholder gains and target ownership to depend on the type of acquirer, we find weak evidence that target managerial ownership drives up the premium for acquisitions by public firms but not by private firms. Institutional ownership in the target firm leads to higher premiums for public acquirers but has no impact on premiums when the acquirer is a private firm. It could well be that private firms make acquisitions only if the target management is cooperative, possibly because of private gains from the acquisition, and such cooperation from target management weakens the efforts of institutional investors to increase the premium. Supporting this perspective, we find that no private equity acquisition in our sample is hostile.

The remainder of the paper is organized as follows. In Section 2, we describe our sample of acquisitions by private and public firms. In Section 3, we compare target gains for acquisitions by private firms and by public firms. We also compare the target gains for acquisitions by different types of private firms. In Section 4, we control for target and deal characteristics. Section 5 examines the relation between premium differences and ownership concentration at public firms. In Section 6, we examine whether premium differences are related to target managerial and institutional ownership. We conclude in Section 7.

2. The sample of acquisitions

We collect our sample of acquisitions from the Securities Data Company's (SDC) US Merger and Acquisition Database. To obtain a sample where offers are most comparable between types of acquirers, we collect all completed majority acquisitions for the period 1980–2005 between US public targets and US bidders in which the acquirer owns 100% of the shares of the target after the deal. We exclude all transactions with nonoperating targets, without disclosed deal value, and labeled as spin-offs, recaps, self-tenders, exchange offers, repurchases, minority stake purchases, acquisitions of remaining interest, or privatizations. We check the Lexis-Nexis database for announcement press releases for the private bidders and we exclude all cases where the bidder is a group of individual investors. We further require each target firm to match on the Center for Research in Securities Prices (CRSP) and Compustat databases and to have a share code indicating a public firm (10, 11). We follow Schwert (1996) and require that the acquisition from first bid to completion takes place in no more than 1 year. Finally, we want to focus on a sample of cash-only offers to have an apples-to-apples comparison between deals that involve private bidders and those that involve public bidders. Excluding noncash deals results in a final sample of 1667 deals where 453 deals involve a private bidder and 1214 deals have a public bidder according to SDC. Though all results reported in tables use this sample, we have also estimated our regressions using broader samples. All the conclusions we draw from our regression analysis hold if we include failed offers, other forms of payment (including all-equity offers), groups of individual investors, or offers for majority interests where the bidder ends up with less than 100% of the target shares.

Table 1 shows the distribution of the number and aggregate value of the acquisitions through time. The fraction of acquisitions each year made by private companies is highest at the end of the 1980s and in recent years. The dollar amounts of the acquisitions by private companies are extremely large in 1988, 2004, and 2005 compared to any other year. The fractions of the total value of acquisitions by private bidders are large in 2004 and 2005 compared to most other years in the sample. In these 2 years, the value of the acquisitions by private companies averages 28.3% of the total value of acquisitions. With the exception of the 2003–2004 and 2004–2005 periods, there is no other 2-year period for which that fraction exceeds 20%.

Though we do not report the results in a table, we investigate the distribution of the acquisitions across industries. The fraction of acquisitions in manufacturing industries is greater for public firm bidders (43.1%) than for private firm bidders (35.8%). The second-most-important group of industries in the sample is the group of service industries (22.4% of acquisitions by public firms and 24.3% of acquisitions private firms). Among the other industries, acquisitions of financial firms are less prevalent for private bidders (11.9% of all acquisitions by private firms) than for public firms (15.2%), but acquisitions of firms in the retail industry are more prevalent for private firms (13.0%) than for public firms (5.7%).

Table 1

Number of deals and aggregate deal value by type of bidder over time. The sample includes all SDC completed cash-only merger and acquisition deals between a US bidder and a US public target announced between 1980 and 2005 that result in 100% ownership by the bidder. The aggregated deal value is in CPI-adjusted 2005 millions of dollars.

Year	All bidders		Public bidders		Private bidders		Private bidders % of all deals		Private equity bidders % of private bidder deals	
	n	Deal value	n	Deal value	n	Deal value	Deals	Deal value	Deals	Deal value
1980	3	1190	3	1190	0	0	0	0	–	–
1981	7	4209	5	3981	2	228	29	5	0	0
1982	9	328	8	318	1	10	11	3	0	0
1983	3	80	2	77	1	3	33	3	100	100
1984	15	8812	11	6220	4	2592	27	29	25	53
1985	59	61,617	50	57,100	9	4517	15	7	33	20
1986	91	50,910	72	43,822	19	7088	21	14	63	82
1987	60	20,532	45	17,380	15	3153	25	15	60	41
1988	99	79,754	64	65,561	35	14,194	35	18	71	51
1989	64	33,728	44	29,716	20	4012	31	12	35	27
1990	25	4689	23	4415	2	275	8	6	50	84
1991	19	2873	14	2672	5	201	26	7	40	73
1992	17	4679	13	4310	4	369	24	8	25	59
1993	26	6649	20	6186	6	463	23	7	50	86
1994	59	36,365	47	33,934	12	2431	20	7	25	7
1995	97	36,017	76	34,323	21	1694	22	5	24	11
1996	88	46,111	66	42,029	22	4082	25	9	41	38
1997	114	57,324	84	49,593	30	7731	26	13	63	60
1998	127	60,979	88	48,760	39	12,219	31	20	38	42
1999	146	75,784	104	64,511	42	11,274	29	15	64	81
2000	120	96,954	83	89,180	37	7774	31	8	51	56
2001	93	33,427	74	28,786	19	4641	20	14	32	81
2002	79	20,807	57	17,161	22	3647	28	18	50	80
2003	80	20,531	47	17,149	33	3382	41	16	73	70
2004	79	67,338	54	45,735	25	21,603	32	32	72	98
2005	88	89,693	60	67,713	28	21,980	32	25	54	81
Total	1667	921,382	1214	781,821	453	139,561	27	15	52	66

Table 1 also reports the distribution of acquisitions across types of private firms. To identify the type of private firm acquirer, we search the Lexis-Nexis database for press releases around the announcement period of each of the deals that (according to SDC) involves a private bidder. We divide the private acquirers into private equity acquirers and private operating company acquirers. By private equity acquirers, we mean all private entities that are not private operating companies. The largest private equity transaction in our sample is the acquisition of Sungard Datasystems in 2005 for almost $11 billion by a consortium that includes Blackstone and KKR. The largest acquisition by a private operating company is the 1988 acquisition of Koppers Company by BNS, Inc., for $2.8 billion (in 2005 CPI-adjusted dollars).

As noted before, some acquisitions are made by groups of investors. The largest acquisition by a group of investors is the acquisition of Park Communications for $938 million (in 2005 CPI-adjusted dollars). The acquisition took place through an auction with five qualified bidders. The main acquiring investors, Donald Tomlin and Dr. Gary Knapp, were the principals of an acquisition company, PAI. Throughout the paper, we exclude groups of investors from the private firm acquirers. Alternative approaches would be to include these investor groups among the private equity acquirers or to create a third group of private firm acquirers. Results when we define private equity acquirers to include private investor groups are similar to the results reported here and we conclude that no insights would be gained by having a third group of private firms.

3. Gains to target shareholders for public bidders and private bidders

We use the CRSP database to collect daily return data for our sample of targets. To measure the premium received by the target, we estimate size and book-to-market portfolio-adjusted buy-and-hold abnormal returns from 42 days before the *first* bid to completion (FBC premium) using the returns on the 25 Fama-French size and book-to-market portfolios (our results are similar if we use market-model cumulative abnormal return (CAR) measures). As Schwert (1996) notes, this approach to estimating the premium has the advantage of including all of the days when the offer to the target shareholders might have changed as well as any pre-bid runup. With this measure of the premium, it cannot be argued that somehow we find differences in premiums because takeover contests proceed differently for private bidders than they do for public bidders.

There is an obvious problem with using a premium measure estimated over a long period of time in that such a measure is sensitive to misspecification of the benchmark return (see Kothari and Warner, 2007). We therefore also estimate target shareholder gains over short event windows using standard event study methods (see, e.g., Brown and Warner, 1985) since such estimates are relatively insensitive to benchmark returns. We compute CARs using market-model abnormal returns based on the CRSP value-weighted index. Market-model parameters are estimated from day -379 to day -127 relative to the first acquisition announcement day as in Schwert (1996). Such a measure is much less sensitive to benchmark specification (see Brown and Warner, 1985), but it would be biased and incomplete if there are systematic differences in how information about acquisition likelihood and terms is revealed to the market before and after the bid announcement between private and public acquisitions.

The first row of Panel A of Table 2 shows the mean and median abnormal returns for the FBC premium. The average premium for acquisitions by public firms is 46.5%. In contrast, the average premium for acquisitions by private firms is 34.4%. The difference is similar for the medians. Consequently, shareholders of firms acquired

Table 2

Target return measures for different bidder types:

The sample includes all SDC completed cash-only merger and acquisition deals between a US bidder and a US public target announced between 1980 and 2005 that result in 100% ownership by the bidder. Panel A reports mean and median [in brackets] return measures for the full sample (All) and for subsamples consisting of private bidders, public bidders, and their difference. Panel B reports mean and median [in brackets] return measures for each private bidder type. The p-value for each difference between the mean [median] return for the private bidder type and public bidders is reported. The last two columns report the difference in mean [median] returns and its significance level across the private bidder types. All reported p-values are based on t-tests for differences in the mean and on Wilcoxon tests for differences in the median. The variable FBC (WBC) is the Fama-French size and book-to-market portfolio-adjusted buy-and-hold return from 42 trading days prior to the announcement of the first (winning) bid to the completion date. The variable MFBC (MWBC) is the cumulative abnormal return from 42 trading days prior to the announcement of the first (winning) bid to the completion date, based on market-model parameters. The variables CAR3, CAR5, and CAR11 are, respectively, the 3-, 5-, and 11-day cumulative abnormal returns around the announcement day, based on market-model parameters. The variable FFRET is the Fama-French size and book-to-market portfolio-adjusted buy-and-hold return from 1 day before the announcement date to the completion date of the transaction. RUNUP is the market-adjusted buy-and-hold return from 63 days prior to the announcement to 6 days prior to the announcement.

Panel A: Return measures for private versus public bidders

	All bidders	Private bidders	Public bidders	Private-public	
				Difference	p-Value
FBC	0.4322 [0.3685]	0.3444 [0.2841]	0.4650 [0.3956]	−0.1206 [−0.1115]	0.000 [0.000]
MFBC	0.4002 [0.3556]	0.3273 [0.2895]	0.4274 [0.3776]	−0.1002 [−0.0881]	0.000 [0.000]
WBC	0.4248 [0.3626]	0.3371 [0.2781]	0.4576 [0.3888]	−0.1205 [−0.1107]	0.000 [0.000]
MWBC	0.3938 [0.3465]	0.3130 [0.2824]	0.4240 [0.3742]	−0.1110 [−0.0918]	0.000 [0.000]
CAR3	0.2747 [0.2181]	0.2206 [0.1775]	0.2948 [0.2361]	−0.0743 [−0.0585]	0.000 [0.000]
CAR5	0.2851 [0.2268]	0.2239 [0.1806]	0.3080 [0.2463]	−0.0841 [−0.0657]	0.000 [0.000]
CAR11	0.3045 [0.2528]	0.2398 [0.2042]	0.3287 [0.2705]	−0.0888 [−0.0663]	0.000 [0.000]
FFRET	0.2990 [0.2345]	0.2528 [0.1925]	0.3162 [0.2496]	−0.0634 [−0.0572]	0.001 [0.001]
RUNUP	0.0909 [0.0490]	0.0837 [0.0414]	0.0936 [0.0533]	−0.0099 [−0.0119]	0.546 [0.456]

Panel B: Return measures by private bidder type

	Private equity bidders	Difference from public p-value	Private operating bidders value	Difference from public p-value	Private equity-private operating	
					Difference	p-Value
FBC	0.2847 [0.2620]	0.000 [0.000]	0.4093 [0.3504]	0.114 [0.058]	−0.1246 [−0.0884]	0.002 [0.005]
MFBC	0.3004 [0.2860]	0.000 [0.000]	0.3566 [0.2943]	0.096 [0.053]	−0.0562 [−0.0083]	0.228 [0.344]
WBC	0.2793 [0.2607]	0.000 [0.000]	0.3999 [0.3230]	0.093 [0.061]	−0.1206 [−0.0622]	0.002 [0.004]
MWBC	0.2832 [0.2707]	0.000 [0.000]	0.3453 [0.2877]	0.050 [0.050]	−0.0621 [−0.0170]	0.162 [0.184]

(Continued)

Table 2 (*Continued*)

Panel B: Return measures by private bidder type

	Private equity bidders	Difference from public *p*-value	Private operating bidders value	Difference from public *p*-value	Private equity-private operating	
					Difference	*p*-Value
CAR3	0.2064 [0.1816]	0.000 [0.000]	0.2360 [0.1749]	0.016 [0.000]	−0.0296 [0.0067]	0.257 [0.828]
CAR5	0.2080 [0.1760]	0.000 [0.000]	0.2413 [0.1898]	0.008 [0.000]	−0.0333 [−0.0138]	0.215 [0.506]
CAR11	0.2179 [0.1932]	0.000 [0.000]	0.2638 [0.2109]	0.018 [0.001]	−0.0459 [−0.0177]	0.119 [0.242]
FFRET	0.2251 [0.1840]	0.000 [0.001]	0.2830 [0.1955]	0.267 [0.136]	−0.0580 [−0.0115]	0.073 [0.193]
RUNUP	0.0652 [0.0209]	0.151 [0.154]	0.1039 [0.0624]	0.658 [0.737]	−0.0386 [−0.0415]	0.164 [0.166]

by public firms receive about 35% more than shareholders of firms acquired by private firms. In the second row, we show estimates of the premium using CARs from the market model (MFBC premium) from 42 trading days before the first bid to the completion date of the transaction. In this case, shareholders of firms acquired by public firms receive 30.6% more than shareholders acquired by private firms. The abnormal return of the target from 42 days before the announcement of the bid by the *winning* firm to completion (i.e., WBC and MWBC) is similar.

We next turn to estimates of shareholder gains obtained from narrow windows around the announcement date (unless we say otherwise, the announcement date is always the date at which the winning bid is announced). Using a CAR for a 3-day window (CAR3), we find that shareholders of firms acquired by public firms earn 29.5% on average over the 3 days around the announcement of the acquisition. In contrast, shareholders of firms acquired by private firms earn 22.1%, or 25.2% less than if the bidder were public. We find similar results using a 5-day window (CAR5) and an 11-day window (CAR11).

To evaluate the relevance of the short event-window premium estimates, it is useful to evaluate whether information revealed in the runup period and the post-runup period differs between types of acquirers. We therefore calculate abnormal returns for the runup period (RUNUP) and from the day before the announcement date to the close of the acquisition using size and book-to-market portfolio-adjusted buy-and-hold returns (FFRET). The results are similar using market-model CARs. Table 2 shows that the target shareholder returns from announcement to the close of the acquisition are significantly lower for acquisitions made by private firms than for acquisitions made by public firms. The absolute value of this difference is similar to that of the announcement returns and is economically large as well. In contrast, there is no difference in RUNUP. It follows that focusing on the 3-day abnormal return does not lead us to understate the premium paid by private firms compared to public firms.

We now turn to the differences across types of private acquirers. Given the interest in acquisitions by private equity firms, such a comparison is important and helps in explaining why target shareholders gain less when a private company makes an acquisition since private operating companies are more similar to public acquirers than are private equity companies. Panel B of Table 2 shows estimates of the acquisition premium by the two types of private acquirers. The average FBC premium is 28.5% for private equity acquirers. This premium is significantly lower than the premium paid by the public acquirers and is roughly 6% points less than the sample average for all private acquirers. Strikingly, target shareholder premiums are 63.3% higher if an offer is by a public firm rather than by a private equity firm. Given these numbers, private operating companies must pay more than private equity firms. We find that private operating companies pay a 40.9% premium on average. With the FBC premium measure, there is no significant difference between the average premium paid by private operating companies and public firms—but there is a significant difference in the medians.

As we did in Panel A, we provide alternative estimates of the gains to the target shareholders. For acquisitions by private equity firms, the results are all consistent with the results obtained for the FBC premium. However, the same cannot be said for the results for private operating companies. All other estimates of target shareholder premiums show that the mean premium is significantly lower when the firm is acquired by a private operating company relative to when it is acquired by a public firm.

The last two columns of Panel B show that there is no significant difference between target shareholder premiums paid by private equity firms versus private operating companies except when we use premiums estimated from the pre-runup period to completion and use market-to-book and size portfolios as benchmarks.

If private equity firms cannot typically exploit operating synergies from their acquisitions, we would expect that target firms that have the potential for synergies would be acquired by operating firms and would have a higher premium. In contrast, firms without the potential for synergies would be acquired by private equity firms and would have a lower premium. It follows from the results in Panel B of Table 2 that the lack of synergies could help explain the lower announcement returns for acquisitions by private equity firms compared to acquisitions by public firms and private operating firms. However, such a conclusion is highly sensitive to how premiums are measured. Except for the long windows using the market-to-book and size portfolios, there is no evidence of a difference in target premiums between acquisitions by private operating firms and acquisitions by private equity firms. To further check the role of synergies, we estimate the premiums for acquisitions by firms that are in the same two-digit SIC code industry as the target and for acquisitions by firms that are not in the same two-digit SIC code industry. Though we do not report the results in a table, in general we find that the within-industry acquisitions have insignificantly different premiums from the diversifying acquisitions within both the public and private bidder groups. (For private nonoperating bidders, an SIC code industry classification might be meaningless.)

Lastly, we estimate the premiums for each half of the sample period, though we do not reproduce the results in a table. In particular, we estimate premiums for the 1980–1992 and 1993–2005 periods. When considering the CAR3 premium measure, we observe an increase in the average premium from the earlier to the later period for both public bidders and private bidders; however, the increase in the private bidder deals is only attributable to the private operating companies, so that the CAR3 premium actually falls for private equity acquirers. There is evidence that the FBC premium is lower in the second half of the sample for private equity acquirers and is unchanged for acquisitions by public firms.

4. Can target characteristics explain the difference in premiums?

In this section, we investigate whether private firms acquire different types of firms and structure deals differently than public firms and whether these differences explain the difference in target premiums. We focus on target and deal characteristics that the empirical and theoretical literatures have found important. We first explore these characteristics at the univariate level in Section 4.1 and then continue with multiple regression analyses in Section 4.2.

4.1. Univariate comparisons of target and deal characteristics

Panel A of Table 3 compares target characteristics for public and private bidders. The first variable we consider is the market value of target equity (MVE) 63 trading days prior to the announcement measured in CPI-adjusted 2005 dollars. We compute this value from CRSP data. We find that public acquirers make significantly larger acquisitions. There is evidence that target shareholders gain less when their firm is larger (see, e.g., Officer, 2003), so the fact that public firms make larger acquisitions increases the puzzle of why premiums are higher for acquisitions by public firms than for acquisitions by private firms. We next consider a measure of leverage (DEBT) equal to the ratio of the book value of debt to the sum of the book value of debt and the market value of equity. Firms acquired by private acquirers are substantially more levered than firms acquired by public firms. To the extent that more highly levered firms have a weaker bargaining position since they do not have the option to recapitalize to defend against the takeover attempt, we expect acquisitions by private firms to benefit target shareholders less. However, it could also be that leverage facilitates more concentrated ownership of the target and hence forces a successful acquirer to offer a greater premium (see, e.g., Stulz, 1988).

Firms acquired by private firms have a significantly lower Tobin's q (Q) than firms acquired by public acquirers. A lower Tobin's q could be explained by low growth opportunities. As emphasized by Jensen (1986), firms with low growth opportunities but high cash flows are prone to agency problems of free cash flow, so that private equity buyers can create value by providing an organizational form where these

Table 3

Summary statistics on target and deal characteristics

The sample includes all SDC completed cash-only merger and acquisition deals between a US bidder and a US public target announced between 1980 and 2005 that result in 100% ownership by the bidder. Panel A reports mean and median [in brackets] values for target characteristics. Accounting variables are from Compustat. The market value of equity (MVE) is from CRSP calculated as the CPI-adjusted (2005 dollars) price of the stock times the number of shares outstanding 63 days prior to the announcement date. Debt-to-assets (DEBT) is calculated as the book value of debt divided by the sum of the book value of debt and the market value of equity. Tobin's q (Q) is defined as the firm market value divided by the book value of assets. Industry-adjusted Tobin's q (IAQ) is defined as Tobin's q minus the median two-digit SIC code industry value of this variable. Age (AGE) is the number of months that the firm has been listed on CRSP. Sales growth (ΔSALES) and employee growth (ΔEMPLOYEE) are both based on the 3-year compounded annual growth in sales and number of employees. R&D is the expense on research and development divided by the book value of assets. Intangible assets (INTANGIBLE) is calculated as the fraction of the firm's assets minus net PPE and minus current assets, divided by the book value of assets. Operating cash flow (OCF) is defined as sales minus costs of goods sold, sales and general administrative expenses, and change in net working capital, divided by book value of assets. ARET_12 is the market-adjusted buy-and-hold return for the 12 months prior to the runup period. TARLIQ is the liquidity of the market for corporate control for the target firm's industry and is defined as the value of all corporate control transactions for $1 million or more reported by SDC for each year and two-digit SIC code divided by the total book value of assets of all Compustat firms in the same two-digit SIC code and year. STDEVAR and STDEV are defined, respectively, as the standard deviation of the market-model residuals and raw returns from day −379 to day −127 relative to the announcement date. STOCKLIQ is the measure of stock illiquidity of Amihud (2002). SEGMENTS is the number of business segments reported on Compustat. FOCUS is an indicator variable equal to one if SEGMENTS is equal to one. NASDAQ is an indicator variable equal to one if the target firm is listed on the Nasdaq exchange. In Panel B, mean (and median for continuous variables in brackets) values are reported for deal characteristics. The deal value (CPI-adjusted 2005 $ million) (DEALVALUE) is the total value of consideration (cash) paid by the acquirer, excluding fees and expenses. TENDER, DIVERSIFY, MBO, TOEHOLD, HOSTILE, BANKRUPT, DEFENSE, TARLOCK, BIDLOCK, TARTERM, and BIDTERM are indicator variables from SDC equal to one if the deal, respectively, is a tender offer, involves a bidder that holds 0.5% or more of the target stock prior to the announcement, is hostile, includes a bankrupt target, includes a defensive tactic, includes target or bidder lockup provisions, or includes target or bidder termination fees. COMPETE is an indicator variable equal to one if another deal for the same target is announced in SDC during the 12 months prior to the announcement date. INITBID is an indicator variable equal to one if the announcement of the offer is followed by an offer by another firm, while no bids took place during the 12 months before the announcement. The variable DAY is the number of calendar days between the announcement date and the completion date.

Panel A: Target characteristics

	All bidders	Private bidders	Public bidders	Private-public Difference	p-Value	Private equity bidders	Difference from public p-value	Private operating bidders	Difference from public p-value	Private equity-private operating Difference	p-Value
MVE	324.5862 [93.9366]	199.4723 [70.5135]	371.2720 [104.0371]	−171.7997 [−33.5236]	0.000 0.000	262.4093 [93.0717]	0.031 0.117	131.0248 [54.6712]	0.000 0.000	131.3845 [38.4005]	0.006 0.000

(Continued)

Table 3 (*Continued*)

	All bidders	Private bidders	Public bidders	Private-public Difference	p-Value	Private equity bidders	Difference from public p-value	Private operating bidders	Difference from public p-value	Private equity-private operating Difference	p-Value
DEBT	0.1961	0.2259	0.1849	0.0409	0.000	0.2393	0.000	0.2112	0.068	0.0281	0.144
	[0.1473]	[0.1841]	[0.1332]	[0.0509]	0.001	[0.2104]	0.000	[0.1617]	0.091	[0.0487]	0.172
Q	1.4726	1.2629	1.5509	−0.2880	0.000	1.2880	0.000	1.2356	0.000	0.0524	0.405
	[1.1769]	[1.0732]	[1.2134]	[−0.1402]	0.000	[1.1545]	0.000	[1.0361]	0.000	[0.1184]	0.026
IAQ	−0.0168	−0.1658	0.0389	−0.2047	0.000	−0.1684	0.001	−0.1630	0.000	−0.0054	0.933
	[−0.1043]	[−0.1872]	[−0.0667]	[−0.1205]	0.000	[−0.2059]	0.000	[−0.1679]	0.001	[−0.0380]	0.632
AGE	136.3761	137.0309	136.1318	0.8991	0.899	145.4534	0.334	127.8710	0.340	17.5824	0.135
	[91.0000]	[99.0000]	[90.0000]	[9.0000]	0.141	[102.5000]	0.082	[98.0000]	0.639	[4.5000]	0.284
ΔSALES	0.1704	0.1173	0.1920	−0.0746	0.001	0.1146	0.003	0.1205	0.013	−0.0059	0.840
	[0.0975]	[0.0699]	[0.1070]	[−0.0371]	0.000	[0.0672]	0.005	[0.0766]	0.004	[−0.0093]	0.843
ΔEMPLOYEE	0.0784	0.0476	0.0910	−0.0434	0.015	0.0596	0.207	0.0326	0.003	0.0270	0.336
	[0.0345]	[0.0186]	[0.0434]	[−0.0248]	0.001	[0.0164]	0.004	[0.0214]	0.019	[−0.0050]	0.822
R&D	0.0419	0.0224	0.0491	−0.0267	0.000	0.0173	0.000	0.0279	0.001	−0.0106	0.096
	[0.0000]	[0.0000]	[0.0000]	[0.0000]	0.000	[0.0000]	0.000	[0.0000]	0.000	[0.0000]	0.989
INTANGIBLE	0.1869	0.1995	0.1822	0.0173	0.113	0.2142	0.029	0.1836	0.921	0.0306	0.107
	[0.1228]	[0.1280]	[0.1204]	[0.0076]	0.246	[0.1368]	0.033	[0.1228]	0.673	[0.0140]	0.065
OCF	0.0766	0.1066	0.0654	0.0412	0.002	0.1242	0.000	0.0875	0.314	0.0367	0.113
	[0.0933]	[0.1029]	[0.0904]	[0.0126]	0.001	[0.1222]	0.000	[0.0890]	0.861	[0.0332]	0.000
ARET_12	−0.0514	−0.0304	−0.0592	0.0288	0.417	−0.0404	0.614	−0.0196	0.489	−0.0209	0.746
	[−0.1418]	[−0.1297]	[−0.1433]	[0.0136]	0.615	[−0.1286]	0.454	[−0.1460]	0.998	[−0.0175]	0.591
TARLIQ	0.0691	0.0674	0.0697	−0.0023	0.632	0.0757	0.389	0.0584	0.038	0.0173	0.033
	[0.0449]	[0.0454]	[0.0446]	[0.0008]	0.548	[0.0470]	0.012	[0.0367]	0.086	[0.0103]	0.001
STDEVAR	0.0367	0.0383	0.0361	0.0022	0.078	0.0367	0.670	0.0400	0.040	−0.0033	0.137
	[0.0317]	[0.0319]	[0.0315]	[0.0004]	0.159	[0.0320]	0.353	[0.0317]	0.222	[0.0003]	0.809
STDEV	0.0376	0.0390	0.0371	0.0020	0.112	0.0376	0.701	0.0406	0.063	−0.0030	0.177
	[0.0327]	[0.0330]	[0.0326]	[0.0004]	0.231	[0.0329]	0.371	[0.0330]	0.352	[−0.0030]	0.812
STOCKLIQ	0.5698	0.9312	0.4343	0.4969	0.040	0.8831	0.197	0.9837	0.060	−0.1007	0.812
	[0.0388]	[0.0790]	[0.0288]	[0.0502]	0.000	[0.0489]	0.006	[0.1175]	0.000	[−0.0686]	0.000
SEGMENTS	1.3868	1.4208	1.3733	0.0475	0.318	1.4911	0.052	1.3333	0.532	0.1577	0.050
	[1.0000]	[1.0000]	[1.0000]	[0.0000]	0.141	[1.0000]	0.006	[1.0000]	0.428	[0.0000]	0.010

Note: this page presents the tail of the preceding panel (FOCUS, NASDAQ) followed by *Panel B: Deal characteristics*. Each cell shows the mean with the [median] in brackets; comparison columns (4)–(7) additionally report two p-values shown as (p₁, p₂), one on the value line and one on the median line.

Variable	(1)	(2)	(3)	(4)	(5)	(6)	(7)
FOCUS	0.7546 [1.0000]	0.7277 [1.0000]	0.7652 [1.0000]	−0.0375 [0.0000] (0.147, 0.450)	0.6741 [1.0000] (0.008, 0.435)	0.7944 [1.0000] (0.377, 0.036)	−0.1203 [0.0000] (0.006, 0.027)
NASDAQ	0.6635 [1.0000]	0.6777 [1.0000]	0.6582 [1.0000]	0.0195 [0.0000] (0.139, 0.453)	0.6314 [1.0000] (0.004, 0.429)	0.7281 [1.0000] (0.391, 0.044)	−0.0968 [0.0000] (0.007, 0.028)

Panel B: Deal characteristics

Variable	(1)	(2)	(3)	(4)	(5)	(6)	(7)
DEALVALUE	552.7184 [157.8988]	308.0815 [108.9949]	644.0039 [180.4255]	−335.9224 [−71.4306] (0.000, 0.000)	388.9164 [135.1475] (0.001, 0.018)	220.1688 [91.4598] (0.000, 0.000)	168.7476 [43.6877] (0.010, 0.000)
TENDER	0.4877 [0.0000]	0.3466 [0.0000]	0.5404 [1.0000]	−0.1938 [−1.0000] (0.000, 0.000)	0.3263 [0.0000] (0.018, 0.000)	0.3687 [0.0000] (0.000, 0.000)	−0.0424 [0.0000] (0.345, 0.344)
DIVERSIFY	0.5279 [1.0000]	0.7020 [1.0000]	0.4629 [0.0000]	0.2391 [1.0000] (0.000, 0.000)	0.9619 [1.0000] (0.000, 0.000)	0.4194 [0.0000] (0.000, 0.000)	0.5425 [1.0000] (0.000, 0.000)
MBO	0.0516 [0.0000]	0.1854 [0.0000]	0.0016 [0.0000]	0.1838 [0.0000] (0.000, 0.000)	0.3347 [0.0000] (0.000, 0.000)	0.0230 [0.0000] (0.234, 0.235)	0.3117 [0.0000] (0.000, 0.000)
TOEHOLD	0.0984 [0.0000]	0.1236 [0.0000]	0.0890 [0.0000]	0.0347 [0.0000] (0.048, 0.035)	0.1483 [0.0000] (0.016, 0.005)	0.0968 [0.0000] (0.039, 0.000)	0.0515 [0.0000] (0.094, 0.096)
HOSTILE	0.0204 [0.0000]	0.0088 [0.0000]	0.0247 [0.0000]	−0.0159 [0.0000] (0.011, 0.041)	0.0000 [0.0000] (0.015, 0.255)	0.0184 [0.0000] (0.719, 0.711)	−0.0184 [0.0000] (0.045, 0.036)
BANKRUPT	0.0060 [0.0000]	0.0110 [0.0000]	0.0041 [0.0000]	0.0069 [0.0000] (0.188, 0.104)	0.0127 [0.0000] (0.103, 0.000)	0.0092 [0.0000] (0.538, 0.576)	0.0035 [0.0000] (0.721, 0.722)
DEFENSE	0.0138 [0.0000]	0.0088 [0.0000]	0.0157 [0.0000]	−0.0068 [0.0000] (0.229, 0.288)	0.0000 [0.0000] (0.053, 0.046)	0.0184 [0.0000] (0.451, 0.322)	−0.0184 [0.0000] (0.045, 0.036)
TARLOCK	0.0024 [0.0000]	0.0000 [0.0000]	0.0033 [0.0000]	−0.0033 [0.0000] (0.046, 0.221)	0.0000 [0.0000] (0.000, 0.000)	0.0000 [0.0000] (0.777, 0.764)	0.0000 [0.0000] (—, —)
BIDLOCK	0.1200 [0.0000]	0.0574 [0.0000]	0.1433 [0.0000]	−0.0859 [0.0000] (0.000, 0.000)	0.0381 [0.0000] (0.381, 0.000)	0.0783 [0.0000] (0.046, 0.397)	−0.0402 [0.0000] (0.070, 0.066)
TARTERM	0.5141 [1.0000]	0.5011 [1.0000]	0.5189 [1.0000]	−0.0178 [0.0000] (0.517, 0.517)	0.5085 [1.0000] (0.769, 0.768)	0.4931 [0.0000] (0.002, 0.010)	0.0154 [1.0000] (0.744, 0.744)
BIDTERM	0.0744 [0.0000]	0.0795 [0.0000]	0.0725 [0.0000]	0.0070 [0.0000] (0.636, 0.629)	0.0763 [0.0000] (0.841, 0.838)	0.0829 [0.0000] (0.484, 0.483)	−0.0067 [0.0000] (0.794, 0.793)
COMPETE	0.0906 [0.0000]	0.0839 [0.0000]	0.0931 [0.0000]	−0.0092 [0.0000] (0.553, 0.561)	0.0720 [0.0000] (0.264, 0.301)	0.0968 [0.0000] (0.605, 0.588)	−0.0247 [0.0000] (0.347, 0.343)
INITBID	0.0258 [0.0000]	0.0375 [0.0000]	0.0214 [0.0000]	0.0161 [0.0000] (0.103, 0.065)	0.0466 [0.0000] (0.081, 0.025)	0.0276 [0.0000] (0.601, 0.568)	0.0190 [0.0000] (0.285, 0.289)
DAY	104.5525 [88.0000]	120.1722 [109.0000]	98.7241 [79.0000]	21.4482 [30.0000] (0.000, 0.000)	129.7415 [120.5000] (0.025, 0.000)	109.7650 [98.0000] (0.017, 0.002)	19.9765 [22.5000] (0.002, 0.002)

problems are less likely to flourish. The difference is also strong when we compute an industry-adjusted q (IAQ) by subtracting the yearly median q of firms in the same two-digit SIC code. Firms acquired by private bidders have a lower Tobin's q relative to their industry median than firms acquired by public bidders. The lower q is not the result of recent poor performance.

Younger firms typically have a higher Tobin's q, but there is no difference in target firm age (AGE) measured in months since listing on CRSP between public and private acquirers, so that age seems an unlikely explanation for the difference in Tobin's q. There are, however, significant differences in other proxies for growth opportunities, suggesting that the difference in Tobin's q is consistent with higher growth opportunities of firms acquired by public bidders. We show data for the last 3 years of sales growth (ΔSALES) and the last 3 years of employment growth (ΔEMPLOYEE). These measures are often used as proxies for growth opportunities. Firms acquired by public firms have greater sales growth and greater employment growth than firms acquired by private firms. They also have higher R&D expenditures, but there is no difference in the ratio of intangible assets to total assets (INTANGIBLE).

Finally, we find evidence that firms taken over by private firms have greater operating cash flows (OCFs) divided by total assets, where OCF is defined as in Moeller et al. (2004) as Sales less COGS less SGA less ΔNWC (the fraction of OCF over book assets is winsorized at the 1% level in the regression analysis). Such evidence is consistent with the view that private equity firms can create value by returning free cash flow to shareholders. We find no difference in the cumulative 12-month market-model residual (ARET_12), making it unlikely that the premium for acquisitions by private firms is lower because the acquisition premium is incorporated to a greater extent into the stock price for such acquisitions compared to acquisitions by public firms. We examine more directly if there is a difference in stock returns close to the acquisition and find that there is none. As a final check of this possibility, we investigate whether the asset liquidity measure (TARLIQ) of Schlingemann et al. (2002) differs between acquisitions by public versus private acquirers. This measure captures the intensity of the market for corporate control and asset sales in an industry. If an industry has great asset liquidity, stock prices might be higher to reflect possible future acquisition premiums. We find no difference in the measure of asset liquidity between targets of public versus private acquirers. There is also no clear evidence that uncertainty about the value of the targets differs between private firm and public firm targets.

We estimate the Amihud (2002) measure of stock illiquidity (STOCKLIQ), measured as the average ratio of the absolute daily return divided by dollar daily volume. A higher value of this measure means that a stock's market is less liquid. We find that targets acquired by private firms have a much less liquid common stock than firms acquired by public firms. Targets acquired by private firms have a similar number of business segments (SEGMENTS) as targets acquired by public firms. A large fraction of targets consists of firms that trade on NASDAQ, but that fraction is the same across private and public bidders.

Panel B of Table 3 shows deal characteristics. All information is obtained from SDC, unless otherwise noted. We find that the dollar value of the deals (DEAL-VALUE) measured in CPI-adjusted 2005 dollars is significantly higher for targets of public firm acquirers versus private firm acquirers. Public bidders are more likely to be involved in tender offers (TENDER) than private bidders. Tender offers tend to be associated with higher premiums (see, e.g., Huang and Walkling, 1987). It is not surprising that more acquisitions by private firms are management buyouts (MBO). Studies of MBO (DeAngelo et al., 1984; Kaplan, 1989) find no evidence that such buyouts are underpriced. Betton and Eckbo (2000) provide evidence that premiums are lower for acquirers with toeholds. Private firms are more likely to have a toehold (TOEHOLD) than public firms. Across our entire sample period, the proportion of hostile acquisitions (HOSTILE) is greater for public bidders than for private bidders, although there is no difference in the proportion of hostile offers between public and private acquirers for the 1990–2005 period (reflecting the decrease in hostile acquisitions among public acquirers). Under 1% of all targets are bankrupt (BANKRUPT) at the time of acquisition and the proportion of bankrupt targets is not different for public and private bidders. Targets of acquisitions by public firms are more likely to use defensive tactics (DEFENSE)—in fact, no target of a private firm in our sample uses defensive tactics according to SDC.

Burch (2001) finds that target lockups are associated with higher target gains. We only find target lockups (TARLOCK) for targets of public firm acquirers. In contrast, bidder lockups (BIDLOCK) are significantly more likely for acquisitions by public firms. Officer (2003) shows that target termination fees result in significantly higher premiums. We find that targets of public firm acquirers are just as likely to have a termination fee as targets of private firm acquirers, so that this lack of difference in the frequency of target termination fees (TARTERM) is unlikely to explain the difference in premiums. There is also no difference in the incidence of bidder termination fees (BIDTERM) across bidder types.

We use two measures of competition. The first measure (COMPETE) indicates whether there was a previous offer for the target prior to the winning bid. Such a situation is equally likely for private bidders as for public bidders. The second measure (INITBID) indicates whether the initial bid, when it is the winning bid, is followed by an offer by another firm. We find that such an outcome is weakly more likely for offers made by private firms. Finally, in contrast to conventional wisdom we find that it takes almost a month longer on average for a private acquisition to be completed than for a public one. The variable DAY is the number of elapsed calendar days from announcement date to the completion date.

Table 2 also shows the difference between target and deal characteristics for acquisitions by private equity firms and by private operating firms. The private equity firms acquire larger targets. Targets of private equity buyers have a more active market for corporate control. The targets of acquisitions by private equity firms have more business segments than the targets of acquisitions by private operating firms. Presumably, having more segments decreases potential synergy gains with the acquirer.

There is no difference in sales growth and employment growth between firms acquired by private operating companies and private equity firms. Acquisitions by private equity firms are more likely to be MBOs, to have a toehold, and to take longer. There are fewer hostile acquisitions by private equity firms than by private operating firms.

4.2. Regression analysis

Our comparison of target and deal characteristics suggests that there are many reasons why shareholders of targets acquired by private firms might receive a different premium than shareholders of targets acquired by public firms. To investigate whether these differences in target and deal characteristics can explain why public acquirers pay more than private acquirers, we estimate multiple regressions. We use abnormal returns as the dependent variable and the target and deal characteristics as explanatory variables. We include an indicator variable for acquisitions by private equity firms (PEBIDDER) and another one for acquisitions by private operating companies (POBIDDER). If target and deal characteristics explain the difference in abnormal returns, these indicator variables should be insignificantly different from zero in our multiple regressions.

Table 4 shows the regression estimates. We first discuss the results for regression (1) which uses the FBC premium. Both indicator variables are significantly negative, showing that acquisitions by private firms have significantly lower premiums than acquisitions by public firms. The indicator variable is -0.1868 for acquisitions by private equity firms, significant at the 1% level. Everything else constant, private equity firms pay a premium lower by 18.7% of pre-bid firm equity value than public companies. In contrast, the indicator variable for acquisitions by private operating companies is -0.0597, significant only at the 10% level. The two indicator variables have significantly different coefficients at the 1% level using an F-test. The estimated indicator variables are of the same magnitude as the premium differences shown in Table 2. Consequently, controlling for firm and deal characteristics does not seem to reduce the average premium difference between acquisitions by private firms versus public firms. We find that target shareholders realize smaller gains when their firm is larger, has a higher industry-adjusted Tobin's q, and has performed better over the past year. In addition, target shareholders gain more when the target firm has more leverage, the acquisition is hostile, the successful bidder follows another bid, and the acquisition is a tender offer.

Regression (2) uses the 3-day announcement abnormal return, CAR3, as the dependent variable. The private bidder indicator variables are significant at the 1% and 5% level, respectively, and much closer in absolute value than in regression (1). An F-test shows that the difference between the indicator variables is not statistically significant. Though the indicator variable for private equity bidders is large in absolute value in model (1) compared to the FBC premium estimate of Table 2, the 3-day announcement abnormal return is similar in absolute value to the indicator variable in model (2). In contrast to regression (1), leverage is insignificant and the COMPETE variable is negative and insignificant. Surprisingly, the bidder lockup variable is positive and significant in regression (2) but not in regression (1). There is no evidence that

Table 4

Multiple regression analysis

The sample includes all SDC completed cash-only merger and acquisition deals between a US bidder and a US public target announced between 1980 and 2005 that result in 100% ownership by the bidder. The dependent variable in model (1) is the Fama-French size-and market-to-book-adjusted compounded return from 42 days before the announcement date of the first bid to the completion date (FBC) and in model (2) it is the 3-day abnormal announcement return (CAR3). PEBIDDER (POBIDDER) is an indicator variable equal to one if the bidder is a private equity (operating) firm. The market value of equity (MVE) is from CRSP calculated as the price of the stock times the number of shares outstanding 63 days prior to the announcement and is in S&P500-adjusted 2005 dollars. All remaining variables are defined in the header of Table 3. ARET_12 is measured relative to the winning (first) bid when CAR3 (FBC) is the dependent variable. Regressions include year and industry (two-digit SIC code main classifications) dummy variables. p-Values are in brackets and are based on heteroskedasticity-consistent standard errors. Coefficients denoted with *, **, or ***, are significant at the 1%, 5%, or 10% level, respectively.

	(1) FBC	(2) CAR3
PEBIDDER	−0.1866* [0.000]	−0.0853* [0.000]
POBIDDER	−0.0600*** [0.095]	−0.0611** [0.012]
ln(MVE)	−0.0263** [0.016]	−0.0133*** [0.064]
IAQ	−0.0201*** [0.078]	−0.0250* [0.003]
DEBT	0.1419** [0.034]	0.0161 [0.746]
OCF	−0.0152 [0.869]	0.0433 [0.481]
TARLIQ	−0.1635 [0.209]	−0.1375*** [0.070]
ARET_12	−0.0700* [0.001]	−0.0599* [0.000]
HOSTILE	0.1866* [0.001]	0.1345* [0.001]
COMPETE	0.0897** [0.042]	−0.1010* [0.000]
INITBID	0.0347 [0.517]	−0.0382 [0.234]
TENDER	0.0770* [0.005]	0.0853* [0.000]
TARTERM	0.0388 [0.198]	0.0085 [0.651]
TOEHOLD	−0.0263 [0.466]	0.0100 [0.622]
STDEVAR	0.1974 [0.819]	0.4391 [0.515]
BIDLOCK	0.0072 [0.825]	0.0376*** [0.056]
Constant	0.7082* [0.000]	0.2051** [0.028]
Obs.	1662	1662
Adj. R^2	0.119	0.127

introducing target and deal characteristics is helpful in explaining the lower target shareholder gains of acquisitions by private firms.[4]

---

[4] All results presented in Table 4 are robust to the exclusion of or controlling for private equity club deals. We define club deals as those deals with a private bidder comprised of two or more private equity firms. Our sample includes 43 club deals with an average target CAR3 (FBC) of 17.0% (13.7%). If we exclude club deals, the coefficients on PEBIDDER and POBIDDER in the FBC (CAR3) regression are −0.1838*** (−0.0729***) and −0.0591* (−0.0609**), respectively. Alternatively if we add a control variable for club deals (i.e., a dummy variable equal to 1 for club deals and 0 otherwise), the coefficients on PEBIDDER and POBIDDER in the FBC (CAR3) regression are −0.1834*** (−0.0737***) and −0.0599* (−0.0610**), respectively. The club deal coefficients are negative, however only the coefficient in the CAR3 regression is significantly different from zero. Furthermore, our Table 4 results are robust to the consideration of only the 1990–2005 period, when the majority of club deals occur.

To investigate the stability of the estimates over time, we estimate the regressions in Table 4 for two periods of 13 years each (not reported). The coefficient on the private equity indicator variable is negative and significant for both periods and increases by roughly 50% in absolute value from the earlier period to the later period. The private operating dummy is significantly negative except with the FBC premium in the 1980–1992 period.

We also estimate the regressions of Table 4, but do not report them, with an additional dummy variable for target management involvement with the bidder using SDC data. The reason we do not focus on these regressions in the reported table is that it seems difficult to evaluate the extent of target management involvement, making the variable perhaps somewhat subjective. We find that the gains of target shareholders are not significantly different for deals that include management involvement compared to other acquisitions. Controlling for management involvement has no effect on the estimates of the private bidder indicator variables.

Ordinary least squares regressions are vulnerable to departures from normality. To evaluate the strength of our results, we also estimate median and robust regressions that put less weight on extreme observations. These regressions (not reported) do not change our conclusions, but they yield lower estimates of the premium difference between public and private bidders. The estimates for PEBIDDER are roughly 14% and 4% in absolute value, respectively, for the FBC premium and the CAR3 abnormal return, and statistically significant with p-values mostly below 1%. The estimates for POBIDDER are between 3% and 4% in absolute value for both premium measures, but only statistically significant when explaining the variation in the 3-day abnormal return.

Finally, to be sure that our findings are not sensitive to our examination of cash-only deals, we estimate the regressions of Table 4 using all offers instead of just cash offers, but do not report the results in a table. The sample increases from 1667 to 3957 observations due primarily to offers that include equity by public firms. There are only 120 acquisitions by private firms that include some equity and they are much more prevalent in the first half of our sample period. We estimate the regressions first without controlling for the form of payment. The indicator variable for private equity firms is negative and significant at the 1% level across all eight specifications and has a magnitude of roughly 0.174 (0.043) in absolute value when the FBC premium (CAR3) is used. The private operating dummy is consistently negative with an average magnitude of 0.048 (0.023) when the FBC premium (CAR3) premium is the dependent variable, although it is only significant at the 10% level for models (1), (2), and (4) and is not significant for the other models. Such regressions are difficult to justify since the literature concludes that the form of payment is highly correlated with the premium paid (Huang and Walkling, 1987). When we add an indicator variable for all-cash offers, both the private equity and private operating indicators are negative and statistically significant across all eight specifications. For the FBC premium (CAR3) the average magnitudes are -0.178 (-0.076) and -0.05 (-0.045) for private equity and private operating bidders, respectively. Consequently, whether we include noncash offers in the regressions or not, target shareholders earn less when they are acquired by a private bidder.

5. Bidder characteristics and the gains to target shareholders for public bidders and private bidders

So far we have shown an economically large and statistically significant difference in target shareholder gains between acquisitions by private firms and acquisitions by public firms. Observable target and deal characteristics do not explain this difference. We now investigate whether the lower shareholder gains in acquisitions by private firms can be explained by differences in bidder characteristics. In contrast to public acquirer deals, such an investigation is necessarily limited by the fact that there is not much information available on private acquirers. Nevertheless, private acquirers have concentrated ownership. If a private acquirer is a private operating company, it cannot have diffuse ownership because its stock is not publicly listed. If a private acquirer is a private equity firm it can have many investors, but decisions are made by a managing partner whose high-powered incentives are closely aligned with those of investors. We therefore investigate the hypothesis that private firms pay less for targets because their managers have better incentives to maximize firm value than managers of diffusely held public corporations. This difference in incentives makes it less likely that managers of private firms will make acquisitions that benefit them at the expense of other shareholders in their company.

In contrast, managers of public companies can benefit from acquisitions even if these acquisitions do not benefit shareholders. For instance, Bebchuck and Grinstein (2007) find that managerial compensation increases as the firm becomes larger, so that mergers that increase firm size can increase managerial compensation even if they destroy shareholder wealth. Consistent with this view, Harford and Li (2007) find that managers of bidder firms are better off in 3-quarters of the acquisitions that are associated with decreases in shareholder wealth. As managers' stakes in the firm increase, we expect managers to become less likely to make acquisitions that adversely impact shareholders. Managers of public companies also gain prestige and perks if they manage larger companies. There is also the possibility, suggested by Harford et al. (2007), that some shareholders do not care when managers of a public firm overpay to buy another public company because they have stakes in both companies.

If private firms pay less for acquisitions than do public firms because their ownership is more concentrated, we would expect the difference in target shareholder gains between private and public acquirers to be less when ownership of the public acquirer is more concentrated. To test this hypothesis, we collect ownership data for the public bidders in our sample from Compact Disclosure. We collect the most recent information on ownership for officers and directors prior to the announcement date. Since we are only able to access Compact Disclosure data starting in 1990, we do not have managerial ownership information for the 1980s portion of our sample. We then estimate our target shareholder gain regressions using different samples of public firms to estimate the coefficient on the private firm indicator variables. The samples of public firms differ by their level of managerial ownership. A priori, there seems to be no reason why the synergy gains of public firm acquisitions would be related to the managerial ownership of the acquiring firm. Consequently, the synergy gain explanation for the difference in premium between public firm acquisitions and private firm acquisitions does not appear capable of explaining a relation between the premium difference and the managerial ownership of public acquirers.

When we compare the target shareholder gains associated with private firm acquisitions to the shareholder gains of public firm acquisitions in Table 5 for different levels of public firm managerial ownership using the FBC premium estimate (regressions (1), (3), (5), (7), (9), and (11)), we find that the difference in the premium is highest when private bidders are compared to public bidders in which managerial ownership is less than or equal to 1%. The regressions in Table 5 use all the control variables used in the regressions in Table 4, but we do not reproduce the estimates for the coefficients on these variables as they are irrelevant for our discussion. In our sample of firms for which managerial ownership is available, 281 firms out of 628 have managerial ownership less than or equal to 1%. For private equity bidders, the indicator variable is −0.2851 and significant at the 1% level. For private operating bidders, the premium paid is significantly different when compared to acquisitions by

Table 5

Multiple regressions by public bidder managerial ownership

The sample includes all SDC completed cash-only merger and acquisition deals between a US bidder and a US public target announced between 1990 and 2005 that result in 100% ownership by the bidder. Six subsamples are formed by grouping all private bidder deals with the subset of public bidder deals with managerial ownership (own) within the range specified for the model. The dependent variable in models (1), (3), (5), (7), (9), and (11) is the Fama-French size- and market-to-book-adjusted compounded return from 42 days before the announcement date of the first bid to the completion date (FBC) and in models (2), (4), (6), (8), (10), and (12) it is the 3-day abnormal announcement return (CAR3). The regressions use but do not report the control variables used in the regressions of Table 4. p-Values are in brackets and are based on heteroskedasticity-consistent standard errors. Coefficients denoted with *, **, or ***, are significant at the 1%, 5%, or 10% level, respectively.

	Public bidder managerial ownership	Return	PEBIDDER	POBIDDER	Constant	Obs.	Adj. R^2
(1)	0 ≤ own ≤ 1%	FBC	−0.2851* [0.000]	−0.1479** [0.025]	1.0179* [0.001]	628	0.152
(2)	0 ≤ own ≤ 1%	CAR3	−0.1413* [0.000]	−0.1119* [0.003]	0.3644*** [0.059]	628	0.149
(3)	0 ≤ own ≤ 5%	FBC	−0.2496* [0.000]	−0.1068** [0.048]	0.8307* [0.002]	788	0.140
(4)	0 ≤ own ≤ 5%	CAR3	−0.1064* [0.000]	−0.0754** [0.022]	0.3600** [0.024]	788	0.143
(5)	5% < own ≤ 15%	FBC	−0.1876* [0.004]	−0.0707 [0.269]	0.5561** [0.048]	468	0.117
(6)	5% < own ≤ 15%	CAR3	−0.0961** [0.018]	−0.0611 [0.165]	0.4913** [0.031]	468	0.108
(7)	15% < own ≤ 25%	FBC	−0.1401*** [0.095]	0.0165 [0.838]	0.4559 [0.302]	400	0.095
(8)	15% < own ≤ 25%	CAR3	−0.0930*** [0.063]	−0.0476 [0.367]	0.5762 [0.133]	400	0.105
(9)	25% < own ≤ 50%	FBC	−0.1785*** [0.072]	−0.0467 [0.634]	0.4689 [0.149]	402	0.078
(10)	25% < own ≤ 50%	CAR3	−0.0548 [0.156]	−0.0100 [0.819]	0.3809** [0.044]	402	0.111
(11)	50% < own	FBC	−0.0850 [0.400]	0.0288 [0.761]	0.8855* [0.006]	392	0.116
(12)	50% < own	CAR3	−0.0360 [0.422]	−0.0084 [0.851]	0.4058** [0.043]	392	0.122

public firms with managerial ownership less than or equal to 1% or 5%. The decrease in the absolute value of the indicator variable is not monotonic across categories of public acquirers with higher managerial ownership, but the indicator variable is always lower than in regression (1) and it is significant at only the 10% level in regressions (7) and (9). Not surprisingly, there are fewer public bidders available for regressions (7), (9), and (11): 53 for regression (7), 55 for regression (9), and 45 for regression (11).

When we compare private equity bidders to public bidders with managerial ownership in excess of 50% in regression (11), which are the public firms for which managerial incentives come closest to the managerial incentives in private equity firms, the absolute value of the indicator variable is less than one-third of its value in regression (1) and is insignificant. There are a variety of firms with greater than 50% managerial ownership, but in most cases these firms are controlled by one individual investor (e.g., Kirk Kerkorian at MGM Mirage).

We perform the same comparisons using the 3-day abnormal return in regressions (2), (4), (6), (8), (10), and (12). For the 3-day abnormal return regressions, there is a monotonic decrease in the absolute value of the indicator variable as private equity bidders are compared with public bidders with increasing managerial ownership. We find that the private equity indicator variable is not significant when the managerial ownership of the public firm exceeds 25%. Again, the magnitude of the absolute value of the indicator variable when public firms have more than 50% managerial ownership is less than a third of its value when public firms have less than or equal to 1% managerial ownership. The estimates of the absolute value of the indicator variable for private operating firms exhibit the same monotonically decreasing pattern as do the private equity coefficients and are only significant when compared to public bidders with managerial ownership less than or equal to 1% or 5%.

Another way to shed light on the importance of managerial agency problems as a potential explanation for the difference in target shareholder gains is to investigate how this difference holds up as the size of the public acquirer varies. One would expect that managers have more discretion in large companies because the costs of collective action for shareholders are larger. We therefore predict that the difference in target shareholder gains between private and public acquirers is smaller for smaller public acquirers. Table 6 (we again omit the coefficients on control variables) shows that this is the case. We estimate our regressions restricting the public acquirers to size quartiles since, not having the size of private acquirers, we cannot use a bidder size variable as is common in regressions seeking to explain acquisition abnormal returns. When we use the FBC premium, the indicator variable for private equity firm acquisitions is significant for all size quartiles and its magnitude is directly related to the public bidder size quartile as predicted. For operating firms, the indicator variable is only significant for the two largest quartiles and again there is a direct relation between the magnitude of the estimates and the size quartile. When we turn to the 3-day abnormal returns, CAR3, we find that the same patterns hold for both private equity firms and private operating companies except that the private equity coefficient is statistically insignificant for the smallest size quartile.

Table 6

Multiple regressions by public bidder size quartiles

The sample includes all SDC completed cash-only merger and acquisition deals between a US bidder and a US public target announced between 1980 and 2005 that result in 100% ownership by the bidder. Four subsamples are formed by grouping all private bidder deals with each size quartile (Q1-Q4) of public bidder deals. Size quartiles are based on public bidder CPI-adjusted (2005 dollars) MVE for the 3 months prior to the announcement date. The dependent variable in models (1), (3), (5), and (7) is the Fama-French size- and market-to-book-adjusted compounded return from 42 days before the announcement date of the first bid to the completion date (FBC) and in models (2), (4), (6), and (8) it is the 3-day abnormal announcement return (CAR3). The regressions use but do not report the control variables used in the regressions of Table 4. *p*-Values are in brackets and are based on heteroskedasticity-consistent standard errors. Coefficients denoted with *, **, or ***, are significant at the 1%, 5%, or 10% level, respectively.

	Public bidder size quartile	Return	PEBIDDER	POBIDDER	Constant	Obs.	Adj. R^2
(1)	Q1 (smallest)	FBC	−0.1038** [0.040]	0.0226 [0.644]	0.9989* [0.000]	709	0.104
(2)	Q1 (smallest)	CAR3	−0.0282 [0.242]	−0.0072 [0.804]	0.2545** [0.047]	709	0.134
(3)	Q2	FBC	−0.1860* [0.000]	−0.0467 [0.309]	0.3355 [0.100]	708	0.129
(4)	Q2	CAR3	−0.0827* [0.002]	−0.0488 [0.127]	0.3251*** [0.053]	708	0.128
(5)	Q3	FBC	−0.2229* [0.000]	−0.1016** [0.028]	0.5247** [0.036]	712	0.137
(6)	Q3	CAR3	−0.1175* [0.000]	−0.0842* [0.004]	0.3714* [0.008]	712	0.132
(7)	Q4 (largest)	FBC	−0.2711* [0.000]	−0.1619* [0.000]	0.9191* [0.000]	711	0.161
(8)	Q4 (largest)	CAR3	−0.1236* [0.000]	−0.1110* [0.001]	0.3591* [0.009]	711	0.124

The evidence suggests that the gains to target shareholders from being acquired by a private firm are similar to the gains to these shareholders if their firm were acquired by a small public firm but not by a large public firm. Moeller et al. (2004) find that targets receive larger premiums from larger public bidders. The results in this paper point to agency costs as an explanation for the premium differentials between public and private bidders.

It is often argued that institutional investors reduce the impact of managerial agency problems. We collect institutional ownership data for the public bidders from Compact Disclosure and compare the gains of target shareholders in acquisitions by private firms to the gains of target shareholders in acquisitions by public firms with different levels of institutional holdings. Though we do not report the results in a table, we find that the private firm indicator variables in our regressions do not vary much as the institutional investor threshold for the public firm comparison group increases. In fact, the private equity indicator variable is significant at less than 1% across all institutional ownership categories using the same ownership cutoffs as in Table 5 and has an average magnitude of −0.23 and −0.11, respectively, for the FBC premium and the CAR3 abnormal return. With respect to the 3-day CAR premium measure, the private operating indicator variable averages 0.077 in absolute value and is significant at least at the 5% level. For the FBC premium estimate, the private operating firm indicator variable has an average coefficient of 0.093 in absolute value and is statistically significant for four of the six institutional ownership bins.

If managers of private firms have better incentives to maximize shareholder wealth, we would expect them to be less likely to overpay and hence more likely to walk away from a deal than managers of public firms. We find that there indeed is a striking difference. For a broad sample from 1980 to 2005 that includes withdrawn deals, private bidders withdrew 37.4% of their offers. In contrast, only 16.9% of the public bidder offers were withdrawn. A concern with withdrawn deals is that the private equity firms that withdraw an offer might really never have been competitive with their offer, so that a withdrawn deal is not necessarily one where the private bidder walks away because the deal became too pricey. Nevertheless, private bidders seem more willing to make offers that do not succeed. Further, we would expect that when public and private bidders compete for a target, public firms would be more likely to win. We find that this is the case for our sample of 1667 completed cash-only deals. We have 75 contests with both private and public bidders. Public bidders win in 57 contests and private bidders win in 18 contests.

6. Can the incentives of target managers explain the return difference?

A concern mentioned in the press is that managers of private firms have two advantages over managers of public firms. First, they are not subject to the greater monitoring that comes from having to report quarterly results and dealing with the laws and regulations that affect public firms. At a time when there is much discussion about the costs of Sarbanes-Oxley, managers of private firms are not affected by these costs. Second, managers of private firms can earn an outsized payoff when the firm is taken public. It would therefore not be surprising if private bidders could convince managers of public firms to be acquired in exchange for keeping their jobs and receiving a share of the payoff when the acquired firm goes public. In this view, target managers might be less diligent in getting the best possible deal for their shareholders. Existing empirical evidence is supportive of the view that managers at times have incentives to obtain greater personal benefits from an acquisition at the expense of their shareholders. In particular, Hartzell et al. (2004) show that target abnormal returns are less when the target's CEO receives large personal benefits from the acquisition.

As managerial ownership in the target firm increases, the postacquisition payoff from an acquisition by a private bidder becomes smaller relative to the loss in premium resulting from acquiescing to a low premium offer. We therefore expect less of a difference in abnormal returns between bidder types for targets with high managerial ownership. We also predict it to be harder for target managers to acquiesce to a low premium if their firm has high ownership by institutional investors. To test these predictions, we collect managerial ownership and institutional ownership for the target firms from Compact Disclosure. As before, based on availability, we are only able to collect this data starting in 1990.

We find little difference in managerial ownership between targets of private firms and targets of public firms. Mean managerial ownership is 19.9% for targets of private firms and 19.2% for targets of public firms. This difference is not significant. The median difference is also insignificant (12.7% vs. 10.5%). These results suggest that private acquirers do not systematically target firms with low managerial ownership. When it comes to institutional ownership, we again find no significant difference in the means (32.4% for targets of private firms versus 37.0% for targets of public firms) or medians (28.5% vs. 28.4%).

Table 7 shows regression estimates using the firms for which we have target insider and institutional ownership data (the coefficients for the control variables are omitted). We find that the private bidder indicator variables have higher absolute values than those in Table 4. Regression (3) adds target insider ownership and target institutional ownership to the regression. We find that both ownership measures have a significant positive coefficient. The economic significance of the coefficients seems small: going from zero to the mean or from the mean to twice the mean increases the premium by roughly 2.6% of preannouncement firm value for managerial ownership and by 4.1% for institutional ownership. Strikingly, however, the ownership variables have no impact whatsoever on the estimates of the private bidder indicator variables. It is conceivable that the relation between the ownership variables and the target gains is nonlinear. To address this possibility, we add the square of the ownership variables in regression (5). The squared ownership measures are not significant, and multicollinearity renders insignificant the level ownership measures as well, but the private bidder indicator variables are unaffected.

In regression (7), we allow for a differential effect of insider and institutional ownership for acquisitions by private equity firms and private operating firms. Since we now interact the respective private bidder indicators with ownership measures, we demean the ownership variables to maintain the interpretation of the private bidder intercept coefficients (see Aiken and West, 1991). Though we find that target managerial ownership is associated with significantly higher premiums for acquisitions by public firms, an F-test shows that this effect disappears when considering offers by private acquirers. In other words, the total impact of insider ownership is essentially zero for acquisitions by either type of private firm. Similarly, target institutional ownership is associated with higher premiums when the acquirer is a public firm, but an F-test shows that target institutional ownership is not related to target shareholder gains when the acquirer is a private firm. These results suggest that target managerial and institutional ownership play a different role in private deals than in public deals. A plausible explanation is that private equity transactions take place when target managers are in favor of the acquisition, in which case their influence either makes institutional investors powerless to push for a higher premium or agreeable to the premium offered.

Regressions (2), (4), (6), and (8) use the 3-day abnormal return instead of the FBC premium. The ownership variables are not significant (except for a positive coefficient for demeaned institutional ownership and a negative coefficient for institutional

Table 7

Multiple regressions with target ownership measures

The sample includes all SDC completed cash-only merger and acquisition deals between a US bidder and a US public target announced between 1990 and 2005 that result in 100% ownership by the bidder. The dependent variable in models (1), (3), (5), and (7) is the Fama-French size- and market-to-book-adjusted compounded return from 42 days before the announcement date of the first bid to the completion date (FBC) and in models (2), (4), (6), and (8) it is the 3-day abnormal announcement return (CAR3). INSIDE (INSTITUTION) is the fraction of ownership held by managers (institutions) in the target firm. DINSIDE and DINSTITUTION are the demeaned values of INSIDE and INSTITUTION. The regressions use but do not report the control variables used in the regressions of Table 3. p-Values are in brackets and are based on heteroskedasticity-consistent standard errors. Coefficients denoted with *, **, or ***, are significant at the 1%, 5%, or 10% level, respectively.

	(1) FBC	(2) CAR3	(3) FBC	(4) CAR3	(5) FBC	(6) CAR3	(7) FBC	(8) CAR3
PEBIDDER	-0.2135*	-0.1008*	-0.2221*	-0.1052*	-0.2235*	-0.1047*	-0.2210*	-0.1027*
	[0.000]	[0.000]	[0.000]	[0.000]	[0.000]	[0.000]	[0.000]	[0.000]
POBIDDER	-0.0789***	-0.0698**	-0.0796***	-0.0700**	-0.0808***	-0.0689**	-0.0849**	-0.0722*
	[0.074]	[0.022]	[0.071]	[0.021]	[0.067]	[0.024]	[0.048]	[0.009]
INSIDE			0.1321***	0.0796	0.1841	0.1187		
			[0.057]	[0.122]	[0.339]	[0.332]		
INSTITUTION			0.1151***	0.0554	0.2035	-0.0468		
			[0.057]	[0.165]	[0.272]	[0.713]		
INSIDE^2					-0.0709	-0.0540		
					[0.752]	[0.723]		
INSTITUTION^2					-0.1077	0.1276		
					[0.586]	[0.350]		
DINSIDE							0.1917**	0.0895
							[0.022]	[0.153]
DINSIDE X PEBIDDER							-0.2437	-0.0457
							[0.125]	[0.658]
DINSIDE X POBIDDER							-0.2056	-0.0380
							[0.225]	[0.776]

(Continued)

Table 7 (Continued)

	(1) FBC	(2) CAR3	(3) FBC	(4) CAR3	(5) FBC	(6) CAR3	(7) FBC	(8) CAR3
DINSTITUTION							0.1136***	0.0795***
							[0.096]	[0.091]
DINSTITUTION X PEBIDDER							0.0186	-0.1227***
							[0.882]	[0.076]
DINSTITUTION X POBIDDER							-0.0557	-0.0281
							[0.739]	[0.831]
Constant	0.6010*	0.3734**	0.5855*	0.3588**	0.5633*	0.3658**	0.6612*	0.4210*
	[0.005]	[0.013]	[0.006]	[0.018]	[0.008]	[0.019]	[0.003]	[0.009]
Obs.	1226	1226	1226	1226	1226	1226	1226	1226
Adj. R^2	0.110	0.113	0.113	0.115	0.112	0.114	0.112	0.113

ownership interacted with private equity). However, the signs of the insider ownership variables and the interactions in regression (8) are consistent with the findings in regression (7).

7. Conclusion

In this paper, we find that target shareholders gain both statistically and economically if a public firm makes the acquisition. Using a premium measure that includes the pre-bid period as well as the period from the first bid to completion as in Schwert (1996), we find that target shareholders earn 35% higher premiums if a public firm makes the acquisition rather than a private firm. Target shareholders earn 63% higher premiums with public bidders rather than private equity bidders.

We investigate why target shareholder wealth gains differ so much between public and private acquirers. Although private operating companies pay less than public firms for most of our premium measures, the difference between these two types of acquisitions is much smaller than the difference between acquisitions by private equity firms and public companies. This evidence suggests that bidders of operating companies pay more for acquisitions because they expect to benefit from synergies. However, observable differences in targets cannot explain the differences in premiums paid.

Managerial ownership in the bidder and the target seems to play an important role in explaining the differences in premiums across organizational forms of the acquirer. There is no significant difference between premiums paid by private equity firms and public firms when the public firms have high managerial ownership. The difference in abnormal returns is highest between acquisitions made by private equity firms and those by public acquirers with low managerial ownership. As the managerial ownership of the public bidder increases, so that the ownership of the public acquirer becomes more similar to the ownership of the private acquirers, the difference in abnormal returns between the two types of bidders becomes small and insignificant. We also find that, whereas high target managerial and institutional ownership are associated with higher premiums for acquisitions by public firms, this is not the case for acquisitions by private firms, suggesting that private firm acquisitions are more likely to involve cooperation by managers to facilitate the acquisition. An outcome variable consistent with these differences in incentives is the sharply greater willingness of managers of private equity firms to walk away from an acquisition than managers of public firms.

Why is it that targets do not wait for a public firm to make a bid and why is it that public firms do not always outbid private firms when such firms make a bid? One would not expect public firms to be willing to pay large premiums for just any firm. It is therefore plausible that unobservable target characteristics can explain why some firms only attract the attention of private bidders or are ultimately more valuable for private equity bidders. Such firms could have little potential for synergy gains. It could also be that these unobservable target characteristics have to do with a greater willingness of target management to be acquired by a private firm than a public firm. Further research should help resolve the issue of whether target characteristics we do not observe in this study help explain the premium difference.

References

Aiken, L. S. and S. G. West, 1991, *Multiple Regression: Testing and Interpreting Interactions*, Sage Publications, Newbury Park, CA.

Amihud, Y., 2002, "Illiquidity and Stock Returns: Cross-Section and Time-Series Effects," *Journal of Financial Markets*, 5, 31–56.

Bebchuck, L. A. and Y. Grinstein, 2007, "Firm Expansion and CEO Pay," Harvard Law School Working Paper #53, Harvard University, Cambridge, MA.

Berle Jr., A. A. and G. C. Means, 1932, *The Modern Corporation and Private Property*, MacMillan, New York.

Betton, S. and B. Eckbo, 2000, "Toeholds, Bid Jumps, and Expected Payoffs in Takeovers," *Review of Financial Studies*, 13, 841–882.

Brown, S. and J. Warner, 1985, "Using Daily Stock Returns, the Case of Event Studies," *Journal of Financial Economics*, 14, 3–31.

Burch, T. R., 2001, "Locking Out Rival Bidders: The Use of Lockup Options in Corporate Mergers," *Journal of Financial Economics*, 60, 103–141.

DeAngelo, H., L. DeAngelo and E. M. Rice, 1984, "Going Private: Minority Freezeouts and Stockholder Wealth," *Journal of Law and Economics*, 27 (2), 367–402.

Harford, J. and K. Li, 2007, "Decoupling CEO Wealth and Firm Performance: The Case of Acquiring CEOs," *Journal of Finance*, 62, 917–950.

Harford, J., D. Jenter and K. Li, 2007, "Conflicts of Interests Among Shareholders: The Case of Corporate Acquisitions," Unpublished Working Paper, University of Washington.

Hartzell, J. C., E. Ofek and D. Yermack, 2004, "What's in It for Me? CEOs Whose Firms are Acquired," *Review of Financial Studies*, 17, 37–61.

Huang, Y. and R. Walkling, 1987, "Target Abnormal Returns Associated with Acquisition Announcements: Payment, Acquisition Form, and Managerial Resistance," *Journal of Financial Economics*, 19, 329–349.

Jensen, M., 1986, "Agency Costs of Free Cash Flow, Corporate Finance and Takeovers," *American Economic Review*, 76, 323–329.

Jensen, M., 1989, "Eclipse of the Public Corporation," *Harvard Business Review*, 67, 61–75.

Kaplan, S., 1989, "The Effects of Management Buyouts on Operating Performance and Value," *Journal of Financial Economics*, 24, 217–254.

Kothari, S. P. and J. Warner, 2007, "Econometrics of Event Studies," In E. Eckbo (Ed.), *Handbook of Corporate Finance*, vol. 1, Elsevier/North-Holland, Amsterdam, pp. 1–36.

Lehn, K. and M. Zhao, 2006, "CEO Turnover After Acquisitions: Are Bad Bidders Fired?," *Journal of Finance*, 56, 1759–1811.

Moeller, S., F. Schlingemann and R. Stulz, 2004, "Firm Size and the Gains from Acquisitions," *Journal of Financial Economics*, 73, 201–228.

Officer, M., 2003, "Termination Fees in Mergers and Acquisitions," *Journal of Financial Economics*, 69, 431–467.

Schlingemann, F. P., R. M. Stulz and R. A. Walkling, 2002, "Divestitures and the Liquidity of the Market for Corporate Assets," *Journal of Financial Economics*, 64, 117–144.

Schwert, G., 1996, "Markup Pricing in Mergers and Acquisitions," *Journal of Financial Economics*, 41, 153–192.

Stulz, R., 1988, "Managerial Control of Voting Rights: Financing Policies and the Market for Corporate Control," *Journal of Financial Economics*, 20, 25–54.

Chapter 9

THE UNDERPRICING OF PRIVATE TARGETS[*]

JOHN W. COONEY

Rawls College of Business, Texas Tech University, Lubbock, Texas, USA

THOMAS MOELLER

Neeley School of Business, Texas Christian University, Fort Worth, Texas, USA

MIKE STEGEMOLLER

Rawls College of Business, Texas Tech University, Lubbock, Texas, USA

Contents

* We thank Craig Dunbar, the referee of this paper, Andres Almazan, Chris Barry, Scott Bauguess, Dan Bradley, Alex Butler, Chitru Fernando, Brad Jordan, Sandy Klasa, Steve Mann, Ron Masulis, Vassil Mihov, Jeffry Netter, Micah Officer, Ajai Singh, and seminar participants at the 2006 Frank Batten Young Scholars Conference at the College of William & Mary, the 2006 Lone Star Finance Symposium at Southern Methodist University, the 2007 FMA European Conference, Baylor University, California State University—Fullerton, Texas Christian University, Texas Tech University, and the US Securities and Exchange Commission for helpful comments. Thomas Moeller wishes to thank the Luther King Capital Management Center for Financial Studies at the Neeley School of Business at TCU for its financial support for this research.

This article originally appeared in the *Journal of Financial Economics,* Vol. 93, pp. 51–66 (2009).
Corporate Takeovers, Volume 1
Edited by B. Espen Eckbo
DOI: 10.1016/B978-0-12-381983-3.00009-5

Abstract

We examine acquisitions of private firms with valuation histories and find a positive relation between acquirer announcement returns and target valuation revisions. Similar to other studies, acquirer announcement returns are positive, on average. However, positive acquirer announcement returns are mainly driven by targets that are acquired for more than their prior valuation. This relation is consistent with pricing effects associated with target valuation uncertainty and behavioral biases in negotiation outcomes.

Keywords

private acquisitions, withdrawn IPOs, valuation uncertainty

JEL classification: G24, G34

1. Introduction

The evidence of positive announcement returns to acquirers of private targets is pervasive and robust, yet explanations are sparse. In this paper, we examine the relation between valuation changes of private firms and the announcement returns of their public acquirers. Using a sample of acquisitions of private firms that withdraw an initial public offering (IPO), we calculate the change in firm value from the planned IPO to the acquisition and find a positive relation between this valuation revision and acquirer announcement returns. On average, acquirers have a statistically and economically significant announcement return of 7.6% when the valuation revision is positive, but only a statistically insignificant 0.7% when the revision is negative. Thus, in our withdrawn IPO sample, positive returns are mainly driven by acquisitions in which there has been an increase in the value of the target. We find a similar positive relation between valuation revisions and acquirer announcement returns in a sample of private targets with valuations from venture capitalists (VCs).

Two examples illustrate what we observe. In its 28 June 2002 IPO registration statement, NOMOS Corp. had an estimated value of $87.4 million. NOMOS subsequently withdrew its IPO registration citing unfavorable market conditions. On 27 October 2003, North American Scientific announced its purchase of NOMOS for $51.6 million, a valuation revision of −41%. (See Appendix A for the calculation of NOMOS' IPO valuation and acquisition price.) In the three days around the acquisition, North American Scientific's cumulative abnormal announcement return (*Acquirer CAR*) was −5.2%. In another transaction, Titan Corp. announced on 27 March 2000 the acquisition of AverStar, Inc. for $205 million, 36% more than its 30 July 1999 IPO valuation of $151 million. The *Acquirer CAR* for Titan was 7.6%.

Several papers document positive returns to acquirers of private targets. Fuller et al. (2002) find positive abnormal announcement returns in a sample of repeat acquirers of private targets, as do Moeller et al. (2004) in a large, relatively unrestricted sample, and Faccio et al. (2006) in non-US acquirers. Other papers find a relation between the method of payment and acquirer returns. Chang (1998) shows that acquirers benefit when the owners of closely held private targets become blockholders of the acquirer in stock acquisitions. Officer et al. (2008) find that the acquirer's use of stock as a method of payment mitigates the negative effects of information asymmetry on acquirers and results in positive announcement returns. Our finding of a positive relation between changes in the target's value and acquirer announcement returns provides new insights into the pricing of private acquisitions and the associated gains to public acquirers. We consider two potential explanations for our finding: (1) behavioral biases in negotiation outcomes commonly known as prospect theory and (2) pricing effects associated with target valuation uncertainty.

We base our first explanation for the positive relation between target valuation revisions and acquirer announcement returns on the relation's similarity to the partial adjustment effect found in IPO underpricing (Hanley, 1993). As in Loughran and Ritter's (2002) application of prospect theory (Kahneman and Tversky, 1979) to IPOs, we contend that owners of the target evaluate the acquirer's offer in relation to the target's prior valuation.[1] When the acquirer's offer is high relative to this prior value, the target is less likely to bargain aggressively to increase the acquisition price, thereby increasing the benefits accruing to the acquirer. Conversely, when the acquirer's offer is relatively low, the target will be more aggressive in takeover negotiations, yielding lower benefits to the acquirer. This behaviorally induced difference in the target's negotiation aggressiveness should result in high (low) acquirer announcement returns when the target's valuation revision is positive (negative).

The target valuation uncertainty hypothesis assumes that managers of both the acquirer and target are risk-averse, are less diversified than market participants, prefer skewness, and believe that the prior valuation is an important indicator of the target's market value.[2] During negotiations over the acquisition price, managers of both firms estimate the expected value of the target (i.e., the value that market participants are expected to attribute to the target as part of the acquirer) and its distribution. The prior valuation of the target should affect the distribution in two ways. First, valuation uncertainty should be higher the larger the absolute difference between the prior valuation and the expected value of the target. Since managers are risk-averse and the target's valuation uncertainty is transferred to the acquirer, larger absolute valuation revisions should result in higher target underpricing and greater gains to the acquirer. Second, the distribution of target values should be positively (negatively) skewed when the prior valuation is above (below) the target's expected value. As the purchaser, the acquirer prefers positively skewed distributions, while the target, as seller, prefers negatively skewed distributions. This implies lower target underpricing and smaller gains to the acquirer when the target's prior valuation is greater than its expected value and higher target underpricing and greater gains to the acquirer when the target's prior valuation is less than its expected value.[3]

For example, suppose the target's prior valuation is $150 and both acquirer and target managers estimate the expected value of the target to be $200. The $50 difference in values implies substantial valuation uncertainty, requiring a discount in

---

[1] Other explanations of the IPO partial adjustment effect are less applicable. For example, Benveniste and Spindt (1989), assuming the presence of many potential investors, predict a partial adjustment effect from a need to compensate IPO investors for the provision of favorable private information. Since the typical private acquisition has only one bidder, a similar rationale is unlikely to explain acquirer returns.

[2] These assumptions come from the existing literature. Jones and Rhodes-Kropf (2004) assume that venture capitalists can manage only a small number of investments and therefore hold significant idiosyncratic risk. Amihud and Lev (1981), among others, assume that managers are risk-averse. Conine and Tamarkin (1981) assume investors prefer positive skewness. Mitton and Vorkink (2007) find that underdiversified investors hold positively skewed portfolios. For our main sample, the target was valued in conjunction with its planned IPO. Lowry and Schwert (2004) note, "the vast majority of public information is in fact fully incorporated [in the initial price range and final offer price]" and "the IPO pricing process is *almost* efficient."

[3] Since acquirer managers are less diversified than market participants are, idiosyncratic risk and skewness affect the acquisition price more than the target's expected value. We define target underpricing as the difference between the target's expected value and the acquisition price. Greater target underpricing should result in higher acquirer announcement returns, other things equal.

the acquisition price to a level below the expected value, for example, $180. Since the prior valuation is lower than the expected value, the distribution of values should be negatively skewed—the prior valuation of $150 implies that target values much below $200 are more likely than values much above $200. Thus, the target must offer a further discount in the acquisition price, for example, $170, to compensate the acquirer for the downside risk associated with the negative skew. We should empirically observe a $20 increase in value ($150–$170), $30 of target underpricing ($200–$170), and a positive acquirer announcement return. If the prior valuation is $250, instead of $150, there is still a $50 difference in the two values, but now there is a positive skew in the distribution of target values. The higher probability of a value much above $200 increases the target's risk of accepting too low a price. The acquirer prefers the positive skew and is willing to pay a higher price for the target than in the first example, for example, $190. Hence, we should observe a $60 decrease in value, $10 of underpricing, and a smaller acquirer announcement return. Thus, the target valuation uncertainty hypothesis predicts a positive relation between the target's valuation revision and acquirer gains. This positive relation should be stronger for positive, rather than negative, valuation revisions. For positive valuation revisions, a higher valuation revision implies more valuation uncertainty and causes the distribution to become more negatively skewed. Both factors should increase target underpricing and gains to the acquirer. However, for negative revisions, the effects are opposite: a larger negative revision requires more underpricing to compensate for increased valuation uncertainty, but less underpricing due to increased positive skewness.

We provide two tests of the prospect theory and target valuation uncertainty hypotheses. First, we investigate the impact of firm-specific and market-wide valuation changes. The relation between market returns and acquirer announcement returns is positive under prospect theory. Since acquirers and targets can hedge the portion of target valuation uncertainty and skewness associated with market returns, there should be no relation between market returns and acquirer announcement returns under the target valuation uncertainty hypothesis. We find a consistently significant positive relation between firm-specific target valuation revisions and acquirer returns and only weak evidence of a positive relation between target valuation revisions resulting from market-wide price changes and acquirer returns. Thus, this evidence favors the target valuation uncertainty hypothesis.

Second, VCs, as experts in pricing private firms, may place less weight on prior valuations and more weight on their own current valuation. Thus, VC ownership of the target should reduce the impact of prior valuations on target valuation uncertainty and skewness. Similarly, Loughran and Ritter (2002) contend that VCs might be less affected by the behavior biases of prospect theory. Therefore, both the target valuation uncertainty and prospect theory explanations predict that the relation between valuation revisions and acquirer announcement returns should be less positive when the target is VC-backed. Consistent with this prediction, we find that the effect of target valuation revisions on acquirer announcement returns is significantly smaller when VCs own a portion of the target.

In summary, this paper contributes to our understanding of the valuation effects of private firm acquisitions. Similar to other studies, we find positive announcement returns to public acquirers of private targets. Yet in our sample, these positive returns are mainly driven by private targets that experience positive valuation revisions. We explore two explanations for this positive relation between target valuation changes and *Acquirer CAR*—behavioral biases and target valuation uncertainty. Our evidence favors the target valuation uncertainty explanation. Furthermore, target valuation revisions dominate a broader measure of riskiness in explaining positive acquirer announcement returns. While we examine only a small portion of private acquisitions, our results may apply more broadly as most private firms have some valuation history, even if it is not observable to researchers. Finally, our finding suggests that a relation similar to the IPO partial adjustment effect is present in mergers and acquisitions.

Section 2 presents the data and descriptive statistics. Our main empirical results are in Section 3. Section 4 presents robustness tests, Section 5 verifies our main empirical result with a larger sample of targets with prior valuations by private equity and VC firms, and Section 6 concludes.

2. Data description

This section describes our sample, provides a description of the acquisition process for a subset of our firms, and explains the calculation of our variables.

2.1. Sample selection

We collect 1119 withdrawn US IPOs from 1996 to 2005 from Thomson SDC Platinum's New Issues database. The beginning of our sample coincides with the availability of electronic filings on the Securities and Exchange Commission's (SEC) EDGAR database. We match the CIDGEN, a firm-specific number assigned by SDC, and the SDC CUSIP of the firms in the withdrawn IPO sample to the universe of acquisitions in the Thomson SDC Mergers & Acquisitions (SDC M&A) database from 1996 to 2005. We also visually inspect for matching names between the sample of withdrawn IPOs and the acquisitions database. This process produces 710 matching transactions out of the 1119 withdrawn IPOs. We likely miss some acquisitions of withdrawn IPO firms with our matching procedure, namely instances when the target changes its name and identifying numbers between the IPO withdrawal and the acquisition.

From the 710 matches, we remove 399 transactions for the following reasons: the target is publicly traded at the time of the acquisition (146 firms); the target is acquired as part of a joint venture (four firms); the acquirer purchases less than 50% of the target or does not own 100% of the target after the acquisition (249 firms). These screens leave 311 transactions, of which 100 involve a nonpublic acquirer.

Of the remaining 211 acquisitions, we require the target's original or amended IPO registration statement to have the filing price range (i.e., an estimate of the IPOs offer price), the anticipated number of primary and secondary shares in the offering, the number of shares outstanding after the planned IPO, and financial statements listing the target's total assets and stockholders' equity. These requirements eliminate 91 firms. We also collect the name of the book underwriter and VC ownership from the IPO registration statements. We eliminate 52 observations due to: confounding events of seven acquirers (e.g., simultaneous acquisition announcements), one target being in bankruptcy, one transaction being misclassified (i.e., in substance, the target purchased the acquirer), seven transactions having missing information (e.g., price paid for the target by the acquirer), one target being a Real Estate Investment Trust and one a subsidiary of another firm, one substantial restructuring of the target in the period between the IPO withdrawal and acquisition, five acquisitions occurring before the IPO registration date, and 28 acquirers not having data on the Center for Research in Security Prices (CRSP) data sets. The resulting sample contains 68 private firms that file with the SEC for an IPO, withdraw their registration, and are subsequently acquired by a publicly traded firm.[4]

There are four possible outcomes for firms that withdraw an IPO. They can (1) be acquired by a publicly traded firm, (2) refile and complete an IPO, (3) be acquired by a private firm, or (4) stay private. Our data show that publicly traded firms acquire about 19% (211/1119) of withdrawn IPOs while the target is still private. The frequency of refiling and completing an IPO is lower. Dunbar (1998) and Dunbar and Foerster (2008) find that less than 10% refile and complete an IPO. We find the median time from the last IPO filing (i.e., the last filing with the SEC for the planned IPO containing valuation information) to acquisition is 243 days with a maximum of about six years. Dunbar and Foerster (2008) find the median time from withdrawal to re-IPO is 663 days, with a maximum of about ten years. Thus, the percentages of withdrawn IPOs that are acquired by publicly traded firms or that re-IPO are likely higher than shown above since the final outcomes of some firms are still undetermined.

2.2. Calculation of the IPO valuation and target's valuation revision

Our main variable, *Valuation revision*, compares the estimated value of the target at the time of its planned IPO to the acquisition price. We estimate the target's *IPO Valuation* as the target's implied value of equity plus book value of liabilities as of the

---

[4] Fifteen of the acquirers in our sample file Form S-4 with the SEC. Form S-4 is frequently required when the acquirer issues stock in connection with the acquisition. In general, the S-4s do not emphasize the target's withdrawn IPO, although ten mention the failed IPO explicitly. In four cases the bidder and target are already negotiating while the target is still in registration for its IPO, six targets conduct informal auctions, and two deals have multiple bidders. The target's board justifies the merger with, among other reasons, the failed IPO coupled with the difficulty of raising funds in two cases, only the failed IPO in two cases, and only the difficulty of raising funds in one case. The board suggests that the merger is a "better deal" than the IPO in four cases.

last IPO registration statement before the withdrawal. The implied value of equity is the product of the number of shares of common stock outstanding before the IPO and the average of the high and low filing prices. We use the pre-IPO shares outstanding, which is calculated as the number of shares to be outstanding after the IPO minus the number of primary shares to be issued in the IPO, so that the IPO value and acquisition price are comparable. (Since the acquisition does not raise capital, we do not include the expected proceeds of the IPO in the calculation of *IPO Valuation*.) We calculate the book value of liabilities as the firm's total assets minus stockholders' equity. *Valuation revision* equals *Acquisition price* divided by *IPO Valuation* minus one. We calculate *Acquisition price* from information in LexisNexis and SEC filings. It is the sum of cash, acquirer stock (valued two trading days before the announcement using CRSP), and assumed liabilities. In most of our analysis, we log *Valuation revision* to reduce the influence of outliers.

2.3. Descriptive statistics

Because our sample is unique, we provide descriptive statistics in Table 1 and compare them to the private acquisition literature. *Acquirer CAR* is the cumulative return in excess of the CRSP equal-weighted index[5] for the three days centered on the acquisition announcement, which is the earlier of the announcement date found on LexisNexis or that reported by SDC.[6] The mean *Acquirer CAR* is 2.8%, which is similar to the CARs of 2.1%, 1.5%, and 3.8% reported in Fuller et al. (2002), Moeller et al. (2004), and Officer et al. (2008), respectively.

The mean *Acquisition price* for the target is $219 million, which is similar to the mean target value of $244 million reported in Officer et al. (2008), but larger than the $105 million reported in Officer (2007). The mean *IPO Valuation* is $333 million. *Valuation revision* has a mean of −2.6% and median of −33.0%, implying that the typical target's acquisition price is less than its estimated value at the time of the proposed IPO.

The average acquirer market value of equity two trading days before the takeover announcement, *Acquirer size*, is $10.2 billion, which is larger than the acquirer equity value of $3.2 billion in Officer et al. (2008). The average *Relative size*, the ratio of *Acquisition price* minus assumed liabilities to *Acquirer size*, is 27.6%. The median value of *Fraction stock*, the fraction of the transaction paid with stock from the SDC M&A database, is 69.8%. Compared to Officer (2007) and Officer et al. (2008), our transactions are relatively large and use stock more frequently.

---

[5] Using the CRSP value-weighted index return, CRSP Nasdaq equal-weighted index return, or CRSP Nasdaq value-weighted index return instead of the CRSP equal-weighted index return does not affect our main results.

[6] The LexisNexis and SDC announcement dates are identical, except for three observations where the LexisNexis date is one day earlier than the SDC date. The 3-day window we use to calculate acquirer CAR captures both dates.

Table 1

Descriptive statistics

This table contains descriptive statistics for our sample of 68 firms that file an IPO registration statement, withdraw, and are subsequently acquired by a public firm from 1996 to 2005. *Acquirer CAR* is the 3-day cumulative abnormal return for the acquirer around the acquisition announcement in which expected returns are measured with the CRSP equal-weighted index. *Acquisition price* is the announced acquisition price for the target, including cash, acquirer stock, and assumed liabilities, as collected from LexisNexis and SEC filings. The value of acquirer stock is calculated two trading days before the acquisition announcement. *IPO Valuation* uses data gathered from the last SEC filing for the planned IPO and is equal to the target's implied value of equity plus the book value of liabilities on the target's balance sheet. The implied value of equity is the product of the common stock outstanding before the planned IPO and *IPO Filing price*, which is the average of the planned IPOs high and low filing prices. *Valuation revision* is equal to *Acquisition price* divided by *IPO Valuation* minus one. *Acquirer size* is the acquirer market value of equity two trading days before the acquisition announcement. *Relative size* is *Acquisition price* minus assumed liabilities divided by *Acquirer size*. *Fraction stock* is the fraction of consideration paid in stock as collected from SDC. *VC Ownership* is the fractional ownership of venture capitalists in the target as gathered from the last SEC filing for the planned IPO. *VC Ownership* is assumed to be zero if the last SEC filing for the planned IPO occurred more than five years before the acquisition announcement. *CM-Rank* is the Carter and Manaster (1990) rank of the lead IPO underwriter, as updated by Loughran and Ritter (2004). *IPO Filing proceeds* is *IPO Filing price* times the anticipated number of shares to be issued with the IPO as gathered from the last SEC filing for the planned IPO.

	(1) Mean	(2) Median	(3) Minimum	(4) Maximum	(5) Standard deviation
Acquirer CAR	0.028	0.010	−0.286	0.402	0.116
Acquisition price ($ million)	219	124	3	3300	419
IPO valuation ($ million)	333	192	26	4075	604
Valuation revision	−0.026	−0.330	−0.983	4.933	1.163
Acquirer size ($ million)	10,217	942	9	296,161	38,259
Relative size	0.276	0.087	0.001	2.074	0.474
Fraction stock	0.533	0.698	0.000	1.000	0.461
VC ownership	0.264	0.248	0.000	0.909	0.264
CM-Rank	7.8	8.0	3.0	9.0	1.4
IPO filing price ($)	12.1	12.0	6.0	22.0	3.3
IPO filing proceeds ($ million)	98	49	6	2739	328

VC Ownership is the sum of venture capital and private equity firm's fractional target ownership as of the last IPO filing. We combine venture capital and private equity ownership because they serve similar roles in the private firm and because it is difficult in the ownership data to distinguish between the two types of firms. Hereafter, we denote both as VC firms. We assume that *VC Ownership* is zero if there are more than five years between the last IPO filing and the acquisition date. In these situations, we assume that the VCs have liquidated their equity position prior to the acquisition.[7]

---

[7] Venture partnerships have finite lifetimes of usually ten years (Gompers and Lerner, 1999). In Section 4.2, we redefine *VC Ownership* to assume that the venture capital ownership is still present beyond five years.

On average, VCs own 26.4% of the target. Further, 65% of our firms have at least some VC participation. This percentage is higher than the 41% reported by Poulsen and Stegemoller (2008) in their sample of private takeovers. However, it is similar to the 56% VC-backing in IPOs in 1999, reported by Gompers and Lerner (2001), who show a rapidly increasing trend in VC-backed IPOs. In summary, although we highlight some differences, our unique sample appears to be largely representative of private firm acquisitions.

CM-Rank is Loughran and Ritter's (2004) updated Carter and Manaster (1990) ranking of the lead underwriter for the planned IPO. The median *CM-Rank* is eight, with nine being the maximum. Thus, prestigious investment banks lead the withdrawn IPOs in our sample. *IPO Filing price* is the average of the high and low filing prices as of the last IPO filing. *IPO Filing proceeds* is the product of *IPO Filing price* and the anticipated number of shares to be issued in the IPO. Means for *IPO Filing price* and *IPO Filing proceeds* are $12.1 and $98 million, respectively.

Dunbar and Foerster (2008) examine a sample of 1473 firms from 1985 to 2000 that file for an IPO and then withdraw their IPO registration. Of their sample, 138 firms refile and complete an IPO. Dunbar and Foerster (2008) find that having high prestige underwriters and VC-backing are important factors in predicting the probability the firm will successfully return to the IPO market. For example, they show that the firms that refile and complete an IPO have a mean Carter and Manaster (1990) lead underwriter rank of 7.4 and 25% are VC-backed. For the firms that do not refile and complete an IPO, the mean Carter and Manaster (1990) rank is 6.5 and only 13.5% of these firms are VC-backed. Compared to the Dunbar and Foerster (2008) sample of firms that re-IPO, our sample firms have similarly prestigious underwriters, but are more frequently VC-backed. Since our sample period begins during a period of increased VC-backing for IPOs (Gompers and Lerner, 2001), it is not surprising that our sample has a higher fraction of VC-backed firms. Overall, this finding suggests that prestigious underwriters and VC-backing are important factors in withdrawn IPO firms being successful acquisition candidates.

Table 2, Panel A, presents the distribution of last IPO filings and acquisition announcements by year. Slightly more than half of our firms file their last IPO registration statement in 1999 or 2000, the peak of the Nasdaq bubble. Conversely, there is only one observation in 2003 and none in 2005. Since there is a high number of IPO withdrawals in 1999 and 2000, we investigate the effects of this clustering in Section 4.1. Acquisition announcements are more evenly distributed across our sample period.

In Table 2, Panel B, we report the number of observations in the top six target industries. Unless otherwise noted, we define "industry" using the Fama and French 49-industry classification. Approximately half of the targets and one-third of the acquirers come from the Computer Software and Business Services industries. This distribution of targets is similar to that in Fuller et al. (2002) and Officer et al. (2008). Overall, our targets and acquirers are from 18 and 22 different industries, respectively. The acquirer and target are in the same industry in 31 of the 68 acquisitions.

Table 2

Observations by year and industry

This table presents the number of observations by year and top six target industries for our sample of 68 firms that file an IPO registration statement, withdraw, and are subsequently acquired by a public firm from 1996 to 2005. Panel A, column 1, shows the number of observations based on the date of the last SEC filing for the planned IPO; column 2 contains the number of observations based on the acquisition announcement date. Panel B, column 1, shows the number of target firms per industry for the top six industries; column 2 contains the number of acquirers. We classify the industry of our sample firms using the Fama and French 49-industry classification.

Panel A. Year	(1) Last SEC filing for IPO	(2) Acquisition date
1996	5	0
1997	8	7
1998	8	7
1999	13	9
2000	22	11
2001	4	11
2002	4	4
2003	1	10
2004	3	5
2005	0	4
Observations	68	68
Panel B. Industry	(1) Target	(2) Acquirer
Computer software	17	15
Business services	16	7
Retail	4	5
Electronic equipment	4	4
Banking	4	3
Medical equipment	4	2

We control for industry characteristics, such as industry liquidity index and industry return. We also use industry dummy variables in unreported regressions, but they do not affect our results.

3. Results

In this section, we test whether valuation changes of the target affect acquirer announcement returns.

3.1. Univariate analysis

In Table 3, we split our sample into terciles based on *Valuation revision*. Acquisitions with larger target valuation revisions have significantly higher *Acquirer CARs*.

Table 3

Acquirer cumulative abnormal return and target valuation revision

This table presents means, medians, and number of observations for *Acquirer CAR*, separated by terciles of *Valuation revision* for our sample of 68 firms that file an IPO registration statement, withdraw, and are subsequently acquired by a public firm from 1996 to 2005. Tercile breakpoints for *Valuation revision* are, from lowest to highest, less than or equal to -65%, between -65% and -6%, and greater than or equal to -6%. The first *p*-value in column 4 is from a *t*-test of difference in means between columns 1 and 3; the second *p*-value is from a Wilcoxon test of difference in medians between columns 1 and 3. All variables are defined in previous tables.

	(1) Valuation revision bottom tercile	(2) Valuation revision middle tercile	(3) Valuation revision top tercile	(4) *p*-Value (1) versus (3)
Mean	-1.6%	3.1%	7.0%**	0.0232**
Median	-2.5%	3.3%	3.2%**	0.0220**
Number of observations	23	22	23	

**Denotes significance at the 0.05 level.

The mean (median) *Acquirer CAR* in the highest tercile is 7.0% (3.2%) compared to -1.6% (-2.5%) in the lowest tercile, and the differences are significant at the 0.05 level. Of our 68 observations, 21 have positive valuation revisions. The mean (median) *Acquirer CAR* for targets with positive revisions is 7.6% (3.2%), and both numbers are statistically different from zero at the 0.05 level (not shown in table). In contrast, the mean (median) *Acquirer CAR* for the 47 targets with negative revisions is only 0.7% (0.0%), both not different from zero. The differences in means and medians between these two groups are significant at the 0.05 and 0.10 levels, respectively. We also calculate the correlation of *Valuation revision* and *Acquirer CAR*. Confirming the other univariate tests, the correlation coefficient equals 0.32 and is significant at the 0.01 level. Thus, acquisitions of targets with positive valuation revisions are associated with higher acquirer announcement returns.

3.2. Determinants of valuation revision

We examine the determinants of *Valuation revision* to understand better the cause for its positive relation with *Acquirer CAR*. A target's value can change between its IPO filing date and acquisition announcement date for at least two reasons. First, the fundamental value of the target can change due to adjustments in expected cash flows or discount rates. Second, the value change can reflect the inherent uncertainty of valuing private firms. Prospect theory predicts a positive relation between valuation revisions and target underpricing without regard to the reason for the change in target value. The target valuation uncertainty hypothesis relies on the second reason to explain this positive relation. To assess the relative importance of these two reasons for target value changes, we regress *Log valuation revision*, that is, the natural log of (1 + *Valuation revision*), on proxies for changes in fundamental value and the target's valuation uncertainty.

The target's fundamental value should change with market movements and IPO withdrawal should cause distressed targets to suffer a decline in value between the last IPO filing and the acquisition. Thus, we proxy for the change in the target's fundamental value with *Industry return since last IPO filing* (the compounded value--weighted return of the target's industry from the last IPO filing to two trading days before the acquisition announcement) and two firm-specific target distress variables: *Debt to assets target* (the target's liabilities divided by total assets) and *Distressed target* (a dummy variable equal to one when the target's earnings before interest, taxes, and depreciation are less than its interest expense). Data for these two variables are from 35 S-4 or 8-K acquirer filings linked to the acquisition. For the 33 observations without these filings, we use the information from the target's last IPO filing. If the change in the value of the target reflects changes in the target's fundamental value, there should be a positive relation between *Industry return since last IPO filing* and *Log valuation revision* and a negative relation between the target distress variables and *Log valuation revision*.

Under the target valuation uncertainty hypothesis, targets with a high absolute *Log valuation revision* should have high valuation uncertainty. To test, we calculate two additional, broader proxies for target valuation uncertainty: the standard deviations of the price-to-earnings and price-to-assets multiples of a matched group of public firms, $\sigma(Price\text{-}to\text{-}assets\ multiple\ target)$ and $\sigma(Price\text{-}to\text{-}earnings\ multiple\ target)$. The matched public firms must be in the same industry and have a contemporaneous (based on the calendar year of the acquisition announcement) equity market value between 50% and 200% of the equity value of the target. The public firm's equity value is the numerator, and book value of total assets is the denominator in the price-to-assets multiple and net income is the denominator in the price-to-earnings multiple. We exclude negative price-to-earnings multiples. If there is a positive relation between the absolute *Log valuation revision* and the target's valuation uncertainty, there should also be a positive relation between the absolute *Log valuation revision* and the target's standard deviation of multiples.

Log valuation revision is the dependent variable in Table 4. Consistent with *Log valuation revision* reflecting changes in the target's fundamental value, *Industry return since last IPO filing* is positive with *p*-values of approximately 0.10 in each model, and both distress variables are negative and significant at the 0.01 level. Both $\sigma(Price\text{-}to\text{-}assets\ multiple\ target)$, column 1, and $\sigma(Price\text{-}to\text{-}earnings\ multiple\ target)$, column 2, are significantly positive at the 0.01 level. In untabulated analyses, we re-estimate the regression in column 1 separately for positive and negative valuation revisions and for above and below median revisions. (For this and our remaining analysis, we use σ (*Price-to-assets multiple target*) as a measure of valuation uncertainty because it allows the use of all 68 observations, is better behaved than price-to-earnings, and

Table 4

Regression results for log valuation revision

This table presents regression results for our sample of 68 firms that file an IPO registration statement, withdraw, and are subsequently acquired by a public firm from 1996 to 2005. The dependent variable is *Log valuation revision*, which is the natural log of (1 + *Valuation revision*). σ(*Price-to-assets multiple target*) and σ(*Price-to-earnings multiple target*) are the standard deviations of valuation multiples of size, industry, and year-matched public firms, measured as of the calendar year of the acquisition announcement date. The first multiple is the market value of equity scaled by total assets; the second is the market value of equity scaled by net income. *Debt to assets target* is the target's liabilities divided by its total assets. *Distressed target* is a dummy variable equal to one if the target's earnings before interest, taxes, and depreciation are less than its interest expense in the same year. The previous two accounting variables are measured as of the calendar year of the acquisition announcement date, if available, or if unavailable, from the most recent IPO filing by the target prior to its withdrawal. *Industry return since last IPO filing* is the compounded value-weighted return of the target's industry from the last SEC filing for the planned IPO to two trading days before the acquisition announcement. We use the 49-industry returns from http://mba.tuck.dartmouth.edu/pages/faculty/ken.french/. All other variables are defined in previous tables. *p*-Values, based on heteroskedasticity-adjusted standard errors, are in brackets.

	(1)	(2)
σ(Price-to-assets multiple target)	1.296*** [0.000]	
σ(Price-to-earnings multiple target)		0.086*** [0.003]
Debt to assets target	−0.660*** [0.001]	−0.693*** [0.000]
Distressed target	−0.718*** [0.001]	−0.896*** [0.002]
Industry return since last IPO filing	0.695* [0.100]	0.791 [0.101]
Intercept	−1.217*** [0.002]	−1.086** [0.020]
F-statistic	17.51***	15.21***
Adjusted R²	0.4775	0.3956
Number of observations	68	67

***, **, *Denote significance at the 0.01, 0.05, and 0.10 levels, respectively.

does not require deleting comparable firms with negative earnings.) The coefficient for σ(*Price-to-assets multiple target*) is always positive and is statistically significant in three of the four subsamples (the *p*-value is 0.12 in the subsample of only positive revisions).

The positive relation between *Log valuation revision* and σ(*Price-to-assets multiple target*) with positive and above median valuation revisions is consistent with *Log valuation revision* reflecting target valuation uncertainty, but the positive relation for negative and below median valuation revisions is inconsistent with this view. This result may be an artifact of sample selection biases. The withdrawn IPOs with the most negative valuation revisions are likely never acquired, possibly excluding those observations in which *Log valuation revision* and target valuation uncertainty are most likely to be negatively related. Alternatively, *Log valuation revision* may measure other aspects of valuation uncertainty not captured by σ(*Price-to-assets multiple target*).

3.3. Regression analysis

We next consider the relation between *Log valuation revision* and *Acquirer CAR* in a multivariate setting including common control variables from the acquisitions literature. We include *Relative size* as a control variable because Faccio et al. (2006) and Asquith et al. (1983) find a positive relation between acquirer announcement returns and relative size in private and public acquisitions, respectively. Moeller et al. (2004) find that larger acquirers earn approximately 2% lower announcement returns than do smaller acquirers. They interpret this finding as evidence of hubris (Roll, 1986). Thus, we include *Log acquirer size*, the natural log of *Acquirer size*.

Fuller et al. (2002) and Faccio et al. (2006) find higher acquirer returns when the acquirer uses stock to purchase the private target. Further, Officer et al. (2008) show that using stock as a method of payment mitigates asymmetric information about the target and leads to more positive acquirer returns. However, Moeller et al. (2004) find no difference between stock and cash deals. To test the effects of payment with stock in our sample, we include *Stock* as a dummy variable equal to one if *Fraction stock* is higher than 95%.

Lang et al. (1989) show that acquirers with high Tobin's Q gain more than acquirers with low Tobin's Q. Thus, we include *Acquirer Q* which is the acquirer's total assets minus book value of equity plus market value of equity, all divided by total assets. Total assets and book value of equity are from Compustat as of the year preceding the acquisition, and acquirer market value of equity is as of two trading days before the takeover announcement. We also control for the acquisition activity of the target's industry with *Liquidity index target industry*. Similar to Schlingemann et al. (2002), this variable is the value of all acquisitions in the SDC M&A database (removing repurchases, self-tender offers, and deals with the same acquirer and target name) divided by the total book value of assets for firms in the same two-digit Standard Industrial Classification (SIC) during the same year. Ratios larger than one are set equal to one.[8]

Acquirer CAR is the dependent variable in Table 5. The coefficient of *Log valuation revision* in column 1 equals 0.036 and is significant at the 0.01 level.[9] Of the control variables, only *Log acquirer size* is significant at the 0.10 level and the coefficient is negative. *Stock* is never significantly positive in any of our regressions.[10] Because of

---

[8] We construct a discount measure similar to Officer (2007) using a portfolio of industry, size, and time-matched public firms. We also construct a blockholder formation variable (Chang, 1998) similar to Officer et al. (2008). We include the discount and blockholder variables in unreported regressions. Both variables are insignificant and do not significantly influence our other variables.

[9] We determine significance levels using heteroskedasticity-consistent standard errors with a small sample adjustment based on White (1980) and MacKinnon and White (1985).

[10] In unreported regressions we interact *Stock* with *Log valuation revision*, change the definition of *Stock* to equal one if the method of payment is at least 50% stock, and if it is 100% stock. In no specification do our results match the positive relation between stock and returns to acquirers of private targets found in most of the literature.

Table 5

Regression results for acquirer cumulative abnormal returns

This table presents regression results for our sample of 68 firms that file an IPO registration statement, withdraw, and are subsequently acquired by a public firm from 1996 to 2005. The dependent variable is *Acquirer CAR*. Our main regression is in column 2. The independent variables include *Log valuation revision* and *Relative size*. *Log acquirer size* is the natural log of *Acquirer size*. *Stock* is a dummy variable equal to one if the fraction of consideration paid in stock is greater than 95%. *Acquirer Q* is the acquirer's total assets minus book value of equity plus market value of equity, all scaled by total assets. *Liquidity index target industry* is the value of all corporate control transactions divided by the total book value of assets for firms in the same two-digit SIC code during the same year. *VC* is a dummy variable equal to one if the last SEC filing for the planned IPO indicates that the target is backed by venture capital. *VC* is equal to zero if the last SEC filing for the planned IPO occurred more than five years before the acquisition announcement. *Log valuation revision × VC* is the interaction of *Log valuation revision* and *VC*. Column 1 omits the two VC-related variables. In column 3, we replace *Log valuation revision*, in both the continuous variable and its interaction with *VC*, with *Industry adjusted log valuation revision*, the natural log of [*Acquisition price* divided by [*IPO Valuation × (1 + Industry return since last IPO filing)*]], and add *Industry return since last IPO filing*. Column 4 includes controls for underwriter quality and time between IPO filing and acquisition. *Low rank underwriter* is a dummy variable equal to one if the IPO underwriter's *CM-Rank* is less than eight. *Log valuation revision × Low rank underwriter* is the interaction of *Log valuation revision* and *Low rank underwriter*. *Long time* is a dummy variable equal to one if the number of days between the last SEC filing for the planned IPO and the acquisition announcement date is more than 365. *Log valuation revision × Long time* is the interaction of *Log valuation revision* and *Long time*. The only explanatory variables in column 5 are σ(*Price-to-assets multiple target*), *Debt to assets target*, *Distressed target*, and *Industry return since last IPO filing*. We add acquisition-related control variables in column 6 and *Log valuation revision* and *Log valuation revision × VC* in column 7. The regression in column 8 includes all explanatory variables. Variables that are not described here are defined in previous tables. *p*-Values, based on heteroskedasticity-adjusted standard errors, are in brackets.

	(1)	(2)	(3)	(4)	(5)	(6)	(7)	(8)
Log valuation revision	0.036*** [0.005]	0.067*** [0.000]		0.079*** [0.010]			0.074*** [0.004]	0.090*** [0.009]
Industry adjusted log valuation revision			0.063*** [0.001]					
Relative size	0.022 [0.600]	0.017 [0.631]	0.020 [0.556]	0.027 [0.432]		0.041 [0.342]	0.020 [0.524]	0.025 [0.487]
Log acquirer size	-0.015* [0.088]	-0.015* [0.067]	-0.012 [0.158]	-0.014 [0.103]		-0.004 [0.611]	-0.010 [0.218]	-0.010 [0.233]
Stock	-0.026 [0.353]	-0.032 [0.257]	-0.036 [0.208]	-0.049 [0.115]		-0.005 [0.850]	-0.025 [0.380]	-0.042 [0.139]
Acquirer Q	0.000 [0.378]	0.000 [0.511]	0.000 [0.428]	0.000 [0.780]		0.000 [0.130]	0.000 [0.348]	-0.000 [0.648]

	(1)	(2)	(3)	(4)	(5)	(6)	(7)	(8)
Liquidity index target industry	0.079 [0.618]	0.134 [0.373]	0.143 [0.333]		0.078 [0.616]	0.017 [0.928]	0.078 [0.653]	−0.008 [0.967]
VC	−0.064** [0.030]	−0.067** [0.029]	−0.067** [0.029]		−0.057 [0.077]	−0.020 [0.537]	−0.054 [0.127]	−0.056 [0.118]
Log valuation revision × VC	−0.049** [0.013]				−0.053** [0.015]		−0.059** [0.018]	−0.056** [0.013]
Industry adjusted log valuation revision × VC		−0.059*** [0.006]	−0.059*** [0.006]					
Low rank underwriter					0.032 [0.333]			0.016 [0.639]
Log valuation revision × Low rank underwriter					−0.009 [0.671]			−0.005 [0.837]
Long time					−0.060** [0.043]			−0.062** [0.045]
Log valuation revision × Long time					−0.017 [0.491]			−0.024 [0.320]
σ(Price-to-assets multiple target)					0.076** [0.022]	0.059 [0.103]	0.004 [0.901]	0.011 [0.760]
Debt to assets target					0.041 [0.250]	0.035 [0.379]	0.057* [0.068]	0.053* [0.056]
Distressed target					−0.043 [0.138]	−0.033 [0.292]	0.001 [0.968]	0.011 [0.756]
Industry return since last IPO filing			0.077* [0.077]		0.067 [0.142]	0.061 [0.209]	0.066 [0.205]	0.075 [0.125]
Intercept	0.147* [0.075]	0.190** [0.019]	0.161** [0.050]	0.198** [0.028]	−0.079 [0.136]	−0.034 [0.703]	0.086 [0.245]	0.114 [0.186]
F-statistic	2.35**	4.53***	4.70***	4.41***	3.28**	2.46**	3.70***	4.36***
Adjusted R²	0.1360	0.1976	0.1970	0.1969	0.1485	0.1176	0.2320	0.2200
Number of observations	68	68	68	68	68	68	68	68

***, **, *Denote significance at the 0.01, 0.05, and 0.10 levels, respectively.

our relatively small sample size, we do not want to overemphasize this result. Further, the information within the target's IPO registration statement, especially valuations by investment banks, would likely reduce the type of asymmetric information that Officer et al. (2008) rely on to explain the positive influence of stock payments in their analysis.

Our main regression in column 2 adds controls for VC-related effects. *VC* is a dummy variable equal to one if *VC Ownership* is greater than zero. Gompers and Xuan (2006) find that announcement returns to acquirers of VC-backed private targets are less positive than those of non-VC-backed private targets. They interpret this result as VC-backed private targets having a greater price negotiating ability than those that are not VC-backed. VC-backing could also reduce target underpricing due to monitoring and certification effects (see Barry et al., 1990; Megginson and Weiss, 1991, for similar arguments in an IPO setting). *VC* should have a negative sign.

With respect to prospect theory, Loughran and Ritter (2002) contend, "... VCs, with their years of experience at taking firms public, might be less susceptible to psychological factors affecting their aggressiveness in bargaining." However, they find no evidence of this contention in a sample of IPOs and there is some evidence that institutional investors are also subject to behavioral biases (e.g., Crane and Hartzell, 2008). Alternatively, VCs' pricing expertise can reduce the influence of the prior valuation on target valuation uncertainty and skewness and therefore reduce the positive relation between valuation revision and acquirer return. We add *Log valuation revision × VC* and predict a negative coefficient.

In column 2 of Table 5, the coefficient for *VC* is −0.064 with a *p*-value of 0.03. VC participation appears to reduce target underpricing, consistent with greater negotiating power, monitoring, and certification effects. The significantly negative coefficient for *Log valuation revision × VC* indicates that the relation between valuation revision and acquirer returns is weaker in the subsample of VC-backed targets. This result supports the hypothesis that VC-backed targets are less susceptible to the psychological effects of prospect theory. Alternatively, the impact of prior valuations on valuation uncertainty and skewness can be lower with VC-backed targets. *Log valuation revision* remains positive and is significant at the 0.01 level after the inclusion of *VC* and *Log valuation revision × VC*.

Eighteen of our targets that received VC funding before their last IPO filing also received VC funding after their last IPO filing, thus providing a more recent valuation and potentially reducing the relevance of the target's earlier IPO valuation. Therefore, one reason for the negative sign for *Log valuation revision × VC* could be the inclusion of these 18 observations. In an untabulated regression, we exclude the 18 observations and re-estimate our main regression with the remaining 50 observations. *VC* and *Log valuation revision × VC* remain negative, but are now insignificant with *p*-values of 0.21 and 0.22, respectively. *Log valuation revision* remains positive with a coefficient of 0.069 and is significant at the 0.01 level. We also examine the 18 observations with additional VC funding and estimate the same regression as in column 1 (not shown in table). The coefficient for *Log valuation revision* is positive and significant at the 0.05 level, but has a point estimate of only 0.012. The lower point estimate suggests that subsequent equity valuations reduce the relevance of the prior IPO valuation and provide an alternative explanation for the negative relation between *Log valuation revision* × *VC* and *Acquirer CAR*.

In column 3, we investigate the impact of firm-specific versus market-related changes in target value. Similar to the argument in Loughran and Ritter (2002) for IPOs, the relation between market returns and *Acquirer CAR* should be positive under prospect theory. Since acquirers can hedge the portion of target valuation uncertainty and skewness associated with market returns, there should be no relation between market returns and *Acquirer CAR* under the target valuation uncertainty hypothesis.

We decompose *Log valuation revision* into the parts due to firm-specific value changes and market returns. Specifically, we calculate the firm-specific value change as the natural log of (*Acquisition price* divided by *Industry adjusted IPO valuation*). *Industry adjusted IPO valuation* is the product of *IPO Valuation* and (1 + *Industry return since last IPO filing*). We then re-estimate our main regression using *Industry adjusted log valuation revision* as the continuous variable and in interaction with *VC*, and include *Industry return since last IPO filing* as a proxy for the market return. *Industry adjusted log valuation revision* is positive and significant at the 0.01 level, and *Industry return since last IPO filing* is positive and significant at the 0.10 level. Similar to our main regression, *VC* and *Log industry adjusted IPO valuation* × *VC* are significantly negative at the 0.05 and 0.01 levels, respectively. Hence, the effects of target valuation revisions and VC presence are insensitive to market returns. We also adjust valuation revision using the CRSP value-weighted Nasdaq return and a multiples-based return.[11] Overall, the results (not shown in table) are similar to those presented in column 3, but the Nasdaq and multiples return variables are weaker than *Industry return since last IPO filing* with *p*-values of 0.13 and 0.98, respectively. In addition, *Industry return since last IPO filing* is insignificant in the regression specifications presented in columns 5–8. Thus, the significance of market returns in determining *Acquirer CAR* is sensitive to the return measurement and regression specification, casting some doubt on the importance of prospect theory as an explanation for the effect of target valuation revisions on *Acquirer CAR*.

Like interim VC valuations, dated IPO valuations and the prestige of the IPO underwriter could influence the relative importance of the IPO valuation. If low-ranked underwriters provide lower quality and less informative IPO valuations, then a valuation from a low-ranked underwriter should have less influence on the managers' estimates of the target's value distribution than a valuation from a high-ranked underwriter. According to the target valuation uncertainty hypothesis, the relation between *Log valuation revision* and *Acquirer CAR* when the target has a low-ranked underwriter should be weaker than for targets with high-ranked underwriters.

---

[11] The multiples-based return is the percentage change of the mean valuation multiple of industry, size, and year-matched portfolios of publicly traded firms from the time of the last IPO filing to the acquisition.

Likewise, a long period between the last IPO filing and acquisition makes the IPO valuation less reliable. Similarly, under the prospect theory hypothesis, less relevant IPO valuations should be weaker "anchors."

In column 4, we add *Low rank underwriter*, a dummy variable equal to one if the IPO underwriter's *CM-Rank* is less than eight (the sample median), and *Long time*, a dummy variable equal to one if more than 365 days pass between the last IPO filing and the acquisition announcement. We also include the interactions of these two variables with *Log valuation revision*. Consistent with our predictions, the point estimates of the interactions of *Log valuation revision* with *Low rank underwriter* and *Long time* are negative. Yet, except for *Long time*, the new variables are insignificant. Estimates for the remaining variables are similar to column 2. Because *Low rank underwriter, Long time*, and their interactions with *Log valuation revision* have little effect on the estimates of our main variables of interest, we conduct most of our remaining tests without them.[12]

In column 5 of Table 5, we test the relation between *Acquirer CAR* and our measures for valuation uncertainty, distress, and market movements from Table 4. The coefficient on $\sigma(Price\text{-}to\text{-}assets\ multiple\ target)$ is positive and significant at the 0.05 level, consistent with risk-averse managers discounting the target's price when valuation uncertainty is high. The target's *Industry return since last IPO filing* and the distress variables are insignificant. We add the acquisition-related control variables in column 6. No variable in this model is significant, but the coefficient of $\sigma(Price\text{-}to\text{-}assets\ multiple\ target)$ is positive, with a p-value of 0.103. We add *Log valuation revision* and *Log valuation revision* $\times$ *VC* in column 7. As in our main regression, these two variables are significantly positive and negative, respectively. *Debt to assets target* becomes significant at the 0.10 level. Adding *Log valuation revision* and *Log valuation revision* $\times$ *VC* reduces the coefficient of $\sigma(Price\text{-}to\text{-}assets\ multiple\ target)$ from 0.059 to 0.004 and the variable is insignificant (p-value of 0.90). The reduced significance for $\sigma(Price\text{-}to\text{-}assets\ multiple\ target)$ could be due to multicollinearity. Nonetheless, *Log valuation revision* dominates our broader measure of riskiness in explaining acquirer announcement returns. Its explanatory power suggests that *Log valuation revision* captures important effects not previously considered in the acquisitions literature.

Finally, we include all of the variables from previous model specifications in column 8. Despite the large number of explanatory variables relative to the number of observations, *Log valuation revision* and *Log valuation revision* $\times$ *VC* are still significant at the 0.01 and 0.05 levels, respectively.

---

[12] We also examine the effect of switching investment banks on *Log valuation revision* to see if improving (lowering) the quality of the investment bank after the withdrawal increases (decreases) the valuation revision. We find that 33 firms switch investment banks between the withdrawal and the acquisition and that there is a positive relation between the change in investment bank reputation and *Log valuation revision*. We are unable to distinguish whether choosing a better investment bank increases the target valuation or whether better target performance attracts better investment banks.

Log valuation revision is positive and significant in all regressions in Table 5, with a point estimate of 0.067 in our main regression in column 2. The interaction of *Log valuation revision* and *VC* has a point estimate of −0.049. These coefficients imply that in a comparison of two otherwise identical transactions with VC-backing, one with a 20% increase in target valuation and one with a 75% decrease (roughly the 0.75 and 0.25 percentiles of *Valuation revision*), *Acquirer CAR* is about 2.8% higher for the transaction with the 20% increase in valuation. The 2.8% represents an increase in value of $27 million for the median acquirer. With the median *Acquisition price* of $124 million, the $27 million represents target underpricing of about 18% (= 27/(124 + 27)), which is similar in magnitude to IPO underpricing and the marketability discount of private firms (Officer, 2007). For firms without VC-backing the implied underpricing is larger at about 44%.

In summary, our multivariate regressions show a significant positive relation between target valuation revisions and acquirer returns. The analyses provide support for the target valuation uncertainty hypothesis and somewhat weaker evidence for the prospect theory explanation.

4. Robustness and alternative explanations

In this section, we address several concerns that could affect our results and explore alternative explanations for the relation between *Log valuation revision* and *Acquirer CARs*.

4.1. Nasdaq bubble, target size, and positive versus negative valuation revisions

One concern is that unusually large price movements associated with the Nasdaq bubble unduly influence our results. An IPO that is withdrawn during this period and acquired after the bubble years is likely to have an acquisition price much lower than its IPO valuation, resulting in a negative *Valuation revision*. If there is also a less favorable reception for acquisitions after the bubble period, low acquirer announcement returns are likely. The combination of these two features could lead to a spurious positive relation between *Acquirer CAR* and *Log valuation revision*. We perform two tests to address this issue.

In column 1 of Table 6, we eliminate 17 observations in which the last IPO filing is in 1999 or 2000 and the acquisition announcement is after 2000 and re-estimate regression (2) from Table 5. For these 17 firms, the median value for *Valuation revision* is −74.7% compared to −19.0% for the 51 other firms, which is significantly different at the 0.05 level. Our results remain qualitatively unchanged after exclusion of these 17 firms. In an untabulated regression, we add two dummy variables to our main regression to account for any influence of the Nasdaq bubble. The first dummy equals one if the acquisition announcement is between 1996 and 1998 and the second equals one if the announcement is in 1999 or 2000. Neither dummy is

Table 6

Robustness

This table presents regression results for our sample of 68 firms that file an IPO registration statement, withdraw, and are subsequently acquired by a public firm from 1996 to 2005. The dependent variable is *Acquirer CAR*. All other variables are defined in previous tables. Regression results in column 1 exclude 17 takeovers in which the last SEC filing for the planned IPO is filed in 1999 or 2000 and in which the takeover announcement occurred after 2000. The results in column 2 exclude seven takeovers in which *Relative size* is less than 1%. In columns 3 and 4, we split the sample into positive and negative valuation revisions, respectively. *p*-Values, based on heteroskedasticity-adjusted standard errors, are in brackets.

	(1)	(2)	(3)	(4)
Log valuation revision	0.053*** [0.002]	0.080*** [0.000]	0.205* [0.058]	0.061** [0.027]
Relative size	0.061* [0.084]	0.015 [0.677]	0.005 [0.962]	0.000 [0.989]
Log acquirer size	−0.006 [0.513]	−0.015 [0.181]	−0.053* [0.051]	−0.016 [0.114]
Stock	−0.008 [0.814]	−0.037 [0.251]	0.037 [0.582]	−0.047 [0.158]
Acquirer Q	0.000 [0.733]	0.000 [0.575]	0.000 [0.720]	0.003** [0.046]
Liquidity index target industry	0.105 [0.497]	0.087 [0.591]	−0.061 [0.878]	−0.062 [0.754]
VC	−0.072** [0.021]	−0.071** [0.020]	0.103 [0.279]	−0.057 [0.200]
Log valuation revision × VC	−0.047** [0.042]	−0.059*** [0.010]	−0.314* [0.069]	−0.039 [0.176]
Intercept	0.109 [0.203]	0.203** [0.050]	0.354 [0.144]	0.203** [0.048]
F-statistic	2.12*	6.17***	4.03**	5.81***
Adjusted R^2	0.1517	0.2111	0.2638	0.0976
Number of observations	51	61	21	47

***, **, *Denote significance at the 0.01, 0.05, and 0.10 levels, respectively.

significant. The results for the remaining variables are similar to those presented for our main regression.

Jarrell and Poulsen (1989) show that acquisitions have little impact on the value of the acquirer if the acquirer is large and the target is relatively small. Therefore, *Acquirer CARs* can be noisier when *Relative size* is small. In column 2 of Table 6, we exclude seven observations in which *Relative size* is less than 1%. *Log acquirer size* becomes insignificant, but the results for the remaining variables are largely unchanged from those in Table 5, column 2. In untabulated regressions, we exclude transactions in which *Relative size* is less than 5% and less than 10%. *Log valuation revision* remains positive and significant at the 0.01 level. Overall, our results are robust to the exclusion of relatively small targets.

The target valuation uncertainty hypothesis states that the relation between *Log valuation revision* and *Acquirer CAR* will be stronger for positive revisions than negative revisions. However, a "lemons problem" (Akerlof, 1970) could strengthen the relation between *Log valuation revision* and *Acquirer CAR* for targets with large negative valuation revisions. Most of these targets experience a negative capital market event in the IPO withdrawal (Dunbar and Foerster, 2008). The owners of these firms could find it difficult to raise necessary capital or exit their investment. Investors may react negatively to acquisitions of these targets because they believe that acquirers overestimate their ability (Roll, 1986) to turn these targets around (Clark and Ofek, 1994). Therefore, in columns 3 and 4 of Table 6, we split the sample into positive and negative valuation revisions. *Log valuation revision* is positive and significant for both subsamples with a higher point estimate for the subsample of positive valuation revisions. However, there is no statistical difference in the coefficients for *Log valuation revision* in the two subsamples—possibly due to the small sample size. Overall, these regressions provide some weak evidence in support of the target valuation uncertainty hypothesis.

4.2. Additional robustness tests

Due to a small sample size, outliers could unduly influence our results. We address this concern by first performing an analysis of residuals for our main regression, column 2 of Table 5, and identifying the five most influential outliers. We then sequentially delete the most, three most, and five most influential outliers, and re-estimate our main regression on the smaller samples. In all three cases, *Log valuation revision* remains positive and significant at the 0.01 level. *VC* and *Log valuation revision* $\times$ *VC* remain significantly negative in all three cases. The results for the remaining variables are largely unchanged. We also eliminate 26 transactions in which the absolute dollar gain to the acquirer is greater than the amount paid for the target. Our results remain qualitatively the same, except for *VC* and *Log valuation revision* $\times$ *VC*, which become insignificant with p-values of 0.69 and 0.22, respectively. We also re-estimate our main regression using *Valuation revision*, that is, we do not take logs, and change the interaction variable to *Valuation revision* $\times$ *VC*. *Valuation revision* is positive and significant at the 0.01 level, *VC* is negative with a p-value of 0.18, and *Valuation revision* $\times$ *VC* is negative and significant at the 0.05 level. Therefore, neither the particular specification of valuation revision, nor outliers appear to drive our main results.

VC is determined by examining ownership data contained in the target's last IPO filing. Ideally, *VC* would be determined at the time of the acquisition, but ownership data for private targets is rarely available at that time. In the IPO filings, we find that 44 firms have VC ownership. SDC's VentureXpert shows that 18 of these 44 firms receive additional VC funding after the IPO withdrawal. There are 24 sample firms that have no VC funding as of, or after, the last IPO filing date. Since we are unable to discern otherwise, we assume that VC ownership as of the last IPO filing is maintained until the acquisition date, except when the time between the last IPO filing and the acquisition date is more than five years. In that case, we assume the VC has liquidated its equity position by the acquisition date. We re-estimate our main regression assuming that VC ownership is present beyond the five years. The results are similar to those reported in column 2 of Table 5.

4.3. Sample selection bias

Withdrawn IPOs can have two possible successful conclusions: the firm can re-enter the IPO market successfully or a public firm can acquire it. Both accomplish the primary goals of most IPOs: the shares of the firm become liquid and the firm gets access to capital. Because we focus on one of these successful conclusions to withdrawn IPO filings, we have a sample bias in the sense that it does not include private firms that withdraw their IPOs and stay private. Does this bias affect our results?

It could be that only the more successful withdrawn IPO firms are acquired. If markets perceive the acquisition of a successful target as better news for the acquirer than the acquisition of a struggling target, then our finding of a positive relation between target valuation revisions and acquirer returns might be a spurious result of our sample selection criteria. To address this issue, we first note that firms in our sample mostly decline in value between their attempted IPO and acquisition. Therefore, although we cannot compare these firms to the set of withdrawn IPOs that remain private, it does not appear that our firms are unusually successful. In addition, well-performing firms should be able to re-enter the IPO market. However, even if our sample firms are unusually successful, it is not obvious (apart from the explanations provided in our paper) why a bidder that acquires a well-performing target will experience a higher announcement return than a bidder that acquires a poorly performing target. If the acquisition price is fair, both well- and poorly-performing targets add or subtract the same value to the acquirer.

An additional bias could result from observing only those targets that have a disclosed deal value. As noted in Rodrigues and Stegemoller (2007), acquirers are not legally required to disclose target financial data, or even the deal value, for targets below a certain relative size threshold unless the transaction can otherwise be classified as material or is not made in the course of normal business. Thus, of the deals that do not require disclosure, acquirers may report only the most beneficial transactions. We address this bias by eliminating transactions with *Relative size* less than 1%, 5%, or 10%, as described in Section 4.1, and *Log valuation revision* remains positive and significant at the 0.01 level.

In summary, our finding of a positive relation between target valuation revisions and acquirer returns in a sample of private acquisitions is robust to various specifications of our main model and does not appear to be driven by obvious sample selection biases. In addition, acquirer announcement returns are related to target valuation changes due to firm-specific and (more weakly) market movements. While we cannot definitively distinguish what causes our results—valuation uncertainty or behavioral biases—they are consistent with both explanations.

5. Evidence from venture capital valuations

Given the specificity of our main sample and the resulting limitations in generalizing our results, we expand our analysis to other acquisitions of private firms with available prior valuations. The SDC VentureXpert database provides some postround valuations of private firms receiving venture capital or private equity financing (hereafter "VC valuations"). We extract from the Mergers & Acquisitions portion of the VentureXpert database all transactions from 1996 to 2005 of targets that are private at the time of the acquisition announcement and whose acquirer is publicly traded on the NYSE, Nasdaq, or American Stock Exchange. This step provides 1109 acquisitions. We use the last VC valuation in our analysis and require a valuation of at least $25 million (the smallest target in our main sample has an IPO valuation of $26 million), a corresponding transaction in the SDC M&A database with the acquirer purchasing 100% of the target, and the deal not being in our main sample of withdrawn IPOs. Of the remaining 300 firms, we exclude 53 transactions due to the following confounding events: simultaneous announcements of (1) other acquisitions or divestitures (37 deals), (2) a double-digit percentage change in earnings, a double-digit percentage loss of employees or sales, or a triple-digit percentage increase in sales (13 deals), or (3) seasoned equity offerings or repurchases (three deals). We exclude 33 transactions in which the acquirer's stock price as of two trading days before the acquisition announcement is less than five dollars due to the noise inherent in low-price firms (e.g., distress, risk, high volatility).[13] Finally, we exclude deals that have data limitations: three deals have no acquisition announcement on LexisNexis; there is no acquisition price in the SDC M&A database or in LexisNexis for ten deals; we cannot compute *Acquirer Q* for three transactions; and four transactions have no information regarding the method of payment (either in LexisNexis or SDC). Our final sample consists of 194 firms.

We expect a decreased ability to find significant results in this sample for three reasons. First, the results from our main sample of withdrawn IPOs suggest that *Log valuation revision* for VC-backed acquisitions (the entirety of this new sample) is less influential on *Acquirer CAR* than for non-VC-backed acquisitions. Second, we are skeptical of the VC valuations because they are self-reported and there are incentives for VCs to report biased values. We find some evidence for biases: 61% of firms have positive valuation revisions in this sample compared to 31% in our main sample. Third, the values provided by the VC firms do not contain the same amount or quality of information as the IPO valuations in our main sample, which have undergone a significantly more rigorous information gathering process than those in this sample. The lower quality and level of information contained in the VC valuation is important for both the valuation uncertainty hypothesis (managers are not likely to place much weight on the prior valuation) and prospect theory (target managers may be "less anchored" on this value).

In column 1 of Table 7, we re-estimate regression (1) from Table 5 using this alternative sample. We do not include *VC* and *Log valuation revision* × *VC* as in our main regression since all targets have VC funding. In column 2, we account for the

---

[13] Inclusion of these acquirers reduces the significance of the results. Seven acquirers have share prices below five dollars in our main sample. Excluding these acquirers from our main sample does not significantly affect our results.

Table 7

Deals with venture capital valuations

This table presents regression results for a sample of 194 firms that receive a valuation from a venture capital or private equity firm and are subsequently acquired by a public firm from 1996 to 2005. The dependent variable is *Acquirer CAR*. *VC Valuation*, from the SDC VentureXpert database, is the latest postround valuation of the private firms that receive venture capital or private equity financing. Regression results in column 2 exclude acquisitions in which the *VC Valuation* was in 1999 or 2000 and the acquisition announcement occurred after 2000. *Log valuation revision* is the natural log of (1 + *Valuation revision*). *Valuation revision* is equal to *Acquisition price* divided by *VC Valuation* minus one. *Log industry adjusted valuation revision* is the natural log of {*Acquisition price* divided by [*VC Valuation* × (1 + *Industry return since VC valuation*)]}. *Industry return since VC valuation* is the compounded value-weighted return of the target's industry from the date of the *VC Valuation* to two trading days before the acquisition announcement. All other variables are defined in previous tables. *p*-Values, based on heteroskedasticity-adjusted standard errors, are in brackets.

	(1)	(2)	(3)
Log valuation revision	0.012** [0.033]	0.018** [0.020]	
Log industry adjusted valuation revision			0.015*** [0.007]
Relative size	−0.234*** [0.002]	−0.284*** [0.001]	−0.246*** [0.001]
Log acquirer size	−0.008* [0.087]	−0.011** [0.037]	−0.009** [0.029]
Stock	−0.001 [0.937]	−0.004 [0.877]	−0.001 [0.951]
Acquirer Q	0.001 [0.274]	0.001 [0.261]	0.001 [0.304]
Liquidity index target industry	0.000 [0.997]	0.019 [0.863]	0.018 [0.867]
Industry return since VC valuation			0.004 [0.651]
Intercept	0.066* [0.098]	0.092* [0.061]	0.074** [0.043]
F-statistic	2.00*	1.83*	1.93*
Adjusted R^2	0.0303	0.0376	0.0326
Number of observations	194	129	194

***, **, *Denote significance at the 0.01, 0.05, and 0.10 levels, respectively.

Nasdaq bubble by eliminating 65 firms in which the VC valuation is in 1999 or 2000 and the acquisition announcement is after 2000. In column 3, we adjust for industry returns from the VC valuation date to the acquisition date, similar to the procedure used in column 3 of Table 5. As in regression (1) of Table 5, the log valuation variable is positive and significant at the 0.05 level or better in all three regression specifications.

Remarkably, we obtain an almost identical point estimate for *Log valuation revision* as compared to our main regression. In column 2 of Table 5, the point estimate of *Log valuation revision* is 0.067. Subtracting 0.049, the coefficient of *Log valuation revision* × *VC*, suggests a coefficient of 0.018 on *Log valuation revision*. In Table 7, the coefficient of *Log valuation revision*, depending on regression specification, ranges from 0.012 to 0.018. *Relative size* is significantly negative using the VC valuation sample, while it is insignificant using our main sample. This difference could be due to more relatively small firms in the VC valuation sample; the mean relative size is 8.6% for the VC valuation sample compared to 27.6% in our main sample. Our claim that the

VC valuation sample suffers from lower data quality is supported by the adjusted R^2s. Using the VC valuation sample, the adjusted R^2s range between 0.03 and 0.04, while it is 0.14 in regression (1) of Table 5.

In sum, this evidence provides further support for the influence of prior valuations on the pricing of private targets and acquirer announcement returns. It raises the question of whether this effect influences private acquisitions more generally and other transactions, for example, acquisitions of public targets.

6. Conclusions

We provide new insights into acquirer announcement returns. We show that private targets experiencing positive valuation changes between their last SEC filing before their withdrawn IPO and subsequent acquisition are more underpriced and that acquirers benefit. Our findings are similar to the partial adjustment effect in IPOs and our paper is the first to show this partial adjustment effect in private acquisitions. Additional analysis on a sample of targets with valuations by private equity and VC firms confirms our results.

Pricing effects associated with target valuation uncertainty appear to be important in explaining announcement returns for acquirers of private firms. We find somewhat weaker support for a behavioral explanation for our results based on prospect theory. Although not observable to researchers, most private targets likely have received valuations prior to their acquisitions. Thus, it is possible that similar pricing effects are present in most private acquisitions and in many other negotiation outcomes. Theoretical models linking target underpricing, acquirer announcement returns, target valuation revisions, and target valuation uncertainty would be useful in further interpreting our empirical results.

Appendix A: Calculation of the IPO valuation and acquisition price for NOMOS Corporation

On 29 April 2002 NOMOS filed Form S-1 with the SEC for its anticipated IPO. Filing prices and shares were first included on its first amendment to Form S-1 filed on 5 June 2002. NOMOS filed a second amendment to Form S-1 on 19 June 2002. Then on 28 June 2002 NOMOS filed a posteffective amendment to Form S-1, which contains the last valuation information prior to withdrawal. Finally, NOMOS filed Form RW on 18 July 2002 withdrawing the registration for its IPO, citing adverse market conditions. On 27 October 2003 North American Scientific, Inc. announced that it was purchasing NOMOS Corp. for 5.3 million shares of stock and $12 million in cash. North American Scientific, Inc.'s closing stock price was $7.47 two trading days before the announcement, resulting in an acquisition price of $51.6 million.

We use the following information from the 28 June 2002 posteffective amendment to Form S-1 to calculate *IPO Valuation*:

High filing price	$12
Low filing price	$10
Primary shares	2,500,000
Secondary shares	0
Shares outstanding after offering	9,620,987
Total assets as of 31 March 2002	$16,092,000
Preferred stock as of 31 March 2002	$6,279,000
Stockholders' equity as of 31 March 2002	$723,000

IPO valuation = Implied value of equity+book value of liabilities.
Implied value of equity = (($12 + $10)/2) (9,620,987−2,500,000) = $78,330,857.
Book value of liabilities[14]= $16,092,000−$6,279,000−$723,000 = $9,090,000.IPO valuation = $78,330,857+$9,090,000 = $87,420,857.

[14] In general, we calculate book value of liabilities as book value of assets minus book value of stockholders' equity. Thus, book value of liabilities includes preferred stock if preferred stock is not included in the total given for stockholder equity (as in the case of NOMOS). However, NOMOS planned to convert its preferred stock into common stock in conjunction with its IPO and the 9,620,987 shares outstanding after the offering include these converted shares. Therefore, we subtract the preferred stock to determine book value of liabilities. We make similar calculations for the 19 other targets that planned to convert preferred stock to common stock. The remaining targets do not have preferred stock, do not plan to convert it to common stock, or include the preferred stock in stockholders' equity.

Appendix B: List of acquisitions of withdrawn IPOs

Acquirer name	Target name	Last SEC filing date	Acquisition announced
Cardiac Science, Inc.	SurVivaLink Corp.	08/01/1996	02/14/2001
Imation Corp.	Cemax-Icon, Inc.	08/14/1996	05/14/1997
Agouron Pharmaceuticals, Inc.	Alanex Corp.	10/15/1996	04/29/1997
Cardinal Health, Inc.	MediQual Systems, Inc.	10/15/1996	05/27/1997
Lightbridge, Inc.	Coral Systems, Inc.	12/19/1996	09/09/1997
Millennium Pharmaceuticals, Inc.	ChemGenics Pharmaceuticals, Inc.	01/14/1997	01/20/1997
KeyCorp	Champion Mortgage Holdings	02/10/1997	06/16/1997
Pharmacopeia, Inc.	Molecular Simulations, Inc.	02/10/1997	02/04/1998
Aspect Telecommunications	Voicetek Corp.	02/14/1997	04/01/1998
Roto-Rooter, Inc.	Vitas Healthcare Corp.	09/23/1997	12/19/2003
Registry, Inc.	Hunter Group, Inc.	10/02/1997	11/14/1997
RCN Corp.	Erols Internet, Inc.	12/05/1997	01/21/1998
Cendant Corp.	Credentials Services Intl., Inc.	12/17/1997	04/13/1998
JDS Uniphase Corp.	Epitaxx	05/13/1998	10/04/1999
PepsiCo, Inc.	Tropicana Products, Inc.	07/17/1998	07/20/1998
Verio, Inc.	Hiway Technologies, Inc.	07/20/1998	07/29/1998
Hain Food Group, Inc.	Natural Nutrition Group, Inc.	08/03/1998	04/05/1999
Giant Group Ltd.	Periscope Sportswear, Inc.	08/10/1998	12/04/1998
Texas Regional Bancshares	Riverway Holdings, Inc.	08/11/1998	09/17/2001
Orchid BioSciences, Inc.	LifeCodes Corp.	09/03/1998	10/01/2001
Mercer Insurance Group	Fin. Pacific Ins. Group, Inc.	11/13/1998	05/02/2005
Becton Dickinson & Co.	Clontech Laboratories, Inc.	03/02/1999	04/27/1999
eBay, Inc.	Butterfield & Butterfield Corp.	04/02/1999	04/26/1999
AppliedTheory Corp.	CRL Network Services, Inc.	06/17/1999	12/06/1999
Goldman Sachs Group, Inc.	Hull Group, Inc.	07/06/1999	07/09/1999
Briggs & Stratton Corp.	Generac Portable Products, Inc.	07/19/1999	03/01/2001
Hoovers, Inc.	Powerize.com, Inc.	07/28/1999	07/12/2000
Titan Corp.	AverStar, Inc.	07/30/1999	03/27/2000
Sonic Automotive, Inc.	FirstAmerica Automotive, Inc.	08/09/1999	08/25/1999
eMusic.com, Inc.	Tunes.com, Inc.	08/17/1999	11/30/1999
Macromedia, Inc.	Andromedia, Inc.	09/24/1999	10/07/1999
Genesco, Inc.	Hat World, Inc.	09/28/1999	02/05/2004
TDK Corp.	Headway Technologies, Inc.	10/08/1999	03/08/2000
Globix Corp.	ComStar.net, Inc.	11/22/1999	08/23/2000
Dollar Tree Stores, Inc.	Dollar Express, Inc.	02/22/2000	04/05/2000
Quokka Sports, Inc.	Total Sports, Inc.	02/23/2000	07/21/2000
Wind River Systems, Inc.	Embedded Support Tools Corp.	02/24/2000	02/28/2000
Covad Communications Group, Inc.	Bluestar Communications Group	03/20/2000	06/16/2000
Celgene Corp.	Signal Pharmaceuticals, Inc.	03/22/2000	06/30/2000
Overture Services, Inc.	AltaVista Co.	04/10/2000	02/18/2003
Lions Gate Entertainment Corp.	Artisan Entertainment, Inc.	04/18/2000	10/24/2003

(Continued)

Appendix B (*Continued*)

Acquirer name	Target name	Last SEC filing date	Acquisition announced
SONICBlue, Inc.	ReplayTV, Inc.	05/01/2000	02/01/2001
MatrixOne, Inc.	Synchronicity, Inc.	05/09/2000	06/07/2004
Ariba, Inc.	SupplierMarket.com	05/11/2000	06/26/2000
Sun Microsystems, Inc.	LSC, Inc.	05/31/2000	02/02/2001
AirGate PCS, Inc.	IPCS, Inc.	07/19/2000	08/29/2001
PC Connection, Inc.	MoreDirect.com, Inc.	07/21/2000	03/26/2002
interWAVE Communications	Wireless, Inc.	08/17/2000	03/19/2001
Open Text Corp.	Corechange, Inc.	08/18/2000	02/26/2003
Broadbase Software, Inc.	ServiceSoft, Inc.	08/25/2000	09/18/2000
ScreamingMedia, Inc.	Stockpoint, Inc.	09/05/2000	07/23/2001
Peregrine Systems, Inc.	Extricity, Inc.	09/25/2000	03/12/2001
Lion Bioscience AG	NetGenics, Inc.	09/27/2000	01/14/2002
JD Edwards & Co.	Youcentric, Inc.	10/10/2000	08/15/2001
eFunds Corp.	Clearcommerce Corp.	10/10/2000	01/12/2005
Microsoft Corp.	PlaceWare, Inc.	11/13/2000	01/21/2003
Click Commerce, Inc.	Webridge, Inc.	01/30/2001	03/18/2004
Itron, Inc.	Silicon Energy Corp.	07/18/2001	01/21/2003
Marathon Oil Corp.	Khanty Mansiysk Oil Corp.	08/29/2001	04/22/2003
Tom Brown, Inc.	Matador Petroleum Corp.	09/10/2001	05/07/2003
Schering-Plough Corp.	Neogenesis Pharmaceuticals, Inc.	02/06/2002	01/20/2005
United Defense Industries, Inc.	United States Marine Repair	04/25/2002	05/28/2002
Paychex, Inc.	Advantage Payroll Svcs. Inc.	06/07/2002	09/18/2002
North American Scientific, Inc.	NOMOS Corp.	06/28/2002	10/27/2003
Chicos FAS, Inc.	White House, Inc.	06/24/2003	07/31/2003
Allied Capital Corp.	Financial Pacific Co.	05/14/2004	06/30/2004
Friedman Billings Ramsey Group	First NLC Fin. Services, Inc.	06/07/2004	01/11/2005
Encore Medical Corp.	Empi, Inc.	08/04/2004	08/09/2004

References

Akerlof, G., 1970, "The Market for 'Lemons': Quality Uncertainty and the Market Mechanism," *Quarterly Journal of Economics*, 84, 488–500.

Amihud, Y. and B. Lev, 1981, "Risk Reduction as a Managerial Motive for Conglomerate Mergers," *Bell Journal of Economics*, 12, 605–617.

Asquith, P., R. Bruner and D. Mullins, 1983, "The Gains to Bidding Firms from Merger," *Journal of Financial Economics*," 11, 121–139.

Barry, C., C. Muscarella, J. Peavy and M. Vetsuypens, 1990, "The Role of Venture Capital in the Creation of Public Companies: Evidence from the Going-Public Process," *Journal of Financial Economics*, 27, 447–471.

Benveniste, L. and P. Spindt, 1989, "How Investment Bankers Determine the Offer Price and Allocation of New Issues," *Journal of Financial Economics*, 24, 343–361.

Carter, R. and S. Manaster, 1990, "Initial Public Offerings and Underwriter Reputation," *Journal of Finance*, 45, 1045–1067.

Chang, S., 1998, "Takeovers of Privately Held Targets, Methods of Payment, and Bidder Returns," *Journal of Finance*, 53, 773–784.

Clark, K. and E. Ofek, 1994, "Mergers as a Means of Restructuring Distressed Firms: An Empirical Investigation," *Journal of Financial and Quantitative Analysis*, 29, 541–565.

Conine T., Jr., and M. Tamarkin, 1981, "On Diversification Given Asymmetry in Returns," *Journal of Finance*, 36, 1143–1155.

Crane, A. and J. Hartzell, 2008, "Is There a Disposition Effect in Corporate Investment Decisions? Evidence from Real Estate Investment Trusts," Unpublished Working Paper, University of Texas.

Dunbar, C., 1998, "The Choice Between Firm-Commitment and Best-Efforts Offering Methods in IPOs: The Effect of Unsuccessful Offers," *Journal of Financial Intermediation*, 7, 60–90.

Dunbar, C. and S. Foerster, 2008, "Second Time Lucky? Withdrawn IPOs that Return to the Market," *Journal of Financial Economics*, 87, 610–635.

Faccio, M., J. McConnell and D. Stolin, 2006, "Returns to Acquirers of Listed and Unlisted Targets," *Journal of Financial and Quantitative Analysis*, 41, 197–220.

Fuller, K., J. Netter and M. Stegemoller, 2002, "What Do Returns to Acquiring Firms Tell Us? Evidence from Firms that Make Many Acquisitions," *Journal of Finance*, 57, 1763–1793.

Gompers, P. and J. Lerner, 1999, "An Analysis of Compensation in the US Venture Capital Partnership," *Journal of Financial Economics*, 51, 3–44.

Gompers, P. and J. Lerner, 2001, "The Venture Capital Revolution," *Journal of Economic Perspectives*, 15 (Spring), 145–168.

Gompers, P. and Y. Xuan, 2006, "The Role of Venture Capitalists in the Acquisition of Private Companies," Unpublished Working Paper, Harvard University.

Hanley, K., 1993, "The Underpricing of Initial Public Offerings and the Partial Adjustment Phenomenon," *Journal of Financial Economics*, 34, 231–250.

Jarrell, G. and A. Poulsen, 1989, "The Returns to Acquiring Firms in Tender Offers: Evidence from Three Decades," *Financial Management*, 18 (Autumn), 12–19.

Jones, C. and M. Rhodes-Kropf, 2004, "The Price of Diversifiable Risk in Venture Capital and Private equity," Unpublished Working Paper, Columbia University.

Kahneman, D. and A. Tversky, 1979, "Prospect Theory: An Analysis of Decision Under Risk," *Econometrica*, 47, 263–291.

Lang, L., R. Stulz and R. Walkling, 1989, "Managerial Performance, Tobin's q, and the Gains from Successful Tender Offers," *Journal of Financial Economics*, 24, 137–154.

Loughran, T. and J. Ritter, 2002, "Why Don't Issuers Get Upset About Leaving Money on the Table in IPOs?," *Review of Financial Studies*, 15, 413–443.

Loughran, T. and J. Ritter, 2004, "Why has IPO Underpricing Changed Over Time?," *Financial Management*, 33 (Autumn), 5–37.

Lowry, M. and W. Schwert, 2004, "Is the IPO Pricing Process Efficient?," *Journal of Financial Economics*, 71, 3–26.

MacKinnon, J. and H. White, 1985, "Some Heteroskedasticity-Consistent Covariance Matrix Estimators with Improved Finite Sample Properties," *Journal of Econometrics*, 29, 305–325.

Megginson, W. and K. Weiss, 1991, "Venture Capitalist Certification in Initial Public Offerings," *Journal of Finance*, 46, 879–903.

Mitton, T. and K. Vorkink, 2007, "Equilibrium Underdiversification and the Preference for Skewness," *Review of Financial Studies*, 20, 1255–1288.

Moeller, S., F. Schlingemann and R. Stulz, 2004, "Firm Size and the Gains from Acquisitions," *Journal of Financial Economics*, 73, 201–228.

Officer, M., 2007, "The Price of Corporate Liquidity: Acquisition Discounts for Unlisted Targets," *Journal of Financial Economics*, 83, 571–598.

Officer, M., A. Poulsen and M. Stegemoller, 2008, "Target-Firm Information Asymmetry and Acquirer Returns," Review of Finance, forthcoming.

Poulsen, A. and M. Stegemoller, 2008, "Moving from Private to Public Ownership: Selling Out to Public Firms Versus Initial Public Offerings," *Financial Management*, 37, 81–101.

Rodrigues, U. and M. Stegemoller, 2007, "An Inconsistency in SEC Disclosure Requirements? The Case of the "Insignificant" Private Target," *Journal of Corporate Finance*, 13, 251–269.

Roll, R., 1986, "The Hubris Hypothesis of Corporate Takeovers," *Journal of Business*, 59, 197–216.

Schlingemann, F., R. Stulz and R. Walkling, 2002, "Divestitures and the Liquidity of the Market for Corporate Assets," *Journal of Financial Economics*, 64, 117–144.

White, H., 1980, "A Heteroskedasticity-Consistent Covariance Matrix Estimator and a Direct Test for Heteroskedasticity," *Econometrica*, 48, 817–838.

Chapter 10

GAINS IN BANK MERGERS: EVIDENCE FROM THE BOND MARKETS*

MARÍA FABIANA PENAS

Department of Finance, CentER-Tilburg University, 5000 LE Tilburg, The Netherlands

HALUK UNAL

Robert H. Smith School of Business, University of Maryland, College Park, Maryland, USA

Contents

* We would like to thank an anonymous referee, Lawrence Ausubel, Robert Bliss, Mark Carey, Bart Danielsen, Robert DeYoung, Doug Evanoff, Armando Gomez, Edward Kane, Robert Marquez, James Moser, Steven Ongena, Nagpurnanand Prabhala, John Teall, Larry Wall, and seminar participants at the Federal Reserve Bank of Chicago's May 2000 Bank Structure Conference, 2001 North American Summer Meetings of the Econometric Society, University of Maryland, Federal Reserve Bank of Atlanta, Federal Reserve Bank of New York, Depaul-Fed Chicago seminar series, Federal Deposit Insurance Corporation, 2001 European Finance Association Meetings, Free University Amsterdam, University of Tilburg, and University of Amsterdam for their helpful comments and suggestions

This article originally appeared in the *Journal of Financial Economics*, Vol. 74, pp. 149–179 (2004).
Corporate Takeovers, Volume 1
Edited by B. Espen Eckbo
DOI: 10.1016/B978-0-12-381983-3.00010-1

Abstract

We present evidence that the adjusted returns of merging banks' bonds are positive and significant across premerger and announcement months. The cross-sectional evidence indicates that the primary determinants of merger-related bondholder gains are diversification gains, gains associated with achieving too-big-to-fail status, and, to a lesser degree, synergy gains. We obtain the same finding when we examine the acquiring banks' credit spreads on new debt issues both before and after the merger. We also provide the first study that shows acquirers benefit by the lower cost of funds on postmerger debt issues.

Keywords

bank mergers, bondholder gains, too big to fail

JEL classification: G21, G28, G34

1. Introduction

Corporate mergers can affect bondholders in several ways. If the merger is synergistic, both bondholders and shareholders gain because firm value can increase by achieving economies of scale and scope and by eliminating less-efficient management (see Jensen and Ruback, 1983). In nonsynergistic mergers, bondholders can still gain if the merger reduces cash flow volatility and leads to a lower risk of default (see, e.g., Galai and Masulis, 1976; Higgins Schall, 1975; Lewellen, 1971).

In the case of bank mergers there are at least two additional layers of complexity. First, the federal deposit insurer might consider the combined bank too big to fail (TBTF) as a result of the merger. This strategy allows all uninsured liabilities to have de facto insurance coverage and thereby maximizes the value of the implicit guarantees received from the government. Second, unlike nonfinancial firms, banks are subject to regulatory capital requirements. As a result, shareholders cannot simply increase leverage to make up for a merger that coinsures bondholders. Hence, even with no TBTF, bondholders could gain and shareholders could lose as bondholders expropriate some of the gains associated with the acquisition.

To the best of our knowledge, no study has examined changes in required returns on banks' debt around the time of a merger. In this paper, we examine first the reaction of nonconvertible bond prices of both the acquiring and target banks around merger announcements, and then changes in the credit spread of the acquiring institution's new debt issues after the merger. Our results contrast sharply with those reported for mergers of nonfinancial firms. We observe that bondholders of both acquirer and target banks realize significant positive risk- and maturity-adjusted returns around the merger announcement month. During the seven consecutive premerger months and the announcement month, bondholders realize positive returns. The sum of cumulative adjusted bond returns is 4.3% for target banks during this period, significantly exceeding the acquiring banks' bond returns of 1.2%. Overall, our findings indicate that bond market participants perceive the bank merger as a default risk-reducing event.

Our cross-sectional tests focus on identifying the factors that determine the merger announcement-month risk- and maturity-adjusted bond returns. Our analysis shows that all three possible rationales (diversification, TBTF, and, to a lesser degree, synergy) account for increased bondholder returns. The acquiring banks of our sample do not significantly increase their leverage ratios postmerger. This finding supports the argument that bank bondholders might benefit from the coinsurance effect. However, after we control for degree of diversification, geographic overlap, and expected changes in leverage and asset quality following merger, our analysis shows that the incremental asset size is a positive and significant determinant of the announcement-month returns.

We also find that bond returns do not increase monotonically with the asset size of the firm involved in the merger, which is consistent with the existence of TBTF gains. Bondholders of medium-size banks (those that can push the combined bank's asset size above the TBTF threshold asset size) realize the highest returns whereas bondholders of mega-banks (those that can be considered TBTF at the time of merger) and smaller banks earn relatively lower adjusted returns.

We provide evidence that the relation between announcement-month abnormal equity returns and adjusted bond returns is positive and significant, which rules out the possibility that bondholders gain at the expense of equity holders. This evidence is consistent with both the TBTF and synergy rationales. In fact, we also find that the positive effect of the incremental size on adjusted bond returns is larger for in-state mergers, which can be explained by the realization of larger synergies and greater market power in this type of mergers.

When we examine changes in credit spreads, our findings substantiate those of the bond-return analysis. We find that credit spreads are higher for those acquirers that attain less diversification (less reduction in equity volatility for the acquirer). After we control for bond characteristics, market conditions, and changes in the balance-sheet variables due to leverage and nonperforming loans, we find that only the medium-size banks realize significant credit-spread reductions. We estimate that the average decline in credit spreads for this group is around 15 basis points. We observe no significant credit-spread reduction in mergers that involve acquirers that can be considered very large banks or small banks. Again, we attribute this result to the existence of TBTF gains in bank mergers.

The paper is organized as follows. Section 2 estimates and provides an analysis of bondholder returns around the merger announcement month. Section 3 estimates the changes in credit spreads of the acquiring banks' new debt issues after the merger announcement. Section 4 concludes the paper.

2. Analysis of bondholder returns

2.1. Sample and data

We construct the sample merger cases for the analysis of bond returns by using the Mergers and Acquisitions database of the Securities Data Company (SDC). We obtain the merger announcement dates from the SDC database and double-check the dates by using ProQuest, which gives us access to the *Wall Street Journal* database of articles and abstracts.

We include merger cases in our study if they meet the following criteria:

1. The merger case is completed during the 1991-1997 period. We exclude more-recent mergers because the Lehman Brothers Fixed Income Database, the data source for monthly returns, ends in March 1998.
2. Both acquirer and target are commercial banks. To avoid any possible effects that are special to thrift institutions, we exclude those cases that involve the takeover of a savings and loan institution.
3. The target bank's assets are equal to at least 5% of the acquiring bank's assets before the merger. Similar to Houston et al. (2001), we enforce this threshold so

that we pick up those merger cases in which the target is large enough to affect the security prices of the acquirer.

4.   The acquirer has not announced the purchase of another commercial bank or savings and loan during the period beginning 3 months before and ending 2 months after the merger announcement. We impose this restriction to minimize the possible contamination of the merger announcement by news of other merger announcements by the same bank.

Next, we use the Lehman Brothers Fixed Income Database to check whether nonconvertible bonds are available for both the acquirer and the target banks identified in the first step. We include bonds if they meet the following criteria:

1.   The Lehman Brothers Database has consecutive returns for 5 months around the announcement date either for the acquirer or the target that are based on "live" trader-quoted prices. We exclude matrix prices because these prices can be unreliable (Warga and Welch, 1993).
2.   Bonds are not rated BB+ or below. We use this restriction because there is no matching index.
3.   Bonds do not have a maturity less than, or equal to, 4 years. This restriction ensures that the cross-sectional variation in returns is not affected by some banks having only short-maturity bonds, which by definition have low sensitivity to changes in default risk.
4.   Return observations are not problematic. The data errors of the Lehman Brothers Database are well known (Elton et al., 2001) and require that we examine data for unusually high or low returns. We eliminate 6 monthly observations, those are lower than -9% (-14.6%, -9.64%, -28.48%, and -10.01%) and those that are higher than 9% (23.29% and 11.23%).

These selection criteria produce a list of 282 bonds corresponding to 66 merger cases. Out of the 66 cases, 48 have bond returns only for the acquirer, three have bond returns only for the target, and 15 have bond returns that meet our selection criteria for both the acquirer and the target banks. Appendix A presents the list of sample merger cases with their corresponding announcement dates.

2.2. Risk- and maturity-adjusted bond returns

We follow Warga and Welch (1993) by using a risk- and maturity-adjusted holding-period return procedure that allows us to measure the abnormal gains realized by the merging-banks' bondholders around the merger announcement. The procedure involves calculating the difference between the monthly raw bond return and the return of an index, with rating and maturity characteristics that are similar to those of the specific bond.

We use the corporate indexes from the Merrill Lynch US domestic bond series. Merrill Lynch has 24 corporate indexes, which are divided into AAA, AA, A, and BBB ratings, and within each rating, into 1-3 years, 3-5 years, 5-7 years, 7-10 years, 10-15 years and greater than 15 years. We use weighted averages and treat as a single bond with a single bond return the risk- and maturity-adjusted returns of multiple bonds issued by the same bank. We base the weight of each bond on the amount outstanding on the merger announcement date. We follow this procedure to avoid biases that could be caused by a few firms having many outstanding bonds.

We estimate adjusted returns for each month of a 12-month event period around the announcement month for each case. The event month is numbered zero and the event window period begins in month $t = -12$ and ends in month $t = 12$. When there are multiple bonds, to have the highest possible number of observations for the 25-month event period, we include those bonds that have the longest series of returns that meet the criteria specified above. Our final sample comprises 192 bonds that correspond to the 66 cases.

Table 1 reports our findings. The adjusted bond returns are positive for most months for both the acquirer and the target banks around the merger month. For target banks, the largest positive adjusted return (1.27%) occurs 6 months before the merger. The next two-largest significant returns are realized in month -3 (0.67%) and the announcement month (0.7%). The positive returns run consecutively for 7 months before the merger for the bondholders of the merging banks. However, the acquiring banks' bondholders realize only 1.24% during this period plus the announcement month, whereas the target bank bondholders realize an impressive 4.33% adjusted return. Furthermore, the announcement-month return for the target banks (0.7%) is significantly higher than the return for the acquiring banks. This finding is consistent with Billet et al. (2004), who for a large sample of nonfinancial mergers during the 1979-1997 period, also find average target excess bond returns significantly exceed the average acquirer excess returns.

Figure 1 plots the separate cumulative adjusted bond returns for acquirer and target banks. The plots demonstrate a gradual increase in bond returns for both groups, starting roughly 8 months before the announcement month. Although the target banks' bondholders experience the first sharp increase in bond prices approximately 6 months before the merger, the acquiring banks' bond prices start to rise gradually 8 months before the merger. We also observe that the differential gain is sustained following the announcement month.

Figure 1 also shows that the market anticipates mergers. Both Kane (2000) and Houston et al. (2001) show that acquisitions are largely anticipated, since many banks are known for their growth-through-acquisition strategies. This anticipation is particularly important in the midst of a consolidation wave (Calomiris, 1999). On July 16, 1991, the *Wall Street Journal* reported that the Chemical and Manufacturers Hanover merger news had ignited a powerful rally in bank bonds on July 15, 1991 (Mitchell and Raghavan, 1991). The article also stated that "Prices of bonds issued by several of the big New York money center banks jumped as much as three points, which amounts to

Table 1

Risk- and maturity-adjusted bond returns for acquirer and target banks

We calculate risk- and maturity-adjusted returns as the difference between monthly bond returns and the return of a Merrill Lynch bond index with similar rating and maturity characteristics as for the specific bond. We obtain bond returns from Lehman Brothers Database. Our index data is the corporate indexes from Merrill Lynch US domestic bond series. We calculate cumulative bond adjusted returns (CAR) as the sum of the bond adjusted returns.

Event month	Acquirer						Target					
	Mean	Std. Dev.	t-Statistics for mean	% pos.	CAR	Obs (N)	Mean	Std. Dev.	t-Statistics for mean	% pos.	CAR	Obs. (N)
−12	0.178	0.764	1.725*	51.79	0.178	56	−0.339	0.833	−1.523	40.00	−0.339	15
−11	−0.030	1.143	−0.193	62.50	0.148	56	−0.493	1.739	−1.134	35.29	−0.832	17
−10	−0.023	1.156	−0.147	49.09	0.125	55	−0.375	1.493	−1.035	27.78	−1.207	18
−9	0.019	0.707	0.204	48.21	0.144	56	−0.003	1.330	−0.008	50.00	−1.210	16
−8	0.173	0.935	1.375	58.93	0.318	56	−0.039	2.068	−0.076	52.94	−1.249	17
−7	0.127	0.707	1.342	56.14	0.445	57	0.123	1.998	0.253	50.00	−1.126	18
−6	0.029	0.505	0.424	57.89	0.473	57	1.272	2.316	2.265**	83.33	0.146	18
−5	0.121	0.784	1.167	51.72	0.595	58	0.641	1.852	1.428	38.89	0.788	18
−4	0.234	0.793	2.306**	56.45	0.829	62	0.381	0.809	1.943*	55.56	1.169	18
−3	0.360	1.233	2.296**	60.32	1.188	63	0.666	1.196	2.296**	66.67	1.835	18
−2	0.149	0.624	1.880*	65.08	1.337	63	0.382	1.488	1.059	44.44	2.217	18
−1	0.149	0.634	1.849*	68.25	1.486	63	0.159	0.633	1.038	66.67	2.376	18
0	0.074	0.868	0.671	52.38	1.560	63	0.704	1.045	2.777**	72.22	3.080	18
1	0.057	0.525	0.858	58.73	1.617	63	0.232	0.586	1.636	72.22	3.313	18
2	0.288	0.703	3.203***	69.35	1.906	62	0.221	1.161	0.786	61.11	3.534	18
3	0.040	0.618	0.508	53.23	1.946	62	0.230	0.642	1.474	55.56	3.764	18
4	−0.012	0.528	−0.171	45.16	1.934	62	0.177	0.536	1.324	64.71	3.941	17
5	0.146	0.537	2.089**	53.33	2.080	60	0.048	0.512	0.360	43.75	3.988	16
6	0.201	0.665	2.279**	65.52	2.281	58	0.418	0.948	1.709	68.75	4.407	16
7	0.041	0.462	0.667	55.17	2.322	58	−0.333	0.965	−1.336	31.25	4.074	16
8	0.023	0.596	0.285	61.11	2.345	54	−0.087	0.379	−0.859	33.33	3.987	15
9	0.074	0.486	1.092	53.85	2.419	52	−0.041	0.231	−0.639	35.71	3.946	14
10	−0.011	0.620	−0.130	47.06	2.408	51	−0.051	0.216	−0.810	30.77	3.896	13
11	0.050	0.510	0.681	56.00	2.458	50	0.271	0.945	0.994	69.23	4.167	13
12	−0.012	0.345	−0.253	42.00	2.445	50	0.440	1.141	1.337	61.54	4.607	13

*, **, and *** indicate significance at the 0.10, 0.05, and 0.01 levels, respectively. The significance levels are based on a two-tailed test.

about $30 for a bond with a $1000 face amount. In contrast, prices of most other investment-grade corporate bonds ended little changed or modestly lower yesterday, as did prices of US. Treasury bonds, municipal bonds and mortgage-backed securities .... The bonds of some large regional banks also rose on speculation that more mergers will occur among those concerns as well." Clearly, one crucial merger event can signal market participants to impound their anticipations in the bond prices

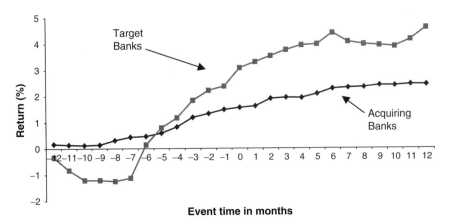

Fig. 1. Risk- and maturity-adjusted bond cumulative returns around the bank merger announcements. We compute debt returns from traded-quoted prices of the Lehman Brothers Database. We adjust each return by subtracting the return of an equivalent Merrill Lynch bond index that matches bond maturity and rating. We first average returns across all bonds belonging to the same firm, then across firms.

of the possible merger partners. In any case, Figure 1 is consistent with bond markets perceiving bank mergers as a default-risk-reducing transaction.

2.3. Cross-sectional analysis of bond returns

Bank mergers can increase bond value through synergy and diversification gains (see Berger et al., 1999; Pilloff and Santomero, 1998 for a review of the evidence). However, Akhavein et al. (1997) and Demsetz and Strahan (1997) report that high leverage ratios and riskier loan portfolios offset the risk-reducing potential of diversification at large bank holding companies (BHCs). Thus, diversification and synergy gains should be examined after controlling for asset risk and leverage.

In contrast to nonfinancial mergers, an additional consideration in bank mergers is the TBTF effect. Evaluation of the regulators' TBTF strategy has become more relevant since the passage of the FDIC Improvement Act of 1991 (FDICIA). To mitigate the TBTF policy, FDICIA requires regulators to act promptly and find a low-cost resolution in the handling of insolvent banks. However, Kane (2000) reports that FDICIA left the door open for the TBTF strategy by authorizing "a systemic risk exception for cases where least-cost resolution would have serious adverse effects on economic conditions or financial stability." Therefore, bondholders must also assess whether or not the merged bank will reach a size that will include it in the "systemic risk" class.

To investigate these possible sources of bondholder gains, we estimate the following regression equation, using the bond returns of both acquirer and target banks:

$$
\begin{aligned}
\mathrm{AR}_i = {} & b_0 + b_1\mathrm{CVOL}_i + b_2\mathrm{INOUT}_i + b_3\mathrm{CNPL}_i + b_4\mathrm{CLEV}_i + b_5\mathrm{LISIZE}_i \\
& + b_6\mathrm{INOUT}_i \times \mathrm{ISIZE}_i + b_7\mathrm{DBIG}_i + b_8\mathrm{DSML}_i + e_i,
\end{aligned}
\tag{1}
$$

where AR is the announcement-month risk- and maturity-adjusted bond return for acquirer or target bank i, and CVOL controls for the gains due to the diversification effect. Similar to Dennis and McConnell (1986), we use equity volatility to capture this effect. DeLong (2001) also uses the correlation coefficient between the acquiring bank's and the target bank's historical stock returns to classify bank mergers as synergistic or diversifying. We define CVOL as the percentage change between the portfolio volatility of the merging banks and the own-bank's equity return volatility before the merger.

We construct this variable by first calculating the volatility of a portfolio that contains equity of the acquirer and target banks in proportion to their asset size. That is,

$$VOL_P = \sqrt{w_A^2 VAR_A + w_T^2 VAR_T + 2 w_A w_T COV_{AT}}, \qquad (2)$$

where VAR is the variance of weekly equity returns 1-year prior to the merger announcement date for the bank, w is the bank's weight, and A, T, and P denote the acquirer, target, and combined bank, respectively; COV is the covariance between the weekly equity returns of the acquirer and the target bank during the 12-month period preceding the merger announcement.

We interpret VOL_p as the expected volatility that incorporates the diversification gains to be attained after the merger. We take the percentage change in the equity return volatility of the combined bank (VOL_P) relative to the merging bank's equity return volatility (VOL_i) and denote this variable as $CVOL_i$. We construct VOL_i as the standard deviation of weekly returns 1-year prior to the merger announcement of bank i, whose bondholders' returns are being explained. Therefore, $CVOL_i$ captures the change in equity volatility expected by the bondholders at the time of the merger. A higher CVOL value implies less diversification and we expect the sign of CVOL to be negative.

The binary variable INOUT takes the value of one if the merger is between banks with headquarters in different states, and zero otherwise. This variable allows us to capture geographic diversification gains, and we expect its sign to be positive. However, the INOUT variable can also show a negative sign if an out-of-state merger creates fewer opportunities for increased market power (Prager and Hannan, 1998) or less cost savings. The latter assumption draws on Houston and Ryngaert (1994), and Houston et al. (2001), who find, by means of a geographic overlap index, that stock price reaction is greater for mergers with greater overlap. The opportunity to realize cost savings is significant for this type of merger because there is a greater potential to close redundant local branches.

We introduce CNPL to control for any merger-related changes in asset portfolio quality that might change the bond's default risk. The variable CNPL is the percentage change in the ratio of nonperforming loans (nonaccrual loans and loans 90 days or more past-due) to total assets of the combined bank relative to the merging bank's nonperforming loans ratio. The ratio for the combined bank is calculated by consolidating the two banks' balance sheets for the year ending before the merger announcement. A higher CNPL implies that the nonperforming loans should rise after the merger. Therefore, CNPL should be negatively related to adjusted bond returns (AR).

We let CLEV control for merger-related changes in leverage ratios. This variable measures the percentage change in the leverage ratio (book value of liabilities over the sum of book value of liabilities, preferred stock, and market value of common stock) of the combined bank relative to the merging bank's leverage ratio. We calculate the leverage ratio for the combined bank by consolidating the two banks' balance sheets for the year ending before the merger announcement. Like CNPL, a higher CLEV value implies higher expected default risk and this should be negatively related to AR.

Choosing a proxy to capture the TBTF effect is not straightforward. The incremental size attained by the merger seems to be a natural proxy. Therefore, we use as an explanatory variable LISIZE, the logarithm of the incremental size attained by the bank in the merger. However, this variable can measure the impact of other factors. For example, Demsetz and Strahan (1997) show that large BHCs are better diversified than small BHCs. Furthermore, the benefits of the creation of internal markets could increase with the size of the bank (see Houston et al., 1997; Stein, 1997). Thus, asset size can capture gains unrelated to TBTF.

One way to tighten the TBTF test is to allow for the existence of banks that already have TBTF status before the merger. These banks should not gain any benefits by merely increasing their size. The tests should also allow for smaller institutions that are far enough away from the TBTF threshold, and therefore should not realize size-related gains. In contrast, the medium-size banks, which rapidly approach or pass the TBTF threshold as a result of a merger, should be the true beneficiaries of this policy.

In Equation (1), the construction of variables DBIG and DSML reflect these concerns. DBIG is a binary variable that takes the value of one when the acquiring bank's asset size is more than 2% of assets of all depository institutions at the end of the year prior to the announcement, and zero otherwise. Eight banks (listed in Appendix C) fall into this category. The second variable, DSML, is also a binary variable that takes the value of one when the bank's asset size is less than 0.35% of industry assets. Eighteen banks fall into this latter category. The coefficients of these two variables test differences between the corresponding group's and the medium-size banks' ARs. Thus, DBIG represents those banks that are already TBTF before merging, and DSML represents those that are sufficiently distant from being TBTF. The TBTF hypothesis predicts that the coefficients of these two variables will be negative.

We also include an interaction term of LISIZE with INOUT. If the effect of the incremental size on bond returns depends on synergies that are stronger for in-state mergers, then we expect this variable to have a negative sign.

2.4. Results

We obtain our data on balance-sheet variables from the quarterly Consolidated Financial Statements (FR-Y9 reports) that each US bank holding company files with the Federal Reserve Board. Our data on equity returns and capitalization come from the Center for Research in Securities Prices (CRSP) files.

Our sample consists of 72 observations, comprising 54 acquirers and 18 targets, and resulting in 57 merger cases. From the 63 acquiring banks included in the estimation of bond returns, we exclude nine cases from the cross-sectional analysis because of missing equity returns in the CRSP equity returns file for the target.

Table 2 reports the descriptive statistics. In Table 2, columns (1)-(3) divide the sample into three groups, representing the mega-size (BIG), medium-size (MID), and small-size (SML) institutions. We express asset size values in constant (December 2000) dollars. We observe that on average, medium- and small-size banks merge with banks that have asset sizes roughly equal to their own. Although in medium-size mergers the combined bank's asset size reaches $100 billion on average, the combined size in mergers between the small-size institutions reaches only $27 billion. On the other hand, the mega-size institutions, which have an average premerger asset size of $178.5 billion, are likely to merge with medium-size institutions.

In Table 2, we are also interested in the comparison between the small- and medium-size groups. As a result of the merger, small-size banks reduce nonperforming loans and leverage and attain the highest reduction in equity volatility (diversification). In contrast, the medium-size banks increase their nonperforming loans and leverage and do not diversify as much as does the small-size group. Nevertheless, medium-size banks realize a significantly higher return than do the smaller banks.

Table 3 reports the estimates of Equation (1). In almost all specifications we observe that the degree of diversification attained in the merger is a significant determinant of the bondholder returns. The proxy variable CVOL shows that the higher the reduction in the expected volatility of equity, the better-off the bondholders. This result is stronger than the findings reported by Asquith and Kim (1982) and Dennis and McConnell (1986) for nonfinancial mergers and shows that bondholders in bank mergers benefit from diversification.

In most specifications, INOUT is positive and significant, capturing the positive effect that geographic diversification has on bond returns. The control for portfolio quality, CNPL, is negative as we expected, though either marginally significant or not significant at all. The change in the leverage ratio, CLEV, is not significant.

The remaining variables show that bondholders favor increases in bank size. Column (1) reports that the incremental size attained in the merger (LISIZE) is positive and significant. We also see that DSML is negative and significant, which implies that the small-size banks' adjusted bond returns are significantly lower than the medium-size banks' adjusted bond returns. On the other hand, DBIG has a negative but insignificant sign. The interaction term of LISIZE with INOUT turns out to be negative and significant. Together with the positive sign of LISIZE, this finding implies that for an identical increase in size, gains to bondholders are higher if the merger is in-state. This result provides some support for the synergy hypothesis, given the potential for increase in market power and cost reductions is stronger for in-state mergers. Column (2) replaces LISIZE with the logarithm of the ratio of the incremental size attained in the merger to the premerger size (LSRAT). This variable has a positive and significant sign.

Table 2

Descriptive statistics for the returns sample

BIG represents those banks with a premerger size greater than 2% of banking industry assets. SML represents the banks with a premerger size less than 0.35% of banking industry assets. MID are those banks with a premerger size less than 2% but more than 0.35% of industry assets at the beginning of the merger year. ACQ denotes the acquirer bank. TAR represents the target bank. AR is the risk- and maturity-adjusted return for the event month. We calculate this return as the difference between monthly bond returns and the return of a Merrill Lynch bond index with similar rating and maturity characteristics as for the specific bond. Bond returns are obtained from Lehman Brothers Database. ISIZE is the incremental size attained in the merger expressed in billions of December 2000 dollars. LISIZE is the natural log of ISIZE. SRAT is the ratio of the incremental postmerger size over the premerger size. LSRAT is the natural log of SRAT. INOUT is a binary variable that takes the value of one if the merger is out of state and zero otherwise. CVOL measures the percentage change between the portfolio volatility of the merging banks and the own-bank's equity return volatility before the merger. CNPL measures the percentage change between the nonperforming loans to total assets of the merging banks and the own-bank's ratio before the merger. CLEV measures the percentage change between the consolidated leverage ratio (book value of liabilities over the sum of book value of liabilities and market value of equity) of the merging banks and the own-bank's leverage ratio before the merger.

	BIG Mean (Std.)	MID Mean (Std.)	SML Mean (Std.)	ACQ Mean (Std.)	TAR Mean (Std.)	Total Mean (Std.)
AR (%)	0.20 (0.27)	0.36 (1.16)	−0.11** (0.64)	0.07[a] (0.94)	0.70 (1.04)	0.23 (1.00)
OSIZE (Bill $)	178.35*** (58.33)	49.63 (24.02)	14.32*** (4.51)	57.90 (58.25)	46.71 (35.49)	55.10 (53.46)
ISIZE (Bill $)	63.10 (66.33)	41.97 (64.58)	13.09*** (15.30)	16.53[b] (21.92)	98.80 (84.89)	37.10 (58.06)
SRAT	0.42 (0.52)	0.88 (1.64)	1.06 (1.38)	0.29[b] (0.29)	2.63 (2.16)	0.88 (1.49)
LISIZE	10.62** (1.01)	9.63 (1.46)	8.68** (1.40)	8.96[b] (1.24)	11.12 (0.93)	9.50 (1.50)
LSRAT	−1.43 (1.07)	−1.07 (1.32)	−0.83 (1.43)	−1.63[b] (0.88)	0.69 (0.74)	−1.05 (1.32)
INOUT	0.75 (0.46)	0.74 (0.44)	0.50* (0.51)	0.69 (0.47)	0.67 (0.49)	0.68 (0.47)
CVOL (%)	−5.91 (10.41)	−9.01 (7.23)	−12.14 (18.17)	−7.67[c] (7.97)	−14.78 (17.00)	−9.45 (11.24)
CNPL (%)	1.60 (6.17)	4.26 (21.91)	−6.94 (28.61)	2.34 (17.52)	−2.37 (35.01)	1.16 (22.96)
CLEV (%)	−0.29 (1.01)	0.38 (1.65)	−0.34* (1.26)	0.21 (0.78)	−0.12 (2.78)	0.13 (1.52)
N	8	46	18	54	18	72

*, **, ***Test the differences in means between the MID and BIG and the MID and SML groups at the 10%, 5%, and 1% significance levels, respectively. [a], [b], [c] Test the differences in means between the ACQ and TAR groups at the 10%, 5%, and 1% significance levels, respectively.

Table 3

Determinants of risk- and maturity-adjusted bond returns in bank mergers

The observations correspond to 54 acquirers and 18 targets. AR is the risk- and maturity-adjusted return of the event month. We calculate this return as the difference between monthly bond returns and the return of an index with similar rating and maturity characteristics to the specific bond. We obtain bond returns from Lehman Brothers database. Our index data is the corporate indexes from the Merrill Lynch US domestic bond series. CVOL measures the percentage change between the portfolio volatility of the merging banks and the own-bank's premerger equity return volatility. INOUT is a binary variable that takes the value of one if the merger is out of state and zero otherwise. CNPL measures the percentage change between the consolidated ratio of nonperforming loans to total assets of the merging banks and the own-bank's premerger ratio. CLEV measures the percentage change between the consolidated leverage ratio (book value of liabilities over the sum of book value of liabilities and market value of equity) of the merging banks and the own-bank's premerger leverage ratio. LISIZE is the logarithm of the incremental size attained by the own-bank in the merger expressed in constant (December 2000) million dollars. LSRAT is the logarithm of the ratio of incremental size over premerger size. DBIG_x is a binary variable that takes the value of unity when the bank's premerger size is greater than x% of banking industry assets. DSML_y is a binary variable that takes the value of unity when the bank's premerger size is less than y% of banking industry assets. DTBTF_z is a binary variable that takes the value of unity when the bank's premerger size is less than z% of banking industry assets, and its postmerger size is more than z%, zero otherwise. Coefficient estimates have heteroskedasticity-consistent standard errors. *t-Statistics* appear in parentheses below each coefficient estimate.

	(1)	(2)	(3)	(4)	(5)	(6)
Constant	−3.877*** (−2.846)	0.985** (2.054)	−4.057*** (−3.012)	0.1246 (0.5697)	−3.608*** (−2.606)	0.0509 (0.250)
CVOL	−0.013* (−1.849)	−0.014** (−2.082)	−0.013* (−1.715)	−0.0124* (−1.7174)	−0.015** (−2.208)	−0.016** (−2.232)
INOUT	3.138** (2.159)	1.627 (1.417)	3.236** (2.249)	−0.3233 (−1.270)	3.163** (2.058)	−0.2815 (−1.186)
CNPL	−0.008* (−1.946)	−0.006* (−1.763)	−0.008** (−2.016)	−0.0065 (−1.5310)	−0.007* (−1.953)	−0.004 (−1.470)
CLEV	−0.030 (−0.518)	−0.034 (−0.5703)	−0.040 (−0.653)	−0.0724 (−1.160)	−0.014 (−0.273)	−0.080 (−1.267)
LISIZE	0.465*** (2.787)	—	0.487*** (2.913)	—	0.431*** (2.591)	—
INOUT × LISIZE	−0.376** (−2.178)	−0.222 (−1.608)	−0.387** (−2.262)	—	−0.3754** (−2.053)	—
LSRAT	—	0.326** (2.491)	—	—	—	—
DBIG_2	−0.422 (−1.359)	0.077 (0.298)	—	—	—	—
DSML_0.35	−0.394** (−2.251)	−0.873*** (−2.867)	—	—	—	—
LISIZE × DBIG_2	—	—	−0.047 (−1.470)	—	—	—
LISIZE × DSML_0.35	—	—	−0.049** (−2.218)	—	—	—
DTBTF_2	—	—	—	1.2252** (2.444)	—	—
DBIG_2.5	—	—	—	—	−0.166 (−0.827)	—
DSML_0.45	—	—	—	—	−0.361** (−2.179)	—
DTBTF_2.5	—	—	—	—	—	1.380** (2.565)
Adjusted R^2	0.257	0.158	0.267	0.244	0.244	0.285
F-stat	4.077***	2.666**	4.231***	5.572***	3.862***	6.655***
Number of obs.	72	72	72	72	72	72

*, **, and *** indicate significance at the 0.10, 0.05, and 0.01 levels, respectively.

Other papers have found that similar size variables are significant to explain abnormal equity returns. For example, Kane (2000) reports that abnormal equity returns are positively related to target size. James and Weir (1987) and DeLong (2001) report that abnormal equity returns are positively related to the relative size of target to bidder. Therefore, asset size seems to have a positive effect on both bond and equity returns.

In sum, the results in columns (1) and (2) show that the medium-size banks' bondholders benefit the most from bank mergers, and that the relation between size and adjusted bond returns is not monotonic.

To further validate this result, column (3) examines how increases in size relate to the initial size of the merging bank. We construct two new variables, DBIG × LISIZE and DSML × LISIZE. For the banks that are already TBTF before merging, the increase in size should not be significant. For the small-size banks, as long as they merge with small-size banks, the incremental size should also not affect adjusted bond returns either, since these banks are too far away from the TBTF threshold. Therefore, we expect the sign of the interaction terms to be negative, which would show that it is the medium-size banks that benefit when merging, and that this benefit increases with the size of the partner. Consistent with this expectation, we observe that the coefficient on the incremental size (LISIZE) is positive and the coefficients on the interaction terms are negative. This finding provides additional support for the argument that medium-size banks benefit the most from increases in size.

In column (4) we try another specification. We replace the size variables with the binary variable DTBTF that equals one if the bank jumps into the TBTF category after the merger but was not TBTF premerger (it was smaller than 2% of industry assets before the merger and becomes larger than 2% after) and equals zero otherwise. The advantage of this variable over the other size variables is that it also takes into account the possibility of a small bank merging with a very large one and therefore getting nearer the TBTF threshold. The new binary variable is positive and significant and indicates that the banks that become TBTF after the merger gain, on average, more than either the banks that did not jump into the TBTF category after the merger or the banks that were already TBTF before the merger.

2.5. Robustness checks

2.5.1. Changing the size cutoff levels

The size cutoff levels, which we set at greater than 2% of banking industry assets and smaller than 0.35% of industry assets, are ad hoc choices. To conduct robustness checks on different cutoff levels for these binary variables, we first replace the small-size bank threshold, 0.35%, with 0.45%. For the TBTF threshold, we use two additional cutoff levels—greater than 2.5% and 1.5% of industry assets, respectively. In column (5) of Table 3, we report the results only for the 2.5% and 0.45% thresholds. The findings of Section 2.4 are robust to the choice of all cutoff levels. Small-size banks' adjusted bond returns are significantly lower than the medium-size banks' bond returns, even if we change the threshold from 0.35% to 0.45%.

We find similar results when we try the new thresholds for the specification that uses the DTBTF variable. The dummy variable is always positive and significant. In Table 3, column (6), we report the regression for the 2.5% threshold. We note that the explanatory power of the specification increases as we narrow the TBTF group (adjusted R^2 is 0.05 for the 1.5% threshold, 0.24 for the 2%, and 0.28 for the 2.5%). Thus, the positive and significant coefficients for the DTBTF variables in specifications (4) and (6) provide strong evidence that those banks which jump into the TBTF category realize higher adjusted returns compared to those that do not.

2.5.2. Adjustment for the clustering problem

The reported standard errors in Table 1 and the cross-sectional regressions might suffer from a clustering problem (overlapping in calendar time of some merger announcements). As Appendix A shows, among the bidders in Table 1 there are nine cases with two mergers announced in the same month, two cases with three mergers announced in the same month, and one case with four mergers announced in the same month. For targets, there are three cases with two mergers announced in the same month. In the cross-sectional regressions there are 11 cases with two mergers announced in the same month, two cases with three mergers announced in the same month, two cases with four overlaps, one case with five overlaps, and one case with six overlaps. Such clustering of announcement dates requires adjustments both in Table 1 standard errors and in the cross-sectional regressions.

To correct the standard errors reported in Table 1, we follow the technique summarized in Collins and Dent (1984) and Campbell et al. (1997). Jaffe (1974) introduced this technique, which eliminates the clustering problem by building portfolios of the securities that experience the same critical event at the same point in calendar time. Mean and standard deviation of returns are then calculated across portfolio and security returns, which do not face a clustering problem. The new significance levels obtained using this approach yield qualitatively similar results as those reported in Table 1.

To handle the clustering problem in cross-sectional regressions, we follow White (1980) to obtain a heteroscedasticity- and cross-correlation-consistent covariance matrix. This approach corrects the covariance matrix of the least-square estimators similar to White's derivation of the heteroscedastic consistent estimator. Following White's technique we, estimate the matrix:

$$S_0 = \frac{1}{n} \sum_{i=1}^{n} \sum_{j=1}^{n} e_i e_j x_i x_j', \tag{3}$$

where $e_i\, e_j = 0$ if i, j occur in different calendar months. We then estimate

$$\text{Var}_{\text{OLS}} = n(X'X)^{-1} S_0 (X'X)^{-1}, \tag{4}$$

and check that the matrix is nonnegative definite. Finally, we use the matrix elements to determine the significance of the least-squares estimators. We observe that our results remain unchanged as a result of this correction, with the two exceptions that the ratio of nonperforming loans becomes more significant and CVOL becomes marginally significant.

2.6. Results on equity returns

As noted above, regulatory constraints on banks' leverage ratios can account for the positive adjusted bondholder returns. To examine the change in the leverage ratio for our sample of banks, we follow Kim and McConnell (1977). We compare the leverage ratio (book value of liabilities over book value of assets) of the consolidated balance sheet of bidder and target the year before the merger with the same ratio for the acquirer after 2 years. We find that the merging banks are highly leveraged premerger and that they do not increase the leverage ratios in any significant manner following the merger. We find that in 58% of the cases there is a decrease in leverage at the end of the year in which the merger becomes effective. The average decrease in the leverage ratio is 0.31%, which is statistically significant. When we compare the first year after the merger (instead of the year of the merger) with the premerger situation, we find a decrease in 54% of cases, but the change in the premerger leverage ratio is −0.34%, which is not statistically significant.

Overall, our results support the hypothesis that merging banks do not increase leverage in a significant way following the merger. However, if only the coinsurance effect was at work, this hypothesis would predict that bondholders would gain and equity holders would suffer as a result of the acquisition. A number of studies report increases in combined equity value around the merger announcements (see, e.g., Cornett and Tehranian, 1992; Houston et al., 2001; Kane, 2000). Houston, James, and Ryngaert show further that the combined returns increase significantly over time, with the 1991-1996 deals showing superior performance relative to the 1985-1990 deals. In contrast, Hannan and Wolken (1989), Houston and Ryngaert (1994), Pilloff (1996), and DeLong (2001) do not report significant combined returns. However, their findings may be due to choosing mergers completed before 1991 (Hannan and Wolken, Houston and Ryngaert, and Pillof) or for not allowing separately for the post-1991 period (DeLong).

To analyze equity return behavior for our sample banks and compare equity returns with the monthly bond returns, we obtain monthly equity returns from CRSP. Following Houston et al. (2001), we calculate abnormal returns as the difference between monthly bank equity returns and the CRSP value-weighted market index return. Figure 2 plots the cumulative abnormal equity returns for acquirer and target banks separately. As with the adjusted bond returns shown in Figure 1, we observe a gradual increase in equity returns for both groups, starting 8 months before the announcement month. The abnormal returns are positive in most months for both groups, with the largest positive abnormal return for the target banks occurring on the announcement month. We note that these results support the earlier studies that examine equity return behavior around bank merger announcements.

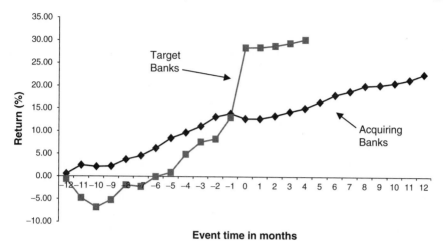

Fig. 2. Market adjusted equity cumulative returns around the bank merger announcements. We compute market-adjusted equity returns as the difference between monthly equity returns and the return on the CRSP value-weighted portfolio. The majority of our sample target banks' shares stop trading, as mergers become effective 4 months after the announcement month.

The observation that both equity holders and bondholders realize positive returns around the merger indicates that bank mergers do not shift wealth between these two claimholders. On the contrary, it appears that both types of claimholders gain from bank mergers. To formally test the relation between bondholder and equity holder gains, we estimate the following regression equation for the same sample of acquirers and targets as described in Section 2.3:

$$AR_i^B = 0.136 + 0.03AR^E$$
$$(0.09) \quad (0.01) \ Adj_j R^2 = 0.12, \quad N = 72. \tag{5}$$

AR^B and AR^E denote the adjusted bond returns and abnormal equity returns, respectively, for each acquirer or target. The heteroskedasticity-consistent standard errors appear in parentheses. The adjusted R^2 is 12% for the 72 observations included in the sample. We observe that the relation between bond and equity returns is positive and significant at the 5% level. This finding validates our expectation that bondholder gains are not realized at the expense of shareholders. Moreover, this result is evidence that bank mergers create value, and is consistent with both the synergy and TBTF hypotheses.

3. Analysis of changes in credit spreads of the acquiring banks

In this section, we examine the credit spreads of new debt issues of the acquiring bank before and after the merger. The main question is whether or not the cost of funding changes for the acquiring bank after the merger.

3.1. Sample and data

From the merger cases analyzed in the previous section, we select those in which (1) the acquirer issues fixed-rate nonconvertible debt not more than 2 years before the announcement date, and (2) the combined bank issues debt within 2 years after the merger becomes effective. These restrictions yield 25 cases. To this sample we add four mergers that were announced in 1998. We also add nine cases that we exclude from the bond-return analysis for not having complete price data in the Lehman Brothers Database. This brings our sample size to 38 cases.

We obtain bond data from the SDC's New Issues database. The number of bonds issued during this 4-year period varies across cases. As a rule, we take the five bonds issued nearest the respective dates. However, we find that in most cases, there are fewer than five issues that have our required characteristics within 2 years before or after a merger. Our sample results in 176 fixed-rate nonconvertible debt issues for 38 different merger cases. In six of these 38 cases, the acquirer buys more than one bank in a short period of time. For these cases we include all bonds issued both before the first announcement and after the last merger effective date. Appendix B reports the details for each case.

In addition to yield-to-maturity, we obtain from the SDC database data that include the issue date, credit rating, seniority, issue size, maturity, and years of call protection. Appendix B reports the average rating of the acquiring bank before the merger and the acquirer's average rating postmerger for each case.

We assign a numerical value to individual bond ratings, using the following scale: AAA+ = 1, AAA = 2, AAA− = 3, AA+ = 4, AA = 5, AA− = 6, A+ = 7, A = 8, A− = 9, BBB+ = 10, BBB = 11, BBB− = 12, and BB+ = 13. Thus, the larger the value, the worse the rating. We observe that in only eight out of 38 cases, the acquirer's average rating postmerger is worse than its premerger rating.

Appendix B also reports the average credit spreads of the acquiring banks both before and after the merger. We calculate credit spread as the difference between the yield at issue and the yield of a US. Treasury security of comparable maturity. Consistent with the ratings behavior, the average credit spreads also decline during the postmerger period. We note that in 27 out of 38 cases the average credit spread after the merger is lower than it is before the merger announcement.

3.2. Credit spreads

To investigate the determinants of the credit spreads (SPREAD) we use the following *ex ante* credit-spread model:

$$
\begin{aligned}
\text{SPREAD}_{it} = {} & c_0 + c_1 \text{MAT}_{it} + c_2 \text{CP}_{it} + c_3 \text{JN}_{it} + c_4 \text{IS}_{it} + c_5 \text{TR}_{it} + c_6 \text{FI}_{it} \\
& + c_7 \text{VOL}_{it} + c_8 \text{NPL}_{it} + c_9 \text{LEV}_{it} + c_{10} \text{ACSZ}_i + c_{11} M \times \text{DBIG}_{it} \\
& + c_{12} M \times \text{DSML}_{it} + c_{13} M \times \text{DMID}_{it} + e_{it}.
\end{aligned} \tag{6}
$$

The intuition underlying the above model is that after controlling for the market conditions, a bond's credit spread is determined by bond- and bank-specific characteristics. This structure follows the models used by Flannery and Sorescu (1996), Gande et al. (1999), and Morgan and Stiroh (2001). Equation (6) augments the standard variables with those that capture possible merger-related gains. It also tests for the existence of size-related credit-spread changes.

In our model, we first control for differences in credit spreads that can be caused by differences in maturity, callability, and seniority of the issues made by the acquiring bank i at time t. Variables MAT and CP are the log of the number of years to maturity and the log of the number of years with call protection, respectively, and JN is a binary variable that takes the value of one if the issue has a junior standing, and zero if it is a senior debt issue. We expect MAT and JN to be positively related with SPREAD, because credit spreads rise with maturity and the junior status of the bond. However, we expect CP to be negatively related to SPREAD, because a longer call protection period implies less chance of callability and hence less value of the call option.

We next control for differences in spread caused by differences in the liquidity of the bonds of a particular name. We follow Hancock and Kwast (2001) and use the logarithm of the issue size, IS, as a proxy for liquidity, assuming that higher liquidity is achieved by a higher issue size. If there are liquidity differences in our sample bond issues and if IS captures the liquidity effect, then we expect SPREAD will be negatively related with IS.

To control for aggregate variations of the credit spreads, we include CS, the difference between the yield on bonds of firms that provide financial services and the 10-year Treasury rate. We obtain the yield index from Merrill Lynch. It excludes bonds from banks and thus avoids a possible endogeneity problem. We expect CS to have a positive sign.

The next set of variables in Equation (6) measures the impact of the merger on bond spreads. The variable VOL captures the diversification effect, and is calculated as follows. For all the bonds issued by the acquiring bank before the merger, VOL is the standard deviation of weekly equity returns 1 year prior to the issue date. For the bonds issued immediately after the merger becomes effective, VOL is the standard deviation of a portfolio that contains the equity of both the acquirer and the target banks in proportion to their asset size, as described in Equation (2). Therefore, a higher value of VOL for the postmerger period implies that a bank attains less diversification after the merger. Thus, we expect credit spreads and VOL to be positively related.

The variable NPL denotes the percentage of nonperforming loans to total assets of the quarter previous to the bond issue date, and includes the nonaccrual loans and loans 90 days or more past-due. We calculate LEV, our leverage measure, as the ratio of the book value of debt to the market value of assets. We define the market value of assets as the sum of the book value of liabilities and preferred stock the quarter prior to the issue date and the market value of common stock the day before the bond issue date. Both NPL and LEV control for asset quality and capital structure changes that occur with the acquisition of another bank. We expect NPL and LEV to be positively related to credit spreads.

The last control variable is the acquirer's premerger log asset size, ACSZ. This variable is constant for all observations that correspond to the same case, and assesses whether or not the bond markets treat large-size banks favorably. Because previous studies show that size and credit spreads are negatively related (see Flannery and Sorescu, 1996; Morgan and Stiroh, 2001), we expect that ACSZ will have a negative sign.

We set the binary variable M equal to one for bonds issued after the merger, and zero for bonds issued before the announcement. This variable captures changes in an acquirer's credit spread that are due to merger-related changes in the acquirer's size. We note that the model controls for other merger-related changes such as asset quality, diversification, and leverage. In addition, as a robustness check, we also include the bond's rating in Equation (6). Thus, the binary variable M captures the remaining significant factor in the merger event, which is the change in the asset size of the acquirer. According to the TBTF hypothesis, this variable should be negatively related to the credit spreads. However, as long as ratings do not adjust immediately to the new information, a negative sign could also be due to the bank being more profitable and less likely to default after the merger. It could also be the case that this dummy variable is capturing reductions in volatility that are not captured by our noisy volatility estimates (equity volatility measures are very noisy and are measured with considerable error). Therefore, we devise a tighter test of the TBTF hypothesis. As we did in Section 2, we examine the significance in the reduction in credit spreads for banks that belong to different size groups. Thus, we introduce the interaction terms of M with the indicator variables DBIG, DMID, and DSML, where DBIG and DSML have the same definitions as in Equation (1). Appendix C provides a list of the banks that fall into the DBIG category. DMID is a binary variable that takes the value of one if the bond belongs to a bank whose assets represent less than 2% but more than 0.35% of industry assets before the merger, and zero otherwise. When DBIG and DMID are interacted with the merge binary variable, M, the coefficients of these binary variables indicate the average decrease in spreads for each of the size groups. Since the TBTF hypothesis predicts that small banks and mega-banks should not benefit from increasing their size, but that medium-size banks will benefit, we should observe that only the coefficient of $M \times$ DMID is significant and negative.

3.3. Results

Table 4 shows the descriptive statistics of the pre- and postmerger bond and firm characteristics. We find that for our sample of acquiring banks before the merger, the number of bond issues (82) is slightly lower than the issues of the combined banks (94). The average size of the issue is also smaller during the premerger period.

In Table 5 we report the regression results when we use the White (1980) estimator for the covariance matrix. The specification in column (1) corresponds to Equation (6). As expected, we find that the credit spreads vary positively and significantly with

Table 4

Descriptive statistics for the yield sample

This table presents summary statistics of the bond characteristics for 82 premerger and 94 postmerger bond issues of the acquiring banks. SPREAD is credit spread, which we define as the yield of the bond minus the yield of a Treasury bond with similar maturity. We construct RATING according to the following scale: AAA+ = 1, AAA = 2, AAA− = 3, AA+ = 4, AA = 5, AA− = 6, A+ = 7, A = 8, A− = 9, BBB+ = 10, BBB = 11, BBB− = 12, and BB+ = 13. JUNIOR is one if the bond is subordinated and zero otherwise. Premerger volatility is measured as the standard deviation of the acquiring bank's weekly equity return 1 year before the issue date for bonds issued premerger. We measure the postmerger volatility of the combined bank as the standard deviation of the portfolio of the merging banks' equity returns during the year preceding the merger announcement. NPL is the percentage of nonperforming loans over total assets. LEVERAGE is percentage of book value of liabilities to market value of assets, which we define as book value of liabilities and preferred stock plus market value of common stock. We average the variables within each merger case and then across cases.

	Acquiring bank (premerger)			Combined bank (postmerger)		
	Mean	Median	Std.	Mean	Median	Std.
Spread	0.9	0.8	0.4	0.7	0.7	0.3
Rating	8.8	9.0	1.8	8.6	8.6	1.5
Maturity	9.7	10.0	3.9	8.9	9.3	5.1
Years of call protection	9.1	10.0	3.7	8.3	8.5	4.3
Junior	0.7	1.0	0.4	0.5	0.5	0.4
Issue size ($ million)	165.6	150.0	79.5	176.3	150.0	108.2
Volatility	3.6	3.5	1.1	3.3	3.0	1.2
NPL	1.2	0.9	0.9	1.0	0.6	0.8
Leverage (%)	88.0	89.6	5.5	84.4	85.9	5.6
Total assets ($ billion)	64.8	38.5	73.9	110.3	68.6	124.1
Number of bond issues	82			94		

maturity and seniority, and negatively with the number of years of call protection. The issue size variable, IS, is not significant. The control for aggregate variations in the credit spreads, CS, has the expected positive sign and is highly significant. The variables that control for firm characteristics are significant and have the expected signs. We see that spreads increase with leverage and the percentage of nonperforming loans.

The coefficient of VOL is significant and positive, indicating that credit spreads are higher for those banks that attain less diversification (as measured by a higher value of VOL). This finding is consistent with diversification being one of the reasons for the decrease in spreads after a merger, and corroborates the findings for adjusted bond returns in Section 2.

The coefficient of ACSZ is negative and significant in all specifications, which implies that on average, the larger banks pay a lower credit spread in their bond issues. This result supports the findings of Flannery and Sorescu (1996) and Morgan and Stiroh (2001). We also observe that the coefficient of M is negative and significant,

Table 5

Determinants of the credit spread

The dependent variable is credit spread, which we define as the yield of the bond minus the yield of a Treasury bond with a similar maturity. Independent variables are MAT (log of years of maturity), CP (log of years with call protection), JN (one if the bond is subordinated, zero otherwise), IS (log of size of the issue), CS (difference between Merrill Lynch index of bond returns for the financial sector, excluding banks and the 10-year Treasury rate), VOL (volatility of bank's equity return 1 year before the issue date for bonds issued before the merger and volatility of the portfolio of the two merging banks for bonds issued after the merger), LEV (market value of leverage), NPL (percentage of nonperforming loans over total assets), RTG (rating), ACSZ (acquirer's premerger size), M (one if issued postmerger, zero otherwise), DBIG_x (one if the bond is issued by a bank whose premerger assets are greater than x% of industry assets, zero otherwise), DSML_y (one if the bond is issued by a bank whose premerger assets are smaller than y% of industry assets, zero otherwise), and DMID_x_y (one if the bond belongs to a bank whose premerger assets are smaller than x% but more than y% of industry assets, zero otherwise). We construct RTG according to the following scale: AAA+ = 1, AAA = 2, AAA− = 3, AA+ = 4, AA = 5, AA− = 6, A+ = 7, A = 8, A− = 9, BBB+ = 10, BBB = 11, BBB− = 12, and BB+ = 13. Coefficient estimates have heteroskedasticity-consistent standard errors. t-Statistics appear in parentheses below each coefficient estimate.

	(1)	(2)	(3)	(4)	(5)	(6)	(7)
C	−0.152 (−0.541)	−0.672** (−2.163)	0.073 (0.246)	−0.328 (−1.133)	−0.671** (−2.155)	−0.331 (−1.149)	−0.238 (−0.758)
MAT	0.456*** (5.963)	0.429*** (6.305)	0.458*** (6.017)	0.440*** (6.239)	0.433*** (6.424)	0.443*** (6.424)	0.452*** (6.328)
CP	−0.250*** (−2.723)	−0.223*** (−2.592)	−0.264*** (−2.813)	−0.243*** (−2.691)	−0.226*** (−2.650)	−0.245*** (−2.778)	−0.254*** (−2.769)
JN	0.102** (2.052)	0.050 (1.003)	0.111** (2.257)	0.069 (1.353)	0.045 (0.918)	0.065 (1.272)	0.057 (1.120)
IS	0.012 (0.402)	0.017 (0.584)	0.024 (0.706)	0.026 (0.801)	0.020 (0.683)	0.028 (0.862)	0.033 (0.959)
CS	0.632*** (11.129)	0.620*** (10.719)	0.626*** (11.277)	0.618*** (10.852)	0.619*** (10.785)	0.618*** (10.960)	0.608*** (10.671)
VOL	0.060*** (2.963)	0.062*** (3.199)	0.068*** (3.549)	0.067*** (3.671)	0.062*** (3.273)	0.068*** (3.764)	0.064*** (3.477)
LEV	0.011*** (3.325)	0.010*** (2.839)	0.010*** (3.369)	0.009*** (2.853)	0.009*** (2.700)	0.009*** (2.667)	0.009*** (2.704)
NPL	0.076** (2.379)	0.058* (1.770)	0.075** (2.417)	0.062* (1.931)	0.059* (1.836)	0.063** (1.978)	0.077** (2.323)
RTG	—	0.043*** (3.174)	—	0.032** (2.293)	0.048*** (3.546)	0.039*** (2.724)	0.033** (2.248)
ACSZ	−0.110*** (−5.234)	−0.080*** (−3.620)	−0.131*** (−4.000)	−0.107*** (−3.403)	−0.081*** (−3.679)	−0.107*** (−3.603)	−0.115*** (−3.413)
M	−0.082*** (−2.880)	−0.090*** (−3.173)	—	—	—	—	—
M*RTG	—	—	—	—	−0.013*** (−3.653)	—	—

M*DBIG_2	—	—	0.025 (0.512)	0.005 (0.113)	—	—
M*DMID_2_0.35	—	—	−0.155*** (−4.359)	−0.148*** (−4.278)	—	—
M*DSML_0.35	—	—	−0.036 (−0.512)	−0.059 (−0.772)	—	—
M*RTG*DBIG_2	—	—	—	—	−0.004 (−0.065)	—
M*RTG*DMID_2_0.35	—	—	—	—	−0.020*** (−5.058)	—
M*RTG*DSML_0.35	—	—	—	—	−0.010 (−1.221)	—
M*DBIG_2.5	—	—	—	—	—	0.026 (0.463)
M*DMID_2.5_0.45	—	—	—	—	—	−0.138*** (−3.757)
M*DSML_0.45	—	—	—	—	—	−0.104 (−1.579)
Adjusted R^2	0.77	0.78	0.78	0.79	0.80	0.79
Number of observations.	176	176	176	176	176	176

*, **, and *** indicate significance at the 0.10, 0.05, and 0.01 levels, respectively.

which indicates that an acquiring bank significantly reduces its cost of debt in the postmerger period after controlling for several significant factors. The specification in column (2) adds the bond's rating, RTG, to Equation (6). With this addition, the seniority variable loses significance but the merger variable keeps its significance.

The coefficients of $M \times \text{DBIG}$ and $M \times \text{DSML}$ in columns (3) and (4) are not significant, indicating that the changes in credit spreads of mega-banks and small banks are not material. In contrast, the coefficient of $M \times \text{DMID}$ shows that when banks in the medium-size group acquire another bank, they experience an average decrease of 15.5 basis points (or 14.8 basis points when RTG is included in specification (4)). We attribute this decrease to the increase in size attained in the merger.

Columns (5) and (6) in Table 5 investigate the impact of mergers on the rating-sensitivity of credit spreads. We construct a new variable, $M \times \text{RTG}$. When we include this variable in the regression with the RTG variable, $M \times \text{RTG}$ measures the merger-related change in the sensitivity of credit spreads to changes in ratings. We expect the sign of $M \times \text{RTG}$ to be negative as our sample banks approach the TBTF threshold after the merger. Column (5) shows that this result obtains.

Furthermore, we construct the variables $M \times \text{RTG} \times \text{DBIG}$, $M \times \text{RTG} \times \text{DMID}$, and $M \times \text{RTG} \times \text{DSML}$ to examine which specific size group experiences the larger reduction in the rating-sensitivity of credit spreads. Consistent with the TBTF, the results in column (6) show that it is the medium-size banks that experience a significant decline. The other two groups do not show any significant decline.

As a robustness check we re-estimate the specification in column (4) given in Table 5 by using different thresholds. We use the same cutoff points explained in Section 2.5.1 and our results remain qualitatively the same. In column (7) we report the specification with the 2.5% and 0.45% thresholds. For all thresholds, the coefficients of $M \times \text{DBIG}$ and $M \times \text{DSML}$ are not significant, indicating that the changes in credit spreads of mega-banks and small banks are not material. In contrast, the coefficient of $M \times \text{DMID}$ (for the new thresholds) shows that when banks in the medium-size group acquire another bank, they experience a significant decrease in their cost of funds.

These findings support the results of our bond-return analysis in Section 2 and provide additional evidence indicating that a potential benefit of bank mergers to acquirers is lower cost of new debt issues. However, this benefit is not uniform across size groups. The findings show that medium-size banks that can push the combined bank-asset size beyond the TBTF threshold after the merger reduce their cost of funds more than mega-banks and small banks.

4. Conclusion

This paper examines bond returns and bond credit spreads around the announcement of bank mergers during the 1991-1998 period. We show that bondholders of bidder and target banks gain significant positive bond returns in the months leading to the merger announcement. We also provide evidence that the relation between announcement-month bond and equity returns is positive and significant. This finding supports the argument that bank mergers are not shifting wealth from shareholders to bondholders. Our cross-sectional regressions identify diversification, TBTF, and, to a lesser degree, synergy as possible sources of these gains.

We support these observations by showing that on average, the credit spreads in the acquiring bank's new bond issues decline significantly following the merger. After we control for bond and bank characteristics, the decline is significantly explained by the degree of diversification attained and whether or not the banks attain TBTF status as a result of the merger. Thus, this paper shows, for the first time, that one significant benefit to the acquirer is lower cost of funds on debt issues postmerger.

Appendix A: Sample merger cases

The samples used in the statistical analyses contain different number of banks depending on data availability. The sample code column indicates the sample to which the bank belongs. Code 1 refers to banks included in calculating the risk- and maturity-adjusted returns. Code 2 refers to the banks included in the cross-sectional regressions of the adjusted returns. Code 3 refers to banks included in the credit-spread sample.

Appendix A

Announce. date	Effective date	Sample code	Acquirer name	Size (mill. $)	Sample code	Target name	Size (mill. $)
5/15/91	1/2/92	1	First Maryland Bancorp., MD	7800		York Bank and Trust Co., PA	1400
6/3/91	3/2/92	1	Banc one Corp., OH	30,336		First Illinois Corp., IL	1654
6/17/91	9/19/91	1,2,3	First Union Corp., NC	39,600		Southeast Banking Corp., FL	11,248
7/15/91	12/31/91	1,2,3	Chemical Banking Corp., NY	74,130	1,2	Manufacturers Hanover Corp., NY	61,239
7/22/91	12/31/91	1,2,3	NCNB, NC	69,100	1,2	C&S/Sovran, VA	49,075
8/12/91	4/22/92	1,2,3	Bank America Corp., CA	95,161	1,2	Security Pacific Corp., CA	78,602
9/13/91	3/16/92	1,2	Society Corp., OH	15,418	1,2	Ameritrust Corporation, OH	10,848
10/11/91	4/1/92	1,2,3	Boatmen's Bancshares Inc., MO	17,469		First Interstate of Iowa Inc., IO	1235
10/28/91	6/18/92	1,2,3	Comerica Inc., MI	13,300		Manufacturers Ntl. Corp., MI	12,507
10/30/91	5/4/92	1,2	National City Corp., OH	24,170	1,2	Merchants National Corporation, IN	5806
11/12/91	4/30/92	1,2	Mercantile Bancorp., MO	7398		Ameribanc Inc., MO	1228
12/30/91	11/2/92	1,2	Banc One Corp., OH	46,293		Affiliated Bankshares, CO	2728
1/20/92	4/30/92	1	South Trust Corp., AL	10,000		First American Bank of Georgia, GA	1240
1/27/92	7/1/92	1,2	Dauphin Deposit Corp., PA	3613		FB & T Corp., PA	648
3/4/92	1/15/93	1,2	Keycorp, NY	23,156		Puget Sound Bancorp., WA	4784
3/5/92	10/1/92	1,2,3	Boatmen's Bancshares Inc., MO	17,635		Sunwest Financial Services, NM	3362
3/18/92	10/15/92	3	NBD Bancorp., MI	29,514		INB Financial Corp., IN	6556
5/18/92	12/7/92	1,2	Barnett Banks Inc., FL	32,886		First Florida Banks Inc., FL	5434
7/30/92	1/15/93	3	Integra Financial Corp., PA	8847		Equimark Corp., PA	2868
7/30/92	2/17/93	1	South Trust Corp., AL	10,158		Prime Bancshares, GA	665
8/20/92	2/10/93	1,2,3	Norwest Corp., MN	40,293		Lincoln Financial Corp., IN	2250
9/21/92	3/1/93	3	First Union Corp., NC	47,720		Dominion Bancshares Corp., VA	8911
11/9/92	6/1/93	1,2,3	First Bank System, MN	17,319		Colorado National Bankshares, CO	2976
12/28/92	5/4/93	3	First Fidelity Bancorp., NJ	30,000		Northeast Bancorp Inc., MD	2764
1/29/93	8/11/93	1,2,3	Bank of New York, NY	40,909		National Community Banks, NJ	4018
3/30/93	9/1/93	1,2,3	Meridian Bancorp Inc., PA	12,208		Commonwealth Bancshares Corp., PA	2067
4/21/93	8/13/93	1,2	Huntington Bancshares, OH	13,895		Commerce Banc Corp., WV	897
7/27/93	1/17/94	1	Norwest Corp., MN	47,800		First United Bank Group Inc., NM	3477
8/2/93	3/16/94	1,2	CoreStates Financial Corp., PA	23,699		Constellation Bancorp., NJ	2415

Date	Ref	Acquirer, State	Assets	Date	Ref	Target, State	Assets
9/20/93	3	Marshall & Ilsley, WI	7850	5/31/94	3	Valley Bancorporation, WI	4394
9/29/93	1,2,3	First Bank System, MN	23,527	3/25/94	1,2,3	Boulevard Bancorp Inc., IL	1564
10/1/93	1,2,3	Society Corp., OH	27,040	3/1/94	1,2,3	Keycorp, NY	32,433
11/3/93	1,2,3	Banc One Corp., OH	76,500	8/15/94	1,2,3	Liberty National Bancorp of Louisv., KY	4686
11/19/93	1,2	CoreStates Financial Corp., PA	22,800	6/27/94	1,2	Independence Bancorp Inc., PA	2727
1/28/94	1,2,3	Bank America Corp., CA	186,933	9/1/94	1,2,3	Continental, IL	21,789
3/21/94	1,2	First Fidelity Bancorp., NJ	34,403	11/29/94	1,2	Baltimore Bancorp., MD	2305
5/9/94	1,2,3	Fleet Financial Group Inc., MA	46,000	1/27/95	1,2,3	NBB Bancorp Inc., MA	2451
7/1/94	1,3	First Bank System, MN	26,330	1/24/95	1,3	Metropolitan Financial Corp., OH	7855
7/1/94	3	Union Planters Corp., TN	6967	12/20/94	3	Grenada Sunburst System, MI	2463
8/18/94	1,2	Boatmen's Bancshares Inc., MO	28,292	3/1/95	1,2	Worthen Banking, AR	3568
8/30/94	1,2	Meridian Bancorp Inc., PA	14,782	2/26/96	1,2	United Counties Bancorp., NJ	1661
9/22/94	1,2,3	Mercantile Bancorp, MO	12,238	6/12/95	1,2,3	Central Mortgage Bancshares, MO	627
2/21/95	1,2,3	Fleet Financial Group Inc., MA	48,727	11/30/95	1,2,3	Shawmut Corporation, CN	32,399
2/21/95	3	First American Corp., TN	7757	11/1/95	3	Heritage Federal Bancshares, KY	516
5/8/95	1,2	US Bancorp, OR	21,400	12/27/95	1,2	West One Bancorp., IH	8793
6/19/95	1,2,3	First Union Corp., NC	96,741	1/2/96	1,2,3	First Fidelity Bancorp Inc., NJ	35,400
7/10/95	1,2,3	PNC Corp., PA	62,094	1/2/96	1,2,3	Midlantic Corp., NJ	13,634
7/12/95	3	NBD, MI	47,756	12/1/95	1,2	First Chicago Corp., IL	72,378
7/19/95	1,2	Banc One Corp., OH	86,783	1/2/96	1,2	Premier Bancorp., LA	5505
8/4/95	1,2	Mercantile Bancorp., MO	16,019	1/2/96	1,2	Hawkeye Bancorp., IO	1951
8/7/95	1,2	First Bank System, MN	32,712	2/16/96	1,2	Firstier Financial Inc., NB	3580
8/25/95	1,2	Boatmen's Bancshares Inc., MO	32,367	1/31/96	1,2	Fourth Financial Corp., KS	7556
8/28/95	3	Chemical Banking Corp., NY	185,281	3/31/96	3	Chase Manhattan Corp., NY	118,756
8/28/95	1,2	National City Corp., OH	32,144	5/3/96	1,2	Integra Financial Corp., PA	14,811
9/22/95	1	Republic New York Corp., NY	41,637	3/1/96	1	Brooklyn Bancorp Inc., NY	4139
10/10/95	1,2,3	CoreStates Financial Corp., PA	29,032	4/9/96	1,2,3	Meridian Bancorp, Inc., PA	14,563
10/18/95	1,2	Wells Fargo Corp., CA	53,374	4/1/96	1,2	First Interstate, CA	55,067
10/23/95	1,2	Regions Financial Corp., AL	13,848	3/1/96	1,2	First National Bancorp. of Gainesv., GA	3112
12/12/95	1,2,3	Bank of Boston Corp., MA	46,083	7/29/96	1,2,3	Baybanks Inc., MA	11,525
12/19/95	1	Fleet Financial Group Inc., MA	72,100	5/3/96	1	National Westminster Bancorp., NY	31,000
1/10/96	1	Firstar Corp., WI	18,784	7/12/96	1	Jacob Schmidt Co., MN	1295
8/30/96	1,2,3	NationsBank, NC	192,308	1/6/97	1,2,3	Boatmens Bancshares Inc., MO	40,683

(Continued)

Appendix A (Continued)

Announce. date	Effective date	Sample code	Acquirer name	Size (mill. $)	Sample code	Target name	Size (mill. $)
9/16/96	12/31/96	1,2,3	Crestar Financial Corp., VA	18,488		Citizens Bancorp., MD	4180
11/4/96	7/2/97	1,2	Southern National Corp., NC	21,400		United Carolina Bancshares Corp., NC	4366
3/14/97	10/1/97	1,2	Marshall & Ilsley, WI	14,763		Security Capital, WI	3658
3/20/97	8/1/97	1,2	First Bank System, MN	36,000	1,2	US Bancorp., OR	33,213
5/5/97	9/30/97	1,2,3	Huntington Bancshares Inc., OH	21,604		First Michigan Bank Corp., MI	3564
6/24/97	12/16/97	1,2,3	Wachovia Corp., NC	47,491	1,2	Central Fidelity Banks Inc., VA	10,570
7/21/97	12/1/97	1,2,3	First Union Corp., NC	143,000	1,2	Signet Banking Corp., VA	11,853
8/29/97	1/1/98	1,2,3	NationsBank, NC	264,562	1,2	Barnett Banks, FL	44,005
10/20/97	6/12/98	1,2,3	Banc one Corp., OH	113,127		First Commerce, LA	9311
11/18/97	4/28/98	1,2,3	First Union Corp., NC	157,274	1,2	CoreStates, PA	47,591
12/1/97	3/31/98	3	National City Corp., OH	54,684		First of America Bank Corp. of Kal., MI	21,691
12/8/97	5/1/98	3	First American Corp., TN	10,600	1,2	Deposit Guaranty Corp., MS	6800
4/13/98	10/2/98	3	Banc One Corp., OH	115,901		First Chicago NBD Corp., IL	114,804
4/13/98	9/30/98	3	NationsBank, NC	314,503		Bank America Corp., CA	265,436
6/8/98	11/2/98	3	Norwest Corp., MN	96,094		Wells Fargo Corp., CA	94,820
7/1/98	11/20/98	3	Star Banc Corp., OH	13,856		Firstar Corp., WI	19,972

Appendix B: Number, average rating, and average credit spread of the bond issues by the acquiring bank and the combined bank

Acquirer	Target	Acquiring bank (premerger)			Combined bank (postmerger)		
		Number of issues	Average rating	Average credit spread	Number of issues	Average rating	Average credit spread
Norwest Corp.	Wells Fargo Corp.	4	6.0	0.4	3	7.0	0.2
Banc One Corp.	First Chicago NBD Corp./First Commerce	5	6.2	0.6	1	7.0	1.4
Bank America Corp.	Security Pacific Corp.	4	9.0	1.8	4	8.8	0.9
Society Corp.	Keycorp	1	10.0	0.9	4	9.3	0.5
Chemical Banking Corp.	Manufacturers Hanover Corp.	1	10.0	1.6	5	9.2	0.9
Bank America Corp.	Continental	4	8.8	0.9	5	8.4	0.6
Fleet Financial Group Inc.	Shawmut Corporation/NBB Bancorp Inc.	3	11.0	1.0	1	10.0	0.6
First Union Corp.	First Fidelity Bancorp Inc.	3	9.0	0.9	2	9.0	0.8
CoreStates Financial Corp.	Meridian Bancorp, Inc.	1	9.0	0.7	1	9.0	0.6
NBD	First Chicago Corp.	1	7.0	0.6	2	8.0	0.3
Chemical Banking Corp.	Chase Manhattan Corp.	4	8.8	0.8	5	8.2	0.7
NationsBank	Bank America Corp.	3	7.3	0.8	5	7.0	1.0
Star Banc Corp.	Firstar Corp.	2	9.0	0.4	2	9.0	0.8
National City Corp.	First of America Bank Corp.	2	8.0	0.5	4	8.0	0.7
NationsBank	Barnett Banks	2	7.0	0.7	2	6.0	0.2
First Union Corp.	CoreStates/Signet Banking Corp.	3	8.7	0.4	3	8.0	1.2
NationsBank	Boatmens Bancshares Inc.	3	8.0	0.5	3	7.7	0.6
Banc One Corp.	Liberty National Bancorp.	2	6.5	0.7	2	7.0	0.8
Comerica Inc.	Manufacturers Ntl. Corp.	1	9.0	1.0	1	9.0	1.0
NBD Bancorp.	INB Financial Corp.	1	6.0	0.7	1	6.0	0.6
Norwest Corp.	Lincoln Financial Corp.	5	7.0	0.6	5	6.0	0.4
First Union Corp.	Dominion Bancshares Corp./Southeast Banking C.	2	8.0	1.6	2	9.5	0.9

(Continued)

Appendix B (Continued)

Acquirer	Target	Acquiring bank (premerger)			Combined bank (postmerger)		
		Number of issues	Average rating	Average credit spread	Number of issues	Average rating	Average credit spread
Bank of New York	National Community Banks	4	9.0	0.8	5	8.0	0.4
First Fidelity Bancorp.	Northeast Bancorp Inc.	1	10.0	1.4	1	11.0	0.8
Union Planters Corp.	Grenada Sunburst System	2	12.5	1.4	1	12.0	0.9
PNC Corp.	Midlantic Corp.	3	7.7	0.3	1	8.0	0.0
Crestar Financial Corp.	Citizens Bancorp.	1	10.0	0.8	1	10.0	1.0
Marshall & Ilsley	Valley Bancorporation	1	8.0	0.7	2	7.0	0.4
Bank of Boston Corp.	Baybanks Inc.	1	11.0	0.8	1	8.0	0.2
NCNB	C&S/Sovran	2	9.0	1.5	5	8.4	0.7
Integra Financial Corp.	Equimark Corp.	1	11.0	1.2	1	11.0	1.1
First American Corp.	Heritage Federal Bancshares	1	12.0	1.1	1	12.0	0.9
Meridian Bancorp Inc.	Commonwealth Bancshares Corp.	1	11.0	1.0	1	10.0	0.7
Huntington Bancshares Inc.	First Michigan Bank Corp.	2	9.0	0.2	2	9.0	0.5
Wachovia Corp.	Central Fidelity Banks Inc.	2	4.5	0.4	3	6.3	0.9
Mercantile Bancorp.	Central Mortgage Bancshares	1	12.0	1.4	3	10.0	0.6
Boatmen's Bancshares Inc.	Sunwest Financial Services/First Interstate of Iowa	1	9.0	1.4	1	9.0	0.9
First Bank System	Metropolitan Financial/Boulevard Bancorp/Colorado National Bankshares	1	10.0	0.9	2	9.0	0.7
Total		82			94.0		

Appendix C: Banks in each size category

C.1.   Returns sample

Bank's asset size is more than 1.5% of industry assets at the end of the year preceding the announcement of the acquisition: (13 cases). NationsBank (at the time of the merger with Barnett Banks and Boatmens), First Union (at the time of the merger with Corestates, Signet Banking and First Fidelity), BankAmerica (at the time of the merger with Security Pacific and Continental), Security Pacific (at the time of the merger with BankAmerica), Banc One (at the time of the merger with First Commerce, Liberty National and Premier Bancorp), Chemical (at the time of the merger with Manufacturers Hanover), and Chase Manhattan (at the time of the merger with Chemical).

Bank's asset size is more than 2% of industry assets at the end of the year preceding the announcement of the acquisition: (eight cases). NationsBank (at the time of the merger with Barnett Banks and Boatmens), First Union (at the time of the merger with Corestates and Signet Banking), BankAmerica (at the time of the merger with Security Pacific and Continental), Banc One (at the time of the merger with First Commerce), and Chase Manhattan (at the time of the merger with Chemical).

Bank's asset size is more than 2.5% of industry assets at the end of the year preceding the announcement of the acquisition: (five cases). NationsBank (at the time of the merger with Barnett Banks and Boatmens), First Union (at the time of the merger with Corestates and Signet Banking), and BankAmerica (at the time of the merger with Continental).

C.2.   Credit-spread sample

Acquirer's asset size is more than 1.5% of industry assets at the end of the year preceding the announcement of the acquisition: (12 cases). BankAmerica/Security Pacific, BankAmerica/Continental, Chemical/Chase Manhattan, NationsBank/Boatmens, NationsBank/Barnett Banks, NationsBank/BankAmerica, First Union/CoreStates, Norwest/Wells Fargo, Banc One/First Chicago, Chemical/Manufacturers, First Union/First Fidelity, Banc One/Liberty National.

Acquirer's asset size is more than 2% of industry assets at the end of the year preceding the announcement of the acquisition: (seven cases). BankAmerica/Security Pacific, BankAmerica/Continental, Chemical/Chase Manhattan, NationsBank/Boatmens, NationsBank/Barnett Banks, NationsBank/BankAmerica, First Union/CoreStates/Signet Banking.

Acquirer's asset size is more than 2.5% of industry assets at the end of the year preceding the announcement of the acquisition: (six cases). BankAmerica/Continental, Chemical/Chase Manhattan, NationsBank/Boatmens, NationsBank/Barnett Banks, NationsBank/BankAmerica, First Union/CoreStates/Signet Banking.

References

Akhavein, J., A. Berger and D. Humphrey, 1997, "The Effects of Megamergers on Efficiency and Prices: Evidence from a Bank Profit Function," *Review of Industrial Organization*, 12, 95–139.

Asquith, P. and E. Kim, 1982, "The Impact of Merger Bids on the Participating Firms' Security-Holders," *Journal of Finance*, 37, 1209–1228.

Berger, A., R. Demsetz and P. Strahan, 1999, "The Consolidation of the Financial Services Industry: Causes, Consequences, and Implications for the Future," *Journal of Banking and Finance*, 23, 135–194.

Billet, M. T., T. H. King and D. C. Mauer, 2004, "Bondholder Wealth Effects in Mergers and Acquisitions: New Evidence from the 1980s and 1990s," *Journal of Finance*, 59, 107–135.

Calomiris, C., 1999, "Gauging the Efficiency of Bank Consolidation During a Merger Wave," *Journal of Banking and Finance*, 23, 615–621.

Campbell, J., A. W. Lo and A. C. MacKinlay, 1997, *The Econometrics of Financial Markets*, Princeton University Press, Princeton, NJ.

Collins, D. W. and W. T. Dent, 1984, "A Comparison of Alternative Testing Methodologies Used in Capital Market Research," *Journal of Accounting Research*, 22, 48–84.

Cornett, M. M. and H. Tehranian, 1992, "Changes in Corporate Performance Associated with Bank Acquisitions," *Journal of Financial Economics*, 31, 211–234.

DeLong, G., 2001, "Stockholder Gains from Focusing Versus Diversifying Bank Mergers," *Journal of Financial Economics*, 59, 221–252.

Demsetz, R. S. and P. Strahan, 1997, "Diversification, Size, and Risk at Bank Holding Companies," *Journal of Money Credit and Banking*, 29, 300–313.

Dennis, D. K. and J. J. McConnell, 1986, "Corporate Mergers and Security Returns," *Journal of Financial Economics*, 16, 143–187.

Elton, E. J., M. J. Gruber, D. Agrawal and C. Mann, 2001, "Explaining the Rate Spread on Corporate Bonds," *Journal of Finance*, 61, 247–277.

Flannery, M. and S. Sorescu, 1996, "Evidence of Bank Market Discipline in Subordinated Debenture Yields: 1983-1991," *Journal of Finance*, 51, 1347–1377.

Galai, D. and R. Masulis, 1976, "The Option Pricing Model and the Risk Factor of Stock," *Journal of Financial Economics*, 3, 53–81.

Gande, A., M. Puri and A. Saunders, 1999, "Bank Entry, Competition, and the Market for Corporate Securities Underwriting," *Journal of Financial Economics*, 54, 165–195.

Hancock, D. and M. L. Kwast, 2001, "Using Subordinated Debt to Monitor Bank Holding Companies: Is It Feasible?," *Journal of Financial Services Research*, 20, 147–187.

Hannan, T. H. and J. D. Wolken, 1989, "Returns to Bidders and Targets in the Acquisition Process: Evidence from the Banking Industry," *Journal of Financial Services Research*, 3, 5–16.

Higgins, R. C. and L. D. Schall, 1975, "Corporate Bankruptcy and Conglomerate Merger," *Journal of Finance*, 30, 93–113.

Houston, J. F. and M. D. Ryngaert, 1994, "The Overall Gains from Large Bank Mergers," *Journal of Banking and Finance*, 18, 1155–1176.

Houston, J. F., C. M. James and D. Marcus, 1997, "Capital Market Frictions and the Role of Internal Capital Markets in Banking," *Journal of Financial Economics*, 46, 135–164.

Houston, J. F., C. M. James and M. D. Ryngaert, 2001, "Where Do Merger Gains Come from? Bank Mergers from the Perspective of Insiders and Outsiders," *Journal of Financial Economics*, 60, 285–331.

Jaffe, J. F., 1974, "Special Information and Insider Trading," *The Journal of Business*, 47, July, 410–428.

James, C. and P. Weir, 1987, "Returns to Acquirers and Competition in the Acquisition Market: The Case of Banking," *Journal of Political Economy*, 95, 355–370.

Jensen, M. and R. Ruback, 1983, "The Market for Corporate Control: The Scientific Evidence," *Journal of Financial Economics*, 11, 5–50.

Kane, E., 2000, "Incentives for Banking Megamergers: What Motives Might Regulators Infer from Event-Study Evidence?," *Journal of Money Credit and Banking*, 32, 671–701.

Kim, E. H. and J. J. McConnell, 1977, "Corporate Merger and the Co-Insurance of Corporate Debt," *Journal of Finance*, 32, 349–365.

Lewellen, W. G., 1971, "A Pure Financial Rationale for the Conglomerate Merger," *Journal of Finance*, 27, 521–537.

Mitchell, C. and A. Raghavan, 1991, "Bank Bonds Show Powerful Price Gains on News Chemical, Manufacturers Hanover Plan to Merge," *Wall Street Journal*, July 16, C17.

Morgan, D. P. and K. J. Stiroh, 2001, "Market Discipline of Banks: The Asset Test," *Journal of Financial Services Research*, 20, 195–208.

Pilloff, S. J., 1996, "Performance Changes and Shareholder Wealth Creation Associated with Mergers of Publicly Traded Banking Institutions," *Journal of Money Credit and Banking*, 28, 294–310.

Pilloff, S. J. and A. Santomero, 1998, "The Value Effects of Bank Mergers and Acquisitions," In Y. Amihud and G. P. Miller (Eds.), *Bank Mergers and Acquisitions*, Kluwer Academic Publishers, Boston.

Prager, R. and T. Hannan, 1998, "Do Substantial Horizontal Mergers Generate Significant Price Effects? Evidence from the Banking Industry," *Journal of Industrial Economics*, 46, 433–452.

Stein, J., 1997, "Internal Capital Markets and the Competition for Corporate Resources," *Journal of Finance*, 52, 111–134.

Warga, A. and I. Welch, 1993, "Bondholder Losses in Leveraged Buyouts," *Review of Financial Studies*, 6, 959–982.

White, H., 1980, "A Heteroskedasticity-Consistent Covariance Matrix Estimator and a Direct Test for Heteroskedasticity," *Econometrica*, 48, 817–838.

Chapter 11

DO TENDER OFFERS CREATE VALUE? NEW METHODS AND EVIDENCE[*]

SANJAI BHAGAT

Leeds School of Business, University of Colorado, Boulder, Colorado, USA

MING DONG

Schulich School of Business, York University, Toronto, Ontario, Canada

DAVID HIRSHLEIFER

Fisher College of Business, Ohio State University, Columbus, Ohio, USA

ROBERT NOAH

Cambridge Finance Partners, LLC, Cambridge, Massachusetts, USA

Contents

* We thank the editor, Bill Schwert; two anonymous referees; Daniel Asquith, Randolph Beatty, Bernard Black, James Brickley, Henry Cao, Nick Crew, Wayne Ferson, Ruth Friedman, Stuart Gilson, David Heike, Steve Kaplan, Dick Kazarian, Seongyeon Lim, Andrew Lo, Uri Lowenstein, Gershon Mandelker, Wayne Marr, Derek Oler, Timothy Opler, Jeff Pontiff, Ed Rice, Matt Richardson, Scott Richardson, Richard Roll, Anil Shivdasani, René Stulz, Sheridan Titman, Garry Twite, Ivo Welch, J. Fred Weston, Jerold Zimmerman, and seminar participants at the University of Arizona, University of British Columbia, University of Chicago, Clemson University, University of Michigan, University of Missouri, University of Rochester, Southern Methodist University, University of Southern California, Tulane University, University of Washington at Seattle, Yale University, York University, the U.S. Federal Trade Commission, the Securities and Exchange Commission, the American Finance Association Meetings in Anaheim, California, the Econometric Society Meetings in Boston, Massachusetts, the Northern Finance Association meetings in Banff, Canada, and the Western Finance Association Meetings in Santa Monica, California for valuable comments.

This article originally appeared in the *Journal of Financial Economics*, Vol. pp. 76, 3–60 (2005).
Corporate Takeovers, Volume 1
Edited by B. Espen Eckbo
Copyright © 2005 Elsevier B.V. All rights reserved.
DOI: 10.1016/B978-0-12-38-1983-3.00011-3

Abstract

Conventional techniques of estimating takeover value improvements measure only a fraction of the total gain and include revelation about bidder stand-alone value. To address these biases, we develop the probability scaling method, which rescales announcement date returns; and the intervention method, which uses returns at intervening events. Perceived value improvements are larger than traditional methods indicate. We cannot reject the hypothesis that bidders on average pay fair prices. Combined bidder-target stock returns are higher for hostile offers, lower for equity offers, and lower for diversifying offers. These effects reflect revelation about bidder stand-alone value, not differences in gains from combination.

Keywords

tender offers, value improvements, truncation dilemma, revelation bias, agency problems

JEL classification: G12, G34

1. Introduction

This paper uses stock price data to estimate value improvements from takeovers, when value improvements are defined as changes in the discounted value of bidder and target cash flows brought about by the combination. Attempts to estimate the value effects of takeovers face two challenges. The first is the truncation dilemma. Given that not all takeover bids succeed, a short event window that extends only a few days past the bid announcement date estimates only a fraction of the value effects that would be brought about by a successful transaction. A long window that extends through successful completion of the transaction can capture the market's assessment of the full effect of takeover on value. However, this comes at the cost of introducing much greater noise and return benchmark errors.

The second challenge, the revelation bias, is that the bidder's return on the announcement date reflects not just news about the value to be derived from combination, but also news about the stand-alone value of the bidder. For example, firms sometimes deliberately time the announcement of takeover bids to be simultaneous with unrelated announcements.[1] More important, the very fact that a firm makes a bid will usually convey information to investors about the bidder's stand-alone value.

To address these issues, we estimate the stock market's perception of value improvements from tender offers using both conventional abnormal stock returns at the time of the initial bid and two new approaches. In our comprehensive 1962–2001 sample, all approaches imply substantial value improvements. Furthermore, the new methods imply estimates of shareholder value improvement that are much larger than those implied by traditional methods.

The first method, the probability scaling method (PSM), uses returns associated with the announcement of the initial bid. As in most past studies, the return cumulation window extends only a short time after the event. PSM then adjusts returns derived from this short window upward to reflect the probability that the offer will fail. It addresses the truncation dilemma by exploiting ex post information about frequency of success to capture the missing slice of the gains from takeover.

The second approach, the intervention method (IM), extracts information about value improvement from the stock returns associated with intervening events such as the announcement of a competing bid. Like PSM, IM addresses the truncation dilemma through appropriate scaling of returns. At the same time, IM also addresses the revelation bias, which taints estimates of the gain to takeover in past market and

---

[1] The *Wall Street Journal* reported: "It's Wall Street's version of 'Wag the Dog.' Over the past week, both Mattel and Coca-Cola have announced acquisitions on the same day they also issued warnings about disappointing earnings. ... No one is suggesting that either company unveiled its acquisition solely to divert attention from its problems. ... But it is also clear that the acquisitions, like the [Iraq] bombings, helped shift attention away from other less favorable developments." The article gives other examples as well (Wall Street Journal, 1998, p. C1).

accounting studies. A disadvantage of IM is that it relies heavily on the subsample in which an intervening event occurs such as arrival of a competing bid.

The main contributions of this paper are the development of the probability scaling and the IMs, and the use of these methods both to estimate value improvements from tender offers and to explore what economic factors affect takeover gains and revelation effects. We find that value improvements from tender offers are on average perceived by investors to be positive and substantially larger than estimates from previous studies. Conventional combined abnormal returns and the PSM estimate are positive in 71% of the sample (694 out of 976 transactions). In the competing bid subsample, the IM estimate is positive in over 93% of the sample (132 out of 141 competing bid transactions). In both the general and the competing bid samples, the conclusion that takeover improvements are on average positive and substantial is robust with respect to several alternative model specifications and plausible variations in the estimated parameters, and it holds in all subperiods. Using traditional event-period weighted-average returns as in Bradley et al. (1988), hereafter BDK-88, yields a combined mean (median) improvement of 5.3% (3.7%) of combined bidder-target value. PSM estimated value improvements tend to be considerably larger, a mean of 7.3% (median 4.6%) of combined value.

Estimated value improvements are particularly large in the competing bid subsample. The average estimated IM improvement in this sample is approximately 13.1% (12.4%) of combined bidder and target value. Using PSM, the average improvement is 14.7% (9.7%). Again these numbers are greater than the estimates of 9.0% (7.6%) using conventional combined abnormal returns in the competing bid subsample.[2]

Using a traditional announcement period estimation method, we find that bidders on average pay a significantly higher premium for the shares they purchase in the offer than the improvement in target share value under bidder control. In contrast, using both of the new methods developed here, we cannot reject the null hypothesis that the payment is on average fair.

Furthermore, our methods can disentangle more specifically than the traditional method how economic forces affect the takeover market. We find that friendly offers, equity offers, and diversifying offers are associated with lower combined bidder-target stock returns. A conventional interpretation would be that the gains from combination are smaller for firms involved with these types of transactions. However, our new methods indicate that these effects reflect differences in revelation about stand-alone value, not differences in the gains from combination.

---

[2] Another reason that the traditional method can understate the true value improvement is that stock prices of acquirers could already reflect an expectation that acquirers will undertake new projects including mergers. For example, an acquisition could be part of a merger program, and market reaction to a takeover bid only captures the surprise relative to expectations (Schipper and Thompson, 1983). However, our probability scaling method shows that the portion of the value improvement that investors learn about at takeover announcement date is substantially underestimated by traditional methods.

For example, cash offers on average are associated with higher bidder, target, and combined abnormal returns than equity or mixed-payment offers. In contrast, based on the IM, cash offers do not create higher value improvements than mixed or equity offers. These findings indicate that the apparent superiority of cash offers in creating shareholder value is an illusory consequence of a more negative revelation effect for the bidder for equity or mixed offers than for cash offers. This suggests an adverse selection in the use of equity as a medium of exchange in takeovers. Also, our finding does not support the hypothesis that the use of cash reveals to investors a general propensity for the bidder's management to waste cash on bad projects.

Similarly, we find that the revelation effect is more favorable for hostile than for friendly offers. On average the market revises upward (downward) its stand-alone valuation of bidders that make hostile (friendly) bids. (The phrase "stand-alone" is used here to mean "not combined with the current target." It does not preclude the possibility that the market perceives bidder value as potentially coming from combination with a different target.) This is consistent with investors interpreting hostile bids as indicating that the bidder has strong cash flow prospects as a stand-alone entity or better alignment of managers' interests with shareholders' interests in the bidder firm or both.

Furthermore, conventional combined returns, PSM value improvements, and bidder returns tend to be lower in diversifying acquisitions. The finding of lower bidder returns indicates that the conclusions of Morck et al. (1990) continue to apply in a data set that includes the turn of the millennium. In sharp contrast, IM estimates of value improvements are similar across these categories. The relative superiority of same-industry acquisitions with PSM (which does not filter out revelation effects) compared with IM (which does) indicates that same-industry acquisitions are associated with more favorable revelation about the bidder than cross-industry acquisitions.

This finding suggests that investors perceive diversifying acquisitions as indicating poor investment opportunities within the bidder's own industry or that management is prone to more severe agency problems. It further suggests that updating about the quality of the bidder's investment opportunities or management, not about the advantages of the combination, leads to lower returns in diversifying transactions.

We also identify some factors that do affect the gains from combination, not just revelation about stand-alone value. For example, using all three approaches, acquisition of a smaller target by a large bidder on average creates a smaller value improvement, measured as a fraction of combined value, than combinations of similar-size firms. But measured relative to the value of the target, the mean estimated improvement is larger for such transactions. These findings are consistent with the importance of both synergies and target-specific improvements such as removal of bad management. Although the business press has raised concerns about combinations of similar-size firms, these two results do not give any clear indication that bidder-target parity in tender offers is a bad thing.

Furthermore, bidder announcement period returns and total value improvements are negatively related to bidder Tobin's Q. In the earlier samples of Lang et al. (1989) and Servaes (1991), returns to bidder and targets were higher when high Q bidders acquired low Q targets. Our finding is consistent with the finding of Dong et al. (2003) that bidders with low book equity/market equity ratios (which tend to be negatively correlated with Q) on average have more negative announcement period returns. Target announcement period returns are negatively related to target Q, consistent with previous literature.

In summary, the methods offered here affect several conclusions about tender offers. In addition to the quantitative conclusion that tender offers produce greater gains than previously estimated, our approach offers conclusions that contrast with those of conventional methods about how means of payment is related to value improvements; what offer hostility indicates about bidder agency problems; whether diversifying acquisitions harm value or just reveal adverse information about stand-alone firm prospects; and whether bidders pay too much. In other words, these methods affect qualitative as well as quantitative inferences about tender offers.

Section 2 develops an empirical measure of value improvements. Section 3 describes the tender offer data. Value improvement estimates of tender offers are presented in Section 4. Section 5 concludes.

2. Measurement of takeover value improvement

Before developing our empirical measure of value improvements, we note the motivation for our methods, and formulate the hypotheses.

2.1. Motivation

A large previous literature uses stock return data to estimate shareholder gains from takeovers, usually in the form of separate estimates of bidder or target gains. Such estimates reflect the gain from combination and also depend on how this surplus is divided between bidder and target.[3] To estimate the total gains from combination, BDK-88 examine a market value-weighted average of abnormal returns of paired bidders and targets in successful takeovers. They examine an event window that extends to 5 days after the initial announcement of the ultimately successful bid. Because substantial uncertainty remains about ultimate success of the bid, the short event window provides an estimate of only a fraction of the market's assessment of the total value gains from takeover. BDK-88 find that the market value-weighted average of bidder and target abnormal returns for successful takeovers during the period 1962–1984 is positive and stable over this period, with an average increase of 7.4% of combined bidder/target market value. This is their estimate of magnitude of synergistic gains from takeover.

Ideally, as recognized by BDK-88, an event window that extends from (well before) the initial announcement through final successful resolution should be used to capture

---

[3] Numerous studies find significant and large positive average abnormal returns for target shareholders. Jensen and Ruback (1983), Jarrell et al. (1988), and Schwert (1996) review this evidence. In contrast, abnormal returns or takeover bidders tend to average fairly close to zero.

the full value effects of takeover. Takeover contests often take as long as three to 6 months between first announcement and final resolution. Such long periods introduce a great deal of noise arising from random price movements and errors owing to mis-estimation of benchmark returns. Long periods also raise issues of the correct way to compound.[4] Empirically, Andrade et al. (2001, p. 110) report a slightly higher average return for the $[-20,$ close] announcement window than using a $[-1, +1]$ window. However, the return estimate becomes noisy as the window extends to the resolution of the takeover bid (with an average window length of 142 days), and this estimate cannot be reliably distinguished from zero.

A short postannouncement window minimizes such noise and benchmark error, because significant security-specific news arrives on a single day, whereas (if only factor risk is priced) the risk premium for a single day is negligible. However, a short window estimates only a fraction of the full value effect of a successful transaction.[5] This is the truncation dilemma.

Several authors have emphasized a second problem for estimating the value effects of takeovers (Bradley et al., 1983; Jensen and Ruback, 1983; Jovanovic and Brag-uinsky, 2002; Roll, 1986). The announcement of an offer and its form reveal bidder information not just about the gain from combination, but also about the bidder's stand-alone value. As a result, takeover-related returns do not provide a pure measure of the gain to shareholders from takeover.

For example, the occurrence of a bid could convey the good news that a bidder expects to have high cash flows, the bad news that the bidder has poor internal investment opportunities, or the bad news that the bidder's management has empire-building propensities.[6] Similarly, the premium offered can convey good or bad news about the bidder's stand-alone prospects. Also, the "lemons problem" with equity issuance implies that the use of equity as a means of payment will convey bad news about the bidder's assets in place, and that the use of cash will convey good news.[7] In contrast, free cash flow and agency problems suggest that the announcement of a

---

[4] The market model is biased to the extent that bids occur after the bidder has experienced abnormally good times (Franks et al., 1991). Barber and Lyon (1997) and Kothari and Warner (1997) study problems of misspecification associated with the use of long-horizon returns and the effectiveness of alternative benchmarks.

[5] A familiar problem, which is not our primary focus, is that a short preevent window omits the effects of probability revisions associated with information leaking out prior to the official public announcement date. Furthermore, we estimate market perceptions of value improvements. These perceptions are sometimes incorrect; see, for example, the model of Shleifer and Vishny (2003), tests of market misvaluation based upon postacquisition long-run stock returns (Andrade et al., 2001; Hou et al., 2000; Loughran and Vijh, 1997; Mitchell and Stafford, 2000; Moeller et al., 2004a,b; Rau and Vermaelen, 1998), and through contemporaneous measures (Dong et al., 2003).

[6] See, for example, Jovanovic and Braguinsky (2002). The Wall Street Journal (1998, p. C1) describes the viewpoint of analysts that "[e]xecutives who see slowing growth often look outside their companies for acquisition opportunities."

[7] See Myers and Majluf (1984), Hansen (1987), Fishman (1989), and Eckbo et al. (1990), as well as the evidence of Travlos (1987) and Franks et al. (1991).

cash bid could reveal that the firm has excess cash flow relative to profitable internal investment needs and that management is likely to waste that cash on poor investments.

It follows that the market value-weighted average of bidder and target equity returns provides a biased estimate of the long-run total equity holder gain from takeover. We term the error in these estimates arising from managers' information about stand-alone value the revelation bias.

Revelation effects should be distinguished from signaling, the special case in which the bidder modifies his acquisition decision for the purpose of influencing short-term market perceptions. In general bidder actions will convey information to the market, regardless of whether the bidder seeks to alter market beliefs. Our approach can accommodate, but does not require, that signaling motives be an important consideration in the decision of whether to make an acquisition. Even if signaling motives are not relevant, the decision to make an offer will in general reveal information possessed by the bidder.[8]

This paper describes empirically abnormal stock returns associated with announcement of tender offers in a sample that extends to the turn of the millennium, and offers new methods of estimating value improvements from takeover which address the truncation dilemma and the revelation bias in stock market studies.[9] By controlling for these biases, our new methods imply much larger value effects than traditional techniques suggest, and imply different conclusions about the sources of takeover value improvements. These methods could be useful in other contexts as well for estimating the full value effects of corporate events and for disentangling revelation effects from value effects of discretionary corporate actions.

Both new approaches address the truncation dilemma. Suppose, for example, that the event window is truncated 5 days after announcement. Then the market price at the endpoint still reflects substantial uncertainty on the part of investors about ultimate success of the offer or of any follow-up offer. The problem the financial economist faces is to infer the total value improvement effect from this fragment of it, much as an anthropologist infers the height of a hominid based on a fossilized leg bone.

---

[8] An alternative to stock market evidence is to examine accounting or other performance measures following completed transactions. Several studies have drawn different conclusions about whether takeovers on average increase or decrease combined fundamental value (e.g., Bhagat et al., 1990; Healy et al., 1992; Kaplan and Weisbach, 1991; Mueller, 1985). Although such studies are informative, they usually do not quantify the total discounted value effect of takeovers. More important, these studies are potentially subject to problems of noise, benchmark error, and revelation bias analogous to those of stock market-based studies. For example, in regard to revelation bias, an offer could be associated with future accounting improvements, which would have occurred even without a takeover.

[9] Andrade et al. (2001) and Moeller et al. (2004a,b) have described several aspects of the returns to takeovers including recent years. Andrade et al. (2001) draw a similar overall conclusion to ours, that takeovers have on average been perceived as value increasing. Moeller et al. (2004a,b) also find positive mean returns, but emphasize the negative dollar returns of large bidders during the 1998–2001 period.

The PSM adjusts returns for the possibility that the transaction is not completed. Ex post data are used to estimate the probability, given that a bid has taken place, that the bidder ultimately succeeds in acquiring the target, and the probability that some other bidder ultimately takes over the target. Based on these probabilities, the announcement period returns of bidder and target are magnified to measure the total perceived value effect of a completed transaction. (For an independent development of a related approach, see Luo (2003). His study examines whether managers take into account stock price reactions to the initial offer in deciding whether to complete the transaction.)

The IM addresses both the revelation bias and the truncation dilemma by focusing on the returns at the time of a different event, the arrival of a competing bid. Because the arrival of a second bidder has a large effect on the probability of the initial bidder's success, the abnormal return observed for the initial bidder at this event implicitly reflects the size of the potential takeover value improvement. (The term "value improvement" in this paper refers to joint bidder and target shareholder gains. Owing to possible wealth redistributions among other stakeholders such as employees and customers, this need not coincide with value to society as a whole.) Furthermore, this event does not occur at the discretion of the initial bidder; it is an external intervention. This is crucial, because, as such, the arrival of a competing bid reveals little or nothing about the stand-alone value of the initial bidder. The IM calculates the value improvement implicit in the observed initial bidder return when a competing bid intervenes.

There are two key inputs to this calculation. The first is the amount by which the arrival of a competing bid reduces the probability that the first bidder succeeds in acquiring the target. The second is the amount that the arrival of a competing bid increases the expected price that the first bidder would pay should it win the contest. (A third relevant input, the initial shareholding of the first bidder in the target, turns out to be relatively unimportant.) Each of these quantities can be estimated from ex post data. Holding constant these parameters, the abnormal return at the time of arrival of a competing bid is a decreasing function of the size of the takeover improvement, that is, it is worse to lose a big improvement than a small one. Inverting this relationship, the size of the takeover improvement can be inferred from the observed abnormal return. A numerical illustration is provided in Appendix A.

Intuitively, the challenge for estimating value improvements is that two very different possibilities are consistent with a negative move in the first bidder's stock price upon the arrival of a competing bid. First, the acquisition could increase the first bidder's value, and arrival of the second bid conveys the bad news that this value is less likely to be realized by the first bidder. Second, the acquisition could decrease the first bidder's value, but the arrival of the second bidder conveys the bad news that the first bidder will on average pay a higher premium in the event that he succeeds. To disentangle these effects, we model the relation between these parameters and stock prices.

The methods that we use require some simplifying assumptions. Conventional methods make even stronger assumptions, though these assumptions are not explicit.

For example, to interpret returns as value improvements using conventional weighted average event-date returns implicitly assumes that a short window can capture the whole value effect, and that there is no revelation bias. In this respect our approach has an important virtue relative to the conventional approach: It makes assumptions explicit. Doing so allows us to quantify explicitly the robustness of the conclusions to relaxing different simplifying assumptions.

IM estimates depend on how competition affects the likelihood of offer success and bid premiums. Several previous papers examine related issues. Betton and Eckbo (2000) estimate outcome probabilities in multiple bid tender offers as a function of offer premium, toehold, and the method of payment. An extensive theoretical literature considers the role of competing bidders in takeovers (Bulow et al., 1999; Eckbo et al., 1990; Fishman 1988, 1989; Ravid and Spiegel, 1999).

Also, some previous papers have examined stock price reactions to events that interfere with takeover completion. These have focused either on testing for collusion and the effects of antitrust enforcement or on documenting the abnormal returns associated with the interfering event. Eckbo (1983) finds negative abnormal stock returns in merger bidders and targets on the announcement of an antitrust complaint. Bradley et al. (1983) find a negative stock price reaction for a bidder upon announcement of a competing bid. Eckbo (1992) analyzes cross-sectional determinants of the market response to government antitrust challenges of merger bids. He does not find that such policies deter collusive takeovers. BDK-88 find that targets receive a greater share of the value gains since the enactment of federal and state takeover legislation, and that offers with competing bids are associated with a more negative bidder abnormal return. Hietala et al. (2003) estimate takeover gains in a case study of competition in the 1994 acquisition of Paramount by Viacom. In contrast with these papers, our focus here in developing the IM is on extracting the size of value improvements from stock price reactions in a large sample of tender offers.

2.2. Hypotheses

The primary issue to be examined is whether takeovers on average increase the joint value of the bidder and target firms. According to the Roll's (1986) hubris hypothesis, no value improvement results from takeover; takeovers occur because of positive valuation errors by bidding managers. Agency problems can also lead bidding managers to pay more for targets than they are worth (e.g., empire building and misuse of free cash). We therefore call the hypothesis of zero value improvement the strong agency/hubris hypothesis. If the strong agency/hubris hypothesis obtains, the expected value of the target to the bidder is the pretakeover market price of the target. If bidding costs are neglected, then the bidder makes negative profits equal in magnitude to the total premium paid for the purchased shares.

Because tender offers are frequently for less than 100% of outstanding shares, estimated bidder profits will depend on the assumptions made about the price paid for remaining shares given that control is obtained. For two reasons, the most natural assumption is that the same price is paid for holdouts as for the shares purchased in the tender offer.[10] First, fair-price antitakeover amendments require paying at least this much to minority shareholders. Second, even if a successful bidder is able to expropriate minority shareholders, such dilution opportunities should be fully reflected in the initial bid price, so that holdout shareholders on average receive the same price as tendering shareholders (Grossman and Hart, 1980).

Let α refer to the fraction of the target's shares owned by the first bidder prior to the bid. Let V_0^T be the nontakeover value of the target. Let V^C be the combined posttakeover value of the first bidder and the target if the first bidder succeeds in acquiring the target, when this value is inclusive of any nonequity payments to shareholders as a result of the offer. Let the nontakeover value of the bidder be denoted V_0^B. Let V^I be the value improvement from takeover. Then

$$V^I \equiv V^C - V_0^B - V_0^T(1 - \alpha). \tag{1}$$

The first term on the right-hand side is the total discounted value of cash flows going to bidder and target shareholders if the combination occurs. The last two terms subtract the total value if there is no takeover. This is the sum of the values of the bidder and the target less the value of the bidder's stake in the target (which would otherwise be double-counted).

Letting a bar denote an expected value, the strong/agency hubris hypothesis asserts that the average value improvement is zero, that is,

$$\bar{V}^I(\theta) = 0, \tag{2}$$

where θ is the market's information set.

Some theoretical models predict that in the absence of dilution of minority shareholders, bidders will not on average profit on shares purchased in the offer (Grossman and Hart, 1980; Hirshleifer and Titman, 1990; Shleifer and Vishny, 1986). Even if a successful bidder loses money on these shares, he could still profit from the acquisition by increasing the value of the shares accumulated prior to the offer (Shleifer and Vishny, 1986). The prediction that the bidder profits on shares purchased in the tender offer is termed the underpayment hypothesis, as opposed to the overpayment hypothesis. The overpayment (underpayment) hypothesis implies that the bid price on average is greater (less) than the value of the target shares to the bidder. Let $(1 - \alpha)$ B be the total amount ultimately paid (in the form of either cash or securities) by a successful first bidder for shares purchased in or subsequent to the tender offer. For convenient comparison, this definition scales B to be the notional price that would be paid if the bidder began with zero toehold and proceeded to purchase 100% of the firm.

---

[10] Comment and Jarrell (1987) present evidence consistent with this assumption. More recently, it is not unusual for holdout investors to receive a package of securities with face value equal to the cash offer to initially tendering investors.

The amount paid by the bidder for the target (the price) includes the amount of cash paid to target shareholders and the market value of any security claims upon the combined firm given to target shareholders. The overpayment and underpayment hypotheses can then be expressed as

$$(1 - \alpha)(\bar{B} - V_0^T) \gtrless \bar{V}^I, \tag{3}$$

where $\bar{B}$ denotes the expected value of the amount the initial bidder pays should he succeed. Dividing both sides by $V_0^C \equiv (1 - \alpha)V_0^T + V_0^B$ gives

$$(1 - \alpha)\left(\frac{\bar{B}}{V_0^T} - 1\right)\left(\frac{V_0^T}{V_0^C}\right) \gtrless \frac{\bar{V}^I}{V_0^C}. \tag{4}$$

This condition describes whether the bid premium exceeds the value improvement, both measured relative to the initial combined bidder and target value.

2.3. The probability scaling method of estimating value changes

Let θ_0 be all public information known prior to the first bid. Let θ_1 be all public information known just after the first bid. Let θ_2 refer to information known just prior to the arrival of a competing bid. Let θ_3 also contain the information conveyed by the competing bid. Let dates $t = 0, 1, 2$, and 3 refer to dates at which $\theta = \theta_0, \theta_1, \theta_2$, and θ_3, respectively. Subscripts of 0, 1, 2, and 3 will denote expectations formed conditional on these information sets.

Let $\bar{V}^I$ be the posttakeover improvement in combined value, as described in Equation (1), conditional on the first bidder succeeding. Let ϕ_t denote the probability of success of the first bidder in acquiring the target given θ_t (ϕ_0 is the probability of a first bidder appearing and succeeding). Let $\bar{B}_t$ be the expected price paid by the first bidder should he win as assessed at date t, let ϕ_t^L be the probability that a first bid occurs and a later bidder subsequently wins, and let $\bar{B}_t^L$ be the expected price paid by such a winning bidder as foreseen at date t. A "1" subscript to variables indicates expected values formed after the arrival of the initial bid.

The conventional approach to estimating value improvements reflects the probabilities of acquisition by current or later bidders, ϕ_0 and ϕ_0^L, but does not estimate the probabilities. To provide meaning to this, some interpretation is needed. One possible interpretation that allows the conventional approach to be viewed as a value improvement is that the potential value improvements that would be brought about by the two potential bidders are equal, and that the probability that acquisition will be consummated by one or the other bidder is one. The latter assumption is strong and clearly counterfactual. In the PSM, we will relax this assumption.

Let z be the sum of the stand-alone values of the first bidder and the target. As is implicit in the conventional approach, we assume that the average size of the improvement brought about by combination of a target with either the initial bidder or a later one is equal. Then the combined value of the first bidder and the target at date 0 is

$$V_0^C = z + \phi^0 \bar{V}^I, \tag{5}$$

where $\phi^0 \equiv \phi_0 + \phi_0^L$ is the market's assessment of the probability that the target is acquired by a potential bidder in the future. For simplicity, in this analysis we consider date 0 to be far enough in advance of the initial bid announcement that little market anticipation of the offer exists. Thus, the ex ante probabilities that a bidder appears and wins (ϕ_0 and ϕ_0^L) are close to zero. This implies that the prior expected target payoff is just the stand-alone value V_0^T, and the prior expected bidder payoff is just the stand-alone value V_0^B. As documented by Palepu (1986), takeovers are low probability events that are hard to predict far in advance. More generally, the approach can be modified to allow for partial anticipation of offers, but given Palepu's evidence it is unlikely that doing so would affect the results substantially.

After the arrival of the initial bid, the market assigns a value $\phi_1 + \phi_1^L$ to the probability that the target is acquired by a bidder. Therefore, the combined value of the first bidder and the target becomes

$$V_1^C = z + (\phi_1 + \phi_1^L)\bar{V}^I. \tag{6}$$

It follows that the combined fractional market value improvement in the bidder and target is

$$R_1^C \equiv \frac{V_1^C - V_0^C}{V_0^C} = \frac{(\phi_1 + \phi_1^L)\bar{V}^I}{V_0^C}, \tag{7}$$

so normalizing the value improvement by combined value,

$$\frac{\bar{V}^I}{V_0^C} = \frac{R_1^C}{\phi_1 + \phi_1^L}. \tag{8}$$

This formula provides a simple implementation of the PSM. We refer to the value improvement on the left-hand side estimated from this PSM formula as the probability-adjusted improvement ratio, or IR^{PSM}.

2.4. The intervention method of estimating value changes

We now describe the IM for estimating value improvements. The IM addresses the revelation bias as well as the truncation dilemma. However, it is based on a smaller subsample of returns (the competing bid subsample). The first step is to calculate the bidder's abnormal return between dates 1 and 3 in terms of the market's expectation of the value improvement $\bar{V}^I(\theta_t)$ at these dates. Then (using empirical estimates of unconditional and conditional probabilities of success and expected premiums, abnormal returns, and other parameters) we invert the relationship to infer $\bar{V}^I(\theta_t)$.

For expositional simplicity, the model examines raw returns. For standard reasons, in implementing the model empirically abnormal returns are used.

Consider the arrival of the competing bid at date 3. Let the market's assessment of the component of bidder's value not derived from the takeover be y. y will not equal the preoffer value of the bidder as assessed by the market if the initial offer conveyed information about the bidder. We assume that the arrival of a competing bid is uninformative about the stand-alone value of the first bidder, so that y is the same at dates 1, 2, and 3 (before and after the arrival of the competing bid). Let $R_3 \equiv (P_3 - P_1)/P_1$ be the date 3 return associated with information θ_3, where P_1 is the bidder's stock price just after the initial bid, and P_3 is the price based on θ_3 after a competing bid arrives. So,

$$P_3 = P_1(1 + R_3). \tag{9}$$

Let $\bar{V}^{\mathrm{I}}(\theta_1), \bar{V}^{\mathrm{I}}(\theta_3), \bar{B}(\theta_1)$, and $\bar{B}(\theta_3)$ be abbreviated as $\bar{V}_1^{\mathrm{I}}, \bar{V}_3^{\mathrm{I}}, \bar{B}_1$, and $\bar{B}_3$, respectively. To relate $\bar{V}(\theta)$ to the observables P_3 and P_1, note that

$$P_1 = y + \bar{\pi}_1 \quad \text{and} \quad P_3 = y + \bar{\pi}_3, \tag{10}$$

where $\bar{\pi}_t$ is the bidder's expected profit from takeover conditional on information θ_t:

$$\bar{\pi}_1 = \phi_1 \left[\alpha \bar{V}_1^{\mathrm{I}} + (1 - \alpha)(\bar{V}_1^{\mathrm{I}} + V_0^{\mathrm{T}} - \bar{B}_1) \right] \quad \text{and}$$
$$\bar{\pi}_3 = \phi_3 \left[\alpha \bar{V}_3^{\mathrm{I}} + (1 - \alpha)(\bar{V}_3^{\mathrm{I}} + V_0^{\mathrm{T}} - \bar{B}_3) \right]. \tag{11}$$

We assume that the arrival of the competing bid at date 3 does not provide any information about the value improvement that the first bidder can effect through takeover.[11] Hence, $\bar{V}_3^{\mathrm{I}} = \bar{V}_1^{\mathrm{I}} = \bar{V}^{\mathrm{I}}$. The robustness of the results with respect to this assumption is analyzed in Section 4.5.[12] The unobservable y can be eliminated from Equation (10), and the result combined with Equation (11), giving

$$\bar{V}^{\mathrm{I}} = \frac{P_3 - P_1}{\phi_3 - \phi_1} - (1 - \alpha)V_0^{\mathrm{T}} + \frac{(1 - \alpha)(\phi_3 \bar{B}_3 - \phi_1 \bar{B}_1)}{\phi_3 - \phi_1}. \tag{12}$$

---

[11] This would obtain under the strong agency/hubris hypotheses. More generally, the arrival of either an initial bid or competing bid could reveal information about target value. However, the evidence regarding the information conveyed by an initial bid is mixed. Bradley et al. (1983) find that average cumulative abnormal returns of targets are approximately zero among targets of failed offers that are not later acquired. It is thus possible that no permanent informational revaluation is associated with the initial bid.

[12] This assumption is consistent with private information possessed by the second bidder. This could be information about a private component of its valuation of the target (e.g., a synergy unique to the second bidder). The second bidder can also possess information superior to that of investors about common value components (e.g., gains from remedying target management failure), so long as investors do not perceive the second bidder's information as adding to that of the first bidder.

Dividing both sides of Equation (12) by V_0^C gives

$$\frac{\bar{V}^{\mathrm{I}}}{V_0^C} = \frac{R_3\left(P_1/V_0^C\right)}{\phi_3 - \phi_1} + (1-\alpha)\left[\lambda\left(\frac{\bar{B}_1}{V_0^T}\right) + (1-\lambda)\left(\frac{\bar{B}_3}{V_0^T}\right) - 1\right]\left(\frac{V_0^T}{V_0^C}\right), \tag{13}$$

where

$$\lambda \equiv \frac{\phi_1}{\phi_1 - \phi_3}. \tag{14}$$

We call the quantity on the left-hand side of Equation (13) the IM improvement ratio, or $\mathrm{IR}^{\mathrm{IM}}$. It is the market's estimate of the percentage improvement in the combined value of the bidder and target. In principle, every parameter in Equation (13) can be given an i superscript to denote the ith takeover contest. However, we begin by developing the method in its most basic form by estimating certain parameters as sample means under the assumption that they are the same across contests. Under this approach, the terms $\bar{B}_1/V_0^T$ and $\bar{B}_3/V_0^T$ can be estimated as

$$\frac{\bar{B}_1}{V_0^T} = \frac{1}{n_1}\sum_{i=1}^{n_1}\left[\frac{B^i}{\left(V_0^T\right)^i}\right] \tag{15}$$

and

$$\frac{\bar{B}_3}{V_0^T} = \frac{1}{n_3}\sum_{i=1}^{n_3}\left[\frac{B^i}{\left(V_0^T\right)^i}\right], \tag{16}$$

where n_1 is the number of initial offers and n_3 is the number of contests in which a competing bid occurs. Similarly, ϕ_1 and ϕ_3 can be estimated as the fraction of initial bids that succeed in the overall sample and in the subsample in which a competing bid occurs, respectively. A more sophisticated approach is to estimate separate transaction-specific expected bid premiums, by regression analysis, and probabilities of success using the logit model of Table 3 (see Section 4.2).

The model provides intuitively reasonable comparative statics. For example, assuming that the competing bid causes a drop in probability of success ($\phi_3 < \phi_1$), a more negative stock return on announcement of a competing bid indicates a larger value improvement. If the arrival of a competing bid implies that a much higher bid is needed to succeed, then for a given stock price reaction to the bid, the value improvement is smaller.

The quantities R_3, P_1/V_0^C, and α can be calculated directly and are specific to the takeover contest, to derive the value improvement ratio $\mathrm{IR}^{\mathrm{IM}}$. The IM makes no assumption whatsoever as to whether improvements are specific to changes in the bidder or the target or involve joint synergies.

The strong agency/hubris hypothesis implies that this ratio is zero. The overpayment and underpayment hypotheses are tested by comparing the average bid premium with the average estimated improvement given in Equation (4).

The conventional approach is based on a variety of strong assumptions. For example, the conventional approach assumes that combined bidder/target returns reflect only the gains from the specific transaction, instead of the possibility of other acquisitions should the given transaction fall through. The conventional approach also assumes that revelation effects of the initial bid are zero. Furthermore, a conventional short-window return approach in effect implicitly assumes that, immediately after the initial offer, investors believe the offer will succeed with certainty.

Our implementation of the IM also makes several simplifying assumptions, some of which could be closer to the truth than others. Where our approach differs from the conventional approach is in making the relevant assumptions explicit. Doing so has the virtue of allowing assumptions to be evaluated critically and suggesting how to test for robustness of the specification. The assumptions we apply are that the arrival of a competing bid does not cause investors to modify their assessment of the stand-alone value of the first bidder; that success of the initial bid is unrelated to the size of the value improvement; that a bidder whose offer fails is not able to locate and purchase another similar target at the same price; and that the unsuccessful initial bidder does not sell its toehold to a later bidder. Section 4.5 discusses and provides four modified versions of the model to evaluate quantitatively the effects of relaxing different assumptions. In brief, we find that the conclusion that value improvements are on average positive is highly robust.

The IM takes into account that an intervention sample (such as a competing bid sample) could have different characteristics from a general sample of bidders and targets. This is reflected in its allowing for firm-specific estimates of various input parameters. We control for ex ante differences between initial bidders that later are in competition with competing bids and initial bidders that are not using several bidder and offer characteristics. These include whether the offer is hostile, the bidder's initial toehold, the initial bid premium, and the relative size of the bidder and target (see Section 4). Nevertheless, if these controls are imperfect, a question remains of the extent to which value improvements in a competing bid subsample are representative of value improvements in a general sample.

3. Data

While the conventional method and the new methods developed here all apply to mergers as well as tender offers, in this paper we focus our empirical tests on a comprehensive sample of tender offers during 1962–2001. Our focus on tender offers is in the tradition of a large literature (e.g., Betton and Eckbo, 2000; Bhagat et al., 1990; Bradley et al., 1988; Lang et al., 1989).

The initial tender offer data set was constructed from two sources. The first consists of 559 tender offers that were announced during the period October 1958 through December 1984. "It contains almost every tender offer made in the 1958–1984 period where at least one firm (the target or a bidder) was listed on the NYSE or Amex ... at some time between July 1962 and December 1984."[13] This study investigates the wealth effects of a tender offer on both bidders and targets. We therefore restricted the sample to the 327 tender offers in which the bidder and target were both listed on the NYSE or Amex. Additional data-availability and data-consistency requirements reduced the sample size within the 1962–1984 subperiod to 292.[14]

The second data source consists of all tender offers from 1985 to 2001, obtained from the Securities Data Company (SDC) Mergers and Acquisitions database. There were 778 tender offers with both the target and the acquirer publicly traded on the NYSE, Amex, or Nasdaq. After excluding 33 offers, the resulting number of tender offers from 1985 to 2001 in our data set is 726.[15] All stock price data are obtained from CRSP and accounting data from Compustat.

To compile a history of the events that occur subsequent to a tender offer that might affect the probability of success of the bid, we manually searched the *Wall Street Journal Index* for the 292 target firms during 1962–1984 and used the online service *Dow Jones Interactive* to search the *Wall Street Journal* for information on the 726 target firms during 1985–2001, for a total of 1018. For these 1018 tender offers, we searched for the following information: litigation by the target firm or its shareholders, litigation by the bidding firm or its shareholders, and a second bidder.

Table 1 records the frequency of the 1018 attempted tender offers during 1962–2001 (see also Figure 1). Using the criterion of success considered by Bradley et al. (1983) that the bidder acquires at least 15% of target shares in the tender offer, 690 or 68% of these offers were successful. Out of these 1018 offers, 221 were considered hostile by the target management. A second bidder entered the contest in 147 tender offers. Target management litigated in 232 cases. Finally, 731 of these 1018 offers were all-cash offers.

Figure 2 describes the percentage of successful and unsuccessful offers, the percentage of offers that had at least two bidders, the percentage offers considered hostile by target management, and the percentage of all cash offers during different periods.

---

[13] The quotation is from the write-up for the data set compiled by Michael Bradley, Robert Comment, Anand Desai, Peter Dodd, and Richard Ruback. We thank these authors for providing us with their data.

[14] Twelve tender offers were announced prior to July 1962. The daily Center for Research in Security Prices (CRSP) tape does not contain returns prior to this date. Our verification of tender offer announcements and name changes led to some minor changes in the database.

[15] In eight tender offers, the acquirer made a subsequent tender offer for the target, and in these cases only the initial tender offers were included. We also excluded 11 tender offers in which the bidder announced multiple takeovers at the same time. For both target and acquirer, the SDC firm names and Committee on Uniform Securities Identification Procedures (CUSIP) numbers were matched with firms in the CRSP database. For 33 of the tender offers, CRSP data were not available either because of the required time period (e.g., a firm was delisted prior to the tender offer event) or the failure to match the firm reported by SDC with a firm in the CRSP database.

Table 1

Number of attempted offers, successful offers, offers that involved two or more bidders, offers that were considered as hostile by target management, and offers in which the target litigated against the acquisition attempt

Sample contains tender offers in which both bidder and target were listed on the NYSE, Amex, or Nasdaq during 1962–2001.

Year	Number of attempted tender offers	Number of successful offers (when the bidder acquired at least 15% of target shares)	Number of attempted offers that had at least two bidders	Number of attempted offers considered hostile by target management	Number of attempted offers in which the target litigated	Number of all cash offers
1962	1	0	0	0	0	1
1963	9	5	1	2	0	9
1964	4	3	0	1	0	4
1965	11	9	1	2	1	10
1966	13	7	2	4	1	12
1967	18	8	11	8	4	16
1968	31	20	13	9	8	16
1969	10	6	3	1	2	4
1970	8	6	0	2	3	6
1971	2	2	0	0	0	1
1972	8	5	0	1	2	6
1973	17	6	2	4	5	16
1974	22	9	5	6	5	21
1975	12	5	3	3	9	11
1976	19	8	3	6	6	17
1977	18	8	5	3	4	18
1978	21	6	5	6	7	14
1979	19	8	4	11	9	16
1980	4	2	2	2	1	4
1981	13	5	9	10	8	3
1982	13	12	0	2	3	2
1983	10	9	2	4	2	0
1984	9	8	1	2	0	1
1985	40	19	7	12	15	29
1986	59	38	8	14	15	51
1987	42	32	5	9	12	38
1988	73	43	17	23	29	61
1989	42	24	6	11	15	31
1990	20	12	1	1	5	15
1991	12	8	2	1	8	3
1992	10	8	0	1	3	7
1993	17	13	2	2	6	11
1994	34	25	4	9	10	30
1995	42	36	3	12	13	30
1996	46	41	2	6	6	30
1997	65	46	8	13	5	38
1998	56	46	2	6	5	42

(*Continued*)

Table 1 (*Continued*)

Year	Number of attempted tender offers	Number of successful offers (when the bidder acquired at least 15% of target shares)	Number of attempted offers that had at least two bidders	Number of attempted offers considered hostile by target management	Number of attempted offers in which the target litigated	Number of all cash offers
1999	74	65	4	6	4	53
2000	61	51	1	5	1	37
2001	33	26	3	1	0	17
1962–2001	1018	690	147	221	232	731

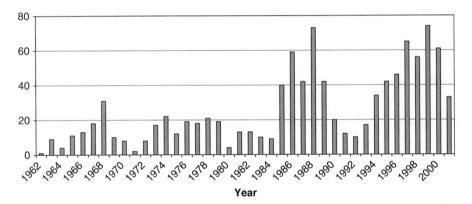

Fig. 1. Number of attempted tender offers. Sample includes 1018 tender offers in which both bidder and target were listed on the NYSE, Amex, or Nasdaq during 1962–2001.

3.1. Returns to bidders and targets

Table 2 summarizes the returns to bidder and target shareholders (with both companies listed on NYSE, Amex, or Nasdaq) during 1962–2001. Let the target and bidder returns be denoted R^{T} and R^{B}, respectively, and let

$$\omega \equiv \frac{(1 - \alpha)V_0^{\mathrm{T}}}{V_0^{\mathrm{C}}}. \tag{17}$$

Then CIBR, the combined initial bid return, is a weighted average of bidder and target abnormal returns,

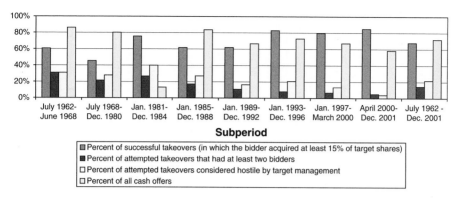

Subperiod

☐ Percent of successful takeovers (in which the bidder acquired at least 15% of target shares)
■ Percent of attempted takeovers that had at least two bidders
☐ Percent of attempted takeovers considered hostile by target management
☐ Percent of all cash offers

Fig. 2. Sample description. Sample contains 1018 tender offers in which both bidder and target were listed on the NYSE, Amex, or Nasdaq during 1962–2001.

$$\mathrm{CIBR} = \omega R^{\mathrm{T}} + (1 - \omega)R^{\mathrm{B}}. \tag{18}$$

This is based on a conventional short postannouncement window returns (day −5 to +5). We define the dollar return for the target as its market value 6 days before the first bid multiplied by the target cumulative abnormal return (CAR); similarly for the bidder and combined dollar returns. Statistical significance is measured using the parametric Z-test as described by Dodd and Warner (1983) and the nonparametric Fisher sign test.

During this 40-year period, the average return to bidding shareholders has been a statistically insignificant 0.18%. The bidder median dollar return is an economically insignificant −$1.2 million. During this same 40-year period, target shareholders enjoyed a statistically and economically significant average return of 30.0% and median dollar return of $41.2 million.

We describe returns to targets and bidders over various subperiods in Table 2 and Figures 3 and 4. The first three subperiods are as in BDK-88: July 1962 through June 1968 is the pre-Williams Act period; July 1968 through December 1980 is the post-Williams Act but pre-Reagan period; and 1981–1984. The 4-year subperiods 1985–1988, 1989–1992, and 1993–1996 correspond roughly to presidential political cycles. Also, the 1981–1988 period was a highly active takeover market, aided perhaps by pro-merger policies of the Reagan administration. Some commentators have argued that the late 1980s and early 1990s, corresponding to our 1989–1992 subperiod, were a time when deals were not economically attractive but were being done for the sake of doing the deal. The Nasdaq and several other broad stock indexes peaked in March 2000, and many observers regard this period as close to the peak of the new economy stock bubble and a turning point of US financial markets.

We therefore divide the most recent portion of our sample periods between January 1997-March 2000 and April 2000-December 2001 subperiods.

Our results for bidder returns, target returns, and a value-weighted average for bidders and targets (the combined return), for the first three subperiods (July 1962-

Table 2

Stock returns over various subperiods in attempted tender offers

CAR is the market-model CAR for the target, bidder, or combined. The CARs are measured over the period 5 days before the first bid through 5 days after in Panel A, and over longer windows in Panel B. Target dollar return is target market value (6 days before the first bid) times target CAR; similarly for bidder and combined dollar returns. Combined CAR (CIBR) is a weighted average of target and bidder CARs, where their weights are their market values as a fraction of the total target and bidder market value. Combined dollar return is the sum of target and bidder dollar returns. The target mean dollar return and the bidder mean dollar return in Panel A may not sum to the combined dollar return because of missing data for target or bidder in some cases. Binomial p is the significance level for the two-tail Fisher sign test that tests whether the median CAR is different from zero. Sample contains 1018 tender offers in which both bidder and target were listed on the NYSE, Amex, or Nasdaq during 1962–2001. All dollar figures are in millions of 2001 dollars.

	Subperiod								Total
Statistics	July 1962–June 1968	July 1968–December 1980	January 1981–December 1984	January 1985–December 1988	January 1989–December 1992	January 1993–December 1996	January 1997–March 2000	April 2000–December 2001	July 1962–December 2001
Panel A: Five-day stock returns									
Number of attempted tender offers	71	176	45	214	84	139	210	79	1018
Bidder									
Mean CAR (%)	3.29	0.05	−1.42	−0.49	−1.78	0.98	0.97	−0.81	0.18
Z-statistic	5.47	0.48	−1.74	−1.00	−3.00	1.22	1.83	−1.01	0.91
Median CAR (%)	1.62	−0.17	−1.72	−1.15	−1.04	0.91	−0.30	−0.56	−0.30
% Positive	63.6	48.8	31.8	44.4	41.7	52.9	48.3	46.8	47.8
Binomial p	0.04	0.81	0.02	0.12	0.16	0.55	0.68	0.65	0.17
Mean dollar return	15.1	23.3	−63.4	−53.4	−56.9	89.5	−190.0	−225.0	−59.2
Median dollar return	9.9	−0.7	−6.8	−2.9	−8.1	4.0	−2.0	−3.6	−1.2
Target									
Mean CAR (%)	17.96	27.97	31.90	25.61	29.08	31.92	33.18	44.78	30.01
Z-statistic	29.65	49.62	28.71	51.06	30.97	40.10	46.70	27.17	110.39
Median CAR (%)	17.79	22.99	31.61	21.89	28.25	29.27	29.46	39.81	26.10
% Positive	94.0	93.6	93.3	93.0	89.2	94.2	96.2	97.4	94.0
Binomial p	0.00	0.00	0.00	0.00	0.00	0.00	0.00	0.00	0.00
Mean dollar return	87.9	74.0	379.7	138.9	178.2	200.0	155.0	201.9	155.0
Median dollar return	51.2	32.3	91.1	37.3	27.9	44.1	46.2	47.2	41.2

Combined (CIBR)

Mean CAR (%)	7.45	6.40	8.12	5.19	3.59	5.05	4.61	3.57	5.27
Z-statistic	10.60	11.64	8.04	11.73	4.48	8.78	8.31	2.25	23.57
Median CAR (%)	6.42	4.20	8.22	3.97	1.76	4.04	2.93	3.00	3.69
% Positive	87.3	73.0	75.0	71.7	59.8	77.4	68.1	58.7	71.1
Binomial p	0.00	0.00	0.00	0.00	0.10	0.00	0.00	0.17	0.00
Mean dollar return	103.3	99.0	321.3	84.6	124.3	291.6	−248.6	−25.3	53.1
Median dollar return	77.9	26.7	44.2	22.8	5.4	55.5	35.4	21.3	32.0
Statistics									

Window: from I days prior to the first bid announcement through one day after

	T = 90	T = 60	T = 30	T = 15	T = 10	T = 5	T = 1
Panel B: Longer window stock returns							
Bidder							
Mean CAR (%)	−0.15	0.22	1.11	0.95	0.83	0.70	0.28
Z-statistic	0.81	0.96	2.81	2.94	2.96	3.24	2.31
Median CAR (%)	0.26	0.68	0.42	0.43	0.31	0.16	0.08
% Positive	50.4	51.3	51.2	53.0	52.1	50.6	50.7
Binomial p	0.82	0.43	0.47	0.06	0.19	0.73	0.68
Target							
Mean CAR (%)	38.92	38.47	36.39	33.06	31.27	28.89	24.47
Z-statistic	49.88	59.90	78.67	98.00	110.17	133.64	172.45
Median CAR (%)	37.04	35.35	32.79	29.01	28.21	24.68	20.07
% Positive	88.2	91.5	93.9	94.8	93.9	95.0	93.5
Binomial p	0.00	0.00	0.00	0.00	0.00	0.00	0.00
Combined (CIBR)							
Mean CAR (%)	6.65	6.88	7.12	6.23	5.88	5.32	4.28
Z-statistic	11.28	13.49	18.68	22.26	24.90	29.42	36.57
Median CAR (%)	7.05	7.09	6.35	4.76	4.44	3.75	2.95
% Positive	62.9	67.2	70.7	72.6	73.4	72.4	74.8
Binomial p	0.00	0.00	0.00	0.00	0.00	0.00	0.00

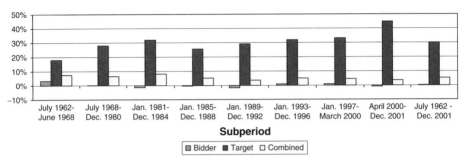

Fig. 3. Mean shareholder returns. Announcement period return is the market-model cumulative abnormal return for the target, bidder, or combined, over the period 5 days before the first bid through 5 days after. Combined return is the weighted average of target and bidder returns, when their weights are their market values as a fraction of the total target and bidder market value. Sample contains 1018 tender offers in which both bidder and target were listed on the NYSE, Amex, or Nasdaq during 1962–2001.

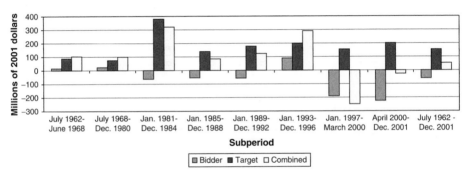

Fig. 4. Mean dollar returns. Target dollar return is target market value (6 days before the first bid) multiplied by target CAR; similarity for bidder and combined dollar returns. CAR is the market-model cumulative abnormal return for the target, bidder, or combined, over the period 5 days before the first bid through 5 days after. Combined return is the weighted average of target and bidder CARs, when their weights are their market values as a fraction of the total target and bidder market value. Sample contains 1018 tender offers in which both bidder and target were listed on the NYSE, Amex, or Nasdaq during 1962–2001.

June 1968, July 1968-December 1980, 1981-1984) are consistent with the findings of BDK-88. Table 2 indicates that during 1985–1988 the bidding shareholders earn a statistically insignificant mean return of −0.49% (median return of −$2.9 million). During this same period, the target shareholders received a statistically and economically significant return of 25.61% (median return of $37.3 million).

The late 1980s and early 1990s (1989–1992) were not kind to bidders; mean return of −1.78% (median dollar return of −$8.1 million). Bidding shareholders generally fared better in the 1993–1996 subperiod; mean return of 0.98% (median dollar return of $4.0 million). The mean combined returns during 1993–1996 was 5.05% (median dollar return of $55.5 million). In the most recent subperiods, bidders suffered wealth losses, although targets realized gains. The mean combined dollar returns were negative in the two post-1997 subperiods (−$248.6 million and −$25.3 million, respectively), apparently because of big losses among bidders that were relatively large. Moeller et al. (2004a,b) find even larger losses to large bidders in their mergers and tender offers sample during 1998–2001. They have relatively few tender offers in their large loss sample. The 1997–2000 mean dollar losses in our tender offer sample are of the same order of magnitude as the dollar gains in the 1993–1996 period.

4. Estimates of value improvements

This section describes the estimation procedures for value improvements using the probability scaling and IMs, and discusses the determinants of value improvements.

4.1. Parameter inputs for the probability scaling and intervention methods

We start with estimation procedures for parameter inputs for the probability scaling and IMs. Both methods require an estimate of the probability that the first bidder is successful. The IM further requires inputs of the average price (relative to the target's preoffer price) at which the first bidder wins, the size of the bidder relative to the initial combined value, the size of the target relative to the initial combined value, and the fraction of the target's equity owned by the first bidder.

4.1.1. Probability of first bidder success

To use the PSM, we need to estimate the probability that the first bidder is successful. Furthermore, because one of our objectives is to address the revelation bias, we need to identify an intervention that changes the probability of the first bidder succeeding, and that is not at the discretion of the first bidder. Litigation by the target, entry of a second bidder, and objection by a regulatory agency are examples of such exogenous events. Our focus is on the arrival of a competing bid, which is a major event for the initial bidder.

To estimate how the market's perception of probability of success is affected by the arrival of a competing bid, we need estimates of the market's perception of probability of success both prior to the competing bid (an unconditional estimate) and subsequent to the bid (a conditional estimate). We therefore estimate both a logit model that conditions only on information known to the market prior to the arrival of the competing bid and a logit model that, in addition, conditions on the arrival of the bid.

Table 3 provides estimates of such models. The dependent variable equals 1 if the first bidder is successful and 0 otherwise. The explanatory variables include the dummy variables for litigation, competing bid, and hostile, the first bidder's toehold α, effective bid premium, and the relative size of the bidder and target. Walkling (1985) and Schwert (2000) find some of the variables used here to be significant determinants of tender offer success.

Table 3

Logit model estimates of the probability of success of the first bidder unconditionally (Models A1 and A2) and conditional on whether a competing bid occurs (Model B)

Sample size is 1018 and contains tender offers during 1962–2001 in which both target and bidder were listed on NYSE, Amex, or Nasdaq. Hostile equals 1 if the target management opposes the first bidder, 0 otherwise. Alpha is fraction of the target held by the first bidder. Effective premium is initial bid price offered relative to the prebid market price of the target, multiplied by the percentage of target shares sought by the bidder through the tender offer. Litigation equals 1 if the target files a lawsuit against the first bidder, 0 otherwise. Competing bid equals 1 if a competing bidder arrives, 0 otherwise. Relative size is bidder prebid market value relative to target prebid market value excluding bidder's toehold.

Independent variable	Coefficient	p-Value
Model A1		
Litigation	−0.488	0.012
Hostile	−1.655	0.000
Alpha	−0.349	0.432
Effective premium	0.011	0.000
Relative size	0.003	0.052
Constant	0.936	0.000
Pseudo $R^2 = 0.1460$		
Percentage predicted = 76.8%		
Model A2		
Hostile	−1.885	0.000
Alpha	−0.449	0.309
Effective premium	0.011	0.000
Relative size	0.003	0.042
Constant	0.881	0.000
Pseudo $R^2 = 0.1408$		
Percentage predicted = 75.4%		
Model B		
Litigation	−0.321	0.114
Competing bid	−1.751	0.000
Hostile	−1.404	0.000
Alpha	−0.614	0.168
Effective premium	0.012	0.000
Relative size	0.002	0.100
Constant	1.101	0.000
Pseudo $R^2 = 0.1969$		
Percentage predicted = 79.9%		

Model A does not condition on whether a competing bid has occurred; Model B does. In measuring bidder returns, we consider both a shorter and a longer window. The short window consists of the period 1 day before and the day of the first competing bid announcement for the target. The long window consists of the period 1 day after the first bid to the day of the first competing bid announcement for the target. For the short window, the market is likely by this time to have learned about the occurrence of litigation related to the initial bid if such litigation was going to occur. At the start of the longer window that begins immediately after the arrival of the initial bid, the market is unlikely to have observed the occurrence of litigation even if it later occurs. Thus, for the short window Model A1 is appropriate, and for the longer window Model A2 is appropriate.

The results indicate that target management opposition, entry of a second bidder, and the effective premium are determinants of bidder success (opposition and competition having negative effects) and, with somewhat lower significance, target litigation and relative size. Thus, the arrival of a competing bid does have an important effect on offer success. Because target opposition is a matter of degree (see Schwert, 2000), whereas the arrival of a competing offer is a discrete event, the latter seems a more appropriate subject for the IM.

4.1.2. Parameter inputs for the probability scaling method

Estimating the PSM improvement ratio IR^{PSM} requires that returns be grossed up by the sum of the probabilities that the first bidder succeeds and that a later bid succeeds. This requires the following inputs: ϕ_1 is the probability of success of the first bidder. In the full sample of 1018 cases the first bidder is successful in 690 instances. For both PSM and IM, we apply transaction-specific estimates using Logit Model A2 in Table 3. ϕ_1 can also be estimated globally as 0.6778 using a simple sample average. ϕ_1^L is the probability that a later bid succeeds in acquiring the target. We derive an estimate of this probability from Betton and Eckbo (2000) to be 0.1463.

4.1.3. Parameter inputs for the intervention method

The IM value improvement ratio IR^{IM} is estimated based on Equation (13). We consider bidder abnormal returns around the announcement of a competing bid. The abnormal returns are computed using the market model as the benchmark. For the short return cumulation window used here, the choice of benchmark is unlikely to affect results materially (Brown and Warner, 1985). The market model is estimated using returns from day -170 through day -21, where day 0 is the announcement of the first bid in the *Wall Street Journal*. The equally weighted CRSP index is used as the market index.

During a 2-day period consisting of the day of the publication of the news of the second bid in the *Wall Street Journal* and the day before, the mean abnormal return for the first bidder is -0.44% (median, minimum, and maximum are -0.42%, -11.71%, and 12.57%, respectively). The mean return for the period from 1 day after the publication of the news of the first bid in the *Wall Street Journal* to the day of the publication of the news of the second bid is -3.58% (median, minimum, and maximum are -1.96%, -99.81%, and 40.31%, respectively).

The 2-day mean average abnormal return on the date of arrival of a competing bid is close to zero. But as we have shown, the arrival of a competing bidder has powerful effects on mean premiums and on success probabilities. The event-date return reflects two offsetting effects. The higher average premium a winning first bidder will have to pay given a competing bid is bad news, but the reduced probability of success resulting from a competing bid can be good news if the market expects a successful bidder to overpay. Because the IM disentangles these possibilities, a zero return, for example, can map into substantial value improvements.

If the market is efficient, and if no news about a competing bid arrives until the day that the bid occurs, then the abnormal return expected from date 1 (immediately after the initial bid) through date 2 (just before the competing bid) will on average be zero. Thus, Equation (13), which gives IR^{IM} in terms of R_3, the return from date 1 through date 3, also applies with a return from date 2 through date 3, or by choosing some starting date between date 1 and date 2.

There is a trade-off in using different periods. If news about a competing bid sometimes arrives between date 1 and 2, calculating the return based on the earlier starting point has the advantage of including the effects of such anticipation of the event. However, calculating the abnormal return over a longer period has the disadvantage of introducing noise arising from normal stock price fluctuations and from benchmark estimation errors. We therefore estimate the return to be substituted for R_3 in Equation (13) based on the two different periods: the 2-day event period (mean −0.43%) and the period from immediately after announcement of the initial bid through announcement of the second bid (mean −3.58%).

We require the following further inputs (all transaction-specific except as otherwise indicated): P_1/V_0^C in Equation (13) is the size of the bidder relative to initial combined value. The mean (median) figure is 0.656 (0.690). V_0^T/V_0^C in Equation (13) is the size of the target relative to combined value prior to the initial offer. The mean (median) figure is 0.368 (0.327). ϕ_1 is the probability of success of the first bidder. In our sample the first bidder is successful in 690 out of 1018 contests. Hence ϕ_1 is estimated as $690/1018 = 0.6778$. We also apply alternative transaction-specific estimates using Logit Model A1 or A2 in Table 3. ϕ_3 is the probability of success of the first bidder given the arrival of a competing bidder. In our sample, there are 147 cases in which a competing bidder arrives, with the first bidder successful in 38 instances. Hence ϕ_3 is estimated as $38/147 = 0.2585$. We also apply alternative transaction-specific estimates using Logit Model B in Table 3. α is the fraction of the target's equity owned by the first bidder. For the 141 tender offers in our competing bid subsample to which we can apply IM, the mean (median) α is 2.41% (0%). For our whole sample of tender offers, the mean bidder ownership is 6.13%, the median ownership is 0%, and only 220 of the 1018 bidders own any shares in the target at the time they make the bid. $\bar{B}_1/V_0^T$ is the average price (relative to the target's preoffer price) at which the first bidder wins in the full sample, and we also employ alternative transaction-specific estimates derived by using a regression technique. The estimate based on sample mean is 1.407. Finally, $\bar{B}_3/V_0^T$ is the average price at which the first bidder wins given the arrival of a competing bidder, and we also employ alternative transaction-specific estimates derived by using a regression technique. The estimate based on sample mean is 1.514.

4.2. Estimated value improvements

In the competing bid subsample, we use several alternative methods to estimate input parameters for IM. The calculations apply Equation (13) using estimated parameters ϕ_1, ϕ_3, $\bar{B}_1/V_0^T$, and $\bar{B}_3/V_0^T$. When these parameters are estimated using sample means and R_3 in (13) is estimated over the 2-day event period as described above (hereafter, the baseline parameter specification), the mean (median) IR^{IM} is 13.1% (12.4%). The discounted combined value as assessed by the market thus is 13.1% more valuable as a result of the takeover. This evidence is inconsistent with the strong agency/hubris hypothesis of zero value improvements in tender offers. Given that the distribution of IR^{IM} is not especially skewed, and 132 of 141 IR^{IM}s are greater than zero, the conclusion that the expected value improvement is significantly greater than zero is highly robust ($p < 0.001$ by a sign test). A histogram of IR^{IM} is provided in Figure 5.

We also estimate separate transaction-specific probabilities of success using the logit model of Table 3 to obtain individual probability estimates for each of the 147 transactions. Similarly, instead of assuming that the expected bid premium that will be paid (relative to preoffer price) in the event that the first bidder succeeds is independent of the transaction, we estimate regression models relating the price paid in successful transactions to the same independent variables used in Logit Models A1, A2, and B (excluding effective premium). This generates a corresponding set of regression models.

These results (unreported) are consistent with the conclusion that value improvements on average differ from zero and are generally positive. For example, when ϕ_1 and ϕ_3 are, respectively, estimated using Logit Model A1 and A3 in Table 3, and $\bar{B}_1/V_0^T$ and $\bar{B}_3/V_0^T$ are estimated using regression models similar to Model A1 and B in Table 3 (excluding effective premium), the mean (median) value improvement is 14.8% (13.8%), which is similar to the estimates obtained using our baseline parameter specification. Appendix B further verifies the robustness of this conclusion with respect to alternative estimates of the input parameters. In what follows, we draw our numerical inference on the IM estimate using our baseline parameter specification.

In Table 4, market-based estimates of the expected combined value improvement from takeover (relative to combined bidder-target value) are labeled CIBR, IR^{PSM}, and IR^{IM}. The average estimated CIBR associated with the arrival of an initial bid during 1962–2001 is approximately 5.27% (median of 3.69%) of combined bidder/target value.

Using PSM, the average estimated value improvement, IR^{PSM} is larger, approximately 7.28% (median of 4.63%) of combined bidder/target value. The average difference between the IR^{PSM} and CIBR estimates relative to combined value is 2.02% (median of 0.22%), with 63.4% of the differences being positive.

We also use a proxy for the revelation bias, the difference $IR^{PSM} - IR^{IM}$. IR^{PSM} reflects the change in underlying value that would be associated with takeover success but also includes revelation effects. IR^{IM} contains only the underlying value effect, not the revelation effect. The difference is therefore a proxy for the revelation bias.

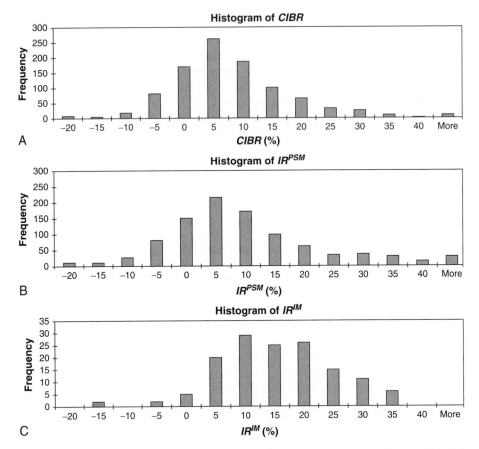

Fig. 5. Histograms of value improvement measures. Sample contains 1018 tender offers in which both bidder and target were listed on the NYSE, Amex, or Nasdaq during 1962–2001. In addition, for IR^{IM} the sample is restricted to cases in which there was a competing bid for the target. CIBR, combined initial bid return; IR^{PSM}, improvement ratio based on probability scaling method; IR^{IM}, implicit market estimates of the value to the bidder of the takeover.

According to Table 4, the overall revelation bias is not significantly different from zero. However, there is variation in revelation effects across time, degree of hostility, and means of payment.

4.3. Determinants of value improvements and revelation effects

We describe several possible determinants of value improvements, and the variables we use as proxies for these determinants. In Tables 5–7, we present univariate results of how value improvements are related to these determinants. In Table 8, we present multivariate regression results.

Table 4

Implicit market estimates of the value improvement as a result of the takeover (IR^{IM}), combined initial bid returns (CIBR), and probability-adjusted combined initial bid returns (IR^{PSM}) by subperiod

All improvement ratios are expressed as a percent of target and bidder market values. CIBR = target CAR × (target market value/target and bidder market values) + bidder CAR × (bidder market value/target and bidder market values). CAR is the market model CAR for the target or bidder over the period 5 days before the first bid through 5 days after. IR^{PSM} = CIBR/(probability the first bidder succeeds unconditionally + probability a later bidder succeeds). The probability of success of the first bidder is estimated from Logit Model A2 in Table 3. The probability that a later bid succeeds is estimated from Betton and Eckbo (2000) and is 0.1463. Parameter inputs for IR^{IM} are estimated using sample means (the baseline specification). Binomial p is the significance level for the two-tail Fisher sign test that tests whether the median is different from zero. Sample contains tender offers in which both bidder and target were listed on the NYSE, Amex, or Nasdaq during 1962–2001. In addition, for IR^{IM} the sample is restricted to cases in which there was a competing bid for the target.

Statistics					Subperiod				
	July 1962–June 1968	July 1968–December 1980	January 1981–December 1984	January 1985–December 1988	January 1989–December 1992	January 1993–December 1996	January 1997–March 2000	April 2000–December 2001	Total July 1962–December 2001
IR^{IM}									
Mean (%)	15.62	12.90	12.09	14.48	11.54	10.86	10.49	10.98	13.05
Median (%)	15.79	12.33	8.51	14.26	9.24	9.99	9.70	11.48	12.38
% Positive	100.0	100.0	91.7	89.2	88.9	90.9	85.7	100.0	93.6
Binomial p	0.00	0.00	0.01	0.00	0.04	0.01	0.01	0.13	0.00
Sample size	18	36	12	37	9	11	14	4	141
CIBR									
Mean (%)	7.45	6.40	8.12	5.19	3.59	5.05	4.61	3.57	5.27
Median (%)	6.42	4.20	8.22	3.97	1.76	4.04	2.93	3.00	3.69
% Positive	87.3	73.0	75.0	71.1	59.8	77.4	68.1	58.7	71.1
Binomial p	0.00	0.00	0.00	0.00	0.10	0.00	0.00	0.17	0.00
Sample size	63	159	44	212	82	137	204	75	976
$IR^{IM} - CIBR$									
Mean (%)	7.06	4.94	−3.30	3.21	6.53	7.43	0.66	9.05	4.04
Median (%)	8.57	4.53	−2.37	3.71	7.36	8.37	2.66	4.47	3.74

(Continued)

Table 4 (Continued)

Statistics	July 1962–June 1968	July 1968–December 1980	January 1981–December 1984	January 1985–December 1988	January 1989–December 1992	January 1993–December 1996	January 1997–March 2000	April 2000–December 2001	Total July 1962–December 2001
				Subperiod					
% Positive	83.3	66.7	41.7	56.8	77.8	72.7	64.3	50.0	64.5
Binomial p	0.01	0.07	0.77	0.51	0.18	0.23	0.42	1.00	0.00
Sample size	18	36	12	37	9	11	14	4	141
IR^{PSM}									
Mean (%)	11.01	8.86	13.24	7.82	5.07	6.38	5.82	3.82	7.28
Median (%)	8.42	5.49	8.82	5.16	2.07	5.19	3.22	3.17	4.63
% Positive	87.3	73.0	75.0	71.7	59.8	77.4	68.1	58.7	71.1
Binomial p	0.00	0.00	0.00	0.00	0.10	0.00	0.00	0.17	0.00
Sample size	63	159	44	212	82	137	204	75	976
$IR^{PSM} - CIBR$									
Mean (%)	3.57	2.46	5.12	2.63	1.47	1.33	1.21	0.25	2.02
Median (%)	1.25	0.46	1.08	0.35	0.01	0.38	0.10	0.00	0.22
% Positive	81.0	63.5	75.0	67.0	51.2	74.5	56.9	42.7	63.4
Binomial p	0.00	0.00	0.00	0.00	0.19	0.00	0.00	0.09	0.00
Sample size	63	159	44	212	82	137	204	75	976
$IR^{PSM} - IR^{IM}$ (estimated revelation bias)									
Mean (%)	-2.75	-2.14	17.25	5.10	-1.53	-6.65	6.11	-7.88	1.67
Median (%)	-4.98	-1.71	15.90	2.94	-5.35	-5.45	4.79	-3.88	1.10
% Positive	44.4	44.4	83.3	62.2	44.4	27.3	57.1	50.0	52.5
Binomial p	0.81	0.62	0.04	0.19	1.00	0.23	0.79	1.00	0.61
Sample size	18	36	12	37	9	11	14	4	141

4.3.1. Friendly versus hostile offers

Academics and other commentators have proposed two different economic roles for takeovers: discipline/removal of bad target managers and exploitation of business synergies. Hostile offers are supposed to be associated with removal of bad target managers, and friendly offers with exploitation of business synergies. To examine these issues we include the hostile dummy defined in Section 3 as an independent variable.

Panels A and B of Table 5 indicate that combined returns to bidders and targets, as measured by CIBR and IR^{PSM}, are on average considerably higher in hostile than in friendly offers. In the overall sample (Panel A), the mean CIBR of hostile offers is 8.43%, versus 4.38% for friendly offers. The mean IR^{PSM} of hostile offers is 16.34%, versus 4.75% for friendly offers. For both measures, the difference between hostile and friendly offers is significant at the 1% level. However, Table 5 indicates that hostile bidders earn lower announcement period returns than friendly bidders.[16] Target announcement period returns in hostile offers are also not higher than in friendly offers. This suggests that hostile bidders that are large (small) relative to targets earn higher (lower) announcement period returns.

The difference between friendly and hostile offers is much larger for IR^{PSM} than for CIBR because hostile bids are less likely to succeed. In consequence, the traditional CIBR method biases returns toward zero more for hostile bids more than for friendly bids. Thus, the PSM indicates an even greater difference between friendly and hostile bids than what is indicated by traditional methods. Large friendly/hostile differences in IR^{PSM} are also present in the competing bid subsample of Panel B. The multivariate results in Table 8 also confirm that IR^{PSM} is significantly positively related to hostility (we do not run regressions with IR^{IM} as the dependent variable, owing to the small competing bid sample size).

In contrast with the large friendly/hostile differences in IR^{PSM}, in Panel B of Table 5 the IM measure (IR^{IM}) indicates that hostile offers are not associated with significantly higher value improvements than friendly offers. Because IM estimates filter out revelation effects, the different behavior of the IR^{PSM} and IR^{IM} estimates indicates that friendly and hostile offers convey different information to investors about bidder stand-alone value.

Panel B of Table 5 indicates that hostility is related to a larger (more positive) revelation effect $IR^{PSM} - IR^{IM}$ (significant at the 1% level). There is a positive revelation effect of hostile offers (6.06%, significant at the 1% level) and a negative revelation effect of friendly offers (−4.42%, significant at the 1% level). The average upward revision in the market's assessment of the stand-alone value of hostile bidders is consistent with the hypothesis that hostile bids are taken by the market as an indicator of strong cash flow prospects or organizational capabilities on the part of

---

[16] The hostile coefficient in the bidder CAR regression in Table 8 is negative but not significant at conventional levels, consistent with Schwert (2000) and Moeller et al. (2004a,b).

Table 5

Implicit market estimates of the value improvement as a result of the takeover (IR^{IM}), combined initial bid returns (CIBR), probability-adjusted combined initial bid returns (IR^{PSM}), and cumulative abnormal returns (CARs) for hostile and nonhostile; cash, stock, and mixed payments; pre-Williams Act (pre-July 1968) and post-Williams Act; and pre-March 2000 and post-March 2000

The value improvement estimates CIBR, IR^{PSM}, IR^{IM}, and CAR are defined in the legend of Table 4. In Panel A, the sample contains 1018 tender offers in which both bidder and target were listed on the NYSE, Amex, or Nasdaq during 1962–2001. In Panel B, the subsample contains tender offers with a competing bid for the target. The mean estimated revelation bias (IR^{PSM} − IR^{IM}) does not necessarily equal the difference in means between the IR^{PSM} and IR^{IM} entries because of different sample size for IR^{PSM} and IR^{IM}. The median of IR^{PSM} − IR^{IM} generally does not equal the difference in medians between the IR^{PSM} and IR^{IM} entries. *t*-Statistic is the student's *t*-value that tests whether the mean is different from zero. Binomial *p* is the significance level for the two-tail Fisher sign test that tests whether the median revelation bias is different from zero.

Statistics	Hostile	Nonhostile	Cash	Mixed	Stock	Pre-Williams Act	Post-Williams Act	Pre-March 2000	Post-March 2000
Panel A									
CIBR									
Mean (%)	8.43***	4.38***	5.79#,***	4.42#◆◆◆	−0.54◆◆◆,***	7.45*	5.11*	5.41	3.57
Median (%)	7.06***	3.04***	4.14#,***	3.12#,◆◆◆	−0.40◆◆◆,***	6.42***	3.52***	3.78*	3.00*
Sample size	213	763	701	202	39	63	913	901	75
IR^{PSM}									
Mean (%)	16.34***	4.75***	7.97#,***	5.83#◆◆◆	−0.50◆◆◆,***	11.01**	7.02**	7.57**	3.82**
Median (%)	13.68***	3.27***	5.30#,***	3.72#◆◆◆	−0.45◆◆◆,***	8.42***	4.41***	4.78**	3.17**
Sample size	213	763	701	202	39	63	913	901	75
Bidder CAR									
Mean (%)	−0.95**	0.49**	0.76##,**	−0.77##	−2.73**	3.29***	−0.04***	0.27	−0.81
Median (%)	−1.15**	−0.17**	0.05##,**	−0.78##	−1.68**	1.62***	−0.44***	−0.29	−0.56
Sample size	214	782	716	205	41	66	930	917	79
Target CAR									
Mean (%)	28.80	30.35	31.60#,***	28.26#◆◆◆	12.35◆◆◆,***	17.96***	30.86***	28.77***	44.78***
Median (%)	25.99	26.10	28.14#,***	25.52#◆◆◆	11.52◆◆◆,***	17.79***	28.01***	25.30***	39.81***
Sample size	220	787	723	205	44	67	940	929	78
Panel B									
IR^{IM}									
Mean (%)	13.59	12.31	13.49	10.99	16.55	15.62	12.68	13.11	10.98
Median (%)	14.03	10.94	13.64#	9.59#◆	16.28◆	15.79	11.69	12.38	11.48

Sample size	82	59	100	24	8	18	123	137	4
CIBR									
Mean (%)	10.35*	7.19*	9.52	7.20	3.72	8.56	9.08	9.22	1.94
Median (%)	10.46**	6.41**	7.81*	5.81	−1.18*	8.26	7.65	7.65	6.01
Sample size	82	60	101	24	8	18	124	138	4
IR^{PSM}									
Mean (%)	19.65***	7.93***	15.50*	11.63	3.34*	12.87	14.96	15.03	3.10
Median (%)	18.30***	7.08***	10.64**	6.73◆	−1.21◆·**	9.32	10.50	10.10	6.60
Sample size	82	60	101	24	8	18	124	138	4
IR^{PSM} − IR^{IM} (estimated revelation bias)									
Mean (%)	6.06***	−4.42***	2.06**	0.64◆	−13.21◆·**	−2.75	2.32	1.95	−7.88
t-Statistic	2.98	−2.75	1.24	0.18	−2.70	−0.81	1.50	1.36	−0.72
Median (%)	5.42***	−4.01***	1.77***	−3.38◆	−11.76◆◆·***	−4.98	1.70	1.10	−3.88
Binomial p	0.02	0.07	0.37	0.54	0.29	0.81	0.47	0.61	1.00
Sample size	82	59	100	24	8	18	123	137	4
Bidder CAR									
Mean (%)	−1.51**	1.74**	−0.20	1.75	−4.15	2.63	−0.58	−0.14	0.04
Median (%)	−1.43**	0.71**	−0.59**	0.75◆◆	−5.15◆·**	0.46	−0.95	−0.79	5.95
Sample size	83	61	102	25	8	20	124	140	4
Target CAR									
Mean (%)	30.68	28.48	31.99***	25.61◆·**	8.00◆◆·***	19.75**	31.35**	29.18*	49.89*
Median (%)	28.77*	22.40*	28.37#·***	21.47#·◆	3.78◆·***	21.06**	28.37**	27.37	33.94
Sample size	84	61	103	24	9	20	125	141	4

*, **, and *** indicate significant difference between the two subgroups (hostile and nonhostile, cash and stock, pre- and post-Williams Act, pre- and post-March 2000) at the 10%, 5%, and 1% levels, respectively. #, ##, and ### indicate significant difference between cash and mixed subgroups at the 10%, 5%, and 1% levels, respectively. ◆, ◆◆, and ◆◆◆ indicate significant difference between stock and mixed subgroups at the 10%, 5%, and 1% levels, respectively.

the bidder.[17] Alternatively, the negative revelation about friendly bidders and the positive revelation about hostile bidders may derive from the fact that hostile offers are more prone to be cash and friendly offers more prone to be equity or mixed payment. We discuss revelation effects associated with means of payment below.

Although there are differences in stockholder returns between friendly and hostile offers, the thrust of this evidence is that both hostile and friendly offers are associated with substantial value improvements in takeovers. Thus, overall, this evidence indicates that both disciplinary synergistic roles for takeover are important.

4.3.2. Cash versus mixed versus equity offers

In general, as in Myers and Majluf (1984), issuance of equity can convey adverse information about the firm's existing assets in place. Several models of means of payment in takeovers imply an adverse selection problem associated with greater use of equity. Under an adverse selection approach, the use of cash could provide the favorable revelation that equity is not used. On the other hand, a cash offer could reveal that the firm has cash in excess of its internal investment needs and is likely to squander that cash on poor investments should the bid fail (Jensen, 1988; Stulz, 1990). This implies a negative revelation effect. An alternative story is that paying with cash indicates a good management that is willing to commit itself to discipline in future investments. This would imply a favorable revelation about managerial quality.

Table 5 indicates an ordering in which cash offers on average create greater CIBR and IR^{PSM} value improvements than mixed offers, and mixed offers greater than stock offers. Most of the comparisons are significant at the 1% level. Similarly, in the multivariate analysis of Table 8, in the regressions with dependent variables CIBR and IR^{PSM}, the coefficient on cash (equity) is significantly positive (negative).

Owing to the smaller sample sizes in Panel B, there is less power to detect differences. Nevertheless, a pattern that emerges clearly is that the value improvement difference between equity and mixed payment offers is much smaller using the IM. In consequence, the revelation bias $IR^{PSM} - IR^{IM}$ is much more negative for stock than for cash offers (difference in means significant at the 5% level, difference in medians significant at the 1% level), and more negative for stock than for mixed offers (difference in means significant at the 10% level, difference in means significant at the 5% level). The point estimates also indicate a more negative revelation bias for mixed offers than for cash offers (substantial for medians), though the difference is not significant. In other words, greater use of equity is associated with more negative revelation about bidder stand-alone value. Thus, our evidence is consistent with the adverse selection theory's implication that the use of equity is an adverse indicator of

---

[17] Despite the favorable revelation about stand-alone value, investors presumably understand that successful hostile offers can be very expensive for the bidder, so no presumption is made that the announcement period returns for hostile offers are positive. See Footnote 16.

firm value, and is not consistent with the argument that the use of cash reveals a propensity of bidding management to waste free cash flow.

4.3.3. Focused versus diversifying transactions

We define an acquisition as same-industry versus cross-industry (i.e., nondiversifying versus diversifying) according to whether the target firm has the same or a different SIC code from the bidder. We consider both three- and four-digit Compustat SIC codes.

A large literature debates the extent to which diversifying acquisitions are associated with more severe bidder agency problems. The agency theory of diversification suggests lower true value improvements, and especially lower bidder returns, in cross-industry transactions than in same-industry transactions.

The data provide support for the notion that same-industry acquisitions create greater value than cross-industry acquisitions. In Table 6, bidder returns and value improvement measures are generally lower in diversifying acquisitions. Similarly, in the multivariate analysis of Table 8, the coefficient estimates for the same-industry dummy are significantly positive for most of the value measure columns.

The evidence for bidder returns confirms that the conclusions in the earlier sample of Morck et al. (1990) extend to the turn of the millennium. The finding for combined value improvements indicates that the lower bidder returns in diversifying acquisitions do not derive solely from redistribution to targets. The results also indicate that the greater gains to same-industry acquisitions identified in stock mergers by Maquieira et al. (1998) applies in tender offers. Our findings provide an interesting contrast with those of Moeller et al. (2004a,b), who find diversification to be insignificant as a predictor of bidder announcement period returns in public acquisitions. The sample of Moeller et al. (2004a,b) includes mergers as well as tender offers, and our study covers a longer sample period. Also, they define industry using SDC SIC codes, whereas we define industries using Compustat SICs. Kahle and Walkling (1996) argue that Compustat SIC codes are better specified than CRSP SIC codes.

Although Table 6 indicates same-industry acquisition are generally associated with higher bidder and combined returns than cross-industry acquisitions, Panel B indicates that IR^{IM} is about the same in the two groups, indicating similar value improvements from combination. The $IR^{PSM} - IR^{IM}$ block indicates the reason: Same-industry acquisitions are associated with more favorable revelation than cross-industry acquisitions. This suggests that investors perceive diversifying acquisitions as indicating that management is prone to agency problems such as wasteful investment, whereas same-industry acquisitions indicate managerial discipline and expertise. These results do not indicate any great pessimism on the part of investors about the value of combination in diversifying transactions. Instead, they indicate that the low returns associated with these transactions derive from adverse updating about the quality of the bidder and its management.

Table 6

The effect of diversification on value improvements

Same industry is measured two ways. First, the same four-digit Compustat standard industrial classification (SIC) codes for the target and bidder. Second, the same three-digit Compustat SIC codes for the target and bidder. The implicit market estimates of the value improvement as a result of the takeover (IR^{IM}), combined initial bid returns (CIBR), probability-adjusted combined initial bid returns (IR^{PSM}), and cumulative abnormal returns (CARs) are defined in the legend of Table 4. In Panel A, the sample contains 1018 tender offers in which both bidder and target were listed on the NYSE, Amex, or Nasdaq during 1962–2001. In Panel B, the subsample contains tender offers with a competing bid for the target. The mean estimated revelation bias ($IR^{PSM} - IR^{IM}$) does not necessarily equal the difference in means between the IR^{PSM} and IR^{IM} entries owing to the different sample size for IR^{PSM} and IR^{IM}. The median of $IR^{PSM} - IR^{IM}$ generally does not equal the difference in medians between the IR^{PSM} and IR^{IM} entries. t-Statistic is the student's t value that tests whether the mean is different from zero. Binomial p is the significance level for the two-tail Fisher sign test that tests whether the median revelation bias is different from zero.

	Four-digit SIC		Three-digit SIC	
Statistics	Same industry	Cross-industry	Same industry	Cross-industry
Panel A				
CIBR				
Mean (%)	6.23*	4.96*	6.20*	4.87*
Median (%)	4.62**	3.31**	4.60**	3.26**
Sample size	254	715	307	662
IR^{PSM}				
Mean (%)	8.26	6.97	8.17	6.91
Median (%)	5.39*	4.12*	5.37**	4.02**
Sample size	254	715	307	662
Bidder CAR				
Mean (%)	0.76	0.00	0.87	−0.11
Median (%)	0.92**	−0.47**	0.77**	−0.51**
Sample size	260	729	314	675
Target CAR				
Mean (%)	29.45	30.34	30.84	29.77
Median (%)	28.37	25.84	29.18*	25.19*
Sample size	263	736	317	682
Panel B				
IR^{IM}				
Mean (%)	12.65	13.16	12.29	13.33
Median (%)	12.77	11.88	12.47	12.14
Sample size	31	109	38	102
CIBR				
Mean (%)	11.01	8.51	11.66*	8.10*
Median (%)	12.13	7.28	11.81**	6.98**
Sample size	31	110	38	103
IR^{PSM}				
Mean (%)	19.13	13.52	20.16**	12.76**

(Continued)

Table 6 (*Continued*)

Statistics	Four-digit SIC		Three-digit SIC	
	Same industry	Cross-industry	Same industry	Cross-industry
Median (%)	14.17*	8.96*	16.46**	8.33**
Sample size	31	110	38	103
$IR^{PSM} - IR^{IM}$ (*estimated revelation bias*)				
Mean (%)	6.48*	0.39*	7.87***	−0.55***
t-Statistic	1.91	0.25	2.63	−0.35
Median (%)	5.72*	−0.02*	6.52***	−1.17***
Binomial *p*	0.15	1.00	0.07	0.77
Sample size	31	109	38	102
Bidder CAR				
Mean (%)	1.25	−0.50	2.01*	−0.90*
Median (%)	1.53*	−0.95*	1.74**	−0.99**
Sample size	31	112	38	105
Target CAR				
Mean (%)	29.55	29.95	30.39	29.67
Median (%)	30.91	25.85	30.22	24.67
Sample size	31	113	38	106

*, **, and *** indicate significant difference between same- and cross-industry tender offers at the 10%, 5%, and 1% levels, respectively.

4.3.4. Relative market values of bidder and target

Some argue that so-called mergers of equals are hard to implement successfully.[18] This suggests that acquisitions of small targets by large bidders will tend to generate greater improvement per dollar spent on acquisition than combinations of similar-size firms. It could also be argued that in unequal acquisitions, the business benefits of possessing the target can be leveraged across a larger set of operations, again yielding greater gains per dollar spent on acquisition.

In the univariate analysis, we place transactions in four relative size categories: bidder/target market value ratio <0.7 (small bidder), $0.7 < X < 1.5$ (same relative size), $1.5 < X < 5.0$ (big relative size), and $5.0 < X$ (largest relative size). We use a continuous variable, the logarithm of relative size, in the regressions.

Table 7 shows that acquisitions in which the bidder is relatively large compared with the target improve value (as a fraction of combined value) significantly less. The regression results in Table 8 confirm this finding: Value improvement measures are inversely related to the relative size of the bidder versus the target. In contrast, when

---

[18] See, for example, *The Economist*, January 9, 1999, p. 15: "Nor does it [success] require similarity of size: mergers of equals seem to be especially tricky, perhaps because they disrupt two strong corporate cultures, and they often throw up intractable problems of leadership." (The use of the term mergers in the quoted remark seems to be generic, not exclusive of tender offers.)

Table 7

The relation between value improvements and relative size

The implicit market estimates of the value improvement as a result of the takeover (IR^{IM}), CIBR, probability-adjusted combined initial bid returns (IR^{PSM}), and CARs are defined in the legend of Table 4. In Panel A, the sample contains 1018 tender offers in which both bidder and target were listed on the NYSE, Amex, or Nasdaq during 1962–2001. In Panel B, the subsample contains tender offers with a competing bid for the target.

	Ratio of bidder size to target size			
	<0.7	0.7–1.5	1.5–5.0	>5
Panel A				
CIBR				
Mean (%)	14.95	11.79	6.87	1.40
Median (%)	12.79	11.88	6.19	1.51
Sample size	85	126	240	525
IR^{PSM}				
Mean (%)	22.06	17.19	9.11	1.68
Median (%)	16.68	15.45	7.03	1.73
Sample size	85	126	240	525
Bidder CAR				
Mean (%)	3.75	2.26	−1.16	−0.47
Median (%)	1.74	1.81	−1.53	−0.41
Sample size	85	127	240	526
Target CAR				
Mean (%)	18.96	21.92	29.21	34.59
Median (%)	16.92	20.02	25.11	30.22
Sample size	85	126	241	527
Panel B				
IR^{IM}				
Mean (%)	25.87	16.74	9.71	5.93
Median (%)	26.73	16.75	9.64	5.39
Sample size	22	31	61	27
CIBR				
Mean (%)	16.77	12.01	7.69	2.13
Median (%)	19.08	11.61	6.29	2.12
Sample size	22	32	61	27
IR^{PSM}				
Mean (%)	27.51	20.10	12.16	3.60
Median (%)	26.40	14.83	8.14	3.40
Sample size	22	32	61	27
Bidder CAR				
Mean (%)	1.22	0.97	−1.34	−0.50
Median (%)	−0.10	−0.25	−2.08	0.05
Sample size	22	32	61	27
Target CAR				
Mean (%)	22.25	23.30	32.36	38.65
Median (%)	23.82	21.36	30.09	30.62
Sample size	22	32	61	27

takeover gains are measured relative to the value of the target (not reported here), the mean estimated improvement is largest when a target is acquired by a much larger bidder. Despite concerns raised in the business press about mergers of equals, it is not clear from these two pieces of evidence that parity of bidder and target size in a tender offer is a bad thing.

Previous research on relative size has focused on its effects on bidder returns. Asquith et al. (1983) find that merger bidder returns decrease with the relative size of the bidder versus target. In a recent sample, Moeller et al. (2004a) report that, after controlling for bidder size, relative size is unrelated to the returns of bidders acquiring public firms. Our evidence indicates that relative size is also related to total (combined) value improvements.

If the gains from combination are derived solely from target improvements such as removal of bad management, then a larger relative size of the bidder would not increase the gains relative to the size of the target. Thus, our finding suggests that there are gains from combination involving synergies between bidder and target. Something about the target, perhaps a unique technology, can be leveraged to provide a firm-wide benefit to the bidder. However, the fact that greater relative size of the bidder implies smaller value gains relative to combined value suggests that there are limits to this leveraging. To some extent the gains do seem to come from changes specific to the target instead of general synergies.

4.3.5. Tobin's Q

Lang et al. (1989) and Servaes (1991) find that takeover gains are related to bidder and target Q ratios. Following Martin (1996), we define Q as the sum of market value of equity, long-term debt, short-term debt, and preferred stock divided by book value of equity, calculated as of the fiscal year-end preceding the takeover announcement date.

To investigate how value improvements are related to bidder and target Tobin's Q ratios, we run value improvement regressions, including Q ratios in the list of independent variables, as well as separate regressions of bidder and target returns on takeover characteristics. The results are reported in the last four columns of Table 8. Bidder announcement period returns (CAR) and total value improvements are negatively related to bidder Q, and target announcement period CAR is negatively related to target Q. The effect of Q in our sample is economically significant. In Table 8, the coefficient of bidder Q is -0.38, meaning for an increase of 1 unit of bidder Q, bidder return decreases by -0.38%. Because the standard deviation of Q is 3.26 (the average bidder Q is 1.88), Q is associated with nonnegligible variation in return. Our results are robust to winsorizing bidder and target Qs.

Our bidder returns finding is consistent with the fact (e.g., Brown and Ryngaert, 1991; Fuller et al., 2002, Moeller et al. 2004a,b; Travlos, 1987) that stock bidders have lower announcement period returns, because stock bidders tend to have higher Q (Martin, 1996) and lower book/market ratios (e.g., Dong et al., 2003).

However, this finding is different from those of Lang et al. (1989) and Servaes (1991). In their earlier sample, bidder returns were higher when high Q bidders

Table 8

Least squares regression results of combined initial bid returns (CIBR), probability-adjusted combined initial bid returns (IR^{PSM}), and cumulative abnormal returns (CARs) against various takeover-specific variables (*t*-statistics in parentheses)

The value improvement estimates CIBR and IR^{PSM} are defined in the legend of Table 4. Industries are classified according to three-digit Compustat standard industrial classification (SIC) codes. Sample contains tender offers in which both bidder and target were listed on the NYSE, Amex, or Nasdaq during 1962–2001. Hostile equals 1 if the offer is viewed as hostile by target management, 0 otherwise. Cash equals 1 if the offer is all cash, 0 otherwise. Stock equals 1 if the offer is all stock, 0 otherwise. Pre-Williams Act equals 1 if the offer was made prior to July 1968, 0 otherwise. Post-March 2000 equals 1 if the offer was made after March 2000, 0 otherwise. Same industry equals 1 if the bidder and target are in the same three-digit Compustat SIC code industry, 0 otherwise. Relative size = acquirer market value/target market value. Tobin's Q = (market value of equity + long-term debt + short-term debt + preferred stock)/total assets.

Variable	Dependent variable					
	CIBR	IR^{PSM}	CIBR	IR^{PSM}	Bidder CAR	Target CAR
Hostile	0.50 (0.63)	6.93 (6.62)	1.05 (1.12)	7.63 (6.00)	−1.63 (−1.83)	5.93 (2.46)
Cash	2.31 (2.97)	3.17 (3.12)	2.69 (3.05)	3.86 (3.22)	2.28 (2.71)	2.77 (1.22)
Stock	−5.12 (−3.14)	−6.34 (−2.96)	−4.81 (−2.20)	−5.20 (−1.76)	−2.41 (−1.16)	−16.05 (−2.86)
Pre-Williams Act	1.00 (0.76)	1.55 (0.89)	2.98 (0.84)	7.18 (1.49)	4.54 (1.34)	−1.04 (−0.11)
Post-March 2000	2.74 (2.37)	3.24 (2.14)	2.31 (1.72)	2.48 (1.36)	−0.05 (−0.04)	11.22 (3.24)
Same industry	1.60 (2.42)	1.85 (2.13)	1.37 (1.78)	1.47 (1.42)	2.11 (2.89)	0.79 (0.40)
Log of relative size	−2.74 (−14.51)	−3.35 (−13.53)	−2.53 (−11.14)	−3.10 (−10.06)	−0.36 (−1.69)	3.58 (6.13)
Log of target size	−0.69 (−3.05)	−0.65 (−2.21)	−0.65 (−2.41)	−0.50 (−1.38)	−0.61 (−2.40)	−1.16 (−1.69)
Bidder Tobin's Q			−0.28 (−2.66)	−0.39 (−2.73)	−0.38 (−3.72)	−0.16 (−0.57)
Target Tobin's Q			0.12 (0.74)	0.14 (0.62)	0.13 (0.83)	−0.97 (−2.26)
Constant	11.78 (7.27)	12.61 (5.93)	11.64 (6.13)	11.93 (4.63)	2.71 (1.50)	28.47 (5.84)
Sample size	935	935	634	634	636	635
Adjusted R^2	0.2206	0.2699	0.2242	0.2751	0.0530	0.1147

acquired low Q targets. The difference in results suggests that the takeover boom of the 1990s had a different character from that of the 1980s. Our finding also contrasts with that of Moeller et al. (2004a,b) that there is no economically significant relation between bidder Q and returns in acquisitions of public firms. Their sample differs from ours in several ways. It includes only successful acquisitions, includes merger bids as well as tender offers, and covers a shorter time period than our sample.

Also, Table 8 indicates that higher target Tobin's Q is associated with lower target announcement stock returns. This is consistent with recent findings for target book/market ratios (see Dong et al., 2003), and with earlier findings of Lang et al. (1989) and Servaes (1991).

4.3.6. Time dependence of value improvements

The Williams Act of 1968 and associated legislation requiring disclosure and delaying completion of tender offers makes it easier for competitors to investigate the target after an initial bid (Jarrell and Bradley, 1980). One would expect, as a result, that the set of bidders who are willing to make an initial offer would be narrower. Post-Williams transactions thus should be associated with higher value improvements. Several authors have shown large changes in premiums and several other takeover-related variables beginning at approximately this time (though explanations differ as to the source of these changes). To assess the effect of the Williams Act, we create a dummy variable for pre-Williams (July 1962–June 1968) and post-Williams subperiods.

In addition, commentators have claimed that the US financial market environment has changed after March 2000, when the Nasdaq and several other broad stock indexes peaked. We examine whether a shift in value gains occurred after March 2000 by using a dummy for pre- and post-March 2000.

Based on Table 4, it appears that 1989–1992 was a period of unusually low value improvements from takeover (based on CIBR and IR^{PSM}; the sample size for IR^{IM} for this period is too small to be meaningful). There is no indication that the takeover boom of the mid-1990s was associated with high percentage value improvements. Based on our estimates, the dollar value increase associated with the mid-1990s transactions was large. However, transactions in the late 1990s and the post-March 2000 period were associated with large wealth losses, because of the tremendous value losses to some relatively large bidders. These results are broadly consistent with the findings of Moeller et al. (2004a) (whose focus was on absolute bidder size).

In Table 5, it appears that value improvements were higher prior to the Williams Act than subsequent to the act. However, based on Table 8, there is no significant difference between the pre- and post-Williams amendment periods under any of the two value improvement measures. This suggests that the difference in takeover gains between these subperiods found in Table 5 was likely the result of shifts in takeover characteristics that are captured as explanatory variables in the multivariate analysis, such as a relatively high proportion of cash offers and smaller bidders prior to the Williams Act.

Table 5 also indicates a massive increase in target announcement period abnormal returns in the post-March 2000 period: from 28.77% to 44.78% (means), and from 25.30% to 39.81% (medians). This finding is reinforced by the target return regression in Table 8, in which the coefficient on the post-March 2000 category variable is substantial ($11.24, t = 3.24$). This indicates that the increase in target returns goes above and beyond what would be predicted by shifts in the regression explanatory variables.

Table 5 also indicates (significant with the PSM measure) that, after March 2000, combined returns (CIBR and IR^{PSM}) decreased. In contrast, the first two regressions in Table 8 suggest that combined returns increased after March 2000. However, as the next two regressions indicate, after controlling for bidder and target Tobin's Qs, the post-March 2000 dummy is not significant for CIBR or IR^{PSM}. These findings indicate that the post-March 2000 decrease in combined returns can be explained fully by shifts in the explanatory variables.

4.3.7. Do bidders pay too much?

To measure over- or underpayment, it is convenient to measure bid premiums relative to combined bidder/target value, according to the overpayment condition Equation (4). The results in Table 9 highlight that the new methods have an important effect on inferences. If we estimate value improvements using CIBR, the combined abnormal stock return, we find that in the competing bid subsample bidders on average significantly overpaid, by 5.1% (median 3.0%), with almost 65% of the 135 observations indicating overpayment. This difference is significant at the 1% level. However, CIBR captures only a fraction of the total takeover gains and is subject to revelation bias. Using either the IM or the PSM, the mean value improvement is not statistically different from the mean premium paid in these multiple bidder offers. So we cannot reliably reject the null that the payment is on average fair. In the competing bid subsample, both of the new methods developed here indicate that about half of the 135 initial bidders overpaid. Because value improvements are large, it appears that most of the bid premiums can be explained by value improvements.

There is a possible sample selection bias in the IM. The IM examines initial bidder returns when a competing bidder enters, but if the initial bidder offers too much on his first bid, this will tend to discourage competitors from arriving. Thus, a bidder who offers a generous initial offer will possibly not end up in the multiple-bidder sample. On the other hand, other things equal, the arrival of a competitor raises the amount that a first bidder with given valuation will have to pay. Thus, we doubt that there is more overpayment in single-bidder contests than in multiple bidder contests. This view is consistent with evidence on competitors' stock returns (see BDK-88).

4.4. Robustness of IM, PSM, and traditional measures to window length

All of the methods we apply are influenced by the length of the window selected. Longer windows capture more fully any anticipation of the event and a greater fraction

Table 9

The difference between value improvement measures and toehold-adjusted bid premium

Value improvement measures include the implicit market estimates of the value improvement as a result of the takeover (IR^{IM}), combined initial bid returns (CIBR), and probability-adjusted combined initial bid returns (IR^{PSM}). These value improvement estimates are defined in the legend of Table 4. p-Value of mean is the significance level for the student's t value that tests whether the mean is different from zero. Binomial p is the significance level for the two-tail Fisher sign test that tests whether the median is different from zero. The difference between value improvement and toehold-adjusted bid premium (ToePrem) is equal to the difference between the right-hand side and the left-hand side of Equation (4) in the text. $ToePrem = (1 - \alpha) \times$ (bid premium) $\times$ target market value/combined bidder and target market value, where α is the fraction of prebid target shares held by the bidder. Sample contains tender offers in which both bidder and target were listed on the NYSE, Amex, or Nasdaq during 1962–2001. In addition, for IR^{IM} the sample is restricted to cases with a competing bid for the target. All improvement ratios are expressed as a percentage of combined target and bidder market value.

Statistics	Subperiod								Total
	July 1962–June 1968	July 1968–December 1980	January 1981–December 1984	January 1985–December 1988	January 1989–December 1992	January 1993–December 1996	January 1997–March 2000	April 2000–December 2001	July 1962–December 2001
CIBR-ToePrem (full sample)									
Mean (%)	−0.11	−4.41	−2.34	−4.26	−3.53	−1.05	−1.53	−1.96	−2.66
Median (%)	0.35	−2.33	−4.73	−3.13	−2.61	0.57	−1.62	−0.84	−1.93
% Positive	54.2	34.5	27.3	31.8	30.9	54.7	42.2	47.3	40.0
p-Value of mean	0.91	0.00	0.31	0.00	0.00	0.21	0.02	0.20	0.00
Binomial p	0.60	0.00	0.00	0.00	0.00	0.31	0.03	0.73	0.00
Sample size	59	145	44	211	81	137	204	74	955
IR^{PSM}-ToePrem (full sample)									
Mean (%)	3.70	−1.71	2.77	−1.62	−2.04	0.29	−0.33	−1.70	−0.59
Median (%)	3.46	−0.23	−1.82	−1.59	−1.04	1.19	−0.93	−0.78	−0.48
% Positive	64.4	49.0	45.5	42.2	39.5	58.4	45.6	47.3	48.0
p-Value of mean	0.02	0.17	0.32	0.07	0.06	0.74	0.67	0.28	0.14
Binomial p	0.04	0.87	0.65	0.03	0.07	0.06	0.23	0.73	0.22
Sample size	59	145	44	211	81	137	204	74	955
IR^{IM}-ToePrem (competing bid subsample)									
Mean (%)	5.46	0.03	−2.47	−7.27	3.86	−0.90	−3.38	7.79	−1.45

(Continued)

Table 9 (Continued)

Statistics	July 1962–June 1968	July 1968–December 1980	January 1981–December 1984	January 1985–December 1988	January 1989–December 1992	January 1993–December 1996	January 1997–March 2000	April 2000–December 2001	Total July 1962–December 2001
				Subperiod					
Median (%)	6.42	1.67	−7.09	−3.82	2.32	3.14	−2.07	6.64	−0.07
% Positive	82.4	58.1	16.7	29.7	66.7	54.5	42.9	100.0	49.6
p-Value of mean	0.00	0.99	0.76	0.02	0.21	0.84	0.30	0.08	0.27
Binomial p	0.01	0.47	0.04	0.02	0.51	1.00	0.79	0.13	1.00
Sample size	17	31	12	37	9	11	14	4	135
CIBR-ToePrem (competing bid subsample)									
Mean (%)	−1.15	−3.51	0.83	−10.48	−2.67	−8.32	−4.03	−1.26	−5.06
Median (%)	−0.62	−1.74	−7.04	−5.74	−1.64	−5.60	−3.14	4.47	−2.95
% Positive	47.1	35.5	33.3	27.0	33.3	36.4	42.9	50.0	35.6
p-Value of mean	0.67	0.04	0.92	0.00	0.26	0.12	0.19	0.89	0.00
Binomial p	1.00	0.15	0.39	0.01	0.51	0.55	0.79	1.00	0.00
Sample size	17	31	12	37	9	11	14	4	135
IR^{PSM}-ToePrem (competing bid subsample)									
Mean (%)	3.41	−0.25	14.78	−2.17	2.33	−7.55	2.73	−0.10	0.91
Median (%)	3.34	0.37	6.50	−1.13	−0.48	−5.24	2.98	5.06	0.56
% Positive	58.8	54.8	75.0	48.6	44.4	45.5	57.1	50.0	54.1
p-Value of mean	0.37	0.90	0.09	0.52	0.63	0.17	0.50	0.99	0.56
Binomial p	0.63	0.72	0.15	1.00	1.00	1.00	0.79	1.00	0.39
Sample size	17	31	12	37	9	11	14	4	135

of the effects of event-resolution. The cost of a longer event window is greater noise and benchmark error. To evaluate whether the value improvements derived by IM and PSM are higher than those implied by traditional approaches, we consider different window lengths.

Using traditional methods, with a $(-5, +5)$ event window where date 0 is the date of the initial bid, the mean (median) weighted average of the bidder and target returns using value weights is 5.27% (3.69%), with 71% of the returns being positive (see Table 2, Panel A). In the older sample of BDK-88, the mean initial return relative to combined market value is 6.93%. Thus, there was a decline in mean returns in the decade following the BDK study.

A reasonable starting point that would account for prepublic announcement anticipation of the event would be in the order of 30–40 days. See, for example, Figure 1 of Schwert (1996). Using a longer window that begins 30 days prior to the initial offer and runs through final announcement of the transaction, we obtain a mean (median) bidder and target weighted return of 7.12% (6.35%). The corresponding measure beginning 90 days prior to the initial offer is 6.65% (7.05%).

The combined CARs for these initial returns for different windows are summarized in Table 2, Panel B. Even with long event windows prior to the event, the mean CAR based on the initial bid is at most only 7.1%, as compared with 13.1% using the IM. These results imply that the gains from takeover are considerably greater than the (already substantial) gains estimated in previous studies.

The use of a long window such as 60 or 90 days is probably suboptimal. While such a window ensures that any preevent information leakage is captured in the return, it also greatly increases noise. In this case, as we lengthen the window, the mean CAR increases up to a 30-day window. But moving from a 15- to a 30-day window leads to a smaller fraction of positive abnormal returns, suggesting that the problem of noise starts to become severe in the longer window.

Furthermore, the use of a $(-1, 0)$ window by IM for the arrival of the competing bid also potentially misses some runup. In unreported results, we find that a longer precompeting bid window is associated with even higher IR^{IM} estimate.

4.5. Robustness with respect to model specifications

We next consider the robustness of our conclusions about value improvements with respect to our model specifications.

4.5.1. Competing bidder information

The arrival of a competing bid may convey information about either the stand-alone value of the target or its value to the initial bidder, a different kind of revelation effect (see Section 2.4). This is likely to have only a minor effect on IM estimation (see Footnotes 11 and 12). More important, the IM mitigates this problem relative to previous studies by focusing on competing bids, because much of the private information possessed by bidders about targets likely already is conveyed by the initial offer.

If the arrival of a competing bid causes an upward revision in the assessed valuation of the first bidder, then ceteris paribus the first bidder's abnormal return R_3 will be higher. By constraining $\bar{V}_3 = \bar{V}_1$, our estimates would tend to wrongly attribute any such higher abnormal return to the reduced probability of the initial bidder succeeding. Thus, the estimated value improvement would be biased downward, providing a conservative estimate. Thus, the inference that takeovers are on average associated with positive underlying value improvements is strengthened.

To analyze this issue directly, suppose that $\bar{V}_3^I = K\bar{V}_1^I$, $K \geq 1$, that is, the arrival of a competing bid causes an upward revision in the assessed valuation by the first bidder of owning the target. We abbreviate $\bar{V}_1^I$ as $\bar{V}^I$ in the following. Substituting into Equations (9)–(11), and solving gives

$$\frac{\bar{V}^I}{V_0^C} = \frac{R_3\left(P_1/V_0^C\right)}{K\phi_3 - \phi_1} - (1 - \alpha)\left(\frac{\phi_3 - \phi_1}{K\phi_3 - \phi_1}\right)\left(\frac{V^T}{V_0^C}\right)$$
$$+ (1 - \alpha)\left(\frac{V^T}{V_0^C}\right)\frac{\phi_3\left(\bar{B}_3/V_0^T\right) - \phi_1\left(\bar{B}_1/V_0^T\right)}{K\phi_3 - \phi_1}. \tag{19}$$

As suggested in Section 2.4, K is likely to be close to one. The implied IR^{IM} estimates, which are increasing in K, are provided in the first two columns of Table 10. This

Table 10

This table provides a sensitivity analysis for IR^{IM}, the value improvement as a result of the takeover, with respect to parameter values in several variations of the basic model

Columns 1 and 2 describe the effects of varying K, the ratio of the expected posttakeover value of the target to the first bidder conditional on a competing bid arriving to the unconditional expected value. Columns 3 and 4 vary γ, the probability that after failure the first bidder will seek and acquire an identical target. Columns 5–7 vary $Pr(S^2|\theta_3)$, the probability that a second bidder wins given that he enters the contest, to allow for the benefits derived by a defeated first bidder from selling his initial shareholding to a competing bidder. Column 6 is based on the actual first bidder initial shareholding, and Column 7 is based on an initial shareholding of 0.15. Parameter inputs for computation of IR^{IM} are derived from regression/logit Models A1 and B (see Table 3).

K (1)	IR^{IM} (%) Mean/median (2)	γ (3)	IR^{IM} (%) Mean/median (4)	$Pr(S^2|\theta_3)$ (5)	IR^{IM} (%) Mean/median (6)	IR^{IM} (%) Mean/median (7)
1.00	14.8/13.8	0.0	14.8/13.8	0.0	14.8/13.8	13.2/12.1
1.10	15.8/15.2	0.2	14.5/13.5	0.1	14.9/13.8	14.1/12.7
1.20	17.5/16.9	0.4	14.3/14.1	0.3	15.3/14.2	15.7/14.1
1.30	18.4/19.0	0.6	14.0/14.6	0.5	15.6/14.3	17.1/16.0
1.40	19.0/20.8	1.0	13.4/14.3	0.7	15.9/14.8	18.5/18.2

simulation supports the conclusion of positive average value improvements; large values of K lead to implausibly high values for $\bar{V}^{\mathrm{I}}/V_0^{\mathrm{C}}$.

4.5.2. Future acquisitions

The basic analysis assumes that success or failure of the offer has no effect on any future acquisitions that the bidder could make. More generally, if the first bidder fails to acquire the target, a similar target could thereafter be successfully acquired at a price similar to what he would have paid if he had been successful in acquiring the original target. If so, the stock price reaction to failure of the initial bid would be muted. A bidder whose offer fails is not certain to make an additional acquisition as a consequence of failure. (No difficulty arises if the bidder intends to make other acquisitions regardless of the outcome of the first contest. The calculation of the stock price reaction associated with the arrival of a competing bid needs modification only if future acquisitions depend on the success or failure in the current contest.) We model this possible dependence by allowing for some probability that failure of the offer will cause the bidder to try to acquire another comparable target at the same expected price.

There are several possible reasons why this probability is less than one. First, alternative targets may seem less attractive to bidding management. For example, under Roll's hubris hypothesis, a bidder's first offer will be to the target he overvalues the most. Second, a manager may change his mind about the desirability of acquisition. Third, he may retire or be replaced before he locates another target. Fourth, if acquisition is undesirable, the initial offer may rouse large shareholders or the board to oppose further attempts.

Suppose that value improvements in takeovers are positive. Then when the arrival of a competing bid reduces the probability of success, the bidder has a good chance of succeeding in another acquisition, so the actual bidder return will be greater than that implied by the basic model of Section 2. This higher return implies that $\mathrm{IR}^{\mathrm{IM}}$ will underestimate the actual improvement. Similarly, if value improvements are negative, $\mathrm{IR}^{\mathrm{IM}}$ will overestimate the improvement. So long as failure could lead to another comparable acquisition, the basic method biases $\mathrm{IR}^{\mathrm{IM}}$ toward zero but leaves its sign unchanged. (More generally, the sign could be incorrect, but this requires a rather special scenario. For example, if the improvement is always zero in the initial contest, but after an initial failure the bidder always makes a negative net present value acquisition, then the stock return will be lower than the calculation in Section 2. The negative stock return, in combination with the reduction in probability of success associated with the arrival of a competing bid, would tend to be attributed to a positive value improvement.) A robustness check is provided by reestimating $\mathrm{IR}^{\mathrm{IM}}$ in a model in which, given failure, there is a probability γ that the bidder will make another acquisition attempt of equal quality to the first.

Suppose that the first bidder can find another identical target with probability γ after failure to acquire the first target. Then Equation (11) becomes

$$\bar{\pi}_1 = [\phi_1 + \gamma\phi_1(1 - \phi_1)][\alpha\bar{V}^I + (1 - \alpha)(\bar{V}^I + V_0^T - \bar{B}_1)] \tag{20}$$

and

$$\bar{\pi}_3 = [\phi_3 + \gamma\phi_1(1 - \phi_3)][\alpha\bar{V}^I + (1 - \alpha)(\bar{V}^I + V_0^T - \bar{B}_3)]. \tag{21}$$

So,

$$\frac{\bar{V}^I}{V_0^C} = \frac{R_3(P_1/V_0^C)}{\delta_2} - (1 - \alpha)\left(\frac{V_0^T}{V_0^C}\right)$$
$$+ (1 - \alpha)\left[\left(\frac{\delta_1 + \delta_2}{\delta_2}\right)\left(\frac{\bar{B}_3}{V_0^T}\right) - \left(\frac{\delta_1}{\delta_2}\right)\left(\frac{\bar{B}_1}{V_0^T}\right)\right]\left(\frac{V_0^T}{V_0^C}\right), \tag{22}$$

where $\delta_1 \equiv \phi_1[1 + \gamma(1 - \phi_1)]$ and $\delta_2 \equiv (\phi_1 - \phi_3)(\gamma\phi_1 - 1)$. IR^{IM} decreases as a function of γ, but the effect is weak. As shown in Columns 3 and 4 of Table 10, the estimated value improvement is still positive and substantial for plausible values of γ. The effect of γ on IR^{IM} would be stronger if, after a second failure, the bidder again had a probability of turning to a third target and so on.

4.5.3. Sale of shares to another bidder

We now allow for the possibility that an unsuccessful initial bidder can sometimes profit by selling his holdings to a successful competing bidder. Let $\Pr(S^2|\theta)$ denote the probability of arrival and success of the second bidder, and let β denote the expected winning bid of the second bidder. Then so long as $\beta > V_0^T$ (so that it pays for the unsuccessful initial bidder to sell to the later bidder),

$$\bar{\pi}_1 = \phi_1[\alpha\bar{V}^I + (1 - \alpha)(\bar{V}^I + V_0^T - \bar{B}_1)] + \alpha\Pr(S^2|\theta_1)(\beta - V_0^T) \tag{23}$$

and

$$\bar{\pi}_3 = \phi_3[\alpha\bar{V}^I + (1 - \alpha)(\bar{V}^I + V_0^T - \bar{B}_3)] + \alpha\Pr(S^2|\theta_3)(\beta - V_0^T). \tag{24}$$

So,

$$\frac{\bar{V}^I}{V_0^C} = \frac{R_3(P_1/V_0^C)}{\phi_3 - \phi_1} - (1 - \alpha)\frac{V_0^T}{V_0^C} + (1 - \alpha)\frac{\phi_3(\bar{B}_3/V_0^T) - \phi_1(\bar{B}_1/V_0^T)}{\phi_3 - \phi_1}\left(\frac{V_0^T}{V_0^C}\right)$$
$$- \left\{\frac{\alpha[(\beta/V_0^T) - 1][\Pr(S^2|\theta_3) - \Pr(S^2|\theta_1)]}{\phi_3 - \phi_1}\right\}\left(\frac{V_0^T}{V_0^C}\right). \tag{25}$$

As a rough approximation, we replace β with our estimates of the expected price paid by a successful first bidder conditional on the arrival of a competing bidder, $\bar{B}_3$. The unconditional probability of a second bidder winning is the probability that a second bidder arrives multiplied by the probability given arrival that the second bidder wins, $\Pr(S^2|\theta_1) = \Pr(\text{Competing bid occurs}) \Pr(S^2|\theta_3)$. $\Pr(\text{Competing bid occurs})$ is estimated as 147/1018. Thus, only one of the other two probabilities is a free variable. IR^{IM} for different possible values of $\Pr(S^2|\theta_3)$ is given in Columns 5–7 of Table 10. A benchmark value for this variable is 0.5, the case in which, given the arrival of a competing bidder, the first and second bidder have equal probabilities of winning. Column 6 gives the estimated improvement ratio with the bidders' actual initial shareholdings in the target. Column 7 provides alternative numbers assuming larger initial shareholdings. For plausible parameter values, the estimated value improvement is robust with respect to the possibility of sale of the initial bidder's toehold.

4.5.4. Valuation/success correlation

Finally, the success of the initial bidder is likely to be positively correlated with the value improvement, because a high valuation first bidder will probably be willing to offer more. The logit-based probability estimates, which generated similar results to simple estimates based on ex post sample fractions, address this issue to the extent that explanatory logit variables such as the initial bid premium are correlated with the first bidder's valuation. In any case, the potential bias is a subtle one, because IM estimates are based on the change in probability of success when a competing bid occurs. Even if probabilities were misestimated across transactions, it is not clear that there would be any important, systematic misestimation in the changes in probabilities.

The most plausible presumption is probably that the arrival of a competitor has a smaller impact on probability of success when the valuation is high. Then for a high valuation first bidder, the drop in probability of success is overestimated, which implies that IR^{IM} is an underestimate. (The negative abnormal return is attributed excessively to the drop in probability of success instead of to a large value improvement.) Conversely, for low (but positive) valuation firms, the drop in probability of success is underestimated, so that IR^{IM} is an overestimate. Under these conditions, this potential bias changes the relative magnitude of IR^{IM} for different firms, but it does not imply any obvious bias in overall sample averages.

Similarly, it can plausibly be argued that if improvements are common across bidders, a high value improvement increases the probability that a competing bid arrives. Again, the potential bias implied by this effect is subtle, because the ex ante probability of a competing bid is overestimated for some contests and underestimated for others. (If the true improvement is high, the arrival of a competing bid would be less of a surprise than our calculations indicate. For such contests, the improvement is underestimated. If the true improvement is low, the arrival of a competing bid would be more of a surprise than our calculations indicate. For such contests, the improvement is overestimated. The effect on overall sample averages is unclear.) It therefore seems unlikely that these effects would have much effect on inferences about value improvements.

In summary, several robustness checks with respect to several possible modeling variants confirm that the conclusion of positive average value improvements provided using the basic model is highly robust. For plausible parameter values, all estimates of the average value improvement are positive and substantial.

5. Summary and conclusions

Despite an extensive literature, the issue of whether tender offers increase or decrease combined average bidder and target value has remained unresolved. Past stock market-based studies have provided valuable information consistent with positive average improvements. However, the conventional event study approach is subject to two estimation problems. The first, the truncation dilemma, arises when the announcement of the event does not ensure successful completion of the event. This forces the investigator to choose between truncated event windows that measure only a part of the value effect of a successful transaction and long windows that introduce severe noise and benchmark errors.

The second problem is that event-related returns are infected with a bidder revelation bias (Bradley et al., 1983; Jensen and Ruback, 1983; Jovanovic and Braguinsky, 2002; Roll, 1986). Tender offer bids are sometimes announced concurrently with other disclosures, and a bid could in itself reveal information about the value of the bidder not arising from the combination, such as the bidder's stand-alone cash flow prospects or the empire-building propensities of management.

This paper estimates whether and by how much tender offers are perceived by investors as improving combined equity value. We offer an approach to estimating perceived value improvements, the PSM, that addresses the truncation dilemma. Furthermore, we offer an approach that addresses both the truncation dilemma and the bidder-revelation bias. This approach, the IM, is based on a model of the stock returns of an initial bidder when a competing bid occurs.

We apply both the traditional method and the two new methods to a sample of tender offers during 1962–2001. Perceived value improvements are much larger than traditional methods indicate. As a result, even though the conventional method indicates that bidders on average overpay, using our new methods we cannot reject the hypothesis that bidders on average pay fair prices for targets.

Furthermore, our methods provide more specific guidance than the traditional method about how economic forces affect the takeover market. We identify several effects (higher combined bidder-target stock returns for hostile offers, lower for equity offers, and lower for diversifying offers) that reflect differences in revelation about bidder stand-alone value, not gains from combination. In other words, it is not that investors perceive that combination creates less underlying value in equity than in cash transactions, but that payment with equity is bad news about bidder stand-alone value (in the spirit of the adverse selection model of Myers and Majluf (1984), but inconsistent with the hypothesis that cash payment reveals a general propensity for the bidder management to waste cash). It is not that investors perceive hostile transactions as creating greater underlying value than friendly ones, but that the announcement of a hostile offer is better news about the quality of bidder management than announcement of a friendly one. And it is not that investors perceive diversification as reducing underlying value, but that diversification conveys bad news about the bidder's stand-alone prospects (such as poor internal investment opportunities).

We also identify some economic factors that do affect the gains from combination, not just revelation about stand-alone value. Using all three approaches, acquisition of a smaller target by a large bidder on average creates a smaller value improvement, measured as a fraction of combined value, than combinations of similar-size firms. But measured relative to the value of the target, the mean estimated improvement is larger for such transactions. These findings are consistent with the importance of both synergies and target-specific improvements such as removal of bad management.

Furthermore, bidder announcement period returns and total value improvements are negatively related to bidder Tobin's Q, in contrast with evidence from the earlier samples of Lang et al. (1989) and Servaes (1991). Target announcement period returns are negatively related to target Q, consistent with previous literature.

All else equal, the evidence of positive value improvements, and that improvements are larger than estimates based on traditional methods, tends to oppose highly restrictive regulation of takeovers. There are, however, other important policy considerations related to takeovers, such as possible errors in market perceptions, possible redistributions of wealth from stakeholders such as customers and employees, the disciplinary or distortive effects of the ex ante threat of takeover, and the ex ante costs of locating targets.

The PSM and the IM can be applied to test the relation of value improvements to other possible determinants. For example, these methods could be used to address whether the arrival of white knights blocks superior hostile acquisitions. These new methods could also be applied to other corporate activities that are announced but are not always carried through, such as repurchase programs, planned asset sales, planned development of new products, and acquisition programs.

Appendix A: Numerical illustration of the probability scaling and intervention methods

The basic ideas of the probability scaling method (PSM) and intervention method (IM) can be illustrated by numerical examples.

A.1. The probability scaling method

Consider a bidder who does not own any shares of the target. Suppose that the stand-alone value of the target is 100, the stand-alone value of the bidder is 200, and the transaction will create a value improvement of 40. Suppose that prior to the initial bid the market assesses the probability of a bid to be close to zero and that just after the initial bid the probability of offer success is perceived to be 0.6. Then the stock market's assessment of the combined bidder-target expected value prior to the initial bid is approximately $100 + 200 = 300$.

Just after the initial bid, this assessment is revised to $100 + 200 + 0.6(40) = 324$. The combined bidder-target equity return is therefore $324/300 - 1 = 8.0\%$. This is only a fraction of the percentage value improvement associated with a completed takeover, which is $40/300 = 13.3\%$ of combined value.

The PSM grosses up the equity return by the probability of success, which gives the total value gain of a virtual completed transaction, $8.0\%/0.6 = 13.3\%$ of combined bidder-target value.

The actual implementation of PSM also takes into account that the target return reflects the market's belief about the likelihood that the target will be acquired by any bidder, not just the first bidder. Section 2.3 derives PSM in detail.

A.2. The revelation bias

We now illustrate the revelation bias inherent in the conventional approach to estimating takeover value improvements. To begin with, let there be no value improvement from successful takeover, so that stand-alone and posttakeover discounted value of target cash flows are both $100. Suppose that prior to the initial bid, the market estimates the stand-alone value of the bidder to be $200. Suppose that a bid reveals favorable news to the market about stand-alone bidder value, so that the postinitial bid market assessment of stand-alone bidder value is $250. The $50 discrepancy is the effect the bid has on the market's assessment of stand-alone value.

The stock market's assessment of combined bidder-target value prior to the initial bid is $100 + 200 = 300$. Just after the initial bid, this assessment is revised to $100 + 250 = 350$. The combined bidder-target equity return will therefore be $350/300 - 1 \approx 16.7\%$. If the revelation effect of the initial bid is ignored, the researcher will wrongly attribute this return to an expected value improvement of $0.166 \times \$300 = \$50$ (50% of target value), when in fact the improvement is zero. As Roll (1986) points out, even a modest revelation bias for the bidder can create a large overestimate of the value improvement from takeover measured relative to target value, because on average bidders are much larger than targets.

A.3. The intervention method

Given that competition reduces a first bidder's probability of success, ceteris paribus its stock price will drop if its value improvement is large compared with the expected price that will be paid, and will rise if the value improvement is less than the expected purchase price. Thus the stock price reaction to a competing bid provides information about the value improvement. However, holding probability of success constant, competition should hurt the first bidder to the extent that he is forced to pay more when he wins. The challenge for the IM is to disentangle these two effects.

After the initial bid, the market's assessment of stand-alone bidder value is $250. We will compare a case of positive value improvement, in which the value of the target managed by the bidder is $140, with the case of zero improvement, in which the posttakeover net present value of target cash flows if managed by the bidder is $100.

A.3.1. Positive value improvement

Suppose that, at the time of the initial offer, the probability of the initial bidder succeeding is 0.6, but that, if a competitor makes a bid, this probability is only 0.4. (These overall probabilities take into account the possibility that a competing bid could be forthcoming.) Suppose that, at the time of the initial offer, the expected price that the first bidder will have to pay if he succeeds is $120, but that, if a competitor arrives, this expected price paid by the first bidder rises to $130. We assume that, regardless of the bidder's method of payment, the expected price ($120 or $130) refers to the actual price paid by the bidder at the time of completion of the deal. Based on this information, the stock price of the bidder after announcing his offer rises to $250 + 0.6 (140 - 120) = 262$. If a competitor appears, the first bidder's stock price retreats to $250 + 0.4(140 - 130) = 254$. Thus, the first bidder's stock return on the arrival of a competing bidder is $(254 - 262)/262 \approx -3\%$.

The initial bidder's stock return reflects the facts that, when a competing bid arrives, (1) the first bidder will have to pay more if he succeeds, and (2) the first bidder has a lower probability of succeeding. Clearly point (1) contributes negatively to the first bidder's return. Point (2) also contributes negatively to the stock return here, because a lower probability of success prevents the bidder from realizing profits. These profits are the difference between the improvement brought about by the first bidder and the expected price paid. Thus, the first bidder's stock return on the arrival of a competing bid reflects the market's assessment of the value improvement that the first bidder can bring about. Specifically, the larger the improvement, ceteris paribus, the more negative the return. And if the improvement is smaller than the expected price, then point (2) will contribute positively to the bidder's return.

A.3.2. Zero value improvement

These points are illustrated by making one change in the example. Suppose that the takeover does not improve value, so the value of the target when acquired is the same as its stand-alone value of $100. Replacing $140 with $100 in the above calculations shows that the bidder's stock return on the arrival of a competing bidder is 0%. The negative effect of the higher price that will be paid in the event of success is offset by the positive effect of an increased probability of failure.

The IM uses ex post data to estimate the various parameters of this numerical example: the unconditional probability of success of an initial bidder, the probability of success given the arrival of a competitor, the unconditional expected price paid by an initial bidder given that he succeeds, and the expected price he pays if he succeeds given that a competing bid occurs. Given these parameters (along with the initial shareholding of the bidder in the target), the value improvement from the takeover implies a specific stock return for the first bidder. It is therefore possible to infer the size of the value improvement from the observed stock return.

The above discussion is based on the distinction between creation of value and revelation of information about value. An action can create value as a direct result of revealing value; this in no way obviates the need to distinguish the two concepts. For example, if a takeover bid conveys to the market the idea that the bidder's prospects are good, customers or suppliers could be more willing to deal with the firm (e.g., Titman, 1984). If so, even a manager whose sole objective is to maximize fundamental value could expend resources to reveal information. Nevertheless, the value created by a corporate action is in general different from the value revealed. Generally, these quantities can have different orders of magnitude and need not have the same sign. Thus, the increase in stock price associated with a corporate action is an invalid measure of the effect of that action on underlying value. Furthermore, even if the announcement of a takeover bid makes market perceptions more favorable, and this change in perceptions in turn increased underlying value significantly, this value increase is not an actual benefit from combination, but a benefit of favorable revelation.[19] The IM accommodates, but does not require, possible effects of value revelation on fundamental value; it accommodates, but does not require, signaling motivations; and it estimates only those value improvements that result from combination of the two firms, not those that result from revelation about stand-alone value.

Appendix B: Robustness of IM results with respect to alternative parameter estimates

We analyze the robustness of the conclusion that the mean value improvement ratio is positive with respect to the parameter estimates for $\bar{R}_3$, ϕ_1, ϕ_3, $\bar{B}_1/V_0^{\mathrm{T}}$, and $\bar{B}_3/V_0^{\mathrm{T}}$. We conduct two experiments. First is a sensitivity analysis of $\mathrm{IR}^{\mathrm{IM}}$ with respect to the probability of success unconditionally, ϕ_1, and conditional on a competing bid, ϕ; with respect to the expected price paid unconditionally, $\bar{B}_1/V_0^{\mathrm{T}}$, and conditional on a competing bid, $\bar{B}_3/V_0^{\mathrm{T}}$; and with respect to the mean first bidder stock return on announcement of a competing bid, $\bar{R}_3$. Second, we compare our results with those implied by samples studied by Bhagat et al. (1990) and Betton and Eckbo (2000).

We examine the effect of shifting each of these estimated parameters simultaneously in the direction of lower $\mathrm{IR}^{\mathrm{IM}}$. This check is stringent, because there is no reason to

---

[19] In the numerical example, the increase in the market's stand-alone valuation of bidder from 200 to 250 could reflect not the direct effect on expectations of more favorable information, but the fact that the bidder's higher stock price could in itself help it to generate greater cash flows as a stand-alone entity.

expect estimation errors all to boost the IR^{IM}. The results indicate that the conclusion that value improvements are on average positive is not very sensitive to shifts in parameter estimates. Even if all four of the estimated parameters are shifted by 12% of their respective mean values, the mean estimated IR^{IM} remains positive.

A limitation of the IM is that it provides value estimates only in those contests for which the intervention (competing bid) actually occurs. If contests that did not enter the intervention sample are different, the returns to the first bidder in such contests upon arrival of a competing bid would be systematically different from the first bidder returns in the actual competing bid sample. While it is impossible to address this issue conclusively, the conclusion of positive value improvements with respect to the estimated stock returns is extremely robust. The sensitivity to $\bar{R}_3$ provides an indication of whether the conclusions we derive are likely to be sample-specific. We recalculated IR^{IM} substituting fictional alternative values for $\bar{R}_3$ for all first bidders. Both the mean and median value improvements remain positive even for an abnormal return as high as +3.5%, and a majority are positive even for an abnormal return as high as +7%. (Intuitively, the reason that the estimates remain positive even when intervention returns are high is that the mean bid premiums are substantial. Thus, even if the value improvement is positive, if it is smaller than the expected price to be paid, the arrival of a competing bid and the associated reduction in the probability of the first bidder succeeding can be good news.) These robustness checks support the conclusion that value improvements are on average positive and substantial.

The conclusion of positive average value improvements applies in other samples as well. Bhagat et al. (1990) (BSV) analyze an exhaustive sample of hostile takeover contests in the United States during 1984 through 1986 when the purchase price was $50 million or more. Their sample consists of 61 contests: 50 targets were acquired and 11 remained independent. The first bidder was successful in 29 of the 61 contests. Competing bids were observed in 30 of the 61 contests. The first bidder prevailed in the face of a competing offer in nine instances.

The above figures indicate that in the BSV sample, ϕ_1, the probability of success of the first bidder in the full sample, is 29/61 or 0.4754. Also, ϕ_3, the probability of success of the first bidder in the presence of a competing bidder, is 9/30 or 0.3000. Similarly, we estimate $\bar{B}_1/V_0^T$, and $\bar{B}_3/V_0^T$ implied by the BSV sample. We then substitute these parameter estimates into the IR^{IM} formula transaction by transaction in our full data set to generate an alternative set of IR^{IM}s.

The estimated input parameters from the BSV sample period (1984–1986) are fairly similar to those of this study. When the BSV sample parameter estimates are substituted into the IR^{IM} formula Equation (13), the inference about IR^{IM} is unchanged, that the mean IR^{IM} is positive. Simultaneously substituting the BSV estimates for $\bar{B}_1/V_0^T$, $\bar{B}_3/V_0^T$, ϕ_1, and ϕ_3 with other mean parameters generates a mean (median) IR^{IM} of 9.0 (9.9).

Betton and Eckbo (2000) examine a sample of tender offers from 1971 to 1990. They report that, in their sample, the unconditional probability of bidder success was 0.6386 and conditional on a competing bid was only 0.1682. The unconditional expected premium was 56.96% and conditional on a competing bid was 85.60%. Applying these figures to our overall sample transaction by transaction in the IR^{IM} formula gives an average IR^{IM} of 17.5% (15.3%). This is somewhat higher than the estimates of about 13–15% using our own sample.

To summarize, in this appendix we have performed robustness checks by varying estimated parameters, both individually and simultaneously, and by using parameter estimates obtained from the BSV and the Betton and Eckbo (2000) samples. These analyses all confirm that value improvements were on average positive.

References

Andrade, G., M. Mitchell and E. Stafford, 2001, "New Evidence and Perspectives on Mergers," *Journal of Economics Perspectives*, 15, 103–120.

Asquith, P., R. Bruner and D. Mullins, 1983, "The Gains to Bidding Firms from Merger," *Journal of Financial Economics*, 11, 121–139.

Barber, B. and J. Lyon, 1997, "Detecting Long-Run Abnormal Stock Returns: The Empirical Power and Specification of Test Statistics," *Journal of Financial Economics*, 43, 341–372.

Betton, S. and B. E. Eckbo, 2000, "Toeholds, Bid Jumps, and Expected Payoffs in Takeovers," *Review of Financial Studies*, 13, 841–882.

Bhagat, S., A. Shleifer and R. Vishny, 1990, "Hostile Takeovers in the 1980s: The Return to Corporate Specialization," *Brookings Papers on Economic Activity*, 1–72.

Bradley, M., A. Desai and E. H. Kim, 1983, "The Rationale Behind Interfirm Tender Offers: Information or Synergy?" *Journal of Financial Economics*, 11, 141–153.

Bradley, M., A. Desai and E. H. Kim, 1988, "Synergistic Gains from Corporate Acquisitions and their Division between Stockholders of Target and Acquiring Firms," *Journal of Financial Economics*, 21, 3–40.

Brown, D. T. and M. D. Ryngaert, 1991, "The Mode of Acquisition in Takeovers: Taxes and Asymmetric Information," *Journal of Finance*, 46, 653–669.

Brown, S. J. and J. B. Warner, 1985, "Using Daily Stock Returns: The Case of Event Studies," *Journal of Financial Economics*, 14, 3–32.

Bulow, J., M. Huang and P. Klemperer, 1999, "Toeholds and Takeovers," *Journal of Political Economy*, 107, 427–454.

Comment, R. and G. Jarrell, 1987, "Two-Tier and Negotiated Tender Offers: The Imprisonment of the Free-Riding Shareholder," *Journal of Financial Economics*, 19, 283–310.

Dodd, P. and J. B.Warner, 1983, "On Corporate Governance: A Study of Proxy Contests," *Journal of Financial Economics*, 11, 401–438.

Dong, M., D. Hirshleifer, S. Richardson and S. H. Teoh, 2003, "Does Investor Misvaluation Drive the Takeover Market?" Dice Center Working Paper 2003-7, Fisher College of Business, Ohio State University; Wharton School, and York University, http://papers.ssrn.com/sol3/papers.cfm?abstract_id = 393021.

Eckbo, B. E., 1983, "Horizontal Mergers, Collusion, and Stockholder Wealth," *Journal of Financial Economics*, 11, 241–273.

Eckbo, B. E., 1992, "Mergers and the Value of Antitrust Deterrence," *Journal of Finance*, 47, 1005–1029.

Eckbo, B. E., R. Giammarino and R. Heinkel, 1990, "Asymmetric Information and the Medium of Exchange in Takeovers: Theory and Evidence," *Review of Financial Studies*, 3, 651–676.

Fishman, M., 1988, "A Theory of Preemptive Takeover Bidding," *Rand Journal of Economics*, 19, 88–101.

Fishman, M. J., 1989, "Preemptive Bidding and the Role of Medium of Exchange in Acquisitions," *Journal of Finance*, 44, 41–58.

Franks, J., R. Harris and S. Titman, 1991, "The Post-Merger Share-Price Performance of Acquiring Firms," *Journal of Financial Economics*, 29, 81–96.

Fuller, K., J. Netter and M. Stegemoller, 2002, "What do Returns to Acquiring Firms Tell Us? Evidence from Firms that Make Many Acquisitions," *Journal of Finance*, 57, 1763–1793.

Grossman, S. and O. Hart, 1980, "Takeover Bids, the Free-Rider Problem, and the Theory of the Corporation," *Bell Journal of Economics*, 11, 42–64.

Hansen, R. G., 1987, "A Theory for the Choice of Exchange Medium in Mergers and Acquisitions," *Journal of Business*, 60, 75–95.

Healy, P. M., K. G. Palepu and R. S. Ruback, 1992, "Does Corporate Performance Improve After Mergers?" *Journal of Financial Economics*, 31, 135–175.

Hietala, P., Kaplan, S. and D. Robinson, 2003, "What is the Price of Hubris? Using Takeover Battles to Infer Overpayments and Synergies," *Financial Management*, 32, 5–31.

Hirshleifer, D. and S. Titman, 1990, "Share Tendering Strategies and the Success of Hostile Takeover Bids," *Journal of Political Economy*, 92, 295–324.

Hou, K., P. Olsson and D. Robinson, 2000, "Does Takeover Increase Stockholder Value?" Unpublished Working Paper, Fisher College of Business, Ohio State University, and Fuqua School of Business, Duke University, http://papers.ssrn.com/sol3/papers.cfm?abstract_id=246151.

Jarrell, G., M. Bradley, 1980, "The Economic Effects of Federal and State Regulations of Cash Tender Offers," *Journal of Law and Economics*, 23, 371–407.

Jarrell, G., J. Brickley and J. Netter, 1988, "The Market for Corporate Control: The Empirical Evidence Since 1980," *Journal of Economic Perspectives*, 2, 49–68.

Jensen, M., 1988, "Takeovers: Their Causes and Consequences," *Journal of Economic Perspectives*, 2, 21–48.

Jensen, M. and R. Ruback, 1983, "The Market for Corporate Control: The Scientific Evidence," *Journal of Financial Economics*, 11, 5–50.

Jovanovic, B. and S. Braguinsky, 2002, *Bidder Discounts and Target Premia in Takeovers*, Unpublished Working Paper 9009, National Bureau of Economic Research, Cambridge, MA.

Kahle, K. and R. Walkling, 1996, "The Impact of Industry Classifications on Financial Research," *Journal of Financial and Quantitative Analysis*, 31, 309–335.

Kaplan, S. and M. Weisbach, 1991, "The Success of Acquisitions: Evidence from Divestitures," *Journal of Finance*, 47, 107–138.

Kothari, S. P. and J. Warner, 1997, "Measuring Long-Horizon Security Price Performance," *Journal of Financial Economics*, 43, 301–339.

Lang, L., R. Stulz and R. Walkling, 1989, "Managerial Performance, Tobin's Q, and the Gains from Successful Tender Offers," *Journal of Financial Economics*, 24, 137–154.

Loughran, T. and A. Vijh, 1997, "Do Long-Term Shareholders Benefit from Corporate Acquisitions?" *Journal of Finance*, 52, 1765–1790.

Luo, Y., 2003, "Do Insiders Learn from Outsiders? Evidence from Mergers and Acquisitions," Unpublished Working Paper, Goldman, Sachs & Co., http://papers.ssrn.com/sol3/papers.cfm?abstract_id=361520.

Maquieira, C. P., W. L. Megginson and L. Nail, 1998, "Wealth Creation Versus Wealth Redistributions in Pure Stock-for-Stock Mergers," *Journal of Financial Economics*, 48, 3–33.

Martin, K. J., 1996, "The Method of Payment in Corporate Acquisitions, Investment Opportunities, and Management Ownership," *Journal of Finance*, 51, 1227–1246.

Mitchell, M. and E. Stafford, 2000, "Managerial Decisions and Long-Term Stock Price Performance," *Journal of Business*, 73, 287–320.

Moeller, S., F. Schlingemann and R. Stulz, 2004a, "Firm Size and the Gains from Acquisitions," *Journal of Financial Economics*, 73, 201–228.

Moeller, S., F. Schlingemann and R. Stulz, 2004b, "Wealth Destruction on a Massive Scale? A Study of Acquiring-Firm Returns in the Recent Merger Wave," *Journal of Finance*, forthcoming.

Morck, R., A. Shleifer and R. Vishny, 1990, "Do Managerial Objectives Drive Bad Acquisitions?" *Journal of Finance*, 45, 31–48.

Mueller, D., 1985, "Mergers and Market Share," *Review of Economics and Statistics*, 47, 259–267.

Myers, S. and N. Majluf, 1984, "Corporate Financing and Investment Decisions When Firms Have Information that Investors Do Not Have," *Journal of Financial Economics*, 13, 187–221.

Palepu, K., 1986, "Predicting Takeover Targets: A Methodological and Empirical Analysis," *Journal of Accounting and Economics*, 8, 3–35.

Rau, P. and T. Vermaelen, 1998, "Glamour, Value, and the Post-Acquisition Performance of Acquiring Firms," *Journal of Financial Economics*, 49, 223–254.

Ravid, S. A. and M. Spiegel, 1999, "Toehold Strategies, Takeover Laws, and Rival Bidders," *Journal of Banking and Finance*, 23, 1219–1242.

Roll, R., 1986, "The Hubris Hypothesis of Corporate Takeovers," *Journal of Business*, 59, 197–216.

Schipper, K. and R. Thompson, 1983, "Evidence on the Capitalized Value of Mergers Activity for Acquiring Firms," *Journal of Financial Economics*, 11, 85–119.

Schwert, G. W., 1996, "Markup Pricing in Mergers and Acquisitions," *Journal of Financial Economics*, 41, 153–192.

Schwert, G. W., 2000, "Hostility in Takeovers: In the Eyes of the Beholder?" *Journal of Finance*, 55, 2599–2640.

Servaes, H., 1991, "Tobin's Q and the Gains from Takeovers," *Journal of Finance*, 46, 409–419.

Shleifer, A. and R. Vishny, 1986, "Large Shareholders and Corporate Control," *Journal of Political Economy*, 96, 461–488.

Shleifer, A. and R. Vishny, 2003, "Stock Market Driven Acquisitions," *Journal of Financial Economics*, 70, 295–311.

Stulz, R., 1990, "Managerial Discretion and Optimal Financing Policies," *Journal of Financial Economics*, 26, 3–27.

Titman, S., 1984, "The Effect of Capital Structure on a Firm's Liquidation Decision," *Journal of Financial Economics*, 13, 137–152.

Travlos, N. G., 1987, "Corporate Takeover Bids, Method of Payment, and Bidding Firms' Stock Returns," *Journal of Finance*, 42, 943–963.

Walkling, R., 1985, "Predicting Tender Offer Success: A Logistic Analysis," *Journal of Financial and Quantitative Analysis*, 20, 461–478.

Wall Street Journal, 1998, "Heard on the Street," December 18.

PART 5

WHERE DO MERGER GAINS COME FROM? INDUSTRY WEALTH EFFECTS OF TAKEOVERS

Chapter 12

HORIZONTAL MERGERS, COLLUSION, AND STOCKHOLDER WEALTH*

B. ESPEN ECKBO

University of British Columbia, Vancouver, British Columbia, Canada

Contents

* This paper, which is based on my University of Rochester dissertation, has benefitted greatly from the "visible hands" of my thesis committee: Gregg A. Jarrell, Michael C. Jensen, and G. William Schwert. I have also received helpful comments from Fisher Black, Claudio Loderer, Avner Kalay, Wayne Mikkelson, Rex Thompson, Jerry Warner, the participants of the finance and industrial economics workshops at New York University, University of British Columbia, and University of Chicago, and the referee, Eugene Fama. The financial support of the Norwegian School of Economics and Business Administration, and the Center for Research in Government Policy and Business at the University of Rochester, is gratefully acknowledged

This article originally appeared in the *Journal of Financial Economics*, Vol. 11, pp. 241–273 (1983).
Corporate Takeovers, Volume 1
Edited by B. Espen Eckbo
DOI: 10.1016/B978-0-12-381983-3.00012-5

Abstract

This paper tests the hypothesis that horizontal mergers generate positive abnormal returns to stockholders of the bidder and target firms because they increase the probability of successful collusion among rival producers. Under the collusion hypothesis, *rivals* of the merging firms benefit from the merger since successful collusion limits output and raises product prices and/or lowers factor prices. This proposition is tested on a large sample of horizontal mergers in mining and manufacturing industries, including mergers challenged by the government with violating antitrust laws, and a "control" sample of vertical mergers taking place in the same industries. While we find that the antitrust law enforcement agencies systematically select relatively profitable mergers for prosecution, there is little evidence indicating that the mergers would have had collusive, anticompetitive effects.

Keywords

horizontal merger, market power, collusion, efficiency, antitrust, market concentration doctrine

JEL classification: G34, D43, L41, K21

1. Introduction

The merger literature contains a substantial amount of evidence indicating that stock-holders of merging firms earn positive abnormal returns from merger activity.[1] A standard interpretation of this evidence is that control over the target firm's resources enables the successful bidder to initiate a revaluation of its own (as well as the target's) shares by implementing a higher valued operating strategy. Following this view, the stockholder gains reflect an increase in the expected spread between the merging firms' future revenues and costs. However, the more difficult issue of whether the gains predominantly originate in cost-side effects ("productive efficiency" theories) or in revenue-side effects ("market power" theories) has remained unanswered. Indeed, despite the widespread public concern with allegedly anticompetitive consequences of mergers, reliable evidence on the importance of market power theories in the context of this particular corporate activity is almost nonexistent.

This paper examines a necessary condition for the proposition that horizontal mergers have collusive, anticompetitive effects. In our context, the central characteristic of the collusion theory is its implication for merger-induced changes in relative product (and factor) prices. However, noting that changes in product prices induce changes in the market value of firms trading at these prices, we instead focus on the abnormal stock returns to the merging firms and their *horizontal rivals*. There are several reasons why this focus is of particular interest. For example, the potential social welfare loss from postmerger collusion on price can be entirely offset by an increase in competition on nonprice variables, such as product quality and service. While product prices are not necessarily sensitive to changes in nonprice competition, under the efficient markets/rational expectations hypothesis stock prices reflect the combined effect of all changes in the firm's expected future cash flows. At a minimum, it is this combined effect which should govern a decision to challenge the merger under antitrust laws. Furthermore, while it is difficult to obtain a precise estimate of the *time* of the merger's impact on product prices, it is well established that stock prices react quickly to public merger announcements. Moreover, while there exists no generally acceptable theory generating "normal" or expected values of product prices, the finance literature provides a model for equilibrium expected stock returns. Finally, the availability of stock price data encourages the use of sample sizes which would be infeasible if we were to rely on product prices, or other firm or industry specific characteristics.

With a sample of 259 horizontal and vertical mergers in mining and manufacturing industries, of which 76 were challenged by the government under claims they "monopolized" product markets, we find that the collusion hypothesis is generally rejected by the data. Rather, the evidence is consistent with the proposition that antitrust policy over the past two decades in part has protected relatively high-cost from relatively low-cost

---

[1] A brief discussion of some of this evidence, and how it relates to the findings of this paper, is given in Section 4.

producers by restricting the opportunity to implement lower cost production techniques by means of merger. This conclusion, which is also to some extent supported by Stillman (1983), casts serious doubt on the validity of a "consumer protection" rationale for this form of government intervention in the market for corporate control.

The paper is organized as follows: Section 2 discusses the testable implications of the collusion hypothesis. Section 3 describes the procedure used to select the merger sample and the portfolio of horizontal rivals for each merger. Section 4 contains the empirical results, and relates the evidence to the findings of previous work. Section 5 concludes the paper.

2. Testable implications of the collusion hypothesis

Merger-related anticipated changes in product or factor prices translate into merger-related abnormal performance by the direct competitors of the bidder and target firms. Below, the implications of the collusion hypothesis are stated in terms of this abnormal performance in response to two consecutive public announcements, each significantly changing the probability that the merger will take place. The first is the merger proposal announcement, the second is the announcement that a "Section 7" complaint against the merger has been (or will be) filed by the Federal Trade Commission (FTC) or the Antitrust Division of the Justice Department.[2]

2.1. Implications for the performance of the rivals

The traditional collusion argument presumes the incentive to coordinate the production rates of the individual rivals within an industry is a function of the costs of monitoring the collusive agreement. Using Stigler's (1964) theory of oligopoly, a horizontal merger can reduce the monitoring costs by reducing the number of independent producers in the industry. The fewer the members of the industry the more "visible" are each producer's actions, and the higher is the probability of detecting members who try to cheat on the cartel by increasing output. The higher this probability, the lower the expected gains from cheating, and the more stable (and profitable) is the cartel in the short run.[3]

---

[2] Section 7 of the Clayton Act prohibits one corporation from acquiring the stock or assets of another "if the effect of such acquisition may be substantially to lessen competition or tend to create a monopoly." The merger proposal and the antitrust complaint announcement dates are taken from the *Wall Street Journal*. In the remainder of the paper, the phrase "antitrust challenge" refers to the antitrust complaint.

[3] Of course, in the absence of government supported entry barriers (such as patents, licences, tariffs, etc.), the collusion argument assumes the degree of resource specialization in the industry is sufficient to slow down the entry process. See, for example, Stigler (1950) for a discussion of the minimum necessary conditions for merger-for-monopoly (or oligopoly) to take place. Note also that the collusion hypothesis does not necessarily presume a *complete* cartelization of the industry. A subset of firms may find it optimal to form a cartel agreement after the merger has been completed and produce a marginal output (or input) restriction on their own, a scenario which is analytically equivalent to the classical "dominant firm" or "price umbrella" model.

   Since effective collusion generates monopoly (or monopsony) rents, the collusion hypothesis implies that the horizontal rivals of the merging firms should earn positive abnormal returns around the merger proposal announcement. The same conclusion holds for rivals expected to remain outside the collusive agreement, in particular since these firms will not bear the costs of restricting output (they are "free-riding" on the higher product price). Conversely, the rivals should earn negative abnormal returns in response to the news of a subsequent antitrust complaint, provided the complaint is expected to significantly increase the costs of collusion (e.g., by prohibiting the merger from taking place). Such a complaint announcement will reverse the expectations of increased monopoly (monopsony) rents caused by the earlier merger proposal.

2.2. *Productive efficiency and implications for regulation*

The above implications of the collusion hypothesis are *necessary* but not sufficient to conclude a given merger is truly anticompetitive. As indicated in Table 1, a pattern of abnormal returns to the merging firms and their rivals which is consistent with collusion can also be consistent with productive efficiency. The latter hypothesis represents a class of theories predicting an increase in the market value of the merging firms due to the implementation of a more cost-efficient production/investment policy after the merger is consummated.[4] In general, the efficiency hypothesis does not restrict the sign of the abnormal returns to the rivals. To see why, note that with productive efficiency each of the two merger-related announcements can have a product/factor price effect and a possibly offsetting *information effect*. That is, the intensified competition in product and factor markets (the merging firms are being replaced by a more competitive corporate entity) tends to result in lower product prices

Table 1

The sign of the abnormal returns to the merging firms and their horizontal rivals as predicted under the collusion and efficiency hypotheses

Hypothesis	Announcement of merger proposal		Announcement of antitrust complaint	
	Merging firms	Rivals	Merging firms	Rivals
Collusion	Positive	Positive	Negative	Negative
Productive efficiency	Positive	Unrestricted	Negative	Unrestricted

[4] The productive efficiency hypothesis covers a wide range of possible specific reasons for merger, among others, realization of technological complimentarities, replacement of inefficient management teams, utilization of unused corporate tax credits, and avoiding bankruptcy costs. A general review of traditional nonmonopolistic hypotheses of merger motivation can be found in Steiner (1975).

and higher factor prices. This price effect causes a negative change in the market value of the rivals at the time of the proposal announcement, and a positive (reversed) effect at the time of the antitrust complaint. On the other hand, since the production technologies of close competitors are (by definition) closely related, the news of a proposed efficient merger can also signal opportunities for the rivals to increase *their* productivity.[5] Similarly, the news of the antitrust complaint can signal a significant restriction in the future merger opportunities of the rivals (cf. "landmark" cases). For each of the two announcements the total wealth impact on the rivals is the sum of the product/factor price effect and the (possibly offsetting) information effect, leaving no necessary restriction on the sign of the rivals' abnormal returns under the efficiency hypothesis.[6]

For the purpose of drawing normative conclusions concerning merger regulation, a further limitation of the tests should be emphasized. The collusion and efficiency hypotheses are not mutually exclusive, which means the observed security value changes resulting from a given merger can represent the sum of simultaneous positive and negative effects due to collusion and efficiency. In principle, the dollar value of the efficiency gains realized *within* the merging firms can outweigh the negative social welfare effects of collusion. Therefore, even a pattern of abnormal returns to the rivals which is *truly* consistent with the collusion hypothesis is not sufficient evidence to conclude that public regulation of the merger will increase social welfare. On the other hand, and this constitutes the basic motivation of the paper, evidence which according to Table 1 is inconsistent with collusion, but consistent with value-maximizing behavior on the part of the merging firms, implies that blocking the merger will reduce social welfare. Essentially, such evidence would indicate that the social efficiency gains created by the merger are sufficient to outweigh the potential welfare loss from collusion. Consequently, based on a sample of challenged mergers, it is possible to use the implications in Table 1 to examine whether the antitrust law enforcement

---

[5] For example, the proposal announcement may disseminate information which enables the rivals to imitate the technological innovation motivating the acquisition. If such innovation activity requires merger, then the stock prices of the rivals will be bid up in anticipation of the expected gains from the future merger activity. Interestingly, Jarrell and Bradley (1980) present evidence consistent with the proposition that the introduction of public disclosure laws has resulted in extensive dissemination of technological information associated with tender offers, thereby significantly reducing the private gains from company takeovers. Note also that if the technological innovation is scale increasing, then imitation by the rivals will further reduce the product price (and increase prices of specialized inputs). In fact, merger waves may be a race by imitators to lower their costs in response to this continuing price decrease.

[6] In principle, one could discriminate between the collusion and efficiency theories by examining the abnormal returns to the merging firms' corporate customers and suppliers of inputs. For example, relative to the proposal announcement, corporate customers and suppliers should lose under the collusion hypothesis and gain under the efficiency hypothesis. However, tests based on this notion are difficult since it is necessary to identify customers and suppliers who cannot switch their purchases/sales to other industries at a low cost.

agencies have followed a policy of systematically blocking socially desirable, efficient mergers.[7]

3. Data sources and sample design

3.1. Selection of mergers

The sample of *unchallenged* mergers was drawn from the FTC's *Statistical Report on Mergers and Acquisitions*. This annual publication lists all completed mergers in mining and manufacturing industries where the target firm has an asset (book) value of $10 million or more. A corresponding sample of *challenged* mergers was drawn from the American Bar Association's *Merger Case Digest* and from the Commerce Clearing House *Trade Regulation Reporter*. These two sources contain a complete list and a short description of all cases brought by the Justice Department (JD) and the FTC under Section 7 of the Clayton Act since 1917. Table 2 lists the number and mean asset (book) values of the mergers in the population and in the sample. The sample period starts in 1963 to allow use of daily stock returns on the University of Chicago CRSP tape. The sample is smaller than the population, primarily because of the basic requirement that security returns should be available for at least one of the merging firms as well as for one or more identifiable horizontal rival. Fifty-five of the 65 horizontal (and all 11 vertical) challenged mergers in the sample satisfy the additional data requirement necessary to reestimate the abnormal performance of the portfolio of rivals (defined below) around the antitrust complaint announcement date. Table 3 lists the outcome of these 55 horizontal Section 7 cases. Sixteen mergers were cancelled by the merging parties as a result of the complaint. Furthermore, in 20 of the 55 cases a settlement between the merging parties and the prosecuting agencies was reached under which divestiture was agreed. Nine mergers were tried, convicted and ordered to divest. Only 7 of the 55 cases were dismissed, and 3 cases are still pending in court. In other words, 45 of the 55 mergers were effectively blocked by the JD and the FTC.

3.2. Selection of horizontal rivals

The analysis focuses on the major industry(-ies) of the target firm. For horizontal mergers, a rival of the target is also a rival of the bidder, although the products in question do not necessarily represent the major activity of the bidder. Each target firm

---

[7] Note, however, that although we can determine the extent to which the law enforcement agencies challenge efficient mergers, the methodology is insufficient to fully address the more basic issue of determining the overall social welfare implications of the current antitrust policy towards mergers. That is, a policy which actually results in the challenge of efficient mergers is obviously costly but can nevertheless be socially optimal if the threat of a challenge also deters a sufficient number of collusive mergers from even entering the state of a merger proposal.

Table 2

The number of "large" horizontal and vertical mergers in mining and manufacturing industries in the period 1963–1978, and the mean asset value of the merging firms in the total population and in the sample[a]

Year of merger completion antitrust complaint[b]	Number of horizontal mergers								Number of vertical mergers							
	Population				Sample				Population				Sample			
	Unchallenged mergers	Challenged by FTC	Challenged by JD	Total	Unchallenged mergers	Challenged by FTC	Challenged by JD	Total	Unchallenged mergers	Challenged by FTC	Challenged by JD	Total	Unchallenged mergers	Challenged by FTC	Challenged by JD	Total
1963	6	3	2	11	1	0	0	1	8	0	0	8	0	0	0	0
1964	12	2	9	23	10	0	4	14	10	0	1	11	7	0	0	7
1965	9	0	7	16	5	0	3	8	7	1	1	9	2	0	1	3
1966	9	4	4	17	8	1	2	11	7	2	2	11	4	1	0	5
1967	7	3	4	14	5	2	3	10	13	0	0	13	7	0	0	7
1968	10	5	8	23	7	3	4	14	12	0	2	14	7	0	0	7
1969	12	6	3	21	7	4	3	14	12	1	3	16	5	0	3	8
1970	8	3	4	15	2	1	1	4	4	0	1	5	1	1	0	2
1971	7	3	6	16	1	1	1	3	1	1	0	2	0	0	1	1
1972	15	3	7	25	6	3	2	11	9	1	0	10	3	0	0	3
1973	19	4	6	29	11	1	4	16	7	1	0	8	2	1	0	3
1974	20	4	3	27	18	1	1	20	3	1	0	4	3	1	0	4
1975	5	3	3	11	3	0	2	5	2	0	0	2	2	0	0	2
1976	14	2	2	18	11	2	0	13	4	0	1	5	3	0	1	4
1977	26	3	3	32	17	1	3	22	4	0	0	4	3	0	0	3
1978	21	7	7	35	13	6	6	25	13	0	2	15	8	0	1	9
1963–1978	200	55	78	333	126	26	39	191	116	9	12	137	57	5	6	68

Mean asset value ($ millions) 1963–1978[c]

	Unchallenged	Challenged by FTC	Challenged by JD	Total	Unchallenged	Challenged by FTC	Challenged by JD	Total	Unchallenged	Challenged by FTC	Challenged by JD	Total	Unchallenged	Challenged by FTC	Challenged by JD	Total
Target firm	$65	$146	$184	$105	$84	$120	$183	$108	$61	$27	$121	$65	$50	$24	$67	$50
Bidder firm	$541	$830	$911	$675	$638	$994	$779	$714	$1063	$546	$483	$978	$769	$192	$416	$696

[a] A "large" merger is one where the asset value of the target firm is at least $10 million. The population of completed, "large" mergers is found in the Federal Trade Commission's *Statistical Report on Mergers and Acquisitions 1979*. Typically, 10–20% of the annual number of mergers in mining and manufacturing industries is classified as "large." In addition to the population of 200 horizontal and 116 vertical unchallenged mergers in the sample period there were 1086 "large" conglomerate mergers. The population of *challenged* mergers is found in the American Bar Association's *Merger Case Digest*, and in the Commerce Clearing House *Trade Regulation Reporter*. To arrive at the population of challenged mergers in the table, cases involving a series of mergers are counted only once. Also, if a specific case has both horizontal and vertical aspects, it is counted once as horizontal. The classifications are taken from the court descriptions. During the sample period the total number of Section 7 cases was 343, including 14 purely conglomerate mergers. The mining and manufacturing restriction excludes, among others, 65 mergers between banks or bank holding companies.

[b] The unchallenged mergers are counted relative to the year of completion of the merger, while the challenged mergers are counted relative to the year of the complaint.

[c] Taken from the FTC *Report* and the Compustat file.

Table 3

55 horizontal Section 7 cases between 1963 and 1978, classified by prosecuting agency by method of settlement and by average number of trading days between case-related events

| | Number of cases | | Average number of trading days | | | |
| | | | Merger proposal to complaint | | Complaint to final judgement[a] | |
Outcome of merger and method of settlement	JD	FTC	JD	FTC	JD	FTC
Merger cancelled[b]	13	3	90	88	58	2
Convicted and divestiture ordered	1	8	13	421	686	1101
Case settled and divestiture agreed[c]	10	10	302	350	515	342
Case dismissed[d]	6	1	790	139	590	0
Case still pending	2	1	283	65	-	-
Sum and aggregate averages	32	23	302	318	337	556

[a]The "final judgement" date is the day of the first *Wall Street Journal* reference to the outcome of the case.
[b]"Final judgement" for this merger category represents "cancellation."
[c]"Final judgement" for this merger category represents "settlement."
[d]"Final judgement" for this merger category represents "dismissed."

was assigned to a set of products using firm-specific information in the Standard and Poor's *Registry of Corporations*, Dun and Bradstreet's *Million Dollar Directory*, and Moody's *Industrial Manual*. This set of products was represented by four-digit SIC industry codes and by a number system identifying *single* products whenever any particular four-digit SIC code contained, according to the *Standard Industrial Classification Manual 72*, a broad range of commodities.[8] As a result, most of the well-known ambiguities associated with the SIC classification system were eliminated. More than 170 different four-digit industries are represented by the sample, with typically one or two mergers per industry. The single most frequently represented industry is Oil and Gas Extraction (SIC 1311) with 24 horizontal and 4 vertical mergers taking place in this industry alone.

---

[8] For example, in one particular case the target firm produced primarily brake shoes and car wheels. According to the SIC manual, brake shoes and car wheels are classified under SIC code 3321 (Gray Iron Foundries). However, industry 3321 also contains several products which cannot be considered close substitutes for brake shoes and car wheels. To account for this the products of this specific target were represented by industry 3321 (1, 2), where (1, 2) identifies the two central products in that industry. In another example, the target firm produced almost exclusively storage batteries. Industry 3691 consists only of this product. Furthermore, industry 3692 contains only primary batteries which can be a close substitute for storage batteries. Consequently, this target was assigned to both industry 3691 and 3692, with no additional product specific reference necessary. Using this system a maximum of four different four-digit SIC codes and ten individual product numbers for each SIC code were assigned to each target firm in the sample. Whenever there was reasonable doubt that the SIC code contained a fairly homogenous group of products, the method of identifying the central products by the number system 1 through 10 was used. A complete list of these products, as well as the identity and classification of the merging firms, can be found in Eckbo (1981).

To identify the horizontal rivals of a target firm a list of all firms on the CRSP file associated with the four-digit SIC code(s) assigned to the target was obtained.[9] Whenever the industry code(s) of the target had not been supplemented by reference to specific products, all firms on this list which had stock returns available in the required estimation period (defined below) were labeled "horizontal rivals." Otherwise, information in Standard and Poor's *Registry* was used to delete the firms on the list which did not produce at least one of the specific products associated with the target's four-digit SIC code(s). This laborious selection procedure was designed to minimize the possibility of including *irrelevant* firms in the target's portfolio of horizontal rivals. Inclusion of irrelevant firms which, by definition, are unaffected by the merger event, will bias the estimated wealth impact of the merger toward zero. Note, however, that exclusion of *relevant* firms (perhaps firms which are not listed on the CRSP file, or firms in other industries producing close substitutes) is a potential problem only to the extent that the actual number of identified rivals per target firm is small, possibly leading to imprecise estimates of abnormal returns. Table 4 lists the number of identified horizontal rivals across several subsamples of the total data base. The 259 mergers are, on average, associated with 11 rivals per merger (range 1–56, median 5).

Table 4

The size of the merger sample and the number of horizontal rivals per merger relative to the merger proposal date

	Sample	No. of listed bidders	No. of listed targets	No. of mergers	No. of rivals per merger		
					Range	Mean	Median
I	*Total data base 1963–1978*	217	107	259	1–56	11	5
	Unchallenged	151	73	183	1–56	13	6
	Challenged	66	34	76	1–29	5	3
II	*Horizontal mergers*	159	86	191	1–56	12	6
	Unchallenged	102	57	126	1–56	15	7
	Challenged	57	29	65	1–29	5	4
	Challenged by FTC	25	11	26	1–26	6	4
	Challenged by JD	32	18	39	1–29	5	4
III	*Vertical mergers*	58	21	68	1–52	9	4
	Unchallenged	49	16	57	1–52	10	4
	Challenged	9	5	11	1–19	6	4
	Challenged by FTC	4	2	5	1–12	6	4
	Challenged by JD	5	4	6	1–19	5	3

[9] The CRSP tape assigns a single four-digit SIC code to each firm, and the date the code became effective. The code is intended to represent the major product line of the firm.

4. Empirical results

4.1. The performance of the merging firms

Table 5 and Figures 1 and 2 show the cumulative average abnormal returns (*CAAR*) earned by bidder and target firms relative to the merger proposal and antitrust complaint announcements. Following much of the tradition in information event studies, the *CAAR* is computed by first estimating the following "market" model for each individual firm,

$$\tilde{r}_{it} = \alpha_i + \beta_i \tilde{r}_{mt} + \tilde{\varepsilon}_{it}, \tag{1}$$

where $\tilde{r}_{it}$ and $\tilde{r}_{mt}$ are the daily, continuously compounded rates of return of firm i and the value-weighted market portfolio. Equation (1) is an adequate representation of the process generating equilibrium expected returns if security returns follow a stationary, multivariate normal distribution.[10] The regression coefficient β_i reflects systematic comovements of security i's return with the return on the market portfolio, while the serially uncorrelated, zero mean error term $\tilde{\varepsilon}_{it}$ picks up the impact of nonmarket factors (such as firm- or industry-specific information events) and random price fluctuations. The coefficients α_i and β_i are estimated using OLS regression and stock returns from the 400 days surrounding the announcement day (day 0), always excluding day -50 through 50.[11] Within this -50 through 50 period the abnormal returns to security i over day τ, conditional on the observed return on the market portfolio, is computed as the forecast error, $\tilde{r}_{it} - (\hat{\alpha}_i + \hat{\beta}_i \tilde{r}_{mt})$. Denoting CAR_i as the daily forecast errors of security i cumulated over the period of interest, *CAAR* is then computed as the cross-sectional average of CAR_i.[12]

---

[10] See Fama (1976, ch. 3) for a discussion of the market model. Schwert (1981) reviews several studies and methodological issues based on the event-time methodology.

[11] Specifically, two sets of coefficients were estimated, $(\hat{\alpha}_i^b, \hat{\beta}_i^b)$ using 150 days of returns prior to the event only, and $(\hat{\alpha}_i^a, \hat{\beta}_i^a)$ using the same number of observations after the event. Thus, we are taking into account the fact that the event itself may significantly affect the systematic risk (β_i) of the firm. Since the OLS estimates are biased and inconsistent in the presence of nonsynchronous trading (i.e., when returns are not measured over a fixed time interval which is identical for all securities), α_i and β_i were also reestimated using the procedures suggested by Scholes and Williams (1977). The results of tests based on the Scholes-Williams estimators were indistinguishable from the OLS based results, and are therefore not reported.

[12] Throughout the paper we report three central statistics summarizing the cross-sectional distribution of the cumulative *standardized* abnormal return of security i ($CSAR_i$). $CSAR_i$ is computed as CAR_i, only that each daily forecasting error is divided by an unbiased estimate of its standard deviation. Since we are assuming normally distributed security returns, it follows that $W_i = CSAR_i / \sqrt{T}$ is distributed Student t with $L - 2$ degrees of freedom (where T and L are the number of trading days in the periods of cumulation and estimation, respectively). Since the variance of W_i is $(L - 2)/(L - 4)$, and provided the mergers are independent events, it follows that $Z = \bar{W}\sqrt{N(L - 4)/(L - 2)}$ is approximately unit normal for large sample size N, where $\bar{W}$ is the cross-sectional average of W_i. We use a two-sided t-test based on Z to assess the significance of *CAAR*. Since the Z-test can fail if security returns are not normally distributed, or if some mergers have a positive impact while others have a negative and off-setting impact, we also report the percent *P1* of the N mergers with $W_i > 0$ and the percent *P2* with $W_i > 0$ at the 5% level of significance. Under the hypothesis of zero abnormal returns, $E(P1) = 50\%$ and $E(P2) \le 5\%$. Noting that $\text{var}(P1) = (0.5)(0.5)/N$ and $\text{var}(P2) = (0.05)(0.95)/N$, we use a two-sided t-test on *P1* and a one-sided t-test on *P2* to assess significance.

Table 5

Abnormal returns to *Bidder* and *Target* firms in horizontal mergers relative to the merger proposal and antitrust complaint announcements

1963–1978 merger sample	Announcement	Sample size	Summary statistic[a]	Period relative to the *Wall Street Journal* announcement (day 0)						
				(−20, 10)	(−10, 5)	(−3, 3)	(−1, 1)	0	(0, 3)	(3, 10)
I Bidders										
Unchallenged	Merger proposal	102	CAAR (Z)	1.58 (1.48)	1.29 (1.54)	0.58 (0.69)	0.07 (−0.12)	0.11 (0.39)	−0.06 (−0.03)	0.27 (0.80)
			P1	52.9	57.8	58.8*	52.9	53.9	56.9	52.0
			P2	5.9	6.9	7.8	8.8**	8.8**	5.9	5.9
Challenged	Merger proposal	57	CAAR (Z)	4.85*** (3.43)	2.68*** (2.61)	2.12*** (3.45)	1.20*** (2.98)	0.22 (0.18)	0.86* (1.88)	1.63** (2.44)
			P1	66.7**	64.9**	66.7**	64.2**	47.4	66.7**	59.6
			P2	8.8	7.0	12.3***	17.5***	8.8	10.5*	5.3
	Antitrust complaint	49	CAAR (Z)	1.00 (0.66)	−0.85 (−0.46)	−0.28 (0.321)	−0.72 (−0.91)	−0.73** (−2.26)	−0.49 (−0.06)	1.00 (1.35)
			P1	61.2	46.9	51.0	46.9	36.7**	53.1	49.0
			P2	10.2*	10.2*	6.1	4.1	8.2	4.1	6.1
II Targets										
Unchallenged	Merger proposal	57	CAAR (Z)	14.08*** (6.97)	12.35*** (8.63)	8.91*** (9.23)	6.24*** (9.97)	3.13*** (10.17)	2.66*** (4.70)	0.46 (0.90)
			P1	70.2***	68.4***	64.9***	59.6	50.9	49.1	45.6
			P2	29.8***	29.8***	33.3***	33.3***	33.3***	21.1***	8.8
Challenged	Merger proposal	29	CAAR (Z)	25.03*** (12.61)	18.58*** (12.74)	11.74*** (12.80)	10.2*** (15.22)	3.82*** (7.99)	2.10*** (2.79)	1.82 (1.52)
			P1	89.7***	86.2***	72.4***	72.4***	58.6	55.2	65.5
			P2	65.5***	58.6***	62.1***	65.5***	48.3***	31.0***	6.9
	Antitrust complaint	17	CAAR (Z)	−4.53* (−1.74)	−9.60*** (−3.77)	−8.62*** (−4.72)	−9.27*** (−7.61)	−4.63*** (−7.20)	−5.95*** (−4.08)	−1.03 (−1.08)
			P1	35.3	23.5**	23.5**	17.6***	29.4*	35.3	47.1
			P2	17.6***	5.9	0.0	5.9	5.9	11.8	5.9

[a]*CAAR*, percent cumulative average abnormal returns; *P1*, the percent of the sample with positive cumulative abnormal returns; *P2*, the percent of the sample with significantly (at the 5% level) positive cumulative abnormal returns; *Z*, test statistic on the cumulative average standardized abnormal returns. *, **, *** indicate the hypothesis of zero abnormal returns [under which $E(CAAR) = 0.0\%$, $E(P1) = 50\%$ and $E(P2) < 5\%$] is rejected on a 10%, 5%, or 1% level of significance.

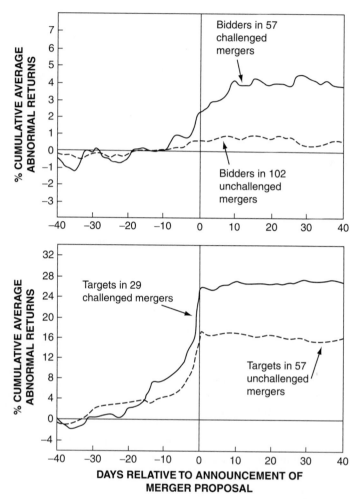

Fig. 1. Daily cumulative average abnormal returns to *bidder* and *target* firms in horizontal mergers relative to the merger proposal announcement date in the period 1963–1978.

Focusing first on the *unchallenged* mergers, the results in Table 5 indicate that the 102 bidder firms typically earn positive but small and generally insignificant abnormal returns over the seven periods surrounding and including the merger proposal announcement. Target stockholders, however, realize on average 14.08% abnormal returns over the 31 trading days in the −20 through 10 period, and 3.13% over the announcement day alone. These returns are more than six standard deviations from zero, and the significance is generally confirmed by the percent positive and percent significantly positive tests. Thus, while we cannot conclude that the typical bidder in the unchallenged sample is made significantly better off as a result of the proposal

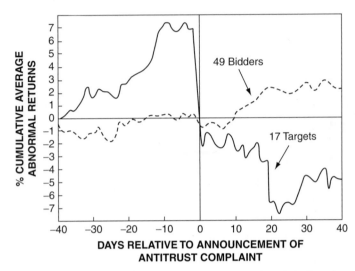

Fig. 2. Daily cumulative average abnormal returns to *bidder* and *target* firms in horizontal mergers relative to the antitrust complaint announcement date in the period 1963–1978.

announcement, target stockholders clearly earn large economic rents from this event. The evidence is generally consistent with the proposition that the mergers are the result of investments undertaken by value-maximizing firms, which is a necessary condition for both the collusion and productive efficiency hypotheses.[13]

This conclusion is even more apparent from the sample of *challenged* mergers. Relative to the merger proposal announcement, the 57 bidders in Table 5 earn on average 4.85% abnormal returns over the −20 through 10 period (with a Z-statistic of 3.43) and 1.20% over the 3 days surrounding the announcement day. The latter abnormal return is significantly different from zero at the 1% level according to both the Z-test and the P2-test, and at the 5% level according to the P1 test. The corresponding returns to target stockholders are 25.03% and 10.2%, respectively, both strongly

[13] A test of the *general* validity of the value maximization hypothesis goes beyond the scope of this paper and would require inclusion of a larger fraction of unsuccessful merger proposals in the data base. See, for example, Dodd (1980), Malatesta (1983), and Schipper and Thompson (1983) for a more comprehensive examination of this issue in the context of mergers. The above results are similar to the findings of Mandelker (1974), Ellert (1976), and Langetieg (1978) (which use monthly security returns and predominantly conglomerate mergers), but contrast with the finding of both Dodd and Malatesta that stockholders of bidder firms systematically lose from merger activity. Interestingly, Schipper and Thompson find that (bidder) firms show positive abnormal performance at the time when they announce the decisions to undertake entire acquisition *programs*, which indicates that the market may have capitalized much of the rents from merger activity even prior to the first public announcement of the merger proposal. Finally note that (ignoring the issue of statistical significance) the uneven distribution of abnormal returns between the merging firms is consistent with a much more even distribution of the *dollar* gains from the merger, since the bidder is typically several times larger (measured by asset value) than the target.

significant according to all three tests. Generally, it appears as if stockholders of bidder and target firms in challenged (horizontal) mergers earn larger abnormal returns than do the corresponding firms in unchallenged mergers.[14]

The significantly negative abnormal performance by bidder and target firms in response to the antitrust complaint announcement indicates that the challenge typically comes as a surprise and is expected to be costly for the merging firms. On average, bidders lose 0.73% and targets 4.63% on the day of the complaint, the latter abnormal return is seven standard deviations from zero.[15] The finding of negative abnormal returns to either of the merging parties is not particularly surprising in light of the fact that the government was successful in blocking most of the challenged mergers in the data base (Table 3). For our purpose, this evidence is important because it is consistent with the proposition that the complaint announcement signals an unanticipated increase in the costs of collusion. Following the discussion in Section 2, we can therefore expect a complaint against a truly collusive merger to cause a drop in the market value of the horizontal rivals of the merging firms as well.

4.2. The performance of the horizontal rivals

The horizontal rivals of a given merger are simultaneously affected by the merger announcement. To account for any contemporaneous cross-correlation of returns, the rivals of each merger are pooled into one (equal-weighted, constant composition) industry portfolio. Thus, subscript i in Equation (1) now refers to the portfolio of rivals of the ith merger. The estimation and test procedure is identical to the one presented in the previous section.

From Table 6 and Figure 3 it is apparent that the rivals of the 126 *unchallenged* horizontal mergers in the data base systematically earn small but positive abnormal returns over the 7 days surrounding and including the day of the merger proposal. The *CAAR* over this period is 0.76% ($Z = 2.59$), which is statistically significant at the 5% level across all three significance tests.[16] Following the predictions in Table 1, this

---

[14] A similar picture emerges from the evidence in Ellert (1976). Note that the significance levels in the challenged sample can be overstated if the law enforcement agencies systematically use the abnormal returns to the merging firms as a basis for a decision to challenge, since one can always expect some merger proposal announcements to produce significantly positive abnormal returns merely by chance.

[15] The mean number of trading days between the proposal and the complaint announcements is 80, based on 15 of the 17 targets in Figure 2 (the mean across all 17 targets is 225). The positive cumulative average abnormal returns for the targets prior to the complaint announcement are in part explained by the fact that three of these 17 targets had their proposal announcement within 10 days prior to the complaint. The *CAAR* of -0.73% ($Z = -2.26$) earned by the 49 bidders on the complaint day can be compared to the negative performance of -1.67% ($t = -4.31$) shown by the convicted "buying" (bidder) firms in the sample used by Wier (1983). As pointed out by Wier, these losses generally represent a combination of expected case-related expenses and loss of economic rents.

[16] 23 of the 126 mergers took place in the oil and gas industry, which is probably one of the most competitive industries in the sample. These 23 cases were associated with an average abnormal performance of 1.42% ($Z = 2.36$) over the $-3, 3$ period.

B. E. Eckbo

Table 6

Abnormal returns to *rivals* of target firms in horizontal mergers relative to the merger proposal and antitrust complaint announcements

1963–1978 Merger sample	Announcement	Sample size	Summary statistic[a]	Period relative to the *Wall Street Journal* announcement (day 0)						
				(−20, 10)	(−10, 5)	(−3, 3)	(−1, 1)	0	(0, 3)	(3, 10)
I Total sample										
Unchallenged	Merger proposal	126	CAAR (Z)	1.10 (1.20)	1.17** (2.23)	0.76** (2.59)	−0.07 (−0.08)	0.03 (0.00)	0.16 (0.97)	0.39 (0.98)
			P1	55.6	56.3	58.7***	53.2	50.8	55.6	48.4
			P2	10.3***	11.9***	11.1***	4.0	4.8	5.6	6.3
Challenged	Merger proposal	65	CAAR (Z)	2.45*** (3.02)	0.91* (1.87)	0.90** (2.25)	0.44 (1.20)	0.19 (0.71)	0.89*** (2.75)	0.96*** (2.60)
			P1	61.5*	46.2	52.3	53.8	50.8	58.5	58.5
			P2	15.4***	9.2*	9.2	4.6	4.6	12.3***	12.3***
	Antitrust complaint	55	CAAR (Z)	1.78 (1.29)	0.78 (0.49)	0.28 (0.43)	0.37 (0.97)	0.15 (0.53)	0.16 (0.23)	0.48 (0.59)
			P1	58.2	45.5	49.1	47.3	63.6**	38.2*	56.4
			P2	5.5	9.1	7.3	3.6	3.6	7.3	10.9**
II Common industry sample										
I Unchallenged	Merger proposal	53	CAAR (Z)	−0.08 (−0.25)	0.73 (1.15)	0.60* (1.69)	−0.10 (0.34)	0.11 (0.46)	0.20 (0.82)	0.20 (0.22)
			P1	49.1	54.7	62.3*	56.6	56.6	62.3*	45.3
			P2	9.4*	13.2***	9.4*	3.8	5.7	7.5	7.5
Challenged	Merger proposal	24	CAAR (Z)	4.51*** (4.06)	2.44*** (3.07)	1.73*** (2.87)	0.59 (1.34)	0.24 (0.83)	1.65*** (3.49)	1.82*** (3.07)
			P1	75.0**	62.5	62.5	62.5	58.3	79.2***	66.7
			P2	29.2***	16.7***	16.7***	4.2	4.2	20.8***	20.8***
	Antitrust complaint	18	CAAR (Z)	−2.21* (−1.70)	−1.26 (−1.40)	−0.47 (−1.03)	−0.14 (−0.44)	−0.13 (−0.55)	−0.30 (−0.99)	−0.36 (−0.90)
			P1	33.3	22.2**	22.2**	33.3	55.6	33.3	44.4
			P2	5.6	5.6	5.6	0.0	0.0	5.6	11.1

[a]*CAAR*, percent cumulative average abnormal returns; *P1*, the percent of the sample with positive cumulative abnormal returns; *P2*, the percent of the sample with significantly (at the 5% level) positive cumulative abnormal returns; *Z*, test statistic on the cumulative average abnormal returns. *, **, *** indicate the hypothesis of zero abnormal returns [under which $E(CAAR) = 0.0\%$, $E(P1) = 50\%$ and $E(P2) < 5\%$] is rejected on a 10%, 5%, or 1% level of significance.

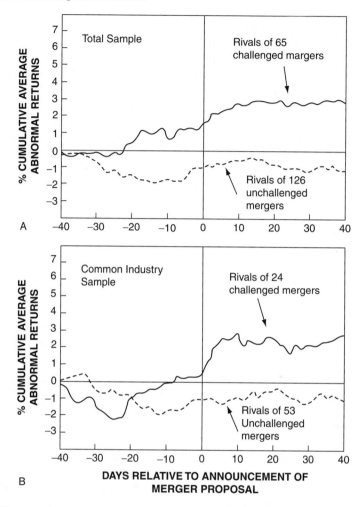

Fig. 3. Daily cumulative average abnormal returns to *rivals* of target firms in horizontal mergers relative to the merger proposal announcement date in the period 1963–1968.

performance is consistent with both the collusion and the productive efficiency hypotheses. Under the latter, the merger proposal announcement signals new information indicating that the resources of the rivals can be more efficiently employed. To provide a perspective on the likely relevance of the collusion hypothesis in the context of unchallenged mergers, however, we compare the performance of the rivals of this merger category to the performance of rivals of challenged mergers. The idea is that if we reject the collusion hypothesis for the sample of challenged mergers (for which we have both a merger proposal and antitrust complaint announcement), then we have a "benchmark" for the size of the proposal-related abnormal returns to the rivals which is "admissible" under the efficiency hypothesis.

With this in mind, note the difference between the performance of rivals of challenged and unchallenged horizontal mergers around the proposal announcement emerging from Table 6. Rivals of challenged mergers earn 2.45% ($Z = 3.02$) abnormal returns over the -20 to 10 period, while the corresponding returns to rivals of unchallenged mergers is 1.10% ($Z = 1.20$). Combined with the results from the previous section (and ignoring the potential selection bias problem mentioned in footnote 14), it appears as if the antitrust law enforcement agencies typically challenge mergers where the merging firms *and* their horizontal competitors earn relatively large abnormal returns in response to the merger proposal announcement. This impression is further supported by the results for the "common industry" sample, where we measure the average impact on the rivals of challenged versus unchallenged mergers holding the underlying industry of the merging firms constant. That is, the common industry sample contains only the challenged mergers in the total data base for which there is also an unchallenged merger taking place in the same industry. The *CAAR*s to the rivals of the 24 challenged mergers satisfying this requirement is 4.51% ($Z = 4.06$) over the -20 through 10 period relative to the merger proposal. The abnormal return over the -3 through 3 interval is 1.73% ($Z = 2.87$). The abnormal performance over these two periods is significantly positive at the 1% level using the standardized abnormal returns (Z) test or the percent significantly positive ($P2$) test. In contrast, the rivals of the 53 unchallenged mergers in this particular sample earn -0.08% ($Z = 0.25$) and 0.60% ($Z = 1.69$) over the same event periods. This is clearly consistent with the proposition that the law enforcement agencies systematically challenge the mergers *within a particular industry* which have the largest wealth impact on the rivals.

Put in perspective, the magnitude of some of the numbers in Table 6 are remarkable. To illustrate, in Section 4.1 we found that the average bidder and target firm in challenged mergers earned 4.85% and 25.03% abnormal returns over the -20 through 10 period relative to the merger proposal announcement. Using the average asset sizes listed in Table 2, and assuming the firms are all equity financed, the typical challenged merger generated net gains of approximately $100 million to the merging firms' shareholders. Furthermore, over the same time period this challenged merger caused a 2.45% increase in the value of the average horizontal competitor (Table 6). Since the average number of competitors in this sample is 5, this amounts to an additional wealth effect of $150 million or more if the typical rival is of the same asset size as the average bidder. If these gains indeed are wealth transfers from consumers or sellers of inputs, it is no mystery why we observe an extensive government interference in the market for corporate control.

However, the evidence on the antitrust complaint announcement in Table 6 and Figure 4 does not support the collusion (wealth transfer) hypothesis. Recall from Section 4.1 that the complaint announcement caused a significant reduction in the value of the target and (to a lesser extent) of the bidder firm. Under the collusion hypothesis, we should therefore see a decline in the value of the rivals in response to

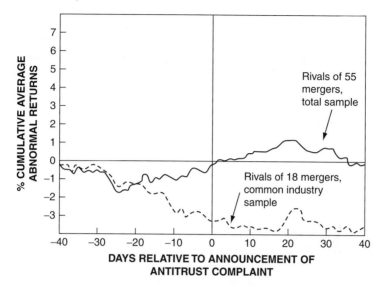

Fig. 4. Daily cumulative average abnormal returns to *rivals* of target firms in horizontal mergers relative to the antitrust complaint announcement date in the period 1963–1978.

this unanticipated increase in the costs of collusion. Based on the total sample of challenged mergers, there is no evidence whatsoever in Table 6 indicating that the complaint announcement reduces the expected future net cash flows to the rivals. The evidence is less conclusive when we focus on the common industry sample. The sign of the abnormal returns in this sample is uniformly negative across all the seven subperiods relative to the complaint; however, the significance levels are too low to reject the hypothesis of zero abnormal performance with any degree of confidence.[17]

---

[17] To gauge the sensitivity of this conclusion to alternative specifications of the return generating process, abnormal returns were also computed using a simple "mean-adjusted return" model, that is, $\tilde{r}_{it} = \bar{r}_i + \tilde{v}_{it}$, where $\bar{r}_i$ is the mean of $\tilde{r}_{it}$, and a "two-factor" model being the market model (Equation 1) with an industry index as an additional explanatory variable. Use of these two models also leads to a rejection of the collusion model. For the mean-adjusted return model the magnitudes of the abnormal returns were almost indistinguishable from the magnitudes reported in the paper. Inclusion of the industry index in the market model, however, significantly reduced the size of the abnormal returns to the rivals at the time of the proposal announcement. The industry index contained all listed firms in the target firm's two-digit SIC industry (-ies), (excluding, of course, the merging firms and the identified horizontal rivals). Given the typically broad range of products in a two-digit SIC industry, this index should contain a reasonable amount of "distant" competitors not expected to be affected by the merger events. The fact that the *CAAR* was significantly reduced as a result of the index can indicate that the abnormal returns to the rivals in Table 6 simply reflect a general, good performance shared by all "distant" competitors and which has little to do with the merger per se. A more likely explanation, however, is that the two-digit SIC index actually contained previously unidentified close competitors, in which case subtracting the returns to the index amounts to "throwing the baby out with the bath water." See Eckbo (1981) for further details on the computation and results of the two-factor model.

The collusion hypothesis can also be examined from a somewhat different angle. Let $P(B)$ be the percent of the sample of horizontal, challenged mergers where the rivals earn negative abnormal returns at the time of the antitrust complaint announcement ("event B"). Furthermore, let $P(B|A)$ be the percent experiencing B conditional on the event that the same rivals earned positive abnormal returns at the time of the merger proposal ("event A"). Under the collusion hypothesis, and based on a sample containing a mixture of efficient and collusive mergers, we should observe $P(B|A) > P(B)$. Moreover, the more significant the abnormal returns in event A, the larger should $P(B|A)$ be relative to $P(B)$.

The results in Table 7 do not support this dependence proposition. That is, we generally cannot reject the hypothesis that $P(B|A_i) = P(B|A_j) = P(B)$, $(i, j = 1, \ldots, 4)$, which is what we should expect if the events B and A are independent.[18] In other words, rivals of challenged mergers earning positive abnormal returns at the 10%, 5%, or 1% significance level at the time of the proposal announcement do *not* appear to have a higher probability of earning negative abnormal returns at the time of the complaint than what is expected by chance. This conclusion is perhaps most spectacular for sample III and IV where we constrain the bidder and target firms to earn positive abnormal returns around the proposal announcement. For example, in sample IV we have constrained the rivals and the merging firms to satisfy *all* the implications of the collusion model as they appear in Table 1 for the merger proposal announcement. Nevertheless, we still cannot say that $P(B|A)$ is significantly larger than $P(B)$ as a result of these constraints.[19] Jointly with the evidence in Table 6, we are therefore rejecting the collusion hypothesis for the challenged mergers. Furthermore, albeit on a less formal basis, it is tempting to argue that since the unchallenged mergers produced a much smaller impact on the rivals at the time of the proposal announcement than did challenged mergers, the collusion hypothesis is probably even less relevant for the unchallenged sample. A further examination of the unchallenged mergers is given in Section 4.4. below.

Finally, notice the general absence of *negative* abnormal performance by the rivals around the proposal announcement. Thus, if horizontal mergers typically take place to realize scale economies, then the resulting expansion of the merging firms' share of the market is on average not sufficient to make the rivals significantly worse off. Incidentally, this result is also inconsistent with the so-called "predatory pricing" theory. That is, we have found no evidence indicating that the mergers will lead to a monopolistic

---

[18] The smaller $P(A)$, that is, the fewer the number of mergers satisfying A, the less meaningful is the operation of conditioning B on A. In the extreme case where A contains a single merger, $P(B|A)$ can only take two values, 0% or 100%. There are several such cases in Table 7, and they should be disregarded for purposes of statistical inference.

[19] The impression emerging from Table 7 that A and B are indeed independent events was also supported by regressions of the rivals' abnormal returns at the complaint announcement on (a constant term plus) the rivals' proposal-related abnormal returns: The regression coefficient was uniformly insignificantly different from zero.

Table 7

The percent of the horizontal challenged mergers where the rivals earn negative abnormal returns around the antitrust complaint announcement conditional on having earned positive abnormal returns around the merger proposal, $(P(B|A))^a$

	Event period[b]	P(B)	(P(A₁))	P(B|A₁)	(P(A₂))	P(B|A₂)	(P(A₃))	P(B|A₃)	(P(A₄))	P(B|A₄)
I	*Total sample; N = 55[c]; σ = 6.7[c]*									
	(−20, 10)	41.8	(54.5)	56.7	(14.5)	50.3	(10.9)	51.4	(3.6)	50.0
	(−10, 5)	54.5	(43.6)	58.5	(10.9)	83.5	(10.9)	67.0	(1.8)	100.0
	(−3, 3)	50.9	(47.3)	46.1	(7.2)	50.0	(5.5)	65.5	(0.0)	-
	(−1, 1)	52.7	(41.8)	52.2	(1.8)	100.0	(1.8)	0.0	(0.0)	-
II	*Common industry sample; N = 18; σ = 11.8*									
	(−20, 10)	66.7	(72.2)	61.5	(27.8)	80.0	(22.2)	75.2	(11.1)	50.5
	(−10, 5)	77.8	(61.1)	72.7	(22.2)	100.0	(22.2)	75.2	(5.6)	100.0
	(−3, 3)	77.8	(61.1)	81.8	(11.1)	100.0	(11.1)	100.0	(0.0)	-
	(−1, 1)	66.7	(61.1)	54.5	(0.0)	-	(0.0)	-	(0.0)	-
III	*Sample I with A₁ imposed on bidders; 29 ≤ N ≤ 31; 9.0 ≤ σ ≤ 9.3[d]*									
	(−20, 10)	36.7	(70.0)	52.4	(23.3)	43.0	(16.7)	40.1	(3.3)	0.0
	(−10, 5)	54.8	(51.6)	69.0	(6.5)	100.0	(6.5)	49.0	(0.0)	-
	(−3, 3)	48.4	(48.3)	47.0	(3.2)	100.0	(3.2)	100.0	(0.0)	-
	(−1, 1)	48.3	(38.0)	45.3	(0.0)	-	(0.0)	-	(0.0)	-
IV	*Sample I with A₁ imposed on bidders and targets; 11 ≤ N ≤ 15; 12.9 ≤ σ ≤ 15.2[c]*									
	(−20, 10)	40.0	(73.3)	54.6	(26.7)	50.8	(26.7)	50.8	(0.0)	-
	(−10, 5)	69.2	(53.9)	85.7	(15.4)	100.0	(7.7)	100.0	(0.0)	-
	(−3, 3)	69.2	(61.5)	50.1	(7.7)	100.0	(7.7)	100.0	(0.0)	-
	(−1, 1)	54.6	(36.4)	24.7	(0.0)	-	(0.0)	-	(0.0)	-

[a] A₁ denotes "positive abnormal returns around the merger proposal announcement"; A_2 is "A_1 at the 10% level of significance"; A_3 is "A_1 at the 5% level of significance"; A_4 is "A_1 at the 1% level of significance"; B denotes "negative abnormal returns around the antitrust complaint announcement."

[b] For $P(B)$ and $P(B|A)$, day 0 is the day of the first reference in the *Wall Street Journal* to the antitrust complaint; for $P(A)$ it is the first, *WSJ* reference to the merger proposal.

[c] The standard deviation of $P(B)$, σ, is calculated as $\sqrt{(50)(50)/N}$, under the assumption that $P(B)$ is binomially distributed with mean 50%. N is the sample size.

[d] Of the total sample of 55 horizontal challenged mergers, only 49 have a listed bidder at the time of the merger proposal.

[e] Of the total sample of 55 horizontal challenged mergers, only 29 have a listed bidder *and* target at the time of the merger proposal.

"price war" between the merging firms and their rivals.[20] Expectations of predatory behavior by the merged firm would have resulted in negative abnormal performance by the rivals at the time of the proposal announcement. Rather, the evidence indicates that the stock returns to rival producers move closely together, and that the good news for the merging firms typically also signals good news for the rivals. Using the framework of Section 2, this result is consistent with the prediction of the efficiency hypothesis, under which the merger proposal announcements convey production-cost related information of value to the close competitors of the bidder and target firms.

4.3. Federal trade commission versus justice department cases

In Table 8 we have split the total sample of the 65 challenged, horizontal mergers in Table 6 into two groups according to whether the JD or the FTC initiated the complaint. Rivals of mergers challenged by the FTC earn essentially zero abnormal returns around the merger proposal announcement, followed by a *significantly positive* abnormal return of 0.74% ($Z = 2.34$) on the day of the antitrust complaint announcement. According to the percent positive test, the probability that the latter performance is a result of pure chance is less than 1%. This evidence strongly contradicts the collusion hypothesis and gives some support to a "rival producer protection" rationale for the behavior of the FTC toward these mergers.[21]

Furthermore, Table 8 reveals that of the two prosecuting agencies it is only the JD which, on average, challenges mergers where the rivals earn significantly positive abnormal returns in response to the proposal announcement.[22] The rivals of the 39 JD cases in Table 8 earn 3.05% ($Z = 2.62$) over the -20 through 10 period, 1.49% ($Z = 2.68$) over the 7 days surrounding the announcement day, and 1.29% ($Z = 3.28$) from day 0 through day 3. The percent positive, and percent significantly positive tests yield somewhat lower significance levels than the standardized abnormal returns test, except for the 0.3 period. The fact that the same rivals do not show significantly negative

---

[20] See McGee (1980) for a review of predatory pricing and various (generally unsuccessful) attempts to test this theory.

[21] Although the issue of *why* the FTC should choose to protect the rivals of the merging firms goes beyond the scope of this paper, it is tempting to cite Posner's (1969) assertion that the FTC is significantly impaired in its task of promoting the public interest by the Commission's dependence on Congress. He claims that FTC investigations are initiated 'at the behest of corporations, trade associations, and trade unions whose motivation is at best to shift the costs of their private litigation to the taxpayer and at worst to harass competitors' (p. 88). Posner's antitrust "porkbarrel" model is certainly not contradicted by the evidence on the performance of the Commission presented here.

[22] Separate examination of the returns to the *merging* firms revealed no significant difference between the performance of firms challenged by the Federal Trade Commission and by the Justice Department. Since the alleged antitrust violations in one particular industry tend to be allocated to the same agency (i.e., the agencies "specialize" in certain industries), the apparent difference between the performance of rivals in FTC and JD cases could simply be the result of an arbitrary allocation of industries between the two agencies, as opposed to reflecting systematic policy differences.

Table 8

Abnormal returns to *rivals* of target firms in horizontal, challenged mergers relative to the merger proposal and antitrust complaint announcements: federal trade commission versus justice department cases

1963–1978 Merger sample	Announcement	Number of mergers	Summary statistic[a]	Period relative to the *Wall Street Journal* announcement (day 0)						
				(−20, 10)	(−10, 5)	(−3, 3)	(−1, 1)	0	(0, 3)	(3, 10)
Challenged by Federal Trade Commission	Merger proposal	26	CAAR (Z)	1.55 (1.57)	0.32 (0.76)	0.02 (0.27)	−0.02 (−0.61)	0.25 (0.41)	0.28 (0.33)	0.72 (0.90)
			P1	57.7	42.3	42.3	46.2	53.8	46.2	53.8
			P2	19.2***	7.7	3.8	0.0	3.8	7.7	11.5
	Antitrust complaint	23	CAAR (Z)	1.77 (1.15)	0.55 (0.46)	−0.66 (0.13)	0.67 (1.33)	0.74** (2.34)	0.27 (0.77)	0.75 (1.06)
			P1	65.2	52.2	43.5	52.0	87.0***	47.8	65.2
			P2	0.0	4.3	4.3	0.0	8.7	4.3	8.7
Challenged by Justice Department	Merger proposal	39	CAAR (Z)	3.05*** (2.62)	1.31* (1.79)	1.49*** (1.68)	0.74** (2.04)	0.16 (0.58)	1.29*** (3.28)	1.12** (2.59)
			P1	64.1*	48.7	59.0	59.0	48.7	66.7**	64.1*
			P2	10.3*	10.3*	12.8**	7.7	5.1	15.4***	12.8**
	Antitrust complaint	32	CAAR (Z)	1.79 (0.72)	0.95 (0.26)	0.52 (0.45)	0.15 (0.15)	−0.28 (−1.29)	0.09 (−0.35)	0.28 (−0.13)
			P1	53.1	40.6	53.1	43.8	46.9	31.3**	50.0
			P2	9.4	12.5*	9.4	6.3	0.0	9.4	12.5*

[a]*CAAR*, percent cumulative average abnormal returns; *P1*, the percent of the sample with positive cumulative abnormal returns; *P2*, the percent of the sample with significantly (at the 5% level) positive cumulative abnormal returns; *Z*, test statistic on the cumulative average standardized abnormal returns. *, **, *** indicate the hypothesis of zero abnormal returns [under which $E(CAAR) = 0.0\%$, $E(P1) = 50\%$ and $E(P2) < 5\%$] is rejected on a 10%, 5%, or 1% level of significance.

abnormal performance around the complaint announcement leads to a rejection of the collusion hypothesis also for this particular sample. The evidence is consistent with the proposition that both the JD and the FTC tend to attack efficient horizontal mergers.[23]

4.4. Horizontal versus vertical mergers

The collusion hypothesis is based on a reduction—through merger—of the number of independent producers in the industry. By definition, vertical mergers do not necessarily lead to this particular change in industry structure. Therefore, there are *a priori* less reasons to expect vertical mergers to produce results consistent with collusion. This suspicion is confirmed by the abnormal performance of rivals of target firms in vertical mergers shown in Table 9. Table 9 reveals no evidence indicating that the average vertical mergers in the total sample—challenged or unchallenged—were expected to have collusive, anticompetitive effects. Specifically, we cannot say with any degree of confidence that the rivals on average earn significantly positive abnormal returns around the merger proposal followed by significantly negative abnormal returns in response to the antitrust complaint. Thus, the data supports the widely accepted view that vertical mergers take place for efficiency reasons.[24]

Given the results for the total sample of vertical mergers in Table 9, it is tempting to view the performance of the rivals of this merger category as a "benchmark" for what to expect under the efficiency hypothesis. For this purpose we use the "common industry" sample in Table 9, comparing the performance of rivals of horizontal and vertical mergers taking place in the same industries. That is, for a given portfolio of rivals we are measuring the impact of vertical and horizontal unchallenged mergers,

[23] These results can be compared to the evidence in Stillman (1983) who examines the collusion hypothesis by estimating the daily abnormal performance of rivals of defendant firms in 11 horizontal Section 7 cases between 1964 and 1972. Based on the first *Wall Street Journal* reference to the merger proposal, as well as the dates of substantive court decisions on the cases, he finds no evidence that these events had any significant impact on the rivals. He therefore concludes that the challenged mergers (i) were not expected to produce collusion, and (ii) would have been efficient. Stillman selects his sample of horizontal rivals by consulting court records and internal government memoranda prepared by the prosecuting agencies. A reexamination of 10 of his cases which are included in our data base revealed a picture similar to the one observed in Table 8: "Our" rivals of his Justice Department cases earn abnormal returns of 5.07% ($Z = 2.01$) over the period -20 through 10 surrounding the merger proposal, while the corresponding performance by "our" rivals of his FTC cases was 0.56% ($Z = -0.17$). No significantly negative abnormal return was found in response to the complaint announcement. Thus, the *main* conclusion based on Stillman's sample remains the same whether one uses his or our procedure for selecting horizontal rivals.

[24] We continue to find that bidder and target firms in challenged mergers earn higher abnormal returns around the proposal announcement than bidders and targets in unchallenged mergers. Note that since we are focusing exclusively on the horizontal rivals of the *target* firm, we cannot exclude the possibility that the vertical mergers in the data base significantly affect other firms in the industry of the *bidder*. A two-stage monopolist can choose on which stage in the vertical chain to exercise the monopoly power. A complete study of vertical mergers should include an examination of the industries of both merger partners in order to fully test the collusion hypothesis on this particular category of mergers.

Table 9

Abnormal returns to *rivals* of target firms in *vertical* mergers to the merger proposal and antitrust complaint announcements

1963–1978 Merger sample	Announcement	Number of mergers	Summary statistic[a]	(−20, 10)	(−10, 5)	(−3, 3)	(−1, 1)	0	(0, 3)	(3, 10)
I Total sample										
Unchallenged	Merger proposal	57	CAAR (Z)	−0.37 (0.65)	−0.01 (0.94)	−0.09 (0.69)	0.39 (−1.16)	0.01 (−0.32)	−0.39 (−0.20)	−0.77 (−0.66)
			P1	43.9	54.4	56.1	40.4	47.4	43.9	40.4
			P2	8.8	3.5	3.5	3.5	7.0	3.5	3.5
Challenged	Merger proposal	11	CAAR (Z)	1.80 (0.31)	1.97 (1.16)	1.42 (0.99)	0.28 (0.38)	−0.40 (−1.06)	0.29 (0.48)	−1.11 (−0.96)
			P1	45.5	63.6	63.6	63.6	27.3*	54.5	45.5
			P2	0.0	9.1	0.0	0.0	0.0	0.0	0.0
	Antitrust complaint	11	CAAR (Z)	−1.58 (−1.05)	1.93 (0.52)	−0.08 (−0.35)	−1.08 (−1.61)	−0.52 (−1.19)	0.25 (−0.07)	0.06 (0.48)
			P1	36.4	54.5	45.5	45.5	54.5	36.4	45.5
			P2	0.0	9.1	0.0	0.0	0.0	0.0	9.1
II Common industry sample										
Vertical unchallenged	Merger proposal	19	CAAR (Z)	2.57 (1.61)	2.80** (2.48)	1.52** (2.02)	0.08 (−0.27)	0.11 (−0.01)	0.69 (1.22)	−0.21 (−0.26)
			P1	68.4	78.9**	68.4	47.4	52.6	57.9	42.1
			P2	5.3	5.3	5.3	0.0	10.5	10.5	0.0
Horizontal unchallenged	Merger proposal	53	CAAR (Z)	1.24 (1.10)	1.52** (2.44)	1.05** (2.30)	−0.01 (0.08)	0.03 (−0.10)	0.31 (0.96)	0.10 (0.53)
			P1	58.5	60.4	56.6	56.6	49.1	58.5	45.3
			P2	13.2***	15.1***	11.3**	5.7	5.7	7.5	7.5

Period relative to the *Wall Street Journal* announcement (day 0)

[a]CAAR, percent cumulative average abnormal returns; P1, the percent of the sample with positive cumulative abnormal returns; P2, the percent of the sample with significantly (at the 5% level) positive cumulative abnormal returns; Z, test statistic on the cumulative average standardized abnormal returns. *, **, *** indicate the hypothesis of zero abnormal returns [under which $E(CAAR) = 0.0\%$, $E(P1) = 50\%$, and $E(P2) < 5\%$] is rejected on a 10%, 5%, or 1% level of significance.

respectively. The abnormal returns are very similar across the two merger categories. Specifically, we can reject the hypothesis that vertical mergers have a different industry impact than horizontal mergers in *any* of the seven periods relative to the proposal announcement. This evidence further supports our earlier argument that the gains to the rivals of the horizontal, unchallenged mergers reported in Table 6 represent discounted future cost-savings made possible by information in the proposal announcement.

5. Summary and conclusions

In this paper we estimate daily abnormal returns to major horizontal competitors of target firms around merger proposal and antitrust complaint announcements, in order to examine whether the merger gains emanate from collusion. The basic proposition is that the rivals can expect to benefit from the news of a horizontal merger which significantly reduces the costs of enforcing a tacit collusive agreement within the industry of the merging firms. Furthermore, subsequent news that the merger is challenged by the government under Section 7 of the Clayton Act will reverse the expectations of monopoly rents, causing the rivals to show negative abnormal performance.

The observed sequence of abnormal returns across the proposal and complaint announcements does not appear to follow this particular pattern predicted by the collusion hypothesis. We *do* find that the rivals of the 65 horizontal challenged mergers in the data base on average earn significantly positive abnormal returns at the time of the merger proposal announcement. For example, the 31-day return from day -20 through day 10 is 2.45% and more than three standard deviations from zero. However, while the subsequent news of the antitrust complaint causes a reduction in the market value of the merging firms, the rivals on average show *positive* abnormal performance of 1.78% (approximately one standard deviation from zero) over the 31 days surrounding this event. There is a small, but *significantly* positive effect of complaints initiated by the FTC. We also find the performance of the rivals at the time of the antitrust complaint to be statistically independent of the corresponding performance around the merger proposal, which further contradicts the collusion hypothesis. Alternatively, the results are consistent with the productive efficiency hypothesis, under which the positive proposal-related performance shown by the rivals of the challenged mergers reflects discounted future cost-savings made possible by information signaled through the proposal announcement.

Three other important conclusions follow from the paper. First, we find that the regulatory activity of both the JD and the FTC is characterized by the imposition of a regulatory tax on the *most profitable* mergers. That is, rivals of the 65 horizontal challenged mergers earn on average larger abnormal returns at the time of the merger proposal than do rivals of the 126 horizontal unchallenged mergers in the data base. This is true whether or not the two merger categories take place in the same industries.

A similar result is observed for the merging firms: Both bidder and target firms in challenged mergers perform better than their counterparts in unchallenged mergers, relative to the merger proposal announcement. The failure of the data to confirm the collusion model implies that the regulatory tax distorts the allocation of corporate resources by making some efficient mergers unprofitable.[25]

Second, we find no significant evidence that proposed horizontal mergers are expected to *reduce* the value of the competitors of the merging firms. Thus, if mergers typically take place to realize efficiency gains, we cannot conclude that the "synergy" effect is expected to produce a significant expansion of the merging firm's share of the market along with an increase in industry rate of output. If scale economies are involved, then these seem on average to be insufficient to make the rivals worse off. Furthermore, the same evidence contradicts the argument that the merging firms were expected to initiate a (monopolistic) "predatory" price war after consummation of the merger.

Finally, we find that the performance of rivals of horizontal *unchallenged* mergers is indistinguishable from the performance of rivals of *vertical* unchallenged mergers, given the mergers take place in the same industries. To the extent that vertical mergers are unlikely to have collusive effects (such mergers do not necessarily reduce the number of independent firms in the industry), this is consistent with the proposition that also the horizontal unchallenged mergers in the sample were expected to be efficient.

These conclusions are based on a sample of mergers which, if anything, is biased *toward* the collusion hypothesis. On average, 80–85% of all horizontal and vertical mergers in mining and manufacturing industries during the sample period involved bidder and target firms with smaller asset sizes than the *smallest* merger in the sample studied here. Furthermore, a large part of the sample consists of mergers actually *accused* of "monopolizing" markets. Given this bias it is difficult to imagine a different merger sample of comparable size and importance which would yield evidence that systematically favors the collusion hypothesis.

References

Dodd, P., 1980, "Merger Proposals, Management Discretion and Stockholder Wealth," *Journal of Financial Economics*, 8, 105–137.

Eckbo, B. E., 1981, *Examining the Anti-Competitive Significance of Large Horizontal Mergers, Center for Research in Government Policy and Business Thesis Series CTS-1*, University of Rochester, Rochester, NY.

Ellert, J. C., 1976, "Mergers, Antitrust Law Enforcement and Stockholder Returns," *Journal of Finance*, 31, 715–732.

Fama, E. F., 1976, *Foundations of Finance*, Basic Books, New York.

---

[25] The issue remains, however, whether the social cost of this tax is more than compensated for by the deterrent effect of the regulatory policy on potentially collusive mergers.

Jarrell, G. A. and M. Bradley, 1980, "The Economic Effects of Federal and State Regulations of Cash Tender Offers," *Journal of Law and Economics*, 23, 371–407.

Langetieg, T. C., 1978, "An Application of a Three-Factor Performance Index for Measure Stockholder Gains from Merger," *Journal of Financial Economics*, 6, 365–383.

Malatesta, P. H., 1983, "The Wealth Effect of Merger Activity and the Objective Function of the Merging Firms," *Journal of Financial Economics*, 11, this issue.

Mandelker, G., 1974, "Risk and Return: The Case of Merging Firms," *Journal of Financial Economics*, 1, 303–335.

McGee, J. S., 1980, "Predatory Pricing Revisited," *Journal of Law and Economics*, 23, 289–330.

Posner, R., 1969, "The Federal Trade Commission," *University of Chicago Law Review*, 37, 47–89.

Schipper, K. and R. Thompson, 1983, "Evidence on the Capitalized Value of Merger Activity for Acquiring Firms," *Journal of Financial Economics*, this issue.

Scholes, M. and J. Williams, 1977, "Estimating Betas from Non-Synchronous Data," *Journal of Financial Economics*, 5, 309–327.

Schwert, G. W., 1981, "Using Financial Data to Measure Effects of Regulation," *Journal of Law and Economics*, 24, 121–158.

Steiner, P. O., 1975, *Mergers: Motives, Effects, Policies*, University of Michigan Press, Ann Arbor, MI.

Stigler, G. J., 1950, "Monopoly and Oligopoly by Merger," *Papers and Proceedings, American Economic Review*, 40, 23–34.

Stigler, G. J., 1964, "A Theory of Oligopoly," *Journal of Political Economy*, 72, 44–61.

Stillman, R., 1983, "Examining Antitrust Policy Towards Horizontal Mergers," *Journal of Financial Economics*, this issue.

Wier, P., 1983, "The Costs of Antimerger Lawsuits: Evidence from the Stock Market," *Journal of Financial Economics*, this issue.

Chapter 13

SOURCES OF GAINS IN HORIZONTAL MERGERS: EVIDENCE FROM CUSTOMER, SUPPLIER, AND RIVAL FIRMS[*]

C. EDWARD FEE

Department of Finance, Eli Broad College of Business, Michigan State University, East Lansing, MI 48824, USA

SHAWN THOMAS

Katz Graduate School of Business, University of Pittsburgh, Pittsburgh, Pennsylvania, USA

Contents

[*] We thank Murillo Campello, Charlie Hadlock, Jun-Koo Kang, Ken Lehn, Anil Makhija, Mike Ryngaert, an anonymous referee, and seminar participants at the University of Arkansas, the University of Kansas, the University of Pittsburgh, Tulane University, and the 2003 Western Finance Association Meeting for helpful comments and suggestions. We thank Jeremy Kopp and Hong-Yan Li for excellent research assistance. Any errors remain our own.

This article originally appeared in the *Journal of Financial Economics*, Vol. 74, pp. 423–460 (2004).

Abstract

We investigate the upstream and downstream product-market effects of a large sample of horizontal mergers and acquisitions from 1980 to 1997. We construct a data set that identifies the corporate customers, suppliers, and rivals of the firms initiating horizontal mergers and use this data set to examine announcement-related stock market revaluations and postmerger changes in operating performance. We find little evidence consistent with increased monopolistic collusion. However, we do find evidence consistent with improved productive efficiency and buying power as sources of gains to horizontal mergers. The nature of the buying power gains, that is, rents from monopsonistic collusion or improved purchasing efficiency, is also investigated.

Keywords

mergers; acquisitions; collusion; buying power

JEL classification: G34, D43, L41

1. Introduction

Managers of firms undertaking horizontal mergers and acquisitions often cite improved productive efficiency as the primary source of anticipated gains to mergers.[1] On the one hand, improved efficiency in production or distribution or both could arise from greater realization of economies of scale, elimination of overlapping facilities, etc. On the other hand, antitrust authorities frequently posit that horizontal mergers enable the merging firms to gain at the expense of customers and suppliers by allowing the merging firms an opportunity to engage in anticompetitive collusion. For instance, merged firms could more easily collude with rival firms to restrict output to monopoly levels and raise prices at the expense of their customers (see Stigler, 1964). Similarly, merged firms could collude with rivals to restrict aggregate purchases to monopsony levels and thereby lower input prices at the expense of their suppliers (see Robinson, 1933).

Merging firms could gain from pooling their purchasing, without necessarily engaging in anticompetitive monopsonistic collusion with rivals. For instance, merging firms could realize purchasing efficiencies if they reduce their input usage or obtain quantity discounts from suppliers. Merging firms could also be able to use their combined purchasing to induce suppliers to compete on price to sell to the combined firm. Further, if the supplier industry is not already competitive, then pooled purchasing and the competition that it induces could allow the merging firms to effectively countervail anticompetitive practices upstream, as noted by Galbraith (1952) and Snyder (1996). If the most efficient suppliers are likely to win such price competitions, then the result is a more efficient allocation of industry resources postmerger. This is in clear contrast to the efficiency implications of anticompetitive collusion.

The gains from increased buying power or anticompetitive collusion are not mutually exclusive of improved productive efficiency. However, gains from buying power or monopolistic collusion are distinct from efficiency gains in that they are expected to affect not only the postmerger performance of the merging firms but also the performance of other firms that share a product-market relationship with the merging firms. In this paper, we investigate the relative importance of buying power (both the anticompetitive monopsonistic variety and the efficiency-increasing variety) and monopolistic collusion as sources of gains to mergers. We construct a data set that identifies the important corporate customers, suppliers, and rivals of a large sample of firms that announced horizontal mergers and acquisitions between 1980 and 1997. This approach, originally suggested by Eckbo (1983), allows us to examine both the valuation impact at announcement and subsequent changes in operating performance for firms both upstream and downstream of the merged firms.[2] To our knowledge, no

---

[1] While our sample includes both mergers and tender offers, for expository purposes, we refer to all deals as mergers in this paper.

[2] Eckbo (1983, p. 245) writes, "In principle, one could discriminate between the collusion and efficiency theories by examining the abnormal returns to the merging firms' corporate customers and suppliers of inputs."

previous paper has examined the effects of horizontal mergers on actual corporate customers and suppliers in a large sample setting.

As in previous studies that examine anticompetitive collusion as a motivation for mergers, we find evidence that rival firms experience positive abnormal returns at merger announcements but do not experience negative abnormal returns when antitrust authorities challenge the mergers. This pattern of abnormal returns appears inconsistent with the conjecture that the market views gains to mergers as largely stemming from anticipated increased collusive activity (of either the monopolistic or monopsonistic variety).[3] We also report insignificant stock price reactions for customer firms at merger announcements and negligible postmerger changes in customer operating performance. These results hold even for those corporate customers that appear to be particularly reliant on the merging firms for their purchases. Taken together, the findings for rivals and customers suggest increased anticompetitive collusion is not a significant source of gains to the mergers in our sample.

We find that, on average, suppliers experience significant declines in cash-flow margins immediately subsequent to downstream mergers. This result suggests that some form of buying power is an important source of gains in horizontal mergers. However, this finding alone does not allow us to determine whether the gains are related to anticompetitive or to efficiency-increasing manifestations of buying power. To gain additional insight into the nature of these purchasing gains, we examine the effects of mergers on different types of suppliers (e.g., retained vs. terminated) and in different industry contexts (e.g., concentrated vs. fragmented). This analysis yields several interesting results.

We find that the net effect of a merger on a particular supplier appears to depend heavily on the supplier's ability to retain its product-market relationship with the merged entity. Specifically, those suppliers that are terminated subsequent to a customer merger experience negative and significant abnormal returns at the merger announcement and significant cash-flow deterioration postmerger. In contrast, those firms that are retained as suppliers experience significant gains in market share and insignificant abnormal returns or changes in operating performance. These results suggest that merging firms could realize gains by pitting their preexisting suppliers against one another in a price competition to remain suppliers postmerger. Given that winning suppliers do not appear to suffer, we interpret these results as more consistent with efficiency-increasing buying power than monopsonistic collusion given that all suppliers would likely be expected to suffer negative effects under the formation of an effective monopsony.

Multivariate analysis confirms the above asymmetric effects of mergers on suppliers' operating performance and also reveals other interesting cross-sectional

---

[3] We use the terms "monopolistic collusion" and "monopsonistic collusion" to refer to anticompetitive collusion in the output and input markets, respectively. To our knowledge, none of the mergers in our sample resulted in only one surviving industry firm. Thus, we could have alternatively chosen the terms "oligopolistic collusion" and "oligopsonistic collusion."

patterns in the effects of mergers on supplier firms. In particular, suppliers that are relatively more reliant on the merging firms for sales revenue (i.e., suppliers that face potentially higher costs of switching output to another industry or customer) experience significantly larger reductions in cash-flow margins subsequent to the merger. In addition, buying power effects are more pronounced when the merging firms operate in industries that are relatively concentrated. Moreover, greater concentration in the suppliers' industry is also associated with larger reductions in cash-flow margins for suppliers. The regressions also confirm anecdotal evidence that, in our sample period, buying power effects are particularly important in mergers among retailers. Finally, for the subsample of deals in which the merging firms operate in concentrated industries, we find that supplier postmerger cash-flow reductions are significantly related to merging firm postmerger cash-flow increases (and cost of good sold reductions), which is consistent with increased buying power representing a significant source of gains to mergers in these settings.

The above patterns are strongly evident in supplier operating performance changes but not nearly as evident in announcement period abnormal returns. One explanation for this seeming inconsistency is that the market anticipates that the observed operating performance changes will be temporary in nature. That is, the market anticipates that, in the long run, upstream firms might undertake strategic actions such as mergers of their own to counteract the buying power effects of downstream consolidation. Consistent with this explanation, we generally find the strongest evidence of supplier operating performance changes in the year immediately following the merger, with less significant changes in subsequent years.

This paper proceeds as follows. In Section 2, we develop the hypotheses to be tested. We describe our sample construction and methodology in Section 3. We report results in Section 4 and offer a concluding discussion in Section 5.

2. Hypothesis development and related literature

Table 1 describes the potential sources of gains to horizontal mergers and details the predicted effects of events increasing the probability of a merger on the merging firms as well as their rivals, customers, and suppliers.[4] Although the various gains are not entirely mutually exclusive, each source of gains, in general, has a different implication as to how the respective firms are expected to be affected by the merger. We exploit this fact to help distinguish gains coming purely from improvements in productive efficiency from those coming from buying power or monopolistic collusion.

---

[4] These predictions apply to anticipated changes in operating performance following mergers as well as stock market reactions to events that increase the probability of a merger. Predictions under the productive efficiency and monopolistic collusion hypotheses, particularly those related to merging firms and rivals, are from Eckbo (1983) and Eckbo and Weir (1985). The predicted stock market reactions to an event that decreases the probability of a merger are generally of the opposite sign.

Table 1

Predicted effects of events increasing the probability of a merger on merging firms, rivals, customers, and suppliers

These predictions apply to anticipated changes in operating performance that follow mergers as well as stock market reactions to events that increase the probability of a merger. Predictions under the productive efficiency and monopolistic collusion hypotheses, particularly those related to merging firms and rivals, are from Eckbo (1983) and Eckbo and Weir (1985). The predicted stock market reactions to an event that decreases the probability of a merger are generally of the opposite sign. For instance, an antitrust challenge suggests the loss of potential market power rents to the merging firms and their rivals and should be accompanied by a negative reaction (provided the market expects the gains to the merger to stem from the increased ability to engage in anticompetitive collusion).

Hypothesis	Merging firms	Rivals	Customers	Suppliers
Productive efficiency: Improved efficiency in operating (excluding purchasing), marketing, or distribution activities	Positive (lower operating, marketing, or distribution costs)	Positive or negative (positive information or competitive disadvantage)[a]	Zero to positive (customers unaffected or cost savings passed along in lower prices)	Zero (suppliers unaffected)[b]
Monopolistic collusion: Increased ability of industry competitors to coordinate a reduction in output and higher prices	Positive (monopoly rents)[c]	Positive (monopoly rents)[d]	Negative (lower quantity and higher prices)	Zero to negative (suppliers unaffected or decreased output leads to lower input demand)
Buying power: Monopsonistic collusion: Increased ability of industry competitors to coordinate lower input prices	Positive (monopsony rents)[c]	Positive (monopsony rents)[e]	Zero to negative (customers unaffected or lower quantity and increased prices)[g]	Negative (lower prices)[f]
Purchasing efficiencies/ countervailing power: Opportunity to switch purchases to more efficient suppliers or increase supplier industry competition or both[h]	Positive (lower input costs)	Positive or negative (lower input costs or competitive disadvantage)	Zero to positive (customers unaffected or cost savings passed along in lower prices)	Positive or negative (lower prices but perhaps greater quantity for retained suppliers)[i]

[a]Rivals' stock prices could rise on a merger announcement if the stock market infers that industry participants are undervalued or that rivals could realize efficiency gains through future mergers of their own, a possibility supported by the findings of Song and Walkling (2000). Alternatively, rivals could experience negative effects if the merging firms gain a competitive advantage that rivals are not expected to replicate.
[b]While suppliers are not expected to be directly affected under the productive efficiency hypothesis, suppliers could indirectly benefit from improved downstream efficiency. For instance, all else equal, improved merging firm efficiency could provide the merging firms a competitive advantage over their rivals and increase sales, which would require greater input purchases. This assumes that the supplier does not lose an equal amount of revenue as a result of reduced purchases from the rivals of the merging firms.
[c]Under certain assumptions, the abnormal returns to bidders could be informative for determining the relevance of the hypotheses. In particular, both collusion hypotheses would likely predict positive returns to both bidders and targets as well as positive combined returns. Consider, for example, the case of an industry

consisting of one potential target and two identical potential acquirers engaged in costless bidding. Because the gains to collusion are largely output-price-related and do not reflect any productive synergies, even the losing bidder will realize them. Neither potential acquirer would have any incentive to bid more than the initial target value plus the anticipated gains to the target under the new pricing structure. This positive externality implies that shareholders of the winning bidder along with those of the target and the losing bidder will be able to realize gains in the values of their holdings.

[d]Rival firms would be expected to suffer if the merger permits the merging firms to engage in predatory pricing following the merger.

[e]An alternative hypothesis to monopsonistic collusion is that mergers increase the likelihood of anticompetitive upstream behavior, such as forcing suppliers to charge higher prices to rivals or to not sell to rivals, as the Federal Trade Commission charged in its 1996 complaint against Toys 'R' Us. Under this possibility, returns to rivals would be negative, not positive.

[f]While some individual suppliers might be expected to experience net gains in response to merging firm purchasing efficiencies or the exercise of countervailing power, it is relatively less likely that any suppliers would benefit under monopsonistic collusion. Under classical stories of monopsony, the firms forming the monopsony simply offer the monopsony price regardless of supplier identity.

[g]A monopsonist is unlikely to pass along its cost savings to consumers. If the output market is competitive, then the monopsonist will sell its reduced output (largely due to the purchase of fewer inputs) at the market price. If the monopsonist has power in the output market, then its reduced output will, all else equal, raise prices and harm customers.

[h]One form of purchasing efficiency is the case in which merging firms reevaluate their supplier relationships and switch their purchases to the most efficient suppliers. Alternatively, purchasing efficiencies could arise if the merging firms reduce their per unit input usage or suppliers can realize economies from serving larger customers. Countervailing power refers to cases in which downstream consolidation effectively countervails a concentrated, and *ex ante* imperfectly competitive upstream industry. Unlike monopsony collusion, countervailing power is an efficiency-increasing outcome. One unique implication of the countervailing power hypothesis is that effects on suppliers should generally be more negative for concentrated upstream industries.

[i]Effects could be asymmetric with retained suppliers benefiting and terminated suppliers suffering.

Reductions in production, distribution, marketing, and other costs that arise from greater realization of economies of scale, elimination of overlapping facilities, etc., are commonly given as sources of gains to horizontal mergers.[5] We refer to the idea that the gains to mergers reflect such anticipated improvements as the productive efficiency hypothesis. To aid exposition and help distinguish among the various sources of gains that we consider, we refer to all merger gains that do not come at the expense of firms sharing a product-market relationship with the merging firms as productive efficiency gains. Efficiency gains in purchasing activities are not included in productive efficiency gains as we have defined this term.

As outlined in Table 1, the main prediction of the productive efficiency hypothesis is that of positive announcement returns and increases in postmerger cash-flow margins for merging firms. The implications for rival firms are unclear. Rivals' stock prices could rise on a merger announcement if the stock market infers that industry partici-

---

[5] Clearly, horizontal mergers could also be motivated by the gains to replacing inefficient management or to exploiting a temporary misvaluation of an industry competitor.

pants are undervalued or that rivals could realize efficiency gains through future mergers of their own. Alternatively, rivals could experience negative effects if the merging firms gain a competitive advantage that rivals are not expected to replicate. Customers would likely either benefit, if some of the cost savings are passed along in lower prices, or be unaffected. Given the distinctions that we are making between improved purchasing efficiency and improved efficiency in other areas of operation, suppliers would not be directly affected if the sole source of gains to horizontal mergers is improved productive efficiency as we have defined it.[6]

Existing evidence on the importance of productive efficiency as a source of gains to mergers comes largely from papers that examine announcement effects on merging firms and subsequent changes in merging-firm operating performance. As cataloged in Bruner (2002), many previous papers have documented positive revaluations for horizontal merger announcements. However, empirical evidence on changes in cash flows around horizontal mergers is mixed; for example, see Ravenscraft and Scherer (1987), Healy et al. (1992), Ghosh (2001), and Heron and Lie (2002).

As in Stigler (1964), horizontal mergers could allow the merged firms to more easily collude with rival firms to restrict output to monopoly levels and thus raise prices at the expense of their customers. We refer to this idea as the monopolistic collusion hypothesis. Under the monopolistic collusion hypothesis, we would expect that merging firms and rivals would benefit and customers would suffer given that the primary result of an effective monopoly is reduced output and increased prices.[7] While a reduction in downstream production and input use could negatively affect suppliers, the importance of these effects is unclear.

Eckbo (1983) and Stillman (1983) point out that a positive reaction by rivals to merger announcements is not, by itself, sufficient evidence to accept the monopolistic collusion hypothesis. As we outline in Table 1, such a reaction is also possible under the productive efficiency hypothesis if the market believes that the rivals can also realize efficiency gains through future takeovers, a possibility supported by the

---

[6] While suppliers are not expected to be directly affected under the productive efficiency hypothesis, suppliers could indirectly benefit from improved downstream efficiency. For instance, all else equal, improved merging-firm efficiency could provide the merging firms a competitive advantage over their rivals and increase sales, which would require greater input purchases. This assumes that the supplier does not lose an equal amount of revenue because of reduced purchases from the rivals of the merging firms.

[7] Rival firms would be expected to suffer if the merger permits the merging firms to engage in predatory pricing following the merger. Under certain assumptions, the abnormal returns to bidders could be informative in determining the relevance of the hypotheses. In particular, both collusion hypotheses would likely predict positive returns to both bidders and targets, as well as positive combined returns. Consider, for example, the case of an industry consisting of one potential target and two identical potential acquirers that are engaged in costless bidding. Because the gains to collusion are largely output-price related and do not reflect any productive synergies, even the losing bidder will realize such gains. Neither potential acquirer would have any incentive to bid more than the initial target value plus the anticipated gains to the target under the new pricing structure. This positive externality implies that shareholders of the winning bidder and those of both the target and the losing bidder will be able to realize gains in the values of their holdings. We thank the referee for bringing this possibility to our attention.

findings of Song and Walkling (2000). However, to the extent that an antitrust challenge lowers the probability of merger completion, challenge announcements should negatively affect rivals' stock prices under the collusion hypothesis, a prediction that is inconsistent with the data in Eckbo (1983).[8] Our data allow us to distinguish between the productive efficiency and the monopolistic collusion hypotheses by separating out the effects of mergers on those firms expected to be most directly affected by the collusive activity, that is, customers. In the interest of updating the findings of prior studies, we report rivals' reactions to merger announcements and challenges.

With regard to the upstream effects of horizontal mergers, both economic theory and anecdotal evidence suggest that there are several channels through which combined purchasing could lead to merger gains as a result of lower input prices. We refer to the general idea that merging firms can combine their purchasing activities and obtain lower input prices as the buying power hypothesis. Unlike monopolistic collusion, buying power can be either efficiency increasing or efficiency decreasing. For this reason, we discuss several variations of the general buying power hypothesis. While these hypotheses have several predictions in common, as we outline in Table 1, we rely on somewhat subtle but important differences in the predictions of the respective hypotheses for suppliers to help ascertain which, if any, are consistent with the data.

Under all forms of the buying power hypothesis, the gains to the merging firms come, at least in part, at the expense of some their upstream suppliers. A recent example of a merger in which buying power was expected to lead to substantial cost savings was the Hewlett-Packard-Compaq deal. A significant portion of the estimated $2.5 billion to $3 billion in annual savings was expected to come from more aggressive dealings with suppliers. An analyst following the firm postmerger described the change in tactics by saying, "HP beats up its suppliers on price. They used to be the nice guy, but now they play rough."[9] As we explain below, "playing rough" is quite different from "playing unfairly" and cannot in and of itself be taken as evidence of anticompetitive behavior.

We refer to the idea that horizontal mergers increase anticompetitive upstream behavior as the monopsonistic collusion hypothesis. Under this hypothesis, we would expect rivals to benefit and suppliers to suffer because the primary implication of monopsonistic collusion is enhanced coordination among industry competitors to obtain lower input prices.[10] The effect of mergers on customers under this hypothesis,

---

[8] Other studies that utilize a similar approach include Stillman (1983), Eckbo (1985, 1992), Eckbo and Weir (1985), and Schumann (1993).

[9] See Crayton Harrison, "One year later, Hewlett-Packard, Compaq offer role model for mega-mergers," *The Dallas Morning News*, May 4, 2003.

[10] An alternative hypothesis to monopsonistic collusion is that mergers increase the likelihood of anticompetitive upstream behavior (e.g., forcing suppliers to charge higher prices to rivals, to not sell to rivals, etc.), as the Federal Trade Commission charged in its 1996 complaint against Toys 'R' Us. Under this alternate hypothesis, returns to rivals would be negative, not positive.

if any, would tend to be negative. The reason for this prediction is that a true monopsonist would generally not pass cost savings along to consumers. If the output market is perfectly competitive, then the monopsonist will sell its reduced output (as a result of reduced input purchases) at the market price. As Blair and Harrison (1993) describe, absent competition in the output market, a monopsonist will have power in the output market and thus its reduced output will, all else equal, raise prices and harm customers.

Merging firms and their rivals are more likely to establish an effective monopsony when they face a supplier industry that is fragmented and competitive. However, supplier industries are often not perfectly competitive and suppliers can exercise market power of their own. In these circumstances, increased downstream buying power need not be economically harmful and could increase efficiency as in the Galbraith (1952) theory of countervailing power. For instance, if upstream firms are colluding to restrict output and keep prices above competitive levels prior to the merger, then the increased purchasing power accompanying combined purchasing could induce members of the upstream cartel to break ranks and compete on price.

Merging firms could realize purchasing efficiencies if they reduce their per-unit input usage or obtain quantity discounts from suppliers. We refer to the idea that merger-induced increased buying power permits firms to gain purchasing efficiencies or to countervail an anticompetitive upstream industry as the purchasing efficiency/countervailing power hypothesis. Under this hypothesis, the effect of mergers on suppliers could be either positive or negative, depending upon how the efficiencies are gained. For example, total profits in the supplier industry could increase, all else equal, if production is switched to lower cost producers even though output prices fall. The prediction of this hypothesis with regard to rivals is indeterminate. If rivals can also gain lower input prices following the merger, then the effects are positive. If not, then rival firms could be at a competitive disadvantage. The effect of mergers on customers under the purchasing efficiency/countervailing power hypothesis depends on the extent to which the cost savings are passed along and hence is also unclear, but probably biased toward the positive side.

Recent theoretical models (see, e.g., Gal-Or, 1999; Inderst and Wey, 2002; Snyder, 1996) and anecdotal evidence both suggest that the effects of increased buying power on supplier firms could be asymmetric. If the merging firms pit their preexisting suppliers against one another in a price competition to remain suppliers postmerger, then the most efficient suppliers are likely to win this competition. For example, Staples executives are quoted in relation to their announced intention to buy Office Depot in 1997 that "all the [supplier] relationships we have now are open to change and renegotiation."[11] In a specific example, prior to their proposed merger, Staples bought pencil sharpeners from Panasonic while Office Depot bought them from Hunt

---

[11] See Roger Lowenstein, "Inside the Staples deal: Chaos upstream," *The Wall Street Journal*, March 20, 1997.

Manufacturing. These respective suppliers inferred from statements by Staples management that only the supplier submitting the lowest bid would be retained. Staples and Office Depot expected to cut their combined input prices by nearly $150 million per year through such enhanced supplier competition.

If the above type of tournament were common, then the purchasing efficiency/ countervailing power hypothesis would predict asymmetric effects on suppliers. On balance, suppliers that are retained might not be harmed by the merging firms' increased buying power; that is, they could sell a higher quantity but at a lower price. However, those suppliers that lose the bidding competition might suffer. While some individual suppliers might be expected to experience net gains in response to merging firm purchasing efficiencies or exercise of countervailing power, it is relatively less likely that any suppliers would benefit under monopsonistic collusion. Under classical stories of monopsony, the firms forming the monopsony simply offer the monopsony price regardless of supplier identity.

Many of the previous papers examining the product-market effects of horizontal mergers have relied on changes in product prices around mergers for inferences. Thus, these papers are often limited to specific industries or clinical settings for which price data can be obtained. For example, Knapp (1990) and Kim and Singal (1993) present evidence relating to airline mergers; Prager and Hannan (1998) present evidence from bank mergers; Barton and Sherman (1984) present evidence from the microfilm market; and Chipty and Snyder (1999) present evidence from the cable television industry.[12]

Our approach of inferring the implications of mergers by examining the effects on customers and suppliers is not entirely new. However, most previous studies have employed this approach in intraindustry or clinical settings, as in the price data studies. For instance, Mullin et al. (1995) examine the market reaction of customers to various events associated with the US Steel dissolution suit that began in 1911, and Mullin and Mullin (1997) examine the reaction of customers to US Steel's 1906 acquisition (by long-term lease) of Great Northern Railway's iron ore properties. Bittlingmayer and Hazlett (2000) examine the effects of antitrust actions against Microsoft on portfolios of firms that produce complements or substitutes for Microsoft's products. In a recent paper, Karceski et al. (2003) examine the reaction of borrowers to banking mergers.

The only other paper we are aware of that examines the reactions of customers and suppliers to merger announcements in a large cross-sectional setting is Shahrur (2002). While we identify individual companies with actual product-market relationships, Shahrur uses the benchmark input-output matrices for the US economy to identify upstream and downstream industries. We view the two approaches as complementary in the sense that the input-output approach is able to identify a large pool of potential customers and suppliers, while our approach is able to identify those individual firms

---

[12] For evidence on the importance of buying power in the pharmaceutical industry, see Ellison and Snyder (2001).

that have actual, significant product-market relationships with the merging firms.[13] An additional methodological difference between the papers is that we examine changes in operating performance as well as stock price reactions. While the two papers are in agreement on a number of points, there are some significant differences in the conclusions drawn regarding the importance of buying power. In particular, Shahrur (2002) reports negative average abnormal returns to suppliers on takeover announcements but positive returns to suppliers for the subset of deals in which merging firm combined abnormal returns are positive. He interprets this finding as evidence against what he refers to as the buyer power hypothesis. The analysis in the present paper, however, suggests that some forms of buying power are, in fact, important.

3. Data

3.1. Sample construction

Our sample of horizontal mergers is drawn from the universe of mergers and acquisitions proposed between January 1, 1980 and December 31, 1997 and included in the Securities Data Corporation (SDC) Mergers & Acquisitions database.[14] We include in our sample all deals that meet the following criteria.

1. The bidder did not previously own a majority interest in the target and was seeking to obtain a majority interest through the transaction.
2. The announcement date of the proposed merger or tender offer can be determined via a search of newswires and newspapers archived in Dow Jones Interactive.[15]
3. The bidder and target are both domestic, publicly traded firms with sufficient data from the Center for Research in Security Prices (CRSP) to calculate announcement period abnormal returns.
4. The bidder and target are not financial or regulated firms [primary CRSP Standard Industrial Classification (SIC) code not 6000-6999, 4000-4099, 4500-4599, or 4800-4999].
5. The bidder and target have data available in Compustat on both a consolidated and industry-segment basis (active and research files).

---

[13] Given that the effects of horizontal mergers are probably greatest on direct competitors, current customers, and current suppliers, differences between our papers' conclusions discussed below could reflect the differences in our respective samples. For instance, a merger between two regional firms would not be expected to have a large impact on rivals that operate in another region. While our sample of rivals is subject to this same weakness, our customer and supplier samples are not. Eckbo (1983) avoids this problem by examining cases in which antitrust complaints state explicitly that the merging firms operate nationally.

[14] We choose to end our sample in 1997 because we require 3 years of postmerger operating performance for sample firms and because a change in segment reporting standards effective for 1998 makes segment definitions potentially inconsistent before and after the change.

[15] The search terms are "(bidder name or target name) and (merg$ or acqui$ or bid or offer)." To facilitate the calculation of announcement period abnormal returns, we exclude deals for which the only public information about the deal is an article reporting that an offer had been rejected.

6. The bidder and target report at least one industry segment each with the same four-digit SIC code (excluding financial and regulated industries).

There are 554 proposed transactions that met the sample formation criteria, and summary statistics for these deals are presented in Table 2. As reported in Panel A, considerable heterogeneity is evident in the frequency and magnitude of deals by year. Given the distinctions that are often drawn regarding merger and acquisition activity in the 1980s versus the 1990s, note that roughly two-thirds of our sample observations are from the 1990s. The average ratio of target firm market value of equity to bidding firm market value of equity (both reported in 1997 dollars) is 45% for our sample of deals. As reported in Panel B, we aggregate deals into broad industries based on the four-digit SIC code of the overlapping segments and using the industry definitions of Fama and French (1997).[16] The industries with the most merger activity over our sample period are energy, business services, retail, health care, electronic equipment, and wholesale. Mergers in these industries account for 51.26% of the mergers in our sample.

Panel C further describes characteristics of the deals in our sample. From newswire searches we determine whether the deal was completed, whether a bid was made for the target in the 6 months preceding the announcement of our sample deal, and whether the deal was challenged by the antitrust authorities.[17] There are 391 deals that were eventually completed. In 10.47% of all deals, the target had received a previous offer or had entertained merger talks with another party. Regulatory authorities challenged 39 of the deals on antitrust grounds. For each transaction we also collect data from SDC on the proposed consideration (cash, stock, mixed), the deal attitude (hostile or friendly), and any toehold (preoffer ownership stake in the target) held by the bidder.[18] The most frequent method of payment in the deals was bidder stock (44.40% of deals).

---

[16] The merging firms in our sample are quite focused, with over 65% of bidders and 77% of targets reporting only one industry segment. In the cases such that more than one segment overlaps, we identify the industry in which the merging firms have the largest combined sales.

[17] To determine if there was a previous bid for the target, we search for stories in the 6 months before the merger announcement date that indicate that the company was in merger talks or received a takeover proposal. We define a deal as challenged if the Justice Department or Federal Trade Commission (FTC) brought suit or threatened to sue to block the deal, or if the firms voluntarily restructured the deal or entered into a consent agreement to satisfy regulatory demands. The search terms that we use to identify challenged mergers are "(bidder name or target name) and (FTC or federal trade or justice or hart$ or antitrust)." As a check on the accuracy of our procedure to identify challenged deals, we cross-reference our results with the FTC and Justice Department's joint "Annual Report to Congress Pursuant to Subsection (j) of the Clayton Act Hart-Scott-Rodino Antitrust Improvements Act of 1976" for fiscal year 1997 (20th report). Our news search is able to accurately identify every case in which a deal in our sample for that year was mentioned in the report. We are unable to secure these reports for every year in our sample, but this check provides us with confidence in the accuracy of our news-searching algorithm.

[18] Information on toeholds is not reliably available from SDC prior to 1984. For deals that were missing this information from SDC, we relied on announcement stories to determine the existence and size of any toehold.

Table 2

Sample description

The sample includes all proposed mergers and acquisitions initiated between 1980 and 1997 that are covered in the Securities Data Corporation (SDC) database and that also meet the following criteria: Bidder did not previously own a majority of target and was seeking to obtain a majority interest through the transaction; announcement date of the deal can be determined via a search of Dow Jones Interactive (DJI); bidder and target are both domestic, publicly traded firms with sufficient data in CRSP to calculate announcement period abnormal returns; bidder and target are not financial or regulated firms [primary CRSP Standard Industrial Classification (SIC) code not 6000-6999, 4000-4099, 4500-4599, or 4800-4999]; bidder and target have data available in Compustat on both a consolidated and industry-segment basis (active and research files); and bidder and target report at least one industry segment each with the same four-digit SIC code (excluding financial and regulated industries). MVE is market value of equity obtained from CRSP and is reported in 1997 dollars. Industries in Panel B are defined as in Fama and French (1997). Searches of DJI determine if deals were challenged by antitrust authorities, were ultimately completed, and involved a prior bid for the target firm. Information regarding type of consideration, deal attitude, and toehold is obtained from SDC.

Year	Deals	Percentage	Average bidder MVE ($ millions)	Average target MVE ($ millions)	Target MVE/ bidder MVE
Panel A: Frequency of deals by year					
1981	12	2.17	5287.27	2803.10	0.59
1982	12	2.17	1733.12	639.54	0.73
1983	7	1.26	306.82	170.85	0.61
1984	18	3.25	964.70	328.99	0.56
1985	28	5.05	2126.70	861.45	0.77
1986	25	4.51	1590.74	521.30	0.35
1987	26	4.69	2434.67	378.31	0.61
1988	40	7.22	2048.17	282.20	0.60
1989	28	5.05	3857.75	1261.65	0.47
1990	17	3.07	2999.62	177.37	0.28
1991	22	3.97	540.50	60.10	0.34
1992	19	3.43	1236.00	157.39	0.18
1993	38	6.86	934.51	465.79	0.52
1994	50	9.03	2486.86	358.31	0.38
1995	67	12.09	2498.92	352.52	0.34
1996	64	11.55	3177.91	514.65	0.34
1997	81	14.63	2495.52	547.65	0.47
All Deals	554	100	2302.33	516.09	0.45
Panel B: Frequency of deals by industry					
Energy	69	12.45	1369.26	726.73	0.51
Business Services	64	11.55	2976.85	279.18	0.33
Retail	54	9.75	2422.37	418.88	0.48
Health care	37	6.68	1701.83	407.30	0.44
Electronic equipment	31	5.60	2513.84	586.86	0.36
Wholesale	29	5.23	826.56	206.86	0.37
Other	270	48.74	2573.40	598.09	0.44
Panel C: Deal characteristics					
Challenged	39	7.04	2054.00	417.51	0.45
Completed	391	70.58	2440.38	454.67	0.34

(*Continued*)

Table 2 (*Continued*)

Year	Deals	Percentage	Average bidder MVE ($ millions)	Average target MVE ($ millions)	Target MVE/ bidder MVE
Cash consideration	163	29.42	2336.41	580.14	0.46
Stock consideration	246	44.40	2350.66	545.28	0.50
Mixed consideration	145	26.17	2233.36	432.87	0.42
Hostile	59	10.65	2341.42	444.74	0.39
Toehold	71	11.84	2455.51	739.52	0.71
Previous bid	58	10.47	3472.82	1136.35	0.52

Bidders had toeholds in 11.84% of the deals, and the average preoffer ownership stake in the target for these deals was 12.96%.

3.2. Identifying corporate suppliers, customers, and rivals

FASB No. 14 required firms to report certain financial information for any industry segment that comprised more than 10% of consolidated yearly sales, assets, or profits between 1977 and 1997.[19] In addition, the identity of any customer representing more than 10% of the total sales of a firm had to be disclosed, as well as the segment that was primarily responsible for these sales. This customer information is contained in the Compustat industry-segment files, but not in an immediately usable format. What is generally listed is an abbreviation of the customer's name, which can vary across reporting firms and years. For example, in 1987 Dean Foods Co. lists customer American Stores Co. as "AMER STORES," while Advo Inc. lists American Stores Co. as "AM STR."

To link the customer abbreviations with full company data, we use the following procedure. First, using an algorithm that compares the number and order of the letters in the abbreviation with those in the company names listed on CRSP (historical name structure), we identify the four company names from CRSP that are most likely to correspond to the abbreviation. In cases in which visual inspection determines an almost certain, distinct match, we link the abbreviation with the CRSP name and permanent identification number. In several instances more than one company name appears to correspond with the abbreviation, and in these cases we identify the customers using the Compustat industry-segment information. For example, Grist Mill Co., a manufacturer of fruit snacks and granola products, lists as its 1997 customers the abbreviations "LUCKY," "KROGER CO," "GRT A&P TEA," and "SAFEWAY INC." Our matching program produces Lucky Chance Mining Company Inc., Lucky Lanes Inc. (a bowling center), and Lucky Stores Inc. (which reports food stores as its only industry segment for 1997) as potential matches for "LUCKY."

---

[19] Effective 1998, SFAS No. 131 now governs required segment disclosures.

It seems unlikely that a mining company would be a large customer of a food producer, and given that Lucky Lanes Inc. ceased operations in 1979, we link "LUCKY" with Lucky Stores Inc. in our database. Finally, for those abbreviations that still lack matches using the above methods, we use the *Directory of Corporate Affiliations* to determine if the reason that we were unable to find a match for a particular abbreviation is that the abbreviation corresponds to a subsidiary of a publicly traded firm. For example, for instances in which abbreviations for Burger King (previously a wholly owned subsidiary of Pillsbury Co.) are given as a customer between 1980 and 1987, we match these abbreviations with Pillsbury Co.

While some discretion is involved in matching customer abbreviations with firm identities, we are conservative in concluding that an abbreviation is in fact a match. While we code some firms as probable matches, we choose to exclude these firms from the analysis if it is not possible to confirm the firm is a match by comparing the abbreviation with previous years' customer descriptions or by using the above-mentioned references. We choose this conservative approach because we feel the potential costs of misidentifying noncustomer firms as customers are greater than the potential costs of failing to identify a limited number of actual customers.

We use the resulting database to identify customers of the merging firms in our sample and then invert the database to identify suppliers. We include in our supplier sample all firms listing either the bidder or target as a customer in either of the 2 fiscal year-ends prior to the merger announcement date. We include only customers of the merging firms' overlapping segments in the analysis because these customers would most likely be directly affected by the merging firms' increased market power. For the average deal in our sample, we identify 1.09 supplier firms and 0.40 customer firms with the necessary data to calculate announcement period abnormal returns.

The nature of the reporting requirements suggests that the suppliers identified will generally be smaller than the merging firms and that the customers will generally be larger than the merging firms. The mean supplier market capitalization is $326.6 million, the mean combined market capitalization of the merging firms is $2.8 billion, and the mean customer market capitalization is $19.4 billion. This implies that the database could be more optimally suited to testing the buying power hypotheses than the monopolistic collusion hypothesis (i.e., the relative importance of the product-market relationship is probably greater for the suppliers we identify than it is for the customers). However, we believe that there is still considerable information content in the customer data and hence analyze both the customer and supplier data.

The data we use to identify industry rivals for the merging firms is also from the Compustat industry-segment files. We identify rivals as any firms, besides the bidder and target, which report at least one segment for the year before the merger in a four-digit SIC code industry group in which the bidder and target overlap.[20] For the

---

[20] In several instances, firms identified as suppliers are also identified as rivals. Most of these cases arise for mergers involving integrated petroleum firms. Therefore, we exclude from the supplier database any firm that is also listed as an industry rival.

average deal in our sample, we identify 75.55 rival firms with the necessary data to calculate announcement period abnormal returns.

3.3. Calculating announcement period abnormal returns

We use standard event study methodology to calculate abnormal returns for the bidder and the target as well as any firm identified as a rival, supplier, or customer of the bidder or target. The market model parameters are estimated over the 200 trading day period starting at day -240 relative to the announcement date. We require at least 100 trading days over the estimation window for a firm to be included in the sample. Cumulative abnormal returns are calculated over the 3-day window centered on the announcement date, and all tests of significance are performed using standardized prediction errors.[21] As in Bradley et al. (1988), we calculate abnormal returns for the value-weighted portfolio of the bidder and target as a measure of total combined gains to the merging firms, and we adjust these returns for any premerger stake in the target held by the bidder.

To facilitate examination of cross-sectional differences, we treat each rival, customer, and supplier as one observation in the calculation of abnormal returns. However, the returns to rivals and, to a lesser extent, customers, and suppliers for a given transaction could be correlated.[22] Thus, we also report results treating all rivals, customers, and suppliers, respectively, as equally weighted portfolios for a given transaction.

---

[21] Given concerns about the effects of information leakage on our results, we also estimate abnormal returns over a window designed to capture any leakage. For each target, we identify two dates: an agreement (announcement) date for the deal in our sample and a leakage date. The leakage date for the target is the first mention that the target might be a deal candidate. We find this date by going back 6 months from the announcement date to identify any stories that indicate that the target received a takeover proposal, was involved in merger talks, or considered putting itself up for sale. If we find such a story, we go back an additional 6 months looking for any prior stories. We take as the leakage date the date of the earliest such story that does not come more than a year before the announcement of our sample deal. Combined abnormal returns to the merging firms over the window from the leak date until 1 day after the announcement date are 3.62% versus 3.06% over the 3-day announcement window. Thus, by using the announcement window we are somewhat understating the overall gains to the deals. However, given potential concerns regarding calculating supplier, customer, and rival abnormal returns over long windows that might include confounding events, we report results for merging firms (and suppliers, customers, and rivals) using only the 3-day window around the announcement of our sample deal.

[22] Mergers might be expected to routinely follow periods of significantly positive abnormal returns (runups) or significantly negative abnormal returns (declining industries), and these return patterns are likely to be similar among suppliers, merging firms, customers, and rivals. This would impart a systematic bias in our market model intercepts for each of the firms we examine and would overstate the correlations between the abnormal returns of the various firms. Thus, we also calculate abnormal returns by replacing the estimated market model intercept with the risk-free rate multiplied by one minus the beta from the market model; for example, see Houston and Ryngaert (1997). Results using these alternative abnormal returns are nearly identical to those reported in the paper.

3.4. Measuring changes in operating performance

We use a matching-firm approach to facilitate comparisons of industry-adjusted pre- and postmerger operating performance and to control for mean reversion in operating performance measures. The operating performance changes are examined only for merging firms that complete their transactions and the respective customers and suppliers of these firms. Matching firms are chosen for each of the merging firms and their suppliers and customers on the basis of industry, asset size, and prior operating performance along the lines suggested by Barber and Lyon (1996) and implemented by Loughran and Ritter (1997).

The specific matching algorithm is as follows. We first identify all firms on Compustat that are not in our sample (i.e., a bidder, target, supplier, or customer) and that have cash flow (defined as operating income before depreciation, item 13) to sales (item 12) data available for the same years as our sample firms (i.e., we require that matching firms have data available for the same time window around the merger as our sample firms). From these firms, we identify those firms with the same two-digit SIC code as our sample firm, asset size at the end of year -1 relative to the merger between 25% and 200% of the sample firm, and cash flow to sales between 90% and 110% of the sample firm. From these firms we choose as the matching firm the company with the cash flow to sales ratio closest to that of our sample firm. If no matching firm is available that meets these criteria, we relax the industry screen to require only a match of the one-digit SIC code. If there is still no match, we eliminate the industry matching requirement and match on size and performance. Finally, if no match is available after eliminating the industry matching requirement, we eliminate the size requirement and match purely on performance. Of the 1311 firms for which we seek matches, 932 have matches at the two-digit level, 248 at the one-digit level, 114 using size and performance, and 17 using only performance.

Our primary measure of operating performance is the cash flow to sales ratio.[23] We calculate this ratio for our sample firms and for the matching firms for 1 year prior to the merger and for each of the 3 years following the year in which the merger is completed. For bidders and targets, we sales-weight each firm's ratio in the year prior to the merger to estimate premerger combined performance. We weight the performance measure for the respective matching firms of the bidder and target in a similar fashion in all years to create a benchmark measure. For each year, we define the industry-adjusted performance measure as the sample firm's ratio minus the benchmark ratio. Because of skewness and the potential influence of outliers when using accounting ratios, we follow Loughran and Ritter (1997) and focus on median values.

---

[23] Because of merger-related accounting practices, we believe this a more informative measure than cash flow to book assets. As an alternate measure of operating performance, we consider the cash flow to market value of assets measure of Healy et al. (1992). However, several recent papers have pointed out potential complications in using this measure; see, for example, Kaplan et al. (1997), Ghosh (2001), and Heron and Lie (2002). In particular, this measure could be biased upward by systematic post-merger stock price declines.

4. Empirical results

4.1. Merging firms

In Panel A of Table 3, we report the announcement period abnormal returns for the merging firms in our sample. For our entire sample, we show a positive average combined abnormal return to the bidder and target of 3.06% over the 3-day announcement window. This is significant at the 1% confidence level using a *t*-test on standardized prediction errors, and a sign test indicates that significantly more firms experience positive (368) than negative (186) combined returns. This finding of positive average combined returns is consistent with the bulk of previous research on mergers and acquisitions (see Bruner, 2002, for a summary of the evidence). Also consistent with previous research, we show that the gains to the merger are limited to target shareholders. Target shareholders experience a positive 18.77% revaluation on the announcement date (significant at the 1% level), while bidders experience a −0.58% return (significant at the 10% level).[24]

We also report in Panel A of Table 3 results for several subsamples of deals for which product-market effects are expected to be prominent. To gauge the effect of mergers in concentrated industries, we identify a subsample of deals for which the premerger industry Herfindahl Index is greater than 2000.[25] The Herfindahl Index is calculated as the sum of the squared market shares of the firms that operate a business segment in the industry. A higher Herfindahl indicates greater industry concentration. For example, an industry in which there are five market participants each with equal market share corresponds to an industry Herfindahl of 2000. We also identify those deals that result in a significant change in industry concentration as indicated by a merger-induced change in the industry Herfindahl Index that exceeds 100 (ΔIndustry Herf. > 100). Finally, we also examine the subset of challenged mergers because these are the transactions identified by regulatory authorities as potentially anticompetitive. All three subsamples of mergers tell roughly the same story with regard to announcement effects on bidders and targets. Combined-firm gains are significantly positive and in the 3-5% range for all subsamples. Target gains are always significantly positive, while bidder gains are indistinguishable from zero in all cases.

Industry-adjusted operating performance changes for merging firms are presented in Panel B of Table 3. We report changes from the year prior to the merger to each of the 3 years following the merger, as well as for the median of the 3-year postmerger

---

[24] As outlined in footnote 7, the absence of positive bidder returns suggests the merging firms' gains are not expected to stem from the capture of monopoly or monopsony rents.

[25] Market concentrations are calculated for the industry in which the bidder and target have an overlapping segment in the year prior to the merger. These measures are calculated on a segment level basis at the four-digit SIC code level. In the cases such that the bidder and target overlap in more than one industry, the statistics apply to the industry in which they have the largest combined sales.

Table 3

Average abnormal returns and changes in median industry-adjusted operating performance for merging firms

Abnormal return is the abnormal return for a 3-day window centered on the merger announcement date and calculated from a market model estimated over the period from 240 to 41 days before the merger announcement. We require at least 100 trading days over the estimation window to calculate abnormal returns. Combined abnormal returns are calculated using a value-weighted portfolio of the bidder and target. Changes in median industry-adjusted operating performance are calculated as postmerger industry-adjusted operating performance minus year −1 industry-adjusted operating performance. Cash flow to sales is defined as the ratio of operating income (item 13) to sales (item 12). Cost of goods sold to sales is defined as the ratio of cost of goods sold (item 41) to sales (item 12). Industry Herf. > 2000 are those deals that occurred in industries (four-digit SIC code) in which the premerger Herfindahl Index was greater than 2000. ΔIndustry Herf. > 100 are those deals that resulted in a change in the industry Herfindahl Index that exceeded 100. Challenged deals are the subset of transactions identified by regulatory authorities as potentially anticompetitive. t-Statistics for abnormal returns are based on tests that the standardized prediction errors are equal to zero. Significance of the number of positive versus number of negative is calculated using a sign test. Significance of changes in median industry-adjusted operating performance is assessed using a Wilcoxon signed-rank test.

	Subsample of deals			
	All	Industry Herf. > 2000	ΔIndustry Herf. > 100	Challenged
Panel A: Abnormal returns				
Combined abnormal returns				
Abnormal return	3.06%	3.48%	4.03%	4.83%
t-Statistic	9.58***	4.34***	5.84***	4.26***
Positive, negative	368, 186***	76, 39***	80, 35***	28, 11***
Target abnormal returns				
Abnormal return	18.77%	19.29%	20.38%	20.32%
t-Statistic	17.84***	8.71***	5.89***	6.57***
Positive, negative	468, 86***	98, 17***	102, 13***	35, 4***
Bidder abnormal returns				
Abnormal return	−0.58%	0.37%	0.14%	−0.76%
t-Statistic	−1.83*	−0.14	0.30	−0.36
Positive, negative	254, 300*	53, 62	57, 58	18, 21
Panel B: Changes in median industry-adjusted cash flow to sales				
Year −1 to year +1	0.38%	1.11%***	0.80%**	0.96%
Positive, negative	190, 164	46, 30*	47, 28**	13, 7
Year −1 to year +2	0.15%	1.01%	0.91%	−0.35%
Positive, negative	170, 167	39, 34	38, 35	9, 11
Year −1 to year +3	−0.00%	0.43%	−0.12%	−0.45%
Positive, negative	153, 153	35, 31	35, 35	8, 12
Year −1 to median postmerger	0.18%	1.00%*	0.91%*	0.26%
Positive, negative	181, 173	42, 34	41, 34	10, 10
Panel C: Changes in median industry-adjusted cost of goods sold to sales				
Year −1 to year +1	−0.22%	−0.78%*	−0.73%*	−1.55%

(*Continued*)

Table 3 (*Continued*)

	All	Subsample of deals		
		Industry Herf. > 2000	ΔIndustry Herf. > 100	Challenged
Positive, negative	172, 182	32, 44	29, 46*	7, 13
Year −1 to median postmerger	0.00%	−0.64%	−1.09%*	−0.53%
Positive, negative	177, 177	34, 42	31, 44	8, 12

***, **, and * denote significance at the 0.01, 0.05, and 0.10 level, respectively.

period.[26] Significance levels for performance changes are calculated using a Wilcoxon signed-rank test. We find evidence of significant operating performance improvements for merging firms in the two subsamples related to industry concentration but not for all mergers as a group. For those deals in concentrated industries, merging firms experience statistically and economically significant improvements in cash-flow margins (year −1 to median postmerger) of 1.00%. For those deals that result in a significant change in industry concentration, this change is 0.91%.[27] Mergers challenged by antitrust authorities do not lead to improvements in operating performance, which is perhaps consistent with concessions being granted to antitrust authorities to win approval of the mergers, which mitigate the gains to the deals.

The changes in cash-flow margins are most pronounced for the year immediately subsequent to the merger and appear to be relatively temporary in nature. This pattern might be expected if the improvements in merging firm performance are related to increases in market power that prompts the affected firms to undertake countervailing actions, for example, upstream or downstream consolidation. Along these lines, news articles suggest that the series of large mergers among defense contractors in our sample period put a good deal of pressure on these firms' suppliers, causing the suppliers to seek mergers in response.[28] Similarly, price pressure resulting from supermarket mergers reportedly was a driving factor leading to subsequent consolidation in the dairy industry.[29]

In an effort to better identify the ultimate sources of the cash-flow gains to merging firms, we also examine changes in several other operating performance measures, including cost of goods sold to sales; selling, general, and administrative expenses to

[26] When only 2 years of postmerger performance are available, postmerger performance will be the average of year +1 and year +2. When only 1 year of postmerger performance is available, postmerger performance is simply year +1 performance.

[27] The results for the two industry concentration subsamples are not independent. Each subsample has 115 deals and 60 deals are common to both subsamples.

[28] See Steven M. Sears, "Rohr CFO cites industry consolidation pressure," Dow Jones News Service, September 11, 1997.

[29] See Paul Schnitt, "Supermarket consolidation forcing merger strategies in dairy industry," KRTBN Knight-Ridder Tribune Business News, Sacramento Bee, November 14, 1999.

sales; net working capital to sales; and employees to sales. To conserve space, we report only limited results from this analysis. As can be seen from Panel C of Table 3, firms in the industry concentration subsamples experience significant reductions in industry-adjusted cost of goods sold to sales consistent with increased buying power resulting in reduced input costs. Otherwise, no significant changes are evident in any of the other performance measures for the entire sample or the subsamples.[30]

4.2. Rivals

Evidence on the abnormal returns to rivals on merger announcements is presented in Table 4. Panel A presents abnormal returns for rival portfolios at merger announcement, and Panel B presents abnormal returns to rivals on announcement of regulatory action. As previous authors have indicated (see, e.g., McAfee and Williams, 1988), detecting the effects of a merger on a rival could be difficult if that rival operates in multiple lines of business. Thus, we perform our analysis on both the overall group of rivals as well as on those rivals conducting business in only one four-digit SIC code industry (referred to as single-segment rivals). We present results for rival portfolios comprised of single-segment rivals only, as well as rival portfolios comprised of single- and multiple-segment rivals. Consistent with Eckbo (1983), we find that, for our entire sample of deals, rivals exhibit stock price increases on merger announcements. We observe positive and significant stock price reactions in the three subsamples (challenged mergers, mergers in concentrated industries, and mergers resulting in large changes in industry concentration) as well.[31] These positive returns to rivals could reflect either expected gains to anticompetitive collusion or efficiency. Notably, the size and statistical significance of the abnormal returns to rivals are generally greater for the tests using portfolios of single-segment rivals.[32]

We report evidence on the returns to rivals on announcements of regulatory action in Panel B of Table 4. If the positive returns in Panel A reflect an expectation by the market that collusion among industry rivals is more likely, then an announcement that the merger is being blocked by antitrust authorities should result in a negative reaction for rivals as outlined in Eckbo (1983). The Hart-Scott-Rodino Antitrust Improvements

---

[30] These results are available from the authors upon request.

[31] Song and Walkling (2000) find that the response of rivals to merger announcements depends upon the degree to which the announcement is unanticipated. Thus, we create a subsample of mergers that are potentially the least anticipated. This subsample includes only deals in which there are no premerger leaks of information or rumors concerning the potential acquisition of the target and for which there is no other acquisition in the same four-digit SIC code as the sample transaction in the year prior to the announcement. Returns to rivals of deals that meet the criteria for the surprise subsample are positive and similar to the other reported subsamples.

[32] Schumann (1993) finds that small rivals experience positive abnormal returns, while large rivals experience insignificant abnormal returns. We show a similar pattern of returns. Specifically, rivals with small market share (>5%) have abnormal returns of 0.40% (significant at the 5% level), and rivals with large market share (>5%) have abnormal returns of 0.02% (insignificant).

Table 4

Abnormal returns to rivals on merger announcement and regulatory action

Rivals are identified as those firms in the same four-digit SIC industry as the overlapping segments of the merging firms, as identified in the Compustat industry-segment file. Single-segment rivals are those that report only one industry segment. Abnormal return is the abnormal return for a 3-day window centered on the merger announcement date and calculated from a market model estimated over the period from 240 to 41 days before the merger announcement. We require at least 100 trading days over the estimation window to calculate abnormal returns. Abnormal returns to a rival portfolio are the equally weighted returns of all rivals for a given deal. t-Statistics are based on tests that the standardized prediction errors are equal to zero. Challenged deals are the subset of transactions identified by regulatory authorities as potentially anticompetitive. Blocked deals are either those in which regulators sued to block the deal or cases in which the merging firms cancelled for regulatory reasons. Industry Herf. > 2000 are those deals that occurred in industries (four-digit SIC code) in which the premerger Herfindahl Index was greater than 2000. ΔIndustry Herf. > 100 are those deals that resulted in a change in the industry Herfindahl Index that exceeded 100. Significance of the number of positive versus number of negative is assessed using a sign test.

		Subsample of deals		
Panel A	All	Challenged	Industry Herf. > 2000	ΔIndustry Herf. > 100
Abnormal returns on announcement for rival portfolios: single-segment only				
Abnormal return	0.54%	1.13%	2.01%	2.53%
t-Statistic	3.17***	1.76*	2.02**	2.78***
Positive, negative	275, 257	22, 15	51, 45	57, 37**
Abnormal returns on announcement for rival portfolios: single- and multiple-segment				
Abnormal return	0.24%	1.21%	0.67%	1.10%
t-Statistic	1.84*	1.75*	0.38	1.67*
Positive, negative	292, 259	25, 14	60, 52	68, 44**

		Subsample of deals	
Panel B	Blocked	Industry Herf. > 2000	ΔIndustry Herf. > 100
Abnormal return on regulatory action for rival portfolios: single-segment only			
Abnormal return	1.14%	2.61%	2.31%
t-Statistic	2.08*	1.89	2.71**
Positive, negative	7, 4	3, 0	3, 0
Abnormal return on regulatory action for rival portfolios: single- and multiple-segment			
Abnormal return	0.73%	2.34%	1.33%
t-Statistic	1.43	1.12	1.06
Positive, negative	7, 4	2, 1	5, 1

***, **, and * denote significance at the 0.01, 0.05, and 0.10 level, respectively.

Act of 1976 requires that parties engaged in significant mergers file their plans in advance with regulatory authorities. Hence, regulators are aware at an early stage of many mergers that, prior to the act, they would have had to sue to cancel after the fact. Thus, regulators and firms are frequently able to negotiate changes in the terms of mergers before the fact, thereby preventing many lawsuits. Defining an event date for antitrust actions settled in this manner is difficult. Thus, we restrict our attention to the 11 deals in our sample for which either regulators sued to block the deals or the merging firms announced they were canceling the deals as a result of regulatory reasons. We refer to these deals as blocked deals.

Consistent with the findings of Eckbo (1983), we do not find negative average abnormal returns to rivals on challenge dates for the sample of all blocked deals or for either of the concentration-related subsamples, a result that is generally inconsistent with the collusion hypotheses. In fact, in some cases the returns to rivals are significantly positive. We are not sure as to the reason for the positive returns in these cases. One possibility is that the market believes that, being stymied in acquiring one target, a bidder could try again by choosing a different, perhaps smaller, target in the same industry. We are hesitant, however, to draw any strong conclusions because of the small sample of blocked deals.

4.3. Customers

As we outline in Table 1, the monopolistic collusion hypothesis unambiguously predicts that horizontal mergers will have negative effects on corporate customers. Table 5 presents results for the customers of merging firms. For the entire sample of deals with customers, we find no evidence that customers experience negative stock market reactions at announcement or changes in industry-adjusted operating perform-ance subsequent to upstream mergers. This result is strongly inconsistent with the monopolistic collusion hypothesis. This result also suggests that customers are not generally harmed significantly by monopsonistic collusion because a monopsonist would lower output, which, absent a perfectly competitive output market, would increase prices. Further, this result suggests that the corporate customers in our sample do not realize significant benefits in the form of cost savings passed along by merging firms.

Table 5 also presents results for customers for several subsets of mergers in which product-market effects are expected to be most evident. Mergers in concentrated industries or mergers that increase concentration significantly do not appear to nega-tively impact customer firms.[33] We also examine the effect of a merger on those customers that appear particularly reliant on the merging firms for inputs and, hence, might face high costs of switching their purchases to other firms. We define reliant customers as firms for which purchases from the bidder or target or both represent more than 5% of cost of goods sold. Even among these reliant customers, we find no negative effects of upstream mergers. Regressions (unreported) explaining customer

---

[33] The small sample sizes for some of the cuts, particularly challenged mergers, stem from the nature of the reporting requirements; that is, challenged mergers are likely to be between large firms, and these firms are less likely to have any customers representing at least 10% of their sales.

Table 5

Abnormal returns and changes in median industry-adjusted operating performance for customers

Customers are identified from the Compustat industry-segment file. Abnormal return is the abnormal return for a 3-day window centered on the merger announcement date and calculated from a market model estimated over the period from 240 to 41 days before the merger announcement. We require at least 100 trading days over the estimation window to calculate abnormal returns. Abnormal returns to a customer portfolio are the equally weighted returns of all customers for a given deal. t-Statistics are based on tests that the standardized prediction errors are equal to zero. Changes in median industry-adjusted operating performance are calculated as postmerger industry-adjusted operating performance minus year -1 industry-adjusted operating performance. Customer portfolio changes in industry-adjusted operating performance are averaged over each deal. Cash flow to sales is defined as the ratio of operating income (item 13) to sales (item 12). Industry Herf. > 2000 are those deals that occurred in industries (four-digit SIC code) in which the premerger Herfindahl Index was greater than 2000. ΔIndustry Herf. > 100 are those deals that resulted in a change in the industry Herfindahl Index that exceeded 100. Challenged deals are the subset of transactions identified by regulatory authorities as potentially anticompetitive. Reliant customers are defined as firms for which purchases from the either the bidder or target represented more than 5% of cost of goods sold. Significance of changes in median industry-adjusted operating performance is assessed using a Wilcoxon signed-rank test. Significance of the number of positive versus number of negative is assessed using a sign test.

		Subsample of deals		Subsample of customers	
	All	Industry Herf. > 2000	ΔIndustry Herf. > 100	Challenged	Reliant customer
Panel A: Abnormal returns to individual customers					
Abnormal return	-0.12%	0.16%	-0.16%	-0.57%	1.11%
t-Statistic	-1.01	0.12	-0.49	0.51	0.36
Positive, negative	105, 113	26, 22	25, 23	3, 2	15, 16
Panel B: Abnormal returns to customer portfolios					
Abnormal return	0.04%	0.20%	-0.13%	-0.57%	1.37%
t-Statistic	-0.53	0.29	-0.39	0.51	0.36
Positive, negative	66, 73	17, 11	18, 13	3, 2	12, 12
Panel C: Changes in individual customer median industry-adjusted cash flow to sales					
Year -1 to year $+1$	-0.04%	-0.69%	-0.88%		0.00%
Positive, negative	61, 65	14, 16	10, 15		9, 8
Year -1 to year $+2$	0.07%	-0.24%	-0.89%		-0.97%
Positive, negative	62, 60	13, 16	9, 15		6, 10
Year -1 to year $+3$	0.28%	0.56%	0.29%		1.24%
Positive, negative	59, 54	16, 13	12, 11		10, 5
Year -1 to postmerger median	0.13%	-0.22%	-0.62%		0.00%
Positive, negative	67, 59	15, 15	11, 14		9, 8
Panel D: Changes in customer portfolio median industry-adjusted cash flow to sales					
Year -1 to postmerger median	0.05%	0.11%	-0.23%		-0.19%
Positive, negative	42, 41	10, 8	8, 8		5, 5

***, **, and * denote significance at the 0.01, 0.05, and 0.10 level, respectively.

firm abnormal returns and changes in operating performance reveal no significant relationship between these variables and returns to merging firms, changes in merging firm cash flows, deal characteristics, or customer firm characteristics (e.g., reliant customer).[34]

The results for customers complement those for rivals in rejecting the monopolistic collusion hypothesis. While we interpret these results as an indication that horizontal mergers do not generally have anticompetitive downstream effects, they alternatively could suggest that the US regulatory regime is effective at deterring anticompetitive mergers.[35]

4.4. Suppliers: univariate results

Univariate evidence on the effects of mergers on upstream firms is presented in Table 6. Panels A and B present abnormal returns results for individual suppliers and supplier portfolios, respectively. Panels C and D present operating performance results for individual suppliers and supplier portfolios, respectively. Individual suppliers experience an average abnormal return of −0.30% at announcement, which is not distinguishable from zero. However, a sign test reveals that significantly more individual suppliers experience negative reactions than positive. For the entire sample, individual suppliers and supplier portfolios have negative industry-adjusted changes in cash flow to sales around the merger. These changes are statistically significant (for individual suppliers) at conventional levels only for the first year subsequent to the merger. This pattern is similar to that observed for the merging firms themselves; that is, in those instances in which operating performance improvements for the merging firms are documented, these improvements appear temporary in nature. In addition, small, negative stock price changes for suppliers could be interpreted as evidence that the market expects that the buying power effects will be mitigated in the longer term.

Results for the subsamples of deals are also reported in Table 6. In addition to the previously defined subsamples, we introduce another subset of deals. Based on a systematic Dow Jones Interactive news search for stories mentioning buying power effects in the context of our sample deals, many of these mergers apparently took place in industries that meet the retail classification of Fama and French (1997).[36] For example, in the context of the acquisition of Broadway Stores by Federated Department Stores, a consultant is quoted as saying, "Bigger size gives you greater buying

---

[34] These results are available upon request from the authors.

[35] Eckbo (1992) finds little evidence consistent with anticompetitive collusion in a sample of mergers in Canada that occurred under a relatively lax antitrust regime, suggesting that regulatory overhang perhaps is not the primary explanation for similar findings for US firms.

[36] The search terms are "bidder name and target name and (merg$ or acqui$) and (buying power or buyer power or purchasing power or supplier$ or saving$ or reduction$)." The following SIC codes comprise the Fama and French (1997) retail classification: 5200-5736, 5900-5999.

Table 6

Abnormal returns and changes in median industry-adjusted operating performance for suppliers

Suppliers are identified from the Compustat industry-segment file. Abnormal return is the abnormal return for a 3-day window centered on the merger announcement date and calculated from a market model estimated over the period from 240 to 41 days before the merger announcement. We require at least 100 trading days over the estimation window to calculate abnormal returns. Abnormal returns to a supplier portfolio are the equally weighted returns of all suppliers for a given deal. t-Statistics are based on tests that the standardized prediction errors are equal to zero. Changes in median industry-adjusted operating performance are calculated as postmerger industry-adjusted operating performance minus year -1 industry-adjusted operating performance. Supplier portfolio changes in industry-adjusted operating performance are averaged over each deal. Cash flow to sales is defined as the ratio of operating income (item 13) to sales (item 12). Industry Herf. > 2000 are those deals that occurred in industries (four-digit SIC code) in which the premerger Herfindahl Index was greater than 2000. ΔIndustry Herf. > 100 are those deals that resulted in a change in the industry Herfindahl Index that exceeded 100. Challenged deals are the subset of transactions identified by regulatory authorities as potentially anticompetitive. Retail are those deals that occurred in industries included in the retail classification of Fama and French (1997). Supplier Ind. Herf. > 2000 are those suppliers that operated in concentrated industries as indicated by a Herfindahl Index greater than 2000. Terminated suppliers are those suppliers that were listed as suppliers before a deal but not after. Significance of changes in median industry-adjusted operating performance is assessed using a Wilcoxon signed-rank test. Significance of the number of positive versus number of negative is assessed using a sign test.

	All	Subsample of deals				Subsample of suppliers	
		Industry Herf. > 2000	ΔIndustry Herf. > 100	Challenged	Retail	Supplier industry Herf. > 2000	Terminated suppliers
Panel A: Abnormal returns to individual suppliers							
Abnormal return	−0.30%	−0.34%	−0.14%	−0.79%	−0.19%	0.57%	−0.48%
t-Statistic	−1.38	−0.96	−0.70	−1.57	−0.85	1.08	−1.67*
Positive, negative	279, 330**	104, 137**	96, 122*	60, 81*	78, 96	29, 32	132, 174**
Panel B: Abnormal returns to supplier portfolios							
Abnormal return	−0.19%	−0.14%	0.68%	−0.46%	1.53%	0.05%	−0.24%
t-Statistic	−0.62	0.63	0.78	−0.80	0.88	−0.33	−1.02
Positive, negative	75, 82	15, 14	23, 25	9, 16	13, 14	38, 55*	41, 56
Panel C: Changes in individual supplier median industry-adjusted cash flow to sales							
Year −1 to year +1	−0.62%*	−3.12%	−1.29%*	−0.10%	−0.93%**	−0.30%	−1.81%**
Positive, negative	222, 255	20, 23	68, 85	48, 48	59, 81*	95, 101	117, 162***
Year −1 to year +2	−0.28%	−0.50%	−0.09%	0.42%	−1.68%*	−0.21%	−1.01%

(Continued)

Table 6 (*Continued*)

	Subsample of deals					Subsample of suppliers	
	All	Industry Herf. > 2000	ΔIndustry Herf. > 100	Challenged	Retail	Supplier industry Herf. > 2000	Terminated suppliers
Positive, negative	210, 222	19, 22	68, 71	50, 39	57, 71	84, 91	114, 134
Year −1 to year +3	−0.56%	−1.81%	−1.81%	0.40%	−0.43%	−1.11%*	−1.11%
Positive, negative	188, 202	17, 20	59, 68	43, 38	55, 59	72, 85	105, 120
Year −1 to postmerger median	−0.84%	−2.31%	−1.29%	0.55%	−0.64%*	−1.13%**	−1.85%**
Positive, negative	225, 252	19, 24	71, 82	54, 42	66, 74	87, 109	122, 157**
Panel D: Changes in supplier portfolio median industry-adjusted cash flow to sales							
Year −1 to postmerger median	−1.68%	−2.31%	−2.22%	−0.48%	−6.01%**	−2.32%**	−2.98%*
Positive, negative	46, 55	7, 12	11, 19	6, 6	5, 14*	24, 42**	36, 51

***, **, and * denote significance at the 0.01, 0.05, and 0.10 level, respectively.

power with vendors. Larger chains are more feasible than smaller ones."[37] Thus, we examine results for the suppliers of merging retailers separately.

The abnormal returns results for the various deal subsets weakly suggest that buying power could be an important factor for some types of deals. For instance, sign tests reveal that deals in concentrated industries, deals that result in a significant increase in concentration, and deals that are subsequently challenged by antitrust authorities lead to significantly more individual suppliers experiencing negative reactions than positive. However, none of the average abnormal returns for the deal subsamples is significant at conventional levels.

Operating performance effects appear larger in the deal subsamples than for the entire sample of deals. For example, mergers that increase concentration and mergers in the retail industry are associated with significant negative changes in operating performance for suppliers. Again, these operating performance changes seem most pronounced for the period immediately following the merger.

The final two columns of Table 6 introduce two new subsamples not previously described. These subsamples are based on supplier characteristics expected to influence the effect of a downstream merger on a particular supplier. First, we identify those suppliers that operate in relatively concentrated industries. Theory suggests that this concentration could permit profits in excess of those in perfectly competitive industries. Thus, the potential for pressuring suppliers to reduce prices is perhaps greater in these contexts. Portfolios of suppliers that operate in concentrated industries do experience significantly more negative reactions than positive reactions, which is weakly consistent with suppliers in concentrated industries being more susceptible to the countervailing effects of downstream mergers. However, neither the magnitude of the supplier reaction nor the reactions of individual suppliers significantly support this conclusion. The operating performance results support the countervailing power hypothesis. Suppliers in concentrated industries experience significant reductions in cash flows subsequent to the downstream mergers. The changes in operating performance for this subsample are most pronounced for the period from year -1 to year $+3$ in contrast to the other subsamples in which operating performance changes are more pronounced for the years immediately surrounding the deal.

As detailed in Table 1, merging firms could realize purchasing efficiencies by pitting their suppliers in a price competition to sell to the combined firm and thereby generally switching their purchasing from less efficient to more efficient suppliers. If this sort of competition is prevalent, then the purchasing efficiency/countervailing power hypothesis would predict an asymmetric effect of mergers on suppliers. As a concrete example of such asymmetries, articles that appear in the business press near the time that the Hewlett-Packard-Compaq deal was announced indicated that suppliers of HP might be winners and suppliers of Compaq might be losers when the two firms consolidated their purchasing.[38]

---

[37] See Tom Abate, "Macy's buying emporium," San Francisco Examiner, August 15, 1995.

[38] For example, see Terho Uimonen, "H-P, Compaq merger may cause grief in Asia—outsourcing consolidation, job cuts are expected," *The Asian Wall Street Journal*, September 6, 2001.

We identify those suppliers that appear to be terminated following completion of a deal based on Compustat industry-segment data from year +1 relative to the merger. The figures in the last column of Table 6 indicate that those individual suppliers that diminish in importance following the merger experience significant negative abnormal returns. Further, a sign test reveals that significantly more individual suppliers that depart postmerger experience negative abnormal returns around the merger announcement than experience positive abnormal returns. The median change in industry-adjusted cash flow to sales for the suppliers that are listed before but not after the merger is -1.85% and is significant at the 5% level. Again, these results suggest that buying power effects could be, in part, influenced by supplier industry and firm characteristics, which is somewhat inconsistent with buying power gains stemming from monopsonistic collusion.

4.5. Suppliers: multivariate results

Table 7 presents multivariate regressions that explain individual supplier abnormal returns and changes in median industry-adjusted operating performance. Given the strength of the operating performance results relative to the abnormal returns results above, we devote the bulk of our multivariate analysis to explaining operating performance changes. A regression explaining supplier abnormal returns is included for completeness and to confirm the univariate results above.

The dependent variable for Columns (1)-(5) of Table 7 is the year -1 to postmerger median change in cash flow to sales. In Column (1), we include as an independent variable the fraction of total supplier sales that are to the bidder and target. The estimated coefficient on this variable is negative and significant. This result is exactly what one would expect under the buying power hypothesis if this variable is, as constructed, a good measure of how reliant the supplier is on the merging firms for sales revenues and, hence, supplier switching costs.

In Column (2), we add a binary variable (terminated supplier) that takes a value of 1 if a supplier is terminated postmerger. Consistent with the univariate results, terminated suppliers experience significantly greater cash-flow reductions postmerger than retained suppliers. Column (3) adds our indicators for significant downstream industry concentration as well as for mergers that result in a significant increase in downstream concentration. This column also adds an indicator variable that takes a value of 1 if the supplier firm's industry has a Herfindahl Index greater than 2000. As in the univariate results, suppliers seem to suffer more when they operate in relatively concentrated industries; for example, when there are greater initial supplier rents for the merging firms to capture. The coefficient on downstream concentration is negative and significant, while the coefficient on a merger-induced increase in downstream concentration is negative but not significant.

In Column (4), we add two variables related to the characteristics of the deal. The first of these is a binary variable indicating whether the merger took place in the retail

Table 7

Regressions of supplier abnormal returns and changes in median industry-adjusted cash flow

Changes in supplier median industry-adjusted cash flow to sales are calculated as median postmerger industry-adjusted cash flow to sales minus year −1 industry-adjusted cash flow to sales. Percentage of sales to merging firms is the percentage of total supplier sales that were to the merging firms in the year prior to the merger. Terminated supplier is a binary variable equal to one for suppliers that were listed as suppliers before a deal but not after. Industry Herf. > 2000 is a binary variable equal to one where the premerger Herfindahl Index for the industry was greater than 2000. Supplier industry Herf. > 2000 is a binary variable equal to one for deals in which the supplier's industry has a Herfindahl Index greater than 2000. ΔIndustry Herf. > 100 is a binary variable equal to one for deals that resulted in a significant change in industry concentration. Retail is a binary variable equal to one for deals that occurred in industries included in the retail classification of Fama and French (1997). Challenged is a binary variable equal to one for the subset of transactions identified by regulatory authorities as potentially anticompetitive. Abnormal return is the abnormal return for supplier firms over a 3-day window centered on the merger announcement date. Merged firm cash flow to sales are the changes in industry-adjusted cash flow to sales around the merger. Merging firms' abnormal returns are the combined abnormal returns to the merging firms and are calculated using a value-weighted portfolio of the bidder and target. Probability completed is the likelihood that an announced deal is completed as estimated by a logit regression model that explains completion using various deal characteristics. t-Statistics based on the white-adjusted standard errors are in parentheses.

Specification	(1)	(2)	(3)	(4)	(5)	(6)
Dependent variable	Cash flow to sales	Cash flow to sales	Cash flow to sales	Cash flow to sales	Cash flow to sales	Abnormal returns
Percentage of sales to merging firms	−0.356 (−1.92)*	−0.404 (−2.15)**	−0.397 (−2.10)**	−0.434 (−2.30)**	−0.434 (−2.28)**	0.030 (1.27)
Terminated supplier		−0.083 (−2.15)**	−0.084 (−2.19)**	−0.091 (−2.38)**	−0.091 (−2.32)**	−0.004 (−0.70)
Supplier industry Herf. > 2000			−0.071 (−1.97)**	−0.049 (−1.34)	−0.050 (−1.33)	−0.002 (−0.23)
Industry Herf. > 2000			−0.096 (−1.70)**	−0.097 (−1.84)*	−0.097 (−1.82)*	0.006 (0.67)
ΔIndustry Herf. > 100			−0.010 (−0.23)	−0.049 (−1.45)	−0.049 (−1.41)	0.008 (1.00)
Retail				−0.082 (−2.26)**	−0.081 (−2.21)**	0.003 (0.38)
Challenged				0.074 (1.55)	0.074 (1.55)	−0.011 (−1.33)
Merged firm cash flow to sales					0.036 (0.10)	
Merging firm abnormal returns						0.021 (0.34)
Probability completed						0.039 (1.50)
Intercept	0.036 (1.33)	0.092 (2.27)**	0.132 (2.95)***	0.155 (3.21)***	0.154 (3.16)***	−0.034 (−1.81)*
R^2	0.020	0.030	0.039	0.053	0.053	0.014
Number of observations	476	476	476	476	476	609

***, **, and * denote significance at the 0.01, 0.05, and 0.10 level, respectively.

industry. Consistent with the anecdotal evidence that buying power effects are significant in retail mergers, retail mergers are associated with more negative changes in supplier operating performance, all else equal. The second variable, which indicates whether a deal was challenged, is positive but not significant. This is perhaps not too surprising given that the upstream effects of mergers have not traditionally been the major concern of US antitrust authorities.[39]

Finally, in Column (5), we add to the regression a measure of the change in operating performance for the merging firms. On the one hand, if the merging firms retain a large portion of their buying power savings, one might expect this variable to be negatively related to supplier operating performance. On the other hand, if buying power savings are largely passed along to ultimate consumers, one would expect little or no correlation. More consistent with the latter possibility, the coefficient on tthis variable is small and insignificant (t = 0.10). This finding suggests that, in most cases, any increased buying power associated with horizontal mergers probably enhances ultimate consumer welfare.

The results of a regression explaining supplier abnormal returns are reported in Column (6) of Table 7. Because announcement period stock returns will be related to the probability that a given deal is eventually completed, we control for the likelihood of completion by estimating this probability from a logit regression and including the predicted probability in the abnormal returns regression. The independent variables used to predict the probability of completion were deal consideration, deal attitude, magnitude of a toehold on the part of the bidder, and the presence of a competing bid. In short, none of the independent variables (including merging firm abnormal returns) is significant in Column (6) except the intercept. This result is consistent with the supplier stock return results reported above and could suggest that the market does not expect the buying power effects to be sustainable.

4.6. Supplier subsample regressions

In Table 7, we find no association between supplier operating performance changes and merging firm operating performance changes, a result that is perhaps consistent with merging firms passing along the majority of any buying power gains to their ultimate customers. In Table 8, we further investigate the empirical validity of this interpretation by examining results for several of the previously defined subsamples.

The results for the subsamples are, in general, similar to those for the full sample with all but one (Industry Herf. > 2000) variable that is significant in Table 7 also significant (and of the same sign) in at least one specification of Table 8. However, the subsample analysis does produce one interesting finding. Specifically, changes in

---

[39] See OECD (1999) for evidence that European regulators are much more concerned with these effects, however.

Table 8

Regressions of supplier changes in median industry-adjusted cash flow for subsamples of deals

Changes in supplier industry-adjusted cash flow to sales are calculated as median postmerger industry-adjusted cash flow to sales minus year −1 industry-adjusted cash flow to sales. Percentage of sales to merging firms is the percentage of total supplier sales that were to the merging firms in the year prior to the merger. Terminated supplier is a binary variable equal to one for suppliers that were listed as suppliers before a deal but not after. Industry Herf. > 2000 is a binary variable equal to one for deals in which the premerger Herfindahl Index for the industry was greater than 2000. Supplier industry Herf. > 2000 is a binary variable equal to one for cases in which the supplier's industry has a Herfindahl Index greater than 2000. ΔIndustry Herf. > 100 is a binary variable equal to one for deals that resulted in a significant change in industry concentration. Retail is a binary variable equal to one for deals that occurred in industries included in the retail classification of Fama and French (1997). Challenged is a binary variable equal to one for the subset of transactions identified by regulatory authorities as potentially anticompetitive. Merged firm cash flow to sales are the changes in industry-adjusted cash flow to sales around the merger. Merged firm cost of goods sold to sales are the changes in industry-adjusted cost of goods sold to sales around the merger. t-Statistics based on the White-adjusted standard errors are in parentheses.

Specification	(1)	(2)	(3)	(4)	(5)
Subsample of deals	Industry Herf. > 2000	ΔIndustry Herf. > 100	Challenged	Retail	Industry Herf. > 2000
Percentage of sales	−0.828	−0.546	−0.411	−0.196	−0.760
to merging firms	(−1.34)	(−1.90)*	(−1.46)	(−0.61)	(−1.75)*
Terminated supplier	−0.151	−0.18	−0.217	−0.125	−0.042
	(−1.35)	(−2.48)**	(−1.98)**	(−2.05)**	(−0.48)
Supplier industry	0.061	−0.089	−0.456	−0.13	−0.048
Herf. > 2000	(0.83)	(−0.65)	(−0.58)	(−2.63)***	(−0.76)
Industry		−0.098	−0.199	−0.315	
Herf. > 2000		(−1.31)	(−1.33)	(−1.40)	
ΔIndustry	0.025		−0.009	0.105 (0.42)	−0.050
Herf. > 100	(0.26)		(−0.06)		(−0.47)
Retail	−0.429	−0.146	−0.149		−0.494
	(−3.32)***	(−1.68)*	(−1.32)		(−2.69)**
Challenged	0.006 (0.06)	0.081 (1.12)		−0.142	0.002 (0.02)
				(−0.55)	
Merged firm	−3.790	−0.750	−0.076	−0.927	
cash flow to sales	(−2.97)***	(−0.84)	(−0.03)	(−1.00)	
Merged firm cost					2.66 (1.89)*
of goods sold to sales					
Intercept	0.172 (1.30)	0.187 (1.12)	0.308 (2.24)**	0.120 (1.28)	0.261 (1.67)
R^2	0.287	0.083	0.073	0.104	0.395
Number of observations	43	153	96	140	43

***, **, and * denote significance at the 0.01, 0.05, and 0.10 level, respectively.

supplier cash-flow margins are significantly negatively associated with changes in merging firm cash-flow margins for the subsample of deals that occur in concentrated industries, which is consistent with gains to the merging firms coming at least in part at the expense of suppliers. Further, a regression of the change in supplier cash-flow margins against the change in merging firms cost of goods sold to sales ratios and the other control variables reported in Column (5) reveals a significant positive relation for the Industry Herf. > 2000 subsample. Taken together, these results suggest that reduced input costs (coming at the expense of suppliers) are an important source of the gains to merging firms in concentrated industries and, moreover, that merging firms are able to retain some of the cost savings instead of passing them along to ultimate customers. Given anticompetitive collusion is facilitated by industry concentration, this result could be interpreted as evidence of monopsonistic collusion. However, the lack of significant negative effects on customers casts some doubt on this interpretation.

4.7. Further evidence on supplier retention

Given the demonstrated importance of remaining a supplier postmerger, we examine the determinants of supplier retention and performance differences between retained and terminated suppliers. Panel A of Table 9 presents the results of a logit regression that explains supplier retention. The dependent variable takes a value of 1 if the supplier is retained and 0 otherwise. Being a supplier to only the target firm (as opposed to being a supplier to only the bidding firm) significantly reduces the probability that the supplier will continue to supply the merged firms. Suppliers who list both the bidder and target are more likely to remain postmerger than those listing only one of the two. Also, suppliers that consistently supplied either the bidder or the target for each of the 2 years prior to the merger are more likely to remain as suppliers to the merged firm. The fraction of sales to the bidder and target is positively related to the probability of remaining as a supplier. All else equal, concentration in the supplier industry does not appear to influence the probability that a particular supplier remains.

The results of Panel B describe the economic effects of the retention decision on suppliers. While terminated suppliers experience more negative abnormal returns than retained suppliers, the difference in abnormal returns at the merger announcement is not significant. We also examine changes in median industry-adjusted cash flow to sales for retained and terminated suppliers. While retained suppliers experience negligible changes in operating performance, terminated suppliers experience significant deterioration in cash flows. The difference in cash flow to sales changes between retained and terminated suppliers is 2.31%, and this difference is highly significant. Finally, we examine changes in relative postmerger market share for suppliers, for which postmerger market share is calculated from year -1 to year $+2$ relative to the merger. For those suppliers that are retained, the average change in market share over the 3 years around the merger is 2.52% (significant at the 5% level), whereas suppliers that depart experience only a 0.68% (insignificant) change in market share. Further, the difference in market share changes between the two groups is significant at the 10% level ($t = 1.88$).

Table 9

Retained versus terminated suppliers

Panel A presents the results of a logit regression where the dependent variable is equal to 1 if a supplier is retained after a merger and 0 otherwise. The sample for this analysis is comprised of suppliers with nonmissing industry-adjusted changes in operating performance around completed mergers. Supplier to target is a binary variable set to one if the supplier listed only the target firm as its customer prior to the merger. Supplier to bidder and target is a binary variable set to one if the supplier listed both the bidding and target firms as customers prior to the merger. Consistent supplier is a binary variable set equal to one if the supplier listed either the bidder or the target as a customer for each of the 2 years prior to the merger. Percentage of sales to merging firms is the percentage of total supplier sales that were to the merging firms in the year prior to the merger. Supplier industry Herf. > 2000 is a binary variable equal to one for cases in which a supplier operates in an industry with a Herfindahl Index greater than 2000. Relative size is the ratio of supplier assets to combined merging firm assets. Panel B contrasts the abnormal returns and operating performance of retained and terminated suppliers. Abnormal return is the abnormal return for supplier firms over a 3-day window centered on the merger announcement date. Changes in median supplier industry-adjusted cash flow to sales are calculated as median postmerger industry-adjusted cash flow to sales minus year −1 industry-adjusted cash flow to sales. Market shares changes represent the supplier's change in market share (at the four-digit SIC code level) around the merger where postmerger market share is calculated in year +2 relative to the merger. These measures are based on the sales of the largest industry segment reported by the supplier firm. Significance of differences in abnormal returns and market share is assessed using a t-test. Significance of differences in changes in median industry-adjusted operating performance is assessed using a Wilcoxon signed-rank test.

Panel A: Logit regression explaining retention of suppliers

	Supplier to target	Supplier to bidder and target	Consistent supplier	Percentage of sales to merging firms	Supplier industry Herf. > 2000	Relative size	Intercept	Pseudo R^2, number of observations
Coefficient	-2.06	3.39	0.97	2.61	-0.05	-1.00	-0.97	0.14
t-Statistic	(-5.68)***	(4.47)***	(4.67)***	(3.76)***	(-0.26)	(-1.26)	(-4.97)***	476

Panel B: Performance differences between retained and terminated suppliers

	Retained	Terminated	Difference
Abnormal returns	-0.13%	-0.48%*	0.35%
Change in median industry-adjusted cash flow to sales	0.46%	-1.85%***	2.31%**
Change in market share	2.52%***	0.68%	1.84%*

*** , ** , and * denote significance at the 0.01, 0.05, and 0.10 level, respectively.

5. Conclusion

We investigate the upstream and downstream product-market effects of a large sample of horizontal mergers and acquisitions from 1980 to 1997. We construct a data set that identifies the corporate customers, suppliers, and rivals of firms initiating horizontal mergers, and we use this data set to examine announcement-related stock market revaluations and postmerger changes in operating performance. For the merging firms themselves, we find positive and significant abnormal returns at merger announcement. Also, several subsamples of merging firms are found to significantly increase postmerger cash flows and reduce cost of goods sold. These findings are consistent with mergers generating gains for the merging firms. However, as detailed in Table 1, these findings alone do not allow us to identify the nature of the gains. Thus, we also examine the effects of mergers on customers, suppliers, and rivals.

We find that customers experience insignificant stock market reactions at announcement and negligible changes in industry-adjusted operating performance subsequent to upstream mergers. These results continue to hold for mergers in concentrated industries and for mergers that result in a significant increase in concentration. Further, the results are similar for customers that *ex ante* appear particularly reliant on the merging firms for inputs and thus would be expected to face the greatest switching costs. Finally, as in previous studies, we also find evidence that rival firms experience positive abnormal returns at merger announcements but do not experience negative abnormal returns when antitrust authorities challenge the mergers. Taken together, the customer and rival results are strongly inconsistent with the monopolistic collusion hypothesis.

The evidence for the merging firms and their suppliers is generally consistent with some form of increased buying power being an important source of gains to mergers. For instance, several subsamples of merging firms are found to reduce their cost of goods sold to sales postmerger while their suppliers as a group experience negative and significant reductions in cash flow to sales immediately subsequent to a downstream merger. In addition, a sign test reveals that significantly more individual suppliers experience negative announcement period returns than positive. Suppliers that are relatively more reliant on the merging firms for sales revenue experience significantly larger reductions in cash-flow margins subsequent to the merger. Furthermore, buying power effects are more pronounced when the merging firms operate in industries that are relatively concentrated.

While all of the supplier results summarized above are consistent with the general notion of buying power being a potentially important source of gains to horizontal mergers, these results do not allow us to determine the nature of these gains; that is, monopsonistic collusion or purchasing efficiencies/countervailing power. Because the two buying power hypotheses have somewhat similar predictions, we rely on somewhat subtle but important distinctions between the hypotheses to further identify the nature of the buying power gains.

The monopsonistic collusion hypothesis suggests all potential suppliers could suffer from a downstream merger, and the purchasing efficiencies/countervailing power hypothesis predicts potentially asymmetric effects on suppliers. Specifically, suppliers that are retained postmerger might not be harmed on balance by the merging firms' increased buying power; that is, they could sell a higher quantity but at a lower price. Those suppliers that lose a bidding competition might suffer. Thus, while some individual suppliers might be expected to experience net gains in response to merging firm purchasing efficiencies or the exercise of countervailing power or both, it is relatively less likely that any suppliers would benefit under monopsonistic collusion.

Empirically, we do find that the net effect of a merger on a particular supplier appears to depend heavily on the supplier's ability to retain its product-market relationship with the merged entity. Specifically, those firms that are terminated as suppliers subsequent to a merger experience negative and significant abnormal returns at the merger announcement and significant deterioration in cash flows postmerger. In contrast, those firms that are retained as suppliers experience significant gains in market share and insignificant abnormal returns and changes in operating performance. Following the reasoning above, we interpret these results as somewhat more consistent with efficiency-increasing buying power than monopsonistic collusion.

We also find that suppliers that operate in concentrated industries experience larger performance declines after a downstream merger. This result is consistent with an efficient form of countervailing power lowering rents in the supplier industries. Further, we find that customers experience insignificant announcement returns. This finding is more consistent with purchasing efficiencies/countervailing power than monopsonistic collusion because monopsonistic collusion can often negatively affect customers as well as suppliers.

In general, our overall results suggest that horizontal mergers' effects on suppliers and merging firms appear to be somewhat temporary in nature. Specifically, merging firm improvements in operating performance and supplier operating performance deterioration appear to be strongest in the first year after the merger. One plausible explanation for this finding is that, in the longer term, upstream firms can undertake strategic actions of their own to counter the increased buying power of their customers; for example, mergers to consolidate the supplier industry. Empirically validating this conclusion is a potentially fruitful topic for future research. Finally, we believe our methodology to identify product-market relationships could be of independent interest to other researchers and that this data could be useful in answering many types of questions beyond those addressed in the present study.

References

Barber, B. and J. Lyon, 1996, "Detecting Abnormal Operating Performance: The Empirical Power and Specification of Test Statistics," *Journal of Financial Economics*, 41, 359–399.

Barton, D. and R. Sherman, 1984, "The Price and Profit Effects of Horizontal Merger: A Case Study," *The Journal of Industrial Economics*, 33, 165–177.

Bittlingmayer, G. and T. Hazlett, 2000, "Dos Kapital: Has Antitrust Action Against Microsoft Created Value in the Computer Industry?" *Journal of Financial Economics*, 55, 329–359.

Blair, R. and J. Harrison, 1993, *Monopsony: Antitrust Law and Economics*, Princeton University Press, Princeton, NJ.

Bradley, M., A. Desai and E. Kim, 1988, "Synergistic Gains from Corporate Acquisitions and Their Division Between the Stockholders of Target and Acquiring Firms," *Journal of Financial Economics*, 21, 3–40.

Bruner, R., 2002, "Does M&A Pay? A Survey for the Decision-Maker," *Journal of Applied Finance*, 12, 48–60.

Chipty, T. and C. Snyder, 1999, "The Role of Firm Size in Bilateral Bargaining: A Study of the Cable Television Industry," *The Review of Economics and Statistics*, 81, 326–340.

Eckbo, B. E., 1983, "Horizontal Mergers, Collusion, and Stockholder Wealth," *Journal of Financial Economics*, 11, 241–273.

Eckbo, B. E., 1985, "Mergers and the Market Power Doctrine: Evidence from the Capital Market," *Journal of Business*, 58, 325–349.

Eckbo, B. E., 1992, "Mergers and the Value of Antitrust Deterrence," *Journal of Finance*, 47, 1005–1029.

Eckbo, B. E. and P. Wier, 1985, "Antimerger Policy Under the Hart-Scott-Rodino Act: A Reexamination of the Market Power Hypothesis," *Journal of Law and Economics*, 28, 119–149.

Ellison, S. and C. Snyder, 2001, "Countervailing Power in Wholesale Pharmaceuticals," Unpublished Working Paper, Massachusetts Institute of Technology.

Fama, E. and K. French, 1997, "Industry Costs of Equity," *Journal of Financial Economics*, 43, 153–193.

Galbraith, J., 1952, *American Capitalism: The Concept of Countervailing Power*, Houghton, Mifflin, NY.

Gal-Or, E., 1999, "Mergers and Exclusionary Practices in Health Care Markets," *Journal of Economics and Management Strategy*, 8, 315–350.

Ghosh, A., 2001, "Does Operating Performance Really Improve Following Corporate Acquisitions?" *Journal of Corporate Finance*, 7, 151–178.

Healy, P., K. Palepu and R. Ruback, 1992, "Does Corporate Performance Improve After Mergers?" *Journal of Financial Economics*, 31, 135–175.

Heron, R. and E. Lie, 2002, "Operating Performance and the Method of Payment in Takeovers," *Journal of Financial and Quantitative Analysis*, 37, 137–155.

Houston, J. and M. Ryngaert, 1997, "Equity Issuance and Adverse Selection: A Direct Test Using Conditional Stock Offers," *Journal of Finance*, 52, 197–219.

Inderst, R. and C. Wey, 2002, "Buyer Power and Incentives," Unpublished Working Paper, London School of Economics.

Kaplan, S., M. Mitchell and K. Wruck, 1997, "A Clinical Exploration of Value Creation and Destruction in Acquisitions: Organizational Design, Incentives, and Internal Capital Markets," Working Paper 5999, National Bureau of Economic Research.

Karceski, J., S. Ongena and D. Smith, 2003, "The Impact of Bank Consolidation on Commercial Borrower Welfare," Unpublished Working Paper, University of Florida.

Kim, E. and V. Singal, 1993, "Mergers and Market Power: Evidence from the Airline Industry," *The American Economic Review*, 83, 549–569.

Knapp, W., 1990, "Event Analysis of Air Carrier Mergers and Acquisitions," *The Review of Economics and Statistics*, 72, 703–707.

Loughran, T. and J. Ritter, 1997, "The Operating Performance of Firms Conducting Seasoned Equity Offerings," *Journal of Finance*, 52, 1823–1850.

McAfee, R. and M. Williams, 1988, "Can Event Studies Detect Anticompetitive Mergers?" *Economics Letters*, 28, 199–203.

Mullin, G., J. Mullin and W. Mullin, 1995, "The Competitive Effects of Mergers: Stock Market Evidence from the U.S. Steel Dissolution Suit" *RAND Journal of Economics*, 26, 314–330.

Mullin, J. and W. Mullin, 1997, "United States Steel's Acquisition of the Great Northern Ore Properties: Vertical Foreclosure or Efficient Contractual Governance?" *Journal of Law, Economics, and Organization*, 13, 74–100.

OECD, 1999, *Buying Power of Multiproduct Retailers. Series Roundtables on Competition Policy DAFFE/ CLP(99)21*, Organisation for Economic Co-operation and Development, Paris.

Prage, R. and T. Hannan, 1998, "Do Substantial Horizontal Mergers Generate Significant Price Effects? Evidence from the Banking Industry," *Journal of Industrial Economics*, 46, 433–452.

Ravenscraft, D. and F. Scherer, 1987, *Mergers, Selloffs, and Economic Efficiency*, Brookings Institution, Washington, DC.

Robinson, J., 1933, *The Economics of Imperfect Competition*, Macmillan and Co., London.

Schumann, L., 1993, "Patterns of Abnormal Returns and the Competitive Effects of Horizontal Mergers," *Review of Industrial Organization*, 8, 679–696.

Shahrur, H., 2002, "Industry Structure and Horizontal Takeovers: Analysis of Wealth Effects on Rivals, Suppliers, and Corporate Customers," Unpublished Working Paper, Georgia State University.

Snyder, C., 1996, "A Dynamic Theory of Countervailing Power," *RAND Journal of Economics*, 27, 747–769.

M Song and Walkling, R., 2000, "Abnormal Returns to Rivals of Acquisition Targets: A Test of the 'Acquisition Probability Hypothesis' " *Journal of Financial Economics*, 55, 143–171.

Stigler, G., 1964, "A Theory of Oligopoly," *Journal of Political Economy*, 72, 44–61.

Stillman, R., 1983, "Examining Antitrust Policy Towards Horizontal Mergers," *Journal of Financial Economics*, 11, 224–240

Chapter 14

INDUSTRY STRUCTURE AND HORIZONTAL TAKEOVERS: ANALYSIS OF WEALTH EFFECTS ON RIVALS, SUPPLIERS, AND CORPORATE CUSTOMERS[*]

HUSAYN SHAHRUR

Bentley College, Waltham, Massachusetts, USA

Contents

Abstract | 606
Keywords | 606
1. Introduction | 607
2. Hypotheses development and related literature | 609
  2.1. Productive efficiency hypothesis | 609
  2.2. Collusion hypothesis | 611
  2.3. Buyer power hypothesis | 612
3. Data sources, takeover sample, suppliers, and corporate customers | 613
  3.1. Takeover sample | 613
  3.2. Benchmark input-output accounts | 616
  3.3. Rivals, suppliers, and corporate customers | 616
4. Methodology and results | 619
  4.1. Measuring abnormal returns | 619
  4.2. Abnormal returns to the merging firm and their rivals, customers, and suppliers | 619
  4.3. Regional bias | 625

[*] This paper is based on my dissertation completed at the J. Mack Robinson College of Business, Georgia State University. I gratefully acknowledge the guidance of my dissertation committee: Gerald Gay, Martin Grace, Jayant Kale (chair), Omesh Kini, and Stephen D. Smith. I would also like to thank Vladimir Atanasov, Conrad Ciccotello, Sudip Datta, Atul Gupta, Ping Hu, Shane Johnson, Richard Phillips, Carter Rakovski, Kartik Raman, Len Rosenthal, Chip Ruscher, Chip Ryan, Myron Slovin, Ajay Subramanian, Anand Venkateswaran, Chip Wiggins, and seminar participants at the 2002 Financial Management Association meetings, the 2002 Southern Finance Association meetings, the Atlanta Finance Workshop, Bentley College, and Louisiana State University for helpful comments and suggestions. I especially would like to thank an anonymous referee for suggestions that have greatly improved the paper. I am grateful to Joseph Fan and Larry Lang for providing the conversion tables of the IO-SIC codes. Christine Chen provided excellent research assistance.

This article originally appeared in the *Journal of Financial Economics*, Vol. 76, pp. 61–98 (2005).
Corporate Takeovers, Volume 1
Edited by B. Espen Eckbo
Copyright © 2004 Elsevier B.V. All rights reserved.
DOI: 10.1016/B978-0-12-381983-3.00014-9

Abstract

We examine the wealth effects of horizontal takeovers on rivals of the merging firms, and on firms in the takeover industry's supplier and customer industries. Inconsistent with the collusion and buyer power motives, we find significant positive abnormal returns to rivals, suppliers, and corporate customers for the subsample of takeovers with positive combined wealth effect to target and bidder shareholders. Overall, our findings suggest that the average takeover in our sample is driven by efficiency considerations. However, we find evidence suggesting that horizontal takeovers increase the buyer power of the merging firms if suppliers are concentrated.

Keywords

takeovers, mergers, efficiency, collusion, buyer power

JEL classification: G34, D42, D43, L41, K21

1. Introduction

What are the motives for the recent wave of horizontal takeovers? A growing body of research suggests that takeovers are driven by efficiency considerations in response to changes in optimal firm boundaries that are brought about by unexpected economic changes (see, e.g., Comment and Schwert, 1995; Jensen, 1993). Mitchell and Mulherin (1996) find evidence consistent with the argument that major economic changes shape the takeover and restructuring markets (see also Andrade and Stafford, 2004; Andrade et al., 2001; Mulherin and Boone, 2000). In addition to this efficiency view, there is a long-standing proposition that horizontal takeovers are attempts by the merging firms to expropriate wealth from customers and suppliers: a horizontal takeover can increase the likelihood of collusion in the takeover industry, which would benefit the merging firms at the expense of their customers and suppliers (e.g., Stigler, 1964). Finally, a third line of reasoning suggests that horizontal takeover can help the merging firms lower their input costs by creating a larger firm with increased buyer power vis-à-vis its suppliers (e.g., Snyder, 1996).

We test the efficiency, collusion, and buyer power theories using a sample of 463 horizontal mergers and tender offers during the period from 1987 to 1999. We examine the wealth effects of takeover announcements on firms in supplier industries in order to test the buyer power motive. In addition, along with the independent study of Fee and Thomas (2004), our paper is the first large-sample study that tests the collusion motive by examining the takeover wealth effects on supplier and customer firms. This approach was originally suggested by Eckbo (1983) who states, "In principle, one could discriminate between the collusion and efficiency theories by examining the abnormal returns to the merging firms' corporate customers and suppliers of inputs." Thus, our approach complements the methodology in Eckbo (1983) and Stillman (1983), who test the collusion motive by examining the wealth effects of merger and antitrust announcements on rival firms.

We use the benchmark input-output (IO) accounts for the US economy to identify both firms in industries that supply inputs to the takeover industry (suppliers), and firms in industries that use the output of the takeover industry (corporate customers). Consistent with prior research on takeovers, we find that the announcement of a takeover is associated with a positive average combined wealth effect (CWE) to target and bidder stockholders (see, e.g., Andrade et al., 2001; Jarrell et al., 1988; Jensen and Ruback, 1983). In addition, we find that rivals and corporate customers earn positive abnormal returns during the takeover announcement period, while suppliers experience an adverse stock price effect.

To further investigate the announcement period abnormal returns, we partition our sample into two subsamples depending on whether the takeover yields a positive or negative CWE to the target and bidder. It is likely that efficiency, collusion, and buyer power motives drive takeovers with positive CWEs. For a subsample of such takeovers (about 60% of the sample takeovers), we find significant positive abnormal returns to rivals, suppliers, and corporate customers, a result that is consistent with the efficiency motive. Inconsistent with the collusion and buyer power motives, takeovers that create wealth for the merging firms also appear to benefit both customers and suppliers.

For the subsample of takeovers with negative CWEs, we find significant negative abnormal returns to rivals, suppliers, and corporate customers. If agency problems drive some of these value-destroying takeovers (see, e.g., Datta et al., 2001; Harford, 1999; Morck et al., 1990), the evidence suggests that the wealth destruction has negative effects on suppliers and customers as well. However, the economically and statistically significant negative average abnormal return to rival firms is also consistent with the view expressed in Mitchell and Mulherin (1996) that takeovers are the "message bearers" of the fundamental changes facing the takeover industry.

We conduct a cross-sectional analysis to examine the determinants of abnormal returns to the merging firms, rivals, suppliers, and corporate customers. Under the market concentration doctrine, the anticompetitive effect of a collusive merger should be higher for takeovers characterized by a larger takeover-induced increase in concentration (see Eckbo, 1985, 1992). Contrary to the prediction of the collusion hypothesis, we find that the merger-induced increase in the concentration of the takeover industry is negatively related to abnormal returns to the merging firms and their industry rivals, and is not related to the abnormal returns to suppliers and corporate customers. Thus, our study extends the findings of Eckbo (1983, 1985, 1992), which do not support the collusion motive, to the recent wave of horizontal consolidations. Our results suggest that the lenient antitrust policy in recent years relative to the sample period in Eckbo (1983, 1985, 1992) does not appear to have resulted in predominantly anticompetitive takeovers.[1]

Galbraith (1952) suggests that an increase in the concentration of the buying industry can result in a countervailing power that enables buyers to pressure their suppliers. Recent theoretical research such as Snyder (1996, 1998) and Stole and Zwiebel (1996) suggest that, by increasing its size, a buyer can lower the costs of inputs bought from monopolistic or oligopolistic supplier industries. Consistent with this buyer-size effect, we find that the CWE to the target and bidder is higher if suppliers are concentrated and the merger results in a large firm relative to the independent target and bidder firms. The adverse effect of this increased buyer power on concentrated suppliers is pronounced if the merger is between firms that are large relative to the takeover industry.

Finally, we find that the higher the percentage of the supplier industry's output sold to the takeover industry, the higher is the magnitude of abnormal returns to suppliers. We also find that the more important the takeover industry's output as an input to the customer industry, the higher is the magnitude of abnormal returns to customers. Among other things, this evidence suggests that the stock market reaction to takeover

---

[1] Eckbo (1983, 1985, 1992) examine the collusion hypothesis using samples of horizontal takeovers for the 1963–1978 and 1963–1981 periods, respectively. See Kwoka and White (1999) for a discussion of the changes in US antitrust policies.

announcements takes into account the economic fundamentals that relate the takeover industry to supplier and customer industries.

Fee and Thomas (2004) also independently examine the effect of horizontal takeovers on rivals, suppliers, and corporate customers. However, one of the major differences between our paper and that of Fee and Thomas (2004) lies in the methodology each paper uses to identify suppliers and customers. We use the IO tables to identify downstream and upstream industries. Fee and Thomas (2004) identify the merging firms' key suppliers and customers by relying on data disclosed in accordance with FASB No. 14, which requires firms to disclose the identity of any customer representing more that 10% of the firm's total sales. Despite this and other major differences between the two papers, Fee and Thomas (2004) also find evidence that is inconsistent with the collusion theory, and that is to some extent consistent with the buyer power motive. Therefore, our two studies complement each other in the goal of improving our understanding of the motives for horizontal takeovers.

This paper proceeds as follows. In Section 2, we review the literature and develop our hypotheses. Section 3 provides details of the sample and the methodology used to identify suppliers and corporate customers. The event study results are reported in Section 4. Section 5 develops our cross-sectional hypotheses and presents the results of our regression analysis. Section 6 concludes the paper.

2. Hypotheses development and related literature

We use abnormal returns for the takeover announcement period in order to examine the significance of the wealth effects of horizontal takeovers on rivals, suppliers, and corporate customers. In this section, we discuss the implications of the productive efficiency, collusion, and buyer power hypotheses on announcement period abnormal returns. Note that there are other possible motives for takeovers such as agency problems (e.g., Jensen, 1986), hubris (Roll, 1986), and market misvaluations (Shleifer and Vishny, 2003), among others. In this paper, we test motives that are specific to horizontal takeovers and have direct implications for firms in supplier and customer industries. Table 1 presents a summary of the predictions of the various hypotheses discussed below.

2.1. Productive efficiency hypothesis

One view that governs horizontal takeovers is that they result in productive efficiency. Related empirical evidence is consistent with related takeovers generating more operating synergies than diversifying mergers (see, e.g., Healy et al., 1992; Maksimovic and Phillips, 2001; Maquieira et al., 1998). An increase in productive efficiency has implications for the merging firms and their rivals, suppliers, and corporate customers. First, the merging firms are expected to capture inframarginal rents that result from the posttakeover increase in efficiency. Second, as suggested by Eckbo (1983), the effect

Table 1

Summary of predictions

This table summarizes the predictions of the various hypotheses regarding the signs of announcement period abnormal returns to the merging firms and their rivals, customers, and suppliers.

	Productive Efficiency	Collusion	Buyer power
Merging firms	Positive	Positive	Positive[a]
	More-efficient production will result in higher inframarginal rents to the merging firms	Higher likelihood of collusion will result in increased monopoly rents to the merging firms (Eckbo, 1983)	Lower input prices due to intensified competition among suppliers (Snyder, 1996)
Rivals	Unrestricted	Positive	Positive[a]
	Positive: information regarding industrywide restructuring.	Higher likelihood of collusion will result in increased monopoly rents to rival firms (Eckbo, 1983)	Lower input prices due to more-intense competition among suppliers (Snyder, 1996)
	Negative: more-intense competition in the industry due to a new, more-efficient combined firm (Eckbo, 1983)		
Customers	Unrestricted[b]	Negative	Unrestricted[c]
	Positive: scale-increasing mergers.	Higher input prices due to higher likelihood of collusion in the takeover industry	*Positive*: benefit from lower input costs for merging firms.
	Negative: scale-decreasing mergers		
			Negative: supplier underinvestment
Suppliers	Unrestricted[b]	Negative	Negative[a]
	Positive: scale-increasing mergers.	Restricted output in the takeover industry results' lower demand for suppliers' output	The increased buyer power of the merging firms will intensify competition among suppliers (Snyder, 1996)
	Negative: scale-decreasing mergers and/or more-efficient combined firm		

[a]Efficient mergers can be of the scale-increasing or the scale-decreasing types (see, e.g., Andrade and Stafford, 2004; Eckbo, 1992). If the merger is expansionary in nature, it should benefit customers. Suppliers can benefit from a scale-increasing merger as long as the positive effect of expansion is not outweighed by the adverse effect of the increased efficiency of the combined firm. Finally, an efficient merger of the scale-decreasing type can hurt customers and suppliers.
[b]Snyder (1996) shows that by creating a larger buyer, a horizontal merger can result in more-intense competition among suppliers, which will benefit the merging firms and their rivals at the expense of suppliers.
[c]Customers may benefit from the increased buyer power if some of the gains resulting from lower input prices are passed on to them because of competition in the takeover industry. Customers can also suffer if the increased buyer power induces suppliers to underinvest.

of an increase in efficiency on rivals is unrestricted. On the one hand, rival firms can be negatively impacted since the efficiency-increasing takeover is expected to result in more-intense industry competition. On the other hand, the takeover can signal that an industrywide increase in productivity is available to rival firms. Rivals can also benefit if the takeover increases the probability that they will be acquired (see, e.g., Eckbo, 1983; Song and Walkling, 2000).

Third, efficiency-driven horizontal takeovers have two effects on suppliers. An increase in productive efficiency results in a decrease in marginal costs, which will result in lower prices and higher output levels, thereby increasing the demand for the factors of production. However, the increase in productive efficiency can result in a lower demand for inputs because of a more-efficient use of the factors of production. The net effect can either be a decrease or an increase in input prices. Therefore, the effect of the announcement of a horizontal takeover on suppliers is unrestricted.

Finally, the increase in productive efficiency can result from two types of mergers: scale-increasing or scale-decreasing mergers (Andrade and Stafford, 2004; Eckbo, 1992). A scale-increasing merger will result in higher output levels and lower output prices. The effect of a scale-decreasing merger on output levels and prices will depend on the level of the takeover efficiency gains. As a result, customers can either benefit or suffer at the announcement of a takeover. As summarized in Table 1, under the productive efficiency hypothesis, the merging firms should experience a positive price effect at the takeover announcement; the wealth effects of horizontal takeovers on rivals, suppliers, and customers are unrestricted.

2.2. Collusion hypothesis

A horizontal takeover reduces the number of firms in the takeover industry. Thus, it lowers the costs to monitor collusion and increases the ability of industry rivals to collude (Stigler, 1964). Eckbo (1983) tests the collusion theory by examining the effect of the takeover on rival firms, which are expected to benefit from a collusive merger. Inconsistent with the collusion hypothesis, Eckbo finds that rival firms do not appear to be negatively impacted at the antitrust announcements that challenge the takeovers. Stillman (1983), Eckbo (1985, 1992), Eckbo and Wier (1985), Banerjee and Eckard (1998), and Song and Walkling (2000) also find evidence that is inconsistent with the collusion hypothesis.[2]

Our study extends the methodology of Eckbo (1983) to include supplier and customer industries.[3] The collusion theory suggests that gains from horizontal takeovers are the result of higher output prices and lower input prices. Thus, this theory

---

[2] Kim and Singal (1993) and Singal (1996) find evidence consistent with both the efficiency and the collusion motives for a sample of airline mergers during the period 1985–1988.

[3] Mullin et al. (1995) extend the methodology in Eckbo (1983) to include corporate customers. They find that the announcement of an antitrust challenge to the combination of eight steel companies in 1901 was associated with positive abnormal returns to railroads, for which steel is a major input.

predicts that horizontal takeovers will hurt firms in supplier and customer industries. In addition, an increase in the likelihood of collusion results in higher monopoly rents that will benefit the merging firms and their industry rivals (Eckbo, 1983). As outlined in the second column of Table 1, under the collusion hypothesis, the announcement of a takeover should be associated with positive abnormal returns to the merging firms and their rivals, while suppliers and corporate customers should experience an adverse wealth effect.

2.3. Buyer power hypothesis

Galbraith (1952) suggests that an increase in the concentration of the buying industry can result in a countervailing power that enables buyers to pressure their suppliers. Ellison and Snyder, (2001) divide the theoretical research on the buyer-size effect into two categories. The first category includes theories that examine the effect of the size of a buyer on its bargaining power vis-à-vis a monopoly supplier (see, e.g., Chipty and Snyder, 1999; Stole and Zwiebel, 1996). These studies show that there are plausible conditions under which a large buyer is charged a lower input price. The second category focuses on tacitly colluding suppliers instead of a monopoly supplier. For example, Snyder (1996, 1998) shows that a merger between two buyers will increase their ability to intensify competition among colluding suppliers. The extent to which large buyers enjoy lower prices is examined in both inter and intraindustry empirical studies. Interindustry studies find that industry profits are negatively correlated with proxies for the buyer power of downstream industries (see, e.g., Schumacher, 1991). Intraindustry studies find evidence consistent with large buyers enjoying lower input prices (see, e.g., Ellison and Snyder, 2001).

One common implication of all buyer power models is that a horizontal merger is expected to benefit the merging firms at the expense of firms in the supplier industry. In addition, Snyder (1996) shows that rival firms will benefit from the intensified post-takeover competition among suppliers, which is caused by the increased buyer power of the merging firms. Finally, while most buyer power models are silent with regard to the effect of the increased buyer power on customers, the business press often suggests that buyer power can benefit consumers. For example, commenting on the recent consolidation in the cable industry, Frank and Solomon, (2002) state, "Programmers like Walt Disney and Viacom, which supply cable companies with channels, are using their increasing power to charge cable companies higher fees for programs. Cable companies need equal reach, and influence as 'gatekeepers' to the public, to resist the cost increases." However, Dobson et al. (1998) suggest that customers can also suffer from a horizontal merger if the increased buyer power induces suppliers to under-invest. As summarized in the third column of Table 1, under the buyer power hypothesis, the merging firms should benefit at the takeover announcement, while suppliers are expected to experience an adverse stock price effect. According to Snyder (1996), rivals should benefit at the takeover announcement. The effect of an increase in buyer power on customers is unrestricted.

3. Data sources, takeover sample, suppliers, and corporate customers

3.1. Takeover sample

We use the Worldwide M&A Section of the Securities Data Company (SDC) database to obtain our horizontal takeover sample. We define a horizontal takeover as one between a target and a bidder that share the same four-digit primary SIC code. Kahle and Walkling (1996) find that one major source of the inaccuracy of Compustat industry classifications is that the Primary SIC Code data item is based on the current primary SIC code of a given firm, and thus does not account for the fact that a large number of firms change their primary SIC code over time. We use Compustat's Historical SIC Code data item, which represents the history of primary SIC codes for any particular firm. Since Compustat reports the historical primary SIC code from 1987 onward, and given our interest in the recent wave of horizontal takeovers, we restrict our sample to the period beginning on January 1, 1987 and ending on December 31, 1999.

Our sample includes successful mergers and tender offers. Including only successful takeovers may bias our results against the collusion hypothesis as long as regulators block some potentially anticompetitive mergers. We believe that this problem is considerably mitigated given the lenient US antitrust policy during the sample period (see Kwoka and White, 1999). Thus, we view our test of the collusion hypothesis as a test to whether the relative leniency in antitrust policy in recent years has allowed potentially collusive mergers to be completed.

A takeover is considered successful if the bidder acquires at least 15% of the total number of target shares outstanding at the time of the announcement. The 15% cutoff is used following Kale et al. (2003). Although the efficiency hypothesis requires that the merger be fully consummated, the collusion and buyer power hypotheses can be at work even if the bidder acquires only a fraction of the total number of shares outstanding. Therefore, excluding transactions with a fraction of target shares acquired less than 100% can bias our results against the collusion and buyer power hypotheses. We also repeat our analysis for the subsample of consummated takeovers and find qualitatively similar results (the subsample includes 416 mergers and tender offers). We exclude takeovers in which the bidder holds more than 15% of the target's total shares outstanding prior to the takeover announcement, and transactions including financial firms (SIC codes between 6000 and 6999). We also require that both the target and the bidder be public domestic firms, have stock returns for the estimation period on the Center for Research in Security Prices (CRSP) tapes, and be covered by Compustat.

The above restrictions result in a sample of 352 mergers and 111 tender offers. The mean (median) market capitalization of bidder firms is $5996 million (688 million). The mean (median) market capitalization of target firms is $526 million (100 million). Table 2 shows the distribution of our sample by year and industry classification at the two-digit SIC code level. The table shows a pattern of industry clustering similar to

Table 2

Distribution of sample by year and industry classification

The sample consists of 463 horizontal takeovers during the period 1987–1999. A takeover is considered horizontal if the bidder and the target have the same primary four-digit SIC code. The takeover sample is obtained from the Worldwide M&A section of the Securities Data Company (SDC). This table displays the distribution of the sample by year and industry classification. *Takeover Intensity* is the number of firms that were involved in horizontal takeovers during the sample period divided by the total number of firms in the corresponding industry.

Industry description	SIC code	1987	88	89	90	91	92	93	94	95	96	97	98	99	Total	% of total	Takeover intensity
Agricultural services	7	0	0	0	0	0	0	0	0	0	1	0	0	0	1	0.2	11.8
Metal mining	10	0	0	0	0	1	0	0	0	0	1	1	2	0	5	1.1	4.2
Oil and gas extraction	13	3	0	0	4	1	0	0	6	2	1	9	3	1	30	6.5	6.1
Mining of nonmetallic minerals	14	0	0	0	0	0	0	0	0	0	0	0	1	0	1	0.2	5.3
Building construction	15	0	0	0	0	0	0	0	0	0	0	1	0	0	1	0.2	1.5
Food and kindred products	20	0	1	0	0	0	1	0	0	0	0	2	1	0	5	1.1	2.1
Textile mill products	22	0	0	0	0	0	2	0	0	0	0	0	0	0	2	0.4	3.0
Apparel	23	0	0	0	0	0	0	0	0	0	0	0	1	0	1	0.2	1.1
Lumber and wood products	24	0	0	0	0	0	0	0	0	0	1	0	0	1	2	0.4	3.9
Furniture and fixtures	25	0	0	0	1	0	0	0	0	1	0	0	0	0	2	0.4	4.2
Paper and allied products	26	0	0	0	0	0	0	1	0	0	0	0	0	0	1	0.2	1.2
Printing and publishing	27	0	0	0	0	0	0	0	1	1	1	0	1	0	4	0.9	3.1
Chemicals and allied products	28	0	0	1	0	2	0	0	4	7	5	2	4	4	29	6.3	5.5
Petroleum refining	29	0	0	0	0	0	0	0	0	0	0	1	0	0	1	0.2	2.4
Rubber and plastics	30	2	0	0	1	0	0	0	0	1	1	1	0	0	6	1.3	4.8
Leather	31	0	0	0	1	0	0	0	0	0	0	0	0	0	1	0.2	4.3
Stone, clay, and glass	32	1	1	0	0	0	0	0	0	0	0	0	1	0	3	0.6	4.0
Primary metal	33	0	2	0	0	1	0	1	0	0	0	1	1	0	6	1.3	4.4
Fabricated metals	34	0	0	0	1	0	1	0	0	1	1	1	1	0	6	1.3	4.1
Industrial machinery	35	1	2	2	0	1	1	2	1	5	4	4	4	3	30	6.5	4.8
Electronical machinery	36	1	2	0	0	2	3	1	4	0	3	6	11	9	42	9.1	6.1
Transportation equipment	37	1	0	0	0	0	0	0	2	0	1	1	1	1	7	1.5	4.3
Instruments	38	2	2	1	1	1	0	1	3	4	3	6	2	3	29	6.3	5.5

Industry														Total	%	
Miscellaneous manufacturing (39)	1	0	0	0	0	0	0	0	0	0	0	1	0	3	0.6	1.8
Railroad transportation (40)	0	0	0	0	0	0	0	0	0	0	0	1	0	3	0.6	7.7
Passenger transportation (41)	0	0	0	0	0	0	0	0	0	1	0	0	0	1	0.2	16.7
Motor freight transportation (42)	0	0	0	0	0	0	0	0	0	0	0	2	1	2	0.4	2.8
Water transportation (44)	0	0	0	0	0	0	0	0	0	0	0	1	0	1	0.2	3.8
Transportation by air (45)	3	0	0	0	0	0	1	1	0	1	1	9	1	9	1.9	11.7
Transportation services (47)	0	0	0	0	0	0	0	0	0	0	0	1	1	1	0.2	3.0
Communications (48)	1	0	0	2	0	0	2	6	3	5	6	38	8	38	8.2	8.6
Electric, gas, and sanitary services (49)	0	1	0	0	0	0	1	1	0	1	0	13	6	13	2.8	5.1
Wholesale trade-durable goods (50)	0	0	0	1	0	0	2	0	2	2	1	11	0	11	2.4	3.4
Wholesale trade-nondurable goods (51)	0	0	0	0	0	0	0	0	1	1	1	3	0	3	0.6	2.0
Building materials (52)	0	0	0	0	1	0	1	0	0	0	0	2	0	2	0.4	7.5
General merchandise stores (53)	0	1	1	1	0	0	1	1	1	1	1	9	1	9	1.9	12.7
Food stores (54)	0	0	2	0	0	0	0	0	1	0	2	7	0	7	1.5	8.9
Automotive dealers (55)	0	0	0	0	0	0	0	0	0	1	1	2	0	2	0.4	6.3
Apparel and accessory stores (56)	0	0	0	1	0	0	0	1	0	0	0	3	1	3	0.6	5.3
Home furniture (57)	0	0	0	0	0	0	0	0	1	0	1	3	0	3	0.6	5.7
Eating and drinking places (58)	0	0	0	0	0	0	1	0	1	2	1	7	1	7	1.5	4.0
Miscellaneous retail (59)	1	1	0	1	0	0	2	1	2	2	3	14	0	14	3.0	6.5
Hotels and rooming houses (70)	0	0	0	0	0	0	0	0	0	0	2	4	1	4	0.9	8.0
Personal services (72)	0	0	0	0	0	0	0	0	0	0	1	2	1	2	0.4	8.0
Business services (73)	3	4	4	2	3	1	3	4	5	4	13	71	8	71	15.3	5.5
Automotive repair (75)	0	0	2	0	0	0	0	0	0	1	1	2	0	2	0.4	9.3
Motion pictures (78)	0	4	0	0	0	0	0	1	1	0	3	8	0	8	1.7	6.5
Amusement (79)	0	0	0	0	0	0	0	0	1	1	3	8	0	8	1.7	7.0
Health services (80)	0	0	0	2	0	2	5	3	4	4	4	18	0	18	3.9	8.3
Social services (83)	0	0	1	0	0	0	0	0	0	0	0	1	0	1	0.2	5.4
Engineering and related serviced (87)	0	0	0	0	0	1	1	1	0	0	0	2	1	2	0.4	0.7
Total	19	18	12	18	14	14	22	41	42	51	76	85	51	463	100.0	
% of total	4.1	3.9	2.6	3.9	3.0	3.0	4.8	8.9	9.1	11.0	16.4	18.4	11.0	100.0		

that reported in Andrade et al. (2001). For example, 15.3% of the sample takeovers involve firms in the business services industry. Despite this industry clustering, the sample covers 142 four-digit SIC codes, which represent about one-third of the total number of four-digit SIC codes of publicly traded firms. The last column of Table 2 provides a measure of the intensity of takeover activity for each of the takeover industries, and is equal to the number of industry firms that were involved in horizontal takeovers during the sample period divided by the total number of firms in the industry. The mean, median, maximum, and minimum values of the takeover intensity variable are 5.5, 5.1, 16.7, and 0.7, respectively. This range of values suggests that the takeover industries vary considerably in the takeover activity they have experienced during the sample period.

Since we define a horizontal takeover based on primary SIC codes, it is important to examine the importance of the business derived from the primary segment relative to the overall operations of the merging firms. We use the Compustat Industry Segment (CIS) tapes to collect data on the segments in which the sample targets and bidders operate. We find that 90% of targets and 77% of bidders are single-segment firms. We also find that 95% of targets and 90% of bidders have more than 75% of their sales derived from their primary segment. Thus, the typical firm in our sample is focused and derives most of its business from the takeover industry.

3.2. Benchmark input-output accounts

The Bureau of Economic Analysis at the US Department of Commerce publishes the benchmark IO accounts for the US economy every 5 years. The accounts are based primarily on data collected from economic censuses conducted by the Bureau of Census. In this study, we rely on the *Use* table of the benchmark accounts. For any pair of supplier and customer industries, the Use table reports estimates of the dollar value of the supplier industry's output that is used as input in the production of the customer industry's output.

3.3. Rivals, suppliers, and corporate customers

In the construction of the portfolios of rivals, suppliers, and corporate customers described below, we only consider single-segment firms covered by CRSP and Compustat. We restrict our analysis to single-segment rival, supplier, and customer firms for three reasons. First and foremost, this restriction increases the power of our tests since many diversified firms will have segments in industries that are not affected by the takeover (McAfee and Williams, 1988). Second, in the case of supplier and customer firms, this restriction will result in the exclusion of firms that have segments operating in the takeover industry. This is important in the event that the takeover announcement releases information that affects the valuation of any firm that operates in the takeover industry (see, e.g., Song and Walkling, 2000). Finally, this restriction will also result in the exclusion of rival firms that operate in the supplier and/or the customer industry. Note that we repeat our analysis using all firms covered by Compustat and find results that are qualitatively similar to those reported here.

We define corporate customers as firms that operate in industries that buy the output of the takeover industry. For each pair of customer-takeover industries, we define two variables: *Customer Input Coefficient* and *Takeover Percentage Sold*, where *Customer Input Coefficient* is the dollar amount of the takeover industry's output sold to the customer industry divided by the customer industry's total output, and *Takeover Percentage Sold* is the percentage of the takeover industry's output sold to the customer industry. The *Customer Input Coefficient* measures the importance of the takeover industry's output in the production of the customer industry's output, and the *Takeover Percentage Sold* measures the importance of the customer industry as a buyer of the takeover industry's output.

Since most takeover industries sell their output to a large number of industries, for each takeover industry we examine two important industries from the list of customer industries with publicly traded firms. The *Main Customer* industry is the industry with the highest *Takeover Percentage Sold*. Simply put, among customer industries, this industry buys the highest percentage of the takeover industry's output. The *Dependent Customer* industry is the customer industry with the highest *Customer Input Coefficient*. In other words, the *Dependent Customer* industry is the industry whose production depends on the takeover industry's output more than any other customer industry.

In order to account for the relatively low dependence of some of the identified customer industries on the takeover industry's output, we only consider customer industries with a *Customer Input Coefficient* greater than 1%. This cutoff results in 334 (366) *Main Customer* (*Dependent Customer*) industries. We also repeat our analysis for 3% and 5% cutoffs and find qualitatively similar results. The 3% cutoff results in 176 (294) *Main Customer* (*Dependent Customer*) industries. The respective numbers for the 5% cutoff are 134 and 236. Table 3 displays descriptive statistics for the variables *Customer Input Coefficient* and *Takeover Percentage Sold*.

We define suppliers as firms that operate in industries that supply the inputs used in the production of the takeover industry's output. For each pair of supplier-takeover industries we define two variables. *Takeover Input Coefficient* is the dollar amount of the supplier industry's output sold to the takeover industry divided by the takeover industry's total output. This variable measures the importance of the supplier industry's output in the production of the takeover industry's output. *Supplier Percentage Sold* is the percentage of the supplier industry's output sold to the takeover industry. This variable measures the importance of the takeover industry as a buyer of the supplier industry's output.

As in the case for customers, for each takeover industry we examine two important industries from the list of supplier industries with publicly traded firms. The *Main Supplier* industry is the supplier industry with the highest *Takeover Input Coefficient*. Simply put, this industry supplies the main input to the takeover industry. The *Dependent Supplier* industry is the supplier industry with the highest *Supplier*

Table 3

Descriptive statistics for the variables used to identify customer and supplier industries

The sample consists of 463 horizontal takeovers during the period 1987–1999. A takeover is considered horizontal if the bidder and the target have the same primary four-digit SIC code. Customer and supplier industries are identified using the benchmark IO accounts for the US economy. For each pair of customer and takeover industries, *Customer Input Coefficient* is the dollar amount of the takeover industry's output sold to the customer industry divided by the total output of the customer industry. *Takeover Percentage Sold* is the percentage of the takeover industry's output sold to the corporate customer industry. The *Main Customer Industry* is the customer industry with the highest *Takeover Percentage Sold*. The *Dependent Customer Industry* is the customer industry with the highest *Customer Input Coefficient*. Only customer industries with *Customer Input Coefficient* greater than 1% are included. For each pair of supplier and takeover industries, *Takeover Input Coefficient* is the dollar amount of the supplier industry's output sold to the takeover industry divided by the takeover industry's total output, expressed in percentage terms. *Supplier Percentage Sold* is the percentage of the supplier industry's output sold to the takeover industry. The *Main Supplier Industry* is the supplier industry with the highest *Takeover Input Coefficient*. The *Dependent Supplier Industry* is the supplier industry with the highest *Supplier Percentage Sold*. Only supplier industries with *Supplier Percentage Sold* greater than 1% are included. All figures are expressed in percentage terms.

	N	Mean	Median	25th percentile	75th percentile
Main customer industry					
Customer input coefficient	334	9	3	1	7
Takeover percentage sold	334	14	5	2	14
Dependent customer industry					
Customer input coefficient	366	12	6	3	13
Takeover percentage sold	366	14	5	2	14
Main supplier industry					
Supplier percentage sold	316	13	7	2	15
Takeover input coefficient	316	9	6	4	11
Dependent supplier industry					
Supplier percentage sold	399	25	17	8	37
Takeover input coefficient	399	9	3	1	7

Percentage Sold. In other words, this industry's percentage of output sold to the takeover industry is higher than that of any other supplier industry.

Since some of the identified supplier industries do not sell a significant fraction of their output to the takeover industry, we include in our analysis supplier industries with a *Supplier Percentage Sold* greater than 1%. This cutoff results in 316 (399) *Main Supplier* (*Dependent Supplier*) industries. We also repeat our analysis using 3% and 5% cutoffs and find qualitatively similar results. The 3% (5%) cutoff results in 218 (195) *Main Supplier* and 360 (337) *Dependent Supplier* industries. Table 3 presents descriptive statistics for the variables *Takeover Input Coefficient* and *Supplier Percentage Sold*.

The Compustat database classifies industries by SIC codes, whereas the Use table is constructed using the IO six-digit coding system. In order to convert four-digit SIC codes to six-digit IO codes, we use the conversion table used by Fan and Lang (2000). They construct this table by using conversion tables published by the Bureau of

Economic Analysis.[4] In order to identify suppliers and corporate customers, we use the 1987, 1992, and 1997 tables for takeovers that occur during the periods 1987–1989, 1990–1994, and 1995–1999, respectively. For the 1997 tables, we use the 1997 annual updates of the 1992 benchmark tables. We also find similar results after repeating our analysis using the 1987, 1992, and 1997 tables for takeovers that occur during the periods 1987–1991, 1992–1996, and 1997–1999 periods, respectively.

4. Methodology and results

4.1. Measuring abnormal returns

We estimate abnormal returns to firm i at date t (AR_{it}) as

$$AR_{it} = R_{it} - \alpha_i - \beta_i R_{mt}, \tag{1}$$

where R_{mt} is the return on the CRSP value-weighted index on day t, R_{it} is the realized return to firm i on day t, and α_i and β_i are parameters estimated using a market model. We also find similar results after repeating the analysis that pertains to the bidder and the portfolio of the bidder and target after constraining the market model intercept to equal zero (see Schwert, 1996). We use an estimation period of 250 days starting on day -300 relative to the takeover announcement date. We require a minimum of 100 daily returns, otherwise the firm is omitted. The takeover announcement date is the date on which either the target or the bidder makes a public announcement regarding the takeover, and is obtained by searching the Dow Jones Interactive database. Following Bradley et al. (1988), we estimate CWE as the cumulative abnormal return (CAR) to a value-weighted portfolio of the bidder and target. The weights are the respective market values of the equity of bidder and target firms for day -10 relative to the announcement date. The target equity market value excludes the value of target shares held by the bidder prior to the announcement. To estimate CARs to rivals, suppliers, and corporate customers, we follow the literature by forming equally weighted portfolios to account for any contemporaneous cross-correlation of returns (see, e.g., Eckbo, 1983; Song and Walkling, 2000). We follow the methodology of Mikkelson and Partch (1988) to test for the statistical significance of CARs. We also test for the significance of the percentage of positive CARs using a nonparametric generalized sign test. This test uses the fraction of positive CARs in the estimation period as the fraction under the null hypothesis instead of assuming 50%.

4.2. Abnormal returns to the merging firm and their rivals, customers, and suppliers

We first examine the abnormal returns to the merging firms. We find that targets earn significant positive abnormal returns at the takeover announcement. The mean CAR to

---

[4] Because of the importance of this conversion table to our study, we manually check its accuracy. We could not identify any case in which the table results in industry misclassification.

target firms is 15.89% ($t = 72.69$) for the $(-1, 0)$ window. For the same window, the mean bidder CAR is -0.61% ($t = -4.06$). The CWE of the sample takeover averages 2.25% ($t = 15.44$) for the $(-1, 0)$ window and 3.52% ($t = 7.36$) for the $(-10, 10)$ window. These results are consistent with the extant evidence on the significance of wealth gains in takeovers (see, e.g., Andrade et al., 2001; Jensen and Ruback, 1983). We also find that the percentage of positive CWE is about 61% over the $(-10, 10)$ window, indicating that a significant proportion of the sample takeovers (about 39%) have a negative CWE.

Table 4 presents abnormal returns for rival, customer, and supplier portfolios. As shown in Panel A, rival firms earn an average CAR of 0.39% ($t = 2.91$) for the $(-2, 2)$ window. The positive average CAR to rival firms is consistent with the evidence in Eckbo (1983) and Song and Walkling (2000), among others. The average CAR to supplier and customer portfolios are insignificant for the shorter window $(-1, 0)$. For the longer window $(-10, 10)$, the CAR to the portfolio of firms in the *Main Customer* (*Dependent Customer*) industry averages a significant 0.50% (1.00%). The CAR to *Main Supplier* (*Dependent Supplier*) industry portfolios averages a significant -0.48% (-0.95%). The proportion of portfolios of *Main Supplier* (*Dependent Supplier*) industries with positive CAR is a significant 45.25% (45.11%).

The evidence in Panel A of Table 4 suggests that for the overall sample, rivals and customers gain while suppliers lose at the takeover announcement. The results for supplier and customer portfolios are somewhat consistent with the positive but insignificant CAR that Eckbo (1983) reports for the rivals of firms involved in vertical mergers, that is, for firms that are in principle the customers or suppliers of the merging firms.

At first sight, the results in Panel A of Table 4 appear to be consistent with both the efficiency as well as the buyer power hypothesis but inconsistent with the collusion hypothesis. However, we report above that a significant proportion of the sample takeovers results in negative CWE. Since the productive efficiency, collusion, and buyer power hypotheses predict a positive CWE, we follow Berkovitch and Narayanan (1993) by splitting our sample into value-creating and value-destroying takeovers, depending on whether a takeover has a positive or negative CWE. An analysis of the two subsamples will enable us to further differentiate among the various competing hypotheses. The results reported in Panels A and B of Table 4 are based on a CWE measured over the $(-2, 2)$ window. Since CWE is measured with error, we discuss in Section 4.5 the validity of this measure to sort takeovers, and the robustness of our conditional results.

In Panel B of Table 4, we report CARs to rivals, customers, and suppliers for the subsample of takeovers with a positive CWE. Compared to the overall sample, the CARs to rivals and customers are significantly higher. The mean CAR to rival firms is 0.43% ($t = 3.85$) for the $(-1, 0)$ period, compared to 0.08% for the overall sample (the difference between the two means is significant at the 1% level using a t-test). The mean CAR to *Main Customer* (*Dependent Customer*) industry portfolios is a significant 1.89% (1.76%) for the $(-10, 10)$ window. The CAR to *Main Supplier* (*Dependent Supplier*) industry portfolios averages a significant 1.06% (1.28%) for the $(-10, 10)$ window.

Table 4

Announcement period abnormal returns to rivals, customers, and suppliers

This table reports cumulative abnormal returns (CARs) to *Rivals*, *Main Customer*, *Dependent Customer*, *Main Supplier*, and *Dependent Supplier* industries. The sample consists of 463 horizontal takeovers during the period 1987–1999. Supplier and customer industries are identified using the benchmark IO accounts for the US economy. For each takeover industry, the *Main Customer Industry* is the industry that buys the highest percentage of the takeover industry's output. The *Dependent Customer Industry* is the industry whose production depends on the takeover industry's output more than any other customer industry. The *Main Supplier Industry* is the industry that supplies the main input to the takeover industry. The *Dependent Supplier Industry* is the supplier industry whose percentage of output sold to the takeover industry is higher than that of any other supplier industry. A customer industry is included in the sample if its total dollar amount spent on the input bought from the takeover industry represents more than 1% of its total output. A supplier industry is included in the sample if it sells more than 1% of its total output to the takeover industry. CARs to rivals, suppliers, and customers are estimated using equally weighted portfolios of single-segment firms in the corresponding industry. Panel A reports CARs for the overall sample. Panel B (Panel C) reports CARs for the subsample of takeovers with positive (negative) *Combined Wealth Effect*, which is the cumulative abnormal return to a value-weighted portfolio of the bidder and target for the $(-2, 2)$ window. Panel D (Panel E) reports CARs to the rival, supplier, and customer portfolios that only include firms whose headquarters are located in either the target or bidder headquarter region (state). A nonparametric generalized sign test is used to test for the percentage of positive CARs.

Panel A: CAR (%) to the overall sample of takeovers

	Rivals		Main customer industry		Dependent customer industry		Main supplier industry		Dependent supplier industry	
No. of portfolios:	455		334		366		316		399	
Mean (median) no. of firms:	43 (19)		82 (42)		21 (7)		34 (31)		24 (9)	
Window	Mean (*t*-stat)	% positive (z-stat)	Mean (*t*-stat)	% positive (z-stat)	Mean (*t*-stat)	% positive (z-stat)	Mean (*t*-stat)	% positive (z-stat)	Mean (*t*-stat)	% positive (z-stat)
$(-1, 0)$	0.08 (0.90)	51.21 (−0.65)	0.19 (1.30)	51.17 (−0.11)	0.12 (1.35)	51.91 (−0.99)	−0.02 (−0.72)	49.20 (−1.07)	0.18 (1.21)	50.12 (−0.60)
$(-2, 2)$	0.39*** (2.91)	54.07 (0.57)	0.30* (1.82)	48.80 (−1.20)	0.21 (1.29)	49.03* (−1.94)	−0.05 (−1.08)	48.41 (−1.29)	0.28 (0.71)	48.37 (−1.30)
$(-10, 10)$	0.52 (1.55)	53.41 (0.29)	0.50* (1.73)	52.10 (0.00)	1.00*** (2.70)	51.52 (−0.99)	−0.48** (−2.05)	45.25** (−2.42)	−0.95** (−1.99)	45.11*** (−2.60)

(*Continued*)

Table 4 (Continued)

	Rivals		Main customer industry		Dependent customer industry		Main supplier industry		Dependent supplier industry	
	Mean (t-stat)	% positive (z-stat)	Mean (t-stat)	% positive (z-stat)	Mean (t-stat)	% positive (z-stat)	Mean (t-stat)	% positive (z-stat)	Mean (t-stat)	% positive (z-stat)
(10, 20)	0.01 (−0.72)	48.79 (−1.68)	0.05 (−0.12)	48.80 (−1.21)	0.31 (1.02)	52.45 (−0.78)	0.09 (0.01)	42.85*** (−3.32)	−0.15 (−1.20)	44.61*** (−2.80)

Panel B: CAR (%) to the subsample of takeovers with positive combined wealth effect

	Rivals		Main customer industry		Dependent customer industry		Main supplier industry		Dependent supplier industry	
No. of portfolios	271		199		222		186		237	
Window	Mean (t-stat)	% positive (z-stat)	Mean (t-stat)	% positive (z-stat)	Mean (t-stat)	% positive (z-stat)	Mean (t-stat)	% positive (z-stat)	Mean (t-stat)	% positive (z-stat)
(−1, 0)	0.43*** (3.85)	57.56* (1.88)	0.50*** (3.24)	58.29* (1.85)	0.52*** (2.74)	55.96 (0.84)	0.04 (0.03)	50.00 (−0.48)	0.59*** (3.11)	56.12 (1.44)
(−2, 2)	1.25*** (7.17)	64.94*** (4.31)	0.79*** (4.24)	52.26 (0.15)	0.76*** (2.87)	52.75 (−0.11)	0.42* (1.91)	53.76 (0.55)	1.37*** (4.34)	55.27 (1.18)
(−10, 10)	1.95*** (5.52)	61.62*** (3.21)	1.89*** (4.86)	60.30** (2.42)	1.76*** (3.04)	55.50 (0.71)	1.06** (2.31)	53.76 (0.55)	1.28*** (3.12)	56.96* (1.70)
(10, 20)	0.07 (−0.06)	48.34 (−1.16)	0.04 (0.60)	51.26 (−0.14)	0.7 (1.18)	54.13 (0.30)	0.32 (0.80)	44.62* (−1.95)	0.24 (−0.14)	46.84 (−1.42)

Panel C: CAR (%) to the subsample of takeovers with negative combined wealth effect

	Rivals		Main customer industry		Dependent customer industry		Main supplier industry		Dependent supplier industry	
No. of portfolios	184		135		144		130		162	
Window	Mean (t-stat)	% positive (z-stat)	Mean (t-stat)	% positive (z-stat)	Mean (t-stat)	% positive (z-stat)	Mean (t-stat)	% positive (z-stat)	Mean (t-stat)	% positive (z-stat)
(−1, 0)	−0.41*** (−3.22)	42.93*** (−3.05)	−0.25* (−1.71)	42.96** (−2.25)	−0.46 (−1.19)	45.83** (−2.38)	−0.10 (−1.13)	46.92 (−1.26)	−0.39* (−1.81)	41.98*** (−2.55)

	Rivals		Main customer industry		Dependent customer industry		Main supplier industry		Dependent supplier industry	
	Mean (t-stat)	% positive (z-stat)	Mean (t-stat)	% positive (z-stat)	Mean (t-stat)	% positive (z-stat)	Mean (t-stat)	% positive (z-stat)	Mean (t-stat)	% positive (z-stat)
(−2, 2)	−0.85*** (−4.16)	36.96*** (−4.68)	−0.41*** (−2.94)	34.81*** (−4.14)	−0.64 (−1.50)	43.06*** (−3.05)	−0.72*** (−4.01)	38.46*** (−3.19)	−1.29*** (−4.16)	38.27*** (−3.50)
(−10, 10)	−1.67*** (−4.53)	39.67*** (−3.94)	−1.50*** (−3.57)	40.00*** (−2.94)	−0.12 (0.55)	45.83** (−2.38)	−2.76*** (−6.16)	31.54*** (−4.77)	−4.23*** (−6.97)	27.78*** (−6.17)
(10, 20)	−0.06 (−1.06)	50.00 (−1.13)	0.07 (−0.90)	45.19* (−1.73)	−0.29 (0.18)	48.61* (−1.71)	−0.15 (−0.79)	42.31** (−2.31)	−0.71 (−1.63)	41.36*** (−2.71)

Panel D: CAR for the (−10, 10) window to portfolios that include firms whose headquarters are located in either the target or bidder headquarter region

Number of portfolios:	Rivals		Main customer industry		Dependent customer industry		Main supplier industry		Dependent supplier industry	
Overall sample	435		311		337		298		355	
Negative CWE	255		188		202		175		213	
Mean (median) number of firms:	19 (7)		27 (15)		9 (4)		12 (9)		12 (5)	

Sample	Rivals		Main customer industry		Dependent customer industry		Main supplier industry		Dependent supplier industry	
	Mean (t-stat)	% positive (z-stat)	Mean (t-stat)	% positive (z-stat)	Mean (t-stat)	% positive (z-stat)	Mean (t-stat)	% positive (z-stat)	Mean (t-stat)	% positive (z-stat)
Overall sample	0.78** (2.47)	52.00 (0.00)	0.47 (1.21)	52.41 (0.47)	0.09 (1.05)	51.37 (0.27)	0.16 (−0.92)	47.44 (−1.41)	−0.34 (−0.81)	44.62** (−2.22)
Positive CWE	1.68*** (4.60)	58.44** (2.08)	1.35*** (2.73)	57.98** (1.98)	1.03** (1.99)	54.49 (1.14)	1.70** (2.23)	56.97* (1.72)	1.82*** (2.73)	53.80 (0.78)
Negative CWE	−0.63** (−2.05)	41.56*** (−2.89)	−0.89* (−1.67)	43.90* (−1.74)	−1.38** (−2.24)	46.43 (−1.56)	−2.28*** (−3.93)	33.88*** (−4.19)	−3.53*** (−4.92)	30.89*** (−4.48)

Panel E: CAR for the (−10, 10) window to portfolios that only include firms whose headquarters are located in either the target or bidder headquarter state

Number of portfolios:	Rivals		Main customer industry		Dependent customer industry		Main supplier industry		Dependent supplier industry	
Overall sample	363		265		247		264		257	
	205		156		147		151		154	

The CARs for the negative CWE subsample are presented in Panel C of Table 4. Rival firms appear to lose at the takeover announcement. The average CAR to rival firms is -1.67% ($t = -4.53$) for the $(-10, 10)$ window. The proportion of portfolios of rivals with positive CARs is 39.67% ($z = -3.94$), compared to 58.67% for the positive CWE subsample. In addition, both customers as well as suppliers suffer significantly at the announcement of a negative CWE takeover. Over the $(-10, 10)$ period, the CAR to a portfolio of firms in the *Main Customer* industry averages -1.50% ($t = -3.57$), and the proportion of positive CAR is 40% ($t = 2.94$). The CAR to the *Main Supplier* (*Dependent Supplier*) industry portfolio averages a significant -2.76% (-4.23%) for the $(-10, 10)$ window. In order to verify whether the pattern of abnormal returns reported in Table 4 is not particular to the specific customer and supplier industries examined, we repeat our analysis for the main five customer and supplier industries. The results of this analysis are qualitatively similar to those reported here. Further, it is possible that the takeover can result in less- or more-pronounced wealth effects on supplier and customer industries if the target and/or bidder have segments in these industries. We find that excluding such takeovers does not significantly affect our results.

Note that in many of the cases reported in Table 4, the statistical and economic significance of the average CAR increases as we augment the window. This increase in CAR can be due to at least three factors. First, extending the window to include preannouncement days should capture any leakage of information about the takeover (see Jarrell et al., 1988). Second, since the sample includes completed takeovers, the likelihood that the takeovers will be completed should be increasing in the time of the announcement. Finally, it may take few days for information to be impounded in small-firm stock prices (see Lo and Mackinlay, 1990). In order to check whether the results for longer windows are not an artifact of the model of abnormal returns we use, we report CAR for the (10, 20) window. In most cases, the average CAR for this window is statistically insignificant.

In short, for the positive CWE subsample, rivals, customers, and suppliers gain at the announcement of the takeover. On the other hand, for the negative CWE subsample, the pattern is reversed: rivals, suppliers, and customers lose significantly at the takeover announcement.[5] Thus, the overall evidence in this section is inconsistent with the collusion and buyer power hypotheses and in fact, suppliers and customers appear to gain from horizontal takeovers that result in a positive CWE to merging firms. Our results are consistent with takeovers resulting in increases in productive efficiency and/or releasing information about overall industry restructuring. Further, the magnitude of the negative CAR to customers, suppliers and, especially, to rival firms for the negative

---

[5] The effect of the takeover announcement on rivals, suppliers, and customers may be related to the method of financing. For example, stock financing can signal that other firms in the takeover industry and/or related industries are overvalued. However, we do not find support for this hypothesis. We find that the abnormal returns to rivals, suppliers, and corporate customers are not significantly related to the method of financing. This result is consistent with the evidence in Betton and Eckbo (2000), who find that the effect of the method of financing appears to be subsumed by the effect of bidder toeholds in the target.

CWE subsample suggests that the announcements of some of these takeovers release negative information regarding the future prospects of the takeover industry.

4.3. Regional bias

In the previous section, we find evidence consistent with the productive efficiency hypothesis. It is possible, however, that our results are biased against the collusion and buyer power hypotheses since the rival, customer, and supplier portfolios include firms that may operate anywhere in the US market. For instance, if the merging firms operate exclusively in one region, under the efficiency hypothesis it is more likely for informational effects to affect the valuation of firms that operate in another region than it is for changes in market power or buyer power. Note that Eckbo (1983) deals with this issue by selecting a sample of mergers between firms that were operating nationally as stated in the court records for antitrust cases. We address this issue using the following approach.

Since domestic firms are not required to disclose information on where they do business within the US market, it is not possible to accurately determine the extent to which they operate in a given market. Therefore, following the literature, we use the headquarter state (Compustat data item ADD3) as the state in which the firm core business is located (see, e.g., Coval and Moskowitz, 1999).[6] In order to further determine whether the headquarter state is a good indicator of the firm's main area of operations, we search the Factiva database and Moody's industrial, OTC industrial, and transportation manuals for information regarding the operations of the merging firms at the time of the takeover. We find that among the cases for which there is some information regarding the geographical operation of targets and bidders that do not appear to operate nationally (72% of targets and 57% of bidders), the headquarter region or state as listed in Compustat is generally described to be the area where the firm's main operations are based.

We repeat our event study analysis for portfolios that only include "regional" firms, those firms whose headquarters are located in either the target or bidder headquarter region. We follow the SDC database by dividing the domestic market into six main regions: Northeast, Southeast, Southwest, Mideast, Midwest, and West.[7] We also repeat the analysis for portfolios that only include "state" firms, firms

---

[6] Coval and Moskowitz (1999) use the location of the headquarters to examine the effect of geographical proximity in investment managers' portfolio choices. Generally, the headquarter state is not the same as the state of incorporation, which is chosen more for regulatory considerations than operational reasons.

[7] The following states are included in each of the regions. Northeast: Connecticut, Delaware, District of Colombia, Massachusetts, Maine, New Hampshire, New Jersey, New York, Pennsylvania, Rhode Island, and Vermont. Southeast: Florida, Georgia, Kentucky, Mississippi, North Carolina, South Carolina, Tennessee, and Virginia. Southwest: Arizona, Arkansas, Louisiana, New Mexico, Oklahoma, and Texas. Mideast: Illinois, Indiana, Michigan, Ohio, West Virginia, and Wisconsin. Midwest: Iowa, Kansas, Minnesota, Missouri, Nebraska, North Dakota, and South Dakota. West: Alaska, California, Colorado, Hawaii, Idaho, Montana, Nevada, Oregon, Utah, Washington, and Wyoming.

whose headquarters are located in either the target or bidder headquarter state. Since some the target and bidder firms in our sample were operating nationally, and considering the potential bias discussed above, we view the approach of including only regional or state firms to be a conservative one as related to the examination of the collusion and buyer power hypotheses.

The results of this analysis are reported in Panel D (regional firms) and Panel E (state firms) of Table 4. We only report CARs for the (-10, 10) window since the results for other windows are qualitatively similar. For the most part, the CARs reported in the two panels are qualitatively similar to those reported in Panels A, B, and C, especially for the subsamples of takeovers with positive and negative CWE. In particular, we find that takeovers with positive (negative) CWE are associated with positive (negative) abnormal returns to the portfolios of rivals, customers, and suppliers.

We also take a less conservative approach and identify "national" takeovers as takeovers in which both the target and bidder were described explicitly in any of the sources that we searched as firms that operate nationally. We find 83 such takeovers. The remaining takeovers are classified as regional takeovers. We then repeat our analysis for portfolios that include all firms and regional firms for national takeovers and regional takeovers, respectively. The results of this analysis are qualitatively similar to those reported in Panels D and E of Table 4.

4.4. Joint tests

The most notable result that we report in Table 4 is that the positive CWE takeovers are associated with positive CARs to rivals, customers, and suppliers. Given the joint nature of the predictions of the various hypotheses, we test whether the positive CARs are the results of joint positive wealth effects. Thus, we conduct tests that are based on the joint signs of abnormal returns to the various portfolios. In particular, we test whether the proportion of takeovers that result in joint positive wealth effects to the merging firms and their rivals, suppliers, and customers is significantly higher than that expected by chance. We also conduct similar tests to further examine the collusion and buyer power hypotheses. Thus, we compute the proportion of takeovers that have joint wealth effects that are consistent with each of the two hypotheses. We use a standard Z test to examine the statistical significance of each of the proportions. We use the estimation period residual series to estimate the proportions under the null hypotheses.

Table 5 shows the results of joint tests that are based on CARs for the (-2, 2) window. The results for other windows are very similar, and are therefore not reported. For customers (suppliers), we use the *Dependent Customer* (*Dependent Supplier*) industry portfolios since the resulting sample sizes are larger. Using the *Main Customer* and *Main Supplier* industry portfolios yields qualitatively similar results. The results are highly consistent with the productive efficiency hypothesis. In particular, we find that the proportion of takeovers with joint positive CARs to the merging firms and their rivals, suppliers, and customers is significantly higher than that of the estimation period.

Table 5

Joint tests

This table reports the proportions of takeovers with particular joint signs of abnormal returns to the merging firms and their rivals, customers, and suppliers. The sample includes 463 horizontal takeovers during the period 1987–1999. Customer and supplier industries are identified using the benchmark IO accounts for the US economy as described in Table 4. Abnormal returns are estimated using a market model. Abnormal returns to rivals, suppliers, and customers are estimated using equally weighted portfolios of single-segment firms in the corresponding industry and cumulated over the $(-2, 2)$ window. Combined wealth effect (CWE) is the cumulative abnormal return to a value-weighted portfolio of the bidder and target for the $(-2, 2)$ window. Regional (state) firms are firms whose headquarters are located in either the target or bidder headquarter region (state). A standard Z test is used to test for the statistical significance of the proportion of takeovers with a particular pattern of abnormal returns, where the proportion under the null hypothesis is that of the estimation period.

	Signs of abnormal returns under the various hypotheses		
	Efficiency	Efficiency, collusion, or buyer power	Efficiency, or buyer power
Merging firms	Positive	Positive	Positive
Rivals	Positive	Positive	Positive
Customers	Positive	Negative	Positive
Suppliers	Positive	Negative	Negative
Panel A: Overall sample			
Portfolios include all firms	16.03%***	6.73%	7.69%
(312 portfolios)	(5.21)	(1.28)	(1.46)
Portfolios include regional firms	15.81%***	5.51%	8.09%
(272 portfolios)	(3.24)	(0.57)	(1.86)*
Portfolios include state firms	14.49%***	6.07%	8.41%
(214 portfolios)	(2.58)	(0.97)	(1.43)
Panel B: Subsample with positive CWE			
Portfolios include all firms	26.74%***	11.23%	12.83%
(187 portfolios)	(4.79)	(0.74)	(1.21)
Portfolios include regional firms	27.22%***	9.49%	13.92%
(158 portfolios)	(3.92)	(0.28)	(1.58)
Portfolios include state firms	25.00%***	10.48%	14.52%
(124 portfolios)	(3.31)	(0.63)	(1.14)

The symbols * and *** indicate statistical significance at the 10% and 1% levels, respectively (Z-values are in parentheses).

As reported in Panel A of Table 5, the overall (unconditional) proportion of takeovers that result in joint positive CARs to the various portfolios is a significant 16.03%. Conditional on a positive CWE, the respective proportion is 26.74%, significantly higher than the 14.44% of the estimation period. The pattern of abnormal returns that is consistent with both the production efficiency and the buyer power hypotheses is weakly supported by the results reported in the last column of Table 5. Further, the results of the joint tests do not support the collusion motive. As reported in Panel B of Table 5, the results of the analysis of portfolios that only include regional or state firms are very similar. In (unreported) results, we find that for the negative CWE subsamples, the only pattern of abnormal returns that is supported by the joint tests is that of joint negative CARs to the various portfolios.

4.5. CWE-based classification

In the previous analysis, we use the combined wealth variable (CWE) to classify takeovers into value-creating and value-destroying deals. Since CWE is measured with error, it can result in misclassifications of takeovers into the two groups. Therefore, we conduct additional analysis to examine the robustness of the conditional results reported in Tables 4 and 5, and the validity of CWE as an instrument to classify takeovers.

First, we identify characteristics of value-creating and value-destroying takeovers. Consistent with the findings in Harford (1999), we find that the median cash-to-sales ratio for bidders in the negative CWE subsample (17.7%) is significantly higher than the corresponding median (7.4%) for bidders in the positive CWE subsample. Further, consistent with the evidence in Maloney et al. (1993), we find that the median leverage for bidders of the negative CWE takeovers (15%) is significantly lower than the corresponding median for bidders of the positive CWE takeovers (21%). The cash and leverage results are consistent with the free cash flow theory of Jensen (1986), and suggest that agency problems appear to be more severe in bidder firms involved in negative CWE takeovers. Note that in the cash and leverage analyses, we focus on bidders since most of the negative wealth effects to the combined target and bidder are due to the negative abnormal returns to bidder firms. Finally, following Lang et al. (1989), we classify the sample bidders and targets into high q and low q firms, where the value of 1 is used as a cutoff point. We find that the proportion of takeovers in the positive CWE subsample in which a high q bidder acquires a low q (15.7%) is significantly higher than that of the negative CWE subsample (8.2%).

Second, partial anticipation of the takeover event can result in CWE not representing the true value of the takeover synergies. To address this issue, we classify the sample bidders into expected and unexpected bidders using the methodology outlined in Harford (1999). We repeat our analysis for the subsample of 139 unexpected bidders, and find a pattern of abnormal returns that is qualitatively similar to that reported in Tables 4 and 5.

Third, we analyze takeovers that are less likely to be misclassified. Assuming that the CWE measurement error is not correlated with the true synergies resulting from the takeover, it is more likely that takeovers with higher and lower CWE represent value-creating and value-destroying deals, respectively. Therefore, we repeat our analysis after excluding takeovers in the top CWE quartile of the negative CWE subsample, and in the bottom CWE quartile of the positive CWE subsample. The results of this analysis are qualitatively similar to and of higher magnitude than those reported in Tables 4 and 5.

Finally, we examine whether our results are sensitive to the window over which CWE is measured. We obtain qualitatively similar results after measuring CWE over the $(-1, 0)$, $(-1, 1)$, $(-5, 5)$, and $(-10, 10)$ windows. We also account for the fact that some targets may have received unsuccessful bids during the period preceding the successful bid. Thus, we define a contest as the set of bids that the target has received after at least 1 year of hiatus. We then use a window that starts 5 days prior to the first announcement of a contest and ends 5 days after the announcement of the successful bid. The corresponding results are qualitatively similar to those reported in Tables 4 and 5.

5. Cross-sectional analysis

In the previous section, we report evidence suggesting that the average horizontal takeover in our sample is driven by efficiency considerations. The main objective of this section is to test for the presence of collusion and buyer power motives in the cross-section by examining the relation between the various abnormal returns and industry structures. In Section 5.1, we develop the cross-sectional hypotheses. Section 5.2 describes the construction of our dependent variables. In Section 5.3, we report and discuss our results.

5.1. Cross-sectional hypotheses

5.1.1. Concentration of the takeover industry

Firms earn zero economic profits in the long run in perfectly competitive markets. Therefore, if the takeover results in efficiency gains, one should expect that the wealth captured by the merging firms would be higher in less-competitive takeover industries. In addition, the takeover can indicate that industrywide efficiency is available to other industry rivals, which can retain more of the wealth gains if the industry is not perfectly competitive. It follows that customers and suppliers of imperfectly competitive industries will benefit relatively less from the productive efficiency created through takeovers. Following the literature, we use the degree of concentration as a proxy for imperfect competition. Thus, the productive efficiency hypothesis predicts a positive (negative) relation between the concentration of the takeover industry and the abnormal returns to the merging firms and their industry rivals (suppliers and corporate customers). When testing this hypothesis, it is important to control for the degree of foreign competition in the takeover industry since studies such as Domowitz et al. (1986) and Katics and Petersen (1994) find that imports appear to intensify competition in concentrated industries.

If the takeover is anticompetitive, a higher degree of concentration in the takeover industry will lead to a higher likelihood of collusion and hence higher monopoly rents, which will benefit the merging firms and their rivals, and hurt suppliers and corporate customers. In addition, the effects of a collusive merger will be more pronounced if the takeover-induced increase in concentration is higher (Eckbo, 1985, 1992). Therefore, the collusion hypothesis predicts that both, the concentration of the takeover industry and the takeover-induced change in concentration, are positively (negatively) related to the abnormal returns to the merging firms and rivals (suppliers and corporate customers).[8]

5.1.2. Concentration of customers

Based on the buyer power model in Snyder (1996), the presence of a large buyer reduces the ability of sellers to collude. Under this theory, the presence of concentrated customers can mitigate the anticompetitive effects of a collusive takeover. Therefore, the collusion hypothesis predicts a negative (positive) relation between the concentration of corporate customers and the abnormal returns to the merging firms (corporate customers). On the other hand, if the takeover yields productivity gains, more of this gain will be translated into profits if the customer industry is concentrated because of lower advertising and other selling expenses (Ravenscraft, 1983) that will benefit the merging firms and their customers. Thus, the efficiency hypothesis predicts a positive relation between the concentration of corporate customers and the abnormal returns to the merging firms and corporate customers.

5.1.3. Concentration of suppliers

In all the buyer power models discussed above, the size of the buyer is relevant only if the supplier industry is not perfectly competitive. Therefore, in order for the takeover to result in higher buyer power for the merging firms, the supplier industry should be sufficiently concentrated in order to sustain collusion. Further, according to Snyder (1996), rival firms will benefit from a horizontal takeover since the increased buyer power will lead to more-intense competition in an imperfectly competitive supplier industry. Therefore, the buyer power hypothesis predicts a positive (negative) relation between the concentration of suppliers and the abnormal returns to the merging firms and their industry rivals (suppliers).

5.2. Measurement of independent variables

The construction of our concentration measures requires detailed data pertaining to the market shares of firms in the takeover, supplier, and customer industries. Following the

---

[8] See Eckbo (1985, 1992) for a more comprehensive discussion regarding the relations between industry concentration and takeover-induced change in concentration, and abnormal returns to the merging firms are rivals. Eckbo (1992) uses arguments based on the relation between industry concentration and the elasticity of industry demand. For the most part, the predictions in Eckbo (1985, 1992) imply that only the predicted impact of the takeover-induced change in concentration is clearcut and can differentiate between the efficiency and collusion hypotheses.

literature, we use Compustat to obtain market share data (see, e.g., Lang and Stulz, 1992; Song and Walkling, 2000). We use the sales-based Herfindahl index to measure the concentration of the takeover industry. We use sales data for the fiscal year preceding the year of the announcement. The takeover-induced change in concentration, *Change in Herfindahl Index*, is measured as $2\,{}^*\mathrm{MS}_b\,{}^*\mathrm{MS}_t$, where MS_b (MS_t) is the bidder (target) market share. If either the bidder or the target is a diversified firm, we use the CIS tapes to obtain sales data for the primary SIC code.

In order to measure the concentration of corporate customers, we estimate the sales-based Herfindahl index as

$$\text{Customer concentration} = \sum_{i=1}^{n} S_i^2, \tag{2}$$

where S_i is the estimated percentage of the takeover industry's output sold to firm i, and n is the number of firms in all customer industries. We estimate S_i by multiplying the sales of firm i by the *Customer Input Coefficient* that corresponds to the firm's industry, and dividing by the takeover industry's total output. Following Ravenscraft (1983), we construct *Supplier Concentration* as the weighted average of the Herfindahl indices for all supplier industries, where the weight for the jth supplier industry is the dollar amount of this industry's output used as input to produce one dollar of the takeover industry's output. In the regression analysis of the CAR to the *Main* and *Dependent Supplier* industry, we use the Herfindahl index of the respective industry.

To control for import competition, we follow Mitchell and Mulherin (1996) and construct *Foreign Competition* as the takeover industry's total imports divided by its total supply. Following the extant literature, in our regression analysis of the CWE variable, we use the control variables described below.

(i)   *Offer Includes Stock* is a dummy variable that equals 1 if the bid includes stock financing, and 0 otherwise (see, e.g., Travlos, 1987).

(ii) *Relative Size* is the ratio of the market capitalization of the target to that of the bidder, with both values being measured 10 days prior to the announcement of the takeover (see, e.g., Mulherin and Boone, 2000; Servaes, 1991).

(iii) *Hostile Takeover* is a dummy variable that equals 1 if the transaction is characterized by the SDC database as a hostile takeover, and 0 otherwise [see Schwert (2000) for an extensive analysis of the effects of hostility in takeovers].

5.3. Cross-sectional results

In this section, we report the results on the determinants of CARs to the merging firms and their rivals, suppliers, and corporate customers. We cumulate the various abnormal returns over the 5-day period surrounding the takeover announcement. The results of the analyses for the $(-1, 1)$ and $(-5, 5)$ windows are qualitatively similar to those reported below. All dependent variables are trimmed at the 1st and 99th percentiles to mitigate the effect of outliers on our results. Trimming the data at the 1st and 99th means dropping all observations that are lower (higher) than the value at the 1st (99th) percentile. We find similar results after trimming the dependent variables at the 5th and 95th percentiles. We also find qualitatively similar results after winsorizing the dependent variables at the 1st and 99th percentiles, where "winsorizing" means setting the lower- and uppermost percentiles equal to values at the 1st and 99th percentiles, respectively.

To correct for heteroskedasticity, we use weighted least squares (WLS) regressions, where the weight is the inverse of the standard deviation of the estimation period residuals. We also repeat our analysis using ordinary least squares (OLS) regressions and the maximum likelihood estimation (MLE) procedure of Eckbo et al. (1990).[9] The OLS results are qualitatively similar to those reported here. We only report the MLE results for the cross-sectional analysis of the CWE variable since the results for rivals, customers, and suppliers are not substantially different from those based on WLS and OLS estimation. We also repeat our cross-sectional analyses for rivals, customer, and supplier portfolios that include only regional (state) firms, or firms whose headquarters are located in either the target or bidder headquarter region (state). For space considerations, we only report the results of our analyses for all firms and state firms. The results for portfolios that include regional firms are very similar to those reported for state firms, and thus are omitted.

5.3.1. Regression of combined wealth effect

In Table 6 we report results of the regression analysis of the CWE variable on the various independent variables. In both the WLS and MLE models, the coefficient on the Herfindahl index of the takeover industry is positive and significant at the 1% level, a result that is consistent with both the productive efficiency and collusion hypotheses. However, inconsistent with the collusion hypothesis, the coefficients on *Change in Herfindahl Index* is not significantly different from zero. To further examine the collusion hypothesis, we interact *Change in Herfindahl Index* with *Herfindahl Index* to test whether the takeover-induced change in concentration has a more significant effect on the combined wealth variable at high levels of pretakeover concentration.

---

[9] Eckbo et al. (1990) show that if managers of the takeover firms have private information regarding the synergies from the takeover and/or the takeover is partially anticipated by market participants, standard ordinary least squares and generalized least squares estimators can be inconsistent. They develop a maximum likelihood estimation procedure that produces consistent estimators. Their cross-sectional model is

$$AR_j = \left[X_j\beta + w \frac{n\left(X_j\frac{\beta}{w}\right)}{N\left(X_j\frac{\beta}{w}\right)} \right] \left[1 - N\left(X_j\frac{\beta}{w}\right) \right] + \varepsilon_j,$$

where AR_j is the abnormal return to firm j, X_j is the vector of independent variables, β is the vector of parameters to be estimated, $n(\cdot)$ and $N(\cdot)$ represent the standard normal density and distribution functions, W represents the standard error of the distribution of managers' private information, and ε_j is the error term.

Table 6

Cross-sectional estimates for the combined wealth gain to target and bidder firms

The dependent variable is *Combined Wealth Effect*, which is the cumulative abnormal return to a value-weighted portfolio of the bidder and target for the $(-2, 2)$ window. The dependent variable is trimmed at the 1st and 99th percentile. The weight used in the weighted least squares (WLS) regressions is the inverse of the standard deviation of the estimation period residuals. Maximum likelihood estimates (MLE) are based on the regression procedure of Eckbo et al. (1990). In the MLE models, W represents the standard error of the distribution of managers' private information. *Herfindahl Index* is the sales-based Herfindahl index of the takeover industry. *Change in Herfindahl Index* is equal to 2 target market share bidder market share. *Takeover Input Coefficient* is the dollar amount of the supplier industry's output sold to the takeover industry divided by the takeover industry's total output. *Supplier Concentration* is the weighted average of the Herfindahl indices of all supplier industries, in which the weight for every supplier industry is the corresponding *Takeover Input Coefficient*. *Customer Concentration* is equal to $\sum_{i=1}^{n} S_i^2$, where S_i is the estimated percentage of the takeover industry's output sold to firm i. *Foreign competition* is the takeover industry's total imports divided by its total supply. *Relative Size* is the market value of equity of the target divided by that of the bidder. *Offer Includes Stocks* is a dummy variable that equals 1 if the bid includes stock. *Hostile Takeover* is a dummy variable that equals 1 if the takeover is characterized as hostile by SDC.

	WLS		MLE	
	(1)	(2)	(3)	(4)
Intercept	1.15 (1.28)	0.92 (0.73)	−3.96*** (−6.00)	−3.18*** (−3.45)
Herfindahl Index	13.51*** (3.29)	12.27*** (2.96)	15.06*** (2.67)	13.85** (2.40)
Change in Herfindahl Index	7.04 (0.23)	5.54 (0.18)	5.38 (0.11)	5.16 (0.10)
Herfindahl Index × Change in Herfindahl Index	−52.35 (−0.75)	−42.38 (−0.60)	−42.66** (−2.36)	−42.68** (−2.14)
Supplier Concentration		4.23 (0.26)		2.47 (0.06)
Supplier Concentration × Relative Size		31.20* (1.75)		31.46 (1.57)
Customer Concentration	14.39*** (2.86)	13.97*** (2.70)	12.83 (1.52)	13.26* (1.79)
Foreign Competition	4.13 (1.27)	3.40 (1.01)	3.43 (0.79)	3.21 (0.67)
Herfindahl Index × Foreign Competition	−42.98** (−2.32)	−41.98** (−2.27)	−42.09* (−1.84)	−41.52 (−1.62)
Relative Size	2.62*** (5.78)	1.05 (1.04)	8.08*** (5.10)	6.51 (1.04)
Offer Includes Stock	−3.78*** (−4.95)	−3.67*** (−4.79)	−4.23*** (−3.84)	−4.39*** (−3.75)
Hostile Takeover	8.56*** (3.85)	8.52*** (3.84)	9.43* (1.89)	5.46 (1.23)
W			34.71*** (6.33)	33.02*** (4.33)
Number of observations	452	452	452	452
Adjusted R^2	0.19	0.19		

The symbols *, **, and *** indicate statistical significance at the 10%, 5%, and 1% levels, respectively (*t*-values are in parentheses).

As shown in the MLE results, the coefficient on this variable is negative and statistically significant. This result is inconsistent with the collusion hypothesis and consistent with the evidence in Eckbo (1992), who reports a negative relation between abnormal returns to the merging firms and the change in concentration in a sample of challenged mergers.

Further, while the coefficient on *Foreign Competition* by itself is insignificant, the coefficient on the interaction between *Herfindahl Index* and *Foreign Competition* is negative and significant. This evidence suggests that foreign competition seems to increase the competition in concentrated takeover industries, leading to lower takeover gains to the target and bidder combined. Note that since our regressions include interaction terms, the total marginal effect of a change in any given variable will obviously depend on the values of the variables with which it is interacted. When interpreting each coefficient separately, we focus on the case in which the value of the interacted variable is close to zero. For example, since the coefficient on the interaction between *Foreign Competition* and *Herfindahl Index* is negative and significant, our interpretation of the positive relation between *Herfindahl Index* and the combined wealth variable is only valid for industries with low foreign competition. In fact, the positive relation between the two variables weakens as foreign competition increases.

In Models 2 and 4 of Table 6, the coefficients on the supplier concentration variable are insignificant. We also interact this variable with *Relative Size*, which is used as a proxy for the size of the combined firm relative to the independent target and bidder. The positive and significant coefficient on the interaction between *Supplier Concentration* and *Relative Size* is consistent with the buyer power hypothesis; a takeover that results in a large combined firm relative to the independent target and bidder firms results in higher buyer power if suppliers are concentrated. In unreported regressions, we find insignificant the coefficient on the interaction term between *Supplier Concentration* and the *Change in Herfindahl Index*, which is used to proxy for the importance of the merger relative to the takeover industry. This result suggests that the takeover does not have to be large relative to the takeover industry in order to increase the buyer power of the merging firms. However, we should expect that the size of the takeover should be relevant when we examine the wealth effects on suppliers.

In addition, the coefficients on *Customer Concentration* are positive and statistically significant. This evidence is consistent with the productive efficiency hypothesis. The effects of the control variables on the CWE variable are consistent with the extant literature. Finally, the value for W, which represents the standard error of the distribution of managers' private information in the MLE procedure, is positive and significant. This result is consistent with the rationale underlying the econometric model of Eckbo et al. (1990).

5.3.2. Regression of abnormal returns to rivals

Our results on the determinants of the CAR to rival firms are reported in Table 7. We report regression results for CARs to portfolios that include all rivals (Model 1), and to portfolios that include only state rivals (Model 2). In both models, the coefficient on *Herfindahl Index* is positive but statistically insignificant. The coefficient on *Change in Herfindahl Index* is negative and significant in Model 1, and negative with a *t* statistic of −1.52 in Model 2. These results are inconsistent with the collusion hypothesis,

Table 7

Weighted least squares regression of cumulative abnormal returns to rival firms

The sample includes 463 horizontal takeovers during the period 1987–1999. The dependent variable is the cumulative abnormal return to an equally weighted portfolio of rival firms for the $(-2, 2)$ window. Abnormal returns are estimated using a market model. The weight used in the weighted least squares regressions is the inverse of the standard deviation of the estimation period residuals. State Rivals are rival firms whose headquarters are located in either the target or bidder headquarter state. The dependent variable is trimmed at the 1st and 99th percentile. Rivals are all single-segment firms operating in the takeover industry. *Herfindahl Index* is the Herfindahl index of the takeover industry. *Change in Herfindahl Index* is equal to 2 target market share bidder market share. *Takeover Input Coefficient* is the dollar amount of the supplier industry's output sold to the takeover industry divided by the takeover industry's total output. *Supplier Concentration* is the weighted average of the Herfindahl indices of all supplier industries, where the weight for every supplier industry is the corresponding *Takeover Input Coefficient*. *Customer Concentration* is equal to $\sum_{i=1}^{n} S_i^2$, where S_i is the estimated percentage of the takeover industry's output sold to firm i. *Foreign competition* is the takeover industry's total imports divided by its total supply. *Combined Wealth Effect* is the cumulative abnormal return to a value-weighted portfolio of bidder and target firms over the $(-2, 2)$ window.

	All rivals	State rivals
	(1)	(2)
Intercept	0.73* (1.71)	−0.14 (−0.20)
Herfindahl Index	1.44 (0.76)	1.88 (0.53)
Change in Herfindahl Index	−77.96* (−1.86)	−2.99 (−1.52)
Herfindahl Index × *Change in Herfindahl Index*	95.18 (1.14)	−254.49 (−1.11)
Supplier Concentration	−11.02* (−1.76)	5.96 (0.57)
Supplier Concentration × *Change in Herfindahl Index*	1000.54*** (2.82)	1162.57** (2.35)
Customer Concentration	0.39 (0.17)	−2.99 (−0.72)
Foreign Competition	1.62 (1.10)	1.61 (0.70)
Herfindahl Index × *Foreign Competition*	−17.54* (−1.86)	−15.71 (−0.83)
Combined Wealth Effect	0.08*** (6.15)	0.08*** (3.61)
Number of observations	445	355
Adjusted R^2	0.09	0.04

The symbols *, **, and *** indicate statistical significance at the 10%, 5%, and 1% levels, respectively (*t*-values are in parentheses).

which predicts a positive relation, and remarkably consistent with the evidence in Eckbo (1985, 1992). The coefficient on the interaction between *Foreign Competition* and *Herfindahl Index* is negative and significant in Model 1. This evidence suggests that foreign competition can intensify competition in concentrated takeover industries, and thus can lead to lower expected takeover gains for firms in these industries.

The coefficient on the interaction between *Change in Herfindahl Index* and *Supplier Concentration* is positive and statistically significant in both models. This evidence suggests that rival firms benefit from the takeover between two large industry firms only when their suppliers are concentrated. This result is consistent with Snyder (1996). Fee and Thomas (2004) discuss the monopsonistic collusion variation of the buyer power hypothesis. Under this hypothesis, firms in the takeover industry can more easily collude in the posttakeover period to reduce their input prices. Our evidence that rivals seem to benefit from an increase in the buyer power only if suppliers are concentrated is inconsistent with this hypothesis and consistent with the evidence in Fee and Thomas (2004). Finally, as shown in both models, the coefficient on the CWE variable is positive and highly significant. Since the combined wealth variable is correlated with some of the independent variables as reported in Table 6, we repeat our results after excluding this variable and find similar results.

As reported in Table 2, the takeover intensity varies considerably across the takeover industries. Since under the productive efficiency hypothesis takeover announcements may release information regarding overall industry restructuring, it is important to control for the extent to which a takeover announcement came as a surprise. Thus, in the spirit of Song and Walkling (2000), we construct a variable that is equal to the number of months since the announcement of the last horizontal takeover within the industry. Including this variable in the regressions of the CAR to rivals produces an insignificant coefficient and does not change the results pertaining to the other independent variables.

5.3.3. Regression of abnormal returns to customers

Table 8 displays results of regressing the CAR to customers on the various explanatory variables. Models 1 and 2 (3 and 4) present results for the customer portfolios that include all customers (state customers). In addition to the explanatory variables discussed above, we add *Customer Input Coefficient*. Recall that this variable captures the dependence of the customer industry on the input bought from the takeover industry. We expect that a higher *Customer Input Coefficient* should be associated with a higher magnitude of abnormal returns to customers. To test this hypothesis, in addition to *Customer Input Coefficient*, we add *Customer Negative CAR Dummy*, a dummy variable that equals 1 if the dependent variable is negative, and we interact this variable with *Customer Input Coefficient*. The coefficient on *Customer Input Coefficient* is positive and significant. Further, the coefficient on the interaction between *Customer Input Coefficient* and *Customer Negative CAR Dummy* is significantly negative in all models except Model 3. In Models 1, 2, and 4, the sum of the two coefficients, which represents the coefficient on *Customer Input Coefficient* for the negative CAR range, is negative and statistically significant using an *F*-test. These results suggest that in the positive CAR range, an increase in *Customer Input Coefficient* results in higher abnormal returns to corporate customers, while in the negative CAR range, an increase in the *Customer Input Coefficient* results in lower abnormal returns to corporate customers.

The results presented in Table 8 do not support the collusion hypothesis. The coefficients on *Change in Herfindahl Index* are insignificant in all reported models. Further, the interaction between *Change in Herfindahl Index* and the Herfindahl index of the takeover industry is either insignificant (Models 1 and 4) or positive and

Table 8

Weighted least squares regression of cumulative abnormal return to customers

The sample includes 463 horizontal takeovers during the period 1987–1999. The dependent variable is the cumulative abnormal return (CAR) on an equally weighted portfolio of customer firms for the (−2, 2) window. The weight used in the weighted least squares regressions is the inverse of the standard deviation of the estimation period residuals. The dependent variable is trimmed at the 1st and 99th percentile. *State Customers* are customer firms whose headquarters are located in either the target or bidder headquarter state. The *Main Customer* industry is the industry that buys the highest percentage of the takeover industry's output. The *Dependent Customer* industry is the industry whose production depends on the takeover industry's output more than any other customer industry. *Customer Input Coefficient* is the dollar amount of the takeover industry's output sold to the corporate customer industry divided by the total output of the corporate customer industry. A customer industry is included in the sample if its *Customer Input Coefficient* is greater than 1%. *Customer Negative CAR Dummy* is a dummy variable that equals 1 if the dependent variable is negative. *Herfindahl Index* is the Herfindahl index of the takeover industry. *Change in Herfindahl Index* is equal to 2 target market share bidder market share. *Customer Concentration* is equal to $\sum_{i=1}^{n} S_i^2$, where S_i is the estimated percentage of the takeover industry's output sold to firm i. *Foreign competition* is the takeover industry's total imports divided by its total supply. *Combined Wealth Effect* is the cumulative abnormal return to a value-weighted portfolio of the bidder and target for the (−2, 2) window.

	All customers		State customers	
	Main customer (1)	Dependent customer (2)	Main customer (3)	Dependent customer (4)
Intercept	0.92*** (10.44)	1.62*** (12.01)	2.80*** (9.52)	4.28*** (7.54)
Customer Negative CAR Dummy	−1.86*** (−20.16)	−2.83*** (−20.53)	−5.18*** (−16.77)	−8.32*** (−15.16)
Customer Input Coefficient	1.73** (2.55)	2.51** (2.43)	1.55** (2.12)	1.80** (3.35)
Customer Input Coefficient × Customer Negative CAR Dummy	−3.86*** (−4.73)	−3.60*** (−2.94)	−0.42 (−1.32)	−3.67** (−2.12)
Herfindahl Index	−0.97* (−1.88)	−1.79** (−2.35)	−2.75* (−1.67)	0.39 (0.11)
Change in Herfindahl Index	1.62 (0.35)	−7.73 (−1.15)	0.68 (0.05)	−1.48 (−0.03)
Herfindahl Index × Change in Herfindahl Index	4.99 (0.51)	31.23** (2.13)	38.10** (2.43)	27.81 (1.37)
Customer Concentration	2.59*** (2.58)	−0.17 (−0.12)	1.77 (0.37)	−2.24 (−0.20)
Foreign Competition	−0.81* (−1.82)	−1.06 (−1.59)	−1.07 (−0.71)	0.88 (0.28)
Herfindahl Index × Foreign Competition	6.60* (1.87)	11.95** (2.27)	1.82 (0.21)	−1.45 (−0.06)
Combined Wealth Effect	0.01** (2.01)	0.00 (0.83)	0.02 (1.29)	0.03** (2.43)
Number of observations	327	357	260	242
Adjusted R^2	0.63	0.60	0.54	0.52

The symbols *, **, and *** indicate statistical significance at the 10%, 5%, and 1% levels, respectively (*t*-values are in parentheses).

significant (Models 2 and 3), supporting our earlier conclusion that horizontal takeovers do not appear to be driven by collusion motives. The negative and significant coefficient on *Herfindahl Index* in Models 1, 2, and 3 is consistent with the hypothesis that concentrated industries can retain more of the wealth created which leads to customers benefiting less from the takeover gains. The positive and significant coefficient on the interaction between *Foreign Competition* and *Herfindahl Index* in Models 1 and 2 is consistent with the hypothesis that imports intensify competition in highly concentrated takeover industries which benefits customers. Finally, the positive and significant coefficient on the CWE is inconsistent with the collusion hypothesis, which predicts a transfer of wealth from customers to the takeover industry.

5.3.4. Regression of abnormal returns to suppliers

The results on the determinants of the CAR to suppliers are reported in Table 9. Models 1 and 2 (3 and 4) present results for supplier portfolios that include all suppliers (state suppliers). Since abnormal returns to any supplier industry should be related to the percentage of the industry's output sold to the takeover industry, we add *Supplier Percentage Sold* to our regressions. Recall that this variable measures the importance of the takeover industry as a buyer from the supplier industry. We expect that higher *Supplier Percentage Sold* should be associated with a higher magnitude of abnormal returns to suppliers. To test this hypothesis, we include *Negative Supplier CAR Dummy* and interact this variable with *Supplier Percentage Sold*. The results reported in Models 1, 2, and 3 that pertain to these variables suggest that for takeovers that result in positive (negative) CARs to the suppliers, an increase in the percentage of output sold to the takeover industry results in higher (lower) abnormal returns.

The results in Table 9 are inconsistent with the collusion hypothesis. The coefficients on *Herfindahl Index*, *Change in Herfindahl Index*, and the interaction between these two variables are statistically insignificant in all reported models. In order to test the buyer power hypothesis, we add to the regressions *Weighted Supplier Concentration*, which is the Herfindahl index of the respective supplier industry weighted by *Supplier Percentage Sold*. The concentration measure is weighted by *Supplier Percentage Sold* to account for the importance of the takeover industry as a buyer to the respective supplier industry. Although the coefficient on *Weighted Supplier Concentration* is statistically insignificant, the coefficient on the interaction between this variable and *Change in Herfindahl Index* is negative and statistically significant in Models 1, 2, and 4. This evidence suggests that the increased buyer power of the combined firm results in significantly lower CAR to suppliers if the takeover is large relative to the takeover industry *and* the supplier industry is highly concentrated. This finding is consistent with the evidence in Fee and Thomas (2004), who find that suppliers that operate in more-concentrated industries experience larger declines in postmerger operating performance. Finally, the positive and significant coefficient on CWE in Models 1, 3, and 4 indicates that suppliers seem to benefit more from takeovers that result in higher combined wealth.

Table 9

Weighted least squares regression of cumulative abnormal returns to suppliers

The sample includes 463 horizontal takeovers during the period 1987–1999. The dependent variable is the cumulative abnormal return (CAR) on an equally weighted portfolio of supplier firms for the (−2, 2) window. The weight used in the weighted least squares regressions is the inverse of the standard deviation of the estimation period residuals. The dependent variable is trimmed at the 1st and 99th percentile. *State Suppliers* are supplier firms whose headquarters are located in either the target or bidder headquarter state. The *Main Supplier* industry is the industry that supplies the main input to the takeover industry. The *Dependent Supplier* industry is the supplier industry whose percentage of output sold to the takeover industry is higher than that of any other supplier industry. *Supplier Percentage Sold* is the percentage of the supplier industry's output sold to the takeover industry. *Supplier Negative CAR Dummy* is a dummy variable that equals 1 if the dependent variable is negative. *Herfindahl Index* is the Herfindahl index of the takeover industry. *Change in Herfindahl Index* is equal to 2 target market share bidder market share. *Weighted Supplier Concentration* is the Herfindahl index of the corresponding supplier industry, weighted by *Supplier Percentage Sold*. *Foreign Competition* is the takeover industry's total imports divided by its total supply. *Combined Wealth Effect* is the cumulative abnormal return to a value-weighted portfolio of the bidder and target firms for the (−2, 2) window.

	All suppliers		State suppliers	
	Main supplier (1)	Dependent supplier (2)	Main supplier (3)	Dependent supplier (4)
Intercept	1.13*** (10.89)	1.98*** (8.64)	1.94*** (6.83)	4.89*** (6.78)
Supplier Negative CAR Dummy	−2.21*** (−22.44)	−3.92*** (−18.67)	−4.33*** (−13.96)	−9.19*** (−12.67)
Supplier Percentage Sold	1.04** (2.11)	2.57** (2.07)	2.89** (2.01)	2.16 (1.14)
Supplier Percentage Sold × Supplier Negative CAR Dummy	−1.49** (−2.33)	−3.74*** (−2.84)	−4.85*** (−2.89)	−1.69 (0.93)
Herfindahl Index	−0.61 (−1.30)	−0.01 (−0.01)	1.08 (0.74)	2.09 (0.56)
Change in Herfindahl Index	−1.87 (−0.44)	13.86 (1.56)	0.32 (0.01)	10.26 (1.43)
Herfindahl Index × Change in Herfindahl Index	5.49 (0.59)	−28.06 (−1.43)	9.48 (0.13)	−252.73 (−0.78)
Weighted Supplier Concentration	−0.94 (−0.78)	2.60 (0.99)	−0.95 (−0.39)	−2.10 (−0.62)
Weighted Supplier Concentration × Change in Herfindahl Index	−381.92* (−1.80)	−1150.51*** (−3.20)	−701.35 (−1.06)	−973.90** (−2.13)
Foreign Competition	0.09 (0.24)	−1.30* (−1.74)	1.81 (1.27)	8.78* (1.81)
Herfindahl Index × Foreign Competition	0.61 (0.26)	−1.37 (−0.30)	−19.33 (−1.06)	−43.62 (−0.78)
Combined Wealth Effect	0.01** (2.24)	0.01 (1.08)	0.06*** (2.79)	0.04** (2.15)
Number of observations	309	391	259	252
Adjusted R^2	0.67	0.59	0.69	0.58

The symbols *, **, and *** indicate statistical significance at the 10%, 5%, and 1% levels, respectively (*t*-values are in parentheses).

6. Conclusion

We examine the relative importance of collusion and buyer power motives using a sample of 463 horizontal takeovers and tender offers during the period 1987–1999. We use the benchmark IO accounts for the US economy to identify firms in industries that supply inputs to the takeover industry (suppliers), and firms in industries that use the output of the takeover industry (corporate customers). We examine the wealth effects of takeover announcements on the merging firms and their rivals, suppliers, and corporate customers. As summarized in Table 10, our findings suggest that efficiency considerations, rather than collusion or buyer power motives, drive the average horizontal takeover in our sample. In particular, consistent with the productive efficiency hypothesis, takeovers that result in positive CWE s to target and bidder firms (about 60% of the sample takeovers) appear to benefit suppliers and corporate customers.

In our cross-sectional analysis of abnormal returns, we find no support for collusion as a motive for horizontal takeovers. We find that the merger-induced increase in the concentration of the takeover industry is not related to the abnormal returns to suppliers and customers, but is negatively related to the abnormal returns to the merging firms and their industry rivals. These results are remarkably consistent with the evidence in Eckbo (1985, 1992), who also finds evidence inconsistent with the collusion hypothesis for a sample of challenged mergers and during an active antitrust period. Our overall evidence suggests that the lenient antitrust policy in recent years does not appear to have resulted in predominantly anticompetitive takeovers, and is consistent with the evidence in Eckbo (1992) regarding the effect of the antitrust overhang.

Table 10

Summary of results

This table displays a summary of the signs of announcement period abnormal returns to the merging firms and their rivals, customers, and suppliers. The sample includes 463 horizontal takeovers during the period 1987–1999. Customer and supplier industries are identified using the benchmark input-output accounts for the US economy as described in Table 4. Abnormal returns are estimated using a market model. Abnormal returns to rivals, suppliers, and customers are estimated using equally weighted portfolios of single-segment firms in the corresponding industry. CWE is the cumulative abnormal return to a value-weighted portfolio of the bidder and target.

	Predictions			Results		
	Productive efficiency	Collusion	Buyer power	Overall sample	Positive CWE takeovers	Negative CWE takeovers
Merging firms	Negative	Positive	Positive	Positive	Positive	Negative
Rivals	Unrestricted	Positive	Positive	Positive	Positive	Negative
Customers	Unrestricted	Negative	Unrestricted	Positive	Positive	Negative
Suppliers	Unrestricted	Negative	Negative	Negative	Positive	Negative

Our results suggest that some takeovers seem to increase the buyer power of the merging firms vis-à-vis their suppliers. In particular, we find that the abnormal returns to suppliers are lower if the merger is between two large firms and the supplier industry is concentrated. This result is consistent with the countervailing power theory of Galbraith (1952) and the theoretical models in Snyder (1996, 1998). Along with the evidence in Fee and Thomas (2004), our results suggest that industry consolidations can help increase the efficiency of upstream industries. This finding suggests that a fruitful area for future research is to examine the effects of the restructuring of one industry on the consolidation of other related industries.

References

Andrade, G. and E. Stafford, 2004, "Investigating the Economic Role of Mergers," *Journal of Corporate Finance*, 10, 1–36.

Andrade, G., M. Mitchell and E. Stafford, 2001, "New Evidence and Perspectives on Mergers," *Journal of Economic Perspective*, 15, 103–120.

Banerjee, A. and E. W. Eckard, 1998, "Are Mega-Mergers Anticompetitive? Evidence from the First Great Merger Wave," *RAND Journal of Economics*, 29, 803–827.

Berkovitch, E. and M. P. Narayanan, 1993, "Motives for Takeovers: An Empirical Investigation," *Journal of Financial and Quantitative Analysis*, 28, 347–362.

Betton, S. and E. B. Eckbo, 2000, "Toeholds, Bid Jumps, and Expected Payoffs in Takeovers," *Review of Financial Studies*, 13, 841–882.

Bradley, M., A. Desai and E. H. Kim, 1988, "Synergistic Gains from Corporate Acquisitions and Their Division Between the Stockholders of Target and Acquiring Firms," *Journal of Financial Economics*, 21, 3–40.

Chipty, T. and C. M. Snyder, 1999, "The Role of Firm Size in Bilateral Bargaining: A Study of the Cable Television Industry," *Review of Economics and Statistics*, 81, 326–340.

Comment, R. and G. W. Schwert, 1995, "Poison or Placebo? Evidence on the Deterrence and Wealth Effects of Modern Antitakover Measures," *Journal of Financial Economics*, 39, 3–43.

Coval, J. D. and T. J. Moskowitz, 1999, "Home Bias at Home: Local Equity Preference in Domestic Portfolios," *Journal of Finance*, 54, 2045–2073.

Datta, S., M. Iskandar-Datta and K. Raman, 2001, "Executive Compensation and Corporate Acquisition Decisions," *Journal of Finance*, 56, 2299–2336.

Dobson, P., M. Waterson and A. Chu, 1998, "The Welfare Consequences of the Exercise of Buyer Power," Unpublished Working Paper, Office of Fair Trading, London.

Domowitz, I., G. Hubbard and B. Petersen, 1986, "Business Cycles and the Relationship Between Concentration and Price-Costs Margins," *RAND Journal of Economics*, 17, 1–17.

Eckbo, E. B., 1983, "Horizontal Mergers, Collusion, and Stockholder Wealth," *Journal of Financial Economics*, 11, 241–273.

Eckbo, E. B., 1985, "Mergers and the Market Concentration Doctrine: Evidence from the Capital Market," *Journal of Business*, 58, 325–349.

Eckbo, E. B., 1992, "Mergers and the Value of Antitrust Deterrence," *Journal of Finance*, 47, 1005–1029.

Eckbo, E. B. and P. Wier, 1985, "Antimerger Policy Under the Hart-Scott-Rodino Act: A Reexamination of the Market Power Hypothesis," *Journal of Law and Economics*, 28, 119–149.

Eckbo, E. B., V. Maksimovic and J. Williams, 1990, "Consistent Estimation of Cross-Sectional Models in Event Studies," *Review of Financial Studies*, 3, 343–365.

Ellison, S. F. and C. M. Snyder, 2001, "Countervailing Power in Wholesale Pharmaceuticals," Unpublished Working Paper, Massachusetts Institute of Technology.

Fan, J. P. H. and L. H. P. Lang, 2000, "The Measurement of Relatedness: An Application to Corporate Diversification," *Journal of Business*, 73, 629–660.

Fee, C. E. and S. Thomas, 2004, "Sources of Gains in Horizontal Takeovers: Evidence from Customer, Supplier, and Rival Firms," *Journal of Financial Economics*, 74, 423–460.

Frank, R. and D. Solomon, 2002, "Cable Industry Mergers? Let's Count the Ways," *The Wall Street Journal, January*, 22, C1.

Galbraith, J. K., 1952, *American Capitalism: The Concept of Countervailing Power*, Houghton-Mifflin, Boston.

Harford, J., 1999, "Corporate Cash Reserves and Acquisitions," *Journal of Finance*, 54, 1969–1997.

Healy, P. M., K. G. Palepu and R. S. Ruback, 1992, "Does Corporate Performance Improve after Mergers?" *Journal of Financial Economics*, 31, 135–176.

Jarrell, G. A., J. Brickley and J. M. Netter, 1988, "The Market for Corporate Control: The Empirical Evidence Since 1980," *The Journal of Economic Perspectives*, 2, 49–68.

Jensen, M. C., 1986, "The Agency Costs of Free Cash Flow: Corporate Finance and Takeovers," *American Economic Review*, 76, 323–329.

Jensen, M. C., 1993, "The Modern Industrial Revolution, Exit, and the Failure of Internal Control Systems," *Journal of Finance*, 48, 831–880.

Jensen, M. C. and R. S. Ruback, 1983, "The Market for Corporate Control: The Scientific Evidence," *Journal of Financial Economics*, 11, 5–50.

Kahle, K. M. and R. A. Walkling, 1996, "The Impact of Industry Classifications on Financial Research," *Journal of Financial and Quantitative Analysis*, 31, 309–335.

Kale, J. R., O. Kini and H. E. Ryan, 2003, "Financial Advisors and Shareholder Wealth Gains in Corporate Takeovers," *Journal of Financial and Quantitative Analysis*, 38, 475–501.

Katics, M. M. and B. C. Petersen, 1994, "The Effect of Rising Import Competition on Market Power: A Panel Data Study of US Manufacturing," *Journal of Industrial Economics*, 42, 277–286.

Kim, H. E. and V. Singal, 1993, "Mergers and Market Power: Evidence from the Airline Industry," *The American Economic Review*, 83, 549–569.

Kwoka, J. E. J. and L. J. White, 1999, *The Antitrust Revolution: Economics Competition and Policy*, Oxford University Press, Oxford.

Lang, L. and R. M. Stulz, 1992, "Contagion and Competitive Intra-Industry Effects of Bankruptcy Announcements," *Journal of Financial Economics*, 32, 45–60.

Lang, L., R. Stulz and R. Walkling, 1989, "Managerial Performance, Tobin's Q, and the Gains from Successful Tender Offers," *Journal of Financial Economics*, 29, 315–335.

Lo, A. and C. Mackinlay, 1990, "When are Contrarian Profits due to Stock Market Overreaction," *Review of Financial Studies*, 3, 175–206.

Maksimovic, V. and G. Phillips, 2001, "The Market for Corporate Assets: Who Engages in Mergers and Asset Sales and are There Efficiency Gains?" *Journal of Finance*, 2019–2065.

Maloney, M., R. McCormick and M. Mitchell, 1993, "Managerial Decision Making and Capital Structure," *Journal of Business*, 66, 189–217.

Maquieira, C., W. Megginson and L. Nail, 1998, "Wealth Creation Versus Wealth Redistributions in Pure Stock-for-Stock Mergers," *Journal of Financial Economics*, 48, 3–33.

McAfee, R. P. and M. A. Williams, 1988, "Can Event Studies Detect Anticompetitive Mergers?" *Economic Letters*, 28, 199–203.

Mikkelson, W. H. and M. M. Partch, 1988, "Withdrawn Security Offerings," *Journal of Financial and Quantitative Analysis*, 23, 119–133.

Mitchell, M. L. and J. H. Mulherin, 1996, "The Impact of Industry Shocks on Takeover and Restructuring Activity," *Journal of Financial Economics*, 41, 193–229.

Morck, R., A. Shleifer and R. Vishny, 1990, "Do Managerial Objectives Drive Bad Acquisitions," *Journal of Finance*, 45, 31–48.

Mulherin, H. J. and A. L. Boone, 2000, "Comparing Acquisitions and Divestitures," *Journal of Corporate Finance*, 6, 117–139.

Mullin, G. L., J. C. Mullin and W. P. Mullin, 1995, "The Competitive Effects of Mergers: Stock Market Evidence from the US Steel Dissolution Suit," *RAND Journal of Economics*, 26, 314–330.

Ravenscraft, D., 1983, "Structure-Profit Relationship at the Line of Business and Industry Level," *Review of Economics and Statistics*, 65, 22–31.

Roll, R., 1986, "The Hubris Hypothesis of Corporate Takeovers," *Journal of Business*, 59, 197–216.

Schumacher, U., 1991, "Buyer Structure and Seller Performance in US Manufacturing Industries," *Review of Economics and Statistics*, 73, 277–284.

Schwert, G. W., 1996, "Markup Pricing in Mergers and Acquisitions," *Journal of Financial Economics*, 41, 153–192.

Schwert, G. W., 2000, "Hostility in Takeovers: In the Eyes of the Beholder," *Journal of Finance*, 55, 2599–2640.

Servaes, H., 1991, "Tobin's Q and the Gains from Takeovers," *Journal of Finance*, 46, 409–419.

Shleifer, A. and R. W. Vishny, 2003, "Stock Market Driven Acquisitions," *Journal of Financial Economics*, 70, 295–311.

Singal, V., 1996, "Airline Mergers and Competition: An Integration of Stock and Product Price Effects," *Journal of Business*, 69, 233–268.

Snyder, C. M., 1996, "A dynamic Theory of Countervailing Power," *RAND Journal of Economics*, 27, 747–769.

Snyder, C. M., 1998, "Why Do Large Buyers Pay Lower Prices? Intense Supplier Competition," *Economics Letters*, 58, 205–209.

Song, M. H. and R. A. Walkling, 2000, "Abnormal Returns to Rivals of Acquisition Targets: A Test of the "Acquisition Probability Hypothesis"," *Journal of Financial Economics*, 55, 143–171.

Stigler, G. J., 1964, "A Theory of Oligopoly," *The Journal of Political Economy*, 72, 44–61.

Stillman, R., 1983, "Examining Antitrust Policy Towards Horizontal Mergers," *Journal of Financial Economics*, 11, 225–240.

Stole, L. A. and J. Zwiebel, 1996, "Organizational Design and Technology Choice Under Intrafirm Bargaining," *American Economic Review*, 86, 195–222.

Travlos, N., 1987, "Corporate Takeover Bids, Method of Payment and Bidding Firm's Stock Returns," *Journal of Finance*, 42, 943–963.

Chapter 15

ABNORMAL RETURNS TO RIVALS OF ACQUISITION TARGETS: A TEST OF THE "ACQUISITION PROBABILITY HYPOTHESIS"[*]

MOON H. SONG

San Diego State University, Department of Finance, College of Business Administration, San Diego, California, USA

RALPH A. WALKLING

Ohio State University, Faculty of Finance, Fisher College of Business, Columbus, Ohio, USA

Contents

[*] The authors are grateful for comments on earlier drafts by participants in finance workshops at the University of Alberta, Case Western University, Columbia University, North Carolina State University, and Purdue University. We also thank Anup Agrawal, Diane Denis, David Denis, Tom George, Kathy Kahle, Games Kenyon, René Stulz, Sunil Wahal, Jim Wansley, the editor (G. William Schwert), and an anonymous referee for helpful comments. Jan Jindra, Christine Lai, Jenny Liu, and Serguei Tichtchenko provided valuable research assistance.

This article originally appeared in the *Journal of Financial Economics*, Vol. 55, pp. 143–172 (2000).

Corporate Takeovers, Volume 1
Edited by B. Espen Eckbo
DOI: 10.1016/B978-0-12-381983-3.00015-0

Abstract

We develop and test the *Acquisition Probability Hypothesis*, which asserts that rivals of initial acquisition targets earn abnormal returns because of the increased probability that they will be targets themselves. On average, rival firms earn positive abnormal returns regardless of the form and outcome of acquisition. These returns increase significantly with the magnitude of surprise about the initial acquisition. Moreover, the cross-sectional variation of rival abnormal returns in the announcement period is systematically related to variables associated with the probability of acquisition. In addition, rivals that subsequently become targets earn significantly higher abnormal returns in the announcement period.

Keywords

acquisition, rivals, tender offer, mergers, collusion

JEL classification: G34, G14, G38, K21, G32

1. Introduction

An extensive literature, beginning with Eckbo (1983, 1985) and extending through Mitchell and Mulherin (1996), finds that rivals of acquisition targets earn significant, positive abnormal returns. The most widely cited explanation is that horizontal mergers eliminate competitors and facilitate collusion among the remaining firms. Yet, Eckbo (1983, 1985, 1992), Stillman (1983), and Eckbo and Wier (1985) all reject the collusion hypothesis, leaving the explanation for positive returns to rivals unclear. Moreover, we have little explanation for the wide cross-sectional variation in abnormal returns to rivals or the finding that only 50–60% of rival firms earn positive abnormal returns.

In this paper, we develop and test an alternate explanation for positive rival returns. Our explanation, the "acquisition probability hypothesis," asserts that rivals earn abnormal returns because of the increased probability that they will be targets themselves. In our model, the appearance of a bidder willing to pay a premium over the market price for a firm is *prima facie* evidence of a valuation differential for at least one firm in the industry. This differential may result from expected synergies or from target management's failure to anticipate and incorporate needed changes. In any case, the appearance of an unexpected acquisition attempt within an industry generates shock waves that cause firm-specific reassessment of the probability of an acquisition attempt for rivals.

The implications of the acquisition probability hypothesis are quite different from those of the collusion hypothesis. For example, acquisitions need not be horizontal to generate abnormal returns to rivals, nor must they be successful. The acquisition probability hypothesis also helps explain the cross-sectional differences in abnormal returns to rivals. Under our hypothesis, revisions in a rival's stock price occur because of *changes* in the perceived probability of acquisition attempts, and these changes vary systematically with individual firm characteristics.

Section 2 reveals the intuition behind the acquisition probability hypothesis and develops testable implications. Section 3 describes the data and methodology of the research. In particular, we develop a procedure to identify unexpected acquisitions within an industry. We then test the implications of the acquisition probability hypothesis on a sample of 141 unexpected acquisitions and 2459 rival firms over the 1982–1991 period. The results, all consistent with the acquisition probability hypothesis, are documented in Sections 4 and 5: (1) rival firms earn positive abnormal returns regardless of the form (horizontal or nonhorizontal) and outcome (successful or unsuccessful) of the initial industry acquisition. Abnormal returns to rival firms are significantly positive in all categories except horizontal acquisitions. (2) The abnormal return to rival firms tends to increase with the magnitude of surprise about an acquisition. (3) The characteristics of target firms are distinct from those of nontargets, but similar to those of rivals that subsequently become targets. (4) Furthermore, the cross-sectional variation in the abnormal returns to rival firms is systematically related to variables associated with the probability of acquisition. (5) The magnitude of returns to rivals is significantly, positively related to the probability of being a target. In addition, the abnormal return for rivals that subsequently become targets is significantly higher than for nontargeted rivals. In separate multivariate tests, we also document that the magnitude of returns to rivals is significantly greater in unregulated firms.

2. Background and hypotheses

Gort (1969) argues that mergers are caused by valuation differentials among market participants, triggered by economic shocks such as changes in technology, industry structure, and the regulatory environment. Since these shocks tend to be industry-specific, acquisitions cluster by industry. Jensen (1988) cites examples that illustrate this point. The sharp rise in interest rates, coupled with the sharp drop in oil prices, were the catalysts of massive restructuring in the oil industry during the early 1980s. The advent of radial tires tripled tire life and (since demand for tires was constant) tripled capacity in the tire industry. Excess capacity within the industry forced restructuring. In each case, an external catalyst (interest rates, oil prices, or technology) led to industry-wide restructuring. Mitchell and Mulherin (1996) detail the clustering of acquisitions within industries and the relation of acquisition waves to external shocks. Acquisition activity is distributed fairly evenly over the 8-year period of their sample; the percentage of acquisition activity occurring in any given year ranges from approximately 10% to 18%. Within specific industries, however, there is noticeable clustering: 50% of the acquisition activity within industries occurs within just 25% of the sample period.

Acquisition activity within an industry is associated with positive abnormal returns to rivals of the targeted firm. Eckbo (1983, 1985) finds that horizontal competitors of target firms earn significantly positive abnormal returns of 0.76% (Z = 2.59) over the 7-day period surrounding the merger proposal date. Eckbo and Wier (1985) report similar announcement period abnormal returns. Stillman (1983) does not aggregate rival firms into a single portfolio but instead reports separate results for the rivals of 11 different mergers. The abnormal return to rivals is positive in nine of the 11 cases analyzed. Mitchell and Mulherin (1996) report abnormal returns of 0.5% to rivals during the month of announcement.

The source of these positive rival returns is unresolved. Increased ease of collusion could explain the positive returns, but Eckbo (1983, 1985, 1992), Eckbo and Wier (1985), and Stillman (1983) reject this hypothesis. Alternative explanations include the signal of positive information about the value of an industry or increased synergies between rivals and subsequent bidders. To date, these explanations for positive returns and the substantial cross-sectional dispersion of these returns have been unexplored. In the paragraphs that follow, we develop a simple model to explain the level and existence of positive abnormal returns to rivals.

2.1. The acquisition probability model

At any point in time, a firm's market value is a weighted average of the values of the firm under current and alternative management(s) where the weights are the probability of the firm being controlled by the various managerial teams. Acquisition attempts will occur when the expected gain from an acquisition attempt exceeds the cost.

External catalysts, such as regulatory changes, technological innovation, changes in consumer tastes, and changes in an industry's cost structures, affect the probability of an acquisition attempt by changing the potential gains to competing managerial teams. An unexpected acquisition within an industry signals that the expected gain from bidding exceeds the cost for at least one firm in the industry. This leads to a revision in the value of rival firms based on their observed characteristics.

Let $p_r(x_1)$ and $E[v_r(x_2)]$ denote, respectively, the probability of rival r becoming a target and the expected return to a rival firm's shareholders, conditional on an acquisition attempt for their firm. x_1 and x_2 represent vectors of characteristics related to the probability of acquisition and firm value. According to the acquisition probability hypothesis, the abnormal return to rival r is

$$\text{AR}_r = \Delta p_r(x_1)E[v_r(x_2)], \tag{1}$$

where Δp_r is the change in the probability of an acquisition attempt for rival r associated with the initial acquisition announcement in its industry.

Analogous to the "information versus synergy" discussion of Bradley et al. (1983), we note that the initial industry acquisition announcement could also signal the existence or increased value of unique industry-specific resources. Under this alternative, the rival's probability of being a target need not change for its value to be affected. Here,

$$\text{AR}_r = E[v_r(x_2)]. \tag{2}$$

Of course, to the extent that the vectors of characteristics x_1 and x_2 overlap, empirical distinction of this alternative and the "acquisition probability hypothesis" is difficult. We note, however, that synergistic gains to rivals need not be realized for announcement period abnormal returns to be affected.

There are many reasons why rival firms are affected differently by external shocks. In the case of changing technology, for example, firms face different costs of adoption, have varying degrees of information about the new process, or have different attitudes towards the risk of new processes. For these reasons and others, the shift in the mean and/or variance of the distribution of potential or actual gains will vary across rival firms, causing cross-sectional variation in their abnormal returns.

External catalysts, which materialize in acquisition activity, cause revisions in the actual or perceived importance of certain firm-specific variables. For example, it is known that managerial ownership is inversely related to the probability of an acquisition attempt (Mikkelson and Partch, 1989; Song and Walkling, 1993). Yet, low managerial ownership by itself is not a reason for acquisition. The impact of managerial ownership on the probability of acquisition is irrelevant to a firm's value unless some economic catalyst suggests that acquisition is profitable. If this catalyst occurs, the importance of managerial ownership is magnified and prices adjust accordingly. Those *attractive* firms that are more easily acquired (i.e., low managerial ownership) receive greater revisions in their market value.

2.2. Implications of the acquisition probability hypothesis

This acquisition probability hypothesis suggests the following testable implications. First, rival firms earn (on average) significantly positive abnormal returns. Unlike the collusion hypothesis, positive abnormal returns for rivals need not be restricted to cases in which the initial acquisition attempt is horizontal or even successful. If an initial acquisition attempt within an industry signals an increased likelihood of a beneficial restructuring for that industry, its rivals will (on average) experience positive abnormal returns regardless of the form of the restructuring (i.e., horizontal or nonhorizontal). Moreover, the initial acquisition need not be successful to cause revisions in the returns to rivals. The appearance of a bid allows shareholders to experience gains, regardless of outcome, by selling on the open market at a revised, presumably higher, price. Second, average abnormal returns to rival firms will be positively related to the degree of surprise associated with the initial acquisition announcement for a particular industry. Third, the cross-sectional variation in the abnormal returns to rival firms will be systematically related to variables associated with the probability of acquisition. The literature suggests that smaller firms, with low managerial ownership, greater debt capacity, and lower growth have an increased probability of acquisition. Fourth, to the extent that the market correctly anticipates acquisition attempts, announcement returns will be higher for those rivals that subsequently become targets. Finally, we also test, but do not feature, another implication: abnormal returns will be lower for regulated firms since government intervention reduces the probability of their being acquired.

3. Data and methodology

Testing the acquisition probability hypothesis requires a list of acquisitions sorted chronologically within each industry, a list of rival firms, and proxy variables to test each of the implications. We begin with a list of acquisition bids compiled from W. T. Grimm's Mergerstat Review for the period from January 1, 1982 through December 31, 1991.[1] This database records formal, publicly announced transfers of ownership of at least 10% of a company's assets or equity where the purchase price is at least $500,000 and where one of the parties is a US company. Over the 1982–1991 period, Grimm reports 1353 acquisition bids. We confirm and in some cases revise the

---

[1] Until 1987, W.T. Grimm and Co. managed this database. Since 1987, Merrill Lynch Business Brokerage and Valuation Services has managed Mergerstat.

first announcement dates through the Wall Street Journal, defining the initial announcement date for a firm as the first indication of control-related discussions
following a minimum 3-month absence of such announcements.

3.1. Target firms and industry classification

We classify each target firm according to its Value Line industry during the quarter
preceding the acquisition announcement. Using Value Line industries enables us to
avoid some of the problems associated with SIC codes: Value Line classifies firms into
approximately 90 different industries, updating classifications as appropriate. Moreover, historical classifications are available.[2] In a subsequent section, rivals will be
defined using Value Line industries. Our purpose here is to identify target firms that
could affect inferences about the acquisition probability of these rivals. Of the 1353
target firms noted by W.T. Grimm, 470 are listed in Value Line, and these firms
comprise our sample for examining industry targets. We later discuss sensitivity tests
using the remaining Grimm targets not covered by Value Line.

3.2. Dormant periods and initial industry targets

Our primary proxy for the degree of surprise about industry acquisition activity is termed
the *dormant period*, the length of time (in months) since a previous acquisition announcement in the same industry. To determine the dormant period, target firms are
sorted chronologically within their Value Line industries. We eliminate regulated industries, including Air Transportation, Electric Utility, Finance and Investment Companies,
Insurance Firms, Savings and Loans, and Natural Gas. In an extension discussed at the
end of the paper, we repeat our methodology and analysis for firms in these industries.
An *initial industry target* is defined as the first firm in an industry to experience
acquisition activity following a minimum 12-month dormant period. *Rivals* are defined
as firms in the same Value Line industry at the time of the initial industry target.

Value Line recognizes changing business environments, creating new or deleting
old industries as appropriate. While Value Line's timeliness is a definite advantage,
changes in industry names must be recognized in our methodology. Where Value Line
combines industry classifications, we use the historical classifications of all firms as
appropriate to calculate the dormant period. For example, the brewing and soft drink
industries were combined in 1987 to form the beverage industry. If an acquisition

---

[2] Kahle and Walkling (1996) report that nearly 40% (80%) of the two- (four-) digit SIC codes of firms
classified by CRSP would be classified differently by Compustat. Moreover, although SIC codes change over
time, Compustat only reports the latest code. Consequently, researchers using historical Compustat data do
not have access to the SIC that existed at the time of interest. We use the classifications reported by Value
Line at the time of the acquisition announcement. We note that geographical location may preclude two firms
in the same industry from actually being rivals. Nevertheless, an acquisition in one part of the country could
still have information content for a distant firm in the same industry.

announcement occurs in the beverage industry after 1987, we trace the history of all firms in the beverage industry to determine whether this is the initial industry announcement. For the initial appearance of an industry, we determine the dormant period by tracing the classification history of the individual firms using the prior industrial classification of these firms.

To calculate dormant periods beginning prior to 1982, we examine the Wall Street Journal Index back to the beginning of 1977 for each firm in a target's Value Line Industry to ascertain whether it was a target. Of course, acquisition activity for smaller firms not covered by our databases could also signal industry activity. To the extent that we misclassify industries or miss initial industry targets, we have biased against finding support for our hypotheses.

Panel A of Table 1 reveals details of the distribution of initial targets for our sample. We identify 141 unregulated initial industry targets. The distribution of initial industry targets over the sample period is fairly uniform, with a slight decline in the 1989–1991 period. This is consistent with the literature. Comment and Schwert (1995), for example, find that 1.5% of their firms receive initial takeover bids each month during 1987–1988, but by 1990 this declines to 0.5% per month. Mitchell and Mulherin (1996) find the lowest level of acquisition activity for their sample in 1989.

Panel B reveals the distribution of industry characteristics for initial industry targets. By design, the minimum dormant period is 13 months; the mean, median, and maximum dormant periods are 38, 31, and 122 months, respectively. To the extent that the dormant period extends beyond the beginning of our data (1977) we understate its length. For example, suppose an initial acquisition occurs in January 1983 and there is no prior acquisition activity for this industry since 1977 (the beginning of our search). We set the dormant period to 72 months, although the actual length is longer. Consequently, the mean dormant period is understated. Consistent with the literature, we use a sales-based Herfindahl index to measure the degree of concentration within an industry. According to the collusion hypothesis, horizontal mergers within more concentrated industries facilitate collusion. By design, the Herfindahl index is constrained between zero and one. The mean and median Herfindahl indices for our sample are 0.14 and 0.16, respectively, indicating relatively low levels of concentration. An alternate measure of concentration is the number of rivals within an industry. A total of 2459 Value Line rivals are associated with the 141 initial industry targets. The number of rivals ranges from 3 to 50 per target firm, with the mean and median being 17 and 15, respectively. Eight of the 2459 rivals were bidders for firms outside their industry at the same time as an initial industry target was announced. Deleting these observations does not affect our results.

The health of an industry is indicative of opportunities for restructuring. Relatively unhealthy industries suggest turnaround opportunities; an initial industry target within an unhealthy industry could have a greater impact on rival firms than initial acquisitions in profitable industries. To test this, we include a measure of industry health in our analysis. Value Line ranks each industry it covers from best (rank $= 1$) to worst (rank $= L$), where L is the number of industries covered in a particular quarter. Since

Table 1

Target firms, rival firms, and dormant periods between initial industry targets over the sample

We identify 1353 target firms from W.T. Grimm for the period 1982–1991. Target firms are then sorted chronologically within their industries as defined by Value Line. The length of time since a previous acquisition announcement in the same Value Line industry is defined as the dormant period.[a] "An initial industry target" is the first firm in an industry to have acquisition activity after a minimum 12-month dormant period without acquisition activity in the industry; 141 unregulated firms meet this criteria. The Herfindahl index is calculated based on sales for each firm in the industry at the time of the initial acquisition announcement. Value Line ranks each of the approximately 90 industries it covers each quarter according to attractiveness to investors. The lowest rank (1) indicates the most attractive industry, and the highest rank (around 90) indicates a relatively unattractive industry. We measure this Value Line rank in the quarter before the initial acquisition announcement.

Panel A. Number of initial industry target firms per year

Year	N
1982	15
1983	14
1984	14
1985	16
1986	15
1987	15
1988	19
1989	11
1990	8
1991	14
Total	141

Panel B. Distribution of industry characteristics for initial industry targets

	Mean	Minimum	Quartile 1	Median	Quartile 3	Maximum
Dormant periods (months)	38	13	19	31	48	122
Herfindahl index of the industry	0.14	0.04	0.11	0.16	0.25	0.70
# Rivals per target firm	17.4	3	9	15	23	50
(total number of rivals is 2459)						
Normalized Value Line industry rank	0.52	0.01	0.31	0.51	0.77	1.00

[a]Before 1982, we check 5 years of reports on each rival firm in the Wall Street Journal Index to ascertain whether it was a target.

the number of industries varies slightly from quarter to quarter, we normalize industry rank by dividing by L. Thus by construction the distribution of relative rank ranges from close to zero to one, with mean and median around 0.5.

3.3. Calculating abnormal returns

We calculate abnormal returns using the market model and standard cumulative abnormal return (CAR) methodology. Since our objective is to explain the cross-sectional variation in rival returns, most of our analysis focuses on individual abnormal returns for each rival firm. Rival firm returns are not independent, however, since they are measured within the same industry over the same time period. Consequently, in discussing the significance of abnormal returns, we also report results after grouping the rivals of each target firm into an equal-weighted portfolio and treating the portfolio as a single observation.

Daily returns for 240 days (covering the period t-300 through t-61) are used to estimate market model parameters for each rival firm and portfolio; day t represents the announcement date for the initial industry target. We require a minimum of 100 daily returns, or the case is deleted. We compute the average abnormal return on day t as the average difference between actual observations and estimated returns for the rival firms analyzed. CARs summarize the price impact over the 2-day period $(-1, 0)$ surrounding the announcement of the initial industry target. Average standardized abnormal returns and average standardized CARs are used to create test statistics.

4. Abnormal returns to portfolios of rivals and the probability of acquisition

4.1. Abnormal returns to target and rival firms

Panel A of Table 2 presents abnormal returns for the entire sample of initial industry targets and their associated rival portfolios over an 11-day window surrounding the initial acquisition announcement. Target abnormal returns average a significant 16.7% for the announcement period $(-1, 0)$. They are also significantly positive beginning with day -4 of the preannouncement period. Abnormal returns to a portfolio of rivals average a significant 0.35% for the announcement period $(-1, 0)$ and a significant 0.56% during the longer period $(-5, +5)$. The percentage of rival portfolios earning positive abnormal returns is 58.2% in the $(-1, 0)$ period and 63.1% in the $(-5, +5)$ period.

Panel B of Table 2 reveals the distribution of abnormal returns for targets and individual rival firms over the period $(-1, 0)$. The average abnormal return to target firms is 16.7%; 87% of all target firms experience positive abnormal returns. The mean abnormal return for rival firms is significant beyond the 1% level ($z = 4.86$), averaging 0.36% for the 2-day period. The range of abnormal returns, however, is quite large; the minimum and maximum 2-day abnormal returns to rivals are -16.0% and 23.4%, respectively. About 52% of rival firms experience positive abnormal returns. Thus, while the mean abnormal return to rival firms is positive and significant, the distribution of returns is dispersed and symmetric around zero.

We also test hypotheses that the proportion of rivals with positive abnormal returns is (a) equal across all 141 observations and (b) equal to 50% in all observations. Chi-square tests, with approximated z-statistics of 9.82 and 9.99, respectively, reject both hypotheses, so there does appear to be a concentration of reaction in some industries. Multivariate tests, reported in later sections, include controls for industry effects.

Table 2

Abnormal returns to target and rival firms

Results are shown for individual target firms and portfolios of rivals. Abnormal returns to rivals are calculated in two ways: the portfolio approach of Panel A aggregates all rivals at the time of a particular initial industry target into one portfolio and treats the returns to this portfolio as a single observation. The individual approach of Panel B treats each rival as a separate observation.

Panel A. Abnormal returns to initial industry targets and portfolios of rival firms

Day	N	Initial target			Rival portfolios $N = 141$		
		AR (%)	z-Stat	% Pos.	AR (%)	z-Stat	% Pos.
−5	141	0.20	0.78	48.2	0.02	0.75	48.9
−4	141	1.09	5.83[a]	54.6	0.12	2.15[b]	58.9
−3	140	1.17	5.37[a]	60.0	0.09	1.15	50.4
−2	138	2.80	15.26[a]	70.3	0.16	2.49[b]	56.7
−1	132	*10.32*	*58.89[a]*	*81.8*	*0.17*	*3.11[a]*	*53.9*
0	141	7.29	29.96[a]	64.5	0.18	3.12[a]	56.9
1	141	0.16	1.15	41.8	0.05	0.62	51.1
2	141	−0.16	0.26	42.6	−0.10	−1.46	44.0
3	140	0.02	−0.72	45.7	−0.00	−0.09	53.9
4	140	−0.49	−2.41[b]	45.0	−0.05	−0.72	45.4
5	141	0.43	1.95[c]	48.9	−0.06	−0.66	46.8
−1, 0	141	*16.74*	*69.20[a]*	*87.2*	*0.35*	*4.41[a]*	*58.2*
−5, +5	141	*21.89*	*37.19[a]*	*91.5*	*0.56*	*3.21[a]*	*63.1*

Panel B. Distribution of abnormal announcement period (−1, 0) returns to target and individual rival firms

Category	N	Mean	Min.	Q1	Median	Q3	Max.	%Pos.
All initial industry target firms	141	16.74	−15.43	2.73	12.76	24.97	97.29	87.2
Individual rival firms	2459	0.36	−16.00	−1.45	0.10	1.95	23.38	52.3

[a]Denotes significance at 1% level.
[b]Denotes significance at 5% level.
[c]Denotes significance at 10% level.

4.2. Motives for initial acquisitions

To shed additional light on the relation between the abnormal return to rivals and the motives behind the initial industry acquisition, we examine the Wall Street Journal for the initial news stories describing the bid for the initial industry target. We identify over 22 phrases repeated frequently in the news articles and reduce these phrases to seven categories of motives. Caution must be applied in interpreting these classifications since the sample sizes of some categories are small. For example, we find only four targets and 62 associated rivals where the financial press explicitly mentions an "industry trend." Nevertheless, our results (available upon request for the sake of brevity) indicate that the highest mean and median abnormal returns to rivals are earned by this category of firms. With one exception, the mean and median returns to rivals (both 1.2%) in the "industry trend" category are more than double the values for the remaining categories. This is true regardless of whether returns to portfolios of rivals or returns to individual rivals are used.

4.3. Abnormal returns across portfolios of rival firms

In Table 3 we begin the analysis of rival abnormal returns conditional on target and bid characteristics. Specifically, we condition the sample on the outcome of the offer, the nature of the bid (horizontal or nonhorizontal), the degree of industry concentration, and the length of the dormant period. We also categorize acquisitions by initial target market value, the level of industry acquisition activity, industry health, the bid premia for the initial industry target, and whether this bid is the first, second, or a subsequent "initial" bid within the industry. Each of these categorizations is linked to the likelihood and potential gain from subsequent acquisition attempts on a rival, the degree of surprise surrounding the initial attempt, or the ease of subsequent collusion within the industry. Since our focus here is on univariate statistical significance across categories rather than explaining the cross-sectional dispersion of individual returns, we report results on (equal-weighted) portfolios of rivals. For each categorization, we report the mean target and mean and median returns to rival portfolios. We also report tests of significance for each subcategory. Except for the difference between the last two dormant-period classifications, tests for differences in abnormal returns to rivals across the subcategories of Table 3 are all insignificant. This includes both t-tests between the various subcategories and a Kruskall-Wallis nonparametric test.

4.4. The outcome and nature of the initial bid

The collusion hypothesis rests on the assumption that merger reduces the number of firms in an industry. This requires a successful, horizontal, acquisition. In contrast, the acquisition probability hypothesis is agnostic with regard to both the completion of the initial acquisition and its form (horizontal or nonhorizontal).

Abnormal announcement period returns experienced by targets of successful and unsuccessful acquisition bids are 21% and 15%, respectively. Mean abnormal returns, however, are insignificantly higher for portfolios of rivals when the initial bid is successful (t-statistic $= 0.16$) and median returns are actually negative for successful offers. Mean and median returns to portfolios of rivals associated with unsuccessful initial targets are significantly positive.

We define horizontal acquisitions as cases in which the initial industry target and its initial bidder share the same three-digit SIC code, as defined by CRSP. We obtain SIC codes for both target and bidder for 70 of the unregulated initial industry targets. Eleven of the initial industry targets are classified as horizontal; 59 are nonhorizontal. The remaining 71 cases, often involving a bid by individuals, are listed as not classified.

Table 3

Distribution of abnormal announcement period $(-1, 0)$ returns to targets and equal-weighted portfolios of rival firms

We identify 1353 target firms from W.T. Grimm for the period 1982–1991. Target firms are then sorted chronologically within their industries as defined by Value Line. The length of time since a previous acquisition announcement in the same Value Line industry is defined as the dormant period. Before 1982, we check 5 years of reports on each rival firm in the Wall Street Journal Index to determine whether it was a target. "An initial industry target" is the first firm in an industry to have acquisition activity after a minimum 12-month dormant period; 141 firms meet this criteria. Results are shown for target firms and portfolios of rivals classified by various criteria. Abnormal returns to rivals are calculated by aggregating all rivals at the time of a particular initial industry target into one portfolio and treating the returns to this portfolio as a single observation.

Category[a]	Target firm returns	Number of portfolios	Average number of firms per portfolio	Mean portfolio return	z-Statistic	Median portfolio return	% Positive portfolios
All firms	16.7	141	17.4	0.35	4.41	0.21	58.2
Successful versus unsuccessful initial targets							
Successful	21.0	44	17.0	0.38	2.67	−0.19	47.7
Unsuccessful	14.8	97	17.6	0.33	3.52	0.29	62.9
Horizontal versus nonhorizontal							
Horizontal	19.4	11	13.0	0.32	1.28	−0.41	36.4
Nonhorizontal	20.3	59	18.9	0.51	3.63	0.45	62.7
Not classified	13.4	71	16.9	0.21	2.41	0.27	57.7
Ranked by Herfindahl index of industry							
$H \leq 0.09$	14.4	24	31.5	0.65	3.88	0.71	79.2
$0.09 < H \leq 0.13$	21.2	27	22.4	0.17	1.18	0.32	59.3
$0.13 < H \leq 0.18$	15.7	30	15.0	0.64	2.65	0.40	63.3
$0.18 < H \leq 0.25$	14.3	30	9.8	0.09	1.29	0.08	53.3
$H > 0.25$	18.0	30	11.8	0.22	1.03	−0.32	40.0
Number of firms in the industry							
Less than or equal to 16	14.3	71	9.2	0.38	3.22	0.17	59.2
Greater than 16	19.2	70	25.8	0.31	3.01	0.27	57.1
Results for various dormant periods							
13–24 months	16.9	58	21.0	0.39	2.97	0.45	62.0
25–36 months	17.8	25	15.6	0.21	1.11	−0.17	48.0
37–48 months	18.3	23	15.8	−0.05	0.18	−0.37	47.8
Above 48	14.6	35	13.9	0.63	3.96	0.67	65.7
Abnormal returns to various initial industry targets for an industry							
First initial industry target	15.5	70	16.3	0.48	4.05	0.28	64.3
Second initial industry target	17.2	43	17.8	0.29	2.24	0.12	51.2
Third and subseq. initial industry targets	19.2	28	19.6	0.12	0.71	0.14	53.6

(*Continued*)

Table 3 (*Continued*)

Category[a]	Target firm returns	Number of portfolios	Average number of firms per portfolio	Mean portfolio return	z-Statistic	Median portfolio return	% Positive portfolios
Level of industry acquisition activity between initial targets							
None	15.7	90	15.9	0.448	4.5	0.32	61.1
One or more targets	18.6	51	20.2	0.166	1.36	0.07	52.9
Target market value (tmval)							
tmval < 74.56 mil	19.6	27	19.5	−0.03	−0.03	−0.32	48.1
74.56 ≤ tmval < 139.55	22.8	29	14.5	0.1	0.66	−0.12	48.3
139.55 ≤ tmval and < 275.70	10.6	28	16.8	0.34	1.65	0.63	64.3
275.70 ≤ tmval and < 774.44	14.5	29	18.3	0.47	2.63	0.29	65.5
777.44 mil ≤ tmval	16.3	28	18.3	0.85	4.93	0.80	64.3
Value line industry rank							
Less than or equal to 0.51	16.7	70	16.5	0.27	2.34	0.18	55.7
Greater than 0.51	16.8	71	18.4	0.42	3.89	0.34	60.1
Target CAR (TCAR)							
TCAR < 1.0%	−3.19	28	19.1	0.60	3.70	0.42	75.0
1.0% ≤ TCAR < 9.0%	4.37	28	16.0	0.01	0.46	0.30	57.1
9.0% ≤ TCAR < 17.3%	13.2	28	15.7	0.38	2.23	0.15	57.1
17.3% ≤ TCAR < 29.7%	22.1	28	18.6	0.42	1.84	0.19	53.6
29.7% ≤ TCAR	46.2	29	17.8	0.33	1.65	−0.27	48.3

[a]Except for the difference between the last two dormant-period classifications, tests for differences in abnormal rival returns across the subcategories of Table 3 are all insignificant. This includes both *t*-tests and a Kruskall-Wallis nonparametric test.

The mean abnormal return to rivals of horizontal targets (0.32%) is insignificantly smaller than the corresponding figure for nonhorizontal rivals (0.51%). Median abnormal returns present a more dramatic difference. Median abnormal returns to rivals are actually negative in horizontal acquisitions. Related to this, a smaller percentage (36.4%) of horizontal portfolios exhibit positive abnormal returns, as compared to 62.7% for nonhorizontal firms. Replications of this analysis using the more homogeneous four-digit SIC codes results in only six horizontal acquisitions but produces similar conclusions. Thus, the existence of positive abnormal returns is not restricted to horizontal acquisitions. Moreover, rival returns are actually lower in the sample of horizontal acquisitions.[3]

4.5. Industry concentration

The collusion hypothesis suggests that higher abnormal returns are earned in more concentrated industries. To examine how the degree of industry concentration affects returns to rivals, we construct a sales-based Herfindahl index for each industry at the time of the initial acquisition announcement. Rivals are then sorted into quintiles based on the Herfindahl index of their industry. Analysis of mean and median returns across quintiles does not reveal a monotonic increase or decrease, but median abnormal returns to rivals are markedly lower and negative for the most concentrated industries (the fifth quintile). Again this result is contrary to that expected by the collusion hypothesis. It is consistent, however, with the acquisition probability hypothesis, which predicts lower probabilities of subsequent acquisition due to antitrust concerns.

Another measure of concentration is the number of rivals per industry. While mean returns are higher for the more concentrated industries (those with fewer firms), the result is affected by extreme values; an opposite ordering is noted for median values.

4.6. Degree of surprise

We have conjectured that the abnormal return to rivals is a positive function of the degree of surprise associated with an initial industry target and that the degree of surprise is related to the length of an industry's dormant period. By construction, the minimum dormant period is 13 months; the maximum dormant period is constrained only by the time period of the sample. We find that mean and median abnormal returns to rivals follow a U-shaped pattern with regard to the length of their industry's dormant period. Mean and median abnormal portfolio returns are largest when the dormant period exceeds 4 years; these returns are significantly higher than cases with dormant periods between 37 and 48 months, which have the smallest abnormal returns. We cannot, however, reject the hypothesis that mean abnormal returns to rivals are equal across all categories of dormant periods.

In spite of the requirement of a minimum dormant period, some industries experience two or more initial industry targets over our sample period. The Air Transportation industry, for example, experienced three separate initial industry targets following dormant periods of 14, 36, and 21 months. It is possible that second and subsequent

---

[3] Betton and Eckbo (1997) find that rivals competing for the same target earn significantly positive abnormal returns around the bid. Analysis of the Grimm Database does not reveal the existence of rival bidders for the same target.

initial industry targets throughout our sample period are at least partially anticipated. We, therefore, also examine results categorized by the order of initial industry targets in an industry.[4] 70 and 43 of our observations are the first and second initial industry targets, respectively, and 28 of our observations are the third and subsequent initial targets. The average abnormal return to portfolios of rival firms associated with the first and second initial industry targets is 0.48% and 0.29%, respectively. The mean abnormal return to third and subsequent initial industry targets declines to 0.12%. Median abnormal returns are 0.28%, 0.12%, and 0.14% for rivals of the first, second, and third and subsequent initial industry targets, respectively. The percentage of rival portfolios experiencing positive abnormal returns is 64% for the first initial industry targets, 51% for the second initial industry target, and 54% for the third and subsequent initial targets. These results are consistent with the greatest change in the probabilities of acquisition attempts occurring at the time of the first initial industry target. Thus, a rival's change in the probability of acquisition, $\Delta p_r(x_1)$ from Equation (1), is smaller following second and subsequent initial targets. An alternative explanation is that targets acquired first in an industry are the firms with the greatest potential for gain, implying that subsequent acquisition activity in our sample is associated with reduced potential for gain. Yet, the abnormal return earned by targets is not declining across this classification. In fact, the abnormal return to initial targets increases slightly across the first, second, and third initial targets.

Alternate measures of surprise, in addition to the length of the dormant period, include the level of acquisition activity in an industry between initial acquisition targets and the size of the initial target firm. Stock prices of rivals in industries with frequent acquisition activity will already incorporate a higher probability of being a target. In 51 of our 141 observations there are one or more acquisitions in the industry between initial industry targets. The mean and median abnormal returns to rivals for these cases are 0.17% and 0.07%, which is significantly smaller than the comparable values of 0.45% and 0.32% for cases without an acquisition attempt between initial industry targets. The size of the initial industry target is also indicative of the magnitude of industry disturbance. Acquisition of a larger target is likely to be more of a surprise than acquisition of a smaller target. Table 3 reveals the abnormal returns to rivals grouped into five quintiles according to initial industry target size. Mean returns to rivals increase monotonically with the size of the target firm. Median returns to rivals increase with the target firm's size in four of five categories.

---

[4] By definition, our data source focuses on large acquisitions involving at least 10% of a firm's shares. We are also able to obtain the percentage of shares sought from Securities Data Corporation for 86 of our 141 initial industry targets. The mean percentages of shares sought in the first, second, and third initial industry targets within an industry are 77.7%, 90%, and 96.5%, respectively. The median percentage of shares sought is 100% for all three categories. Thus, the majority of our sample involves offers for control. Moreover, the inclusion of any small cleanup offers biases against our finding a significant impact on industry rivals.

4.7. Industry health and potential for gain

The potential for gain through acquisition is likely to be related to both industry health and the size of the premium paid for the initial target. Rivals in declining industries present turnaround and restructuring opportunities. Higher premia paid to the initial industry target could indicate greater potential gains from acquiring firms in the industry.

To examine the impact of industry health on returns to rivals we use the Value Line industry rank. The lowest rank (1) indicates the most attractive industry; the highest ranks (around 90) indicate relatively unattractive industries. An acquiring firm, however, unlike most individual investors, can alter a firm's strategies or redeploy its assets. "Unattractive industries" can represent ideal takeover targets. Arguably, the poorest performing (i.e., highest-ranked) industries are most attractive for turnaround given opportunities for restructuring in the industry. The appearance of an external catalyst (initial acquisition) in these industries could indicate a higher level of subsequent acquisition activity and higher rival returns. Although mean and median returns are higher for rivals in poorly performing industries, the differences are insignificant in univariate tests.

Abnormal returns to the initial target can proxy for the potential gain from the acquisition of rivals. To examine the relation between target and rival abnormal returns, we group initial industry targets by quintile according to the target 2-day CAR. The results, shown in Table 3, do not reveal a systematic relation between mean target CARs and their corresponding rival portfolio abnormal returns. Contrary to expectations, median abnormal returns to rivals tend to decline monotonically across quintiles of target abnormal returns. The means from these quintiles are insignificantly different from each other. In a related test, the regression of rival portfolio CARs on target CARs produces an insignificant coefficient. We do not find evidence of a link between the size of the bid premium and rival abnormal returns.

4.8. Are announcement period abnormal returns related to the actual acquisition experience of rivals?

In this section, we examine the market's ability, at the time of the initial industry target, to assess correctly which rivals will subsequently become targets. We examine W.T. Grimm for each of the 2459 rival firms to determine whether they became targets of acquisition after the initial acquisition target for their industry. Results are shown in Table 4.

Sixty-six of the 2459 unregulated rivals, or about 2.6%, are targets of acquisition attempts in the subsequent 12 months. The abnormal return of these rivals (at the initial industry announcement) is 1.36%, which is significantly higher than the 0.32% for the rivals that are nontargets. Nontargets are defined as rivals that do not experience acquisition attempts within 3 years after their initial industry target. The *t*-statistic for this difference is 2.35. Differences in median returns suggest a similar conclusion: 0.81% for rivals targeted within 1 year and 0.06% for nontargets. Rivals that are targeted in the second or third years after the initial industry target earn insignificantly

Table 4

Announcement period abnormal returns to rivals categorized by acquisition activity in the 3 years following the initial industry announcement

Rivals are defined as firms in the same Value Line classification as an initial industry target. An initial industry targets is the first firm in a Value Line industry to be the target of an acquisition attempt following a minimum 12-month dormant period of acquisition activity within the industry. The abnormal return for each firm is defined as the residual from a market model. Abnormal returns are cumulated over the 2-day announcement period $(-1, 0)$, where 0 is the Wall Street Journal announcement date of the initial industry target. t-Statistics for differences from zero are shown in parentheses. Statistics for differences between means and medians across categories are shown in the lower part of the table.

| *Abnormal announcement periods returns $(-1, 0)$* | | | |
Rivals that were subsequently	Mean	N	Median
Nontargets within 3 years	0.32^a (4.26)	2144	0.06
Targets within 1 year	1.36^a (4.26)	66	0.81
Targets within 2–3 years	0.42^b (2.03)	249	0.30
		2459	
Tests for differences in means and medians between			
	t-Statistics	p-Value Kruskal-Wallis	
Targets within 1 year and nontargets	2.35^b	0.04^b	
Targets within 2–3 years and nontargets	0.44	0.25	

[a]Denotes significance at 1% level.
[b]Denotes significance at 5% level.

higher mean and median returns than nontargets. Rivals that are successfully acquired earn a 2-day announcement return of 1.34%, which is insignificantly smaller than the 1.37% earned by rivals subsequently involved in unsuccessful acquisitions. Median results show a similar pattern.

Ex post we know that the probability of acquisition, $[p_r(x_1)]$, changed most dramatically for the rivals that were targets within 1 year. The abnormal returns for these firms are three to four times higher than those of nontargets. Nevertheless, the abnormal returns for nontargets are still positive and significantly different from zero. While this abnormal return to nontargets could reflect the uncertainty about their subsequent acquisition status, it is also consistent with an increase in industry-specific quasi-rents. The initial industry acquisition announcement could signal the existence or increased value of unique industry-specific resources. Our evidence indicates significantly positive abnormal returns to nontargeted rivals and significantly and substantially higher returns to subsequently targeted rivals.

5. Explaining the cross section of returns to individual rivals

In this section, we begin by comparing the characteristics of rivals that subsequently become targets to those that do not using both a univariate and logistic analysis.

We also relate the abnormal return of rivals to firm characteristics associated in the literature with the probability of acquisition. Finally, we examine the relation between abnormal returns to rivals and the probability of acquisition predicted by a logistic regression. Examining individual firms, as opposed to portfolios, allows us to test the importance of firm-specific variables in explaining cross-sectional variation in abnormal returns to rivals.

5.1. Comparing target and rival firms

In the previous section, we find that the market correctly anticipates subsequent acquisition attempts on rival firms. We ask whether these subsequently targeted rivals have a distinct financial profile. A finding that initial and subsequent targets have a distinct financial profile as compared to all rivals would strengthen our understanding of a differential announcement return to rivals based on the probability of acquisition.

Table 5 presents descriptive statistics on initial industry targets and their corresponding rivals. All financial data are obtained from Compustat using fiscal year ends preceding the acquisition attempt on the initial industry target. Ownership data are obtained from the latest Value Line issue covering the rival firm but preceding the acquisition attempt on the initial industry target. We are able to obtain complete financial and ownership data on 106 initial industry targets and 2084 rival firms.

Columns A, B, and C report financial and ownership characteristics for initial industry target firms, all rival firms, and rivals that become targets within 1 year after the initial industry acquisition announcement, respectively. Columns D and E contain t-tests for differences between these categories. T-tests for differences between targets and all rivals (Column D) reveal that on average targets have higher leverage, are significantly smaller in terms of market value of equity and sales and have significantly lower levels of managerial ownership. The latter result occurs despite the known inverse relation between firm size and managerial ownership. Tobin's Q is significantly lower for target firms. We calculate Tobin's Q using the following equation:

$$Q = (S + P + D - \text{NWC})/(\text{TA}), \tag{3}$$

where S is the market value of equity, P is the liquidating value of preferred stock, D is the book value of long-term debt, NWC is the net working capital, and TA is the book value of total assets.

In addition, target firms have insignificantly higher levels of outside block ownership. Growth rates for target firms are insignificantly smaller than for rival firms. These results are generally consistent with previous empirical tests of differences between target and nontarget firms (Hasbrouck, 1985; Mikkelson and Partch, 1989; Palepu, 1986; Song and Walkling, 1993).

5.2. Rivals that subsequently become targets

At the time of the initial industry target, none of the rival firms has experienced acquisition activities in at least the preceding 12 months. After the initial industry

Table 5

Univariate analysis comparing initial industry target firms, all rivals, and rivals that are subsequently targets

Rivals are defined as firms in the same Value Line classification as an initial industry target. An initial industry target is the first firm in a Value Line industry to be the target of an acquisition attempt following a minimum 12-month dormant period of acquisition activity within the industry. We obtain financial and ownership data on 106 initial industry targets; 2084 rival firms are associated with these initial targets. Fifty-one of these rivals become targets themselves within the subsequent year.

	A	B	C	D	E
	Initial industry target firms	All rival firms	Rival firms that are subsequent targets[a]	t-Statistic for differences between rivals and initial industry targets	Rival firms that are subsequently targets and initial industry targets
Sales (millions)	1094.0	2418.4	1779.5	4.90[b]	1.07
Market value of firm (millions)	621.0	1529.0	656.2	6.12[b]	0.18
Growth (3 years geometric avg. of sales)	11.3%	12.3%	17.1%	0.57	0.97
Leverage	27.0%	22.2%	26.0%	−2.47[c]	−0.29
Tobin's Q	0.68	0.89	0.72	4.89[b]	0.57
Managerial ownership	14.2	17.5	16.4	2.11[c]	−0.44
Outside block ownership	7.7	5.5	6.6	−1.54	0.82
N	106	2084	51		

[a]Subsequent targets are those firms that become targets within 1 year after the initial industry target.
[b]Denotes significance at 1% level.
[c]Denotes significance at 5% level.

target, some rivals become targets themselves. Column E presents t-statistics for differences between initial industry targets and rival firms that are subsequently targets. Interesting results emerge. When we compare initial industry targets to rivals that are themselves targets in the next 12 months, all of the significant differences in firm characteristics disappear. Leverage, size, managerial ownership, and Tobin's Q are significantly different in the comparison of all rival firms to their initial industry targets. None of these variables is significantly different in comparisons of initial industry targets to rivals that subsequently become targets. Indeed, all variables but growth (which was insignificant anyway) have mean values for subsequent targets that are closer to the means of initial industry targets.

Table 6 tests these relations in a multivariate context using logistic regression. In the first regression we compare initial industry targets to all rivals, setting the dependent variable equal to one for the initial industry targets. Target firms are significantly smaller and have significantly lower levels of managerial ownership and significantly lower

Table 6

Logistic regressions comparing initial industry target firms, all rivals, and rivals that are subsequent targets

Rivals are defined as firms in the same Value Line classification as an initial industry target. An initial industry target is the first firm in a Value Line industry to be the target of an acquisition attempt following a minimum 12-month dormant period of acquisition activity within the industry. We obtain financial and ownership data on 106 initial industry targets; 2084 rival firms are associated with these initial targets. Fifty-one of these rivals become targets themselves within the subsequent year. The dependent variable equals one if the firm is a target.

	Constant	Growth	Log (market value of equity)	Block-holder ownership (dummy)	Tobin's Q	Managerial ownership (α):	Leverage	Likelihood ratio index	Chi-square df = 6 (p-value)	N
Initial industry targets Firms versus rivals	-1.29^a (-2.29)	0.27 (0.51)	-0.21^b (-2.71)	-0.02 (-0.09)	-0.46^a (-2.22)	-0.01^a (-2.14)	0.65 (1.25)	0.03	22.4 (0.00)	2190
Initial industry targets Firms versus rivals that are targets within 1 year	2.19^c (1.95)	-0.52 (-0.86)	-0.17 (-1.17)	-0.25 (-0.63)	-0.24 (-0.55)	-0.01 (-0.89)	0.31 (0.32)	0.02	3.5 (0.85)	157

[a]Denotes significance at 5% level.
[b]Denotes significance at 1% level.
[c]Denotes significance at 10% level.

levels of Tobin's Q. Growth, block ownership, and leverage are insignificant. These results complement our previous univariate results (Table 5). In the second regression we compare initial industry targets (dependent variable equals one) to rivals that become targets themselves within 1 year. None of the differences remain significant. Thus, initial industry targets have a distinct financial profile as compared to all rivals, but rival firms that subsequently become targets are indistinguishable from the initial targets. The existence of measurable differences in subsequently targeted rivals is consistent with the differential pricing of these firms at the time of the initial acquisition announcement. Section 5.3 addresses the extent to which these target-specific characteristics are priced in the initial announcement returns of rival firms.

5.3. Cross-sectional analysis of rival returns

In Table 7 we regress announcement period abnormal returns on firm and industry characteristics associated with the probability of acquisition. The spirit of this regression is similar to that of Eckbo (1992). Remember that, at the time of the initial industry announcement, the actual identity of subsequent industry targets is unknown. Regression (1) reveals that abnormal returns to individual rival firms decrease with the growth rate of a rival firm's sales. This is consistent with the acquisition probability hypothesis. Palepu (1986) finds that firms with lower growth rates are more likely to be acquired. Rival returns significantly decrease with managerial ownership. This is also consistent with the literature (Mikkelson and Partch, 1989; Song and Walkling, 1993). In spite of its statistical significance throughout the analysis, the size of the coefficient on managerial ownership suggests that it has a relatively minor economic impact.[5] Abnormal returns are insignificantly related to firm size, Tobin's Q, and the existence of a blockholder. Firms with increased leverage earn significantly higher abnormal returns. The latter result is inconsistent with the literature, but consistent with our previous univariate results. Results for this variable are mixed throughout the subsequent regressions.

In regressions (2) and (3), we add industry characteristics. In this case, returns are significantly positively related to the dormant period. Returns increase with industry timeliness (less attractive industries earn higher returns) and are significantly negatively related to the Herfindahl index; the latter result is inconsistent with collusion. The collusion hypothesis, however, relates to the horizontal consolidation of firms within an industry. To determine whether an initial acquisition is horizontal or non-horizontal, we need data on industrial classification of both target and bidder firms. We obtain our SIC codes for target and bidder from CRSP. Too few cases for both

---

[5] Following Morck et al. (1988) and McConnell and Servaes (1990), we allow for a nonlinear impact of managerial ownership using three variables for managerial ownership: the first represents the impact of managerial ownership at levels less than 5%. The second recognizes levels larger than or equal to 5% and less than 25%. The third recognizes levels greater than or equal to 25%. Our results, not shown for brevity, indicate that abnormal returns are insignificantly related to managerial ownership below 5%, significantly negatively related to it between the 5% and 25% levels, and insignificantly related to it at higher levels.

Table 7

OLS regressions relating abnormal returns of individual rival firms to their financial and ownership characteristics and to the predicted probability of being a target

Rivals are defined as firms in the same Value Line classification as an initial industry target. An initial industry target is the first firm in a Value Line industry to be the target of an acquisition attempt following a minimum 12-month dormant period of acquisition activity within the industry. We obtain financial and ownership data on 2084 rival firms associated with these initial targets. We obtain data on the type of proposed acquisition (horizontal or nonhorizontal) for initial acquisition attempts associated with 1062 rivals firms. The dependent variable is the abnormal return for each individual rival over the 2-day announcement period $(-1, 0)$ for the initial industry target.

| | | | Firm characteristics | | | | | | | Industry characteristics | | | | | |
No.	Constant	Predicted probability	Growth	Log size	Block-holder ownership dummy	Tobin's Q	Mgt. ownership (α):	Leverage	Dormant period	Industry rank according to Value Line	Herfindahl index	Dummy for horizontal initial industry target	Adj R^2	F-Stat (p-value)	N
1	0.67 (1.59)		-1.00^a (-2.25)	-0.06 (-1.09)	0.06 (0.34)	0.14 (1.32)	-0.01^a (-1.96)	0.81^a (1.86)					0.00	2.36 (0.03)	2084
2	0.69 (1.56)		-0.90^a (-2.02)	-0.05 (-0.96)	0.04 (0.21)	0.18^b (1.68)	-0.01^a (-2.09)	0.68 (1.55)	0.01^b (1.75)	0.38^c (2.90)			0.01	3.15 (0.00)	2084
3	0.92^a (2.02)		-0.84^b (-1.89)	-0.06 (-1.06)	0.03 (0.15)	0.18^b (1.65)	-0.01^b (-2.14)	0.62 (1.41)	0.01^a (2.04)	0.28^c (2.59)	-1.60^a (-1.96)		0.01	3.23 (0.00)	2084
4	1.91^c (2.89)		-1.42^a (-2.31)	-0.14^b (-1.88)	-0.15 (-0.59)	0.15 (1.03)	-0.01^a (-2.15)	1.15^b (1.77)	0.01 (1.22)	0.31^a (2.15)	-2.26^a (-1.98)	0.37 (0.97)	0.20	3.05 (0.00)	1062
5	-0.036 (-0.195)	8.05^a (2.32)											0.00	5.38 (0.00)	2084
6	0.23 (0.86)	6.54^b (1.85)							0.01^a (2.41)	0.24^a (2.25)	-1.70^a (-2.09)		0.01	5.14 (0.00)	2084

[a]Denotes significance at 5% level.
[b]Denotes significance at 10% level.
[c]Denotes significance at 1% level.

target and bidder are available using Compustat data to check the sensitivity of our results to the source of SIC codes. We have complete data on 1062 unregulated rivals. The results, displayed in regression (4), are similar to the other rows except that size is now significantly negatively related to returns to rivals. The dormant period and the dummy variable for horizontal initial acquisitions are insignificant.

The results are consistent with the determinants of acquisition probability being priced at the time of an initial industry target. That is, abnormal returns to rival firms are significantly related to variables associated with the probability of acquisition attempt. The lack of significant differences in returns across horizontal and nonhorizontal acquisitions is consistent with the acquisition probability hypothesis, but is unexplained by the collusion hypothesis.

5.4. Predicted probabilities and abnormal returns

We also perform a direct comparison of the relation between the abnormal returns to rivals and the predicted probability that these firms will become targets. To accomplish this, we calculate probabilities from the logistic regression comparing targeted to nontargeted rivals and then regress abnormal returns to rivals against these predicted probabilities. The results are shown in regressions (5) and (6) of Table 7.

Using a two-tailed test, the predicted probability of being a target is significantly related to abnormal returns at the 2% level. Note that this interpretation is conservative. The appropriate test for a specific hypothesis (i.e., abnormal returns increase with the predicted probability of being a target) is a one-tailed test. Abnormal rival returns are significantly positively related to this predicted probability in both regressions. According to the acquisition probability hypothesis, abnormal returns should be related to the change in acquisition probability. The logit regression measures the level of acquisition probability. Our results are consistent with the change in abnormal returns being correlated with the level of probability. Returns also continue to be significantly positively related to both the industry rank and the length of the dormant period and significantly negatively related to the Herfindahl index.

5.5. Sensitivity tests and extensions

In our univariate analysis, we noted that acquisition activity within an industry and initial target size are alternate measures of surprise about the initial acquisition announcement. To test the importance of these variables, we replace the dormant period with a dummy variable set equal to one if there has been any acquisition activity in the industry since the previous initial target. The variable enters with a significant negative coefficient; abnormal returns to rivals are significantly smaller when acquisition activity within an industry has been higher. The results, omitted for brevity, are consistent with market anticipation of higher probabilities of acquisition and hence lower changes in these probabilities, $[\Delta p_r(x_1)]$, surrounding an initial industry acquisition announcement. When the dummy variable for acquisition activity and the dormant period are included simultaneously, their coefficients are insignificant. Of course, industries with higher levels of acquisition activity are likely to have smaller dormant periods; both are measures of surprise about an initial industry acquisition announcement. Similarly, adding the initial target's market value to regression (3) results in an insignificant positive coefficient (p-value $= 0.18$).

Our definition of dormant periods is based on target firms covered by Value Line. Of course, shock waves can be transmitted by acquisition activity for related firms not covered by Value Line. Consequently, we identify 883 additional target firms listed by W.T. Grimm. For each of these firms we search the preceding year's Predicast F&S Index to find the primary seven-digit SIC code and industry name and then subjectively assign these firms to the appropriate Value Line industry. In general, our assignment is based on industry name and correspondence of the firm's SIC code with the SIC codes (and industry names) of the Value Line firms. We are able to classify 760 of the 883 firms. These additional targets, while undoubtedly smaller and less newsworthy than our Value Line events, could still produce confounding effects if their acquisition announcements were just prior to those of our Value Line initial industry targets. Firms not covered by Value Line, but ostensibly related to Value Line industries, become targets in the 12 months preceding 54 of our 141 initial industry targets. Nevertheless, sensitivity tests reveal that these cases have very little impact on our results. Mean and median target and rival CARs are insignificantly different between these and the remaining cases. A dummy variable set equal to one for the rival firms associated with these 54 cases is insignificant in each of the regressions of Table 7. The significance and magnitude of the remaining coefficients are practically unaltered by the inclusion of this dummy variable.

Under the acquisition probability hypothesis, we also expect abnormal rival returns to be smaller for regulated industries since regulatory approval reduces their probability of acquisition. To test this, we replicate our methodology using regulated firms. We identify 238 rivals associated with 23 additional initial targets in regulated industries as defined by Value Line, including Air Transportation, Electric Utility, Finance and Investment Companies, Insurance Firms, Savings and Loans, and Natural Gas. Similar results are obtained using Compustat SICs to identify regulated firms, that is, between 4000 and 5000 and between 6000 and 7000.

In multivariate sensitivity tests regressing abnormal returns on a combined sample of regulated and unregulated rivals, a dummy variable set equal to one for regulated industries enters with a negative sign significant beyond the 1% level. (Results are available upon request.) Conclusions regarding the other independent variables are unaltered. The result is consistent with the acquisition probability hypothesis.

6. Summary and conclusions

Previous research finds positive abnormal returns to rivals of acquisition attempts but does not explain their existence. Our explanation, the acquisition probability hypothesis, asserts that rivals earn abnormal returns to the extent that their probability of becoming a target is revised. The acquisition probability hypothesis has implications for explaining the cross-sectional variation in abnormal returns to rivals and, unlike the collusion hypothesis, does not require horizontal or even successful acquisition of target firms for rivals to experience changes in value.

We identify 141 unregulated initial industry acquisition targets and 2459 associated rival firms over the period 1982–1991. Our results, based on both individual rival firms and portfolios of rival firms, indicate that rivals earn significantly positive abnormal returns and that the distribution of these returns exhibits considerable cross-sectional variation. Rivals of initial industry targets involved in nonhorizontal, successful, and unsuccessful acquisitions also earn significantly positive abnormal returns.

Comparison of individual firm characteristics reveals significant differences between the set of initial industry targets and all rival firms, but insignificant differences between initial targets and rivals that become targets within 1 year. Rivals that become targets in the year subsequent to the initial industry acquisition announcement have a financial profile similar to the initial industry target.

Rivals that become targets in the subsequent year earn significantly larger abnormal returns at the initial industry acquisition announcement than untargeted rivals. Multivariate tests reveal that the magnitude of abnormal returns for rival firms changes with variables related to the probability of acquisition attempts. Finally, abnormal returns for rivals are significantly positively related to the predicted probability of acquisition attempts. All of these results are consistent with the acquisition probability hypothesis.

References

Betton, S. and E. Eckbo, 1997, "State-Contingent Payoffs in Takeovers: New Structural Estimates," Unpublished Working Paper, Stockholm School of Economics.

Bradley, M., A. Desai and E. Kim, 1983, "The Rationale Behind Interfirm Tender Offers: Information or Synergy?," *Journal of Financial Economics*, 11, 183–206.

Comment, R. and G. Schwert, 1995, "Poison or Placebo? Evidence on the Deterrence and Wealth Effects of Modern Antitakeover Measures," *Journal of Financial Economics*, 39, 3–43.

Eckbo, E., 1983, "Horizontal Mergers, Collusion, and Stockholder Wealth," *Journal of Financial Economics*, 11, 241–273.

Eckbo, E., 1985, "Mergers and the Market Concentration Doctrine: Evidence from the Capital Market," *Journal of Business*, 58, 325–349.

Eckbo, E., 1992, "Mergers and the Value of Antitrust Deterrence," *Journal of Finance*, 47, 1005–1029.

Eckbo, E. and P. Wier, 1985, "Antimerger Policy Under the Hart–Scott–Rodino Act: A Reexamination of the Market Power Hypothesis," *Journal of Law and Economics*, 28, 119–149.

Gort, M., 1969, "An Economic Disturbance Theory of Mergers," *Quarterly Journal of Economics*, 83, 624–642.

Hasbrouck, J., 1985, "The Characteristics of Takeover Targets, Q and Other Measures," *Journal of Banking and Finance*, 9, 351–362.

Jensen, M., 1988, "Comment on "Characteristics of Hostile and Friendly Takeover Targets", by Morck, R., Shleifer, A., Vishny, R.," In A. Auerbach (Ed.), *Corporate Takeovers, Causes and Consequences*, University of Chicago Press, Chicago.

Kahle, K. and R. Walkling, 1996, "The Impact of Industry Classifications on Financial Research," *Journal of Financial and Quantitative Analysis*, 31, 309–335.

McConnell, J. and H. Servaes, 1990, "Additional Evidence on Equity Ownership and Corporate Value," *Journal of Financial Economics*, 27, 595–612.

Mikkelson, W. and M. Partch, 1989, "Managers' Voting Rights and Corporate Control," *Journal of Financial Economics*, 25, 263–290.

Mitchell, M. and H. Mulherin, 1996, "The Impact of Industry Shocks on Takeover and Restructuring Activity," *Journal of Financial Economics*, 41, 193–229.

Morck, R., A. Shleifer and R. Vishny, 1988, "Management Ownership and Market Valuation: An Empirical Analysis," *Journal of Financial Economics*, 20, 293–316.

Palepu, K., 1986, "Predicting Takeover Targets," *Journal of Accounting and Economics*, 8, 3–35.

Song, M. and R. Walkling, 1993, "Impact of Managerial Ownership on Acquisition Attempts and Target Shareholder Wealth," *Journal of Financial and Quantitative Analysis*, 28, 439–457.

Stillman, R., 1983, "Examining Antitrust Policy Towards Horizontal Mergers," *Journal of Financial Economics*, 11, 225–240.

Chapter 16

WHERE DO MERGER GAINS COME FROM? BANK MERGERS FROM THE PERSPECTIVE OF INSIDERS AND OUTSIDERS*

JOEL F. HOUSTON

Department of Finance, Insurance and Real Estate, Graduate School of Business Administration, University of Florida, Gainesville, Florida, USA

CHRISTOPHER M. JAMES

Department of Finance, Insurance and Real Estate, Graduate School of Business Administration, University of Florida, Gainesville, Florida, USA

MICHAEL D. RYNGAERT

Department of Finance, Insurance and Real Estate, Graduate School of Business Administration, University of Florida, Gainesville, Florida, USA

Contents

* Thanks to C. Ted Fee for providing excellent research assistance. Thanks also to the referee, Jay Ritter, Karen Wruck, and participants at the JFE/Harvard Conference on Clinical Research for their comments.

This article originally appeared in the *Journal of Financial Economics*, Vol. 60, pp. 285–331 (2001).
Corporate Takeovers, Volume 1
Edited by B. Espen Eckbo
Copyright © 2001 Elsevier Science S.A. All rights reserved.
DOI: 10.1016/B978-0-12-381983-3.00016-2

Abstract

Traditional studies fail to find conclusive evidence that bank mergers create value. We analyze a sample of the largest bank mergers between 1985 and 1996. For a subset of this sample, we obtain management estimates of projected cost savings and revenue enhancements. We find that recent mergers appear to result in positive revaluations of the combined value of bidder and target stocks. Although not as large as the present value of management's estimates, with the bulk of the revaluation being attributable to estimated cost savings rather than projected revenue enhancements.

Keywords

mergers and acquisitions, bank mergers

JEL classification: G34, G21

1. Introduction

The academic literature on the value gains from bank mergers creates a troubling paradox. Empirical studies examining the stock market reaction to merger announcements find little evidence of wealth creation, with shareholders of the acquired firm gaining at the expense of shareholders of the acquiring firm (see, e.g., Houston and Ryngaert, 1994). Similarly, there appears to be little or no improvement in the postacquisition operating performance of merged banks relative to industry peers (see, e.g., Berger et al., 1999; Pilloff, 1996). The lack of econometric evidence of efficiency gains is quite surprising given that bank mergers continue at a rapid pace and that an important impetus for consolidation has been the removal of geographic and product market entry restrictions that are generally believed to impede operating efficiency and bank profitability.

One interpretation of this paradox is that the current wave of bank acquisitions reflects either managerial hubris and/or a massive corporate control problem that results in value destruction for acquiring firm shareholders. For example, Ryan (1999) argues that most bank acquisitions are not in shareholders' interests. Gorton and Rosen (1995) argue that the primary motive for bank mergers is empire building by managers who are insulated from the market for corporate control. For a general discussion of the role of managerial hubris in acquisitions, see Roll (1986). An alternative interpretation is that consolidation has improved the operating efficiency of the banking industry, but the corresponding benefits have not been fully captured in previous large sample studies.

In this paper, we try to sort out these issues by taking a closer look at the sources of merger-related gains in banking. Our analysis differs from previous studies of bank acquisitions in two ways. First, we analyze only large bank mergers over a longer time period that includes more-recent mergers. By using only large acquisitions, our sample allows us to detect valuation consequences more readily than a sample including smaller transactions. By analyzing transactions over a period of 12 years (1985–1996), we are able to investigate whether the rationales and wealth consequences of large bank mergers have changed over this time period.

Second, for 41 acquisitions we obtain management's projections of the merger's estimated cost savings and revenue enhancements. These projections allow us to identify management's primary rationale for these acquisitions and also enable us to quantify the likely valuation consequences of the acquisitions. While it is often treacherous to "take management's word for it" on a given matter, we try to verify the credibility of management's claims. In the spirit of recent work by Kaplan and Ruback (1995) and Gilson et al. (2000), we estimate the present value of the incremental earnings that management expects from the merger. We then investigate the relation between these estimated gains and the change in the market value of the stock of the bidder and the target. This analysis indicates the extent to which investors agree with management's projections of cost savings and revenue enhancements, which in turn provides important insights into what the market is looking for when it values bank mergers. To further gauge the credibility of management's projections, we also examine stock analysts' reports shortly after announced mergers to see if analysts concur with management. Finally, we examine postmerger performance to determine if it is consistent with managerial forecasts.

Like previous studies, we find that the market value of the acquiring bank declines and the market value of the acquired bank increases on the announcement of a merger. For the entire sample of 64 mergers, the combined market value of the bidder and target, on average, increases slightly on the announcement of the transaction. Consistent with Becher (1999), we find that a shift has occurred over time. Compared to the 1980s, average abnormal returns have been higher for both bidders and targets in the 1990s. The higher returns have been accompanied by an increased frequency of "in-market" mergers in the 1990s. Interestingly, there has also been a significant increase in the 1990s in the numbers of deals in which management makes an explicit forecast of expected cost savings and/or revenue enhancements.

Focusing on the subsample of 41 mergers that include managerial projections, we find that the primary source of management's expected merger-related gains is cost savings. Revenue enhancements are far less important. Indeed, our valuation of estimated revenue gains account for, on average, only 7% (the median is 0) of the total valuation gains implied by management's estimates. The total implied valuation gains are generally quite large, although the estimated gains are sensitive to the assumptions used with respect to the duration of incremental earnings and the rate used to discount those earnings. Under optimistic assumptions that incremental merger-related earnings are perpetual and grow at the inflation rate, we estimate that the average sample merger should increase the combined value of the bidder and target by 13%.

Looking at the market's reaction to merger announcements, we find that management's projected merger gains explain roughly 60% of the cross-sectional variation in the combined bidder and target stock returns. Interestingly, while valuation estimates of projected cost savings are positively related to the combined stock market returns of the bidder and target, the valuation estimates of projected revenue increases are negatively related to these same stock market returns. Thus, our results suggest that cost savings represent the primary source of gains in the large majority of recent bank mergers and that managerial cost savings projections have significant capital market credibility.

While stock market valuation changes are highly correlated with the valuations we place on management's estimated merger benefits, we are limited in what we can say about whether the magnitude of stock market changes is commensurate with the magnitude of revaluations implied by managerial forecasts. Under the most "optimistic" valuations of management forecasts, stock market value changes appear "too small." When one considers potential errors in the valuation of incremental earnings gains, anticipation of likely takeover deals, and information conveyed by the merger announcement unrelated to merger gains, it is difficult to assess whether the market is fully valuing managerial claims or is heavily discounting them as overoptimistic.

To shed more light on the credibility of managerial forecasts, we examine analysts' reports for our subset of 41 mergers. For the most part, analysts seem to buy into management's cost savings projections. To the extent that cost savings projections are questioned, the analysts are as likely to suggest that the estimates are too conservative as they are to claim them to be too optimistic. Consistent with observed stock market reactions, however, analysts appear to be skeptical about revenue projections. In some cases, analysts also suggest that cost savings are likely to lead to revenue losses that management does not discuss. There are also cases in which management is including cost savings in their forecasts that could be achieved in the absence of the merger. Again, however, it is not clear that this is evidence of managerial hubris. For example, numerous press articles provide examples in which management teams expect some loss of revenue in a merger. Not discussing these likely losses could merely indicate an attempt to downplay merger negatives.

To obtain a final gauge of the credibility of management forecasts, we examine merged banks' postmerger performance by looking at managerial disclosures and press accounts. In the majority of transactions, management claims to have met its cost-cutting targets. Following mergers, we also find increases in merged bank operating performance measures that are correlated with management cost savings estimates.

The remainder of the paper is divided into four sections. Section 2 reviews the previous literature on the gains from bank acquisitions and discusses why the techniques used in large sample studies of bank acquisitions fail to uncover merger gains. Section 3 describes our sample and methodology. Section 4 presents our empirical results and Section 5 summarizes our findings and offers conclusions.

2. Finding value enhancing mergers in banking: review of previous literature

2.1. Rationales for bank mergers

Bank mergers can increase value by reducing costs and/or increasing revenues. Cost reductions can be achieved by eliminating redundant managerial positions, closing overlapping bank branches, vacating redundant headquarters facilities, and consolidating back-office functions like check clearing. Cost-cutting potential may be greater when merging banks have geographic overlap. Bank executives frequently claim that mergers with considerable operations overlap can result in cost savings equal to 30% of the target's noninterest expenses. Revenue enhancements can come from a variety of sources. The most frequently cited source is cross-selling of bank services. For instance, one reason for First Union's acquisition of First Fidelity Bancorporation was to market its brokerage and mutual fund services to First Fidelity's customers. The ability to raise fees and lower interest rates on deposit accounts (and hence raise net interest revenue) is also cited as a motivation for acquisitions. John McCoy of Banc One argued in the 1980s that many banks mistakenly followed strategies such as meeting competitors' fees. McCoy believed that many bank products were price inelastic and that customers would agree to pay more for high-quality, promptly delivered services (see *The American Banker*, October 20, 1987, p. 1).

In spite of these opportunities to create value, implementing these actions is not problem-free. Conflicts over "who is in charge" can delay cost-cutting efforts, and reluctance to lay off staff can eliminate large cost-cutting opportunities. The integration process can also result in losses of bank customers and significant "restructuring costs" such as severance payments and lease buyouts. Customer runoff and integration costs can be magnified when computer glitches slow down the integration process and cause disruption in customer service. Additionally, promised revenue enhancements might not materialize if customers rebel against fee increases or are not interested in the new services offered by an acquiring bank (see *The American Banker*, December 9, 1997, p. 25).

2.2. Review of the past literature

Academic studies of merger-related gains in banking generally follow one of two approaches; see Berger et al. (1999) for an excellent literature review on gains from bank mergers. The first approach examines changes in the merged banks' postmerger accounting profits (ROA or ROE) or operating costs, measured by operating costs per employee or the bank's efficiency ratio (where the efficiency ratio is noninterest expense divided by the sum of net interest income and noninterest income) relative to the premerger pro forma performance of the merging banks. The merger is assumed to generate improved performance if the changes in accounting-based performance are superior to the changes in the performance of comparable banks that were not involved in merger activity. The results of these studies are mixed. For example, Cornett and Tehranian (1992) and Spindt and Tarhan (1992) find increases in postmerger operating performance, while Berger and Humphrey (1992), Pilloff (1996), and Berger (1997) do not.

The mixed conclusions are not surprising given the numerous empirical difficulties associated with these studies. For example, even if mergers improve performance, accounting-based studies can fail to detect it because the lags between the completion of mergers and the realization of operating improvements can be long and varied. Indeed, restructuring and consolidation costs can lead to deterioration in short-term performance even though long-term performance is expected to improve. This problem is compounded by the fact that many banks make multiple acquisitions over a short span of years. To partially combat this problem, studies such as Pilloff (1996) restrict the sample of analyzed mergers to banks with limited acquisition activity around each usable observation. Similar restrictions are placed on the industry benchmark firms.

Unfortunately, the above solution raises the problem of selection bias. Focusing on infrequent acquirers can overweight a sample with mergers that were poorly implemented, because failed acquirers will tend to abstain from future acquisitions while successful acquirers will tend to seek new and bigger deals. The selection bias problem also extends to industry benchmarks. It is difficult to construct benchmarks of nonacquiring banks in a rapidly consolidating industry. Those that do not acquire at all might have some peculiarities that can bias test results. Selection bias problems also go to the question of the timing of acquisitions. Houston and Ryngaert (1997) find that most acquiring banks issue stock to finance their mergers. Banks might be willing to make stock-financed acquisitions only when they are at an earnings peak and foresee future profit declines. In a nonbanking context, Loughran and Ritter (1997) find that equity issuers experience a drop in profitability after an equity issue.

Another problem with using accounting data arises from the accounting rules governing mergers. As Kwan and Wilcox (1999) point out, in mergers involving the use of purchase accounting, the cost basis for the acquired bank's assets is written up to the current market value. As a result, accounting expenses associated with depreciated assets (such as property and equipment) can increase even though the transaction creates real efficiencies. Discretion accorded managers in expensing restructuring charges and loan charge-offs can also cause accounting-based measures to provide a distorted picture of merger-related gains.

The second approach to analyzing merger gains examines the stock price performance of the bidder and the target firm around the announcement of an acquisition (see, e.g., DeLong, 1998; Houston and Ryngaert, 1994; James and Weir, 1987). A merger is assumed to create value if the combined value of the bidder and the target increases on the announcement of the merger. Most studies find negligible evidence of value creation and instead document what appears to be wealth redistribution. The value of the target increases about 15% in the 5 days around the merger announcement and the value of the bidder decreases about 2%. The two effects roughly cancel each other out in terms of revaluation of the joint firms because targets are smaller than bidders.

There are several reasons why stock return evidence fails to find gains from acquisitions even if they exist. First, merger announcements mix information concerning the proposed acquisition with information about the financing of the acquisition. Bank acquisitions tend to be financed by stock issuance. Stock offerings are generally interpreted as signals of the issuer's "overvaluation." Hence, the negative announcement returns to bidding firms could be partly attributable to negative signaling unrelated to the value created by the merger. Consistent with this view, Houston and Ryngaert (1997) find that the returns to bidders are significantly greater in bank mergers financed with cash than mergers financed with stock.

A second shortcoming of abnormal return studies is that, in the midst of a consolidation wave, acquisitions are largely anticipated. Consequently, the positive merger effects on bank value do not appear in announcement-date stock returns. This problem is particularly acute for likely acquisition targets. For example, the Dow Jones News Service of July 17, 1995 highlights a report in Barron's that five bank stocks "thought most likely to be acquired, are starting to look fully valued." Four of these five banks were acquired in the next year. Lehman Brothers and Salomon Brothers in their quarterly bank industry reports frequently provide a list of potential targets (as well as the bidders that are likely to create the greatest value). For example, see the Salomon Brothers industry report "Shop Til You Drop" (August 1997) or the Lehman Brothers industry report "Bank Franchise Value Model" (September 1995). In addition the *American Banker* periodically evaluates the top US bank holding companies and provides an analysis of the range of potential purchase prices for banks that are potential targets in acquisitions, (e.g., see *American Banker*, March 24, 1998, p. 10). On the acquirer side, many banks in the late 1980s and 1990s had well-known strategies of growth through acquisitions. For example, when Banc One announced its acquisition of Valley National in 1992, it had 10 other acquisitions pending.

Capitalization of expected merger gains before the announcement will create an attenuation bias that can shrink positive returns into insignificant average returns for the combined banks on the announcement day. It is not clear how to correct this bias. An approach that we use, also used by Houston and Ryngaert (1994), is to measure announcement returns from the date a bank is identified as a likely target (or bidder) in an acquisition. However, this adjustment accounts only for the preannouncement leakage associated with a specific transaction and not for the fact that a bank can have an ongoing acquisition program or that a bank is perceived as an ongoing potential target. Another approach, employed by Becher (1999), is to expand the event window. When the window is expanded to 30 days before the first takeover announcement, Becher finds improved bidder returns. This could, however, be picking up improvements in the bidder's stock price that motivate the bidder to make a stock-based bid.

A final problem is that the negative announcement return of bidding firms can reflect disappointment that the bidding firm is less likely to be acquired in the future. This clearly has been a factor in several acquisitions in our sample. For example, PNC's acquisition of Meridian Bancorp was criticized by some analysts as destroying value because it lessened the likelihood that PNC would be a takeover candidate. Similar criticisms were made of First Chicago's merger with NBD and Bank of Boston's merger with Bay Banks.

These problems suggest that the combined stock returns of the bidder and target on the announcement of an acquisition can understate any value gains associated with a merger. However, even if there is no attenuation bias in announcement returns, the insignificant returns to the combined banks do not necessarily imply that there are no efficiency gains from bank acquisitions. As Calomiris and Karceski (1999) point out, efficiency gains from acquisitions can flow to bank customers. So, small positive returns to the combined banks can simply reflect the fact that the merged bank captures only a small fraction of the gains. Failure to enact efficiency-enhancing mergers, however, could render the bank less competitive in future years.

While past studies find little significant increase in the combined value of merging banks, there are important cross-sectional differences in abnormal stock returns. For example, Houston and Ryngaert (1997) find that the abnormal returns to the combined bank are positively related to the degree of branch overlap between the two banks, the percent of the acquisition financed with cash or conditional stock, and the profitability of the bidder prior to the acquisition.[1] Likewise, DeLong (1998) finds that focusing

---

[1] Conditional stock offers involve financing the acquisition with common stock, but the number of shares issued is a function of the bidder's future stock price; such offers are a way for bidders to communicate that good news may be revealed before the deal is closed (or of warranting that bad news will not be revealed).

mergers (those that increase either geographic or product focus) increase value, whereas diversifying mergers destroy value. Hence, there is information content in bank merger announcements. We try to exploit this in our analysis by examining the extent to which managerial projections of merger-related gains are incorporated into bank stock prices.

3. Sample and experimental design

3.1. Sample selection

Our sample consists of large bank acquisitions announced during the period 1985–1996. To construct our sample, we obtain from Mergestat and SNL Securities a list of all mergers with a stated deal value (the amount paid for the target's shares) in excess of $400 million in 1985 inflation-adjusted dollars.[2] We include a transaction in our sample if the target's assets are at least 10% of the bidder's assets in the year preceding the merger. This leaves us with a sample of 64 mergers. A list of the mergers in our sample is provided in the Appendix.

We focus on large bank acquisitions for three reasons. First, these are the most important in terms of explaining the bank consolidation process of the 1980s and 1990s. Second, because of their size, it is easier to observe the impact of larger acquisitions on performance. Third, large transactions are more likely to draw analyst and press attention and are therefore more likely to have detailed disclosures associated with them.

We obtain detailed information on the terms of the merger and expected merger-related gains from 8 K filings, proxy statements, press releases, annual reports, news stories, and analyst research reports. News stories are obtained from a search of all sources available on the Dow Jones News Retrieval Service for a time period beginning 1 year prior to the announcement and ending 2 years after the transaction is competed.

We obtain full-page analyst research reports from INVESTEXT, an online service that provides research reports authored by investment analysts from approximately 320 investment banks, brokerage houses, and research firms. For each of the banks in our sample, we conduct an online search for analyst research reports on the company from the date of the announcement of the acquisition to 9 months after the completion of the acquisition.[3] For firms without INVESTEXT reports, we also utilize stock analysts' reports from CIRR microfiche for the years 1985–1989. Between the two sources, we obtain analyst research reports for 59 of the 64 mergers in our sample.

---

[2] Inflation measures are based on the Consumer Price Index obtained from the Federal Reserve Bulletin.

[3] This search provides the table of contents for all research reports. Due to the expense associated with obtaining reports ($1.50 per page), we review the table of contents and obtain reports in which the analyst seems to provide some detailed analysis of the merger transaction. When there is more than one company report from the same analyst during this time window, we obtain the report that follows most closely the announcement of the acquisition. The maximum number of research reports for a given merger is five (Wells Fargo and First Interstate in 1996 and Chemical Bank and Chase Manhattan 1995) and the average number is 2.41.

Stock price information for the bidder and target firms in our sample is from the Center for Research on Securities Prices (CRSP). Accounting information is from banks' annual reports and 10 Ks.

In our empirical analysis we examine the relation between projected merger gains and the degree of geographical market overlap between the target and the bidder. Previous research by Houston and Ryngaert (1994) and Hawawini and Itzhak (1990) finds that the stock price reaction is greater for mergers with greater overlap. These studies conjecture that mergers with significant overlapping operations have a greater potential to realize cost savings because of greater opportunities to close redundant or less-efficient local branches. We measure geographic overlap using the approach developed by Houston and Ryngaert (1994). The overlap measure is constructed by first identifying each bank subsidiary of the target and bidder. Next, using the *McNally and Thomson Bank Directory*, we identify the number of branch offices of each firm in a given city. Using this information, the overlap variable is defined as

$$\text{Overlap} = \frac{\sum_{i=1}^{n} \min(T_i, B_i)}{\sum_{i=1}^{n}(T_i + B_i)}, \tag{1}$$

where n is the total number of cities in which either bank has an office while T_i and B_i are the total number of offices the target and bidder have in city i. This measure of overlap can take on a maximum value of 0.5 when there is complete overlap between the two firms' operations and a minimum value of 0 where there is no overlap. Overlap can be thought of as a crude measure of the percentage of offices of the two banks that could be closed as a result of the merger. To obtain a useful classification of merger types for data analysis purposes, we also classify any merger in which the number of overlapping branches is less than 4% of the target's total branches as a market-expansion merger. We choose this cutoff because it appears to correspond to the cutoff used by SNL Securities when classifying mergers. Specifically, SNL appears to roughly classify mergers as out-of-market when the overlap is less than 0.04. Unfortunately, SNL Securities classifies mergers only after 1989.

The best sources of information on management's estimates of merger-related cost savings and revenue enhancements are press releases, proxy statements pertaining to merger votes, 8 K filings, and analyst reports. Analysts often receive projections from management and pass these on in their reports, and proxy statements often provide estimates to justify the transaction to shareholders. In many cases, management estimates of merger-related gains are very specific, with information on the timing and details of cost savings and revenue gains. For example, the Comerica and Manufacturers National merger proxy in early 1992 predicts that the merger will result in pretax costs savings of $45 million in the first year after completion, $119 million in the second year, and $145 million in the third year. The proxy also notes that the firm anticipates taking a pretax charge of $110 million to cover merger and integration costs such as severance payments, investment banking fees, lease buyouts, and write-downs of redundant software. The after-tax charge is estimated at $76 million.

Unfortunately, not all proxies are as detailed. For instance, many merger proxies will merely state that the firm anticipates saving a certain amount in annual noninterest expenses within the first 2 years. Lacking any additional information in estimating merger gains, we simply assume that the cost savings are spread equally throughout the consolidation process. So, for instance, when MNC Financial estimated $83 million in cost savings over 2 years in its acquisition of Equitable Bancorporation, we assume savings of $41.5 million in the first year and $83 million in the second year. In most cases, the cost savings are given as pretax figures. In these cases, we estimate after-tax savings by assuming that the tax rate is three percentage points above the federal corporate tax rate. This assumption reflects the fact that most banks face a state tax as well as a federal tax. We apply the same rules to estimate after-tax revenue gains.

An additional problem with the forecasts is their tendency to change in the early periods after merger announcements. In some cases, management will give a number early on that might be based on saving a certain percentage of expenses, but the expense number might be based on last year's expenses as opposed to an updated number published in a proxy statement that is based on expenses going 2 years forward. Hence, many proxy estimates are somewhat higher (usually no more than 10–15% higher) than estimates given at press time.

3.2. Valuation of merger benefits

To examine whether management estimates of merger gains are reflected in the stock market's valuation of the merger benefits, we estimate the present value of the after-tax cost savings and revenue gains from the merger. Our estimate of the value of the merger gains follows procedures similar to those employed by Kaplan and Ruback (1995) and Gilson et al. (2000). In particular, for 41 mergers, we have after-tax cost savings and revenue estimates going out 2–4 years. Cost savings and revenue projections are only used if the projections appear to be complete, are explicit in terms of cost and revenue breakdown, and provide a time to completion on the projections. For horizons shorter than 4 years, we extend the forecast by assuming that the cost savings or revenue gains will grow at the rate of expected inflation. The inflation forecasts are based on the Federal Reserve Bank of Philadelphia Blue Chip Indicator Series predictions of 10-year horizon inflation rates. The present value of merger gains equals the present discounted value of the incremental cash flows arising from the acquisition.

For cost savings, incremental cash flows represent cost savings estimates (net of taxes). For projected revenue gains, the incremental cash flows should equal the revenue gains less any increase in operating costs resulting from enhanced revenues (net of taxes). In practice, however, given how management reports revenue gains, no adjustment appears necessary. A good deal of the anticipated revenue gains comes from repricing products (e.g., increased net interest income arising from paying lower rates on deposits). Revenue gains due to repricing should have no impact on operating costs, so no adjustment is necessary. For other sources of revenue gains (e.g., gains

from cross-selling products), any increase in operating expenses appear to be incorporated into the cost figures management provides. For example, First Union's acquisition
of First Fidelity Bancorporation introduced First Union products such as brokerage
service to First Fidelity customers. Arguably, any revenue increase would create some
offsetting costs. Nevertheless, when First Union projected the impact of the merger in its
8 K filing, all costs and revenue changes are listed and flow through to the bottom line
in the earnings projections. In addition, none of the stock analyst reports that we
review make an allowance for extra costs due to extra revenue in their bottom line
projections. Hence, it seems reasonable to assume that any such costs must serve to
reduce cost savings associated with the merger. Fortunately, as we later report, revenue
increases tend to make up a small portion of merger-related gains, hence any error in
estimating the magnitude of net-of-cost revenue enhancements is likely to be small.

Using these after-tax cost savings and revenue estimates going out 4 years, we
estimate the present value of these earnings increments as follows:

$$\text{Estimated present value of merger} = \sum_{t=1}^{3} \frac{\text{CS}_t + \text{Rev}_t}{(1+K)^t} + \frac{\text{CS}_4 + \text{Rev}_4}{(K-I)(1+K)^3} - \text{RC}, \quad (2)$$

where CS_t is the after-tax cost savings estimate in year t after the merger, Rev_t the
after-tax revenue estimate in year t after the merger, K the discount rate (defined
below), I the long-run inflation forecast from the Philadelphia Federal Reserve Bank,
and RC is the after-tax restructuring charge associated with the merger.

The above formula assumes that cost savings and revenue gains increase in perpetuity at a rate equal to the long-term inflation forecast and uses an equity discount
rate that is based on the capital asset pricing model. The risk-free component of the rate
is the 10-year Treasury bond yield to maturity at the time of the merger announcement.
Beta is the Value Line beta of the acquirer. Value Line calculates betas using weekly
data over 5 years and allows for mean reversion of beta toward one. In mergers
reported as "mergers of equals" (where the bidder and target are approximately the
same size), we average the beta of the two banks to get the firm beta. The beta is then
multiplied by an assumed market risk premium of 7% and added to the 10-year T-bond
yield to get the discount rate.[4] The average discount rate for the 41 firms in our sample
is 15.05%.

[4] The 7% risk premium is the approximate arithmetic mean risk premium relative to T-bonds recommended by
Ibbotson and Associates (1999). This discount rate has two appealing aspects. It accounts for the fact that CAPM
tests frequently find that the intercept term is too high and the risk premium too low for fitted data when the risk-
free rate is assumed to be a short-term T-bill. Secondly, it accounts for long-term inflation forecasts built into the
10-year Treasury bond. In a prior draft of this paper, we use a smaller market risk premium suggested by Copeland
et al. (1995) based on the historical geometric average risk premium relative to T-bonds. This results in lower
discount rates and roughly 20% higher present values of incremental merger gains. A troubling aspect of the
discount rate used is that it reflects the cost of equity financing and thus assumes no debt financing associated with
the merger. The discount rate also assumes that cost savings and revenue estimates are of similar risk to the average
cash flows of the firm. Arguably, cost savings are less risky.

The last component of the equation is an estimate of the after-tax restructuring costs associated with the merger. Management generally conveys some estimate of merger integration costs in the form of a merger restructuring charge. The charge is generally an undiscounted estimate of future severance payments, lease buyouts, and write-downs of assets deemed obsolete due to the merger, although most of these costs will be incurred shortly after the merger is completed. However, different banks report their restructuring costs in different ways. For instance, there are cases in which management includes loan loss provisions as part of the restructuring cost. We exclude this item from the charge. It is alleged that some firms aggressively estimate all possible integration costs and use the merger reserve to make future earnings look better. There is little we can do about this. A couple of firms only report costs as they are incurred and do not give a detailed breakdown of how integration costs affect subsequent-year earnings. In the few cases in which management does not take a charge or does not provide an estimate of the charge, we treat the actual merger expense (or charge) reported by the firm in the annual report at the end of the merger year as if it were an ex ante estimate.

4. Empirical results

4.1. Changes in the bank acquisition market: evidence from the full sample of mergers

Table 1 provides descriptive statistics for the entire sample of bank mergers. Since we are interested in whether recent merger activity differs from mergers in the 1980s, we also report descriptive statistics for mergers in two time periods: 1985–1990 and 1991–1996. The financial characteristics of the bidder and target banks indicate no significant differences in the relative size or profitability of bidder or target banks for mergers in the 1980s and 1990s. During both periods, the target assets average about 40% of the bidder's assets. Bidders are, on average, slightly more profitable (as measured by ROA) than targets for the entire sample period and each of the subperiods.

In terms of deal characteristics, there are several significant differences between mergers in the 1980s and 1990s. As shown in Panel B of Table 1, mergers in the 1980s are more likely to be market expansion mergers with less geographical overlap between bidders and targets. Cost savings are also reported more frequently in the 1990s, with 94.5% of the acquirers reporting cost saving estimates in the 1990s versus only 22.2% in the 1980s. The more frequent reporting of cost savings coincides with a reduction in the frequency of market expansion transactions in the 1990s. If one believes that geographic overlap is essential to generate significant cost savings, this could be construed as evidence that acquirers are less likely to make projections for mergers that will not generate much in the way of tangible earnings increases. However, as discussed below, managerial estimates of a merger's impact on costs and/or revenues are much more frequent even for market expansion transactions in the 1990s. Consequently, it is difficult to determine whether more frequent reporting of

Table 1

Descriptive statistics for 64 bank mergers announced during the period 1985–1996

The sample consists of large bank acquisitions in which the market value of the target exceeds $400 million in 1985 dollars and the target's assets equal at least 10% of the bidder's assets. Descriptive statistics are reported for the entire sample as well as for mergers in the 1980s and mergers in the 1990s to show changes in merger characteristics over time. Asset size is measured by the book value of assets for the year preceding the merger announcement. The market value of equity is measured 5 days before any news announcement identifying the firm as being involved in merger activity and equals the number of shares outstanding times the price per share of common stock. ROA is return on assets computed as net income divided by average total assets for the year preceding the merger announcement. Market overlap is a measure of the degree to which the operations of the bidder and target overlap geographically. The maximum value of overlap is 0.5 and the minimum value is 0. Overlap is defined as

$$\text{Overlap} = \frac{\sum_{i=1}^{n} \min(T_i, B_i)}{\sum_{i=1}^{n} (T_i + B_i)},$$

where n is the total number of cities in which either bank has offices and T_i and B_i are the total number of officers the target and bidder have in city i. Market expansion mergers involve mergers in which the amount of branch overlap divided by total target bank offices is less than 0.04. Mergers with cost savings estimates are acquisitions in which the acquiring bank's management provides a cost savings estimate in either the press release, the proxy statement, the 8k filing, or an analyst meeting. Cost savings estimates are only used if the forecasts are explicit about the level of savings and define a time frame for achievement.

	Overall		1985–1990		1991–1996	
	Mean	Median	Mean	Median	Mean	Median
A. Financial characteristics						
Bidder asset size ($ millions)	35,000	22,100	18,400	15,200	47,200	29,300
Target asset size ($ millions)	14,900	6980	7390	5132	20,300	9710
Target assets/bidder assets	0.434	0.351	0.455	0.382	0.419	0.267
Target market value of equity/bidder market value equity	0.387	0.342	0.396	0.346	0.381	0.308
Bidder ROA	0.0107	0.0106	0.0105	0.0107	0.0109	0.0104
Target ROA	0.0087	0.0100	0.0086	0.0095	0.0089	0.0104
Number of observations	64		27		37	
B. Deal characteristics						
Market overlap	0.066	0.028	0.040	0.00	0.084	0.060
Percent market expansion	45.3		62.1		30.4	
Percent using purchase accounting	11		8		14	
Percent with firm cost savings estimates	64		22.2		94.5	

estimates reflects an increased sensitivity of senior management to justify their deals or whether technological and regulatory changes enhanced the opportunity for cost savings and have made the numbers worth reporting.

Table 2 provides the abnormal stock returns for bidders and targets as well as the combined market value change associated with the mergers. Abnormal returns for the bidder and the target are calculated over a period beginning 4 days before the so-called "leak date" and ending on the day after the agreement is announced. The leak date is

Table 2

Announcement-period abnormal returns and combined valuation changes for 64 large bank acquisitions announced during the period 1985–1996

Abnormal returns are net-of-market returns compounded daily over a window running from 4 days before the target (bidder) is identified in the financial press as being involved in merger activity related to the eventual acquisition until 1 day after the merger agreement is announced. Market returns are the return on the CRSP value-weighted market portfolio. Combined abnormal returns are computed as a weighted average of bidder and target returns. The weights are the market value of each firm's equity 5 days before the target (bidder) is identified as being involved in merger activity related to the eventual acquisition. The valuation change is computed by taking the abnormal return to the target multiplied by the target's market value 5 days before the first merger news for the target and adding it to the abnormal return to the bidder multiplied by the bidder's market value 5 days before the first merger news for the bidder.

	All deals	1985–1990	1991–1996
Number	64	27	37
Combined abnormal returns (%)	1.86	0.14	3.11[*]
t-Statistic	2.17	0.17	2.35
Valuation change ($ millions)	165.90	2.27	285.31[*]
Bidder abnormal returns (%)	−3.47	−4.64	−2.61
t-Statistic	−3.87	−5.82	−1.83
Target abnormal returns (%)	20.80	15.58	24.60[*]
t-Statistic	9.13	5.19	7.77

[*]Significantly greater than the corresponding figure for the 1980s at the 10% level.

the first date that the target (bidder) is cited as being potentially involved in takeover activity (e.g., being in takeover talks or putting the bank up for sale). This includes specific rumors that are not denied by the parties involved, but excludes generic articles that the bank might make a good takeover target (bidder). Note that the target leak date often precedes any bidder leak date, because the target may be identified as being in acquisition talks, but the bidder is not identified. When there is no leak date, the leak date is set equal to the announcement date.

To calculate merger event abnormal returns over the announcement window of interest, each day the bank's return less the CRSP value-weighted market index return is calculated. These daily net-of-market returns are then compounded over the window period. To measure the combined-firm merger-related revaluation for each transaction, we multiply the abnormal returns for the target and the abnormal returns for the bidder by the respective market value of each bank 5 days prior to the leak date. We then sum the bidder and target revaluation. To compute the combined return, we divide the combined revaluation of the target and bidder by the combined market value of their common stock (5 days before each bank's "leak date").

Like previous studies, we find a negative and statistically significant abnormal return to acquiring banks and a positive and statistically significant return to acquired banks. However, in contrast with a number of prior studies, we find that the average combined return to the bidder and target is not only positive (1.85%) but significantly different from zero at the 5% level. The average combined return for bidders and targets results in an average $165 million increase in the combined value of the bidder and target. Comparing deals in the 1980s to deals in the 1990s, there is a significant increase in the abnormal returns of the combined banks. Indeed, the combined return for bidders and targets is positive and statistically significant only for the deals in the 1990s. The superior performance in the 1990s is due to increased returns for both the bidder and target banks.

To further investigate the reason for the increase in combined returns, we compare market expansion acquisitions to market overlap transactions. As shown in Table 3, the returns for market overlap transactions are significantly higher than the returns realized for market expansion transactions. This difference is due to the significant increase in the combined returns for market overlap transactions in the 1990s. Notice that the average return increases from 0.89% in the 1980s to 4.77% in the 1990s. In contrast, for market expansion transactions, the combined returns decline slightly in the 1990s relative to the 1980s.

One explanation for the increase in returns for market overlap transactions is that the opportunity for cost savings is greatest for these types of transactions and that the opportunities for cost savings through consolidation of branch operations and back-room operations increased in the 1990s. This view is reflected in several stock analyst reports discussing industry trends (e.g., "Shop till you drop," Salomon Brothers industry report, August 1997) and is also consistent with the idea that in the 1990s there is "overcapacity" in banking in terms of redundant backroom operations and full-service branch offices. Overall, this evidence is consistent with previous empirical work by Houston and Ryngaert (1994) showing that geographically focused mergers offer higher returns than geographically diversifying mergers. While the conjecture is that these increased returns are due to superior cost-cutting opportunities, we investigate this contention by examining management's forecasted merger-related gains for the subsample of 41 mergers.

4.2. Management's view of the sources and magnitude of merger-related gains

Using the methodology described in Section 3, we estimate the value of merger-related cost savings and revenue gains for a sample of 41 mergers in which management provides contemporaneous estimates of cost savings and revenue gains. Table 4 contains descriptive statistics for the banks in the subsample. As shown in Table 4, the characteristics of the mergers in the subsample are similar to the mergers in the larger sample in terms of the relative size and ROA of the target and the bidder. They differ, however, in that these mergers have greater geographic overlap and the abnormal returns on the stock of the combined bidder and target are significantly higher at 3.15% (vs. −0.48% for those not reporting estimates).

Table 3

Descriptive statistics for bank mergers grouped by type of merger during the period 1985–1996

Summary statistics concerning announcement period, abnormal stock returns, cost savings estimates, and market overlap for a sample of 64 larger bank acquisitions grouped by whether or not the merger acquisition extends the bidder's geographical market. Announcement-period abnormal returns are daily net-of-market returns compounded daily over a window running from 4 days before the target (bidder) is identified in the financial press as being involved in merger activity related to the eventual acquisition until 1 day after the merger agreement is announced. Market returns are the return on the CRSP value weighted market portfolio. A merger is defined as a market expansion merger if the number of offices overlapping geographically divided by the total number of target offices is below 0.04. Market overlap is a measure of the degree to which the operations of the bidder and target overlap geographically. The maximum value of overlap is 0.5 and the minimum value is 0. Overlap is defined as

$$\text{Overlap} = \frac{\sum_{i=1}^{n} \min(T_i, B_i)}{\sum_{i=1}^{n} (T_i + B_i)},$$

where n is the total number of cities in which either bank has offices and T_i and B_i are the total number of officers the target and bidder have in city i. Combined abnormal returns are the weighted average of bidder and target returns. The weights are the market value of each firm 5 days before the target (bidder) is identified as being involved in merger-related activity. Cost savings estimates are only used if the forecasts are explicit about the level of savings and define a time frame for achievement.

	Overall sample		1985–1990		1991–1996	
	Mean	Median	Mean	Median	Mean	Median
A. Market expansion						
Number of observations	29		18		11	
Bidder abnormal return (%)	−4.40	−4.68	−4.23	−3.76	−4.93	−4.89
Target abnormal return (%)	16.17	12.45	11.43	8.59	23.93[*]	26.02[*]
Combined abnormal return	−0.045	−0.41	0.57	0.44	−0.82	−0.94
Percent with management cost savings estimates	37.9	–	11.1	–	81.8	–
Market overlap	0.002	0	0.008	0	0.003	0
B. Market overlap						
Number of observations	35		9		26	
Bidder abnormal return (%)	−2.69	−4.28	−5.45	−5.08	−1.73[*]	−2.93
Target abnormal return (%)	24.62	18.18	23.28	19.28	24.88	15.34
Combined abnormal return (%)	3.77	1.40	0.89	0.91	4.77[*]	4.04[*]
Percent with management cost savings estimates	85.7	–	44.4	–	100	–
Market overlap	0.118	0.115	0.116	0.115	0.119	0.126

[*]Significantly different from mean (median) for 1980s at the 10% level.

The higher returns for this subsample are not all that surprising. For all mergers in the subsample, management provides an estimate of the incremental cost savings and/ or revenues the merger is expected to generate. Disclosure of this information could indicate that these mergers are likely to have the largest incremental earnings increases. Alternatively, the acquiring bank's management could face greater

Table 4

Descriptive statistics for 41 bank mergers with management estimates of cost savings and revenue enhancement during the period 1985–1996

The 41 mergers are from a subset of 64 large bank acquisitions preceding the merger announcement. ROA is return on assets computed as net income divided by average total assets for the year before merger announcement. Market value equals the market value of common stock outstanding 5 days before the target (bidder) is identified as being involved in merger activity related to the eventual acquisition. Market overlap is a measure of the degree to which the operations of the bidder and target overlap geographically. The maximum value of overlap is 0.5 and the minimum value is 0. Overlap is defined as

$$\text{Overlap} = \frac{\sum_{i=1}^{n} \min(T_i, B_i)}{\sum_{i=1}^{n} (T_i + B_i)},$$

where n is the total number of cities in which either bank has offices in and T_i and B_i are the total number of officers the target and bidder have in city i. Combined abnormal returns are a weighted average of bidder and target returns. The weights are the market value of each firm's equity 5 days before the target (bidder) was identified as being involved in merger activity related to the eventual acquisition. The abnormal returns for each firm are daily net-of-market returns compounded over a window running from 4 days before the target (bidder) is identified as being involved in merger activity related to the eventual acquisition until 1 day after the merger announcement. The combined market value change of the target and bidder is computed by taking the abnormal return to the target multiplied by the target's market value 5 days before the first merger news for the target and adding it to the abnormal return to the bidder multiplied by the bidder's market value 5 days before the first merger news for the bidder. The estimated present value of merger gains equals the discounted value of management estimated cost savings and revenue gains computed using Equation (2) in the text. In computing the present value of gains, a perpetual growth rate equal to the expected rate of inflation is used. The inflation estimate is from the Philadelphia Federal Reserve Bank. Merger gains are computed net of restructuring changes. After-tax cash flows are discounted using a CAPM-based discount rate.

	Mean	Median
Panel A: Financial characteristics of bidder and target banks		
Bidder asset size ($ millions)	43,300	26,700
Target asset size ($ millions)	18,700	7729
Bidder ROA (%)	1.06	1.04
Target ROA (%)	0.88	1.04
Panel B: Deal characteristics and valuation changes		
Target market value/bidder market value	0.381	0.307
Market overlap	0.091	0.069
Combined abnormal return (%)	3.15	0.64
Bidder abnormal return (%)	−2.94	−4.73
Target abnormal return (%)	24.73	19.23
Combined market value change of target and bidder ($ millions)	265.46	36.54
Estimated present value of merger gains ($ millions)	765.05	369.06
Estimated present value of net cost savings ($ millions)	711.36	367.09
Estimated present value of revenue gains ($ millions)	53.69	0
Estimated present value of merger gains/target market value	0.5207	0.3650
(Estimated present value of merger)/(combined bidder and target market value)	0.1306	0.0950

shareholder scrutiny and therefore may need to justify the transactions by providing detailed cost and revenue estimates. Indeed, it could be argued that more-recent transactions almost always carry estimates because the investment community expects them. Moreover, this heightened scrutiny might force management to be more select-ive in the types of deals that they pursue.

In Panel B of Table 4, we provide estimates of the present value of incremental earnings expected from the merger. We also break out the present value of net cost savings from the merger (the present value of cost savings less the after-tax restruc-turing charge) and the present value of revenue enhancements. The average present value of estimated incremental earnings is $765.05 million and is highly skewed with a median value of $369.06 million. Most of the earnings gains arise from expected net cost savings, with estimated net cost savings averaging $711.36 million. The average estimated gains related to revenue enhancements are only $53.69 million, with a median of 0. In fact, only about 7% of the merger-related gains in the average transaction are related to changes in estimated revenue. Moreover, management reports revenue estimates in only 13 of the mergers in our sample.

The qualitative evidence from analyst reports and news accounts (discussed below) suggests that management is often reluctant to report revenue gains or to justify mergers based on revenue enhancement. For example, in a small number of cases in which management does not report revenue estimates, the press accounts and analyst reports suggest that management believes that enhancements are possible. Interest-ingly, analysts frequently compliment managers for showing that a deal "works," usually meaning that the deal is accretive to per-share earnings within 1 or 2 years, without assuming any revenue enhancements. Hence, it is possible that revenue enhancements are sometimes reported to justify what the investment community feels is a shaky transaction. In either event, the numbers suggest that management views merger gains as arising primarily from cost savings and not from revenue enhancements.

As shown in Table 4, the estimates of merger-related gains are large relative to the premium paid for the target. The average estimated present value of the merger gains as a percentage of the target's premerger market value is 52.07%. On the other hand, the average target's value increases only 24.73% over the announcement window. Nevertheless, the average bidder's value falls by 2.94%. The average estimated present value of the merger gains as a percentage of the combined bidder and target's market value is 13.06%, but the average stock market revaluation of the combined bidder and target is only 3.15%. Indeed, in all but two of the 41 mergers, the estimated value of merger gains exceeds the joint revaluation of the bidder and target.

On the basis of the above evidence, it is tempting to speculate that acquiring bank managers are overly optimistic in their assessments of the gains to be created from mergers. Before investigating this conjecture, it is worth recalling our early discussion of the limitations of bank merger event studies. Since these transactions may have been anticipated by capital markets, observed returns could be biased toward zero. Add-itionally, a bidder can convey negative information whenever it offers to acquire a target with stock. In our sample of 41 transactions with cost estimates, 38 bidders use stock as the sole means of payment. There are also questions regarding the valuation model we employ. It might be overly optimistic to assume that the estimated cost savings and revenue enhancements would never happen without the merger and that real incremental merger gains will last in perpetuity.

Before we address alternative valuation scenarios, the reasonableness of our current estimates can be judged in part by answering two questions. First, are the projected valuation gains explained by factors that should be related to those gains? Second, are the valuation estimates related to the abnormal returns in a manner that is consistent with economic intuition?

We first investigate the determinants of management's estimates of merger-related gains. We attempt to explain the variation in the estimated valuation of total merger-related gains (revenue increases and cost cuts) and in the estimated valuation of net cost savings using a number of variables that are predicted to influence those gains. In each case, the present value estimates are divided by the combined premerger market values of the bidder and target. The explanatory variables are the degree of geographical overlap, the size of the target relative to the bidder, the pretax ROA for the combined target and bidder prior to the merger (adjusted for special items), and the premerger operating efficiency ratio of the merging banks in the year prior to the merger (adjusted for special items). The detailed definitions of the ROA and efficiency ratio are given in Table 5. We expect the estimated cost savings to be positively related to market overlap, the relative size of the target, and the premerger efficiency ratio, and negatively related to the firms' premerger ROA.

The results of this analysis are provided in Table 5. Our valuations of net cost savings and total earnings gains are best explained by the degree of geographical overlap. Regressions including this variable explain about 58% of the variation in the valuation of net cost savings forecasts. The explanatory power of regressions combining cost savings and revenue enhancements is lower. High levels of overlap indicate substantial opportunities for cost savings via elimination of redundant facilities. Since a higher efficiency ratio is associated with higher noninterest expenses, the positive coefficient on the efficiency ratio is consistent with relatively inefficient banks offering the greatest cost savings. The negative coefficient on the combined banks' premerger ROA is also consistent with less-profitable banks offering the greatest cost savings potential. Larger acquisitions also result in larger cost savings estimates.

While the determinants of (estimated) value creation inferred from incremental earnings forecasts appear reasonable, it is still an open question whether the stock market takes these estimates seriously. To address this question, we estimate the cross-sectional relation between target and bidder announcement returns and our estimates of appropriately scaled merger-related gains. The results, reported in Table 6, indicate that our estimates of merger-related gains explain a considerable proportion of the cross-sectional variation in announcement-day returns of the bidder and target.

Panel A of Table 6 reports the results for the target returns. The slope coefficient suggests that target banks receive 36 cents of every dollar of estimated total gains.

Table 5

Determinants of the value of merger gains

Cross-sectional regressions relating the present value of management's estimated cost savings and revenue gains from the bank acquisition to the bidder and target's premerger efficiency ratio and return on assets, the market value of the target relative to the bidder, and the degree of geographic overlap. The sample consists of 41 large bank mergers with management estimates of cost savings or revenue gains over the period 1985–1996 (t-statistics are in parentheses). The estimated present value of the merger equals the discounted value of management's estimated cost savings and revenue gains computed by using Equation (2) in the text and a perpetual growth rate equal to the expected rate of inflation. The inflation estimate is from the Philadelphia Federal Reserve Bank. Merger gains are computed net of restructuring charges. The rate for discounting estimated cost savings and revenues is based on the CAPM. The estimated present value of the cost savings equals the present discounted value of management estimated cost savings net of restructuring charges. The combined efficiency ratio is the sum of labor, equipment, and occupancy costs for both the bidder and the target divided by the sum of the taxable equivalent net interest income and noninterest income from nonrecurring items for the bidder and target. This ratio is computed using accounting information in a year preceding the merger. If the merger is announced in the first half of the fiscal year, the ratio is calculated using prior fiscal year data and if the merger is announced in the second half of the fiscal year, the ratio is calculated for that year. The adjusted pretax ROA begins with profit before tax of the bidder and target combined and then excludes securities gains and other nonrecurring income items and adds book provisions for loan losses, OREO expenses, amortization of intangibles (primarily goodwill), and restructuring charges associated with mergers and reorganizations. This adjusted pretax profit figure is divided by the average total assets for the bidder and target in the year it is calculated. Market value equals the market value of common stock outstanding 5 days before the target (bidder) is identified as being involved in merger activity related to the eventual acquisition. Market overlap is a measure of the degree to which the operations of the bidder and target overlap geographically. The maximum value of overlap is 0.5 and the minimum value is 0. Overlap is defined as

$$\text{Overlap} = \frac{\sum_{i=1}^{n} \min(T_i, B_i)}{\sum_{i=1}^{n} (T_i + B_i)},$$

where n is the total number of cities in which either bank has offices in and T_i and B_i are the total number of officers the target and bidder have in city i.

	Estimated present value of merger/combined market value		Estimated present value of net cost savings/combined market value	
	(1)	(2)	(3)	(4)
Constant	−0.412 (−1.49)	0.216 (2.77)	−0.328 (−1.53)	0.176 (2.68)
Combined efficiency ratio (premerger)	1.046 (1.61)		0.827 (1.63)	
Combined adjusted pretax ROA (premerger)		−8.57 (−2.25)		−7.07 (−2.30)
Target market value/bidder market value	0.105 (1.65)	0.08 (1.34)	0.086 (1.75)	0.071 (1.36)
Market overlap	0.762 (4.68)	0.874 (4.94)	0.809 (5.81)	0.896 (5.67)
Adjusted R^2	0.513	0.517	0.581	0.588

When the gains are broken out into a revenue component and a net cost saving component, the coefficient estimate on cost savings is similar at 0.37 and the coefficient on revenue gains is positive (0.19) but insignificant. Clearly, the important

Table 6

Cross-sectional regression relating bidder and target abnormal stock returns to estimated merger gains

Bidder and target abnormal stock returns are daily net-of-market returns compounded daily over a window running from 4 days before the bidder or target is identified in the financial press as being involved in merger activity related to the eventual acquisition until 1 day after the merger agreement is announced. The sample consists of 41 large bank mergers with management estimates of cost savings or revenue gains during the period 1985–1996. Panel A contains results using announcement-day abnormal returns for the target bank as the dependent variable. Panel B contains results using announcement-day abnormal returns of the bidder bank as the dependent variable. Panel C contains results using announcement-day abnormal returns of the combined bidder and target banks as the dependent variable. The combined bidder and target returns are a weighted average of the bidder and target returns where the weights are each bank's premerger market value (*t*-statistics are in parentheses). Estimated present value of merger gains equals the discounted value of management's estimated cost savings and revenue gains computed using Equation (2) in the text. In computing the value of gains, perpetual growth rate equal to the expected rate of inflation is used. The inflation estimate is from the Philadelphia Federal Reserve Bank. Merger gains are computed net of restructuring changes. Bidder and target market values are the market value of common stock outstanding 5 days before the target (bidder) is identified as being involved in merger activity related to the eventual acquisition. Estimated present value of net cost savings equals the present discounted value of management estimated cost savings net of restructuring charges Estimated present value of revenue enhancements equals the present discounted value of estimated after-tax revenue gains.

Explanatory variable	(1)	(2)	(3)
Panel A: Target abnormal returns			
Constant	0.057 (1.69)	0.058 (1.68)	0.063 (2.16)
Estimated present value of merger gains/target market value	0.361 (5.44)		
Estimated present value of net cost savings/target market value		0.371 (6.86)	0.374 (6.82)
Estimated value of revenue enhancements/target market value		0.191 (0.41)	
R^2	0.492	0.497	0.492
Panel B: Bidder abnormal returns			
Constant	−0.072 (−6.59)	−0.075 (−6.70)	−0.074
Estimated present value of merger gains/bidder market value	0.220 (3.94)		
Estimated present value of net cost savings/bidder market value		0.272 (3.04)	0.252 (3.91)
Estimated value of revenue enhancements/bidder market value		−0.213 (−0.70)	
R^2	0.305	0.335	0.328
Panel C: Combined firm abnormal returns			
Constant	−0.032 (−2.65)	−0.035 (−3.38)	−0.035 (−3.21)
Estimated present value of merger/combined bidder and target market value	0.487 (4.29)		
Estimated present value of net cost savings/combined bidder and target market value		0.579 (5.80)	0.550 (5.90)
Estimated value of revenue enhancements/combined bidder and target market value		−0.427 (−1.30)	
R^2	0.591	0.655	0.641

determinant of the target returns is the net cost savings. When this variable is introduced alone, the regression R^2 remains at 49%.

Panel B reports the results for the bidder returns. For every dollar increase in the total valuation gain estimate, the bidder's value increases 22 cents. When we break out the components of the gain, the bidder's value goes up 27.2 cents for every dollar of our estimated value of net cost savings and falls 21.3 cents for every dollar of estimated revenue valuation gains. The revenue coefficient, however, is not statistically different from zero. Again, the whole story is net cost savings. When this variable is introduced alone, the R^2 of the regression is 33%, about the same as when the revenue variable is included.

Some additional points emerge from the bidder return regressions. Each specification has a significant intercept of about −7%. One interpretation of the intercept is that it is related to news conveyed by the merger announcement that is unrelated to the merger gains. One aspect would be the negative signal of issuing a large quantity of equity in a merger. These are large acquisitions, and the equity issuance literature tends to find larger negative returns for larger equity issues. A second component of the intercept might reflect disappointment that the bidder itself is now less likely to be acquired. The negative coefficient on the valuation of revenue gains is also suggestive. When coupled with the positive coefficient on the valuation of revenue gains for targets, it suggests that bidders anticipating revenue enhancement might be paying for something that will not pay off in the eyes of the market. Again, however, the coefficients on the revenue variables are statistically insignificant. What is encouraging, from a rational bidder perspective, is the coefficient on the net cost savings variable. The stock market is clearly capitalizing management's cost-cutting projections as if the bidder will get a slice of this "synergy." Thus, one hypothesis of mergers that can clearly be dismissed based on these results is the hypothesis that bidders routinely overestimate the cost savings gains and overpay that full amount to targets. If this hypothesis were true, we would expect a negative coefficient on the cost savings variable.

The final set of regressions in Panel C of Table 6 are for the combined bidder and target returns. Once again, cost savings have the greatest explanatory power. Indeed, when we present the value of revenue gains and cost savings separately, the estimated coefficient on revenue gains is significantly negative. The negative coefficient on revenue gains once again suggests the possibility that management includes estimates of revenue gains to justify what investors believe are questionable deals. Our valuation estimate of net cost savings, when entered in the regression alone, explains 64% of the cross-sectional variation in the combined returns of the bidder and target banks. The slope coefficient suggests that a dollar in present value of estimated net cost savings results in about a 55-cent change in the combined value of the bidder and the target. Theoretically, if the stock market fully capitalized the merger wealth effects at announcement, we would expect the coefficient to equal one. However, we know that there is substantial prior anticipation of takeover activity that is already built in the respective banks' stock prices, which could explain why the coefficient is well below one. At the same time, the intercept (-3.53%) is also consistent with negative signaling effects from the merger announcement.

The combined evidence of Tables 4 and 6 could also indicate that management typically overvalues the merger-related gains. This conclusion seems particularly true for revenue estimates that appear to have no influence on returns. As for cost savings, the average valuation of cost savings is much higher than the average combined stock market revaluation of the bidder and target, and the coefficients on the net cost savings variable in the regressions in Panel C of Table 6 are well below one. We should be careful about this interpretation, however, because our valuation estimates do not come directly from management. Indeed, we take the cost and revenue forecasts and infer valuation consequences from those numbers. For instance, management generally forecasts some level of cost savings to be accomplished in 2 years. They rarely state what will happen after that date, though the inference is often that these are permanent cost cuts.

To investigate how alternative assumptions about the future affect our analysis, we use two alternative valuation models. In one model we assume no growth in nominal cost savings and revenue enhancements beyond year 4. In the other model, we assume that the revenue enhancements and cost savings will decline 30% per year after year 4. The rationale for tweaking the valuation models in these ways is based on the idea that any merger savings should be incremental relative to what would occur without a merger. For instance, a merger could provide the impetus for cost-cutting efforts, particularly if one of the organizations involved has been previously lax in that area. Once the changes are made, however, it is possible that the organization can again slip into bad habits and that the incremental merger benefits will be lost over time. Alternatively, it could be argued that even without a merger, competitive pressures would eventually lead an inefficient bank to get its house in order. Hence, the gap between a bank's expense levels with and without the merger will tend to converge through time. Additionally, employing a perpetuity valuation model assumes that the organization "will last forever." This too could be overly optimistic.

Table 7 provides the results for our robustness tests using alternative valuation models. Using the zero perpetual growth assumption, Table 7 shows that the total valuation estimate as a percentage of combined firm value falls from 13% to 10.1%. The estimated slope coefficient in the regression relating the combined revaluation to the value of net cost savings increases to 0.735 and slightly decreases the R^2 of the regression relative to the inflation rate perpetual growth model. The slope coefficient for the newly estimated total valuation gains (including revenues) also increases. The more draconian valuation model assuming a 30% decay rate in incremental earnings produces much smaller estimates of total valuation gains that are only 4.3% of the combined value of the bidder and target. The regression slope coefficients are in excess of one and generate smaller regression R^2s.

It is worth noting that the effect of tweaking the model with lower growth rates is very similar to multiplying the estimated gains with a different scalar. As the gains are multiplied by a smaller factor, the slope coefficient increases and the intercept stays

Table 7

Cross-sectional regressions relating combined bidder and target abnormal returns to valuation estimates of merger gains computed using alternative assumptions about long-term growth

Combined bidder and target abnormal returns are a weighted average of bidder and target abnormal returns where the weight is each bank's premerger market value. Abnormal returns are daily-net-of market returns compounded daily over a window running from 4 days before the bidder or target is identified in the financial press as being involved in merger activity related to the eventual acquisition until 1 day after the merger is announced. The sample consists of 41 large bank mergers with management estimates of cost savings or revenue gains during the period 1985–1996. Panel A contains regression results relating combined abnormal returns to the present value of merger gains assuming no growth in cost savings and revenue gains after 4 years following the merger. Panel B contains regression results relating combined abnormal returns to the present value of merger gains assuming that cost savings and revenue gains erode after 4 years at a rate of −30% (*t*-statistics in parentheses). The estimated present value of merger gains equals the discounted value of management estimated cost savings and revenue gains computed by using Equation (2) in the text, except the perpetual growth rate of incremental earnings after year 4 is set equal to 0 in Panel A and −30% in Panel B. Merger gains are computed net of restructuring charges. Market value equals the market value of common stock outstanding 5 days before the target (bidder) is identified as being involved in merger activity related to the eventual acquisition. The mean value of the present value of merger gains relative to the market value of the bidder and target is 0.101 (10.1%) in Panel A and 0.043 (4.3%) Panel B. The estimated present value of net cost savings equals the present discounted value of management estimated cost savings net of restructuring charges, except the perpetual growth rate of incremental earnings after year 4 is set equal to 0 in Panel A. The mean value of the present value of net cost savings relative to the market value of the bidder and target is 0.094 (9.4%) in Panel A and 0.039 (3.9%) Panel B.

Explanatory variables	(1)	(2)
Panel A: Explaining combined abnormal returns with present value estimates based on perpetual growth of 0%		
Constant	−0.034 (−2.75)	−0.038 (−3.40)
Estimated present value of merger gains/combined bidder and target market value	0.646 (4.86)	
Estimated present value of net cost savings/combined bidder and target market value		0.735 (6.05)
R^2	0.610	0.667
Panel B: Explaining combined abnormal returns with present value estimates based on perpetual growth of −30%		
Constant	−0.035 (−2.99)	−0.039 (−3.46)
Estimated present value of merger gains/combined bidder and target market value	1.558 (5.23)	
Estimated present value of net cost savings/combined bidder and target market value		1.805 (6.03)
R^2	0.577	0.632

about the same. Being slightly less optimistic about the long run (i.e., assuming zero growth) tends to preserve the interpretation that the merger gains are somewhat anticipated (though the coefficient edges closer to one) and that combined returns are reduced due to negative signaling at the announcement of mergers. The more aggressive decay model gives results with respect to the slope coefficient that suggest the valuation estimates are downward biased.

A final way to evaluate management's cost savings and revenue estimates is to determine the market value multiple revaluation for the incremental cash flows. To estimate this multiple we used the third-year after-tax revenue and cost projections. These projections are assumed to represent management's assessment of the "long-run" or steady-state cash flow gains from the merger. We take these projections of nominal incremental cash flows in year 3 and discount the projections back to the time of the merger at the anticipated inflation rate over the 3-year horizon. This gives us steady-state projections in real terms. We then regress the market revaluation of the bidder and target against the steady-state incremental earnings projections. The estimated regression coefficients can be interpreted as the multiple at which the market values incremental cash flows.

The regression results using this methodology are reported in Table 8. For the combined banks, the cash flow multiple for cost saving is about 3.5. In contrast, the multiple for revenue gains is negative. By comparison, banks covered by the Value Line Investment Survey have average-price-to-earnings multiples in the early to mid-1990s in the 8–12 range. Hence, the multiple attached to extra earnings, even in the case of cost savings, is well below market multiples during this time period. Nevertheless, one should keep in mind that the estimate of the multiple assigned to future earnings is not directly comparable to a current earnings multiple. The market revaluation also accounts for the restructuring costs associated with the merger, which typically equal the projected annual cost savings for the merger. Furthermore, the estimated savings used in the regression are based on peak savings that will not be achieved in 2–3 years. When one adjusts for the fact that our estimated multiple does not account for restructuring costs and the time delay in achieving earnings, the results are quite consistent with the regressions based on discounted cash flows, which find that roughly half the estimated cost savings are capitalized into market prices.[5]

4.3. Potential sources of overoptimism in managerial projections

Given the inability of the stock market evidence to provide a conclusive answer regarding the degree of overptimism (except perhaps with respect to revenue estimates) in managerial forecasts, we now turn our attention to management's estimates to find additional insights. There is some reason to believe that management is being too optimistic in certain dimensions of its forecasts (or is at least not being totally

---

[5] To see this, note that if there were no restructuring costs associated with the merger, the market revaluation could be raised by the amount of the restructuring charge. Then the cost savings multiple would be 4.5 rather than 3.5. Also, since there is a time delay in achieving savings, this might artificially shave another point off of our estimated earnings multiple relative to a current earnings multiple. Thus, the reported multiple of 3.5 on 3-year steady-state earnings is more comparable to a multiple of 5.5 if the earnings could be achieved immediately and at no restructuring costs. Comparing a multiple of 5.5 to a bank earnings multiple of 10 suggests that about 55% of the estimated savings are capitalized by the market, which is similar to the regression estimates based on discounted cash flow valuation of cost savings.

Table 8

Cross-sectional regression relating bidder and target abnormal stock returns to estimated after-tax merger-related revenue gains and cost savings in the third year after the merger

Bidder and target abnormal stock returns are daily net-of-market returns compounded daily over a window running from 4 days before the bidder or target is identified in the financial press as being involved in merger activity related to the eventual acquisition until 1 day after the merger agreement is announced. The sample consists of 41 large bank mergers with management estimates of cost savings or revenue gains during the period 1985–1996. Panel A contains results using announcement-day abnormal returns for target bank as the dependent variable. Panel B contains results using announcement-day abnormal returns of the bidder bank as the dependent variable. Panel C contains results using announcement-day abnormal returns of the combined bidder and target banks as the dependent variable. The combined bidder and target returns are a weighted average of the bidder and target returns where the weights are each bank's premerger market value (t-statistics are in parentheses). Estimated real after-tax revenue gains and cost savings for the third year after the merger are taken from management projections and are adjusted for expected inflation. The inflation estimate is from the Federal Reserve Bank of Philadelphia. Bidder and target market values are the market value of common stock outstanding 5 days before the target (bidder) is identified as being involved in merger activity related to the eventual acquisition.

Explanatory variable	(1)	(2)	(3)
Panel A: Target abnormal returns			
Constant	0.081 (1.86)	0.081 (1.95)	0.082 (2.20)
Estimated present value of merger gains/target market value	2.362 (3.43)		
Estimated present value of net cost savings/target market value		2.499 (4.55)	2.504 (4.22)
Estimated value of revenue enhancements/target market value		0.154 (0.03)	
Adjusted R^2	0.379	0.374	0.390
Panel B: Bidder abnormal returns			
Constant	−0.067 (−6.34)	−0.072 (−7.05)	−0.070 (−6.65)
Estimated present value of merger gains/bidder market value	1.399 (3.91)		
Estimated present value of net cost savings/bidder market value		1.870 (3.41)	1.597 (4.09)
Estimated value of revenue enhancements/bidder market value		−2.947 (−1.15)	
Adjusted R^2	0.308	0.338	0.334
Panel C: Combined firm abnormal returns			
Constant	−0.025 (−2.05)	−0.029 (−3.14)	−0.036 (−3.21)
Estimated present value of merger/combined bidder and target market value	3.107 (4.11)		
Estimated present value of net cost savings/combined bidder and target market value		3.963 (6.82)	3.514 (4.98)
Estimated value of revenue enhancements/combined bidder and target market value		−6.089 (−2.21)	
Adjusted R^2	0.589	0.686	0.653

forthcoming about negative aspects of their deals). For example, one of the most important oversights is the fact that management rarely includes an estimate of revenue losses arising from consolidation. Despite the likelihood of occurrence, expected revenue losses are infrequently reported and are rarely mentioned by analysts. In fact, within our sample, expected revenue losses are reported in only one transaction (Wells Fargo's acquisition of First Interstate Bancorp). *The American Banker* (December 9, 1997, p. 25) notes that "customer retention is something that most analysts rarely monitor unless something goes really wrong." Nevertheless, the same article quotes Lehman Brothers analyst Michael Plodwick as saying that "Most banking companies start out by estimating that five percent to ten percent of an acquired bank's deposits will be lost during an in-market transaction ... but usually a little less in an out-of-market deal." Losses are generally greater for in-market transactions because cost-saving branch closures are more likely to lead to customer shifts.

While a 5% (or even 10%) deposit loss does not necessarily imply a 5% revenue loss, a cost-cutting merger that creates a 5% loss of the acquired bank's revenues could easily cut our valuation of merger benefits by about one-third of the gains realized from a typical in-market merger. It is worth noting that some analysts are cognizant of this potential. Specifically, for the analyst reports that we review, at least one analyst forecasts and quantifies significant revenue losses in four separate deals (the mergers of Fleet and Shawmut, Comerica and Manufacturers National, Wells Fargo and First Interstate, and Chemical Bank and Manufacturers Hanover). These four deals were all big cost-saving mergers, which suggest that omitted revenue losses are probably proportional to cost savings. This sort of forecast omission (or overoptimism) would tend to lower the slope coefficient on the present value of net cost savings for our regressions in Table 6.

A second area of overoptimism can occur when management estimates the costs of integrating the two banks. These restructuring charges include items such as severance payments and lease buyouts. As we indicate in Section 3.2, restructuring charge estimates are sometimes omitted by firms. In these cases, we substitute ex post cost disclosures. It appears, however, that when restructuring estimates are given, they frequently underestimate ex post integration costs or actual charges subsequently taken. For 27 firms in our sample, we are able to glean some additional information about actual restructuring costs from the corporate disclosure statements. On average, the actual costs cited by management are 24.2% higher than what was initially estimated. These underestimates of restructuring costs will lead to upward-biased estimates of management's forecasts of the value gained from the merger. We should note, however, that estimates of after-tax restructuring charges in our sample average only about 1% of the combined bidder and target equity values. Hence, a 24% underestimate is not a large source of bias. On the other hand, these numbers do not include operating losses associated with lost customer transactions and misposting of deposits and loan payments to customer accounts. These snafus may occur in the process of integrating back-office computers. These items cost Wells Fargo roughly

$200 million in 1997 in the process of integrating First Interstate Bancorp. Wells Fargo, however, appears to be an outlier in this regard.

A final source of bias in management forecasts is the tendency to include cost savings that would have been realized without a merger transaction. For instance, security analysts note that at least $250 million of the $1.5 billion of cost savings originally forecasted in the Chase Manhattan and Chemical Bank merger were attributable to a cost-cutting program already under way at Chase. Lehman Brothers analyst M.L. Mayo notes that in the NationsBank acquisition of Boatmen's Bancshares, "Boatmen's has lots of low hanging fruit. Even without a merger, Boatmen's earnings could increase by one-fourth to one-third if excess capital were redeployed and efficiency gains achieved." In the case of the merger of First Union and Dominion Bankshares, First Union estimated that $30 million of the cost savings from the acquisition would be due to lower costs associated with real estate workouts once the bank got healthier. Presumably, this would have occurred without the merger.

In each of the items we have just discussed, it is not clear that management is unaware of the biased nature of the forecasts. For instance, strict adherence to accounting rules suggests that restructuring charges should not be taken until the acquirer is certain about the liabilities associated with the merger. Hence, initial charges might cover only the easier-to-estimate integration costs. Lumping in "nonmerger-related" cost savings and failure to discuss what, on average, might be minor revenue losses from an acquisition could also be management's attempt to put the best face on a stock-financed acquisition without making explicitly false claims. These tendencies do, however, tend to exaggerate the valuation estimates we use in this paper.

4.4. Analyst assessments of merger-related gains

Another way to assess merger-related gains and the reasonableness of management's forecasts is to examine analysts' opinions. In order to assess analysts' reaction to each of the bank mergers, we collect detailed analyst reports around the time of each announcement. We are able to find at least one analyst report for 36 of the 41 mergers in our subsample. While the reports vary considerably in their style and level of detail, a few general impressions emerge from reading these reports. These impressions are summarized in Table 9.

In most cases, analysts' primary focus is on the estimated cost savings. In Table 9, we classify each deal according to whether analysts view management's cost savings estimates as realistic, too optimistic, or too conservative. In the vast majority of cases, analysts view management's numbers as being realistic. Moreover, when analysts disagree with management, they appear to be just as likely to view management's numbers as too optimistic as they are to view them as too conservative. Consequently, analysts' forecasted cost savings are not biased in any particular direction on average with regard to management's projections. This rough alignment of analyst and

Table 9

Analysts' assessments of management's ability to achieve their targeted cost savings and revenue targets

Sample consists of 41 large bank acquisitions with management estimates of cost savings or revenue gains during the period 1985–1996.

Buyer	Target	No. of analysts that believe management's cost savings targets are too optimistic	No. of analysts that believe that management's cost savings targets are realistic	No. of analysts that believe management's cost savings targets are too conservative	No. of analysts that believe management's revenue targets are too optimistic	No. of analysts that believe management's revenue targets are realistic	No. of analysts that believe management's revenue targets are too conservative
Bank of New York	Community Banks of NJ						
Bankamerica	Continental Illinois		1				
Bankamerica	Security Pacific		4				
BankBoston	Baybanks		3		1	1	
Barnett Banks	First Florida		1				
BB&T Corp. (Win-Sal) or Southern	United Carolina Bancshares Corp.		1				
Boatmen's Banc-shares	Centerre		2	1			
Boatmen's Banc-shares	Fourth Financial			1			
Chemical Banking	Chase Manhattan		4				
Chemical Banking	Manufacturers Hanover		3	1	3	1	
Comerica	Manufacturers National		4				
Corestates Financial	First Pennsylvania		4			3	1
Corestates Financial	Meridian Bancorp		2				
Crestar Financial Corporation	Citizens Bancorporation (MD)						
First Bank System	FirsTier Financial		1				
First Chicago	NBD		4		3		

Acquirer	Target						
First of America	Security Bancorp	1			1		
First Union	Dominion Bancshares		2				
First Union	Florida National		3	2			
First Union	First Fidelity		1	1	4		
Fleet Financial	Shawmut National	1					
Keycorp	Puget Sound Bancorp		2				
Marshall & Isley	Valley Bancorporation			1			
Mercantile Bancorporation	Mark Twain Bancshares Inc.		1				
MNC Financial	Equitable Bancorporation		3				
National City Corp.	First Kentucky Bancorp	1	1		1	1	
National City Corp.	Integra Financial	1					
National City Corp.	Merchants National	1					
NationsBank	C&S Sovran		1	1			
NationsBank Corp.	Boatmen's Bancshares, Inc.		3		3		
NBD Bancorp	INB Financial		1	1			
PNC Bank	Midlantic Corp.	1	1			1	1
Regions Financial Corp.	First National Bancorp.						
Society Corp.	Ameritrust	1	3	1			
Society Corp.	Keycorp	1	1	1			
Southern National	BB&T Corp.	1	1				
Sovran	Commerce Union	1	1				
U.S. Bancorp (Ore)	West One Bancorp	1				1	
UJB Financial	Summit Bancorporation						
Wells Fargo	First Interstate Bancorp		5		1	4	

management forecasts could reflect management's incentives to report realistic numbers and/or analysts' unwillingness or inability to meaningfully question management's assumptions. It is apparent, from the reports, that analysts regularly take into account management's track record in previous mergers when assessing their likelihood of achieving the projected cost savings of a particular merger.

While analysts focus heavily on cost savings, in some acquisitions they also consider revenue enhancements. Interestingly, as shown in Table 9, analysts more frequently disagree with management about the size of revenue enhancements. When disagreements arise, analysts are more likely to view management's projected revenue enhancements as being too optimistic. Consistent with this view, many analysts seem to heavily discount management revenue forecasts in their proforma earnings models. For example, M.A. Orenbach of Sanford Bernstein in his September 6, 1996 report on the merger between NationsBank and Boatmen's Bancshares writes that "Our practice with respect to revenue enhancements is to haircut management's projections by fifty percent if they seem reasonable (and more if they do not)."

Apart from the estimated cost savings and revenue enhancements, some mergers allegedly provide capital structure benefits. Details regarding this information are reported in Table 10. In four cases, analysts argue that the merger might enable the combined bank to free up excess capital which can be used to either reduce less-profitable assets or to repurchase common stock. However, in only one case (the merger between First Union and First Fidelity) does management actually attempt to quantify the benefits from adjusting the capital structure. It is notable that at least one of the analysts following this merger did not believe that the projected capital structure benefits would be fully realized. In the merger between Chemical and Manufacturer's Hanover, analysts noted that the merger would enable the banks to jointly increase their capital ratio, which would make it easier for the joint bank to be an underwriter in the derivative market.

Not surprisingly, analysts also focus heavily on whether they believe that the bidding firm is overpaying for the target. This information is also summarized in Table 10. The evidence here is somewhat mixed. For our subset of 41 mergers, 36 firms have at least one analyst report. For 12 of the 36 firms, at least one of the analysts believes that the bidder overpaid. For transactions in which at least half of the analysts with an opinion believe the bidder overpaid (11 cases), the average abnormal return for the bidder is −8.65%. We do not know whether analysts' assessments of overpayment are made after the announcement date and are therefore simply a way of explaining the negative return to bidders.

In contrast, for mergers in which the majority of analysts found the purchase price defensible, the average bidder return is −0.04% (the difference is statistically significant at the 1% level). Target returns, however, are not significantly higher in mergers where analysts believe that bidders overpaid (in fact, the average return is slightly lower in deals involving overpayment). The combined target and bidder returns are also significantly lower in transactions in which analysts believe the bidder overpaid.

Table 10

Analysts' assessment of additional motivations for undertaking the acquisition, whether management overpaid for the target, and other considerations involved in the merger

Sample consists of 41 large bank acquisitions with management estimates of cost savings during the period 1985–1996.

Buyer	Target	Unreported revenue enhancements opportunities	Significant capital structure benefits	No. of analysts indicating that management overpaid for the target		Other considerations
				Yes	No	
Bank of New York	Community Banks of NJ				2	
Bankamerica	Continental Illinois				4	
Bankamerica	Security Pacific					
BankBoston	Baybanks				3	Concern that bidder was not a target
Barnett Banks	First Florida	×				
BB&T Corp. (Win-Sal) or Southern	United Carolina Banc-shares Corp.			1	1	
Boatmen's Bancshares	Centerre	×			3	
Boatmen's Bancshares	Fourth Financial				1	
Boatmen's Bancshares	Worthen Banking				2	
Chemical Banking	Chase Manhattan	×			5	
Chemical Banking	Manufacturers Hanover[a]		Raises/improves over-all capital position		5	
Comerica	Manufacturers National				4	
Corestates Financial	First Pennsylvania				4	
Corestates Financial	Meridian Bancorp	×			2	
Crestar Financial	Citizens Bancorporation (MD)					
First Bank System	FirsTier Financial				1	
First Chicago	NBD Bancorp				4	

(Continued)

Table 10 (*Continued*)

Buyer	Target	Unreported revenue enhancements opportunities	Significant capital structure benefits	No. of analysts indicating that management overpaid for the target		Other considerations
				Yes	No	
First of America	Security Bancorp		Benefits from freeing up excess capital	1		Concern that bidder was not a target
First Union	Dominion Bancshares				1	Concern about continued dilution
First Union	First Fidelity		benefits from freeing up excess capital	1	1	Analysts skeptical about capital structure benefits
First Union	Florida National					
Fleet Financial	Shawmut National			2	3	Concern about continued dilution
Keycorp	Puget Sound Bancorp		Benefits from freeing up excess capital		2	
Marshall & Isley	Valley Bancorporation	×			1	
Mercantile Bancorporation Inc.	Mark Twain Bancshares Inc.				3	Concern that bidder wasn't a target
MNC Financial	Equitable Bancorporation				3	
National City Corp	First Kentucky Bancorp			1	1	Concern about continued dilution
National City Corp	Integra Financial			1	1	
National City Corp	Merchants National			2	1	
NationsBank	C&S Sovran				2	
NationsBank Corp.	Boatmen's Bancshares, Inc.		Benefits from freeing up excess capital	2	2	
NBD Bancorp	INB Financial				2	
PNC Bank	Midlantic Corp.			2	1	Analysts thought PNC shareholders would reject offer; concern

				Comment
Regions Financial Corp.				that deal removes PNC as a potential target.
Society Corp. / First National Bancorp.				
Society Corp. / Ameritrust		4		
Keycorp	×	3		Concern that bidder was not a target
Southern National / BB&T Corp.	×	2		
Sovran / Commerce Union		2	2	Concern about continued dilution concern that bidder was not a target
U.S. Bancorp (Ore) / West One Bancorp	×	1		
UJB Financial / Summit Bancorporation		1		
Wells Fargo / First Interstate Bancorp		3		

a Bankamerica merger with Security Pacific often characterized as "disappointing" from Bankamerica's view due to large unforseen liabilities at Security Pacific.

Analysts often address a variety of other factors that are related to potential overpayment. In some cases, there is considerable discussion of the target's credit quality—instances arise in which analysts believe that management can obtain the projected cost savings but worry that the target's loan portfolio will have more potential bad loans than indicated in the bidding firm's forecast. In other cases, analysts are concerned that the acquisition is just one of a series of future dilutive acquisitions. Finally, concerns sometimes arise that the acquisition will prevent the bidder from itself becoming a target.

Overall, our review of analyst reports suggests that the primary source of merger-related gains is cost savings, not revenue growth. Moreover, the evidence is also consistent with at least a portion of the negative return to bidders resulting from overpayment for the target bank.

4.5. Postmerger performance

An additional way to assess management's estimates of merger gains is to examine the relation between changes in operating performance following mergers and management's estimate of merger-related gains. Since merger gains arise primarily from cost savings, we examine the relationship between changes in operating performance and management's estimated cost savings. We measure changes in operating performance by the change in the combined bank's adjusted efficiency ratio and changes in the combined bank's adjusted pretax ROA. The changes are computed by taking the difference between the performance of the bank the year after the merger and the performance of the bank the year prior to the merger. The dating convention can be explained with an example. If the merger was announced in the first half of 1995, we compare performance in 1996 and 1994. If the merger was announced in the second half of 1995, we compare 1997 and 1995. The definitions of the performance measures are given in Table 11. An improvement in the efficiency ratio implies a negative difference, while an improvement in pretax ROA implies a positive difference. Both measures are obtained by eliminating nonrecurring items, such as restructuring charges and asset sale gains, from the calculations. Also, loan loss provisions were excluded due to the tendency of managers to take premerger accounting "big baths." Two firms are omitted from the analysis because they were acquired before we could fully monitor their performance and four banks are eliminated because they made even larger acquisitions than the one we analyze before we could measure their performance.

As shown in Panel A of Table 11, the postmerger operating performance of the banks improves. The average adjusted efficiency ratio declines, while the average pretax ROA increases. The medians of the performance measures are significantly different in both cases. Note also that the results report numbers with and without MNC Financial. MNC is a severe outlier. The company was hit with large-scale nonperforming loans after its merger with Equitable Bancorporation due to widespread

Table 11

Changes in operating performances around bank acquisitions for a sample of 36 bank acquisitions with management estimates of cost savings and revenue gains during the period 1985–1996

Premerger performance measures are for the fiscal year before the merger announcement if the merger is announced in the first half of a fiscal year or in the fiscal year of the merger announcement if the merger is announced in the second half of the fiscal year. Postmerger performance measures are 2 fiscal years after the premerger performance year. Panel A contains descriptive statistics for the performance measures. Panel B contains regression results relating changes in performance to cost saving estimates and premerger performance. Results are presented with and without the MNC Financial acquisition of Equitable Bancorporation because this firm is an extreme outlier (t-statistics are in parentheses). The combined efficiency ratio is the sum of labor, equipment, and occupancy costs for both the bidder and the target divided by the sum of the taxable equivalent net interest income and noninterest income from nonrecurring items for the bidder and target. This ratio is computed using accounting information in the year preceding and the year following the merger (as defined in the Table 10 heading). When possible, restated data are used to insure comparability of firms. The combined adjusted pretax ROA begins with profit before tax of the bidder and target combined and then excludes securities gains and other nonrecurring income items and adds book provisions for loan losses, OREO expenses, amortization of intangibles (primarily goodwill), and restructuring charges associated with mergers and reorganizations. This adjusted pretax profit figure is divided by the average total assets for the bidder and target in the relevant year it is calculated. Second-year cost savings estimates are in dollar terms.

Panel A: Change in performance measure

	Before merger	After merger
Combined adjusted efficiency ratio	0.4179 (0.4165)	0.4069* (0.4051)
Combined adjusted pretax ROA	0.0229 (0.0222)	0.0248* (0.0249)
Combined adjusted efficiency ratio (excluding MNC Financial acquisition)	0.4179 (0.4149)	0.4011* (0.4042)
Combined adjusted pretax ROA (excluding MNC Financial acquisition)	0.0228 (0.0221)	0.0254* (0.0251)

Panel B: Regressions relating changes in performance measures to cost savings measure

	Change in combined efficiency ratio		Change in combined pretax ROA	
	Entire sample	MNC Financial acquisition omitted	Entire sample	MNC Financial acquisition omitted
Constant	0.071 (1.27)	0.076 (1.52)	0.0145 (2.53)	0.0101 (3.64)
Second year cost savings estimate/(average total assets for the post merger year)	0.425 (0.08)	−4.061* (−2.07)	−0.062 (−0.10)	0.364 (1.50)
Combined adjusted efficiency ratio before the merger	−0.198 (−1.44)	−0.199 (−1.62)		
Combined adjusted pretax ROA before the merger			−0.543* (−2.32)	−0.369* (−2.78)
Adjusted R^2	0.023	0.173	0.165	0.233

*Significantly different from the premerger distribution at the 0.01 level based on a Wilcoxon sign rank test.

real estate problems in the Washington DC area in the early 1990s. Facing financial difficulty, it sold its large and profitable MBNA subsidiary for a substantial gain, thereby eliminating it from its operating numbers.

The regressions in Panel B of Table 11 attempt to explain the changes in operating performance. The independent variables are the level of prior performance and a cost savings variable. The cost savings variable is the forecasted cost savings in year 2 of the merger deflated by the merged banks' average assets in the postmerger year. Given that most of these mergers are somewhere between their first year and second year of integration, the variable is an imperfect proxy for the amount of cost savings anticipated at the time the accounting numbers are measured. In spite of this fact, the regressions in Panel B that omit the MNC merger show that changes in performance are related to estimates of cost savings, though the strength of this result is marginal in terms of statistical significance. Not surprisingly, changes in performance are also related to prior performance, with poor prior performance leading to improvement.

4.6. Postmerger performance: qualitative assessment

The improved operating efficiency following the mergers in our sample reinforces the argument that an important motive for bank mergers is cost savings. However, the accounting measures of operating efficiency and profitability do not provide a clear picture of whether management successfully meets their cost savings or revenue targets. Moreover, as discussed in Section 2, and as illustrated by the plight of MNC Financial, accounting numbers do not always give an accurate description of whether management met its merger goals. To better gauge postmerger performance, we examine annual reports and proxy statements in the 3 years following the merger for any discussion of whether management meets its cost savings goals for the merger. We also examine related press accounts in Dow Jones News Retrieval over the same 3-year period. From these various accounts, we classify the merger's performance as being in line with management's original forecast, significantly worse than expected, worse than expected, better than expected, or inconclusive. Expected performance refers to management's original expectations regarding the merger's projected cost savings. Mergers are classified as worse than expected if cost savings fall more than 10% below targets, cost cuts are well behind their initial timetable, news accounts suggest significant negative surprises with respect to customer loss, or integration costs are sufficiently above expectations to merit press coverage. The classifications are reported in Table 12.

In the large majority of cases, the mergers appear to exceed or at least meet management's original expectations. We characterize performance as below expectations in only four of the mergers, and in only one case (the merger between Wells Fargo and First Interstate) is performance significantly worse than expected. It is important to note that the classifications reported in Table 12 only address whether management meets its stated cost reduction targets. In a few instances, these targets are met, yet the combined firm suffers because of other events. For example, the merger

Table 12

Qualitative assessment of postmerger performance for a sample of 41 large bank acquisitions with management estimates of cost savings and revenue gains during the period 1985–1996

Mergers are classified according to the authors' assessments

Buyer	Target	Significantly worse than expected	Worse than expected	Performance roughly in line with management's expectations	Better than expected	Inconclusive
Bank of New York	Community Banks of NJ					×
Bankamerica	Continental Illinois					×
Bankamerica[a]	Security Pacific			×		
BankBoston	Baybanks			×		
Barnett Banks	First Florida				×	
BB&T Corp. (Win-Sal) or Southern National	United Carolina Bancshares Corp.			×		
Boatmen's Banc-shares	Centerre				×	
Boatmen's Banc-shares	Fourth Financial					×
Boatmen's Banc-shares	Worthen Banking					×
Chemical Banking	Chase Manhattan			×		
Chemical Banking	Manufacturers Hanover[a]			×		
Comerica	Manufacturers National		×			
Corestates Finan-cial	First Pennsylvania					×
Corestates Finan-cial	Meridian Bancorp		×			
Crestar Financial Corporation	Citizens Bancor-poration (MD)					×
First Bank System	FirsTier Financial			×		
First of America	Security Bancorp			×		
First Chicago	NBD Bancorp			×		
First Union	Dominion Banc-shares					×
First Union	First Fidelity			×		
First Union	Florida National				×	
Fleet Financial	Shawmut National				×	
Keycorp	Puget Sound Bancorp			×		
Marshall & Isley	Valley Bancor-poration					×
					×	

(Continued)

Table 12 (*Continued*)

Buyer	Target	Significantly worse than expected	Worse than expected	Performance roughly in line with management's expectations	Better than expected	Inconclusive
Mercantile Bancorporation Inc.	Mark Twain Bancshares Inc.					
MNC Financial	Equitable Bancorporation			×		
National City Corp.	First Kentucky Bancorp		×			
National City Corp.	Integra Financial			×		
National City Corp	Merchants National			×		
NationsBank	C&S Sovran				×	
NationsBank Corp.	Boatmen's Bancshares, Inc.				×	
NBD Bancorp	INB Financial				×	
PNC Bank	Midlantic Corp.					×
Regions Financial Corp.	First National Bancorp.					×
Society Corp.	Ameritrust				×	
Society Corp.	Keycorp			×		
Southern National	BB&T Corp.			×		
Sovran	Commerce Union					×
U.S. Bancorp (Ore)	West One Bancorp				×	
UJB Financial	Summit Bancorporation			×		
Wells Fargo	First Interstate Bancorp	×				

[a] Bankamerica merger with Security Pacific often characterized as "disappointing" from Bankamerica's view due to large unforseen liabilities at Security Pacific.

between Bankamerica and Security Pacific is not classified as a failure due to large unknown liabilities inherited from the merger partner. These liabilities existed with or without the merger.

While these numbers are instructive, they should be interpreted with some caution. In a large number of cases, the postmerger performance is inconclusive. Moreover, there is a potential selection bias to the extent that managers report good news more readily than bad news. For example, management might report that it met its cost savings target on schedule but fail to report that revenue losses were much larger than expected.

5. Summary and conclusion

Deregulation and changing technology have dramatically transformed the banking industry over the past two decades enabling many banks to provide a wider range of banking services and to service more customers across a larger geographical area. These same forces are also routinely offered as a justification for the consolidation of the banking industry over this time period. Despite these often-stated rationales for bank mergers, most of the previous academic literature tends to find that the net value created from bank mergers is quite limited.

This paper tries to get at the root of this apparent contradiction by building upon the existing literature in two important ways. First, we consider the estimated value gains from bank mergers over a longer period of time, taking into account more-recent mergers. Second, we calculate the expected net present value of the merger's net benefit for the subset of mergers for which we are able to obtain management's projections of the merger's estimated cost savings and revenue enhancements. These details enable us to assess what management believes to be the primary source of merger gains. By linking management's assessment of the merger's value to stock analysts' reports and the stock market's reaction, we are able to look at each bank merger from the perspective of management, analysts, and investors.

Our results suggest that most of the estimated value gains from bank mergers stem from the opportunity to cut costs by eliminating overlapping operations and consolidating backroom operations. For the typical bank merger, estimated revenue enhancements are significantly less important. Furthermore, both bidder and target bank merger announcement returns are strongly and positively related to managers' estimated cost savings. We also find that more-recent bank mergers (those occurring in the 1990s) are more likely to be accompanied by detailed projections of cost savings, and generate higher abnormal returns than mergers prior to 1990. In this respect our results do not conflict with earlier studies, but they indicate that bank mergers have gotten better over time.

Finally, while we find that the market responds positively to deals with higher projected cost savings, the market also appears to significantly discount management's projections. Merger announcement stock revaluations are well below our present value estimates of merger gains inferred from managerial projections. The explanation for this discount is multifaceted. In part, it reflects prior market anticipation of merger activity and negative signaling associated with stock-financed acquisitions. It could also involve potential error in converting cost savings estimates into valuation gains. There is also evidence, however, that management's initial projections typically understate the costs that are incurred in order to realize the estimated cost savings, and that management typically understates the potential revenue loss that arises as part of the consolidation. These factors can at least partially explain why the market generally discounts management's forecast of the anticipated gains from bank mergers.

Appendix

Our sample consists of 64 bank mergers announced between 1985 and 1996 in which the stated deal value (the amount paid for the target's share) exceeds $400 million in 1985 inflation-adjusted dollars and the target bank's assets are equal to at least 10% of the acquiring bank's assets in the year preceding the merger.

Bidder	Target	Announcement date
Banc One	Marine Corp	07/24/87
Banc One Corp.	American Fletcher Corp.	05/07/86
Banc One Corp.	Valley National Corp.	04/14/92
Bank of New England	Conifer Group, Inc.	08/14/86
Bank of New York[a]	National Community Banks, Inc.	01/29/93
Bankamerica Corp.[a]	Security Pacific Corp.	08/12/91
Bankamerica Corp.[a]	Continental Bank Corp.	01/28/94
BankBoston Corp.[a]	BayBanks, Inc.	12/13/95
Barnett Banks Inc.[a]	First Florida Banks Inc.	05/18/92
BB&T Financial Corp.[a]	Southern National Corp. (NC)[b]	08/01/94
BB&T Corp.[a]	United Carolina Bancshares Corp.	11/04/96
Boatmen's Bancshares Inc.[a]	Centerre Bancorporation	05/04/88
Boatmen's Bancshares, Inc.[a]	Fourth Financial Corporation	08/28/95
Boatmen's Bancshares, Inc.[a]	Worthen Banking Corp.	08/18/94
Citizens & Southern (GA)	Landmark Banking	02/22/95
Chemical Banking Corp.	Texas Commerce Bancshares Inc.	12/15/86
Chemical Banking Corp.[a]	Chase Manhattan Corp.[b]	08/28/95
Chemical Banking Corp.[a]	Manufacturers Hanover Corp.[b]	07/15/91
Comerica Inc.[a]	Manufacturers National Corp.[b]	10/28/91
Corestates Financial Corp.[a]	Meridian Bancorp	10/10/95
Corestates Financial Corp.[a]	First Pennsylvania Corporation	09/18/89
Crestar Financial Corporation[a]	Citizens Bancorporation (MD)	09/16/96
First Bank System, Inc.[a]	FirsTier Financial Inc.	08/07/95
First Chicago Corporation[a]	NBD Bancorp, Inc.	07/12/95
First Fidelity Bancorporation	Fidelcor Inc.[b]	07/31/87
First of American Bank Corporation[a]	Security Bancorp, Inc. (Southgate)	09/12/91
First Union Corp.	Atlantic Bancorporation	06/17/85
First Union Corp.	First Railroad	06/11/86
First Union Corp.[a]	First Fidelity Bancorporation	06/19/95
First Union Corp.[a]	Dominion Bankshares Corp.	09/21/92
First Union Corp.[a]	Florida National Banks, Inc.	03/07/89
Fleet Financial Group Inc.	Norstar Bancorp[b]	03/18/87
Fleet Financial Group, Inc.[a]	Shawmut National Corporation	02/21/95
Hartford National Corp.	Shawmut Corp.[b]	08/26/87
Keycorp[a]	Puget Sound Bancorp	03/09/92
M N C Financial Inc.[a]	Equitable Bancorporation (MD)	07/12/89
Marshall & Isley Corp.[a]	Valley Bancorporation	09/20/93
Maryland National Corp.	American Security Corp.	08/01/86
Mercantile Bancorporation Inc.[a]	Mark Twain Bancshares Inc.	10/28/96

(Continued)

Appendix (*Continued*)

Bidder	Target	Announcement date
Midlantic Corp.	Continental Bancorp	02/21/86
N B D Bancorp Inc.[a]	I N B Financial Corp.	03/18/92
National City Corp.[a]	Merchants National Corp.	10/30/91
National City Corp.[a]	First Kentucky	01/28/88
National City Corp.[a]	Integra Financial Corporation	08/28/95
NationsBank Corp.[a]	Boatmen's Bancshares, Inc.	08/30/96
NationsBank Corp.[a]	C & S Sovran Corp.	07/22/91
P N C Financial Corp.	Citizens Fidelity Corp.	06/30/86
P N C Financial Corp.	Central Bancorporation Inc.	07/31/87
PNC Bank Corp.[a]	Midlantic Corp.	07/10/95
Regions Financial Corporation[a]	First National Bancorp. (GA)	10/23/95
Republicbank Corp.	Interfirst Corp.	12/17/86
Security Pacific Corp.	Rainier Bancorporation	02/24/87
Society Corp.	Trustcorp Inc.	06/19/89
Society Corp.[a]	Keycorp[b]	10/04/93
Society Corp.[a]	Ameritrust Corp.	09/13/91
Sovran Financial Corp.	Citizens and Southern Corp. (GA)[b]	09/27/89
Sovran Financial Corp.	Suburban Bancorp	09/24/85
Sovran Financial Corp.[a]	Commerce Union Corp.	04/27/87
Suntrust Banks Inc.	Third National Corp.	09/02/86
UJB Financial Corp.[a]	Summit Bancorporation (NJ)	09/11/95
US Bancorp[a]	West One Bancorp	05/08/95
Wachovia Corp.	First Atlantic Corp.	06/17/85
Wachovia Corp.	South Carolina National Corp.	06/24/91
Wells Fargo and Company[a]	First Interstate Bancorp	01/24/96

[a]Indicates that we have detailed cost savings and/or revenue enhancement figures.
[b]Indicates that the merger was announced as a merger of equals.

References

Becher, D. A., 1999, "The Valuation Effects of Bank Mergers," Penn State Working Paper.

Berger, A. N., 1997, "The Efficiency Effects of Bank Mergers and Acquisitions: A Preliminary Look at the 1990s Data," In: Y. Amihud, G. Miller (Eds.), *Mergers of Financial Institutions*, Business One-Irwin, Homewood, IL.

Berger, A. N. and D. B. Humphrey, 1992, "Megamergers in Banking and the Use of Cost Efficiency an Antitrust Defense," *Antitrust Bulletin*, 37, 541–600.

Berger, A. N., R. S. Demetz and P. E. Strahan, 1999, "The Consolidation of the Financial Services Industry: Causes, Consequences, and Implications for the Future," *Journal of Banking and Finance*, 23, 135–194.

Calomiris, C. and J. Karceski, 1999, "Is the Bank Merger Wave of the 1990s Efficient? Lessons from Nine Case Studies," In: N. K. Steven (Ed.), *Mergers and Productivity*, University of Chicago Press, Chicago.

Copeland, T., T. Koller and J. Murrin, 1995, *Valuation Measuring and Managing the Value of Companies*, 2nd edition, McKinsey & Company, Wiley, New York.

Cornett, M. M. and H. Tehranian, 1992, "Changes in Corporate Performance Associated with Bank Acquisitions," *Journal of Financial Economics*, 31, 211–234.

DeLong, G. L., 1998, "Domestic and International Bank Mergers: The Gains from Focusing Versus Diversifying," Working Paper, New York University, New York.

Gilson, S., E. S. Hotchkiss and R. S. Ruback, 2000, "Valuation of Bankrupt Firms," *Review of Financial Studies*, 13, 41–74.

Gorton, G. and R. Rosen, 1995, "Corporate Control, Portfolio Choice, and the Decline of Banking," *Journal of Finance*, 50 (5), 1377–1420.

Hawawini, G. and S. Itzhak, 1990, *Mergers and Acquisitions in the US Banking Industry: Evidence from the Capital Markets*, Elsevier Science, Amsterdam.

Houston, J. F. and M. D. Ryngaert, 1994, "The Overall Gains from Large Bankmergers," *Journal of Banking and Finance*, 18 (6), 1155–1176.

Houston, J. F. and M. D. Ryngaert, 1997, "Equity Issuance and Adverse Selection: A Direct Test Using Conditional Stock Offers," *Journal of Finance*, 52, 197–219.

Ibbotson and Associates, 1996, *Stocks, Bonds, Bills and Inflation: 1996 Yearbook*, Ibbotson Associates, Chicago, IL.

James, C. M. and P. Weir, 1987, "Returns to Acquirers and Competition in the Acquisition Market: The Case of Banking," *Journal of Political Economy*, 95 (2), 355–370.

Kaplan, S. and R. S. Ruback, 1995, "The Valuation of Cash Flow Forecasts: An Empirical Analysis," *The Journal of Finance*, 50, 1059–1093.

Kwan, S. and J. A. Wilcox, 1999, "Hidden Cost Reductions in Bank Mergers: Accounting for More Productive Banks," Proceedings of the 35th Annual Conference on Bank Structure and Competition, Federal Reserve Bank of Chicago, May 5, Chicago.

Loughran, T. and J. R. Ritter, 1997, "The Operating Performance of Firms Conducting Seasoned Equity Offerings," *Journal of Finance*, 52, 1823–1850.

Pilloff, S. J., 1996, "Performance Changes and Shareholder Wealth Creation Associated with Mergers of Publicly Traded Banking Institutions," *Journal of Money, Credit and Banking*, 28, 294–310.

Roll, R., 1986, "The Hubris Hypothesis of Corporate Takeovers," *Journal of Business*, 59 (2), 199–216.

Ryan, S. J., 1999, "Finding Value in Bank Mergers," Presentation, Federal Reserve Bank of Chicago Bank Structure Conference, May 5, Chicago.

Spindt, P. A. and V. Tarhan, 1992, "Are There Synergies in Bank Mergers?" Working Paper, Tulane University.

PART 6

OTHER RESTRUCTURING ACTIVITY: BREAKUPS AND HIGHLY LEVERAGED TRANSACTIONS

Chapter 17

CORPORATE RESTRUCTURING: BREAKUPS AND LBOs

B. ESPEN ECKBO

Tuck School of Business at Dartmouth, Hanover, New Hampshire, USA

KARIN S. THORBURN

Tuck School of Business at Dartmouth, Hanover, New Hampshire, USA

Contents

This article originally appeared in B. E. Eckbo (ed.), *Handbook of Corporate Finance: Empirical Corporate Finance*, Vol. 2, Ch. 16, pp. 431–496 (2008).
Corporate Takeovers, Volume 1
Edited by B. Espen Eckbo

Abstract

This chapter surveys the empirical literature on corporate breakup transactions (divestitures, spinoffs, equity carveouts, tracking stocks), leveraged recapitalizations, and leveraged buyouts (LBOs). Many breakup transactions are a response to excessive conglomeration and reverse costly diversification discounts. The empirical evidence shows that the typical restructuring creates substantial value for shareholders. The value drivers include elimination of costly cross-subsidizations characterizing internal capital markets, reduction in financing costs for subsidiaries through asset securitization and increased divisional transparency, improved (and more focused) investment programs, reduction in agency costs of free cash flow, implementation of executive compensation schemes with greater pay-performance sensitivity, and increased monitoring by lenders and LBO sponsors. Buyouts after the turn of the century created value similar to LBOs of the 1980s. Recent developments include club deals (consortiums of LBO sponsors bidding together), fund-to-fund exits (LBO funds selling the portfolio firm to another LBO fund), a highly liquid (until mid-2007) leveraged-loan market, and evidence of persistence in fund returns (perhaps because brand-sponsors borrow at better rates). Perhaps the greatest challenge to the restructuring literature is to achieve a modicum of integration of the analysis across transaction types. Another challenge is to produce precise estimates of the expected return from buyout investments in the presence of limited data on those portfolio companies that do not return to public status.

Keywords

restructuring, breakup, divestiture, spinoff, equity carveout, tracking stock, leveraged recapitalization, leveraged buyout, highly leveraged transaction

JEL classification: G34

1. Introduction

Shocks to the corporate economic environment may give rise to severe organizational inefficiencies. For example, a vertically integrated firm may find that long-term contracts and/or spot market purchases of a key input have become more efficient. Or increased general capital market liquidity may have rendered internal capital markets a relatively costly divisional funding mechanism for conglomerates. High leverage may be optimal as financial innovations and expertise make it less expensive to manage financial distress. Financial innovations and general market liquidity may also render it optimal to securitize an entire division. The result is increased divisional managerial focus. In this chapter, we collectively refer to the transactions that implement these and other changes in asset composition, financial contracting, and ownership structure as "corporate restructurings."

We focus the survey on garden-variety restructuring procedures used to securitize and sell off part of the firm. Takeovers—the perhaps ultimate form of corporate restructuring—are reviewed in Betton et al. (2008). However, we include leveraged buyouts (LBOs) in which the entire firm is acquired by a financial buyer such as a buyout fund. We also deal with issues of financial distress only tangentially, as the evidence surrounding restructurings in bankruptcy are covered Hotchkiss et al. (2008).

It is useful to classify corporate restructurings into two broad groups: breakups and highly leveraged transactions. Breakup transactions focus primarily on the separation of company assets and therefore include divestitures, spinoffs, equity carveouts, and tracking stock. Highly leveraged transactions involve a significant increase of debt in the firm's capital structure, either through a debt-financed special dividend in a leveraged recapitalization or in an LBO.[1]

Corporate restructurings may be initiated by the firm's top-level management, by divisional managers, or by outside sponsors like buyout funds. Occasionally, the restructuring is defensive, arising in response to a control threat from the market for corporate control. Regardless of who initiates the transaction, the parties are seeking to improve operating efficiency, increase cash flow, and, ultimately, enhance firm profitability. In breakup transactions, assets are transferred to higher value users, while highly leveraged transactions involve optimizing capital structure, improving managerial incentives and achieving tax efficiency.

The survey is organized as follows. We begin in Section 2 with a brief discussion of the so-called diversification discount and potential costs of diversification, which motivate many breakup transactions. Sections 3 through Section 6 then detail the structure and consequences of various types of breakup transactions, including

---

[1] We do not survey recapitalizations that do not involve extensive use of leverage. Examples include state privatizations (Megginson and Netter, 2001), conversions from mutual to stock companies (Masulis, 1987), and stock repurchases. Stock repurchases are reviewed in Kalay and Lemmon (2008).

divestitures (Section 3), spinoffs (Section 4), equity carveouts (Section 5), and tracking stock (Section 6). Next we turn to highly leveraged transactions, including leveraged recapitalizations and LBOs. Section 9 concludes the survey.

2. Restructurings and the boundaries of the firm

2.1. Breakup transactions

The economic boundary of the firm may be defined as the point where within-firm transactions start to become more costly than arm's-length (across market) transactions. There are numerous theories for why within-firm transactions may economically dominate market transactions, ranging from transactions costs (Coase, 1937) to agency costs and costs of imperfect contracting and moral hazard (Grossman and Hart, 1986; Hart and Moore, 1990; Jensen, 1986; Jensen and Meckling, 1976; Klein et al., 1978; Williamson, 1985). Alternatives outright ownership of resources include renting (long- or short-term contracts) and "spot" market transactions to ensure continued operations of the firm. These organizational alternatives have different implications for corporate taxes, firm-specific resource specialization and development of appropriable quasi-rents (which in turn lead to bargaining issues and potential for opportunistic behavior), investment decisions, risk-sharing, and financing costs.

An asset such as an operating plant may have greater value as a division of a conglomerate than as a stand-alone "pure play" entity. The degree to which conglomerates generate value depends on the managerial skills and the nature of the resources required to operate efficiently within an industry. The value of using shared resources, such as managerial time and internal capital, differs across firms and industries as well as through time. As the boundaries of the firm change over time, some firms respond by undertaking expansions (mergers and acquisitions), breakups (divestitures, spin-offs), and recapitalizations (leveraged recaps and buyouts). Breakup transactions create value when synergies from conglomeration become negative, that is, when the costs of keeping the company's assets together exceed the benefits from doing so.

As emphasized by Maksimovic and Phillips (2007) the corporate finance literature on conglomeration took off with the discovery of the "conglomerate discount" by Lang and Stulz (1994) and Berger and Ofek (1995). The discount is measured as the difference between the market value of the diversified firm and the sum of the estimated values of the (nontraded) divisions. The latter are estimated using multiples from single-segment (pure play) competitors. Berger and Ofek (1995) report a diversification discount of 13–15% in the 1986–1991 period. Subsequent empirical work has extended and reinterpreted the early results. Maksimovic (2007) conclude that diversified firms *predominantly* behave like value maximizers given their productivity and that internal capital markets tend to facilitate the efficient transfer of resources. However, they also point to ambiguities reflecting econometric issues of endogeneity and self-selection, as well as choice of data, at various steps of the overall test strategy.

The typical breakup transaction reviewed below is shown to generate substantial shareholder value. This evidence is consistent with both the empire-building hypothesis and the value-maximizing self-selection hypothesis for the average observed diversification discount. Whether managers of firms breaking up are value-maximizers or empire-builders, the breakup may be an optimal response to exogenous changes in the economic boundaries of the firm. Reversing costs of excessive conglomeration may be a by-product of downsizing. Diversified firms undertaking breakup transactions are, however, more likely to be facing significant diversification costs than a random sample of conglomerates. Consequently, firms busting up are prime candidates for examining the potential nature of diversification costs.

The literature provides several examples of diversification costs and how they may distort investment. Scharfstein and Stein (2000) describe conditions under which top management inefficiently allocates too much funds to divisions with poor investment opportunities (cross-subsidization). Rajan et al. (2000) argue that investment choices may be distorted because top management cannot commit to future distribution of funds until a surplus has been realized. Goldman (2004) models the resource allocation inside a multidivision firm of a manager with stock-based compensation and shows that the investment incentives improve after a spinoff of a division.

Another potential cost of diversification is related to executive compensation: since the division is a private entity, it is difficult to tie divisional manager compensation directly to the underlying value of the operations under their control. Stock-based compensation policies may be critical to induce optimal investment decisions and to retain managerial talent in a competitive labor market. A separate listing of subsidiary stock resolves such compensation issues, lowering agency costs, and increasing market value.[2]

Breakup transactions may also result because conglomeration accentuates costly information asymmetries between investors and corporate insiders. Nanda and Narayanan (1999) model a diversified firm's decision to divest a division that is undervalued by the market. Outside investors observe the aggregated (conglomerate) cash flow only, while management also observes the divisional cash flows. Without detailed divisional information, the market rationally assigns an average performance to each division. This pooling results in undervaluation of the well-performing division and overvaluation of the poorly performing division. In this situation, it may he optimal to divest the overvalued (underperforming) division in order to lower the cost of capital for the undervalued division.

A related information-based argument is that conglomerates operating in a wide range of industries are more difficult for analysts to value correctly. This is true both because analysts tend to specialize in certain industries and because divisions may be relatively opaque in terms of financial information. A breakup may lead to increased coverage by financial analysts and improved quality of the information available to investors. Liu (2005) further maintains that a breakup allows outsiders more generally to discover firm value at a lower cost. As a result, high-value firms may undertake breakups in order to separate themselves from low-value firms.

Are there too few breakups? Boot (1992) argues that self-interested managers are reluctant to sell assets because a divestiture may signal poor managerial quality. Lang et al. (1995) also point out that managers who value control may be reluctant to sell assets in order to promote operating efficiency alone. In this situation, an active market for corporate control may be required to force more divestitures. Financial distress is another scenario which may force even nonvalue-maximizing managers of financially constrained firms to divest assets in order to raise capital (see also Hotchkiss et al., 2008).

The above arguments emphasize how breakups create value by reversing negative synergies. A divisional or asset sale may also be the result of the demand side: the assets may simply be worth more under the buyer's control. That is, the buyer may be a higher quality manager, and the divisional resources may offer a greater potential for synergies when merged with the acquiring firm. Selling the asset at a premium may serve the interest of all parties involved. Finally, corporate breakups may be forced by direct legal actions under antitrust or bankruptcy court, or by regulatory changes changing the economic boundary of the firm.

2.2. Highly leveraged transactions

In a highly leveraged transaction, the focus of the restructuring is on the economic effects of the leverage increase. Whether undertaking a debt-financed dividend (leveraged recap), or a leveraged purchase of a division or the entire firm (LBO, where the firm goes private), it is the leverage increase rather than any concomitant asset restructuring that provides the main economic motivation for the transaction. As a result, LBOs tend to involve financial (as opposed to strategic) buyers, such as buyout funds.

The literature points to several possible sources of gains in leverage-increasing transactions. Under the classical tradeoff theory of debt (see Frank and Goyal, 2008), firms move to a higher level of debt in order to capitalize on the corporate debt tax shield provided by the (US) tax law. In addition to the potential for corporate tax benefits, the literature emphasizes beneficial managerial incentive and monitoring effects of higher leverage. Some highly leveraged firms may also gain a strategic advantage in product markets. On the other hand, high leverage is not for everyone: under conditions of financial distress, a debt overhang tends to prevent efficient investments (Myers, 1977).

In terms of managerial incentives, Ross (1977) presents a signaling model in which managers who face personal bankruptcy costs signal their private information about higher future expected cash flows by committing to a greater corporate debt level. In the vernacular of Jensen (1986), entrenched managers prefer to overinvest rather than pay out the firm's "free cash flow" as dividends (where free cash flow is defined as corporate liquid funds in excess of what is required to fund all positive net present value projects). A leveraged recapitalization, where the firm increases its debt without retaining the proceeds (thus increasing leverage ratios), reduces Jensen's overinvestment problem by precommitting to disgorge future cash flows in the form of interest payment. Jensen (1986) further argues that the greater risk of financial distress associated with higher leverage also helps discipline managerial investment policies. Stulz (1990) formalizes this intuition and shows that high leverage is particularly valuable when investment opportunities are poor, even if the free cash flow is negative.

Increasing leverage also allows wealth constrained managers to hold a greater percentage of total equity after the transaction is completed. For example, in a leveraged recapitalization, the debt may be paid out as cash dividend to nonmanagerial stockholders and as a stock dividend (or a cash dividend that is immediately reinvested in the firm) to managers. In an LBO, the managers may roll over their equity investment, while other equity-holders are paid out, again increasing managers' fractional equity ownership. The incentive effect of such greater managerial equity ownership helps reduce manager-shareholder conflicts of interest. Garvey (1992) explores the conditions under which leverage and management equity ownership are complementary in reducing the overinvestment problem of free cash flow.[3]

Highly leveraged transactions may also lead to improved monitoring by banks, and by the LBO sponsor who has its own money at risk in the transaction. Jensen (1989) argues that active governance by buyout sponsors and high-powered managerial incentives, combined with the pressure from high leverage, provides an incentive structure that is superior to that of public firms with dispersed ownership and weak governance. He even suggests that the LBO organizational form may "eclipse" the traditional corporate form, a prediction that has yet to be proven (we present evidence on the frequency of LBO transactions in Section 8 below).

Moreover, highly leveraged transactions may cause wealth transfers across the firm's various constituencies. For example, bonds that lack protective covenants may become more junior in the capital structure, resulting in a bondholder loss (benefiting shareholders). It is also possible that incumbent managers participating in an LBO have inside information about the firm's future prospects, expropriating selling shareholders. Muller and Panunzi (2004) argue that the LBO sponsor may be in a position to expropriate minority shareholders by merging the firm with the raider's leveraged acquisition subsidiary. Perotti and Spier (1993) present a model in which the firm gains bargaining power in contracting renegotiations by temporarily increasing leverage. Specifically, after retiring equity through a junior debt issue, shareholders threaten to underinvest in valuable new projects unless employees concede to wage reductions. Finally, there is a growing literature linking leverage to the firm's strategic position in product markets. See the reviews of Maksimovic (1995) and Parsons and Titman (2008), for reviews of this literature.

---

[3] See also Garvey (1995) for an analysis of managerial incentive effects of leverage.

We now turn to a detailed description of the empirical evidence on breakups and highly leveraged transactions. In the course of discussing the evidence, we return to several of the hypotheses outlined above.

3. Divestitures

A divestiture is the sale of a portion of the firm's assets to a third party—typically another company or a private equity fund—in a private transaction. The assets sold may be a division, segment, subsidiary, or product line. In return, the seller typically receives cash, but sometimes also securities or a combination of both. The proceeds from the sale are reinvested in the remaining business or distributed to the firm's claim holders. While eliminating some assets, the selling firm continues to exist in essentially the same form as before. Divestitures may trigger a substantial tax liability: the difference between the proceeds from the sale and the firm's tax basis in the assets is a capital gain or capital loss, which is taxed at the corporate tax rate.

3.1. Transaction volume

In 2006, US corporations announced 3375 divestitures with a total deal value of $342 billion (source: *Mergerstat Review*). The line in Panel A of Figure 1 shows the annual number, and the bars show the total dollar volume of US divestitures over the period 1980–2006. The number of transactions was relatively stable between 1980 and 1995. Since the mid-1990s, however, the divestiture activity has tripled and reached record high levels in 2005–2006.

The most aggressive divester in 2006 was UTEK (26 divestitures), followed by General Electric (17), Clear Channel Communications (11), El Paso (10), and Federated Department Stores (10). Two of the sellers, General Electric and El Paso, were also among the most aggressive divesters in the previous year. In addition, General Electric was listed as the most aggressive US acquirer in 2006 and 2005, with 30 and 28 acquisition announcements, respectively.

The total divestiture activity tracks closely the merger and acquisition (M&A) activity in the economy. Panel B of Figure 1 shows the annual number of US divestitures as a percentage of all US takeovers from 1970 and forward. While the number of divestitures increased sharply in the second half of the 1990s, it fell behind the even greater increase in M&A volume over the same period. This trend was reversed once the takeover activity slowed after the turn of the century. In 2006, divestitures made up 32% of all M&A transactions, somewhat below the annual average of 38% over the whole 1970–2006 period.

3.2. Valuation effects

Panel A of Table 1 shows the stock price reaction of the divesting firm for 18 selected studies with announcement dates in years 1963–1999. The studies typically report the

Number (line) and total transaction value (bars) of divestitures

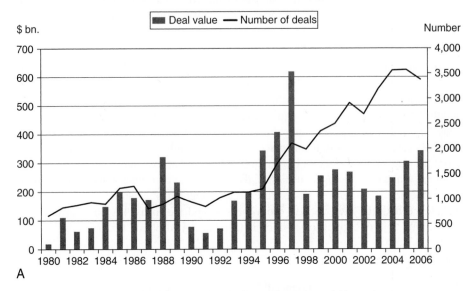

A

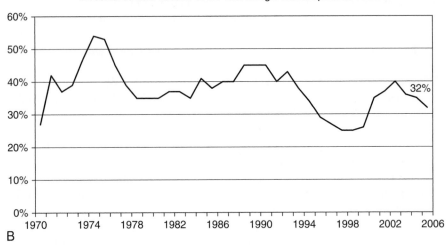

B

Fig. 1. Annual volume of US divestitures, 1970–2006: (A) number (line) and total transaction value (bars) of divestitures; (B) divestitures as a fraction of the US merger and acquisition volume. Source: *Mergerstat Review*.

Table 1

Cumulative abnormal returns (CAR) for divestiture announcement of 3700 sellers and 1243 buyers in 19 selected studies, 1963–1999

Relative size is the average ratio of the sales price of the divested assets to the predeal total assets (TA) and market value of equity (MVE) of the seller and buyer, respectively.

Study	CAR		Relative size		Sample size	Time period	Event window
	Mean (%)	Median (%)	TA (%)	MVE (%)			
Panel A: Seller returns							
Alexander et al. (1984)	0.3				53	1964–1973	[−1, 0]
Linn and Rozeff (1984)	1.6				77	1969–1981	[−1, 0]
Rosenfeld (1984)	2.3				62	1976–1978	[−1, 0]
Jain (1985)	0.5				1062	1970–1979	[−1, 0]
Klein (1986)	1.1				202	1963–1981	[−2, 0]
Hite et al. (1987)	1.5		16		114	1963–1981	[−1, 0]
Hirschey and Zaima (1989)	1.6				170	1975–1982	[−1, 0]
Hirschey et al. (1990)	1.5			38	75	1975–1982	[−1, 0]
Afshar et al. (1992)	0.7			10	178	1985–1986	[−1, 0]
Sicherman and Pettway (1992)	0.9			30	278	1980–1987	[−1, 0]
John and Ofek (1995)	1.5	0.8		39	258	1986–1988	[−2, 0]
Lang et al. (1995)	1.4	0.7	11	69	93	1984–1989	[−1, 0]
Loh et al. (1995)	1.5				59	1980–1987	[−1, 0]
Slovin et al. (1995)	1.7	0.7	33	17	179	1980–1991	[0, 1]
Hanson and Song (2000)	0.6	0.3		27	326	1981–1995	[−1, 1]
Mulherin and Boone (2000)	2.6	1.6		18	139	1990–1999	[−1, 1]
Clubb and Stouraitis (2002)	1.1	0.5		14	187	1984–1994	[−1, 0]
Dittmar and Shivdasani (2003)	3.4		31		188	1983–1994	[−1, 1]
Sample size weighted seller average	1.2		25	27	3700	1963–1999	[−1, 1]
Panel B: Buyer returns							
Jain (1985)	0.5				304	1976–1978	[−1, 0]
Hite et al. (1987)	0.6		19		105	1963–1981	[−1, 0]
Sicherman and Pettway (1992)	0.5				278	1980–1987	[−1, 0]
Datta and Iskander-Datta (1995)	0.0			13	63	1982–1990	[−1, 0]
John and Ofek (1995)	0.4	−0.5		72	167	1986–1988	[−2, 0]
Hanson and Song (2000)	0.5	0.2			326	1981–1995	[−1, 1]
Sample size weighted buyer average	0.5		19	25	1243	1963–1995	[−1, 1]

cumulative abnormal stock return (CAR) over the 2-day interval $(-1, 0)$ where day 0 is the announcement day.[4] The average CAR for the announcements are positive—ranging from 0.3% to 3.4% across the different samples—and almost all of the estimates are statistically significant at the 1%-level (two-sided t-test against zero). The sample-size-weighted average CAR for the combined sample of 3700 divestitures is 1.2%. In sum, the evidence indicates that the average divestiture increases the value of the selling firm.

As further shown in the table, firms sell one-quarter or less of their total assets (TA) in the average transaction. Several studies find that the seller firm announcement returns are increasing in the relative size of the divested assets (Klein, 1986; Mulherin and Boone, 2000; Zaima and Hearth, 1985). It is possible that the returns on asset sales are independent of the size of the assets, so that relatively larger assets have a greater impact on the parent firm's return. This is similar to the effect of the relative size of the target on bidder returns documented in the takeover literature and reviewed in Betton et al. (2008).

Klein (1986) reports that the disclosure of the sales price is central to the market's assessment of the transaction. She finds a positive seller stock price reaction only when the price is disclosed at the initial divestiture announcement. Firms that fail to announce the transaction price have CARs close to zero. The significance of price disclosure is confirmed by Afshar et al. (1992) and Sicherman and Pettway (1992). Clubb and Stouraitis (2002) find that the announcement returns tend to increase with the difference between the sales price and an estimated value of the assets in their current use. Overall, this suggests that the market's valuation of the transaction depends on the sales price relative to the value of the assets when operated by the firm.

The abnormal returns on divestiture announcements are positive also for buyers, although they are of a smaller magnitude than for sellers. For six selected studies with data for the period 1963–1995 and listed in Panel B, the average buyer announcement CAR ranges from 0.0% to 0.6%. The sample-size-weighted buyer ACAR is 0.5% for the combined sample of 1243 divestiture announcements. Sicherman and Pettway (1992) document a size effect in the buyer's stock price reaction similar to that of sellers; that is, buyer returns tend to increase with the relative size of the acquired assets.

While both sellers and buyers appear to gain from a divestiture, most of the gains tend to accrue to the selling (divesting) firm. In each individual transaction, however, the division of the total gains depends on the relative bargaining strength of the two parties. Sicherman and Pettway (1992) use a debt downgrade prior to the asset sale as an indication of a weaker bargaining position vis-à-vis the buyer. As expected, they find significantly lower CARs for sellers whose debt was downgraded prior to the transaction.

---

[4] A typical approach is to estimate the parameters using a single-factor market model over approximately a year prior to the event: $R_{jt} = \alpha_j + \beta_j R_{mt} + \varepsilon_{jt}$, where R_{jt} is the stock return of firm j and R_{mt} is the market return on day t. The abnormal return $AR_{j\tau}$ over event day τ is computed as $AR_{j\tau} = R_{j\tau} - (\hat{\alpha}_j + \hat{\beta}_j R_{m\tau})$, where $\hat{\alpha}_j$ and $\hat{\beta}_j$ are the coefficient estimates from the time-series regression. The cumulative abnormal return is $CAR(\tau_1, \tau_2) = \sum_{\tau=\tau_1}^{\tau_2} AR_{j\tau}$, where τ_1 and τ_2 define the event window relative to the announcement day 0.

Moreover, the value creation is conditional on the successful completion of the divestiture. Hite et al. (1987) show that the seller stock price drops back to its initial level if a previously announced divestiture is canceled. In addition, announcement returns are positive for buyers completing the transaction, but insignificant for buyers in transactions that subsequently fail.

3.3. Drivers of value creation in divestitures

The positive announcement returns for sellers and buyers indicate that divestitures generally create value. We now turn to the evidence on the potential reasons for this value creation.

3.3.1. Increase in corporate focus

The typical divestiture involves sales of assets that are outside of the diversified firm's core business, and it results in an increased focus of the remaining operations. John and Ofek (1995) show that three-quarters of divested segments are unrelated to the seller's core business, defined as its primary four-digit Standard Industry Classification (SIC) code. Moreover, using various measures for firm focus, they find that sellers become more focused after the divestiture. Their focus measures include a sales-based Herfindahl Index across the firm's business segments, the total number of business lines reported by the firm, and whether the divested division is outside the firm's core business.

Schlingemann et al. (2002) find that firms tend to divest noncore segments that are relatively small. Maksimovic and Phillips (2001) and Kaplan and Weisback (1992) show that firms are more likely to sell peripheral assets. Kaiser and Stouraitis (2001) describe how Thorn EMI successfully raises cash by selling unrelated assets, reinvesting the proceeds in the company's core business. In sum, divested assets are typically outside the firm's core business, and the asset sales result in an increased focus of the firm's remaining operations.

John and Ofek (1995) find that the divestment announcement returns are positively related to measures capturing the increase in focus. Moreover, the operating profitability of the remaining assets increases after a divestiture, but only for the firms that become more focused. Denis and Shome (2005) show that large firms downsizing their assets become more focused and increase their operating performance. Berger and Ofek (1999) document average CARs of 7% for focusing-related announcements by diversified firms. Overall, there is substantial evidence that the value creation from divestitures is related to the resulting increase in the selling firm's focus.

3.3.2. Elimination of negative synergies

If the divested segment has negative synergies with other divisions of the diversified firms, the divestiture will create value simply by eliminating these negative synergies. Dittmar and Shivdasani (2003) examine the investment efficiency of divesting firms and find that segment sales are associated with a reduction of the diversification discount. Moreover, they document significant improvements in the investment decisions of the firm's remaining segments after the divestiture. Specifically, the investment level increases for segments that underinvest relative to single-segment firms and decreases for segments that overinvest relative to their peers. They also find that the announcement returns are higher the greater the subsequent reduction in the diversification discount and the greater the improvement in segment investments. Overall, their evidence suggests that divestitures create value by reducing costly cross-subsidization of inefficient investments in the diversified firm.

Colak and Whited (2007) reach a very different conclusion, addressing the endogeneity of breakup decisions. They confirm that firms selecting a divestiture or spinoff are different from their peers: the firms that restructure are typically larger and more diversified, and are in relatively fast-growing industries. Controlling for these differences, they show that although spinoffs and divestitures are associated with improved investment efficiency, these improvements are not directly caused by the restructuring itself.

Kaplan and Weisback (1992) examine whether divestitures are evidence of failed acquisitions. Studying a sample of 271 large firms acquired between 1971 and 1982, they find that 44% of the targets were sold by the end of 1989. Only one-third of the divested segments are classified as failed acquisitions, however, based on accounting profitability and comments by managers and the business press. Kaplan and Weisback (1992) conclude that acquirers sell businesses that they have improved or that they once had synergies with but no longer do. See also Fluck and Lynch (1999) for a model where diversifying acquisitions are made to help finance marginally profitable projects, to subsequently be divested once the projects are profitable and can generate the necessary funds internally.

3.3.3. Better fit with the buyer

As discussed above, a divestiture will create value if the assets are worth more to the buyer than the value in their current use. A buyer could, for example, have substantial synergies or superior management skills. John and Ofek (1995) find that seller announcement returns are higher when the buyer has some comparative advantage in managing the assets, such as a buyer operating in the same industry as the divested division or an LBO group.

Using US Bureau of Census data, Maksimovic and Phillips (2001) examine the effect of asset sales on the productivity at the plant level. They show that divestitures are more likely in business cycle upturns, when the assets are less productive than industry benchmarks, when the selling division is less efficient than the buyer, and when the firm has more efficient divisions in other industries. They conclude that most divestitures result in productivity gains by redeploying assets from relatively low-productivity sellers to higher ability buyers.

Datta et al. (2003) also study the efficiency of the reallocation of assets in divestitures. They use Tobin's q, defined as the ratio between the market value and the replacement cost (here the book value) of the assets, as a proxy for management's capability to manage the assets. They find that the announcement returns are highest for transactions where the buyer has a relatively high q and the seller has a relatively low q, possibly because the assets are transferred to a better managed firm. Overall, the evidence suggests that divestitures create value by transferring assets to higher valuation buyers.

3.4. Corporate governance

3.4.1. Agency issues

Although divestitures may be required to maximize shareholder wealth, some incumbent managements resist such actions. Berger and Ofek (1999) find that announcements of focus-increasing transactions often are preceded by corporate control and incentive-altering events, including management turnover, outside shareholder pressure, changes in management compensation, and unsuccessful takeover attempts. Gillan et al. (2000) describe how Sears announced the divestiture of financial services and refocused on retail first after a long period of poor performance and coincident with substantial pressure from institutional investor activists. This suggests that the restructuring may have been postponed until it could no longer wait.

Consistent with a reluctance to sell assets, the monitoring of and incentives provided to top management are critical to the value created by a divestiture. Tehranian et al. (1987) document significantly higher announcement returns for divesting firms that provide long-term performance plans to their top executives. Hirschey and Zaima (1989) find higher announcement returns for divestitures by companies with concentrated ownership than sales by widely held firms. Also, the returns are higher for firms where insiders are net-buyers of the firm's stock over the preceding 6-month period. Hanson and Song (2000) further show that divestiture gains are increasing in the fraction of outside directors on the board and the percentage equity ownership of the management team. Pointing to the importance of banks as monitors, Hirschey et al. (1990) find some evidence of higher announcement returns for firms with bank debt. Overall, firms with better monitoring and more managerial share ownership seem to make divestitures that create more value.

The proceeds received by the divesting firm may be reinvested in the firm's remaining operations, used to retire debt, or distributed to shareholders. Lang et al. (1995) and Kaiser and Stouraitis (2001) show that the announcement returns are positive when the proceeds are used to pay back debt, but insignificant for firms that reinvest the proceeds. Slovin et al. (1995) also find higher announcement returns when the proceeds are paid out. This suggests that management may employ the funds inefficiently if retained by the firm.

Bates (2005) examines the payout and retention decision for 400 large asset sales between 1990 and 1998. He finds that the probability of retaining the cash proceeds increases in the divesting firm's growth opportunities, measured by its market-to-book ratio. However, firms retaining the proceeds consistently overinvest (have higher capital expenditure) relative to their industry peers. Also, the higher the equity ownership of officers and directors, the more likely it is that the sale proceeds are paid out. The evidence is again consistent with investment inefficiencies associated with retention of proceeds from asset sales.

3.4.2. Financial distress

Several studies indicate that asset sales are used as a way of generating cash when the firm is financially constrained. Divestiture announcements are typically preceded by a period of negative stock returns (Alexander et al., 1984; Hanson and Song, 2003; Jain, 1985) and poor operating performance (Brown et al., 1994; Lang et al., 1995; Schlingemann et al., 2002). Moreover, firms with high leverage are more likely to sell assets (Kruse, 2002; Ofek, 1993). Officer (2007) shows that selling firms have lower cash balances, cash flow, and bond ratings than size- and industry-matched control firms, all of which suggests that the sellers are liquidity constrained. Also, Nixon et al. (2000) find that financially distressed firms prefer a divestiture to a spinoff, which does not generate cash. In addition, Asquith et al. (1992), Ofek (1993) and others show that firms in financial distress frequently sell assets as part of the restructuring process.

The optimal use of proceeds from asset sales changes when the firm is in financial distress. The firm's ability to pay dividends to shareholders is typically limited by debt covenants at this point, and the choice stands between reinvestment in the business or repayment of debt. For a sample of distressed firms, Brown et al. (1994) show that shareholder announcement returns are significantly higher when the proceeds are retained by the firm rather than used to repay debt. Also as expected, bondholder announcement returns are higher when the proceeds are used to pay off debt. They suggest that creditor influence over distressed firms may force asset sales that benefit the firm's creditors at the detriment of shareholders. Datta and Iskander-Datta (1996) find that divestitures by financially distressed firms generate positive announcement returns for bondholders but not for shareholders.

Schleifer and Vishny (1992) argue that financially distressed firms sell assets at depressed prices to lower valuation industry outsiders because higher valuation industry insiders are liquidity constrained. Pulvino (1998) finds that financially constrained airlines sell aircraft at lower prices than their unconstrained competitors. Moreover, Officer (2007) shows that acquisition multiples are lower when the parent firm has experienced negative abnormal stock returns over the year leading up to the sale and when the corporate loan spread above treasury rates are high. Examining firms auctioned in Swedish bankruptcy, however, Eckbo and Thorburn (2008) reject the fire-sale hypothesis: they find little evidence of fire-sale discounts when assets are sold as going-concerns.[5]

Liquidity may be a factor in the decision to sell assets. Kim (1998) documents that managers sell their most liquid assets first, before selling more illiquid assets. Moreover, Mulherin and Boone (2000) and Schlingemann et al. (2002) show that breakup transactions tend to cluster in industries where the aggregate corporate transaction volume is large, that is, in industries with relatively liquid markets for corporate assets.

4. Spinoffs

In a spinoff, a public company distributes its equity ownership in a subsidiary to its shareholders. The distribution is a pro rata dividend, and parent shareholders receive subsidiary stock in proportion to their ownership in the parent firm. The spinoff involves a complete separation of the two firms. After the spinoff, the subsidiary becomes a publicly traded company with a unique ticker symbol and an independent board of directors. In contrast to a divestiture, a spinoff does not generate any cash proceeds for the parent company. Also, since the spinoff involves a public listing of shares, it has higher transaction costs and takes longer time than a divestiture.

A spinoff may be structured as a tax-free transaction if it qualifies under Section 355 of the Internal Revenue Code. Among the most important requirements under Section 355 are (i) the parent must have control of the subsidiary (own at least 80% of the voting rights) prior to the distribution; (ii) the parent must distribute control (at least 80% of the votes) to shareholders and retain no practical control of the subsidiary; (iii) the spinoff must have a valid business purpose; and (iv) the parent or the subsidiary cannot be acquired within 2 years after the spinoff. If the spinoff qualifies under Section 355, there is no tax on the distribution of stock, at neither the parent nor the shareholder level. Most spinoffs in the United States are structured as tax-free transactions.

If a spinoff does not qualify under Section 355, however, the distribution is taxed as a property dividend. The parent recognizes a gain equal to the difference between the fair market value of the subsidiary and the parent's tax basis in the subsidiary, similar to a capital gain. This gain is taxed at the corporate tax rate. Moreover, shareholders pay a dividend tax on the fair market value of the subsidiary (the distributed subsidiary stock).

The condition under Section 355 requiring that the subsidiary is not acquired within 2 years of the spinoff is outside the parent company's control. Yet, a potential acquisition of the subsidiary after a tax-free spinoff would trigger an often substantial tax liability at the parent company level. To transfer the cost of this potential liability to the subsidiary and thus ultimately the acquirer, it is common practice that the subsidiary contractually commits to pay any such future tax liability of the parent, if the subsidiary is acquired within 2 years of the spinoff.

---

[5] See Hotchkiss et al. (2008) for a more detailed review of asset restructurings by financially distressed firms.

Maydew et al. (1999) compare 52 tax-free spinoffs with 218 divestitures in the period 1987–1995. They find that tax costs average 8% of the divested assets. They suggest that managers prefer a taxable assets sale when the sales price is high enough to offset the associated tax cost.

4.1. Transaction volume

Using data from Thompson SDC Platinum (SDC), Figure 2 plots the annual number (line) and total deal value (bars) of spinoffs announced between 1985 and 2007. As shown in Panel A, the number of US spinoffs soared in the second half of the 1990s and reached a peak in year 2000 with over 90 transactions. The aggregate spinoff value peaked in 1999 with a total market capitalization of $144 billion. While the interest for spinoffs plummeted with the burst of the Internet bubble, the deal activity has recently recovered. In 2007, a total of 90 spinoffs were announced in the United States to a total value of almost $80 billion. The largest US spinoffs announced in 2006–2007 were Kraft Foods (market capitalization of $51 billion), Tyco Healthcare Group ($23 billion), Tyco Electronics ($19 billion), Duke Energy Corp-Natural Gas ($15 billion), and Discover Financial Services ($15 billion).

Panel B shows the annual number and total deal value of non-US spinoff transactions. The international volume of spinoffs has been growing relatively steadily since the mid-1990s, reaching an all-time high in 2007, with a total market value of $188 billion across 169 transactions. Some of the largest spinoffs in 2006–2007 outside the United States include Philip Morris International, Switzerland (market value of $108 billion); SK Corp-Petrochemical Business, South Korea ($17 billion); HydroOGK, Russian Federation ($12 billion); and Experian Ltd., the United Kingdom ($11 billion).

4.2. Valuation effects

The results from 19 selected studies estimating shareholder gains from spinoff announcements are listed in Table 2. The samples contain a total of 2052 spinoffs announced between 1962 and 2000. Shareholder average CARs are significantly positive and range from 1.7% to 5.6% across the various studies. The lowest average CAR of 1.7% is for a sample of 156 European spinoffs announced in 1987–2000 and examined by Veld and Veld-Merkoulova (2004). Combining the 19 studies, the sample-size-weighted abnormal announcement return is 3.3%.

The average CAR of 3.3% in spinoffs is higher than the 1.2% average CAR for divestitures reported above. Recall, however, that buyers also tend to experience positive announcement returns in divestitures (average CAR of 0.5%). In contrast, the total gains from a spinoff are reflected in the parent company stock. Thus, some of the difference in announcement returns between spinoffs and divestitures could be explained by buyers sharing in the value creation from the latter transaction.

Number (line) and total transaction value (bars) of U.S. spinoffs

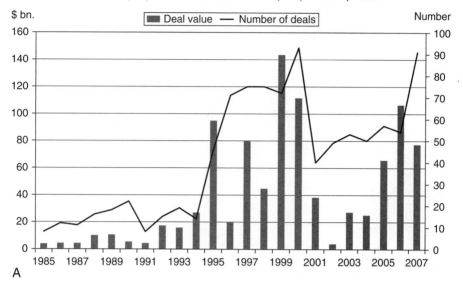

A

Number (line) and total transaction value (bars) of non-U.S. spinoffs

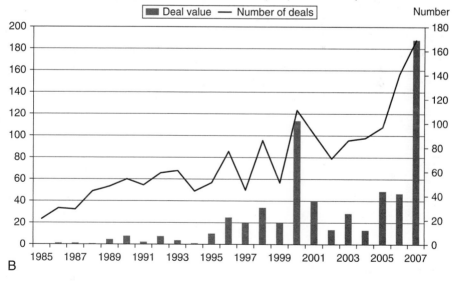

B

Fig. 2. Annual volume of spinoff announcements, 1985–2007. Source: SDC.

Table 2 further shows that the market value of the subsidiary is about one-quarter that of its parent in the average spinoff. As for divestitures, the announcement returns for spinoffs are increasing in the relative size of the subsidiary. Miles and Rosenfeld (1983)

Table 2

Cumulative abnormal returns (CAR) for 2052 spinoffs in 19 selected studies, 1962–2000

Relative size is the ratio of the market value of equity of the spunoff subsidiary and the parent company prior to the spinoff.

Study	CAR		Relative size		Sample size	Time period	Event window
	Mean (%)	Median (%)	Mean (%)	Median (%)			
Miles and Rosenfeld (1983)	3.3			10	55	1963–1980	[0, 1]
Hite and Owers (1983)	3.3			7	123	1963–1981	[−1, 0]
Schipper and Smith (1983)	2.8			20	93	1963–1981	[−1, 0]
Rosenfeld (1984)	5.6				35	1969–1981	[−1, 0]
Vijh (1994)	2.9	2.1	29	18	113	1964–1990	[−1, 0]
Allen et al. (1995)	2.1				94	1962–1991	[−1, 0]
Slovin et al. (1995)	1.3	1.6	33	24	37	1980–1991	[0, 1]
Daley et al. (1997)	3.4	1.4			85	1975–1991	[−1, 0]
Best et al. (1998)	3.4				72	1979–1993	[−1, 0]
Desai and Jain (1999)	3.8		29	18	144	1975–1991	[−1, 1]
Krishnaswami and Subramaniam (1999)	3.1	1.9	31	14	118	1979–1993	[−1, 0]
Mulherin and Boone (2000)	4.5	3.6	22	14	106	1990–1999	[−1, 1]
Gertner et al. (2002)	3.9	2.2	24	19	160	1982–1996	[−1, 0]
Wruck and Wruck (2002)	3.6				172	1985–1995	[−1, 0]
Burch and Nanda (2003)	3.7	3.2	24	20	106	1979–1996	[−2, 1]
Maxwell and Rao (2003)	3.6	2.6	25	19	80	1976–1997	[−1, 0]
Seoungpil and Denis (2004)	4.0	3.1	25	17	150	1981–1988	[−1, 1]
Veld and Veld-Merkoulova (2004)	1.7	0.6			156	1987–2000	[−1, 0]
McNeil and Moore (2005)	3.5		25	23	153	1980–1996	[−1, 1]
Sample size weighted average	3.3		26	18	2052	1962–2000	

show that shareholder CARs are on average greater in spinoffs of subsidiaries with a market value exceeding 10% of the parent company's market value compared to spinoffs of relatively small subsidiaries. In addition, Alli et al. (2001) find insignificant announcement returns for 47 spinoffs that are subsequently withdrawn, as if the market anticipates the withdrawal at the time of the announcement.

The evidence of positive announcement returns for spinoffs is compelling. Some studies also report long-term returns following spinoffs. Cusatis et al. (1993) estimate the buy-and-hold stock returns for parents and subsidiaries spun off in the 1965–1988 period. They find positive average returns for holding periods of 24 and 36 months compared with portfolios of industry and size-matched stocks. McConnell et al. (2001) investigate portfolios of parents and subsidiaries in 89 spinoffs between 1989 and 1995. In contrast to the earlier work, they find little evidence of higher average buy-and-hold returns compared to portfolios matched on size and book-to-market. Also, using the Fama and French (1993) three-factor model as a benchmark, they reject the hypothesis that the portfolios of spinoff companies exhibit abnormal returns.

4.3. Drivers of value creation in spinoffs

4.3.1. Increased corporate focus

As with divestitures, a potential source of value creation in spinoffs is an increase in corporate focus resulting from the elimination of unrelated divisions. Daley et al. (1997) report that the positive announcement returns are limited to spinoffs that increase corporate focus, defined as the parent and subsidiary having different two-digit SIC industry codes. They document substantial improvements in the return on assets for parents in focus-increasing spinoffs, but not for parents where the spunoff subsidiary is in a related industry. Moreover, Desai and Jain (1999) find that focus-increasing spinoffs have significantly higher announcement returns, long-run abnormal stock returns, and improvements in operating performance than do nonfocus increasing spinoffs.

Burch and Nanda (2003) estimate the change in the parent firm's diversification discount from the year prior to the year after the spinoff. They find that the diversification discount is reduced when the spinoff increases corporate focus, but not otherwise. Overall, the evidence suggests that shareholder gains in spinoffs are associated with a subsequent increase in firm focus.

4.3.2. Elimination of negative synergies

The separation of an unrelated business segment may further reduce any negative synergies that exist between the subsidiary and the rest of the firm. Gertner et al. (2002) examine whether spinoffs help eliminate value-reducing cross-subsidization in diversified firms. They show that the subsidiary's investment decisions become much more sensitive to the firm's investment opportunities after the spinoff. Specifically, the total capital expenditure decreases for firms in low Tobin's q industries and increases for firms in high q industries. These changes take place primarily for subsidiaries whose operations are unrelated to the parent's core business and in spinoffs generating higher announcement returns.

Seoungpil and Denis (2004) further find that, prior to the spinoff, parent firms trade at a discount to and invest less in their high-growth (high q) divisions than do their standalone peers. Following the spinoff, however, the diversification discount is eliminated and investments have increased for the high-growth segments. Also, McNeil and Moore (2005) show that subsidiary capital expenditures move toward industry levels after the spinoff, for both previously rationed and subsidized divisions. Announcement returns are greater when parent firms allocate capital in a seemingly inefficient way, defined as rationing high q and subsidizing low q spinoff divisions, as is the reduction in the diversification discount. Overall, the evidence indicates that spinoffs create value by improving the investment decisions in diversified firms.

Allen et al. (1995) propose that spinoffs provide a way to unwind unsuccessful prior acquisitions. They examine a sample of 94 spinoffs in which the spunoff entity previously had been acquired by the parent firm. Their evidence suggests that the original acquisition was value destroying: the average acquisition announcement return is negative both for the acquirer and for the target and bidder combined. Moreover, the spinoff announcement return is positive and negatively correlated to the acquisitions return; that is, the greater the anticipated loss from the acquisition, the larger the expected gain from the spinoff. While not identifying a unique source for the value creation in spinoffs, these results are consistent with the elimination of negative synergies between parent and subsidiary.

4.3.3. Wealth transfer from bondholders

A spinoff may increase shareholder value at the expense of the parent firm's creditors by reducing the TAs of the firm. Also, if the spinoff increases the volatility of the cash flows of the two separate firms the expected payoff to debtholders will decrease, with a corresponding gain to shareholders (Galai and Masulis, 1976). MacMinn and Brockett (1995) further argue that a spinoff could transfer wealth from liability claimants by removing corporate assets from their reach. Nevertheless, the impact of a spinoff on debtholders is limited by the existence of restrictive debt covenants. Hite and Owers (1983) find insignificant bondholder abnormal returns for a sample of 31 spinoff announcements in 1963–1981, as do Schipper and Smith (1983).

In a case study of Marriott, however, Parrino (1997) documents a significant drop in the value of Marriott's bonds following its spinoff announcement. At the same time, shareholder announcement returns were positive, suggesting a wealth transfer from bondholders. Maxwell and Rao (2003) examine monthly bond return data for a sample of 80 spinoffs between 1976 and 1997. They find that parent bondholders tend to experience a price decline after the spinoff announcement. The average abnormal bond return (adjusted for the treasury rate) in the month of the spinoff is −0.9%, and decreasing in the relative size of the spunoff subsidiary. Consistent with a bondholder loss, credit ratings are more likely to be downgraded than upgraded subsequent to the spinoff. They find, however, that the combined value of the publicly traded debt and equity increases, suggesting that a wealth transfer from bondholders could only explain part of the shareholder gains.

4.3.4. Information asymmetries

The aggregation of financial data across divisions may exacerbate informational asymmetries between outside investors and insiders for diversified firms. Krishnaswami and Subramaniam (1999) examine whether spinoffs reduce such information gaps, using the dispersion in analysts' forecasts and analysts' forecast error as a measure for the information asymmetry. They find that spinoffs are more common for firms with relatively high levels of information asymmetry compared to their industry rivals. The announcement returns are higher for firms with a greater degree of information asymmetry, and the information gap tends to decrease after the spinoff. Best et al. (1998) also find that spinoff announcement returns are increasing in financial analysts' earnings forecast errors. Overall, this suggests that one source of value creation in spinoffs is the mitigation of information asymmetries.

Analysts play an important role in producing and disseminating information about the firm. Gilson et al. (2001) study changes in the coverage by financial analysts for a sample of 103 focus-increasing spinoffs and equity carveouts over the period 1990–1995. They document a 45% increase in analyst coverage in the 3 years following a breakup. The new analysts tend to be specialists in the subsidiary's industry. Moreover, the accuracy of the earnings forecast improves by 30–50%, and in particular for the industry specialists. In sum, increases in corporate focus seem to improve the information provided by analysts, in both quality and quantity.

Huson and MacKinnon (2003) further show that analysts tend to revise upwards their short-term earnings forecast in response to a spinoff. Also, idiosyncratic stock return volatility increases following a spinoff, and more so when the spunoff subsidiary is unrelated to the parent firm. They conclude that the stock price becomes more sensitive to firm-specific information, which benefits informed traders relative to uninformed traders.

4.3.5. Clientele effects

Previously combined into a single security, the spinoff creates the opportunity to hold the subsidiary stock separately. This expansion of investors' opportunity set increases liquidity and opportunities for investor diversification. In a sample of 113 spinoffs during 1964–1990, Vijh (1994) finds abnormal stock returns of 3.0% on the spinoff ex date, that is, the day that the subsidiary starts trading separately, accompanied by an increased trading volume. He attributes the positive returns to higher demand for the parent and subsidiary stocks once they have been separated.

Abarbanell et al. (2003) show that institutional investors rebalance their portfolio holdings in parents and their spunoff subsidiaries dependent on the fund's investment style and fiduciary restrictions. However, they find little evidence that such rebalancing trades lead to abnormal price pressures for parents or subsidiaries around the spinoff. Chemmanur and He (2007) examine the trading of institutional investors in 66 spinoffs between 1999 and 2004. They find large imbalances in the postspinoff trading of parent and subsidiary stock: 46% of the trades are in the opposite direction, and trades in the same direction are heavily concentrated in one of the firms. This imbalance increases in the measure of information asymmetry and the difference in beta risk and growth rates between the parent and subsidiary. Overall, spinoffs seem to relax a trading constraint that existed prior to distribution of the subsidiary stock.

4.3.6. Increased probability of a takeover

The fact that it is possible after the spinoff to acquire control of the division through a stock purchase increases the probability that the division will become a future takeover target. The spinoff may also increase the probability that the parent will become a target as the parent is now a smaller and more focused firm. Cusatis et al. (1993) examine 146 tax-free spinoffs over the period 1965–1988 and show that both the parent and the spunoff subsidiary are indeed more likely to become takeover targets, compared to a set of control firms matched on size and industry. They suggest that two pure plays created by a spinoff are more attractive as targets than the combined company. Most of the takeovers occur 2–3 years after the spinoff, possibly to protect the tax-free status of the spinoff. Given the large premiums typically paid in control transactions, they attribute the positive abnormal stock returns at the time of the spinoff to the increased probability of being acquired.

4.4. Corporate governance

Self-interested managers may be reluctant to downsize assets under their control. Ahn and Walker (2007) study the importance of effective corporate governance for firms' decision to spin off a subsidiary. Their sample is 102 spinoffs between 1981 and 1997. They find that firms conducting a spinoff have greater stock ownership by outside board members, and smaller and more heterogeneous boards relative to their peers. Following the spinoff, parent firms increase their market-to-book ratios and reduce the diversification discount. They conclude that effective governance increases the likelihood of a spinoff, which is a value-increasing strategy.

Wruck and Wruck (2002) examine the management team of the spunoff subsidiary. They show that 21% of spinoff top managers are outsiders, while 48% of the insiders are parent company top managers rather than division heads. They argue that subsidiary managers lack the corporate governance expertise required when the former division becomes publicly traded. Announcement returns are highest for spinoff subsidiaries led by a parent firm's top manager and a division head, combining corporate governance and operating expertise.

In a spinoff, the parent management can design the governance structure of the subsidiary without seeking approval from shareholders. Daines and Kausner (2004) find that the charters of spunoff subsidiaries include substantially more takeover defenses than do the charters of a sample of size- and industry-matched IPO firms, where shareholders have a say on the corporate charter. Moreover, the spunoff firms tend to have more takeover protection than do their parents. Thus, it appears that managers prefer more takeover defenses than shareholders do.

Pyo (2007) find that pay-performance sensitivity increases for subsidiary CEOs after a spinoff. The higher the pay-performance sensitivity, the greater the improvements in operating performance postspinoff. Seward and Walsh (1995) propose that the likelihood of becoming a takeover target should be higher for spunoff firms with little CEO equity incentives. They find that the takeover probability—hostile as well as friendly—increases with the CEO's stock and option ownership in the spunoff subsidiary. While not discussed by Seward and Walsh (1995), it is possible that CEOs with relatively low pay-performance sensitivity also adopt more takeover defenses in the spinoff firm.

Allen (2001) examines the postspinoff trades of senior managers, directors, and block-holders in 193 public subsidiaries and their parents over the period 1978–1991. He finds that insiders who trade during the first year following the spinoff earn excess returns of 36% over the subsequent 12-month period. He suggests that insiders take advantage of the spinoff as an opportunity to use private information on the relative prospects of the parent and the subsidiary.

4.5. Splitoffs

A splitoff is similar to a spinoff in that the subsidiary becomes an independent company with a separate stock listing. The splitoff, however, involves an exchange offer, where shareholders are offered to exchange parent company stock for subsidiary stock. Thus, the splitoff effectively resembles a stock repurchase, where the parent company buys back its own shares using subsidiary stock as consideration. As a result of the exchange offer, the ownership structure in the parent and the subsidiary are different postsplitoff (depending on the extent to which parent shareholders participate in the exchange offer). Similar to a spinoff, a splitoff does not generate any new cash to the parent company. The tax treatment is also the same as for a spinoff.

Splitoffs are rare, partly because the valuation of the subsidiary stock is critical for the exchange offer. A splitoff is therefore always preceded by an equity carveout, which helps establish the market value of the subsidiary stock. Recent transactions include McDonald's splitoff of 51% of its interest in Chipotle Mexican Grill, announced in April 2006 and valued at $660 million; Viacom's splitoff of Blockbuster in 2004; and General Motors (GM) splitoff of Hugh Electronics in 2003.

We are unaware of any systematic empirical evidence on splitoffs—reflecting the limited number of transactions.[6] Given the similarity with spinoffs, the research on spinoffs is likely relevant for splitoffs as well. In addition, some value may be created in splitoffs from the repurchase of parent stock, for example, by signaling that the parent stock is undervalued.

5. Equity carveouts

An equity carveout is a partial initial public offering (IPO) of the stock in a subsidiary. The subsidiary gets its own management team and a separate board of directors. It becomes subject to all financial and other reporting requirements of public companies, such as 10-K reports and proxy statements filed with the Securities and Exchange Commission (SEC).[7]

The parent company often retains a controlling interest, creating a public minority interest in the subsidiary. There are several reasons for the retention of a majority ownership of the voting rights: Retention of at least 80% allows consolidation for tax purposes and the opportunity to subsequently undertake a tax-free spinoff, while retention of 50% or more permits consolidation for accounting purposes. Allen and McConnell (1998) show that parent firms on average retain 69% (median 80%) of the subsidiary's shares, while Vijh (2002) reports a median parent ownership of 72%. Of course, since the subsidiary becomes a publicly traded company of its own, the carveout does reduce the parent's control over its former wholly owned subsidiary.

The shares offered in the IPO may be sold either by the subsidiary itself (a primary issue) or by the parent company (a secondary issue). A primary issue has no tax consequence, while a secondary issue is taxable to the parent as a capital gain. Because of this difference in tax treatment, the majority of equity carveouts are primary issues. The parent company may require the proceeds or leave the proceeds in the subsidiary. The proceeds are streamed back to the parent using the following procedure: (i) prior to the carveout, the subsidiary issues a tax-free dividend to the parent in the form of a note (debt obligation); (ii) after the carveout, the proceeds from the IPO are used to repay the note.

5.1. Transaction volume

Figure 3 shows the annual distribution of equity carveouts worldwide from 1985 to 2007, using data from SDC. Most of the carveout transactions are outside the

---

[6] For a case study, see E.I. du Pont de Nemours and Company: the Conoco splitoff (A), HBS 9-202-005.
[7] See Hand and Skantz (1998) for an analysis of the accounting choice for equity carveouts under SAB 51. Allen (1998) describes the equity carveout strategy of Thermo Electron, which carved out 11 subsidiaries during 1983–1995.

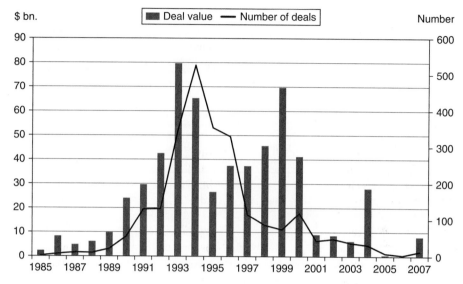

Fig. 3. Annual worldwide volume of equity carveouts, 1985–2007. Source: SDC.

United States. The worldwide carveout volume peaked in the first half of the 1990s, in both numbers and dollar values. The total market value of subsidiary IPOs reached $80 billion in 1993, and there were over 500 equity carveout transactions in 1994. The late 1990s saw a second surge in the dollar volume of carveouts ($70 billion), however, without a corresponding increase in the number of transactions. In recent years, only a handful of equity carveout transactions have taken place each year.

Most large carveouts in 2006/2007 took place outside the United States. The way SDC classifies carveouts, this transaction category also contains subsidiaries carved out by the government (state privatizations). The largest equity carveouts in 2007 include France Telecom SA (IPO proceeds of $3.6 billion); China Agri-Inds Holding Ltd., Hong Kong ($2.5 billion); Bank of Beijing, China ($2.0 billion); Qatar Airways, Qatar; and Kiora Holding Pty Ltd., Australia.

5.2. Valuation effects

Equity carveouts are viewed favorably by the market. Table 3 shows the parent cumulative abnormal announcement stock return for eight selected studies of equity carveouts over the period 1965–2002. The average announcement return is positive and significant across all samples, ranging from 1.2% to 2.7%. The sample-size-weighted average is 1.9% for the total of 1050 cases. The announcement returns for a sample of German firms average 1.7%, which is similar to the returns for US firms (Wagner, 2004). Interestingly, the positive returns found for equity carveouts are in

Table 3

Cumulative abnormal returns for 1050 equity carveout announcements in eight selected studies, 1965–2002

CAR is the parent cumulative abnormal stock return over the event window relative to the announcement of the equity carveout. Relative size is the ratio of the market value of equity of the carved-out subsidiary and its parent company.

Study	CAR		Relative size		Sample size	Time period	Event window
	Mean (%)	Median (%)	Mean (%)	Median (%)			
Schipper and Smith (1986)	1.8			8	76	1965–1983	[−4, 0]
Klein et al. (1991)	2.7				52	1966–1983	[−4, 0]
Slovin et al. (1995)	1.2	1.5	45	31	32	1980–1991	[0, 1]
Allen and McConnell (1998)	2.1		20	14	186	1978–1993	[−1, 1]
Vijh (1999, 2002)	1.9			18	336	1980–1997	[−1, 1]
Mulherin and Boone (2000)	2.3	0.8	37	17	125	1990–1999	[−1, 1]
Hulburt (2003)	1.6	1.1		30	172	1981–1994	[−1, 0]
Wagner (2004)	1.7		32	22	71	1984–2002	[−1, 1]
Sample size weighted average	1.9		33		1050	1965–2002	

stark contrast to announcements of seasoned equity offerings (SEO), upon which the parent stock price typically falls.[8]

The average carved-out subsidiary across the studies in Table 3 has a market value of about one-third that of its parent. As for other breakup transactions, the announcement returns are found to be increasing in the relative size of the carved-out subsidiary (Allen and McConnell, 1998; Vijh, 2002). Vijh (1999) estimates long-term (3-year) abnormal stock returns for both parent companies and the carved-out subsidiaries, and finds that these are insignificantly different from zero using a variety of benchmarks.

5.3. Drivers of value creation in equity carveouts

Equity carveouts separate the subsidiary from its parent. After the carveout, transactions between the two companies must take place at arm's length. As a result, many of the sources of value creation in spinoffs may also create value in carveouts.

---

[8] See Eckbo et al. (2007) for a review of security offerings.

5.3.1. Increased focus

Vijh (2002) examines a sample of 336 equity carveouts between 1980 and 1997. A majority of the motives offered for the carveout by the parent company involve lack of fit and focus, and a desire to restructure the operations. He shows that parents and subsidiaries in carveouts are typically in different industries, and documents that announcement returns are higher on average for carveouts of nonrelated subsidiaries.

The evidence on improvements in operating performance following carveouts is mixed. Hulburt et al. (2002) find that both parents and subsidiaries improve their operating performance relative to their industry peers in the year after the carveout. In contrast, Powers (2003) and Boone et al. (2003) show that the subsidiary operating performance declines after the carveout. Boone et al. (2003) find that the operating performance of the parent company improves only when it has completely divested its ownership in the subsidiary after 4 years.

5.3.2. Financing subsidiary growth

Information asymmetries between the firm and outside investors tend to increase the cost of capital (Myers and Majluf, 1984). Prior to the carveout, outside investors have access to the parent company's financial information, with information at the divisional level being less accessible. This opaqueness may increase the cost of funding divisional-level capital expenditures. Because a public listing of the subsidiary increases the quality of the financial information available to investors, Schipper and Smith (1986) suggest that equity carveouts help finance high-growth subsidiaries. Their data bears this out: in their sample, a frequently stated motive for the carveout is to enable the subsidiary to finance future growth. They also show that carved-out subsidiaries typically have higher price-earnings ratios than their parents, indicating higher growth rates.

Chen and Guo (2005) also report that parent firms prefer equity carveouts and divestitures to spinoffs when revenue growth and book-to-market ratios are high. Vijh (2002) further finds that, over a subsequent 3-year period, both parents and their carved-out subsidiaries do a greater number of SEO than control firms matched by industry and size. In addition, the capital expenditures of the subsidiaries exceed those of their control firms. Overall, it appears that equity carveouts are used to increase financing opportunities and reduce financing costs for high-growth subsidiaries.

Michaely and Shaw (1995) document investment banking fees of 7% for carveouts and 2% for spinoffs in a sample of 61 carveouts and 30 spinoffs between 1981 and 1988. They attribute the higher costs of carveouts to the greater scrutiny and more stringent disclosure standard associated with the continued control by the parent company. They also suggest that, because of the higher costs, carveouts are more attractive to firms with relatively low leverage that hold high-quality assets. Consistent with this, they find that larger less-leveraged parents with relatively large and low-risk subsidiaries tend to prefer a carveout to a spinoff.

5.3.3. Wealth transfers and information asymmetries

Carveouts have the potential for transferring wealth to shareholders from other claim-holders. For example, the separation of assets from the parent possibly reduces the cash flow and collateral available to bondholders. Allen and McConnell (1998) find, however, positive excess bond returns when firms announce a carveout, thus rejecting the bondholder wealth transfer hypothesis.

Nanda (1991) models an equity carveout using the adverse selection framework of Myers and Majluf (1984). In equilibrium, only undervalued parents with overvalued subsidiaries perform carveouts. Thus, carveouts cause a positive announcement effect on average (and there are no wealth transfers).[9] Slovin et al. (1995) examine industry rivals of equity carveout firms. They postulate that the market's misvaluation may apply to all firms in the industry. For a sample of 32 carveouts between 1980 and 1991, they show that industry rivals of the carved-out subsidiaries experience negative announcement returns, consistent with the overvaluation argument. They also report insignificant abnormal returns to parent-company rivals. However, Hulburt et al. (2002) find negative returns for parent-company rivals as well, using a sample of 185 equity carveout announcements over the years 1981–1994. They argue this is evidence against the proposition that parents of carveouts tend to be undervalued.

Vijh (2006) examines the announcement returns to the SEO of 90 subsidiaries and 37 parents following equity carveouts. He documents negative returns to the issuer, but insignificant returns to the nonissuer, whether parent or subsidiary. Using a sample of equity carveouts from 1995 to 2002, Baltin and Brettel (2007) detect traces of market timing for the 1998–2000 "hot-market" period. Overall, the proposition that equity carveouts are designed to sell overvalued equity in the subsidiary receives mixed support.

5.3.4. Follow-on events

Equity carveouts appear to be a temporary organizational form. A majority of equity carveouts are followed by a subsequent event. In Schipper and Smith (1986), two-thirds of 76 carved-out subsidiaries were later reacquired by the parent (23), divested entirely (17), spunoff (4), or liquidated (4). Moreover, Klein et al. (1991) find that 44 of 52 carveouts (85%) are followed by a second event: 25 reacquisitions, 17 selloffs, and 2 spinoffs. Divestitures take place sooner than reacquisitions: three-quarters of the divestitures occur within 3 years of the carveout, compared to one-third of the reacquisitions. Also, the probability of a reacquisition is greater when the parent retains 80% or more of the subsidiary shares.

---

[9] By assuming the carveout's assets in place are sufficiently small relative to those of the parent, Nanda (1991) rules out the possibility that the parent of the carveout is also overvalued (which would result in a negative announcement effect of the carveout). Overvalued parents always prefer to issue their own shares.

Klein et al. (1991) argue that an equity carveout may be the first stage in a divestiture of a subsidiary. As noted above, the listing of the subsidiary's shares reduces informational asymmetries and exposes the subsidiary to the market for corporate control. Perotti and Rossetto (2007) model equity carveouts as a way for the parent to obtain information from the market on the value of the subsidiary as an independent entity. Though costly, the listing generates information about the optimal allocation of ownership of the subsidiary. Thus, the carveout improves the decision to exercise the option to sell or reacquire control, explaining the temporary nature of carveouts.

Gleason et al. (2006) document insignificant announcement returns for carveouts that are later reacquired. However, Klein et al. (1991) show that parents experience significantly positive announcement returns when the follow-on event is a selloff, both at the initial equity carveout and at the subsequent divestiture. Moreover, the probability of becoming a target is higher for carved-out subsidiaries than for a sample of matched firms (Hulburt, 2003). This evidence is consistent with equity carveouts creating value by facilitating future corporate control events.

5.4. Agency issues

Allen and McConnell (1998) argue that some managers avoid selling off assets because their compensation (both tangible and intangible) is tied to the size of the assets they manage. When the financing of the investments require an asset sale, the preference is to sell a minority stake in a subsidiary, maintaining assets under control. For a sample of 188 equity carveouts, they find that parent firms perform relatively poorly prior to initiating a carveout: parents have lower interest coverage ratios, higher leverage, lower operating profitability, and lower return on assets than their industry rivals. In sum, the sample parents of the carveouts were poor performers and cash constrained.

Allen and McConnell (1998) also find that the stock market's reaction to the carveout announcement is determined by the use of the proceeds. Firms announcing that the proceeds will be reinvested in the firm experience insignificant announcement returns, while the average CAR is a significant 7% for firms that will use the proceeds for debt repayment or a dividend. This suggests that the stock market may be concerned with inefficient investment decisions if the firm retains the proceeds. Schipper and Smith (1986) provide further evidence on managers' reluctance to relinquish control of the subsidiary. They document that, in a majority of cases, the president or CEO of the carved-out subsidiary is also a parent company manager.

Powers (2003) suggests that managers use their inside information about the subsidiary prospects in determining what fraction of subsidiary shares to sell to the public. He shows that the subsequent improvement in subsidiary operating performance tends to increase in the size of the ownership stake retained by the parent. Similarly, Atanasov et al. (2005) show that carved-out subsidiaries tend to have lower operating performance than their peers only when parents retain less than 50% ownership.

Their interpretation is very different, however. They suggest that parent managers either self-select the carveout to avoid consolidating the subsidiary's financial results, or transfer wealth from the minority shareholders in nonconsolidated subsidiaries through intercorporate transactions ex post.

6. Tracking stocks

Tracking stock—also called targeted stock or letter stock—is a separate class of parent company common stock whose dividends track the performance of a given division. That is, the holders of the tracking stock are entitled to the cash flow generated by this division, hence determining the value of the stock. The diversified company retains its legal form as one consolidated entity, however, with one and the same board of directors and top management team. There is no legal separation or transfer of assets, and the parent retains control of the division. As a result, the voting rights of the tracking stock is in the parent firm and not in the tracked division. These voting rights typically vary in proportion to the market value of the underlying division, but could also be fixed at the issue of the tracking stock.

There are several ways to distribute tracking stock. It can be issued to current shareholders as a dividend or used as payment in an acquisition. The most common way, however, is to sell the tracking stock in a public offering, raising cash for the parent firm. Once the tracking stock is listed, the underlying division files separate financial statements with the SEC. Thus, tracking stock creates a type of quasi-pure play, where the tracked division files its own financial statements and has its own stock, while still being part of the diversified firm. Since tracking stock is an issue of the company's own stock, it has no tax implications.

6.1. Transaction volume

The first tracking stock was issued by GM in 1984 as part of the payment for Electronic Data Systems (EDS). The new stock, GM-E, allowed the selling shareholders—most notably Ross Perot, who continued in a management position—to participate in the upside of EDS, despite being part of a much larger company going forward. GM issued its second class of tracking stock, GM-H, in 1985 when acquiring Hughes Aircraft. The next company to issue tracking stock was USX, separating its steel division from its oil division (Marathon) in 1991.

In total, 32 US companies have issued some 50 different tracking stocks to date, most of them in the 1990s. The market seems to have lost its appetite for tracking stock since the turn of the century. The most recent issues of tracking stock include Sprint PCS and CarMax Group in 2001, and AT&T Wireless and Disney's Go.Com in 2000. Carolina Group announced an issue in 2002 that was subsequently withdrawn. Internationally, there has been only a handful tracking stock issues, including Sony Communication Network in 2001 (Japan) and Alcatel Optronics (France) in 2000.

6.2. Valuation effects

Announcements of tracking stock are received positively by the market. D'Souza and Jacob (2000) document an average abnormal 2-day announcement return of 3.7% for 37 tracking stocks issued by 14 US companies between 1984 and 1999. Billett and Mauer (2000), Elder and Westra (2000), Chemmanur and Paeglis (2001), and Harper and Madura (2002) also report positive tracking stock announcement ACARs of 2–3%. Notice, however, that, given the limited number of tracking stock issues, these studies use largely the same data.

The evidence on the long-run performance of tracking stock is inconclusive. Examining 19 firms issuing tracking stock, Chemmanur and Paeglis (2001) find that the stock of parent firms underperform industry indexes over a subsequent 3-year period, while the average subsidiary outperforms its industry index. In contrast, Billett and Vijh (2004) document negative buy-and-hold returns for subsidiaries, but insignificant long-term excess returns for parents. Clayton and Qian (2004) further report insignificant long-run stock performance for tracking stock issuers. As discussed below, however, the strongest testament to a poor performance of tracking stock is the fact that they have almost entirely disappeared from the marketplace.

6.3. Drivers of value creation in tracking stock

A tracking stock is akin to a "quasi-pure play." On the one hand, tracking stock allows the firm to retain its internal capital market, file a joint tax return, and share certain fixed costs and resources (Billett and Mauer, 2000; Danielova, 2008). On the other hand, the requirement to file separate financial statements with the SEC provides some degree of separation between a division and its parent. Also, the tracking stock makes it possible to give stock-based compensation to subsidiary managers.

Clayton and Qian (2004) examine whether the separate listings increase the demand for the parent and subsidiary stocks. They document an ex-date abnormal return of 3% for the parent company, suggesting that the quasi-pure-play created by the tracking stock increases investor interest in the firm. However, Elder et al. (2005) fail to find any increase in the liquidity of the parent firm after the tracking stock issue. Instead, firms issuing tracking stock have relatively low stock-market liquidity and greater bid-ask spreads than comparable control firms. Overall, the evidence is inconclusive as to whether tracking stock increases investor demand to hold the diversified firm.

Logue et al. (1996) argue that tracking stock is most useful for firms where the benefits of consolidation and integration outweigh the benefits from a complete separation. However, it is questionable whether tracking stock separates the divisions sufficiently to successfully create a pure-play stock. Not surprisingly, D'Souza and Jacob (2000) show that the returns of tracking stocks are more highly correlated with other common stocks of the same company than with other firms in the same four-digit SIC industry as the tracked division. We now turn to a discussion of the major failure of tracking stock.

6.4. Agency Issues

Under US corporate law, the board of directors has full discretion to transfer assets between wholly owned divisions (within contractual boundaries set by debt covenants). The assets underlying a tracking stock therefore lack legal protection from expropriation by the parent company.[10] Toward the end of the 1990s, firms issuing tracking stock started to explicitly warn investors of the risk of expropriation. For example, in its 1999 prospectus for tracking stock in its online broker, Donaldson, Lufkin, and Jenrette (DLJ) warned of a conflict of interest: "The board of directors may make decisions that favor DLJ at the expense of DLJ direct."

There are several examples of expropriation taking place. When GM in August 1995 announced its plan to spin off its tracking stock in EDS (GM-E), it first required EDS to make a one-time contribution of $500 million to the parent (GM). EDS shareholders challenged this payment in Delaware court—and lost: the court's decision was that the board of directors has full discretion to transfer money within the corporation—tracking stock or not. Similarly, before US Steel spun off the tracking stock in its oil division Marathon in 2001, it first transferred $900 million of debt to Marathon. Not surprisingly, the stock of the steel division soared 19% on the day of this announcement.

The poor legal protection of the assets underlying a tracking stock is likely the major reason for the near-disappearance of this security. In fact, most of the tracking stocks have been reversed over the last decade. In a press release issued on December 16, 1999, Kerry Hoggard, chairman of Fletcher Challenge Ltd., said: "It is clear that the Group's capital structure is seen as complex by investors, is perceived to raise governance issues, and has resulted in a significant structural discount being applied to all our stocks. We cannot allow this to continue, and will move as quickly as possible to a full dismantling of the target share structure."

Billett and Vijh (2004) examine 11 announcements to remove the tracking stock structure. They find significant and positive excess stock returns of 14% to the dismantling announcement. Tracking stock in its current form may very well be a phenomenon of the past.

7. Leveraged recapitalizations

A leveraged recapitalization (henceforth "recap") is a significant payout to shareholders financed by new debt borrowed against the firm's future cash flow. The company remains publicly traded, but with a substantially higher debt level. For a sample of 27 firms completing leveraged recaps over the period 1984–1988, Gupta and

---

[10] Hass (1996) provides an in-depth discussion of the fiduciary duties of the company's directors as they relate to tracking stock.

Rosenthal (1991) find a threefold increase in the average debt-to-total-capital ratio, from 22% of to 67%. Denis and Denis (1993) document that the median ratio of total debt to TAs increases from 45% to 86% for a sample of 39 recaps in 1984–1988. Moreover, studying 42 leveraged recaps between 1985 and 1989, Handa and Radhakrishnan (1991) report that the proposed payout averages 60% of the prerecap market value of equity (MVE).

The cash distribution to shareholders is typically structured as a large, special, one-time dividend. Alternatively, the distribution could be in the form of a share repurchase or exchange offer. Management often forfeit the cash distribution on their shareholdings and instead takes additional stock. Consequently, leveraged recaps typically result in a substantial increase in managerial equity ownership. Handa and Radhakrishnan (1991) document that insider equity ownership increases by three times, while Gupta and Rosenthal (1991) report a doubling of the insider ownership (from 3.8% to 8.4%). In Denis and Denis (1993), the median ownership of officers, directors, and employees soars from 6% to 15%.

Prior to the widespread use of poison pills, leveraged recaps were sometimes used as a defense against a hostile takeover threat. See Denis (1990) for an analysis of leveraged recapitalizations as a takeover defense.

A leveraged recapitalization triggers a tax liability at the investor level. The tax depends on how the payout to shareholders is structured. For a special dividend, the amount distributed from the firm's retained earnings is taxed as a dividend. If the special dividend exceeds the retained earnings on the firm's balance sheet, the remaining cash distribution is a return of capital, treated as a capital gain. If the recap is structured as a share repurchase, the entire distribution is taxed as a capital gain.

The financial accounting for leveraged recapitalizations does not require any step-up of the company's assets. As a result, if the new debt exceeds the book value of the firm's equity, the company's book equity becomes negative following the recap. What appears like an LBO by a private equity sponsor is sometimes structured as a recap. Recap accounting can be used if the buyer acquires less than 94.9% of the firm's stock, and the owners of the minority interest, which must be widely held, are independent from the buyer.

7.1. Transaction volume

Figure 4 shows the annual volume of leveraged recapitalization transactions announcements from 1985 through 2007, using data from SDC. The recap volume has largely followed the ups and downs of the high-yield debt markets. As shown in Panel A, in the United States, leveraged recaps were particularly popular in the late 1980s, with a peak in combined transaction value (bars) of $37 billion in 1988 and 47 recaps (line) in 1989. There was a smaller surge in recapitalization transactions in the period 1997–2000, and then again in 2005, however, without a corresponding increase in transaction size. Panel B shows the non-US volume of leveraged recapitalizations.

Panel A: Number (line) and total transaction value (bars) of U.S. leveraged recapitalizations

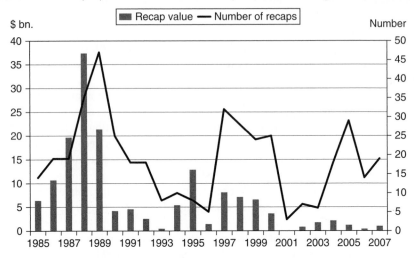

Panel B: Number (line) and total transaction value (bars) of non-U.S. leveraged recapitalizations

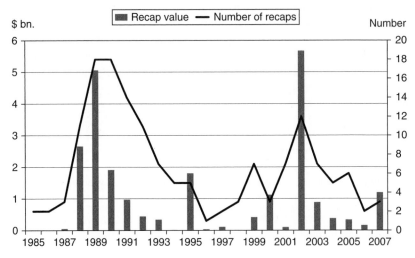

Fig. 4. Annual volume of leveraged recapitalizations, 1985–2007: Panel (A) number (line) and total transaction value (bars) of US leveraged recapitalizations; Panel (B) number (line) and total transaction value (bars) of non-US leveraged recapitalizations. Source: SDC.

The international recap activity is generally lower and involves smaller amounts. Companies announcing leveraged recapitalizations in 2006–2007 include Charter Communications Inc, Palm Inc., Foster Wheeler Ltd., and Acadia Realty Trust.

7.2. Valuation effects

The wealth effects of leveraged recapitalizations are substantial. For a sample of 44 recaps over 1985–1990, Bae and Simet (1998) find a 2-day shareholder ACAR of 5.7%. Moreover, Handa and Radhakrishnan (1991) report an average 2-day abnormal return of 5.5%, and Gupta and Rosenthal (1991) find an average announcement CAR of 5.9%. Moreover, Balachandran et al. (2004) document a 3-day average CAR of 4.4% for a sample of 167 leveraged recapitalizations in Australia between 1989 and 2002.

Since the leveraged recapitalization may be a response to a corporate control threat, several studies measure the returns over a longer event window. Denis and Denis (1993) use a window starting 40 days prior to initiation, defined as the first indication of a takeover or the announcement of the recap, through completion of the recap. They estimate an average abnormal return of 32% (median 26%). Kaplan and Stein (1993) compute the cumulative abnormal stock return starting 40 days prior to the recap announcement, or the day of a hostile bid if there is one, through the recap completion. They find an average CAR of 45% (median 47%) for 12 leveraged recapitalizations between 1985 and 1988.

Kaplan and Stein (1993) further estimate the change in systematic risk of the firm's securities after the leveraged recap. The increase in the equity risk is relatively modest. Using daily returns and market-model estimates, the average equity beta increases by 37% from 1.01 to 1.38 after the recapitalization. They then make two different assumptions about the change in TA risk from the transaction. Assuming that the systematic risk of the assets (asset beta) is constant, the implied debt beta averages 0.65. However, when they assume that the entire market-adjusted premium represents a reduction in fixed costs, the implied debt beta averages 0.40. Overall, leveraged recapitalizations generate substantial shareholder wealth and appears to be associated with a surprisingly small increase in equity systematic risk.

7.3. Drivers of value creation in leveraged recapitalizations

As discussed earlier, the high debt in leveraged recapitalizations reduces the firm's free cash flow and hence managerial discretion over the investment decisions (Jensen, 1986). Denis and Denis (1993) examine the change in operating performance and investments for 29 completed recapitalizations between 1984 and 1988. They document large decreases in the undistributed cash flow (median −31%) and capital expenditures (median −35%), despite improvements in operating performance (median 21%) from the year prior to the year after the recap. Also, the postrecap cash flow covers only two-thirds of the prerecap capital expenditures, forcing a reduction in the level of investments. They further examine the market reaction for capital expenditure announcements and find a significantly negative ACAR over the 5-year period prior to the recapitalization, suggesting a past pattern of overinvestment. Following the recap, the average number of announced investments drops from 1.2 to 0.3 per firm and year, with an average stock market reaction that is insignificantly different from zero. They conclude that the increased debt plays a central role in disciplining managers' investment decisions.

Consistent with these results, Wruck (1994) documents organizational and compensation changes in Sealed Air following its leveraged recapitalization in 1989. She suggests that the financial leverage was used as a tool to improve the internal control systems, which together with the high debt service created an environment that led to enormous performance improvements and value creation.

Peyer and Shivdasani (2001) study the efficiency of the internal allocation of investments after leveraged recapitalizations in 22 multidivisional firms between 1982 and 1994. Prior to the recap, companies allocate investments to high q divisions. Following the recap, however, investments become less sensitive to division q and more sensitive to division cash flow. While this may indicate that the internal allocation of capital becomes less efficient, the total level of capital expenditure declines, as do the firm's diversification discount. Peyer and Shivdasani conclude that the costs of distorted divisional investments are outweighed by the benefits of lower firm-level investments. Overall, leveraged recapitalizations appear to create value by curbing managerial overinvestment and improving operating performance.

Walker (1998) suggests that the benefits from leveraged recapitalizations are transitory, examining 39 recaps between 1985 and 1989. He finds that the recap firms have higher free cash flow prior to the recap than matching firms. However, the prerecap level of capital expenditures is not significantly different from that of its peers. Moreover, operating performance increases from year -1 to $+1$ relative to the special dividend, but reverts in the subsequent years.

A leveraged recapitalization could be used to signal management's private information about the future cash flow of the firm. Healy and Palepu (1995) describe how managers at CUC International successfully undertake a leveraged recap in 1989 to communicate their optimistic beliefs about the firm's future cash flows to investors. Balachandran et al. (2004) examine if the positive information conveyed by a recap extends to other firms in the industry. They find insignificant stock returns for competitors of firms announcing a leveraged recapitalization, suggesting that the content of any new information is unique to the recap firm.

A large fraction of the leveraged recapitalizations in the late 1980s subsequently failed. Denis and Denis (1995) report that 9 (one-third) of 27 firms completing a leveraged recap between 1985 and 1988 became financially distressed. They find that the poor operating performance of the nine distressed firms is in line with that of their industry peers. Moreover, the stock market reacts negatively to announcements of asset sales as well as to economic and regulatory events associated with the demise of the high-yield market. They conclude that the incidence of distress is not related to poorly structured transactions, but rather to unexpected macroeconomic and regulatory developments.

8. Leveraged buyouts (LBO)

An LBO is the acquisition and delisting of an entire company or a division, financed primarily with debt. The buyer is typically a private equity fund managed by an LBO sponsor—or recently sometimes a consortium of funds. The sponsor raises debt to finance the majority of the purchase price and contributes an equity investment from the fund. The equity is injected into a shell company, which simultaneously borrows the debt and acquires the target.

The sponsor relies on the company's cash flow, often supplemented by assets sales, to service the debt. The objective is to improve operating efficiency and grow revenue for a 3- to 5-year period before divesting the firm. Debt is paid down over time and all excess returns accrue to the equity holders. The exit may be in the form of an IPO, a sale to a strategic buyer, or a sale to another LBO fund. While an IPO typically generates a higher valuation, it could take several years for the LBO fund to entirely unwind its holdings through the public markets.

Because of the heavy debt load, a target firm is traditionally characterized by a strong predictable cash flow, supported by a history of profitability. In addition, it is often in a mature industry, with low growth and limited need for additional capital expenditures. The industry scope of LBOs has increased over time, as has the importance of international deals. Also, while the conventional LBO involves a publicly traded target company, a majority of the leverage buyouts are of private firms.

A management buyout (MBO) is an LBO of a segment, a division or a subsidiary of a large corporation in which key corporate executives play a critical role. MBOs are generally smaller than traditional LBOs and, depending on the size of the transaction, a sponsor need not be involved. In the following, MBOs are singled out only if this term is explicitly used to characterize a sample.

8.1. Transaction volume

The leverage buyout activity varies considerably over time. Figure 5 shows the annual number (line) and total deal value (bars) of LBOs announced between 1985 and 2007, using data from SDC. As shown in Panel A, a first surge in US LBO activity occurred in the late 1980s. This is when landmark transactions such as KKR's buyouts of RJR Nabisco (worth $25 billion) and Safeway ($4 billion) took place. The economic recession in 1990–1991, combined with regulatory restrictions on investments in high-yield instruments, the bankruptcy of Drexel Burnham Lambert, and a reduction in new lending by commercial banks, put an abrupt end to this first wave of highly leveraged transactions.

Most of the transactions in the 1990s were LBOs of private companies and divisions. As the availability of debt financing soared in the mid-2000s, the public-to-private transaction reappeared in a second buyout boom. The total value of US LBO transactions announced in 2006 and 2007 amounts to $450 and $410 billion, respectively.

Number (line) and total transaction value (bars) of U.S. leveraged buyouts

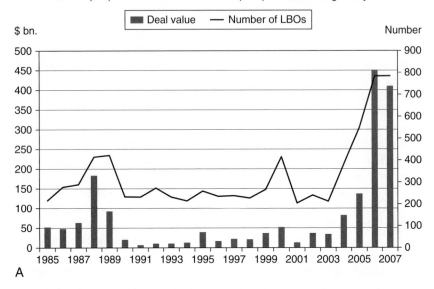

A

Number (line) and total transaction value (bars) of non-U.S. leveraged buyouts

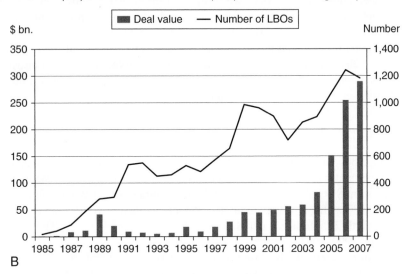

B

Fig. 5. Annual volume of leveraged buyouts, 1985–2007: (A) number (line) and total transaction value (bars) of US leveraged buyouts; (B) number (line) and total transaction value (bars) of non-US leveraged buyouts. Source: SDC.

Recent large US buyouts include Equity Office Properties ($41 billion), HCA ($33 billion), TXU ($32 billion), Harrah's Entertainment ($28 billion), Clear Channel Communications ($27 billion), First Data ($26 billion), SLM ($26 billion), Kinder Morgan ($22 billion), and Hilton Hotels ($20 billion), to mention a few.

Panel B shows the corresponding LBO volume outside the United States. The number of non-US buyouts has grown steadily since the mid-1980s, with a short dip in transaction volume in 2002 after the burst of the Internet bubble. The international LBO volume reached a record high in 2007 with a total deal value of $289 billion across almost 1200 transactions. Large buyouts outside the United States announced in 2006–2007 include BCE, Canada ($51 billion); Alliance Boots, the United Kingdom ($22 billion); BAA, Spain ($22 billion); Altadis, Spain ($18 billion); Thames Water, the United Kingdom ($15 billion); and Vodafone KK, Japan ($14 billion).

Stromberg (2007) estimates the value of firms acquired in LBOs between 1970 and 2007 as a total of $3.6 trillion, three-quarters of which represent LBOs undertaken after 2000. This second wave of large LBOs has spurred a renewed interest in LBOs in academic research. Since the financing market turmoil began in mid-2007, however, only a limited number of large buyouts have been announced in the United States and internationally.

8.2. The LBO capital structure

An LBO is financed with a mix of bank loans, high-yield debt, mezzanine debt, and private equity. The bank debt, which is often syndicated in the leveraged-loan market, is secured and most senior in the capital structure. The interest rate is floating, generally quoted as a spread above the London Interbank Offering Rate (LIBOR). While the maturity varies with the firm's credit profile, it is commonly in the range of 5–8 years and always shorter than that of junior debt. The bank debt has to be amortized before any other claimholders are paid off. At times (but not in 2006/2007), cash sweeps are common, requiring the firm to use any excess cash flow for accelerated amortization of the bank loans.

The bank debt is typically structured as several tranches of term loans (A, B, C, and D), where the holder of Tranche A also provides a revolving credit facility. Term A, the pro rata facility, is sold to traditional banks and is senior to the other tranches. In the second LBO wave, branches B, C, and D had minimal front-end amortization and were primarily sold to institutions and funds. The proportion leveraged bank loans in the capital structure varies, but was around 40% for US buyouts closed in 2006–2007.

The remaining debt is raised from the subordinated debt markets. High-yield debt (junk bonds) is generally subordinated and/or unsecured. Interest is fixed, based on a spread to treasury bonds that varies with credit quality, and expressed as a coupon. This debt has a bullet maturity in 10 years and is as a rule callable at a premium. The high-yield bonds are typically sold to the public in a 144A offering, which requires a road show and hence takes time to close. It is therefore common practice to finance the high-yield portion through a bridge loan at deal closing, repaid within a year with the proceeds from the subsequent bond issue.

As an alternative to high-yield debt, which is publicly traded, the market for second lien loans took off in 2003. These loans are privately placed with hedge funds and Collateralized Loan Obligation (CLO) investors, and are secured in the firm's assets but subordinated to the bank loans. CLOs combine a large number of leveraged loans (first and second lien) into a pool, which itself is sliced in tranches sold to institutional investors. In 2007, the total volume of second lien loans reached $30 billion (source: Standard & Poor's LCD).

The debt multiple is the average ratio of the pro forma total debt to adjusted EBITDA. The source is Standard & Poor's LCD.

Figure 6 shows annual debt multiples, defined as the pro forma ratio of total debt to adjusted EBITDA, in LBO transactions between 1997 and 2007. Debt multiples reached a low in 2001, when the average transaction raised 3.6 times EBITDA in the debt markets. The expansion of the debt markets and aggressive lending practices in 2007 are reflected in a much higher average debt multiple of 6.1 times EBITDA. After the financial market turmoil in mid-2007, however, credit markets are constrained, and debt multiples are considerably lower again.

In periods when access to high-yield debt and bank loans is limited, sponsors resort to mezzanine financing, which replaces or is subordinated to the high-yield bonds. It is sold in a private placement to funds and institutions, thus avoiding any public filing

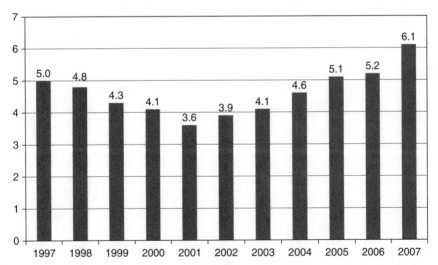

Fig. 6. Annual pro forma debt multiples in LBOs, 1997–2007.

requirements. The mezzanine is a committed financing with individually negotiated terms. It is structured as a debt contract or preferred equity, with warrants and other "equity kickers" attached to increase its total returns. All or part of the interest expense or dividend is often in the form of additional securities rather than cash, so-called pay-in-kind (PIK). The use of mezzanine financing is more widespread in Europe, where the leveraged-loan markets and high-yield bond markets lag those of the United States.

Private equity is the most junior in the capital structure. It typically has voting rights but no dividends. This equity is raised from pension funds, endowments, insurance companies, and wealthy individuals into a fund managed by a private equity partnership (the sponsor). Prominent LBO sponsors include Blackstone, Carlyle, and KKR. Most sponsors are paid a management fee of 2% on the fund's capital and receive a carried interest of 20% of the profits realized by the fund. In addition, some sponsors charge deal fees and monitoring fees to their portfolio companies. See Metrick and Yasuda (2007) for a detailed description and analysis of the fee structure in LBO funds. The capital raised for private equity is setting new record levels. In 2006, private equity funds had an inflow of $225 billion in new capital.

Panel A of Figure 7 shows the average equity contribution in LBOs from 1987 through 2007. The source is Portfolio Management Data. The deals in the end of the 1980s were extremely highly leveraged, with an average equity portion of 8–13% of the total capital. Over the last decade, most LBO transactions have had a substantially higher fraction of equity financing, with equity constituting on average one-third of the capital structure in recent years. Managers are generally required to coinvest in the buyout equity along with the LBO fund. If a manager has been involved in a prior buyout, she is asked to roll over a portion of her equity in the target firm. If it is a first-time LBO, managers may be offered to buy equity at a discount, or receive additional stock and options conditional on certain performance goals.

Panel B of Figure 7 shows the average price multiple in LBOs, defined as the ratio of the purchase price to the adjusted EBITDA, for the period 1997–2007. Average prices have risen from a low average multiple of 6.4 in 2001 to a high of 9.8 in 2007. The total funds raised in the buyout transaction are used for consideration to the seller as well as underwriter fees for the LBO debt (usually 1.5–2.5% of the principal amount) and call premiums on existing bonds.

Axelson et al. (2007) document the financial structure of 153 large US and European buyouts between 1985 and 2006. They find that the leverage of LBO firms is unrelated to debt levels of size- and industry-matched public firms. Instead, the leverage decreases in the interest rates prevailing at the time of the buyout. Prices also decline in interest rates, but are positively related to price multiples in public markets. They conclude that LBO capital structures are largely driven by the economy-wide cost of borrowing rather than firm-specific factors. See also Roden and Lewellen (1995) for an analysis of the structure of the LBO financing package.

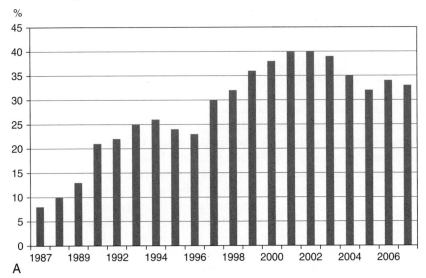

A

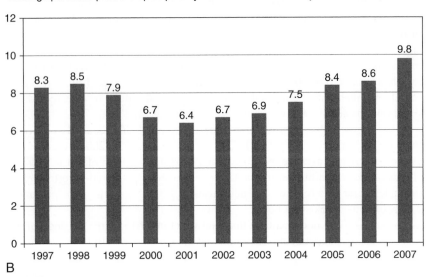

B

Fig. 7. Average annual % equity contribution and purchase multiples in LBOs. Source: Portfolio Management Data.

8.3. Value creation in LBOs

The total value created in an LBO is divided between the selling shareholders and the LBO investors. Table 4 shows the premiums paid in 1058 LBO transactions between 1973 and 2006 as reported by seven selected studies. The premium is defined as the final offer price in excess of the target stock price 20–60 days prior to the announcement of the bid. As shown in the table, the average premium ranges from 27% to 59% across the seven studies, with a sample-size-weighted average of 37%. The median premium ranges from 27% to 42%, with an average of 32%. It appears that premiums are generally somewhat lower in the 2000s compared to the 1980s. The exception is the study by Renneboog et al. (2007) of 177 buyouts in the United Kingdom between 1997 and 2003. They document an average premium of 40% (median 38%), which is higher than the contemporaneous LBO premiums of 27–29% in the United States (Billet et al., 2008; Guo et al., 2008).

Several studies find 2-day average CARs of 16–17% for LBO announcements in the 1980s (DeAngelo et al., 1984; Lehn and Poulsen, 1989; Slovin et al., 1991; Van de Gucht and Moore, 1998). For a sample of 641 LBOs in 1980–2001, Brown et al. (2007) estimate an average announcement CAR of 19%. The announcement return reflects a combination of the market's estimate of the target gains from a deal and the likelihood that the deal succeeds. Overall, the target shareholders tend to make substantial gains in LBOs.

The second part of the equation is the returns realized by the LBO investors. These returns have been difficult to estimate since the buyout targets are taken private and often do not return to public ownership. Kaplan (1989a) estimates a median market-adjusted return of 28% (mean 42%) for investors in 25 MBOs that went public after on

Table 4

Premiums paid in 1058 leverage buyouts for seven selected studies, 1973–2006

The premium is the ratio between the final offer price and the prebuyout stock price less one.

| Study | Premium | | Type of deal | Sample size | Time period | Day of prebuyout stock price |
	Mean (%)	Median (%)				
DeAngelo et al. (1984)	59		LBO	23	1973–1980	−40
Lehn and Poulsen (1989)	36		LBO	257	1980–1987	−20
Kaplan (1989b)	46	42	MBO	76	1980–1985	−40
Harlow and Howe (1993)	45		LBO	121	1980–1989	−20
Renneboog et al. (2007)	40	38	LBO	177	1997–2003	−40
Billet et al. (2008)	27	27	LBO	212	1990–2006	−60
Guo et al. (2008)		29	LBO	192	1996–2006	−20
Sample size weighted average	37	32		1058	1973–2006	

average 2.7 years. Muscarella and Versuypens (1990) examine the equity returns for 58 LBO firms that returned to public status after on average 2.9 years. Comparing the IPO price with the LBO price, they estimate an average annualized rate of raw return of 268%. This return is, however, not significantly different from the return of a hypothetical levered portfolio of S&P500 firms.

More recently, LBO fund return data has been available through self-reporting to Venture Economics. Jones and Rhodes-Kropf (2004) examine quarterly returns of 379 LBO funds formed between 1980 and 1999, using sponsor estimates of value changes. Estimating fund performance measured against the Fama and French (1993) three-factor model, they find fund excess returns (alphas) that are insignificantly different from zero.

Ljunqvist and Richarson (2003) use proprietary data from a large institutional investor. They study the returns to investments for 54 US LBO funds raised between 1981 and 1993, observing the actual cash inflows and outflows of the funds. They find that the LBO funds outperform the stock market and have positive alphas. On a risk-adjusted basis, the excess return of the typical LBO fund is 5% annually. Groh and Gottschalg (2008) also find positive excess returns in a sample of 133 US buyouts over 1984–2004. Their benchmark is a portfolio of public market equivalents matched by systematic risk and timing, and they correct for self-selection.

Kaplan and Schoar (2005) study the returns net of costs for 169 LBO funds raised between 1980 and 2001. They estimate that the median fund underperforms the stock market index, generating 80% (mean 97%) of the return on the S&P500. However, for the subset of sponsors that have been around for at least 5 years, the median perform-ance exceeds the S&P500 by 50% (mean 80%). They show that this performance is persistent, and they suggest that LBO sponsors may have different skills in managing portfolio companies. Phallipou and Gottschalg (2007) examine 739 LBO funds raised in 1980–1993, assuming that unrealized assets have zero value. They find that the funds net of cost underperform the S&P500 by 3% on average and confirm the persistence in LBO fund returns.

For a sample of 50 large UK buyouts over the 1997–2004 period, Acharya and Kehoe (2008) report positive industry-adjusted returns over the life of the deal. The returns are positively correlated to improvements in operating margins and asset growth. In contrast, Nikoskelainen and Wright (2007) find a median return to enter-prise value of −5% (average 22%), adjusted for the return of the FTSE 100 index on the London Stock Exchange. They examine a sample of 321 exited buyouts in the United Kingdom between 1995 and 2004.

Overall, the total gains from LBOs are large, manifested in the substantial premiums paid to target shareholders. However, the evidence is inconclusive as to whether selling shareholders largely capture all the gains in LBOs. Depending on the sample, the benchmark portfolio, and assumptions about the value of assets that are not liquidated, the estimates of LBO fund abnormal returns range from positive to negative.

8.4. Drivers of value creation in LBOs

8.4.1. Operating efficiency

As argued by Jensen (1986), the high leverage in buyouts may result in improved managerial investment decisions for firms with high cash flow and few growth opportunities. Lehn and Poulsen (1989) examine 263 LBOs in the 1980s. They find some evidence that firms with high levels of free cash flow are more likely to go private and that acquisition premiums increase with the target firm's cash flow. They conclude that the mitigation of agency problems associated with free cash flow are a major source of buyout gains.

Opler and Titman (1993) find that LBO targets have a combination of high cash flow and unfavorable investment opportunities (low q), and are more diversified than firms that don't become targets. In addition, buyouts are less likely for firms with high expenditures for research and development (R&D). Similarly, Long and Ravenscraft (1993) show that LBOs typically target firms with R&D expenditures below the industry average. Also, Bae and Simet (1998) find that LBO announcement returns are increasing in the free cash flow of the target firm. In contrast, Servaes (1994) finds no significant difference in the capital expenditure level between target firms in 99 going private transactions and their industry peers. Overall, however, the evidence suggests that the potential for incentive realignment in firms with high levels of free cash flow represents an important factor in the LBO decision.

If leverage successfully curbs overinvestment, this should show in the postbuyout operating performance. Kaplan (1989a) examines the performance of 48 large MBOs between 1980 and 1986. He shows that the firms experience substantial increases in operating income (+42%), reductions in capital expenditure, and improvements of the net cash flow (+96%) over a 3-year period following the buyout. Smith (1990) also reports significant performance improvements for 58 MBOs in 1977–1986. She finds that operating returns, measured as operating cash flow per employee and per dollar of operating assets, increase significantly from the year prior to the year after the buyout. She examines changes in accounting line items and finds no evidence that repair and maintenance expenditures are postponed or that the R&D expenditures are reduced. Instead, the higher margins are a result of adjustments in the management of working capital.

Several other studies document improved operating efficiency after buyouts. Lichtenberg and Siegel (1990) examine data from the Longitudinal Business Database (LBD) of the US Bureau of the Census for 131 LBOs in the period 1981–1986, with a total of 1132 plants. They show that plant total factor productivity (TFP) increases more than the industry average in the years following an LBO. Consistent with this finding, Harris et al. (2005) find an above-industry increase in TFP for UK MBO plants in the 1990s. Moreover, Muscarella and Versuypens (1990) examine the performance of 72 LBO firms that went public again. They show that LBO firms reduce operating costs and experience significant improvements in their operating margins. Also, while there is a dramatic increase in leverage upon completion of the LBO, the debt ratios are gradually reduced before returning to public ownership.

The evidence of improvements in operating performance is weaker for more recent transactions. Guo et al. (2008) examine 94 US public-to-private LBOs between 1990 and 2005. They find that postbuyout gains in operating performance are comparable to or slightly exceed benchmark firms matched on industry and prebuyout characteristics. The cash flow improvements are greater for firms with higher increases in leverage and when the CEO is replaced in the buyout transaction. Moreover, the median returns to LBO investors are 25% (average 57%) adjusted for Fama-French industry portfolio returns. Interestingly, the cash flow improvements and returns to capital are strongly related. However, due to the small magnitude of the cash flow gains, they suggest that recent transactions are not largely motivated by improving the operating efficiency of underperforming firms.

There is a concern that the trimmed organization and reduced capital expenditure may hurt the long-term prospects of LBO firms. Lerner et al. (2008) study a sample of 495 LBO firms that filed at least one successful patent application in the period 1986–2005. They show that firms continue to pursue high-impact patents after going private, concentrating their innovations in areas of historical core strengths. They conclude that LBOs promote a beneficial refocusing of the firm's patent portfolios.

Overall, the results suggest that LBOs target firms with free cash flow, where the leverage could help improve investment decisions by reducing managers' discretionary funds. There is convincing evidence of postbuyout improvements in operating performance and plant productivity. Also, while total capital expenditures decline, critical investments in R&D seem to continue.

8.4.2. Employment

It appears that improvements in operating efficiency are associated with employee layoffs. Kaplan (1989a) finds that the median firm reduces its employee count by 12% relative to the industry from the year prior to the year after the buyout. Muscarella and Versuypens (1990) show that the average employment declines by 0.6% for LBO firms that subsequently went public. This job creation is in the bottom 10% of COMPUSTAT firms. Lichtenberg and Siegel (1990) report that white-collar compensation and employment decline in the years following the buyout. Moreover, for a sample of 33 LBOs in 1980–1984, Liebeskind et al. (1992) report that LBO firms downsize the operations more than comparable firms in terms of number of employees, plants, and total revenues. In addition, there is some evidence that buyouts in the United Kingdom lead to modest declines in employment (Amess and Wright, 2007; Wright et al., 1992).[11]

---

[11] Perotti and Spier (1993) present a strategic model of temporarily high leverage. They show how shareholders, by retiring equity through a junior debt issue, can credibly threaten to underinvest in valuable new projects unless employees concede to wage reductions.

More recent evidence, however, suggests that the decline in LBO employment in existing facilities is outweighed by additional employment in new establishments, defined as new plants, offices, and retail outlets. Davis et al. (2008) examine LBD data for 5000 US targets acquired in private equity transactions between 1980 and 1995. Consistent with previous work, they find that employment drops more in target establishments than in control firms following the buyout. However, the LBO firms create substantially more jobs in new establishments than their peers. They conclude that the private equity sponsors push the target firm to expand in new, higher value directions. Overall, while LBO firms appear to trim their workforce to improve efficiency in existing production facilities, they also create additional job opportunities through new establishments.

8.4.3. Corporate governance

Highly leveraged transactions lead to increased monitoring by banks and the LBO sponsor (who has its own money at stake). Jensen (1989) argues that the combination of active governance by buyout sponsors, high-powered managerial incentives, and pressures from high leverage, provide a corporate governance system and incentive structure that is superior to that of widely held public firms. He predicts that the LBO organization eventually will eclipse the traditional, widely held public companies to become the dominant organizational form. While this has not yet happened, there is little doubt that the LBO organization carries with it a relatively efficient governance structure.

A central governance characteristic of LBOs is a meaningful management equity participation. Kaplan (1989a) shows that the median equity ownership of the top management team increases from 6% to 23% for 76 MBOs in the 1980s. Moreover, Muscarella and Versuypens (1990) report that the most highly paid officer owns 18% of the LBO firm's equity prior to an IPO exit.

The equity ownership of the top management team is also substantial in more recent samples. Kaplan and Stromberg (2008) study 45 LBOs from 1996 to 2004. They find a median equity ownership of 6% for the CEO and 16% for the management team. Nikoskelainen and Wright (2007) report an average equity ownership of 37% (median 35%) for 321 UK buyouts over the 1995–2004 period. Acharya and Kehoe (2008) examine a sample of 59 large buyouts in the United Kingdom between 1997 and 2004. They document an equity ownership including options of 3% for the CEO and 13% for the top management team as a whole. In sum, LBOs provide significant equity-based incentives to top management that help align managerial incentives with shareholders' interests.

Furthermore, the concentration of ownership provides LBO sponsors with a strong incentive to monitor the firm closely. Baker and Wruck (1989) describe the organizational changes at O.M. Scott after its LBO in 1986. The board had five members, of which one was a manager and three represented the buyout sponsor. All board members owned stock. The board met quarterly, and an executive committee monthly.

More importantly, one of the private equity partners served as a liaison between the LBO sponsor and the firm's managers. The operating partner, which functioned as an advisor and a consultant, spent several weeks at O.M. Scott after the buyout closed and was thereafter in telephone contact with the CEO daily. Baker and Wruck (1989) conclude that the close monitoring by the LBO sponsor, combined with the restrictions imposed by the high leverage and significant managerial shareholdings and bonus plans, led to a substantial improvement in O.M. Scott's operating performance and investment policies.[12]

The evidence suggests that LBO sponsors are also active monitors in more recent transactions. Cornelli and Karakas (2008) examine the board structure for 88 UK buyouts sponsored by a private equity firm over the 1998–2003 period. They find that, on average, the board size decreases by 15%, from 6.5 to 5.5 directors after the buyout. Moreover, outside directors are replaced by individuals representing the LBO sponsor, who controls on average 40% of the board seats. Also, the CEO is replaced in half of the buyout transactions.

Acharya and Kehoe (2008) show that LBO sponsors on average own 77% of the equity in their portfolio companies. The average sponsor holds 45% of the seats on a board with eight members that meet monthly. The sponsor engages through weekly, often informal, meetings with management over the due diligence phase and the first 3 months after closing. They also report that two-thirds of the LBO firm's top management is replaced within 100 days of the deal. In sum, buyout sponsors play an important role through active monitoring of the LBO firm.

Cressy et al. (2007) compare the operating performance of private equity-backed LBOs with that of comparable nonbuyout private firms matched on industry and size. Their sample is 122 UK buyouts in 1995–2002. They find a higher postbuyout operating profitability for the LBO firms, and particularly when the sponsor specializes in the target firm industry.

While the monitoring by LBO sponsors is an important governance mechanism in LBOs, managers sometime undertake MBOs without the involvement of a private equity sponsor. Fidrmuc et al. (2008) examine the choice between an MBO and a sponsor-backed buyout across 129 UK LBOs in 1997–2003 and where management stayed in control. They find that MBO targets have lower market-to-book ratios, more cash on hand, and greater managerial ownership. They suggest that managers invite LBO sponsors when they need help to complete a deal, and they conclude that MBOs and sponsor-backed LBOs are complementary transactions.

Cotter and Peck (2001) analyze how the equity ownership of the LBO firm interacts with the structure of the buyout debt. Their sample is 64 LBO firms in 1984–1989, of which a buyout specialist owns majority control in 40 firms (63%). They find that firms controlled by an LBO sponsor use less short-term and/or senior bank debt to finance

---

[12] See also Denis (1994) for an analysis of the organizational changes at Safeway after its leveraged buyout in 1986.

the transaction. Moreover, the LBO firm's operating performance increases with the use of senior debt only in deals where no buyout specialist is involved. They suggest that bank debt, having more restrictive covenants, and debt with shorter maturity, and thus higher debt service, both help motivate and monitor management in the absence of an active buyout specialist. See also Grinstein (2006) for an analysis of how the debt structure is used to commit investors to disciplinary actions against management.

In sum, LBOs are characterized by powerful corporate governance structures. First, management owns a substantial portion of the equity. Second, the ownership is concentrated with an LBO sponsor who actively monitors management. Third, the high leverage puts additional pressure to generate cash flow. Together, these mechanisms provide compelling incentives for managers to improve the efficiency of the LBO firm.

8.4.4. Wealth transfers from debtholders

If the prebuyout bonds lack protective covenants, the LBO firm may issue more senior debt. Bonds that lack protective covenants become more junior in the capital structure, resulting in a reduction in the value of those bonds. Thus, it is possible that some of the buyout gains represent wealth transfers from target firm debtholders. Marais et al. (1989) examine a sample of LBOs between 1974 and 1985. They find positive average CARs for convertible securities and preferred stock, most of which are redeemed as part of the buyout. A majority of the nonconvertible debt claims remain outstanding without renegotiation after the buyout. This debt typically lacks covenants restricting additional borrowing with higher seniority, and there are pervasive downgradings of public debt following successful buyout proposals, suggesting bondholder losses.

Asquith and Wizman (1990) investigate the 1-month return for 199 bonds of LBO targets in the 1980s. They find an average abnormal return of −1% across all bonds. However, these losses are concentrated to bonds with no covenant protection (mean return of −3%). Bonds with strong covenant protection have insignificant returns. Overall, the losses to bondholders are small compared to the total gains accruing to shareholders in the same LBO. Warga and Welch (1993) document an average risk-adjusted LBO announcement return of −7% for 36 bonds. The bondholder losses, however, constitute at most 6% of the shareholder gains. They too conclude that bondholder expropriation is a minor source of gains in LBOs. See also Billet et al. (2008) for an examination of bond returns in LBOs. They suggest that bondholder wealth expropriation has declined with the increased use of change-in-control covenants.

Ippolito and James (1992) propose that LBOs could extract wealth from other stakeholders as well. They examine the termination of pension plans in 169 buyouts in the 1980s. They find that the incidence of pension terminations doubles following LBO announcements. However, many of these terminations are affiliated with plant closings or an adaption to terms offered by the competitors of the LBO firm. Brown et al. (2007) examine the effect of LBOs on the firms' suppliers, using a sample of 157 suppliers of firms undertaking LBOs in 1990–2001. They document an average announcement CAR of -1.3% for the suppliers. Moreover, the negative returns are concentrated to suppliers with substantial relation-specific investments. Thus, some of the LBO gains may come from the financial leverage as a commitment device in negotiations with suppliers and other stakeholders.

Another group of stake holders in the buyout transaction are the LBO bank lenders. Kracaw and Zenner (1996) examine the wealth effects of highly leveraged transactions on the stock prices of lead banks of the leveraged-loan syndicate. They find significantly positive average CARs of 0.5% when the transaction is announced and another 0.4% when the bank financing is agreed upon. Moreover, the bank stock returns are increasing in the size of the highly leveraged transaction. In all, bank lenders are expected to make profits on financing highly leveraged transactions and not the opposite.

Demiroglu and James (2007) investigate whether brand-sponsors borrow at better terms. Examining a sample of 181 LBOs completed between 1997 and 2007, they find that buyouts sponsored by high-reputation partnerships pay narrower loan spreads, have fewer and less restrictive loan covenants, and borrow more at a lower cost from institutional loan markets. In addition, sponsor reputation is positively related to the amount of leverage used to finance the buyout. Moreover, Ivashina and Kovner (2008) study 1582 leveraged loans financing private equity sponsored LBOs between 1993 and 2005. They show that transaction loan spreads decline in the sponsor's relationship (past business) with the bank and the potential for future bank business. In sum, larger LBO sponsors can borrow at better terms. It is possible that this competitive advantage could help explain the persistence in returns across LBO sponsors documented by Kaplan and Schoar (2005).

8.4.5. Wealth transfers from target shareholders

While managers have a fiduciary duty to negotiate fair value in a buyout transaction, as acquirers of shares, they stand to gain from a low transaction value. By understating the true value of the target shares, they expropriate wealth from outside shareholders in the buyout. DeAngelo (1986) examines the accounting choices of 64 NYSE firms proposing an MBO during 1973–1982. Using a variety of tests, she fails to find any evidence that managers systematically understate earnings in the period leading up to the buyout. Perry and Williams (1994) employ a different methodology and a larger sample of 175 MBOs. In contrast, they find evidence of manipulation of the discretionary accruals that lowers the earnings in the year preceding the buyout announcement.

Kaplan (1989b) compares the financial forecasts that firms present at the time of an MBO to subsequent performance. He finds that the actual postbuyout performance generally lags the forecast, rejecting the notion that managers capitalize on inside information in the MBO. Lee (1992) studies a sample of withdrawn MBO proposals to determine whether managers' proposals reveal information beyond the gains from the completed transaction. He finds that stock prices drop back to their prebid level after the withdrawal of the MBO proposal unless another bidder appears. He suggests that the wealth creation in LBOs primarily results from efficiency gains associated with the completed transaction rather than wealth transfers from prebuyout shareholders. Moreover, Ofek (1994) finds that stock prices drop back to their prebuyout level after MBO offers are canceled or rejected by the target boards. Also, there is no subsequent improvement in the operating performance of these firms. Overall, the evidence at large suggests that buyout gains come from other sources than expropriation of selling shareholders.

A relatively new practice is the so-called club deals, where two or more private equity firms jointly sponsor an LBO. The equity portion in recent mega-deals may be too large for a single fund to finance on its own. However, a concern with these deals is that LBO sponsors may collude to limit competition, hence reducing the price paid to target shareholders. Indeed, the US Department of Justice launched an inquiry in late 2006 into the effect of such private equity consortiums on takeover competition.

Officer et al. (2008) examine the collusion argument for a sample of 53 club deals and 133 single-sponsor LBOs completed between 1984 and 2007. Using target abnormal return estimates, they find that club deals are associated with significantly lower premiums than single-sponsor deals. Guo et al. (2008) show that club deals are associated with higher returns on the capital invested in the LBO. However, they also find higher returns for target shareholders, rejecting the proposal of lower prices. Boone and Mulherin (2008) examine 70 club deals and 94 single-sponsor deals over the 2003–2007 period. Based on SEC filings, they show that the level of takeover competition is significantly higher for both types of LBO bidders compared to a control sample of takeovers. Moreover, target abnormal returns are largely the same across the different bidder categories. In sum, there is little evidence that club deals limit bidder competition in LBOs.

Outside investors may play an active role in the buyout, protecting target shareholder interests. Peck (1996) examines block trades in 111 MBO bids between 1984 and 1987. She finds that acquisitions of equity blocks increase around MBO offers, peaking 3 months prior to the offer. The participation of these blockholders increases the probability that the MBO proposal fails and a rival bidder acquires the firm. For a sample of 196 LBOs in 1990–2006, Huang (2008) finds significant increases in hedge fund holdings prior to the bid. He shows that the initial buyout premium increases with the level of hedge fund ownership in the target. Thus, outside investors seem to play an important role in increasing target returns.

8.4.6. Taxes

Interest expenses are deductible and therefore reduce the firm's cost of capital. In the 1980s, management could also choose to step up the value of the assets after the buyout, increasing depreciation deductions. Kaplan (1989b) estimates the value of potential tax benefits created in MBOs using a range of assumptions about the marginal tax advantage to debt and the debt retirement schedule. Depending on the assumptions, the median value of the tax benefits from interest deductions range from 13% to 130% of the premium paid to prebuyout shareholders, or 5–53% of the MVE 2 months prior to the buyout. He finds a strong positive correlation between the total tax deductions and the premium, and suggests that taxes are an important source of gains in LBOs.

See also Schipper and Smith (1991) and Newbould et al. (1992) for further analysis of tax deductions in LBOs. Jensen et al. (1989) estimate that LBOs have a positive overall effect on the tax revenue of the US Treasury. Simulations of the net effect of LBO activity for the US Treasury are found in Chatfield and Newbould (1996).

8.5. Industry effects

Slovin et al. (1991) propose that LBO announcements convey private information about the future prospects of the industry. Examining the stock price reaction of 940 industry rivals of 128 buyouts in the 1980s, they find a significant and positive rival average announcement CAR of 1.3%. The rival returns are greater for rivals that are smaller in size than the target firm. Phallipou and Gottschalg (2008) argue that LBO announcements signal the existence of an industry-wide agency problem, encouraging industry rivals to improve their governance structure too. They document an increase in rival firm options awards, director share ownership, and CEO turnover following LBO activity. It is not clear, however, whether their results are specific to rivals in industries with LBO activity or reflect a general trend in corporate governance.

One of the potential costs with high leverage is that it reduces financial flexibility and makes the LBO firm vulnerable to price competition by rival firms. Chevalier (1995b) examines how an LBO affects the pricing behavior of the LBO firm and its rivals in a local market, using data from the supermarket industry. She shows that prices rise when rival firms are also highly leveraged and LBO firms have higher prices than their competitors. However, prices fall when rival firms have relatively low debt levels and a single competitor controls a large market share. She finds that these low prices increase the probability that the LBO firm will exit, and suggests that rivals attempt to prey on LBO chains.

Phillips (1995) examines how financial leverage interacts with product market decisions for four different industries where a major player initiated an LBO. In three of the industries, characterized by difficult entry and high leverage of rival firms, prices increase and industry output declines with the average industry debt ratio. In the fourth industry, characterized by low leverage of rivals and low barriers to entry, prices fall and industry output increases with the industry debt ratio.

Overall, the evidence indicates that firms' leverage decisions affect industry pricing and output. See also Dasgupta and Titman (1998) for an equilibrium model explaining the interaction between capital structure and product markets, Fulghieri and Nagarajan (1996) for a model on the strategic role of high leverage for deterring entry in monopolistic markets, and Chevalier (1995a) for further evidence. Also, Parsons and Titman (2008) discuss empirical studies on the interactions between leverage and corporate strategy.

8.6. Organizational longevity and exit

Are LBOs a transitory structure or a sustainable corporate form that lasts over a longer period of time? Jensen (1989) argues that the organizational form of an LBO is superior to public ownership for firms in low-growth industries, predicting long-lived LBO companies. In contrast, Rappaport (1990) claims that the lack of financial flexibility will ultimately harm the buyout firm and foresees a prompt return to the public equity markets. Kaplan (1991) examines 183 large LBOs completed between 1979 and 1986. He finds that the median LBO target remains in private ownership for 7 years. Moreover, 45% of the LBO firms return to public ownership at some point. In a sample of 72 reversed IPOs, that is, LBOs that subsequently went public, Muscarella and Versuypens (1990) report that the average firm remains private for 3 years.

Stromberg (2007) studies holding periods and exits for 21,000 buyout transactions in 1970–2007. Of these buyouts 17,000 (80%) were backed by a financial sponsor. Given the large number of transactions in the 2000s, only 40% of the firms in his sample have exited. He finds that 39% of the exits are in the form of a sale to a strategic buyer. One quarter of the exits are a secondary buyout, that is, a sale to another LBO fund—an exit form that has increased in importance over the last decade. IPOs account for 13% of the exits. Moreover, despite the significant leverage used in buyouts, only 6% of exiting firms file for bankruptcy or initiates a financial restructuring. Stromberg (2007) further shows that the median firm stays in LBO ownership for 9 years, and only 8% of the firms are sold within 2 years of the buyout. Overall, the evidence suggests that LBOs are a long-term organizational form for many firms.

Van de Gucht and Moore (1998) use a hazard model to estimate the probability that an LBO firm returns to public ownership for a sample of 343 LBOs over 1980–1992. They show that 27% of the firms reverse through an IPO after 3.5 years on average. Another 9% of the firms are sold to a publicly held company. Almost half of the firms remain private, and 12% file for bankruptcy. Moreover, the likelihood for an IPO is higher when the industry average market-to-book ratio is rising.

Degeorge and Zeckhauser (1993) study the decision to exit a buyout through a public offering for 62 reverse LBOs in the 1980s. They find that the IPO coincides with a peak in the buyout firm's operating performance. The stock of the reverse LBOs outperform comparison firms, however, suggesting that the market anticipates the subsequent decline in operating profitability. They conclude that LBO firms choose to go public when their performance is strong. Holthausen and Larcker (1996) further show that the accounting performance of LBO firms exceeds that of its industry rivals at the time of the IPO and for the following 4 years. See Liu (2005), Cao and Lerner (2006), and Cao (2008) for additional evidence on reverse LBOs.

Halpern et al. (1999) conjecture that there are two types of targets in LBOs. One is the classical public target with little managerial equity and high free cash flow. The other is a target that performs poorly because the manager has too much of her wealth invested in the firm and hence is suboptimally risk-averse. Examining 126 LBOs in 1981–1986, they find that their sample clusters into two groups. The first group has low prior managerial equity and takeover premiums that decrease in managerial equity. Moreover, the buyout is led by an outside sponsor, and the LBO firm is typically sold in an IPO or to a strategic buyer. The second group has high managerial equity and takeover premiums that increase in managerial equity. These buyouts are led by managers, and the LBO firm tends to remain private. In addition, managers in this group typically increase their ownership fraction but decrease the dollar investment in the LBO firm. The authors suggest that a partition into these two different types of target firms better describes the LBO population.

Why did so many deals fail in the early 1990s? Bruner and Eades (1992) examine the failure of Revco in 1988, only 19 months after its LBO. They simulate the ex ante probability of survival, based on historical and predicted cash flows at the time of the deal. They conclude that the company was overleveraged from the closing of the deal, with little probability of successfully servicing its debt. Kaplan and Stein (1993) contend that the buyout market overheated toward the end of the 1980s, resulting in many poorly structured transactions. They find higher price multiples and leverage ratios, increased use of junk bonds with few restrictive covenants, and more money paid up-front to managers and investment banks.

9. Conclusions

In this chapter, we review the extant literature on corporate breakup transactions and highly leveraged transactions. For each individual transaction, we survey techniques, transaction volume, valuation effects, and potential sources of restructuring gains. Corporate breakup transactions are optimal when the separation of the diversified firm's divisions increases firm value. The breakup transactions range from divestitures and spinoffs, which entirely separates a subsidiary from its parent, to equity carveouts and tracking stock, which preserves some parent control. The highly leveraged transactions result in the firm taking on substantial additional debt in its capital structure. This happens in leveraged recapitalizations and in LBOs.

A divestiture is a sale of a division or subsidiary in a private transaction. Asset sales generate cash to the parent firm on the one hand, but trigger a capital gains tax on the other. The average parent firm experiences an abnormal stock return of 1% and the average buyer a CAR of 0.5% when a divestiture is announced. These valuation effects have several explanations: (i) most divestitures involve divisions that are unrelated to the parent firm, increasing the corporate focus of the diversified firm; (ii) the parent firm's investment decisions tend to improve after the divestiture; and (iii) assets are often transferred to a higher valuation buyer. Moreover, it appears that managers are reluctant to sell assets, managers in firms with better corporate governance make better divestment decisions, and the retention of proceeds is associated with inefficient investments.

A spinoff is the separation of a subsidiary through a distribution of the stock to parent shareholders. Spinoffs can be completed without any tax implications, but also do not generate any cash to the parent. The parent stock price increases by 3% on average at the announcement of a spinoff. The value creation comes from: (i) increased corporate focus, (ii) elimination of cross-subsidization leading to improved investment decisions, (iii) reduced information asymmetries, and (iv) a higher probability of becoming a target. Investors rebalance their portfolios when the parent and subsidiary stocks start trading separately. Moreover, parent managers design the subsidiary corporate charter to include more takeover defenses compared to the parent firm itself as well as other IPO firms.

An equity carveout is a partial IPO of the subsidiary, where the parent typically retains a controlling stake. It generates cash (the IPO proceeds) but no tax. The average parent firm experiences an abnormal stock return of 2% at the announcement of an equity carveout. The gains in equity carveouts are attributed to: (i) an increase in corporate focus and (ii) a reduction of the financing costs for high-growth subsidiaries. Equity carveouts are a temporary organizational form, and most carveouts are subsequently reacquired or sold off. It is possible that the carveout generates information about the value of the subsidiary as an independent company, improving the decision to exercise the option to sell out or buy back the subsidiary.

Tracking stock is a separate class of common stock in the parent company, tracking the performance of a given division. The tracking stock generates cash if it is offered to the public and has no tax implication. The average parent CAR is 3% on the announcement of a tracking stock issue. These announcement returns are, however, difficult to explain beyond an initial market infatuation with yet another breakup transaction. The tracking stock is a "quasi-pure" play in that it requires separate divisional SEC filings, but has voting rights in the parent. In fact, tracking stock trades like its corporate sibling divisions rather than its industry. It lends itself for expropriation since the corporate board, without legal remedy, can transfer funds from the tracked division to the rest of the company. As a result of such expropriation, most tracking stock issues have been dissolved.

A leveraged recapitalization is a large special dividend financed by debt, substantially increasing the firm's leverage. The average abnormal stock return is 5% on the announcement of a leveraged recapitalization and 20–30% through closing of the transaction. The gains in leveraged recapitalizations are attributed primarily to the incentive effects of debt: recap firms substantially cut their capital expenditures and increase operating profitability.

An LBO is an acquisition by private investors financed primarily by debt. Premiums paid to target shareholders in LBOs average 37%, and announcement CARs average 16–17%. The LBO gains are attributed to several sources: (i) improved investment and operating efficiencies, (ii) increased equity-based incentives to management, and (iii) strong monitoring by the LBO sponsor. Buyouts of the 2000s seem to have somewhat less improvements in operating efficiency, but in general create value similar to LBOs of the 1980s. Recent developments include club deals (consortiums of LBO sponsors bidding together), fund-to-fund exits (LBO funds selling the portfolio firm to another LBO fund), a highly liquid (until mid-2007) leveraged-loan market, and evidence of persistence in fund returns (perhaps because brand-sponsors borrow at better rates).

In this survey, we have focused on the individual transactions and their associated empirical evidence. This is also how most of the literature progresses. A major drawback of this approach is the resulting lack of analysis of alternatives. That is, when a company self-selects a divestiture, what were reasonable alternative strategies? In what sense was divestiture superior to, say, a spinoff, or an equity carveout? In what sense was going private via an LBO superior to a leveraged recapitalization? Are there systematic differences between public to private LBO transactions and private-to-private restructurings? Ideally, one would use a theoretical model to structure the answers to these types of questions. Perhaps the greatest challenge to the restructuring literature is to achieve a modicum of integration of the analysis across transaction types. Also, it is difficult to evaluate the expected return from buyout investments with only limited data on portfolio companies that do not return to public status within the sample period. We expect these issues to be resolved as both theories and data become more readily available in the future.

References

Abarbanell, J. S., B. J. Bushee and J. S. Ready, 2003, "Institutional Investor Preferences and Price Pressure: The Case of Corporate Spin-offs," *Journal of Business*, 76, 233–261.

Acharya, V. and C. Kehoe, 2008, "Corporate Governance and Value Creation: Evidence from the Private Equity Market," Working Paper, London Business School.

Afshar, K. A., R. J. Taffler and P. S. Sudarsanam, 1992, "The Effect of Corporate Divestments on Shareholder Wealth: The UK Experience," *Journal of Banking and Finance*, 16, 115–135.

Ahn, S. and M. D. Walker, 2007, "Corporate Governance and the Spinoff Decision," *Journal of Corporate Finance*, 13, 76–93.

Alexander, G., P. Benson and J. Kampmeyer, 1984, "Investigating the Valuation Effects of Announcements of Voluntary Corporate Sell-offs," *Journal of Finance*, 39, 503–517.

Allen, J., 1998, "Capital Markets and Corporate Structure: The Equity Carve-outs of Thermo Electron," *Journal of Financial Economics*, 48, 99–124.

Allen, J. W., 2001, "Private Information and Spin-off Performance," *Journal of Business*, 74, 281–306.

Allen, J. W. and J. J. McConnell, 1998, "Equity Carve-outs and Managerial Discretion," *Journal of Finance*, 53, 163–186.

Allen, J. W., S. L. Lummer, J. J. McConnell and D. K. Reed, 1995, "Can Takeover Losses Explain Spin-off Gains?" *Journal of Financial and Quantitative Analysis*, 30, 465–485.

Alli, K., G. B. Ramirez and K. K. Yung, 2001, "Withdrawn Spin-offs: An Empirical Analysis," *Journal of Financial Research*, 24, 603–616.

Amess, K. and M. Wright, 2007, "The Wage and Employment Effects of Leveraged Buyouts in the UK," *International Journal of the Business of Economics*, 14, 179–195.

Aron, D. J., 1991, "Using the Capital Market as a Monitor: Corporate Spinoffs in an Agency Framework," *RAND Journal of Economics*, 22, 505–518.

Asquith, P. and T.A. Wizman, 1990, "Event Risk, Covenants, and Bondholder Returns in Leveraged Buyouts," *Journal of Financial Economics*, 27, 195–213.

Asquith, P., R. Gertner and D. Scharfstein, 1992, "Anatomy of Financial Distress: An Examination of Junk-bond Issuers," *Quarterly Journal of Economics*, 109, 625–658.

Atanasov, V., A. Boone and D. Haushalter, 2005, "Minority Shareholder Expropriation in U.S. Publicly-Traded Subsidiaries," Working Paper, Babson College.

Axelson, U., T. Jenkinson, P. Stromberg and M. S. Weisbach, 2007, "Leverage and Pricing in Buyouts: An Empirical Analysis," Working Paper, Stockholm Institute of Financial Research.

Bae, S. C. and D. P. Simet, 1998, "A Comparative Analysis of Leveraged Recapitalization Versus Leveraged Buyout as a Takeover Defense," *Review of Financial Economics*, 7, 157–172.

Baker, G. and K. H. Wruck, 1989, "The Case of the O M Scott & Sons Company," *Journal of Financial Economics*, 25 (December), 163–190.

Balachandran, B., R. Faff and T.A. Nguyen, 2004, "The Intra-industry Impact of Special Dividend Announcements: Contagion Versus Competition," *Journal of Multinational Financial Management*, 14, 369–385.

Baltin, M. and M. Brettel, 2007, "Equity Carve-outs—A Matter of Time?" Working Paper, Aachen University.

Bates, T. W., 2005, "Asset Sales, Investment Opportunities, and the Use of Proceeds," *Journal of Finance*, 60, 105–135.

Berger, P. G. and E. Ofek, 1995, "Diversifications Effect on Firm Value," *Journal of Financial Economics*, 37 (1, January), 39–65.

Berger, P. G. and E. Ofek, 1999, "Causes and Effects of Corporate Refocusing Programs," *Review of Financial Studies*, 12, 311–345.

Best, R. W., R. J. Best and A. M. Agapos, 1998, "Earnings Forecasts and the Information Contained in Spinoff Announcements," *Financial Review*, 33, 53–67.

Betton, S., B. E. Eckbo and K. S. Thorburn, 2008, "Corporate Takeovers," In B. E. Eckbo (Ed.), *Handbook of Corporate Finance: Empirical Corporate Finance*, vol. 2, Chapter 15, Elsevier/North-Holland, Amsterdam, Handbooks in Finance Series, 291–429.

Billett, M. T. and D. C. Mauer, 2000, "Diversification and the Value of Internal Capital Markets, *Journal of Banking and Finance*, 24, 1457–1490.

Billett, M. T. and A. M. Vijh, 2004, "The Wealth Effects of Tracking Stock Restructurings," *Journal of Financial Research*, 27, 559–583.

Billet, M. T., Z. Jiang and E. Lie, 2008, "The Role of Bondholder Wealth Expropriation in LBO Transactions," Working Paper, University of Iowa.

Boone, A. L. and J. H. Mulherin, 2008, "Do Private Equity Consortiums Impede Takeover Competition?" Working Paper, University of Kansas.

Boone, A., D. Haushalter and W. Mikkelson, 2003, "An Investigation of the Gains from Specialized Equity Claims," *Financial Management*, 32, 67–83.

Boot, A. W., 1992, "Why hang on to losers? Divestitures and takeovers," *Journal of Finance*, 47, 1401–1423.

Brown, D. T., C. M. James and R. M. Mooradian, 1994, "Asset Sales by Financially Distressed Firms," *Journal of Corporate Finance*, 1, 233–257.

Brown, D. T., C. E. Fee and S. E. Thomas, 2007, "Financial Leverage and Bargaining Power with Suppliers: Evidence from Leveraged Buyouts," Working Paper, University of Pittsburgh.

Bruner, R. and K. Eades, 1992, "The Crash of the Revco LBO: The Hypothesis of Inadequate Capital," *Financial Management*, 21 (1, Spring), 35–49.

Burch, T. R. and V. Nanda, 2003, "Divisional Diversity and the Conglomerate Discount: Evidence from Spinoffs," *Journal of Financial Economics*, 70, 69–98.

Cao, J., 2008, "What Role Does Private Equity Play When Leveraged Buyouts Go Public?" Working Paper, Boston College.

Cao, J. and J. Lerner, 2006, "The Performance of Reverse Leveraged Buyouts," NBER Working Paper 12626.

Chatfield, R. E. and G. D. Newbould, 1996, "Leveraged Buyouts: Implications for U.S. Treasury Tax Receipts," *Quarterly Journal of Business and Economics*, 35, 51–65.

Chemmanur, T. J. and S. He, 2007, "Institutional Trading, Information Production, and Corporate Spin-offs," Working Paper, Boston College.

Chemmanur, T. and I. Paeglis, 2001, "Why Issue Tracking Stock," Working Paper, bcedu.

Chen, H.-L. and R.-J. Guo, 2005, "On Corporate Divestiture," *Review of Quantitative Finance and Accounting*, 24, 399–421.

Chevalier, J. A., 1995a, "Capital Structure and Product-Market Competition: Empirical Evidence from the Supermarket Industry," *American Economic Review*, 85, 415–435.

Chevalier, J. A., 1995b, "Do LBO Supermarkets Charge More? An Empirical Analysis of the Effects of LBOs on Supermarket Pricing," *Journal of Finance*, 50, 1095–1112.

Chou, D.-W., M. Gombola and F.-Y. Liu, 2006, "Earnings Management and Stock Performance of Reverse Leveraged Buyouts," *Journal of Financial and Quantitative Analysis*, 41, 407–438.

Clayton, M. J. and Y. Qian, 2004, "Wealth Gains from Tracking Stocks: Long-Run Performance and Ex-Date Returns," *Financial Management*, 3, 83–106.

Clubb, C. and A. Stouraitis, 2002, "The Significance of Sell-Off Profitability in Explaining the Market Reaction to Divestiture Announcements," *Journal of Banking and Finance*, 26, 671–688.

Coase, R., 1937, "The Nature of the Firm," *Economica*, 4, 386–405.

Colak, G. and T.M. Whited, 2007, "Spin-Offs, Divestitures and Conglomerate Investment," *Review of Financial Studies*, 20, 557–595.

Cornelli, F. and O. Karakas, 2008, "Private Equity and Corporate Governance: Do LBOs Have More Effective Boards?" Working Paper, London Business School.

Cotter, J. and S. Peck, 2001, "The Structure of Debt and Active Equity Investors: The Case of the Buyout Specialist," *Journal of Financial Economics*, 59, 101–147.

Cressy, R., F. Munari and A. Malipiero, 2007, "Playing to Their Strengths? Evidence that Specialization in the Private Equity Industry Confers Competitive Advantage," *Journal of Corporate Finance*, 13, 647–669.

Cusatis, P. J., J. A. Miles and J. R. Woolridge, 1993, "Restructuring Through Spinoffs: The Stock Market Evidence," *Journal of Financial Economics*, 33, 293–311.

D'Souza, J. and J. Jacob, 2000, "Why Firms Issue Targeted Stock," *Journal of Financial Economics*, 56, 459–483.

Daines, R. and M. Kausner, 2004, "Agents Protecting Agents: An Empirical Study of Takeover Defenses in Spinoffs," Working Paper, Stanford University.

Daley, L., V. Mehrotra and R. Sivakumar, 1997, "Corporate Focus and Value Creation: Evidence of Spinoffs," *Journal of Financial Economics*, 45, 257–281.

Danielova, A. N., 2008, "Tracking Stock or Spin-Off? Determinants of Choice," *Financial Management*, 37, 125–139.

Dasgupta, S. and S. Titman, 1998, "Pricing Strategy and Financial Policy," *Review of Financial Studies*, 11, 705–737.

Datta, S. and M. Iskander-Datta, 1995, "Corporate Partial Acquisitions, Total Firm Valuation and the Effect of Financing Method," *Journal of Banking and Finance*, 19 (1), 97–115.

Datta, S. and M. Iskander-Datta, 1996, "Takeover Defenses and Wealth Effects on Securityholders: The Case of Poison Pill Adoptions," *Journal of Banking and Finance*, 20 (7), 1231–1250.

Datta, S., M. Iskandar-Datta and K. Raman, 2003, "Value Creation in Corporate Asset Sales: The Role of Managerial Performance and Lender Monitoring," *Journal of Banking and Finance*, 27, 351–375.

Davis, S. J., J. Haltiwanger, R. Jarmin, J. Lerner and J. Miranda, 2008, "Private Equity and Employment," Center for Economic Studies, CES-0807.

DeAngelo, L. E., 1986, "Accounting Numbers as Market Valuation Substitutes: A Study of Management Buyouts of Public Stockholders," *Accounting Review*, 61, 400–420.

DeAngelo, H., L. DeAngelo and E. Rice, 1984, "Going Private: Minority Freezeouts and Stockholder Wealth," *Journal of Law and Economics* (October), 367–402.

Degeorge, F. and R. Zeckhauser, 1993, "The Reverse LBO Decision and Firm Performance: Theory and Evidence," *Journal of Finance*, 48, 1323–1348.

Demiroglu, C. and C. James, 2007, "Lender Control and the Role of Private Equity Group Reputation in Buyout Financing," Working Paper, University of Florida.

Denis, D. J., 1990, "Defensive Changes in Corporate Payout Policy: Share Repurchases and Special Dividends," *Journal of Finance*, 46, 1433–1456.

Denis, D. J., 1994, "Investment Opportunities and the Market Reaction to Equity Offerings," *Journal of Financial and Quantitative Analysis*, 29, 159–177.

Denis, D. J. and D. K. Denis, 1993, "Managerial Discretion, Organizational Structure, and Corporate Performance: A Study in Corporate Performance," *Journal of Accounting and Economics*, 16, 209–237.

Denis, D. J. and D. K. Denis, 1995, "Causes of Financial Distress Following Leveraged Recapitalizations," *Journal of Financial Economics*, 37, 129–157.

Denis, D. K. and D. K. Shome, 2005, "An Empirical Investigation of Corporate Asset Downsizing," *Journal of Corporate Finance*, 11, 427–448.

Desai, H. and P. C. Jain, 1999, "Firm Performance and Focus: Long-Run Stock Market Performance Following Spinoffs," *Journal of Financial Economics*, 54, 75–101.

Dittmar, A. and A. Shivdasani, 2003, "Divestitures and Divisional Investment Policies," *Journal of Finance*, 58, 2711–2743.

Eckbo, B. E. and K. S. Thorburn, 2008, "Automatic Bankruptcy Auctions and Fire-sales," *Journal of Financial Economics*, 89, 404–422.

Eckbo, B. E., R. W. Masulis and Ø. Norli, 2007, "Security Offerings," In B. E. Eckbo (Ed.), *Handbook of Corporate Finance: Empirical Corporate Finance*, vol. 1, Chapter 6, Elsevier/North-Holland, Amsterdam, Handbooks in Finance Series, 233–373.

Elder, J. and P. Westra, 2000, "The Reaction of Security Prices to Tracking Stock Announcements, *Journal of Economics and Finance*, 24, 36–55.

Elder, J., P. K. Jain and J.-C. Kim, 2005, "Do Tracking Stock Reduce Information Asymmetries? An Analysis of Liquidity and Adverse Selection," *Journal of Financial Research*, 28, 197–213.

Fama, E. F. and K. R. French, 1993, "Common Risk Factors in the Returns on Stocks and Bonds," *Journal of Financial Economics*, 43, 3–56.

Fidrmuc, J. P., P. Roosenboom and D. van Dijk, 2008, "Do Private Equity Investors Crowd Out Management Buyouts," Working Paper, Erasmus University, Rotterdam.

Fluck, Z. and A. W. Lynch, 1999, "Why Do Firms Merger and Then Divest? A Theory of Financial Synergy," *Journal of Business*, 72, 319–346.

Frank, M. Z. and V. K. Goyal, 2008, "Tradeoff and Pecking Order Theories of Debt", In B. E. Eckbo (Ed.), *Hand-book of Corporate Finance: Empirical Corporate Finance*, vol. 2, Chapter 12, Elsevier/North-Holland, Handbooks in Finance Series.

Fulghieri, P. and S. Nagarajan, 1996, "On the Strategic Role of High Leverage in Entry Deterrence," *Journal of Banking and Finance*, 20, 1–23.

Galai, D. and R. W. Masulis, 1976, "The Option Pricing Model and the Risk Factor of Stock," *Journal of Financial Economics*, 3, 53–81.

Garvey, G. T., 1992, "Leveraging the underinvestment problem: How high debt and management share-holdings solve the agency costs of free cash flow," *Journal of Financial Research*, 15, 149–166.

Garvey, G. T., 1995, "Debt Finance and the Cost of Management Ownership: Some Elementary Results," *Managerial and Decision Economics*, 16, 37–46.

Gertner, R., E. Powers and D. Scharstein, 2002, "Learning About Internal Capital Markets and Corporate Spin-offs," *Journal of Finance*, 57, 2479–2506.

Gillan, S., J. W. Kensinger and J. D. Martin, 2000, "Value Creation and Corporate Diversification: The Case of Sears Roebuck & Co.," *Journal of Financial Economics*, 55, 103–137.

Gilson, S. C., P. M. Healy, C. F. Noe and K. G. Palepu, 2001, "Analyst Specialization and Conglomerate Stock Breakups," *Journal of Accounting Research*, 39, 565–582.

Gleason, K., J. Madura and A. K. Pennathur, 2006, "Valuation and Performance of Reacquisitions Following Equity Carve-outs," *Financial Review*, 41, 229–246.

Goldman, E., 2004, "The Impact of Stock Market Information Production on Internal Resource Allocation," *Journal of Financial Economics*, 71, 143–167.

Grinstein, Y., 2006, "The Disciplinary Role of Debt and Equity Contracts: Theory and Tests," *Journal of Financial Intermediation*, 15, 419–443.

Groh, A. P. and O. Gottschalg, 2008, "Measuring the Risk-Adjusted Performance of U.S. Buyouts," Working Paper, University of Navarra.

Grossman, S. J. and O. D. Hart, 1986, "The Costs and Benefits of Ownership: A Theory of Vertical and Lateral Integration," *Journal of Political Economy*, 94, 691–719.

Guo, S., E. S. Hotchkiss and W. Song, 2008, "Do Buyouts (Still) Create Value?" Working Paper, Boston College.

Gupta, A. and L. Rosenthal, 1991, "Ownership Structure, Leverage, and Firm Value: The Case of Leveraged Recapitalizations," *Financial Management*, 20, 69–83.

Halpern, P., R. Kieschnick and W. Rotenberg, 1999, "On the Heterogeneity of Leveraged Going Private Transactions," *Review of Financial Studies*, 12, 281–309.

Handa, P. and A. R. Radhakrishnan, 1991, "An Empirical Investigation of Leveraged Recapitalizations with Cash Payout as Takeover Defense," *Journal of Finance*, 2 (June), 731–745.

Hand, J. R. M. and T. R. Skantz, 1998, "The Economic Determinants of Accounting Choices: The Unique Case of Equity Carve-Outs Under SAB 51," *Journal of Accounting and Economics*, 24, 175–203.

Hanson, R. C. and M. H. Song, 2000, "Managerial Ownership, Board Structure, and the Division of Gains," *Journal of Corporate Finance*, 6, 55–70.

Hanson, R. C. and M. H. Song, 2003 "Long-Term Performance of Divesting Firms and the Effect of Managerial Ownership," *JEAF*, 27, 321–336.

Harlow, W. V. and J. S. Howe, 1993, "Leveraged Buyouts and Insider Nontrading," *Financial Management*, 22, 109–118.

Harper, J. T. and J. Madura, 2002, "Sources of Hidden Value and Risk Within Tracking Stock," *Financial Management*, 31, 91–109.

Harris, R., D. S. Siegel and M. Wright, 2005 "Assessing the Impact of Management Buyouts on Economic Efficiency: Plant-level Evidence Form the United Kingdom," *Review of Economic Studies* 87, 148–153.

Hart, O. D. and J. Moore, 1990, "Property Rights and the Nature of the Firm," *Journal of Political Economy*, 98, 1119–1158.

Hass, J. J., 1996 "Directorial Fiduciary Duties in a Tracking Stock Equity Structure: The Need for a Duty of Fairness," *Michigan Law Review*, 94, 2089–2177.

Healy, P. M. and K. G. Palepu, 1995, "The Challenges of Investor Communication: The Case of Cuc International Inc.," *Journal of Financial Economics*, 38, 111–140.

Hirschey, M. and J. K. Zaima, 1989, "Insider Trading, Ownership Structure, and the Market Assessment of Corporate Sell-offs," *Journal of Finance*, 44, 971–980.

Hirschey, M., M. B. Slovin and J. K. Zaima, 1990, "Bank Debt, Insider Trading, and the Return to Corporate Selloffs," *Journal of Banking and Finance*, 14, 85–98.

Hite, G. L. and J. E. Owers, 1983, "Security Price Reactions around Corporate Spin-off Announcements," *Journal of Financial Economics*, 12, 409–436.

Hite, G., J. Owers and R. Rogers, 1987 "The Market for Inter-Firm Asset Sales: Partial Sell-Offs and Total Liquidations," *Journal of Financial Economics*, 18, 229–252.

Holthausen, R. W. and D. F. Larcker, 1996, "The Financial Performance of Reverse Leveraged Buyouts," *Journal of Financial Economics*, 42, 293–332.

Hotchkiss, E. S., K. John, R. Mooradian and K. S. Thorburn, 2008, "Bankruptcy and the Resolution of Financial Distress," In B. E. Eckbo (Ed.), *Handbook of Corporate Finance: Empirical Corporate Finance*, vol. 2, Handbooks in Finance Series, Elsevier/North-Holland, Amsterdam, Chapter 14.

Huang, J., 2008, "When Bad Stocks Make Good Investments: The Role of Hedge Funds in Leveraged Buyouts," Working Paper, Boston College.

Hulburt, H. M., 2003, "Equity Carve-Outs and Changes in Corporate Control," *Journal of Applied Business Research*, 19, 29–40.

Hulburt, H. M., J. A. Miles and J. R. Woolridge, 2002, "Value Creation from Equity Carve-Outs," *Financial Management*, 31, 83–100.

Huson, M. R. and G. MacKinnon, 2003, "Corporate Spinoffs and Information Asymmetry Between Investors," *Journal of Economics and Management Strategy*, 9, 481–503.

Ippolito, R. A. and W. H. James, 1992, "LBOs, Reversions and Implicit Contracts," *Journal of Finance*, 47, 139–167.

Ivashina, V. and A. Kovner, 2008, "The Private Equity Advantage: Leveraged Buyout Firms and Relationship Banking," Working Paper, Boston College.

Jain, P., 1985, "The Effect of Voluntary Sell-Off Announcements on Shareholder Wealth," *Journal of Finance*, 40, 209–224.

Jensen, M. C., 1986, "Agency Costs of Free Cash Flow, Corporate Finance, and Takeovers," *American Economic Review*, 76, 323–329.

Jensen, M. C., 1989, "Eclipse of the Public Corporation," *Harvard Business Review*, (September–October), 61–74.

Jensen, M. C. and W. Meckling, 1976, "Theory of the Firm: Managerial Behavior, Agency Costs, and Capital Structure," *Journal of Financial Economics*, 3, 305–360.

Jensen, M. C., S. Kaplan and L. Stiglin, 1989, "Effects of LBOs on Tax Revenues of the U.S. Treasury," *Tax Notes*, 42, 727–733.

John, K. and E. Ofek, 1995, "Asset Sales and Increase in Focus," *Journal of Financial Economics*, 37, 105–126.

Jones, C. and M. Rhodes-Kropf, 2004, "The Price of Diversifiable Risk in Venture Capital and Private Equity," Working Paper, Columbia University.

Kaiser, K. M. J. and A. Stouraitis, 2001, "Reversing Corporate Diversification and the Use of the Proceeds from Asset Sales: The Case of Thorn Emi," *Financial Management*, 30, 63–102.

Kalay, A. and M. Lemmon, 2008, "Payout Policy," In B. E. Eckbo (Ed.), *Handbook of Corporate Finance: Empirical Corporate Finance*, vol. 2, Handbooks in Finance Series, Elsevier/North-Holland, Amsterdam, Chapter 10.

Kaplan, S., 1989a, "The Effects of Management Buyouts on Operating Performance and Value," *Journal of Financial Economics*, 24 (2, October), 217–254.

Kaplan, S., 1989b, "Management Buyouts: Evidence on Taxes as a Source of Value," *Journal of Finance*, 44, 611–633.

Kaplan, S. N., 1991, "The Staying Power of Leveraged Buyouts," *Journal of Financial Economics*, 29, 287–313.

Kaplan, S. N. and A. Schoar, 2005, "Private Equity Performance: Returns, Persistence, and Capital Flows," *Journal of Finance*, 60, 1791–1823.

Kaplan, S. N. and J. C. Stein, 1993, "The Evolution of Buyout Pricing and Financial Structure in the 1980s," *Quarterly Journal of Economics*, 108, 313–357.

Kaplan, S. N. and P. Stromberg, 2008, "Leverage Buyouts and Private Equity," Working Paper, University of Chicago.

Kaplan, S. N. and M. S. Weisback, 1992, "The Success of Acquisitions: Evidence from Divestitures," *Journal of Finance*, 47, 107–138.

Kim, C. E., 1998, "The Effects of Asset Liquidity: Evidence from the Contract Drilling Industry," *Journal of Financial Intermediation*, 7, 151–176.

Klein, A., 1986, "The Timing and Substance of Divestiture Announcements: Individual, Simultaneous and Cumulative Effects," *Journal of Finance*, 41, 685–696.

Klein, B., R. G. Crawford and A. A. Alchian, 1978, "Vertical Integration, Appropriable Rents, and the Competitive Contracting Process," *Journal of Law and Economics*, 21, 297–326.

Klein, A., J. Rosenfeld and W. Beranek, 1991, "The Two Stages of an Equity Carve-Out and the Price Response of Parent and Subsidiary Stock," *Managerial and Decision Economics*, 12, 449–460.

Kracaw, W. A. and M. Zenner, 1996, "The Wealth Effects of Bank Financing Announcements in Highly Leveraged Transactions," *Journal of Finance*, 51, 1931–1946.

Krishnaswami, S. and V. Subramaniam, 1999, "Information Asymmetry, Valuation, and the Corporate Spin-Off," *Journal of Financial Economics*, 53, 73–112.

Kruse, T. A., 2002, "Asset Liquidity and the Determinants of Asset Sales by Poorly Performing Firms," *Financial Management*, 31, 107–129.

Lang, L. H. P. and R. M. Stulz, 1994, "Tobin's q, Corporate Diversification, and Firm Performance," *Journal of Political Economy*, 102, 1248–1280.

Lang, L., A. Poulsen and R. Stulz, 1995, "Asset Sales, Firm Performance, and the Agency Costs of Managerial Discretion," *Journal of Financial Economics*, 37, 3–37.

Lee, S., 1992, "Management Buyout Proposals and Inside Information," *Journal of Finance*, 47, 1061–1079.

Lehn, K. and A. Poulsen, 1989, "Free Cash Flow and Stockholder Gains in Going Private Transactions," *Journal of Finance*, 44, 771–787.

Lerner, J., M. Sorensen and P. Stromberg, 2008, "Private Equity and Long-Run Investment: The Case of Innovation," Working Paper, Harvard University.

Lichtenberg, F. and D. Siegel, 1990, "The Effects of Leveraged Buyouts on Productivity and Related Aspects of Firm Behavior," *JFE*, 27, 165–194.

Liebeskind, J., M. Wiersema and G. Hansen, 1992, "LBOs, Corporate Restructuring, and the Incentive-Intensity Hypothesis," *Financial Management*, 73–88.

Linn, S. C. and M. S. Rozeff, 1984, "The Corporate Sell-off," *Midland Corporate Finance Journal*, 2, 17–26.

Liu, M. H., 2005, "Information Content of Conglomerate Stock Breakups," Working Paper, University of Kentucky.

Ljunqvist, A. and M. Richarson, 2003, "The Cash Flow, Return and Risk Characteristics of Private Equity," Working Paper, New York University.

Logue, D. E., J. K. Seward and J. P. Walsh, 1996, "Rearranging Residual Claims: A Case for Targeted Stock," *Financial Management*, 25, 43–61.

Loh, C., R. B. Jennifer and H. Toms, 1995, "Voluntary Corporate Divestitures as Antitakeover Mechanisms," *Financial Review*, 30, 41–60.

Long, W. and D. Ravenscraft, 1993, "LBOs, Debt and R&D Intensity," *SMJ*, 14, 119–135.

MacMinn, R. D. and P. L. Brockett, 1995, "Corporate Spin-Offs as a Value Enhancing Technique When Faced with Legal Liability," *Insurance: Mathematics and Economics*, 16, 63–68.

Maksimovic, V., 1995, "Financial Structure and Product Market Competition," In R. Jarrow, V. Maksimovic and B. Ziemba (Eds.), *Finance*, Chapter 27, North-Holland, Series of Handbooks in Operations Research and Management Science, 887–920.

Maksimovic, V., 2007, "Conglomerate Firms and Internal Capital Markets," In B. E. Eckbo (Ed.), *Handbook of Corporate Finance: Empirical Corporate Finance*, vol. 1, Chapter 8, Handbooks in Finance Series, Elsevier/North-Holland, Amsterdam.

Maksimovic, V. and G. Phillips, 2001, "The Market for Corporate Assets: Who Engages in Mergers and Asset Sales and Are There Efficiency Gains?" *Journal of Finance*, 56, 2019–2065.

Marais, L., K. Schipper and A. Smith, 1989, "Wealth Effects of Going Private for Senior Securities," *JFE*, 23, 155–191.

Masulis, R., 1987, "Changes in Ownership Structure: Conversions of Mutual Savings and Loans to Stock Charter," *Journal of Financial Economics*, 18, 29–60.

Maxwell, W. F. and R. P. Rao, 2003, "Do Spin-Offs Expropriate Wealth from Bondholders?" *Journal of Finance*, 58, 2087–2108.

Maydew, E. L., K. Schipper, and L. Vincent, 1999, "The Impact of Taxes on the Choice of Divestiture Method," *Journal of Accounting and Economics*, 28, 117–150.

McConnell, J. J., M. Ozbilgin and S. Wahal, 2001, "Spin-Offs, Ex Ante," *Journal of Business*, 74, 245–280.

McNeil, C. R. and W. T. Moore, 2005, "Dismantling Internal Capital Markets vis Spinoff: Effects on Capital Allocation Efficiency and Firm Valuation," *Journal of Corporate Finance*, 11, 253–275.

Megginson, W. and J. Netter, 2001, "From State to Market: A Survey of Empirical Studies on Privatization," *Journal of Economic Literature*, 39, 321–389.

Metrick, A. and A. Yasuda, 2007, "Economics of Private Equity Funds," Working Paper, Wharton at University of Pennsylvania.

Michaely, R. and W. H. Shaw, 1995, "The Choice of Going Public: Spin-Offs vs. Carve-Outs," *Financial Management*, 24, 5–21.

Miles, J. A. and J. D. Rosenfeld, 1983, "The Effect of Voluntary Spin-Off Announcements on Shareholder Wealth," *Journal of Finance*, 38, 1597–1606.

Mulherin, J. H. and A. L. Boone, 2000, "Comparing Acquisitions and Divestitures," *Journal of Corporate Finance*, 6, 117–139.

Muller, H. M. and F. Panunzi, 2004, "Tender Offers and Leverage," *Quarterly Journal of Economics*, 119, 1217–1248.

Muscarella, C. and M. Versuypens, 1990, "Efficiency and Organizational Structure: A Study of Reverse LBOS," *Journal of Finance*, 45 (5, December), 1389–1413.

Myers, S. C., 1977, "Determinants of Corporate Borrowing," *Journal of Financial Economics*, 5, 147–175.

Myers, S. C. and N. S. Majluf, 1984, "Corporate Financing and Investment Decisions When Firms Have Information That Investors Do Not Have," *Journal of Financial Economics*, 13, 187–221.

Nanda, V., 1991, "On the Good News in Equity Carve-Outs," *Journal of Finance*, 46, 1717–1737.

Nanda, V. and M. P. Narayanan, 1999, "Disentangling Value: Financing Needs, Firm Scope and Divestitures," *Journal of Financial Intermediation*, 8, 174–204.

Newbould, G. D., R. E. Chatfield and R. F. Anderson, 1992, "Leveraged Buyouts and Tax Incentives," *Financial Management*, 21, 50–57.

Nikoskelainen, E. and M. Wright, 2007, "The Impact of Corporate Governance Mechanisms on Value Increase in Leveraged Buyouts," *Journal of Corporate Finance*, 13, 511–537.

Nixon, T. D., R. L. Roenfeldt and N. W. Sicherman, 2000, "The Choice Between Spin-Offs and Sell-Offs," *Review of Quantitative Finance and Accounting*, 14, 277–288.

Ofek, E., 1993, "Capital Structure and Firm Response to Poor Performance: An Empirical Analysis," *Journal of Financial Economics*, 34, 3–30.

Ofek, E., 1994, "Efficiency Gains in Unsuccessful Management Buyouts," *Journal of Finance*, 49, 637–654.

Officer, M. S., 2007, "The Price of Corporate Liquidity: Acquisition Discounts for Unlisted Targets," *Journal of Financial Economics*, 83, 571–598.

Officer, M. S., O. Ozbas and B. A. Sensoy, 2008, "Club Deals in Leveraged Buyouts," Working Paper, University of Southern California.

Opler, T. and S. Titman, 1993, "The Determinants of Leverage Buyout Activity: Free Cash Flow vs. Financial Distress Costs," *Journal of Finance*, 48, 1985–1999.

Parrino, R., 1997, "Spinoffs and Wealth Transfers: The Marriott Case," *Journal of Financial Economics*, 43, 241–274.

Parsons, C. and S. Titman, 2008, "Capital Structure and Corporate Strategy," In B. E. Eckbo (Ed.), *Handbook of Corporate Finance: Empirical Corporate Finance*, vol. 2, Handbooks in Finance Series, Elsevier/North-Holland, Chapter 13.

Peck, S. W., 1996, "The Influence of Professional Investors on the Failure of Management Buyout Attempts," *Journal of Financial Economics*, 40, 264–294.

Perotti, E. C. and K. E. Spier, 1993, "Capital Structure as a Bargaining Tool: The Role of Leverage in Contract Renegotiation," *American Economic Review*, 83, 1131–1141.

Perotti, E. and S. Rossetto, 2007, "Unlocking Value: Equity Carve Outs as Strategic Real Options, *Journal of Corporate Finance*, 13, 771–792.

Perry, S. E. and T. H. Williams, 1994, "Earnings Management Preceding Management Buyout Offers," *Journal of Accounting and Economics*, 18, 157–179.

Peyer, U. C. and A. Shivdasani, 2001, "Leverage and Internal Capital Markets: Evidence from Leveraged Recaptializations," *Journal of Financial Economics*, 59, 477–515.

Phallipou, L. and O. Gottschalg, 2007, "The Performance of Private Equity Funds," Working Paper, University of Amsterdam.

Phallipou, L. and O. Gottschalg, 2008, "Governance Effects of LBO Events," Working Paper, Syracuse University.

Phillips, G. M., 1995, "Increased Debt and Industry Product Markets: An Empirical Analysis," *Journal of Financial Economics*, 37, 189–238.

Powers, E. A., 2003, "Deciphering the Motives for Equity Carve-Outs," *Journal of Financial Research*, 26, 31–50.

Pulvino, T., 1998, "Do Asset Fire-Sales Exist? An Empirical Investigation of Commercial Aircraft Transactions," *Journal of Finance*, 53, 939–978.

Pyo, U., 2007, "Enhancing Managerial Incentives and Value Creation: Evidence from Corporate Spinoffs," *Journal of Economics and Finance*, 31, 341–358.

Rajan, R., H. Servaes and L. Zingales, 2000, "The Cost of Diversity: The Diversification Discount and Inefficient Investment," *Journal of Finance*, 55, 35–80.

Rappaport, A., 1990, "The Staying Power of the Public Corporation," *Harvard Business Review*, 1, 96–104.

Renneboog, L., T. Simons and M. Wright, 2007, "Why Do Firms Go Private in the UK? The Impact of Private Equity Investors, Incentive Realignment and Undervaluation," *Journal of Corporate Finance*, 13, 591–628.

Roden, D. M. and W. G. Lewellen, 1995, "Corporate Capital Structure Decisions: Evidence from Leveraged Buyouts," *Financial Management*, 24, 76–87.

Rosenfeld, J., 1984, "Additional Evidence on the Relation Between Divestiture Announcements and Shareholder Wealth," *Journal of Finance*, 39 (5), 1437–1448.

Ross, S., 1977, "The Determinants of Financial Structure: The Incentive Signaling Approach," *Bell Journal of Economics*, 8, 23–40.

Scharfstein, D. S. and J. C. Stein, 2000, "The Dark Side of Internal Capital Markets: Divisional Rent-Seeking and Inefficient Investment," *Journal of Finance*, 55, 2537–2564.

Schipper, K. and A. Smith, 1983, "Effects of Recontracting on Shareholder Wealth: The Case of Voluntary Spinoffs," *Journal of Financial Economics*, 12, 437–467.

Schipper, K. and A. Smith, 1986, "A Comparison of Equity Carve-Outs and Seasoned Equity Offerings: Share Price Effects and Corporate Restructuring," *Journal of Financial Economics*, 15, 153–186.

Schipper, K. and A. Smith, 1991, "Effects of Management Buyouts on Corporate Interest and Depreciation Tax Deductions," *Journal of Law and Economics*, 34, 295–341.

Schleifer, A. and R. Vishny, 1992, "Liquidation Value and Debt Capacity: A Market Equilibrium Approach," *Journal of Finance*, 47, 1343–1365.

Schlingemann, F. P., R. M. Stulz and R. A. Walkling, 2002, "Divestitures and the Liquidity of the Market for Corporate Assets," *Journal of Financial Economics*, 64, 117–144.

Seoungpil, A. and D. J. Denis, 2004, "Internal Capital Markets and Investment Policy: Evidence of Corporate Spinoffs," *Journal of Financial Economics*, 71, 489–516.

Servaes, H., 1994, "Do Takeover Targets Invest," *Review of Financial Studies*, 7, 253–277.

Seward, J. K. and J. P. Walsh, 1995, "The Acquisition of Restructured Firms: An Illustration of Market," *Journal of Economics and Management Strategy*, 3, 585–603.

Sicherman, N. W. and R. H. Pettway, 1992, "Wealth Effects for Buyers and Sellers of the Same Divested Assets," *Financial Management*, 21, 119–128.

Slovin, M. B., M. E. Sushka and Y. M. Bendeck, 1991, "The Intra-Industry Effect of Going-Private Transactions," *Journal of Finance*, 46, 1537–1550.

Slovin, M., M. Sushka and S. Ferraro, 1995, "A Comparison of the Information Conveyed by Equity Carve-Outs, Spin-Offs, and Asset Sell-Offs," *Journal of Financial Economics*, 37, 89–104.

Smith, A. J., 1990, "Corporate Ownership Structure and Performance," *Journal of Financial Economics*, 27, 143–164.

Stromberg, P., 2007, "The New Demography of Private Equity," Working Paper, Stockholm Institute of Financial Research.

Stulz, R. M., 1990, "Managerial Discretion and Optimal Financing Policies," *Journal of Financial Economics*, 26, 3–27.

Tehranian, H., N. G. Travlos and J. F. Waegelein, 1987, "The Effect of Long-Term Performance Plans on Corporate Sell-Off-Induced Abnormal Returns," *Journal of Finance*, 42, 933–942.

Van de Gucht, L. M. and W. T. Moore, 1998, "Predicting the Duration and Reversal Probability of Leveraged Buyouts," *Journal of Empirical Finance*, 5, 299–315.

Veld, C. and Y. V. Veld-Merkoulova, 2004, "Do Spin-Offs Really Create Value? The European Case," *Journal of Banking and Finance*, 28, 1111–1135.

Vijh, A. M., 1994, "The Spinoff and Merger Ex-Date Effects," *Journal of Finance*, 49, 581–609.

Vijh, A., 1999, "Long-Term Returns from Equity Carve Outs," *Journal of Financial Economics*, 54, 273–308.

Vijh, A. M., 2002, "The Positive Announcement-Period Returns of Equity Carveouts: Asymmetric Information or Divestiture gains?" *Journal of Business*, 75, 153–190.

Vijh, A. M., 2006, "Does a Parent-Subsidiary Structure Enhance Financing Flexibility," *Journal of Finance*, 59, 1337–1360.

Wagner, H. F., 2004, "The Equity Carve-Out Decision," Working Paper, University of Munich.

Walker, M., 1998, "Leverage Recapitalization, Operating Efficiency, and Stockholder Wealth," *Financial Review*, 33, 88–114.

Warga, A. and I. Welch, 1993, "Bondholder Losses in Leveraged Buyouts," *Review of Financial Studies*, 6, 959–982.

Williamson, O. E., 1985, *The Economic Institutions of Capitalism: Firms, Markets, Relational Contracting*, Free Press, New York.

Wright, M., S. Thompson and K. Robbie, 1992, "Management-Led Leveraged Buy-Outs: A European Perspective," *Journal of Business Venturing*, 7, 45–71.

Wruck, K. H., 1994, "Financial Policy, Internal Control, and Performance: Sealed Air Corporation's Leveraged Special Dividend," *Journal of Financial Economics*, 36, 157–192.

Wruck, E. G. and K. H. Wruck, 2002, "Restructuring Top Management: Evidence from Corporate Spinoffs," *Journal of Law and Economics*, 20, S176–S218.

Zaima, J. K. and D. Hearth, 1985, "The Wealth Effects of Voluntary Selloffs: Implications for Divesting and Acquiring Firms," *Journal of Financial Research*, 8, 227–236.

AUTHOR INDEX

A

Abadie, A. 193, 211–212
Abarbanell, J.S. 742
Acharya, S. 186, 197–199
Acharya, V. 764, 767–768
Afshar, K.A. 730
Agrawal, A. 90, 322
Ahn, S. 742
Aiken, L.S. 404
Akbulut, M.E. 70
Akdogu, E. 33, 102, 104
Akerlof, G. 430
Akhavein, J. 448
Aktas, N. 104, 106, 111
Alexander, G. 734
Allen, J.W. 740, 743–744, 746, 748–749
Alli, K. 739
Amess, K. 766
Amihud, Y. 38, 42, 391, 394, 412
Amir, E. 284
Amit, R. 215
Andrade, G. 8, 11, 227–266, 274, 276, 279, 295,
  311, 319, 358, 482–483, 607, 610–611, 616, 620
Ang, A. 283
Ang, J.S. 12, 38, 274, 321
Asquith, P. 27, 36, 89, 361, 367, 423, 451, 515,
  734, 769
Atanasov, V. 749
Axelson, U. 761

B

Bae, S.C. 755, 765
Bagnoli, M. 31, 48
Baird, D.G. 62
Baker, G. 767–768
Baker, M. 84, 95, 97, 164
Balachandran, B. 755–756
Ball, R. 159–160, 162–163
Baltin, M. 748
Banerjee, A. 102, 611

Banz, R. 159
Barber, B. 143, 159, 162, 165–166, 218, 343, 482, 582
Barberis, N. 159
Bargeron, L.L. 25, 66, 71, 77, 379–408
Barry, C. 426
Barth, M.E. 274, 284
Barton, D. 575
Basu, S. 159
Bates, T.W. 25, 66, 68–69, 734
Bauguess, S.W. 93
Beaver, W. 143
Bebchuk, L.A. 30, 56–57, 63, 399
Becher, D.A. 11, 104, 106, 676, 680
Bennedsen, M. 216
Berger, A.N. 448, 675, 678
Berger, P.G. 209, 723, 731, 733
Berkovitch, E. 37, 41, 620
Berle, A.A. Jr., 382
Bernard, V. 149, 166–168
Bertrand, M. 194
Best, R.W. 741
Betker, B.L. 61
Betton, S. 3–123, 200, 395, 485, 491, 501, 505,
  530–532, 624, 659, 722, 730
Bhagat, S. 59–60, 70, 95, 475–532
Bharath, S. 216
Bhattahcaryya, S. 104, 107
Billett, M.T. 89–90, 751–752, 763, 769
Bittlingmayer, G. 110–111
Blair, R. 574
Blanchard, O. 238
Bliss, R.T. 92
Blume, M. 162
Bohren, O. 200
Boone, A.L. 13, 25, 230–231, 276, 311, 319, 361,
  607, 730, 735, 747, 771
Boot (1992), 725
Boudoukh, J. 164
Bradley, M. 27, 29, 36, 60, 66, 70, 77, 355, 373, 479,
  482, 485, 489, 491–492, 517, 526, 542, 581,
  619, 649

SUBJECT INDEX